REF
HD
8066
.A78
2006
v.3

D0212065

FOR REFERENCE

Do Not Take From This Room

ENCYCLOPEDIA OF
U.S. Labor and Working-Class History

VOLUME 3
O–Z
INDEX

Eric Arnesen

EDITOR

Routledge
Taylor & Francis Group
New York   London

Routledge is an imprint of the
Taylor & Francis Group, an informa business

Routledge
Taylor & Francis Group
270 Madison Avenue
New York, NY 10016

Routledge
Taylor & Francis Group
2 Park Square
Milton Park, Abingdon
Oxon OX14 4RN

© 2007 by Taylor & Francis Group, LLC
Routledge is an imprint of Taylor & Francis Group, an Informa business

Printed in the United States of America on acid-free paper
10 9 8 7 6 5 4 3 2 1

International Standard Book Number-10: 0-415-96826-7 (Hardcover)
International Standard Book Number-13: 978-0-415-96826-3 (Hardcover)

No part of this book may be reprinted, reproduced, transmitted, or utilized in any form by any electronic, mechanical, or other means, now known or hereafter invented, including photocopying, microfilming, and recording, or in any information storage or retrieval system, without written permission from the publishers.

Trademark Notice: Product or corporate names may be trademarks or registered trademarks, and are used only for identification and explanation without intent to infringe.

Library of Congress Cataloging-in-Publication Data

Arnesen, Eric.
   Encyclopedia of U.S. labor and working-class history / Eric Arneson.
      p. cm.
   Includes bibliographical references and index.
   ISBN 0-415-96826-7
   1. Labor--United States--History--Encyclopedias. 2. Working class--United States--History--Encyclopedias. 3. Industrial relations--United States--History--Encyclopedias. I. Title. II. Title: Encyclopedia of United States labor and working-class history.

HD8066.A78 2006
331.0973'03--dc22
                                                                                    2006048640

Visit the Taylor & Francis Web site at
http://www.taylorandfrancis.com

and the Routledge Web site at
http://www.routledge-ny.com

CONTENTS

ASSOCIATE EDITORS

Leon Fink
Department of History, University of Illinois at Chicago

Cindy Hahamovitch
Department of History, College of William and Mary

Tera Hunter
Department of History, Carnegie Mellon University

Bruce Laurie
Department of History, University of Massachusetts at Amherst

Joseph McCartin
Department of History, Georgetown University

CONTRIBUTORS

María Graciela Abarca
University of Buenos Aires, Argentina

Ellen S. Aiken
University of Colorado

Lindsey Allen
Independent Scholar

Edie Ambrose
Xavier University

David M. Anderson
Louisiana Tech University

Ronald Applegate
Cornell University

Eric Arnesen
University of Illinois at Chicago

Andrew Arnold
Kutztown University of Pennsylvania

Dexter Arnold
University of Cincinnati

Steve Ashby
University of Indiana

Carl L. Bankston, III
Tulane University

Lucy G. Barber
National Archives and Records Administration

James R. Barrett
University of Illinois at Urbana-Champaign

Kathleen M. Barry
University of Cambridge, UK

Rachel A. Batch
Widener University

Beth Thompkins Bates
Wayne State University

Joshua Beaty
College of William and Mary

Mildred Allen Beik
Independent Scholar

Evan P. Bennett
Independent Scholar

Michael J. Bennett
Independent Scholar

Julie Berebitsky
University of the South

Timothy A. Berg
McHenry County College, Illinois

Aaron Max Berkowitz
University of Illinois at Chicago

Matthew S. R. Bewig
University of Florida

Mary H. Blewett
University of Massachusetts at Lowell

Kevin Boyle
Ohio State University

Lauren H. Braun
University of Illinois at Chicago

Douglas Bristol
University of Southern Mississippi

David Brody
University of California at Davis (emeritus)

Jamie L. Bronstein
New Mexico State University

Edwin L. Brown
University of Alabama at Birmingham

CONTRIBUTORS

Victoria Bissell Brown
Grinnell College

David Brundage
University of California at Santa Cruz

Emily Brunner
University of Chicago

Robert Bruno
University of Illinois at Urbana-Champaign

Nicholas Buchanan
Massachusetts Institute of Technology

Peter H. Buckingham
Linfield College

Stephen Burwood
State University of New York at Geneseo

Robert Bussell
University of Oregon

Jenny Carson
University of Toronto

Theresa A. Case
University of Houston

Kenneth M. Casebeer
University of Miami Law School

James G. Cassedy
National Archives and Records Administration

Marisa Chappell
Oregon State University

Robert W. Cherney
San Francisco State University

Daniel Clark
Oakland University

Catherine Clinton
Independent Scholar

Andrew Wender Cohen
Syracuse University

Peter Cole
Western Illinois University

Stephen Cole
Notre Dame de Namur University

Timothy C. Coogan
LaGuardia Community College, New York

Axel B. Corlu
Binghamton University, State University of New York

Seth Cotlar
Willamette University

Evan Matthew Daniel
Tamiment Library/Robert F. Wagner Labor Archives, New York University

Catharine Christie Dann
College of William and Mary

Colin Davis
University of Alabama at Birmingham

G. V. Davis
Marshall University

Greta de Jong
University of Nevada at Reno

John D'Emilio
University of Illinois at Chicago

Dennis A. Deslippe
Australian National University

Anthony DeStefanis
College of William and Mary

Ileen A. DeVault
Cornell University

Victor G. Devinatz
Illinois State University

Steven Deyle
University of California at Davis

Steven Dike-Wilhelm
University of Colorado

Brian Dolinar
Claremont Graduate University

Colleen Doody
DePaul University

Gregory Downey
University of Wisconsin at Madison

Michael V. Doyle
Skidmore College

Alan Draper
St. Lawrence University

Philip Jacques Dreyfus
San Francisco State University

Melvyn Dubofsky
Binghamton University, State University of New York

Douglas R. Egerton
Le Moyne College

Kathleen L. Endres
University of Akron

Beth English
Princeton University

John Enyeart
Bucknell University

Steve Estes
Sonoma State University

Candace Falk
University of California at Berkeley

Rosemary Feurer
Northern Illinois University

Lisa Michelle Fine
Michigan State University

Leon Fink
University of Illinois at Chicago

Michael W. Fitzgerald
St. Olaf College

John H. Flores
University of Illinois at Chicago

Mary E. Fredrickson
Miami University of Ohio

Joshua B. Freeman
Graduate Center, City University of New York

John D. French
Woodrow Wilson International Center for Scholars

Daniel Geary
University of California at Berkeley

Gregory Geddes
Binghamton University, State University of New York

Erik S. Gellman
Northwestern University

Gene C. Gerard
Tarrant County College, Texas

Kristin Geraty
Indiana University

Larry G. Gerber
Auburn University

Heidi Scott Giusto
Duke University

Lawrence B. Glickman
University of South Carolina

Susan M. Glisson
University of Mississippi

Chad Alan Goldberg
University of Wisconsin

Steve Golin
Bloomfield College

Risa L. Goluboff
University of Virginia

Elliott J. Gorn
Brown University

Thomas M. Grace
Cornell University

George N. Green
University of Texas at Arlington

Jean-Denis Grèze
Independent Scholar

James Green
University of Massachusetts at Boston

Brian Greenberg
Monmouth College

Richard A. Greenwald
Drew University

CONTRIBUTORS

John Grider
University of Colorado

Andrew Gyory
Independent Scholar

Pamela Hackbart-Dean
Georgia State University

Greg Hall
Western Illinois University

Daniel Harper
University of Illinois

Kenneth J. Heineman
Ohio University

John Heinz
Chicago Maritime Society

Jeffrey Helgeson
University of Illinois at Chicago

Danielle Hidalgo
Independent Scholar

Frank Tobias Higbie
University of Illinois at Urbana-Champaign

Matthew Hild
Georgia State University

Adam J. Hodges
University of Houston at Clear Lake

Sean Holmes
Brunel University, United Kingdom

Michael Honey
University of Washington-Tacoma

Adam Howard
University of Florida

Tera Hunter
Carnegie Mellon University

Maurice Isserman
Hamilton College

Maurice Jackson
Georgetown University

Catherine O. Jacquet
University of Illinois at Chicago

Elizabeth Jameson
University of Calgary

Robert F. Jefferson
Xavier University

Richard J. Jensen
University of Nevada at Las Vegas (emeritus)

John B. Jentz
Raynor Memorial Libraries, Marquette University

Edward P. Johanningsmeier
Independent Scholar

Robert D. Johnston
University of Illinois at Chicago

Gwen Hoerr Jordan
University of Wisconsin at Madison

Yevette Richards Jordan
George Mason University

Lisa Kannenberg
The College of Saint Rose

Anthony Kaye
Pennsylvania State University

Brian Kelly
Queens University Belfast, Northern Ireland

Kevin Kenny
Boston College

Andrew E. Kersten
University of Wisconsin at Green Bay

Lionel Kimble, Jr.
Chicago State University

Marta M. Knight
California State University at Sacramento

Steven D. Koczak
New York State Senate Research Service

David Koistinen
American University of Beirut, Lebanon

James C. Kollros
St. Xavier University

Robert Korstad
Duke University

Molly Ladd-Taylor
York University

Clarence Lang
University of Illinois at Urbana-Champaign

Jennifer Langdon-Teclaw
University of Illinois at Chicago

R. Todd Laugen
Metropolitan State College of Denver

Bruce Laurie
University of Massachusetts, Amherst

Mark Lause
University of Cincinnati

John Leggett
Rutgers University

Steven Leikin
San Francisco State University

Karen Leroux
Drake University

Steven C. Levi
Independent Scholar and Author

Alex Lichtenstein
Rice University

Robbie Lieberman
Southern Illinois University

Joseph Lipari
University of Illinois at Chicago

Rebecca S. Lowen
Independent Scholar

Stephanie Luce
University of Massachusetts at Amherst

Jennifer Luff
Service Employees International Union

John M. Lund
Keene State College, University of New Hampshire

Brigid Lusk
Northern Illinois University

John F. Lyons
Joliet College

Robert Macieski
University of New Hampshire

Nancy MacLean
Northwestern University

Anastasia Mann
Princeton University

Geoff Mann
Simon Fraser University

Wendi N. Manuel-Scott
George Mason University

Kathleen Mapes
State University of New York at Geneseo

Sharon Mastracci
University of Illinois at Chicago

Joseph A. McCartin
Georgetown University

John Thomas McGuire
State University of New York at Cortland

Elizabeth McKillen
University of Maine at Orono

Robert C. McMath, Jr.
University of Arkansas

Eden Medina
Indiana University

Ronald Mendel
University of Northampton, United Kingdom

Timothy Messer-Kruse
University of Toledo

Jack Metzgar
Roosevelt University

Steven Meyer
University of Wisconsin at Milwaukee

Gregory M. Miller
University of Toledo

Heather Lee Miller
Historical Research Associates, Inc.

James A. Miller
George Washington University

CONTRIBUTORS

Timothy Minchin
La Trobe University

Samuel Mitrani
University of Illinois at Chicago

Marian Mollin
Virginia Polytechnic Institute and State University

Scott Molloy
University of Rhode Island

Paul D. Moreno
Hillsdale College

Alexander Morrow
University of Oregon

Scott Nelson
College of William and Mary

Caryn E. Neumann
Ohio State University

Mitchell Newton-Matza
Lexington College

Bruce Nissen
Florida International University

Mark A. Noon
Bloomsburg University of Pennsylvania

Stephen H. Norwood
University of Oklahoma

Kathleen Banks Nutter
Smith College

Kathryn J. Oberdeck
University of Illinois at Urbana-Champaign

Edward T. O'Donnell
College of the Holy Cross

Richard Oestricher
University of Pittsburgh

Brigid O'Farrell
Stanford University

Amy C. Offner
Dollars and Sense *Magazine*

John S. Olszowka
Mercyhurst College

Colleen O'Neill
Utah State University

Liesl Miller Orenic
Dominican University

Annelise Orleck
Dartmouth College

Merideth Oyen
Georgetown University

David Palmer
Flinders University, Australia

Karen Pastorello
Tompkins Cortland Community College, New York

Barry Pateman
University of California-Berkeley

Brad Paul
National Policy and Advocacy Council on Homelessness (NPACH)

Ruth Percy
University of Toronto

Michael Perman
University of Illinois at Chicago

Jean Pfaelzer
University of Delaware

Lori Pierce
DePaul University

Michael Cain Pierce
University of Arkansas

Jerald Podair
Lawrence University

Kevin Noble Powers
Georgetown University

David Purcell
University of Cincinnati

Peter Rachleff
Macalester College

Bruno Ramirez
University of Montreal, Canada

Scott E. Randolph
Purdue University

Padma Rangaswamy
South Asian American Policy and Research Institute

David C. Ranney
University of Illinois at Chicago (emeritus)

Gerda W. Ray
University of Missouri at St. Louis

Jonathan Rees
Colorado State University at Pueblo

Steven A. Reich
James Madison University

David M. Reimers
New York University (emeritus)

Ester Reiter
Atkinson College, York University

Rachel R. Reynolds
Drexel University

Christopher Rhomberg
Yale University

Lawrence Richards
University of Richmond

Elizabeth Ricketts
Indiana University of Pennsylvania

Steven A. Riess
Northeastern Illinois University

Howard Rock
Florida International University

John C. Rodrigue
Louisiana State University

Marc S. Rodriguez
University of Notre Dame

Donald W. Rogers
Central Connecticut State University and Housatonic Community College

Gerald Ronning
Albright College

Margaret Rose
University of California at Santa Barbara

Sarah F. Rose
University of Illinois at Chicago

John J. Rosen
University of Illinois at Chicago

Doug Rossinow
Metropolitan State University

Kate Rousmaniere
Miami University

Margaret C. Rung
Roosevelt University

Jason Russell
York University

John Russell
Georgia State University

Francis Ryan
Moravian College

Joseph C. Santora
Essex County College

Ralph Scharnau
Northeast Iowa Community College, Peosta

Ronald W. Schatz
Wesleyan University

Michael Schiavone
Flinders University, Australia

Kevin E. Schmiesing
Acton Institute

Dorothee Schneider
University of Illinois at Urbana-Champaign

Katrin Schultheiss
University of Illinois at Chicago

Rima Lunin Schultz
University of Illinois at Chicago

Carlos A. Schwantes
University of Missouri at St. Louis

CONTRIBUTORS

James Searing
University of Illinois at Chicago

Karin A. Shapiro
Duke University

Paul Siegel
Independent Scholar

Michael W. Simpson
University of Wisconsin at Madison

Joseph E. Slater
University of Toledo

Eric Richard Smith
University of Illinois at Chicago

Michael Spear
City University of New York

Robyn Ceanne Spencer
Pennsylvania State University

Sarah Stage
Arizona State University, West Campus

Howard R. Stanger
Canisius College

Richard Stott
George Washington University

David O. Stowell
Keene State College, University of New Hampshire

Shelton Stromquist
University of Iowa

Thomas Summerhill
Michigan State University

Paul Michel Taillon
University of Auckland, New Zealand

Vanessa Tait
University of California at Berkeley

Clarence Taylor
Baruch College, City University of New York

Kieran W. Taylor
University of North Carolina at Chapel Hill

Michael M. Topp
University of Texas at El Paso

Frank Towers
University of Northern Colorado

Martin Tuohy
National Archives and Records Administration, Great Lakes Branch

Mary C. Tuominen
Denison University

Joseph M. Turrini
Auburn University

Emily E. LaBarbera Twarog
University of Illinois at Chicago

William E. Van Vugt
Calvin College

Susannah Walker
Virginia Wesleyan University

Wilson J. Warren
Western Michigan University

Peter Way
Bowling Green State University

John Weber
College of William and Mary

Edmund F. Wehrle
Eastern Illinois University

Carl R. Weinberg
Indiana University

Robert E. Weir
Mount Holyoke College

Virginia Wright Wexman
University of Illinois at Chicago

Carmen Teresa Whalen
Williams College

Jeannie M. Whayne
University of Arkansas

John White
Independent Scholar

Marcus Widenor
University of Oregon

John Fabian Witt
Columbia University

David Witwer
Lycoming College

Kenneth C. Wolensky
Pennsylvania Historical and Museum Commission

James Wolfinger
Northwestern University

Chris Wonderlich
University of Illinois at Chicago

John Chi-Kit Wong
Washington State University

Robert H. Woodrum
Clark Atlanta University

Gerald Zahavi
State University of New York at Albany

Minna P. Ziskind
University of Pennsylvania

David A. Zonderman
North Carolina State University

ALPHABETICAL LIST OF ENTRIES

THEMATIC LIST OF ENTRIES

Concepts and Developments

Abolitionism
Affirmative Action
American Exceptionalism
American Standard of Living
Anarchism
Anticommunism
Apprenticeship
Arbitration
Artisans
Arts and Crafts Movement
Assembly Line Production
Blacklists
Boycotts
Capital Flight
Catholic Church
Central Labor Unions
Child Care
Child Labor
Civil Rights
Cold War
Collective Bargaining
Company Towns
Convict Labor in the New South
Cooperation
Coxey's Army
Culture, Working-Class
De-Industrialization
Disfranchisement
"Don't Buy Where You Can't Work" Campaigns
Dorr War
Dual Unionism
Education, Labor
Emancipation and Reconstruction
Environmentalism
Family Wage
Film
Five Dollar Day
Foreign Policy
Fourierism

Free-Soilism
Gender
Globalization
Gold Rush
Great Migration
Great Society/War on Poverty (1960s)
Historiography of American Labor History
Hoboes
Housework
Immigration Restriction
Indentured Servitude
Industrial Democracy
Industrial Unionism
Injunctions
Labor Day
Labor Republicanism
Labor Theory of Value
Living Wage
Living Wage Campaigns
Maquiladoras
May Day
Migrant Farmworkers
Music
New Left
New South
New York City Fiscal Crisis (1970s)
No-Strike Pledge
Novels, Poetry, Drama
Operation Dixie
Organized Crime
Pattern Bargaining
Peonage
Philadelphia Plan
Plumb Plan
Politics and Labor, Nineteenth Century
Portal-to-Portal Pay
Protocol of Peace
Racketeering and RICO
Rosie the Riveter
Sacco and Vanzetti
Sexual Harassment
Sharecropping and Tenancy

Legal Cases, Acts, and Legislation

Management

Labor-Management Cooperation
National Civic Federation
National Right to Work Committee
Personnel Management
Pinkerton Detectives
Welfare Capitalism

Organizations

A. Philip Randolph Institute
Actors' Equity Association
African Blood Brotherhood
Alliance for Labor Action
American Alliance for Labor and Democracy
American Labor Party
Association of Catholic Trade Unionists
Black Lung Associations
Black Panther Party
Black Workers Congress
Brookwood Labor College
Bryn Mawr Summer School for Women Workers
   in Industry
Civil Rights Congress
Colored Farmers' Alliance
Communist Party
Conference for Progressive Political Action
Delmarva Poultry Justice Alliance
DRUM, FRUM, ELRUM
Farmer-Labor Party
Future Outlook League of Cleveland
Greenback-Labor Party
Highlander Folk School/Highlander Research and
   Education Center
Home Club
Hull-House Settlement (1889–1963)
Illinois Woman's Alliance
International Labor Defense
International Workers' Order
Jewish Labor Committee
Justice for Janitors
Know-Nothing Party
Ku Klux Klan (Reconstruction and WWI Era)
Labor Research Association
Labor's Non-Partisan League (1936–1944)
League for Industrial Democracy (LID)
League of Revolutionary Black Workers
Liberal Party
Locofoco Democrats
Lowell Female Labor Reform Association (LFLRA)
Loyal Legion of Loggers and Lumbermen
March on Washington Movement
Miners for Democracy
Molly Maguires

National Ad Hoc Committee of Black Steelworkers
National Association for the Advancement of
   Colored People (NAACP)
National Association of Colored Graduate Nurses
National Child Labor Committee
National Consumers League
National Labor Reform Party
National Negro Congress
National Negro Labor Council
National Urban League
New England Labor Reform League
New England Workingmen's Association
Poor People's Campaign
Popular Front
Populism/People's Party
Professional Air Traffic Controllers Organization
Socialist Labor Party
Socialist Party of America
Socialist Trade and Labor Alliance
Socialist Workers' Party
Sons of Liberty
Trade Union Unity League
Unemployed League (1930s)
Union League Movement
Union Summer
Wages for Housework
Women's Trade Union League
Workers Alliance of America
Workers' Defense League
Working Girls' Clubs
Zoot Suit Riots

Periods

Antebellum Era
Civil War and Reconstruction
Colonial Era
Dominance and Influence of Organized Labor: 1940s
Gilded Age
Great Depression: 1930s
Politics and Labor, Twentieth Century
Progressive Era
Revolution and Early National Period
Significant Gains and Missed Opportunities: 1950s
   and 1960s
Unemployment, Insecurity, and the Decline of Labor:
   1970s
Vietnam War
Wage Losses and Union Decline: 1980s through the
   Early 2000s
Worker Mobilization, Management Resistance: 1920s
World War I
World War II

THEMATIC LIST OF ENTRIES

INTRODUCTION

At the dawn of the twenty-first century, the scholarly field of labor history is a large, sophisticated, and diverse one. Prior to the 1960s, economists, political scientists, and historians largely took individual trade unions and the labor movement as the subjects of their academic investigations. Since the 1960s, however, the emergence of the "new labor history" has broadened the investigative lens considerably, embracing countless topics that earlier scholars might not even recognize as belonging to their field. Trade unions and labor movements continue, of course, to be legitimate subjects of exploration, but labor history has come to embrace much more. Initially concerned with grassroots activism, the experiences of the rank and file, and working-class communities and their cultures, the "new labor history"—which by 2006 is no longer very new—is deeply concerned with politics, law, race, ethnicity, gender, law, and migration. The sheer heterogeneity of America's working classes now stands at the heart of much of the field. Historians clearly recognize that just as there was no single working class possessing shared interests, so too was there no single working-class identity, culture, or ideology.

Today, a large and growing number of labor historians and labor studies scholars have produced a large and rich body of literature on a vast array of subjects. The Labor and Working-Class History Association and the Labor Studies Association boast hundreds of members, the field publishes multiple journals, articles on labor's past regularly find their way into non-labor oriented journals, and the themes explored by labor historians are routinely covered in U.S. history textbooks. To a significant extent, labor history, long considered by its practitioners to be a vital component of the larger drama of American history, is recognized as such by the larger field of American historians as well.

The *Encyclopedia of U.S. Labor and Working-Class History* builds upon the past several generations of scholarship to explore numerous dimensions of the working-class past. Its conception of what constitutes labor history is expansive and capacious, its sense of the borders between different fields porous. While attentive to the field's traditional focus on skilled craft and semi-skilled manufacturing workers, it devotes considerable attention to occupations that have only more recently attracted scholarly attention, such as longshoring, domestic service, prostitution, nursing, teaching, hair styling, computer programming, sleeping car portering, housework, and agriculture. It erodes the artificial boundaries between labor history and African-American history, treating the subjects of slavery, the slave trade, slave rebellions, and abolitionism, for instance, as integral to the recounting of the history of American labor. The heterogeneity of the working class is a central theme, with the *Encyclopedia* providing extensive coverage of race and gender divisions and the experiences of a multitude of immigrant groups.

How to Use This Book

Organization

The *Encyclopedia of U.S. Labor and Working-Class History* is organized in a straightforward and easy to use **A to Z format**. Users will find a number of useful features accompanying the entries, including **References and Further Reading** and **See Also** suggestions for easy cross-referencing. The volumes each include a thematic list of entries, in addition to an alphabetical list of entries and a **thorough, analytical index**.

Illustrations

The *Encyclopedia* includes 78 illustrations. These photographs, culled from the archives of the Library of Congress, accompany specific entries, and depict strikes, union meetings, workers, and influential leaders.

INTRODUCTION

Thematic Coverage

The *Encyclopedia of U.S. Labor and Working-Class History* features 662 independent entries ranging in length from 500 to 6,000 words. The topics covered fall into 11 broad categories:

Concepts and Developments: Entries included in this category look in depth at central concepts, ideas, and broad developments in the history of American workers. American exceptionalism, sexual harassment, music, affirmative action, syndicalism, strikebreaking, living wage campaigns, immigration restriction, indentured servitude, and the historiography of labor history are only a few of the subjects treated in this broad-ranging category.

Government Agencies and Committees: Entries falling into this category examine government agencies affecting labor. Among the many covered are the Fair Employment Practice Committee, the LaFollette Civil Liberties Committee, the U.S. Women's Bureau, and the Federal Bureau of Investigation.

Individuals: Entries in this category cover a diverse set of figures intimately involved in labor relations and working-class life over the past two and a half centuries. Familiar figures like Walter Reuther, Jimmy Hoffa, George Meany, and A. Philip Randolph will be found in this section. But the list of key figures includes a host of less familiar names, including labor poet George Lippard, community activist Saul Alinsky, settlement house leaders Florence Kelley and Jane Addams, the mythic figure John Henry, labor troubadour Joe Hill, African-American labor activists Richard L. Davis, Willard Townsend, and Maida Springer, anarchist Lucy Parsons, and labor journalist John Swinton.

Legal Cases, Acts, and Legislation: This category focuses on laws and court cases affecting labor relations and working-class life. Examples in this group include the Chinese Exclusion Acts, the Civil Rights Act of 1964, Aid to Families with Dependent Children (AFDC), the Immigration and Nationality Act of 1965, and the North American Free Trade Agreement.

Management: Business organizations and programs (such as labor-management cooperation, welfare capitalism, and the National Right to Work Committee) are examined in this category.

Organizations: Organizations that are not unions, but nonetheless were working-class associations or bodies that dealt with working-class issues, compose another category. The Socialist Party of America, the Colored Farmers' Alliance, the Populist Party, and the March on Washington Movement fall into this category.

Periods: Lengthy chronological entries provide broad coverage of the principal contours of the evolution of labor systems and labor relations from the colonial era to the present. The period covered in each essay (the colonial era, the antebellum era, the Gilded Age and Progressive Era, the 1940s, and 1980 to the present, for example) conforms to an established periodizaiton or logical block of time corresponding to key developments.

Racial and Ethnic Categories of Workers: Racial and ethnic/immigration groups constitute another category of entries, with coverage of a wide range of groups including the Irish, Mexican and Mexican Americans, French Canadians, and recent immigrants from Southeast and South Asia and Central America.

Regions: Key geographical regions with a defined historical scholarship (including the South, the Pacific Northwest, the Southwest, and California) are explored in this category of entries.

Strikes: Strikes and labor-related conflicts represent a significant group of entries. Well-known events such as the Pullman Strike of 1894, the 1912 Lawrence Textile Strike, the 1937 Memorial Day Massacre, and the J.P. Stevens campaign are examined, as are many lesser known conflicts including the 1881 Atlanta Washerwomen's Strike, the 1919 Bogalusa, Louisiana strike, and the 1891–1892 Tennessee Convict Uprising.

Trade Unions: Numerous entries explore the history of trade unions in the nineteenth and twentieth centuries. While commonly recognized and major unions and union federations such as the United Steelworkers of America, the Knights of Labor, the International Brotherhood of Teamsters, and the Industrial Workers of the World are covered, so too are unions that are not household names, such as the Stockyards Labor Council, the International Fur and Leather Workers Union, and the United Hatters', Cap and Millinery Workers' International Union. Particular attention is paid to unions and labor associations composed of non-white workers and women, including the Brotherhood of Sleeping Car Porters, the United Farm Workers of America, the Southern Tenant Farmers Union, the Women's Trade Union League, and the Coalition of Labor Union Women.

A total of 298 scholars in the United States and Europe have contributed to the *Encyclopedia*. These individuals are specialists in their fields and bring to the project a vast wealth of knowledge and expertise. They share no historiographical or political perspective, and each has approached their subjects as she or he saw fit. Indeed, the interpretations offered are those of the authors and, at times, similar topics are explored from different or even conflicting interpretive positions.

Acknowledgments

Since the actual labor that goes into creating an encyclopedia of this sort is vast and collective, numerous people necessarily contributed significant to bringing this project to fruition. The five associate editors—Leon Fink, Cindy Hahamovitch, Tera Hunter, Bruce Laurie, and Joseph McCartin—are all superb scholars of labor's past who devoted considerable time and energy to conceptualizing the volume, identifying potential authors, and reading, editing, and engaging the arguments of the hundreds of entries in this volume. Without their editorial care and expertise, this project would have been impossible to complete. At Routledge, Mark L. Georgiev helped shape the project in its early stages, while Kristen Holt oversaw the massive logistical operation of contacting authors, answering queries, and shepherding the project through the editorial process. Closer to home, fellow historian Katrin Schultheiss provided her usual and invaluable intellectual support and guidance throughout the project's life, while our children Rachel, Samuel, and William patiently, and sometimes not so patiently, endured my continual thinking-out-loud about the project and countless of its individual subjects. While their interests remained largely fixed on baseball, soccer, and children's fiction—they provided no editorial support but did occasionally ask good questions—I suspect that they learned something about the history of labor and the craft of history in the process. I look forward to the day when they too can use and learn from the *Encyclopedia*.

Eric Arnesen

O

OAKLAND GENERAL STRIKE (1946)

In December 1946, a strike of predominantly female department store clerks sparked a citywide general strike in Oakland, California. More than 100,000 workers struck for 2.5 days, shutting down factories, shipyards, construction, most retail, and virtually all transportation in the city. Local working-class mobilization carried over into the municipal elections of 1947, when a slate of labor-endorsed candidates won four seats on the city council.

Before World War II, Oakland's business and politics had been dominated by a conservative, downtown, commercial elite, led by *Oakland Tribune* publisher Joseph Knowland. In the 1930s, insurgent Congress of Industrial Organizations (CIO) unions emerged in factories and along the waterfront, but much of the local economy remained concentrated in skilled craft production, and the American Federation of Labor (AFL) remained the larger and stronger union federation.

The war however brought thousands of new migrants to work in the defense industries, especially shipbuilding, while the number of employed women in Oakland nearly doubled. By 1945, the city population had increased by almost a third, and the African-American population more than tripled. Many of these workers, previously excluded by race, gender, or skill, suddenly became members of unions that often received them poorly or resisted them altogether. But by the mid-1940s, a more progressive leadership emerged in the local AFL, and the CIO also reached out to new workers in the community.

With mass layoffs in the postwar period and fears of a new open-shop and wage-cutting drive by employers, union leaders focused on organizing new members, including workers in the historically anti-union downtown retail sector. By the fall of 1946, the AFL Department and Specialty Store Employees' Union, Local 1265, had recruited a majority of workers at Kahn's, a large department store, and at Hastings, a men's store. After management refused to recognize the union, the employees at the stores, the majority of them women, voted to strike. Local Teamsters' Union drivers refused to transport goods to or from the struck stores, which soon ran low on inventory and faced serious losses of business in the Christmas shopping season.

The employers then turned to the local government. Downtown business leaders met with local law enforcement officials, who agreed to provide security to allow the stores to bring in $500,000 worth of merchandise using an out-of-town, nonunion trucking firm. Union leaders got word of the plan, and on Saturday night, November 30, about 70 special pickets surrounded the stores. By Sunday morning, December 1, some 250 police arrived, equipped with shotguns and tear gas. Strikers and union leaders watched as police cars and motorcycles escorted convoys of strike-breaking trucks delivering goods to the stores.

The response on the streets was immediate: That morning a car men's union officer stopped a passing streetcar and removed its controls, halting traffic through the area. Crowds gathered downtown over the next 2 days, as local AFL union leaders met and voted almost unanimously for a general strike. On Tuesday morning an estimated 100,000 AFL members from 142 unions walked off their jobs, and CIO members, though not called out, honored AFL picket lines (public utilities, organized by CIO unions, remained in service).

Crowds ranging from 5,000–20,000 people assembled downtown in largely peaceful demonstrations around the stores. Strikers and sympathizers sang and danced to guitars or music played from union loudspeakers in what was described as a carnival-like atmosphere. The unions officially referred to the strike as a holiday, while union picket captains kept order and exhorted people to remain nonviolent. For 2.5 days thousands of working people in Oakland, migrants, women, members of ethnic minorities, and veterans of economic depression and war, all came forward to claim their right to the city.

Meanwhile local AFL union leaders began negotiating with the city manager and the business elite. As the talks went on, the Oakland unions experienced mounting pressure from their international unions to end the general strike. On the second Teamsters' vice-president Dave Beck ordered his members to return to work, and with that the employers broke off negotiations. The unions settled with the city manager that the police would no longer be used to break legal picket lines, and each party issued separate statements. The AFL unions officially ended the strike on Thursday morning, December 5, and a CIO mass meeting, set for that evening to decide whether to join the strike, was never held.

In the general strike, the AFL unions successfully resisted the business elite's attempt to use police force to break their movement. However they were unable to resolve the Kahn's and Hastings' dispute, and the striking women clerks would remain out for several more months. As the limits of the initial settlement became clear, local AFL and CIO unions came together the following spring to endorse a slate of pro-labor candidates in the 1947 city elections. In a record voter turnout, four of the five candidates won election despite a vicious red-baiting campaign led by the *Oakland Tribune*.

Without a majority on the nine-member city council however, the new councilors failed to move much of their agenda. The progressive period in local politics ultimately came to an end on the issue of public housing. In 1949, the city council voted to approve a plan to build 3,000 units of federally subsidized public housing, backed by the AFL and CIO unions and the NAACP. Intense opposition from real estate, landlords, and property-owning interests however led to a

bitterly contested recall election in which only two of the progressive councilors survived. By 1951, the conservative majority on the council had rescinded the program of public housing.

In the immediate postwar period, citywide general strikes broke out in a number of American cities, including Pittsburgh, Houston, Stamford, Connecticut, and Rochester, New York. In Oakland the 1946 general strike represented a peak of popular class solidarity and action, but the union movement had yet to overcome gender and racial divisions or find ways of sustaining mobilization across a wider political arena.

CHRISTOPHER RHOMBERG

References and Further Reading

Lipsitz, George. *Class and Culture in Cold War America: "A Rainbow at Midnight."* New York: Praeger, 1981.

Rhomberg, Chris. *No There There: Race, Class, and Political Community in Oakland.* Berkeley: University of California Press, 2004.

Self, Robert O. *American Babylon: Race and the Struggle for Postwar Oakland.* Princeton, NJ: Princeton University Press, 2003.

Wolman, Philip. "The Oakland General Strike of 1946." *Southern California Quarterly* 57, 2 (1975): 147–179.

OCCUPATIONAL SAFETY AND HEALTH ADMINISTRATION (OSHA)

Since its creation in 1970, the Occupational Safety and Health Administration (OSHA) has significantly improved workplace safety. OSHA has also dramatically altered workplace dynamics by granting workers the right to participate in creating a safe workplace. Yet OSHA has also faced nearly constant attacks from employers and advocates of deregulation.

Workplace Safety before OSHA

Prior to OSHA workplace safety and health were regulated almost entirely at the state level. Factory inspections, workers' compensation, and other safety laws passed in the late nineteenth and early twentieth centuries were not only often relatively weak but also varied markedly from state to state. Inspectors could generally enter only after an accident had already taken place, or if a worker had filed a formal complaint, court orders were required to force companies to correct violations, and some state departments of labor refused to inform workers of hazards without company authorization. Moreover even in 1969, state safety inspectors were outnumbered two to one by fish and game wardens. State safety and compensation laws also did not cover farm and domestic workers—which in effect meant that they did not protect many female workers—nor could they effectively track victims of occupational diseases when they moved, especially in the case of such diseases as silicosis that develop over decades.

The two major federal safety programs were similarly weak. The U.S. Bureau of Mines gained the power to inspect mines in 1941 and the power to set and enforce safety standards only in 1952, after decades of lobbying by the United Mine Workers of America (UMWA). Likewise under the Walsh-Healey Act of 1936, the U.S. secretary of labor could set safety standards for companies that did more than $10,000 worth of business annually with the federal government; but even as late as 1969, the federal government was inspecting less than 5% of the 75,000 eligible workplaces annually.

Workers themselves had only a limited ability to improve workplace safety before OSHA. Occasionally skilled workers and unionized workers used wildcat strikes to demand safer working conditions, such as extra escape shafts in mines. Coal miners and lumber workers generally stopped working for the day when a fellow worker died in an accident, and miners also routinely left mines when they feared an explosion or a cave-in. But even unionized workers could not force employers to install safer technologies; for instance although hatmakers won rest breaks to limit their exposure to mercury salts, they could not change the work process to remove the salts entirely.

Workplace Safety Becomes a Public Issue

In the late 1960s, several different factors brought public attention to the issue of workplace safety. While union administrations continued to pay little attention to health and safety issues during the 1950s and 1960s, workers themselves became far more active in demanding a safe workplace. Rank-and-file workers in the United Auto Workers, UMWA, and the Teamsters led wildcat strikes over such issues as speedups, unsafe mine conditions, the lack of black lung compensation laws, and participation in contract negotiations. Workers' demands were further strengthened by the Farmington mine explosion of 1968, which killed 78 miners, and by a 29% rise in workplace injuries from 1961–1970. Increasing scientific knowledge about industrial hazards and the

newly formed environmental movement also helped raise public concern about industrial malfeasance and workplace hazards and mobilize support in Congress.

Public concern over workplace safety was strong enough in the 1960s that both Presidents Lyndon Johnson and Richard Nixon saw a federal occupational health and safety law as a key means of solidifying working-class support and introduced bills to Congress. Although the business lobby managed significantly to dilute the final bill signed by Nixon in December 1970 from the Democratic version introduced in 1968, the "safety bill of rights" still covered 56 million workers in 3.5 million workplaces: All workers except for those who are self-employed or work on their family farm, those who work in industries covered by other federal safety laws, or those who work for state or local governments.

OSHA Basics

The OSHA has two main regulatory functions: To set standards and to conduct safety inspections of workplaces. Under OSHA employers must provide workers with access to their medical records, information about exposure to toxic substances, and any necessary personal protective equipment; employers must also explain hazards to workers. Additionally employers with more than 10 employees must keep records of all accidents, treatments, hazardous situations, or other safety-related activities and promptly report to OSHA all fatalities or accidents that result in the hospitalization of four or more employees; OSHA then investigates the workplace for safety violations. During these inspections, OSHA can assess fines for willful violations (such as knowingly and intentionally committing a violation or making no effort to eliminate a known hazard), repeat violations, failure to correct violations, and falsifying reports.

Industry-specific standards have been one of the most effective yet controversial aspects of OSHA's work. Early on OSHA adopted consensus standards created by industry groups; unions unsurprisingly critiqued these standards as too lax. The OSHA also began work on specific hazard standards, such as asbestos, benzene, and byssinosis (a dust disease that afflicts cotton workers), but work on these standards progressed very slowly. Each standard begins with a proposal by the National Institute for Occupational Safety and Health (NIOSH) or a petition from outside parties, such as unions; OSHA then forms an advisory committee with representatives from labor, business, and the public. After publishing the proposed regulation, taking comments, holding a public hearing, and accepting legal briefs, OSHA finally issues the new standard. The new standard can be appealed to an independent board or challenged in court, as in the case of the benzene standard, which was vacated by the Supreme Court in 1980 for failing to incorporate economic factors or address a "significant risk" to workers. Large companies, which hold most of the relevant data, have often withheld research from NIOSH and OSHA or successfully weakened the standard through the advisory committee or comment periods. Despite these challenges and frequent critiques from the labor movement, specific standards have greatly improved workers' safety—for instance virtually ending byssinosis in the United States.

The OSHA's inspection work has also faced intense criticism over the years. The OSHA has struggled with regulations that do not cover all potential safety violations and a limited force of inspectors—generally less than 2,000—that allows it to inspect only around 2% of workplaces per year. Labor unions have faulted OSHA for generally levying only small fines that do not serve as an effective deterrent and adhering rigidly to safety regulations, while employers have called for OSHA to focus on the most dangerous workplaces. Particularly in OSHA's first decade, small businesses—which make up the majority of firms covered by the OSH Act and which rarely have the detailed safety programs of large firms—complained that they faced excessive scrutiny from inspectors. Yet the OSH Act has significantly changed the balance of power in the workplace by granting workers the right to complain confidentially to OSHA about workplace conditions, contest the amount of time OSHA allows employers to fix violations, and participate in OSHA inspections, all without the fear of retaliation by employers; employers also started incorporating health and safety provisions into contracts. Furthermore in 1990, Congress raised OSHA's fines—from $1,000 to $7,000 for serious violations and from $10,000 to $70,000 for willful and repeat violations—to encourage employers to take safety more seriously.

Through OSHA unions have become much more engaged with health and safety issues. Several unions have written occupational health provisions into contracts—the United Rubber workers won a contract requiring management to help finance university research on benzene and leukemia, while other unions have won the establishment of union-management safety committees. Unions have also played a vocal role in fighting for specific OSHA standards, such as noise, vinyl chloride, coke-oven emissions, and cotton dust.

Attacks on OSHA

By the early 1980s, OSHA faced a storm of criticism from employers; in particular employers complained that OSHA did not focus its inspections on the workplaces where the most accidents occurred. Under pressure from the Reagan administration, Congress, and the Supreme Court, OSHA incorporated nonregulatory and voluntary approaches during the 1980s and 1990s and in particular limited its focus on small businesses and concentrated inspections on the most dangerous workplaces. The Voluntary Protection Program, which started in 1982, exempted firms with exemplary safety records from routine inspections and prioritized them for regulation variances. The Reagan administration also pressured OSHA to establish joint management-labor health and safety committees; some unions supported these committees, since they offered a means of addressing issues not yet covered by OSHA regulations.

During the Clinton and George W. Bush administrations, OSHA faced not only budget cuts but also repeated attempts to weaken the agency. In the mid-1990s, some congressional Republicans tried unsuccessfully to force OSHA to incorporate cost-benefit and risk-assessment analysis into existing and new standards, exempt most workplaces from inspection, ban unannounced inspections, and abolish NIOSH. Moreover despite OSHA's nearly 20 years of research on ergonomics standards, Congress prohibited the agency from issuing either proposed or final standards for several years in the mid-to-late 1990s. After OSHA finally published the ergonomics standards in 2000, which covered more than 100 million workers at 6.1 million worksites and would help prevent 460,000 musculoskeletal disorders per year, George W. Bush signed a congressional repeal of the standards. Moreover although one of OSHA's major contributions was to include workers in the safety process—an approach that has been very successful in improving worker health—this approach has been greatly weakened. Under the Strategic Partnership Program, OSHA has created over 50 advisory committees that entirely exclude labor unions. The OSHA has also continued to emphasize voluntary and cooperative approaches rather than inspections and enforcement, canceled work on more than 20 incomplete rules, and issued no major new standards since the overturned ergonomics standard in 2000.

The OSHA also faces challenges in protecting workers during the current era of labor-market restructuring and globalization. The decline of unions and the concomitant rise of telecommuting and subcontracting leave workers with less supervision and training, fewer rights, poorer work conditions, and often little or no health care. Since most OSHA laws have focused on full-time workers in large workplaces, OSHA is somewhat ill-equipped to cope with this changing workplace. Moreover globalization has distributed dangerous work to ill-supervised workplaces in countries that have a weak or absent union movement, few worker rights, and weak safety and health regulations. Despite the profound challenges that OSHA faces, OSHA has undoubtedly greatly improved worker safety: By 2001, workers were 40% less likely to be injured on the job than in 1971, and 60% less likely to die.

SARAH F. ROSE

References and Further Reading

Asher, Robert. "Organized Labor and the Origins of the Occupational Health and Safety Act." *Labor's Heritage* 3, 1 (1991): 54–76.
Bain, Peter. "Human Resource Malpractice: The Deregulation of Health and Safety at Work in the USA and Britain." *Industrial Relations* 28, 3 (1997): 176–191.
Berman, Daniel. *Death on the Job: Occupational Health and Safety Struggles in the United States.* New York: Monthly Review Press, 1978.
Donnelly, Patrick. "The Origins of the Occupational Safety and Health Act of 1970." *Social Problems* 30, 1 (1982): 13–25.
McGarity, Thomas O., and Sidney A. Shapiro. *Workers at Risk: The Failed Promise of the Occupational Safety and Health Administration.* Westport, CT: Praeger Publishers, 1993.
Noble, Charles. *Liberalism at Work: The Rise and Fall of OSHA.* Philadelphia, PA: Temple University Press, 1986.
Szasz, Andrew. "Industrial Resistance to Occupational Safety and Health Legislation." *Social Problems* 32, 2 (1984): 103–116.

See also **Federal Coal Mine Health and Safety Act; Walsh-Healey Public Contracts Act**

OCEAN HILL-BROWNSVILLE STRIKES (1968)

On May 9, 1968, a community school board in the predominantly black and Puerto Rican Ocean Hill-Brownsville section of Brooklyn, New York, seeking to test its powers, sent termination letters to 19 white educators, most affiliated with the union that represented the city's public school teachers, the United Federation of Teachers (UFT). The UFT's attempts to obtain their re-instatement would culminate in three racially divisive citywide teachers' strikes in the

fall of that year that left permanent scars on New York's racial landscape.

Origins of the Ocean Hill-Brownsville Controversy

The roots of the Ocean Hill-Brownsville dispute lay in the failure to integrate the New York public education system in the wake of the 1954 *Brown v. Board of Education* Supreme Court decision. By the mid-1960s, the city's schools were more segregated than they had been at the time of that decision, a result of racialized housing patterns and white resistance. In response black parents began to demand a greater voice in the operation of public schools in their neighborhoods. This movement for community control of education also drew support from Manhattan-based elites, including Mayor John V. Lindsay, and Ford Foundation President McGeorge Bundy. During the summer of 1967, the foundation provided funding for an experiment in community control of schools in Ocean Hill-Brownsville. A local board composed largely of black neighborhood residents was elected, but its powers were defined vaguely.

The local board quickly clashed with the UFT, and its president, Albert Shanker. The union was young, having been in existence only since 1960, and its leaders viewed community control of education as a threat to their hard-won collective bargaining gains. The UFT moreover was over 90% white, giving its disagreements with the local board over control of hiring, termination, and curriculum in the Ocean Hill-Brownsville schools an uncomfortable racial subtext. The power struggle between the union and the Ocean Hill-Brownsville local board escalated during the 1967–1968 school year. Middle- and working-class whites in the city, many residing outside Manhattan in the outer boroughs of the Bronx, Brooklyn, Queens, and Staten Island, began to voice support for the UFT, interpreting community control as an unwarranted special benefit accorded blacks. By the spring of 1968, the union and the local board were on a collision course.

In early May the local board met to select a group of white educators to be terminated. Many, including Fred Nauman, a UFT chapter chairman, were active in the union and/or critical of the Ocean Hill-Brownsville community-control experiment. None had received the notice and hearings that were customary in cases involving termination from positions in the New York City public school system. The letters were delivered to the educators on May 9.

The Ocean Hill-Brownsville Strikes

Shanker and the UFT sought to frame their battle to re-instate the terminated educators as one involving labor rights, and not race. The dispute, Shanker insisted, was solely about due process: Workers were entitled to fair hearings when their job security was threatened. He averred that the UFT would fight to protect the procedural rights of all members regardless of race. Supporters of the Ocean Hill-Brownsville local board in the black community however argued that substance, and not procedure, was at stake. They viewed community control of education as a civil rights issue and the UFT's invocation of due process as a canard. They blamed the terminated educators for undermining an experiment in educational reform that offered hope to disadvantaged minority children. Union bureaucrats, they claimed, were impeding the cause of racial justice.

On August 26, a trial examiner appointed by the New York City Board of Education ordered that the group of terminated educators, now reduced to 10 by voluntary transfers, be reinstated. After the Ocean Hill-Brownsville local board refused to comply and Mayor Lindsay declined to press the issue, the UFT struck all of the city's public schools on September 9, the first in a series of three strikes that would last until mid-November. Twice, on September 10 and 29, the union entered into agreements with Lindsay and the board of education under which the disputed teachers would return to their classrooms. The Ocean Hill-Brownsville local board, which had not been a party to the agreements, sabotaged them. During the summer the local board had hired a group of young, procommunity-control replacement teachers to take the places of the UFT teachers in the event of a strike in the fall. The two groups clashed in the Ocean Hill-Brownsville classrooms after the strike settlements brought them together. In addition community activists harassed the union teachers on their return to Ocean Hill-Brownsville. The settlement agreements broke down, and the strikes resumed.

By October Shanker was demanding not only the reinstatement of his teachers, but also the discontinuation of the Ocean Hill-Brownsville community-control experiment in its entirety. This stance inflamed the city's African-American population. Despite his *bona fides* as a supporter of civil rights—Shanker had participated in the 1963 March on Washington and Freedom Summer in 1964, and was a friend and ally of Martin Luther King, Jr.—the UFT president was denounced as a racist in black neighborhoods. For his part Shanker accused the local board of fomenting anti-Semitism when a flyer defaming Jews was placed in the mailboxes of white Ocean Hill-Brownsville teachers. He had the flyers reprinted and distributed throughout the city in an effort to galvanize support for the UFT. Since most of the disputed teachers were Jewish, the flyers carried special resonance in that community and led to an upsurge in antiblack sentiment there.

The strikes were especially difficult for black unionists in the city, who were caught between the competing imperatives of race and class. The UFT's Black Caucus attempted to chart a middle course, affirming its loyalty to the union while also supporting community control, satisfying neither side. Black members of District Council 37, American Federation of State, Country, and Municipal Employees (AFSCME); Local 1199 of the Drug and Hospital Workers; and District Council 65 of the Retail, Wholesale, and Department Store Union, criticized New York Central Labor Council President Harry Van Arsdale for his support of the UFT. On November 13, they staged a sit-in at Van Arsdale's office demanding that he use his influence to save community control in Ocean Hill-Brownsville. The protesters announced that they now identified as blacks first and unionists second, a painful reminder of the power of race to transcend even the most institutionalized class loyalties, both in the labor movement and the city at large.

Settlement and Aftermath

The black unionists' sit-in provided the immediate impetus to settle the third and final strike. By November striking white teachers and African-American counterdemonstrators were confronting each other daily in the streets surrounding the city's public schools, racial epithets flying. White middle-class opinion had swung sharply against Mayor Lindsay, who was perceived as an apologist for black militancy. Shanker, whose membership was beginning to feel the effects of almost 2 months without work, and who was facing a growing procommunity-control movement within his union, also had reason to seek a settlement.

The final strike ended with an agreement, reached on November 17, which generally favored the UFT. The disputed teachers were returned to their classrooms, and the Ocean Hill-Brownsville schools placed under the supervision of a state trustee. The settlement also continued the suspension of the local board that had begun during the strikes. By 1970, Shanker and the UFT had succeeded in ending the Ocean Hill-Brownsville community-control experiment.

The Ocean Hill-Brownsville strikes left a legacy of racial bitterness in New York that would linger for decades. It shifted the city's political culture rightward, helping to forge a race-based coalition of outer-borough white Catholics and Jews who elected Mayors Edward Koch (1978–1990) and Rudolph Giuliani (1994–2002); both had strained relationships with New York's black community. Outer-borough whites with memories of the Ocean Hill-Brownsville crisis provided the electoral support for municipal budget cuts, social service reductions, and anticrime measures during the Koch and Giuliani administrations that targeted black New Yorkers. These whites also appropriated the rhetoric of community control, which had been employed by African-Americans during the Ocean Hill-Brownsville strikes, for their own purposes. They defeated plans for integrated housing in the Forest Hills neighborhood of Queens (1972) and integrated education in Brooklyn's Canarsie section (1972–1973) with local-control arguments borrowed from Ocean Hill-Brownsville.

By the 1980s, the effects of residential, educational, and economic isolation had turned the Ocean Hill-Brownsville community inward. New black leaders like Al Sharpton, who had been a participant in the Ocean Hill-Brownsville dispute as a youth, were emerging to confront white New York across an urban chasm now defined almost entirely by race. The Ocean Hill-Brownsville strikes symbolized the angry intersection of labor and racial politics in New York and the failure of class-based interracialism to take hold in the city.

JERALD PODAIR

References and Further Reading

Cannato, Vincent J. *The Ungovernable City: John Lindsay and His Struggle to Save New York*. New York: Basic Books, 2001.

Edgell, Derek. *The Movement for Community Control of New York City's Schools, 1966–1970: Class Wars*. Lewiston, NY: Edwin Mellen Press, 1998.

Gittell, Marilyn, and Maurice Berube, eds. *Confrontation at Ocean Hill-Brownsville*. New York: Praeger, 1969.

Gordon, Jane Anna. *Why They Couldn't Wait: A Critique of the Black-Jewish Conflict over Community Control in Ocean Hill-Brownsville, 1967–1971*. New York: Routledge Falmer, 2001.

Hampton, Henry, and Steve Fayer. *Voices of Freedom: An Oral History of the Civil Rights Movement from the 1950s through the 1980s*. New York: Bantam Books, 1990.

Jacoby, Tamar. *Someone Else's House: America's Unfinished Struggle for Integration*. New York: Free Press, 1998.

Perlstein, Daniel H. *Justice, Justice: School Politics and the Eclipse of Liberalism*. New York: Peter Lang, 2004.

Podair, Jerald E. *The Strike That Changed New York: Blacks, Whites, and the Ocean Hill-Brownsville Crisis*. New Haven, CT: Yale University Press, 2002.

Ravitch, Diane. *The Great School War—New York, 1805–1973: A History of the Public Schools as Battleground of Social Change*. New York: Basic Books, 1974.

Urofsky, Melvin. *Why Teachers Strike: Teachers' Rights and Community Control*. Garden City, NY: Doubleday, 1970.

See also **Shanker, Albert**

O'CONNOR, JESSIE LLOYD (FEBRUARY 14, 1904–DECEMBER 24, 1988)
Labor Journalist and Activist

Born in Chicago, O'Connor grew up in the well-to-do Chicago suburb of Winnetka, heir to a considerable fortune of both money and liberal tradition. Her father, William Bross Lloyd, was known in the early part of the twentieth century as one of the millionaire Socialists. His family owned, among other profitable properties, a portion of the *Chicago Tribune*. Her mother, Lola Maverick Lloyd, was part of the Texas Maverick family, prominent in the cattle industry. She was also a founder of both the Women's Peace Party and the Women's International League for Peace and Freedom. O'Connor's paternal grandfather was Henry Demarest Lloyd, the nineteenth-century social critic and author of the 1894 classic, *Wealth against Commonwealth*.

In 1925, O'Connor graduated magna cum laude from Smith College with a degree in economics. While in London during the General Strike of 1926, she was greatly disturbed by the conditions under which workers labored and lived as well as by the inaccurate reports of the General Strike in the mainstream press. As she continued to travel around Europe, including several months spent in the Soviet Union, she began publishing articles as a freelancer.

Back in America by 1929, O'Connor signed on as a reporter for the left-wing news bureau, the Federated Press. One of her Federated Press coworkers was the young labor journalist Harvey O'Connor (1897–1987), later the author of several corporate exposes, including *Mellon's Millions* (1933); the two married in 1930 and spent the next 57 years working together for social justice.

As a reporter for the Federated Press, O'Connor covered the 1929 Gastonia, North Carolina, textile workers' strike as well as the 1931 coal miners' strike in Harlan County, Kentucky. The dispatches she sent back were vivid but never patronizing descriptions of the grinding poverty and exploitative work conditions she saw during both strikes, a model of what was then known as "revolutionary reportage."

The O'Connors moved to Pittsburgh in 1931, opening a branch office of the Federated Press in that notoriously anti-union city. A year later the couple went to the Soviet Union, spending several months assisting fellow American and radical journalist Anna Louise Strong in establishing a pro-Communist English language paper, the *Moscow Daily News*. They returned to the United States just as the New Deal got under way and turned their journalistic talents to covering the growing demands of organized labor.

In 1935, Jessie Lloyd O'Connor made headlines of her own and caused an uproar when she used her voice as a stockholder to denounce the unfair labor practices of U.S. Steel at the annual stockholders meeting—the same year that her husband Harvey O'Connor published *Steel-Dictator*, a critical examination of the U.S. Steel Corporation. She also became an active member of the American League against War and Fascism (ALAWF). Growing out of the World Congress against War held in Amsterdam in 1932, the ALAWF formed in the United States in 1933, speaking out against fascism as well as in support of labor during the heady days of the Popular Front during the 1930s.

By 1939, the O'Connors were living in the famed settlement Hull-House, which following the 1935 death of founder Jane Addams, was in the process of charting a new course under a series of head residents. During the tenure of the controversial head resident Charlotte Carr from 1937 to 1943, Hull-House activities were increasingly directed toward the concerns of labor.

On both the national and local levels, O'Connor was active in a number of organizations, including the League of Women Shoppers (LWS). Founded in New York City in 1935, the LWS was dedicated to using women's power as consumers on behalf of the interests of labor, a coming together of the middle-class base found in the National Consumers' League and the focus on union-made goods found in the Women's Union Label Leagues. The LWS opened a Chicago branch only a month after the Memorial Day Massacre outside of Republic Steel's Chicago plant in which 10 workers were killed and more than a hundred wounded during a peaceful demonstration in support of the Steel Workers' Organizing Committee. Thus when O'Connor joined the LWS and was elected as secretary of the Chicago branch, she was well aware of the limits of the Wagner Act in the face of police

brutality. Inspired by the organization's motto, "Use Your Buying Power for Justice," the LWS supported a variety of labor actions around the country. To support their activities, they raised funds through rummage sales and in O'Connor's Chicago branch, a mink coat raffle. Secretary O'Connor relied on her journalism experience to churn out press releases, meeting notices, and letters of appeal to various constituencies.

As a resident of Hull-House during World War II, the lifetime pacifist O'Connor was like many torn between her pacifism and the fight against fascism. She increasingly directed her considerable energy and talents toward even more locally defined issues, such as affordable housing and safe streets in her immediate Chicago neighborhood while maintaining her active role in the LWS, serving as vice-president and president of the Chicago League until its demise in 1943. After a 3-year (1945–1948) stint in Texas while Harvey served as publicity director for the Oil Workers' International Union, the O'Connors moved to Little Compton, Rhode Island, where they opened their spacious oceanfront home to a variety of activists, offering respite and financial assistance in particular to several civil rights activists and the many victims of McCarthyism. They, too, felt the effects of the virulent anticommunism of the 1940s and 1950s. The FBI began active surveillance of the O'Connors in 1939, the same year that both denied any connection to the Communist party in official correspondence with the Dies Committee, also known as the House Un-American Activities Committee (HUAC), which in the early 1950s revoked the O'Connors' passports for several years. Nonetheless O'Connor continued her activism as part of the National Committee for the Progressive party (1949–1952) and as a cofounder of the National Committee to Abolish HUAC. Until her death in 1988, this tireless crusader for social justice continued actively to protest American corporate growth overseas, antilabor policies at home, and was an early opponent of the Vietnam War. Using her personal wealth and her journalism, O'Connor supported the cause of American labor for six decades.

KATHLEEN BANKS NUTTER

Selected Works

Lloyd, Jessie. *Gastonia: A Graphic Chapter in Southern Organization*. 1930.
O'Connor, Harvey, Jessie Lloyd O'Connor, and Susan Bowler. *Harvey and Jessie: A Couple of Radicals* (1987).

See also **Gastonia Strike (1929); House Un-American Activities Committee/Dies Committee; Hull-House;**

Labor Press; Lloyd, Henry Demarest; Memorial Day Massacre (1937); National Consumers' League; Popular Front; Union Label

O'HARE, FRANK P. (APRIL 23, 1877–JULY 16, 1960)
Socialist and Editor

Francis Peter O'Hare moved to St. Louis from Iowa as a young boy with his family. He grew to maturity in the rough-and-tumble Irish ghetto of Kerry Patch, taking a job as a water boy during the building of the St. Louis railroad depot during the turbulent year of 1892, his only actual experience in the working class in a long life dedicated to the creation of a cooperative commonwealth. In the late 1890s, he fell under the influence of successive business mentors imbued with the spirit of Progressivism and then became a Socialist after studying popular works grounded in Marxism, the weekly *Appeal to Reason* newspaper, and material from a correspondence course on political economy.

While attending an *Appeal*-sponsored training school for socialist agitators, O'Hare wooed and wed fellow student Kate Richards. The happy couple spent their honeymoon and several years beyond making speeches and organizing locals for the Socialist party of America (SP). Studying the roots of injustice first hand in the American Southwest and Northeast interested them more than Marxist theories, which enabled them to communicate effectively with landless farmers, cotton pickers, miners, and other workers. They became proponents of an Americanized Marxism light on theory and passionate about a peaceful, evolutionary approach to bringing about a socialist millennium. After speaking at an experimental socialist encampment (derived from religious and Populist camp meetings) in Grand Saline, Texas, Frank O'Hare perfected the encampment idea, supervising huge weeklong gatherings between harvest and planting in rural Oklahoma and elsewhere. Such SP-orchestrated activities helped to set down socialist grass roots in the Southwest and recruited thousands of converts to party membership and even greater numbers who voted regularly for SP candidates. Under Frank O'Hare's leadership, Oklahoma became a bastion of socialist strength, with more members per capita then any other state.

In 1911, the O'Hare's moved to St. Louis to revive a moribund socialist monthly tabloid, the *National Rip-Saw*. The paper began to feature original muckraking articles on the exploitation of workers, humorous essays, and columns by the party's leading lights. Frank eschewed public speaking to oversee the *Rip-Saw* and the career of Kate O'Hare, who had become second only to perennial SP standard bearer Eugene Debs as a drawing card on the booming socialist lecture circuit. He sent his wife out on a punishing schedule of speaking engagements paid for by party locals with subscriptions to the tabloid, leaving him in charge of their four children for much of the time. After Debs joined the *Rip-Saw*, Frank O'Hare put the aging working-class hero on a schedule similar to his wife's, thus bringing relations to a boil with the two people he admired most in the movement. O'Hare did not hesitate to wield the editor's blue pencil (even on Debs's copy) to keep the paper neutral on such party controversies as the Barnes sex scandal and the expulsion of members of the Industrial Workers of the World for advocating violence and sabotage (direct action) in strikes. By 1916, the *National Rip-Saw* stood second only to *Appeal to Reason* in circulation among socialist papers.

American participation in World War I created a crisis in the SP with the overwhelming majority of members choosing to resist government mobilization. Frank O'Hare was one of the few party leaders to see that a revolutionary stand by an evolutionary organization in a wartime emergency would bring on a catastrophe. Seeking to spare his family from persecution, he moved them to Florida to participate in a communal scheme, only to have Kate take a high-profile tour of the country. Her principled and outspoken opposition to the war led to arrest and imprisonment after a patently unfair trial. With the SP press shut down by the government, the public came to view Socialists as disloyal. Hoping to counteract the drumbeat of hostility, Frank O'Hare published a newsletter dedicated to publicizing his wife's cause.

Once her sentence had been commuted by President Woodrow Wilson, the O'Hares moved to Girard, Kansas, to restart the *Rip-Saw*, an effort highlighted by a largely successful publicity campaign to embarrass the government into freeing other political prisoners. The Children's Crusade (as they called it) led to the O'Hares' expulsion from the SP because their campaign did not have the advance blessing of party leaders. In the changed atmosphere of the early 1920s, the *Rip-Saw* lost money. To save the tabloid Frank O'Hare renamed it *American Vanguard* and began to publish at New Llano Colony, a socialist commune in Louisiana. He and his wife worked at cross purposes there, with Kate choosing to focus on prison reform and Frank trying to renew his life-long commitment to publicizing socialism. Together they published a series of articles exposing the scandalous conditions in American prisons and the exploitation of prisoners for private profit through sweatshops behind bars. While the campaign led to changes in prison labor, the colony pulled the plug on the *Vanguard,* and Kate O'Hare sued Frank for divorce.

Frank O'Hare returned to St. Louis in 1925, where he lived in poverty for most of 35 years. He worked for Federated Press in New York during the early 1930s and Oscar Ameringer's *American Guardian* later in the decade, but quarrels with his associates led to his dismissal from both concerns. O'Hare contributed to the book review section and the editorial page of the *St. Louis Post-Dispatch* on and off for years. He filled his time corresponding with old comrades and friends from the movement, writing a memoir that went unpublished, and working on fanciful inventions, all of which he failed to patent, since he wished to have nothing to do with the government. A passionate advocate of public housing and transportation, beautification projects, and above all civil rights in the 1950's, O'Hare defied segregation laws in St, Louis, insisting that the monthly civic luncheons he hosted be open to all, including African-Americans, a fitting climax to a lifetime of challenging social and political conventions.

PETER H. BUCKINGHAM

References and Further Reading

Basen, Neil K. "Kate Richards O'Hare: The 'First Lady' of American Socialism, 1901–1917." *Labor History* 21 (spring 1980): 165–199.

Buckingham, Peter H., ed. *Expectations for the Millennium: American Socialist Visions of the Future.* Westport, CT: Greenwood, 2002.

———. *Rebel against Injustice: The Life of Frank P. O'Hare.* Columbia: University of Missouri Press, 1996.

Buhle, Paul. *Marxism in the United States.* New York: Verso, 1991. (revised ed.)

Green, James R. *Grass-Roots Socialism: Radical Movements in the Southwest, 1895–1943.* Baton Rouge: Louisiana State University Press, 1978.

Miller, Sally M., *From Prairie to Prison: The Life of Kate Richards O'Hare.* Columbia: University of Missouri Press, 1993.

National Rip-Saw (continued as *Social Revolution, Social Builder,* and *American Vanguard*). 1911–1917; 1920–1924 (microfilm).

O'Hare, Frank P. "The Oklahoma Vote." *International Socialist Review* 9 (1909): 519–520.

———. Personal Papers. St. Louis: Missouri Historical Society.

———. "The Red Card Organization and State Election Law." *International Socialist Review* 12 (1912): 668–669.

Salvatore, Nick. *Eugene V. Debs, Citizen and Socialist.* Urbana: University of Illinois Press, 1982.

Weinstein, James. *The Decline of Socialism, in America, 1912–1925.* New York: Vintage, 1969.

See also **Debs, Eugene V.; Socialist Party of America; World War I**

OPERATION DIXIE

Operation Dixie was the name given by the Congress of Industrial Organizations (CIO) to the organizing drive that it conducted across 12 southern states from 1947–1953. The CIO made tremendous organizing gains in the 1930s and 1940s, but the South remained an area of low unionization in relation to the industrialized North. Low union density in the South was viewed as a significant problem for unions. Southern workers were generally paid less than their northern counterparts. Unions felt that the continued existence of a low-wage, nonunion region in the United States could lead to the transfer of work from the North to the South. Operation Dixie was conceived to address this issue.

United Mine Workers (UMW) veteran Van Bittner was appointed director of Operation Dixie by CIO president Philip Murray, with Textile Workers' Union of America (TWUA) official George Baldanzi appointed as deputy director. The organizing drive officially lasted until 1953, but it was beset by challenges that in many ways stalled it in its first year of operation. The South was not completely bereft of a union presence, and southern workers had engaged in forms of industrial action prior to Operation Dixie. The 1934 textile strike was an example of such activity. The strike occurred in states outside the South, but it was perhaps more important to the South, since the textile industry was the region's major industry. The strike has been viewed as a failure by various commentators. While hundreds of thousands of southern workers participated in the strike, many of them were blacklisted for strike activity. Indeed many commentators have attributed the reluctance of southern textile workers to unionize during Operation Dixie to memories of what they experienced during the 1934 strike. Southern capitalists were perhaps the most vehemently anti-union employers in the United States, and the pattern of opposition to unions exhibited in the 1934 strike would reoccur during Operation Dixie.

The CIO was run by people from the industrialized northern states, and many of the organizers used in Operation Dixie were from these states. This fact often meant that organizers were unprepared for the social and cultural realities of the South. For example issues of race were perhaps that greatest challenge faced by the CIO organizers. White textile workers showed a willingness to organize but were often opposed to joining a union with African-American workers. Appeals to white racial identity—or whiteness—were an extremely effective method used by southern employers when challenging CIO organizing efforts. Employers produced misleading propaganda materials that implied that the CIO unions had a problack orientation and the threat that this orientation might pose for white workers. African-American workers in the South proved quite receptive to unionizing and joined unions in the face of considerable intimidation from both white workers and employers.

The South, while beset by racial segregation, was also divided by social class. Textile employers often exerted considerable influence over the lives of their workers beyond the workplace. Workers were expected to show a deferential attitude toward mill owners and others in the community who were in positions of authority. Local sheriffs and clergy helped ensure that textile mill owners were able to maintain a dominant position in their communities. Co-operation between mill owners, local politicians, and community leaders, such as the local clergy, proved effective in blunting the effectiveness of Operation Dixie. Northern union organizers were almost universally viewed as Communists, and joining a CIO union could be associated with godlessness.

The Democratic party was dominant in the South, but it was hardly receptive to the labor movement. Unions in the North had often made both organizing and legal gains with the assistance of Democratic legislators, and the labor movement was a key part of the Democratic party in northern states. In the South the party identified itself as being proworker but not necessarily pro-union. This meant that the CIO unions could not be assured of the assistance of Democratic politicians in the South and that they would indeed encounter some opposition from them. Workers in the South identified with the Democratic party, but their interaction with the party was informed by complex cultural and social norms—such as appeals to whiteness—that were not always well-understood in other parts of the United States.

Operation Dixie was also impacted by a number of difficulties within the labor movement itself. American unions, while often perceived by the public as a monolithic entity, were hardly unified in the immediate post-Second World War years. The CIO had been in existence only since 1935, and while it had made great strides with organizing industrial workers, launching Operation Dixie was a major undertaking for the organization. It hoped to organize 1 million southern workers in the first 12 months of Operation Dixie, which was a highly ambitious figure. The CIO was not a single, large, industrial union; it was instead a federation of different unions that had their own organizing functions. Despite this the congress chose to use a centralized organizing structure during Operation Dixie.

The different unions that were part of the CIO and Operation Dixie had similarly differing experiences with the South. Of all of the CIO unions, the stakes were particularly high for TWUA. The TWUA had a presence in the South, and it participated in the 1934 textile strike. The union was aware that the low-wage South was a threat to its membership in the North, and the future viability of the union may have been dependent on the success of organizing southern workers. Other CIO unions supported Operation Dixie, but the immediate futures of these unions were not so closely linked to the success or failure of Operation Dixie as was the future of the TWUA.

The CIO was in competition with the American Federation of Labor (AFL). The AFL had also organized some textile workers in the South, but the federation did not feel that an industrywide campaign was necessarily the best method of organizing in the South. For the CIO the industrywide pattern of bargaining was the objective. The AFL leadership, including AFL President George Meany, was suspicious of the political leanings of CIO union leaders. It was not unusual for AFL leaders to associate the CIO with communism. American employers were well aware of the conflict between the two labor federations, and this unfortunate division in the crucial immediate postwar years contributed to the failure of Operation Dixie.

The CIO unions also had challenges with the message that they were conveying to southern workers. They emphasized the voice that workers could gain in the workplace through union membership, but they did not always suggest that southern workers would receive wages equal to those received by their counterparts in the North. This was perhaps a curious strategy, since workers were usually receptive to the idea that union membership would bring significant economic gains, and unions often emphasized that such gains could be had through unionization. Arguments in favor of workplace democracy and having a voice at work were consequently insufficient inducements to encourage more southern workers to challenge the obstacles that they faced and opt for membership in a CIO union.

While Operation Dixie officially lasted until 1953, its demise was evident by 1947. In that year Congress passed the Taft-Hartley Act. Among its provisions was Section 14b, which enabled individual states to pass right-to-work laws. Florida had passed such a law as early as 1944, but anti-unionism effectively became institutionalized in the South as successive southern states passed right-to-work legislation. The small gains that the TWUA made during the early stages of Operation Dixie were quickly diminished following the passage of Taft-Hartley. The CIO unions increasingly chose to devote organizing resources to states where there was a greater chance of success.

The failure of Operation Dixie had a major, long-term impact on the American labor movement. The South continued to be a low-wage, nonunion region in the years following the end of the organizing drive. Southern states consciously used this low-wage, nonunion status as a method of enticing northern employers to relocate to the South. This process was initially referred to in the South as Balancing Agriculture with Industry (BAWI), and it effectively drew industry to the South. The worst fears of the CIO were confirmed as well-paying, unionized jobs were lost to the southern states. Such unions as the United Auto Workers were ultimately affected by the failure of Operation Dixie, since new auto plants were eventually built in the South as employers, primarily auto manufacturers from other countries, sought to take advantage of the low wages and low union density in southern states.

The fact that the South continued to be a nonunion region meant that the labor movement was effectively constrained to a few states in the north and west. By the end of twentieth century, half of the union members lived in just over half-a-dozen states. The virtual exclusion of the unions from the South meant that they were not really a truly national movement but rather a regionally based movement that claimed a national mandate. This reality can be linked to the failure of Operation Dixie. Operation Dixie, though of relatively short duration, was consequently a moment of high but unrealized ambition for American labor.

JASON RUSSELL

References and Further Reading

Brattain, Michelle. *The Politics of Whiteness: Race, Workers, and Culture in the Modern South*. Princeton, NJ: Princeton University Press, 2001.

Griffith, Barbara S. *The Crisis of American Labor: Operation Dixie and the Defeat of the CIO*. Philadelphia, PA: Temple University Press, 1988.

Minchin, Timothy J. *What Do We Need a Union for? The TWUA in the South, 1945–1955*. Chapel Hill: University of North Carolina Press, 1997.

See also **Congress of Industrial Organizations**

ORDER OF RAILWAY CONDUCTORS
See **Railroad Brotherhoods**

ORDER OF UNITED AMERICAN MECHANICS

Founded in Philadelphia on July 8, 1845, the Order of United American Mechanics (OUAM) mixed trade union activism with moral reform and nativist politics. It sought to protect skilled workers' status and living standards by reinforcing mutual bonds between labor and small business and by combating foreign competition. The OUAM's links to evangelical moral reformers and political nativists undermined opportunities for cross-ethnic alliances among workers in the mid-nineteenth century.

The turn to nativism by American workingmen occurred as immigration from Ireland and Germany increased. In the industrializing cities of New England and the mid-Atlantic, immigrants competed for unskilled jobs in hauling and carting and in the sweatshops that cropped up next to traditional craft enterprises. By the mid-1840s, immigrants comprised a significant voting block in major cities. The OUAM fared best in large cities where sweatshops and immigration had visibly undermined the dominance of native-born craftsmen in work and politics.

The founders of the OUAM came from skilled crafts, such as carpentry and printing. They included several men, such as carpenter George F. Turner, who were active in the nativist American Republican party.

The American Republican party originated in 1843 in response to Catholic efforts to dilute Protestant religious instruction in the public schools. In the summer of 1844, Philadelphia experienced two riots against Irish Catholics. The riots grew out of the school controversy but also played on skilled workers' concerns about the role of immigrants in "deskilling" the textile industry.

American Republicans exploited an anti-Irish backlash to win Philadelphia's 1844 municipal elections. American Republicans, like the later Know Nothing party, wanted to restrict immigrant-voting rights, lengthen the naturalization period, maintain Protestant ascendancy in public education, and otherwise curb the influence of Catholic immigrants in public life. Along with Philadelphia, American Republicans won elections in New York City and Boston, where they allied with the Whig party. American Republicans did best in Philadelphia, where they survived until the late 1840s.

Growing out of this surge in nativism, the OUAM restricted membership to American-born, white males aged 18 and up who belonged to productive trades. Those deemed nonproducers included merchants, bankers, and white-collar professionals. The order rejected foreign-born applicants and encouraged its members to boycott immigrant shops and the products of foreign labor.

Founded at Philadelphia's Jefferson Temperance Hall, the OUAM shared much in common with working-class evangelical reform organizations. Several OUAM founders also belonged to the Washingtonians, a workers' temperance organization that, unlike the more upper-class American Temperance Society, sought to reform hardened drinkers rather than outlaw alcohol entirely. Closely tied to evangelical churches, the Washingtonians and the OUAM tackled workers' insecurity over the decline of skills and living standards by encouraging sober habits and an industrious work ethic. Taking as its motto "honesty, industry, and sobriety," the OUAM penalized members for drinking, Sabbath breaking, patronizing brothels, swearing, and other perceived moral lapses. Members monitored each other's behavior and reported violations. The OUAM included liquor dealers in its category of nonproducers who were barred from membership. It also sponsored lectures and reading rooms for worker education. After the Civil War the OUAM's moral reformism, minus its nativism, found expression in the Knights of Labor.

The OUAM borrowed practices from an earlier nativist secret fraternity, the Society of Red Men, and from the Freemasons, to which several OUAM leaders belonged. The OUAM's initiation ceremony, elaborate rituals, and its sickness and burial plans resembled those of other voluntary societies. In its capacity as a trade union, secrecy helped protect OUAM members from anti-union employers and reinforced the solidarity needed to sustain strikes and boycotts.

Although it occasionally engaged in strikes, the OUAM emphasized the mutual interests between workers and businessmen, especially those uniting the masters of small workshops and skilled mechanics. Rather than conceive of labor as a class arrayed against capital, the OUAM thought of workers as members of a broad producing mass fighting self-seeking parasites who enriched themselves by violating ethical codes in the marketplace and politics. Encouraging members to restrict business to other members, or at the least to native-born businessmen, fit the producerist agenda of securing a fair return for labor and protecting avenues for advancement that would enable wage earners to become independent proprietors in later life.

In 1845, the OUAM spread from Philadelphia to neighboring New Jersey and Delaware. Two years later it appeared in New York City. By 1850, the OUAM had at least 10,000 members in the Philadelphia area and claimed chapters throughout New England and the mid-Atlantic, with a total membership approaching 60,000.

In 1853, the order launched the Junior OUAM as a vehicle for training future members. Other offshoots included the Daughters of America, founded in 1875, and the Loyal Legion, a uniformed auxiliary, established in 1886.

Although never at the forefront of strikes, the OUAM supported turnouts by skilled workers. Among their most successful efforts was an 1853 strike for higher wages staged by 2,000 Baltimore ironworkers. Strikers affiliated with the OUAM staged rallies and organized pickets at those foundries refusing to increase pay. The OUAM chapters in other cities contributed to a strike fund that helped carry the day for Baltimore's iron molders.

The OUAM involvement came at the price of ethnic solidarity. Baltimore's German ironworkers, approximately one-third of the workforce, acted through a separate ethnic association and occasionally clashed with OUAM members. At the city's 1853 elections, temperance candidates who sympathized with the strikers and who practiced the OUAM's brand of moral reform won an upset victory. The next year the OUAM supported the nativist Know Nothing party as it swept to power in Baltimore, Philadelphia, and most other major American cities.

In the mid-1850s, the Know Nothings absorbed the energy of working-class nativists. Shortly thereafter nativism waned as sectionalism and free soil consumed workers' attention. Although the OUAM declined as an effective labor organization, it survived as an organization and overlapped with post-Civil War nativist societies.

FRANK TOWERS

References and Further Reading

Laurie, Bruce. *The Working People of Philadelphia, 1800–1850*. Philadelphia, PA: Temple University Press, 1980.
———. *Artisans into Workers: Labor in Nineteenth-Century America*. New York: Hill and Wang, 1989.
Stevens, Albert C. *The Cyclopedia of Fraternities*. Detroit, MI: Gale Research Company, 1966. (reprint, 1907)

See also **Artisans; Know-Nothing Party**

O'REILLY, LEONORA (FEBRUARY 16, 1870–APRIL 3, 1927)
Working Women's Society, Knights of Labor, and Women's Trade Union League

Leonora O'Reilly grew up in the last quarter of the nineteenth century on the Lower East Side of New York where she developed an activist spirit, became a member of the Socialist party, and dedicated her life to work for radical industrial reform. When O'Reilly was 1-year-old child, her father died. Her mother went to work in a factory, soon joining the Knights of Labor (KOL). At age 11 O'Reilly began working in a shirtwaist factory. In 1886, at 16 years of age, she also joined the KOL, becoming one of a small group of women who organized the Working Women's Society (WWS).

The WWS comprised both working-class and middle-class women seeking to improve the working conditions of laboring women. The members attempted to bridge their cross-class differences even as they focused their energies in different directions. The primary activity of the middle-class members was to educate female consumers and to influence them to buy goods produced by companies that paid their workers a fair wage. The work of the WWS laid the foundation for the National Consumers' League (founded in 1890). O'Reilly and the other working-class women in the WWS directed their efforts toward organizing workers, advancing protective legislation, and supporting strikes. O'Reilly did however take advantage of the educational and cultural opportunities offered by the middle-class members, including joining the Social Reform Club, a group comprising of upper-middle-class radicals who supported the labor movement. In 1894, several of these members, who were also associated with the Henry Street Settlement, offered O'Reilly the opportunity to stop working in the factory for a year to participate in settlement work.

At Henry Street, O'Reilly initiated a vocational skills program that she hoped would help younger girls avoid factory work. She taught girls in the settlement's model shirtwaist factory how to sew a complete garment and operated a cooperative where they could sell their results. The cooperative failed after a short time, unable to compete with the cheaper factory-produced clothing. O'Reilly completed a domestic arts degree at the Brooklyn Pratt Institute in 1900. For the next decade she taught sewing to garment workers, first at the Brooklyn settlement, Asacog House, and then at the Manhattan Trade School for Girls.

O'Reilly also worked to organize female laborers. In 1897, together with some of the Henry Street settlement reformers, she assisted female garment workers in forming the short-lived United Garment Workers' (UGW) Local 16. In 1903, O'Reilly joined the newly formed and American Federation of Labor-(AFL)-affiliated Women's Trade Union League (WTUL) with the hope of continuing her organizing work.

O'Reilly, frustrated by the class tensions that plagued the WTUL throughout its existence, had a tumultuous relationship with the organization. The divisions over goals and strategies between the more conservative middle-class members and the more radical working-class members caused O'Reilly to resign for short periods on several occasions. Her initial dissatisfaction with the organization stemmed from her perception of its middle-class members' patronizing attitude toward female workers. She sought to change this dynamic by recruiting Asacog House reformer Mary Drier and her sister Margaret Drier (Robins) to join the league. Though both women were wealthy, O'Reilly believed they were true supporters of working women and the movement to organize. All three held leadership roles within the WTUL and helped shape its work.

O'Reilly worked earnestly for the WTUL for a dozen years. She served for a time as vice-president of the New York branch under Mary Drier and was one of the league's most dynamic speakers. For a number of years she traveled across the country, speaking for the cause of organized labor almost daily, including a talk at a mass meeting in support of the New York garment workers' strike in December 1909. After 146 workers died in the Triangle Shirtwaist Fire in 1911, O'Reilly served as chairman of the WTUL committee on fire protection, which conducted a study and made recommendations calling for the enactment and enforcement of laws to improve safety conditions in factories. In 1915, she served as the league's delegate to the International Congress of Women (ICW) meeting in The Hague, where she spoke about the experiences of female laborers. After her trip however, O'Reilly became frustrated with the class tensions within the league and with the male-dominated AFL's lack of support for the WTUL and female suffrage. As a result she reduced her involvement with the league.

O'Reilly had long coupled her work within the labor movement with agitations for female suffrage. As a Socialist she believed that giving workingwomen the vote would help to diminish the disparity of economic and political power in society. In 1907, she joined Harriot Stanton Blatch's newly formed

Equality League of Self-Supporting Women, established to persuade workingwomen to support female suffrage. She served as the league's first vice-president. Four years later in 1911, O'Reilly and WTUL colleague Rose Schneiderman organized the Wage-Earners' League for Women Suffrage (WELWS), creating a short-lived suffrage association that was exclusively comprised of workingwomen. O'Reilly served as its president.

While her health remained strong, O'Reilly was active in a number of social and political reform organizations during the early twentieth century. In 1909, she was one of the founders and first committee members of the National Association of Colored People. In 1914, she helped to establish the Industrial Section of the New York Woman Suffrage party as a cross-class alliance dedicated to female suffrage and trade unionism. O'Reilly served as its chair through 1916. The following year she worked for the Irish revolution. In 1919, she again served as the WTUL delegate to the ICW, this time held in Washington DC. During the congress Eleanor Roosevelt invited O'Reilly and the other U.S. delegates to lunch where they impressed Roosevelt with their views on labor reform. When O'Reilly's health began to fail in 1920, she retired from most public activity, though she did teach a course on the theory of the labor movement at the New School for Social Research in 1925.

O'Reilly died of heart disease at the age of 57.

GWEN HOERR JORDAN

References and Further Reading

Orleck, Annelise. *Common Sense and a Little Fire: Women and Working-Class Politics in the United States, 1900–1965.* Chapel Hill: University of North Carolina Press, 1995.

Shively, Charles. "O'Reilly, Leonora." In *Notable American Women, 1607–1950: A Biographical Dictionary*, edited by Edward T. James, Janet Wilson, and Paul S. Boyer. Cambridge, MA: Belknap Press of Harvard University Press, 1971.

Tax, Meredith. *The Rising of the Women: Feminist Solidarity and Class Conflict, 1880–1917.* New York: Monthly Review Press, 1980.

See also **Knights of Labor; National Consumers League; Schneiderman, Rose; Triangle Shirtwaist Fire; Women's Trade Union League**

ORGANIZED CRIME

The term organized crime refers to groups involved in criminal conspiracies marked by their scale of complexity and their length of existence. The term is often used to describe the Italian-American mafia, but it also can refer to various other types of groups with a range of different ethnic backgrounds and types of structures, from outlaw motorcycle gangs to neighborhood street gangs. The nature of organized crime shifted dramatically in the 1920s, as a result of Prohibition and as the criminal gangs that emerged in that era began to assert influence over some union officials. The relationships that emerged between some union officials and organized crime figures were complex combinations of exploitation and cooperation. Certain unions operating in particular economic sectors were particularly prone to suffer from this kind of corruption. Finally the ability of organized crime groups to gain influence over some unions gave crime figures a new source of economic power and facilitated a range of profitable criminal activities.

The history of organized crime begins in the cities of the late 1800s and includes the activities of neighborhood-based street gangs, vice entrepreneurs, and political machines. Street gangs were loosely organized groups based on location and ethnicity. They had a fluid membership and a weak leadership structure. Though street gang members engaged in crime, much of it involved nonutilitarian violence, such as turf battles, whose goal was not profit but to demonstrate the toughness of the gang members. Another limitation of these groups stemmed from the fact that street gang members often moved on to other types of activity as they reached adulthood. Because of their nonprofit-centered focus, some have referred to street gangs as cultural gangs. Vice entrepreneurs in contrast engaged in relatively little violence and instead focused on profit-making crimes. They provided goods and services that were illegal but for which there still remained significant demand. Such victimless crimes, also known as moral crimes, have always been a central economic function of organized crime. Vice entrepreneurs ran houses of prostitution, gambling establishments, or provided illegal substances. They might hire individual members of street gangs for various kinds of tasks, such as debt collection or to work as bouncers, but the role of gang members in these enterprises remained limited. For vice entrepreneurs the main threat to their livelihood came from law enforcement, and so they paid protection to the police and by extension to the machine politicians who controlled the police. Thus this early form of organized crime, sometimes referred to as a syndicate of vice, was dominated by the machine politicians who played the dominant role. Essentially the machine politicians and the police levied an unofficial tax on the illegal activity of the vice entrepreneurs, who made payoffs in order to avoid arrest.

Prohibition (1920–1933) changed the dynamics of organized crime. The Eighteenth Amendment ratified in 1919 and enforced through the Volstead Act passed that same year made the production and sale of alcohol illegal. The law created a huge new illicit market in the United States, and liquor providers, known as bootleggers, proliferated. The profits involved in bootlegging also spurred a great deal of violence as groups and individuals struggled to control local markets in a lucrative business that stood outside existing avenues of legal adjudication. Prohibition created a new economic environment for organized crime.

It was the graduates of the street gangs, such men as Alphonse Capone, Arthur Flegenheimer (also known as Dutch Schultz), and Meyer Lansky, who proved most adept at seizing the opportunities offered by Prohibition. In an era of lawlessness and violence, they were specialists in violence, who created a new type of criminal gang. Unlike the street gang or cultural gang, these new criminal groups were profit-centered with a more permanent membership. Sometimes called entrepreneurial gangs, they strictly controlled nonutilitarian violence and maintained a more formal leadership structure. Ethnic divisions were often blurred; for instance Capone's gang included Jews, Italian-Americans, and even a prominent Welshman, Murray Humphreys, in a leadership position. After dominating the illegal alcohol market by driving out less-violent competitors, entrepreneurial gangs also came to demand protection payments from vice entrepreneurs. Before Prohibition vice entrepreneurs had paid politicians and police to avoid arrest; now they paid criminal gang leaders to avoid being killed. This kind of organized crime arrangement, where an entrepreneurial gang plays the pivotal role, is referred to as a syndicate of power. Violence or the threat of violence now gave the gangster the ability to tax illegal activity.

Capone's gang and others of its type established dominance over illegal activity in the territory that they controlled. The process of taxing and monitoring that illegal activity is referred to as licensing. Individuals engaged in illegal activity, from gambling to supplying illegal substances, cannot go to the police for protection, and so they are vulnerable to extortion by groups with a greater access to violence. But licensing also involves a form of extralegal governance. For instance a criminal gang provides a way to resolve disputes for parties who cannot turn to such conventional resources as the courts. These licensing arrangements can also involve protection from law enforcement. Often an entrepreneurial gang has established more effective relations with the civil authorities, perhaps through more consistent and larger payoffs than an individual illegal entrepreneur can maintain. From the perspective of local law enforcement, it often makes sense to support a kind of long-term working arrangement with a group or an individual who can maintain order among illegal entrepreneurs. Thus someone engaged in illegal activity who seeks to avoid making licensing payments might face legal as well as extralegal punishment.

The Italian-American mafia represents a version of an entrepreneurial gang, and it emerged as a distinctly organized group during this Prohibition Era. The term mafia itself has its origins in Sicily, where it referred in general to a set of values that celebrated manliness and self-reliance. By the mid-1800s, men who were thought to embody those values and who established tightly knit groups of armed followers were known as *mafiosi*. In the lawless environment of Sicily, the *mafiosi* and their followers offered a form of protection and justice to the local population. Out of these groups emerged a secret society organization, the mafia, whose members took an oath of secrecy and pledged loyalty to their leader.

The term mafia began to appear more frequently in the United States at the turn of the twentieth century in Italian-American communities, where immigrants apparently recreated an organization that they had heard about in the old world. This early form of an Italian-American mafia was inward looking and traditionalist in outlook, dominated by conservative, older men, sometimes referred to as "mustache Petes." The opportunities provided by Prohibition helped change the character of this mafia, as a more Americanized generation took leadership positions in the mafia. In New York City for example Charles (Lucky) Luciano assumed control of the mafia after the death of two more traditionalist leaders in what was known as the Castellammarese War (1930–1931). Although born in Sicily, Luciano had come to the United States at the age of 10 and had acculturated to American society far more than previous mafia leaders. He also had strong connections outside the insular world of the Italian immigrant community; one of his closest associates was the Jewish organized crime figure Meyer Lansky.

Luciano changed the structure of the mafia in ways that facilitated profit-making criminal activity. Membership remained restricted to men of Italian descent, but the formal structure he created centered less on a celebration of traditional values and more on the need to avoid disputes and thus increase profits. Each mafia family was divided into several crews, each crew overseen by a *capo* or captain. Individual members of the crew developed a circle of associates and sought out whatever criminal opportunities they could. These members used their mafia status as a way to intimidate potential rivals and victims but also as a source for networks of potential, reliable contacts who could help arrange more complicated schemes. The mafia's structure provided peaceful ways to adjudicate the inevitable disputes that emerged in such schemes and in this way protected their profit-making potential. In exchange a mafia member gave a share of his earnings to his *capo*, who in turn passed some of that share to the boss of the family.

A loose national structure for the mafia provided a way to facilitate even larger schemes. New York had five independent mafia families that co-existed, but in the rest of the country, there was one family per city. A group known as the Commission in New York helped coordinate endeavors involving different families from Cleveland to the East Coast. The Commission provided a peaceful way to adjudicate disputes that arose between families. The family based in Chicago, known as the Outfit, provided the same service for mafia organizations in the rest of the country. Periodically a national conference attended by mafia leaders from across the country would be held to address important issues. New York State Troopers stumbled on one such conference at Apalachin in 1957, and the publicity surrounding their discovery helped fuel public awareness about the mafia.

The mafia and other entrepreneurial gangs became involved in labor racketeering by the late 1920s. In Chicago, New York, and elsewhere some union officials described efforts by gangsters to gain control of their labor organizations through threats of violence. Vulnerable to kidnapping and assassination, with little hope of effective protection from the police, many union officials faced the choice of giving in to such threats or trying to fight back, and fighting back often involved making some kind of arrangement with a rival criminal gang. In Chicago for instance officials from the Teamsters and other unions facing threats from Capone's gang turned for help to another gang run by Roger Touhy. In New York City's garment district, locals in the Amalgamated Clothing Workers' Union made regular payments to a leading Jewish organized crime figure, Louis "Lepke" Buchalter.

But if some union leaders made deals with criminal gangs out of fear, others made arrangements with organized crime groups for more complex reasons. Testimony at criminal trials in the 1940s and much later highlights the ways in which some union officials turned to organized crime figures for support in organizing efforts and aid against political rivals in their own organizations. Roy Williams, president of the Teamsters from 1981–1983, cited many such benefits from his long relationship with the Kansas City *mafioso* Nick Civella. In such cases fear, ambition, respect, and a kind of friendship all might co-exist in a relationship that could span several decades. Perhaps

the best-known example of a union leader with mafia ties was James R. Hoffa, president of the Teamsters' Union from 1957–1971. An illegal FBI wiretap recorded his Detroit mafia contact, Anthony Giacalone, describing Hoffa less in terms of a victim than of an equal partner. "Listen, they ain't nobody sharp enough for Jimmy Hoffa. In this town or any other town. He's going to use everybody, every SOB in the world."

The influence of these organized crime groups has mostly been limited to particular unions in particular sectors of the economy. Typically organized crime has exercised a role in sectors marked by smaller, entrepreneurial firms, where the ease of entry for new firms had often brought fierce competition among the businesses. In these sectors there usually was a long history of corruption and collusion that predated the entry of organized crime. Unions whose jurisdictions cover such sectors suffered disproportionately from problems with corruption. This includes the four national unions, the Teamsters, the Laborers, the Longshoremen, and the Hotel and Restaurant Workers, which the President's Commission on Organized Crime (1983–1986) described as "substantially influenced and/or controlled by organized crime" (President's Commission, *The Edge*, 1986). However local unions operating in such sectors might be controlled by organized crime even if the national union to which they were affiliated maintained sterling reputations for honest, democratic administrations. For example organized crime groups allegedly controlled Local 102 of the International Ladies' Garment Workers' Union (ILGWU) in New York's Garment District even though its parent union championed anticorruption efforts in the American Federation of Labor (AFL).

Organized crime groups benefited in a number of ways from their ability to control some union leaders. Vincent Cafaro, a member of New York's Genovese Crime Family, explained to a Senate Committee in 1988, "We got our money from gambling, but our real power, our real strength came from the unions" (*Organized Crime 25 Years After Valachi,* 1988). In particular industries, such as construction or the garment trades, mafia control over some of the strategic unions gave organized crime figures an important economic niche. Companies with mafia connections could reap a number of competitive advantages by avoiding certain union restrictions. Or with mafia guidance, the unions could be used to enforce cartel arrangements that reserved the most lucrative business opportunities for certain companies. In New York in the 1980s, for example, a group of contractors with mafia ties monopolized concrete construction work worth $2 million–$15 million. Mafia-controlled union leaders ensured that if an outside company tried to take on one of those jobs, it would suffer a range of crippling labor problems.

In addition organized crime groups found other ways to profit from their ability to control some union leaders. Sometimes union officials were required to pass on a share of their salaries to a mafia leader. In other cases money was drained out of union treasuries through a variety of devices, from no-show union jobs to padded bills and fake expense vouchers. New opportunities emerged with the proliferation of union pension plans and health benefits in the post-World War II Era. The ability to influence the management of those funds gave organized crime groups access both to new sources of revenue and potential investment capital. For instance the Teamsters' Union Central States Pension Fund made loans to individuals with mafia connections, and those individuals in turn gave mafia figures a share of the profits from their businesses. In one example money was skimmed from the daily take of several Las Vegas casinos that were built on the basis of such arrangements with Central States' Pension Fund loans.

DAVID WITWER

References and Further Reading

Abidinsky, Howard. *Organized Crime.* Chicago: Nelson-Hall Publishers, 1994.

Block, Alan. *East Side-West Side: Organizing Crime in New York, 1930–1950.* Swansea, Wales: University College of Cardiff, 1980.

Cohen, Andrew Wender. *The Racketeer's Progress: Chicago and the Struggle for the Modern American Economy, 1900–1940.* New York: Cambridge University Press, 2004.

Haller, Mark. "Illegal Enterprise: A Theoretical and Historical Interpretation." *Criminology* 28 (May 1990): 207–235.

Nelli, Humbert S. *The Business of Crime: Italians and Syndicate Crime in the United States.* New York: Oxford University Press, 1976.

New York State Organized Crime Task Force. *Corruption and Racketeering in the New York City Construction Industry: The Final Report.* New York: New York University Press, 1990.

President's Commission on Organized Crime. *The Edge: Organized Crime, Business, and Labor Unions.* Washington, DC: U.S. Government Printing Agency, 1986.

Reuter, Peter. *Racketeering in Legitimate Industries.* Washington, DC: Rand, 1987.

U.S. Senate, Permanent Subcommittee on Investigations. *Twenty-Five Years after Valachi.* Washington, DC: U.S. Government Printing Office, 1988.

Witwer, David. *Corruption and Reform in the Teamsters Union.* Chicago: University of Illinois Press, 2003.

———. "The Scandal of George Scalise: A Case Study in the Rise of Labor Racketeering in the 1930s." *Journal of Social History* 36, 4 (summer 2003): 917–940.

See also **International Brotherhood of Teamsters; McClellan Committee Hearings; Racketeering and RICO**

O'SULLIVAN, MARY KENNEY (1864–1943)
Cofounder, Women's Trade Union League

Mary Kenney O'Sullivan, a bookbinder, was the first female organizer for the American Federation of Labor (AFL), cofounder of the Women's Trade Union League (WTUL), and a factory inspector. O'Sullivan was born in Hannibal, Missouri, on January 8, 1864, the daughter of Irish immigrants, Michael Kenney, a railroad machinist, and Mary Kelly. She left school after the fourth grade and went to work as a dressmaker's apprentice. When she was 14, her father died, leaving O'Sullivan responsible for her invalid mother. She found work in a bookbindery, supporting both herself and her mother the next several years as they moved from Hannibal to Keokuk, Iowa, eventually settling in Chicago in the late 1880s.

In her unpublished autobiography, O'Sullivan makes clear her growing frustration with the conditions of labor faced by working women at the end of the nineteenth century. As in many skilled trades, improvements in technology allowed for the increased mechanization of bookbinding, thus increasing the employment of women. But like many women, as O'Sullivan became more skilled at her craft, she chafed at being relegated to the lesser skilled, lower paid jobs reserved for female employees in bookbinderies. Hoping to improve working conditions, O'Sullivan turned to trade unionism. She joined the Women's Federal Labor Union No. 2703, an AFL affiliate and was elected to the Chicago Trades and Labor Assembly. But there, too, O'Sullivan was frustrated as she confronted time and time again the ambivalence of many male trade unionists regarding the involvement of female workers in organized labor. Many male labor leaders advocated a family wage, claiming at the same time that women's increased participation in the workforce at lower wages drove down wages for all. But O'Sullivan knew that as the sole support of herself and her mother she was hardly atypical. She increasingly saw trade unionism for women as the remedy, arguing that the benefits of improved working conditions and higher wages for women could only improve conditions and wages for all workers.

However around 1890, when she formed the Women's Book Bindery Union No. 1, O'Sullivan found her greatest support in Chicago's growing social-reform community. A lifelong advocate of temperance, O'Sullivan was dismayed that the only place she could initially find to hold meetings for her fledging union was above a Chicago saloon. Jane Addams, cofounder of Chicago's legendary settlement

Hull-House, offered the young organizer meeting space as well as the money to print the first notices. Soon O'Sullivan and her mother moved into Hull-House, joining other working- and middle-class women in a cooperative housing venture known as the Jane Club. Within this supportive environment, she expanded her organizing efforts to include female garment makers as well as female bookbinders.

She soon came to the attention of AFL President Samuel Gompers, and in 1892 he hired O'Sullivan as the first female organizer for the AFL. After first organizing female collar makers in Troy, New York, she spent several months in Boston, Massachusetts, where she organized women in the shoe and garment industries and in the bookbinding trade. In Boston, as she had in Chicago, O'Sullivan quickly formed alliances with the male-dominated trade union movement, speaking before that city's Central Labor Union. She also found much support within the city's social reform community, particularly at Denison House, part of the College Settlement Association. Despite her commitment to trade unionism for women, O'Sullivan was nonetheless increasingly frustrated in her efforts to organize women. Social constraints of the day that deemed such activity as inappropriate hampered her work as did the continued ambivalence of many male labor leaders, and she was disappointed at the numbers of women she was able to organize. The AFL was disappointed, too, and 6 months after appointing her, decided it was not cost-effective to keep a female organizer in the field. O'Sullivan returned to Hull-House in Chicago and worked with social reformer Florence Kelley to secure passage of the 1893 Illinois Factory Bill that regulated the employment of women and children. Her 1894 marriage to local labor organizer and *Boston Globe* labor editor John O'Sullivan brought her back to Boston. Together the O'Sullivans had four children, one of whom died in infancy, and were active members in the Boston labor scene. O'Sullivan continued to focus on the organization of women and expanded her connections within the city's social-reform community, using both Denison House and the Women's Educational and Industrial Union, founded by middle- and upper-class women in 1878 to assist working women, as her bases of operation. Throughout the 1890s, O'Sullivan organized female shoe workers, garment workers, and weavers. However when her husband died in 1902, O'Sullivan had to support herself and her three young children, and she found work as the manager of a model tenement in Boston and as the director of a girls' summer camp sponsored by Denison House.

Even without the critical support of her husband, O'Sullivan was still determined to organize female workers into viable trade unions. In 1903, she and

several others came together at the annual AFL convention, held that year in Boston, and formed the WTUL, a cross-class alliance of trade unionists and social-reform workers, both men and women. The WTUL's stated mission was to organize female workers into existing trade unions, advocate for protective labor legislation, and provide education for female workers. Soon branches were established in Boston, New York, and Chicago. In its early years, O'Sullivan was secretary and vice-president of the National WTUL as well as a leader in the Boston branch. However this cross-class alliance was fraught with turmoil from the beginning, and O'Sullivan was soon dismayed both by the ever-present class tensions between the middle- and upper-class female allies and the working-class women and by the continued refusal of the AFL officially to recognize the WTUL. O'Sullivan resigned from the WTUL, primarily in response to that organization's refusal to support the 1912 Lawrence textile strike because the AFL had not sanctioned it. Two years later she became one of five female factory inspectors for the newly created Massachusetts Board of Labor and Industries, a post she held until 1934. She died on January 18, 1943 after a lifetime of working to improve the conditions of life and labor for workingwomen such as herself.

KATHLEEN BANKS NUTTER

Selected Works

Nutter, Kathleen Banks. *The Necessity of Organization: Mary Kenney O'Sullivan and Trade Unionism for Women, 1892–1912*. New York: Garland Press, 2001.
O'Sullivan, Mary Kenney. Unpublished autobiography. Boston, MA: Records of the National Women's Trade Union League, Schlesinger Library, Radcliffe College.

See also **Addams, Jane; American Federation of Labor; Gompers, Samuel; Hull-House Settlement; Kelley, Florence; Lawrence Strike (1912); Women's Trade Union League**

OWEN, ROBERT DALE (1801–1877)
Worker's Rights Activist and Abolitionist

Born in 1801, in Glasgow, Scotland, Robert Dale Owen was the eldest son of noted Welsh textile magnate and social reformer Robert Owen, whose passion and originality regarding the uplift of the emerging industrial working class strongly influenced Robert Dale Owen's life and career. Educated at the New Lanark School his father had founded, as well as by private tutors, Owen completed his education with 4 years of college-level work at the progressive school of Philipp Emanuel von Fellenberg in Hofwyl, Switzerland. He later credited his educational experiences at New Lanark and in Hofwyl for impressing on him the importance of education to any program of social reform.

Owen spent most of his adult life after 1825 in the United States and involved himself in political, communitarian, abolitionist, and other efforts to bring about reforms to capitalism and to ameliorate the harm it wrought on industrial workers. Owen was a leader of the Working Men's party in New York, an early feminist, a Democratic member of Congress, a diplomat, and an abolitionist. Owen largely retired from public life after the Civil War and died at his summer home in Lake George, New York, a year and 1 day after his second marriage.

Owen immigrated to the United States in 1825 and immediately began his career as an American reformer by helping his father create the Utopian community of New Harmony, Indiana. This communitarian experiment in cooperative production was based on the elder Owen's theories and experiences at New Lanark. New Harmony, only one of literally hundreds of such ventures during the nineteenth century, lasted until 1827, when it failed. At New Harmony Owen once again taught school, edited the *New Harmony Gazette*, and met the reformer and freethinker Frances Wright, with whom he enjoyed a close personal and professional partnership for some 10 years. After New Harmony Owen journeyed to Wright's Nashoba community, a Utopian experiment near Memphis, Tennessee, dedicated to racial equality and the emancipation of slaves. Following a brief return to Europe and a stint in New Harmony, Owen followed Wright to New York City and became the editor of the *Free Enquirer*, an anticlerical, freethinking journal that he ran from 1828 to 1832. Like his father Owen had long disavowed religion; now, he argued against the institutions of church and marriage and in his book *Moral Physiology* promoted contraception, both as a way to relieve poverty and a means for the emancipation of women. Needless to say Owen became a *bête noire* of the conservative, evangelical establishment of the period.

Along with Wright, Owen soon became an intellectual leader of one faction of the Working Men's party of New York, through which he pressed his "state guardianship" plan for public education. In contrast to party founder Thomas Skidmore, who advocated radical measures to redistribute property, Owen urged the establishment of free boarding schools modeled after Hofwyl, where children of all classes would be educated in an atmosphere of social equality.

In addition to instruction in reading, writing, mathematics, history, and the like, Owen proposed that all students be trained in agriculture and a useful trade. This, Owen believed, would yield in the students an understanding of the dignity of labor and a reduction in class stratification. After the elections of 1829, when the Working Men won several races, Owen joined forces with two former Tammany Hall politicos, Noah Cook and Henry Guyon, to form an alliance that forced Skidmore out of the party. Much to Owen's chagrin, Cook and Guyon soon turned on him and ejected him from the party in 1830. This marked the end of Owen's participation in radical labor politics.

After a short stay in Europe, Owen returned to New Harmony, now a midwestern town rather than a Utopia, married, and began a reformist political career that lasted through the Civil War. Owen served three terms in the Indiana General Assembly, from 1835 to 1838, where he managed to secure increased funding for the state's public schools. After two unsuccessful campaigns, in 1842 he was elected to the U.S. House of Representatives as a Democrat and served in Congress from 1843 to 1847. While in Washington he drafted the bill for the founding of the Smithsonian Institution, and as a member of its organizing committee, he insisted that the institution engage in public education as well as scientific research. Elected to the Indiana Constitutional Convention in 1850, Owen played a key role in securing property rights for married women and widows and in the adoption of a common public school system. Returned to the Indiana Assembly in 1851, Owen introduced and succeeded in passing a state law liberalizing divorce in Indiana. In 1853, President Franklin Pierce appointed Owen as U.S. *chargé d'affaires* to the Kingdom of Naples.

After leaving that post and returning to the United States in 1858, Owen again took up the cause of working people and became a leading proponent of the abolition of slavery. His September 17, 1862, letter on the subject to Abraham Lincoln was credited by Treasury Secretary Salmon Chase as a key influence on the president's evolving thinking toward emancipation, which came a few days later. In 1863, Secretary of War Edwin Stanton appointed Owen chairman of the American Freedman's Inquiry Commission to investigate and report on the condition and prospects of the newly freed slaves. Owen's book, *The Wrong of Slavery*, was one result of that work. Though an abolitionist, Owen urged only gradual enfranchisement of the freed slaves and a reconstruction effort led by military officers that foreshadowed congressional reconstruction.

Though not himself a member of the working class, Owen's broad sympathies for the poor and exploited were sincere and deeply felt. His reformist impulses, from advocacy of cooperative production to women's rights and emancipation, were consistently geared toward the amelioration of the living conditions of working people. His ideas regarding public education and feminism were especially prescient, and many of them became mainstream thinking in the decades after his death.

MATTHEW S. R. BEWIG

References and Further Reading

Hugins, Walter. *Jacksonian Democracy and the Working Class*. Stanford, CA: Stanford University Press, 1960.
Leopold, Richard William. *Robert Dale Owen: A Biography*. Cambridge, MA: Harvard University Press, 1940.
Owen, Robert Dale. *Threading My Way*. London, UK: Trubner, 1874.
———. *The Wrong of Slavery*. Philadelphia, PA: Lippincott, 1864.
———. *Emancipation Is Peace*. New York: 1863.
———. *Moral Physiology*. New York: 1830.
———. *Popular Tracts*. New York: 1830.
Owen, Robert Dale, and Horace Greeley. *Divorce: Being a Correspondence between Horace Greeley and Robert Dale Owen*. New York: 1860.
Pancoast, Elinor, and Anne E. Lincoln. *The Incorrigible Idealist: Robert Dale Owen in America*. Bloomington, IN: Principia Press, 1940.
Pessen, Edward. *Most Uncommon Jacksonians*. Albany: State University of New York Press, 1967.
Schlesinger, Arthur M., Jr. *The Age of Jackson*. Boston, MA: Little, Brown, 1945.
Wilentz, Sean. *Chants Democratic*. New York: Oxford University Press, 1984.

OXNARD STRIKE (1903)

The Oxnard Strike of 1903 was the first successful agricultural strike in southern California and was organized by the first biracial union in the state, the Japanese-Mexican Labor Association (JMLA). Following the strike the JMLA petitioned the American Federation of Labor (AFL) for a charter. The AFL issued the charter but forbade the union from admitting Asians. Refusing to join the AFL without their Japanese allies, the Mexican branch of the JMLA was denied AFL institutional support and soon disintegrated. Consequently the Oxnard Strike highlights the correlation between race and class in southern California's agricultural production, provides a window into European-Americans' distinct racial attitudes toward Japanese and Mexicans, and demonstrates that racial discrimination could divide workers within the American labor movement.

The town of Oxnard lies within Ventura County and was named after the entrepreneurs who established the American Beet Sugar Company (ABSC)

in 1898 and the Bank of Oxnard (1899), which loaned money to growers producing beets for the ABSC. Drawing first on Chinese and due to the Chinese Exclusion Act (1882), numerous Japanese and Mexican laborers, the ABSC refined nearly 200,000 tons of beets in 1903. Paralleling the rise of the beet industry was a class structure in which most racial minorities held undesirable occupations and earned little remuneration. Within Ventura County Euro-Americans owned 95% of the farms and held the highest paying labor positions; they were the only permanent workers within the sugar factory and tended to work as department heads, supervisors, and personal staff. Meanwhile 50% of Japanese and Mexicans and 65% of Chinese worked as farmhands, while another 18%–33% of these minorities worked as unskilled-laborers. Residential patterns further divided the lives of most Euro-Americans from racial minorities. Within Oxnard, Japanese and Mexicans tended to live in ethnic enclaves on the east side of town while German and Irish farmers and Jewish families lived on the west side. However while most minorities worked as laborers, a small but influential number of minorities were middle-class. Some of these minorities worked as labor contractors, obtaining workers for growers. In return for their services, minority contractors received a portion of their workforce's wages and thus profited from minority labor. Yet as a result of ethnoracial affinities, racial discrimination, residential separation, the correlation between contractors' and laborers' wages, and perhaps the influence of the Japanese Socialist Movement, minority contractors often demanded high rates of pay for their workforces.

Responding to these circumstances, the Bank of Oxnard, Bank of A. Levy, and the ABSC, organized the Western Agricultural Contracting Company (WACC) in 1902. Working with growers seeking to undercut minority contractors, by February of 1903, the WACC controlled 90% of the local labor contracts, reduced minority contractors' commissions, prevented contractors from negotiating directly with farmers, and required minority laborers to pay the WACC a contracting fee. In order to manage their diverse workforce, the WACC created a Japanese department under Inosuke Inose, a former contractor who managed a WACC affiliated store and held stock in the ABSC; and a Mexican department under Albert Espinosa, a skilled beet worker.

On February 11, 1903, roughly 500 Japanese and 200 Mexicans convened to form the JMLA. Composed of contractors, laborers, and Japanese students working as temporary laborers, the JMLA represented three segments of the agricultural workforce united against the WACC. Led by President Baba Kozaburo (a former labor contractor ousted by the WACC); secretary of the Japanese branch, Y. Yamaguchi (a boarding student recruited from San Francisco); and secretary of the Mexican branch, J. M. Lizarras (perhaps a former labor contractor), the JMLA represented its biracial membership through its two branches, attention to linguistic needs (union meetings were multilingual), and creation of solidarity symbols (the union's emblem depicted a rising red sun, a pair of clasped hands, and the initials JMLA). Seeking to unseat the WACC, to bargain with farmers directly, and to raise wages, the JMLA agreed to stop working through the WACC and thus went on strike. By March hundreds of WACC laborers had defected to the JMLA, raising its membership to 1,200, about 90% of the agricultural workforce.

During the third week of March, the WACC facilitated the creation of a competing minority union, the Independent Agricultural Labor Union (IALU), which claimed to seek a congruent relationship between employers and employees. The IALU's board of directors included Inose and other influential Japanese residents who remained aligned with the WACC. Local newspapers, such as the *Daily Democrat,* commended the new union. To the JMLA's disdain, the IALU began recruiting workers on behalf of growers. Tensions erupted on March 23 when a group of JMLA workers attempted to place their union's emblem on an IALU caravan. Immediately after shots were fired from several directions, two Japanese and two Mexicans were hit; one Mexican, Luis Vasquez, was killed. Most local newspapers blamed the shooting on the JMLA. The *Los Angeles Times* suggested that Mexicans were the principal perpetrators of the violence. The JMLA issued a statement to the press claiming they had not been armed during the altercation, that WACC laborers were armed by local hardware stores, that no JMLA member had been arrested, and critiqued the police for failing to arrest the shooters. Only the Oxnard *Courier* and the *Los Angeles Herald* printed the statement; the *Times* refused.

After the shooting a Euro-American ranch owner was arrested for Vasquez's murder, tried, and after 2 days of contradictory testimonies, cleared of any wrongdoing. Incensed the JMLA's strike turned militant. The JMLA unionists intimidated non-JMLA laborers and aggressively recruited others. By the end of March, the WACC, local growers, and the JMLA agreed to negotiate. Given the strength of the JMLA (their membership stood at 1,300; the WACC's at 60), after only a few days of debate, the JMLA gained control of over 5,000 acres of farmland, secured the right to negotiate with farmers directly, and obtained a minimum wage of $5.00 per acre of beets (nearly double the WACC wage). On March 30, the strike ended. About 2 months later, Lizarras appealed to the AFL for a charter, inviting the most influential union in the United States to take a position on minority unionists. The AFL President Samuel Gompers granted the charter but stipulated that the union could not admit Asians. On June 8, the Mexican branch of the JMLA rejected the AFL's racialist offer, exalted Japanese unionists, and stated they would accept only a racially inclusive charter committed to the abolition of racial discrimination. The Mexican branch never received this charter, and the JMLA later dissolved.

JOHN H. FLORES

References and Further Reading

Almaguar, Tomas. *Racial Fault Lines: The Historical Origins of White Supremacy in California.* Berkeley: University of California Press, 1994.
———. "Racial Domination and Class Conflict in Capitalist Agriculture: The Oxnard Sugar Workers' Strike of 1903." *Labor History* 25, 3 (1984). Reprinted in *Working People of California,* edited by Daniel Cornford. Berkeley: University of California Press, 1995.
Gomez-Quinones, Juan. "The First Steps: Chicano Labor Conflict and Organizing 1900–1920." *Aztlan: Chicano Journal of the Social Sciences and Arts* 3 (1972): 13–49.
Ichioka, Yuji. *The Issei: The World of the First-Generation Japanese Immigrants, 1885–1924.* New York: The Free Press, 1988.
Yoneda, Karl. "100 Years of Japanese Labor History in the USA." In *Roots: An Asian American Reader.* Amy Tachiki, Eddie Wong, and Franklin Odo, eds. Los Angeles: The Regents of the University of California, 1971.

See also **American Federation of Labor; Chinese Exclusion Acts**

P

P-9 STRIKE

The pronounced downward slide of the U.S. labor movement that began with Ronald Reagan's firing of more than 10,000 striking members of the Professional Air Traffic Controllers Organization (PATCO) in the summer of 1981 has continued unabated for more than a quarter century. Declining in size, density, and influence, unions have appeared powerless to resist corporate decisions to close factories, outsource work, eliminate jobs, rewrite job descriptions, renege on pension commitments, increase workers' shares of health-care costs, slash wages, and more (or is it less?). Strikes have almost disappeared as an expression of workers' power, while unions' political clout is dismissed by Democrats and Republicans alike.

Alongside the PATCO disaster, for many commentators, the Austin, Minnesota, Hormel strike of 1985–1986 has come to symbolize these developments. In 1991, Barbara Koppel's film *American Dream* won the "Best Documentary" Academy Award, cementing the strike's iconic status. It told the story of how 1,700 workers, employed in a state-of-the-art plant by a profitable corporation untouched by foreign competition, were backed against a wall. Their refusal to knuckle under to their employer's demands for concessions led to a prolonged strike. When Hormel chose to re-open five months into the strike and the governor of Minnesota (a "prolabor" Democrat) sent in the National Guard to breech the picket lines, the strike was broken. Faithful union members lost their jobs, their cars, their homes, even their families.

While this is all some commentators and filmmakers might see—or want audiences to see and students to learn—there was much more to the P-9 Strike that earns it its place in labor history. In the midst of the management push for concessions, what we can now recognize as the first stage of the corporate neoliberal agenda, Hormel workers, members of United Food and Commercial Workers Union (UFCW) Local P-9 ("P" for "Packinghouse"), their families, and their supporters offered an embodiment of resistance, a living, breathing vision of a democratically controlled union, driven by its members, with a passionate commitment to justice, and a willingness to explore new, creative strategies and tactics. Inspired by their example, more than 3,000 local unions sent aid to P-9 and tens of thousands of activists made pilgrimages to Austin.

After having co-operated with Hormel management's demands for new job descriptions, payment systems, and chain speeds as the price for getting a new plant built in Austin in the late 1970s to early 1980s, P-9 members rediscovered their historical roots as the Independent Union of All Workers of the 1930s and drew their line in the sand when they were asked to accept a 23% pay cut. "If not now, when? If not here, where? If not us, who?" they asked. They reached out to their fellow meatpackers at seven other Hormel plants scattered around the country, they called on workers in other industries to support their campaign to bring labor solidarity and financial pressure (via a strategy developed by Ray Rogers and his Corporate Campaign, Inc.) to bear on Hormel, and they called on each other to stand firm. Some became traveling speakers (the so-called road warriors), visiting unions, schools, and community organizations from coast to coast. Others made Christmas toys, wrote songs and poems, painted murals, walked miles on picket lines, and joined protests at other factories, in other communities, even in other countries. They found a stunning variety of ways to tell their stories, express their struggle for justice, and seek connection with other workers facing similar challenges.

And through it all, they learned about political economy, labor history, power, and most of all, about themselves.

Inspired by the P-9ers' examples, thousands of workers sent money, visited Austin, and committed to a boycott of Hormel products and the financial institutions that bankrolled the company. In 33 cities, they organized themselves into support committees. At some times, in some places, their networks of support were mobilized to help other workers in addition to the Hormel strikers. And at some times, in some places, encouraged by the Hormel strikers' example and emboldened by their new networks, they stood up to their own employers' demands for concessions and their own unions' insistence that resistance was futile. Rank-and-file militancy spread within many unions, taking a variety of forms—caucuses, election slates for local, even national, offices, new publications, and alliances with workers in other unions.

The United Food and Commercial Workers' national union leadership deepened its opposition to Local P-9 and its struggle. It urged meatpackers around the country to accept the necessity for a "controlled retreat," and as P-9's movement grew, so did the UFCW's determination that it had to nip this movement in the bud. It insisted that workers at other Hormel plants had to continue to work in the face of P-9's requests that they engage in sympathy strikes; they opposed the boycott of Hormel products; they urged unions that wanted to send aid to the strikers to send it to the national union rather than directly to the local or through one of the support committees; they did not organize political pressure on the governor of Minnesota when he began to consider sending in the National Guard. Finally, they put Local P-9 in trusteeship and called the strike off. Most important, they had signaled to Hormel from the outset of the conflict that if it could just outlast the local union, it would get to deal directly with the national union. With the support of other national union bureaucracies that also feared the threats posed by oppositional movements within their own organizations, the UFCW was able to strangle the movement that Local P-9 represented.

The defeat had high costs—the loss of jobs, pensions, homes, cars, and even families. But even in defeat, the P-9 strikers, the more than a thousand who had held firm, and their many supporters had written a chapter in labor history whose importance becomes clearer and clearer the more time passes. They demonstrated that the course of economic neoliberalism, with its skyrocketing inequality, terrifying insecurity, and competitive individualism, did not have to emerge out of Ronald Reagan's America. They showed that rank-and-file workers could run a democratic union; build a movement culture and a network of solidarity; threaten entrenched power in corporate boardrooms, state capitols, and union bureaucracies; educate themselves about the place of workingwomen and workingmen in U.S. history; and transform themselves into human beings for whom the idea that "an injury to one is an injury to all" could become a watchword for everyday life, even in the United States.

PETER RACHLEFF

References and Further Reading

Brecher, Jeremy, and Tim Costello, eds. *Building Bridges: The Emerging Grassroots Coalition of Labor and Community*. New York: Monthly Review Press, 1990.
Green, Hardy. *On Strike at Hormel*. Philadelphia: Temple University Press, 1990.
LaBotz, Dan, ed. *A Troublemakers' Handbook*. Second edition. Detroit: Labor Notes, 2005.
Lynd, Staughton. *Solidarity Unionism*. Chicago: Charles H. Kerr, 1992.
Rachleff, Peter. *Hard-Pressed in the Heartland: The Hormel Strike and the Future of the Labor Movement*. Boston: South End Press, 1993.
Slaughter, Jane. *Concessions and How to Beat Them*. Detroit: Labor Notes, 1983.

See also **Independent Union of All Workers**

PACIFIC NORTHWEST

Work life in the Pacific Northwest in the nineteenth and early twentieth centuries was shaped by an economy based primarily on the production of a few basic commodities, geographical isolation from distant markets, and an enormous land area inhabited by a comparatively small non-Indian population that tended to concentrate its residence in a handful of urban areas. Even the largest population center, Portland, until surpassed by Seattle in 1910, was exceedingly small in comparison to San Francisco, Saint Louis, or Chicago. In 1880, at the beginning of a chaotic decade that witnessed dramatic expansion of the Pacific Northwest economy and the rising prominence of organized labor, Portland could boast of

8,000 residents (on a good day). That number compared to 149,000 residents for San Francisco, 299,000 for Chicago, and 310,000 for Saint Louis. In fact, the entire Pacific Northwest—Oregon, Washington, and Idaho combined—in 1880 had a population of just 282,000, or fewer people than resided in either Chicago or Saint Louis. It is little wonder that during its formative years, organized labor in the Pacific Northwest often marched to a different beat, one that might appear jarringly out of step with national trends and leadership.

Until completion of a northern transcontinental railroad in 1883 at last made long-distance travel relatively easy, the Pacific Northwest remained physically remote from the East Coast and Midwest and chronologically divergent from the nation's mainstream of history. When the nation's founders signed the Declaration of Independence in Philadelphia in July 1776, the Pacific Northwest remained a blank spot on the map of North America. Outsiders knew nothing about its high mountain ranges, dense coastal rain forests, and rolling interior plains. No one living in Europe or along America's East Coast could say whether woolly mammoths might still roam its bunchgrass prairies until the explorers Lewis and Clark entered the region in 1805 after a two-year trip from Saint Louis. Civil War battles had little direct impact on the Pacific Northwest or its sparsely populated landscape, though the region did welcome as new residents numerous refugees fleeing Missouri's own bitter guerrilla warfare.

To reach the Oregon Country during the decades of overland travel by wagon—from the 1840s through the 1860s—required four to six months of hard travel across the prairies and high mountains beyond the Mississippi River. The transcontinental railroad radically redefined the space separating the Pacific Northwest and Chicago or St. Louis to an easy journey of just five or six days, easy at least for affluent passengers easily able to afford a bed in a luxury sleeping car and dinner in the diner.

Driving the Pacific Northwest economy were the products of farm, forest, fishery, and mine. By contrast, local manufacturing, apart from the big-four industries, was of little importance economically. Commodities were god, beginning with the fur trade in the 1780s. Legions of fur traders and trappers revealed some of the treasures that Mother Nature had hidden within the Pacific Northwest, yet their contribution to settlement or economic development of the region was minimal at best. The men who depended wholly on Mother Nature to supply the commodity basic to their economic survival understood clearly that wilderness lands transformed into farms, ranches, and towns doomed any future commerce in furs by forcing trappers and traders to retreat to an ever-shrinking wild domain. Thus, the fur trade belongs to the premodern regional economy that existed before the 1870s and 1880s and development of regional and transcontinental railroad connections.

From the 1880s until the 1930s, most jobs within the region involved harvesting grain and other products of farm and ranch, catching and canning fish, cutting and milling lumber, and digging and processing coal and various metals. Such jobs invariably placed a big premium on physical prowess and mobility and thus encouraged formation of a regional workforce composed to a large degree of itinerant single males who worked in gangs for a daily or weekly wage. The power of human muscle, rather than hard-won proficiency in a craft, was the attribute employers prized most. Most manual laborers acquired the needed dexterity on the job rather than through any formal program of apprenticeship or education. The number of workers engaged in skilled crafts was small by comparison.

It was not uncommon for an army of seasonal workers to follow the grain harvest across the rolling fields of eastern Oregon and Washington in late summer and then migrate to the busy wharves of Seattle and Portland to help load seagoing ships with grain and other commodities. Many men of muscle had no families and no permanent homes, other than the missions, flophouses, and saloons of the large cities in which they often spent the slack winter season. Hardscrabble mining towns and the meager timber camps located deep in the Northwest forests were often as isolated as the region's numerous sheep and cattle ranches, and a large portion of the population was seasonal and transient. Seattle in 1920 ranked at the top of the nation's list of cities of 25,000 or more with the greatest percentage of male residents. No wonder its shame (or badge of distinction) was a large, thriving, and notorious red-light district.

Child labor was never a serious problem in the Pacific Northwest, and that may have been related in part to the preponderance of adult males in the regional workforce, men who did not hesitate to prove their masculinity in a barroom brawl but feared and loathed the power of employers to reduce their wages by any number of tricks, including hiring child labor. Because the region's first intense phase of industrial development dated only from the 1880s, well after the East Coast and Midwest had begun flexing their bulging industrial muscle, organized workers and their territorial and state legislators were able to anticipate and address perceived mistakes made in the older states—but only to a limited degree and because so much work in the Pacific Northwest required far more muscle than children possessed. Even with child labor laws and a few other basic labor regulations in place, life on the job in the Pacific Northwest was no better, and in some cases much worse, than in the states that industrialized earlier. Logging and mining, along with railroading, were three of the most dangerous industries anywhere—"more dangerous than war" was the way one scholar described the appalling rate of accidents and death in the Northwest timber industry.

A primary exception to a regional work life dominated by muscular and mobile males was the highly seasonal canning industry. During the summer fruit and vegetable harvest, the numerous canneries of the Willamette, Hood, Walla Walla, Yakima, and Wenatchee river valleys employed large numbers of women—workers prized less for their muscle power than for their manual dexterity and short-term availability. The same pattern defined the seasonal cannery work on the Columbia River, Pacific Coast, and Puget Sound required to process each year's salmon catch. Again, these jobs required mainly manual dexterity and seasonal availability. The region's early seafood canneries also employed Chinese males, who, beginning in the 1880s, were systematically excluded from jobs in most other Northwest industries.

The racial and ethnic composition of the Pacific Northwest workforce tended to fluctuate over time. Violent protests by Euro-American workers affiliated with the Knights of Labor in the 1880s dramatically reduced the number of Chinese males employed in Northwest industries. Many left the region to return to China or to seek a more congenial job climate in California, though some remained in domestic service or to grow plots of vegetables for sale to local purchasers. In the 1890s, Japanese workers migrated to the Northwest and found employment as maintenance-of-way workers on railroads, among other industrial jobs. Industrial workers in the twentieth century included immigrants from the Philippines and Mexico. Many of the first African-American workers in the Pacific Northwest were recruited from the East and Midwest as strikebreakers in coal camps that once dotted the foothills of the Cascades east of Seattle and Tacoma. As such, they often had to endure an ugly mix of racial prejudice and economic rage from Euro-American workers they displaced.

Organized labor in the Pacific Northwest tended to mirror the peculiarities and prejudices of the local workforce. Labor unions among locomotive engineers and other skilled workers dated back to the 1860s, but for the next two decades, they remained weak and confined largely to the region's relatively small number of skilled workers, if they survived at all.

The decade of the 1880s witnessed the first large-scale unionization of workers in the Pacific Northwest. For a time, the Knights of Labor grew powerful and prominent, especially in the cities of Portland, Tacoma, Seattle, and Spokane. The local Knights built their imposing edifice primarily from the rotted timber of anti-Chinese prejudice. In mid-decade, the Knights' regional leaders (who belonged to a secret West Coast radical organization) carefully orchestrated a campaign of violence that drove nearly a thousand Chinese residents out of Tacoma. It is unlikely that a single person of Chinese ancestry remained behind. The Knights sought, but failed, to do likewise in Seattle and Portland. Apart from their success in Tacoma and some of the outlying coal camps, the local Knights generated mostly bad publicity for themselves.

Out of the wreckage of the Knights of Labor's debacle in the 1880s derived, nonetheless, some enduring features of the Northwest labor movement. Foremost was long-term bias against Asian workers. Second, and perhaps paradoxically, was a strain of economic and social idealism that influenced Northwest politics for decades—at least through the 1930s. In a related way, some disappointed but yet idealistic labor activists formed various socialist and anarchist utopian colonies on Puget Sound in the 1880s and 1890s. They believed that by example they could transform an ailing industrial society. Finally, the idea of organizing workers by industry at a time when the newly formed American Federation of Labor (AFL) promoted labor organization by craft remained very popular in the Pacific Northwest and led to numerous philosophical debates, if not outright clashes, among local labor activists.

There clearly was a tie between Knights of Labor idealism and activism in the mining region tributary to Spokane, Washington. In newly established metal mining camps east of Spokane and across the border in the rugged mountains of northern Idaho, conflict between mine labor and owners over wage reductions and worsening working conditions flared into open violence in 1892. In these isolated one-industry towns, as in the camps of the timber industry, conditions of life were harsh and employers ruled with iron-fisted autocracy. In such circumstances, workers sought economic security through exclusion of low-wage Asian labor and union membership and its promise of collective action. When violence in 1892 resulted in the jailing of local union leaders, they used their idle time in prison to organize a new regional union called the Western Federation of Miners. Later it became the International Union of Mine, Mill and Smelter Workers, or the Mine-Mill Union. But even after it merged with the United Steelworkers of America in

1967, many of its members never forgot that the Mine-Mill Union had been "born in jail."

Because the number of craft workers remained low in the Northwest (with its emphasis on commodity production), skilled unions affiliated with the American Federation of Labor effectively ignored a large percentage of the region's workforce. However, various industrial unions emerged from the wreckage of the Knights of Labor to address that need in the early twentieth century. By far, the most famous was the Industrial Workers of the World (IWW), organized in Chicago in 1905 by members of the Western Federation of Miners and other dissident industrial unions and federations.

Shaped by the rough-and-tumble world of commodity producers in the American West, the Industrial Workers of the World openly embraced radical solutions to the perceived ills of society and did not shy away from seeking to organize "the unorganizable"—the itinerant harvest hands, timber and sawmill workers, and any other vulnerable workers who supported its uncompromising mission to radically transform industrial society.

During the years from 1890s until the aftermath of World War I in the early 1920s, the Pacific Northwest witnessed several outbursts of industrial violence that tainted the way many people perceived organized labor. Twice in the 1890s, the Coeur d'Alene mining district of northern Idaho erupted in violence that resulted in military occupation and indiscriminate jailing of union leaders and their sympathizers. A violent postscript to the 1899 violence occurred in late 1905, when Harry Orchard assassinated the former Idaho governor Frank Steunenberg. When captured a few days later, Orchard claimed that top leaders of the Western Federation of Miners had hired him to retaliate for Steunenberg's role in suppressing the 1899 violence. In a celebrated trial in Boise, the Idaho capital, the newly elected senator, William E. Borah, battled with the defense attorney Clarence Darrow. It became such a high-profile media event that even President Theodore Roosevelt weighed in with his opinions. In the end, Darrow won acquittal. Two of the defendants, Charles H. Moyer and George Pettibone, soon faded from public consciousness, but the third, William D. Haywood, who once worked as a metal miner in Silver City, Idaho, remained prominent as the leader of the Industrial Workers of the World, or Wobblies.

Industrial violence next erupted on the streets of Spokane in 1909, when Wobbly protesters engaged in illegal public speaking and were imprisoned. Soon, every train entering the city brought a fresh supply of speakers, and thereby the IWW flooded and overwhelmed the city's jails. They focused their wrath on the dishonest employment agencies in Spokane that found harvest jobs for itinerant workers but colluded with employers to keep a constant stream of workers churning through the system—all for a fee that enriched the agencies and their accomplices on the region's farms and ranches.

The Washington legislature passed a law banning such practices, but it proved weak and poorly enforced. During World War I, the author Zane Grey visited the wheat fields of eastern Washington and wrote a potboiler called *The Desert of Wheat* that pits honest farmers against vile and incendiary Wobblies determined to undermine the nation's fight against Germany and other enemy nations.

Even before Americans joined the fight in April 1917, anti-Wobbly violence boiled out of control in the sawmill town of Everett, Washington, in 1916. Again, on the occasion of the first anniversary of the end of the war, anti-Wobbly violence erupted in Centralia, Washington, in November 1919. Earlier that year, the Seattle General Strike of February 1919 had made the public edgy, and the "Centralia Massacre" further contributed to growing antilabor sentiment in the Pacific Northwest.

As elsewhere, the 1920s were lean years for organized workers in Washington, Oregon, and Idaho. The big-four industries loomed as large in the regional economy as ever, but something vital had changed when roads began to connect once isolated mine and timber camps to nearby cities and when itinerant harvest hands could purchase cheap used cars and motor to and from work. Apparently, to some workers "automobility" became an acceptable substitute for social mobility. The Wobbly message based on disinheritance seemed less compelling than before as workers were able to develop some semblance of family life where formerly that had been impossible. Throughout the 1920s, Wobblies still published updated versions of their little red songbook, and itinerants traveling by stealing aboard empty boxcars still gathered around hobo campfires to sing familiar refrains, but their numbers were shrinking because of the automobile and increasing miles of all-weather roads.

Because of its dependence on production of commodities sold to distant markets, the economy of the Pacific Northwest appeared to ride a roller coaster of boom and bust, one for which the operator was invisible or located in some faraway place. Maybe there was no operator. It was easy to think that way during the depression that lasted from 1893 to 1897, the worst the nation had ever experienced, or from 1929 to 1941, which was even worse.

During the widespread joblessness of the 1893 depression, workers of the Northwest found no economic or social safety net in place to sustain them during the hard times. It was "survival of the fittest," which sometimes meant relocating to the capacious shores of Puget Sound, building a hut of driftwood, and eating clams for free for the taking—for breakfast, lunch, and dinner. As one optimist phrased it, when the tide is out the table is set, though one worker claimed to have eaten so many clams he could feel the tide rise and fall in his stomach.

Other idled workers took a more direct approach and in Seattle, Tacoma, and Portland formed one of the industrial arms that organized around the United States in the spring of 1894. Popularly known as "Coxey's Army" (for the original organizer in Ohio), the protest had elements of a media craze. But it had a serious side, too: to present a "petition in boots" to Congress on May 1, 1894, to urge members to pass legislation designed to put the jobless to work building good roads—something the nation greatly needed during the heyday of railroad domination of the means of transportation.

Coxey's original army did march down Pennsylvania Avenue as promised, but police arrested him when he attempted to present his petition to Congress. Most of the armies from the West Coast never did reach the Capitol, though the one from Tacoma gave the nation a momentary scare when its weary members grew tired of walking and stole a train in Montana, racing off toward Capitol Hill with the United States Army in hot pursuit. Rounded up and herded into makeshift prison camps in Helena, the Montana capital, some determined members built rafts and attempted to continue down the Missouri River to achieve their original goal.

Nothing came of the Northwest's Coxey protest, or did it? In 1944, on the fiftieth anniversary of his original protest, an elderly Jacob Coxey mounted the Capitol steps and finally read the petition he had been barred from presenting to Congress earlier. The document sounded both quaint and thoroughly dated. In the Northwest as elsewhere, the New Deal response to the Great Depression of the 1930s put the jobless to work building roads, beautifying parks, fighting insect infestations of the national forests, painting post office murals, and accomplishing a host of other assignments.

By far, the biggest New Deal projects were the building of the Bonneville and Grand Coulee dams on the Columbia River. These federal projects provided thousands of construction jobs and became showcases for the merits of managing the once wild river. The newly established Bonneville Power Administration hired the labor troubadour Woody Guthrie to compose a series of songs extolling the virtues of the big dams.

Organized labor, which struggled through the 1920s, gained a valuable boost in the 1930s from New Deal legislation that encouraged workers to organize. So many did organize that the House of Labor proved too small to contain both the craft and industrial unions, which had a strong base of support in the Pacific Northwest. A result was the formation of the Congress of Industrial Organizations (CIO). Labor rivalry and conflict erupted at several locations until the two overarching labor organizations resolved their differences and merged in 1954 as the AFL-CIO.

One of the most powerful leaders of an AFL union during the split was Dave Beck of Seattle, who rose with the trucking industry and the expanding network of good roads that fostered its growth to become the national head of the Teamsters' Union. Alas, although Beck's rapid rise gained him widespread fame as a tough and effective AFL union leader, his downfall was equally dramatic. He went to federal prison for income tax evasion in 1962.

At the end of the twentieth century and the start of the twenty-first, the industrial base of the Pacific Northwest looked dramatically different than it had a hundred years earlier: commodity production had been overshadowed by manufacturing, but not the region's traditional manufacturing of heavy logging equipment and aircraft. Boeing, which rose to prominence as an aircraft manufacturer during the frenzied days of World War II production, continued to produce renowned aircraft, but by the 1990s, the Puget Sound region had become more clearly identified with Microsoft and its software programs than with Boeing's jetliners. In fact, Boeing relocated its corporate headquarters from Seattle to Chicago in 2001.

This story had a parallel in the region's once almighty timber industry. At various times during the twentieth century, both Oregon and Washington ranked as the nation's top timber producers. Production remained high during the 1940s and 1950s, stimulated by World War II and the baby boom and the resulting new home construction afterward. Timber jobs were numerous and paid good wages. But then production leveled out before starting to decline. In a sign of things to come, one of the region's top timber producers, Georgia-Pacific, relocated its headquarters from Portland to Atlanta in 1982, much as Boeing would do two decades later. Second- and third-growth trees matured faster in the moist, warm climate of the South—not to mention that unions were less powerful in the South than in the Pacific Northwest.

The 1980s were grim for timberworkers. Environmental restrictions made it more difficult and costly to harvest trees, and an economic slump and heightened competition from Canadian timber caused dozens of sawmills to close permanently—taking down with them many a one-industry town. The mills that remained modernized with high-technology equipment (including lasers and computers) that greatly reduced the number of people needed to turn forest giants into two-by-fours.

It was the same story down on the farm in the 1980s. Where the annual grain harvest had once required two or three dozen itinerant harvest hands to run threshing machines, care for approximately 30 horses needed to pull each reaper, and then sack grain by hand, two or three people could do the job. The combine operator, usually the owner of the ranch, operated an air-conditioned, stereo-equipped machine, while one or two truck drivers (often teenagers eager for a good-paying summer job) drove the golden harvest to the local grain elevator.

In many places the traditional commodity-based economy simply vanished. Not a single fish cannery remained along the Columbia River. Once where dozens of them each year produced millions of cans of salmon to feed working people of Ireland, England, and many other distant places, not even the buildings remained. In some places only a few half-submerged pilings remained to mark the one-time site of busy production. The seafood industry, except for some small-scale shellfish canners, largely disappeared from the Pacific Northwest.

Gone, too, were the Cascade coal towns of Washington after a peak of production in 1919. Most of the once great silver mines of northern Idaho closed in the 1980s, and the former gritty smelter town of Kellogg struggled to re-invent itself as an Alpine ski resort to tap the almighty tourist dollar. With a Superfund site in the neighborhood, that would prove no easy sell.

Organized labor, which had been concentrated in traditional manufacturing industries, along with newer ones like Boeing, had yet to gain a real foothold among high-tech and tourist-industry workers that now accounted for a preponderance of Pacific Northwest jobs. Because organized labor tended to ally with the Democratic Party, the decline of its political clout was particularly dramatic in Idaho, which became perhaps the single most Republican state in the Union. The Democratic Party formerly found a congenial base in the state's once numerous mine and timber towns, but the currents of economic change eroded that base until scarcely a remnant remained.

At the turn of the twenty-first century, the Pacific Northwest still possessed two economies, as it had for at least two decades. The traditional commodity-producing and manufacturing economy in which organized labor once was strongest had declined at least since the early 1980s. At the same time, the high-tech and tourist-based economy grew ever stronger, and here organized labor had yet to make significant inroads. Unless something dramatic changes, the future for organized labor in the Pacific Northwest should look like the immediate gloomy past

CARLOS A. SCHWANTES

References and Further Reading

Schwantes, Carlos A. *Hard Traveling: A Portrait of Work Life in the New Northwest*. Lincoln: University of Nebraska Press, 1994.
———. *Radical Heritage: Labor, Socialism, and Reform in Washington and British Columbia, 1885–1917*. Seattle: University of Washington Press, 1979.

PAINE, THOMAS (1737–1809)
Writer, Advocate for Democracy and Reform

Thomas Paine was one of the few leaders of America's founding generation who emerged out of and remained a hero for the Atlantic world's working class. Born in 1737 in Thetford, about 75 miles from London, the young Paine's formal education ended at the age of 12 when he followed his father into the staymaker's trade, making whalebone corsets for middle-class and aristocratic women. Paine briefly established his own shop in 1758, but when that failed, he spent most of the next 10 years working sporadically as a teacher, tax collector, and staymaker until he finally found steady work in 1768 as an excise officer in Lewes. Up until this point in his life, there is little evidence that Paine had engaged in any organized political activity.

That quickly changed when Paine joined the Headstrong Club in Lewes, a town with a tradition of political radicalism that extended back to the English Civil War of the 1640s. In this club, Paine was introduced to a tradition of English Republicanism that advocated sweeping reforms that would make the English government more representative and less corrupt. He became involved with the popular Wilkite movement in the late 1760s and wrote his first political pamphlet in 1772 calling for the rationalization of the system of excise collection. By 1774, however, his career as a budding reformer was cut short when he lost his job and declared bankruptcy. In the fall of 1774, he sought out Benjamin Franklin in London and secured his assistance in starting over again in the New World.

Soon after his arrival in Philadelphia, Paine found work editing the *Pennsylvania Magazine*, and through that employment he came into contact with a flourishing and diverse community of political radicals. As the crisis with England intensified, a coalition of urban workers, Enlightenment scientists, and progressive-minded professionals took control of Pennsylvania's political system. These people found common cause in their opposition to British tyranny, and together they crafted a political persuasion that Paine would soon masterfully articulate in his first American pamphlet, *Common Sense*. In 1775 and 1776, the Philadelphia militia had been taken over by workingmen who radically democratized that institution. They insisted on electing their officers, and by making the hunting shirt their official uniform, they challenged the class hierarchies that had previously structured the militia's ranks. Paine's *Common Sense* echoed the anti-authoritarian populism of these militia men, sarcastically referring to the king as the "Royal Brute" and arguing that hereditary power often supplied "an ass for a lion." Many of Paine's working-class compatriots also took part in what historians have called "the artisan Enlightenment," a movement of self-educated workers who embraced the radical social implications of Newtonian science. Their study of science had taught them that the world operated according to a set of universal laws that any person, regardless of their social position, could discern through their faculties of reason. Where kings and aristocrats had traditionally claimed unique access to truth, an increasing number of Philadelphia's working people came to believe with Paine that the broad mass of the people, through their use of reason and common sense, could best generate the laws that governed their society. In a language that echoed the populist humor and assertiveness of the radicalized community around him, Paine's *Common Sense* funneled that community's resentments and aspirations into the growing movement for national independence.

Tom Paine's experiences during the War for Independence testify to the complexities of class in the late eighteenth century. Thanks in part to his support of the radically democratic Pennsylvania Constitution of 1776, Paine remained a hero for a patriot rank and file that appreciated his support for political measures that served their interests. And although the Patriot leadership class looked with suspicion upon the growing politicization of ordinary Americans, in the early years of the war, they embraced Paine as an effective spokesperson for their cause. At George Washington's request, for example, Paine wrote a stirring set of essays (*The Crisis Papers*) that strengthened public support for the war during those "times that try men's souls." By the 1780s, however, Paine's ability to bridge the leadership class and the patriot rank and file had dwindled. At the root of his political fall from grace lay an ideological divide between Paine and his fellow Americans. Paine was unusual in the 1780s in that he endorsed both highly democratic political arrangements and free market economics. Most supporters of the free market were established leaders who resisted political democratization, while most supporters of a more participatory and inclusive political system advocated a "moral economy" that would use price controls and other economic restrictions to protect laborers from the vagaries of the market. Although Paine's 1780s amalgam of democracy and free market capitalism would become mainstream in America by the early nineteenth century, when he boarded a ship bound for England in 1787, he had ceased to be a major public figure.

Paine re-emerged on the world stage in 1790, when he wrote the *Rights of Man* (part 2 appeared in 1792) in defense of the revolution in France and in support of democratization in Britain. These pamphlets were perhaps the most widely read tracts of the 1790s, and the working-class political movements that emerged in Britain at this time embraced Paine as a leading spokesman for their cause. In part 2 of *Rights of Man*, Paine sketched out a plan for a welfare system that would supply pensions for elderly and injured workers as well as their widows. This plan was to be financed by a progressive tax system with a top tax rate of 100%. In 1794, Paine published the *Age of Reason*, a scathing attack on established religion that interpreted it as a way for elites to gain the allegiance and subservience of ordinary people. He followed this deist tract with his most radical piece, *Agrarian Justice*, which argued that commercial society had made poverty an increasingly "hereditary" state. To remedy this systemic inequality, Paine claimed that each person should have their natural right to property restored by the state in the form of monetary payments made to every person, male and female, when they reached the age of 21 and then for every year after they had reached the age of 50. Paine's unprecedented claim that this economic support from the government should be claimed as "a right" and not as a form of charity marked a major departure from his 1780s endorsement of the free market and gained him the admiration of working people throughout the Atlantic world.

Throughout the nineteenth century, various groups of American labor activists, freethinkers, and abolitionists joined together to commemorate his birthday and re-affirm their support for Paine's revolutionary ideas. Such supporters, however, were always a minority. His association with deism and the French Revolution earned him the powerful enmity of established leaders in both Europe and America. When he returned to America in 1802, he was pilloried in the press as the leader of an international conspiracy to overthrow all religion, abolish private property, and destroy the American government. He was welcomed by a small community of Democrats in New York City, but the Americans who threw stones at his carriage as he rode through New Jersey best exemplified the extent to which the world's first self-proclaimed democracy had turned against the eighteenth century's most effective advocate of democratization.

SETH COTLAR

References and Further Reading

Fast, Howard. *Citizen Tom Paine*. New York: Grove Press, 1983.
Foner, Eric. *Tom Paine and Revolutionary America*. New York: Oxford University Press, 2004.
Foner, Eric, ed. *Thomas Paine: Collected Writings*. New York: Library of America, 1995.
Kaye, Harvey. *Thomas Paine and the Promise of America*. New York: Hill & Wang, 2005.

PARSONS, ALBERT (1848–1887)

Albert R. Parsons was born in Alabama in 1848 to parents who had moved there from New England. Orphaned as a boy, he moved to Texas to live on his brother's ranch. He apprenticed as a printer and then talked his way into a Confederate cavalry unit after the Civil War started.

When it ended, Parsons returned to east Texas and started his own newspaper in Waco, which he used to advocate for the cause of the freedmen. In 1868, he began a dangerous career as a radical Republican politician and militia colonel until 1872, when Reconstruction effectively ended in Texas. In 1873, Parsons, who had wed a woman of color named Lucy, left Texas to ply his trade in Chicago.

The Texan found work as a printer at the Chicago *Times* and soon became interested in the controversy over unemployment relief; he decided that the city's socialists were valiantly fighting for the poor but were being excoriated by the press just as the Republicans had been condemned for advocating racial justice in Texas. This cause set Parsons on a course that would in the next decade make him an agitator of international renown until he was convicted and executed for being an accessory to the Haymarket bombing of May 4, 1886, an explosion that led to the deaths of seven police officers.

Albert Parsons began to win a hearing from Chicago's workers when he gave a stirring speech in July 23, 1877, a day before the great railroad strike erupted in Chicago.

His speech, calling for those in the "grand army of starvation" to join the "grand army of labor," was so sensational that the newspapers and police blamed Parsons for the unrest and violence that followed the strike. Despite being fired, blacklisted, red-baited and threatened with lynching, Parsons persisted in his work, becoming the leading campaigner for the Workingmen's Party and the Socialistic Labor Party. Indeed, he believed he would have been elected to the city council as a socialist in 1879 but that he had been cheated out of office by a fraudulent count.

This experience was one of several that turned Parsons away from the electoral path to socialism. In 1881, he helped found the International Working People's Association after he had joined company with German immigrant revolutionaries like his fellow Chicagoan August Spies. In 1884, Parsons began to edit a paper called *Alarm* with his wife, Lucy—a paper that expressed the same call for social revolution and the same need for armed struggle Spies espoused in the German socialist publications he managed.

During the mid-1880s, Albert Parsons became a notorious agitator and orator in Chicago. His fame then spread to other Midwestern cities as well, where he was often asked to speak. By 1885, the Parsonses rejected the electoral path to socialism, embraced a homegrown brand of anarchism, and called for the use of guns and dynamite bombs in the coming struggle with the employers, the police, and the military.

At the same time, Parsons played an active role in the Knights of Labor and in various other movements aimed at organizing workers and gaining the eight-hour day. He viewed shorter hours as a reform the employers would never accept, but he also thought the demand had radical implications because the achievement of eight hours would offer workers the freedom to educate themselves and to conceive of a society based on co-operation instead of competition. Militant unions and a radical labor movement were essential in the process, as Parsons described it. Revolutionary workers' organizations would be the cells that would compose a new communal social organism without oppressive employers, laws, armies, and police forces.

In early 1886, Parsons emerged as a leading figure in the eight-hour strike movement that culminated on May 1 of that year and hit with the greatest force in Chicago. He had just returned to the city on May 4 when he was asked to speak at a rally called by the anarchists to protest the death of four strikers killed by the police the night before. He refused at first and then changed his mind. He delivered a rousing talk condemning the employers and the police and then left the area with his wife and children before the bomb exploded.

After the bombing, comrades persuaded Parsons to flee Chicago, fearing that he would be hunted down and killed. He left for a two-month exile and then returned to Chicago to stand trial with the seven other anarchists accused of aiding and abetting the bombing. His lawyer, William Black, had convinced Parsons that he would be acquitted because no evidence connected him to the bombing. Black was wrong, however. Parsons was convicted of being an accessory to murder and sentenced to death.

In his final speech to the court, Parsons held forth for more than nine hours over a two-day period, offering a litany of complaints about his trial in particular and injustice in general. His words were published by his wife, Lucy, and circulated by anarchists and socialists around the world in working-class districts from Barcelona to Havana, where the name Albert Parsons became as well known as the names of Abraham Lincoln and John Brown.

While in prison, Parsons became a kind of celebrity, much quoted in the mainstream and labor press. His stature grew even greater when leading men in Illinois, believing Parsons was innocent of murder, urged him to beg the governor for clemency so that his sentence could be commuted to life in prison. But Parsons refused to serve jail time for a crime he had not committed—a stance that seemed heroic to many observers, especially to those active in the labor and radical movements of that time.

Albert Parsons was executed, along with three German comrades, on November 11, 1887, and buried next to them in Waldheim Cemetery outside of Chicago, a site that would become a hallowed one to radical pilgrims for decades afterward.

In the remaining years of her life, Lucy Parsons (who died in 1941) worked tirelessly to keep her husband's memory alive. During the Cold War years, Albert Parsons became a forgotten figure from a chapter in "labor's untold story" until the mid-1980s, when his story was revived and then featured in many historical studies, as well as in three plays and a novel.

JAMES GREEN

References and Further Reading

Avrich, Paul. *The Haymarket Tragedy*. Princeton: Princeton University Press, 1984.
Duberman, Martin. *Haymarket: A Novel*. New York: Seven Stories Press, 2001.
Foner, Philip S., ed. *The Autobiographies of the Haymarket Anarchists* (1886). New York: Humanities Press, 1969.
Green, James. *Death in the Haymarket: A Story of Chicago, the First Labor Movement, and the Bombing That Divided Gilded Age America*. New York: Pantheon, 2006.
Nelson, Bruce C. *Beyond the Martyrs: A Social History of Chicago's Anarchists, 1870–1900*. New Brunswick, NJ: Rutgers University Press, 1988.
Parsons, Lucy, ed. *Famous Speeches of the Eight Chicago Anarchists in Court*. 1910. Reprint, New York: Arno Press, 1969.
Roediger, David, and Franklin Rosemont, eds. *The Haymarket Scrapbook*. Chicago: Charles H. Kerr, 1986.

PARSONS, LUCY (1853–1942)
Anarchist

Lucy Parsons became the best-known anarchist speaker in the United States in the three decades after her husband, Albert, was executed in Chicago on November 11, 1887, for allegedly conspiring in a bombing plot that killed seven policemen in Chicago's Haymarket Square on May 4, 1886. During her husband's confinement on death row, Lucy Parsons traveled to cities all over the nation and spoke to many sympathetic labor groups; after his death, she traveled to England, where she was received like a celebrity by radical and union groups. In the next two decades, Parsons continued her speaking and publishing activities, reviving the memory of Albert Parsons and the four other anarchists executed for the bombing, men who came to be known as the Haymarket martyrs. In these years, only Emma Goldman rivaled Lucy Parsons's fame as an anarchist agitator and a champion of free speech.

Lucy Parsons said that she was born Lucy Gonzalez in 1853 to a Hispanic mother and a Creek Indian father and that she was raised on her uncle's ranch in Texas. However, neither her birth date nor her parentage can be confirmed, and it seems likely that Lucy was born on a plantation in Hill County, Texas, and that her mother was a slave of African descent.

In any case, it is clear that Parsons was living around Waco, Texas, during the violent years of federal reconstruction in that area and that she knew of atrocities committed against newly freed blacks. This is most likely the setting in which she met Albert Parsons, while he was active as a radical Republican fighting for the rights of emancipated blacks.

Albert Parsons and Lucy were married in Austin, Texas, in 1872. The couple left Texas the following year and settled on the North Side of Chicago, where she worked as a dressmaker.

During the last half of the 1870s, Albert Parsons became a noted labor organizer and socialist campaigner in Chicago, and during the early 1880s, as he moved toward revolutionary socialism and anarchism, Lucy joined him in a highly public career of radical education and agitation.

Soon after the birth of her first child, a boy, in 1879, Lucy plunged into organizing female workers in Chicago as an activist in the Working Women's Union, where she met other talented women organizers like Elizabeth Rodgers and Lizzie Swank. Lucy Parsons increased her involvement after she gave birth to daughter in 1881, the same year the International Working People's Association (IWPA) was formed by her husband and other social revolutionaries.

By 1884, Lucy Parsons was active in the Chicago IWPA's American Group while she wrote articles and helped her husband produce the paper *Alarm*, an ultramilitant publication in which the writers and editors advocated the use of force, including dynamite, as a means of abolishing what they called wage slavery. Indeed, she became an especially passionate advocate of "propaganda by deed"—the use of force by revolutionaries acting on behalf of the oppressed. Lucy Parsons was a prominent speaker at weekly rallies held by the IWPA, whose members called themselves anarchists, and in noisy street demonstrations such as the one on Thanksgiving Day in 1885, Parsons led a "poor people's march" into the neighborhoods of the wealthy shouting denunciations at the rich in the name of the hungry.

When the national movement for the eight-hour day gathered force in April 1886, Lucy Parsons joined the Chicago anarchists in mobilizing unskilled, immigrant workers into the anarchist-led bodies of the city's Central Labor Union. She was especially active in organizing the women workers in the sewing and tailoring shops of the North and West sides. Parsons was attending such a meeting on the night of May 4, 1886, when she and her husband left to go to Haymarket Square, where Albert was asked to address a crowd of workers assembled by the anarchists to protest the killing of four strikers by the police at the McCormick Works the night before. Lucy brought her two young children to the square that night and left together with Albert when he finished his speech and a rainstorm threatened. They were socializing in a nearby saloon when the bomb exploded on Desplaines Street and changed their lives forever.

Lucy Parsons's efforts to commemorate her husband's life and work took many tangible forms, including her publication of *The Life of Albert Parsons* and *Famous Speeches of the Haymarket Anarchists*, both widely disseminated around the world for 30 years after the anarchists' deaths on November 11, 1887, and her solicitation of funds for a monument on the grave site of Albert and his comrades in Waldheim Cemetery near Chicago, a memorial unveiled in 1893.

Parsons remained a militant anarchist until around 1900, at which point she no longer advocated the use of force and joined other radicals who were attempting to create a revolutionary workers' movement based on nonviolent direct action.

For this reason, Parsons was a prominent speaker at the founding convention of the Industrial Workers of the World (IWW) in 1905. During the next decade, she was a prominent figure in the effort to gain free speech for workers and was arrested many times in her efforts to exercise that right.

During the 1920s, Parsons became active in the Communist Party's International Labor Defense group, taking up the cause of the radicals Sacco and Vanzetti. She lived to speak at the fiftieth anniversary of the anarchist hangings in 1937, when she connected those deaths to those of the 10 strikers killed by the Chicago police in the Memorial Day massacre earlier that year. Though blinded in her old age, Lucy became a revered figure to the radicals, organizing the new unions of the Congress of Industrial Organizations in Chicago during the late 1930s. On May Day, 1941, she waved to bystanders as she rode on a float constructed by the CIO Farm Equipment Workers Union. It would be her last May Day. She died on March 7, 1942, when her home caught fire. Lucy Parsons was buried next to her husband at Waldheim Cemetery.

JAMES GREEN

References and Further Reading

Ashbaugh, Carolyn. *Lucy Parsons: American Revolutionary*. Chicago: Illinois Labor History Society, 1976.

Avrich, Paul. *The Haymarket Tragedy*. Princeton, NJ: Princeton University Press, 1984.

Green, James. *Death in the Haymarket: A Story of Chicago, the First Labor Movement, and the Bombing That Divided Gilded Age America*. New York: Pantheon, 2006.

Roediger, David, and Franklin Rosemont, eds. *The Haymarket Scrapbook*. Chicago: Charles H. Kerr, 1986.

See also **Parsons, Albert**

PATERSON (NJ) SILK STRIKE (1913)

The 1913 Paterson, New Jersey, silk strike was the biggest and longest Paterson strike. Led by the Industrial Workers of the World (IWW), and aided by poets and artists from New York City, it demonstrated solidarity and discipline. The strike was a high-water mark of the pre-WWI American left, and its outcome contributed to the decline and breakup of the left.

The 1913 strike was one of a series by Paterson silk workers, stretching back to the 1880s and forward to the 1930s. Silk weavers, who constituted the majority

Bus load of children of Paterson, N.J., strikers (silk workers) in May Day parade - New York City. Library of Congress, Prints & Photographs Division [LC-USZ62-52620].

of the workforce in the silk industry, came from textile centers in Europe to Paterson, because the pay was better than in Europe. They brought pride in their craft with them, and experience in labor struggles and socialist and anarchist ideas.

Before 1913, strikes in Paterson were frequent and short. Typically, weavers in a shop would walk out, usually to protect their wages or working conditions. Sometimes, dyers helpers would shut down their plant, to raise wages. Occasionally, as in a 1894 ribbon weavers strike, a 1902 dyers helpers strike, and a 1912 broad-silk weavers strike, a whole branch would go on strike.

In 1913, for the first and last time in Paterson, the trades joined together. The silk workers had learned from their defeats in 1902 and 1912 that if they didn't stick together, they would lose. This lesson was re-inforced by IWW speakers—Elizabeth Gurley Flynn, Bill Haywood, and Carlo Tresca—who came to Paterson after a successful 1912 textile strike in Lawrence, Massachusetts.

The initial aim in 1913 was to defend the status quo in loom assignments. The Doherty mill had raised the number of looms assigned to each broad-silk weaver from two to four, and broad-silk weavers began the strike. When the dyers helpers joined, they brought an emphasis on an eight-hour day. Then the ribbon weavers also joined, to protest the tactics of the Paterson

municipal government in arresting IWW speakers and peaceful pickets.

Observers of the strike were amazed by the strikers' disciplined nonviolence, despite police provocations, which included over two thousand arrests and the closing of the strikers' meeting halls. Observers were also struck by the democratic spirit of the strike, the way strikers—including women—actively joined in decision making, rather than blindly following their local leaders or IWW speakers. Finally, observers were impressed by the solidarity among the different ethnic groups, the Italian, Jewish, German, and English silk workers.

The strike began on February 25; by mid-March, 23,000 silk workers (out of a total of 25,000) had joined the strike, and the silk mills and dye houses in Paterson were entirely shut down. But the larger Paterson silk mills and the dye houses had annexes in Pennsylvania. These annexes, which the manufacturers began building in the 1890s to escape the militancy of Paterson workers, enabled them to hold out in 1913, despite the fact that production was halted in Paterson. The Paterson silk workers and the IWW sent people to Pennsylvania to persuade local workers to strike. But the resulting strikes in Allentown and Hazelton were brief. The Paterson silk manufacturers, using the annexes in Pennsylvania, were able to limp through the strike.

Unable to win a quick victory, the Paterson strikers organized themselves for the long haul. Community organizations, especially the local chapters of the Sons of Italy and the (Jewish) Workmen's Circle, donated money and food. Socialists in New York and New Jersey aided the strike. With the help of the IWW, the strikers reached out to Greenwich Village writers and artists, who came to Paterson to see the strike and were moved by it. John Reed (later known for his coverage of the Bolshevik Revolution) came to Paterson and was arrested and sent to jail. Margaret Sanger (later known as the advocate of birth control) went to Hazleton and was also arrested and sent to jail. In Paterson, Sanger and Flynn talked birth control to the women strikers and the wives of the men strikers.

The most spectacular result of the cooperation between Paterson silk workers and New York artists was the Pageant of the Paterson Strike. The Pageant took place in Madison Square Garden on June 7. The Garden was sold out. There were 1,100 strikers who played themselves, the strikebreakers, and the police; many strikers, responding to Reed's questions, had previously helped develop the script. John Sloan, already famous as a painter of the "Ash Can" school, painted the backdrop, a giant silk mill. Robert Edmund Jones, later Eugene O'Neill's set designer, designed a center aisle through the audience, down which the strikers ran at the end of the first act, screaming, "Strike! Strike! Strike!"

The audience became passionately involved in the Pageant, and the press acknowledged its power. But in July, worn down by the long strike, silk workers began to return to work. The strike was lost. For the strikers, it was only a partial defeat. They succeeded in preventing the manufacturers from going ahead with four looms, and they lived to strike again, albeit in smaller numbers; in 1919, the weavers won an eight-hour day.

But left-wing supporters of the strike turned on each other after the 1913 defeat. Socialists blamed the IWW. The IWW, which had been on the rise in the eastern United States, was essentially finished there. Haywood and Flynn quarreled, with Flynn blaming the Pageant for the loss of the strike. Many historians have accepted her judgments. Others have argued that the Pageant succeeded in its original aim, which was to publicize the strike in New York, and that the strike was lost not because of the Pageant, but because the manufacturers, with their annexes in Pennsylvania, were even stronger than the strikers.

For a brief moment, in Paterson, the great hopeful energies of the strikers, the IWW, and the young radicals from the Village came together, creatively and powerfully. Then, for Paterson and for the American left, the moment passed.

STEVE GOLIN

References and Further Reading

Dubofsky, Melvin. *We Shall Be All: A History of the Industrial Workers of the World.* Chicago: University of Illinois Press, 1969.
Flynn, Elizabeth Gurley. *The Rebel Girl: An Autobiography.* New York: International Publishers, 1973.
Golin, Steve. *The Fragile Bridge: Paterson Silk Strike, 1913.* Philadelphia: Temple University Press, 1988.
Scranton, Philip B., ed. *Silk City: Studies of the Paterson Silk Industry.* Newark: New Jersey Historical Society, 1985.

See also **Industrial Workers of the World**

PATTERN BARGAINING

After a decade of massive organizing campaigns, the American labor movement emerged from World War II with secure national strongholds in the auto, steel, and meatpacking industries. Unions aspired to uniform bargaining standards with all the employers in each industry; recalcitrant employers in fragmented industries resisted. Thus, unions developed pattern bargaining as a hybrid strategy to enforce industry bargaining by presenting common contract demands at each company within an industry. Particularly in manufacturing, pattern bargaining became a defining feature of unions' collective identity, and the United Auto Workers (UAW) and the United Steelworkers (USW) waged strikes to "protect the pattern." But during the 1980s and 1990s, unions learned that the universal gains won during a flush economy could turn to collapsing dominoes of losses when ailing companies dragged down the pattern for entire industries.

Since the advent of collective bargaining in the United States, laborites had argued that unions could function as rationalizing agents in fragmented industries by harmonizing wages and work rules and forcing employers to co-ordinate with each other. Common contract standards would preclude ruinous wage undercutting as a competitive strategy for employers, and unionists hoped to help stabilize boom-and-bust cycles, particularly in industries like textiles and coal. In the 1930s, New Deal policy makers embraced this reasoning. The National Industrial Recovery Act (NIRA) created ad hoc industrial councils to set production, price, and wage standards, and a range of World War II-era federal agencies, from the National War Labor Board to the War

Manpower Commission, arbitrated disputes between unions and employers and promulgated shop-floor rules and wage settlements.

The apotheosis of this vision was multi-employer, industrywide bargaining. However, federal policy imposed industry bargaining only during crisis. American businesses, scarcely reconciled to New Deal legislation obliging them to recognize unions, tolerated industry bargaining but showed little interest in continuing it when federal mandates expired. A few industries stood out as exceptions: clothing manufacture, full-fashioned hosiery, and railroads sustained national bargaining between unions and industry associations for some years after World War II. The Teamsters came close to achieving a sectoral agreement. In 1964, solid organizing and strategic bargaining enabled the Teamsters to win a national master contract covering most motor freight carriers.

Thwarted at industry bargaining, unions came up with pattern bargaining. Obliged to deal bilaterally with individual employers, unions simply devised their own industry standards and then bargained for them. This required national co-ordination among locals and a centrally directed bargaining policy. To achieve a national pattern, unions generally selected the dominant firm in an industry as its target, negotiated the best possible settlement, and then turned to smaller competitors to insist acceptance of similar terms. The Steelworkers showed the way. After settling with industry leader U.S. Steel in 1937, the Steelworkers waged organizing campaigns at Little Steel firms like Bethlehem and Republic. After winning union recognition, the Steelworkers demanded and won similar contracts with Little Steel, in what came to be called "me-too" agreements. The potency of pattern bargaining is suggested by employers' efforts to ban it; in 1953, employers unsuccessfully lobbied to prohibit the practice in amendments to the Taft-Hartley Act. Congress of Industrial Organizations (CIO) unions embraced the tactic and pursued patterns in auto, rubber, farm equipment, aerospace, and meatpacking.

Features of pattern bargaining included master agreements with employers covering all plants and work locations; common expiration dates for each master contract; and successorship provisions binding the employer to include a union recognition covenant as a condition of sale for its plants and operations. Contracts generally required a master wage schedule, thus obviating regional wage variations. Unions needed strong centralized authority to enforce the pattern on locals; workers at a well-performing plant could be tempted to break off and bargain independently, while underperforming plants needed solidarity to sustain contract standards. Employers coordinated

closely as well, generally meeting privately to exchange notes and plot strategy, while maintaining a public façade of bilateral bargaining. Moreover, pattern bargaining required a high degree of unionization within an industry. By the 1960s, workers in auto and steel enjoyed a predictable cycle of steady contract improvements.

Pattern bargaining was most entrenched and sustained in auto and steel, with less durable instances in other mass production sectors like farm equipment and meatpacking. Workers in diverse industries adopted variants. Airline pilots established strong craft density within an incompletely unionized sector and achieved an industry pattern. New York City public unions representing workers from teachers to clerks to police officers formed a bargaining council to negotiate with the city and insist on the same percentage wage increase for all municipal workers.

As unionization rates nosedived across the economy beginning in the 1980s, the advantage in pattern bargaining shifted from unions to employers. In steel and auto, recession and overcapacity combined to bankrupt manufacturers, which promptly demanded contract concessions from their unions. Employers borrowed the unions' logic and insisted that concessions granted to one employer must be extended to all. Manufacturing unions faced a spiral of givebacks that dismantled contract edifices built over a generation. Further, the pattern disadvantaged entire industry sectors contending with nonunion competitors; thus, nonunion Japanese and European auto assembly plants in the United States all shared a widening competitive edge over Detroit's Big Three auto firms. In other sectors, different competitive pressures eroded union density and bargaining power. Deregulation of trucking swiftly produced a new low-cost nonunion trucking sector that undercut Teamster signatories and eviscerated the master freight agreement; in meatpacking, anti-union slaughterhouses gradually overtook the once dominant union firms. Janitors were a marked exception to the general decline. The Justice for Janitors campaign, launched in the late 1980s, systematically organized cleaning contractors in urban markets and, upon achieving market density, won marketwide agreements and in some cases forced contractors to bargain in industry associations.

JENNIFER LUFF

References and Further Reading

Backman, Jules, and A. L. Gitlow. "Evolution of National Multi-Employer Collective Bargaining." *Southern Economic Journal* 18, no. 2 (October 1951): 206–218.
Dubofsky, Melvin. *The State and Labor in Modern America.* Chapel Hill: University of North Carolina Press, 1994.

Ready, Kathryn J., and Peter Cappelli. "Is Pattern Bargaining Dead? A Discussion." *Industrial and Labor Relations Review* 44, no. 1 (October 1990): 152–165.

Seltzer, George. "Pattern Bargaining and the United Steelworkers." *Journal of Political Economy*. 59, no. 4 (August 1951): 319–331.

See also **Collective Bargaining; National Industrial Recovery Act; National War Labor Board (WWII); Steel and Iron; Teamsters for a Democratic Union**

PEONAGE

Peonage is a form of coerced labor that emerged in the southeastern United States after the emancipation of African-American slaves. The English term "peonage" originally derived from the Spanish *peon*, meaning foot soldier. Before being imported into the United States, peonage referred to a type of involuntary servitude based on a laborer's indebtedness to a creditor. This hybrid of free labor and chattel slavery was prevalent in European colonies in Latin America and the Philippines. In 1850, the first instances of such peonage arose in the United States with the conquering of the New Mexico territory at the end of the Mexican-American war.

After the Civil War ended in 1865, American peonage became most closely identified with the plight of indebted African-American farmworkers in the South. Although the Thirteenth Amendment to the U.S. Constitution outlawed slavery and involuntary servitude in 1865, white southerners attempted to return their former slaves to a system of labor as close to chattel slavery as possible. Southern legislatures passed so-called Black Codes to authorize peonage practices. Though varying by state, the Codes generally restricted the labor choices of freed slaves and ensured a steady labor force for southern landowners. They prohibited freedpeople from renting agricultural land and from working in nonagricultural trades. They also required blacks to carry written proof of lawful employment to avoid arrest for vagrancy. Although the federal Bureau of Freedmen, Refugees, and Abandoned Lands protected former slaves in many ways, its requirement that they sign yearly labor contracts with landowners who were often their former masters bolstered white power.

After Union military officials invalidated the Black Codes in late 1865 and early 1866, Congress passed a number of federal civil rights statutes and an antipeonage statute. Congress also proposed, and the states ratified, the Fourteenth Amendment in 1867 and the Fifteenth Amendment in 1870. A web of both social customs and racially neutral laws nonetheless emerged to strengthen involuntary servitude in the South. By the late 1800s, a new system of labor had emerged. African-Americans seeking a modicum of autonomy rented land through sharecropper or tenant farmer agreements. Despite the improvement this represented over gang labor, the system remained oppressive as legal barriers severely hampered renters' profits. Losses fell disproportionately on tenants due to crop lien statutes, which funneled profits directly to pay white landlords and merchants who lent supplies. Sharecroppers, who paid landlords with shares of crops, had a more difficult time. Both tenants and sharecroppers were so indebted to landlords that crop profits did not even cover their debt, let alone the ability to forego additional loans.

Additional state legislation made it difficult for southern African-Americans to choose their employment freely. One common law among southern states prohibited an employer from enticing a laborer away from a job. Another—the criminal surety law—allowed courts to hire out African-Americans who failed to pay their fines. Employers had their own employees convicted of often trumped-up petty offenses in order to obtain cheap and guaranteed labor in return. Convict leasing, while not unconstitutional per se, was a publicly administered version of the surety system. Emigrant agent licensing laws required labor recruiters to pay exorbitant fees in southern states. By 1900, additional laws emerged to help entrench the peonage system. Modified contract labor laws made it a crime for a laborer to fraudulently sign and break a labor contract. Southern states inferred a fraudulent signing from the very act of breaking the contract.

In addition to labor-specific laws, many other laws encouraged peonage by curtailing the mobility of African-American workers. Hitchhiking laws, for example, forbade a free mode of transportation for workers to reach other sources of employment. Vagrancy laws afforded law enforcement considerable discretion to arrest African-Americans and put them to work.

The oppressive atmosphere in the South provided fertile ground for peonage and prevented simple legal solutions from eradicating the deeply rooted problem. In a society committed to defending white supremacy, southern landowners supported by white officials could effectively ignore federal laws that may have protected African-American laborers. By the 1890s, white southerners had largely disfranchised African-Americans, barring them from positions of power. White planters could also rely on rural isolation to prevent workers from discovering other sources of work and from asserting their legal rights. They could also resort to beatings, lynching, and property expropriation to instill fear in African-American laborers.

African-Americans attempted to escape their peon status by moving between farms or between states. They also resisted by shirking on loans, by resorting to violence, and by occasionally obtaining their own property. Legal challenges, however, were largely beyond their means.

Historians have long debated the extent of the southern peonage system in the late nineteenth century. Some argue that the tenant system did not operate to the detriment of African-Americans in some areas of the South. The evidence is clear, however, that a significant amount of agricultural peonage existed in the South before 1900. Peonage also flourished during this period in rural industries like turpentine, lumber, naval stores, and railroad construction.

The Progressive Campaign against Peonage

By the time the first public campaign against peonage emerged, the Thirteenth Amendment and the Peonage Act of 1867 had lain dormant for more than a quarter of a century. At the turn of the twentieth century, peonage caught the attention of American progressives bent on eradicating a bevy of social ills. Even as white progressives in both the North and the South tolerated increased white-on-black violence and the general deterioration of the status of African-Americans, they deemed peonage—with its overtones of chattel slavery—beyond the pale of a civilized nation.

In the North, a progressive press exposed the problem of peonage, portraying it as proof of the South's backward and pariah status. Progressives like Ray Stannard Baker wrote exposés on southern peonage, and Oswald Garrison Villard—grandson of the abolitionist William Lloyd Garrison—attacked peonage in the newspapers much as his grandfather had critiqued chattel slavery.

White southern liberals played critical roles in exposing Progressive Era peonage. Fred Cubberly, a Florida Commissioner, filed the first test case of the federal peonage statute. In Alabama, Erastus Parsons, the grandson of a former state governor, instituted habeas corpus proceedings to free a peon, and Judge Thomas Jones, a patrician former Alabama governor himself, impaneled a grand jury to investigate peonage.

In the African-American community, leaders united in their opposition to peonage despite differences on other issues. Even Booker T. Washington, usually seen as an accommodationist in contrast to such civil rights activists as W. E. B. DuBois, joined in the antipeonage crusade. Washington secretly funded litigation and provided information about peonage practices to the northern press.

The federal government under President Theodore Roosevelt responded to public outcries against peonage with litigation. Not only was peonage the subject of much opprobrium, but it also enabled Roosevelt's Republican Justice Department to embarrass the largely Democratic white South. By 1905, the Justice Department had prosecuted more than 100 peonage cases.

The Justice Department's first test case reached the Supreme Court in 1905. Although *Clyatt v. United States* did not result in a conviction, the Court upheld as constitutional the Peonage Act of 1867. In 1911, *Bailey v. Alabama* struck down a contract labor law for violating the Thirteenth Amendment's prohibition on involuntary servitude. A third case, *United States v. Reynolds* in 1914, ruled unconstitutional Alabama's criminal surety system, whereby indigents convicted of misdemeanors were subject to criminal penalties if they ceased working for the sureties who had paid their fines.

Despite these decisions, the federal government ultimately did little to help black peons. Statutes limited the reach of federal law enforcement, as they only allowed for prosecutions of involuntary servitude based on debt. Although some state courts struck down laws facilitating peonage, other states took advantage of the narrowness of Supreme Court decisions to maintain peonage laws. Still other states, notably Florida and Georgia, defiantly repassed statutes virtually identical to those struck down. The juries of southern states were similarly recalcitrant. Almost always all white, most juries would refuse to convict local white planters of peonage.

Federal investigations after 1906 emphasized the plight of immigrants rather than that of blacks. Many immigrants were lured to the South by promises of high wages but found themselves in debt working as peons in railroad and turpentine camps. The United States sought to avert international embarrassment from these stories of European immigrants. Assistant Attorney General Charles Wells Russell and Mary Grace Quackenbos, a wealthy New York attorney and the first female special assistant U.S. attorney, traveled across the South to investigate peonage among immigrants.

Pressure from white southern congressmen contributed to the new emphasis on immigrants. These congressmen criticized the Justice Department's focus on African-American peonage in the South. Congress accordingly passed a bill calling for an investigation into nationwide peonage among immigrants.

The resulting Immigration Commission Report concluded that peonage had existed in the United States in 1907 but that it had largely been eliminated by 1911.

The belief that peonage was not a serious problem stemmed from two related impulses. The first, generally espoused by southerners, was that the South opposed peonage, viewing it as a vestige of the past and an outlier practice. The second was that, as a general matter, progressives in the North and South had faith in the power of public exposure. They believed changing public opinion—rather than battling to punish landowners—would easily end peonage. The Alabama judge Thomas Jones reflected this belief when he obtained several peonage convictions but gave light sentences and recommended pardons for some of the guilty.

Interwar Period

From the start of World War I through the 1920s, 1.5 million African-Americans escaped oppressive conditions in the rural South and headed to northern and southern cities. Their departure strengthened the resolve of many southern planters to retain remaining workers through oppressive peonage practices. Though peonage clearly endured in this environment after 1914, its exact scope was unknown. The remoteness of rural peonage practices made measuring the problem difficult. Although written complaints poured into the Department of Justice and the NAACP after 1909, isolated and often illiterate victims had difficulty making their complaints heard.

Sporadic exposés during the interwar period suggested the persistence of peonage across the South. The case of John Williams, the notorious "murder farmer" of Jasper County, Georgia, exposed a southern planter willing to murder laborers who might testify about peonage. Williams, who was sentenced to life in prison for the murder of an African-American laborer, inspired a former governor, Hugh Dorsey, to publish a pamphlet documenting a horrific picture of peonage across rural Georgia.

In another notorious incident, the federal government appeared to sponsor the establishment of peonage camps after the flooding of the Mississippi River in 1927. Camps providing shelter for those displaced by the flood forced African-American refugees to work on river levees and for white landowners. Secretary of Commerce Herbert Hoover and the Red Cross denied these allegations, which the NAACP documented through its own investigations.

During the Great Depression, farm mechanization and bankruptcies, a labor surplus, and federal agricultural policies decreased the need for farmworkers. Though peonage may have declined in the 1930s as a result, high-profile incidents of forced labor proved its existence. In Arkansas, Paul D. Peacher was charged in 1937 with slavery under an 1866 Slave Kidnapping Act for forcing 20 striking African-Americans to stay in jail-like conditions and work on his farm. Another infamous Depression-era case involved a Georgia farmer who chased escaped peons to Chicago in 1939. The African-American lawyer William Henry Huff interceded on behalf of the escaped peons. He created the Abolish Peonage Committee to publicize the case and pressure the federal government to prosecute. Ultimately, a federal judge threw out the charges against the farmer.

The World War II Campaign against Peonage

During World War II, southern planters renewed efforts to maintain coercive control over African-American laborers despite the many who fled north for lucrative industrial jobs. Landowners fearful of labor scarcity used coercion to force remaining workers to stay rather than higher wages to induce them to do so. As the rural South became less isolated, however, planters found it increasingly difficult to restrict worker movement and hide egregious practices from federal authorities.

Within this context, the federal government revitalized its antipeonage work. Building on the peonage and slave kidnapping statutes, the Thirteenth Amendment, and additional civil rights statutes, Justice Department lawyers in the newly established Civil Rights Section instituted numerous investigations. One particularly widespread incident occurred in 1942 on the United States Sugar Corporation's Florida sugar plantations. The federal prosecution ultimately failed when an all-white grand jury refused to indict. As a general matter, the Civil Rights Section sought to expand the meaning of peonage under federal statutes to include cases that did not implicate a debt. Despite these efforts, the debt element of statutory peonage remained and limited some prosecutions.

The Supreme Court supported Justice Department efforts to eradicate peonage with its wartime decisions. In *Taylor v. Georgia* and *Pollock v. Williams*, the Court re-affirmed its 1911 decision striking down coercive contract laws. *United States v. Gaskin* ruled that the arrest of a person with intent to force him into labor to repay a debt violates the Thirteenth Amendment, even if no labor is actually performed.

Other civil rights organizations contributed to federal efforts to end peonage during the 1940s. The Justice Department often received reports of peonage from groups that had conducted their own investigations. The Workers Defense League (WDL), for example, repeatedly exposed peonage in Florida, Texas, South Carolina, Georgia, and Tennessee. The NAACP also brought peonage complaints to the government's attention.

Peonage after World War II

Reports of peonage and federal prosecutions of the practice declined during the 1950s. Nevertheless, it is likely peonage changed in form rather than entirely disappeared. One sign that peonage persisted was the WDL's success in persuading the United Nations to create a Commission on Forced Labor. Another came in 1951, when a white social activist from Florida named Stetson Kennedy testified to that Commission about the problem of peonage in the United States.

Whatever the scope of the peonage problem since 1950, the types of victims and circumstances clearly changed. Peonage became more closely associated with immigrants, who generally replaced African-Americans as the poorest farmworkers. One study of peonage from 1961 to 1963 found the highest incidence in California, likely due to the prevalence of Mexican migrant labor in the state. The study also found incidents of peonage in 29 other states.

A tool used in this new type of peonage was the traditional one of the unconscionable labor contract. The United States government undertook to formalize the use of alien farmworkers in both the Bracero and H-2 workers programs. Despite these federal efforts, several exposés revealed the continued threat of peonage to foreign farmworkers. In 1961, Edward Murrow's CBS documentary titled *Harvest of Shame* focused national attention on the problem. In 1969, a *New Republic* article by Robert Coles and Harry Huge spotlighted peonage in Florida.

After the 1950s, peonage also changed by expanding to nonrural industries. Sweatshops, particularly in the garment industry, and prostitution rings became fertile ground for peonage and other forms of involuntary servitude. In the late 1980s, the Supreme Court clarified the definition of involuntary servitude under the Thirteenth Amendment. In *United States v. Kosminksy*, the Court said the law, though not requiring a laborer to be indebted, did require an objective determination of coerced labor. The Justice Department continued to prosecute peonage and involuntary servitude under this definition into the twenty-first century. Newer laws protecting immigrants from peonage have augmented the federal government's ability to address the problem.

RISA L. GOLUBOFF

References and Further Reading

Bernstein, David E. *Only One Place of Redress: African Americans, Labor Regulations, and the Courts from Reconstruction to the New Deal.* Durham, NC: Duke University Press, 2001.

Brodie, Sydney. "The Federally-Secured Right to Be Free from Bondage." *Georgetown Law Journal* 40 (March 1952): 367–398.

Carr, Robert K. *Federal Protection of Civil Rights: Quest for a Sword.* Ithaca, NY: Cornell University Press, 1947.

Cohen, William. "Negro Involuntary Servitude in the South: 1865–1940: A Preliminary Analysis." *Journal of Southern History* 42 (February 1976): 31–60.

Daniel, Pete. *The Shadow of Slavery: Peonage in the South, 1901–1969.* New York: Oxford University Press, 1973.

Goluboff, Risa L. "The Thirteenth Amendment and the Lost Origins of Civil Rights." *Duke Law Journal* 50 (2001): 1609–1685.

———. "'Won't You Please Help Me Get My Son Home': Peonage, Patronage, and Protest in the World War II Urban South." *Law and Social Inquiry* 24 (1999): 777.

Hahamovitch, Cindy. *The Fruits of Their Labor: Atlantic Coast Farmworkers and the Making of Migrant Poverty, 1870–1945.* Chapel Hill: University of North Carolina Press, 1997.

Hahn, Steven. *A Nation under Our Feet: Black Political Struggles in the Rural South from Slavery to the Great Migration.* Cambridge: Belknap Press, 2003.

Hamilton, Howard Devon. "The Legislative and Judicial History of the Thirteenth Amendment: The Inception of the Thirteenth Amendment." *National Bar Journal* 9 (1951): 26.

———. "The Legislative and Judicial History of the Thirteenth Amendment: What Is Not Involuntary Servitude." *National Bar Journal* 10 (1952): 7.

Jones, Jacqueline. *The Dispossessed: America's Underclasses from the Civil War to the Present.* New York: 1992.

Novak, Daniel Novak. *The Wheel of Servitude: Black Forced Labor after Slavery.* Lexington: University Press of Kentucky, 1978.

Cases and Statutes Cited

Bailey v. Alabama, 219 U.S. 219 (1911)
Clyatt v. United States, 197 U.S. 207 (1905)
Pollock v. Williams, 322 U.S. 4 (1944)
Taylor v. Georgia, 315 U.S. 25 (1942)
United States v. Gaskin, 320 U.S. 527 (1944)
United States v. Kozminski, 487 U.S. 931 (1988)
United States v. Reynolds, 235 U.S. 133 (1914)
Peonage Act of 1867, ch. 187, 14 Stat. 546 (1867)
Slave Kidnapping Act of 1866, ch. 86, 14 Stat. 50 (1866)

See also **African-Americans; Convict Labor in the New South; Emancipation and Reconstruction; Migrant Farmworkers; Sharecropping and Tenancy; Slavery; South; Thirteenth Amendment**

PEOPLE'S PARTY
See **Populism/People's Party**

PERKINS, FRANCES (1880–1965)
Department of Labor

Born in 1880, Frances Perkins attended Mount Holyoke College, graduating in 1902. After teaching for several years, the Boston native went to New York City in 1909 to study for a master's degree at Columbia University. Finishing her degree the next year, she joined the Consumers' League of New York, an organization devoted to raising labor standards for working women and children.

Perkins personally witnessed the Triangle Shirtwaist Factory fire on March 25, 1911, where 146 garment industry workers, mostly young, immigrant women, died trying to escape a factory fire. A determined Perkins went to work for the Factory Investigating Commission (FIC), created in June 1911 by the New York legislature to investigate working conditions in the state's manufacturing. While working for the Commission, Perkins became close friends with the FIC's two major political figures, State Senator Robert F. Wagner Sr. and State Assembly Majority Leader Alfred E. ("Al") Smith. Perkins also lobbied for the passage of a 54-hour workweek bill for New York's factory women workers, which became law in March 1912. These experiences convinced her that labor legislation constituted the most effective means of helping labor, although Perkins also supported trade unionism.

In 1919, the newly elected governor, Al Smith, appointed Perkins to New York's Industrial Commission. For the next 10 years (except from 1921 through 1923) Perkins gained invaluable experience overseeing New York's workers' compensation system, as well as mediating strikes.

When Franklin D. Roosevelt became Smith's successor in 1929, he appointed Perkins the state's first female industrial commissioner. Previously cool to Roosevelt because of his perceived superciliousness, a surprised Perkins soon formed a close working relationship with the new governor. She also provided subtle, but effective, assistance to reformers working for a minimum wage bill for workingwomen in New York, which passed in early 1933. She also became a major critic of President Herbert Hoover's attempts to alleviate the growing depression and convinced Governor Roosevelt to form a governmental committee that sought to stabilize New York's unemployment situation.

Perkins became the first women member of the U.S. cabinet when the newly elected President Franklin D. Roosevelt appointed her head of the nation's Department of Labor in March 1933. Confirmed by the Senate, Perkins faced widespread skepticism among both business and labor interests doubtful about a woman's ability to manage the nation's labor affairs. Within the next two years, however, Secretary Perkins won grudging admiration as an effective, if sometimes prickly, arbitrator between management and labor, helping to settle disputes in San Francisco and Minneapolis. Her attempt to reconcile skilled and unskilled laborers failed, however, and the American Federation of Labor (AFL) remained separate from the Congress of Industrial Organizations (CIO) until 1955.

While not directly involved with the Wagner Act, Perkins shepherded through Congress the passage of the Social Security Act of 1935 and the Walsh-Healey Public Contracts Act of 1936, which required federal contractors to meet minimum wage standards.

The passage of the 1938 Fair Labor Standards Act (FLSA) perhaps proved the most significant triumph for Perkins, since it provided the first federal floor wage requirements for workers in the United States. The secretary of labor prepared the groundwork for the FLSA by holding seven national minimum wage conferences from 1933 through 1937, which brought together business leaders, labor leaders, and government officials to discuss the issue. Perkins lobbied for the FLSA after President Roosevelt introduced the law to Congress in May 1937. A significant feature of the final bill, enacted in June 1938, gave the administration of the FLSA to Department of Labor officials.

Although organized labor never warmed to Perkins, business interests became increasingly hostile to her. When Perkins delayed the deportation of the controversial longshoremen leader Harry Bridges in 1938, the House Judiciary Committee considered a motion for impeachment. While Perkins testified before the Committee, the motion never reached Congress.

Perkins continued to serve as secretary of labor after President Roosevelt secured his third term in 1940. Her influence, however, diminished as President Roosevelt's tendency to create myriad administrative agencies during World War II meant that Perkins possessed little control over the United States' wartime labor situation. The secretary of labor did ensure that labor standards established during the New Deal did not end.

Forced to resign by President Harry S Truman in July 1945, Perkins published her surprisingly balanced memoirs, *The Roosevelt I Knew*, the next year. The former cabinet officer continued her active career, most notably teaching at Cornell University's School of Labor and Industrial Relations until her death in 1965.

JOHN THOMAS MCGUIRE

References and Further Reading

Martin, George. *Madam Secretary: Frances Perkins*. Boston: Houghton Mifflin, 1976.
Perkins, Frances. *The Roosevelt I Knew*. New York: Viking, 1946.

See also **Department of Labor; Triangle Shirtwaist Fire**

PERLMAN, SELIG (1888–1959)
Labor Intellectual

Best known to labor historians for his collaboration with his mentor, John R. Commons, on the classic *The History of Labour in the United States* (1918), Selig Perlman emerged from Jewish immigrant origins to become one of the most influential labor intellectuals of the early twentieth century. Born to a small merchant family in Bialystock, Russia, Perlman passed from Jewish day school to a Russian gymnasium to a brief period studying medicine with other politically radical Russian émigrés in Italy before a fortuitous connection with the visiting American socialist, William English Walling, provided the invitation to emigrate to the United States and, shortly thereafter, enroll at the University of Wisconsin.

Combining a sharp-edged theoretical disposition with a commitment to empirical research, Perlman soon substantially advanced contemporary understandings of the workers' movement in America and elsewhere. His undergraduate thesis, "History of Socialism in Milwaukee," completed after one year of coursework, reflected an initial continuity of intellectual and political commitments. Espousing the revisionist "opportunism" of Eduard Bernstein, Perlman extolled Victor Berger and the Milwaukee socialists for the triumph of "realism" over "revolutionism" in labor and political circles. Pursuing graduate training at Wisconsin under Commons and Richard T. Ely, Perlman assimilated Commons's emphasis on the role of marketplace forces (as opposed to class conflict at

the point of production) as influences on workers' behavior. His dissertation, published as the last part of volume two of Commons' *History of Labour* (1918), emphasized the skilled worker's view of job control as a kind of property right. Next, Perlman's *A History of Trade Unionism in the United States* (1922), begun as an update of Ely's *The Labor Movement in America* (1886), continued this emphasis on trade unionism as a worker's form of market protection. Rather than contending over ownership of the means of production, Perlman insinuated, American workers sought to insulate themselves from cheap goods and cheap labor through the power of collective bargaining agreements.

Ultimately ensconced in his own teaching position at the University of Wisconsin's economics department and School for Workers, Perlman produced his most influential work, *A Theory of the Labor Movement* (1928). At once offering a summary historical reflection on worker movements in Russia, Germany, and Britain, as well as the United States, Perlman here developed the concept of "job consciousness—with a limited objective of wage and job control" as the characteristic way that American labor, in contradistinction to European "class consciousness," defended workers' economic security. The reasons that a European-style "class consciousness" continually failed to take root in the United States, enumerated Perlman, included the mobility of the wage-earning class, with outlets both in the "West" and in lower-level managerial positions; early access of workers to the ballot and identification with the larger public; and massive immigration, making for "the most heterogeneous laboring class in existence" (pp. 165–169). Another prominent theme of *A Theory* was Perlman's pointed reflection on the continual struggle of "organic labor" against "dominance by the intellectuals." Instead of an American exceptionalism, à la Werner Sombart, Perlman's intellectual-versus-worker paradigm implied a "Soviet" exceptionalism, with "backward" Russia the one country where the "will to power" of intellectuals within the workers' movement had prevailed. Outside the Soviet Union, he argued, built-in tensions between the two social groups persisted (with intellectuals weakest of all in the United States), but the trade unionists, mature and well-organized, tended increasingly to shape both industrial and political action in their own pragmatic, nonrevolutionary image. Perlman's personal experience had likely made him particularly aware of the social standing and role of the intellectual. An outsider both as an immigrant and a Jew to American academic culture, he also enjoyed relatively little direct contact with the American labor organizations—let alone the ordinary workers—he wrote about. In the circumstances, his assimilation of American pragmatism (one combined with a particular reading of Jewish law) likely led him to a mistrust of all abstract faiths and utopian political projections. Always conscious of the anti-Semitic slights around him, in his later years, Perlman turned his focus to the plight of European Jews, and, but for health reasons, would have accepted a chair at Hebrew University of Jerusalem in the mid-1950s.

LEON FINK

References and Further Reading

Fink, Leon. "'Intellectuals' versus 'Workers': Academic Requirements and the Creation of Labor History." *American Historical Review* 96 (April 1991): 395–421.

Perlman, Mark. "Selig Perlman." In *American National Biography*, volume 17. New York: Oxford University Press, 1999, pp. 353–355.

Perlman, Selig. *A Theory of the Labor Movement*. 1928. Reprint, Philadelphia: Porcupine Press, 1979.

PERSONNEL MANAGEMENT

Broadly conceived, personnel management encompasses any effort by supervisors to direct employees, but the term is largely associated with the maturation of industrial capitalism and construction of formal employee policies. It involved the establishment of specialized activities within public and private institutions, which created rules and procedures for employee relations, including hiring, training, promotion, discipline, and dismissal. In the mid- to late nineteenth century, business firms blended informal employee relations practices with more formal employee policies, often relying on both personal decisions and impersonal rules to govern employees. By 1880, specialized personnel offices and staff positions began to appear in large corporate entities, such as John Wanamaker's department store, but few businesses followed suit until the 1910s and 1920s, and many of these offices remained small. Narrowly conceived, they often focused on record keeping. In 1883, the Pendleton Act created the U.S. Civil Service Commission to oversee implementation of a merit system in the federal government. Although hiring remained decentralized within agencies, the commission became the government's central personnel agency. During the Great Depression, the establishment of specialized personnel offices accelerated—perhaps in response to the expansion of unions—both in the public and private sector. One study estimated that the number of personnel departments doubled in companies employing more than 250 people between 1929 and 1935, and the Department of Agriculture established the first federal department personnel office in 1925, with

many agencies following in the 1930s. By 1939, the federal government had a Council of Personnel Administration consisting of agency personnel directors who discussed common issues, such as union relations, and sought to unify personnel practices.

Scholars offer myriad explanations for the creation of personnel administration. For some, the emergence of this field is largely a function of size; as organizations, especially corporations, grew larger and more complex, firm owners sought ways to standardize employee relations practices, standardizing them across far-flung divisions. Often drawing on theories articulated by the sociologist Max Weber, this view stressed the way that bureaucracies—with their functional division of labor, hierarchical organization, and impersonal rules—became the most efficient way of conducting business. Explanations placing more emphasis on human agency and internal pressures focused on the role that middle-level managers played in creating new functions as a means of expanding career options and their professional authority. Scholars influenced by Marxism argued that the emergence of personnel administration reflected a management effort to assert greater control and discipline over labor, particularly as a means of combating high employee turnover rates in the early twentieth century, strikes, and union power. Turning this interpretation on its head, some students of personnel management maintained that unionization and collective bargaining, with its reliance on contracts and rules, encouraged management to adopt more formal personnel management procedures. Harkening back to a Weberian model, those who attempted to blend these two interpretations suggested that both managers and workers desired a more predictable environment based on standard employee procedures and policies. Finally, some more politically inclined scholars asserted that government regulations and legislation, such as affirmative action, led firms and public agencies to develop personnel offices to administer these regulations.

Scientific Management, Welfare Work, and Gender

As an occupation, personnel management has strong ties to Progressive Era movements and deep roots in engineering and social welfare work. Like many Progressive Era reformers, some early personnel management proponents valued technical expertise, efficiency, and standardization. While others in the field prized these concepts, and demonstrated a characteristic Progressive proclivity to support intervention, they were equally influenced by moral concerns. They conceived of personnel management as an opportunity to humanize industrial capitalism and improve the life of workers by stressing the personal, over technocratic, aspects of personnel work.

Frederick W. Taylor's influential scientific management theories, and the movement spawned by them, contributed to the early formation of a technically oriented form of personnel work. Drawing on the new field of engineering and its foundation in mathematics and emphasis on scientific method, Taylor and his followers sought to increase worker efficiency through the application of scientific principles to the management of labor. While not specifically designed for personnel management, Taylor's theories nonetheless encouraged devotees to apply scientific management to employee relations. Harlow Person, for instance, a member of the Society to Promote the Science of Management (renamed the Taylor Society after Taylor's death), devised the first college course for employment managers, offering it at Dartmouth College's Amos Tuck School of Administration and Finance in 1915. Frank and Lillian Gilbreth, members of the American Society of Mechanical Engineers and two founders of the Society to Promote the Science of Management, conducted experiments on how to reduce worker fatigue and increase productivity. One company, Plimpton Press, which had introduced Taylorism into its workplace, established a separate employment department in 1910 with Jane C. Williams as its manager. Her department had multiple responsibilities ranging from matching workers to appropriate jobs, training, orientation, and grievance work to maintaining a library, offering financial advice, and providing a lunchroom. These developments coalesced into an employment management movement, which gathered force in the 1910s and initially stressed the need to match workers' mental and physical traits with appropriate jobs.

Williams's diverse tasks suggested the welfare roots of personnel management. Sometimes referred to as "industrial betterment," this movement attracted reformers eager to soften the industrial experience. At times influenced by the Social Gospel movement, proponents focused on improving the lives and raising the morale of workers. To this end, they favored the implementation of recreation, health, and educational programs and the establishment of other employee services, such as dining rooms. Usually labeled welfare departments or offices, their heads perceived themselves as operating between line and staff positions and as mediators balancing the needs of management and workers. The National Cash Register Company established the first recorded welfare office

in 1897, with Lena H. Tracy as its head. Several other large companies, such as Filene's Department Store, Westinghouse Electric, and H. J. Heinz Co., subsequently created their own offices. A study by the National Civic Federation reported 2,500 firms with welfare offices by 1914, many of them headed by women. At about the same time, the term "employment management" began to replace the phrase "welfare work."

Notably, personnel work offered women access to white-collar managerial positions. Usually referred to as social or welfare secretaries, women who ran welfare offices frequently had backgrounds in vocational guidance, social reform, and teaching. Other women came to personnel administration through training in psychology. Lillian Gilbreth, for example, became an early advocate of applying psychology to management. Like Gilbreth, Person supported the blending of social and behavioral sciences, especially the emerging field of industrial psychology, with scientific management and its engineering emphasis.

Industrial psychology, pioneered by Hugo Münsterberg, who came to Harvard from Germany in 1892, suggested that mental tests could match the best person with the best job and that an ideal psychological environment could increase worker output. During World War I, the federal government significantly supported this program by hiring psychologists, such as Walter Dill Scott, who developed intelligence and occupation aptitude tests for both the military and industry.

This reliance on psychology served as a bridge between the hard scientific basis of personnel administration and its softer origins in welfare reform, a split that further revealed the gendered dimension of personnel work. Both men and women acted as proponents of the scientific and welfare versions of personnel management, but men and a masculine discourse generally dominated the scientific management movement, and women and a feminine discourse tended to be more prominent in welfare reform efforts. Scientific management's emphasis on rationality and efficiency was portrayed in masculine terms and contrasted to the more feminine versions of employee welfare work, which was conveyed as focusing on emotional well-being. Tensions over the masculine and feminine forms of personnel management, including ongoing efforts of women to break into management careers dominated by men and equally powerful attempts by managers to make the field more manly as a means of gaining professional legitimacy, led to significant fragmentation of the personnel movement in the early twentieth century. It also suggested the struggle this field and its practitioners faced as it attempted to build professional authority.

Professionalization

In a sign of the field's desire to carve out a specific identity and to professionalize, employment management associations and journals began to appear in the 1910s. The National Association of Corporation Schools (NACS), created in 1913, became the first national organization to examine personnel management explicitly. It began publishing a bulletin in 1914. In 1922, NACS merged with the National Association of Employment Managers, to form the National Personnel Association, which eventually became the American Management Association (AMA). Ostensibly a neutral, professional organization, the AMA nonetheless had strong ties to large corporations, such as Standard Oil, DuPont, and General Electric, and in the 1920s showed a distinctively anti-union bias. Its journal underwent several name changes, calling itself *Personnel Administration*, *Personnel*, and finally *HR Focus* in 1991. In 1919, many of the same companies associated with AMA had organized a Special Conference Committee, chaired by the former personnel director for Standard Oil, to coordinate personnel policies and labor relations activities. A few years later, they formed the Personnel Research Federation to promote industrial psychology. The Federation's *Personnel Journal* (formerly the *Journal of Personnel Research*) was published until 1996. Although none of these associations called overtly for the hostile suppression of unions, they promoted employee representation plans, such as company unions, with a clear aim to undermine worker support for labor organizations.

In the public sector, managers, who generally did not deal with the same union issues as their private-sector counterparts, had their own professional organizations and journals. Public personnel managers tended to join the Society for Personnel Administration, which published *Personnel Administration*, starting in 1938. In 1972, the journal merged with *Public Personnel Review* to become *Public Personnel Management*. By the 1940s, journals with the term "human relations" in the title began to appear, and in the 1980s, "human resources" became more prevalent.

The human relations school of management, which many personnel administrators eagerly embraced in the 1930s and 1940s, provided personnel work with closer ties to the academy and cemented personnel management to the social and behavioral sciences.

It emerged from a series of experiments conducted by the Harvard sociologist Elton Mayo and others at Western Electric's Hawthorne plant in the 1920s. These experiments reflected the increased attention paid to management issues by academics and the desire by many in the field to marry psychology and sociology to personnel administration. Drawn to the writings of the German sociologist Emile Durkheim, Mayo believed that organizations should be viewed as social systems in which individual problems and group dynamics could easily undermine morale, and hence productivity. Supervisors therefore needed to recognize that worker behavior was often guided by emotional sentiments seemingly disconnected from the actual job performed. To maximize morale and increase productivity, line managers would need to diagnose and address workers' psychological and social problems. Mayo's more personal approach to management appealed to personnel specialists with a reformist orientation and those wishing to enhance the field's professional credibility. It also connected management studies more firmly to the academy, as evidenced by the University of Chicago's Committee on Human Relations in Industry (1943), which collaborated with Sears, Roebuck and Company on numerous studies. This management school also spawned a plethora of publications, including Fritz J. Roethlisberger and William S. Dickson's book *Management and the Worker* (1939), which became the most widely distributed text on Mayo's brand of human relations. Personnel offices often sought to train line managers in the art of human relations, which encouraged managers to improve their interpersonal skills so that they could counsel and communicate more effectively with subordinates. As part of a larger industrial democracy movement, human relations seemed to humanize management in a way that the technocratic Taylor system had not.

Critics complained that human relations merely masked power relations within firms and ignored legitimate worker complaints about work conditions and pay. Moreover, they argued, the underlying aim of human relations was to force the worker to adjust to a hierarchical work environment, rather than encourage a more democratic workplace. Many perceived it as an effort to undermine unions. A simultaneous stress, starting in the 1920s, on creating employee representation programs as a means of promoting industrial democracy often led to the establishment of company unions, which was further evidence to critics of the conservative aims of these efforts. Although some human relations experts sought to include unions in programs, labor organizations often expressed skepticism of its value as an empowering source for workers.

Personnel Management in the Post-World War II Era

Labor relations specialists often found themselves organized as a subset of a personnel office, particularly after passage of the National Labor Relations Act in 1935. Overall, however, personnel offices concentrated on training, benefits, job classification, and payroll. Developments in post-Mayo management schools reinvigorated the field's academic orientation but also put new emphasis on the growing white-collar workforce of the widening service sector. These theories included the management guru Peter Drucker's "management by objectives," Douglas MacGregor's "Theory Y," which stressed worker self-actualization, and "Theory Z," an American interpretation of familial management styles practiced in postwar Japan. Simultaneously, scholars sought to reconstruct a science of administration, using cybernetics, economics, and math. Although critical of Taylor's scientific management, the most prominent organizational theorist, Herbert Simon, applied mathematical and economic models and used theories drawn from political science, sociology, and psychology in an effort to construct an overarching theory of bureaucratic rationality.

The proliferation of new federal regulations regarding workplace equity also contributed to shifts in the field. In the 1970s, personnel departments began to take over administration of affirmative action programs and implement sensitivity training. They also acquired a new nomenclature, calling themselves "human resources" rather than personnel departments. A major exception to this occurred in 1976, when the government created the Office of Personnel Management to replace the U.S. Civil Service Commission.

Under increasing economic pressure to become leaner, many corporations began to lay off middle-level managers in the 1980s and 1990s, and human resource specialists found themselves particularly vulnerable. Weaker unions and a political environment less conducive to enforcing personnel regulations made it more difficult for human resource employees to justify their positions. In many cases, companies put more responsibility on line managers to oversee employment issues, suggesting a return to the more decentralized, less formal structure characteristic of nineteenth-century firms. Nevertheless, formal personnel functions continue to exist in large and small companies and in government agencies. The fluctuating fortune of personnel management suggests the ways in which this concept continues to make and remake itself as an integral aspect of an organizational society.

MARGARET C. RUNG

References and Further Reading

Eilbert, Henry. "The Development of Personnel Management in the United States." *Business History Review* 33 (Autumn 1959): 344–364.

Gillespie, Richard. *Manufacturing Knowledge: A History of the Hawthorne Experiments*. Cambridge: Cambridge University Press, 1991.

Jacoby, Sanford M. *Employing Bureaucracy: Managers, Unions, and the Transformation of Work in American Industry, 1900–1945*. 1985. Reprint, New York: Columbia University Press, 2004.

———. *Modern Manors: Welfare Capitalism since the New Deal*. Princeton, NJ: Princeton University Press, 1997.

Jacques, Roy. *Manufacturing the Employee: Management Knowledge from the 19th to 21st Centuries*. London: Sage Publications, 1996.

Licht, Walter. "Studying Work: Personnel Policies in Philadelphia Firms." In *Masters to Managers: Historical and Comparative Perspectives on American Employers*, edited by Sanford M. Jacoby. New York: Columbia University Press, 1991.

Rung, Margaret. *Servants of the State: Managing Diversity and Democracy in the Federal Workforce, 1933–1953*. Athens: University of Georgia Press, 2002.

Strom, Sharon Hartman. *Beyond the Typewriter: Gender, Class, and the Origins of Modern American Office Work, 1900–1930*. Urbana: University of Illinois Press, 1992.

Waring, Stephen. *Taylorism Transformed: Scientific Management Theory since 1945*. Chapel Hill: University of North Carolina Press, 1991.

Wren, Daniel. *The Evolution of Management Thought*. 4th ed. New York: John Wiley & Sons, Inc., 1994.

PESOTTA, ROSE (NOVEMBER 20, 1896–DECEMBER 7, 1965)
Anarchist, Labor Organizer, Trade Union Officer

Rose Pesotta was born Rachelle Peisoty in Derazhnya, Ukraine, Russia. Her parents, Itsaak (Isaack) and Masya, were prosperous grain merchants, and Pesotta grew up in an Orthodox Jewish home relatively untouched by the vicious anti-Jewish pogroms so many experienced during this time in the shtetls of the Russian Empire. Educated at home as well as at a local private girls' school, by the time she was a teenager, Pesotta was fluent in Yiddish, Hebrew, Ukrainian, and Russian. She was also by her teens active in the radical Russian anarchist movement, well read in and heavily influenced by the work of Mikhail Bakunin, Peter Kropotkin, and Pierre Joseph Proudhon. Seeking to escape a planned marriage, Pesotta immigrated to America before the age of 17, joining her sister Esther in New York City just before Thanksgiving, 1913. During processing by immigration agents, her name was changed to Rose Pesotta, and she soon found work in New York City's booming garment industry, a trade she returned to repeatedly for the next 50 years.

By the time Pesotta became a garment worker and joined the International Ladies' Garment Workers' Union (ILGWU), the union had endured the bitter strike of 1909–1910 known as "The Uprising of the 20,000" and the 1911 Triangle Factory Shirtwaist Fire with the tragic loss of 146 workers, most of them young women, barely out of their teens, and like Pesotta, Russian Jewish and Italian immigrants. While conditions within the New York City garment industry were still far from ideal, much needed reforms had occurred in the wake of the Triangle fire, and Pesotta credited the union for much of it. She was soon active in her local, part of a significant anarchist minority. In 1920, she was elected to the executive board of Local No. 22, and throughout the 1920s, she served on several strike committees at the same time that she attended various worker education programs, including the Bryn Mawr Summer School for Women Workers and Brookwood Labor College in Katonah, New York. For Pesotta, trade unionism was the most effective vehicle to not only improve workers' conditions but also to advance the principles of anarchism she held so dear. Since her arrival in America in 1913, Pesotta had also been active in the vibrant anarchist movement in New York City and suffered personally the government repression during the Palmer Raids of 1919–1920 when her then fiancé, a fellow Russian immigrant and anarchist Theodore Kushnarev, was deported along with hundreds of others. But Pesotta continued her active involvement in anarchists' circles and devoted much time and energy working during the 1920s on behalf of Nicola Sacco and Bartolomeo Vanzetti, two Italian immigrant anarchists charged with murder and robbery and executed in 1927.

As a committed anarchist, Pesotta was also virulently anti-Communist, and it was her efforts to expel Communist union members within her local, combined with her engaging personality, that brought her to the notice of the ILGWU leadership, who made her an organizer by the end of the 1920s. With the onset of the Great Depression in 1929, whatever gains the ILGWU had made were quickly eroded as the garment industry, too, felt the impact of this worldwide economic devastation. Pesotta would later remember this as a time when thousands of New York City garment workers went hungry for lack of work. Those who did find work experienced conditions similar to those in the sweatshops of the early part of the twentieth century. However, with the election of Franklin Roosevelt in 1932 and the New Deal reforms beginning with the National Industrial Recovery Act that aimed at putting Americans back to work, the ILGWU seized the prolabor moment and increased its organizing efforts across North America. In 1933, the union hired Pesotta as a full-time organizer, and she was soon organizing Mexican women garment workers in Los Angeles as well as their counterparts in Montreal, Puerto Rico, Boston, and Cleveland. She also helped striking United Auto Workers in their 1936 sit-down strikes in Akron, Ohio, and Flint, Michigan. An effective organizer who spoke to the workers as a worker herself, Pesotta was equally adept at getting press attention during the numerous strikes she oversaw during the 1930s. News photographs from the time repeatedly show a smiling Pesotta, fashionably dressed, holding a picket sign in her white-gloved hands. Her success in the field brought her recognition within the hierarchy of the ILGWU, and at the union's 1934 convention, Pesotta was elected as one of 24 vice presidents, the only woman then serving, and the third woman ever elected to that position in ILGWU history. While she enjoyed a close, if sometimes volatile, working relationship with her mentor, the ILGWU president David Dubinsky, Pesotta was frequently frustrated in her role as an officer in a union in which the rank and file was predominately female and the leadership was decidedly male dominated. Her frustration was further compounded by the tension between her anarchist principles and her leadership role, however limited it was by her sex. In 1942, she resigned her position as a full-time organizer and returned to her trade, working as a dressmaker in a New York City shop. Two years later, she resigned from the ILGWU executive board—the same year she published her own account of her years as an organizer and union officer. That memoir, *Bread upon the Waters* (1944), was immediately well received, translated into several other languages, and remains a vivid look at organizing and union politics during the 1930s.

Although in her later years she worked briefly for the Anti-Defamation League of B'nai B'rith and the American Trade Union Council for Histadrut, the Israeli labor organization, it was through her work as a union dressmaker that Pesotta supported herself until her retirement in 1963. She spent her last years living in the recently opened ILGWU cooperative housing complex at Penn South in New York City and remained politically active until shortly before her death in 1965. Pesotta's biographers emphasize the apparent contradictions of her life—she was a warm and engaging woman, beloved by many in the rank and file, while in her personal life, she experienced several disappointing, even heartbreaking love affairs, including with Powers Hapgood. Although she initially welcomed the opportunity to join the

ILGWU, in doing so she often came into conflict with her strong anarchist beliefs at the same time she battled the male domination of the union she served for 50 years.

KATHLEEN BANKS NUTTER

Selected Works

Pesotta published two memoirs, the above-mentioned *Bread upon the Waters*(1944) and *Days of Our Lives* (1958), which focuses on her earlier years in Russia; her papers are held by the New York Public Library.

References and Further Reading

Leeder, Elaine. *Gentle General: Rose Pesotta, Anarchist and Labor Organizer*. Albany: State University of New York Press, 1993.

See also **Anarchism; Brookwood Labor College; Bryn Mawr Summer School for Women Workers in Industry; Dubinsky, David; Hapgood, Powers; International Ladies' Garment Workers' Union (ILGWU) (1900–1995); National Industrial Recovery Act; Triangle Shirtwaist Fire; Uprising of the 20,000 (1909)**

PETERSON, ESTHER (1906–1997)
Labor Organizer, Educator, Lobbyist, and Political Activist

Working with a group of labor reformers in the 1940s and 1950s, Esther Peterson helped develop an economic agenda to enable women to achieve equality at work and accommodate responsibilities at home. Peterson skillfully moved this agenda forward at the U.S. Department of Labor, where she was the highest-ranking woman in the Kennedy administration. Her major accomplishments there included the groundbreaking work of the first President's Commission on the Status of Women and the passage of the 1963 Equal Pay Act, thus laying the groundwork for major shifts in employment policy and a renewed feminist movement that brought about fundamental changes in society.

The daughter of Anna and Luther Eggertsen, Peterson grew up in Provo, Utah, where her Danish grandparents had settled. She was raised in a strong Mormon community and graduated from Brigham Young University. In 1930, she moved to New York City, where she received a master's degree from Columbia Teachers' College and married Oliver Peterson, a socialist who introduced her to the labor movement.

During the 1930s, Peterson taught at a private girls' school in Boston, but also at the YWCA and the Bryn Mawr Summer School for Women Workers. She became an organizer for the American Federation of Teachers and in 1939 was hired in the education department of the Amalgamated Clothing Workers of America (ACWA). Peterson became the first legislative representative for the ACWA in 1944, working closely with then Congressman John F. Kennedy.

In 1948, her husband joined the Foreign Service as one of the new labor attachés. For the next 10 years, and now with four children, the Petersons lived in Sweden and Brussels, where Esther worked with European trade unions and the International Confederation of Free Trade Unions (ICFTU). In 1952, during the McCarthy Era, Oliver was accused of Communist activities. Although eventually cleared of all charges, he was soon diagnosed with cancer and never fully regained his health, shifting more financial responsibility to Esther.

The Petersons returned to the United States in 1958, and Esther became the first woman lobbyist for the AFL-CIO, in the Industrial Union Department. She renewed her working relationship with Kennedy and was an early labor supporter for his presidential campaign. She was appointed director of the Women's Bureau (1961–1964) and assistant secretary for labor standards (1961–1968), U.S. Department of Labor. Building on her trade union work, she then served in the administrations of Presidents Johnson and Carter as an advisor on consumer affairs and as a delegate to the United Nations in the Clinton administration. She also worked with private industry and helped develop the UN's Guidelines for Consumer Protection.

Esther Peterson's contributions to the labor movement and to workingwomen were firmly grounded in her family's commitment to education, hard work, and helping others and strongly shaped by her husband's progressive politics. Her leadership in what Dorothy Sue Cobble, in *The Other Women's Movement*, calls "labor feminism" further reflected Peterson's experiences with collaborative and cross-class organizations like the Bryn Mawr Summer School, where she was influenced by women and men from the Progressive Era and Roosevelt's New Deal. She never lost sight of workingwomen's needs as she struggled to balance her own work and family life. She strongly supported protective legislation for women, opposed the Equal Rights Amendment, and advocated for increases in the minimum wage and expansion of the labor laws to include domestic and other low-paid workers. She argued that women's lives were undervalued at home and in the workplace, and she championed the union women's approach to solutions through both government and collective bargaining.

The President's Commission on the Status of Women (PCSW) was the culmination of union women's activities over 30 years. The commission was an idea discussed in the 1940s when Peterson served on a labor committee that advised the Women's Bureau on a range of workingwomen's issues. She wanted the PCSW's focus to be broad, covering employment as well as the civil and political efforts of women, and inclusive. The 26 commissioners came from all walks of life, chaired by Eleanor Roosevelt, and the advisory committees eventually numbered over 250 people. For the first time, federal attention focused on problems of African-American women.

The final PCSW recommendations were extensive but reflected the tensions of the time over women's multiple roles. They called for equal opportunity and protective legislation while seeking improvements for women in a wide range of areas including training, child care, and benefits for maternity, social security, and unemployment. The Commission brought together women from the many different feminist movements, who went on to work toward sex and race equality in a multitude of ways.

As the PCSW was getting under way, Peterson's backing was also important for the equal pay bill introduced by Congresswoman Edith Green. While union women had long advocated the idea of equal pay for comparable work, they compromised on this narrower legislation guaranteeing equal pay for equal work, which became law in 1963. The heated debate over the legislation opened a discussion on sex discrimination in employment that was greatly expanded by the 1964 Civil Rights Act and the decades of legislation and court cases that followed. As protective laws were dismantled under this new framework, Peterson no longer opposed the Equal Rights Amendment but renewed her commitment to improving labors standards for all workers. In her 90s, however, she was quick to note that the family problems of workingwomen had yet to be solved.

Peterson went on to bring her formidable political skills and her ability to reach across barriers of race, gender, and class to consumer issues. When she took these issues back to the labor movement, she found little interest, although she considered them important for working families. Internationally recognized for her work on behalf of consumers, she championed legislation for truth in lending, unit pricing, meat and poultry inspection, and occupational safety. In 1981, Esther Peterson was awarded the Presidential Medal of Freedom, the United States' highest civilian honor.

BRIGID O'FARRELL

References and Further Reading

Cobble, Dorothy Sue. *The Other Women's Movement: Workplace Justice and Social Rights in Modern America.* Princeton, NJ: Princeton University Press, 2004.
Kessler-Harris, Alice. *In Pursuit of Equity: Women, Men, and the Quest for Economic Citizenship in Twentieth-Century America.* New York: Oxford University Press, 2001.
Kornbluh, Joyce L., and Brigid O'Farrell, eds. "You Can't Giddyup by Saying Whoa: Esther Peterson Remembers Her Organized Labor Years." *Labor's Heritage* 5, no. 4 (Spring 1994): 38–59.
Laughlin, Kathleen. *Women's Work and Public Policy: A History of the Women's Bureau, U.S. Department of Labor, 1945–1970.* Boston: Northeastern University Press, 2000.
The National Women's History Project, Biography Center. "Esther Peterson." www.nwhp.org/tlp/biographies/peterson/peterson_bio.html.
O'Farrell, Brigid, and Joyce L. Kornbluh. *Rocking the Boat: Union Women's Voices, 1915–1975.* New Brunswick, NJ: Rutgers University Press, 1996.
Peterson, Esther. Papers, Oral History Interviews, Additions. The Arthur and Elizabeth Schlesinger Library, Harvard University, Cambridge, MA. http://oasis.harvard.edu.
Peterson, Esther, with Winifred Conkling. *Restless: The Memoirs of Labor and Consumer Activist Esther Peterson.* Washington, DC: Caring Publishing, 1995.

PETRILLO, JAMES CAESAR (1892–1984)
President, American Federation of Musicians (AFM), 1940–1958

One of the most powerful and well-known labor leaders of his era, after World War II James Petrillo publicly exemplified the "labor czar." Petrillo's primary focus was ensuring jobs for musicians, and his battle against recording companies, radio stations, and movie theaters' use of recorded, or "canned," music was the defining issue of his career. While Petrillo helped solidify and extend the AFM's position as a strong, national union, his most pervasive legacy may be the Musician's Performance Trust Fund, which has employed musicians for free, public concerts since 1948.

Petrillo was born on the West Side of Chicago, and despite the lack of a formal education, he used a combination of toughness and talent to rise to influence in the musicians' union. As a youth, he began playing the trumpet in a Hull-House band, but he "lost his lip" early and was an undistinguished musician. He found his calling in union politics, however, after joining the Chicago Federation of Musicians (CFM), Local 10 of the AFM, in 1918. His first assignment for the CFM was to organize musicians playing in Chinese restaurants, and his success and acuity at this difficult task propelled him to the local's vice presidency in 1919. The early 1920s were a period of intense factional fighting for control of the CFM. After Local 10's president was severely beaten, and a bomb exploded in the union's offices, Petrillo was elected president in 1922. The CFM remained a contentious organization, with in-fighting and strong disagreements expressed in violence. As president, Petrillo survived a bomb blast at his home, gunfire attacks on his car, and being kidnapped to hold office for 40 years.

Despite early violence and controversy, Petrillo was an aggressive and effective leader of the CFM. In 1927, he led Chicago theater musicians on the biggest strike in AFM history to date. Petrillo's attorneys, including Clarence Darrow, defeated an injunction in court, and the union won the strike only four days later. Petrillo also changed the union's relationship with radio stations, signing the first union contract with a radio station, forcing the station to pay musicians who had previously played without payment, and negotiating for stations to hire "standby" musicians. Petrillo also brought musicians working in Chicago hotels into the AFM, and by the 1930s, the CFM controlled most of the musical jobs in the city. After staving off a Congress of Industrial Organizations (CIO) organizing drive in Chicago by lowering CFM membership fees, Petrillo took on his next issue: battling "canned" music. In 1937, Petrillo made a move to ban CFM musicians from making recordings or transcriptions without the consent of the union's executive board. The ban never transpired; instead, radio stations using the recordings agreed to hire staff musicians. Petrillo's bold action was in sharp contrast to AFM leaders' policy regarding canned music, of which he was an outspoken critic. Technological displacement had been a major problem for the AFM since 1926, when the first "talking" movie appeared. During the 1930s, the AFM, under its president, Joseph Weber, fought the increased use of recorded music, with a publicity campaign claiming it "debased" musical performance. In contrast, Petrillo argued that musicians needed to fight for a cut of the recorded music business profits. He claimed that musicians were unique in creating the very product that made them obsolete and that they had the right to protect themselves and their jobs from technological displacement. By the late 1930s, Petrillo's message resonated within the AFM, and he became president in 1940.

In 1942, as AFM president, Petrillo announced a national ban on recording and transcription by AFM musicians, with the exception of recordings for the armed services. The aim of the ban was to force the music entertainment industry to compensate musicians for their recordings. Record companies were difficult foes because they had large stockpiles of previously recorded material to turn to and also faced a shortage of resources for new recordings due to the war. By 1944, however, the AFM had won concessions from the record producers in the form of the Recording Trust Fund, in which every sale of recorded music included a small fee paid to the AFM. The AFM distributed this revenue to unemployed musicians to offer free public concerts. Although this practice was deemed illegal in 1946, Petrillo launched a second, similar recording ban in 1948 that resulted in a new fund, the Musicians' Performance Trust Fund (MPTF). Since 1948, the MPTF has provided millions of dollars' worth of free public concerts in cities throughout the United States.

Petrillo's successes made him a postwar icon: he was the highest-paid labor leader in the country, was featured on the cover of *Time* magazine twice, and played a widely publicized duet with Harry Truman at the 1948 AFM convention. At the same time, he became a target of Congress, and Petrillo and the AFM's bargaining tactics came under investigation. In 1946, Congress passed the Lea Act (commonly known as the "Anti-Petrillo" Act), a precursor to Taft-Hartley. The Lea Act barred musicians from collectively bargaining with recording companies, forcing radio stations to hire standby musicians, or receiving funds for recordings previously aired. After the Supreme Court ruled the Lea Act constitutional in 1947, the AFM leadership reluctantly accepted the law, but after membership pressure forced them to challenge the Act again in later years, it was repealed in 1980.

Although Petrillo's reign did survive congressional action, by the mid-1950s he was facing a number of new challenges from within the AFM itself. Some musicians, particularly those working in the California film industry, complained that the MPTF surcharge made them vulnerable to foreign competition. In 1958, they formed a rival union, the Musicians Guild of America (MGA), which threatened to split the union. In addition, black musicians, the vast majority of whom had historically been segregated in subsidiary locals, challenged the AFM to integrate the locals. Faced with a rebellious membership, Petrillo stepped down in favor of his handpicked successor, Herman Kenin, in 1958. Four years later, Petrillo was voted out of the Local 10 presidency when a group of musicians calling themselves Musicians for Democracy won the CFM election emphasizing issues of democracy, health plans, and racial integration. Petrillo survived to play an encore, however, when in 1964 he was anointed head of the

AFM's Civil Rights Commission. Over the next decade, the Commission oversaw the integration of AFM locals, although racial divisions within the union remained a problem. Petrillo retired from the union in 1975, and passed away in 1980.

CHRIS WONDERLICH

References and Further Reading

Leiter, Robert. *The Musicians and Petrillo*. New York: Bookman Associates, Inc., 1953.

Seltzer, George. *Music Matters: The Performer and the American Federation of Musicians*. Metuchen, NJ: The Scarecrow Press, 1989.

See also **American Federation of Musicians**

PHELPS DODGE COPPER STRIKE (1983–1984)

When the Phelps Dodge Copper Strike began in the early morning hours of July 1, 1983, members of organized labor were optimistic that they would prevail, as they always had in recent memory. Every time their three-year contract expired, they would walk out, shut down the mines for a few weeks, and ultimately force the company to grudgingly give organized workers what they had demanded in the first place. Everyone seemed to play by an unwritten set of rules. However, when the 1983 strike ended a year or so later, labor, including some of the largest and most powerful unions in the United States, was left licking its wounds and wondering how it had suffered one of its worst setbacks since the Great Depression. Some observers claim that the Phelps Dodge copper strike resulted in the largest decertification of union locals in American history, and they are probably right.

The coalition of 13 unions that represented workers employed at Phelps Dodge's massive Morenci and Ajo, Arizona, mines, mill, and smelter complexes had begun to informally prepare to negotiate a new contract to replace the one that would expire at midnight, June 30, 1983. Phelps Dodge had begun to

Production. Copper (refining). Copper ingots on conveyors at a large copper refining operation. Large amounts of copper are produced for the war effort at the El Paso, Texas plant of Phelps-Dodge Refining Company. Library of Congress, Prints & Photographs Division, FSA/OWI Collection [LC-USE6-D-009687].

prepare, too. The copper giant publicly and repeatedly announced that because the price of copper had fallen so low in 1982, it would demand major changes in the workers' wage and benefits package, notably the elimination of the union's hard-won cost of living increase, or COLA.

For unions, COLA became a rallying cry. Give back COLA, labor warned, and you will return to the dark days of autocratic rule by copper bosses. For Phelps Dodge's senior management, desperate because it felt squeezed by runaway inflation on one hand and the plummeting price of copper on the other, eliminating COLA became the surest and fastest way to trim the cost of producing copper in the United States so that its big Arizona and New Mexico mines could compete successfully with low-cost copper streaming out of Chile.

Less publicly, Phelps Dodge leaders began to take formal steps to work through a strike of any length. Quietly, they were changing the rules of engagement, though periodically they publicly warned organized labor what it would do if workers refused to accept the elimination of COLA in the contract scheduled to be implemented on July 1, 1983. The company bible was a newly published compendium instructing management how to operate during strikes. The book was conceived and endorsed by the labor economist Herbert Northrup of the University of Pennsylvania's prestigious Wharton School of business. Richard T. Moolick, the company no-nonsense president, purchased paperback copies of the thick "how-to" guide and made certain they circulated among key personnel. Giving management an additional measure of confidence was President Ronald Reagan's recent firing of the striking airline controllers. The nation's conservative political climate definitely favored management.

One particularly dramatic event occurred in the spring of 1982 when Phelps Dodge temporarily closed its Arizona mines for several months, citing the abysmally low price of copper. During that same time, Chairman George Munroe toured the company's production sites and held open forums in which he used charts and graphs to lay out the company's dire economic predicament for its workers. Cynical union workers openly questioned the company's explanation, and the union protested that management should not speak to workers without going through union spokespersons. Decades of contentious labor relations made any dialogue between Phelps Dodge and its unionized workers difficult at best.

Labor did not believe that the economic picture was as gloomy as the eloquent Munroe made it sound. Further, with the mines remaining closed for several months, it was easy for labor spokespersons to claim that the company was maneuvering to drain workers' bank accounts and thus make them lean and hungry to work through any call to strike. Phelps Dodge always denied that, but there is no denial that the company was quietly working to implement Northrup's suggestions of how to work through a strike. The company had in place a master plan to work through the strike if organized labor walked off the job as promised on July 1. Labor seems to have believed it was all a bluff.

Though workers struck on July 1 as predicted, nothing else went as predicted for organized labor. The company continued to operate its plants with supervisory personnel and a growing number of unionized workers who decided they needed the money to feed their family and pay bills. Some families split down the middle, with one brother defiantly crossing the union picket line while the other loudly cursed his sibling as a "son of a bitch."

The strike remained a standoff until one night late in July, when someone never identified fired a bullet through the side of the Ajo home of Keith Tallant, one of the union workers who conspicuously defied the union by crossing its picket line. The bullet lodged in the brain of his sleeping two-year-old daughter, who had to be rushed to a hospital in Phoenix for lifesaving neurological surgery. For the Democratic governor of Arizona, Bruce Babbitt, this was a wake-up call. He had tried to stay out of the conflict, but when he visited the little girl in the hospital, he felt new urgency to somehow mediate the mounting conflict.

The situation grew more tense in early August when Phelps Dodge announced that it would soon begin hiring permanent replacement workers and that the die-hard strikers would be out of jobs. It was one thing to use supervisory personnel, or even independent-minded union members, but to hire outsiders was more than strikers in Morenci and Ajo could take. A loud and menacing crowd of strikers converged on the Phelps Dodge general office building in Morenci and forced visibly-shaken managers to agree to a 10-day shutdown of Phelps Dodge's flagship property. President Moolick immediately flew to Arizona from the company's New York offices and angrily berated his Morenci managers for cowardly yielding to labor's threats. He publicly promised that the property would re-open at the end of the forced 10-day shutdown.

Working behind the scenes, Phelps Dodge managers pushed Governor Babbitt to be prepared for the worst when the Morenci complex re-opened. Babbitt, shaken by the course of events, publicly maintained that he was not in Phelps Dodge's employment, but behind the scenes he began readying the Arizona

National Guard for strike duty. The state's military rumbled into the mining town in a mighty show of force, and the plant re-opened as scheduled on August 20.

President Moolick always maintained that as far as he was concerned, the strike ended when the Morenci plant restarted. Labor would never concede that point. Instead, it launched several legal battles with the company, none of which ever forced the copper giant to yield anything in the long run. It also vented its wrath on Governor Babbitt, whom one prominent spokesperson for the Steelworkers union now referred to as "Governor Scabbitt."

According to federal labor law, workers on the job were eligible to vote on union representation exactly one year after the beginning of the strike. They did so under the watchful eyes of federal mediators, and the overwhelming majority of replacement workers at every facility voted the union out—more than 30 union locals died that day. It was a humiliating defeat for organized labor. But workers who had for the past year been cursed and spat at by union brothers and sisters on the picket line had no love left for the unions. At the beginning of the twenty-first century, the Morenci complex, with the largest open-pit copper mine in North America, still remained nonunion. Phelps Dodge shut down its Ajo complex in 1984.

Organized labor attempted for several more years to publicly shame and humiliate Phelps Dodge leaders, but it was to no avail. Phelps Dodge did not produce a product it sold directly to the public, and thus the public outside the Arizona copper towns took almost no notice of the struggle. Even the Steelworkers eventually gave up on the strike. Labor was left with nothing but bitter memories.

CARLOS A. SCHWANTES

References and Further Reading

Kingsolver, Barbara. *Holding the Line: Women in the Great Arizona Mine Strike of 1983*. Ithaca, NY: ILR Press/ Cornell University Press, 1996.
Rosenblum, Jonathan D. *Copper Crucible:How the Arizona Miners' Strike of 1983 Recast Labor-Management Relations in America*. 2nd ed. Ithaca, NY: Cornell University Press, 1998.

PHILADELPHIA JOURNEYMEN CORDWAINERS STRIKE (1806)

The Philadelphia shoemakers strike of 1806 resulted in the prosecution and trial of its leadership. Because the case involved the application of British common law in postrevolutionary America, Caesar A. Rodney, a prominent Delaware jurist and later U.S. attorney

general, defended the workers, in a case touching on the applicability of English common law in the United States.

The published proceedings of the trial offer a rare documentary snapshot of a vibrant labor organization early in American history. The union's origins and its name—the Federal Society of Journeymen Cordwainers—imply origins among those shoemakers involved in supporting the 1796 strike of the Federal Society of Journeymen Cabinet and Chair-Makers. Frequent labor disputes created well-practiced procedures; when the union voted to "strike" specific shops, it sent "tramping committees" to patrol those workplaces against "scabs." Several employers resorted to legal action to break the 1806 strike.

The legal foundations for *Commonwealth v. Pullis* grew from the definition of such associations as "criminal conspiracy" under English common law. In the late eighteenth and early nineteenth century, parliamentary "Combinations Acts" explicitly extended this to place workers' organizations beyond the law. Prosecutors believed that the parliamentary action had clarified the meaning of common law as prohibiting labor organizations, while the Jeffersonians doubted the applicability of the common law here. The strikers argued that the employers regularly made binding arrangements as to the price of the product and that workers should have an equal right to make similar arrangements as to the price of what they contributed to the process, their labor. The conviction of the strikers, though it only involved a nominal fine, established just such a distinction between the rights of capital and the rights of the only capital workers themselves controlled.

This 1806 strike cast a long judicial shadow. Although *Commonwealth v. Hunt* (1842) in Massachusetts accepted the legitimacy of unions, it left ambiguity as to strikes. Although the courts gradually accepted strikes, the *de facto* legalization of labor activities in the 1930s also implied the legal regulation of what would and would not be acceptable practices. More broadly, "criminal conspiracy" remains a legally ambiguous area by which the authorities have continued to take action against combination of citizens.

MARK LAUSE

References and Further Reading

Tomlins, Christopher L. *Law, Labor, and Ideology in the Early American Republic*. Cambridge, England; New York: Cambridge University Press, 1993.
The Trial of the Boot & Shoemakers of Philadelphia: On an Indictment for a Combination and Conspiracy to Raise Their Wages. Philadelphia: Printed by B. Graves, for T. Lloyd and B. Graves, 1806. Reprinted *A Documentary History of American Industrial Society*, edited by John R.

Commons, Ulrich B. Phillips, Eugene A. Gilmore, Helen L. Sumner, and John B. Andrews. With preface by Richard T. Ely and introduction by John B. Clark. Cleveland: The A. H. Clark Company, 1910–1911, reprinted New York: Russell & Russell, 1958.

Turner, Marjorie Shepherd. *The Early American Labor Conspiracy Cases, Their Place in Labor Law; a Reinterpretation.* San Diego, CA: San Diego State College Press, 1967.

PHILADELPHIA PLAN

Named for the city where it was first put into practice, the Philadelphia Plan required contractors bidding on government construction projects to set goals and targets for the number of minority workers. Signed by Assistant Labor Secretary Arthur Fletcher on June 27, 1969, the administrative order was the product of decades-long civil rights agitation and policy innovation. The Philadelphia Plan was a significant chapter in the development of federal affirmative action legislation.

Background: Racial Discrimination in the Building Trades

With the Philadelphia Plan, the federal government targeted one of the most racially exclusive sectors of the labor movement. This was especially the case in the highest-paying skilled trades, in which contractors—especially in union strongholds in the urban North and West—depended on union hiring halls to furnish the best-trained workers for each job. Entrance to these trades required years of union-sponsored apprenticeship and technical training, and building trades unions preferred to fill these slots with family and friends. Thus, it was easy for unions in trades that had been white from the beginning, such as steamfitting, electrical installation, and sheet metal work, to reproduce a white membership. But even in older trades such as carpentry and masonry, which had a tradition of African-American craftsmen (especially in the South), whites were disproportionately represented. Jim Crow decreased the number of black craftsmen in the South, and labor unions ensured that subsequent generations of blacks would find it increasingly difficult to gain access to training and work in these trades in the North. By 1961, less than 1% of the nation's building trades apprentices were African-American. Instead, racial minorities were disproportionately concentrated in the lowest-paying trades that did not require tremendous skill—namely common laborers and hod carriers.

Before the 1960s, African-Americans had resisted organized labor's racial practices with little success. Prior to the World War I Great Migration, African-Americans responded to union exclusion on an individual basis, typically by strikebreaking and working for open-shop contractors. In the interwar years, however, resistance increasingly became a collective endeavor. Black craftsmen attempted to put pressure on white unions by forming their own unions, associations, and training programs. Whenever possible, they sought assistance from any organization that was willing to offer support—whether it came from moderate groups such as the Urban League or a radical organization such as the Communist Party. But these efforts were usually no match for powerful building trades unions, and African-Americans realized that their best hopes rested with state intervention.

The federal government meekly intervened on behalf of African-Americans on several occasions. From 1935 to 1937, the Public Works Administration (PWA) attempted to secure jobs for black construction workers by implementing a quota plan on its projects. But while the PWA produced short-term gains for a small number of blacks, the agency's program did nothing to address the issue of union membership and apprenticeships and therefore did not expand the black workforce in construction in the long run. The World War II Fair Employment Practice Committee (FEPC), with its weak enforcement mechanisms, produced similar results. Finally, the President's Committee on Government Contracts, established by Eisenhower in 1953, and the President's Committee on Equal Employment Opportunity, established by Kennedy in 1961, sounded good in theory but did little in practice to increase the number of minority construction workers.

All the while, union construction workers benefited from increased government spending in national defense and heavy construction. The Interstate Highway System, Housing Act, and Area Redevelopment Act, among others, helped provided steady jobs for union construction workers. Moreover, the unions' ability to restrict the labor supply ensured that these jobs would command high wages. This trend would continue with the construction boom of the 1960s.

The 1960s: Protest and Policy

The construction industry's long history of racial discrimination made it a prime target for civil rights activists and policy makers in the 1960s. Between 1963 and 1967, the Congress of Racial Equality

(CORE) and the National Association for the Advancement of Colored People (NAACP) staged protests and pickets at federally funded construction sites in Cleveland, St. Louis, Philadelphia, New York City, Newark, Oakland, and Washington, DC. These protests caught the attention of government officials. In 1963, violent protests at the site of a partially built school in Philadelphia prompted President Kennedy to issue Executive Order 11114, which ambiguously called upon contractors to take "affirmative action" with regard to black workers on government projects. In 1965, President Johnson issued Executive Order 11246, which shifted the development and enforcement of affirmative action programs to the Department of Labor's Office of Federal Contract Compliance (OFCC).

For the next two years, the OFCC moved toward a workable application of affirmative action. In 1966, it took a major step when it established the pre-award program for construction, in which the OFCC would first review a contractor's employment "system" *before* the government awarded a contract. The Department of Labor experimented with different pre-award affirmative action plans in St. Louis, San Francisco, and Cleveland before settling on the Philadelphia Plan in 1967. The Philadelphia Plan required contractors bidding on government jobs to submit "manning timetables" listing the number of minority workers they intended to employ on each aspect of the project. Before a contract was signed, a compliance committee examined the lowest bidder's employment practices—including periodic on-site head counts and evaluations.

The Philadelphia Plan met immediate resistance. The AFL-CIO and its Building Trades Department protested the federal intervention. Organized labor claimed that they were being unfairly singled out by the government and that the plan would discriminate against deserving whites. For most of the twentieth century, labor leaders in the construction trades could accurately assert that their unions' national policies did not condone racial discrimination. Instead, they attributed the paucity of minority workers in the skilled trades to economic realities and a general lack of interest. Nevertheless, building trades unions tried to head off government action by developing their own minority recruitment programs. In 1963, they teamed up with national contractor associations and established the Joint Committee on Equal Employment Opportunities to increase minority representation in apprenticeship programs on the industry's, and not the government's or civil rights movement's, terms. In 1965, these efforts were intensified as local building trades unions began working with groups such as the Urban League to establish joint apprenticeship programs—special outreach programs aimed at recruiting minority youths for union apprenticeship programs.

Unions and contractors were not alone in protesting the Philadelphia Plan. The National Association of Manufacturers and conservative Republicans objected to the Plan as well because they believed that affirmative action programs violated the Civil Rights Act of 1964. Dissent also came from within the ranks of the Johnson administration. The opposition proved to be too much, and in November 1968, General Comptroller Elmer Staats ruled that the Philadelphia Plan was illegal.

The Nixon administration revived the Philadelphia Plan. Scholars have debated Nixon's motives in implementing a pioneering affirmative action program in federal employment. Most agree that support for the plan was in large part political—putting the Democratic Party in the awkward position of having to choose between the labor movement and the civil rights movement. The Nixon administration also had a keen interest in lowering construction costs. By the late 1960s, large corporations and open-shop organizations complained that building trades unions benefited from artificially high wages derived from their restrictive apprenticeship programs and the Davis-Bacon Act. Nixon could anticipate that the Philadelphia Plan would both expand the labor supply and enervate organized labor's position in the industry. Finally, some have argued that Nixon was motivated by his opposition to discrimination and his hope to quell urban unrest.

Regardless of Nixon's personal motives, his Department of Labor was largely responsible for the administrative order. Although his prime interest was increasing the construction industry's labor supply, George Shultz, Nixon's secretary of labor, also considered himself a supporter of African-American civil rights. In the spring of 1969, he re-organized his department and gave Assistant Secretary of Labor Arthur Fletcher, one of the administration's highest-ranking African-Americans, his blessing in retooling the Philadelphia Plan. Meanwhile, a new wave of protests and counterprotests struck in Philadelphia, Pittsburgh, and Chicago—creating the added urgency of heading off potentially explosive racial conflicts in American cities.

Under Fletcher's revised Philadelphia Plan, the OFCC surveyed local conditions and established a target range, expressed in percentages rather than numbers, for each trade. Contractors bidding on federal projects exceeding $500,000 were required to meet these "goals" and "timetables." Mindful of the first Philadelphia Plan's fate, Labor Department officials took pains to emphasize that the Plan did not implement numerical quotas and that the revised Plan simply required contractors to show good faith in hiring minorities. Although opponents continued to cry foul, this time the Philadelphia Plan withstood legal challenges. And although the Plan originally only applied to five counties in eastern Pennsylvania, it was extended in 1970 to cover all government contracts exceeding $500,000. The Plan was amended again in 1971 to include women.

Ultimately, the Philadelphia Plan did little to increase the numbers of minorities and women in the building trades. Some black unionists and civil rights leaders criticized the Plan for not providing for adequate apprenticeships for black youths and for not upgrading older workers. The architects of the Plan underwrote it with the assumption that the construction industry would maintain the vitality of the 1960s boom. However, government construction spending plummeted throughout the 1970s, creating hard times for construction workers and framing civil rights employment legislation as a zero-sum game between blacks and whites. Indeed, the increase in minority and female construction workers since 1969 owes more to the weakened position of building trades unions than it does to the Philadelphia Plan.

The most significant legacy of the Philadelphia Plan is its contribution to affirmative action employment policies. Although Nixon distanced himself from anything that hinted at quotas shortly after approving the order, the Equal Employment Opportunity Commission built upon affirmative action tools such as goals, timetables, and quotas throughout the 1970s. The debates that engulfed the Philadelphia Plan continue to swirl around the issue of affirmative action.

JOHN J. ROSEN

References and Further Reading

Graham, Hugh Davis. *The Civil Rights Era: Origins and Development of National Policy: 1960–1972*. New York and Oxford: Oxford University Press, 1990.

Kotlowski, Dean J. "Richard Nixon and the Origins of Affirmative Action." *The Historian* 60, no. 3 (Spring 1998): 523–541.

Palladino, Grace. *Skilled Hands, Strong Spirits: A Century of Building Trades History*. Ithaca, NY and London: Cornell University Press, 2005.

Sugrue, Thomas J. "Affirmative Action from Below: Civil Rights, the Building Trades, and the Politics of Racial Equality in the Urban North, 1945–1969." *Journal of American History* 91, no. 1 (June 2004): 145–173.

PHILADELPHIA PRINTERS STRIKE (1786)

During the British occupation of New York City, journeymen printers there formulated a scale of wages, but no job action seems to have taken place. In the spring of 1786, though, Philadelphia masters prepared to reduce wages, and 26 journeymen printers signed a formal protest to the plan coupled to an insistence that the old scale be maintained. They left work and refused to return until the masters agreed to pay the old scale, the equivalent of 20 shillings or one Spanish dollar per day. Participants included old colonial printers, former Continental soldiers such as Samuel Lecount, and future leaders of the local trade unions that began emerging a decade later.

The strikers seem to have acted with the tacit support of Benjamin Franklin, the aged but mentally alert and open-minded patron of the "art preservative" in the New World. Franklin had arranged a citywide scale of prices and wages in 1754 and favored a uniform scale. During the prerevolutionary resistance, the war, and the postwar conditions of the Confederation, real estate and rents had soared and food prices had risen steadily. Still, the strikers were not interested in a pay increase or a permanent trade union but in maintaining the scale of Franklin's day and the legacy of master-worker fraternalism. The outcome of the strike is difficult to tell, but it did not result in a uniform citywide scale and surely varied from shop to shop.

In March 1788, a number of the veterans of this strike met with their employers in Franklin's home to establish a more permanent society to cooperate in managing the local craft. Believing in a common artisan interest that united employers and employees, Franklin left a codicil in his will setting aside funds to loan enterprising journeymen to help them become self-employed. After his death in 1790, the association adopted the name of the "Franklin Society."

Through the Franklin Society, the artisan standards of the 1786 strike continued to inspire the hired men. The expansion of the workplace and the introduction of boys and "two-thirds" journeymen eroded the quality of apprenticeship standards and craft labor, as well as wages. Increasingly, they imposed modern hierarchies in production that reduced hired craftsmen to a merely more skilled kind of wage labor. A defense of artisan standards became inseparable from the drive toward self-organization among the hired hands. After a short-lived Typographical Society in New York, journeymen there started a "Franklin Typographical Society" in 1798, and Boston journeymen launched a Franklin Society in 1802. Hired men in the Philadelphia craft formed a mutual aid Asylum Company in 1799 and the Philadelphia Typographical Society in 1802. By 1815, local printers unions had also appeared at Baltimore, Albany, New Orleans, and Washington.

MARK LAUSE

References and Further Reading

Lause, Mark A. *Some Degree of Power from Hired Hand to Union Craftsman in the Preindustrial American Printing Trades, 1778–1815.* Fayetteville: University of Arkansas Press, 1991.

Rosemont, Henry P. "Benjamin Franklin and the Philadelphia Typographical Strikers of 1786." *Labor History* 22 (Summer 1981): 398–429.

PHILADELPHIA TRANSIT STRIKE (1944)

Philadelphians living on Broad Street would have seen a remarkable sight if they had peered out their windows at 4:00 a.m. on August 1, 1944. Buses, a dozen or more, stood idle in the middle of the street, some with their engines still running. Elsewhere, trolleys sat in their carbarns and subways at their stations, waiting for drivers who would not come. Thousands of people across the city stood at their trolley stops waiting, probably impatiently, before returning home to call City Hall and the Philadelphia Transportation Company (PTC) to ask what was wrong. Operators started off by telling each person that "No cars are moving anywhere in the city" but soon became so overwhelmed that they quit answering the phones. By noon, with the newspapers' morning editions having hit the streets, everyone understood what had happened: PTC workers had gone on strike to prevent black promotions to the traditionally white position of driver, and the nation's third largest war production center was at a standstill. The PTC strike, the largest racially motivated "hate" strike of World War II, ultimately lasted six days, ending only when the U.S. Army, following the orders of President Franklin Roosevelt, took over the transit system and ordered everyone back to work under penalty of conscription for failure to return.

The Philadelphia transit strike had its origins in the racial tensions that plagued urban centers across the United States during the war. From Mobile to Detroit to Philadelphia, American cities had to come to grips with migration patterns that drained the South's rural population while adding millions of residents to ill-prepared metropolitan areas. In Philadelphia, the black population jumped from 250,000 in 1940 to 375,000 in 1950. New arrivals found the city inhospitable: they were forced into the city's worst housing, their children attended segregated schools, and studies showed that as many as 90% of area businesses openly discriminated in their hiring practices. While any discrimination was bad, the company that disturbed black Philadelphians the most was the PTC. African-Americans had worked for the transit company for decades, but only in positions of menial labor. They were not allowed to drive transit vehicles or interact with the public. This policy angered African-Americans because the PTC was a semi-public company that received taxes as well as fares from the black community. PTC discrimination was, according to the *Pittsburgh Courier*, "tantamount to discrimination by the City of Philadelphia."

When black employees pressed PTC management to change its policies, they were told the company could not promote African-Americans without the consent of the Philadelphia Rapid Transit Employees Union (PRTEU)—a company union unaffiliated with the American Federation of Labor (AFL) or the Congress of Industrial Organizations (CIO). PRTEU leaders worked closely with the company, demanding the PTC reserve the best jobs for whites in exchange for wages some 10% below national standards. Management and its white workers were happy with this arrangement, and the black employees knew they would never overturn Jim Crow without help.

They found support in three places: the National Association for the Advancement of Colored People (NAACP), the Transport Workers Union (TWU—a CIO affiliate), and the Fair Employment Practice Committee (FEPC). The NAACP staged protest marches and petition drives and generally energized the black community so that all African-Americans saw their vital stake in overturning PTC segregation. The TWU, which had supported African-American access to transit jobs in New York City, won a representation election against the PRTEU in the spring of 1944 that guaranteed organized labor would no longer stand in the way of black rights. And the FEPC, which Roosevelt had established in 1941 to combat discrimination in war plants, held hearings that determined the company and the PRTEU were illegally imposing a Jim Crow system on the workforce. That system, the FEPC ordered, had to end by August 1, 1944.

White workers were angered by the campaign against their supposed right to control transit jobs and began a movement to stop integration at the PTC. They circulated fliers in the carbarns, telling white workers they had to form a "white supremacy movement" to protect their jobs and held meetings on PTC property, where they swore they would go on strike rather than work with African-Americans. The PTC happily allowed this movement to grow because it could halt the TWU. In contract talks, the CIO union had demanded a 15% pay raise and a better pension, which management knew would cost millions. But PTC leaders also knew the Smith-Connally Act forbade wartime strikes and gave the government the power to abrogate any contract and toss out a union if it led a strike against a war production company. So management used its workers' racism to try to undermine the CIO union and consequently set the stage for the war's worst hate strike on August 1, 1944.

The strike itself was relatively short, lasting less than a week. Since Philadelphia was such a vital war production center, making everything from ammunition to uniforms, President Roosevelt could not let the stoppage drag on. He sent in five thousand heavily armed troops on August 5 to break the strike with force if necessary. The strikers, who knew they would be drafted if they stayed out, returned to work a couple of days later. African-Americans, with the support of the federal government, won their campaign to secure driving jobs at the PTC. Their victory cracked Jim Crow in an important local industry and opened the way for many African-Americans to get driving jobs. A month after the strike's end, the FEPC reported that blacks were doing well in their new jobs and that the company had two more trainees in the process of becoming drivers. By October, the number of black drivers had doubled from the original eight to 16, and within a year, the PTC counted some nine hundred black employees, including drivers, conductors, and a member of the publicity staff. The PTC became a valuable employer for the black community.

The Philadelphia transit strike was only one of many hate strikes that swept America during World War II. Tense race relations in the nation's cities led to walkouts at shipyards, aircraft factories, and transit companies across the United States. The Philadelphia strike stopped production for a week, slowing the war effort and costing the local economy some 4.6 million hours of lost production. But in the end, the strike failed as a combination of black activism, CIO support, and federal intervention ensured African-Americans equal access to the best jobs at the PTC.

JAMES WOLFINGER

References and Further Reading

Hill, Herbert. *Black Labor and the American Legal System: Race, Work, and the Law.* Madison: University of Wisconsin Press, 1985.

Meier, August, and Elliott Rudwick. "Communist Unions and the Black Community: The Case of the Transport Workers Union, 1934–1944." *Labor History* 23 (Spring 1982): 165–197.

Spaulding, Theodore. "Philadelphia's Hate Strike." *The Crisis* 51 (September 1944): 281–283, 301.

Winkler, Allan. "The Philadelphia Transit Strike of 1944." *Journal of American History* 59 (June 1972): 73–89.

See also **American Federation of Labor; Congress of Industrial Organizations; Fair Employment Practice Committee; Smith-Connally Act; Transport Workers Union**

PINKERTON DETECTIVES

Six railroad corporations financed the 1855 Chicago opening of Allan Pinkerton's North West Police Agency. Renamed Pinkerton's National Detective Agency three years later, it became the world's largest and most notorious supplier of paid labor spies and strikebreakers. Pinkerton's so dominated public imagination that the title "Pinkertons" was often used to denote any labor detectives.

Allan Pinkerton, a Scottish immigrant and abolitionist, pioneered spying on U.S. railroad workers in the 1850s. Called "spotters," the Pinkerton operatives watched workers, especially conductors, for offenses such as socializing with passengers, keeping ticket money from ticket sales, or sleeping on the job. During the Civil War, Allan Pinkerton worked undercover for General George McClelland and claimed to have foiled an assassination attempt against President Abraham Lincoln. Parlaying his wartime exploits into national fame, Pinkerton, with his sons Robert and William, added offices in New York and Philadelphia. In addition to general detective work for diverse clients, the agency provided three antilabor services to large employers: labor spies, strike guards, and strikebreakers. In 1873, the Pinkerton spy James McParlan infiltrated the Molly Maguires, a militant group of Irish miners in the Pennsylvania coalfields, and became a lodge officer. Exposed after two years, McParlan gave dramatic testimony that resulted in the execution of 13 men. Most spying was not dramatic, but Pinkerton's approach stressed the value of elaborate subterfuge and patience in labor espionage.

In addition to labor spies, Pinkerton's also provided strike guards and strikebreakers. The corporations claimed that the guards were to protect company property and prevent violence. In practice, the strike guards worked under the employer's direction to prevent picketing and embolden strikebreakers. Local officials often deputized private guards during strikes, but the guards remained accountable only to the employer. Pinkerton strikebreakers were often armed, too, and ready to club or shoot strikers.

When Allan Pinkerton died in 1884, his sons continued the agency. By then, many railroad and coal corporations had established in-house railroad police or coal and iron police. They still called on Pinkerton's, however, for undercover work and additional men during strikes. Many new strikebreaking agencies, such as Pearl L. Bergoff, Baldwin-Felts, and Waddell-Mahon, opened in the 1880s, and some, like Thiel's, were headed by former Pinkerton operatives.

Pinkerton's prided itself on the distinction between its detectives, who were said to be carefully recruited and trained, and its guards and strikebreakers, who were hired hurriedly, selected mostly for strength, and employed only while disorder continued. According to Frank Morn, Pinkerton operatives may have been involved in the never-solved 1886 Haymarket bombing in Chicago, and there were increasing reports of Pinkertons shooting at workers in the late 1880s. In the 1890s, Pinkertons helped break mine strikes in Idaho, Arizona, Alabama, and Pennsylvania.

The best-known use of Pinkertons was at Homestead, Pennsylvania (1892), where the appearance of a barge of armed Pinkertons provoked a battle with unionists that left 13 people dead. The Pinkertons retreated temporarily, but lethal conflict at the formerly peaceful strike served as a pretext for mobilizing the Pennsylvania National Guard. Trade unionists, socialists, Populists and many others were outraged over the use of Pinkertons at Homestead and urged curbs on private police. The Knights of Labor had demanded the prohibition of detectives in labor disputes since 1885, and working people had campaigned for state Anti-Pinkerton Acts since 1886.

Anti-Pinkerton Acts typically prohibited the importation of armed guards or detectives for strike work. Private police, often deputized for strike work, were paid and directed by the employer. When a Pinkerton committed a crime, it was virtually impossible to prosecute him because he left town quickly. Private police removed the advantage won by unionists who had built local political power. Even when elected officials, as at Homestead, refused to mobilize armed force, the corporations could order it by telegraph. Congress passed an Anti-Pinkerton Act immediately after Homestead, and workers won Anti-Pinkerton Acts in 24 states by 1899. The agencies, however, easily circumvented the law by tactics such as transporting strikebreakers separately from weapons.

Allan Pinkerton had been a relentless self-promoter who wrote 17 books with lurid titles such as *Strikers, Communists, Tramps, and Detectives* (1878). Pinkerton amplified the hostile late nineteenth-century stereotypes of unionists and unemployed workers. These caricatures of subversive violence both emphasized the need for Pinkertons and justified what the public tended to see as corporate mercenaries. Pinkerton was also a founding member of the International Association of Police Chiefs (IACP), a professional association in which he advocated inculcating police leadership with the outlook and techniques of the detective agencies.

Pinkerton's expanded in the twentieth century despite union objections, newspaper exposés, and government investigations. Historians often attribute the rise of private police in the United States to the relative weakness of public police. The private forces, however, continued to expand in the twentieth century despite the growth of additional public law enforcement bodies. In the 1921 paper workers' strike, for example, Pinkertons patrolled the village of Corinth alongside the recently created New York State Police.

Pinkerton's was the largest supplier of labor spies, with 27 offices and 300 clients for whom it did anti-labor work in 1935. General Motors was its largest client. From 1934 to mid-1937, 52 United Auto Workers members were Pinkerton spies. A Pinkerton was the president of the Chevrolet local in Flint, and another was vice president of the Fisher Body local in Lansing. General Motors also hired Pinkertons to spy on William Green, John P. Frey, Homer Martin, Walter Reuther, and others.

The National Labor Relations Act (1935) changed the legal context for private policing by legalizing unionization efforts. The La Follette Committee on Civil Liberties' exposure of private police in industry echoed many of the revelations of the earlier Homestead report and Commission on Industrial Relations report. In its early years, however, the National Labor Relations Board (NLRB) heard complaints of labor spying and sometimes ordered the re-instatement of workers who had been dismissed. In 1937, in response to the changed political climate, Pinkerton's board of directors formally ended industrial espionage.

NLRB regulations did not, however, put an end to either espionage or commercial strikebreaking. Private detectives and corporate police adopted new techniques using high technology, ingenious legal tactics, and public relations to defeat unionization efforts. Infamous in the nineteenth century, private police are even more pervasive in the twenty-first century.

GERDA W. RAY

References and Further Reading

Auerbach, Jerold S. *Labor and Liberty: The La Follette Committee and the New Deal.* Indianapolis, IN and New York: The Bobbs-Merrill Company, Inc., 1966.

Mackay, James A. *Allan Pinkerton: The First Private Eye.* New York: J. Wiley & Sons, 1997.

Morn, Frank. *"The Eye That Never Sleeps": A History of the Pinkerton National Detective Agency.* Bloomington: Indiana University Press, 1982.

Smith, Robert Michael. With a Foreword by Scott Molloy. *From Blackjacks to Briefcases: A History of Commercialized Strikebreaking and Unionbusting in the United States.* Athens: Ohio University Press, 2003.

See also **Homestead Strike (1892); Molly Maguires; Strikebreaking**

PITTSTON COAL STRIKE (1989–1990)

In 1989–1990, Pittston coal miners waged a 10-month strike that galvanized the labor movement as striking miners engaged in the largest labor civil disobedience campaign in recent history, including a mine occupation reminiscent of the 1930s sit-down strikes.

The Pittston strike exemplified efforts by major American corporations to break out of traditional collective bargaining procedures that had been established in the post-World War II era. Pittston, in the late 1980s and early 1990s the leading U.S. coal exporter, sought to end pattern bargaining, common in auto, steel, rubber, earthmoving equipment, and mining, where one company would negotiate a contract with its union and other companies would follow the pattern and negotiate basically the same terms. Pittston refused to sign the contract the union negotiated with the Bituminous Coal Operators Association, demanding an end to company payments into the industrywide health insurance fund for retirees, cuts in pension and health-care coverage for working miners, work rule changes, and the right to open new mines without union representation.

In January 1988, Pittston terminated its health benefits to 1,500 retired and disabled miners and widows, ended pension contributions for working miners, and eliminated arbitration of unresolved grievances. The United Mine Workers of America (UMWA) miners worked without a contract for 14 months while continuing to negotiate, and then from April 1989 to February 1990, 1,700 workers struck Pittston mines in Virginia, Kentucky, and West Virginia. The retirees' health care became a galvanizing issue, creating a tremendous sense of unity among the miners—not a single miner crossed the union's picket lines throughout the strike—and fostering community support throughout the mine towns. Legally, the strike was an "unfair labor practice strike" called over company violations of labor law, which prohibited the company from permanently replacing the strikers.

The UMWA president, Richard Trumka, elected in 1982 with pledges to rebuild and unify the faltering, divided union, threw the resources of the international union behind the strike and turned it into a national cause célèbre within the embattled labor movement. The union declared that the Pittston struggle was more than just a strike but was a "people's movement." The filmmaker Barbara Kopple produced *Out of Darkness*, which combined strike footage with a history of the mineworkers' union, and Anne Lewis produced the film *Justice in the Coalfields*.

The union determined to wage a sustained nonviolent civil disobedience campaign, drawing on the lessons of the civil rights movement. Union staff, trained by peace activists in the principles of nonviolent resistance, spread out across the eastern coalfields to train the Pittston miners. Richard Trumka declared in "Out of Darkness" in the midst of the strike, "Labor law is formulated for labor to lose. If you play by every one of those rules, you lose every time. So what it forces you to do, is to change the way you've operated." Vice President Cecil Roberts echoed this sentiment, saying, "They didn't think that a predominately white, mountain, rural workforce would ever follow the teachings of Dr. King. But they did. Dr. King says there is nothing more invigorating than being in jail for a cause that you believe in. And I think that's absolutely right. There's nothing wrong with going to jail when you're trying to change an unjust system or an unjust law."

The civil disobedience campaign was kicked off by women, calling their strike support group the Daughters of Mother Jones, who staged a two-day sit-in at Pittston headquarters. Subsequently, the miners began a series of sit-downs blocking the roads to the mines. In the course of the strike, over 3,000 people were arrested; many miners and family members were arrested multiple times for a total of over 5,000 arrests. The union formed Camp Solidarity, a tent city near Castlewood, Virginia, for the over 50,000 supporters who came to show their solidarity. The miners and family members wore camouflage to symbolize their resistance and to make it difficult for the police to identify protesters accused of picket-line violence.

On April 30, 1989, 12,000 miners and supporters rallied in solidarity, hearing speeches from UMWA leaders, rank-and-file miners, and Reverend Jesse Jackson. In June 1989, 46,000 miners in 11 states declared "memorial days" and struck in solidarity with the Pittston miners. The miners were forced to return to work when the international union was advised the strikes violated the Taft-Hartley Act's prohibition on sympathy strikes.

The union also waged a corporate campaign, picketing Shawmut Bank, which had the Pittston board member William Craig as its vice president, and influencing unions and supporters to withdraw deposits. A Pittston workers' solidarity committee in Boston succeeded in pressuring the Boston, Cambridge, and Somerville city councils to withdraw city funds. Craig was forced to resign his position with Shawmut Bank. The miners received additional moral support and publicity when an international delegation including a representative from Polish Solidarność (Solidarity) arrived in October 1989. At the height of the strike, the union received 15 to 20 requests for speaking engagements a week, and rank-and-file miners traveled the country publicizing their strike.

By July, union leaders had been thrown in jail for refusing to order the miners to end the civil disobedience campaign, and court fines against the union passed $4 million. When the company refused to back off its demands, in September the union escalated its civil disobedience campaign. Dubbing their plan "Operation Flintstone" in tribute to the 1936–1937 UAW sit-down strike in Flint, Michigan, 99 miners and one pastor marched into the Moss 3 mine and occupied it. For three and a half days, thousands of miners and supporters demonstrated outside the mine, but faced with an imminent police assault, the miners ended their sit-in.

On New Year's Day, 1990, the union reached a tentative agreement that gave some concessions but saved the workers' pensions and retirees' health coverage, and on February 20, the Pittston miners ratified the contract, ending their 10-month strike. The company agreed to petition the courts to drop the $64 million in fines, and the fine was tossed out in a unanimous decision by the U.S. Supreme Court in 1993.

UMWA President Trumka declared the union had overcome the combined efforts of the company and the courts to eliminate the union, and the entire labor movement celebrated its first major victory since President Reagan fired 11,359 striking air traffic controllers and crushed the PATCO union in 1981.

STEVEN ASHBY

References and Further Reading

Beckwith, Karen. "Collective Identities of Class and Gender: Working-Class Women in the Pittston Coal Strike." *Political Psychology* 19, no. 1 (1998): 147–167.
Birecree, Adrienne M. "The Importance and Implications of Women's Participation in the 1989–90 Pittston Coal Strike." *Journal of Economic Issues* (March 1996): 187–210.
Brisbin, Richard A. Jr. *A Strike like No Other Strike: Law and Resistance during the Pittston Coal Strike of 1989–90.* Baltimore: Johns Hopkins University Press, 2002.
Green, James. "Camp Solidarity: The United Mine Workers, the Pittston Strike, and the New 'People's Movement.'" In *Building Bridges: The Emerging Grassroots Coalition of Labor and Community*, edited by Jeremy Brecher and Tim Costello. New York: Monthly Review Press, 1990.
Green, James. "Planting the Seeds of Resurgence: The United Mine Workers Strike Pittston Coal in 1989." In *Taking History to Heart: The Power of the Past in Building Social Movements*. Amherst: University of Massachusetts Press, 2000.
Moore, Marat. "Ten Months That Shook the Coalfields: Women's Stories from the Pittston Strike." *Now and Then: The Appalachian Magazine* 7, no. 3 (Fall 1990): 6–12.
Puette, William J. "Labor Buried Alive: The Mine Workers' Pittston Strike." In *Through Jaundiced Eyes: How the Media View Organized Labor*. Ithaca, NY: ILR Press, 1992.

See also **Trumka, Richard L.**

PLUMB PLAN

Named for the railroad union attorney Glenn E. Plumb, the Plan aimed to nationalize U.S. railroads in the aftermath of World War I. Railroad labor unions led the campaign for nationalization, and the Plan became a rallying point for broader progressive forces in the labor movement. Despite widespread support from railroad workers, who had seen benefits from temporary federal control of the railroads during the war, the Plan fell victim to the Red Scare that soon followed the Armistice.

During World War I, private control of the roads had seriously hampered the national coordination needed to boost industrial production and transport war supplies. Moreover, there was a labor shortage, as higher wages drew workers out of the largely non-union, low-wage railroad repair shops. These problems led the Wilson administration to seize control of the railroads in December 1917, temporarily putting them in the hands of the U.S. Railroad Administration (USRA). Co-ordination improved under federal control. Under pressure from workers, commissions set up under the USRA granted substantial wage increases and protection for union organization, which shot up during 1918. Late that year, the Railway Employees Division (RED) of the American Federation of Labor (AFL), which represented unionized shopcraft workers, conducted a referendum asking workers whether they wanted government control of railroads to continue after the Armistice: 99% said yes.

Glenn Plumb, who served as attorney for the four railroad operating brotherhoods, thought that public railroad ownership could deliver justice for workers, lower rates for shippers and passengers, and reduce class conflict. Under his plan, the government would charter a public corporation to run the railroads. It would buy out the current owners with a combination of cash and government bonds. The board of directors would consist of 15 members, five elected by railroad workers, five elected by railroad management, and five appointed by the president to represent the public. If revenue exceeded expenses, the surplus would be split evenly between the federal government and the employees. The 50%

"dividend" going to the employees, however, would be divided between the "operating officials" and the workers, and the former would receive twice the rate of the latter. The government would use its share to extend and maintain the roads and to create a fund to retire the bonds used to buy the roads. If the government share was more than 5% of gross operating revenue, the Interstate Commerce Commission (ICC) would be obliged to reduce passenger and freight rates by this amount. With lower rates and possibly lower revenue the next year, workers and managers would presumably be motivated to be more efficient; if they succeeded in lowering costs, they would continue to receive a dividend. It would be, as Plumb put it, "scientific management under democratic control."

Since President Wilson pledged that he would return the roads to private control and a privatization bill sponsored by Senator Albert Cummins (R-IA) gained momentum in 1919, the Plumb Plan League swung into action. Led by Arthur Wharton, the head of the RED, the League included on its executive board officials of the railroad brotherhoods, who remained outside of the AFL. Its newspaper, *Railroad Democracy: The Plumb Plan Weekly* (later renamed *Labor*), eventually reached some 500,000 readers. The League charged one dollar per year for membership, organized six hundred local chapters, and sponsored speaking tours. In a bid to widen its base, League leaders named the AFL chief, Samuel Gompers, honorary president in the summer of 1919, though without his consent. While this move angered Gompers, who viewed nationalization as a dangerous move in the direction of Bolshevism, the League won a political victory when delegates at the national AFL convention in January 1920 passed a resolution that endorsed railroad nationalization. Their vote reflected the wave of working-class militancy that swept the United States after the Armistice, as an unprecedented four million workers went on strike.

It was in this heated context that in August 1919, Thetus W. Sims (D-TN) introduced a bill in the House of Representatives to put the Plumb Plan into effect. Though the Plumb Plan was far from Bolshevist, Plumb was attacked as a dangerous radical, and the Sims bill was buried. Meanwhile, the Senate passed the Cummins bill, with a provision outlawing railroad strikes, and in January, the House passed a similar bill, sponsored by John Esch (R-WI). The conference bill, without the antistrike provision, was approved in February 1920 as the Transportation Act, which formally returned the railroads to private control.

CARL R. WEINBERG

References and Further Reading

Davis, Colin J. *Power at Odds: The 1922 National Railroad Shopmen's Strike*. Urbana and Chicago: University of Illinois Press, 1997.

Foner, Philip S. *History of the Labor Movement in the United States: Postwar Struggles, 1918–1920*. New York: International Publishers, 1988.

Keating, Edward. *The Story of "Labor": Thirty-Three Years on the Rail Workers' Fighting Front*. Washington, DC: Darby Printing (?), 1953.

Kerr, K. Austin. *American Railroad Politics, 1914–1920: Rates, Wages, and Efficiency*. Pittsburgh, PA: University of Pittsburgh Press, 1968.

Olssen, Erik. "The Making of a Political Machine: The Railroad Unions Enter Politics." *Labor History* 19 (Summer 1978): 273–296.

Plumb, Glenn E. "Labor's Solution of the Railroad Problem." *The Nation* 109 (August 19, 1919): 200–201.

Plumb, Glenn E., and William G. Roylance. *Industrial Democracy: A Plan for Its Achievement*. New York: B W. Huebsch, Inc., 1923.

POLITICS AND LABOR, NINETEENTH CENTURY

To understand working-class politics in nineteenth-century America, we must understand how the American political and class systems changed. Contrary to De Tocqueville, mass democratic electoral politics did not emerge directly out of the American Revolution but slowly through struggles over generations. Indeed, suffrage did not become universal until the last third of the twentieth century. And a workforce in which the largest occupational categories in 1800 were slaves, farmers, farmhands, domestics and unpaid household workers, artisans, and sailors changed to a workforce with a majority of blue-collar wage earners. Working-class politics involved struggles for interests of an evolving working class within the polity and struggles to gain full inclusion in that polity.

Undemocratic America

In 1800, somewhat over half of the adult white male population (and perhaps one fifth of the adult population) could vote (Keyssar, p. 24). No other country had suffrage this wide, yet the United States was still profoundly undemocratic. The daily lives of a majority of the people violated basic criteria for democratic rights: proprietorship over the individual's "own person and capacities" (Macpherson, p. 263).

Three categories of adults—composing at least two thirds of the adult population—could not expect American law to recognize their title to their persons or their labor: slaves, Indians, and women. African-Americans—almost all slaves—composed nearly one fifth of the population. Indians, like African-Americans, had virtually no enforceable legal standing. Yet, native peoples still controlled more than three quarters of the territory of what would become the United States and may have still numbered as much as one fifth of the white population. While the law recognized white women, the doctrine of *femme couvert* legally subsumed women under their fathers and husbands. Most women also did not own property or the products of their labor.

Even among white males, proprietorship over persons and capacities varied. Indentured servants, still numerous in the late 1700s, were short-term slaves. Free white males who did not own property (as about half of them did not) faced legal and customary restrictions. Many of their commonest occupations restricted the right to quit. Sailors could not leave their ship without permission of the captain and faced life-threatening corporal punishment if they questioned the authority of officers. Agricultural workers (the largest category of waged labor) often signed annual contracts under which their employer held their wages as a bond until completion of the contract. If they quit or were fired, they forfeited all of their accumulated wages.

Thus, the daily lives of a substantial majority of working Americans in 1800 did not match any substantive understanding of freedom. Directly or indirectly, much of nineteenth-century politics reflected the contradictions between that daily reality and the promises of our founding revolutionary documents.

Three underlying factors shaped how those contradictions would be translated into the formal political arenas of parties, elections, and policy making: the heritage of European colonialism, the rules for political activity set out in federal and state constitutions, and a highly tribalized religiosity.

Heritage of Colonialism

The United States would not have existed but for the world-changing impact of European colonialism. However, within the resulting Atlantic economy, British North America occupied a niche that shaped subsequent political development differently from the rest of the hemisphere. British North America contained no land appropriate for sugarcane and no precious metals, the two greatest sources of colonialist wealth and plunder. While slave societies developed around the Chesapeake and in the coastal Carolinas,

other parts of British North America had few slaves. North American slavery remained a sideshow to the sugar colonies until the nineteenth century cotton boom. Because slave owners did not dominate, British North America disproportionately attracted European immigrants. The northern colonies and some western parts of the southern colonies became the most substantial white majority societies in the hemisphere.

As a result, by the American Revolution a bifurcated political culture combined reverence for the rights of Englishmen with defense of undemocratic racial hierarchy in an uneasy co-existence of political tendencies representative of metropole and colonial periphery. This contradiction fundamentally shaped and eventually dominated antebellum politics and influences American political culture to this day. Working-class politics emerged in a society where racial hierarchy and regional alignments functioned (and still function) as crosscutting axes to political divisions based on bourgeois versus proletarian.

Rules of the Political Game

If the colonial heritage structured American political culture, the constitutional heritage structured party politics and electoral behavior. Our constitution drafters left us with a political system markedly different from most other electoral democracies.

Chosen in a winner-take-all election conducted separately from legislative elections, and holding power at the behest of this national electorate rather than by maintaining a parliamentary majority, the American president resembles a constitutional monarch more than a parliamentary prime minister. The president nominates key government personnel unilaterally (subject to congressional approval, rarely refused until quite recently), in contrast to the parliamentary alliance building typical of prime ministers. The president similarly operates far more unilaterally than a prime minister in setting policy goals, suggesting budgetary priorities, and conducting foreign policy.

The principle of separation of powers, of which the separate election of president and legislature is a prime example, also means that effective governance demands simultaneous majority coalitions in several political institutions and at several levels. Power in American government is decentralized as well as divided among three branches of the national government. States select congressmen and senators. Maintaining national legislative majorities in both houses of Congress thus demands cultivation of political influence within the states. State constitutions, with rare exceptions, mirror the national constitution.

All successful American political parties have adapted to the logic of this constitutional structure. Since no party could remain politically credible for long without capturing the executive, and no party could actually govern without dual legislative majorities, parties defined themselves as engines for manufacturing and holding majority electoral coalitions, not as bearers of a coherent ideological vision. They became patchworks of constituencies. Most of what critics and reformers have lamented about American party politics ever since—the emphasis on personalities rather than issues, the intellectual shallowness and inconsistency of electoral appeals, and the preoccupation with winning at all costs—are a result of the strategic logic embedded in the constitutional structure.

This constitutional system presented working people with a double political dilemma. First, they needed to gain entrance. Second, they needed to negotiate within the party structures that constitutional rules dictated. Although activists frequently tried to flout the constitutional logic by organizing labor parties, such parties could never exercise significant political influence beyond the local level and could never sustain themselves for long periods. But working-class voters rarely had sufficient political clout to effectively pressure major party politicians to shape party programs around working-class demands.

Religious Identities

Finally, a distinctive religious heritage shaped cultural and political life. Many of the colonies had been founded by religious dissenters (Puritans in New England, Quakers in Pennsylvania, Catholics in Maryland) or attracted others (Baptists, Methodists, German Evangelicals and Lutherans). Several founding sects attempted to establish their denominations within their own colonies, aggravating conflicts between denominations. Well before mass party politics emerged in the nineteenth century, there had been a tradition of ethnoreligious conflict. Party coalitions developed in part around this tradition. As the Second Great Awakening stimulated both religiosity and the proliferation of religious sects, ethnoreligious identity became the most consistent determinant of partisan loyalties. Ethnoreligious and regional identities, which divided workers, frequently trumped other concerns.

Mechanics

Prior to the Jacksonian Era, formal politics had largely been a gentlemen's hobby, but in the major seaports, working people—who made up the overwhelming majority—exercised influence both through crowd activity and through organization among skilled workers. Enough artisans could meet the property qualification for suffrage to constitute a sizable constituency—a "Mechanics Interest."

However, commercialization and industrialization divided the old Mechanics Interest after the 1790s. Journeymen began organizing separately from the Revolutionary Era Mechanics Societies. Journeymen's societies successfully pressured employing masters to raise wages, maintain customary work rhythms, and hire only union members. In response, masters locked out workers and took union leaders to court under British common law doctrines of conspiracy in restraint of trade. More than two dozen such trials took place between 1805 and the 1830s, accompanied with packed courtrooms, popular pamphleteering, mass demonstrations, and political debates in city councils and state legislatures. The controversies around these trials symbolized the increasing bitterness of the larger conflict that provoked them. After the verdict in an 1836 trial of journeymen tailors in New York City, activists plastered the city with a "coffin handbill" denouncing the judge for burying liberty and equality and implicitly threatening his safety.

Decades of such conflict politicized and radicalized urban artisans and laborers, a process heightened by the self-conscious agitation of a scattering of European political exiles—United Irishmen, Luddites, Jacobins—and native Paineite radicals. By the end of the 1820s, radical artisans attempted to organize the world's first labor parties.

Workingmen's Parties

Workingmen's Parties startled political observers in Philadelphia and New York City in 1829, despite their amateur leadership and rudimentary organization. The Philadelphia Party ran poorly in its first campaign in 1828 but garnered about 20% of the vote in Philadelphia County the following year. The New York City Party did even better, with 31% in the 1829 state assembly races electing Ebenezer Ford, a carpenter.

Publicity of these initial successes inspired a frenzy of imitators and opportunists. Working people organized dozens of local Workingmen's Parties in the next year or two, and in some cities, ambitious politicians launched workingmen's tickets of doubtful authenticity, hoping to capture votes with the popular label. None lasted more than two or three years.

Yet despite their brief flare, they crystallized popular sensibilities about the implications of capitalist development and the potential of mass electoral mobilization. American politics would never be the same. The Workies made a larger public conscious of how commercialization, industrialization, and the transportation revolution had begun to alter the American political economy. A world of workers and bosses had started to replace a world of farmers, sailors, merchants, slaves, and planters. The Workies looked to the state to remedy their problems with the new political economy. The proper role of the state in economic life has been a staple of American politics ever since. The Workies also suggested that politics was too important to be left to gentlemen. Working people, who had often ignored elections even when they were eligible to vote, discovered politicians and voting booths.

The Workies also helped politicians discover the people. They demonstrated the electoral potential of a populist style pitting the People against the Enemies of the People—Tory bosses, Masonic cabals, the slave power conspiracy, and later economic royalists or secular humanist intellectuals.

Emergence of the Second American Party System

The Workies also benefited from fortuitous timing. Party competition had disappeared during the previous decade with the collapse of the Federalists. The Workingmen appeared just as political entrepreneurs sought new rhetoric and constituencies around which to build a second party system.

The Workingmen suggested possibilities both to incipient Jacksonian Democrats and proto-Whigs. Organizers of Jackson's 1828 presidential campaign successfully re-invented the wealthy and well-educated Tennessee military hero as a backwoods man of the people fighting for just plain folks against an Eastern establishment. Jackson—an Indian fighter, slave owner, and advocate of the creditor rather than the debtor faction in Tennessee politics—had no history of sympathy for the downtrodden, but he did harbor hostility toward the pretensions of seacoast elites, and he was willing to play the part. The Jacksonians won decisively amidst unprecedented turnout.

Both parties responded to this demonstration of how populist style could mobilize voters, and both also recognized that successful mass mobilization demanded a party organization run by political professionals. Their competition for voters undermined elite resistance to white manhood suffrage. By the 1840s, voter turnout reached the highest levels in American history, often topping 80% in national and state elections.

The Whigs defined themselves against Jackson by combining an economic program for capitalist development with an emphasis on respectability and Protestant morality. Their economic program anticipated the belching smokestacks and full dinner pails of late nineteenth-century McKinley Republicans: a national bank for monetary regulation and capital formation, a federally funded infrastructure to facilitate movement of goods, and high tariffs to protect American workers and manufacturers from foreign competition. The Whig formula: economic growth, prosperity for all, plentiful high-wage jobs plus moral stewardship with enforced Sabbath observance, prohibition, and Bible reading in the public schools.

Democrats built a coalition capable of winning national elections even after Jackson no longer headed the ticket by combining diverse groups repelled by the Whigs. The majority of slave owners opposed the Whig economic program. They feared that European nations that bought their cotton might retaliate against American tariffs, and protection for American industry meant higher prices for manufactured goods. A more fundamental concern intensified these objections: any program that strengthened the capacities of the national government strengthened the one institution that could threaten slavery.

Others threatened either by Whig economics or Whig morality joined slaveholder opponents of federal power: Catholics, Protestant sects that also feared persecution, secularists, drinkers and other enthusiasts of sensual pleasures, noncommercial farmers who viewed capitalist development as a threat rather than an opportunity, labor unionists embittered by conservative judges, and entrepreneurs who thought of themselves as outsiders or had local rather than national economic interests.

Two slogans—"personal liberty" and "white men's democracy"—united the diverse Democratic coalition around an assertively laboristic rhetoric. Not until New Deal Democrats did any major political party match Jacksonian claims as friends of labor or their appropriation of a language of class anger. Whigs countered that their formula for prosperity made them the true friends of labor.

That both major parties consciously competed so strenuously and self-consciously for a labor vote is at first glance surprising. The emerging working class of industrial wage earners, journeymen, urban day laborers, and servants still constituted a small percentage of the national electorate—not much more than 10% in 1840—and that minority, divided like other Americans by region, race, ethnicity, and religion, could hardly function as a politically cohesive group. But laboristic rhetoric meant more than an appeal to labor as a potential constituency. It symbolized widespread concerns about capitalist development.

Working People and the Second Party System

Many labor activists responded skeptically to the laboristic appeals of Jacksonians and Whigs. The former Philadelphia Workingman William English complained how "once a year politicians call us *men*; ... once a year we are the *intelligent, virtuous, orderly working men*. But then they want our *votes*." His colleague, John Ferral, accused both Democrats and Whigs of trying "to lure...working people into the meshes of their nets" (Pessen, pp. 123–124). Yet both, like most labor leaders, campaigned for the Democrats, attracted by antibank and antimonopoly diatribes, and by willingness of some urban Democratic politicians to defend workers' right to strike and support legislative goals like 10-hour-day laws. President Van Buren's 1840 executive order establishing the 10-hour day for workers in federally funded projects seemed like tangible evidence that Democrats' proworker language had substance.

But while labor activists tended to support the Democrats, working-class voters divided their votes between the two major parties. In part, this reflected the regional and ethnoreligious identities of working people. That region, ethnicity, and religion are the most reliable statistical predictors of partisan behavior in this era makes it appear that class concerns were irrelevant to antebellum politics. But that argument is hard to reconcile with other evidence about antebellum politics and culture—the widespread labor unrest of the 1830s and the 1850s, the popularity of literature darkly critical of capitalist development, and the eagerness of political campaigners to use explicitly class-tinged rhetoric. After the Bible, the two best-selling books in the antebellum United States were both critiques of America's labor systems: Harriet Beecher Stowe's *Uncle Tom's Cabin* and George Lippard's surrealist denunciation of capitalist exploitation, *The Quaker City*. Or consider the response of an Ohio congressman to a Whig colleague's speech about the harmony of interests between capital and labor (Ashworth, pp. 88–91):

Well this is very fine.... I suppose the capitalist will have no objection to exchanging situations with the laborer; that he will give up his capital to the laborer...his lands... the key to his costly sideboard, and the freehold to his rich wines, gold goblets, cut glass decanters...and he, the capitalist will enter the field of toil and sweat and there labor from morning till night.... And when shall such an example as this take place...when the lion and the lamb shall sit down in peace.

It seems more likely that class concerns mattered to working-class voters but that workers did not agree about which party best addressed those concerns. For example, Whig promises of tariff protection looked like job protection for some workers but higher living costs to others. In iron cities like Pittsburgh and in New England cotton mill towns, working people tended to vote Whig because tariffs offered protection from British competition threatening their livelihoods. In New England shoe towns, where tariff protection was less important, working-class voters were not as likely to vote Whig. In Philadelphia and Boston, both strongly Whig cities, correlations between the property values or wealth of each ward and the percent voting for Whigs or Democrats show a statistically significant tendency for voters in the poorer wards to vote more Democratic than the rest of the city, even when Whigs carried the cities overwhelmingly.

Overall, the Democrats' proworker rhetoric may have given them a slight edge among working-class voters, especially where Democratic politicians went beyond laboristic rhetoric to actively support workers. But industrial workers represented too small a percentage of the national electorate and were too divided by region, race, religion, ethnicity, and sectoral economic interests to form a cohesive voting bloc, except in a few scattered local elections.

Politics of Race and Slavery

The second party system depended on a bipartisan evasion that eventually scuttled it. Whig and Jacksonian leaders agreed to keep discussion of slavery out of the electoral arena. Some did so because they valued preservation of the Union above all else; some because they hoped slavery might gradually disappear without conflict; some because they believed a successful national party needed to draw votes on both sides of the Mason-Dixon line and could only do so by avoiding the issue. The congressional "gag rule," as its opponents called it—a procedural agreement to automatically table without discussion all petitions and proposals relating to slavery—symbolized the evasion.

But industrialization and capitalist development undermined this gentlemen's agreement. Mechanical production of cotton textiles produced an explosive worldwide demand for cotton. The American South was the best cotton-growing land on earth. King Cotton made southern slavery more profitable than it had ever been, dashing illusions that slavery might peacefully fade away. The cotton boom fueled the entire economy and stimulated westward expansion. In the first two hundred years of European settlement in North America, few Euro-Americans had moved more than two hundred miles west of the Atlantic coast. In the next 50 years, they would sweep across the continent. Each time a new territory petitioned for statehood, Congress had to revisit slavery. In an economy driven by cotton mills and cotton factories in the fields, slavery could not be kept out of party politics.

Repeated political crises over territorial expansion kept the issue of slavery in the consciousness of citizens, who also felt vaguely threatened by capitalist development. For example, leapfrogging slave territory threatened free white farmers' access to prime land (because slave owners could outbid them for the best acreage) when they were already nervous about the growing commercialization of agriculture.

The expansion of slavery also threatened to muddy the color line that had helped to maintain the loyalty of non-slaveholding and poor whites. The Jeffersonian ideal of a yeoman republic envisioned a society where a majority of white families owned land and those who didn't had reasonable hope of doing so. Within this ideology, whiteness corresponded with financial independence from the wills of others. The color line marked both a cultural and a material boundary. But with the rapid increase in waged labor that accompanied industrialization, an ever-growing portion of the white population faced what they insistently called wage slavery: lifelong financial dependence on employers and daily submission to the will of another, work regimes that uncomfortably mirrored the situation of chattel slaves. Both industrialization and the expansion of slavery thus served to intensify the racialization of American culture and the perception of slavery as degrading and threatening.

Working People and the Politics of Slavery and Race

Working people divided bitterly over slavery and race. For example, both the mobs who attacked abolitionist meetings and the victims of those attacks were disproportionately working class. On the one hand, many working-class radicals interpreted the growth of wage labor as a Tory counter-revolution designed to undermine their revolutionary birthright. They argued that industrialists and slave owners—lords of the loom and lords of the lash—collaborated in this plot to expand exploitation. All working people, regardless of race, legal status, ethnicity, or religion, should unite against their oppressors. Yet, given the racialized nature of American political culture, it is not surprising that even many white workers who preached a radically democratic version of American republicanism saw potentially emancipated slaves not as allies but as a barbarian horde that would further weaken their position against industrialists.

George Henry Evans, a New York City printer, organizer of the Workingmen's Party, and editor of the *Workingmen's Advocate*, had been the only editor in New York to defend the slaves' right to revolution after the 1831 Nat Turner Uprising. White workers shared blame for the loss of life in Virginia, Evans argued, because they had allowed slavery to persist by not actively fighting for abolition. But by the 1840s, Evans had become an anti-abolitionist convinced that northern industrialists had joined the abolitionist movement to shift popular attention away from the white slaves of the North.

Other labor radicals went further than Evans, trying to ally with southern politicians against northern industrialists. Mike Walsh, an Irish-American union organizer, editor, and New York City congressman, sought an alliance with John C. Calhoun, whom he viewed as an American equivalent of the British "Tory Socialists" who had sponsored factory inspection and other reforms in Britain.

Slaves and White Southerners

Perhaps the only cohort of working people who had absolutely no disagreement or confusion over the slavery question were African-Americans. About one American in five was African-American in 1790, about one in seven in 1860. However, because nearly every African-American performed menial labor regardless of age or sex, African-Americans represented about twice as large a percentage of the labor force as the population. The cotton they grew was decisive to the growth of the entire economy. They literally carried the rest of America on their backs.

Slaves resisted in small and individual ways such as shirking and tool breaking, and in large, collective actions such as mass escapes and rebellions. Free blacks, often linked to slave rebels, organized annual race conventions, armed vigilance committees against slave catchers, and decisive support for white abolitionists. William Lloyd Garrison's famous *Liberator* could not have gotten off the ground in 1831 without black support. When its first issue rolled off the presses, Garrison had only one hundred white subscribers.

During the course of the nineteenth century, slave rebellions also suggested a growing political self-consciousness among black working people. Many colonial slave revolts had been rooted in African cultural traditions and ethnic solidarities. They were as much mass escapes seeking refuge in Maroon communities as political assaults on the slave system. But the largest slave rebellions and conspiracies of the nineteenth century—the 1800 and 1802 Virginia conspiracies, the 1811 Louisiana revolt, Denmark Vesey's 1823 plot in Charleston, and the Virginia uprising of Nat Turner's followers in 1831—were all self-consciously revolutionary political movements seeking to overthrow the slave system. To a striking degree, the ideological visions of their leaders mirrored those of white labor activists—Paineite radical democracy and millenarian evangelical Protestantism.

Thus, despite their exclusion from formal electoral politics, African-American working people were self-conscious and decisive political actors. Their resistance made it impossible for other Americans to avoid recognition that slavery depended on systematic mobilization of coercive violence. Slave resistance undermined the moral claim of the United States as the democratic city on the hill and inspired other critics of the shortcomings of American democracy. The violence visited on slave rebels also dramatized the claims of antislavery activists trying to convince non-slave-owning whites that slavery threatened their liberties as well.

It is difficult to judge how consistently such arguments resonated with southern white working people. As W. E. B. DuBois noted, the "psychological wage" of white supremacy gave poor white southerners an emotional investment in slavery. Many poor white men wanted to join the planter class more than they wanted to overthrow it. But generations of conflict between Tidewater and Upcountry had also fostered a long tradition of class antagonism within the white South. Carriers of this tradition, such as the Kentucky abolitionist Cassius Clay or the North Carolina artisan Rowan Hinton Helper, who published an antislavery tract in 1857, tried to convince white working people that slavery robbed them of economic opportunity and liberty. Both had a following, especially in the Upper South and in cities with cohorts of immigrant workers and labor unions such as Baltimore, Richmond, and New Orleans. But proslavery mobs burned the printing presses of men like Clay who tried to rouse southern workers to fight

the planter class, threatened the lives of iconoclasts like Helper, and terrorized political activists who attempted to campaign for the Free Soil or Republican parties. While intense electoral competition between Democrats and Whigs gave southern politics a democratic appearance, in a region where black and white opponents of the slave regime faced overwhelming violence and terror, overt working-class political opposition to the slave regime had no chance of even getting started.

Free Soil and the Rise of the Republican Party

But a militarized South, with ubiquitous armed slave patrols pursuing runaway slaves into free territory, with militant advocates of slaveholder rights seemingly bent on nationalizing slavery, suggested to white northern workers that slavery no longer was someone else's problem. This sense that southern firebrands wanted to nationalize slavery enhanced the political capital of moderate antislavery politicians. While the abolitionists' moral critiques of slavery had never come close to winning a majority of the northern public, moderate antislavery politicians hoped to combine those who opposed slavery on moral grounds with those willing to fight the Slave Power—the slaveholding class—out of self-interest. As one Michigan Free Soiler put it, they had to show voters "that their *bread and butter* depends upon their doing right" (Formisano, p. 214).

The Republicans' 1856 campaign slogan—"Free Soil, Free Labor, Free Men"—embodied that strategy. Free labor, Republicans argued, could not compete with slave labor. Only in Free Soil states, states that outlawed slavery, could free labor thrive, and only where free labor thrived could workingmen be free. Recruiting savvy political veterans from both major parties, the Republicans combined what had been most appealing in both Jacksonian and Whig appeals to working people. They married the Jacksonians' paeans to honest workingmen and democratic self-reliance with Whig economics and promises of full employment and upward mobility.

Like all successful American parties, the Republican Party consciously built a diverse coalition. They cultivated nativists and prohibitionists, balanced tickets, and promised spoils. But they nonetheless conveyed a sense of idealism and integrity that perhaps made platitudes about honest labor seem meaningful. Republicans, after all, had done something unusual in American political history: they had taken an unequivocal position on the most controversial issue of their day.

Republicans did not run well among unskilled workers, disproportionately Irish Catholics and Germans (also two thirds Catholic). They carried too much of the scent of militant Protestantism and nativism. But they ran well among northern skilled workers. Lincoln got as many as two thirds of the votes of skilled workers in such industrial cities as Pittsburgh and Cincinnati, although he averaged only 40% of the national popular vote. Radical labor activists, from German Marxists to aging Workingmen, increasingly saw the abolition of slavery as a prerequisite to any successful response to the labor question of industrial capitalism.

Working People and the Politics of War and Reconstruction

Civil War draft resisters argued that the Civil War, like most wars, was a rich man's war and a poor man's fight. They objected to the draft law's provisions allowing the well-to-do to escape service by paying substitutes. Some objected to risking life and limb to free the Negroes. In New York City in 1863, where Irish and African-American workers had long harbored mutual hostility, draft riots became murderous pogroms against people of color.

But the war also kindled a remarkable surge of working-class political idealism, a sense that the working class was being called to a great moral purpose and that out of suffering would come a society that offered the working class something closer to the promises of its founding documents.

Perhaps the most startling evidence of political purpose was the conduct of African-American young men. Long before Lincoln had committed himself to emancipation, slaves became convinced that the war would usher in the day of Jubilee. Wherever Union lines moved close enough to suggest the possibility of successful flight, they abandoned the plantations. Men of military age begged a reluctant army to train and arm them so they could fight their oppressors. By war's end, perhaps a quarter of the male slaves of military age had escaped slavery to join the Union army, guaranteeing a ready supply of enthusiastic infantrymen just when draft resistance had seemed to threaten the war effort and withdrawing a pool of the most valuable labor power from the Confederate economy. W. E. B. DuBois called this mass flight the largest general strike in American history.

Lincoln, the first poor boy to reach the presidency, understood how to dramatize that sense of mission. His Gettysburg Address redefined the war for the Union as it was to a war for what it should be—"government of the people, by the people, for the people." His second inaugural address clothed the political project he had posed at Gettysburg in the evangelical language of sin, suffering, and redemption.

In the mid- and late 1860s, this idealism of the War years, combined with an inflationary spiral, stimulated the greatest outpouring of labor activism since the 1830s. The Boston machinist Ira Steward, the theorist and promoter of the eight-hour day, summarized a widespread sentiment among northern workers at the end of the war: "the workingmen of America will in future claim a more equal share in the wealth their industry creates...and a more equal participation in the privileges and blessings of those free institutions, defended by their manhood on many a bloody field of battle." Steward urged radical Republicans to turn their eyes northward: "[L]et our dinner tables be reconstructed," he declared.

Steward helped to refine a working-class interpretation of republicanism that had been percolating among Paineite labor radicals, utopian labor reformers, and evangelical millenarians for much of the previous century: the political struggle for human rights and democratic government and the conflict between producers and nonproducers, who lived off the value produced by other men, were essentially the same. In the next generation, this producer republicanism would culminate in the national ascendancy of the Knights of Labor. Working-class political activists imagined that labor republicanism would politically unite an emerging working-class majority who would use the American political system to emancipate wage slaves just as they had emancipated chattel slaves.

Producer Republicanism and Gilded Age Politics

At the end of the Civil War, the prospects for restructuring American politics around the question of wage labor, as the Republicans had done around slavery, seemed much better than they would be in retrospect. Although still small and fragile, labor unions had expanded significantly. What had begun as a war to prevent secession had been transformed into a war to abolish an undemocratic labor system. Surely, labor activists believed, their fellow Americans could be made to see that liberty and justice for wage slaves was merely an extension of the principles for which they had just fought and died. Who could have imagined just 30 years ago that the small circles of abolitionists who risked their lives whenever they spoke in public would live to see slavery abolished?

Rising working-class discontent would make "the labor question," as it came to be called, one of the central topics of public discourse for the next 50 years, but would-be worker politicians found it far harder to translate discontent into political power than to raise the question. Major parties occasionally selected labor leaders as candidates, a few prominent national politicians expressed sympathy for industrial workers, and some big-city machine politicians courted labor by restraining strikebreaking by police and local judges, but such pockets of support were too scattered and episodic to significantly shape national party agendas.

Discontented workers, disgusted with the unwillingness of the Republicans and Democrats to address their concerns, frequently tried to run labor candidates on Labor, Socialist, Greenback, and Populist tickets. Such efforts followed a recurring pattern. Following peak moments of industrial conflict, they often did surprisingly well, emerging out of nowhere with sufficient electoral clout to challenge the major parties and occasionally win a few offices. Thus, the Massachusetts Labor Reform Party elected 22 state legislators in 1869 and polled 15% of the state vote the following year. The Greenback-Labor Party received over one million votes in 1878, ran particularly strongly in industrial cities like Pittsburgh, and elected the union leader Martin Foran to Congress from Cleveland and the future Knights of Labor grand master workman Terence Powderly as mayor of Scranton. Socialists elected local officials and state legislators in Chicago, St. Louis, Milwaukee, Detroit, and Louisville during the 1870s. Local labor parties associated with the Knights of Labor also displayed electoral strength in the mid-1880s. Their 1886 mayoral candidates drew more than a third of the votes in New York and Chicago and won elections in several smaller cities. Populists in the 1890s ran competitive races in many industrial and mining towns.

Such surges of labor protest voting demonstrated that working-class discontent ran deep, but almost invariably such surges turned out to be one-hit wonders, quickly fading into insignificance in subsequent efforts. The labor organizations that spawned them could rarely sustain their own organizational base through fluctuations in the business cycle, so labor party resources frequently disappeared. Even at their peaks, the most powerful national labor organizations represented too few members to win elections outside their strongest bastions. The Knights' peak membership reached over 700,000 in 1886, but nearly 11.5 million people voted in the 1888 presidential election. Even if turnout among Knights eligible to vote had been 100%, and even if they had all voted as a bloc, they could not have represented more than 5% of the national electorate.

Given the structure of American politics, minor parties, which might have slowly built support within a parliamentary system, seemed impotent after the initial flush of enthusiasm faded, even where they had local victories. Labor activists elected in local races found themselves undermined by incumbent opponents and officials and outflanked by hostile state and national governments. They could not deliver on the expectations of their voters. Accomplishing anything demanded compromise and political alliance, but skeptics about independent political action pointed out that this necessity suggested they should bargain for concessions within the major parties.

Finally, their electoral base usually had prior major party partisan preferences based on regional and ethnocultural identities. At peak moments of industrial conflict and agitation, significant numbers of working-class voters might put such identities aside temporarily, but as emotions calmed, and as third-party politicians could not deliver on millenarian expectations, let alone even minimal pork-chop benefits, the lure of returning to the power and security of a major party home became compelling.

A Century of Working-Class Politics in Retrospect

What did a century of working-class political action accomplish? For many activists and for many historians sympathetic to working people, the answer was frustrating. Explicitly prolabor parties went down to inevitable defeat, while joining major parties seemed at best to offer limited gains. The structures of political power seemed nearly as impermeable to working-class influence at the end of the century as at the beginning. Neither major party offered workers more than episodic support or more than occasional tangible material benefits—no social security, unemployment insurance, workmen's compensation, food stamps, public housing, enforceable safety standards, enforceable statutory limits on employer demands, or right to collective bargaining. Indeed, by the end of the century, the rapid increase in such anti-union devices as court injunctions, yellow-dog contracts, and heavily armed private company armies made union membership more dangerous than it had been for the members of journeymen's societies who had faced conspiracy indictments at the beginning of the century. Every year, police, troops, and armed company guards killed peaceful and unarmed strikers. Between the Gilded Age and the 1930s, more Americans died in the class war of the picket line than died in the shooting war with Spain. Not until the New Deal would working people achieve significant influence on public policy or the right to organize without having to fear for their lives.

Yet in other ways, working-class political agitation had improved working-class life. Democratic values had become sacrosanct in American political culture—even though practices still didn't always match. Slavery had been abolished and de jure universal male suffrage achieved—although many African-American southerners would not have de facto voting rights until the 1970s. Women's suffrage would follow within the next 20 years. A century of agitation had lowered the length of the average working day by three or four hours. Workers would rarely tolerate forms of intimidation common in 1800: corporal punishment in the workplace, long delays in wage payment designed to make them compliant for fear of losing accumulated pay, restrictions on freedom of movement.

Working-class politics had also shaped American culture. By 1900, virtually everyone in America knew what people meant when they used words like union, strike, boycott, scab, picket line, or solidarity. Such cultural knowledge provided a basis for struggle by subsequent generations of American working people. The "labor question" would be at the core of Progressivism and the New Deal.

Yet, for all the benefits they provided, Progressive and New Deal reforms would certainly have disappointed such nineteenth-century labor activists as the Workingmen Thomas Skidmore or George Henry Evans or advocates of producer republicanism like Ira Steward. They would have recognized the value of these reforms. But they would have argued that the social bargain of the New Deal, while granting important social welfare benefits and the right to organize, still left working people in a subservient dependence on their employers. In a new century, with the victories of the New Deal era seemingly relentlessly rolled back, perhaps American working people need to relearn a key lesson of these nineteenth-century labor radicals: meaningful democracy is incompatible with sharply unequal economic power.

RICHARD OESTREICHER

References and Further Reading

Ashworth, John. *"Agrarians" and "Aristocrats": Party Political Ideology in the United States, 1837–1846.* Cambridge: Cambridge University Press, 1987.

Formisano, Ronald. *The Birth of Mass Political Parties: Michigan, 1827–1861.* Princeton, NJ: Princeton University Press, 1971.

Keyssar, Alexander. *The Right to Vote: The Contested History of Democracy in the United States.* New York: Basic Books, 2000.

Lipset, Seymour Martin, and Gary Marks. *It Didn't Happen Here: Why Socialism Failed in the United States.* New York: W. W. Norton, 2000.

Macpherson, C. B. *The Political Theory of Possessive Individualism: Hobbes to Locke.* Oxford: Oxford University Press, 1964.

Montgomery, David. *Beyond Equality: Labor and the Radical Republicans, 1862–1872.* New York: Alfred A. Knopf, 1967.

———. *Citizen Worker: The Experience of Workers in the United States with Democracy and the Free Market during the Nineteenth Century.* Cambridge: Cambridge University Press, 1993.

Oestreicher, Richard. "Urban Working-Class Political Behavior and Theories of American Electoral Politics, 1970–1940." *Journal of American History* 74 (March 1988): 1257–1286.

POLITICS AND LABOR, TWENTIETH CENTURY

In the first two thirds of the twentieth century, organized labor moved from the margins of American politics to a position of power and influence, its rise facilitated by a series of carefully crafted strategies and bitterly fought battles. As American public life shifted to the right in the 1970s, 1980s, and 1990s, labor's standing tumbled, so that by the end of the century, it was once again on the margins, seemingly incapable of influencing politics and policy in any significant way.

The late nineteenth century had been a particularly difficult period for the labor movement. Unprecedented economic change fostered profound conflict at workplaces across the nation. Yet when working people tried to protect or advance their interests through collective action, they often faced fierce resistance from the combined power of capital and the state. Employers regularly secured court injunctions declaring particular strikes illegal. When workers violated those injunctions, government officials enforced the court orders with massive shows of force. Time and again, federal troops and state militias intervened in strikes the courts had prohibited, shattering walkouts at gunpoint, arresting strike leaders, and even battling workers in the streets. "All the machinery of the state stands ready to protect and further the interests of capital," complained a pro-union observer, "while labor is absolutely without law, a law unto itself, save when it commits some act, to be dealt with as a criminal."

Unionists had no single solution to the dilemma they faced. Some argued that business and government were so hopelessly intertwined that only revolutionary action could tear them asunder. Others favored a democratic evolution to socialism, a perspective that was gaining a substantial following in the working class at the turn of the century, thanks in part to the relentless agitation of the Socialists' dynamic spokesman, Eugene V. Debs. Still other labor activists favored government regulation of the capitalist economy and the creation of a welfare state. The fledgling American Federation of Labor (AFL), meanwhile, argued that there was no point in trying to restructure the American political economy. Instead, union members should adopt a more modest goal, pressuring politicians to rewrite the laws that constrained union action so that labor might pursue its self-interest as it saw fit.

The AFL president, Samuel Gompers, reduced his strategy to a simple dictum: "Reward your friends," he famously said, "and punish your enemies." In practice, however, the AFL did not maintain the nonpartisanship that Gompers claimed to favor. Although the Republican Party had a progressive wing, most of its major figures opposed labor law reform. In the Democratic Party, the balance was much the opposite. Democratic conservatives, such as Grover Cleveland, were more than willing to lend their weight to corporate interests. But by the first decade of the twentieth century, party leaders were willing to endorse the AFL's demands. In exchange, Gompers brought the federation into alliance with the Democrats. In both the 1908 and 1912 presidential elections, for instance, the AFL worked closely with the Democratic National Committee to mobilize the working-class vote, and federation officials campaigned on behalf of the Democratic candidates.

The AFL's mounting involvement in Democratic affairs brought Federation officials into contact with the Party's growing progressive wing. It was not always an ideal match. Gompers's primary political aim was to reduce government involvement in labor's affairs, whereas progressives generally supported greater government action, albeit on behalf of working people rather than on behalf of business interests. So Gompers opposed calls for a law mandating an eight-hour workday, state-supported health-care plans, federal mediation of labor conflicts, and a minimum wage, all reforms progressives strongly supported. But other unionists were drawn to the progressives' expansive view of government power. Many connections occurred on a local level, where labor activists joined with settlement house workers, socially minded lawyers such as Felix Frankfurter and Frank Walsh, ethnic politicians such as Al Smith, some socialists, and even a handful of liberal businessmen to promote progressive causes. In the course of the Wilson administration, however, the labor-progressive alliance shifted from the streets of Chicago and New York to the highest levels of government.

When Woodrow Wilson was elected president in 1912, he was not considered a champion of labor.

His first three years in office did little to change that impression. But as Wilson faced re-election and the possibility of war in 1916, he shifted his administration's labor policy dramatically. First came a burst of progressive reform, including a limited minimum wage law and a long-awaited prohibition on child labor. Then, after the United States entered World War I, Wilson launched what one historian has called "a mini-legal revolution" in collective bargaining. Desperate to bring order to a chaotic wartime economic mobilization, the president created a National War Labor Board (NWLB) to adjudicate industrial disputes. Directed by a cadre of progressives, the board used its power to support workers' right to unionize without employer interference, to promote workplace democracy through formal systems of shop-floor representation, to extend the eight-hour day and the minimum wage to more industries, and to provide women workers with equal pay for equal work. Such vigorous government policy helped to trigger a surge in union membership from 3 million workers in 1917 to over 5 million in 1920, a 70% increase in three years. Suddenly, Samuel Gompers's circumscribed vision of the state's proper role appeared hopelessly antiquated—a relic of another age.

But the bold experiments of the war years did not last. In 1919, businessmen and their conservative allies launched a political offensive that shut down the NWLB, reversed the labor movement's great surge forward, and triggered a Red Scare so ferocious that it eviscerated the radical left. By the early 1920s, organized labor was reeling, whipsawed by a Republican ascendancy that had no interest in its agenda, a judiciary once again willing to wield the cudgel of injunctions, and a business community determined to re-assert its absolute authority over the workplace. Badly battered by labor's dramatic turn of fortunes, Gompers drew the AFL back from its engagement with party politics, a policy endorsed by his successor, William Green, who assumed control of the Federation after Gompers's death in 1924. Labor's progressives, meanwhile, desperately tried to open new political avenues, but their most ambitious effort—Robert La Follette's 1924 third-party campaign for the presidency—ended in crushing defeat.

The severe setbacks of the 1920s did not destroy the progressive ideal, however. With the collapse of the NWLB, its advocates returned to their settlement houses, unions, law offices, college campuses, and congressional offices, policy makers in exile. But they maintained the network they had built during the Wilson Administration. And through that network they sharpened the ideas that had shaped the wartime labor program. In the midst of the 1920s boom, to talk of economic rationalization through federal support of unionization, workplace democracy, and the expansion of the welfare state must have seemed like an academic exercise. When the boom gave way to a massive depression, though, the progressives were perfectly positioned to resurrect their program.

In the early days of the Great Depression—1930, 1931, and 1932—the progressive bloc promoted its ideas primarily through congressional allies such as New York's Robert Wagner, Wisconsin's Robert La Follette, and Nebraska's George Norris. The 1932 presidential election shifted the balance of power from Capitol Hill to the White House. Like Woodrow Wilson before him, Democrat Franklin Roosevelt enjoyed substantial support from organized labor during the campaign. But that support was hardly decisive, and when FDR took office, he was not beholden to labor interests. He desperately needed a labor policy, however, and the progressives had one to offer. So Roosevelt integrated the network into his administration. The connections ran from Secretary of Labor Frances Perkins through the presidential aides Tommy Corcoran and Benjamin Cohen to Roosevelt's informal advisor Felix Frankfurter, back to Senator Wagner and other New Deal congressmen and finally to select union leaders, most notably the United Mine Workers (UMW) president, John L. Lewis, and Sidney Hillman of the Amalgamated Clothing Workers of America (ACWA).

It took the progressive network almost three years to consolidate its position within the administration. Roosevelt endorsed the right of workers to form unions free of employer interference with Section 7 (a) of the 1933 National Industrial Recovery Act (NIRA), but weak enforcement undermined the measure's effectiveness. By the winter of 1935, it was clear that Section 7(a) was not working. Senator Wagner therefore introduced a replacement bill designed to put the power of the federal government behind workers' rights. In concept, the bill embodied the progressive idea that unionization would regularize industrial relations and thus help to rationalize the American economy. What's more, progressives argued, unionized workers would have the leverage necessary to win higher wages, which would boost purchasing power and foster the economic growth an economy mired in depression so obviously needed. In practice, Wagner's bill followed the model established during World War I: creating a federal agency—the National Labor Relations Board (NLRB)—empowered to protect workers as they organized unions.

At first, FDR did not endorse the bill. But as it moved through Congress in the spring of 1935, he added his support. The National Labor Relations Act (NLRA) became law on July 5, 1935. The progressives' moment had arrived.

For the next two years, politics, policy, and direct action fused in a fashion it never had before. When AFL leaders refused to launch a nationwide organizing campaign to bring unionization to the nation's core industries, Lewis and Hillman abandoned the AFL to create their own federation, the Congress of Industrial Organizations (CIO). To make sure that the CIO had the political support it needed to take on corporate America, Lewis and Hillman threw themselves and their unions into Roosevelt's 1936 re-election campaign. Lewis funneled over $500,000 of Mine Workers' money—an unprecedented sum—into Democratic coffers. Union organizers worked tirelessly to bring working-class voters to the polls. And Lewis himself campaigned for Roosevelt across the country, his efforts capped by a joint appearance with the president in the heart of Pennsylvania's coal country days before the election. When Roosevelt swept the election—carrying 46 of 48 states—Lewis knew the CIO was ready to move. "We...must capitalize on the election," he told his executive board shortly after the votes were counted. "The CIO was out fighting for Roosevelt....We wanted a president who would hold the light for us while we went out and organized."

That is precisely what they got. On the last day of December 1936, autoworkers in Flint, Michigan, began their epic sit-down strike. From that spark, the CIO fire spread across industrial America, its advance aided by sympathetic New Dealers such as the Michigan governor, Frank Murphy, who refused to use force to evict the sit-down strikers, and the progressives who staffed the new National Labor Relations Board. In the course of 1937, union membership increased by three million as the CIO organized workers in some of the nation's most powerful companies, among them General Motors and U.S. Steel. There were also some stinging defeats that year. But by the beginning of 1938, organized labor had become a major power in the American economy, its dramatic rise—and future prospects—tied intimately to the New Deal state.

Just how intimately the two were tied became clear over the next decade. As the militancy of 1937 began to fade, the CIO came to rely more heavily on its allies at the NLRB to advance the union cause. There were still dramatic strikes—CIO unions shut down both Bethlehem Steel and the Ford Motor Company in 1941, for instance—but it was as much NLRB pressure as mass protest that forced the firms to recognize their workers' right to unionize. The United States' entry into World War II at the end of 1941 strengthened the connection. Patriotic fervor demanded that the labor movement pledge not to strike for the duration. In exchange for that critical concession, the federal government guaranteed unions "maintenance of membership." That is, if a union had a contract with an employer when the war began, all new hires would automatically become union members after 15 days on the job. As a result, union membership shot up by five million during the war, thanks not to union action but to government policy.

Both AFL and CIO unions benefited from the Democrats' support for unionization; in fact, the AFL grew more quickly than the CIO in the late 1930s and early 1940s. Still, AFL leaders kept their distance from Roosevelt and the Democrats. The CIO, in contrast, strengthened the ties it had forged in the crucible of 1936. It was partly a practical matter, of course, a quid pro quo for all that the New Dealers had done for the labor movement. But it was more than that. The CIO had its share of bread-and-butter unionists, who wanted nothing more from their unions that higher wages and shorter hours. But the CIO was also home to a vast array of progressives who hoped that the labor movement might promote a range of reforms. National health care, public housing, federal aid to education, civil rights, national economic planning, even the nationalization of key industries: CIO activists supported these and many more causes. And at least as long as Franklin Roosevelt was alive, most of them believed that the Democratic Party offered the only real avenue for advancing their agendas.

So the CIO integrated itself into the Democratic Party machinery. Union leaders such as Sidney Hillman took seats on the Party's policy-making committees, while local labor activists filled positions in the Party's state and city councils. In the 1944 presidential election, Sidney Hillman built an elaborate campaign structure, the CIO Political Action Committee (PAC), that raised campaign contributions from every union local, produced reams of campaign literature, crafted radio advertisements, and sponsored get-out-the vote drives—all on behalf of Roosevelt and the Democrats. Dissent was not an option. When John L. Lewis announced that he would not support FDR's re-election bid in1940, his fellow unionists abandoned him. Eight years later, the CIO's left-wing faction rallied behind Henry Wallace rather than the Democratic nominee, Harry Truman; Lewis's successor as CIO president, Philip Murray, responded by purging the leftists from the federation.

Many historians have concluded that the CIO's commitment to the Democratic Party in the 1940s was a fundamental error. As they tied themselves to the Democrats, they argue, CIO leaders were forced to subordinate their agenda to that of the Party. This was particularly damaging by the late 1940s, when the Cold War forced mainstream politics to the right.

Party loyalty and political calculation demanded that CIO spokespersons back away from the most radical of their demands—such as the nationalization of industry—in favor of the Democrats' increasingly watered-down reformism. Murray's purging of the left was but one result of the Faustian bargain the CIO had struck, the historians say. And with that bargain, the great hopes of the 1930s simply faded away.

The argument has much to recommend it. American politics certainly did drift to the right in the years immediately after World War II, and as it did so, CIO leaders were forced to soften their militant edge. One example illustrates the point. In early 1949, Walter Reuther, the president of the United Automobile Workers, proudly told a union audience, "I am not particularly interested when people talk about free enterprise. I am a believer in a planned economy." Two years later, as McCarthyism swept the nation, Reuther felt compelled to declare that he "believe[d] strongly in the free enterprise system." Reuther had not changed, but the times had. Because the Democrats were sure of labor's support, moreover, Party leaders did not have to give labor everything it wanted. Instead, they could treat unions as simply another constituent group, one part of a larger coalition whose expectations had to be managed.

But the argument can be taken too far. For all the limitations that post-World War II politics imposed, the unions of the CIO and, after their 1955 merger, the AFL-CIO wielded enormous influence in the 1950s and 1960s. Democratic presidents regularly consulted with union leaders. Labor officials held a number of important political appointments. Arthur Goldberg, for instance, moved from the staff of the United Steelworkers to become John Kennedy's secretary of labor and from there to the United States Supreme Court, while Walter Reuther's administrative assistant, Jack Conway, helped to direct Lyndon Johnson's War on Poverty. Most important, labor lobbyists were instrumental in passing into law some of the most important reforms of the postwar era, including the creation of Medicare and Medicaid, the expansion of Social Security, and the destruction of the southern system of segregation, a triumph secured by the Civil Rights Act of 1964 and the Voting Rights Act of 1965. On its own terms, this is an imposing list of accomplishments. Given labor's position at the start of the twentieth century, it is truly remarkable.

Despite its political sophistication, however, organized labor was ill-prepared for the shocks that shook the movement in the late 1960s and 1970s. Trouble began in the latter half of the 1960s, when the era's searing political conflicts began to dissolve the electoral coalition that the New Dealers had assembled in the 1930s. At the same time, a combination of war-induced inflation, rising foreign competition, and declining investor confidence loosened the United States' once iron grip on manufacturing. The problems deepened in the 1970s, as a series of unprecedented events pushed up prices on basic goods while an influx of foreign goods cut deeply into American corporations' market share. By the end of the decade, profit margins were tumbling. Desperate to reverse the decline, corporate executives began the restructuring that would strip the United States of much of its manufacturing base.

But the business community understood that restructuring alone was not sufficient. If profits were to be improved, they argued, the federal government had to abandon the New Deal system, which they insisted had become a drag on innovation and investment. To that end, the corporate elite allied itself with the growing conservative movement of the late 1970s, itself an amalgam of tax rebels, free marketers, supply-siders, religious and cultural conservatives, and aggressive cold warriors. Like the New Dealers of the 1930s, the conservatives traded on the economic crisis of the 1970s to take control of the federal government. In January 1981, Ronald Reagan took the oath of office as president of the United States—and the conservative revolution began in earnest.

For the next 20 years, the revolution pummeled the labor movement. The assault was multisided. As major manufacturing firms downsized their operations, unions lost thousands upon thousands of members. The Reagan and Bush administrations, meanwhile, turned government policy against unionization. Reagan signaled the shift during the famous PATCO strike of 1981, when the president fired 11,500 striking air traffic controllers. The more significant change resulted from Reagan and Bush appointing conservatives to the NLRB. The appointees greatly widened management's power to resist union organization and demands, stripping away many of the protections the New Dealers had put in place a half century earlier. Many corporations with unionized workforces used their new leverage to demand that their workers accept wage cuts and reduced fringe benefits. Companies without unions felt free to intimidate those workers who dared to consider organizing or even to complain about working conditions. According to one study, one of every 20 workers who demanded union representation in the1980s lost his or her job.

Together, these blows crippled labor's political power. Obviously, the labor movement had no leverage with the Republicans, who now dominated Washington. But the problem extended to the Democratic Party as well. By the end of the twentieth century, only 13% of the American workforce was unionized, down from its mid-1950s peak of 35%. With its base reduced so dramatically, the union movement no longer had the ability to marshal a huge bloc of voters or invest vast sums of money in political campaigns. Consequently, Democratic officials no longer believed it necessary to support even the most basic demands of the union movement, a point driven home in 1993, when the Democratic president, Bill Clinton, pushed the North American Free Trade Agreement through Congress, despite labor's vociferous opposition. That was perhaps the most telling symbol of labor's precipitous political decline. A movement that had once promised to reward its friends and punish its enemies found itself in the closing years of the twentieth century with far too many enemies to punish and few friends to reward.

KEVIN BOYLE

References and Further Reading

Dubofsky, Melvyn. *The State and Labor in Modern America.* Chapel Hill and London: University of North Carolina Press, 1994.

Fraser, Steven. *Labor Will Rule: Sidney Hillman and the Rise of American Labor.* New York: The Free Press, 1991.

Greene, Julie. *Pure and Simple Politics: The American Federation of Labor and Political Activism, 1881–1917.* New York: Cambridge University Press, 1998.

Lichtenstein, Nelson. *State of the Union: A Century of American Labor.* Princeton, NJ: Princeton University Press, 2002.

McCartin, Joseph. *Labor's Great War: The Struggle for Industrial Democracy and the Origins of Modern American Labor Relations, 1912–1921.* Chapel Hill: University of North Carolina Press, 1997.

Zieger, Robert. *The CIO 1935–1955.* Chapel Hill: University of North Carolina Press, 1995.

POOR PEOPLE'S CAMPAIGN

While it is sometimes regarded as the disappointing final chapter of the civil rights movement, the Poor People's Campaign of 1968 signaled a shift in protest politics from legal reform to economic transformation. Frustrated by the limits of earlier civil rights victories and the government's flagging support for Great Society social programs, Martin Luther King Jr. initiated the Poor People's Campaign, which he envisioned as a series of disruptive protests in the nation's capital that would force Congress and the president to take action to end poverty. After King's April 4, 1968, assassination, his associates in the Southern Christian Leadership Conference (SCLC) proceeded with the campaign, and for six weeks, three thousand poor blacks, whites, Chicanos, Puerto Ricans, and Native Americans made their home in

Poor People's March at Lafayette Park and on Connecticut Avenue. Library of Congress, Prints & Photographs Division, U.S. News & World Report Magazine Collection [LC-DIG-ppmsca-04302].

Resurrection City, a symbolic protest community of plywood and canvas huts constructed near the Reflecting Pool at the Lincoln Memorial. Bogged down by mud and infighting, harassed and infiltrated by police and government agents, and largely ignored by the public, the SCLC disbanded the city and ended the Poor People's Campaign when its demonstration permit expired in June.

Origins of the Poor People's Campaign

From the earliest days of his leadership of the civil rights movement, King had been rhetorically committed to economic justice. As a young pastor of a middle-class congregation in Montgomery, Alabama, he provided leadership to the historic bus boycott that had its most direct impact on female domestic workers and laborers. Overseas visits to Africa and India in the late 1950s exposed King to the colonial dimensions of poverty and inequality, and his addresses at union conventions indicate that he valued the labor movement's role in bettering the wages and conditions for working people. But in the months following his unsuccessful open housing campaign in Chicago during the summer of 1966, King spoke more frequently and with greater urgency about the need for a redistribution of economic and political power. King believed that President Lyndon B. Johnson had sacrificed his War on Poverty and other domestic

reforms for an expanded war in Vietnam. He was also frustrated by the limitations of earlier civil rights victories that may have ended legal discrimination but did little to guarantee true equality. As dozens of cities erupted in spontaneous violence during the summer of 1967 and Black Power militants challenged his leadership, King spoke openly about the need for the movement "to find a kind of middle road between riots and timid supplication." What was needed was "a method of dislocating the functioning of a city without destroying life and property," he told the National Advisory Commission on Civil Disorders that fall.

King Proposal Meets Resistance

The Poor People's Campaign proved to be a tough sell, even among King's coworkers and closest confidants. In the weeks after he announced plans for the campaign at a December 4 press conference, SCLC staff grumbled privately that the goals for the protests were unclear and that a Washington mobilization would pull them from their ongoing work in Cleveland, Chicago, and Grenada, Mississippi. The longtime advisor Bayard Rustin broke publicly with King and warned that the demonstrations would damage the Democratic Party's showing in the 1968 elections and sink the pending civil rights bill banning housing discrimination. NAACP officials predicted that the protests would lead to violence and even more repressive countermeasures.

In the early weeks of 1968, a more sinister opposition sprang into action, as the FBI stepped up its long-standing campaign against King. At the FBI director J. Edgar Hoover's urging, clandestine informants infiltrated SCLC regional offices, gathered information on the organization's supporters, and spread rumors intended to divide the movement. Welfare recipients considering the trip to Washington were warned that their benefits would be cut, and organizational allies of the SCLC were told of the group's alleged mishandling of funds. Agents leaked exaggerated threats of violence to panicky Washington city officials, fueling their deepest fears of an invading mass of poor people. As an overwhelmingly white organization with few agents who could convincingly pass as poor black people, the FBI welcomed the cooperation of military intelligence units that had their own extensive spy operations. With the important exception of the Community Relations Service Division of the Department of Justice, which provided SCLC leaders valuable advice and logistical assistance, a constellation of local and federal government bodies lined up to contain, if not destroy, the Poor People's Campaign.

On the Way to Washington

King's efforts to mobilize support for the campaign in the weeks before its scheduled late April kickoff stiffened his resolve. Traveling by chartered airplane and driving along backcountry roads, King delivered dozens of addresses at rural churches and community centers across Mississippi, Alabama, and Georgia. In the tiny Delta town of Marks, Mississippi, King spoke at a Head Start center that had received no federal assistance in its two years of existence. He repeated the campaign's demands that the federal government provide jobs or a guaranteed income for every adult, and he listened somberly as African-American women spoke of their need for shoes and better schools for their children.

Between scheduled stops in Mississippi, King addressed a rally on March 18 in support of the Memphis sanitation workers, who had been on strike for more than a month over the city's refusal to recognize their union. He was moved by the black workers' spirit. Their struggle reminded King of his early days in the civil rights movement and embodied the goals of the Poor People's Campaign. Despite the protests of SCLC staff, who feared that he was stretching himself too thin, King agreed to the strike leaders' request that he return to the city to lead a nonviolent protest march. That march, on March 28, ended abruptly in violence. Acts of vandalism by youthful protesters were met with brutal retaliation by the police; one protestor was killed and dozens were wounded. King's FBI enemies and their media allies used the news to cast doubt on his reputation as a nonviolent leader and to suggest that the Washington protests promised more of the same, but on a larger scale. On his return to Memphis a few days later, King was felled by an assassin's bullet.

The Poor People's Campaign

In the wake of King's death, his close friend Ralph D. Abernathy assumed the leadership of the SCLC and the Poor People's Campaign. Ironically, the tragic events in Memphis re-energized the campaign; the number of volunteers pledging to come to Washington exceeded expectations and the SCLC suddenly found itself awash in donations. On April 29, Abernathy led an advance group of one hundred poor people to Washington, where they met with government officials and made their demands public. Following a meeting with Secretary of State Dean Rusk, Abernathy declared these initial efforts a success: "I think this is the most fruitful three days ever seen in the history of this city. The leaders here for the first time heard the cries and groans of the poor people speaking in their own language, unpolished—an outpouring from the souls of poor people. The poor are no longer divided. We are not going to let the white man put us down any more. It's not white power, and I'll give you some news, it's not black power, either. It's poor power and we're going to use it." Meanwhile, nine caravans of poor people from as far away as Seattle and Los Angeles prepared for their cross-country trips. From Marks, Mississippi, where King had spoken just a few weeks earlier, a 50-person delegation began its slow journey across the Deep South on several wagons pulled by teams of mules. Several hundred Mexican-Americans affiliated with the *Alianza de Pueblos Libres* and the Crusade for Justice traveled from New Mexico and Colorado, while staff members from the Highlander Center and the Appalachian Volunteers organized a contingent of white and black poor people from Tennessee, Kentucky, and West Virginia.

The Poor People's Campaign officially began on May 12 with a Mother's Day march cosponsored by the SCLC and the National Welfare Rights Organization. Coretta Scott King led demonstrators through Washington neighborhoods that had been devastated just weeks before in the riots that followed her husband's murder. Speaking to an audience of five thousand people at the Cardozo High School stadium, she called for the repeal of recent amendments to the Social Security Act that had raised eligibility standards and cut benefits for women and children. The following day, Abernathy officially opened Resurrection City, and arriving protestors began moving in to their new homes on the National Mall.

Over the next five weeks, protestors took part in dozens of demonstrations around the capital, most of which targeted government agency heads and congressional leaders. Protesters were usually greeted by sympathetic officials who discussed pending legislation but offered no firm commitments or concessions. For fear of alienating white supporters, the SCLC had agreed to refrain from the disruptive protests King had promised the previous year, at least until the June19 mass demonstration that was to be the highlight of the Poor People's Campaign. Billed as "Solidarity Day," the event drew more than 50,000 people to the foot of the Lincoln Memorial, where they heard speeches by Abernathy, the United Auto Workers president Walter Reuther, and Coretta King. Reporters drew comparisons to the 1963 March on Washington for Jobs and Freedom, contrasting the mood of frustration and anger with the earlier march's "exhilarating sense of hope and promise."

The momentum provided by the strong showing on Solidarity Day arrived too late to save the Poor People's Campaign. Resurrection City had descended into chaos, and SCLC failed to provide the camp with the necessary leadership. Paid provocateurs and gang members intimidated visiting journalists and protesters. Residents complained about poor food and muddy conditions created by many consecutive days of rain, and they noted that several of the SCLC's top leaders slept at the Pitts Motor Hotel. Untrained young men serving as marshals provided inconsistent security, and incidents of violence, though exaggerated by the dozens of clandestine operatives inside the City, grew more frequent. The Mexican-American leader Reies Lopez Tijerina criticized Abernathy and the SCLC for ignoring the nonblack coalition members and declined to move his delegation to Resurrection City, choosing instead to stay at a nearby private high school. The daily demonstrations at government offices grew progressively combative, but they were unfocused. In the days following Solidarity Day, police shot tear gas into the campsite in response to several incidents of rock throwing. With their permit from the National Park Service due to expire, SCLC and Justice Department officials devised plans for a face-saving retreat. On June 24, about 200 protesters, including Ralph Abernathy, were arrested at Capitol

Hill, while 120 more who remained in Resurrection City were arrested without major incident. Sporadic protests continued late into the summer, but the media turned its attention to the upcoming Republican and Democratic national conventions.

Though the SCLC left Washington without gaining any substantial concession from the government, the Poor People's Campaign marked a departure from earlier civil rights protests in that it placed economic justice at the center of its demands. In this sense, the campaign had much in common with the contemporaneous protests of African-American cafeteria workers at North Carolina universities, who went on strike for an end to racist employment practices, and black workers in Detroit, who launched a series of wildcat strikes that would hobble the auto industry during the late 1960s. The Poor People's Campaign also laid the groundwork for subsequent SCLC solidarity work on behalf of factory workers and municipal employees in Atlanta and hospital workers in Charleston, South Carolina. For nonblack participants, the Poor People's Campaign signaled the growing maturation of the Chicano, Puerto Rican, and Native American movements, all of which gained visibility in the 1970s. Their struggles, like those of the black workers, were built upon earlier civil rights victories, while aiming to complete the unfinished business of the 1960s social protests—a radical reordering of the U.S. economy.

KIERAN W. TAYLOR

References and Further Reading

Berry, Faith. "The Anger and Problems and Sickness of the Poor of the Whole Nation Were in This One Shantytown." *New York Times*, 7 July 1968.

Branch, Taylor. *At Canaan's Edge: America in the King Years, 1965–68*. New York: Henry Holt, 2006.

Franklin, Ben A. "Abernathy Declares 'Poor Power' Will Change Policies and Priorities of U.S." *New York Times*, 2 May 1968.

Garrow, David J. *Bearing the Cross*. New York: William Morrow, 1986.

Loftus, Joseph A. "Dr. King Suggests 'Camp-In' in Cities." *New York Times*, 24 October 1967.

McKnight, Gerald D. *The Last Crusade*. Boulder, CO: Westview Press, 1998.

Semple, Robert B. Jr. "Mood of the Marchers: Patience Worn Thin and a Feeling This Is the Last Chance." *New York Times*, 20 June 1968.

See also **Rustin, Bayard**

POPULAR FRONT

Throughout its existence in the roughly 1934 to 1939 period, the Popular Front (also translated as "People's Front") promoted coalitions and fostered organization building by the political left. Although not without problems, the resulting coalitions in the United States led to notable political achievements. Calls for a united front against fascism were raised in the early 1930s, but only with the Communist Party's official abandonment of organizing toward revolution and accompanying outreach to non-Communists was a movement against the growth of international fascism initiated. The Popular Front, which began as a diplomatic strategy by the Communist International (Comintern) to secure the Soviet Union against Nazi Germany and fascist Italy, grew outside the Communist Party's immediate control, although heavily influenced by the Party's cadres. Ultimately Communist in origin, the resulting Popular Front reached across party, class, and professional lines from working class to upper class, from labor to law. The achievements and shortcomings of this strategy and its effects remain disputed among historians.

The 1932 World Congress Against War in Amsterdam, where less than half the delegates were Communist Party members (830 of 2,196), was an early attempt to forge coalitions against the growth of fascism, but the Comintern only backed this effort in March 1933. The League's significance lies in its early appeal for united action against fascism. It took many more months to formalize the unity, but when it was codified, it assumed a Communist cast as the League Against War and Fascism became a vehicle for the Communist Party.

Student Communists and Socialists were also at the forefront of co-operation, uniting in organizing antiwar strikes. The Communist Party, though, continued to insist that only it held the model for realizing world socialism and fiercely attacked other opponents on the left even while working with them in the League Against War and Fascism. This marriage between leftist factions was always precarious, with frequent sniping and an eventual ban on party affiliation in League work.

Not until Hitler's seizure of power and suppression of the German left did the Comintern officially endorse a united effort against fascism. Previously, it had feared such a strategy would inhibit the revolutionary potential of a Communist movement stemming from the political right's accruing of power. The rise of the Nazis and their threat to left-wing parties shook the foundations of Communist initiatives. Adolf Hitler crushed the political left in Germany, where the strongest Communist movement outside of Russia had been seated, and the Comintern reconsidered its approach. French, German, and Polish Communist leaders issued a joint communiqué offering alliances to social democrats in mid-February 1933, two weeks after Hitler became chancellor.

Throughout 1933, the Comintern also observed capitalist opposition to President Franklin Roosevelt's New Deal programs.

Then at Nantes, France, on October 24, 1934, the Communists endorsed a Popular Front when the French Communist Maurice Thorez spoke before the French Communist Party. The Comintern approved of Thorez's plan in January 1935, and later in the summer at the Seventh Congress of the Comintern, the Bulgarian Georgi Dimitroff suggested the need for a people's front in order to combat the rising threat of fascism, which was promising to undo the Russian revolution. Dimitroff's policy was adopted officially by the Comintern for all Communist parties shortly after.

The new policy urged co-operation among left-wing parties in the defense of liberal democracy even while the Communist goal of monopoly over the left remained the same as before.

The coalitions resulting from the Communists' abandonment of revolutionary rhetoric and their co-operation with other left and liberal forces were loosely knit. Many activities in this period involving Communists remained informal alliances like the New Deal's center-left coalition of grassroots supporters in which the Communist Party spent more time building other pro-New Deal groups than building itself. The new strategy fostered Communist popularity as membership increased throughout the period, while other left-wing parties lagged behind. The apparent moderation and embrace of Americanism also made the Communist Party more palpable, or at least less subversive in appearance, to the mainstream. But despite these gains, turnover of party membership ran at 50% throughout the era.

The Popular Front never achieved the sort of critical mass the strategy hoped for, and it has even been suggested by some historians that the change to a more moderate united front strategy limited the possibility of making the types of political gains the Communists had achieved during the strike wave of 1934. Still, the Party secretary Earl Browder credited the Party's membership achievements to its work in American labor, which benefited greatly from Communist help after 1935, which placed communists at the forefront of the labor movement even when they faced discrimination. The three largest unions in the American Federation of Labor (AFL) all backed the formation of the Congress of Industrial Organizations (CIO) in 1935, and the CIO's John L. Lewis, an anti-Communist, tapped into Communist experience by inviting Party activists to organize for the new labor organization. Having backed off from creating their own union organization, the Trade Union Unity League, and opposing dual unionism, the Popular

Front Communists became valuable organizers for the CIO. A symbiotic relationship developed between Party members and unions. The strength of the steel and autoworkers unions, in particular, owed much to the Communists' Popular Front strategy. Hopes for a Farmer-Labor Party were not realized, but with the American Labor Party (ALP), the Communists attempted to build a powerful national force. While that also failed, the ALP, with Communist aid, played a pivotal role in the elections of Fiorello LaGuardia and Vito Marcantonio.

Another achievement of the Popular Front was the advancement of desegregation among the African-American community. The Communist Party stood at the forefront of black empowerment among organizations not officially affiliated with civil rights. In New York City, where the Communist Party was strongest, Communists permitted interracial couples in its co-operatives, integrated toilet facilities at Party functions, and racially mixed audiences at the Greenwich Village club, Café Society. The interracial environment benefited jazz culture with its many black performers and forged valuable ties within and outside the black community. The Communist Party was also the only major opponent to mobilize against the Italian invasion of Ethiopia. Many black non-Communist leaders, benefiting from the assistance of Party cadre, began to speak positively of Communist work.

Gender relations were far more contentious. By 1936, 25% of the Communist Party members were women, who reached around one third of the membership in 1940. Recent research by Kate Weigand suggests that women were also benefiting from the Communist work through "opportunities, education, and self-confidence they probably could not have found elsewhere" and also from the periodic defense of women's rights by the Communist Party secretary Earl Browder. Auxiliary organizations under women's leadership formed to bolster other Popular Front organizations, but as auxiliaries they also reflected the limits of women's participation. Through these experiences, women began to develop a more radical gender consciousness and criticize the Party's gender divisions, which eventually resulted in Party attempts to pressure male cadres to behave more generously toward their female equals. Still, the failure to commit to women's uplift also marked Popular Front practice.

The long-lasting legacy of the Popular Front period, however, was antifascism, which earned the Communist Party support from the left around the world long after the Second World War concluded. The fascism the Popular Front intended to confront is still not easily defined, but the Communist Party put forth a Marxist reading that construed fascism as the dangerous and militant last gasp of capitalism. While the enemy itself remained vague, the initiative attracted many non-Communists into the coalition. In the United States, antifascist organization building was manifested as a series of campaigns and layers of coalitions. Antifascism offered the American left a unifying theme it had long desired. Divisions remained, but the Popular Front fomented a semblance of cohesion where there had been many fissures before.

No other event characterized this more than the Spanish Civil War (1936–1939), the era's most celebrated cause. The right-wing rebellion by Francisco Franco and half of the Spanish army against a Popular Front government provoked an international outcry among the political left. Communists, Socialists, anarchists, and many nonaligned individuals in the United States and elsewhere formed aid organizations in defiance of their governments and in cooperation with Spanish Republican leaders. A number of small strikes against freighters carrying alleged war material to Spain in late summer of 1938 were among the most obvious actions by American workers, but hundreds of unions across the country donated money, goods, and supplies to the ailing Spanish Republicans. The furriers union, for example, donated fur coats, and the International Ladies' Garment Workers' Union (ILGWU) donated clothing. Many more liberal Americans also rallied to the cause with donations and support. The Communist Party was central to the campaign, but it would have gone nowhere without broad support.

This Spanish aid movement was also instrumental in provoking a shift from the Popular Front to the Democratic Front. The difference was largely semantic, and few of the Popular Front's proponents even in the Communist Party understood the change, but the Comintern nonetheless issued statements altering the policy in early 1937. The main difference lay in monied opponents of fascism now being included in the People's Front coalition. Spanish Loyalist organizations had already brought out some of America's wealthiest scions to the side of Spanish aid. The change in Comintern policy caught up with then current practice.

Interest in Spain had waned by early 1939 as defeat loomed. The Spanish war ended in March, preceding the official end of the Popular Front by six months, a shift ushered in by the Hitler-Stalin Pact in September 1939. At that point, the Soviet Union, isolated by the western nations, submitted to a nonaggression pact with Germany as a measure of security in the coming world war. While this ended the Comintern's People's Front and led to massive resignations from the Communist Party, the Popular Front itself ceased to disappear. Aid organizations that emerged out of the Spanish, Chinese, and Czech crises refocused on the growing refugee crisis rising from the onset of World War II, and unions built by the Party gathered strength. With the entry of the United States into the conflict as an ally of the USSR following Pearl Harbor, the Popular Front was renewed, albeit with bitterness against Communists for the 1939–1941 interval. Now, though, a virtual consensus on antifascism was reached. Communist Party membership never reached Popular Front levels, however, even as the new united front against fascism after Pearl Harbor became institutionalized in the culture.

The Communists themselves were never satisfied with the results of the Popular Front efforts and should not be the final judges of that movement's achievements or failures.

ERIC R. SMITH

References and Further Reading

Brown, Michael, Randy Martin, Frank Rosengarten, and George Snedeker, eds. *New Studies in the Politics and Culture of U.S. Communism*. New York: Monthly Review Press, 1993.

Cohen, Robert. *When the Old Left Was Young: Student Radicals and America's First Mass Student Movement, 1929–1941*. Oxford: Oxford University Press, 1993.

Denning, Michael. *The Cultural Front: The Laboring of American Culture in the Twentieth Century*. New York: Verso, 1996.

Klehr, Harvey. *The Heyday of American Communism: The Depression Decade*. New York: Basic Books, 1984.

Levenstein, Harvey A. *Communism, Anticommunism, and the CIO*. Westport, CT: Greenwood Press, 1981.

Naison, Mark. *Communists in Harlem during the Depression*. Urbana: University of Illinois Press, 2005.

Ottanelli, Fraser. *The Communist Party of the United States: From the Depression to World War II*. New Brunswick, NJ: Rutgers University Press, 1991.

Ryan, James G. *Earl Browder: TheFailure of American Communism*. Tuscaloosa: University of Alabama Press, 1997.

Weigand, Kate. *Red Feminism: American Communism and the Making of Women's Liberation*. Baltimore: Johns Hopkins Press, 2001.

See also **American Labor Party; Communist Party; Congress of Industrial Organizations; International Ladies' Garment Workers' Union (ILGWU) (1900–1995); Sit-Down Strikes (1937); United Electrical, Radio, and Machine Workers of America**

POPULISM/PEOPLE'S PARTY

"Populism," in its historical American meaning, refers to the People's or Populist Party, which emerged out of a movement of farmers and workers in the 1890s. The Populist label has also been applied to many popular movements or tendencies, both progressive and reactionary, in the United States, Europe, and Latin America. This essay focuses on the historical third-party movement and its antecedents.

To characterize Populism as a "movement" is to say it was not a spontaneous outburst in response to economic or social ills but rather an organized effort by people who considered themselves to be oppressed. The People's Party arose out of several organizations of farmers and workers in the 1880s and 1890s. These sometimes disparate groups shared the "common sense" of working people at the time that producers—anyone whose labor creates value—deserve to enjoy the fruits of their labor. Farmers, sometimes in collaboration with the Knights of Labor (KOL), established economic co-operatives, but they were also drawn to electoral politics, where they sought redress through legislation.

Birth of a Movement

Hard times made folks consider extraordinary measures. Although the health of the American economy was relatively good in the 15 years following the Civil War, farm commodity prices declined at a much steeper rate than the overall deflation rate. Between the 1870s and mid-1890s, the price farmers received for their wheat, corn, or cotton dropped by over half. Wages for workers outside of agriculture declined, but not so precipitously. Then the bottom fell out in 1893 with what contemporaries called the "Great Depression."

At the same time, farmers and workers saw that a wealthy few controlled strategic resources such as credit, transportation, and wholesale trade, while federal monetary policies further depressed prices. If "producerism" gave them a way of expressing why hard work should be rewarded, the spread of monopoly and contraction of the money supply helped explain why that was not happening.

Hard times and the ideological "lense" of producerism made people angry, but the mobilization of millions into a national movement required more than strong feelings. In the 1870s and especially the 1880s, farmers and workers formed community-based organizations, adapting the organizing techniques of voluntary associations including churches, fraternal organizations, and early farmer and labor organizations. Women as well as men participated. In Kansas and elsewhere, women who had honed their leadership skills in churches and groups like the Women's Christian Temperance Union emerged as spokespersons.

Farmers and workers met to discuss common problems, practice familiar rituals, and plan strategies. To offset the economic power of monopolists, they created marketing and purchasing cooperatives. Believing that their enemies controlled government, they pressed upon the major parties legislative demands to benefit the people.

Who and where were these people? They were, by and large, small property holders—farmers, mainly, but also artisans, railroad workers, miners, rural doctors, and preachers, and even some small-business owners. Their organizations were strongest in the South, the Great Plains (from Texas to the Dakotas), and the Mountain West. Ethnically, they were mainly of European descent, although in the South, black farmers joined racially separate organizations. Heroic efforts to unite southern producers across the racial divide had only limited success. Most black "farmers" were actually tenants, sharecroppers, or laborers, and those in the last two categories were employees of farm owners. In several states, the Knights of Labor made serious efforts to organize this marginalized group.

In the 1880s, farm organizations spread across the South and West, mobilizing an army of potential recruits for political insurgency. Several went by the name of "Farmers' Alliance." One began in upstate New York in 1877 but was transplanted to Chicago in 1880 by the farm editor Milton George, who used his newspaper to recruit members in the Midwest. The most successful group, commonly known as the "Southern" Alliance, began in central Texas, also in 1877. Its membership was restricted to whites. A parallel "Colored" Alliance began in Texas in the 1880s. A fourth group, the Agricultural Wheel, sprang up in the lower Mississippi Valley, led by the Canadian-born machinist Isaac McCracken. As a young man, McCracken had joined the Blacksmiths and Machinists' Union, where he met Terence Powderly, later the grand master workman of the Knights of Labor. Upon moving to Arkansas, he worked as a railroad machinist and farmed. McCracken was an effective organizer and a forceful advocate of independent political action.

After a shaky start, in the mid-1880s, the Texas-based Alliance launched an ambitious program of centralized co-operatives and an equally ambitious plan to expand across the South and into the Plains states. The architect of these schemes was Charles W. Macune, a small-town doctor and editor. An inveterate joiner and organizer, Macune was at the right spot at the right time. By the end of the 1880s, his organization, now officially the National Farmers Alliance and Industrial Union, had over 1.5 million members in more than 20 states.

Traveling organizers were instrumental in the rapid spread of the farmers' movement. While most were rural community leaders—often preachers or teachers—some had learned organizing skills in the union movement. Many of these were Knights of Labor, and membership overlapped between the Knights and the Alliance. Indeed, cooperation between farmers and workers in successful railroad strikes in Colorado (1884) and the Southwest (1885) swelled the ranks of both groups. The Alliance and Knights cooperated nationally to advance a common agenda, but relations between Alliance leaders and Powderly ranged from cool to hostile.

Toward the People's Party

From its inception, the Alliance was political, though officially nonpartisan. Some of its earliest leaders were veterans of third-party movements of the 1870s. Their political program reflected a producerist tradition that affirmed private ownership of property but was grounded in the belief that monopoly power had stifled the fair working of capitalism. The legislative program they devised was intended to ensure access to land, credit, transportation, and an expanding money supply, thereby ensuring equal opportunity and abolishing special privilege.

The fullest development of the Populists' agenda was the platform adopted at the People's Party's 1892 convention. While several streams converged in this document, its origin is traceable to the 1886 legislative demands of the Texas Alliance. That document was heavily indebted to the 1878 preamble to the Knights of Labor's constitution, which in turn drew from 1867 manifestos of the National Labor Union.

This political agenda could not be easily implemented in a system where the dominant parties opposed even modest economic reform. Reformers faced a difficult choice: should they press their claims as a political interest group and force one or both parties to adopt their plan, or should they form a new party? The answer depended, in part, on how the major parties responded.

In December 1889, these choices were debated at a joint meeting of the Alliances and the Knights of Labor. Westerners, many of them veterans of earlier third-party movements, argued for a new party. Most southerners preferred to apply pressure within their region's dominant Democratic Party. The St. Louis meeting adjourned with no consensus on strategy but with agreement on a platform that re-affirmed the unity of farmers and labor and demanded federal action to protect access to land, control monopolies (in part through public ownership of railroads), and currency reform. There was also support for schemes to provide federal loans to farmers based on the value of their land (popular in the West) or their crops (the southern Subtreasury Plan).

In 1890, recent history and major party reaction dictated different strategies in the West and the South. Many key western leaders had long since left the old parties, and leaders of the dominant Republican Party scoffed at the demands presented to them. In the South, white reformers had to contend with the recent history of Reconstruction and Democrats' skillful use of the race issue. Nevertheless, the dominant reaction among southern Democratic officeholders to the "Alliance Yardstick" was to pledge their support, whether they meant it or not.

In 1890, both approaches seemed to work. In Kansas and elsewhere in the West, the Alliance and the Knights joined forces to create independent parties, and Colorado followed suit in 1891. Kansas independents won most of the congressional elections and controlled the legislature, where they elected the farm leader William Peffer to the Senate. In Colorado, the labor editor Davis Waite later won the governorship. Four southern states elected governors with ties to the Farmers' Alliance, and three fourths of the region's congressmen (all Democrats) endorsed the Alliance agenda. Much the same happened in Iowa, where because of close competition between Republicans and Democrats, *both* major parties pledged their support.

But pressure for a new party continued to build. Soon after the 1890 elections, southern Democrats reneged on their promises. Despite an Alliance directive not to join the caucus of any party that did not support its demands, all but one of the congressmen elected with Alliance support joined the Democrats in organizing the House. The exception was Georgia's Tom Watson.

When delegates convened again in St. Louis in February 1892, the stage was set for creation of a party with strong southern representation. The North Carolina Alliance leader Leonidas Polk chaired the meeting. A version of the now-familiar platform was adopted, including a stirring preamble written by Ignatius Donnelly of Minnesota. The People's Party was launched. Polk was the likely presidential candidate, but he died before the Party's convention in July. Instead, in Omaha the Populists nominated James B. Weaver, a veteran of the Union Army and of third-party campaigns (he was the Greenback Party's presidential nominee in 1880).

Weaver won 22 electoral votes, the first by any third-party candidate since the Civil War. But the prospects for future success were not encouraging.

His only victories came in the western heartland of third-party movements. In only one southern state (Alabama, with strong union support) did Weaver win even a third of the votes. The Party barely scratched in the Northeast and did little better in the industrial belt stretching from Illinois to Pennsylvania.

Clearly, the People's Party would be hard pressed to win national elections and implement its program. The American system of elections created huge obstacles for new parties. Populists were divided among themselves on issues such as prohibition and women's suffrage, and leaders of the old parties brought the weight of culture to bear on citizens who considered defecting. Also, in those western states where Populists had already won elections, they now had records to defend, some of them not attractive.

The depression that struck the nation in 1893 made President Grover Cleveland hugely unpopular, but the Populists could not capitalize on their position as champions of the downtrodden. Not even the Pullman Strike in 1894 galvanized the Party's potential base. Even in Illinois, where the American Railway Union leader Eugene V. Debs campaigned for the Party, Populists were badly beaten. So the Populists faced yet another decision: stick with their platform and stay in the field as an independent party, or cooperate with a major party.

In 1892 and 1894, Populists in some states had formed alliances with the weaker of the two major parties—Democrats in the West and Republicans in the South. North Carolina Populists successfully fused with Republicans in 1894, sending Marion Butler to the Senate. Co-operation or "fusion" with a major party was not unusual for third parties in nineteenth-century America, but for a movement that viewed itself as being above petty partisanship, such tactical shifts could confuse and demoralize grassroots Populists and leave fusionists open to charges of selling out.

Then there was the silver issue. The Populist agenda included aggressive proposals for an expanded and more flexible money supply. Elements in both major parties began pressing for coinage of silver as a means to the same end. It was a weak substitute but a strong political tactic, particularly after President Cleveland forced repeal of the Sherman Silver Purchase Act through Congress. By 1894, western Populists were increasingly drawn to the silver issue and to collaboration with Democratic silverites, including William Jennings Bryan of Nebraska. The silver craze also swept southern Democratic parties, but many southern Populists, having left the Democratic Party at great cost, were loath to rejoin the fold.

The issue came to a climax in 1896 when Bryan, having received the Democrats' presidential nomination, was put forward for the Populist nomination as well. Neither Debs nor Peffer, though opposing his nomination, would agree to challenge him. In a highly charged convention, the People's Party nominated Bryan while rejecting his Democratic running mate in favor of Tom Watson. Although the convention endorsed the full Omaha Platform, by nominating Bryan, Populists conceded that silver was the issue of the campaign. National fusion with the Democrats meant local confusion. In the South, some Populists were simultaneously co-operating with Republicans, while most of their western counterparts were making common cause with Democrats.

Bryan carried the South and most of the West in a losing battle, but as a Democrat. Only in a few western states did the Populist contribution make a difference. Fusion agreements brought some local victories to the Populists in 1896 and 1898, but the Party's career as an independent force was over.

Bryan would dominate Democratic politics for two more decades, and when Democrats regained control of both Congress and the White House in 1912, he played a major role in passage of several bills that were heavily indebted to the Populist agenda, with former Populists in Congress in support.

ROBERT C. MCMATH, JR.

References and Further Reading

Argersinger, Peter H. *The Limits of Agrarian Radicalism: Western Populism and American Politics.* Lawrence: University Press of Kansas, 1995.

Clanton, Gene: *Congressional Populism and the Crisis of the 1890s.* Lawrence: University Press of Kansas, 1998.

Destler, Chester McArthur. *Henry Demarest Lloyd and the Empire of Reform.* Philadelphia: University of Pennsylvania Press, 1963.

Goldberg, Michael Lewis. *An Army of Women: Gender and Politics in Gilded Age Kansas.* Baltimore: Johns Hopkins University Press, 1997.

Goodwyn, Lawrence. *Democratic Promise: The Populist Moment in America.* New York: Oxford University Press, 1976.

Hunt, James L. *Marion Butler and American Populism.* Chapel Hill: University of North Carolina Press, 2003.

Kazin, Michael. *A Godly Hero: The Life of William Jennings Bryan.* New York: Knopf Publishing Group, 2006.

Larson, Robert W. *Populism in the Mountain West.* Albuquerque: University of New Mexico Press, 1986.

McMath, Robert C. Jr. *American Populism: A Social History, 1877–1898.* New York: Hill and Wang, 1993.

Ostler, Jeffrey. *Prairie Populism: The Fate of Agrarian Radicalism in Kansas, Nebraska, and Iowa, 1880–1892.* Lawrence: University Press of Kansas, 1993.

Pollack, Norman. *The Just Polity: Populism, Law, and Human Welfare.* Urbana: University of Illinois Press, 1987.

Sanders, Elizabeth. *Roots of Reform: Farmers, Workers, and the American State, 1877–1917.* Chicago: University of Chicago Press, 1999.

Shaw, Barton C. *The Wool-Hat Boys: Georgia's Populist Party.* Baton Rouge: Louisiana State University Press, 1984.

PORTAL-TO-PORTAL PAY

Portal-to-portal pay is compensation from the time a worker enters the workplace until he or she leaves. It covers such "nonproductive" activities as travel, eating, resting, preparatory work, waiting, and sleeping. The issue originally arose in coal mining in the 1930s. Traditionally, miners were paid only "face-to-face pay" for the time they spent at the mine's face. However, in 1941, a federal district court held that travel from the mine's portal to its face constituted work. Thereafter, portal-to-portal pay became a key union demand in bargaining negotiations and a subject of litigation for nonunion workers. Key controversies arose from weaknesses in the 1938 Fair Labor Standards Act (FLSA). Although it set a minimum wage and required time-and-a-half compensation for overtime work, the FLSA did not define what constituted "work time" and gave the Wage and Hour Administration of the U.S. Department of Labor no power to resolve controversies. Thus, the FLSA opened the way for a series of court battles over what comprised compensable work. These cases and the Portal-to-Portal Pay Act of 1947 revealed conflicts between Congress, federal courts, employers, and unions regarding labor law, custom, and collective bargaining contracts.

In two key cases, *Jewell Ridge Coal Corp. v. Local 6167, UMWA* (1945) and *Anderson v. Mt. Clemens Pottery Co.* (1946), the Supreme Court extended the reach of portal-to-portal pay. *Jewell Ridge* arose from the bitter 1943 United Mine Workers of America (UMWA) bituminous coal strike. Desperate for a resolution that would raise miners' pay without undercutting the Little Steel Formula for collective bargaining agreements, the War Labor Board and the UMWA head, John L. Lewis, agreed that miners would be paid for travel time. Companies objected that the agreement voided both customary labor relations and collective bargaining agreements. In the resulting *Jewell Ridge* case, the Court held that its definition of work time superseded custom and contract.

In *Anderson v. Mt. Clemens*, the Court's three-part opinion created the conditions for a national controversy. The Court held that under the FLSA, travel and preparatory time were compensable unless the amount was very small; the Court's own standards for work time overwhelmed custom and contract; and employers bore the burden of proof for compliance with the Court's decision. Workers seized on this decision and on the fact that employers found in violation of the FLSA were liable for back wages plus damages of 100%. A spate of lawsuits for unpaid portal-to-portal wages met objections from employers, which complained that the courts had illegitimately redefined "working time" and that portal-to-portal claims would amount to over $5 billion in liability. In response, Congress passed the 1947 Portal-to-Portal Pay Act, which restricted judges' jurisdiction in disagreements over the definition of "working time," preventing them from contravening a labor contract or customary labor relations.

The Portal-to-Portal Pay Act highlighted a congressional movement to protect against employer liability and to emphasize collective bargaining. Thus, the law was a companion to the 1947 Taft-Hartley Act, which made illegal organized labor's most effective direct-action tactics. The Portal-to-Portal Act also contributed to the growing distance between the fortunes of union and nonunion workers. Subsequently, workers traditionally unpaid for "nonproductive" duties could win portal-to-portal pay only through collective bargaining contracts.

JEFFREY HELGESON

References and Further Reading

Dubofsky, Melvyn, and Warren Van Tine. *John L. Lewis: A Biography*. New York: Quadrangle/The New York Times Book Co., Inc., 1977. (See especially pp. 421–437 and pp. 456–461.)

Murray, Paul R. "The Portal-to-Portal Pay Problem: Origin and Solution." Master's thesis, Stanford University, 1947.

Schultz, Bud, and Ruth Schultz. *It Did Happen Here: Recollections of Political Repression in America*. Berkeley: University of California Press, 1990, pp. 382–383.

Ullom, Harry H. "Portal-to-Portal Pay." Master's thesis, University of Texas, 1949.

Watkins, T. H. *Righteous Pilgrim: The Life and Times of Harold L. Ickes, 1874–1952*. New York: Henry Holt & Co., 1990, pp. 753–759.

Cases and Statutes Cited

Anderson v. Mt. Clemens Pottery Co., 328 U.S. 680 (1946). Rehearing denied October 14, 1946.

Jewell Ridge Coal Corp. v. Local 6167, United Mine Workers, 325 U.S. 161 (1945). Rehearing denied June 18, 1945.

Tennessee Coal, Iron, and Railroad Co. v. Muscoda Local No. 123, 5 Cir., 135 F.2d 320 (1943). Rehearing denied 5 Cir., 137 F.2d 176.

Tennessee Coal, Iron, and Railroad Co. v. Muscoda Local No. 123, 40 F. Supp. 4, USDC, ND Ala. (August 13, 1941)

Tennessee Coal, Iron, and Railroad Co. v. Muscoda Local No. 123, 321 U.S. 590 (1944). Rehearing denied May 29, 1944.

Fair Labor Standards Act, 52 Stat. 1060, 29 U.S.C. 201, et seq., 29 U.S.C.A. 201 et seq.

Labor-Management Relations Act of 1947; 29 USC Sec. 141–197 [Title 29, Chapter 7, United States Code]

Portal-to-Portal Pay Act of 1947; Public Law 49, 80th Congress, 1st Session

See also **Fair Labor Standards Act; Lewis, John L.; National War Labor Board (WWII); Taft-Hartley Act; United Mine Workers of America**

POSTAL STRIKE (1970)

The national postal wildcat strike of March 1970 is one of the most impressive strikes in all of American history. Despite a multitude of obstacles, more than 200,000 postal workers not only successfully struck, but they also forced a significant change in their status, their rights, their working conditions and earning power, and their own collective organization. Their actions compelled every branch of the federal government (legislative, executive, and judicial) to recognize the legitimacy of union power. This strike was one of the key events that signaled the arrival of public employees into the ranks of organized labor.

What makes this strike and its success so surprising? It occurred in the midst of a war, with hundreds of thousands of American soldiers away from home and dependent on the delivery of packages and messages from their families. Likewise, their loved ones relied on the mail to receive messages from their sons and daughters in the military. Older Americans depended on the postal service for their social security and pension checks. A strike would have an immediate disruptive impact on the lives of millions. Any strike by postal workers, or other federal employees, would have been illegal. Postal workers were (dis)organized into nine different unions, seven of which were granted some degree of recognition (but not formal collective bargaining rights) and two of which were not. Most of the unions were not affiliated with the AFL-CIO, and some of them had openly hostile relationships with each other. Postal workers and their organizations were also legally prohibited from participating in organized political activity. Postal workers' pay was so low that some of them qualified for food stamps and welfare assistance, hardly the basis for the building up of savings that might tide a worker and his family over during a strike. Last, postal workers were the most diverse workforce in the country, their ranks including urban African-Americans and small-town white southerners, veterans and college degree holders. That they would act in a unified, collective, militant fashion seemed—and seems today—amazing.

Yet many of the same factors pushed them in the direction of taking action. The Vietnam War itself, opposition to the war, and debate over the war functioned to politicize everyday life in America, not just on college campuses but also in post offices and working-class neighborhoods. As energy prices and interest rates spiked upward, workers asked whether the war was bringing them economic security or increased risk. African-Americans, Chicanos, and women, their expectations and aspirations raised by the civil rights movements and seemingly historic pieces of legislation, chafed when they bumped into glass ceilings and limited opportunities. Postal workers knew that the vast American populace depended on their labor, and they felt empowered by that. While the multiplicity of unions made monolithic organization unlikely, the tight fit of particular unions to their members (such as specific crafts, on the one hand, or the all-black National Alliance of Postal Employees, on the other) gave rank-and-file workers a sense of ownership of their organizations, an access to direct voice. The low pay prompted postal workers to take risks, even to the point of possibly losing their jobs, while the diversity of the workforce brought the influence of progressive ideologies and social movements into the inner life of the unions. By the spring of 1970, only the lid of legal restriction seemed to hold down the bubbling cauldron of discontent and militancy.

On March 12, 1970, frustrated by continuing inaction by Congress on a series of proposals, New York City letter carriers at a regular monthly union meeting demanded that their leaders conduct a strike vote. Despite the opposition of both the national and local presidents of the National Association of Letter Carriers, five days later, on St. Patrick's Day, the New York local voted to strike and put up pickets. Although the local president had not even communicated with his counterpart at the Manhattan-Bronx Postal Union (which represented inside workers), the latter organization's leadership chose to encourage their members not to cross the letter carriers' picket lines. At 5 a.m. on Wednesday, March 18, the strike was on, and within a day, it was 100% effective in New York City. Over the next few days, the strike spread, first to the Northeast, then to the Midwest, and then to the West Coast, having its greatest strength in large cities. Court orders and injunctions were ignored, as some 200,000 joined the strike. Fearing that police action would only exacerbate the situation, the government and postal officials refrained from arresting union leaders. Their efforts to use National Guardsmen to sort and deliver the mail were disastrous. Finally, after a week, a combination of threatened fines and promises of wage increases and health benefits brought the strike to an end.

This strike brought profound changes to postal workers and the post office. Over the next month, union representatives and the postmaster general reached an agreement that included a 6% wage increase retroactive to December 1969, a commitment to encourage Congress to pass legislation enabling collective bargaining, with the promise of another 8% wage increase at that point, a compression of the wage schedule so that workers could reach top levels much more quickly, and a promise of amnesty for all strikers and union leaders. Congress then followed through with the sweeping Postal Reorganization Act, creating a quasi-corporate United States Postal Service (USPS) and providing postal employees with full organizational and collective bargaining rights under the National Labor Relations Act, except for the right to strike (replaced by binding arbitration). At the same time, some of the unions moved toward merger. In July 1971, five of the unions joined together to create the American Postal Workers' Union, the National Association of Letter Carriers and the Rural Letter Carriers Association merged, while the National Association of Post Office Mail Handlers, which had been within the Laborers' International Union, chose to remain so. For the next three decades, these three unions would approach the USPS from a position of consolidated strength, at times bargaining jointly, even if they remained organizationally separate.

Union cohesion and militancy in the Post Office were promoted by the generation that had lived through the 1970 strike. Many of them became the first officers of their local unions, bargaining local agreements and recruiting new members. As they moved into retirement, locals and the national union honored them and their recollections and stories would be told and retold at banquets and in local union publications. The national postal wildcat strike became the foundational narrative of postal workers' unionism, no matter which union they belonged to, no matter what town or city they worked in.

PETER RACHLEFF

References and Further Reading

Aronowitz, Stanley, and Jeremy Brecher. "The Postal Strike." In *Root and Branch: The Rise of the Workers' Movements*, edited by Root and Branch. Greenwich, CT: Fawcett, 1975.

Rachleff, Peter. *Moving the Mail: From a Manual Case to Outer Space*. Morgantown, WV: The Work Environment Project, 1982.

Walsh, John, and Garth Mangum. *Labor Struggle in the Post Office: From Selective Lobbying to Collective Bargaining*. Armonk, NY: M. E. Sharpe, 1992.

See also **American Postal Workers' Union**

POWDERLY, TERENCE (1849–1924)
Knights of Labor

Terence Powderly led the Knights of Labor (KOL), the largest working-class organization of the nineteenth century, for 14 years, from 1879 to 1893. His reign was defined by controversy, and many scholars have blamed him for the order's demise. Portrayed by some as moralistic, disloyal, dictatorial, and even pusillanimous, Powderly's detractors, then and now, argued that his commitment to acquiring a more equitable distribution of wealth did not match his dislike of strikes, distrust of political action, and opposition to radicalism. Essentially, this anti-Powderly narrative portrays him as increasingly out of step with the men and women he represented and thus unable or unwilling to fashion a powerful industrial union movement at the very moment corporate capitalism took off. Others have come to Powderly's defense, pointing out that he was well respected and labor's first media superstar, a man who built a diverse and strong organization. Powderly's character, and his perceived inability to lead, in actuality had little to do with the decline of the Knights of Labor. Rather, the organization declined as a result of divisions among workers on issues of race, ideology, and skill. The presence of powerful corporate foes who had the support of politicians, judges, police forces, state militias, and the army also hurt the Knights of Labor.

Born in Carbondale, Pennsylvania, on January 22, 1849, the deeply Catholic Powderly left school at 13, worked on the railroad, and in 1866 began an apprenticeship as a machinist in Scranton. Politics sparked his interests during the 1870s. Identifying with his Irish immigrant father, he joined the popular Irish Land League movement, which sent money across the Atlantic and lobbied U.S. leaders to defend the Irish people against British imperialism. Closer to home, Powderly often supported the Republicans but, in 1878, he did join the Greenback Labor movement. Beginning in 1879, he served six years as mayor of Scranton.

Powderly's career as mayor coincided with his election to the position of grand master workman of the KOL. He likely joined the Knights in the mid-1870s, but the exact date is difficult to pinpoint as the order was secret until 1882. Philadelphia tailors founded the KOL in 1869, and by 1876, it welcomed unskilled laborers throughout Pennsylvania. When Powderly won the order's top spot in 1878, he insisted upon abandoning secrecy and organizing as many workers as possible, and building a highly democratic organization. Power flowed from the bottom up, as local and district assembly leaders ran day-to-day affairs. The Knights welcomed immigrants, African-Americans, and women into their ranks, although Chinese workers were excluded. Throughout its existence, the KOL claimed over 12,000 local assemblies in roughly 3,000 communities. At its peak, between 1885 and 1886, the order grew from 110,000 workers to 729,000. By the end of the decade, however, there were 250,000 Knights. Defenders of Powderly point to the lack of centralization, the emerging differences between skilled and unskilled workers, and simultaneous strikes as some of the reasons he cannot be blamed for the order's ultimate failure. No one person, they suggest, could have managed a relatively new national labor movement in this era of industrial expansion and class struggle with a small treasury and limited power.

Such a position makes sense when one considers that in 1885 alone the Knights were involved in a protest against Chinese immigrants in Rock Springs, Wyoming, engaged in a coal strike in Indiana, and embroiled in a confrontation with Jay Gould's railroad managers throughout the Midwest and Southwest.

Ultimately, the event that continues to define Powderly's career as a labor leader was his handling of the Haymarket Affair in 1886. On May 4, a group of citizens from the greater Chicago area gathered to protest acts of police brutality perpetrated against striking workers at the McCormick reaper plant. During the protest at Haymarket Square, four police officers died when a bomb exploded. The police responded by shooting into the crowd. Eight men were found guilty of conspiracy to commit murder, and eventually the state of Illinois hanged four of them. The state had little or no evidence to arrest the eight men; all eight were condemned, rather, for their anarchist beliefs. Although most Knights favored cooperativism, socialism, or a type of social democracy, as opposed to anarchy, they understood this trial as an attack on their right to protest.

Powderly chose to distance himself from those on trial, fearing that the KOL's public image would be injured. His decision came just as Knights started to lose strikes and skilled workers were considering whether or not they should join Samuel Gompers's new union for craftsmen. Under Powderly, the order had adopted the motto, "An injury to one is the concern of all." To many of his followers, he betrayed this guiding principle. In 1893, radicals defeated Powderly as their candidate won the office that had made the machinist from Scranton a national celebrity.

After losing his position as grand master workman, Powderly worked as commissioner general of immigration and performed various tasks within the Department of Labor until his death in 1924.

JOHN ENYEART

References and Further Reading

Oestreicher, Richard. "Terence Powderly, the Knights of Labor, and Artisanal Republicanism." In *Labor Leaders in America*, edited by Melvyn Dubofsky and Warren Van Tine. Urbana: University of Illinois Press, 1987.

Phelan, Craig. *Grand Master Workman: Terence Powderly and the Knights of Labor*. Westport, CT: Greenwood Press, 2000.

Weir, Robert E. *Beyond Labor's Veil: The Culture of the Knights of Labor*. University Park: Pennsylvania State University Press, 1996.

———. *Knights Unhorsed: Internal Conflict in a Gilded Age Social Movement*. Detroit: Wayne State University Press, 2000.

See also **Haymarket Affair (1886); Knights of Labor**

PRESSER, JACKIE (1926–1988)
President, International Brotherhood of Teamsters

President of the International Brotherhood of Teamsters (IBT) from 1983 until the time of his death in 1988, Presser's career highlighted the way in which corruption, organized crime, and government investigation combined to shape this union. Presser rose through the ranks of the Teamsters thanks partly to his ties to organized crime figures, but also through his role as an informant for the Federal Bureau of Investigation (FBI). In 1988, the federal government used both his election as IBT president in 1983 and his informant reports to support an effort to impose a trusteeship over the IBT.

The grandson of Jewish immigrants, Presser was born in Cleveland in 1926. His father, William Presser, had become a union organizer during the 1930s and eventually led an organization of workers who serviced vending machines. Through that organization, Presser's father developed relationships with Jewish and Italian-American organized crime figures; he would later be described as an associate of the Cleveland Mafia. In the early 1950s, James R. Hoffa helped bring the elder Presser's union into the IBT and then supported the Ohio Teamster leader's rise through the Teamsters hierarchy. As a Hoffa loyalist who also enjoyed strong ties to Hoffa's successors, William Presser held a number of important offices in the Teamsters, including serving as an IBT vice president with a seat on the General Executive Board. He was, therefore, well positioned to do favors for his

organized crime connections and to promote his son Jackie's career in the Teamsters. With his father's help, Jackie first became an organizer with the Teamsters in 1952, and then in 1966, he gained a charter for a new local, Local 507, which would organize industrial and warehouse workers. His father arranged to transfer members from other locals into Local 507, and it grew into the largest Teamsters local in Cleveland. Finally, the father provided his son with one final boost. In 1976, William Presser resigned his post as vice president of the IBT, and Jackie was chosen to take his place.

Having gained a seat on the IBT's General Executive Board, Jackie Presser sought next to become the general president of the union. In seeking that goal, he engaged in a dangerous but ultimately successful strategy. Publicly, Jackie Presser represented himself as part of a new generation of Teamster leadership interested in improving the union's public relations, but privately he cultivated the same organized crime connections that his father had developed. Presser assured prominent Mafia figures that they could gain more money from his leadership of the union, thus making them allies in his political efforts to achieve the IBT's top position. At the same time, beginning in 1974, Presser became an informant for the FBI, providing the Bureau with information about organized crime's influence in the union. Presser's relationship with the FBI brought him a measure of protection from prosecution. It also allowed him to sabotage his rivals within the Teamsters leadership by providing damaging information about their activities. In this way, the federal government developed a criminal case involving Roy Williams, Presser's predecessor as president of the Teamsters Union. When Williams resigned after being indicted, representatives of the Cleveland Mafia met with other Mafia leaders in Chicago and New York urging them to support Presser's election. To what degree that support played a pivotal role remains open to question, but the union's General Executive Board did vote unanimously for Presser to succeed Williams. Still playing a double game, Presser reported on the Mafia's support for his election to his FBI handlers.

Presser assumed the presidency of the IBT during a difficult time in the union's history. Congress had passed legislation deregulating the trucking industry, and the new economic environment undercut the union dramatically. Membership numbers declined as the union-organized proportion of the trucking industry shrank. The recession of 1981–1983 exacerbated these declines, and under Presser's leadership, members were asked to accept a series of concessionary contracts that proved very unpopular. Angry dissidents within the union depicted Presser, who earned over $500,000 a year from his various union positions, as out of touch with the needs of the members. For his part, Presser spoke of the need to move the union into new areas of organizing, calling for more vigorous efforts to bring in public employees and workers in high-technology industries.

Presser's position became more tenuous in 1986, when the Justice Department indicted him on charges of embezzling union funds through providing no-show jobs. The case brought to light the FBI's tangled relationship with Presser, when it surfaced that Bureau officials had misled their counterparts in the U.S. Attorney's Office and the Department of Labor about Presser's status. One FBI agent would later serve time in prison for perjury as a result of his efforts to shield Presser from prosecution. But less than a week after his indictment, Presser won re-election by a roll call vote of delegates at the IBT Convention, overwhelming the candidate supported by the dissident group, Teamsters for a Democratic Union, by a vote of 1,729 to 24. Nor were his fellow Teamster officials the only ones to rally around the embattled Presser. In the face of news of an impending federal effort to impose a trusteeship over the troubled union, the leadership of the AFL-CIO welcomed the Teamsters back into a labor federation from which it had been ousted in the 1950s because of its corruption. The recently indicted Presser was given a seat on the AFL-CIO's executive council.

A year later, in 1988, the Justice Department filed a civil suit using the Racketeer Influenced and Corrupt Organizations (RICO) statute and asking a federal court to impose a trusteeship over the Teamsters. The department claimed that organized crime controlled the union's top leadership. The suit drew on evidence that included Presser's informant reports and trial testimony by Mafia figures involving Presser's 1983 election to the union presidency. Less than two weeks after that suit was filed, Presser died from cardiac arrest, having been ill for some time with brain cancer.

DAVID WITWER

References and Further Reading

Brill, Steven. *The Teamsters*. New York: Simon and Schuster, 1978.
Crowe, Kenneth C. *Collision: How the Rank and File Took Back the Teamsters Union*. New York: Charles Scribner's Sons, 1993.
La Botz, Dan. *Rank and File Rebellion: Teamsters for a Democratic Union*. New York: Verso, 1990.
Neff, James. *Mobbed Up: Jackie Presser's High-Wire Life in the Teamsters, the Mafia, and the FBI*. New York: Dell Publishing, 1989.

See also **International Brotherhood of Teamsters; Organized Crime; Racketeering and RICO**

PRINTING AND PUBLISHING INDUSTRY

Johannes Gutenberg introduced printing methods using movable type in Germany in 1440, while William Caxton imported the first printing presses into England in 1490. Together, these modern printing methods quickly spread throughout Europe's major cities. In Colonial America, the first independent weekly newspaper appeared in 1721, while the first daily emerged in 1783. By the end of the nineteenth century, newspapers were published in all major U.S. cities.

Technological developments could be characterized by stability and evolution during the industry's first 250 years. Printing presses moved from hand to steam power, and from single sheet to continuous roll, while the setting of type evolved from hand to mechanical typesetting, after Ottmar Mergenthaler invented a keyboard-based mechanical typesetter, the Linotype, around 1890. Additional developments in stereotyping (enabling multiple presses to produce a single copy of a newspaper) and photoengraving (reproducing photographs) enhanced both the productivity and physical appearance of printed matter, but together none of these processes radically departed from previous technologies—they still brought paper into contact with inked type. Aided by larger business, social, and demographic changes, they did, however, contribute to the rapid growth of the industry into the twentieth century.

For most of the nineteenth century, printing was concentrated in large cities, notably New York, Philadelphia, Chicago, and Boston. As late as 1900, they accounted for 40% of newspaper printing and 50% of all book and job work. Until 1880, book and job work (commercial printing) was only a small side business in newspaper shops. After 1880, commercial work became a distinct printing sector. Unlike newspaper offices that were larger, hierarchical, often monopolistic and, during the twentieth century, part of larger chain organizations, commercial shops were smaller, engaged in intense local competition, earned thin profit margins and produced nonstandardized batch work using skilled printers. Compared with the emerging mass production industries, printing industry firms were smaller in size.

Changes in industry structure by 1880 led to greater complexities in the production processes in newspapers and commercial shops. The labor process experienced a growing division of labor. These shifts went furthest in the larger newspaper offices. Moreover, aggregate changes in the industry and the larger economy created tensions between labor and management. Work relations became more impersonal, and journeymen printers experienced decreased mobility owing to greater capital requirements, increased firm size, and capitalist control of resources. The historical pattern of reciprocity between labor and management had eroded.

Printers: Work Culture, Unions, and Control over the Labor Process and Labor Market

The vast majority of printers were native-born white men with German parentage. They were highly skilled. Their job duties—setting type by hand—required a high degree of literacy. Both craft workers and proprietors shared a common cultural heritage, with many proprietors starting out as journeymen printers. Women worked in the printing industry, but they were more likely to be employed in book binderies doing semiskilled jobs, and in clerical positions. Only 5.7% of the industry's manufacturing workforce was composed of women in the mid-twentieth century.

The printers' work culture was rooted in the nature of work and spread across the country by itinerant or "tramp" printers. At its core were the principles of mutuality, respectability, and independence. The culture promoted solidarity and control over work. Journeymen printers began organizing during the last quarter of the eighteenth century in support of "price lists" (unilaterally determined prices of labor accepted or rejected by employers) and benevolence. By the late nineteenth century, as industry and economic transformations altered the context in which printers lived and worked, a new work culture formed that resembled Selig Perlman's "job consciousness."

Until the mid-nineteenth century, printers' unions were highly unstable and short-lived, moving in lock-step with economic conditions. But printers had organized "chapels" during the 1830s as key workplace institutions that regulated the trade, adjudicated disputes, and imbued apprentices with craft values. Chapel governance gave printers considerable authority over daily affairs at the point of production and provided them with a strong institutional foundation that would eventually support permanent unionism by the mid-nineteenth century. Chapels also retained a high degree of autonomy from unions for many years. The "father of the chapel," later the "chapel chairman," presided over chapel affairs, which also included the regulation of personal and professional conduct. Workplace disputes over union-promulgated rules were adjudicated by peers and chapel chairs. Printers considered these disputes to be internal governance issues, such that most workplace grievances were resolved inside the chapel and union free of employer involvement. Later, an "external" procedure, typical of modern grievance procedures, emerged as a complement to this "internal" one once collective bargaining emerged around 1900. Chapel chairs' roles expanded to include policing the labor contract.

Not until 1852 did local printing unions combine to create a national union, the National Typographical Union (NTU). In 1869, the International Typographical Union (ITU) replaced the NTU when it admitted Canadian locals to membership. The main purpose of national federation was to regulate travelers and uphold craft standards. Aside from a traveling card system, the ITU remained a decentralized union until the 1880s when, as a result of steady growth and activist locals, the ITU initiated a series of changes to wrest control from locals. Among the most significant institutional changes were the creation of a national strike fund; referenda voting procedures; a salaried professional staff, including organizers and district representatives; a benefit fund; and the negotiation of a series of arbitration agreements with the publishers' association between 1901 and 1922.

Inside the ITU, the compositors composed the majority of members and wielded great influence. This created tension and frustration among the other printing crafts inside the quasi-craft ITU. Between 1889 and 1903, five separate crafts split from the ITU to create their own national unions. Because they still shared common interests, these unions formed local allied printing trades councils to coordinate activities and cooperate in areas such as bargaining, union label enforcement, and concerted activities. Despite cooperative efforts, there existed sometimes bitter rivalries and other differences that made printing unions ill suited to deal with industry and technological changes after 1960.

Union democracy nonetheless was a key institutional characteristic of the ITU. Rooted in secret groups, factions, and cliques that formed in defense against employer blacklists, anti-unionism, and abusive foremen, the ITU's formal two-party political system debuted in 1912. The "Wahneta" party tended toward conservatism, while the "Progressives" were more militant. These different orientations were reflected in labor relations practices depending on which party was dominant. That is, when the Wahnetas ruled, the ITU negotiated national arbitration agreements and maintained peaceful labor relations. On the other hand, when Progressives were in power, they took a more militant stand in labor relations and voted to end the arbitration agreements in 1922. Still, legacies of local union autonomy often protected local labor relations traditions.

The ITU sought to regulate the workplace and the labor market through a variety of policies and practices. Abusive foremen were problematic, so the ITU passed two significant "laws" designed to rein in their excesses. In 1899, it required that all foremen be union members (an ITU law that, in many places, continued after the passage of the Taft-Hartley Act in 1947), and in 1890, it promulgated the Priority Law, which limited foremen discretion in hiring and discharge and granted printers the right to choose their substitutes in their absence. In essence, Priority established a high degree of both job control and due process for printers. Combined with the closed shop and an ITU overtime law designed to spread work to other ITU members, these laws went well beyond other unions' control over jobs. Moreover, they were part of internal union governance.

Printers' demands for shorter hours were part of a larger process to gain control over the external labor market. The quest for shorter hours that began during the latter part of the nineteenth century came easier for newspaper printers than it did for commercial printers. The main reason was the mechanization of typesetting. Linotypes and similar machines reduced the need for certain tasks, facilitated a shift from piece rates to wage payments for operators, and reduced hours. National arbitration agreements contributed to labor peace. While there was some technological displacement, printers' fears of widespread job loss never materialized owing to reduced production costs, increased productivity, especially at larger newspapers, and an overall increase in demand for labor. The ITU successfully won jurisdiction over these machines and encouraged members to acquire skills to operate them. While some additional divisions of labor occurred (for example, proofreader, advertising, and machinist classifications), the ITU preserved overall skill levels and jurisdiction, wages supplanted piece rates, and the workday was reduced without conflict.

In the commercial branch, the ITU's drive for shorter hours was generally met with resistance. During the second half of the nineteenth century, in response to labor organization, printing employers formed separate local and national organizations. Even though these organizations operated in the same labor markets, their product markets were different. New York and Chicago were at the forefront of employer organization. The American Newspaper Publishers Association formed in 1887 but did not address labor matters until the Linotype's introduction in the 1890s. In the commercial branch, the United Typothetae of America (UTA) formed in 1887 to fight unions and the ITU's demand for the nine-hour day. Battles over shorter hours were episodic in nature and lasted into the early 1920s. In 1898, the UTA and three major printing unions established the "Syracuse Agreement," which initially created the 57-hour workweek but gradually reduced hours to 54 by 1899.

But as soon as the ink dried, the ITU began pushing for an eight-hour workday or 48-hour workweek. This action pushed the UTA toward an aggressive open-shop stance and led to a strike in 1906 in which the ITU succeeded and the UTA lost 45% of its membership. After World War I, printers again sought reduced hours. A joint labor-management conference agreed to a 44-hour workweek beginning May 1, 1921, with pay rates unchanged. Strikes broke out when some shops refused to accept these terms. This time, commercial employers were more successful; many shops became nonunion. Another significant outcome of these strikes was that, until 1935, the workweek in newspaper offices was shorter (44 hours) than in commercial shops (48 hours). Moreover, wages were higher in newspaper offices than in commercial shops, and higher in printing than manufacturing in general. Printing industry wages generally held firmer than manufacturing wages during economic downturns. In general, industry wages were locally determined and, given the decentralized nature of the industry, highly variable.

Between the Civil War and World War I, employers attempted to redesign the labor process to lessen costs, increase speed, raise output, and reduce union power. Employers subdivided tasks, tried different payment schemes, and implemented new machinery, but union compositors used their strategic position in the labor process to preserve their skill and control over the labor process. They formed strong unions, often allied with other printing trades, passed and vigorously enforced union laws and regulations, and bargained collectively for shorter hours, better working conditions, and higher wages. But after World War II, union fortunes began to change for the worse in the face of new technologies, industry restructuring, unfavorable public policies, and a climate that was becoming increasingly hostile to unions.

The Postwar Consolidation of the Printing Industry

The number of daily newspapers held steady between 1950 and 1980, at roughly 1,750, but reached an all-time low by 2000. The decline was largely the result of consolidations and the shuttering of afternoon papers. Independently owned newspapers declined from 1,300 in 1953 to about 700 by 1980 and to fewer than 300 by 2000. Large, publicly traded media companies and chain ownership came to dominate the industry. By the late 1990s, chains controlled 77% of daily newspapers and over 80% of circulation. Over the course of the twentieth century, but with roots in the late nineteenth century, locally owned family ownership gave way to chain and publicly traded media corporations endowed with great amounts of resources.

In commercial printing, three significant industry changes occurred after 1960. First, there was a movement toward firm re-organization through chain ownership and mergers and acquisitions. This led to larger, multiplant operations and a move toward decentralization to avoid unions. Second, there was an outmigration of firms from traditional downtown printing centers. This trend spawned the growth in the number of nonunion firms operating outside city limits and the decline of master collectively bargained agreements. Third, and the most significant factor that impacted both the newspaper and commercial branches, companies rapidly introduced new computer-based technologies. These technologies, centered primarily in composing rooms, greatly increased productivity but also raised production costs. As part of this switch from "hot type" to "cold type," employers searched for ways to lower production costs. They saw unions as both contributing to high costs and as obstacles to lowering production costs.

New Technology and Union Decline

The origins of the industry's rapid technological transformation date to 1945, when newspaper employers experienced a surge in strikes for higher wages as wartime wage freezes were lifted. Higher wages and production interruptions caused costs to rise and led firms to find new methods to lower costs. One solution was a new composition technique called photocomposition, a revolutionary electronic technology that was four to six times faster than mechanical machines. Installed first at the Quincy (Massachusetts) *Patriot-Ledger* in 1953 to weaken the ITU, photocomposition machines automatically justified type and set it to film instead of lead. This cold type method employed less-skilled and lower-paid operators, many of whom were women. But because many employers feared the ITU, few photocomposition machines were installed until the early 1960s. This fear was justified in 1963 when an ITU-led strike over jurisdiction over these machines closed seven New York City dailies for 114 days.

Employers moved more aggressively toward cold type after a recession in the late 1950s and new competition for advertising revenues from television and magazines squeezed profits. Sandwiched between rising production costs and falling revenues, employers sought to reshape the labor process once more. With photocomposition, photoengraving and stereotyping became superfluous. Offset printing press technologies, however, maintained the skill levels of press operators. A technological revolution beginning in the early 1960s dramatically reduced production costs and the quantity and quality of labor demanded to manufacture newspapers. The center of this revolution was the composing room. Responses to the new technology ranged from controversy, conflict, and capitulation. By the early 1980s, the diffusion of the new technology was complete.

The most common responses to the new technology were workforce reductions by attrition and buyouts, and the decertification of bargaining units. The ITU negotiated an 11-year lifetime job security (automation) pact with New York City publishers in 1974. Similar agreements followed at other newspapers. In essence, these long-term contracts guaranteed jobs for printers doing other tasks in exchange for management's freedom to implement new technology. Attrition would humanely eventually shrink the workforce.

The effect on ITU and union membership was severe and predictable. ITU membership was stable until about 1969, but between 1970 and 1982, active rolls fell by over 40%, while the ranks of apprentices dropped by over 70%. Despite these membership losses, total industry employment fell by only 13%. In absolute numbers, ITU union membership (including retirees and apprentices) declined from 90,000 to 43,000. The Graphic Communications International Union, a union of press operators and allied printing workers with the bulk of its membership in commercial printing, saw its membership fall from 220,000 to 154,000 between 1969 and 1983. Total printing union membership peaked in 1969 at 309,000 but fell by one third by 1983, while printing industry union density declined from 39% in 1959 to less than 20% by 1986. Newspaper industry union density dropped from about 18% in 1975 to under 10% by 2000.

Changes in the labor process have reduced skill levels for most printing crafts. Since the early 1930s, for those crafts that have not been obliterated by new technologies, there has been a steady convergence of skills toward the lowest-skilled mailer classification. The effect of this secular shift has been a re-ordering of power from craft workers and their unions to employers. Aside from falling union membership and density rates, other outcomes reflect this power shift.

Between 1964 and 2004, there were eight printing union mergers that have been completed and a handful of others that failed. The Communications Workers of America and the International Brotherhood of Teamsters are the two most significant international unions that represent printing industry workers, with many of the old crafts now divisions within these unions. Related to these mergers have been interunion jurisdictional rivalries that have historically hindered printing industry labor solidarity.

Strikes in the newspaper industry peaked in 1978 and, following larger industrial relations trends, have become quite rare. When they have occurred since then, as they did in New York, Pittsburgh, Detroit, and Seattle, they were often contentious and damaging to both sides. Unions also have made many numerous concessions in work rules and economics as a result of these strikes and contract settlements. For example, there have been reductions in "featherbedding" staffing levels, continuing implementation of new technologies, changes in the distribution and delivery of newspapers, an increased use of independent contractors, less lucrative retirement and health protections, and a movement toward merit pay systems in newsrooms. Since 1970, printing industry production workers' wages have fallen relative to those of manufacturing workers in general, while newspaper production workers saw their wages fall below manufacturing wages for the first time in 1996.

Technology has always played a critical role in the printing industry. From Gutenberg's press to the Internet, the communication of news and information continues to inform, educate, and entertain. But technological evolutions and revolutions also have reshaped the labor process, inverting power relationships on both the shop floor and in larger society. The once mighty printing unions have been weakened greatly, while the autonomous and high-skilled craft printer has become a wage worker with much less control over his or her work, and often employed in a large, publicly traded media corporation.

HOWARD R. STANGER

References and Further Reading

Dertouzos, James N., and Timothy H. Quinn. *Bargaining in Response to the Technology Revolution: The Case of the Newspaper Industry*. R-3144-DOL. Santa Monica, CA: Rand, 1985.

Giebel, Gregory. "Corporate Structure, Technology, and the Printing Industry." *Labor Studies Journal* (Winter 1979): 228–251.

Jackson, Robert Max. *The Formation of Craft Labor Markets*. Orlando, FL: Academic Press, 1984.

Kalleberg, Arne L., and Michael Wallace et al. "The Eclipse of Craft: The Changing Face of Labor in the Newspaper Industry." In *Workers, Managers, and Technological Change: Emerging Patterns of Labor Relations*, edited by Daniel B. Cornfield. New York: Plenum Press, 1987, pp. 47–71.

Lipset, Seymour M., Trow, Martin, and Coleman, James. *Union Democracy: The Internal Politics of the ITU*. Garden City, NY: Anchor Books, Doubleday and Company, Inc., 1956.

Loft, Jacob. *The Printing Trades*. New York: Farrar and Rinehart, Inc., 1944.

Neiva, Elizabeth MacIver. "Chain Building: The Consolidation of the American Newspaper Industry: 1953–1980." *Business History Review* 70 (Spring 1996): 1–42.

Picard, Robert G., and Jeffery H. Brody. *The Newspaper Publishing Industry*. Boston: Allyn and Bacon, 1997.

Porter, Arthur R. Jr. *Job Property Rights: A Study of the Job Controls of the International Typographical Union*. New York: King's Crown Press, 1954.

Scott, Daniel T. *Technological Change and Printing Industry Unions, 1958–1983*. Doctoral Dissertation, New School for Social Research, 1986.

Sleigh, Stephen R. *On Deadline: Labor Relations in Newspaper Publishing*. Bayside, NY: Social Change Press, 1998.

Stanger, Howard R. *Cooperation, Conciliation, and Continuity: The Evolution of a Modern Grievance Procedure in the Columbus Typographical Union No. 5, 1859–1959*. Doctoral Dissertation, Ohio State University, 1994.

———. "Newspapers: Collective Bargaining Decline amidst Technological Change." In *Collective Bargaining in the Private Sector*, edited by Paul F. Clark, John T. Delaney, and Ann C. Frost. Urbana-Champaign, IL: Industrial Relations Research Association, 2002.

PROFESSIONAL AIR TRAFFIC CONTROLLERS ORGANIZATION

The Professional Air Traffic Controllers Organization (PATCO) was founded on January 11, 1968, when several hundred air traffic controllers from around the United States met at a hotel near New York's John F. Kennedy International Airport. The controllers worked for the U.S. federal government's Federal Aviation Administration (FAA). Their jobs were to direct airplane traffic into, out of, around, and between airports all over the United States. Their union grew out of their dissatisfaction with forced overtime, belligerent supervisors, inadequate equipment, and high stress. During the 1970s, PATCO became one of the most militant unions in the federal service. It led a strike in August 1981 that was ultimately broken by President Ronald Reagan in one of the most important events in late twentieth-century U.S. labor history.

The formation of PATCO owed to rapidly burgeoning air travel in the 1960s and the spread of union organization in the federal sector following President John F. Kennedy issuance of Executive Order 10988 in 1962, which cleared the way for limited collective bargaining for federal workers. After several false starts, in the fall of 1967, controllers in the New York metropolitan region together with allies in Chicago, Atlanta, and later, Los Angeles, settled on a plan for a national organization of air traffic controllers. The leading forces in that effort were two New York controllers, Michael J. Rock and John F. Maher. Initially, Rock, Maher, and other controllers were divided over whether the new organization should be a union or an employees association. In a desire to build an organization with broad appeal, they opted not to place the word "union" in their organization's name. To help attract members, they invited the famous trial attorney F. Lee Bailey to serve as chairman of their organization. Bailey helped PATCO attract thousands of members in its first few months and gave the organization publicity. But Bailey never desired to lead a union, and his growing differences with the PATCO's board ultimately led to his departure from the organization in 1970.

Between 1968 and 1970, PATCO transcended its early ambivalence and developed into a militant union. Its first job action, a work-to-rule protest mounted in July 1968 called "Operation Air Safety," drew attention to controllers' chronic state of overwork. Snarling air traffic across the country, the protest attracted both public and congressional sympathy. A second job action, a sick-out launched in several key air facilities in 1969, led to worsening relations between PATCO and the FAA. The FAA's subsequent efforts to weaken PATCO triggered a 19-day national sick-out that began on March 25, 1970. The sickout amounted to a strike (privately, PATCO leaders referred to it as such) held in defiance of federal law. The sick-out never involved more than one quarter of the FAA's workforce, yet it led to weeks of chaos in the national air transit system before a federal injunction finally ended the job action. The FAA initially fired dozens of strike leaders. Significantly, however, the FAA later rescinded all but one of its firings as a part of President Nixon's effort to woo union leaders to support his policies and his re-election.

The deal between the Nixon administration and labor paved the way for PATCO's re-organization. John F. Leyden, who led New York area controllers during the sick-out, became PATCO's president in 1970. His rise coincided with PATCO's affiliation with the Maritime Engineers Beneficial Association (MEBA), a small but politically powerful affiliate of the AFL-CIO. Through MEBA's intervention, PATCO won recertification as a union eligible to represent federal employees. In October 1972, PATCO won election as exclusive representative for air traffic controllers and won its first collective bargaining contract in 1973.

In its early years, PATCO won significant victories for its members, including an early retirement/second career program that offered medically disqualified controllers to retrain for new jobs; an immunity program, which allowed controllers and pilots to anonymously report near midair collisions in hopes that such reporting would lead to safety reforms; a relaxation of the FAA's white-shirt-and-necktie dress code; and free familiarization flights in airline cockpit jump seats. Soon PATCO developed a loyal membership of over 13,000 members and enjoyed a higher dues-paying membership rate than any other union in the open-shop federal sector.

Yet controllers' gains were limited by federal law, which prohibited bargaining over wages and benefits in the federal sector. PATCO creatively circumvented the law by using a series of slowdowns to pressure the FAA to reclassify its members in 1976 into higher scales of the government service (GS) code. Yet, that strategy was not repeatable. In subsequent years, a series of developments placed PATCO under intense pressure. The organization saw an influx of militant Vietnam-era veterans who were disenchanted with the government. Inflation began to eat at the value of its members' salaries and benefits, and federal workers' wages and salaries began to fall behind rising prices. Meanwhile, government deficits made politicians increasingly tough negotiators. These developments came to a head in 1978 negotiations with the FAA, which yielded a three-year contract that deeply disappointed PATCO members.

The disappointment of 1978 led Leyden to initiate a strike-preparation program to give the union a stronger hand during its planned 1981 negotiations. That program saw PATCO create a strike fund and a network of anonymous strike leaders who could direct the organization should its elected leaders be arrested during a strike. Leyden was nonetheless reluctant to wage an illegal walkout. His well-known position was not shared by members of the union's executive board. In January 1980, a majority of his board announced that they would support the union vice president, Robert Poli, a former Cleveland area controller, against Leyden in upcoming union elections. Leyden angrily resigned his office, and Poli immediately acceded to the union's presidency.

During 1980 and 1981, Poli prepared PATCO for the 1981 negotiations and a potential strike. In hopes of strengthening PATCO's position, Poli endorsed Ronald Reagan in the waning days of the 1980 presidential campaign after Reagan promised PATCO members that he would consider their needs carefully if he were elected. Negotiations with the Reagan administration did not result in a contract acceptable to PATCO, however, and in 1981, the union led an illegal strike against the federal government on August 3, 1981. When PATCO strikers did not return to work after two days on strike, they were permanently replaced and PATCO was broken. During its 13-year existence, PATCO helped illustrate what was possible—and impossible—for a militant federal government workers' union to achieve.

JOSEPH A. MCCARTIN

References and Further Reading

Hurd, Rick, and Jill Kriesky. "The Rise and Demise of PATCO Reconstructed." *The Industrial and Labor Relations Review* 40 (October 1986): 115–123.

Nordlund, Willis J. *Silent Skies: The Air Traffic Controllers' Strike*. Westport, CT: Praeger, 1998.

Northrup, Herbert R. "The Rise and Demise of PATCO." *Industrial and Labor Relations Review* 37 (January 1984): 167–184.

Round, Michael. *Grounded: Reagan and the PATCO Crash*. New York: Garland Publishing, 1999.

Shostak, Arthur B., and David Skocik. *The Air Controllers' Controversy: Lessons from the PATCO Strike*. New York: Human Sciences Press, 1986.

PROFESSIONAL AIR TRAFFIC CONTROLLERS ORGANIZATION STRIKE (1981)

The disastrous 1981 walkout by the Professional Air Traffic Controllers Organization (PATCO) was one of the most important strikes in American labor history, marking the onset of a period of virulent anti-unionism. The strike was staged by roughly three quarters of the largely white male workforce of nearly 16,000 air traffic controllers employed by the U.S. government's Federal Aviation Administration (FAA) and was held in defiance of laws that prohibit strikes by federal workers. It was broken when President Ronald Reagan issued orders to fire strikers 48 hours into the walkout. Reagan's act in turn helped legitimize the permanent replacement of strikers by private-sector employers in the 1980s.

The 1981 strike grew out of a decade of contentious relations between PATCO and the FAA that followed the founding of the union in 1968. Controllers, who provided guidance and coordination to the nation's air traffic system, objected to the stressful nature of their jobs and believed they deserved compensation comparable to that of airline pilots, who worked for private employers. The FAA, meanwhile, opposed PATCO's demands and strove for a regimented work culture that many controllers detested. In many ways, these adversaries had been on a collision course since 1978 when PATCO agreed to a contract that disappointed controllers and the FAA

began a more aggressive effort to weaken the union's power.

Still, the 1981 strike might have been avoided had not two developments occurred. First, PATCO's longtime president, John Leyden, resigned from office in January 1980 when his executive board decided to endorse a rival, the PATCO vice president Robert Poli, for the union presidency. Unlike Leyden, Poli was prepared to launch an illegal strike if his members saw it as necessary to achieve PATCO's bottom-line contract demands. Second, Ronald Reagan was elected president. In October 1980, PATCO endorsed Reagan's candidacy after Reagan promised to respond to controllers' job-related concerns. Ironically, this promise elevated controllers' expectations going into the 1981 negotiations and helped pave the way for the strike.

As negotiations began in 1981, controllers sought a shorter workweek, compensation for on-the-job training, and other improvements in their stress-filled working conditions. Importantly, they also sought higher salaries. Federal law prohibits unions from negotiating over wages, yet PATCO demanded a $10,000 across-the-board wage increase for controllers. Ultimately, the salary demand proved to be a public relations blunder. At a time of rising unemployment, high inflation, and concession bargaining by industrial unions, even some in organized labor proved less than enthusiastic about defending PATCO's contract demands once the strike began.

The PATCO strike was initially set for June 22, 1981. But the strike was postponed on that day when the union was unable to muster 80% support for the strike among working controllers. Robert Poli thus accepted a tentative contract offer from Secretary of Transportation Drew Lewis that improved controllers' compensation, a precedent-setting concession by the government according to many observers since the government was legally forbidden to collectively bargain over salaries.

But the FAA's June 22, 1981, offer fell far short of PATCO's demands. After re-assessing the situation, PATCO's executive board recommended that the membership reject the tentative contract and hold a second strike vote. Controllers overwhelmingly complied with the board's recommendations and rejected the contract by a wide margin in a mail ballot. Negotiations between Poli and Lewis resumed on July 31, but quickly stalemated. The union held a strike vote on the night of August 2, 1981, meeting its 80% support goal. The walkout began at 7 a.m. EST on August 3, 1981.

The government and leading air carriers were well prepared for the walkout. Air traffic proceeded without major incident, though with thousands of flights canceled in a pattern predetermined by the FAA and the airlines. Meanwhile, injunctions were issued in jurisdictions across the country, leading to the subsequent arrest of several strike leaders for contempt of court orders that demanded that controllers return to work. President Reagan issued a televised ultimatum that gave controllers until August 5 to reclaim their jobs. Failing to do so, they would be fired. More than 11,500 strikers ignored Reagan's warning and saw their employment terminated. The AFL-CIO protested this union-busting act. But threatened sympathy strikes by other unions in support of PATCO never materialized. Public opinion tended to support Reagan's hard-line response to the walkout. When no major midair collisions occurred, and air traffic volume began inching up, it became clear that Reagan had won, though at a considerable cost to air carriers, taxpayers, and the national economy. PATCO was subsequently decertified as a union.

Reagan's busting of PATCO reverberated widely through the American economy in the following years and marked a turning point in the history of U.S. labor relations. Although the courts had long ruled that the 1935 Wagner Act allowed the permanent replacement of economic strikers, few large employers had actually exercised this option before 1981. Flagrant union busting was widely viewed as unethical and un-American. Reagan changed that. In the years after the PATCO strike, Phelps-Dodge, Hormel, and other large companies joined a growing list of private employers that simply replaced strikers.

The rise of the permanent replacement tactic clearly dampened workers' willingness to strike. Between 1947 and 1980, the Bureau of Labor Statistics annually reported at least 180 strikes involving more than 1,000 workers each. Since 1982, the number of such strikes has never once reached even one half that level. Figures show a sharp decline from the 235 strikes involving roughly one million workers in 1979 to a record low of 17 walkouts involving only 73,000 workers in 1999. The PATCO strike and the use of permanent replacement workers that it legitimized were not alone responsible for this trend. The threat of plant closings and other factors also played a role in the diminishing use of organized labor's oldest weapon. But more than any other single event, the PATCO strike signaled a profound decline in organized labor's power in the late twentieth-century United States.

JOSEPH A. McCARTIN

References and Further Reading

Nordlund, Willis J. Silent Skies: The Air Traffic Controllers' Strike. Westport, CT: Praeger, 1998.

Round, Michael. Grounded: Reagan and the PATCO Crash. New York: Garland Publishing, 1999.

Shostak, Arthur B., and David Skocik. The Air Controllers' Controversy: Lessons from the PATCO Strike. New York: Human Sciences Press, 1986.

PROGRESSIVE ERA

The Progressive Era has the reputation for being one of the great eras of social and political reform in American history. While scholars debate the period's precise chronology, most historians pinpoint the age from the turn of the century to World War I as the high point of a progressive impulse that transformed the country. Historians argue vigorously over whether this impulse was unitary and coherent enough to be called "Progressivism," or whether it was a collection of related but fundamentally different political movements. Regardless of the terminology that might be used, the wave of reforms that came during or immediately after this period was indeed impressive and included—among many others—the first wave of constitutional amendments since the Civil War: the income tax, the direct election of senators, prohibition, and woman suffrage.

Traditional scholarly interpretations of Progressivism have placed the middle class at the center of these reform efforts—and with good reason, as reform efforts from antimonopoly efforts to prohibition had significant middling constituencies. However, historians have tried to situate labor more fully at the forefront of the period's most significant events. We can now see that workers were both the motive force behind and the subjects of crucial reform legislation. Moreover, much of what happened during "the Progressive Era" fell outside the dramas of Progressive reform—and this was particularly the case in relation to the lives of the mass of workers who lived during the first two decades of the twentieth century.

The Main Contours of Social and Economic Change

The primary social changes of the period were mass migration and immigration, and the rise of large corporations. We cannot tell the stories of these changes without putting workers front and center.

Numbers alone tell an important part of the story: Because these trends began in the late nineteenth century, it is best to discuss the period from roughly the end of the Civil War to the end of World War I. For example, from 1870 to 1920 more than 10 million Americans migrated from farm to city, while another

20 million—a great number, for the first time, from Southern and Eastern Europe—came to the United States as immigrants.

Most of these migrants ended up working within manufacturing, making the United States for the first time the most powerful economy in the world. The number of employees within the manufacturing sector skyrocketed from 2.5 million in 1870 to 11.2 million in 1920 (or nearly 40% of the workforce). An increasing number of these employees worked in gigantic factories owned by huge corporations like U.S. Steel. The growth of these big business behemoths was also explosive, with quasi-monopolies formed in industries ranging from meatpacking to textiles to tobacco—particularly during the great merger movement that swept the economy between 1897 to 1904.

Under a regime of laissez-faire capitalism, the lives of workers in corporate factories were often relentlessly bleak. Bells rang and whistles blew before sunrise to announce the start of what, not unusually, was a 10- to 12-hour workday. Work conditions could be extremely hazardous, with accidental death and dismemberment frequent and almost always poorly compensated. Although wages generally grew over the period, seasonal and cyclical unemployment made the lives of all but the most privileged workers insecure.

Despite the prevalence of this kind of work experience, however, it is incorrect to generalize too much about American workers during this period. While the above description fits the lives of millions of male immigrants, the single most numerous occupation during the period was actually that of domestic servant. Agricultural employment remained supreme in much of the South and West, particularly for African-Americans. And the majority of employees in the country actually continued to work in relatively small businesses.

Still, when commentators invoked the problem of labor in the early twentieth century, they spoke primarily of "what it meant to work in a large-scale, mechanized, rationally managed, corporate system of production."

Growth of Unions: American Federation of Labor and Industrial Workers of the World

Workers responded to these conditions with the first sustained and long-lasting drive for unionization in American history. The primary organization vehicle for workers was the American Federation of Labor (AFL), although other more radical unions such as the Industrial Workers of the World (IWW) also played crucial roles in the era's unionizing ferment.

The American Federation of Labor became the only truly national union in the country after the demise of the Knights of Labor during the 1890s. The AFL, however, had a distinctly different approach to organizing from that of the Knights. The Knights were, by philosophy if not always in practice, an industrial union that sought to include the skilled and unskilled, women and men, and workers of all races. The AFL, on the other hand, generally limited its recruiting to skilled workers; it also refused to admit the storekeepers and reformers who had provided much of the community-based support for the Knights of Labor. And while the AFL began with a commitment to racial egalitarianism, it quickly accepted the segregation common in the skilled trades. The AFL also poured out its hostility upon immigrants, particularly those from Asia; at the turn of the century, for instance, the Federation published a pamphlet titled *Some Reasons for Chinese Exclusion. Meat vs. Rice. American Manhood against Asiatic Coolieism. Which Shall Survive?*

Despite its severe limitations, the AFL brought genuine gains to many American workers during an era that witnessed one of the most virulent anti-union offensives on the part of employers. Between 1897 and 1903, its membership shot up from 400,000 to nearly three million. The AFL also began to admit some industrial unions, such as the United Mine Workers (UMW) and the International Ladies' Garment Workers' Union (ILGWU). The group's expansion did temporarily come to a halt when corporate elites used violence and the power of the courts to launch an effective movement for the open shop. Yet the attempt to suppress the AFL ironically benefited the organization, providing legitimacy to its self-characterization as the primary voice for American workers.

Much of the AFL's success was due to the tireless energy, ambition, and vision of Samuel Gompers. Gompers was elected annually to serve as the organization's president every year, except one, from the group's formation in 1886 until his death 1924. Born in London in 1850, the Jewish Gompers began his work life at the age of 10 as a shoemaker before taking on his father's trade of cigar making. The family moved to New York City in 1863, and the following year Gompers joined the Cigar Makers' International Union. He became president of his local in 1875 and vice president of the international union in 1886.

That same year Gompers also helped form the AFL. Throughout the 1890s, the moderate Gompers battled socialists for influence within the organization, although Gompers was himself actually never completely unsympathetic to socialism. Yet through the turn of the century, he decisively rejected not only that movement's radicalism but also its emphasis on political action. Although Gompers later brought the AFL into a close connection to the Democratic Party, he remained convinced that politicians were treacherous and that workers could ultimately only rely on themselves. By 1900, Gompers's position as AFL chieftain was firm.

Gompers and the AFL were class conscious, believing in a fundamental divide between workers and employers. Yet they accepted the prevailing economic structure, seeking to get—in Gompers's famous words—more and more and more out of the coffers of capitalists. The AFL's main rival to this "pure and simple" unionism, in contrast, sought an outright overthrow of capitalism.

Formed in Chicago in 1905, the Industrial Workers of the World made little doubt of its revolutionary commitments—and its disdain for the AFL. The IWW preamble declared:

> The working class and the employing class have nothing in common....Between these two classes a struggle must go on until the workers of the world organize as a class, take possession of the means of production, abolish the wage system, and live in harmony with the Earth...

> The trade unions foster a state of affairs which allows one set of workers to be pitted against another set of workers in the same industry, thereby helping defeat one another in wage wars....Instead of the conservative motto, "A fair day's wage for a fair day's work," we must inscribe on our banner the revolutionary watchword, "Abolition of the wage system."

> It is the historic mission of the working class to do away with capitalism.

The Wobblies, as they came to be known—the origin of the label is unclear—had distinctive centers of regional strength. Growing out of brutal struggles in western mines, the IWW effectively organized many of the West's miners as well as the region's migratory labor stream of lumbermen and agricultural harvest workers. The Wobblies went out of their way to organize cross-racially, although their claims to speak for the entire working class were sometimes belied by the hyper-masculinity common in migratory work camps. Yet the IWW proved its success among women workers, too, claiming several remarkable successes among northeastern textile employees. In the process, the Wobblies became a cause célèbre among bohemian intellectuals, with the cross-fertilization between Greenwich Village rebels and organic working-class intellectuals producing some of the most interesting cartoons and songs of the entire American working-class tradition. The IWW also became the object of often deadly and extralegal vigilantism from employers and local authorities who used jailing, murder, and terrorism to combat Wobbly fights for free speech and workers' rights.

The Wobblies always prided themselves on a decentralized, even anarchist organizational structure. Yet, like the AFL, they too had a guru. William Haywood was The Bad Man of the labor movement, especially compared to the clean and respectable Gompers. Born in Salt Lake City in 1869, Haywood began mining work when nine years old—the same age that he also lost use of his right eye while whittling a slingshot. He joined the Western Federation of Miners (WFM) in 1896, and by 1900, he had joined the WFM's executive board and was soon helping direct the union's response to violent warfare in Colorado's mining districts.

In 1905, Haywood helped found the IWW; the following year he was arrested along with two associates for his alleged involvement in the assassination of the Idaho ex-governor, Frank Steunenberg (authorities tracked him down in a brothel). In one of the most celebrated criminal court cases of the era, Haywood was declared not guilty—although the leading authority on the case, J. Anthony Lukas, has made a tentative case for Haywood's guilt.

In 1908, Haywood was ousted from his WFM leadership position and quickly gravitated toward the Wobblies' espousal of socialism and direct workers' action. By 1915, he had become the IWW's official leader. A large physique and a booming voice, along with a visceral fearlessness, enabled "Big Bill" to inspire followers and intimidate his enemies in the class struggle. Upset at the IWW's continued class warfare during World War I, the federal government lowered the boom, and Haywood served a year in Leavenworth on charges of violating the Espionage and Sedition Acts. While out of jail on appeal, the Supreme Court rejected his case, and Haywood fled to Moscow; many Wobblies believed that he had betrayed their cause to save his own skin. He died desperate and lonely in 1928. Half of his ashes were buried in the Kremlin, with the remainder making their way back to Chicago for internment near a monument to the Haymarket anarchists who had initially helped inspire Haywood's activism.

An Era of Great Strikes

Especially because of the efforts of Samuel Gompers and the AFL, during the Progressive Era the national union movement became institutionalized for the first time in American history. The AFL's moderate stance often led to attempts at conciliation, with certain segments of labor and capital both recognizing the value of industrial peace. Such growing harmony, however, never solidified, and the first two decades of the twentieth century have instead a well-deserved reputation as an age of often-violent labor conflict.

The number of strikes dramatically increased between 1900 and 1917. Each conflict of course had its own texture and significance. Two particularly important strikes, however, well illustrate the differing approaches of the AFL and the IWW—as well as the growing political power of labor.

When the 1902 anthracite strike in Pennsylvania began, it appeared that powerful mine owners held all the cards in their attempt to beat back the largely Southern and Eastern European immigrant workforce. Yet by the end of the five-month strike, the president of the United States had broken a potent precedent to intervene on behalf of workers.

The United Mine Workers was the primary organizing force in the anthracite (hard coal) districts of northeastern Pennsylvania. While not recognized by the mine owners, the UMW had successfully pressed for a 10% wage increase after a brief 1900 strike. This settlement was extended through April 1902. At that time, the UMW insisted on a 20% wage increase, an eight-hour day, fair weighing of the coal its miners extracted, and recognition of the union. George F. Baer, the mine owners' representative, refused to bargain at all, despite the union's offer of arbitration.

In May 1902, 150,000 miners put down their picks and shovels. As the strike extended through the summer, the price of coal quadrupled, and citizens began to fret about their inability to heat their homes during the winter. As calls for presidential intervention mounted, Theodore Roosevelt and the Republican senator Mark Hanna convinced the mine owners to meet with union officials at the White House. John Mitchell, the UMW president, impressed the president, but Roosevelt was furious at the intransigent heads of the coal companies. Finally, with threats of violence in the air, Roosevelt made plans to send in federal troops to operate the coalfields. Just before the implementation of such radical—albeit temporary—nationalization, Roosevelt's secretary of war, Elihu Root, convinced J. P. Morgan, the New York financier who was effectively in charge of the mines, to get the mine owners to stand down. They agreed to arbitrate, and the miners returned to work in late October.

President Roosevelt then appointed the Anthracite Coal Strike Commission to investigate and work out a solution. With the skillful aid of Clarence Darrow and Henry Demarest Lloyd, Mitchell and the UMW successfully made their case that many miners lived in abject poverty and that the companies did little to make this deadly occupation safer (513 miners were killed in the nine-county anthracite region in 1901 alone). Low wages made child labor a necessity for family survival. The Commission found this testimony compelling and, while it did not grant the UMW official recognition—a crucial blow to the union—it did significantly increase the wages and decreased the hours of the miners. Even more significantly, the president had, for the first time in American history, weighed in on a labor dispute—and vindicated the rights of workers.

There was, however, no such story of conciliation in the 1912 great uprising in Lawrence, Massachusetts. In January of that year, 10,000 women, men, and children left their jobs after 500 Italian employees of the American Woolen Company found their pay shortchanged. The IWW had previously not conducted any significant labor struggles in the East, but a fledgling Wobbly local gained leadership of the strike and created a festive culture of opposition. Four days into the conflict, police turned icy fire hoses on the workers, but this merely energized the strikers. Several weeks later, the police raided the train depot in Lawrence, where IWW "Rebel Girl" Elizabeth Gurley Flynn was organizing a transport of children out of the increasingly violent city. Officers attacked the women and children and then detained them at police headquarters. National public opinion was becoming riveted on Lawrence, although citizens found it difficult to figure out which side best exemplified law-breaking anarchism.

The root cause of the strike, as in the anthracite region, was simple: wages well below poverty level. Male breadwinners could not earn enough money to support a family in even the most rudimentary fashion, and the textile mills were full of women and children—without whose wages it would have been impossible for families to pay for food and shelter. When mill owners cut wages and hours after the state of Massachusetts passed a 54-hour-per-week work law for women, family survival was once again threatened. The mill owners held so much power that even AFL-affiliated skilled workers were unable to organize. Yet the solidarity that the IWW generated was impressive enough that, by mid-March, it enabled the workers to declare victory. Yet, because of the legitimacy they granted the system of capitalist wage slavery, the IWW would not authorize the signing of contracts. So although the Wobblies reaped a massive public relations triumph from the Lawrence strike, their local collapsed the next year, and there would be no further Wobbly contributions to the long and bitter struggle to organize the textile industry there.

The Realm of the Political

We should, however, resist the temptation to see such acrimonious strikes as the primary pattern of labor relations. Arguably of even greater significance was the increasingly friendly relationship between the house of labor and national political figures. While the federal judiciary retained a basic hostility to the organization of workers, Theodore Roosevelt and Woodrow Wilson increasingly courted "responsible" unionists. The result was the origin of the tight connection between unions and the Democratic Party that has continued to this day. While many critics have pointed to the great costs to workers of putting all their eggs in the Democratic basket, during the Progressive Era, the unions' political strategy brought unprecedented legislative gains.

The roots of labor's political activity were at the local level, where unionists, and even members of independent working-class parties, were elected to city councils throughout the country. Trade unionists became an important constituency for reform-minded mayors such as Hazen Pingree of Detroit and Tom Johnson of Cleveland. In San Francisco, the most powerful municipal labor movement in the nation took over city hall in 1901 and held power until a corruption scandal led to the mayor Eugene Schmitz's downfall six years later. Workers produced a kind of working-class progressivism that focused on issues relating to the eight-hour day for public employees, fairer taxation, and municipal ownership of utilities.

The increasing success of working-class local politics in part flowed from the pressure exerted by the period's powerful socialist movement. Indeed, socialism was more respectable and influential during the Progressive Era than at any time in American history. The charismatic presidential candidate Eugene Debs received nearly one million votes in the 1912 election—6% of the total. That same year, more than a thousand socialists won state and local office, while socialist members of Congress Morris Hillquit of New York and Victor Berger of Milwaukee helped ensure that at least a mild version of the class struggle appeared in a good number of the nation's newspapers.

Although the mainstream of the American socialist movement was moderate by European standards, its potential radicalism helped pave the way for the relationship between mainstream politicians and members of the AFL. For instance, Theodore Roosevelt—who was, at best, suspicious of unions—warned that if business elites and members of Congress did not heed the legitimate claims of respectable workers' advocates like Samuel Gompers, they would face the revolutionary specter of socialism.

The primary obstacle to such a rapprochement between labor and government was the federal judiciary. As Melvyn Dubofsky has noted, "it was unelected judges with lifetime tenure who determined national labor policy more often and more decisively than elected public officials did" (Dubofsky, 1994, p. 37). These judges, heavily influenced by a highly individualistic vision of political economy, by and large declared war on organized labor. Judges, declaring that unions violated the prohibition on restraint of trade found in the 1890 Sherman Act (which was designed to regulate monopolistic businesses), routinely used injunctions to cripple strikes. Nor could unions any longer use other effective weapons in their arsenals. In the infamous "Danbury Hatters" case of Loewe v. Lawlor (1908), judges effectively outlawed secondary boycotts, which were meant to pressure companies uninvolved in a particular conflict between workers and an employer not to purchase nonunion or "unfair" products. Gompers v. Buck's Stove and Range Co. (1911) ratified this prohibition of boycotts and sanctioned the jailing of union leaders for daring even simply to speak out against an offending company. The Supreme Court also upheld the "yellow-dog contract," which allowed employers to demand as a condition of hiring that workers never join a union.

This judicial hostility is what ultimately drove AFL leaders to embrace political activism. Gompers and his colleagues continued to retain deep suspicions about the federal government. Yet a "pure and simple" unionism that largely eschewed politics was proving more and more inadequate under the avalanche of unfavorable court decisions. As John Mitchell commented in 1903, "the trade union movement in this country can make progress only by identifying itself with the state."

Starting in 1906 with the presentation of its "Bill of Grievances," the AFL threw itself wholeheartedly into the national political realm. Promising to punish its enemies—and, secondarily, to reward its friends—the AFL attempted at first to maintain its nonpartisanship by supporting candidates who advocated the cause of workers. The result over the next decade was the election of an increasing number of friends of labor, including trade unionists themselves. For example, in 1910, 15 unionists were elected to Congress, including the former United Mine Workers official William B. Wilson, who would become the first secretary of the Department of Labor in 1913.

In 1908, Samuel Gompers made the fateful decision to all but officially endorse William Jennings Bryan, the Democratic nominee for president, after the Democrats embraced the AFL's demand for reform of the injunction system. Bryan suffered defeat, but four years later, the Democrat Woodrow Wilson was elected to the White House. Wilson had only a few years before been extremely antilabor; in 1909, the then governor of New Jersey declared, "I am a fierce partisan of the Open Shop and of everything that makes for industrial liberty." Yet, Wilson's ideology evolved as he recognized the value of the labor constituency. Despite the AFL's preference for Missouri's Champ Clark as the Democratic nominee, the organization fell in behind Wilson and played an active role in his campaign.

Initially, much of the support that Wilson provided to the AFL in return was symbolic, such as when he became the first president to address the organization's annual convention. Yet increasingly, organized labor expected concrete results and, in many ways, it received them. Secretary William Wilson was able to use his position in the Department of Labor to become a strong advocate for unions. President Wilson appointed a left-wing radical, Frank Walsh, to head the United States Commission on Industrial Relations (CIR). The CIR, which held public hearings from 1913 to 1915 in an attempt to solicit information that would lead to a reconciliation of labor and capital, issued a final report that was, in the words of the labor historian Melvyn Dubofsky, "perhaps the most radical document ever released by a federal commission." The report recommended strong governmental support for union organizing efforts, as well as for a variety of government programs to meet the crises of poverty and unemployment. Procapitalist and more moderate "public" members of the CIR wrote dissenting minority reports, however, and in the end, the cautious Wilson refused to embrace Walsh's call for social democracy.

What labor did get under the first Wilson administration, however, was first and foremost the Clayton Antitrust Act of 1914. While the Clayton Act had many components that had nothing to do with unions, its most important provisions, at least rhetorically, proclaimed that labor was not "an article of commerce" and upheld the legitimacy of unions and strikes. Because it also seemed to promise relief from judicial injunctions, Gompers declared the law labor's "Magna Carta." Yet in practice, the law was ambiguous enough to allow judges to continue to intervene in ways destructive to unions—an outcome that Congress and Wilson were likely comfortable with as they sought to please labor without making radical changes in the American political economy.

Still, labor could point to genuine reasons to be pleased with Woodrow Wilson. In 1914, the president sent the military to Colorado after the Ludlow massacre, one of the most infamous events in American labor history. After many violent interchanges with the workers, militia and coal company police associated with John D. Rockefeller's Colorado Fuel and Iron Company raked a tent camp of strikers with machine-gun fire and then burned the camp to the ground. The 25 murdered workers included a dozen women and children who suffered a particularly horrifying death. In response, Wilson gave clear orders that the federal troops were under no circumstances to help the coal-mine owners protect strikebreakers as they sought to resume production.

Moreover, as Wilson looked toward a close re-election campaign in 1916, he put aside his concern with "class" legislation and signed into law progressive reforms such as the La Follette Seamen's Act of 1915. This bill for the first time regulated the work conditions of sailors. The following year, Wilson signed the Keating-Owens Act, outlawing child labor. In 1916, the president also appointed to the Supreme Court Louis Brandeis, one of the country's most powerful champions of protective labor legislation. Wilson culminated his courting of labor with his approval of the Adamson Act, which granted railroad workers the eight-hour day. Unionists avidly turned out to support Wilson's successful re-election bid, and according to Melvyn Dubofsky, "things had never looked better for organized labor."

Women Workers

While AFL political activism was designed primarily to aid skilled workers, by no means did all labor-oriented politics revolve around the agenda of privileged male workers. Indeed, at the very heart of middle-class as well as working-class Progressivism was the push for protective legislation for women workers, as reformers tried to fathom how to respond to the increase of female factory workers from 324,000 in 1870 to more than two million in 1920.

Those who concerned themselves with the plight of early twentieth-century labor often hoped to pass laws that would limit the hours and provide for a minimum wage for all workers. Yet the Supreme Court made clear in its infamous 1905 case of *Lochner v. New York* that such legislation was a violation of the individual worker's freedom of contract. Three years later, however, the Court proved willing to approve an Oregon maximum-hours law for women workers. In the case of *Muller v. Oregon*, Florence Kelley and Josephine Goldmark of the National Consumers' League joined with Louis Brandeis to argue that overwork not only harmed female employees but also endangered the propagation of the entire human race because of their deleterious effect on women's maternal function.

The Triangle Shirtwaist Fire of 1911, one of the worst industrial disasters in American history—and certainly the most visible during the Progressive Era—tragically highlighted the necessity of such laws. The Triangle Shirtwaist Company employed approximately 600 workers, mainly young immigrant women, in its Greenwich Village factory. These workers generally labored for up to 14 hours per day for meager wages. The massive "Uprising of the 20,000," a gigantic 1909 garment workers' strike, had begun at Triangle; the company then refused to sign on to the collective bargaining agreement that other employers reached with the International Ladies' Garment Workers' Union.

Conditions in the factory well epitomized the dangers facing so many industrial workers—*The Jungle*, Upton Sinclair's 1905 exposé of the Chicago meatpacking industry, being the most famous portrait of these hazards. Flammable textiles filled the factory, but despite the prevalence of smoking and gas lighting, the company did not have on hand any fire extinguishers. When a blaze began on the eighth floor of the building on March 25, 1911, workers from that floor and two floors above were generally able to escape. Those on the ninth floor, however, were trapped, at least partly because of a door that Triangle's owners had locked to prevent theft or unauthorized breaks. New Yorkers looked on with horror as young women who were not incinerated inside the factory jumped to their deaths.

Public reaction to the 146 deaths at Triangle was swift, as was the passage of legislation mandating improved factory safety. Much of the powerful advocacy on behalf of women workers, including in the aftermath of the Triangle disaster, came from the Women's Trade Union League (WTUL). More than any other national organization, the WTUL showed the promise of cross-class solidarity as wealthy women combined with their working-class sisters to support strikes and advocate for the cause of labor. The WTUL also injected a working-class spirit into the struggle for woman suffrage.

Along with a broad circle of female reform groups, the WTUL fought hard for protective labor legislation for women workers. Yet laws that capped hours for women and that mandated a minimum wage did not unproblematically assist their intended beneficiaries. The justification of such laws—whether for reasons of expediency or genuine concern—emphasized women's status as powerless victims who desperately needed aid from the paternal hand of government. The laws at times seemed to sap the energy of female union organizing, and they also served to drive women out of some previously mixed-sex occupations. Contemporary feminists, celebrating individualism, joined the Supreme Court in voicing their concern about the law's stripping individual workers of full personal choice. The response of protective labor law advocates, in turn, emphasized that poor immigrant workers did indeed need protection from their much more powerful employers and that working-class women had needs genuinely different from those of middle-class or elite women. The conflicts over the gendered uses of government presaged the bitter conflicts between women activists that broke out during the 1920s over the Equal Rights Amendment.

Conclusion

Historians have traditionally marked American entry into World War I as the end of the Progressive Era. The fate of labor lends considerable credence to this chronology. Moderate unions entered a new era of official legitimacy as Woodrow Wilson enlisted Gompers and the AFL in the war effort. Yet the IWW, and many socialists, vocally opposed the war; in turn, the government launched an intense wave of repression against those it deemed disloyal. While radicals like Eugene Debs languished in prison, workers unleashed one of the largest strike waves during the bloody year of 1919. The birth of Bolshevik Russia and the entry of women into voting booths dramatically changed the political culture of American class relations.

The immediate aftermath of these conflicts was a renewed government and employer offensive that left organized labor reeling during much of the 1920s. Yet the reforms of the Progressive Era had planted seeds that New Dealers—many of them involved in these early twentieth century struggles—would nurture as the United States entered the even more transformative 1930s.

ROBERT D. JOHNSTON

References and Further Reading

American Federation of Labor. "Some Reasons for Chinese Exclusion. Meat vs. Rice. American Manhood against Asiatic Coolieism. Which Shall Survive?" Washington, DC: American Federation of Labor, ca. 1901.

Brody, David. "The American Worker in the Progressive Age: A Comprehensive Analysis." In *Workers in Industrial America: Essays on the Twentieth Century Struggle*, by David Brody. New York: Oxford University Press, 1980, pp. 3–47.

Buenker, John D. *Urban Liberalism and Progressive Reform*. New York: Norton, 1973.

Dubofsky, Melvyn. *Industrialism and the American Worker, 1865–1920*. 3rd edition. Wheeling, IL: Harlan Davidson, 1996.

———. *The State and Labor in Modern America*. Chapel Hill: University of North Carolina Press, 1994.

———. *We Shall Be All: A History of the Industrial Workers of the World*. 2nd edition. Urbana: University of Illinois Press, 1988.

Dye, Nancy Schrom. *As Equals and as Sisters: Feminism, the Labor Movement, and the Women's Trade Union League*. Columbia: University of Missouri Press, 1980.

Frankel, Noralee, and Nancy Schrom Dye. *Gender, Class, Race, and Reform in the Progressive Era*. Lexington: University Press of Kentucky, 1991.

Gompers, Samuel. *Seventy Years of Life and Labor: An Autobiography*. Edited by Nick Salvatore. Ithaca, NY: ILR Press, 1984.

Greene, Julie. *Pure and Simple Politics: The American Federation of Labor and Political Activism, 1881–1917*. New York: Cambridge University Press, 1998.

Haywood, Big Bill. *Bill Haywood's Book: The Autobiography of William D. Haywood*. 1929. Reprint, Westport, CT: Greenwood Press, 1983.

Kazin, Michael. *Barons of Labor: The San Francisco Building Trades and Union Power in the Progressive Era*. Urbana: University of Illinois Press, 1987.

Kessler-Harris, Alice. *Out to Work: A History of Wage-Earning Women*. New York: Oxford University Press, 2003.

Lukas, J. Anthony. *Big Trouble: A Murder in a Small Western Town Sets Off a Struggle for the Soul of America*. New York: Simon and Schuster, 1997.

McCartin, Joseph Anthony. *Labor's Great War: The Struggle for Industrial Democracy and the Origins of Modern American Labor Relations, 1912–1921*. Chapel Hill: University of North Carolina Press, 1997.

McGerr, Michael E. *A Fierce Discontent: The Rise and Fall of the Progressive Movement in America, 1870–1920*. New York: Free Press, 2003.

McGovern, George S., and Leonard F. Guttride. *The Great Coalfield War*. Boston: Houghton Mifflin, 1972.

Montgomery, David. *The Fall of the House of Labor: The Workplace, the State, and American Labor Activism, 1865–1925*. New York: Cambridge University Press, 1987.

Payne, Elizabeth Anne. *Reform, Labor, and Feminism: Margaret Dreier Robins and the National Women's Trade Union League*. Urbana: University of Illinois Press, 1988.

Painter, Nell Irvin. *Standing at Armageddon: The United States, 1877–1919*. New York: Norton, 1987.

Salvatore, Nick. *Eugene V. Debs: Citizen and Socialist*. Urbana: University of Illinois Press, 1982.

Stromquist, Shelton. *Reinventing "The People": The Progressive Movement, the Class Problem, and the Origins of Modern Liberalism*. Urbana: University of Illinois Press, 2006.

Tax, Meredith. *The Rise of the Women: Feminist Solidarity and Class Conflict, 1880–1917*. New York: Monthly Review Press, 1980.

Woloch, Nancy. *Muller v. Oregon: A Brief History with Documents*. Boston: Bedford, 1996.

Cases and Statutes Cited

Gompers v. Buck's Stove and Range Co. 221 U.S. 418 (1911)

Lochner v. New York 198 U.S. 45 (1905)

Loewe v. Lawlor 208 U.S. 274 (1908)

Muller v. Oregon 208 U.S. 412 (1908)

See also **American Federation of Labor; Danbury Hatters Case: *Loewe v. Lawlor* (1908, 1915); Debs, Eugene V.; Gompers, Samuel; Haywood, William D. "Big Bill"; Industrial Workers of the World; *Lochner v. New York* (1905); Triangle Shirtwaist Fire; Women's Trade Union League**

PROSTITUTION
Sex Work

Prostitution, to which the adage "the world's oldest profession" has often been applied, has been practiced by women, and to a lesser extent men, in America ever since Europeans arrived on the North American continent. Perhaps ironically, because precontact Native Americans possessed strikingly different conceptions of sexuality and property than did their European counterparts, prostitution as we think of it today did not exist prior to European contact. Most Indians, although custom and practice varied from group to group, were relaxed about sex and sexuality, had few proscriptions on sexual experimentation and sexual choice for men and women, and possessed no concept of sexual ownership, making the sale of sex literally impossible. Yet early Western visitors to what would later become the United States often referred to so-called promiscuous Indian woman as whores, a term synonymous in the English language with prostitutes and other sexually immoral women. This assumption allowed white men to justify demands that they either be allowed free access to the Native American women's bodies or be able to buy them as they could lower-class women or women of color in their own societies. It also allowed white women to assume a sense of moral superiority over the supposedly "heathen," uncivilized women and men whose land they were overtaking.

The Puritan religion of a few of the northeastern American colonies condemned all forms of sexual excess and immorality and called on its followers to be clean in both mind and body. Puritan ministers likened the body of a debauched individual, whether man or woman, to the brothel, wherein all manner of unspeakable evils might occur, and redemption was surely lost as a result. Close-knit Puritan communities not only provided materially for their members, minimizing the economic factors that often lead to prostitution, and also ostracized those who crossed sexual taboo lines. A relatively even sex ratio helped channel sexual activity more often than not into marriage. This combination of factors minimized the existence of prostitution in these small New England towns. However, the growth of smaller towns and the influx of new townspeople over the seventeenth and eighteenth centuries resulted in greater social heterogeneity, the fraying of social safety nets, and a decline of ministers' and familial moral sway. Concomitantly, prostitution and other forms of sexual immorality began to rise in these once "pure" communities.

The social and economic situation in the mid-Atlantic colonies, so markedly different from that in New England, ultimately also kept prostitution rates relatively low during the early colonial years. The Europeans who settled in such colonies as Maryland and Virginia held much the same views about sexual morality as did their neighbors to the north; however, skewed sex ratios and residence patterns based on a plantation economy created a situation wherein men vastly outnumbered women and close-knit communities were virtually nonexistent. The practice of indentured servitude drew many young women from Europe and placed them at the mercy of their masters, who often expected sexual favors from them at no cost. In addition to free sexual access to their white servants, white southern men perceived the growing numbers of women of African descent enslaved in these areas as legitimate, free sexual outlets. Although southern colonies banned interracial unions, miscegenation was common among white men and black women.

As urban areas consolidated in the mid- to late-1700s along the Atlantic seaboard, prostitution became an increasingly viable outlet not only for male lust but also for women looking for work. Expanding maritime trade and commerce at ports such as New York and mercantile hubs such as Philadelphia drew sailors and entrepreneurs alike looking for willing female company. Alexander Hamilton reported in 1744 that sexual commerce in New York City was rampant, especially near the battery.

During the French and Indian wars and as the colonies geared up for the War of Independence, soldiers became an increasingly common feature in late eighteenth-century colonial cities, providing a steady trade for prostitutes. During the latter conflict, female camp followers of all classes kept soldiers company and provided such services as laundry, nursing, and cooking; they also quite often worked as prostitutes for the troops, causing concern about the spread of venereal disease among the ranks.

After the American colonies won their independence from Britain and the new United States began its slow but inexorable westward expansion, urban areas such as Philadelphia and New York continued to attract consumers and purveyors of sex. Indeed, sexual commerce exploded in these areas over the nineteenth century. Embracing the liberal and libertine ideals flowing in the young country, male citizens of the City of Brotherly Love during the late eighteenth and early nineteenth centuries frequented the many so-called bawdy houses that peppered the city; women, too, participated in the loose sexual atmosphere of the town. As a result of the promiscuous atmosphere of the time, which permeated all social classes, venereal disease and illegitimate pregnancies were rampant. However, lower-class women—some prostitutes, some not—especially suffered under a system that labeled them (but not the men with whom they had engaged sexually) immoral if they became diseased or pregnant and then abandoned them to an unmerciful urban welfare system. In this atmosphere, prostitution both exemplified sex as a recreational activity and symbolized the dangers of promiscuous sexuality for individuals and society. Prostitution for at least some women, however, remained a viable occupation at this time when wage work for women was sorely limited.

The years from 1820 to 1840 marked a change in the relative autonomy some prostitutes had by that time gained in such cities as New York City. This span of time coincided with a period in women's history that some historians have referred to as the Cult of True Womanhood, wherein respectable women were expected to be religiously pious, sexually pure, and socially subordinate to men in all dimensions of life. Between 1832 and 1838, a series of brothel riots occurred in the city, which, according to the historian Timothy J. Gilfoyle, represented an effort by disgruntled men to regain economic and sexual control over sexually and economically independent women in the city. In 1836, Helen Jewett (the alias of Dorcas Doyen, originally from Maine), an educated, successful, and sought-after prostitute living in a well-known brothel patronized by businessmen and politicians, was murdered by her lover, Richard Robinson, who then tried to incinerate her body to cover the evidence. The press sensationalized Jewett's murder, exposing all of the details of Jewett's life, both sordid and mundane, as well as those of Robinson, who was eventually acquitted of the murder.

Jewett and Robinson riveted public attention; each symbolized Americans' fears of the changing gender roles and relationships of the time. The murdered Jewett, on the one hand, epitomized the proverbial result of walking down the "primrose path," which, respectable folks warned young women, inevitably led to social marginality and, ultimately, death. Yet at the time of her death, Jewett owned clothing and jewelry worth more than $1,500, lived in a fine house, and possessed what most women did not, personal freedom. On the other hand, Robinson represented a new cohort of middle-class young men who were moving to urban areas and seeking employment, and hopefully their fortune, in the professions the city afforded them. Away from the watchful eyes of their communities of origin, supported in their sexual exploits by the homosocial groups in which they socialized, and with spending money in their pockets, these men were part of the newly emerging "sporting male" subculture that quickly thereafter came to be identified with urban life. Both Jewett and Robinson represented unfettered sexuality and the growing independence of young men and women, but the outcomes for their behaviors were radically different. Whereas through his acquittal Robinson received the ultimate validation of sexual license and economic independence, through her murder Jewett received the ultimate punishment for the very same behaviors. Although many New Yorkers clamored for Robinson's punishment, a significant number of others supported Robinson, claiming that Jewett deserved her fate and that no man should be accountable for the death of a whore.

The question of why a woman from such any initially respectable and educated background as Jewett would choose to become a prostitute was one that has perplexed nineteenth- and twentieth-century Americans. William Sanger, the author of *The History of Prostitution* (first published in 1858 and remaining in print well into the twentieth century), asked just that question of over a thousand American prostitutes in the mid-nineteenth century. Expectedly, the largest number answered that economic hardship was the cause. What bothered Sanger and other social reformers of the age, however, was that women gave "inclination," which Sanger explicitly defined to mean sexual desire, as their second most common response. Although, of course, many American women worked outside the home and also had enjoyable sex lives, this last revelation confounded most white, middle-class, Christian Americans who had embraced the domestic ideal of women. The possibility that some women were turning to sex work as a way to engage in sexual activity that they might both enjoy and profit from was a frightening possibility for these Americans, who believed a woman's proper place was in the home (with a man providing for her economically) and that women lacked sexual desire.

The behavior of real American women, many of whom were not middle class, belied this supposed norm of dependence and frigidity. By the late 1870s and early 1880s, mining towns flourished everywhere in the American West. Towns such as Butte, Montana; Cripple Creek, Colorado; Virginia City, Nevada; and Deadwood, South Dakota, grew overnight from small camps to booming cities. Mining was the magnet drawing people to these newly formed communities, and gender and age ratios in these new boomtowns often were skewed toward adult males, to whom canny prostitutes were quickly drawn. Women of all races, classes, and backgrounds headed west looking to make their fortunes (albeit in a bit different manner from the men who preceded them) in the goldfields of California, silver smelters of Nevada, and copper mines of Montana.

Families followed the gold-digging men and women a few years later, creating a more civilized feel and bringing with them the more respectable markers of community—schools, churches, and theaters—which co-existed alongside the less respectable—saloons, gambling halls, and brothels. This mix of frontier and civilization led often to antiprostitution campaigns, wherein respectable, pious men and women, many of whom were members of such reform groups as the Women's Christian Temperance Union, did their best to eradicate prostitution from their midst. Such efforts were typically futile, however, until the Progressive Era. Indeed, western towns came to be known as much for their hard-drinking miners and loggers as for the "sisters of joy" who lived by their sides.

Although frontier life was often hard and many prostitutes died of disease and accidents or were murdered, some women who sold sex in western towns created a decent life for themselves. The truism promoted by social reformers that a prostitute's life span was no more than five years, as she progressed from high-class whore to suicidal drunk, was the exception to the rule. Instead, western prostitutes followed a more common trajectory, entering prostitution when they were young and performing sex work, often in a transient manner, to make ends meet or to get ahead financially before moving on to another occupation or marriage. Some worked as prostitutes until they married and settled down, either in the same vicinity or another western community where their past was not so well known, and resumed a more "respectable" life. Others continued to work in the sex trade after marriage, sometimes as prostitutes, sometimes as madams. Still others, such as Nevada City's Julia Bulette or Seattle's Lou Graham, became prominent members of their communities, contributing time and money to philanthropic causes, business development, and political campaigns.

Just like in other groups of workers, prostitutes throughout the nineteenth and early twentieth centuries functioned within a hierarchy in very different kinds of work environments. The historical sociologist Marion Goldman, who studied prostitution on the Comstock Lode in late nineteenth-century Nevada, found that this stratification resulted from a number of conditions in these women's work lives: whether the unions were clandestine or flagrantly solicited; the subtlety with which a prostitute asked for payment; whether a woman had talents or attributes other than sexual ones; how many men a woman was involved with; whether she was expensive or cheap; and the social class of the men who patronized her. Goldman found that women perceived to be higher class were those whose services were clandestine; who did not openly ask for payment; who were educated or had some talent, such as acting or dancing; and who limited their encounters to one or only a couple upper-class men who could afford her expensive fee.

This hierarchy did not exist only in Nevada. Almost every study of prostitution has outlined a very similar kind of class distinction among sex workers, with local variations. Typically, madams and higher-class prostitutes, especially in the late nineteenth and early twentieth century brothels of New Orleans, New York, Chicago, or San Francisco, lived in sumptuous surroundings where men of means and power, often the most respected and connected persons in their communities, could not only have sex with a beautiful and often well-educated, accomplished woman but also socialize with other wealthy men, conduct business transactions, drink alcohol, dance, and sometimes just sleep. A famous example of this kind of establishment was the Everleigh Club, which was run by Minna and Ada Everleigh (aka Lester), two sisters from Kentucky who left acting careers to open a brothel first in Omaha, Nebraska, and then in Chicago. The Everleigh sisters' opulent house and wealthy clientele made them both famous and rich. When their doors finally closed as a result of pressure from the Chicago Vice Commission and the mayor, rumors circulated that they had made a million dollars in their chosen profession. The exact amount of their profits is unknown, but the sisters did live out the rest of their lives quite comfortably in New York City.

Some elite prostitutes were women who moved in and out of other more respectable occupations, such as acting, dancing, or secretarial work, whom a man might "keep" as a mistress by paying for her rent, clothing, and food in exchange for occasional sexual encounters. Middle-class prostitutes in urban areas often worked together out of apartments or furnished rooms, sharing expenses and arranging "dates" so as not to coincide with each other's schedule; others worked within the "call girl" system whereby a central dispatcher took "orders" and sent the appropriate "dish" out to the client. Lower classes of sex workers typically worked out of small, dirty cribs, where they performed no-frills sex acts as quickly as possible for 50 cents to $5; others walked the streets looking for johns, who would often receive sexual services in their cars or in taxis, or who would take the prostitute to a cheap motel or houses of assignation that rented by the hour.

Another hierarchy among prostitutes was based on race. African-American and other ethnic and immigrant women were at the bottom of the hierarchy. Many black prostitutes earned far less than did white prostitutes, were arrested more often than were whites, and had fewer options for leaving the business than did their white counterparts. Although they functioned at the bottom of the social hierarchy, black prostitutes sometimes were able to use to their advantage deeply held white stereotypes of black men and black women as hypersexual (a stereotype that served not only to justify white male access to black women throughout the nineteenth and twentieth centuries but also to justify white male persecution of black men whom they accused of raping "pure" white women). Vice investigators in both early twentieth-century Chicago and New Orleans, for example, found black women marketing their so-called heated sexual nature to potential white customers.

Althea, a mixed-race Chicago prostitute, promised that she and her colleague could give two undercover cops a better "jazzin" (slang for sex) than a white girl, and she savvily noted that their fee was less than that of white prostitutes. Although they typically made less overall than white women, evidence shows that black women often charged white men more than they charged black men for their sexual services and sometimes catered only to better-paying white customers.

Although African-American women in the United States have suffered sexual exploitation at the hands of white men ever since the first slave ships arrived from Africa, not all black women were at the bottom of the commercial sex work ladder in the nineteenth and twentieth centuries. In southern cities—New Orleans, for example—mixed-race women (typically referred to as octoroons or quadroons, depending on the percentage of African-American blood in their heritage) often commanded larger fees from white men than did their white counterparts. The brothels of such famous mixed-race madams as Lulu White and "Countess" Willie V. Piazza attracted high-class prostitutes and wealthy men and had reputations as being some of the best houses in the city. Perhaps ironically, at a time when racial segregation was becoming institutionalized in the Jim Crow South,

Piazza's house was a "whites only" establishment. Just as ironically, as the historian Alecia P. Long has noted, New Orleans's octoroon prostitutes were able to maintain their political clout through close contact with powerful white men. Many of these women were able to weather the growing storm of institutionalized racism and not only continue to move in high-class social circles but also acquire significant financial and material wealth because of (not in spite of) their mixed-race, prostitute status.

In the early twentieth century, an outcry from social reformers arose against the so-called white slave trade in the United States. Spurred on by anti-immigrant sentiment, most notably against Southern and Eastern European men, many of whom were Catholic or Jewish, white Progressive Era reformers, most of whom came from "old immigrant" families of Northern European, Protestant stock, published numerous tracts warning families to "protect" their young daughters who were coming to the cities from their rural homes. Unsuspecting young virgins were easy prey for the evil men who awaited their arrival in the city, men who would seduce them and then send them off to work as sex slaves, often drugged and always against their will. In response to the growing hysteria among social reformers concerned with white slavery, Congress passed the Mann Act in 1910, which banned the transportation of women across state lines for the purpose of prostitution. Although a sex trade undoubtedly existed, arrests made under the Mann Act turned on its head the belief that ethnic men were selling white women as sex slaves. Instead, more white, native-born men were prosecuted under the Act than any other ethnic group combined; furthermore, the women whom these men were convicted of trafficking in were more often than not women from immigrant ethnic groups or lower classes, not the white, middle-class farm girls reformers had worried about. Indeed, it was Asians who most often filled the ranks of the real sex slaves in American society in the late nineteenth and early twentieth centuries.

Most prostitutes fell somewhere near the bottom of the sex work hierarchy. But the dream of repeating the Everleigh sisters' success lured many women into the sex trade, while low wages and miserable working conditions pushed those same women out of more traditional lower-class jobs, such as domestic work, factory work, or the sewing trades. Indeed, a significant number of prostitutes had formerly been live-in domestic workers, a job that most women loathed because of the long hours and strenuous labor. Many domestic workers chose to become prostitutes, noting that the work was less demanding of their time and effort and that they at least got paid for what their former male employers often expected for free. Although some reformers sympathized with the plight of such lower-class women, many of whom were African-Americans or other ethnic minorities, most of society castigated their greed and accused them of "sinning for silk," a veiled condemnation of their desire to gain upward mobility or cross entrenched color and gender lines through disrespectable means.

Women's tenuous economic status outside of the family or marriage also created situations that forced them into prostitution. The death of a father, husband, or brother who had been the sole provider; one's own sickness or that of a family member; or divorce could easily send a middle-class woman from a life of leisure to one of prostitution. Madeleine, a nineteenth-century prostitute, was born into a middle-class family and was plunged into poverty and ultimately turned to prostitution when her father died suddenly at an early age.

The experiences of Maimie Pinzer, an early twentieth-century East Coast Russian Jew, provide other examples of factors leading to prostitution. Maimie, who by all appearances was an intelligent and motivated young woman, tried hard to be "respectable," even starting her own mimeographing business at one point with a female partner. Nonetheless, she faced constant barriers to landing or keeping a job: chauvinism, sexual harassment, employers' revulsion when they saw that she was missing an eye, and so on. As a result, Maimie often resorted to prostitution to supplement what income she could make through more respectable means or to enjoy a nice meal out when she was hungry. She was also financially hobbled by her unwillingness to remain married to a man for whom she felt no passion, simply because he loved her and usually provided enough income to keep her from needing to prostitute herself. Maimie felt guilty about selling sex for money and saw her willingness to do so as a moral flaw in herself, and yet she was also quite pragmatic about the inequities women like herself faced in urban American in the early twentieth century. Her experience was likely representative of many young women at the time, who blurred the lines between prostitution and what historians have called "treating," wherein a woman traded sexual favors for entertainment, food, or other goods and services. Like Maimie, these women crossed in and out of commercial sex as needed, and often held "regular" jobs and were married, separated, or divorced from men who knew about and accepted, if not promoted, their forays into prostitution.

Nineteenth-century municipal governments and state legislatures in the United States toyed with the idea of legalizing or regulating (and taxing) prostitution. New Orleans's city council, for example, voted in 1857 to tax its prostitutes and to establish a licensing system. The experiment was short-lived for ironic reasons. Madame Emma Pickett reluctantly applied in May 1857 for a license to operate a bordello; two years later, however, she sued the city to recover the fee she had paid for the license. The courts upheld her side of the case and declared the law unconstitutional. Although states such as New York and cities such as San Francisco debated off and on whether to legalize or regulate prostitution in the same manner as England or Paris had in the mid-1800s, only two American cities experimented with such legislation in the nineteenth century: St. Louis, Missouri, which enacted regulated prostitution in 1870 (but then quickly repealed), and New Orleans, which created two limited areas in which prostitution was legal (one that serviced predominantly white clients and one that serviced predominantly black customers). Although these attempts were short-lived, they indicate that many Americans recognized prostitution was a business and its practitioners performing a service, however distasteful middle-class Americans might find it.

The business of prostitution permeated nineteenth- and twentieth-century life much as did any other service industry of the time. Landlords generated huge incomes from properties rented to brothels, often charging exorbitant rents to their disrespectable tenants on the one hand while participating in respectable religious, business, or political roles on the other. Additionally, prostitutes and brothels patronized local laundry services, grocers, florists, seamstresses, milliners, alcohol distributors, and many other merchants and service providers. Finally, the fines and bribes prostitutes paid to municipalities and police officers, along with the money they gave to their madams and pimps, rounded out the informal economy of sex work. Indeed, their financial contribution to local economies was often crucial to community development in some neighborhoods.

Prostitutes have lived by the adage, "Whatever you have to sell, it pays to advertise," doing so through such media as New Orleans's famous *Blue Books* and other such sporting guides to American cities, as well as by sitting in street-side windows displaying their wares, strolling down a boulevard exchanging coy glances with potential customers, or in later times, taking out ads in the *Yellow Pages*. Furthermore, many prostitutes and their panderers have realized that it takes money to make money, investing in clothes, props, and other tools of the trade with which to entice and pleasure their customers.

A major change in the history of prostitution occurred in the first and second decades of the twentieth century. With roots in the earlier purity crusades of the late nineteenth century, Progressive Era antivice campaigns took a new, more scientific approach to eradicating what they now referred to as the "social evil." Reformers from various backgrounds—from fiery ministers to ardent feminists to shrewd politicians—joined together to investigate vice and promote "social hygiene" around the country. The vice commission studies of New York and Chicago were the most prominent, with both of those cities publishing famous reports, both titled *The Social Evil*, in 1902 and 1912, respectively. However, more than 40 cities around the country held their own investigations and published their findings in reports with smaller distribution but perhaps no less impact in their individual communities.

Although prostitutes are stereotypically female, men have also worked as prostitutes in the United States. In the late nineteenth and early twentieth centuries, especially, urban areas exploded in size, providing anonymity and a subculture for homosexual men and women. The presence of gay districts, many of which overlapped with sex districts on the edges of such minority neighborhoods as Harlem or Chicago's Black Belt, provided a new kind of sexual service for interested male customers. As the historian George Chauncey Jr. has revealed, straight male access to the sexual services of both gay-identified and straight-identified men had increased dramatically in New York City by the 1910s and 1920s with streetwalking "fairies" and "wolves" frequenting such areas as Times Square and less conspicuous male prostitutes working out of brothels around the city. Far less common, but available for those willing to pay, male and female prostitutes sometimes serviced female customers. However, such cases were by far the least common. Then, as now, men have consumed the vast majority of sexual services available.

A result of Progressive Era vice reform, among its other municipal outcomes, was what has been called the "closing of the red lights." One of the most famous of these districts, in which the sex trade and other vices were tolerated, if not legal, was New Orleans's Storyville, a district named for the alderman Sidney Story, who proposed the ordinance creating the city's segregated sex district in 1898. The district was "named" in his honor, despite the vehement protests of Story, who was himself against prostitution but believed containment was the only remedy for a vice that most people perceived to be a "necessary evil" and that was unlikely to disappear. The name stuck, though, and Storyville was soon reported to have over two thousand prostitutes working out of over two hundred brothels, cabarets, and other such establishments. Just 20 years later, though, another city ordinance officially closed the district. Although

Storyville still boasted eight hundred prostitutes at that time, it had lost its former glory. The combination of this decline, Progressive Era vice campaigns, and wartime fears of soldiers contracting venereal disease from prostitutes were the nails in Storyville's coffin. Similar impulses nationwide led to widespread closures of vice districts both legal and illegal in just a few years. As a result, prostitution, in effect, went underground.

By 1920, although the red lights had effectively been extinguished, prostitution remained. The sex business, however, changed. Whereas before 1920 prostitution had been a predominantly woman-run and woman-staffed business (with a handful of male owners and male brothels thrown into the mix), after 1920, men increasingly controlled the sale of women's bodies through more organized groups, such as the Mafia, as well as through individual pimps, who provided protection to prostitutes made more vulnerable to prosecution as a result of the Progressive Era reforms. The advent of the automobile and the increasing availability of such technologies as the telephone also transformed sex work after 1920. So-called streetwalkers became more common as johns could pull up and pick them up on the street and either take them to hourly motels or houses of assignation or else receive their services in the privacy of their private vehicles or taxicabs. Call-girl services became more common, too, providing a central phone number to clients and then sending girls out to a home, business, or hotel in response to customers' requests.

Streetwalking, call-girl services, and a few remaining brothels predominated the sex trade throughout the middle of the twentieth century, with massage parlors, peep shows, and burlesque and strip clubs rounding out the kinds of sexual services available to customers. Autobiographies of madams and prostitutes published in the mid-twentieth century and Alfred Kinsey's controversial studies of male and female sexuality published in 1948 and 1953 attested to the continued existence of prostitution between 1920 and 1970, but researchers devoted little study to prostitutes or prostitution during those years, as the U.S. public worried more about the Cold War than about vestiges of the late nineteenth- and early twentieth-century heyday of commercial sex. However, events coalesced in the late 1960s and early 1970s to put prostitution back on the public radar screen. Legalization of the birth control pill in 1960 and then abortion in 1973, freer sexual attitudes surrounding the so-called second sexual revolution, and the "second wave" of feminism dramatically increased women's control over sexuality and reproduction. At the same time, two events returned attention to prostitution in American society: the legalization of prostitution in the perhaps aptly named Storey County, Nevada, in 1971 (four other counties quickly followed suit) and the publication of Xaviera Hollander's *The Happy Hooker* in 1972.

Xaviera Hollander, a Dutch transplant to the United States who proclaimed that she made a fortune on her back and loved every minute of it, represented for many "liberated" women the epitome of a woman's control over her own body and her ability to gain economic freedom through sex work. Similarly, Nevada brothel owners capitalized on their ability to attract male customers and female employees to their establishments by claims to having disease-free, happy hookers who enjoyed all the benefits of more traditional employees. Such claims to prostitutes' choice and control over their work and bodies quickly led to a bitter division among feminists in the 1970s and 1980s. Whereas so-called sex-positive (or pro-sex) feminists usually agreed that not all prostitutes were victims and that some women found pleasure and power in performing sex work, other feminists vehemently denied the ability of any sex worker to claim that she had choice or control, arguing instead that prostitution was the ultimate symbol of men's sexual exploitation of women and therefore must be eradicated completely from society.

Although sex-positive feminists conceded that there was a wide spectrum of reasons that women (and men) chose prostitution—from coercion to choice—they nevertheless wished for prostitutes to be accorded the same status as other workers. Such activists wished to alter negative perceptions of prostitution, referring to the job instead as "sex work" and to its practitioners as "sex workers" and advocating for decriminalization and even regulation of the sex trade. In response to this shift in thinking about the nature of sex work and its practitioners, such organizations as COYOTE (Call Off Your Old Tired Ethics, 1973) and U.S. PROS (U.S. Prostitutes' Collective, 1980) formed to advocate for prostitutes' rights. COYOTE, for example, was founded by Margo St. James in 1973 to work for the repeal of the prostitution laws and an end to the stigma associated with sexual work.

Antiprostitution feminists formed other prostitutes' rights groups, such as WHISPER (Women Hurt in Systems of Prostitution Engaged in Revolt). These organizations coalesced around members who, in opposition to those in pro-sex and pro-sex work organizations, believed all prostitutes were victims and that all prostitution was an indicator of men's sexual exploitation of women.

Although each of these prostitutes' rights organizations had (or has) different—and sometimes oppositional—underlying ideologies and goals, the majority have approximated more traditional types of labor organizations. Legalization and decriminalization, such as had occurred in Nevada, according to U.S. PROS, created "the new sex assembly lines" of the world (West, p. 279) and actually deprived women of their rights by allowing employers and even the state to control their labor. Instead, COYOTE and U.S. PROS (which was formed as part of the larger International Wages for Housework Campaign) advocated complete abolition of laws against prostitute women in order to return women's ability to choose prostitution as a viable business option and maintain control over their working conditions and wages. Prostitutes' rights advocates clearly distinguished between voluntary and forced prostitution, and they also were adamantly against any use of children or unwilling individuals in sex work. However, they argued, adult women who chose to sell sex for money should be accorded the same rights as other service workers. The fact that prostitutes were providing sex instead of clean sheets or someone's dinner, prostitutes' rights advocates proclaimed, should not alter the simple fact that sex workers are workers.

Although the number of prostitutes' rights organizations exponentially increased in the 1970s and 1980s, COYOTE, U.S. PROS, and the like apparently were not, however, the first such organizations for prostitutes. Although the research to date is slim, evidence from late nineteenth-century New Orleans suggests that madams in that city formed a benevolent association, much like those formed for workers in other fields (firemen, police, insurance salesmen, and the like), called the Venus and Bacchus Society. Such formal or informal networks or organizations likely existed in other urban areas that contained large numbers of prostitutes and their affiliated businesses.

At the end of the twentieth century and the beginning of the twenty-first, sex work once again transformed. Traditional prostitution, escort services, stripping, massage parlors, and live sex shows still existed, but new technologies also fostered the rise of phone sex, Internet sex, high-definition pornography, and even virtual sex—all geared (perhaps ironically) toward facilitating solitary masturbation. Additionally, sex workers of both genders saw a rise in the business of bondage and other fetish-oriented services, both heterosexual and homosexual in nature. Transsexual and transvestite sex workers were increasingly obvious, perhaps most notably in their drag performances but also as streetwalkers selling sex to customers.

The Work of Sex

According to such English-language dictionaries as Merriam-Webster's, prostitution is the exchange of sex for money. Most dictionaries do not gender the act of prostitution. A "prostitute," however, is first defined as a woman who sells sex for money. The second definition is a man who does so, especially those who engage in homosexual practices for pay. In both cases, the heteronormative implication is that men—often referred to as "johns," a term that the dictionary defines specifically as coming from the masculine name John—are the customers. No word exists in the English language for a women who purchases sex, whether it be from a man or a woman, although the term "gigolo" refers to a man supported by a woman, usually in return for his attentions, the nature of which the dictionaries never outline (although they explicitly refer to prostitutes as selling sex).

Thus, prostitution is an economic exchange in which women, and to a lesser degree men, provide services to male, and to an almost invisible degree, female customers. Just as, for example, waitresses provide food service to hungry customers or nurses succor suffering patients, prostitutes' labor is the performance of sex acts designed to produce orgasm in their aroused customers. However, despite the labor-intensive and service-oriented nature of sex work and the supposed truism that prostitution is the "oldest profession," labor historians, even those who study women's labors, have devoted considerably less attention to prostitutes and prostitution than they have to other occupations.

Prostitutes engage in a wide variety of sex acts—sometimes pleasurable, often distasteful, meaningless, or violent—with multiple partners for pay on the job. Additionally, they construct a separate sexual persona when off the clock. By doing so, prostitutes are both agents and victims—agents in that they choose to perform certain sex tasks as part of their workaday life but also victims because they must also appeal to (and presumably sate) customers' desire in order to earn a living.

According to prostitutes' historical and contemporary accounts, the fantasies they appeal to and the sex acts they sell represent both savvy marketing and the limits of what they will and will not do as part of their daily work requirements. This might mean offering fellatio instead of intercourse, because the former is less work for equal or the same pay, while refusing to kiss her customer on the mouth, because it would allow him to cross a barrier she maintains while "on the clock." She still must satisfy her customer's need for orgasm by offering the service that will get the job done; yet, she finds ways to maintain her sense of self while doing so. Thinking about prostitutes' work as a task, rather than a value-laden sexual act, reveals that the binary of agent/victim does not necessarily hold up in the commercial sex environment. Sex as work complicates traditional distinctions between prostitutes and other women, most of whom sell or trade their services in some form.

Striking images of Nevada brothels taken in the late twentieth century "read" alongside prostitutes' and madams' autobiographical writing from the same time reveal to labor historians and historians of sexuality alike the importance of the quotidian nature of the work prostitutes perform. Examination of images and memoirs reveals that prostitutes surrounded themselves not only with the tricks of their undoubtedly skilled trade but also with the tools, marketing sexual allure and performance to each customer in assembly-line fashion. Nineteenth- and twentieth-century brothels alike created a fantasy environment for customers. Although fashions undoubtedly changed from the 1880s to the 1980s, the environment in which many prostitutes worked also provided the tricks—red velvet walls, mirrors, erotic images, heart-shaped beds, and an occasional S and M or fetish closet—while each sexual performance space also contained the tools—lotion, condoms, porn, plastic-lined trash cans, the requisite sink, and an occasional bidet.

Furthermore, sex workers saw themselves as business owners and workers, professionals in all senses of that term and with similar hierarchies as other professions. As such, prostitution has had a well-developed work culture and identity. Although sex work encompasses sex tasks and marketed fantasy, it is also on a daily level quite routine and repetitive and, at least internally, contains little of the stereotypical stigma that outsiders attach to the women who do the work. Indeed, most prostitutes view their work as simply a job, which, as does any job, has ups and downs, plusses and minuses, and ins and outs (pun fully intended). Like factory workers, prostitutes have been expected to maximize their labor costs by turning as many tricks as possible in as short a time as possible. Pictures of Nevada brothels, for example, reveal panels of timers with which to regulate exactly how much service a girl would provide for her fee. Although the tricks and tools of the trade have changed over time, the inextricably interconnected nature of sex/sexuality (be it fantasy, sexual performance, or a sexual/work identity in the more modern sense) and work tasks and culture have remained much the same.

HEATHER LEE MILLER

References and Further Reading

Adler, Jeffrey S. "Streetwalkers, Degraded Outcasts, and Good-for-Nothing Huzzies: Women and the Dangerous Class in Antebellum St. Louis." *Journal of Social History* 25, no. 4 (Summer 1992): 737–755.

Butler, Anne. *Daughters of Joy, Sisters of Misery*. Urbana: University of Illinois Press, 1985.

Cohen, Patricia Cline. *The Murder of Helen Jewett: The Life and Death of a Prostitute in Nineteenth-Century New York*. New York: Knopf, 1998.

Delacoste, Frédérique, and Priscilla Alexander, eds. *Sex Work: Writings by Women in the Trade*. 2nd ed. San Francisco: Cleis Press, 1998.

Gilfoyle, Timothy J. *City of Eros: New York City Prostitution and the Commercialization of Sex, 1820–1920*. New York: W. W. Norton, 1992.

———. "Prostitutes in History: From Parables of Pornography to Metaphors of Modernity." *American Historical Review* 104 (February 1999): 117–141.

Mackey, Thomas C. *Criminal Law Reform, Defending Character, and New York City's Committee of Fourteen, 1920–1930*. Columbus: Ohio State University Press, 2005.

Meyerowitz, Joanne. "Sexual Geography and Gender Economy: The Furnished Room Districts of Chicago, 1890–1930." *Gender and History* 2, no. 3 (Autumn 1990): 274–296.

Miller, Heather Lee. "Trick Identities: The Nexus of Work and Sex." *Journal of Women's History* 15, no. 4 (Winter 2004): 145–152.

Mumford, Kevin J. *Interzones: Black/White Sex Districts in Chicago and New York in the Early Twentieth Century*. New York: Columbia University Press, 1997.

Peiss, Kathy. *Cheap Amusements: Working Women and Leisure in Turn-of-the-Century New York*. Philadelphia: Temple University Press, 1986.

Pivar, David. J. *Purity and Hygiene: Women, Prostitution, and the "American Plan," 1900–1930*. Westport, CT: Greenwood Press, 2002.

———. *Purity Crusade: Sexual Morality and Social Control, 1868–1900*. Westport, CT: Greenwood Press, 1973.

Rosen, Ruth. *The Lost Sisterhood*. Baltimore: Johns Hopkins University Press, 1982.

Tong, Benson. *Unsubmissive Women: Chinese Prostitutes in Nineteenth-Century San Francisco*. Norman: University of Oklahoma Press, 1994.

PROTOCOL OF PEACE

On July 7, 1910, the cloakmakers' "Great Revolt" began, as almost 50,000 members of the International Ladies' Garment Workers' Union (ILGWU) in New York City walked off their jobs. As work ground to a halt throughout the city, diverse actors moved to reshape the future of industrial relations. Involvement came from many fronts. Meyer Bloomfield, a prominent Boston social worker and industrial reformer, began an effort to end the strike on behalf of A. Lincoln Filene, the owner of the Boston department store Filene's. Bloomfield, Filene, and others had been involved with "the labor question" for some time by 1910. Both had been active in the national and regional National Civic Federation. Both had experience with the ladies' garment industry and Jewish labor. On July 21, Bloomfield met with manufacturers, to offer his services in settling the strike. The next day, Bloomfield met with Julius Henry Cohen, the lawyer for the manufacturers. On July 21, Bloomfield wrote to the famed Boston attorney Louis Brandeis and explained how he laid the foundation for talks and that Brandeis should come and lead them.

Brandeis left for New York on July 23, writing his brother Alfred that "I was called to N.Y. Saturday p.m. to try to settle the N.Y. Garment Workers' strike." He took with him a "draft of a proposed labor agreement." This draft included several ideas, the most important of which was the request that the union give up its demand for a closed or union shop. Brandeis told the 20 men assembled that they were witnessing an important moment in history, the birth of a new system of industrial relations. Brandeis's proposed settlement called for a novel approach: an industrywide agreement, a limited form of industrial democracy, a "preferential shop," health and safety regulations, a grievance mechanism, and an industry-standard wage policy.

The union at first rejected the new plan, holding out for a closed union shop rather than mere preference for union members. But an injunction barring picketing, coupled with the activities of Filene and Brandeis, forced the ILGWU's General Executive Board to rethink the strike. The union finally officially dropped its demand for the closed shop. And on September 2, the two lawyers for each side met to draw up a settlement. The Protocol established "a kind of industrial self-government" that Brandeis had been trying to establish for some time. There were three parts to the Protocol. First were the normal labor contract issues of hours, wages, and paid holidays. In this regard, the Protocol was better than most contracts of the day, clearly better than garment workers ever saw. The second part involved features unique to the garment industry: abolition of charges for electricity and supplies; the establishment of shop committees to establish a just piece rate; and most revolutionary, a Joint Board of Sanitary Control—a committee made up of representatives of both the union and the association who would oversee working conditions. The third and most important part of the Protocol was the implementation of Brandeis's conceptions of efficiency and industrial democracy.

The centerpiece of Brandeis's program for industrial democracy was clearly the preferential shop, the ban on all strikes and lockouts, and the establishment of grievance and arbitration mechanisms. Crucial was the last clause and agreement, on the preferential shop, which, in effect, recognized the union shop indirectly. As the garment industry expert Benjamin Stolberg states, "The clause was as effective, for the union's purpose, as if the full closed shop had been adopted" because the union could always supply workers.

A central aspect of the Protocol was the attempt to rationalize, standardize, and Taylorize the garment industry. All work stoppages would be eliminated. Work would continue as grievances were arbitrated. As a tripartite agreement between labor, management, and the public, the Protocol steered the industry into the modernity of an industrial consumer society. In exchange for giving union leadership some authority, the Protocol mandated industrial self-management. In essence, the association expected the ILGWU to police its own members for the benefit of the industry. The union was to supply "efficient" workers and ensure continuous and rational production. If the union could do this effectively, workers would benefit. By controlling its own members, the union brought to industry what the manufacturers could not: stability and rationality. One measure for the Protocol's success could be seen in both the unionization that followed and by the new role for union leaders and outside arbitrators. Union leaders could be cheered by swelling membership rolls, as with the increased authority and respectability the Protocol vested in them. In 1910, the New York City cloakmakers represented three fourths of the entire ILGWU membership. The agreement covered 1,796 out of a possible 1,829 shops. By 1912, 90% of all cloakmakers were in the union. Manufacturers could take a measure of hope that the anarchy and chaos of the seasonal wildcat strikes were over as all garment workers were being brought into a disciplined and maturing labor union. The signing of the Protocol of Peace finally institutionalized for the cloakmakers, and then for the whole industry, some of the major features that the shirtwaist workers had struggled for in 1909.

The structure of the Protocol intended to impose efficiency and rationality on a chaotic industry. Bringing industrial hygienists, reformers, shop owners, and workers together, it sought to contribute to the larger discourse on the role of work in the newly forming consumer society and on the rights of management and workers in an industrial society. Most shared the opinion that the current situation was chaotic. The Protocol's answer was the principle of layered bureaucracy, which Protocolists envisioned as an industrial version of our nation's constitutional checks and balances.

At the top of this system stood the Board of Arbitration, which consisted of three members: one from management, one from labor, and Brandeis, who represented the public. All decisions of the Board were binding. Below it was the Committee on Grievances, which consisted of four members, two from each side, which acted as a conciliation agency. This committee heard all grievances filed by either side. A majority vote brought settlement, meaning at least one member from the other side had to switch. Only if a deadlock occurred—which happened, as we will see, all too often—would it go to the Board of Arbitration.

Another remarkable feature of the Protocol was the Board of Sanitary Control. This was a prototypical Progressive Era reform effort. This Board consisted of seven members, two from the union, two from management and the remainder chosen by the four to represent the public. Its first order of business was a systematic investigation into the sanitary conditions of the cloak, suit, and skirt industry. This was one of the first full-scale public health surveys of the industry. The Sanitary Board did not, at first, have enforcement powers. Its power lay in its ability to marshal public outrage against unsanitary conditions. Members of this board had great faith in the public at large, believing that if they only knew the true conditions, they would become outraged and demand action. The most dramatic of these new sources was the authorizing of "sanitation strikes." Under the sanitation provisions of the Protocol, workers would be allowed to strike over unsanitary conditions authorized by the Sanitation Board. In addition, the Board developed a sanitary certificate that shop owners had to hang in their shops to show they were in complete compliance with the sanitary features of the Protocol.

While the machinery of the Protocol was being put into place, Protocolists began to spread the agreement to other sectors of the ladies' garment industry in New York City. To prove their thesis about the Protocol's revolutionary potential, they needed to demonstrate its potential to bring peace to an entire industry. Thus, even before the bugs were worked out of the initial settlement, Brandeis and company were seeking to implement the Protocol in new sectors of the ladies' garment industry.

The union and the association hit on a novel way to organize the industry and thereby spread the protocol to all sectors of the garment industry: an orchestrated general strike. Both sides embarked upon a co-ordinated effort to quickly and painlessly rationalize the industry. First, the association provided the union with a list of all member shops. The union, in turn, pledged to pressure all nonmember shops to join the association. Last, both agreed to a general strike to organize both workers and employers in the industry. The association stated that "unless the union . . .

as a result of the 'general strike' enroll[ed] in its membership the bulk of the workers in the industry" the agreement would certainly fail. It was clear, then, that these strikes were, from their inception, a tool to organize not just the workforce, but the entire industry. By the end of March, the Protocol had come to encompass the entirety of the ladies' garment industry. Reformers and the press heralded these events, but few anticipated the problems that would soon arise. To many outside of the rank and file, the Protocol was a magic bullet, an inoculation against class disruption and an "uncivilized" economy. Blind to the realities of the day-to-day functioning of Protocolism, the public soon moved on to other concerns. While on the surface the Protocol seemed to be functioning as planned, problems were smoldering beneath. The Protocol mechanisms were bureaucracy embodied. The Arbitration Board sped up the centralizing mission of the new labor system that the Protocol had unleashed. It took almost all authority from workers and the shop floor and placed it in centralized and regulated bodies dominated by industrial experts. The Protocol officially ended with the settlement of the 1916 strike, though sections such as the Board of Sanitary Control lasted for decades more.

RICHARD A. GREENWALD

References and Further Reading

Bender, Daniel E. *Sweated Work, Weak Bodies: Anti-Sweatshop Campaigns and Languages of Labor.* New Brunswick, NJ: Rutgers University Press, 2004.

Carpenter, Jesse Thomas. *Competition and Collective Bargaining in the Needle Trades, 1910–1967.* Ithaca, NY: ILR Press, 1972.

Greenwald, Richard A. *The Triangle Fire, the Protocols of Peace, and Industrial Democracy in Progressive Era New York.* Philadelphia: Temple University Press, 2005.

PUBLIC-SECTOR UNIONISM

From the early 1960s to the present, public-sector unions have been the major success story of American labor. From the early 1960s to today, public-sector union density rose from less than 12% to around 40%; meanwhile, from the mid-1950s to today, private-sector union density declined from more than 33% to less than 10%. Also, by the year 2000, about 40% of all union members were public workers. This counters some conventional wisdom about the American working class. Counting those who, for example, clean public schools as "workers" reveals an American working class quite receptive to the labor movement.

Yet the history of public-sector unions is studied much less than the history of private-sector unions.

Perhaps this is because government employees are still stereotyped as bureaucrats, not authentic "workers." But public workers fought long and hard for the right to unionize and did so for the same reasons as private-sector workers. Also, despite their successes, public-sector unions have still not won even the basic right to bargain collectively on a national scale. A sizable minority of states still do not grant any public employees the right to bargain, and many states deny bargaining rights to significant categories of public workers.

Throughout American history, public workers have encountered the claim that governmental labor relations are entirely distinct from private-sector labor relations. In 1920, Senator Charles Thomas (D-CO) stated that the "fundamental idea lying at the foundation of organized labor . . . has been the assumption ...of an antagonism of interest and of purpose between employer and employee....That situation cannot be applied to public employment."

Unionists articulated a different vision. Public workers had "grievances just the same as men in other walks of life," insisted Boston's labor newspaper in 1919. "Government workers who are unorganized can be and are exploited as cruelly as unorganized workers in private industry," echoed the newspaper of the Transportation Workers Union (TWU) in 1942 (Slater, *Public Workers*, pp. 1, 27, 193).

Policy makers still treat public and private employees quite differently. Yet public employees have struggled for over a century to organize into unions to improve wages, hours, and conditions of work and to have an effective voice in their working lives. The question of how these desires should be balanced against concerns of democracy (determining policies based on public choices) and public budgets has been at the center of public-sector labor relations policies.

Studying public-sector unions provides a different picture of labor history, generally depicted solely as a rise and decline of private-sector unions. Further, it demonstrates another way in which American labor was "exceptional." In comparable countries, public workers have long been accorded most or all of the same rights as private-sector workers. It also demonstrates a variety of political strategies and tactics labor has used, largely distinctive to the public sector.

The "False Dawn" and the Boston Police Strike of 1919

Public employees began forming unions in the mid-nineteenth century. Organized public employees were typically members of mostly private-sector unions, for example, skilled workers in naval yards. Public workers in Philadelphia won the 10-hour day after a protest in 1835. In 1867, the National Labor Union unsuccessfully called for the closed shop in public employment. The different tactics public workers would use and the different responses those tactics provoked were highlighted in 1895 when the postmaster general, William Wilson, barred any employee from visiting Washington to influence legislation affecting his or her employment. In 1905, the Chicago Electricity Department signed the first known formal labor contract between a municipal public employer and a union. In 1906, the American Federation of Labor (AFL) created its first national union of government workers, the National Federation of Post Office Clerks.

Public-sector organizing began to take off around the time of World War I. The AFL chartered the American Federation of Teachers (AFT) in 1916, and in 1918, the AFT grew from 2,000 to 11,000 members. In 1917, the AFL established a union for employees of the federal government (the National Federation of Federal Employees), and in that same year, the National Association of Letter Carriers and the Railway Mail Carriers affiliated with the AFL. In 1918, the AFL created the International Association of Fire Fighters (IAFF); from 1918 to 1919 alone, the number of IAFF locals increased from 82 to 262. In 1910, union density in the public sector was around 3.5%; from 1915 to 1921, it went from 4.8% to 7.2%. Combined with an increase in the size of government, this meant that the number of unionized public workers nearly doubled in those years. The AFL welcomed these developments. In June 1919, for the first time the AFL agreed to charter locals of police and soon chartered 37.

But in September 1919, the Boston police strike occurred, a seminal and crippling event that cut short this first, false dawn of public-sector organizing. More than 1,100 police went on strike over wages, hours, working conditions, and the right to form a union. The consequences were devastating. The Boston police commissioner, Edwin Curtis, helped cause the strike by banning police from affiliating with the AFL, claiming that police officers could not have "divided loyalty." Private employers also strongly opposed the police union. Police officers, who had seen almost no increase in pay in 20 years, insisted on their right to affiliate with the AFL and were suspended for so doing, thus triggering the strike.

The strike instantly provoked trouble. As the officers left their posts, crowds gathered to attack them, substitute police officers, and others. For three days, the city suffered from significant lawlessness and violence. A total of around 5,000 state National Guard troops finally intervened, killing nine and wounding 23 others. Although other Boston unions had threatened a general strike in support of the police union, it did not materialize. In the context of other labor radicalism in 1919, the mainstream press opposed the union. Governor Calvin Coolidge capitalized on his harsh treatment of the strikers to launch a career in national politics.

Future public workers were especially unlucky that this strike involved police. In later years, it was used to argue against any public workers being allowed even the right to organize, on the grounds that such rights would lead literally to death and destruction. After the strike, many jurisdictions barred police officers from organizing unions (all police locals were soon destroyed), but further, many other types of unions, including teachers and street cleaners, would be banned. Public-sector union density stagnated through the 1920s. For decades to follow, arguments against public-sector unions echoed those made in Boston. As late as 1963, the Michigan Supreme Court upheld a bar on police unionizing, stressing the need for "undivided allegiance"; President Ronald Reagan cited the Boston strike as a precedent for firing striking members of the Professional Air Traffic Controllers Union (PATCO) in 1981.

Another lingering effect was that public employees now often sought to unionize outside the AFL. Indeed, at the beginning of the twenty-first century, some major public-sector unions remained outside the AFL-CIO: the Fraternal Order of Police, the National Education Association (NEA), and others, such as the National Treasury Employees Union.

Legal Status from the New Deal to the 1960s

America is unique among industrialized democracies in sharply differentiating legal rules for public- and private-sector labor relations, and these rules had a tremendous effect on public-sector unions. Before the 1960s, the law everywhere in the United States prohibited strikes and almost all collective bargaining in government employment, and courts routinely allowed public employers to bar union membership itself. While the National Labor Relations Act (NLRA) of 1935 gave basic protections to private-sector unions, no federal law has ever covered these public-sector unions. Nor, up to the 1960s, did any state laws. Prior to the 1960s, state courts made public-sector labor law, typically endorsing whatever rules public employers imposed. Federal workers were marginally better off, as the Lloyd-La Follette Act of 1912 gave federal employees the right to form unions, albeit not to bargain. This "pre-collective bargaining era" for public workers in the United

States lasted decades beyond when public workers in, for example, Britain and France won bargaining and related rights quite similar to those of private-sector workers in those countries.

Since the 1960s, a majority of states have passed laws allowing some public employees to bargain, but public-sector laws are more restrictive than the NLRA. And even in the twenty-first century, many states refuse to grant bargaining rights to most or all public employees, and only 11 states permit any public employees to strike under any circumstance. Thus, the rules governing public-sector labor relations have always been different from and less generous than private-sector law.

Why was the development of public-sector law so delayed and deformed? First, the Boston strike was a major blow. Second, judges who made the law until at least the early 1960s blended several types of concerns. They were, like many judges in those days, hostile to labor. They also promoted a particular vision of state structure and sovereignty in which judges gave considerable deference to local public employers, partly because courts did not want to be in the business of reviewing personnel decisions. Most broadly, the federalist structure of the American state, with its extreme division of power, had the practical effect of placing the power to make the "law" of labor relations squarely in the hands of local officials, themselves the actual employers. Finally, judges simply assumed that public workers would want to strike and bargain the full range of issues that private workers bargained, even though, from 1920 through the mid-1960s, all public-sector unions had waived the right to strike and in fact strikes by public workers were rare, small in scale, and short. Still, judges uniformly opposed public-sector labor rights, often in vitriolic opinions. Two separate court decisions in the 1940s, from Texas and New York, used the following quote: "To tolerate or recognize any combination of . . . employees of the government as a labor organization or union is not only incompatible with the spirit of democracy but inconsistent with every principle upon which our Government is founded" (*Railway Mail Association v. Murphy* [1943]; *CIO v. City of Dallas* [1946]).

Union Activities in the Pre-Collective Bargaining Era

Public-sector unions existed and were active before bargaining laws began being passed in the 1960s. Public-sector union density ranged from 9% to 13% from the 1930s to the early 1960s. This was a significant total number, as by 1934 there were nearly 3.3 million government workers in the United States (12.7% of all nonagricultural workers). To break down the categories, between the world wars, civilian federal employees were about one fourth of all the public workers. Of state and local government workers, school employees constituted from 33% to 50%. In the 25 years after World War II, state and local governments expanded at up to twice the rate of the federal government. For this period, police and fire services were the largest category of municipal employees aside from school employees.

The period before the 1960s also created the central institutions and determined much of the basic character of the public-sector labor movement. The major players of today have been in place for a long time. In addition to the unions listed above, the American Federation of Government Employees (AFGE) and the American Federation of State, County and Municipal Employees (AFSCME) were formed in the 1930s; by the 1960s, the National Education Association had been converted from an employer-dominated group to a more traditional union. And public-sector unions, then as now, relied heavily on political strategies.

In this era, public-sector unions used various tactics to represent their members. First, they used politics. They supported sympathetic candidates in local elections. They lobbied and made appeals to the public, trying to enlist public pressure to influence public officials who were employers and those who could enact laws and regulations that would protect workers. Civil service and pension laws were major goals. Second, they represented workers in civil service or whatever other types of hearings were available. Third, they helped provide training, information, and other resources for their members. Fourth, they engaged in "informal" bargaining, which sometimes led to quasi-collective agreements.

Such practices were surprisingly common. A 1946 study found that 97 cities had written agreements with employee organizations. And these contracts helped workers: public school janitors represented by the Building Service Employees International Union were typically better paid than their unorganized counterparts. But these agreements were far short of modern, binding collective bargaining, both in their narrow scope and their dubious enforceability. Employers had no obligation—and in many cases arguably no actual legal power—to enter into them. Union efforts in these decades were creative and sometimes effective, but because they lacked institutional rights, they at best achieved mixed success.

For example, the powerful and militant TWU reacted angrily after its main local in New York City was converted into a public-sector union when the city bought the subways in 1940. This act removed collective bargaining rights from thousands of workers. The TWU's reaction included mass protests and huge publicity campaigns. It ultimately won a compromise: a system granting rudimentary bargaining rights, but still with significant restrictions based on its public-sector status.

Civil Service Rules

While unsuccessful in passing bargaining laws before the 1960s, unions did help pass civil service laws. Federal civil service rules originated in the Pendleton Act of 1883. Passed in response to an assassination attempt on President Garfield by a man allegedly disappointed by not receiving a patronage job, the Act attempted to decrease the role of political spoils and increase the role of merit in federal employment. It created civil service exams, barred dismissals of covered employees for political reasons, and created a Civil Service Commission to enforce these rules.

State governments adopted civil service systems for the same reasons as the federal government: to replace the spoils system with the merit system. Illinois actually adopted its law under circumstances remarkably similar to those that led to the Pendleton Act. The state passed the "Optional Civil Service Act for Cities" in 1895, after Mayor Carter Harrison of Chicago was killed by a disappointed office seeker. Illinois then passed a civil service law for state employees in 1905. Other early states included New York, which passed the first such law in 1883, Massachusetts in 1884, Wisconsin in 1905, New Jersey in 1908, California and Ohio in 1913, Kansas in 1915, and Maryland in 1920. By 1948, 25 states had adopted such systems, as had hundreds of cities. Today, essentially all public employers have civil service rules.

These laws initially offered only limited protection: many workers were excluded, and protections were often scant. Still, they brought some standards to hiring (requiring passing civil service exams) and provided some check on arbitrary firing. And today, such laws provide general "just cause" protection in discipline and discharge.

Wisconsin and the Beginning of the Collective Bargaining Era

The end of the old era began with the passage of the first state statute permitting public-sector collective bargaining in Wisconsin in 1959 and 1962. This law was enacted after AFSCME had struggled for over a decade to pass such a bill, finally overcoming the entire history of objections and obstacles to public-sector unions: fears of police strikes; legal doctrines concerning government sovereignty; policy objections to unions bargaining with government; and opposition from private business interests and conservative political leaders.

The law, after the 1962 amendments, provided that covered public workers (most local government employees) had the right to organize into unions and to bargain. If bargaining reached an impasse, a state agency (the Wisconsin Employment Relations Bureau) could conduct mediation at the request of both parties and fact-finding at the request of either party. Later, the law was amended to provide, among other things, for binding arbitration.

The trend continued. Federal employees received limited collective bargaining rights for the first time just after the Wisconsin law was signed in 1962, when President Kennedy issued Executive Order 10988. In the 1960s, states began passing laws that allowed public-sector bargaining and created specific mechanisms to resolve bargaining impasses that did not involve striking. By 1966, 16 states had enacted laws extending some bargaining rights to at least some public workers. In 1978, the Federal Service Labor Management Relations Act of 1978 was adopted for most federal employees; it provides bargaining rights and binding arbitration at impasse.

In the late 1960s, courts finally accepted an argument that public-sector unionists had made for decades: that the First Amendment of the Constitution prevented a public employer from firing or otherwise discriminating against a public employee because of membership in or support of a union. Thus, while some public employees are still without a legal right to bargain, all have a constitutional right to form unions.

The public-sector laws that have developed since the mid-1960s vary tremendously. At the turn of the twenty-first century, there were more than 110 separate state public-sector labor law statutes, augmented by many local ordinances, executive orders, and other authority. Twenty-nine states and the District of Columbia allowed collective bargaining for all major groups of public employees; 13 states allowed only one to four types of public workers to bargain (most commonly teachers and firefighters); and eight do not allow any public workers to bargain. While only 12 states allowed any public workers to strike, 38 states provided some impasse procedures for unionized public workers. Thirty-six states used mandatory or optional mediation; 34 used fact-finding; and 30 had

arbitration as the final step, with 21 states using binding arbitration. Still, a significant minority of states ban bargaining as well as striking, and a few (for example, Virginia) bar any official recognition of a public-sector union.

Political fights over the rights of public workers have continued. In 2004, the governors of Indiana and Missouri unilaterally withdrew executive orders permitting state employees to bargain collectively. After the 9/11 attacks, the Bush administration would not approve a bill creating the Department of Homeland Security (DHS) unless administration officials were empowered to design a new personnel system that could vitiate collective bargaining rights and civil service protections for DHS workers (notably, about 48,000 of these workers had previously enjoyed bargaining rights in predecessor agencies). Even where collective bargaining is allowed for public workers, state legislatures have sometimes narrowed existing laws to restrict the topics over which some public workers can bargain. For example, in the 1990s, Michigan restricted the topics over which teachers' unions could bargain.

The Rise of Public-Sector Unions in the 1960s and Beyond

With a constitutionally protected right to organize, and rights to bargain in an increasing number of states, public-sector unions greatly increased in membership. In 1955, public-sector unions had about 400,000 members; by the 1970s the total was more than 4 million. From 1955 to 1991, the AFT increased its membership from 40,000 to 573,000; AFSCME grew from 99,000 to 1,191,000; and the IAFF grew from 72,000 to 151,000. The Service Employees International Union, which has a large public-sector component, grew from 50,000 to 108,000.

From 1955 to 1991, the total membership of the AFL-CIO only rose from 12,622,000 to 13,933,000. The growth of these unions thus had an impact on the labor movement. The number of public employees in the organization grew from 915,000 (about 5% of total AFL-CIO membership) in 1956 to 1.7 million (about 9%) in 1966. By 1993, around 40% of union members in the United States were in the public sector. By 1997, AFSCME's 1.3 million members made it the second largest union in the AFL-CIO, after the Teamsters. That same year, the AFT claimed 1 million members.

At the turn of the twenty-first century, the highest rates of unionization in the public sector were in local government employment (43.2 % in 2001), with police, teachers, and firefighters leading the way. Notably, police and firefighters were not allowed to strike even where they could bargain and even where other public workers were allowed.

This boom—and the new state public-sector bargaining laws that were inextricably linked to it—had a variety of causes. The increased size of public employment likely played a role, although notably, levels of public employment were not growing much relative to the economy as a whole. The number of government workers nearly doubled in the 1960s and 1970s (with most of the growth in state and local government employment), bringing the total to more than 16 million in 1980. Still, in 1960, public workers constituted 15.4% of nonagricultural employees, and by 1991, this figure was still less than 17%. Continuing experience with stability in private-sector relations and the climate of social change of the 1960s and 1970s also contributed to the new toleration of public-sector unions.

There was also a brief period of relative militance in the public sector. In the later 1960s and 1970s, teachers, sanitation workers, and even police, among others, engaged in job actions and (often illegal) strikes. In some cases, unions won rights with those tactics; in other cases, the actions caused a backlash.

For example, the American Federation of Teachers became engaged in a bitter and divisive job action in the Ocean Hill-Brownville neighborhood of New York in 1968–1969. Civil rights activists and unionists, generally allies by this time, split badly over whether local community groups should be given more authority over schools, including over labor and personnel matters such as transfers.

Perhaps part and parcel of the general tenor of protesting social movements, illegal strike actions decreased considerably in the 1980s and beyond. The PATCO strike of 1981, involving air traffic controllers, was famous (and arguably was the symbolic start of a wider attack on unions), but it was the exception. Intriguingly, studies indicate that at least in many circumstances, passing laws that gave public workers the right to bargain collectively actually decreased the number of illegal strikes by public employees.

Conclusion

Public-sector unions contain a tremendous variety of types of workers: police officers, kindergarten teachers, road maintenance crews, and white-collar semi-professional and professional jobs, among others. Some of these jobs are unique to the public sector (firefighters); some are widespread in the private

sector (secretaries and janitors). Yet public workers remain a coherent category primarily for two reasons. First, they will inevitably behave politically in some way, because their employers are politicians. Second, in the United States, their bargaining rights are different from and more limited than bargaining rights in the private sector, both in what they can bargain over and what may happen when bargaining impasses arise. Although government workers have always had many of the same concerns as those in the private sector, their unions have had far fewer legal rights, and their range of practical action has been much more circumscribed.

Including public workers requires reconceptualizing the periodization of labor history. In the traditional view, 1935 to 1945 was the watershed, with a small core of unions before the New Deal and a mostly successful labor relations regime after World War II. The decline of private-sector labor has undercut this view. But further, the rise of public-sector unions now seems as meaningful as, say, the creation of the Congress of Industrial Organizations (CIO). The significance of the 1960s and beyond comes as much from the workers who entered the labor movement as from those who left it.

This history also shows that the attitudes of employers are crucial to unions. Modern public-sector employers are less aggressively hostile toward unionization than private-sector employers, possibly because of institutional concerns (they are elected) and possibly because civil service rules constrain them.

In 1942, the TWU's newspaper wrote that "government workers who are unorganized can be and are exploited as cruelly as unorganized workers in private industry. Whatever progress government workers have made in recent years they have made only through labor organization." That vision continues to motivate millions of public workers today.

JOSEPH E. SLATER

References and Further Reading

Beadling, Tom, Pat Cooper, Grace Palladino, and Peter Pieragostini. *A Need for Valor: The Roots of the Service Employees International Union, 1902–1992*. Washington, DC: SEIU, 1992.

Berkeley, Miller, and William Canak. "There Should Be No Blanket Guarantee: Employer Opposition to Public Employee Unions." *Journal of Collective Negotiations in the Public Sector* 24 (1995): 17–36.

Burpo, John. *The Police Labor Movement: Problems and Perspectives*. Springfield, IL: Charles Thomas, 1971.

Chickering, Lawrence, ed. *Public Employee Unions: A Study of the Crisis in Public Sector Labor Relations*. San Francisco: Institute for Contemporary Studies, 1976.

Crouch, Winston. *Organized Civil Servants*. Berkeley: University of California Press, 1978.

Eaton, William. *The American Federation of Teachers, 1916–61.* Carbondale: Southern Illinois University Press, 1975.

Edwards, Harry R., Theodore Clark, and Charles Craver. *Labor Relations Law in the Public Sector: Cases and Materials.* 4th ed. Charlottesville, VA: Michie, 1991.

Gammage, Allen, and Stanley Sachs. *Police Unions.* Springfield, IL: Charles Thomas, 1972.

Goulden, Joseph. *Jerry Wurf: Labor's Last Angry Man.* New York: Atheneum, 1982.

Grodin, Joseph, Mary Weisberger, and Martin Malin. *Public Sector Employment.* 2nd ed. St. Paul, MN: Thompson West, 2004.

Johnston, Paul. *Success While Others Fail: Social Movement Unionism and the Public Workplace.* Ithaca, NY: ILR Press, 1994.

Kearney, Richard, and David Carnevale. *Labor Relations in the Public Sector.* 3rd ed. New York: Marcel Dekker, 2001.

Kramer, Larry. *Labor's Paradox: The American Federation of State, County, and Municipal Employees, AFL-CIO.* New York: Wiley, 1962.

Leibig, Michael, and Wendy Kahn. *Public Employee Organizing and the Law.* Washington, DC: BNA, 1987.

Lewin, David, Peter Feuille, Thomas Kochan, and John Thomas Delaney, eds. *Public Sector Labor Relations: Analysis and Readings.* Lexington, MA: Lexington Books, 1988.

Malin, Martin. "Public Employees' Right to Strike: Law and Experience." *University of Michigan Journal of Law Reform* 26 (1993): 313–401.

Murphy, Marjorie. *Blackboard Unions: The AFT and the NEA, 1900–1980.* Ithaca, NY: Cornell University Press, 1990.

Najita, Joyce, and James Stern, eds. *Collective Bargaining in the Public Sector: The Experience of Eight States.* Armonk, NY: M. E. Sharpe, 2001.

Nesbitt, Murray. *Labor Relations in the Federal Government Service.* Washington, DC: BNA, 1976.

Podair, Jerald. *The Strike That Changed New York: Blacks, Whites, and the Ocean Hill-Brownsville Crisis.* Cambridge, MA: Yale University Press, 2003.

Russell, Francis. *A City in Terror: The 1919 Boston Police Strike.* New York: Viking Press, 1975.

Saltzman, Gregory. "Bargaining Laws as a Cause and a Consequence of the Growth of Teacher Unionism." *Industrial and Labor Relations Review* 38 (1985): 335–351.

Shaffer, Robert. "Where Are the Organized Public Employees? The Absence of Public Employee Unionism from U.S. History Textbooks, and Why It Matters." *Labor History* 43 (2002): 315–334.

Slater, Joseph. "Homeland Security vs. Workers Rights? What the Federal Government Should Learn from History and Experience, and Why." *University of Pennsylvania Journal of Labor and Employment Law* 6 (2004): 295–356.

———. *Public Workers: Government Employee Unions, the Law, and the State, 1900–62.* Ithaca, NY: Cornell University Press, 2004.

Spero, Sterling. *Government as Employer.* New York: Remsen Press, 1948.

Spero, Sterling, and John Capozolla. *The Urban Community and Its Unionized Bureaucracies: Pressure Politics in Local Government Labor Relations.* New York: Dunellen, 1973.

Stieber, Jack. *Public Employee Unionism: Structure, Growth, Policy.* Washington, DC: Brookings Institution, 1973.

Urban, Wayne. *Why Teachers Organized.* Detroit: Wayne State University Press, 1982.

Walsh, John. *Labor Struggle in the Post Office: From Selective Lobbying to Collective Bargaining.* Armonk, NY: M. E. Sharpe, 1992.

Wellington, Harry, and Ralph Winter Jr. *The Unions and the Cities.* Washington, DC: Brookings Institution, 1971.

PUBLISHING
See **Printing and Publishing Industry**

PUEBLO REVOLT (1680)

The Pueblo Revolt of 1680 was a coordinated uprising on the part of Pueblo Indians and their Apache and Navajo allies, aimed at ousting Spanish settlers from the northern Rio Grande basin of the province of New Mexico in New Spain. Hundreds of Spaniards and Pueblo natives died, including 21 of the province's 33 missionaries. Nearly every Spanish building and church was destroyed or damaged. The revolt was initially planned for August 11, 1680, but the plot was discovered on August 9, and the general revolt was advanced on August 10. While both sides experienced losses, the Pueblo were the decided victors. For approximately three weeks, natives tortured and killed Spaniards, destroyed and appropriated Spanish property, and pushed the colonizers out of the upper Rio Grande. The rebellion allowed the Pueblo Indians to hold their land as undisputed rulers from 1680 to 1692 and caused a shift in Spanish power from Santa Fe to El Paso.

The revolt has often been referred to as Popé's Rebellion after a San Juan Tewa Indian leader, Pop'ay (Ripe Pumpkin) or El Popé, living at Taos pueblo in August 1680. Claiming that the god Poheyemo appeared to him from the underworld and appointed him as his representative, Popé spread word of his vision from the *kiva* (ceremonial structure) at Taos. His instructions were to kill all the Spaniards and missionaries, destroy all evidence of Christian religion, and return Indians to their former freedom. At the turn of the twenty-first century, historians have placed emphasis on the co-operation between multiple leaders and participants, rather than emphasizing one individual's agency in sparking the revolt.

Many additional explanations for the bloody revolt of 1680 have been offered. Religious disputes, disease, environmental changes, population decline, concentration of settlements, Spanish violence, increased land grants to colonists, disrupted trade, and coerced labor are cited for creating increased tensions and a motive for the uprising. The revolt has often been characterized as a "holy war." Most scholars agree, however, that it was finally the realization of lost territory, culture, and autonomy that created the conditions ready for the revolt of 1680.

Since the arrival of Juan de Oñate and a group of Mexican settlers to northern New Mexico in 1598, the Spanish asserted control over indigenous religion, economy, and culture. The colonizers applied the name Pueblo (referring to the permanent towns of stone or adobe) to native groups who shared an agricultural subsistence economy. This included groups with diversified languages and traditions including the Tewa, Hopi, Zuni, and Acoma. Often using force and coercion, the governor, soldiers, and missionaries exacted labor from the Pueblo people. Nearly every seventeenth-century governor abused power for economic gain. Native labor was used for weaving in workshops, gathering piñon pine nuts, building carts, and driving mules for trade caravans to Mexico City. Many natives also performed duties as servants. Most of this work was without compensation, but even those who received wages were paid well below the standard.

Under the *encomienda* system, the Spanish government granted citizen soldiers-for-hire labor and tribute in return for acting as the state's police force. The Spaniards' demands for grain, livestock, handicrafts, and other goods disrupted the traditional patterns of agriculture and work. Franciscan missionaries demanded indigenous labor for the construction and maintenance of the mission compounds and church structures. Toward the end of the seventeenth century, there were a number of minor and local revolts by the Pueblo in response to Spanish abuses. However, it was not until August 1680 that a full-fledged, coordinated response occurred.

Coordination was a feat in itself, for each Pueblo community was an independent political unit, and within the region native peoples spoke at least six different languages and countless dialects. Period accounts reveal that coordination for the revolt was made possible by close communication between Pueblo leaders. Calendars in the form of knotted cords, representing the days until the attack, were distributed throughout the native settlements. Each day a single knot would be untied, and when there were no knots left, that would be the day of the revolt. Messengers were also sent to spread word to kill all the friars and the settlers on August 11. Two such runners from the Tesuque pueblo were captured on August 9 and revealed the plan to the Spanish. Despite this setback, the Pueblo people were alerted and the rebellion ensued on August 10. Northern Pueblo peoples such as the Tewa, the Northern Tiwa, and the Pecos Indians were the most active in the revolt and suffered the most casualties. Due to the lack of accurate records, the number of Pueblo killed is not known.

In the aftermath of the rebellion, many Pueblo revived native traditions and reconstructed *kivas* and shrines. While the Pueblo leaders maintained control of New Mexico for a decade, internal discord is cited for causing developing factionalism after 1680. A significant number of people residing in New Mexico at the time of the rebellion were *mestizos* who could claim both native and non-native ancestry, and intermarriage with the Pueblo was predominant by 1680. This acculturation and miscegenation blurred alliances both before and after the rebellion and caused additional unrest on the part of Pueblo leaders. In the early 1690s, the Spanish used the internal weaknesses to re-assume control and were largely successful despite a second revolt in 1696.

Sources for understanding the rebellion are contemporary accounts largely written or recorded by Spanish religious and political leaders. These provide an often contradictory and sometimes misleading picture of the events and require careful ethnographic reading. Adding to the written records, scholars have turned to archaeological remains, oral histories, and material culture to provide additional context.

Although interpretations of the rebellion differ, historians agree that it was one of the most successful revolts against a European power in the New World. Natives and non-natives lost their lives and had property destroyed. Yet for over a decade, the Pueblo people maintained control of their homeland. Many speculate that their success inhibited later Spanish attempts to eradicate their culture and forced government and religious officials to adopt less harsh policies toward natives after reconquest.

CATHARINE CHRISTIE DANN

References and Further Reading

Espinosa, J. Manuel, ed. and trans. *The Pueblo Indian Revolt of 1696 and the Franciscan Missions in New Mexico: Letter of the Missionaries and Related Documents.* Norman: University of Oklahoma Press, 1988.

Folsom, Franklin. *Red Power on the Rio Grande: The Native American Revolution of 1680,* Introduction by Alfonso Ortiz. 1973. Reprint, Albuquerque: University of New Mexico Press, 1996.

Gutiérrez, Ramón A. *When Jesus Came, the Corn Mothers Went Away: Marriage, Sexuality, and Power in New Mexico, 1500–1846.* Stanford, CA: Stanford University Press, 1991.

Hackett, Charles Wilson, ed. *Revolt of the Pueblo Indians of New Mexico and Otermín's Attempted Reconquest, 1680–1682.* Trans. Charmion Clair Shelby, 2 vols. Albuquerque: University of New Mexico Press, 1942.

Knaut, Andrew L. *The Pueblo Revolt of 1680: Conquest and Resistance in Seventeenth-Century New Mexico.* Norman: University of Oklahoma Press, 1995.

Preucel, Robert W., ed. *Archaeologies of the Pueblo Revolt: Identity, Meaning, and Renewal in the Pueblo World.* Albuquerque: University of New Mexico Press, 2002.

Reff, Daniel T. "The 'Predicament of Culture' and Spanish Missionary Accounts of the Tepehuan and Pueblo Revolts." *Ethnohistory* 42 (Winter 1995): 63–90.

Weber, David. *What Caused the Pueblo Revolt?* Bedford, MA: St. Martin's Press, 1999.

PUERTO RICANS

Puerto Ricans have immigrated to the United States primarily as working-class labor migrants. Economic change in Puerto Rico left many agricultural and other workers unemployed or underemployed. Men and women migrated in search of work. Meanwhile, U.S. employers recruited Puerto Ricans as a source of low-wage workers. The governments of the United States and Puerto Rico promoted migration through contract labor programs. Policy makers attributed unemployment and poverty to "overpopulation" instead of to economic development policies that provided jobs that were too scarce and wages that were too low. Puerto Ricans also came through networks of family and friends, helping each other to make the trip and to find work and housing. As a result of these labor migrations, predominantly working-class Puerto Rican communities have formed throughout the United States.

Since 1917, Puerto Ricans have come to the United States as U.S. citizens. In 1898, at the end of the Spanish-Cuban-American War, Spain ceded sovereignty over Puerto Rico to the United States, and the United States has retained that sovereignty ever since. Hence, Puerto Rican migration is within the confines of the colonial relationship between the United States and Puerto Rico. U.S. government policies and U.S. businesses have a pivotal impact on Puerto Rico's economy. Initially, Puerto Ricans coming to the United States had an ambiguous status, considered neither citizens nor "aliens." In 1917, the U.S. Congress declared all Puerto Ricans to be U.S. citizens. Although Puerto Ricans arrived in the United States entitled to full citizenship rights, they also arrived as a multiracial and mixed-race people, with a distinct language and culture, who were often recruited as low-wage workers.

Contract Labor and the Puerto Rican Diaspora

From 1900 to 1901, more than 5,000 Puerto Rican men, women, and children were transported from Puerto Rico to Hawai'i to work on sugar plantations. The trip by boat and by train was grueling. Half of the passengers escaped en route, some abandoning ship in New Orleans and others refusing to get back on a ship in San Francisco. Those who landed in Hawai'i found harsh working and living conditions. Employers hoped Puerto Ricans would serve as low-wage workers and undermine the organizing efforts of Japanese workers. Puerto Rican migrants, however, included union activists. Although employers fostered conflict and competition among their diverse workforce along racial and ethnic lines, Puerto Ricans, Japanese, Chinese, Portuguese, Hawai'ians, and Filipinos forged alliances to improve conditions. Along the way, they formed a unique multiethnic local culture, as the anthropologist Iris López describes. In 2000, Hawai'i's Puerto Ricans marked the centennial of their arrival with celebrations.

This early contract labor initiative laid the foundation for future programs and highlights their key dynamics. Policy makers in the United States and Puerto Rico viewed "overpopulation" as the cause of unemployment. They viewed emigration and contract labor programs as a solution. Yet U.S. investments and economic development policies in Puerto Rico displaced workers, causing unemployment. Facing limited opportunities at home, Puerto Ricans migrated in search of work within Puerto Rico, to the United States, and to other countries. U.S. employers hoped to increase profits by lowering labor costs. Government-sanctioned contract labor programs linked workers and destinations, and covered transportation costs, which were then deducted from workers' wages along with other expenses such as food. While some workers returned to Puerto Rico when their contracts expired, others remained in their new destinations, sent for family and friends, and provided the foundations for the Puerto Rican diaspora.

Other contract labor initiatives followed. Although labor migration is often thought of as a male phenomenon, women were recruited as well. In 1904, 50 Puerto Rican women between the ages of 15 and 21 were recruited to work at the St. Louis Cordage Company in St. Louis, Missouri. In 1920, 130 women were recruited to the American Manufacturing Company, a rope factory in Brooklyn, New York. The Arizona Cotton Growers' Association recruited whole families in 1926, and 1,000 made the trip. Finding wages and living conditions far below their expectations and their contracts' provisions, workers protested, trying to force the company to uphold the contracts' provisions. They found support from the Phoenix Central Labor Council, which raised funds, had a bread line, and sent telegrams to the labor leaders Santiago Iglesias in Puerto Rico and William Green in the

United States. During World War I, thousands of Puerto Rican men, recruited to work in war industries and on military bases, found themselves in Louisiana, North Carolina, South Carolina, and Georgia.

These contract labor programs sparked widespread complaints from workers. Nevertheless, policy makers increased their involvement and the scope of contract labor programs. During World War II, the U.S. War Manpower Commission recruited men to work in war industries, including canning plants like the Campbell Soup Company in southern New Jersey, and on the B & O and Pennsylvania Railroads. After the war, a private labor agency brought men to work in agriculture and in the steel industry at the National Tube Company, a division of U.S. Steel in Lorain, Ohio. Puerto Rican women were brought to work as domestics in Chicago and Philadelphia. Policy makers briefly promoted labor contracts for domestics but then turned to labor contracts for seasonal farmworkers, especially along the eastern seaboard. The farm labor program lasted for decades and brought thousands of men each year.

Working-Class Communities between the World Wars

After World War I, New York City became the largest Puerto Rican community, as the population surpassed that in Hawai'i. By 1940, 88% of Puerto Ricans living in the continental United States made the city their home. Philadelphia's Puerto Rican community grew as well. These communities grew through social networks, as family and friends helped each other make the trip and get settled. The cigar maker Bernardo Vega left his hometown of Cayey in 1916 and headed for New York City. In his *Memoirs*, he recalled that aboard the steamship, "the overriding theme of our conversations, however, was what we expected to find in New York City. With our first earnings we would send for our nearest relative." Most came looking for work. When they arrived, networks continued, and both cities became home to vibrant, diverse, working-class communities.

Cigar makers and socialists figured prominently among the migrants to both cities. Many were politically active in Puerto Rico. Born in 1885, Vega participated in Puerto Rico's first large-scale workers' group, the *Federación Libre de Trabajadores*, started in 1899, and he was a delegate to the founding convention of the *Partido Socialista* in his hometown in 1915. Cigar makers labored while the lector read, contributing to an educated and politically active group. In his *Memoirs*, Vega wrote, "As socialists,

we dig our trenches everywhere in the world." He continued his activism in New York City, describing Harlem as "a socialist stronghold," with neighborhood clubs for political, cultural, and sports activities. Like Vega, Jesús Colón was a cigar maker and a socialist, who left Cayey for New York City. Between his arrival in 1917 and his death in 1974, Colón's leadership fostered 25 community organizations, as the historian Linda Delgado reveals. A prolific writer, he produced more than 250 essays and vignettes that depicted the economic and racial struggles of working-class Puerto Ricans and the need to work to improve conditions for the community. As the historian Ruth Glasser documents, working-class musicians also migrated to New York City between the World Wars, with many U.S. veterans among them. Puerto Rican musicians had been recruited for African-American regimental bands during World War I. After the war, many made their way to New York City, displaced from their other economic pursuits and searching for jobs and musical opportunities in the city.

In Philadelphia, cigar makers contributed to the growth of the Puerto Rican community. They constituted part of a pan-Latino, working-class community, as the historian Víctor Vázquez-Hernández portrays. Puerto Ricans found work in the cigar-making shops owned by other Spanish speakers, especially Spaniards and Cubans. Known for their political activism, cigar makers were founders of early Spanish language mutual aid societies, and they played important roles in labor movements. As early as 1877, Philadelphia was home to a Spanish-speaking local of the Cigar Makers' International Union (CMIU).

Farmworkers and Garment Workers

After World War II, Puerto Rican migration increased dramatically, and Puerto Ricans became the first airborne migration. Men and women came in search of work, and government-sponsored labor contracts provided transportation and placements for many. Puerto Ricans found work in areas where unions played a role—in agriculture and food processing, and in the garment and steel industries. As postwar strikes sought to improve wages and conditions, Puerto Ricans were among the labor activists. For example, one year after Puerto Ricans were recruited to Lorain, Ohio, to work in the steel industry, they participated in a strike by the Congress of Industrial Organizations (CIO). As Eugene "Gene" Rivera notes, Puerto Ricans were accused of meeting with Communists during the strike, and the broader community's fears of Communist infiltration continued to affect Puerto Ricans' community-building efforts.

Puerto Rican men became farmworkers, either through the government-sponsored contract labor program or through networks of family and friends. Most worked in New Jersey, Pennsylvania, New York, Connecticut, and Massachusetts, with fewer in other states. Contracts guaranteed wages and specified allowable deductions, hours, and minimum standards for food and housing. Yet workers found contracts violated and conditions harsh, as they struggled to meet their immediate needs and often, to send money home. Some workers left in search of better options, and some sought to improve conditions through organizing.

In 1972, in Connecticut about 100 Puerto Rican tobacco workers formed the ATA, the *Asociación de Trabajadores Agrícolas* (Agricultural Workers Association). As the historian Ruth Glasser explains, the ATA, along with other groups, struggled to improve living conditions, wages, sick and overtime pay, and health care. They challenged the government of Puerto Rico's right to negotiate labor contracts on behalf of workers, and they sought unrestricted access to labor camps for visitors and organizers. During 1973, hundreds of tobacco workers struck to protest the food provided and the firing of workers involved in previous actions. Workers gained free access to the camps. The government of Puerto Rico agreed to stop using misleading radio advertisements to recruit workers, to revise the contract, and to provide more staff to address workers' complaints. Although the ATA affiliated with the United Farm Workers in 1975, the UFW was stretched thin by its efforts in the West, and the mobilization of tobacco workers in Connecticut waned. Still, in light of public scrutiny, the government's contract labor program dwindled from 12,760 workers in 1974 to 5,639 in 1975.

As Puerto Rican women became concentrated in the garment industry in New York City and other urban areas, many became members of the International Ladies' Garment Workers' Union (ILGWU), and some became union activists. By 1947, the ILGWU claimed 7,500 Puerto Rican members and estimated that another 4,000 to 8,000 worked in other small shops. Puerto Rican women found jobs mainly in the lower-skilled and lower-paid segments of the industry, especially dressmaking, skirts, and blouses. In Local 22 Dressmakers, Puerto Rican membership doubled from 8% to 16% between 1945 and 1953, while Jewish membership declined from 63% to 51% and African-American membership remained at 15%. Louise Delgado became a union activist with Local 22, first as a shop-floor representative,

then as an executive board member, and finally as a business agent. Born in Guayama, Puerto Rico, she came to New York City in 1923 at the age of eight, joining her family. Like many other Puerto Rican women, she started in the garment industry by helping her mother with homework. In 1934, she started working in a shop, and she continued in the industry until she retired in 1978. Delgado witnessed the dramatic increase in Puerto Rican women workers in the industry, as well as critical changes in the industry. Garment shops left New York City in search of low wages and higher profits, and the industry increasingly relied on contracting shops that competed for assembly work. The 1958 dressmakers strike addressed some of these industry changes. Puerto Rican women were among the 105,000 striking workers in New York and six nearby states.

Conclusions

The scholarship in Puerto Rican studies is largely interdisciplinary. Scholars have examined many dimensions of Puerto Rican working-class communities, especially in New York City, the largest Puerto Rican community. Writers have depicted Puerto Ricans' struggles for inclusion, the creation of community-based organizations, political activism, and other topics. Ethnographers have examined contemporary issues, including gentrification, identity, and family dynamics, especially focusing on Chicago. Other social scientists have focused on the economic restructuring and de-industrialization of urban areas in the Northeast and Midwest that affected communities where Puerto Ricans had settled. Puerto Rican workers were economically displaced again. Fewer works have explored the historical dimensions. Puerto Ricans' working lives and their interactions with labor unions have thus far received too little attention in both historical and contemporary accounts.

CARMEN TERESA WHALEN

References and Further Reading

Colón, Jesús. *A Puerto Rican in New York and Other Sketches*. New York: Mainstream Publishers, 1961.
———. *The Way It Was, and Other Writings*. Edited by Edna Acosta-Belén and Virginia Sánchez Korrol. Houston, TX: Arte Publico Press, 1993.
Glasser, Ruth. *My Music Is My Flag: Puerto Rican Musicians and Their New York Communities, 1917–1940*. Berkeley: University of California Press, 1995.
Sánchez Korrol, Virginia. *From Colonia to Community: The History of Puerto Ricans in New York City, 1917–1948*. 2nd ed. Berkeley: University of California Press, 1994.

Vega, Bernardo. *Memoirs of Bernardo Vega: A Contribution to the History of the Puerto Rican Community*. Edited by César Andreu Iglesias. New York: Monthly Review Press, 1984.

Whalen, Carmen Teresa. "'The Day the Dresses Stopped': Puerto Rican Women, the International Ladies' Garment Workers' Union, and the 1958 Dressmakers Strike." In *Mapping Memories and Migrations: Locating Boricua and Chicana Histories*, edited by Vicki Ruiz and John Chávez. Forthcoming. Bloomington: Indiana University Press, 2006.

———. *From Puerto Rico to Philadelphia: Puerto Rican Workers and Postwar Economies*. Philadelphia: Temple University Press, 2001.

Whalen, Carmen Teresa, and Víctor Vázquez Hernández, ed. *The Puerto Rican Diaspora: Historical Perspectives*. Philadelphia: Temple University Press, 2005.

PULLMAN STRIKE AND BOYCOTT (1894)

A local walkout on 11 May 1894 by perhaps 2,800 railway car shop workers at Pullman's Palace Car Company south of Chicago, Illinois, expanded by early July 1894 to encompass more than 150,000 railroaders in a boycott of Pullman-built cars on at least 20 railroads across 27 midwestern and western states. The Pullman strike and boycott drew support from militant members of the fledgling American Railway Union (ARU), an industrial union that organized railroad workers across the range of craft lines and occupational hierarchies. Railroad officials whose indebted corporations had fallen into federal court receivership seized the opportunity of the American Railway Union boycott of Pullman cars to discharge and blacklist ARU members, obtain federal judicial injunctions against ARU actions, and use U.S. military force to re-open rail lines and protect strikebreakers. Although ARU supporters kept U.S. troops occupied along several western railroad lines until late August and September 1894, the combination of personal poverty, federal court injunctions, military force, and the imprisonment of ARU leaders and activists by U.S. marshals effectively ended the strike at the Pullman car shops near Chicago and the national boycott of Pullman cars by late July 1894. The Pullman strike and boycott of 1894 continues to hold historical significance not only for the unprecedented magnitude of government military and civil force employed to break the railroaders' industrial organization, but also for the questions it raised about the proper role of the state in labor disputes and the weighing of conservative trade unionism versus the more inclusive industrial unionism of the ARU.

The Pullman Palace Car Company, a manufacturer and leasor of railway sleeping, parlor, passenger, freight, and electric street railway cars, opened car-building shops and an adjacent company-owned town 14 miles south of Chicago along the Illinois Central Railroad on January 1, 1881. Attractive brick row houses, wide streets, utilities, indoor plumbing, and nearby shops and parks offered clean, spacious, healthy rental housing for Pullman car builders, seamstresses, and car repairmen. The town of Pullman quickly attracted international attention as a "model" town that would improve the living conditions of working-class families, thereby raising the moral development and productivity of workers. One study found that the death rate in Pullman was one half the average of the urban slum districts of Chicago, while others lauded company officers uncritically for their apparent attentiveness to the well-being of Pullman resident-workers. A handful of observers during the 1880s and early 1890s, however, identified two fundamental flaws in "the Pullman system": the lack of home ownership and the company's exertion of social control through the invasive deployment of "spotters." A third complaint, mismanagement by foremen and lower-level managers, manifested itself in nepotism, favoritism, and abusive treatment of longtime workers during the late 1880s and early 1890s.

Despite the company's projected image of beauty and order, Pullman craftsmen and laborers employed strikes to protest the loss of subsidized streetcar fares in 1882, shifts from daily wages to piecework, and substantial wage cuts in 1884, 1885, and 1887. The walkouts were isolated in specific departments, failed to achieve their objectives, and betrayed the absence of a broader, sustained culture of organization across crafts. One exception, a May 1886 general strike for an eight-hour workday and a 10% wage increase, not only failed, but also provoked the company president and founder, George M. Pullman, to contribute funds toward the suppression and prosecution of labor activists such as the Haymarket anarchists and the Knights of Labor. In January 1888, wood-carvers struck to protest an abusive foreman, but company officials allowed the men to return. Three years later, freight car department workers struck in January 1891, but after managers ordered the men back, only one returned. A strike by 41 steamfitters and blacksmiths in December 1893 ended in defeat.

The economic depression that shut factory gates and plunged an unprecedented number into unemployment in spring 1893 only hit Pullman factory orders in late summer. Car works managers slashed wages in August 1893 and laid off 3,400 workers by November until just 1,100 remained. The layoffs adversely affected rent collection in the company town, though, so the company began bidding for new construction contracts at a loss, rehired 2,000 shop employees by April 1894, and spread the work among 3,100 workers at the reduced wage rates.

Complaints about abusive foremen increased. In early April, Pullman workers began joining new American Railway Union lodges in Kensington and Grand Crossing. Eventually, 19 local ARU lodges enrolled 4,000 area men and women. An elected grievance committee of 46 members, headed by Thomas W. Heathcoate, identified the investigation and correction of shop abuses, the reduction of rents, and the restoration of pre-depression wage rates as three goals. On 7 May 1894, Heathcoate, the committee, and the ARU vice president, George W. Howard, met Pullman's second vice president, Thomas Wickes, to explain why reducing rents and raising wages would ease the crisis in unpaid rents. Wickes requested a written list of grievances and a second conference in two days. At that second meeting, George Pullman himself appeared after two hours to explain how the shops were operating at a financial loss. Pullman discounted the possibility of restoring wage rates and failed to understand the relationship of high rents to diminished household incomes by justifying the company's right to a reasonable profit from property rental. He did promise to investigate complaints about abusive treatment within the shops. The ARU vice president Howard also obtained a promise from Wickes that no committee member would suffer reprisal.

The following morning, 10 May, three committeemen were laid off by a superintendent, allegedly for lack of work. While Pullman and Wickes knew nothing of the layoffs and the claim of no work may have been legitimate, the workers viewed the layoffs as the latest act of betrayal. That night and into the early hours of the morning, Pullman workers met at Turner Hall in Kensington and authorized a strike. At work the morning of Friday, 11 May 1894, nearly all workers in all departments suddenly walked away from their jobs in a general strike, prompted by a rumor that the company would impose a lockout at noon.

The American Railway Union's vice president and general secretary had counseled Pullman workers that a strike would be premature, due to unfavorable economic conditions and Wickes's promise to investigate shop grievances. Local inexperience in sustaining labor organization also probably factored among the officers' concerns. During the American Railway Union's national convention in Chicago one month later, the ARU vice president Howard recommended that any additional actions be limited to strikes at the Pullman Company's shops at St. Louis, Missouri, and Ludlow, Kentucky, and that a boycott be avoided.

ARU convention delegates, however, were eager to exercise their perceived new strength after an April 1894 strike victory against the Great Northern Railroad. The union, founded in February 1893 by Eugene V. Debs and other former officers of the major railroad brotherhoods on a model of federation long promoted by the Knights of Labor, established many local lodges among western railroaders during the winter of 1893–1894, growing from 96 local lodges in mid-November 1893 to 125 by 1 January 1894 and 453 by early June 1894. Some routes, such as the Chicago, Rock Island, and Pacific Railway, were not well organized, though.

Despite the risks, ARU convention delegates voted 22 June 1894 to initiate a boycott 26 June of all Pullman-built cars and the trains that carried them. Since Pullman cars were pulled in passenger trains on nearly all midwestern and western railroads, a boycott would effectively stall all passenger traffic on most railroads from Ohio to Texas, California, and Washington state. The boycott began in the Illinois Central Railroad yards in Chicago on 26 June. The next day, 5,000 workers refused to switch, brake, or run trains with Pullman cars. Fifteen railroads were stopped. The following day, 40,000 men had shut down almost every line. By 29 June, an estimated 100,000 ARU members and supporters honored the boycott, halting traffic on at least 20 railroads. The Pullman strike and boycott eventually extended through 27 states and affected 41,000 miles of railroad routes.

In Chicago, the General Managers' Association (GMA) represented 24 railroad companies that employed 221,000 workers. Formed in 1886 but feeble until a January 1892 re-organization, the GMA coordinated wage scales for different railway trades and, beginning in March 1893, recruited strikebreakers, dealt with individual brotherhoods, and distributed "blacklists" of railroaders barred from employment. By 1894, the General Managers' Association was positioned to fight and defeat the American Railway Union.

Strike activity in Pullman itself remained remarkably peaceful and orderly, due largely to discipline exerted by strike leaders, a picket line that circled the car works, and material support from Chicago area merchants, politicians, and other sympathizers. Throughout the western states, the American Railway Union exhibited significant power because of widespread disaffection with the inflexible brotherhoods, a tradition of federation across craft divisions that originated with the Knights of Labor's District Assembly 82 on the Union Pacific Railroad during the 1880s, and support from local residents of railroad towns. ARU enforcement of the boycott by interfering with trains carrying U.S. mail, freight, and passengers across state lines prompted the General Managers' Association to enlist U.S. government officials against the union. Limited injunctions against boycott activities were granted by federal judges in New Mexico Territory 27 June and in Chicago 29 June to protect individual railroad companies under federal court receivership protection. Near Blue Island, Illinois, a few miles west of Pullman, a crowd of rowdy, striking brickyard laborers blocked Rock Island Railroad yard traffic on 1 July. On 2 July 1894, the federal judges Peter Grosscup and William A. Woods granted a thorough injunction against all interference with railroad traffic. Later that day, the U.S. marshal John W. Arnold read the injunction twice to a gathering of perhaps 2,000 people at Blue Island. When they seemed unable or unwilling to comprehend the terms of the injunction, Arnold wired for U.S. army troops. In ARU boycott centers throughout the western states, similar confrontations between angry railroaders and incompetent deputy U.S. marshals prompted frantic telegraphs to Attorney General Richard Olney for U.S. troops.

Early in the morning of 4 July 1894, the Fifteenth U.S. Infantry entered Chicago from Fort Sheridan north of the city and took up positions in the railroad yards at Grand Crossing and Blue Island, while the cavalry and artillery occupied the Union Stockyards. Similarly, two companies of the Tenth Infantry entered Raton, New Mexico Territory, on 4 July to intimidate and restrain active ARU participants, while five companies of the Seventh Infantry accompanied deputy U.S. marshals in arresting 48 ARU boycott participants at Trinidad, Colorado. More than one thousand soldiers rode Northern Pacific trains between St. Paul and the Puget Sound 7–9 July to ensure their free passage and the transportation of strikebreakers. At Livingston, Montana, 10 July, a captain in charge of an all-black company of the Twenty-fourth Infantry quelled an especially threatening crowd of perhaps 600 townspeople by striking an aggressive local ARU leader on his head with the blunt side of the captain's saber. Federal troops, sailors, and marines also occupied Los Angeles, Sacramento, San Francisco, and the Central Pacific Railroad line to Ogden, Utah. Military forces compelled submission to the judicial injunctions and civil authorities. Arrests, imprisonment for contempt of court without jury trial, and criminal indictments for conspiracy decimated the union's national and local leadership. Debs, Howard, other union officers, and many ordinary railroaders served jail time.

The Pullman strike and boycott of 1894 brought about the central role of the state as regulator of labor-management conflicts and the submission of labor organizations to state power. Beginning with the Erdman Act of 1898 (originally drafted by Attorney General Richard Olney), Congress would regulate labor relations between railroad workers and employers. Railroaders, long divided and thwarted by craft rivalries, lost a viable industrial union on the western railroads and were relegated to increasingly conservative brotherhoods. Blacklisting by railroad managers kept many ARU members unemployed for years and forced others to seek jobs using assumed names. Along the route of the Northern Pacific Railroad, for example, 1,944 ARU boycott participants were blacklisted by name. Personal sacrifices by those railroaders and Pullman shop workers exacted high prices lasting years after the Pullman strike and boycott ended.

MARTIN TUOHY

References and Further Reading

Buder, Stanley. *Pullman: An Experiment in Industrial Order and Community Planning, 1880–1930.* New York: Oxford University Press, 1967.

Cobb, Stephen G. *The Rev. William Carwardine and the Pullman Strike of 1894: The Christian Gospel and Social Justice.* Lewiston, NY: The Edwin Mellen Press, 1992.

Hirsch, Susan. *After the Strike: A Century of Labor Struggle at Pullman.* Urbana: University of Illinois Press, 2003.

Jebsen, Harry, Jr. "The Role of Blue Island in the Pullman Strike of 1894." *Journal of the Illinois State Historical Society* 67, no. 3 (June 1974): 275–293.

Laurie, Clayton D. "Extinguishing Frontier Brushfires: The U.S. Army's Role in Quelling the Pullman Strike in the West, 1894." *Journal of the West* 32, no. 2 (April 1993): 54–63.

Lindsey, Almont. *The Pullman Strike: The Story of a Unique Experiment and of a Great Labor Upheaval.* Chicago: University of Chicago Press, 1942.

Papke, David Ray. *The Pullman Case: The Clash of Labor and Capital in Industrial America.* Lawrence: University Press of Kansas, 1999.

Pullman Company Archives. Newberry Library, Chicago.

Pullman Company Correspondence, 1892–1912. South Suburban Genealogical and Historical Society, Hazel Crest, IL.

Records of the District Courts of the United States (Record Group 21). National Archives and Records Administration.

Robert Todd Lincoln Collection, Abraham Lincoln Presidential Library, Springfield, IL.

Salvatore, Nick. *Eugene V. Debs: Citizen and Socialist.* Urbana: University of Illinois Press, 1982.

Schneirov, Richard, Shelton Stromquist, and Nick Salvatore, eds. *The Pullman Strike and the Crisis of the 1890s: Essays on Labor and Politics.* Urbana: University of Illinois Press, 1999.

Smith, Carl. *Urban Disorder and the Shape of Belief: The Great Chicago Fire, the Haymarket Bomb, and the Model Town of Pullman.* Chicago: University of Chicago Press, 1995.

Stromquist, Shelton. *A Generation of Boomers: The Pattern of Railroad Labor Conflict in Nineteenth-Century America.* Urbana: University of Illinois Press, 1987.

See also **American Railway Union; Blacklists; Debs, Eugene V.; Knights of Labor; Pullman, George Mortimer; Railroad Brotherhoods**

PULLMAN, GEORGE MORTIMER
(March 3, 1831– October 19, 1897)

George Pullman did not invent railroad sleeping cars, as commonly reported, but his attention to the details of comfort and his technological improvements made sleeping cars economically viable beginning in 1859. Yet, Pullman's inability to recognize his dependence upon the contributions of carpenters, seamstresses, train porters, car cleaners, and others, coupled with paternalistic control of the inhabitants of his namesake company town, caused simmering worker discontent that eventually exploded in the Pullman Strike and Boycott of May–August 1894.

George Pullman was born south of Buffalo, New York, the third of eight children. His father, a carpenter during the Erie Canal's building boom, invented and patented a machine for transporting buildings about 1835. The evangelical fervor of late 1820s western New York pushed his Baptist father to convert to Universalism. Baptists commenced a boycott of the elder Pullman's carpentry business. The father's jobs along the Erie Canal caused frequent absences. Older brothers Henry and Albert began cabinetmaking in Albion, New York, about 1845, and George apprenticed with them and assisted in moving houses. After Albert moved to Grand Rapids, Michigan, in 1850 to manufacture furniture, George became a hands-on supervisor of workmen, unjamming mud-clogged rollers and energetically securing contracts during a canal-widening project.

A chance meeting in Albion in January 1859 with a former Illinois governor's wife drew Pullman into jacking up sections of Chicago's business district. Pullman traveled to Grand Rapids (where Albert was impoverished) and Chicago, where his partnership won the contract to raise the Matteson House Hotel, began ahead of schedule, and raised the five-story structure by five feet over 10 days. Albert joined George and worked alongside the laborers under the building as foreman. In spring 1860, George left Albert in charge of subsequent jobs, ventured out to the gold-mining region near Central City, later Colorado Territory, and bought and operated an ore-stamping mill, a store, and other ventures in partnerships between mid-1860 and spring 1863.

Pullman's entry into railroad sleeping car manufacture began in partnership with the New York State senator Benjamin Field in early 1859. Upon Pullman's arrival in Chicago, he convinced Alton Railroad managers to adopt his innovations and hired a shop mechanic to rebuild two coaches into sleeping cars. The first ran 15 August 1859. His cousin worked as conductor on the cars. In 1867, Pullman's Palace Car Company was chartered and incorporated. Between 1870 and 1880, Pullman erected cars at an acquired factory in Detroit. Albert Pullman supervised craftsmen and laborers as general superintendent, and then second vice president.

Pullman exerted paternalistic control over his younger siblings with some success during the 1850s to 1860s but failed with his own children, wife, and workers during the 1880s to 1890s. The pressures of business, coupled with Pullman's own irascible personality, made him austere and unapproachable. In 1881, Pullman opened a newly built company-owned town and manufacturing plant 14 miles south of Chicago. Most observers lauded the new town, consciously designed to improve the living conditions of working families accustomed to urban slum tenements. In 1885, the economist Richard T. Ely credited Pullman with recognizing the "commercial value of beauty" in the luxurious cars built in Pullman's plant and the broad, tree-lined streets and ornamented red-brick row houses of the adjacent town. However, Ely also found that nepotism, favoritism, company spies, and the suppression of workers' grievances rendered residents silent and unattached and the town "un-American."

Workers did not always remain silent, however. Individual department strikes in 1882, 1884, and 1885 preceded a May 1886 general strike of the Knights of Labor for an eight-hour day. The Haymarket bombing and subsequent prosecution of anarchists prompted Pullman to donate for their conviction and execution. Albert Pullman left the company that same year. Strikes in 1888, 1891, and May 1894 were precipitated by heavy-handed foremen and wage cuts but reflected the underlying discontent with workers' inability to represent their interests collectively. The May 1894 strike, which prompted a 26 June national boycott of Pullman cars by railroad workers loyal to the American Railway Union, brought widespread criticism upon George Pullman for refusing to negotiate, reduce rents, or shift half the financial burden off of the workers. He suffered a "nervous depression" that left him bedridden and ill until autumn 1894 and caused severe strains upon his marriage and family life. Pullman died of a heart attack 19 October 1897. One son, George Jr., briefly worked as a Pullman car inspector in Chicago, and then in New Jersey after his father's death until June 1898. Pullman's enduring legacies more than one hundred years after his death are the National Historic

Landmark Town of Pullman and the George M. Pullman Educational Foundation, which assists college students of limited financial means.

MARTIN TUOHY

References and Further Reading

Buder, Stanley. *Pullman: An Experiment in Industrial Order and Community Planning, 1880–1930*. New York: Oxford University Press, 1967.

Business Records in Pullman Company Archives, Newberry Library.

Ely, Richard T. "Pullman: A Social Study." *Harper's Magazine* 70 (February 1885): 452–466.

"George M. Pullman Educational Foundation." www.pullmanfoundation.org/ (2003–).

"Historic Pullman Foundation." www.pullmanil.org/ (2003–).

Leyendecker, Liston Edgington. *Palace Car Prince: A Biography of George Mortimer Pullman*. Niwot, CO: University Press of Colorado, 1992.

Personal Correspondence, 1874 diary fragment, and 1894 diary in Mrs. C. Phillip Miller Collection, Chicago Historical Society.

Reiff, Janice L. "A Modern Lear and His Daughters: Gender in the Model Town of Pullman." In *The Pullman Strike and the Crisis of the 1890s: Essays on Labor and Politics*, edited by Richard Schneirov, Shelton Stromquist, and Nick Salvatore. Urbana and Chicago: University of Illinois Press, 1999, pp. 65–86.

See also **Haymarket Affair (1886); Knights of Labor; Pullman Strike and Boycott (1894)**

Q

QUILL, MICHAEL J. (SEPTEMBER 18, 1905–JANUARY 28, 1966)
President, Transport Workers' Union

Michael Joseph Quill headed the Transport Workers' Union (TWU) from shortly after its founding in 1934 until his death in 1966. During those years he also held a series of positions in the Congress of Industrial Organizations (CIO), with which the TWU was affiliated, and he served as an elected member of the New York City Council. While the modest size of the TWU—at the time of his death it had 135,000 members—kept Quill from reaching the very top ranks of labor leadership, his radical views, outspokenness, and involvement in New York City politics often brought him into the spotlight of public attention.

Quill's political outlook was shaped by his youthful involvement in the Irish republican movement, which led him to question authority, embrace militancy, and become sympathetic to the political left. Born on a mountain farm in County Kerry, Ireland, to a family that supported the Irish Republican Army (IRA) during the struggle for Irish independence and the subsequent civil war, Quill served with the IRA during the early 1920s. In 1926, he immigrated to the United States and took a job with New York's Interborough Rapid Transit Company. Quill became well known among fellow Irish transit workers through his involvement in various Irish organizations. When an effort began in 1933 to unionize the city's transit industry, which brought together organizers from the Communist party (CP), various groups of discontented workers, and IRA veterans working in transit, Quill joined early. His wealth of contacts in the Irish community, standing as a former republican fighter, and his gift for speaking quickly brought him to the forefront of the union group.

In 1935, Quill became the first elected president of the TWU (there had been an appointed president before him). Two years later when the TWU accepted a charter from the CIO to be a national mass transit workers' union, Quill was elected as the first president of the reconstituted union, giving up his post as head of the New York local though continuing to help lead it. Flush with recognition victories in New York, the TWU began transforming the lives of the city's transit workers, winning shorter hours, better pay, and new benefits, while slowly spreading to other cities.

During the organization of the TWU, Quill drew close to the CP, possibly joining it. Until the late 1940s, he worked closely with the party members who held the other top posts in the transit union and participated in various political campaigns supported by the Communists. (He also remained active in Irish republican causes.) With his sharp wit and position as the head of a national union, Quill emerged within the CIO as one of its best-known left-wing leaders. When in 1938 dissident transit workers charged in testimony before a congressional committee that Quill and other TWU leaders were Communists, Quill retorted in one of his best-known statements that he "would rather be called a Red by the rats than a rat by the Reds." In addition to his union post, Quill served for 8 years on the New York

City Council representing the Bronx, elected twice as a candidate of the left-liberal American Labor party and once as an independent. With the onset of the Cold War, Quill broke ranks with the CP. The changing political atmosphere in the labor movement and the country no doubt influenced him, but two specific issues precipitated his 1948 decision, the insistence by the CP that its union backers support the third-party presidential bid of Henry Wallace in spite of the strong opposition of CIO President Philip Murray, and the party's continuing support for freezing the New York City transit fare, which Quill came to believe would undercut the possibilities for wage hikes. After a bitter civil war within the TWU, Quill succeeded in ousting the union leaders who remained aligned with the CP, retaining his presidency by constructing a new set of alliances that included centrists and conservatives as well as anti-Communist liberals.

In the decades after World War II, the TWU, under Quill, expanded into the airline industry; absorbed railroad workers who had been organized by the CIO; and continued to sign up mass-transit workers. In New York the union faced a series of challenges after its initial organization, including the 1940 city takeover of most private transit lines, which forced the TWU to fight for years to win back its status as an exclusive collective-bargaining agent. During the 1950s, Quill and other TWU leaders were criticized by skilled craft workers who felt they would do better with separate unions for their own groups and during the 1960s, by African-Americans who felt they had insufficient access to better paid jobs and union leadership posts.

Quill gave up his City Council seat in 1949, but he remained prominent in New York affairs as president of the New York City CIO Council. In 1950, he became a vice-president of the CIO as well. Even after his break with the CP, Quill stayed on the left of what became a narrowed spectrum of opinion within the labor movement and the country. In 1955, he was the most prominent critic within the CIO of its decision to merge with the American Federation of Labor (AFL), charging that the constitution of the combined group would allow raiding, racketeering, and racial discrimination. In the 1960s, Quill actively supported the civil rights movement and was an early critic of the Vietnam War. He occasionally described himself as a Socialist and called for the New York subway system to be made free. Though Quill's fiery rhetoric had limited practical impact, it made him stand out in an era of increasingly bland labor leaders and helped keep alive a labor political tradition that openly acknowledged fundamental class conflict.

Though Quill often threatened to strike the New York transit system, he did not lead the TWU to do so until 1966, when he sought a major improvement in wages, especially for more skilled workers, and a militant fight as a way to reunify the union and cement his legacy. The strike, which all but shut down New York City for 12 days, ended in a substantial union victory. Quill, who was jailed, and then suffered a heart attack during the walkout, was the object of fierce public and political criticism as well as support from within the labor movement. He died of heart failure 2 weeks after the strike. Fittingly striking cemetery workers dropped their picket line so that he could be buried.

JOSHUA B. FREEMAN

References and Further Reading

Freeman, Joshua B. *In Transit: The Transport Workers Union in New York City, 1933–1966*. Philadelphia, PA: Temple University Press, 2001.

Quill, Shirley. *Mike Quill—Himself: A Memoir*. Greenwich, CT: Devin-Adair, 1985.

Whittemore, L. H. *The Man Who Ran the Subways: The Story of Mike Quill*. New York: Holt, Rinehart, and Winston, 1968.

See also **American Federation of Labor-Congress of Industrial Organizations; American Labor Party; Communist Party; Transport Workers' Union**

R

RACKETEERING AND RICO

The term "racketeering" came into popular use in the 1920s when it usually referred to the activities of a new generation of organized crime that had emerged during Prohibition. Racketeering often involved labor unions. Examples of labor racketeering included crimes such as extortion from employers and union leaders, embezzlement from union funds, and the creation of various kinds of anticompetitive cartel arrangements. But the word "racketeering" also served as a political tool and was applied by organized labor's opponents to legal but aggressive forms of union activity. Thus, historically, public alarm about the danger of racketeering often has been used to justify new restrictions on organized labor. Concern about the growing economic influence of organized crime through racketeering has also justified significant extensions of the federal government's role in law enforcement. One of the most prominent examples of that trend was the passage in 1970 of a broad, new federal conspiracy law, the Racketeer Influenced and Corrupt Organizations Act (RICO). This law gave federal prosecutors a powerful weapon with which to attack the leadership hierarchy in criminal gangs; it also included civil provisions that allowed the government to assume control of corrupt labor organizations.

Criminal gangs that emerged during Prohibition (1920–1933) became involved in labor racketeering by the late 1920s. They tended to exert influence over unions with particular kinds of jurisdictions—typically labor organizations that operated in economic sectors that had long been marked by anticompetitive forms of collusion among employers and unions. At least since the 1890s, some unions in some sectors of the economy had engaged in such collusive arrangements with employers. In return for closed-shop contracts, unions in construction and the teaming trades and in some of the service sectors agreed to help employers control the level of competition in their industry. Typically unions in these sectors helped employers limit the entry of new firms and policed agreements on prices and customer allocation arrangements. These collusive arrangements tended to appear in industries where the initial start-up capital requirements were so low that new firms could easily enter the marketplace, creating a tendency toward cutthroat competition. Businesses in those sectors turned to organized labor in hopes that it could provide economic stability.

Often unions involved in such activity were also troubled by charges of corruption. To a certain extent, those charges reflected the ways in which union leaders in those settings could easily dominate their members; the union's initial organization stemmed from the leader's relationship with the employers, not on his ability to mobilize the membership. The employers supported the union because of what it offered them, and so there was rarely a need to rally the union's rank and file to man the picket lines. Thus, these unions often lacked the basic democratic mechanisms that encouraged active membership, and that in turn made it more difficult for the members to police their leadership. But charges of corruption also frequently reflected the hostility of outside business interests, which resented the strategic power of unions in these sectors. Indeed, the term "racketeering" itself first emerged in Chicago in the 1920s as a way for anti-union employers to condemn the kinds of collusive arrangements that had allowed some labor organizations to become powerful in certain areas of the city.

The new type of criminal gangs that emerged in the 1920s, during Prohibition, eventually began to assert a role in these kinds of collusive business environments. Union officials in these sectors faced threats of violence and demands for money. Given organized labor's tenuous legal status, particularly in these collusive sectors, union officials lacked the kind of protection that law enforcement would have provided to businesspersons in an industrial sector had they faced similar threats. Also, in places like Chicago, union officials knew that the police regularly colluded with criminal gangs. Thus, typically the gangland murder of union leaders went unsolved and brought no crackdown by police. In such settings, some union leaders chose to make arrangements with criminal gangs. These arrangements might involve appointing gang members or their associates to lower-level union posts. They also might involve agreements to allow a gang to siphon off a portion of the union's funds, perhaps by kicking back a share of the top officers' salaries. With the emergence in the post-WWII era of various benefit funds, arrangements were made in unions such as the Teamsters for organized crime groups to benefit from the financial decisions of some of these funds.

In addition to drawing on the funds of a labor organization, members of criminal gangs found other ways to profit from their ability to dominate some union leaders. One type of racketeering grew out of changes in federal labor laws in the 1930s. In the new political atmosphere of that decade, employers lost two of their most important weapons for combating organized labor. The Norris LaGuardia Act (1932) placed new limits on the abilities of employers to use injunctions against organized labor, while the Wagner Act (1935) made company unions illegal. At the same time, employers faced a wave of militant union organization. Many responded by turning to organized crime groups, which offered them a way to meet this threat. Gangsters provided businesspersons with the opportunity to sign a collective bargaining agreement with a kind of captive union, one controlled by organized crime. Such a collective bargaining agreement would forestall the organizing efforts of legitimate unions while leaving the employer's labor costs virtually unchanged. Workers covered by agreements with such captive unions saw no increase in their wages, no changes in their work conditions, and received no benefits. Indeed, because the employer now deducted union dues from their paycheck, these workers might

actually suffer a decrease in pay. The employer, on the other hand, received tangible benefits. In return for the employer deducting dues and providing other forms of compensation to the corrupt union official, organized crime muzzled any militancy by the workers and blocked efforts by other unions to intercede. The captive union functioned as a new kind of company union.

Even though employers often benefited from this kind of organized criminal activity, businesses were usually depicted by the press and law enforcement as the main victims of labor racketeering. Payments made by businesspersons to criminal figures or corrupt union officials were described as extortion, a legal term for money paid under threat of harm. This term, however, was applied even in circumstances such as the ones described above, or when an employer paid off a corrupt union official in order to gain a more favorable collective bargaining agreement. Using that definition of extortion left union officials appearing as the perennial villains and employers as the hapless victims. It also made labor racketeering appear to result from the ability of powerful unions to threaten the economic well-being of businesses. In this political context, the term "racketeering" itself became a kind of political weapon to use against the growing power of unions in the 1930s, 1940s, and 1950s. Critics of organized labor, such as the newspaper columnist Westbrook Pegler, described legal but aggressive forms of union activity, such as secondary boycotts or even organizational picketing, as forms of racketeering.

This biased depiction of labor racketeering meant that campaigns against organized crime often served as a pretext for efforts to limit the power of labor unions. The McClellan Committee hearings (1957–1959), for example, helped raise awareness about the existence of the Mafia and made labor racketeering an important public issue. But the Committee was dominated by conservative congressmen who used the hearings to promote an anti-union agenda. They sought to raise concern about the connection between organized crime and the Teamsters Union in order to promote anti-union legislation. To protect the nation from the threat of labor racketeering, the McClellan Committee urged Congress to enact new restrictions on the ability of unions to organize and picket. The result was the Landrum-Griffin Act (1959), which among other things banned secondary boycotts and put new limits on organizational picketing.

More recent efforts to confront the threat posed by organized crime and labor racketeering have involved the use of the Racketeer Influenced and Corrupt Organizations statute (RICO) (18 U.S.C. Sections

1961–1968). RICO was passed as one of the sections of the Organized Crime Control Act of 1970. This statute came as part of a wave of legislation at the end of the 1960s that aimed to give federal law enforcement the legal tools it needed to effectively combat organized crime. This same generation of legislation, for instance, created the Witness Protection Program and authorized the use of electronic surveillance by law enforcement. The legislation marked a new federal commitment to waging a war on organized crime. In passing such laws, Congress was responding to warnings about the growth of organized crime issued by the Task Force on Organized Crime of the President's Commission on Law Enforcement and Administration of Justice (1965–1967). The Task Force had specifically warned that the Mafia was using its ability to dominate some unions as a way to infiltrate heretofore legitimate areas of business. Robert Blakey, who drafted the RICO statute, had served on the staff of the Task Force, and he made sure that the new legislation included specific provisions for stopping organized crime's infiltration of the larger economy.

RICO made it a crime to use a pattern of criminal activity or the proceeds of such criminal activity to gain control over an organization (that is, an enterprise) or to run such an enterprise through a pattern of criminal activity. The criminal provisions of RICO function as a broad conspiracy statute that treats organized crime activity as an "enterprise." Originally, the law was understood to target only such criminal activity that brought criminal gangs into legitimate organizations such as unions or a business. But since 1981, the Supreme Court has held that the term "enterprise" can also refer to illegitimate groups, in effect making it possible for the government to prosecute individuals for participating in a criminal group, such as a Mafia family. According to the language of the statute, anyone who infiltrates, participates in, or conducts the affairs of such a RICO-defined enterprise through a pattern of racketeering activity has violated this law.

Establishing a pattern of racketeering activity forms the central part of a RICO prosecution. For the purposes of the statute, such a pattern must involve at least two racketeering acts, with at least one committed since 1970 and the last one occurring within 10 years of its predecessor. These racketeering acts, referred to as RICO predicates, include a long shopping list of federal and state felonies. In this way, the language of the act allows prosecutors to overcome the statute of limitations on crimes and to ignore the jurisdictional divisions between state and federal crimes. In effect, the government can present a jury with the whole career of an individual and a criminal group, bringing together otherwise disparate acts into one large set of conspiracy charges.

The penalties for conviction under RICO are quite severe, another reason why prosecutors like this statute. Each RICO predicate charge carries a possible 20-year sentence, and a defendant can also be charged with participating in the enterprise conspiracy, a separate charge that also carries a 20-year sentence. As a result, organized crime figures convicted under RICO face lengthy prison sentences. To take one example, in *United States v. Salerno* (1986), the government convicted the leaders of several New York organized crime families on charges related to their role in the commission that oversaw Mafia operations along the East Coast. RICO's tough sentencing provisions made each defendant liable for up to 300 years in jail, and although the judge did not impose that full amount, the men were sentenced to 100 years of prison apiece. In addition, RICO includes a powerful forfeiture provision that allows the government to seize any assets gained as a result of the criminal activity engaged in by the defendant.

In the first few years after its passage, RICO went unused, but by the 1980s, prosecutors made it the workhorse in a campaign against organized crime. This campaign was marked by the FBI's effective use of electronic surveillance, which provided a persuasive new kind of evidence for use in organized crime trials. Similarly, the threat of RICO sentences and the availability of an effective Witness Protection Program led to the emergence of significant cooperating witnesses from within ranks of organized crime families. Aladema ("Jimmy the Weasel") Fratianno, who had been the acting boss of the Los Angeles Crime Family, was one of the first of these Mafia turncoats, but many others followed. Their testimony offered juries an insider's view of organized crime and helped bring about some of the most significant convictions in this law enforcement effort. As a result, hundreds of organized crime figures, including many of the top Mafia leaders, have been convicted and sent to jail.

This campaign against organized crime also took advantage of RICO's civil provisions. While the criminal section of RICO is meant to be punitive, the civil section aims to be preventative, to block organized crime's further use of a labor union or a business. To that end, prosecutors can draw on a range of potential remedies that include court orders barring individuals from having any further connection to an organization as well as court-imposed trusteeships.

Civil RICO offers the government a number of advantages. Civil procedure allows prosecutors to build up their case during the pretrial period by requiring the defendant to respond to the prosecutors' requests for depositions and internal documents, providing evidence that the government can later use to demonstrate organized crime's control over the organization. A lesser standard of proof is required for the government to make its case in a civil proceeding, a "preponderance of evidence" as opposed to the requirement of "beyond a reasonable doubt" needed for a criminal conviction. Finally, defendants in such a suit face serious financial consequences should the government prevail. They are liable to treble damages as well as court costs and attorney fees, and that financial threat serves as a powerful incentive to reach a settlement with the government before the case goes to trial.

The Justice Department began to use civil RICO against union corruption in the mid-1980s. By 2004, it had filed a total of 21 civil RICO suits against labor organizations, and in several other cases it has used the threat of such suits to convince unions to make specific internal reforms. Only one case, the government's first suit against Teamsters Local 560 in New Jersey, has ever gone to trial. The government's victory in that case, combined with the consequences that defendants face should they lose, has meant that in all of the subsequent cases, defendants have agreed to settlements before trial. Three of the suits involved international unions, the International Brotherhood of Teamsters (IBT), the Laborers' International Union of North America (LIUNA), and the Hotel Employees and Restaurant Employees' International Union (HERIU). The bulk of the suits were filed against local affiliates of those three international unions and against local affiliates of the International Longshoremen's Union (ILA). The President's Commission on Organized Crime (1983–1986) had named those four internationals (ILA, IBT, HERIU, LIUNA) as the unions most dominated by organized crime. Three other civil RICO suits were filed against local affiliates of international unions with quite the opposite reputations. In those cases, though the international union's leadership enjoyed an honest reputation, the local affiliates in question had long been notorious for their alleged connections to organized crime. The civil RICO suit filed in 1994 against the New York City District Council of Carpenters was one example of such a case.

These suits have resulted in various types of trusteeship arrangements, which have ranged widely in terms of the length of their duration and the kinds of oversight exercised. The shortest trusteeship lasted for 18 months, but others have gone on significantly longer, as much as six years. Often, the consent decrees that result from civil RICO settlements call for some continuation of government oversight, on an open-ended basis, even after the formal trusteeship comes to an end. In the case of the IBT, for instance, the terms of three court officers serving as trustees expired following the certification of the results of the union's 1991 elections. But government oversight continues in the form of an Internal Review Board, which pursues cases of corruption involving Teamster officials. The courts have granted some trustees great authority in conducting the affairs of a union under a civil RICO trusteeship—from negotiating contracts with employers to administering the organization. But other trustees have been limited to a narrower range of activity, from reviewing financial decisions to banning union officials with organized crime connections. In each case, the specifics of the trusteeship emerged out of a combination of what the particular U.S. attorney's office requested, what the union officials in question were willing to settle for, and the decision of the federal judge hearing the suit.

Critics of the use of civil RICO against unions have focused on several issues. Some have noted the apparent lack of a coherent strategy or direction in the government's use of this powerful tool. Individual trustees have operated in isolation from one another, and there has been no effort to develop any kind of guide to policies most likely to rid a union of organized crime influence. Union officials have complained about the costs of paying for government oversight. In some cases, trustees (almost always former federal prosecutors) have earned sums far larger than the allegedly corrupt and piratical union officials who were ousted by the civil RICO suit. Other critics have worried about the ways in which civil RICO challenges the traditional autonomy of labor unions. This threat appears more palpable in cases when a conservative administration filed suit against a national union, such as happened in 1988, when the Reagan administration's Justice Department sued the IBT, then the largest labor organization in the country.

DAVID WITWER

References and Further Reading

Abidinsky, Howard. *Organized Crime*. Chicago: Nelson-Hall Publishers, 1994.

Cohen, Andrew Wender. *The Racketeer's Progress: Chicago and the Struggle for the Modern American Economy, 1900–1940*. New York: Cambridge University Press, 2004.

Crowe, Kenneth. *Collision: How the Rank and File Took Back the Teamsters Union*. New York: Charles Scribner's Sons, 1993.

Jacobs, James B. *Busting the Mob:* United States v. Cosa Nostra. New York: New York University Press, 1994.

———. "The RICO Trusteeships after Twenty Years: A Progress Report." *The Labor Lawyer* 19, no. 3 (2004): 419–485.

New York State Organized Crime Task Force. *Corruption and Racketeering in the New York City Construction*

Industry: The Final Report. New York: New York University Press, 1990.

President's Commission on Organized Crime. *The Edge: Organized Crime, Business, and Labor Unions*. Washington, DC: U.S. Government Printing Agency, 1986.

Reuter, Peter. *Racketeering in Legitimate Industries*. Washington, DC: Rand, 1987.

Summers, Clyde. "Union Trusteeships and Union Democracy." *University of Michigan Journal of Law Reform* 24, nos. 3–4 (1991): 691–707.

Task Force on Organized Crime, President's Commission on Law Enforcement and Administration of Justice. *Task Force Report: Organized Crime, Annotations and Consultants Papers*. Washington, DC: U.S. Government Printing Office, 1967.

Witwer, David. *Corruption and Reform in the Teamsters Union*. Chicago: University of Illinois Press, 2003.

———. "The Scandal of George Scalise: A Case Study in the Rise of Labor Racketeering in the 1930s." *Journal of Social History* 36, no. 4 (Summer 2003): 917–940.

See also **Hotel and Restaurant Employees International Union; International Brotherhood of Teamsters; International Longshoremen's Association; Laborers' International Union of North America; McClellan Committee Hearings; Organized Crime**

RAILROAD BROTHERHOODS

The railroad brotherhoods are a historically significant but underappreciated set of unions that organized workers in the U.S. railroad industry for roughly a century from the 1860s through the 1960s. Probably because of the large number of brotherhood-style railroad unions and their complex interlocking jurisdictions, predominantly craft orientations, explicitly fraternal natures, and conservative (in some notable instances racist) policies, the railroad brotherhoods have not garnered labor historians' sustained attention. Yet, these unions defined the predominant model of unionism in one of the nation's most vital economic sectors, included among their number some of the earliest successful national-level unions, played vital roles in the development of American industrial relations machinery, and were party to groundbreaking social welfare legislation. In the process, four of them—the so-called Big Four brotherhoods of "train service" or "running trades" workers (engineers, conductors, firemen, brakemen)—became the most powerful set of unions in the United States by the era of World War I and remained among the most influential of unions through the first half of the twentieth century.

The railroad brotherhoods are also significant for their standing as "brotherhoods." More explicitly than most other American unions, the railroad brotherhoods constituted themselves as fraternal bodies of workingmen. Borrowing from Masonic fraternalism, widespread in the nineteenth-century United States, the railroad brotherhoods practiced fraternal ritual, emphasized the principles of mutual aid and moral uplift, and made male gender and craft occupational identity central to their organizational cultures. Expressed in the ideals of manhood, brotherhood, and craft pride, this bundle of ideals and practices represented a fraternalistic/mutual-aid logic that helped these unions survive in the hostile political and economic climate of the late nineteenth century while meeting the very real material needs of men who labored in a hazardous industry. The Big Four brotherhoods pioneered this brotherhood style of unionism during the 1870s and 1880s. The rest of so-called standard railroad unions of nonoperating workers of clerks, telegraphers, car repairmen, signalmen, and maintenance-of-way workers and the like patterned themselves after the brotherhoods as they organized from the 1880s onward. Thus, the term "railroad brotherhoods" refers to both the operating and 16-odd nonoperating unions of railroad workers as well as to the distinctive style of unionism they practiced.

Origins and Early Development in the Nineteenth Century

The railroad brotherhoods became known for their conservative, mutual-aid-oriented unionism early on. The first successful national-level union of railway workers began in 1863, following a series of short-lived efforts dating from the mid-1850s, when engineers working on Detroit railroads founded the Brotherhood of the Footboard in response to wage cuts and the imposition of piecework. Led by William D. Robinson, the new union aggressively defended wages and work rules in the course of several strikes. However, in the face of the railroads' fierce opposition and division within the Brotherhood's ranks, the union shifted course in 1868, replacing Robinson with the cautious Charles Wilson as grand chief engineer, changing its name to the Brotherhood of Locomotive Engineers (BLE) and embracing benevolent work among railway workers instead of direct confrontation with capital. The Order of Railway Conductors (ORC), the Brotherhood of Locomotive Firemen (BLF, which changed its name to the Brotherhood of Locomotive Firemen and Enginemen—BLFE—in 1907), and the Brotherhood of Railroad Brakemen (later renamed the Brotherhood of Railroad Trainmen, BRT) followed the Engineers' example, organizing

Locomotive engineer, Saint Louis, Missouri. Library of Congress, Prints & Photographs Division, FSA/OWI Collection [LC-USF33-003027-M4].

themselves in 1868, 1873, and 1883, respectively. The Switchmen's Mutual Aid Association, which came into being in the late 1870s and was succeeded by the Switchmen's Union of North America in 1894, organized brakemen whose duties were confined to switching yards, but it never achieved the kind of power that the Big Four came to enjoy. Competing claims inevitably led to jurisdictional conflict among these unions, most notably between the Trainmen and Switchmen. Nevertheless, all of the operating brotherhoods shared a common policy in their restriction of membership to white men "of good moral character."

During the 1870s and 1880s, the railroad brotherhoods perfected their approach to labor relations and mutual aid. The visiting of sick or injured members and the provision of death and disability insurance grew out of customary workplace mutualism, but the brotherhoods quickly institutionalized these traditions and by the early twentieth century boasted some of the largest union insurance funds. With moral uplift, which ranged from technical instruction to the inculcation of sober and industrious habits, brotherhood leaders emphasized the individual's self-improvement and upward mobility. Combining these fraternal practices, brotherhood leaders such as the Engineers' chief engineer Peter M. Arthur and the Firemen's secretary-treasurer Eugene V. Debs sought to recruit running trades workers while simultaneously presenting their organizations to railroad management as bulwarks against labor radicalism,

arguing that they in fact produced "a better class of railway men." In the aftermath of the railroad strikes of 1877, increasing numbers of managers came to see the brotherhoods of train service workers as plausible partners in labor relations. During the 1880s, with continued periodic labor upheavals and a tight railroad labor market due to rapid expansion of the national railroad network, the brotherhoods negotiated favorable agreements on a number of roads. Together with their craft orientation, this success encouraged the brotherhoods to chart a course separate from that of the larger labor movement, refusing protective alliances with other segments of organized railroad labor and declining affiliation with the American Federation of Labor (AFL).

The Big Four might have enjoyed a monopoly on train service unionism had it not been for continued dissatisfaction with conservative brotherhood-style unionism among segments of running trades workers, especially in the aftermath of the BLE's and BLF's near disastrous strike against the Chicago, Burlington & Quincy Railroad in 1888. Most acute on the frontier of railroad expansion where labor conditions were tightest, this undercurrent animated the rise and fall of industrially oriented railway unionism in the form of the Knights of Labor (KOL) in the 1880s and American Railway Union (ARU), which Eugene Debs led after breaking with the BLF in the 1890s. However, during these years both of these unions engaged in epic confrontations with capital and were destroyed. Indeed, the Pullman strike and boycott of 1894 proved a turning point in railroad labor relations as the ARU buckled under the combined might of the railroad corporations and the national state, ending the possibility of industrial, all-grades unionism on the railroads.

The Big Four proved to be the beneficiaries of this episode as they avoided the boycott and in some instances helped to break it. In the aftermath of the conflagration, figures in the federal government and the railroads took favorable note of the brotherhoods' actions and set about including them in a state-sanctioned system of mediation and arbitration designed to prevent conflicts like the Pullman boycott and to ensure that the railroads remained free of "radical" industrial-style unionism. The ensuing Erdman Act of 1898 provided the framework for the nation's first real system of collective bargaining and the first, if de facto, recognition of the right of unions of the brotherhood variety to exist. Nevertheless, the dream of broader unionism did not die with the ARU, as into the 1930s minorities of running trades workers dissatisfied with the Big Four's conservatism periodically mounted rank-and-file rebellions and experimented with dissident union movements, sometimes uniting with nonoperating workers.

Brotherhood Power during the Progressive Era

With its mediation and arbitration machinery, the Erdman Act enabled the Big Four to wax powerful after 1900. The increasing volume of railroad traffic following the severe 1890s depression placed increasing strain upon railroad workers as they worked longer, more intensive hours and confronted a steadily rising cost of living. Rank-and-file pressure from below and recognition of the need to confront the railroad corporations on a broader basis prompted brotherhood leaders to pursue synchronized industrial action through a series of "concerted movements." However, while they became adept at the quasi-courtlike proceedings of the arbitration process and won important gains, they became ever more disappointed with arbitrators' awards. By 1916, the brotherhoods had sworn off arbitration altogether, choosing instead to band together in the presenting of demands for the eight-hour day in the train service to all the nation's railroads and threatening a national rail strike. The ensuing crisis, coming on the eve of U.S. entry into World War I, forced the intervention of President Woodrow Wilson and the passage of the Adamson Act, the first federally legislated eight-hour

day for nongovernment workers and a significant expansion of the federal government's ability to intervene in and regulate labor relations. While the brotherhoods' achievements during these years testified to their increased power and their ability to win appreciable gains for their members in terms of wages and protective legislation, they also used their power toward such decidedly less laudable ends as the eviction from the train service of black workers through legislative lobbying, contract negotiation, and a series of hateful "race" strikes.

If the period from the late 1890s through 1916 marked the waxing of the Big Four, it also represented a time of continued struggle for the rest of the railroad industry's unions. Never as strategically placed as the workers of the running trades, telegraphers, maintenance-of-way workers, car repairmen, and clerks found it difficult to command the respect of management. Beginning in the mid-1880s, a period of heady expansion and tight labor markets in the railroad industry, unions of nonoperating workers emerged as telegraphers, track foremen, and car repairmen formed local and regional associations oriented toward the provision of mutual aid. By the early 1890s, these organizations had formed into national-level unions: the Brotherhood of Railway Trackmen (later to become the Brotherhood of Maintenance of Way Workers), the Order of Railroad Telegraphers (ORT), and the Brotherhood of Railway Carmen of America. Following the 1890s depression, which severely tested all of the brotherhoods, the Order of Railway Clerks (later, the Brotherhood of Railway and Steamship Clerks, Freight Handlers, Express and Station Employees) joined these unions in 1900. Like the operating brotherhoods, these unions patterned themselves on the fraternal model, initially emphasized benefit work and insurance, and restricted their membership to white men. Unlike the Big Four, the nonoperating brotherhoods did not enjoy the provisions of the Erdman Act (with the exception of the ORT) and at one time or another affiliated with the AFL, a measure of their relative weakness. Thus, while the return of prosperity in the new century enabled the nonoperating brotherhoods to recoup earlier losses and to grow in size, they nevertheless faced an uphill battle in their efforts to win recognition and establish the principle of collective bargaining with railroad management.

In these circumstances, the federal government's World War I takeover of the national railway system catapulted unionism forward and transformed railroad labor relations. As the United States headed into the European conflict during 1917, the nation's railway system, which had failed to expand sufficiently over the previous decade, almost collapsed under the weight of war-related shipping. From the beginning of 1918 through early 1920, as the Wilson administration sought to direct and rationalize railroad service through the United States Railroad Administration (USRA), it also worked to rationalize and stabilize railroad labor relations with the establishment of industrywide grievance and collective bargaining machinery and the explicit prohibition of employer discrimination against union membership. The USRA's impact upon nonoperating workers was particularly significant, permitting its brotherhoods to extend their membership, gain recognition for the first time in many instances, win important wage gains, and sign national agreements standardizing wages and working conditions. With these protections, new railroad unions such as the Railroad Yardmasters of America and the Train Dispatchers Association came into existence, and one insignificant union, the Brotherhood of Railroad Signalmen, which had existed since 1901 as only a local affair, expanded into a truly national union. While the benefits of federal control were not quite as dramatic for the Big Four, they nevertheless took note of the positive impact of the state, particularly as one of their number, William S. Carter of the BLFE, served as director of the USRA's Division of Labor. Concluding that it was in their interest to continue federal railroad control after the war, and moved by the World War I rhetoric of industrial democracy, in 1919 the railroad brotherhoods, led by such "progressives" as the Engineers' Warren Stone, mounted the "Plumb Plan" for permanent nationalization of the railways.

Political and Economic Action during the Interwar Years

Expansive as the brotherhoods' postwar plans for the railroads might have been, the heady World War I years sparked a reaction as both employers and conservative politicians, now in control of Congress and the White House, determined to roll back labor's wartime gains. The Transportation Act of 1920 thus not only returned the railroads to private ownership, but it also remade the structure of railroad industrial relations by introducing the Railroad Labor Board (RLB), a quasi-judicial body empowered to decide labor disputes by itself. Heavy-handed and inconsistent in its handling of arbitration cases, the RLB, together with a sympathetic judiciary, permitted the railroad corporations to beat back union advances through the introduction of company unionism and selective observance of Labor Board decisions. With

the depression of 1920–1921 and the railroad shopmen's strike of 1922, the railroads' "open shop" offensive precipitated a considerable decline in union membership among the nonoperating brotherhoods over the 1920s.

The operating brotherhoods also suffered during these years, but with their continued clout, they led railroad labor's counterattack not in industrial action but rather in the realm of electoral politics. While the Big Four had historically shared organized labor's reluctance to become involved in politics, their experience since the turn of the century had demonstrated the advantage of exercising union influence in the political arena. After Congress dismissed their plan for railroad nationalization, the brotherhoods formed the Conference for Progressive Political Action in 1922, an organization that became the focal point for a wide range of unionists, reformers, farm leaders, and intellectuals. This "progressive bloc" hewed to independent political action, succeeded in electing some labor-friendly congressmen, and in 1924, backed the Wisconsin senator Robert M. La Follette (R-WI) in his unsuccessful insurgent campaign for the presidency. While the brotherhoods failed to install their candidate in the White House, their efforts did pay dividends in revision to the railroad industrial relations statutes. As a part of their broader political action, the brotherhoods had sustained a campaign to abolish the RLB, winning passage of the Railway Labor Act of 1926. Marking the first time Congress recognized the right of workers to join unions without employer interference, the Act established the more cooperative framework that would govern railroad industrial relations into the post-World War II era and would serve as a model for industrial relations legislation in other industries.

As the brotherhoods entered into political action in the first half of the 1920s, they also embarked in a new direction: labor banking. The brotherhoods' foray into the financial industry may have appeared anomalous, but in fact it grew out of their tradition of fraternal mutual-aid unionism, the nation's cooperative movement as it quickened during the Progressive Era, and the World War I experience itself. Inspired by the idea that labor banks held the potential to democratize the American financial system, impressed with the possibility of translating workers' savings into economic and political power, and seeing in labor banks a means of blunting employers' open-shop drive, Warren Stone and the BLE founded the first of its 14 banks, the Brotherhood of Locomotive Engineers National Cooperative Bank, in 1920. The BLE's flagship bank achieved deposits of over $26 million by 1924 and delivered a variety of financial services to union members. However, mismanagement and ill-advised land investments in Florida drew the Engineers deep into debt and led to the collapse of its banks by decade's end. While the brotherhoods' banking ventures ended in disaster, their bold initiatives in the economic and political arenas revealed a real degree of labor dynamism often overlooked in the 1920s.

Dominated by the Great Depression and the New Deal, the decade of the 1930s marked the consolidation of railroad-industrial relations machinery with the Amended Railway Labor Act of 1934. As the Depression deepened, the brotherhoods used their political power to address the problem of railroad unemployment, supporting full-crew, train-limit, and six-hour-day legislation. The measure with the greatest significance was the Railway Retirement Act of 1937, which established a separate system of social security for railroad employees. Together, these railway laws represented important New Deal industrial relations and social welfare legislation that paralleled the better-known Wagner and Social Security Acts and enabled the brotherhoods to secure national agreements covering almost all the industry's operating and most nonoperating employees by the end of the decade.

Decline and Consolidation after World War II

The World War II period and the return of prosperity in the early 1940s enabled the brotherhoods to begin recovering the wage losses they had suffered during the Depression despite the no-strike pledge they adopted for the duration of the war. However, persistent rank-and-file discontent with the application of national agreements and wartime wage stabilization policies animated a series of short wildcat strikes, some resulting in the temporary government seizures of railroads. This undercurrent of wartime labor conflict burst into the open at war's end as the operating and nonoperating brotherhoods presented demands for increased wages, shorter hours, and work rules revisions. Most of these unions settled their issues through the Railway Labor Act machinery, except the BLE and the BRT, which had become frustrated by the tedious process of working through the Act's machinery. On May 23, 1946, after a series of strike votes and emergency conferences and in defiance of warnings from President Harry Truman, Alvanley Johnston of the Engineers and Alexander F. Whitney of the Trainmen led their unions in the only true national railroad strike of the twentieth century. Nevertheless, two days later, the unions capitulated in the face of Truman's seizure of the railroads and threats to draft striking employees into the military. Successive rounds of demands and presidential

seizures in 1948 and 1950 completed railroad labor's part in the broader post-World War II strike wave.

The postwar strike wave marked the railroad brotherhoods' last moment of true national prominence. In the 1950s, even as union membership peaked, the railroad industry entered a period of decline brought on by competition from interstate trucking, intercity busing, and the growth of the airline industry. Increased automation and rationalization of the industry resulted in steadily declining employment, an eroding membership base for the brotherhoods, and a corresponding reduction in union bargaining power. By the 1960s, the brotherhoods were fighting largely defensive battles, attempting to preserve jobs and maintain wages and working conditions. In 1969, with the exception of the Engineers, the operating brotherhoods merged to form the new AFL-affiliated United Transportation Union (UTU). The UTU aimed to end the craft rivalries that had dogged the brotherhoods through their histories and to increase the railroad unions' economic power. In practice, the UTU devoted most of its energies to political and legislative action, a direction suggested by its central role in the creation of the Congress of Railway Unions in 1969, a federation consisting of the UTU, the Maintenance of Way Employees, the Railway and Steamship Clerks, the Hotel and Restaurant Employees International Union, and the Seafarers International Union of North America. Through the 1970s, the UTU lobbied Congress and fought battles in the federal courts, winning from the Supreme Court the right of railroad workers to strike selectively. By the 1980s, reflecting the turning tide against organized labor brought on by Ronald Reagan's presidency, the UTU was focusing on stopping White House efforts to undo the landmark social welfare and protective labor legislation it had helped to bring about earlier in the century.

PAUL MICHEL TAILLON

References and Further Reading

Arnesen, Eric. "'Like Banquo's Ghost, It Will Not Down': The Race Question and the American Railroad Brotherhoods, 1880–1920." *American Historical Review* 99, no. 5 (December 1994): 1601–1633.

Henig, Harry. *The Brotherhood of Railway Clerks.* New York: Columbia University Press, 1937.

Huibregste, Jon R. "A New Type of Capitalist: The Brotherhood of Locomotive Engineers' Financial Scheme, 1920–1927." *New England Journal of History* 56 (1999): 36–49.

McIsaac, Archibald M. *The Order of Railroad Telegraphers: A Study in Trade Unionism and Collective Bargaining.* Princeton, NJ: Princeton University Press, 1933.

Olssen, Erik. "The Making of a Political Machine: The Railroad Unions Enter Politics." *Labor History* 19 (1978): 273–296.

Richardson, Reed C. *The Locomotive Engineer, 1863–1963: A Century of Railway Labor Relations and Work Rules.* Ann Arbor: University of Michigan, 1963.

Robbins, Edwin C. *Railway Conductors: A Study in Organized Labor.* New York: Columbia University Studies in Social Sciences, 1914.

Seidman, Joel. *The Brotherhood of Railroad Trainmen: The Internal Political Life of a National Union.* New York: John Wiley & Sons, 1962.

Stromquist, Shelton. *A Generation of Boomers: The Pattern of Railroad Labor Conflict in Nineteenth-Century America.* Urbana: University of Illinois Press, 1987.

Taillon, Paul. "'To Make Men out of Crude Material': Work Culture, Manhood, and Unionism in the Railroad Running Trades, c. 1870–1900." In *Boys and Their Toys: Masculinity, Technology, and Class,* edited by Roger Horowitz. New York: Routledge, 2001, pp. 33–54.

See also **Adamson Act; American Federation of Labor; American Railway Union; Conference for Progressive Political Action; Debs, Eugene V.; Erdman Act; Hotel and Restaurant Employees International Union; Industrial Democracy; Knights of Labor; Plumb Plan; Pullman Strike and Boycott (1894); Railroad Shopmen's Strike (1922); Railroads; Railway Labor Acts (1920–1934); Railroad Strikes (1877)**

RAILROAD SHOPMEN'S STRIKE (1922)

On July 1, 1922, hundreds of thousands of railroad shopmen went out on a nationwide strike that directly threatened the country's economic and social lifeline. The strike became a titanic struggle among union workers, railroad managements, local state authorities, and the federal government. The course taken by the strike was predicated on the relative strengths and tactics of both strikers and railroad management.

The strike began in protest against a wage cut imposed by a government agency, the Railroad Labor Board (RLB). The RLB had been established under the 1920 Transportation Act. Its major role was to oversee the working conditions and wages of the nation's over 2 million railroad workers. Starting in 1921, the RLB handed down a series of decisions that adversely affected the wages and working conditions of the nation's 400,000 shopmen. The shopmen were the men and women who built and repaired the country's rolling stock. This included locomotives and freight and passenger cars. After the RLB handed down a further wage cut in 1922, the shopmen's union organization, the Railway Employees' Department (RED), ordered its members to stop work on July 1 in protest.

The strikers established picket lines in cities and towns throughout the United States. In railroad towns especially, the battle became one for the hearts and minds of the local populace. Shopmen generally were respected members of railroad towns holding positions as mayors, chiefs of police, aldermen, and the like. With such control, they were able to effectively stop the importation of strikebreakers. In those locales where strikebreakers and armed guards were used, tensions mounted. Shootings became common as both strikers and guards were injured and killed. Such confrontations became common throughout the country. In these same communities, local merchants tended to side with the strikers. Thus, strikers and their families were given free groceries, complimentary tickets, and free rent. There was a darker side to this support where those shopmen who continued to work were marked for retribution. Some of the working shopmen (scabs) were verbally threatened, some were kidnapped and whipped or tar and feathered, and their houses often became sites of vandalism. Critical also to the strikers' success was the support from their wives, daughters, and sweethearts, who gathered badly needed supplies and in some cases stood on the picket line in support. Such support was not universal, however. Some shopmen, especially in the Southeast, refused to let their female supporters get involved. Local police forces also played a supportive role. Armed guards were arrested for carrying concealed weapons. In many cases, such support was predicated on the fact that chiefs of police were trying to maintain their political links to the wider community. Actions during the strike would therefore be remembered during election time.

Community support also attracted the attention of state and federal authorities. Reports by U.S. district attorneys and U.S. marshals highlighted the growing tension. In response, railroad managements were encouraged to apply for injunctions against the strikers. Such injunctions or restraining orders were easily obtained. Once the restraining orders were handed down, U.S. marshals acquired large numbers of deputy marshals to enforce them. These deputy marshals became the protectors of railroad property and strikebreakers and helped escort replacement workers and food and provisions into the railroad shops. Thus, community support of strikers was neutralized by the U.S. marshals.

President Warren Harding and his secretary of commerce, Herbert Hoover, tried hard to mediate a peace agreement between the shopmen and railroad heads. Initially, he appeared successful after a breakaway group of railroad managers agreed to negotiate. But a sizable section refused to sit down with the RED leaders. The most obstructionist were the Pennsylvania Railroad officials. Harding and Hoover were forced to back off and await events. By the second week in August (six weeks into the strike), Hoover

Chicago, Illinois. Grinding down a part of locomotive cylinder housing at the Chicago and Northwestern Railroad shops. Library of Congress, Prints & Photographs Division, FSA/OWI Collection [LC-USW3-012735-D].

reported to Harding that only two weeks of coal supplies were left. In addition, the nation's rolling stock was becoming increasingly dangerous as repairs could not keep up with demand. With little end in sight, President Harding consulted with his attorney general, Harry Daugherty. Harding's decision was to obtain a federal injunction against the strikers. On September 1, Daugherty obtained one of the most sweeping injunctions in U.S. history. The union leaders were enjoined from issuing strike instructions or funds to support the strike. In essence, the injunction destroyed the strike leaders' effectiveness. Facing heavy court fines if they ignored the injunction, the trade union leadership searched for railroads that would sign a peace agreement. Fortunately, a breakaway managerial group had formed. Led by the leaders of the Baltimore and Ohio (B&O) and Seaboard Airline Railroads, a solution was hammered out that recognized the seniority rights of the strikers and allowed them to return to work without any discrimination.

The majority of the railroads, however, refused to bargain with the union leaders. Instead, these railroads were determined to rid themselves of a union presence. Strikers could only return to work as new employees and nonunion members. Over the following months, many strikers were forced back to work under these conditions. But not until 1924 did the union leadership eventually admit defeat and order the remaining strikers back to work.

The shopmen's defeat was a major one. It ended their national power within the railroad industry. The strike also represented the last major industrywide strike until the emergence of CIO unions in the 1930s. Many reasons contributed to the shopmen's defeat. The shopmen were hampered by a lack of unity across race lines. Large number of African-Americans, Hispanics, and Asians labored in the railroad shops but were not allowed entry into the shopmen's unions. Such discrimination tactically weakened the strike because many minority shopmen reasoned that the unions were exclusionary and thus there was little incentive to support the strikers. The Harding administration also played a divisive role. Its appointees to the RLB and its eventual unleashing of a sweeping federal injunction sounded the death knell for the strike. Above all, though, it was railroad management that did much to defeat the strike. Its determination to push hard for wage cuts and thereby confront the shopmen set the tone for the upcoming battle. Managements were determined to return to the prewar period where union representation in the railroad shops was barely discernible. Management paid an enormous cost in defeating the shopmen, thousands of guards were hired, eating and sleeping facilities were set up in railroad shops across the country, and finally, hundreds of thousands of strikebreakers were recruited. Management obviously thought the cost was worth paying, but by the 1930s and World War II, unions returned to shops and this time they stayed.

COLIN DAVIS

References and Further Reading

Davis, Colin J. *Power at Odds: The 1922 National Railroad Shopmen's Strike*. Urbana: University of Illinois Press, 1997.

Hirsch, Susan Eleanor. *After the Strike: A Century of Labor Struggle at Pullman*. Urbana: University of Illinois Press, 2003.

See also **Railroads**

RAILROAD STRIKES (1877)

In the spring of 1877, the United States was still in the grip of a major industrial depression that had begun four years earlier. The depression had devastated organized labor, but labor's demands for a living wage, the right to bargain collectively, and an eight-hour work day, among others, remained—and were even more salient in the midst of widespread unemployment and hunger.

The Railroad Strikes of 1877—known by contemporaries as The Great Strike or Great Upheaval—were one of the most spectacular episodes of urban violence in American history. Triggered by a 10% wage cut instituted by most railroad corporations on July 1, they began on July 16 at the Baltimore and Ohio (B&O) railroad yard in Martinsburg, West Virginia. In Martinsburg, railroad workers dismantled a cattle train upon its entrance to the yard. Uncoupling the cars, the men stated that no more freight trains would be allowed to travel until their wages were restored. This job action by railroad workers quickly elicited support from the Martinsburg community. That evening, a crowd gathered at the town depot and prevented the arrest of the strikers by the police; and the following day, freight traffic was disrupted or stopped by striking railroad workers, and more ominously for railroad companies and ruling elites

in general, people with no wage relationship to the B&O. The strike of railroad workers spread rapidly from Martinsburg, engulfing towns and cities throughout the Northeast and the Midwest, extending as far west as the Pacific coast.

The strike of railroad workers triggered a series of widespread, popular uprisings against the railroads—the nation's pre-eminent industrial enterprise after the Civil War and the symbol of the capitalist nature of the American industrial revolution. Though viewed by most people as the carriers of progress and prosperity, the railroads also engendered considerable hostility: their tracks and trains wreaked havoc in urban communities, obstructing the commercial and social uses of streets and killing and injuring thousands of people every year in various types of accidents. Consequently, crowds composed mostly of workers with no wage relationship to the railroad companies, sprinkled with substantial numbers of middle-class folk, joined striking railroad workers in stopping trains; they also engaged in violent attacks against railroad property.

Given Baltimore's proximity to Martinsburg and its status as the major rail nexus for the B&O Railroad, it was the place of the first major outbreak of violence. On Friday, July 20, the Great Strike erupted in Baltimore. Railroad and civil authorities had already filled Baltimore with hundreds of soldiers in expectation of "trouble," and trouble they got. On Front Street, at the armory housing a regiment of troops called out to protect railroad property, thousands of people collected. Women, children, unemployed men, and people from nearly all walks of life in the city gathered to voice their rage at the troops. Catcalls, threats, and brickbats were hurled at the armory. Fairly soon, portions of the regiment were ordered to leave the armory in order to march to the major railroad depot at Camden station. Their exit and the crowd's response were a deadly mixture: in response to a fusillade of stones, brickbats, and perhaps a gunshot or two, the soldiers opened fire upon the crowd. As different companies of the regiment departed the armory and marched through the streets to Camden station, battles broke out all along the route. Nearly a dozen people lay dead and a score injured (only one soldier suffered serious wounds). Not a single one of the dead or wounded was a railroad striker—testimony to the scope of the hostility big business, railroad corporations in particular, had elicited in the years since the Civil War.

As people in Baltimore and other cities experienced the Great Strike or its beginnings that July weekend, the seminal event of the Strike occurred in Pittsburgh, Pennsylvania. Pittsburgh was home to another railroad giant, the Pennsylvania Railroad Company, and the company held the nearly universal antipathy of the city's working class. Its monopoly on rail and freight traffic into and out of the city had created a deep reservoir of ill-feeling. Antimonopoly sentiment, a set of values with roots stretching back to the eighteenth century, ran deep throughout the country, especially as industrialization created behemoth corporations that crushed small businesses as easily as hapless cows caught on the tracks. Nowhere was antimonopoly sentiment deeper and more widespread than in Pittsburgh. In addition to the city's industrial manufacturing establishments, Pittsburgh was home to the mighty Pennsylvania Railroad Company. Its rolling stock, roundhouses, freight houses, and switchyards covered a vast area by the Union depot, running alongside a ridge.

Pittsburgh's railroad workers knew of the strike in other cities, and they too had suffered a pay cut. The strike started on Thursday, July 19 when a group of trainmen refused to take out any freight trains. At approximately the same time, another event was beginning that was to prove pivotal in the city—and emblematic of the hostility railroad corporations had fostered in countless cities and small towns across the nation—a crowd composed largely of non-railroad workers began to form at the Twenty-Eight Street crossing about one mile from the Union depot. This crowd would play a signal role in what was to follow; indeed, they began to interfere with the movement of trains almost immediately. As trainmen refused to run freight trains and also refused to allow the use of strikebreakers—scabs—the crowd at the crossing grew in size. Indeed, striking railroad workers had to intercede to allow passenger trains to continue to run—a conscious strategy on the part of the strikers so as not to alienate public opinion. As the day ended, hundreds of incoming freight cars lay idle in the Pennsylvania yard. On Friday, July 20, no freight trains were moving into or out of the city. The situation remained the same the next day, July 21. Yet as elsewhere, railroad corporations were successfully soliciting the armed intervention of local, state, and federal authority. Local police forces, in Pittsburgh and other cities, were simply overwhelmed by the size of the strike and the crowds. State militias faced a problem, which was particularly pronounced in Pittsburgh: militiamen were drawn from the city, and they did not want to fire on people who might be their neighbors or coworkers. Efforts to get the Pittsburgh militia to control the strikers—and the ever-growing Twenty-Eighth Street crowd—generally failed. Militiamen either failed to show up when called or they fraternized with the members of the crowd. Consequently, militiamen from Philadelphia were rushed to the city via special trains provided by the railroad company. Of the many features of society revealed in stark relief by the Great Strike of 1877,

none was as apparent as the state's willingness to use armed force against ordinary people on behalf of the interests of private capital.

Strikers and the people of Pittsburgh knew that militiamen from Philadelphia were headed to their city. Arriving on Saturday, July 21, these out-of-town militiamen would prove to be the trigger for the most spectacular and violent episode in the history of the Great Strike of 1877. Unlike their Pittsburgh counterparts, the state militiamen from Philadelphia had few qualms about firing into crowds of people who were anonymous to them. By late Saturday afternoon, there were six hundred Philadelphia troops at the Union depot in the city. News of the arrival of the troops had brought even more people to the yards of the Pennsylvania Railroad. The troops had one goal: clear the tracks so that freight trains could run again. With fixed bayonets, they moved on the crowd of striking railroad workers, Pittsburgh militiamen who were openly fraternizing with their fellow residents, unemployed workers, iron and steelworkers, and women and children who blocked the tracks leading out of the freight yards. The crowd was frankly hostile and refused to be moved; a number of the militiamen charged the crowd, stabbing several people. A barrage of stones and rocks followed, people in the crowd even angrier from the sight of unarmed people being bayoneted by out-of-town soldiers. The command to fire quickly followed the hail of stones. When the firing was over, 20 people lay dead and nearly 30 were wounded. The crowd, numbering in the thousands, sent the six hundred troops fleeing back into the relative safety of a roundhouse. Crowd members began to empty the standing freight cars and then set on fire not only the freight cars, but railroad property in general. A three-mile stretch of railroad property—cars, workshops, lumberyards, and roundhouses—went up in a spectacular blaze that lit up the night sky for many miles. When it was over, 2,000 cars of every sort had been destroyed; nearly 40 buildings of various kinds lay in ashes, and more than 100 locomotives were ready for the scrap heap. The shock of the carnage, both material and human (another 20 people had been killed by the Philadelphia militiamen), was such that the city populace itself largely restored order to its streets by Monday morning.

News of what transpired in Pittsburgh shocked and terrified the nation. Newspaper headlines screamed that "the mob" had nearly burned the city to the ground in its fury to get at railroad property; insurrection threatened the nation and property everywhere was at risk. Yet the railroad workers' strike continued—as railroad workers in scores of other cities went out on strike during or after the events in Baltimore and Pittsburgh. The same weekend that the western terminus of the Pennsylvania Railroad burned to the ground, the Great Strike began in upstate New York, as striking railroad workers in Buffalo, Albany, and elsewhere struck. As was the case nearly everywhere, their strike quickly caused strikes of workers from other economic sectors, as well as people from the middle classes.

Chicago and St. Louis experienced serious urban disorder consequent upon the Great Strike in those cities. In St. Louis, a general strike followed the strike of railroad workers—for several days, the city was ruled by the Workingmen's Party of the United States, as workers in virtually every industry struck and shut the city down. Chicago, the nation's slaughterhouse and a major nexus for all railroads headed west or east, had its own share of Great Strike violence, with at least one pitched battle between troops and working-class crowds claiming the lives of nearly 20 people. In Chicago, as in the nation generally, the Great Strike of 1877 was put down by the armed forces of the state, whether they were local or state militia, or federal troops called out by President Rutherford B. Hayes. Even San Francisco experienced civil strife as a result of the Great Strike, though the working class in that city vented its anger not on railroad corporations, but on the city's Chinese community.

The Great Strike facilitated the demise of Reconstruction. Waning northern interest in the southern "negro problem" was quickly replaced with the "labor problem" terrifyingly illustrated in northern cities during the strikes. The violence of the railroad strikes accelerated the development of the national state. In the years and decades after the strikes, state militias expanded in size and became more efficient, and National Guard armories were built (many of stone) or strengthened. The 1877 strikes both reflected and accelerated the growth of class consciousness among urban industrial workers, regardless of craft or skill. In many locales where the strikes were particularly pronounced, labor parties, albeit short-lived, formed for the fall elections.

DAVID O. STOWELL

References and Further Reading

Bruce, Robert V. *1877: Year of Violence*. Chicago: Quadrangle Books, 1959.

Foner, Philip S. *The Great Labor Uprising of 1877*. New York: Monad Press, 1977.

Roediger, David R. "'Not Only the Ruling Classes to Overcome, but Also the So-Called Mob': Class, Skill, and Community in the St. Louis General Strike of 1877." *Journal of Social History* (Winter 1985): 213–239.

Salvatore, Nick. "Railroad Workers and the Great Strike of 1877: The View from a Small Midwest City." *Labor History* 21, no. 4 (Fall 1980): 522–545.

Schneirov, Richard. "Chicago's Great Upheaval of 1877." *Chicago History* (1980): 3–17.

Stowell, David O. *Streets, Railroads, and the Great Strike of 1877*. Chicago: University of Chicago Press, 1999.

RAILROADS

Work on the railroads was quite diverse, encompassing the most sophisticated industrial work of the nineteenth century as well as the most backbreaking menial labor. At the top of the industrial pyramid were the designers and mechanics who built the engines themselves. In the 1820s and 1830s, the manufacture of most American locomotives took place in England. But by the 1850s, Philadelphia, Baltimore, and Pittsburgh had emerged as locomotive manufacturing centers, largely because of their proximity to iron foundries. Until the 1870s, most locomotives were custom built in locomotive works and shipped to railway companies.

Because of the custom nature of locomotive construction before the American Civil War, every major railroad in the early nineteenth century required extensive repair shops for the rebuilding of broken locomotives and the building of railway cars. A foundry produced custom molds for railway parts. Carpenters, millers, and trimmers fashioned cars. Boilermakers, coppersmiths, tinners, and machinists repaired, rebuilt, and re-assembled these parts to keep railway cars running. After the Civil War, manufacturers' experience with interchangeable parts, particularly in steam engine design, led to a re-organization of repair shops. Manufactured engines in standard models emerged first from the Baldwin Works in Philadelphia. By the 1870s, in New England and the Midwest, and into the 1880s in the South, these standard-sized engines increased in popularity. Parts could be ordered and shipped, diminishing the need for custom-built parts and cheapening the cost of maintaining locomotives and railway cars. Increasingly, repair shops did less and less manufacturing, becoming holding pens for parts and diminishing the need for the diversity of skills in repair shops. By the 1880s, many railway repair shops became white-only enclaves, as black helpers, apprentices, and painters who had been a very visible part of southern shops were closed out of railway work. Conflicts over labor in repair shops were somewhat different than they were for workers who worked on tracks. Repair workers could not simply stop business by stopping work; they had to wait for broken engines and rolling stock to pile up to effectively stop a railway from operating. This inability to fully stop operations would prove crippling in the Shopmen's Strike of 1922. Repair shops were radically

Albuquerque, New Mexico. Working on the fire box of an engine in the Atchison, Topeka and Santa Fe Railroad locomotive shops. Library of Congress, Prints & Photographs Division, FSA/OWI Collection [LC-USW3-020490-D].

altered again in the 1940s (the 1950s in the South) with the widespread adoption of diesel locomotives. Even more so than in the 1880s, repair shops became large repositories for parts, further decreasing the need for bespoke parts or re-engineering. Indeed, many steam repair shops were closed and demolished, replaced with streamlined diesel shops that housed spare parts and a staff of engine mechanics and oilers.

Next in order of skill were the operating brotherhoods: engineers, firemen, conductors, and brakemen. A loose system of apprenticeship governed these trades. Firemen, for example, in charge of keeping a fire in engines, acted as apprentice engineers. Through the 1870s and 1880s, as wood-fired engines were replaced with coal-fired engines, the physical demands of this job decreased while proper firing in these more efficient engines became a more delicate matter. Engineers and firemen were invariably the first to die from exploding boilers, "scalded to death by the steam" in the words of the railway song, "The Wreck of the Old 97." Engineers, meanwhile, maintained control of the engine, setting speed and calling for brakes. Throughout the United States, the romance of railroading focused on the engineer and fireman. Dozens of mountain ballads like "Casey Jones" and "The Wreck of the Old 97" described their exploits, real and imagined. Engineers and firemen, as Walter Licht

has shown, came largely from the ranks of the repair shops and machine shops.

Next among trainmen were conductors and brakemen. A brakeman's job in the mid-nineteenth century involved jumping from car to car to turn hand brakes when called to do so by the engineer. By the 1880s the Westinghouse air brake minimized the dangers of braking and made braking easier. Brakemen were considered apprentice conductors, as both positions involved the management of the train behind the locomotive. Indeed, conductors managed all parts of the train behind the locomotive, including taking tickets and ejecting passengers who tried to "ride the blind" by hiding in the folds of fabric that separated the passenger trains. Conductors often came from the ranks of stagecoach drivers, though many (perhaps most) came from rural backgrounds.

Perhaps because of the diversity of skills and the fixed nature of control of the parts of the locomotive, each of these skilled workers had their own unions, though the Order of Railway Trainmen and the Knights of Labor both sought to draw these workers into industrial rather than craft unions. A narrower craft consciousness may also have emerged from the peculiar industrial structure of early railways, in which rule books governing the behavior of workers became longer and longer, governing nearly every action of trainmen. While working to rule may have helped trainmen push back against the arbitrary power of foremen, it may also have fostered an over-emphasis on rules and order over solidarity and community. The very nature of early trainmen's unions may also have lent a certain closed character to their ideology. Early railway brotherhoods in the mid- to late nineteenth century resembled contemporary fraternities, in which brothers engaged in humiliating and secretive initiations that blended elements of Rosicrucianism and Masonic ritual. Brothers pledged secrecy and undying devotion to the group, exchanged secret handshakes, and pledged to work only with brothers. In a practical sense, these craft unions found it difficult to agree with each other when it came to collective action, most notoriously when engineers refused to support firemen and other trainmen in the Great Upheaval of 1877, and the Southwestern Strikes of 1886.

Railway trainmen have often been associated with radical politics. Whether engineers, firemen, conductors, or brakemen, trainmen saw themselves at the top of the labor hierarchy, both as representatives of labor and as uniquely responsible for the fate of the entire working class. In politics, many were socialists, anarchists, and later communists. Trainmen's constant mobility, both on the train and from job to job, made them particularly important for the growth of radical and working-class movements from the 1860s through the 1930s and 1940s. The Mexican historian Adolpho Gilly, for example, has argued that North American railway engineers and brakemen contributed in important ways to the intellectual ferment that created the Mexican Revolution.

Among railway trainmen, conductors faced the most direct scrutiny because they collected fares on passenger trains. Indeed, the infamous corporate spy (and bungler) Allan Pinkerton got his start spying on conductors to ensure that they did not pocket the fares collected from passengers. By the latter part of the 1850s, Pinkerton created a "detective agency" that promised to ferret out theft and eliminate emerging unions among railroad trainmen. Often the peculiar position of detectives led them to overstate the threat of workers' unions and their own importance in preventing violence. Indeed, during the Civil War, Pinkerton provided inflated figures for Confederate strength behind the lines in the Peninsular Campaign in the Civil War, leading General McClellan to delay his invasion of Richmond and extend the war by four years, a feat that ironically seemed only to expand the renown of the Pinkerton Agency. In 1878, Pinkerton published a highly colored account of railway unions in a book titled "Strikers, Communists,

Tramps, and Detectives," which purported to reveal some of the secret rituals of the railway brotherhoods in the wake of the Great Upheaval of 1877.

By the latter part of the 1870s, George Pullman created the Pullman car, a sleeping car that became a hallmark for luxury. African-Americans by this time had been excluded from the repair shops and from positions as firemen, partly through the actions of white railway brotherhoods. Some African-Americans, however, found positions as servants and cooks on the Pullman cars. Here, too, the connection between trainmen and radical politics was pronounced, as African-American Pullman car porters became important in the growing socialist movement of the early twentieth century, joining the Brotherhood of Sleeping Car Porters in great numbers. Pullman car porters, too, may have been influential in facilitating the so-called Great Migration of African-Americans to northern cities in the early decades of the twentieth century. By bringing black newspapers to the rural South, they may have encouraged thousands to leave the Jim Crow South for the less-segregated northern cities, where job opportunities and a thrilling, urban, largely African-American world beckoned.

The final and largest group among railway workers consisted of the maintainers of track, called section hands or track liners in the nineteenth century, and maintenance-of-way workers in the twentieth. Every railway in regular operation required approximately one worker for every mile of track. Usually gangs of five or more workers were responsible for a stretch of track five or more miles long. Most days, track liners relined track that heavy running or storms had driven out of line. A road boss received orders from the roadmaster, who regularly inspected the road from a handcar. When the roadmaster noted problems on a road, he would drop a wadded note, called a butterfly, near the misaligned track. The butterfly would identify the source of the problem. Track liners relined or replaced track using railway spike hammers that resembled picks. Workers edged the longer, skinnier end of the hammer under the track to lift it. The shorter end would be used to shift the track over and to hammer down spikes. Until as late as the 1960s in the American South, African-American workers relined track by singing songs to co-ordinate the movements of track lining. Sometimes a caller would be appointed to set the pace for workers while workers sang the refrain; other times all workers would sing together. Among these songs was the folk ballad "John Henry," which told of a powerful black man who fought in a rock-drilling contest (or track-lining contest) with a steam drill. Though John Henry defeated the drill, he died just afterward. Such songs co-ordinated labor so that workers jiggered their "dogs" or picks at the same time, but they also warned workers to slow down. The snatches of song sung by track liners ("I got a girl / She works in the yard / She brings me meat / She brings me lard") had tremendous reach through the twentieth century, finding their way into jazz, blues, and rock and roll songs of the 1920s, 1930s, and 1960s. In addition, track lining, co-ordinated with song, may have been an important precursor to African-American step shows performed by black fraternities in the 1910s and 1920s. In modern step shows, five or more black performers hold sticks that they dance around in complex and precise lockstep formations.

African-American workers continued to work as firemen and engineers on timber lines in the South, while many continued as brakemen through the turn of the century. African-Americans served as yard workers as well. When the federal government assumed control over railways during World War I, they re-organized and streamlined routes, turning some positions back to African-Americans, who had been removed between Reconstruction and the turn of the century. After World War I ended, the federal government gave these much-improved routes to private hands. Violence ensued as white workers attacked black workers to regain their position, most visibly in the "race riots" of Memphis in 1919. Despite investigation by the Fair Employment Practice Committee during World War II, black workers were denied full seniority rights and equal opportunities for work. Only with the Civil Rights Act of 1964 were African-Americans accorded something approaching full rights to wages, benefits, and employment opportunities.

SCOTT NELSON

References and Further Reading

Arnesen, Eric. *Brotherhoods of Color: Black Railroad Workers and the Struggle for Equality.* Cambridge, MA: Harvard University Press, 2001.

Davis, Colin J. *Power at Odds: The 1922 National Railroad Shopmen's Strike: The Working Class in American History.* Urbana: University of Illinois Press, 1997.

Gilly, Adolfo. *The Mexican Revolution.* Expanded and revised ed. London: Verso, 1983.

Hunter, Louis C., and the Eleutherian Mills-Hagley Foundation. *A History of Industrial Power in the United States, 1780–1930.* Volume 2: Steam Power. Charlottesville: Published for the Eleutherian Mills-Hagley Foundation by the University Press of Virginia, 1979.

Licht, Walter. *Working for the Railroads: The Organization of Work in the Nineteenth Century.* Princeton, NJ: Princeton University Press, 1983.

Lightner, David L. *Labor on the Illinois Central Railroad, 1852–1900: The Evolution of an Industrial Environment (Dissertations in American Economic History).* New York: Arno Press, 1977.

Luff, Jennifer D. "Judas Exposed: Labor Spies in the United States." Dissertation, College of William and Mary, 2005.

Montgomery, David. *The Fall of the House of Labor: The Workplace, the State, and American Labor Activism, 1865–1925.* New York: Cambridge University Press, 1987.

Nelson, Scott Reynolds. *Iron Confederacies : Southern Railways, Klan Violence, and Reconstruction.* Chapel Hill: University of North Carolina Press, 1999.

Nelson, Scott Reynolds. *Take This Hammer: The Death of John Henry and the Birth of an American Legend.* New York: Oxford University Press, forthcoming, 2006.

Santino, Jack. *Miles of Smiles, Years of Struggle: Stories of Black Pullman Porters.* Urbana: University of Illinois Press, 1989.

Stromquist, Shelton. *A Generation of Boomers: The Pattern of Railroad Labor Conflict in Nineteenth-Century America (Working Class in American History).* Urbana: University of Illinois Press, 1987.

See also **Henry, John; Knights of Labor; Pullman, George Mortimer; Pullman Strike and Boycott (1894)**

RAILWAY LABOR ACTS (1920–1934)

The Railway Labor Act of 1926 represented a breakthrough in state-labor-management relations. It served as a model for both section 7(a) of the National Industrial Recovery Act and the Wagner Act of 1935. Its genesis lay in World War I and the national railroad strike in 1922.

Transportation Act of 1920

American participation in World War I was a boon to the political and economic aspirations of the railway employees and their unions. On December 26, 1918, President Woodrow Wilson issued an executive order asserting federal operational control of the entire railroad industry. Forced to take this action because of severe railroad gridlock in the Northeast and significant rolling stock shortages nationally, the order also opened a new phase in efforts to mediate labor-management disputes in the industry. Under the auspices of the United States Railroad Administration (USRA), railway labor in general, not just the four brotherhoods, made significant advances in wages, work rules changes, membership, and state support in disputes with management. Consequently, they were loath to leave the protection of federal control as Congress debated ending or extending the tenure of the USRA in 1919. Labor threw its considerable weight behind the Plumb Plan, a proposal for nationalizing the railroads. Instead, Congress enacted the Transportation Act of 1920 (also know as the Esch-Cummins Act) that returned the rail carriers to private operation. Though the Senate's version included both a prohibition on strikes by railroad employees and compulsory arbitration of disputes, the compromise arranged by the conference committee contained neither provision and instead represented a compromise between labor's desire to protect wartime gains and the carriers' demand for a return to prewar managerial authority.

For the first time in federal labor legislation, Title III of the Transportation Act included all employees of common carrier railroads operating in interstate commerce, not just the members of the four operating brotherhoods. It called for the creation of a tripartite United States Railroad Labor Board consisting of three members, each representing labor, management, and the public, all appointed by the president and subject to Senate approval. In practice, the public members often sided with the management representatives. The Board was empowered to act as both mediator and arbitrator concerning unresolved disputes over wages and work rules. Conspicuously absent was any power of enforcement beyond the weight of public opinion, a fact re-inforced by the Supreme Court in *Pennsylvania Railroad Co. v. Railway Labor Board*. Subsidiary to the Board was a three-tier system of local, regional, and national Boards of Adjustment to hear grievances arising from disputes over the implementation of agreements. Though the Act required disputants to attempt reconciliation privately, in its five years of life, the Board heard some 13,000 cases. The large number of cases obscured a bitter reality; both unions and management intensely disliked the law. The carriers, especially after 1923, simply ignored Board decisions favorable to their employees. The four operating brotherhoods, with assistance from Secretary of Commerce Herbert Hoover, arrived at a private accommodation with railroad executives to bypass the Board altogether in 1922. Thus, many of the cases heard by the Board involved nonoperating employees, a group fragmented across many small unions, some affiliated with the American Federation of Labor (AFL) and others not, and consequently as a group susceptible to anti-union efforts by management. This situation, a privileged and minority group of employees generally unaffected by the decade's characteristic re-assertion of managerial authority and a majority that enjoyed far less stable wages and work rules, was ripe for a simultaneously catastrophic and transformative strike.

Shopmen's Strike of 1922

In early 1921 and 1922, the Railway Labor Board ordered two wage cuts that affected nonoperating railroad employees more severely than they did the members of the brotherhoods. This action, in combination with persistent management efforts to push company unions, contract shop work to nonunion firms, and install piecework pay schemes, led the leadership of the AFL's Railway Employees Department to call for a national strike by shop workers. They demanded the revocation of the wage reductions and piecework rates.

On July 1, 1922, over 400,000 machinists, boilermakers, Carmen, and other railroad shop workers walked off their jobs in the first national railroad strike since 1894. The Railway Labor Board quickly branded the strike illegal in a 5-2 vote, simultaneously asserting that strikers had voluntarily forfeited their positions and seniority and that their replacements were entitled to all the protections of the law. The leadership of the operating brotherhoods sympathized with the strikers in the abstract, but beyond sporadic walkouts emanating mostly from the behavior of railroad guards, their membership stayed on the job. Widespread violence against persons and property by both sides characterized the strike everywhere. After two attempts by President William Harding to arrange a settlement compromise, rejected in turn by the railroads and then the unions, the weight of the federal government fell behind the carriers.

In September 1922, Attorney General Harry M. Daugherty sought and received from Judge James H. Wilkerson of the United States District Court of Illinois a sweeping injunction. Citing the Sherman Anti-Trust Act, Wilkerson branded the strike a criminal conspiracy and enjoined the unions, their executives, and membership from any strike activity whatsoever. The injunction, combined with the success of the carriers in obtaining strikebreakers and the poor finances of the shop unions, led the shopmen's leadership to reach a settlement with a coalition of moderate eastern railroad executives. The agreement guaranteed the positions and seniority of returning strikers and provided for the creation of a commission to negotiate problems between replacements and returning employees. Approximately 100,000 strikers returned to work under this agreement. However, many carriers, especially in the West, were not party to the agreement and were determined to break both the strike and the shop unions, a desire eventually realized, though in some areas strike activity lingered into 1928. The strike essentially destroyed the various shop unions, and even those strikers who returned to work faced an emboldened management.

Railway Labor Act of 1926

The strike, especially its widespread violence but also the frightening implications of the Wilkerson injunction, revealed the inadequacy of the Railroad Labor Board and the deficiencies in the Transportation Act. Between 1923 and 1926, a number of reform proposals appeared in Congress. The bill that eventually became the Railway Labor Act emerged from several meetings between union and railway leaders at the suggestion of President Calvin Coolidge. Passed with little debate, the bill became law on May 20, 1926.

The Railway Labor Act put the federal government squarely behind the principle of collective bargaining in the railroad industry. The Act eliminated the Railway Labor Board, replacing it with a five-member Board of Mediation, empowered to provide mandatory mediation but not compulsory arbitration. It specified the creation of emergency presidential commissions when disputes appeared intractable and specifically prohibited strikes during the 30-day period mandated for its investigations and deliberations and an additional 30 days thereafter. To speed the resolution of minor disputes—those concerning the interpretation of agreements—the Act instituted a series of adjustment boards, an idea borrowed from the period of federal control. Most important, the Act protected the right of railroad employees to bargain collectively and elect representatives free from employee coercion. For the carriers, the bill protected the company unions that had emerged after the 1922 strike, especially in the shop crafts, and limited the scope of collective bargaining to individual systems.

Railway Labor Act Amendments of 1934

Often ignored in the larger sweep of New Deal-era labor legislation, the 1934 amendments to the Railway Labor Act significantly expanded employee and union protections and gave visible indication of the power of the brotherhoods in the building of a New Deal coalition while simultaneously presaging many of the provisions of the Wagner Act. The amendments emerged amidst a railroad industry financial meltdown that left almost 50 major railroads near or in bankruptcy by 1934. The amendments extended to all railroad workers the employee protections written into the Bankruptcy Act of 1932 and the Emergency Railroad Transportation Act of 1933. Those laws had prohibited carriers in bankruptcy from using yellow-dog contracts, influencing employees in representation decisions, enforcing closed shops (often used to

protect company unions), or refusing to bargain collectively with certified representatives. To these provisions were added a new permanent and bipartisan National Railroad Adjustment Board to handle grievances relating to interpretations of agreements with neutral referees appointed in case of a deadlock. The Act also extended the cooling-off period by an additional 30 days and added specific language rendering the decisions of the Board enforceable in federal court and infractions punishable by fine or imprisonment. Last, it called for a reduction in the membership of the Board of Mediation, itself renamed the National Mediation Board, because it no longer handled grievances, but granted the revamped organization authority to conduct representation elections.

These amendments withstood constitutional challenge in 1937 in *Virginia Railway Co. v. System Federation no. 40, AFL*. Later amended in 1936, 1940, 1951, 1964, and 1970, the basic provisions of the Railway Labor Act remain in place. Though the Act served as a model for later legislation for all workers, its emphasis on arbitration, strike avoidance, and federal intervention continue to mark out railroad labor from the rest of the American union movement.

SCOTT E. RANDOLPH

References and Further Reading

Davis, Colin. *Power at Odds: The 1922 National Railroad Shopmen's Strike.* Urbana: University of Illinois Press, 1997.

Dubofsky, Melvyn. *The State and Labor in Modern America.* Chapel Hill: University of North Carolina Press, 1994.

Eggert, Gerald. *Railroad Labor Disputes: The Beginnings of Federal Strike Policy.* Ann Arbor: University of Michigan Press, 1967.

Lecht, Leonard A. *Experience under Railway Labor Legislation.* New York: Columbia University Press, 1955.

Montgomery, David. *The Fall of the House of Labor: The Workplace, the State, and American Labor Activism, 1865–1925.* Cambridge: Cambridge University Press, 1987.

Rehmus, Charles M., ed. *The Railway Labor Act at Fifty: Collective Bargaining in the Railroad and Airline Industries.* Washington, DC: National Mediation Board, 1977.

Wilner, Frank K. *The Railway Labor Act and the Dilemma of Labor Relations.* Omaha, NE: Simmons-Boardman Books, 1991.

Wolf, Harry D. *The Railroad Labor Board.* Chicago: University of Chicago Press, 1927.

Cases and Statutes Cited

Pennsylvnia Railroad Co. v. Railway Labor Board, 261 U.S. 72 (1923)

Virginia Railway Co. v. System Federation no. 40, AFL, 300 U.S. 515 (1937)

Bankruptcy Act, 47 Stat. 1467 (1933)

Emergency Transportation Act, 48 Stat. 211 (1933)
National Industrial Recovery Act, 48 Stat. 195 (1933)
National Labor Relations Act (Wagner Act), 49 Stat. 449 (1935)
Newlands Act, 38 Stat. 103 (1913)
Railway Labor Act, 44 Stat. 577 (1926)
Railway Labor Act, 48 Stat. 1185 (1934)
Transportation Act (Esch-Cummins Act), 41 Stat. 456 (1920)

RAMSAY, CLAUDE (1916–1986)
President, Mississippi AFL-CIO

Claude Ramsay was born in 1916 on a farm near Fort Bayou, Mississippi, eight miles from the Gulf Coast. He began work at the International Paper plant in Moss Point, Mississippi, in 1939, and advanced rapidly inside the mill until he was drafted in 1942. Ramsay's experience in the Army shook his faith in segregation, and he returned from the war interested in politics. He supported President Harry Truman in the 1948 elections, while the rest of Mississippi defected to the Dixiecrats, who bolted the Democratic Party over civil rights. He became active in his union and was elected president of Paperworkers Local 203 in 1951 and president of the Jackson County Central Labor Council the following year. Ramsay was elected the second president of the recently merged Mississippi AFL-CIO in 1959 because he was regarded as the only candidate who could bring former AFL and CIO local unions together. Both wings of the labor movement perceived him as capable, determined, and deeply committed to unions.

Ramsay made his mark as the president of the Mississippi AFL-CIO. He supported unions, civil rights, and the national Democratic Party in a state that reviled all three. Regarding unions, Mississippi was as hostile and forbidding as any state in the country. Ramsay confronted this anti-union sentiment immediately upon his election as president. Not content with having a right-to-work law on the books, the state legislature decided in 1960 to make the right to work part of the state constitution, which required a referendum by voters. Ramsay led a gallant but losing fight against the proposition. Defeat clarified for Ramsay that the Mississippi AFL-CIO was too weak to defend itself politically. In order to remove anti-union laws and defeat anti-union legislators, the Mississippi AFL-CIO would need allies.

Ramsay found his allies in the emerging civil rights movement. Despite the fact that Mississippi seethed with segregationist sentiment, Ramsay aligned the labor movement with black civil rights groups. Ramsay believed that unions in Mississippi could prevail only if blacks were enfranchised. Antilabor legislators from agricultural Black Belt districts in Mississippi could be defeated only with the help of black voters who lived there. Simple arithmetic led Ramsay to form coalitions with the Mississippi NAACP, fund register-and-vote drives among blacks, and support local civil rights groups.

Ramsay was also deeply engaged in Democratic Party politics. The Mississippi Democrat Party (the Regulars) refused to support the Party's presidential ticket in 1964 because it opposed the national Party's strong civil rights planks. Four years later, in preparation for the 1968 elections, Ramsay and other liberal Democrats in Mississippi formed the Loyalists to challenge the Regulars for control of the statewide Democratic Party. The Loyalists sought to create a bona fide Democratic Party in Mississippi, one that was loyal to the national Party's platform and candidates.

Ramsay's support of unions, civil rights, and the national Democrat Party put him at odds not only with Mississippi's ruling class, but with his own members. Local unions protested Ramsay's stance against segregation, his support for the national Democratic Party, and his alliance with civil rights groups by disaffiliating from the Mississippi AFL-CIO. When they walked out, they took their dues money with them. The Mississippi state council stayed afloat financially only because of subsidies it received from the AFL-CIO in Washington, DC. Even more discouraging for Ramsay were the inroads white supremacy groups, such as the Citizens' Councils, the Ku Klux Klan, and the John Birch Society, made among his members and the public denunciations of the Mississippi AFL-CIO that issued from them. Local unions and their members publicly repudiated Ramsay's leadership because of his outspoken support for black civil rights.

The 1960s were a decade of trial for Ramsay as Mississippi was consumed with making a last, desperate stand to defend segregation. Candidates endorsed by the Mississippi AFL-CIO lost repeatedly, and Mississippi AFL-CIO membership declined precipitously. The ordeal even extended into Ramsay's personal life as his family was harassed and his life threatened. He kept a shotgun in his car and let it be known that he was armed at all times in order to discourage would-be assassins.

As the tumult of the 1960s dissipated, Ramsay began to see results from his efforts to alter the political climate in Mississippi. At the 1968 Democratic national convention, an integrated group of Loyalist delegates from Mississippi were seated in place of the Regulars. Membership to the Mississippi AFL-CIO began to recover as local unions that had disaffiliated in protest to Ramsay's alliance with civil rights groups now rejoined. In addition, Ramsay's alliance with blacks began to pay political dividends. The Mississippi AFL-CIO found political allies among increasing numbers of newly elected black legislators and newly enfranchised black voters.

Ramsay died on January 17, 1986, just one month after retiring as president of the Mississippi AFL-CIO, a post he held for 26 years. In an odd way, his funeral vindicated and symbolized the principles for which he had fought. Black leaders, who would have been denied entry into the funeral home previously, were now in attendance and walked by his casket garlanded in flowers that spelled out "AFL-CIO." Mississippi politicians who did not even bother to solicit the state council's endorsement when Ramsay took office in 1959 now sat in the pews to pay homage to labor's fallen leader. And newspapers in Mississippi that had excoriated him mercilessly for his civil rights activity in the past now hailed him as a prophet and acknowledged in their obituaries that Mississippi was a better place for his courageous efforts.

ALAN DRAPER

References and Further Reading

Draper, Alan. "Claude Ramsay, the Mississippi AFL-CIO, and the Civil Rights Movement." *Labor's Heritage* 4, no. 4 (1992): 4–24.
———. *Conflict of Interests: Organized Labor and the Civil Rights Movement in the South*, 1954–68. Ithaca, NY: Cornell University Press, 1994.
McElvain, Robert S. "Claude Ramsay, Organized Labor, and the Civil Rights Movement in Mississippi, 1959–1966." In *Southern Workers and Their Unions, 1880–1975*, edited by Merl E. Reed, Leslie S. Hough, and Gary M. Fink. Westport, CT: Greenwood Press, 1981, pp. 110–137.
McMillen, Neil R. "The Development of Civil Rights, 1956–1970." In *History of Mississippi*, Volume 2, edited by Richard Aubrey McLemore. Jackson: University and College Press of Mississippi, 1973, pp. 154–197.
Mosley, Donald C. "The Labor Union Movement." In *History of Mississippi*, Volume 2, edited by Richard Aubrey McLemore. Jackson: University and College Press of Mississippi, 1973, pp. 250–273.
Silver, James W. *Mississippi: The Closed* Society. New York: Harcourt, Brace & World, 1964.
Simpson, William. "The Birth of the Mississippi 'Loyalist Democrats.'" *Journal of Mississippi History* 44, no. 1 (1982): 27–44.

RANDOLPH, A. PHILIP (1889–1979)
President, Brotherhood of Sleeping Car Porters

Asa Philip Randolph was one of the most prominent black freedom fighters of the twentieth century. He became the editor of the *Messenger*, a black Socialist weekly; a labor organizer; the president of the Brotherhood of Sleeping Car Porters, the first black labor union to be recognized by a major corporation; the head of the March on Washington Movement; and the convener of the historic 1963 March on Washington for Jobs and Freedom. Randolph was born in 1889 in Crescent City, Florida. His father was an ordained AME minister who, along with his wife, Elizabeth, also ran a tailoring business to help provide for his family. Asa was nurtured in the AME heritage. His father's ministry stressed a social gospel message, emphasizing racial justice. The Reverend James Randolph, Asa recalled, told his parishioners that the AME Church was a black independent institution whose mission, in part, was social. Along with stressing the social gospel, the elder Randolph also taught his son racial pride, informing him of the great black figures such as Nat Turner and Frederick Douglass. A. Philip Randolph was well acquainted with the religious teachings of the Bible. He noted that as a child he would sit and read the Bible, and his mother, Elizabeth, who was considered the disciplinarian in the Randolph household, was very devout. In fact, the church was the center of her world. All of her friends were members of the church, and all of her activities outside of the household were in the church. Thus, Randolph's parents had an important influence in shaping his religious beliefs. Although Randolph would later become critical of conventional religion and certain types of religious leaders, he would not abandon black church culture but incorporate its language in the battles he waged for social justice.

Labor Organizer and Socialist

When Randolph was very young, he and his family moved to Jacksonville, Florida, where the Rev. James Randolph became pastor of a local AME church. Asa and his older brother James would later attend Cookman Institute, one of the first high schools for blacks in Florida. Soon after graduating from Cookman Institute, Randolph worked at odd jobs, including selling insurance premiums and clerking in a grocery store. He eventually decided to migrate to New York City in 1911, seeking a career in acting. In New York, Randolph worked at several occupations, including working as a porter and a waiter on a steamboat. As a result of what he said was job exploitation, he attempted to organize the waiters and other workers on the steamboat. However, when management received wind of his activity, he was fired. He also created an Elevator and Switchboard Operators Union, thereby gaining early experience as a labor

Asa Philip Randolph seated with President Lyndon Johnson. Library of Congress, Prints & Photographs Division [LC-USZ62-104210].

organizer. Randolph also attended the City College of New York, where he took courses in political science, history, and economics, as well as other courses in the humanities and social sciences. It was at City College that Randolph first learned about Socialist and Marxist theory.

Randolph also received an education in politics on the streets of New York. There he heard "soapbox" orators such as Eugene V. Debs and the black Socialist Hubert Harrison preach the gospel of Socialism. Motivated by their class analysis, Randolph became convinced that there were numerous benefits for working-class African-Americans in industrial unionism. After meeting Chandler Owen and acquainting him with Socialism, both men became members of the Socialist Party, arguing that racism was rooted in capitalist exploitation and that Socialism was the best means of liberating the black masses.

In 1917, Randolph and Owen started the first black Socialist journal in the country, the *Messenger*. A number of Harlem radicals wrote for the *Messenger*, including the Rev. George Frazier Miller, the pastor of an Episcopalian church in Brooklyn, New York; W. A. Domingo and Lovett Fort-Whiteman, who would later be two of the first people of African origins to join the American Communist Party; and the journalist George Schuyler. During the early part of its existence, the *Messenger* celebrated the Russian Revolution, supported Socialist candidates for office, pushed for industrial unionism, and advocated a Socialist solution to the race problem in America. One of the most controversial issues addressed by the *Messenger* was World War I. But after 1919, the *Messenger* became anticommunist in tone, indicating Randolph's opposition to forces outside of the country attempting to give direction to the Socialist movement and his opinion that Communists were responsible for the schism within the Socialist Party.

Randolph and Owen opposed the war and used the pages of their magazine to publicize their opposition. They pointed to the hypocrisy of a country that claimed it was fighting to make the world safe for democracy but would not do anything to end the racial terror on its own shores. Randolph and Owen were both arrested for speaking out against the war and charged with violating the Espionage Act.

The Brotherhood of Sleeping Car Porters

During World War I, Randolph created the Brotherhood of Labor, an agency whose mission, in large part, was to educate new black migrants to New York City on the social, economic, and political conditions of the city. Randolph organized a number of trade unions. However, despite his efforts in creating unions, these organizations did not have a long life. Because of his lack of success in creating and maintaining for any significant amount of time a labor organization, by 1924 Randolph decided to give up on labor organizing and instead dedicate his full attention to his magazine. However, he would change his mind about labor organizing when in 1925 he was asked to help the Brotherhood of Sleeping Car Porters (BSCP) in their fight to win the right to collectively bargain with its employer, the Pullman Company.

The Pullman Palace Car Company was created by George Pullman in 1867. The luxurious sleeper train cars consisted of red carpet, wood ornaments, and silver-trimmed oil lamps. On each train, there was a buffet sleeping car, smoking room, chandelier, and other items to make readers feel like they were in a hotel on wheels. Of course, the most important components of Pullman's operations were the porters. Pullman recruited former slaves to perform the various services required on the train to make passengers comfortable. The services included accepting and discharging customers, taking care of luggage, making the beds, changing the linen, cleaning the cars, and waiting on passengers. Apparently, Pullman came to the conclusion that former slaves were the best people to perform these tasks because of their time spent in servitude. Hence, from the start of the Pullman's Company's incorporation, black men were relegated to the job of porter. By the 1920s, the Pullman Company was the largest employer of black men in the United States.

Porters were paid poorly, worked long hours, and were treated badly by management. In fact, a porter's monthly salary was less than a New York City factory worker's. The company expected blacks to be grateful, loyal, and obedient to their employer and management, and they were required to be polite to the passengers regardless of the circumstances. In fact, because they depended on tips to supplement their meager wages, porters dared not challenge rude and disrespectful customers. One of the worst aspects of the job was when porters were compelled into "deadheading" and forced to "double out." Deadheading meant they had to work many hours a month without receiving wages for that time. Doubling out meant that when a porter returned from a long run, he could be ordered to go out on the next train without rest. These and other practices reduced the porters to menial servants. Although the first generation of porters did not express their displeasure about their working conditions, the more educated black men who replaced the former slaves were more willing to articulate their dissatisfaction with their treatment.

Randolph at first was reluctant to get involved in the Brotherhood's struggle to win recognition as the collective bargaining agency for Pullman porters, but after he investigated their grievances, he decided to help lead the campaign for recognition. Under his leadership, several chapters of the BSCP were organized, including New York, Chicago, St. Louis, Kansas City, Seattle, Omaha, Los Angeles, Washington DC, Denver, Boston, Buffalo, and Oakland. The fight to win recognition was a 12-year struggle between the union and the Pullman Company. The company employed a host of intimidating tactics including creating and using a spy network, firing workers, persuading religious leaders and many of the black middle class to publicly denounce the Brotherhood, and organizing a company union to undermine the Brotherhood's legitimacy. The union's membership, which had reached a high of nearly 7,000 in 1928, fell to around 770 by 1932.

However, Randolph and the organizers and members of the BSCP persevered. Randolph and the BSCP did not only turn to porters to win recognition but relied on support from community, labor, and civic organizations. In particular, Randolph requested and received support from many in the various black religious communities. A number of black pastors allowed Randolph to hold BSCP meetings in their churches. When he addressed meetings of porters, Randolph did not speak of Socialism but used the religious oratory with which many in the black community were acquainted.

Finally, in 1937, the union won recognition after the passage of an amendment to the Railway Labor Act in 1934 giving Pullman porters and dining car cooks and waiters the right to organize and collectively bargain. Eventually, the Railroad Mediation Board ordered an election for employee representatives for the porters, and the BSCP overwhelmingly won. By the summer of 1935, the Brotherhood began formal negotiations with the Pullman Company. But it should be noted that while it was because of the Emergency Railroad Transportation Act (ERTA) and the National Industrial Recovery Act (NIRA) that the BSCP eventually received recognition, the fact that Randolph and the members of the BSCP "stayed the course" and did not fold led to the union's victory. Moreover, the BSCP should be seen as more than a labor organization. Randolph and the leaders of the organization interpreted their struggle as a civil rights one. Throughout his public career, Randolph argued that civil rights must be linked to the rights of working people, and in numerous speeches and letters, Randolph contended that the battle for recognition was to win dignity and respect for black people.

The National Negro Congress and the March on Washington Movement

Randolph remained active in the fight for labor and civil rights. In 1935, the National Negro Congress (NNC) was formed to help foster greater collaboration among black political, religious, and civic organizations. Some of the country's most important black leaders were involved in the new organization such as Lester Granger of the Urban League; Adam Clayton Powell Jr. of Abyssinian Baptist Church in Harlem; Alain Locke, a professor of philosophy at Howard University; and Randolph. Randolph was offered and accepted the presidency of the new organization. However, shortly after he accepted the leadership of the NNC, he became involved in a battle with the American Communist Party. The Party was an early supporter of the NNC and had sent a number of delegates to its opening convention. Randolph, in his first presidential address, warned against Communist attempts to take over the organization. Nevertheless, the Communist Party USA (CPUSA) was a major financial contributor to the NNC. In its determination to see that the NNC survive, the Communist Party also provided personnel, who moved into key positions. Eventually, Randolph resigned as president, citing many issues, including the Communist Party's influence over the Congress.

When Nazi Germany began invading and occupying countries in Europe, American industries began contracting with the government to increase production of ships, tanks, guns, and other items for defense. Despite the urgent need for tens of thousands of skilled workers to help in the production of these items, war production companies refused to hire blacks. Moreover, the federal government refused to take steps to end the racial discriminatory actions of these industries. In fact, the administration publicly announced that it would continue to segregate blacks and whites who enlisted in the armed services. In response to the blatant discrimination on the part of industry and the government, Randolph launched the March on Washington Movement (MOWM), which helped organized thousands of people of African origins in the United States to march on the nation's capital in 1941, demanding that President Franklin Delano Roosevelt issue an executive order banning discrimination in the defense industry. The March on Washington Committee was organized and headed by Randolph and consisted of prominent black leaders such as Walter White of the NAACP and Lester Granger of the Urban League. Although Eleanor Roosevelt met with Randolph and White to convince them to call off the march, Randolph refused, insisting that the president agree to ban discrimination in the defense industry. The threat of thousands of black people coming to Washington DC to protest convinced FDR to hold a meeting with Randolph and other march leaders in June 1941. Although the president attempted to convince Randolph to call off the march, he refused unless an executive order was issued. Eventually, FDR agreed, and his close ally, Mayor Fiorello La Guardia of New York, Randolph, and others associated with the White House worked out a compromise. The compromise was Executive Order 8802, which banned employment discrimination in the defense industry and the government. FDR also created a temporary Fair Employment Practice Committee to help ensure that defense manufacturers would not practice racial discrimination. Because of a major victory in forcing the government to take action against discrimination, the first time since Reconstruction, Randolph agreed to call off the march.

Banning Discrimination in the Armed Forces and the Second March on Washington

Randolph's confrontation with FDR would not be the last time he clashed with a U.S. president. He believed that President Harry S. Truman's 1947 call for a peacetime draft was an opportunity to demand an end to discrimination in the armed forces. The leader of the MOWM helped establish the League for Nonviolent Civil Disobedience Against Military Segregation. The group announced a campaign of civil disobedience to force the president to issue an executive order ending segregation in the military. Truman responded by calling a meeting of prominent black leaders, including Randolph; however, nothing was resolved at the meeting. Testifying before the Senate Armed Services Committee considering the draft bill, Randolph warned that if segregation was not ended in the armed services, blacks would refuse to serve. Under pressure from Randolph and other black leaders and fearing losing the black vote in a close election, Truman decided to issue Executive Order 9981 ending discrimination in the United States military.

Randolph's prominence as a civil rights leader faded by the time the modern civil rights movement emerged. New leaders and organizations such as Martin Luther King Jr., Fred Shuttlesworth, and Ralph Abernathy of the Southern Christian Leadership Conference; James Farmer and Bayard Rustin of the Congress of Racial Equality; and John Lewis and Diane Nash of the Student Nonviolent Coordinating Committee moved to the forefront in the fight for racial justice. In addition, Malcolm X and the Nation of Islam gained a great deal of attention, condemning white racism and calling for the separation of races as the solution to the race problem in America. However, Randolph remained a respected figure in the civil rights community. In 1962, Randolph and Bayard Rustin suggested that a march on Washington for Jobs and Freedom be organized. They met with black leaders, and Randolph was selected as the national director of the march while Rustin was chosen as the march's organizer. Civil rights groups, labor unions, civic organizations, and prominent individuals endorsed the endeavor. President Kennedy met with march organizers and expressed fear that violence was going to erupt in the streets, thereby harming the chances of his proposed civil rights bill of passing in Congress. Randolph responded to the president's concern by pointing out to him that blacks were already in the streets and that it would be better for them to come under the influence of civil rights leaders. Thus, the civil rights leaders did not back down from Kennedy.

To ensure a positive tone from speakers of the event, Randolph convinced John Lewis, the head of the Student Nonviolent Coordinating Committee, to alter his speech, which called for a scorched-earth policy to win civil rights. Despite Kennedy's reluctance, on August 28, 1963, 250,000 people came to the nation's capital, making the March on Washington one of the most memorable events in modern American history.

In 1964, Randolph created the A. Philip Randolph Institute to strengthen the ties between labor and civil rights organizations. He contended that the civil rights movement needed the help of labor to help advance economic justice for African-Americans. In 1965, the institute created the A. Philip Randolph Educational Fund to help establish a forum where people could discuss strategies for providing programs for social justice. The Fund was a think tank for the civil rights movement. Due to ill health, Randolph retired from his position as president of the BSCP and vice president of the AFL-CIO executive council. A. Philip Randolph died on May 16, 1979, at the age of 89.

CLARENCE TAYLOR

References and Further Reading

Anderson, Jervis. *A. Philip Randolph: A Biographical Portrait*. New York: Harcourt Brace, 1974.
Arnesen, Eric. "A. Philip Randolph: Labor and the New Black Politics." In *The Human Tradition in American Labor History*, edited by Eric Arnesen. Wilmington, DE: Scholarly Resources, 2003, pp. 173–191.
Fink, Leon. "A Voice for the People: A. Philip Randolph and the Cult of Leadership." In *Progressive Intellectuals and the Dilemmas of Democratic Commitment*, by Leon Fink. Cambridge, MA: Harvard University Press, 1997, pp. 184–213.
Harris, William Hamilton. *Keeping the Faith: A. Philip Randolph, Milton P. Webster, and the Brotherhood of Sleeping Car Porters, 1925–37*. Urbana: University of Illinois Press, 1977.
Pfeffer, Paula F. *A. Philip Randolph, Pioneer of the Civil Rights Movement*. Baton Rouge: Louisiana State University Press, 1990.
Quarles, Benjamin. "A. Philip Randolph: Labor Leader at Large." In *Black Mosaic: Essays in Afro-American History and Historiography*, by Benjamin Quarles. Amherst: University of Massachusetts Press, 1988, pp. 151–177.
Taylor, Clarence. "Sticking to the Ship: Manhood, Fraternity, and the Religious Worldview of A. Philip Randolph." In *Black Religious Intellectuals: The Fight for Equality from Jim Crow to the 21st Century*, by Clarence Taylor. New York: Routledge, 2002, pp. 11–36.

See also **A. Philip Randolph Institute; Brotherhood of Sleeping Car Porters; March on Washington Movement; National Association for the Advancement of Colored People (NAACP); National Urban League**

RETAIL, WHOLESALE, AND DEPARTMENT STORE UNION

Since its establishment in 1937, the Retail, Wholesale, and Department Store Union (RWDSU) was the primary Congress of Industrial Organizations (CIO) union organizing in the distributive industry. Unlike its American Federation of Labor (AFL) counterparts, it focused on department store, wholesale, and warehouse workers, as opposed to food store workers. The RWDSU formed from a split within the AFL's Retail Clerks International Protective Association (RCIPA). It was centered in major metropolitan areas in the United States and Canada, with its strongest locals in New York City. Many of those New York City locals had strong ties with the left and especially the Communist Party. These connections led to conflict within the RWDSU during the Second Red Scare of the late 1940s and early 1950s. Some scholars maintain that these conflicts hindered organized labor's ability to keep up with retail expansion in the suburbs following World War II. The RWDSU also spawned the National Health Care Workers Union, Local 1199, in the 1960s. In 1993, the RWDSU combined with the United Food and Commercial Workers, AFL-CIO, Central Labor Council (CLC).

The Founding of the Union

Two New York City locals of the RCIPA, Local 338 led by Samuel Wolchok and Local 1250 led by

1185

Clarina Michelson, formed the center of what eventually became the RWDSU. Wolchok had a socialist background and was a noted anticommunist. In contrast, Local 1250's origins lay with the Office Worker's Union, supported by the Communist Party-backed Trade Union Unity League (TUUL). These locals, and others, were dissatisfied with the RCIPA's lack of militancy, lack of support for new organizing, and lack of democratic representation in the international. They viewed the RCIPA as failing to take a strong stand on key workplace issues, including the seasonality of employment, late closings, and unpaid overtime. In 1937, the dissenting locals formed the New Era Committee, which presented an opposition slate for RCIPA elections. When this action failed to bring about reform in the union, the New Era Committee applied for and received a charter with the CIO, forming the United Retail Employees of America (UREA). Shortly thereafter, Local 65, representing garment district wholesale and warehouse workers, joined as well. Wolchok served as president of the new union until 1948.

The CIO charter coincided with a wave of sit-down strikes at various retail and department store establishments in New York City, Philadelphia, Providence, and elsewhere. Key demands included union recognition, a 40-hour week, and minimum wage increases. In this context, the UREA administered the CIO's Department Store Organizing Committee (DSOC), originally led by Sidney Hillman. Local 1250 was instrumental in organizing other major New York City department stores, which were chartered as locals of the DSOC. Macy's nonselling staff became Local 1-S, Gimbels and Saks 34th Street were Local 2, Bloomingdale's was Local 3, and Stern's was Local 5. While the union had most of its success in New York City, it also organized major stores in Pittsburgh, Providence, Boston, and Chicago. St. Louis, Toledo, and Detroit also had significant membership in the wholesale, warehouse, and dairy sections. The DSOC was officially dissolved in 1940, and the UREA became the United Retail, Wholesale, and Department Store Employees of America (URWDSEA). After World War II, the name was shortened to the RWDSU.

World War II

During World War II, like most unions, the RWDSU abided by the no-strike pledge. However, the union also saw during this period significant conflict, including a series of strikes, against Montgomery Ward & Co. The union had the support of both the National Labor Relations Board (NLRB) and the War Labor Board (WLB) in its disputes with Montgomery Ward. After a 13-day strike in 1944, President Franklin Roosevelt ordered Montgomery Ward to sign the contract proposed by the WLB. The company declined, so the United States Army took over the company's property and removed the company president. Despite the union's support from the government, the Montgomery Ward strikes divided the union on political grounds. Arthur Osman and 500 stewards from the very left-wing Local 65 publicly criticized the RWDSU leadership for allowing strikes to go forward in violation of the no-strike pledge.

The RWDSU expanded into Canada in 1945, organizing food processing and warehouse establishments in Ontario and Saskatchewan. It grew rapidly in the years following World War II, while Cold War politics weakened and divided the union in the United States.

The Second Red Scare

The New York City department store locals, Local 65, retail Local 830, drugstore employees' Local 1199, and displaymen's Local 144, formed a faction with close ties to the Communist Party in a largely anticommunist international. These political differences generated considerable conflict. This friction came to a head in 1948 when nine of the left-wing locals, which composed half of the RWDSU's membership, seceded from the international and formed their own independent union. The secession was sparked by those locals' refusal to submit the noncommunist affidavits required by the Taft-Hartley Act. In August 1948, Wolchok threatened to seize the noncomplying locals, beginning with Local 1-S (which was willing to comply). Local 1-S voted to secede, followed closely by Locals 2, 3, 5, 1250, 65, 830, 1199, and 144. All but Local 1-S and Local 830 then formed the Distributive Workers Union (DWU) in February 1950, led by Arthur Osman, who was the founder and president of Local 65. At the DWU's founding convention, Osman advocated compliance with the Taft-Hartley law and the filing of noncommunist affidavits. Officers who were members of the Communist Party resigned their memberships, signed and dated the resignations, and put them in vaults. They then filed the affidavits. Many of the leaders were subsequently accused of perjury in connection to the affidavits. A federal grand jury and the Senate Internal Security Subcommittee both accused union officers of maintaining Communist ties subsequent to the filing. The DWU was short-lived. In October 1950, it merged with two left-wing unions that had been purged from the CIO, the Food, Tobacco, Agricultural, and Allied Workers and the United Office and Professional Workers of America, to form the Distributive, Processing, and Office Workers Union of America (DPOWA). Each major city merged its locals into one. Philadelphia had District 76. The New York City locals merged to form District 65, led by David Livingston. In 1954, the DPOWA joined the CIO, and dissident RWDSU locals rejoined the RWDSU.

During the 1950s, the move of department stores to the suburbs posed a major challenge to the RWDSU, now led by Max Greenberg until 1975. As major New York City department stores under union contract closed their doors, suburban branches of these same stores were on the rise. The suburban stores were not unionized. Through the 1950s and 1960s, the RWDSU attempted to bring suburban stores in the Northeast and the Midwest under contract. In this effort, the RWDSU anticipated broader efforts by the AFL-CIO decades later to organize large retailers not located in urban areas that were traditional union strongholds. The RWDSU drive focused on the particular benefits it could offer women workers, such as paid maternity leave and pension and retirement benefits. These efforts had some small successes, but the campaign was largely unsuccessful.

1960s to the Present

In the 1960s and 1970s, RWDSU Local 1199, led by Leon Davis, emerged as a new force in the labor movement. Starting in 1959 and continuing through the 1980s, Local 1199 organized hospital workers, first in New York City and then in other major cities, including Charleston and Philadelphia. 1199 became semi-independent from the RWDSU, constituting itself as the National Union of Hospital and Health Care Employees in 1973.

Factionalism affected the RWDSU again in 1969 when District 65 and 10 other locals in seven states that opposed the international's support for the Vietnam War seceded to form the Distributive Workers of America (DWA). The DWA, led by Cleveland Robinson, then joined the Alliance for Labor Action (ALA), a labor organization formed to challenge the AFL-CIO in 1969. The ALA disbanded in 1971.

Alvin Heaps led the RWDSU from 1976 to 1986. Under his leadership, the RWDSU attempted to reassert control over Local 1199 and re-absorb it wholly into the union. This attempt failed, and in 1984, the National Union of Hospital and Health Care Employees, whose membership was predominantly

African-American and female, left the RWDSU and eventually merged with the Service Employees International Union (SEIU). Women had been an increasing proportion of the membership of the international since World War II, and a significant number of locals had a majority female membership. Women often served as shop stewards and local officers. Regardless, through the history of the union, women were underrepresented at the highest levels of leadership. Heaps's unexpected death resulted in the ascension of Lenore Miller to head the union, the first female president of the union.

MINNA P. ZISKIND

References and Further Reading

Cuneo, Carl J. "The Withering of Trade Union Patriarchy." www.sociology.org/content/vol001.003/cuneo/RWPAT.HTM.

Fink, Leon, and Brian Greenberg. *Upheaval in the Quiet Zone: A History of Hospital Workers' Union, Local 1199.* Urbana and Chicago: University of Illinois Press, 1989.

Kirstein, George G. *Stores and Unions: A Study of Growth of Unionism and Dry Goods and Department Stores.* New York: Fairchild Publications, Inc., 1950.

Ziskind, Minna P. "Citizenship, Consumerism, and Gender: A Study of District 65, 1945–1960." Ph.D. diss., University of Pennsylvania, 2001.

———. "Labor Conflict in the Suburbs: Organizing Retail in Metropolitan New York, 1954–1958." *International Labor and Working-Class History* 64 (Fall 2003): 55–73.

See also **Alliance for Labor Action; Davis, Leon; Sit-Down Strikes (1937)**

REUTHER, WALTER (1907–1970)
President, United Auto Workers

Perhaps more than any other labor leader, Walter Philip Reuther embodied the hopes and limits of organized labor's golden moment. He began his career as a radical organizer in 1930s Detroit. In the mid-1940s, he assumed the presidency of the union he had helped to build, the United Auto Workers (UAW). A man of imposing intellect, boundless energy, and fierce ambition, Reuther used his position to push the boundaries of collective bargaining, strengthen labor's voice in American politics, and promote a host of progressive causes. Despite all his efforts, though, at the time of his death in 1970 the goal closest to his heart—the democratization of industry—remained a dream unfulfilled.

Walter Reuther was born in Wheeling, West Virginia, on September 1, 1907, the second son of German-born working-class parents. His mother,

Anna, was a devout Lutheran; his father, Valentine, a fervent unionist and socialist. Anna and Valentine ran their family like a socialist *Volksverien*, organizing family debates on social issues, stocking their small library with socialist pamphlets, and continually encouraging their children to work for the advancement of the working class. Walter and his siblings—older brother Ted, younger brothers Roy and Victor, and sister Christine—learned their lessons well. By the time they were teenagers, they, too, had become committed socialists, high-minded and moralistic in their commitment to social change.

While Valentine shaped his children's political consciousness, he also urged them to learn trades, the surest route to security for working-class Americans in the early twentieth century. Walter decided to become a tool and die maker. It was a telling choice. Tool and die workers were the most modern of craftsmen, responsible for making the molds and dies manufacturers used to mass-produce goods. To make his way in the trade, a young man had to have an intimate knowledge of the production process, an ability to conceptualize intricate designs, and the dedication to see those designs to completion. Walter loved it. At age 15, he left school to take up an apprenticeship at a Wheeling metal shop. The apprenticeship was supposed to last four years, but after just three, Reuther decided he had learned enough to test his skills on the open market. So he packed up his tools and headed for the world's most modern industrial center: Detroit.

It is hard to imagine a more audacious move. Detroit's auto factories were marvels of integrated manufacturing; up and down vast assembly lines, armies of workingmen and women pieced together thousands of perfectly machined parts, from engine blocks to rumble seats. To keep this complex system running, auto companies hired the best tool and die makers they could find, not untested teenagers fresh from West Virginia. But Reuther walked straight into the premier tool shop in the city, at Henry Ford's fabled Highland Park plant, and talked his way into one of the highest-paying jobs a blue-collar worker could find.

The wonders of mass production did not last long. Just two years after Reuther began working at Ford's, the national economy collapsed. The Great Depression hit the auto industry with particular force: by 1931, Detroit's unemployment rate had climbed to a cataclysmic 30%. Protected by his skill, Reuther held on to his job. But the widespread misery that surrounded him confirmed the political lessons his father had taught him. In the first few years of the 1930s, Walter immersed himself in socialist activities, rushing from meeting to meeting, rally to rally. In

1932, the Depression's worst year, he campaigned relentlessly for the Socialist Party presidential candidate, Norman Thomas. As soon as the election results were in, the Ford Motor Company informed Reuther that he was fired.

There is no firm evidence that Reuther lost job because of his political activity. But his sudden entry into the ranks of the unemployed certainly opened new avenues for his activism. With his younger brother Victor at his side, Walter embarked on a round-the-world educational tour, which culminated in an 18-month stint as a worker in the Soviet Union's Gorki auto plant. The Soviets' attempt to build a workers' state deeply impressed him. Though it is unlikely he ever joined the Communist Party, he and Victor returned to the United States in the spring of 1935 determined to bring a revolution to American industrial relations.

The moment was propitious. The previous year, a group of dissident union leaders broke from the nation's largest labor organization, the American Federation of Labor (AFL), and formed the Congress of Industrial Organizations (CIO) with the intention of bringing unionization to the nation's core industries. Walter's brother Roy had already volunteered as a foot soldier in the campaign, working as an organizer among the autoworkers of Flint, a hardscrabble industrial town 70 miles north of Detroit. Walter and Victor signed on, too, joining other radicals in a left-wing cadre within the fledgling United Auto Workers. With his typical alacrity, Walter launched himself into a leadership position. Within months of his arrival back in Detroit, Reuther had become the president of UAW Local 174 and a member of the union's executive board.

At first, these were largely empty appointments, since the UAW had virtually no members. Then the epic sit-down strikes of 1936–1937 forced two of the three largest automakers—General Motors and the Chrysler Corporation—to recognize the UAW as the representative of their workers. As the UAW's status skyrocketed, so did Reuther's standing. Almost overnight, the radical organizer became a labor leader, sharing responsibility for a 400,000-member union that, because of its strategic position, wielded enormous influence over the American economy.

Reuther used his new authority to advance his vision of a restructured economic order. It is impossible to say when he first encountered the ideas of Thorstein Veblen. He could have encountered them in is father's library. Or perhaps one of his socialist comrades had suggested a few titles to him. Whatever the source, Reuther found in Veblen's 1921 book, *The Engineers and the Price System*, a framework that would shape his thinking for the rest of his life.

Veblen argued that new technology made it possible for the economy to create unlimited abundance. But businesspersons refused to unleash technology's extraordinary abundance, Veblen said. Instead, they manipulated the price system to create scarcity and maximize profit. The key to prosperity, then, was to strip businesspersons of their control over the industrial system and hand it to experts who would serve the public interest.

It is not surprising that a former tool and die maker—steeped in the details of production, trained in the power of planning—would find these ideas appealing. Reuther's particular genius was finding ways to make them palatable to the American public. To that end, Reuther rejected Veblen's choice of ideal experts—engineers—and instead argued that the economic decision making should be shared by representatives of business, labor, and the government: a democratic reconstruction of economic affairs. Rather than call for the complete refashioning of private enterprise, moreover, Reuther proposed piecemeal change, which he invariably linked to an issue of pressing national concern. He first unveiled the strategy in 1941. That year, the Roosevelt administration was desperately preparing for war. But the major airplane manufacturers were refusing to mass-produce military aircraft. There was a simple way to break the bottleneck, Reuther said. Retool auto factories so that they begin making planes. And to make sure the job was done correctly, put the new operation under the joint control of the auto companies, the UAW, and the federal government. In no time at all, promised Reuther, the industry would be manufacturing "500 planes a day." Auto executives objected so strenuously that the proposal quickly died. Yet its originality and sheer audacity won Reuther a string of admirers among Washington's liberal elite. The plan even impressed Franklin Roosevelt, who took to calling Walter "my young, red-headed engineer."

As Reuther built a national reputation, he also embroiled himself in an increasingly fierce battle for control of the UAW. At the time of the sit-down strike, Reuther had allied himself with the union's small but influential communist faction. Shortly thereafter, the alliance shattered. Gradually, Reuther constructed around him a new bloc of supporters, expressly committed to purging the communists from the union. The UAW's left wing responded by charging that Reuther was trying to grab power at any cost. All through the early 1940s the conflict raged, both sides locked in endless rounds of charge and countercharge. As the nation slipped into the Cold War in 1946, the conflict finally tipped Reuther's way. In a bitterly contested campaign, he traded on the growing anticommunist hysteria to win the

UAW's presidency. His opponents claimed his victory was a triumph for the right wing. Reuther saw it differently. "We are the vanguard," he proclaimed in his inaugural speech. "We are the architects of the future, and we are going to fashion the weapons with which we will work and fight and build."

For the next 24 years, Reuther tried to uphold that pledge. Under his direction, the UAW moved collective bargaining far beyond the question of wages rates. Reuther forced auto manufacturers to provide their workers with comprehensive health care, retirement plans, paid vacations, cost-of-living allowances, and in perhaps his greatest coup, supplemental unemployment benefits, which gave autoworkers a substantial portion of their pay while they were laid off. These benefits did not vault UAW members into the middle class, as social commentators often claimed. But they did assure them a level of security unimaginable only a few decades earlier.

Reuther also dramatically increased the UAW's political power. From its founding, the union had worked with the Democratic Party. Reuther strengthened the ties. Thanks to the efforts of Walter's brother Roy, who directed the union's political department, the UAW came to dominate the Michigan Democratic Party, while union funds and personnel poured into the Democrats' national campaigns. In the mid-1950s, moreover, Reuther engineered the merger of the AFL and the CIO, thus creating a potential political bloc of 15 million members. Such efforts opened doors: from Harry Truman onward, Democratic presidents courted Reuther's support and welcomed his counsel. And on one occasion, Lyndon Johnson considered appointing him to a cabinet post.

The UAW president used his influence to promote a host of social reforms. He vigorously supported the extension of the welfare state, hoping he could bring to the United States the "cradle to grave" social provisions Western European nations provided their citizens. He dreamed of rebuilding American cities, replacing crumbling ghettos with gleaming modern homes that the poor could afford. Though he was a committed anticommunist, he favored negotiations with the Soviet Union and campaigned for nuclear disarmament. And he was a devoted ally of the postwar era's greatest social movement, the struggle for racial equality. UAW money helped to underwrite the southern civil rights movement. Union lobbyists fought relentlessly for civil rights legislation. And time and again Reuther lent the cause his voice, even when many white UAW members wanted him to remain silent.

As important as all those commitments were, however, they never displaced Reuther's dream of democratizing the American economy. Throughout his presidency, he searched for ways to put Veblen's ideas into practice. He tried to use collective bargaining, most notably in 1946, when he demanded that General Motors give the UAW a say in setting automobile prices. He traded on national emergencies. When the United States went to war in Korea, for instance, he argued that the economic mobilization be managed by a combination of corporate, union, and government officials. And he dovetailed his proposals with other liberal initiatives, such as Lyndon Johnson's War on Poverty, which he said should be linked to national economic planning. Reuther made such proposals so often that one critic claimed that the UAW president was good for "500 plans a day."

No matter how he packaged them, Reuther's proposals made no headway. Businesspersons firmly rejected any encroachment on the right to manage their corporations as they saw fit. Politicians he considered his friends listened politely to his plans and then slipped them silently into file cabinets, never to be seen again. Even his fellow unionists rejected his ideas, no one more vigorously than the AFL-CIO president George Meany, who swept aside Reuther's ideas as impractical and unnecessary. Many other associates quietly agreed. Talk of democratizing the economy made sense in the depths of the Depression, when corporate America lay prostrate. In the heady economic boom of the 1950s and 1960s, though, such ideas seemed outmoded. The columnist Murray Kempton put the sentiment in print in a 1960s profile of the UAW. Reuther, he said, "seems a little obsolete."

But Reuther refused to see his agenda as a vestige of more radical times. On the contrary, as American public life began to swing to the right in the late 1960s, Walter stepped up his activism. In 1968, he withdrew the UAW from the AFL-CIO, claiming that the labor federation had grown too conservative. He promised to launch an aggressive organizing campaign to bring more workers into the union movement. He belatedly joined the anti-Vietnam War movement. And he renewed his call for democratic economic planning, arguing that the nation must be prepared for the challenges sure to come once the war in Southeast Asia ended.

The furious activities of those years came to a sudden end on May 9, 1970. That evening, Reuther boarded a small private plane for a quick trip to the UAW summer camp at Black Lake, Michigan, a few hours north of Detroit. The plane crashed just short of its landing, killing all aboard. In its obituary, the *New York Times* eulogized Reuther as "a crusader for a better world ... [who] challenged not only labor but the country ... to seek newer and broader horizons." The newspaper then recounted his many accomplishments at the bargaining table and in public life. But it did not note that Reuther's greatest challenge to the status quo—his dream of an economic order made more democratic—remained unmet.

KEVIN BOYLE

References and Further Reading

Barnard, John. *American Vanguard: The United Auto Workers during the Reuther Years, 1935–1970*. Detroit: Wayne State University Press, 2004.

Boyle, Kevin. *The UAW and the Heyday of American Liberalism, 1945–1968*. Ithaca, NY: Cornell University Press, 1995.

Lichtenstein, Nelson. *The Most Dangerous Man in Detroit: Walter Reuther and the Fate of American Labor*. New York: Basic Books, 1995.

REVOLUTION AND EARLY NATIONAL PERIODS

The working classes of Revolutionary and Early National America are not easy to define. There were three separate groups of workers that could be defined as working classes in the Revolutionary and Early National eras. Slaves and free African-Americans constitute the first sector, though the two groups had very different histories. Agricultural laborers, prior to purchase of a farmstead, if they did so, would be the second. The third sector, the one that would evolve into the modern working class and whose strikes, boycotts, and other labor actions would become the root of the American working classes' organization and tactics, was the urban craftsmen, particularly those in the major seaports. (Rural craftsmen tended to be small shop proprietors.)

About 350,000 slaves resided in the 13 colonies prior to the Revolution, 250,000 of which had been imported to the colonies in the eighteenth century. Slavery was legal in every colony prior to the American Revolution, but after the Revolution, it was ended by every state north of the Mason-Dixon Line by the end of the Early National era. In the South, on the other hand, slavery flourished, the slave population increasing to almost four million in 1860. Slaves earned no wages, held little if any private property, paid no rent, and were subject to the total control of the masters under the various slave codes of each state. In the North, most slaves acted as servants within the household and occasionally as workers on the farm or in the craft shop. In the South, where most were concentrated, they worked largely in the tobacco, rice, and (after the 1790s) the cotton fields. There they commonly worked in gang labor, marched to the fields at sunup, and were led to their quarters at sundown. A number in the Deep South worked in a task system that allowed free time once they completed their assigned work, time enough to cultivate a small garden. Their living quarters, garments, and food were provided by masters who had total control over their hours of labor. During the American Revolution, slaves in the South fled by the hundreds to British lines where they were promised freedom. British promises were often broken, but about 20,000 sailed away after the war. In the North they more commonly fought on the side of the Americans, some earning their freedom that way. The free black population tended to be mulatto in the South, doing farm labor and occasionally owning small homesteads. In the North they tended to be isolated unskilled laborers who worked on the docks. A number were artisans, especially carpenters and hairdressers. But slaves are generally believed to be part of a rural precapitalist system of labor and as non-wage earners were peripheral to the development of the American working class.

Farm laborers made up a small percentage of those living in the rural areas of the country (at a time when less than 10% of the country lived in urban centers). For most, the work was temporary, and the realistic goal was to become a landowning farmer. Many farmers in early America were unable to hire free labor and forced to rely on their families, unless they could purchase indentured servants. Because of distance and outlook and scarcity there were few opportunities or incentives to organize, and there is little sense that any kind of collective consciousness or identity grew among free farm laborers. Nor were rural labor organizations or political movements formed until after the Civil War.

Skilled craftsmen lived in rural communities as well as in urban society. In rural communities, they were more likely to be a jack-of-all-trades artisan, such as a joiner who could fix a wheel, mend a coach, or build a chair. There were only a few craftsmen in any farming community, though occasional villages such as that of the Moravians in Rowan County, North Carolina, were known for their craftsmanship, male and female, in leather and textiles.

The core of working-class history in this era is to be found in the skilled and semiskilled urban artisans. American craftsmen were most heavily concentrated in towns and cities, especially the major seaports, where they constituted the largest sector of the population. They worked in a panoply of trades ranging from goldsmithing, silversmithing, and cabinetmaking at the top to baking, butchering, and carpentry in the middle to tailoring and shoemaking at the bottom. The most populous trades were the building crafts, particularly carpentry and masonry, which might employ 40% of the city's craftsmen during the construction season. Tailoring and shoemaking followed in size.

Colonial Heritage

Mid-eighteenth-century artisans could be classified as either wage earners, the beginning of a working class, or master craftsmen, incipient bourgeois entrepreneurs, because in the course of a colonial career, they were often both. Normally, a lad of 13 or 14 would contract with a master craftsman to learn a trade. He boarded with his master, who was responsible for his rudimentary education and clothing as well as teaching the secrets of the trade. Learning the mysteries of the most demanding trades such as cabinetmaking or watchmaking took many hours at the hands of the ablest craftsmen, who passed down knowledge gained from centuries of craftsmanship. The more rudimentary trades, such as shoemaking, with awl and hammer skills, took less time to master. Following release from indentures at 21, he would be a wage earner or journeyman, often working in various cities for master craftsmen. If competent and savvy, he would open his own business. A master's dwelling commonly included a lower-story shop with his family living above.

While the vast majority of artisans in colonial America remained craftsmen throughout their lives, within the middling or lower-middling ranks of society, upward mobility was possible. Expert cabinetmakers, for example, participated directly in colonial trade, shipping thousands of Windsor chairs. Other highly skilled artisans worked closely with merchants in a nascent capitalist economy operating under the rules of British mercantilism. Within the poorest trades, mobility to master craftsman standing was not the rule. Moreover, even masters owning small shoemaker or tailoring shops often earned a subsistence living, with little security in times of personal crisis or economic recession. This was particularly true of Boston, a city ravaged by wars for empire, where many craftsmen sank to subsistence levels. The shoemaker George Robert Twelves Hewes, the last survivor of the Boston Tea Party, was imprisoned early in his career for small debts, such were the perils of his trade. Too, poorer artisans were prey to the scourge of epidemics, especially smallpox and yellow fever that periodically ravaged the nation's seaports.

English guild traditions that limited admission to a trade, controlled prices, supervised craft practice, built elegant headquarters, and provided artisans a respected place in their city's life did not survive the transatlantic crossing. While a few trades established benevolent societies to provide social security and camaraderie for master craftsmen, and some traditions of apprenticeship indentures and workshop practices persisted, colonial America had no guild tradition, nor did it develop one. Artisans, possessing demanding skills and well-fashioned tools, were clearly above the level of laborers on the docks, indentured servants, and the slaves who made up 10% of the population of New York and Philadelphia and nearly half of Charleston. Wearing their noted leather aprons, they dressed in a common manner, kept common hours, and shared common social customs. Yet they were subject to a tradition that classified anyone who performed manual labor, however refined, as beneath the rank of a gentleman.

Lacking breeding, wealth, and education, they were expected to defer to their mercantile and professional betters, who regarded mechanics (as they were commonly known) with a measure of condescension. There were no guilds to mediate that pejorative standing.

On the other hand, the absence of guilds allowed for a more open society in which many artisans gained freemanship. As independent entrepreneurs who owned their shop, freemen were entitled to vote, making up an important part of the political mix of eighteenth-century urban politics. Though they seldom held office above that of constable during the colonial era, they became an important voice in Pennsylvania in the battle between the proprietary interests of the Penn family and those wanting to make Pennsylvania a royal colony, and in New York in the constant play of factions, especially between the Delancey and Livingston factions representing upstate and metropolitan mercantile interests. In the famous Zenger affair of the 1730s, in which the printer William Zenger was tried and acquitted for defaming Governor Cosby, artisans were active both as printers and as citizens. They attended rallies in the streets for Cosby's opponent, William Morris. In Boston, there were fierce political debates over paper money and British impressment with artisan participation.

American Revolution

Thus, by the time of the American Revolution, the largest sector of an emerging incipient working class worked in the cities as artisans and tradesmen. It had its own traditions, dress, and political awareness and was clearly separate from the mercantile and professional classes, as well as the slave and free black underclass. During the Revolution, the role of this class was largely political, while after the Revolution, the political merged with economic strife to forge the origins of the modern working class.

The coming of the American Revolution brought urban artisans to a far more prominent political role than they had ever attained in colonial politics, and perhaps to as prominent a role as labor would achieve for many years. The major events leading to the Revolution—the Sugar Act, the Stamp Act, the Townshend Act, and the Boston (and New York) Tea Party—brought in its wake widescale participation by artisans in every American seaport. This could be seen on the streets in the Sons of Liberty, crowds of artisans, including masters and journeymen, and unskilled laborers and a few small merchants, who gained near control of the cities. They demanded and received the resignation of every stamp collector who had accepted that position, some even having to resign more than once. They enforced the boycott of stamped products, requiring that both the courts and the ports be closed. No merchant dared ship against their will.

In Boston, they were led by the colorful shoemaker Ebenezer McIntosh, who spoke through a trumpet. There had been rival South and North End gangs that had competed with each other on Pope's Day (Guy Fawkes Day), and the events of 1765 saw these crowds become major political players. They were not averse to force, tearing down the warehouses of the stamp distributor Andrew Oliver and then turning upon Lieutenant Governor Thomas Hutchinson, known for years as a conservative, hard-money proponent. They took apart his expensive house brick by brick, stripping the walls and smashing the furniture. They were led in part by Sam Adams and John Hancock, but they were also showing their frustration at the increased poverty of many Bostonian workingmen and the contempt of the upper classes for those who worked with their hands, a contempt that was centuries old. Fears of class warfare turned some of Boston's leaders against the artisans, and McIntosh was arrested and then released. The rapid politicization of the artisans clearly demonstrated that craftsmen had their own concerns and that they were willing to resort to extreme measures. Events leading to Lexington and Concord were largely under the control of the city's elite, but the artisans were there to carry out measures when necessary, as they did most notably at the Boston Tea Party in 1773, when they threw hundreds of chests of the British East India Company's tea into Boston harbor rather than be forced to pay the tax levied on it.

It was, however, in New York and Philadelphia where the working class, represented by the artisans of these two cities, became part of the governing classes. In New York, the beginning was similar to that of Boston, with the Sons of Liberty (Liberty Boys) forcing the resignation of the stamp collector John McHenry, placing a sign denouncing Governor Colden as the chief murderer of their rights and privileges, and destroying the home of Major Thomas James, commander of Fort George. Artisan politicization increased during the Townshend Act, a tax on imports, as craftsmen pressed for a policy of nonimportation and found themselves opposed by many of the city's merchants. Mechanics could gather in large numbers as they did in 1770 to protest the hiring of British sailors to do their work. They also put on their own tea party in 1773. In New York, when British control began to break down in 1774 and 1775, the artisans formed their own committee and demanded more radical action than the city's merchants, for years the political leadership, would agree to authorize. When it came to choosing delegates to the Continental Congress in 1774, the Mechanics Committee decided to put up its own slate of candidates. Ultimately, the economic power of the merchants forced a compromise favoring mercantile opinion, but even so, the city's delegation signed the Continental Association that would ultimately suspend trade with the mother country. In the following two years, artisans continued to have a major voice in the various committees that were formed to govern the city and state. With the former stay maker Tom Paine as a role model, the craftsmen took radical stands, petitioning the state assembly to ensure that the new state constitution was subject to popular ratification, the birthright of every man, and then urging New York's delegates to vote for independence well before the merchants were ready to take that momentous step (Force, pp. 895–898). During the war, New York was the headquarters of British occupation. Many of its residents fled, though some loyalists remained as did a number of slaves, who sought promised freedom within British lines and were carried off to Canada when the British evacuated the city in November 1783.

In Philadelphia, at first artisans were divided. They had been loyal to their patron Benjamin Franklin, a local hero who, though he strongly opposed the Stamp Act as a colonial agent in London, assumed it would be carried out and nominated his friend, the baker John Hughes, to be stamp collector. The result was that artisans were split over the resort to force, and two factions, one led by Joseph Galloway and composed of ship carpenters and other tradesmen (the White Oaks and the Hearts of Oak), stood in front of threatened houses to protect them. The conflict over the issue of royal government was raging with such strength that it divided opponents to the Stamp Act at first. By early November 1765, this had faded and the artisans united. Meanwhile, old

political alliances fell apart, Anglicans and Quakers withdrew or were displaced, and a new Presbyterian artisan-based party appeared in city politics as the pre-industrial working-class elements, similar to those in Boston and New York, claimed an even greater share of power in Philadelphia. By 1770, when they did not persuade merchants to maintain nonimportation, they turned away from mercantile leadership and began running their own artisan candidates for political positions. They won enough elections to force open public galleries in the Assembly and, like New York, when British control broke down, formed their own Committee of Mechanics to bargain with the city's elite. Indeed, it was in Philadelphia that artisans achieved the greatest sense of self-consciousness as an influential political body and the skills to act with political effectiveness. Working with small merchants, they took over the government during the American Revolution and were largely responsible for the radical Pennsylvania constitution that established a unicameral legislature, removed the property requirement for voting in the Commonwealth, and called for free public education. They were able to carry out a revolutionary agenda to an extent greater than any other group of workingmen.

During the War, artisans served as soldiers in the Continental Army, as members of local militia, and on board privateer ships. Many were killed or wounded. Though few attained officer rank, the experience left a strong sense of citizenship and ownership in the new republic that emerged. Egalitarianism replaced the traditions of deference for those who had wagered their lives in search of liberty.

Early Republic

The Early Republic was a golden age for the working classes who had skills. For slaves, free blacks who worked as unskilled laborers on the docks and as domestic servants, and the women who toiled as domestic servants and seamstresses, it was a time of subsistence, an everyday struggle for adequate shelter, firewood, and food, with a cold winter meaning possible famine. Often they had to depend on the charitable institutions of the cities and state as well as private philanthropy for survival.

But for the vanguard of the working class, the Early National era offered increasing opportunities for political involvement and a critical say in the direction of American electoral politics and the legacy of the American Revolution. Second, it gave birth to the American labor movement.

Artisans by and large favored the American Constitution. In New York, for example, they played a major part of the parade in July 1788 to encourage the delegates in Poughkeepsie to ratify the Constitution. They marched in formation by trade with various floats or displays of their craft. To them a strong federal government meant increased protection for American industries and greater trade and commerce, as well as support of a strong American nation.

At the outset of government under the new federal charter, most workingmen who could vote, urban artisans, having given their support to the Constitution and the nation it created, were Federalists. They were no longer elected to high office and no longer as involved in the day-to-day operation of government at the highest levels. However, analysis of voting records indicates that artisans did achieve offices in the cities. Ordinary workingmen were most likely to win election as constables, though men of greater wealth, but still working as master craftsmen, did win a number of seats as aldermen or assistant aldermen.

Most important, however, was the role played by artisans in the battle between Jeffersonians and Hamiltonians for the future direction of the American Republic in the 1790s and early 1800s. While the struggle played out in Philadelphia and Washington, the first American party system formed, as each side attempted to elect representatives either in support of a strong central government with a large national debt, a central bank, and a diverse economy or in favor of a weak central government, agrarianism, egalitarianism, and states' rights. Each assembly election turned into a battle over the Revolution's legacy, with the artisan classes, the largest sector of the city, as the pivotal bloc in urban elections. While artisans were attracted to the Federalist attempt to diversify the economy and protect manufactures, they were wary of Hamiltonian plans to institute English-style factories that they believed would eliminate artisan workshops. They were deeply moved by the Jeffersonian movement's emphasis on equality of citizenship regardless of economic worth or education or birthright versus the Federalist preference for deference to the better educated and well bred. In the 1790s, artisan support went back and forth between the two parties.

Local newspapers, artisans' most useful means of information and communication, and often edited by radical Irish émigrés such as William Duane and James Cheetham, were quick to expose cases in which craftsmen were offended by Federalist attempts to coerce their employees into voting for Federalists. These daily prints, together with stinging broadsides, described instances of insult and disrespect.

Federalist attempts to increase the military and stand up to foreign aggressors did attract the artisan electorate, though the Anglophile allegiances of Federalists lost the support of many artisans, who still regarded the British as the hated enemy. However, when the nation's major foe in the late 1790s became France, artisans were more inclined to give their support to the Federalists.

In the pivotal year of 1800, Jefferson would have to win votes in the Middle Atlantic states if he were to attain the presidency. They lay in Philadelphia, where he managed to win a share of the state's electoral votes. In New York, the Federalists had converted the election into a winner take all of electoral votes. The key to victory was New York City's single slate election. Led by Aaron Burr, the Republicans put together a ballot filled with Revolutionary heroes, and with the support of the artisan community, won the election (having lost in 1799) and gave Jefferson the state's electoral votes and with it, the White House. The switch of allegiance of the artisans, and especially the more numerous poorer artisans living in the city's outer wards, was the key to the Jeffersonians' victory. In the end, there was no way that the Federalists could match the egalitarian Jeffersonian appeal. Many artisans were Revolutionary War veterans. They believed with Jefferson that a ploughman and a professor (Jefferson, 12:15) shared equal capacities in choosing right from wrong, in choosing correct representatives. Federalist deferential expectations were impossible to hide and led to the ultimate demise of that party. Jefferson was also an able politician. While he early wrote disparagingly of the "mobs" of great cities as "sores" on the human body, he later showed gratitude to the urban working classes and won their widespread support (Jefferson, Q. XIX).

The Federalists, while never again winning back the White House, continued to compete for workingmen's votes, forming the Washington Benevolent Society to help them reach out. They were able to win a number of elections, especially during the hard economic times caused by the War of 1812. Many artisans along with sailors were hurt by Jefferson's Embargo of 1807–1808 and other measures restricting trade. War, of course, also cut off trade because of British naval superiority. Republicans appealed to the patriotism of the working classes, asking them to put their national pride above their pocketbook, while Federalists advocated an end to war and the establishment of trade, and with that, employment. The elections were close during those years, but most workingmen did, indeed, stick with the Anglophobe egalitarian Republicans.

Labor Movement

While most historians place the birth of the modern American labor movement in the Age of Jackson with its large unions and the rise of workingman's parties, it is clear that the Early National era, as well, played a significance role. The era saw citywide work stoppages in a number of cities and a large number of strikes, many of which are unrecorded. It also reveals the rise of many journeymen associations with their own constitutions that attempted to win and sustain gains in their wages and hours. The rise of the labor movement can be traced to the fast growth of the American economy in the 1790s and early nineteenth century, largely due to the increased trade and demand brought by the war between France and England and especially the long Napoleonic wars. Of further assistance in growth was the business revolution (Cochran), including improvements such as secure and regular information, insurance, and systematic incorporation procedures; per capita income in the United States rose from 55% to 62% between 1800 and 1840. The greater demand caused by increased population, wealth, and trade led to rapid expansion in a number of artisan trades, most notably shoemaking, cabinetmaking, tailoring, printing, carpentry, and masonry (construction). A cabinetmaker in New York, for example, filled a single order for five thousand Windsor chairs to the West Indies in 1795, all before industrialization.

In this world, employers, though many were master craftsmen, became more committed to the profit and loss of the enterprise than to the paternalistic, family-like craft enterprise. Capital costs increased markedly: printing presses, for example, were well beyond the reach of ordinary journeymen. Consequently, it became less and less common for journeymen to rise to master craftsman standing. Journeymen had to come to the realization that, barring some unlikely opportunity or exceptional ability, they would remain in that station for their entire lives.

Reacting to the situation of becoming a permanent wage-earning class, journeymen in the major American seaports formed associations that would enable them to compete in the marketplace and maintain adequate salaries and working conditions. Trade societies were known in the colonial period, but they were largely associations for fraternity and family benefits in the event of death or disability. They also occasionally lobbied for protective tariffs and participated in civic life. They were mostly composed of master craftsmen, though they may have been open to journeymen as well. The most venerable of these societies, the General Society of Mechanics and Tradesmen of New York City, remains in existence to this day.

The journeymen societies did have provisions for fraternity and for benefits when financially able. However, they had economic motives at heart. A number of constitutions survive. Following the republican spirit, they are very democratic, providing for election of officers and open meetings. They also have key provisions requiring, in the Cordwainers Society, for example, that no member work for a master who employed nonmembers and that all members work for an established wage. The New York Typographical Society had similar provisions: "No member of the society shall work for less than the wages which may be established; neither shall he engage in or continue in any office where there is a journeyman working for less that the established price" (Stevens, p. 42).

When they were strong enough, these journeymen societies would negotiate with the masters, who formed their own societies, and agree to either the price of piecework (cabinetmakers, tailors) or wages and hours (masons and carpenters). They could also appeal to the masters to stop practices that they considered harmful, such as the hiring of underage apprentices at cheap wages. This caused the Topographical Society to write letters to the master printers asking that they respect those working in "the noblest art with which the earth is blest" and pay a decent wage, and not hire "miserable botches" (foreigners willing to work for lower wages) (Barnett, pp. 162–163). They also made appeals to the public to boycott recalcitrant employers and used social ostracism against journeymen who would not join their societies or would work for lower wages.

When appeals and negotiations broke down, journeymen were willing to resort to more coercive methods. A number of journeymen in cabinetmaking and in tailoring formed their own stores where they offered the public their work. In 1819, employers of no less a figure than Duncan Phyle did that, as did 80 other cabinetmakers in New York in 1802. These were not commonly successful, however.

The most common tactic was the strike. Journeymen could walk out on either a particular master or, if necessary, would stage a citywide strike. Some years, disagreements became so common that it threatened construction work in the city as a whole. The most common reasons for the strikes were failure to come to agreement on wages, or, as in the Panic of 1819, attempts by employers to cut wages. Journeymen tailors also went on strike when employers used female labor to do a large share of their work at lower wages.

They argued that "women are incomplete" and unable to work up to the standards of men. Journeymen cordwainers went on a citywide strike in New York over the use of apprentices to replace journeymen ([New York] *Evening Post*, July 13, 1819).

Strikes and walkouts that took place within strong memory of the American Revolution inevitably had a republican flavor. This is spelled out in a strike manifesto by the carpenters of New York in 1809 ([New York] *American Citizen*, April 10, 1809):

> Among the inalienable rights of man are life, liberty and the pursuit of happiness. By the social compact every class in society ought to be entitled to benefit in proportion to his qualifications. Among the duties which individuals owe to society are single men to marry and married men to educate their children. Among the duties which society owes individuals is to grant them just compensation not only for current expenses of livelihood, but to the formation of a fund for the support of that time of life when nature requires a cessation of work.

The American Revolution, in this context, demanded that the working class receive a wage that enabled them to live adequately and retire without the need of public assistance. Society owed a living wage to its workingmen.

Employers were not without weapons in fighting back. They were able to use a surplus of employees and apprentices who wanted to leave their indentures early, as well as Irish immigrants and, in the tailoring trades, female seamstresses, to find cheaper wage labor. In addition, the new marketplace often required the mass production of shoes and furniture at less than highly skilled level: slopwork sold at wholesale. Cheap, less skilled labor was often suitable to their needs. When threatened with a citywide strike against the masters, the master cordwainers (shoemakers) in Philadelphia (1806) and in New York (1810) took the journeymen to court and charged them with a conspiracy against nonmembers under English common law. While the conspiracy cases are open to various interpretations, the argument of the masters was that the attempt to a closed shop by requiring all journeymen to join the Journeymen's Society if they wanted to find work (for no Society member would work for a master who employed a nonmember) was a conspiracy against the freedom of other individuals and the overall good of the community. The journeymen argued that they had the right to organize as any group in society and that that right was necessary as a countervailing force. If, indeed, they were now to be a permanent working class, then they had to be able to offer a strong defense against the strength of the masters. Eventually, in *Commonwealth vs. Hunt*, Judge Leander Shaw would rule that English common law did not apply.

The Revolutionary and Early National eras were critical in the formation of the country's working classes. While relatively small in number, their political and economic struggles, their victories and defeats, would have a lasting impact.

HOWARD ROCK

References and Further Reading

Barnett, George. "The Printers: A Study in Trade Unionism." *American Economic Association Quarterly*, 3d. ser., no. 10 (1909): 162–163.

Cochran, Thomas. *Frontiers of Change: Early Industrialism in America.* New York: Oxford University Press, 1981.

Foner, Eric. *Tom Paine and Revolutionary America.* New York: Oxford University Press, 1976.

Force, Peter, ed. *American Archives.* Washington, DC: 1895. VI, pp. 895–898.

Gilje, Paul A. *Wages of Independence: Capitalism in the Early American Republic.* Madison, WI: Madison House, 1997.

Jefferson, Thomas. Letter to Peter Carr, 1787. *Papers of Thomas Jefferson*, edited by Julian Boyd et al., 12:15. Princeton, NJ: Princeton University Press, 1950.

Jefferson, Thomas. *Notes on the State of Virginia.* 1782. Q. XIX.

Lewis, Johanna Miller. *Artisans in the North Carolina Backcountry.* Lexington: University of Kentucy Press, 1995.

McCusker, John. J., and Russell R. Menard. *The Economy of British America, 1607–1789.* Chapel Hill: University of North Carolina Press, 1985.

Montgomery, Charles F. *American Furniture: The Federal Period, 1788–1825.* New York: The Viking Press, 1966.

Nash, Gary B. *The Urban Crucible: Social Change, Political Consciousness, and the Origins of the American Revolution.* Cambridge, MA: Harvard University Press, 1979.

Rigal, Laura. *The American Manufactory: Artisans, Labor, and the World of Things in the Early Republic.* Princeton, NJ: Princeton University Press, 1998.

Rilling, Donna J. *Making Houses. Crafting Capitalism: Builders in Philadelphia, 1790–1850.* Philadelphia: University of Pennsylvania Press, 2001.

Rock, Howard B. *Artisans of the New Republic: The Tradesmen of New York City in the Early Republic.* New York: New York University Press, 1979.

———. *The New York City Artisan, 1789–1825: A Documentary History.* Albany: SUNY Press, 1989.

Schultz, Ronald. *The Republic of Labor: Philadelphia Artisans and the Politics of Class, 1720–1830.* New York: Oxford University Press, 1997.

Smith, Billie G. *The "Lower Sort": Philadelphia's Laboring People, 1750–1800.* Ithaca, NY: Cornell University Press, 1990.

Stevens, George A. *New York Typographical Union Number Six.* Albany, NY: 1912, p. 42.

Wilentz, Sean. *Chants Democratic: New York City and the Rise of the American Working Class, 1788–1850.* New York: Oxford University Press, 1984.

Young, Alfred F. *The Shoemaker and the Tea Party: Memory and the American Revolution.* Boston: Beacon Press, 1999.

RICE, MONSIGNOR CHARLES OWEN (1908–2005)
United Steelworkers of America

Finding inspiration from the papal encyclicals on social justice written by Leo XIII (*The Condition of Labor*, 1891) and Pius XI (*After Forty Years: Reconstructing the Social Order*, 1931), Monsignor Charles Owen Rice of Pittsburgh helped build the Steel Workers Organizing Committee (SWOC), later renamed the United Steelworkers of America (USWA). The SWOC president, Philip Murray, a devout Catholic and admirer of Leo XIII and Pius XI, found in Rice a friend who helped place the moral authority of the Church behind the union drive of the 1930s.

Born the son of Irish immigrants in New York City in 1908, Charles Owen Rice went to Ireland at the age of four to be raised by relatives following his mother's untimely death. The seven years he spent in Ireland exposed him to the nationalist and religious sectarian violence that culminated in the Easter 1916 rebellion against Great Britain. As the product of an interfaith marriage—his mother had been born Protestant but converted to Catholicism—Rice learned to dislike discrimination and to recoil from the tribal wars he saw in Europe. After his father found decent employment in the booming city of Pittsburgh, Rice returned to America in 1920. His Irish sojourn had drawn him close to the Catholic Church and helped determine his vocation. The influence of his Pittsburgh-based uncle, Joseph Rice, a labor organizer, drew him to the union cause.

Three years after his ordination in 1934, Rice, with the support of the Pittsburgh bishop Hugh Boyle, emerged as a clerical activist. During the late 1930s and 1940s, Rice fought communists in the Congress of Industrial Organizations (CIO) and anti-union corporate executives with equal vigor. Rice, who would be featured in such national magazines as *Time* and *Look*, also helped found the anticommunist Association of Catholic Trade Unionists (ACTU) in 1937.

Following the line of reasoning advanced by Pope Pius XI, Rice regarded atheistic communism and laissez-faire capitalism as the bastard twins of secular humanism. Far from being opposite political and economic systems, Catholic reformers claimed that unfettered capitalism and communism threw aside God in the quest to place man at the center of the universe. Such quests, Rice and Pius XI believed, inevitably led to dictatorship and mass murder as communist and capitalist societies lost any sense of moral restraints.

In 1940, Rice championed Murray's ascension to the presidency of the CIO and criticized the CIO founder, John L. Lewis, for his unwillingness to defend European democracies against Nazi aggression. Whatever the flaws of capitalist democracies such as Great Britain—and there were many, Rice noted—Nazi Germany was a pagan, totalitarian nation bent upon world conquest and had to be resisted. After World War II, Rice played a role in the expulsion of the communist-led United Electrical Workers (UE) from the CIO. Although Rice felt that many American communists were well-intentioned idealists, they still owed too much allegiance to a Soviet Union that did not differ all that much from a defeated Nazi Germany.

Beyond marching on union picket lines, speaking at CIO rallies, writing a labor column for the diocesan newspaper (the *Pittsburgh Catholic*), and conducting worker education classes, Rice operated the St. Joseph House of Hospitality in the Hill District of Pittsburgh. Thousands of dispossessed men seeking food and shelter went through the doors of this Catholic Worker Movement refuge, including a young Polish-American coal miner named Jock Yablonski. Rice filled Yablonski with a crusading zeal. Thirty years later, in 1970, Rice presided over Yablonski's funeral mass after the Mafia-connected United Mine Workers' president Tony Boyle ordered his assassination.

Rice's career as a "labor priest" came to an end following Murray's death in 1952 and the installation in 1950 of a new bishop, John Dearden, who was less tolerant than his predecessors of clerical activists. With the advent of a new Pittsburgh diocese bishop, John Wright, in 1959, Rice received permission to resume his political activism. Wright also transferred Rice to Holy Rosary parish in Homewood—a black ghetto neighborhood that has been chronicled by the novelist John Edgar Wideman.

In the mid-1950s, Rice began to have second thoughts about his anticommunist activism, thoughts that were deepened in the 1960s by the escalating war in Vietnam. As a "ghetto priest," Rice became immersed in the Black Power movement. His association with student antiwar activists, former Marxist foes, and black radicals alienated patriotic, socially conservative Catholics and steelworkers.

In his 1960s and 1970s articles for the *Pittsburgh Catholic*, *Commonweal*, and the *National Catholic Reporter*, Rice largely eschewed union issues to focus on U.S. foreign policy and race relations. When he did discuss unions, it was invariably to criticize the AFL-CIO president, George Meany. Since the merger of the American Federation of Labor (AFL) with the CIO in 1955, Rice felt that Meany had moved organized labor into blind anticommunist extremism while permitting the racially exclusive practices of the AFL's affiliates to continue unchecked.

By 1967, Rice's antiwar activism became consuming. He cochaired the National Mobilization Committee, which, with A. J. Muste and David Dellinger, sought to end U.S. involvement in the Vietnam War. At the local level, Rice served as cochair of the Western Pennsylvania Americans for Democratic Action (ADA). Originally founded in 1947 to combat communist influence within the Democratic Party and the CIO, the ADA by 1968 had moved left. Rice, along with the Western Pennsylvania ADA chair Molly Yard, the future leader of the National Organization for Women (NOW), proved instrumental in re-orienting the ADA's politics. Both dismissed the defection of local and national AFL-CIO leaders from the ADA. In turn, steelworkers barred Rice from entering their union halls.

Rice's allies in the 1960s were largely college-educated professionals. Their influence within the Democratic Party at the local level was limited since working-class Catholics either chose to stay home in 1972 or supported Republican Richard Nixon, rather than vote for George McGovern, their party's antiwar presidential nominee. Such professionals, however, were destined to play major economic and political roles in postindustrial America and the national Democratic Party. In the 1970s, just as the social crisis of the 1960s appeared to have cooled down, Pittsburgh and other industrial cities experienced massive economic dislocation.

In the years before the demise of the Iron City and its rebirth as a center of software engineering and biotechnology, Rice had warned of the decline of the region's manufacturing base. His identification with 1960s-era activists, however, led the very working-class audience that would be the most harmed by economic restructuring to tune him out.

KENNETH J. HEINEMAN

References and Further Reading

Heineman, Kenneth J. *A Catholic New Deal: Religion and Reform in Depression Pittsburgh*. University Park: Pennsylvania State University Press, 1999.

McCollester, Charles, ed. *Fighter with a Heart: Writings of Charles Owen Rice, Pittsburgh Labor Priest*. Pittsburgh: University of Pittsburgh Press, 1996.

McGeever, Patrick J. *Rev. Charles Owen Rice: Apostle of Contradiction*. Pittsburgh: Duquesne University Press, 1989.

Heineman, Kenneth J. "Iron City Trinity: The Triumph and the Trials of Catholic Social Activism in Pittsburgh, 1932–1972." *U.S. Catholic Historian* 22 (Spring 2004): 121–145.

———. "'Model City': The War on Poverty, Race Relations, and Catholic Social Activism in 1960s Pittsburgh." *The Historian* 65 (June 2003): 867–900.

———. "Reformation: Monsignor Charles Owen Rice and the Fragmentation of the New Deal Electoral Coalition in Pittsburgh, 1960–1972." *Pennsylvania History* 71 (Winter 2004): 53–85.

Rice, Charles Owen. "Confessions of an Anti-Communist." *Labor History* 30 (1989): 449–462.

See also **United Steelworkers of America**

RILEY, WILLIAM (MID-1850s–1910s) United Mine Workers of America

Historians know less than they would like about the life of William Riley, a black coal miner and union leader who became a significant local official of the nascent United Mine Workers of America (UMWA) in the early 1890s. Born a slave in the mid 1850s in northeast Tennessee, Riley was elected to the post of UMWA's secretary-treasurer of District 19 (Kentucky Tennessee) in 1891. A product of the Jim Crow South, a world in which African-American literacy rates ranged between 10% and 20%, he, like both of his parents, his children, and his spouses, could read and write.

Prior to his election as secretary-treasurer of District 19, Riley had already achieved a position of prominence among the Newcomb-Jellico miners of Campbell County, having attained the role of checkweighman. Because mining companies paid their laborers by the coal tonnage that they mined, and then often sought to reduce wages by underestimating the tonnage, miners fought to hire their own checkweighman—someone who could independently verify the company weigher's records. When they gained this right, miners invariably elected a person they trusted and thought would stand up to the mining companies. Riley, his fellow miners believed, was such a man.

Riley sought not only to hold particular companies to account, but to improve the working conditions of black and white miners throughout District 19. As secretary-treasurer, he worked as a roving organizer who urged miners to join the UMWA, arranging contracts between coal companies and their employees, organizing and mediating strikes, settling disputes among the miners themselves, and on some occasions, holding the union accountable to its public commitments to inclusiveness. Riley joined the UMWA because of his fervent belief in organized labor and his faith in the interracialism of the UMWA—that all miners, irrespective of race and color, had a place within the UMWA's broad tent. Riley's insistence that black and white workers join forces in labor unions to fight for their rights as working people ran contrary to the philosophies of African-American race leaders around the turn of the twentieth century.

W. E. B. DuBois and his followers believed that leadership of the African-American community fell to the educated elite known as the "Talented Tenth." Others, like Booker T. Washington, urged African-American workers in the South to place their trust in the South's white elite. Following Washington's admonishments, the Nashville black elite would eventually help white coal company owners suppress strikes by Tennessee's black and white miners.

The faith that Riley placed in the interracialism of the UMWA reflected the paucity of alternative allies in the postbellum South. Deeply cognizant of failures of the Republican Party and the severe limitations of the Democratic Party, southern black workers had few places to turn to secure better working conditions. National unions like the UMWA offered black workers the possibility of better pay, safer working environments, and a modicum of protection from the vicissitudes of racial hostility from fellow white miners. But even these organizations were imperfect, as Riley himself acknowledged. On the local level, he found himself regularly confronting white miners who treated their black counterparts abysmally. Riley repeatedly found himself having to renegotiate agreements between white and African-American miners to share positions of authority, like mining supervisor or checkweighman. Miners would agree to share these positions in proportion to their respective numbers, but once a black miner's turn came, white miners frequently reneged on their promises. In addition, as he traveled across District 19, Riley often found himself in difficult straits, finding few places that would give him a place to sleep at night. On the national level, Riley did his best to hold the UMWA to its interracial ideals, offering a motion at the 1892 convention to deny locals their charters if they discriminated against their African-American members. Riley failed in this endeavor, which must have pained him greatly. He knew the value of national oversight in the age of segregation, and when District 19 decided to withdraw from the UMWA and establish a separate southern mining union, Riley refused to stand for re-election as secretary-treasurer. Though he remained a checkweighman for a few more years and remained a labor rights activist, he left both the union and coal mining in 1895, after District 19 lost its charter. At that point, his letters to the *United Mine Workers Journal*, the major extant source of information about William Riley, ceased. At a time when Jim Crow legislation and segregationist mores became ever more entrenched, Riley sought solace and social uplift in the African-American church, becoming a preacher in Clinton, the county seat of Anderson County, Tennessee.

KARIN A. SHAPIRO

References and Further Reading

Lewis, Ronald. "Race and the United Mine Workers' Union in Tennessee: Selected Letters of William R. Riley, 1892–1898." *Tennessee Historical Quarterly* 36 (1977): 524–536.

Shapiro, Karin A. *A New South Rebellion: The Battle against Convict Labor in the Tennessee Coalfields, 1871–1896.* Chapel Hill: University of North Carolina Press, 1998.

———. "William Riley: Southern Black Miners and Industrial Unionism in the Late 19th Century." In *The Human Tradition in American Labor History*, edited by Eric Arnesen. Wilmington, DE: Scholarly Resources, 2004, pp. 69–87.

RIVERA, DENNIS (1950–)
President, 1199/SEIU: New York's Health and Human Service Union

Dennis Rivera was born in Aibonito, Puerto Rico, on August 6, 1950. His father, Daniel Hickey, an Irish-American from Dunkirk, New York, went to Puerto Rico just after the end of World War II to set up a nonunion factory for a manufacturer of women's undergarments. In December 1946, Hickey married Olga Rivera, whose mother supervised the orientation for new employees at the factory. As a youth, Dennis went to parochial school, played basketball and baseball, and attended but did not graduate from the Colegio Universitario de Cayey, affiliated with the University of Puerto Rico.

While he was a college student, Rivera became increasingly engaged in radical politics, especially in opposition to U.S. involvement in the Vietnam War. He was elected president of the Aibonito chapter of the Independentista Party and ran, unsuccessfully, for city councilman. Drawn into the island's labor movement, Rivera led a strike by an insurgent group of sanitation workers and helped found the National Union of Health Care Workers of Puerto Rico. In 1976, Rivera met Concha Mendoza, a medical student at Boston University who was engaged in community service work in San Juan hospitals. He followed her to Brooklyn, where she had accepted a residency at Kings County Hospital, and in June 1977, they married in Red Bank, New Jersey.

Soon after coming to New York, Rivera approached Local 1199, a militant union founded in the radical politics of the early 1930s, for a job. By 1977, 1199 had been organizing for two decades in New York City's voluntary hospitals and had also grown into a national union of hospital and health-care workers representing some 100,000 members in 14 states and the District of Columbia. Rivera's union experience in Puerto Rico convinced an 1199 vice president, Stephen Frankel, to hire him. In September

1977, Rivera went to work as an organizer at Albert Einstein Medical Center in the Bronx, New York.

Rivera joined 1199 at a time of significant transition for the union. In the late 1970s, hoping to more effectively organize health-care workers into a single union nationally, 1199's president, Leon Davis, had opened merger discussions with the Service Employees International Union (SEIU). But Davis suffered a severe stroke in 1979 and had to retire in 1982. Because his successor, Doris Turner, was opposed to 1199's projected merger with the SEIU, an emotionally charged civil war developed within the union soon after she became president.

As the internal struggle heated up, Rivera, who by 1983 was both a Guild Division vice president and head of the union's Latin caucus, joined with other Davis-era union loyalists, in particular, with the executive secretary, Moe Foner, to oppose Turner and support the proposed merger with the SEIU. Rivera became a leader of the Save Our Union opposition and was eventually dismissed by Turner. A disputed union election in 1983, one that involved charges of ballot-box tampering, was followed by failed contract negotiations the next year. These upheavals led, in 1986, to Turner's defeat in union elections monitored by the U.S. Department of Labor and to Rivera's election as Local 1199's executive vice president. In 1989, 1199 members elected Rivera president of the New York union.

Left unsettled by Rivera's victory was 1199's status within the labor movement as well as its still sought-after merger with the SEIU. In 1996, Rivera secured 1199's re-admittance into the AFL-CIO; two years later, he successfully negotiated 1199's affiliation with the SEIU, which established 1199, the National Health and Human Service Employees Union, SEIU, AFL-CIO, as the largest union of health-care workers in the United States. Since Rivera became president, the ranks of 1199 in New York State have tripled, reaching more than 237,000 members. Rivera is also the president of the SEIU New York State Council and chairs the SEIU Health Care Division, leading some 750,000 members in local unions throughout the United States.

Rivera's tenure as president of 1199 has been marked by the same mix of socially conscious idealism and no-nonsense trade unionism or militant pragmatism that distinguished Leon Davis's leadership. Rivera has proved adept at negotiating New York's complex political terrain to secure contracts that not only provide concrete benefits for union members but also often improve the living standards of working people throughout the state. In 1998, 1199 united with the New York Greater Hospital Association, an agency representing hospital management, in an intense public relations effort that successfully lobbied the state's political leaders to apply an increase in the cigarette tax to expand health coverage to one third of New York's 3.2 million uninsured residents. Then, in 2002, Rivera gained Governor George Pataki's agreement to apply the almost $2 billion windfall the state would be receiving when Empire Blue Cross and Blue Shield converted from a nonprofit insurer to a for-profit institution, as well as the money from another increase in the state's cigarette tax, to finance raises and job security for New York City's 55,000 home health aides and nursing home and hospital workers.

Understanding the direct connection between the ability of his union to win good contracts and the politics of health care, Rivera has made 1199 a more active power broker in both the city and state of New York. Since 1989, when 1199 helped David Dinkins in his successful bid for mayor of New York, politicians running for city or state office from either major party have sought 1199's endorsement. In 2002, after Pataki supported the union's plan to finance wage increases and protect members' jobs, 1199 endorsed the Republican governor's bid for re-election. Yet even while making 1199 a potent electoral force, Rivera has remained faithful to the union's tradition of political dissent. In 2001, he was arrested and jailed, along with Robert Kennedy Jr. and other activists, for peacefully protesting the U.S. Navy's continued use of the island of Vieques as a bomb test site. Under Rivera, 1199 has co-operated with environmental and other community-based groups to, as he puts it, "upgrade the opportunities" afforded working people in the United States. To be effective, a labor leader must, in his view, be active in politics and social change.

BRIAN GREENBERG

References and Further Reading

Fink, Leon, and Brian Greenberg. *Upheaval in the Quiet Zone: A History of Hospital Workers' Union, Local 1199.* Urbana: University of Illinois Press, 1989.

Raskin, A. H. "Profiles (Dennis Rivera)." *The New Yorker,* December 10, 1990.

Roberts, Sam. "A New Face for American Labor." *New York Times,* May 10, 1992.

ROBINS, MARGARET DREIER (SEPTEMBER 6, 1868–FEBRUARY 21, 1945)
Women's Trade Union League

Margaret Dreier Robins, leader of the Women's Trade Union League (WTUL), brought working-class women and their middle-class allies together to work for labor concerns.

Robins was born in Brooklyn, New York, as the eldest of five children of German immigrant parents. Her father, Theodor Dreier, made a fortune importing iron, and her mother, Dorothea Adelheid Dreier, undoubtedly inspired her daughter's later activism by volunteering for a number of local charities. A fairly serious young woman, Robins had little interest in the parties and balls that typically occupied women of her position. After graduating from high school in 1885, Margaret—or Gretchen, as she was known to friends—joined the Women's Auxiliary at Brooklyn Hospital. For the next 15 years, the hospital remained her primary civic concern. It would introduce her to the conditions facing the poor.

Robins's path to the labor movement began when Josephine Shaw Lowell recruited her for the Woman's Municipal League (WML), New York's first women's civic committee. As head of the WML's legislative committee, Robins began investigating the relationship between organized prostitution and the city's employment agencies. She recruited Frances A. Kellor to investigate the city's employment agencies, an investigation that led to Kellor's publication *Out of Work* (1905). Kellor's research provided the documentation for a bill to regulate agencies, written by Robins's committee, that became law in 1904. It was Robins's first legislative effort, but her organizing and lobbying success brought her to public attention.

A deeply religious woman, Robins always saw her activism as an expression of her Congregationalist faith. Robins worked with the WML to protect women who were the most vulnerable to exploitation—job seekers, domestic workers, and immigrants. Many of these women were forced into prostitution. To assist them, Robins and Kellor founded the New York Association for Household Research (NYAHR) in 1904. However, Robins's interests quickly expanded. She joined the labor movement for the same protective reasons that drove her to become involved with the WML and the NYAHR.

Persuaded by friends, Robins joined the New York branch of the WTUL in December 1904 and immediately became treasurer. She became its president in March. As Robins's quick ascent indicates, the WTUL was a fairly weak organization at her arrival. It aimed to secure legislation that would better the working conditions, wages, and hours of working women. Robins made the WTUL into a force by recruiting women from the working class and by supporting strikes by women workers. At the same time, her social connections opened the wallets of upper-middle-class sympathizers and enabled the WTUL to become a pivotal player in women's organizations concerned with the problems of working women.

Like many women of her generation with great ambitions, Robins never planned to marry. However, she met and married Raymond Robins, a former Colorado lead miner turned lawyer, within a few months in 1905. The couple, now living in Chicago in the shadow of Jane Addams's Hull-House, saw themselves as a team working through different means for the same goals. While her husband focused on settlement work, Robins headed the Chicago WTUL from 1907 to 1913. Her first public action was to lead a protest parade of about 20,000 workingmen and workingwomen through Chicago to protest the arrest of the labor organizer Bill Haywood and his forced transfer from Colorado to Idaho to stand trial for the murder of a former governor of that state. Robins also served as member of the executive board of the Chicago Federation of Labor from 1908 to 1917. These ties, as well as her connections to Hull-House reformers, placed Robins in a position to enter the growing national discourse about women workers.

In 1907, Robins became the leader of the national WTUL. She would continue as its head until 1922, serving during the league's most influential years. Robins and the WTUL worked to carve out a home for workingwomen in labor institutions. She pushed the group to organize women in trade unions, to educate the public on issues concerning workingwomen, and to seek protective legislation, especially in regards to minimum wages and maximum hours for women workers. Robins herself did much of the publicizing. In 1911, she spent many early morning hours on Chicago street corners telling hotel and restaurant employees arriving for work about a recently enacted 10-hour maximum work law. Unlike many pioneers, she also had a gift for working with others. A notably inspirational woman, Robins mentored many young women unionists, including Agnes Nestor.

Under Robins's direction, the WTUL founded *Life and Labor*, a journal that Robins initially edited and that focused on women's issues. She was also primarily responsible for establishing the Training School for Women Workers, the WTUL's effort to train women workers for leadership in its labor organizations. When this educational experiment ended in 1926, about 40 young women had been prepared for local trade union leadership.

As president of the WTUL during the famed garment strikes of 1909–1911 in New York, Philadelphia, and Chicago, Robins worked with leaders such as New York's Rose Schneiderman to shape the organization into the nation's most effective agency for supporting the rights of working women. During the Hart, Schaffner, and Marx strike in 1910–1911, the Chicago WTUL, under Robins's direction, raised more than $70,000 for the strikers, much of the money coming from Robins's inheritance. Robins secured legal counsel, marched in picket lines, organized relief, worked tirelessly to inform the public about the true conditions of the workers, and recruited influential supporters. The arbitration procedures secured by Robins after the Hart, Schaffner, and Marx strike secured a measure of self-government for workers, eventually established the preferential shop, and later became a landmark in labor history. This success became her most treasured memory.

The male-dominated unions of this era, especially the large American Federation of Labor (AFL), did not generally welcome women workers and typically paid little attention to their concerns. The successes of Robins and the WTUL did not go unnoticed by male unionists, and the strains damaged the labor movement. In 1914, the Hart, Schaffner, and Marx workers belonging to the AFL's United Garment Workers joined the New York workers to form the Amalgamated Clothing Workers Union. The AFL and its leader, Samuel Gompers, blamed Robins and the WTUL for the treasonous actions of the clothing workers. Robins and Gompers, as well as the WTUL and the AFL, never worked well together after 1914.

Robins resigned from the WTUL in 1922 with the intention of focusing on the International Federation of Working Women. She was the prime mover behind the organization. Unfortunately, conflicts between Europeans and Americans over the direction and vision of the group prompted Robins to leave the Federation within a year. Searching about for a new project, Robins and her husband moved to a farm near Brooksville, Florida, with the aim of developing new farming strategies to combat poverty in the area. Unable to cut all ties with the WTUL, she became the chair of its committee on southern work in 1937.

Robins's political activism is typical of women social justice reformers of the early and mid-twentieth century. She supported women's suffrage as furthering democracy. Although she criticized suffragists who failed to take into account the interests of labor, she also joined the Leslie Woman Suffrage Commission to engage in nationwide lobbying for the vote. Robins opposed the Equal Rights Amendment (ERA), as did most women's organizations and activist women before 1970, because of the negative effects of the proposed legislation on laws that protected women workers. She condemned proponents of the ERA as individualistic feminists.

By 1932, Robins had begun to ease her way out of public life in part because of the poor health of her husband. Robins died of pernicious anemia.

CARYN E. NEUMANN

References and Further Reading

Payne, Elizabeth Anne. *Reform, Labor, and Feminism: Margaret Dreier Robins and the Women's Trade Union League*. Urbana: University of Illinois Press, 1988.

See also **Amalgamated Clothing Workers of America; American Federation of Labor; Gompers, Samuel; Haywood, William D. "Big Bill"; Nestor, Agnes; Schneiderman, Rose; Triangle Shirtwaist Fire**

ROCK SPRINGS, WYOMING, STRIKE OF 1885

The strike that Rock Springs, Wyoming, coal miners launched in September 1885 began in violence and ended in defeat. It occurred spontaneously after a clash between Chinese and white miners and played out against the backdrop of a national anti-Chinese movement that originated, and grew especially virulent, in the West. After the completion of the transcontinental railroad in 1869, Rock Springs became the hub of the Union Pacific Railroad's coal-mining operations. Many of the Chinese workers who built the western leg of the transcontinental road subsequently found work in southern Wyoming as miners. The Chinese Massacre, which kindled the 1885 Rock Springs strike, began on September 2 with a dispute between two Chinese miners and two white miners over which pair had been assigned a particularly productive room in one of the mines. When the Chinese stood their ground, a group of white miners beat them and forced them from the mine. The incident sparked a full-scale riot aimed at expelling all Chinese laborers from southern Wyoming. By the end of the day, the mob had killed 28 Chinese, forced hundreds more to flee into the surrounding hills, and burned Rock Springs' Chinatown to the ground. White miners shut down the mines and, as a condition of returning to work, demanded that Union Pacific managers dismiss all Chinese.

The root of white miners' antipathy toward Chinese labor in Rock Springs stretched back to 1875. Jay Gould, then the driving force behind the Union Pacific Railroad, hired Chinese laborers to replace white miners who walked out when the company cut wages without lowering prices at its company stores. The company kept the mines running with Chinese labor and the strike collapsed. Over the next several years, the Union Pacific employed more Chinese miners, despite protests from Wyoming's citizens that its hiring practices displaced and angered white workers and might well lead to violence against the Chinese. By playing Chinese miners off against white miners, Gould kept labor costs low and impeded labor unity.

During the early 1880s, western workers gained strength and began to unionize. In 1884, Union Pacific shopmen, aided by the Knights of Labor, carried out two successful strikes in response to proposed wage cuts. These victories led other Union Pacific employees, including two thirds of Rock Springs' white coal miners, to join the union. Between 1884 and 1885, western workers joined the Knights of Labor in unprecedented numbers. When Charles Francis Adams became president of the Union Pacific Railroad in June of 1884, the growth of the labor movement was his most pressing concern.

The strength of the Knights of Labor derived from its broad organizational base. The union joined unskilled and skilled workers, women and men, blacks and whites. Chinese laborers constituted the lone exception to the union's inclusiveness. The Knights of Labor promulgated race-based justifications for halting Chinese labor immigration that portrayed the Chinese as inherently inferior to whites and unfit for American citizenship. The union's primary motivation, however, was economic. As industrialists brought increasing numbers of Chinese contract laborers into the country and used them to break strikes and undercut white workers' wages, unionists' frustration with competition from Chinese labor mounted. Although expulsion was the strategy that white miners in Rock Springs settled on to combat Chinese labor competition, it was not the only strategy they considered. In testimony investigators gathered after the Chinese Massacre, Chinese miners acknowledged that whites had asked them to join strikes and that they had refused. Unable to speak English, completely dependent on the company's labor contractor for supplies to sustain them, the Chinese were in no position to strike. Moreover, the Chinese were well aware of whites' animosity toward them and hesitated to cast in their lot with those who vilified them. Nonetheless, the unwillingness of Chinese miners to strike fueled white miners' anger against them.

An 1884 coal strike in Wyoming and Colorado forged the final link in the chain of events that led to the 1885 showdown between the Union Pacific Railroad and white miners in Rock Springs. Miners in the company's all-white camp of Carbon, Wyoming, struck, but not those in Rock Springs, where the Union Pacific employed 331 Chinese workers and only 150 whites. Although white miners in Rock Springs sabotaged equipment to express solidarity with the strikers, the fact that the company could operate its Rock Springs mines entirely with Chinese labor kept white miners there from joining the strike. The strikers in

Carbon demanded that the company rescind a recent wage cut, abolish "ironclad contracts" that prohibited union membership, decrease prices at company stores, and dismiss all Chinese miners in Rock Springs. Continuing coal production in Rock Springs eventually weakened the strikers' position, and the strike ended on January 29, 1885, with the company agreeing only to arbitrate the wage issue. Within months, the company hired 40 new Chinese miners in Rock Springs and subsequently dismissed a small number of white miners. Coming on the heels of a strike that had called for an end to Chinese labor, the Union Pacific's decision to hire more Chinese miners posed a direct challenge to the union and amplified the fury that white miners unleashed on the Chinese on September 2, 1885.

After the Chinese Massacre, Union Pacific officials, backed by Wyoming's territorial governor, requested federal troops to restore order and escort unwilling Chinese miners back to Rock Springs. Adams aimed to re-open the mines with or without white miners, using only Chinese labor if need be. He knew, even relished, the response his actions would evoke from unionized whites. Predicting that the Union Pacific was about to have the largest strike it had ever seen, he declared that he wanted "to have it and have it now." Adams intended to portray the Knights of Labor as a radical, unprincipled organization that supported "the murderers and robbers" who had perpetrated the massacre in Rock Springs.

When the mines re-opened on September 21, only one quarter of the Chinese miners reported to work, and many of these retreated rather than run the gauntlet of whites gathered at the pit entrance to intimidate them. The Chinese, angry at being forced to return to Rock Springs, sent spokespersons to ask Union Pacific officials for train passes to California. When officials refused, they asked the company's labor contractor for back wages to buy their own tickets out of Rock Springs. Refused once again, they approached Knights of Labor members for help, hoping that those who most wanted them out of Rock Springs might pay for their departure. One union member suggested that the Chinese strike rather than leave. On the following day, Chinese miners stayed home. In order to force the Chinese back into the mines, the Rock Springs mine superintendent closed the company store, thereby cutting off supplies to Chinese workers, and threatened to turn them out of company housing. The Chinese called off their walkout and returned to work the next day.

With the Chinese back in the mines, only a general strike would have produced a victory for striking miners in Rock Springs. Union Pacific officials feared that would be the union's next step, noting in correspondence that the strikers were receiving considerable encouragement from Knights of Labor officers in Denver and that workers' antipathy toward the company was intense all along the line. In order to discourage engineers, brakemen, firemen, and mechanics from launching a sympathy strike that would shut down the railroad, Union Pacific officials stated publicly that they would turn the line over to the federal government before negotiating with the strikers.

The national body of the Knights of Labor could not support the cause of white miners in Rock Springs without seeming to condone their violence against the Chinese. Events in Rock Springs revealed a major weakness of the union. Its local assemblies were largely autonomous and so could call and conduct strikes in response to local circumstances, without direction or discipline from the national organization. When a partisan grand jury in southern Wyoming claimed that not one white assailant could be identified and issued no indictments, national union officers distanced themselves further from the local assembly in Rock Springs. Terence Powderly, the union's leader, took both national politicians and industrialists to task for perpetuating "the Chinese evil," but he refused to support a general strike.

Although Adams never was able to spring the trap he laid for the Knights of Labor, his strategy prefigured the successful counterattack that capitalists mounted against the union after the Haymarket bombing in 1886. He reflected that, if the organization could have been compelled to stand "in direct alliance with murderers, desperadoes, and robbers, it would have been worth to us almost anything." If the Union Pacific's victory was not as sweet as Adams had hoped, it was victory nonetheless. By the end of October, coal production had risen to near normal in Rock Springs and the company employed twice as many Chinese as it had before the massacre. In mid-November, striking miners admitted defeat.

ELLEN S. AIKEN

References and Further Reading

Bromley, Isaac. *The Chinese Massacre at Rock Springs, Wyoming Territory, September 2, 1885*. Boston: Franklin Press, 1886.

House Reports, 1st Session, 49th Congress, 1885–1886, Vol. 7, Report No. 2044. "Providing Indemnity to Certain Chinese Subjects." Washington, DC: Government Printing Office, 1886.

Klein, Maury. *Union Pacific: The Birth of a Railroad, 1862–1893*. Garden City, NY: Doubleday and Company, Inc., 1987.

Storti, Craig. *Incident at Bitter Creek: The Story of the Rock Springs Chinese Massacre*. Ames: Iowa State University Press, 1991.

Voss, Kim. *The Making of American Exceptionalism: The Knights of Labor and Class Formation in the Nineteenth Century*. Ithaca, NY: Cornell University Press, 1993.

See also **Knights of Labor**

RODGERS, ELIZABETH FLYNN (AUGUST 25, 1847–AUGUST 27, 1939)
Knights of Labor

For almost two decades, from the early 1870s to 1887, Elizabeth Rodgers was one of the early women labor leaders in Chicago and among the first women office-holders in the Knights of Labor. Rodgers fought for the rights of women laborers in the workplace and within the union while also celebrating her role as wife and mother.

Throughout her youth, Rodgers was exposed to the hardships of workers and their efforts to organize. Born Elizabeth Flynn in Ireland in 1847, Rodgers was raised in London, Ontario, Canada, where there was a strong labor movement. As a young woman she married George Rodgers, a socialist and union organizer, and joined him in his agitations. Blacklisted by companies for their activism, the couple was forced to move several times during the 1860s. Rodgers took in boarders to provide for their growing family (which ultimately included 10 children) while her husband sought work as an iron molder.

The family settled in Chicago during the depression of the early 1870s, where Rodgers more directly joined her husband in the organized labor movement. Rodgers helped to organize primarily non-wage earning women and a few domestic servants and seamstresses into the Working Women's Union (WWU). She served as its presiding officer and together with its members, including Lucy Parsons, Lizzie Swank, and Alzina Stevens, met with local businesspersons and their employees to address conflicts over working conditions. Rodgers and the WWU also attempted to organize women workers. They held meetings to educate workers on their rights and protest strategies and joined the larger campaign for the eight-hour day. In 1877, in recognition of her efforts, Rodgers was elected delegate to the predominantly male state trades assembly in Illinois.

Rodgers was among the first women who joined the Knights of Labor when it opened its membership to female workers in 1881. Rodgers was comfortable with the organization's dual and disparate vision of women's role: a worker entitled to equal pay for equal work and a wife and mother responsible for developing moral character in the home and beyond. She took pride in doing her own housework and caring for her children and stood up to those who argued that women labor activists were unsexed. Rodgers acted on her belief that women should be allowed to pursue whatever work she was able to do without restriction. For Rodgers, during the 1880s that meant holding elected and appointed offices within the Knights of Labor.

Rodgers was among the first women to hold a number of official positions for the Knights organization. After joining, she assisted in the transformation of the WWU into the one of the first all-woman local assemblies of the Knights of Labor, Number 1789. Rodgers was elected its master workman and represented her local in District Assembly No. 24, which comprised 50,000 members. In 1885, chartered by the Knights' general master Terence Powderly, Rodgers became a regular organizer. The following year, 1886, when the master workman for the District Assembly 24 died, Rodgers was named to fill the office, becoming the Knights' first woman to hold the position of a district master workman. She was also elected a delegate to the 1886 Knights of Labor national convention. Rodgers attended with her two-week-old daughter.

On May 3, 1886, when laborers rallied in Haymarket Square, Rodgers supported the cause but was critical of the anarchists' rhetoric. After the violence at the event, the Knights of Labor suffered a significant decline, and Rodgers was among those who left the labor movement. She pursued a career in the insurance field. She was among the founders and served as the high chief ranger of a women's auxiliary to the Catholic Order of Foresters (WCOF), a fraternal life insurance society. Rodgers held a salaried position with the WCOF from 1891 to 1908. During her tenure, she received criticism from women labor leaders in Chicago for failing to consider the needs and situation of workingwomen. Complaints included Rodgers's employment of a nonunion printing company to produce the WCOF journal and setting high enrollment fees that prohibited workingwomen from joining the Order. Women leaders within the Chicago Teachers Federation, including Margaret Haley and Catherine Gogin, were among those who ultimately forced Rodgers to leave her office in 1908.

Rodgers died in relative anonymity in 1939 at the age of 92. Though Rodgers's commitment to the labor movement did not extend throughout her life, during her involvement her colleagues recognized her for her contribution to the cause. For that period, Rodgers devoted a tremendous amount of time and energy to the labor movement, pioneering leadership roles for women within the Knights organization. During and beyond her involvement in the labor movement, Rodgers consistently supported a woman's right to work and to earn equal pay for equal work, insisting that this work did not compromise her role as wife and mother.

GWEN HOERR JORDAN

References and Further Reading

Jones, Archie. "Rodgers, Elizabeth Flynn." In *Notable American Women, 1607–1950: A Biographical Dictionary*, edited by Edward T. James, Janet Wilson, and Paul S. Boyer. Cambridge, MA: Belknap Press of Harvard University Press, 1971, pp. 187–188.

Leidenberger, Georg. "Rodgers, Elizabeth Flynn." In *Women Building Chicago 1790–1990: A Biographical Dictionary*, edited by Rima Lunin Schultz and Adele Hast. Bloomington: Indiana University Press, 2001, pp. 762–764.

Levine, Susan. "Labor's True Woman: Domesticity and Equal Rights in the Knights of Labor." *Journal of American History* 70, no.2 (1983): 323–339.

Tax, Meredith. *The Rising of the Women: Feminist Solidarity and Class Conflict, 1880–1917*. New York: Monthly Review Press, 1980.

See also **Knights of Labor**

ROSIE THE RIVETER

After Europe went to war in 1939, American industries awakened from the Great Depression's doldrums. More men—and women—were called back to work or got new jobs in the revived factories, offices, retail outlets, and service industries. After Pearl Harbor, American men marched off to war, leaving a tremendous void in aircraft factories, munitions plants, shipyards, steel mills, and rubber works. Who would take the place of the men in these important defense industries? The answer was Rosie the Riveter.

There were really two Rosie the Riveters. The first was an image created by the War Advertising Council in 1942 as part of the Women in War Jobs/Industry campaign. The second was the real-life person—really millions of women—who worked in the aircraft factories, munitions plants, shipyards, steel mills, rubber works, and defense industries during World War II.

The image of Rosie the Riveter was designed to appeal to white, middle-class women. According to *Advertising and Selling Magazine*, advertisers needed to make a "heroine" out of the "lady of the assembly line." That "heroine" became Rosie the Riveter. Rosie was the embodiment of an American patriotic woman worker ready to do her part to win the war. She was a multimedia personality, appearing in newspapers, magazines, and film. She was the featured personality in advertising, feature stories, and music. Rosie the Riveter the media personality was attractive, white, and energetic. After a long eight-hour shift, she went home to take care of her children and the household, or went out on a date, if she was single. Rosie never challenged her traditional, domestic role. Instead, she merely transferred her traditional skills and responsibilities to the workplace. According to the *Women's Home Companion*, a popular monthly magazine, "Any woman who can run a sewing machine can run almost any factory machine." A *Saturday Evening Post* advertiser emphasized, "Give them [women workers] a rivet gun for a needle, sheets of metal for material, and these war workers will stitch you an airplane wing in half the time it used to take." Moreover, because women had natural child-rearing tendencies, they were temperamentally suited for the endless routine of factory work. As one writer for *Advertising and Selling Magazine* observed, "Repetition, monotonous tasks fail to break down this care taking attitude."

The women who worked in the aircraft factories, munitions plants, shipyards, steel mills, rubber works, and other war-related industries found that the image of Rosie had little to do with the reality of work.

Between 1940 and 1945, the number of female workers—the real-life Rosie the Riveters—increased from 12 million to 18 million. The largest number of American women—19 million—worked in July 1944. The majority of these women had worked outside the home before the war, although not necessarily in manufacturing. Most worked in less lucrative jobs in the service industry, in retail, or as domestics. But when the men went off to war and war production demands continued (indeed accelerated), more and more women shifted over to lucrative manufacturing jobs. Between 1940 and 1944, the number of women employed in manufacturing increased by 141%; the number working as domestics declined by 20%.

During World War II, an additional 6 million women joined the workforce. Most were married; for the first time, married women outnumbered single women in the female labor force in America. One third of these women had children under the age of 14.

Women who worked in defense industries during the war held an array of jobs. A minority of women took jobs once held by men; under the provisions of the National War Labor Board, these women were paid the same or substantially the same as the men. Most women, however, held the lighter jobs, those not traditionally held by men. Whether holding men's jobs or the lighter jobs, the women who worked in the defense industries were paid well, better than they had ever been paid before.

But there was a downside to the real life of Rosie the Riveter. Work was hard, and she often found hostility at work and difficulty finding adequate day care. Nonetheless, most women wanted to keep their jobs after the war. According to a Women's Bureau survey of 300 Baltimore women, the majority wanted to stay on their jobs, but few were given that option. Only about a third of the women kept their war jobs. Most shifted to other positions that paid less or remained unemployed.

The desires of women to stay on the job surprised many. The War Department, for example, never saw women as permanent replacements in industry. "A woman is a substitute, like plastic instead of metal," asserted one War Department brochure. That attitude was shared by industry. Women workers were the first casualties in reconversion cutbacks. In the summer of 1945, about 75% of the women employed in the aircraft and shipbuilding industries lost their jobs.

KATHLEEN ENDRES

References and Further Reading

Anderson, Karen. *Wartime Women: Sex Roles, Family Relations, and the Status of Women during World War II*. New York: Berkley Books, 2001.

Campbell, D'Ann. *Women at War with America: Private Lives in a Patriotic Era*. Cambridge, MA: Harvard University Press, 1984.

Carewe, Sylvia. "Where's the Woman's Angle in This War?" *Advertising and Selling Magazine* (August 1942): 23.

Endres, Kathleen L. *Rosie the Rubber Worker: Women Workers in Akron's Rubber Factories during World War II*. Kent, OH: Kent State University Press, 2000.

Gluck, Sherna Berger. *Rosie the Riveter Revisited: Women, the War, and Social Change*. Boston: Twayne Publishers, 1987.

"The Homefront." http://worldwarii06.tripod.com/id1.html.

Honey, Maureen. *Creating Rosie the Riveter: Class, Gender, and Propaganda during World War II*. Amherst: University of Massachusetts Press, 1984.

McNutt, Paul V. "Wake Up and Work." *Women's Home Companion* (May 1943): 40–41, 85.

"Now, They're Sewing Metal Twice as Fast." *Saturday Evening Post*, June 26, 1943, p. 99.

See also **World War II**

RUSTIN, BAYARD (1912–1987)
Peace and Civil Rights Activist

Born into a working-class African-American family in West Chester, Pennsylvania, Rustin absorbed Quaker ideals of community service and social justice from his maternal grandmother. Moving to Harlem in 1937, he observed at close hand the militant class and racial politics of Depression-era New York and soon joined the Young Communist League. Though he broke with the Communist Party in 1941, Rustin always retained a belief that class was a fundamental divide in American society and that issues of economic inequality were critical matters.

Between 1941 and 1965, Rustin's base of operations was the American peace movement, and he worked first for the Fellowship of Reconciliation under A. J. Muste, and then for the War Resisters League. He organized many protests against the nuclear arms race, particularly the civil defense program in the United States and the aboveground testing of nuclear weapons. Rustin developed close ties with pacifists in Europe and with leaders of anticolonial national liberation movements in Africa, and he planned multinational protests in both Europe and Africa.

Having adopted a Gandhian belief in militant nonviolence, Rustin strove to insinuate the practice of nonviolent direct action into the African-American civil rights movement. In the 1940s, he worked closely with A. Philip Randolph in his March on Washington Movement and in efforts to desegregate the U.S. armed services. He also was among the founders of the Congress of Racial Equality, an interracial organization committed to nonviolent action to achieve racial justice. He was a leader of its Journey of Reconciliation, a 1947 effort to challenge bus segregation in interstate travel in the South. His efforts in both the pacifist and racial justice movements led to many arrests in these decades.

In 1956, Rustin traveled to Montgomery, Alabama, where he quickly formed a close relationship with the Reverend Martin Luther King Jr. Rustin provided King with critical mentoring in the theory and practice of Gandhian nonviolence. He drew up the plans for what became the Southern Christian Leadership Conference, and for several years he was a key confidant of King. A steady refrain in his advice to King was the relevance of economic justice issues to the fight for racial equality.

Throughout these years, Rustin maintained ties with the labor movement, primarily, though not exclusively, through his relationship with A. Philip Randolph. A founder of the organization In Friendship, he worked to mobilize trade union support for the burgeoning civil rights movement in the South. He also used his ties with student groups to recruit volunteers in unionizing drives, such as the efforts of Local 1199 to organize hospital workers in New York City in the 1950s.

A controversial figure because of his Communist past and his homosexuality, Rustin was nonetheless chosen by A. Philip Randolph to be the chief organizer of the 1963 March on Washington, which became one of the signature events of the civil rights movement. The success of the March gave Rustin a public platform that he had never enjoyed before.

In the wake of the March, Rustin increasingly argued that the future of the civil rights movement lay in an alliance with other progressive forces, particularly the organized labor movement. His February 1965 article in *Commentary*, "From Protest to Politics," developed these ideas at length. He urged civil rights activists to shift away from a reliance on protest and instead focus on developing a majority electoral coalition. Rustin viewed organized labor as the key partner for the civil rights movement, and he believed that the black freedom struggle needed to move beyond civil rights toward advocacy of the economic justice measures that were essential for meaningful equality.

With the support of A. Philip Randolph, Rustin left the War Resisters League and in 1965 created a new organization, the A. Philip Randolph Institute, to build bridges between organized labor and the civil rights movement. Largely funded through contributions from individual trade unions and the AFL-CIO, the Institute remained his base of operations for the rest of his life. Through it, Rustin pushed civil rights organizations like the NAACP to lobby for a higher minimum wage and full employment measures, while prodding trade unions, particularly the crafts, to open their training and apprenticeship programs to African-Americans.

Rustin's commitment to a politics of coalition with labor put him at odds with many in the black freedom movement, especially as the movement became more militant in the late 1960s and turned toward black power and black nationalism. For instance, he sided with the United Federation of Teachers, led by Albert Shanker, in its bitter conflict with the Oceanhill-Brownsville community board and its ensuing strike against New York City's public schools. Rustin also dissented from calls for affirmative action as a remedy for racial discrimination, arguing that the key issue was an insufficient number of jobs that paid a living wage. Affirmative action, he often said, would only drive a wedge between the components of a potential majority coalition among progressives.

Rustin also lost much credibility among black and white radicals alike in the late 1960s because of his refusal to break with the Johnson administration over its escalation of the Vietnam War. Even though Rustin saw Johnson's Great Society programs as inadequate to the task of eliminating poverty, he saw them as a step in the right direction. He was unwilling to make the war a litmus test for political affiliation and to abandon access to administration officials. His critics, however, attributed his stance on the war to the dependence of the Randolph Institute on the AFL-CIO and its president, George Meany, staunch supporters of both Johnson and the war.

In the 1970s and 1980s, Rustin used the Randolph Institute to mobilize black trade unionists as a definable bloc, and especially encouraged massive voter registration drives. Increasingly focusing his energy on international human rights work, particularly the plight of refugees, he lobbied within the AFL-CIO to win its support for refugees from Southeast Asia to be admitted into the United States.

JOHN D'EMILIO

References and Further Reading

Rustin, Bayard. *Down the Line: The Collected Writings of Bayard Rustin*. Chicago: Quadrangle Books, 1971.
———. *Strategies for Freedom: The Changing Patterns of Black Protest*. New York: Columbia University Press, 1976.

See also **Communist Party; Muste, A. J.; Randolph, A. Philip**

RUTTENBERG, HAROLD (1914–1998)
Steelworkers Activist

During the 1930s and 1940s, Harold Ruttenberg helped steelworkers in their struggle for a union and then worked as a staffer in the Steel Workers Organizing Committee (SWOC) and the United Steelworkers of America (USWA).

Ruttenberg became interested in the workers' struggle in 1933 and 1934 when he was a student at the University of Pittsburgh. The steelworkers' struggle was embodied by the "Rank and File" movement inside the Amalgamated Association of Iron, Steel and Tin Workers (the AA). That venerable union had a broad jurisdiction in the steel industry, but in practice, it consisted of a few thousand craft workers in odd niches of the industry. The AA's elected leadership under its president Mike Tighe was timid and afraid of being swamped by the thousands of new members from basic steel companies. The newly unionized workers were organized in union locals but had no national leadership of their own. The strange upshot was that four pro-union intellectuals began to play an informal leadership role for the Rank and File workers. The Big Four were Heber Blankenhorn, Stephen Raushenbush, Harvey O'Connor, and Ruttenberg. The Rank and File leaders had a thankless task, for neither they nor their movement had many resources. While many steelworkers wanted to strike, the ad hoc leadership was afraid that a strike without resources or a sympathetic union leadership would be lost and would set back the union movement for years. In the

spring of 1934, the Rank and File leaders settled for a weak presidential commission. Many workers left the movement in disgust, while many of the remaining dissident lodges were expelled by Tighe.

When the Steel Workers Organizing Committee was formed in 1936, Ruttenberg joined that effort. He helped to co-ordinate SWOC's campaign to win over leaders of the steel companies' employee representation programs.

Clinton Golden, SWOC's leader in the eastern states, soon had Ruttenberg appointed to the post of research director. Ruttenberg investigated conditions in the steel industry and the workforce. He was especially interested in the massive unemployment caused by the replacement of the old hand-style sheet mills by modern rolling mills.

In 1942, Ruttenberg and Clinton Golden coauthored *The Dynamics of Industrial Democracy*. The book outlined a series of 37 ideas leading to productive relations between unions and managements. It was based on the idea that even strong unions could get only limited concessions from a company. The only way to get more was to improve the company's productivity. Therefore, provided that management accepted the union's role, the union had to cooperate with management for their mutual benefit. The result would be a laboristic order that benefited all. The authors made it clear that the union needed to control dissidents in its ranks. Industrial democracy did not imply union democracy.

Ruttenberg worked as the assistant director of the steel division of the War Production Board in 1942 and 1943. In 1946, he left the USWA and became a business executive.

JAMES C. KOLLROS

References and Further Reading

Clark, Paul F., Peter Gottlieb, and Donald Kennedy, eds. *Forging a Union of Steel: Philip Murray, SWOC, and the United Steelworkers*. Ithaca, NY: ILR Press, 1987.
Rose, James D. *Duquesne and the Rise of Steel Unionism*. Urbana and Chicago: University of Illinois Press, 2001.

See also **Amalgamated Association of Iron and Steel Workers; Industrial Democracy; United Steelworkers of America**

RYAN, JOSEPH (1884–1963)
International Longshoremen's Association

Joseph Ryan became the head of the International Longshoremen's Association (ILA) in 1927, and in 1943 cemented his control by becoming international president for life. Ryan had started work on New York's waterfront in 1910. An injury a few years later drove him from the docks, but not from the ILA. His speaking and organizational skills made Ryan an attractive prospect. He started out as financial secretary to Local 791, moved up to financial secretary of the ILA's powerful New York District Council, and finally to the position of president in 1927. He long remained a controversial figure both within the ILA and the American Federation of Labor (AFL). The infestation of gangsters in the ILA corresponded with Ryan's presidency. Just like his gangster allies throughout the New York City port, Ryan gained financially from his union position. Through a complex web of official and unofficial organizations, and union dinners, Ryan plundered ILA funds. Ryan was not circumspect in use of the position of president. He wore expensive suits and drove expensive automobiles, had golf club memberships, and enjoyed luxurious vacations around the world. Ryan also took bribes from stevedoring companies to maintain labor peace. Thus, he accumulated large sums of money from ILA funds and by shakedowns of employers.

As Irish and Italian criminal gangs began to dominate the New York waterfront, increasing numbers of gangsters obtained union positions. When questioned about the large numbers of criminals holding union office, Ryan replied that he was merely giving ex-convicts a second chance to rehabilitate. But there was another reason for hiring ex-convicts: they would maintain control over the men. Because of the widespread influence of gangsters throughout the ILA, longshoremen thought twice before challenging the rule of Ryan and other ILA officials.

Ryan's reputation as being friendly to notorious gangsters and accepting employer bribes encouraged West Coast longshoremen to break from the ILA. In 1934, a strike broke out on the West Coast. Led by Australian-born Harry Bridges, the strike pitted not just longshoremen against shippers and stevedores but also seamen, cooks, pilots, and oilers. Ryan visited the West Coast in May 1934. In his usual way of ignoring local sensibilities, he negotiated a settlement of the strike. Ryan, however, had misjudged the temper of the San Francisco men. In a noisy meeting, Ryan was yelled down and forced from the podium. Humiliated, Ryan shot back by dismissing Bridges from union office. But such a tactic could not forestall the militancy of West Coast longshoremen. In 1936, the West Coast longshoremen joined the fledgling CIO and formed a new union, the International Longshoremen's and Warehousemen's Union (ILWU). Ryan's failure to control the West Coast men had culminated in the loss to the ILA of thousands of dues-paying members.

Perhaps Ryan might have been privately pleased to have rid himself of the troublesome West Coast men, but he also had to confront opposition back home in New York. A rank-and-file revolt was evident on the Brooklyn docks. Encouraged by Harry Bridges, thousands of New York longshoremen seemed to be ready to challenge Ryan's control. Pete Panto was the rank-and-file leader in Brooklyn. At last it appeared that an alternative to Ryan's rule was present. In 1939, Panto's threat was nullified after he went missing. Years later, his body was discovered in a lime pit in New Jersey. He had been murdered by Albert Anastasia, the reputed head of Murder Inc. The murder of Panto had a chilling effect on the challenge to Ryan. But after World War II, Ryan was forced once again to fight an insurgency within the ILA. A series of wildcat or unofficial strikes broke out in 1945, 1948, and 1951. Each time, a small cadre of ILA officials in New York rose up to challenge Ryan. Nurturing the confrontation was increasing dissatisfaction with Ryan's negotiating ability with stevedores and shippers. Ryan was perceived as a weak bargainer and was labeled with the nickname "nickel-and-dime Ryan." When compared to the wages and benefits of the West Coast longshoremen, this was plainly evident. Under the leadership of Harry Bridges, the ILWU negotiated wages and working conditions that the New York longshoremen could only dream of. Also influencing the ILA insurgents was World War II. Returning veterans to the industry were not so intimidated as before. There existed a keen sense of injustice and anger at the continuing loss of democracy within the ILA. Communist activity on the docks also fed this resistance, as did the efforts of labor priests, led by Father John Corridan.

The 1945, 1948, and 1951 strikes placed Ryan on the defensive. Just as problematic, stevedores and shippers lost confidence in Ryan's ability to deliver peace and accept relatively low wages. Following the 1951 strike, Ryan's control was fast eroding. Calls for a public investigation of the ILA heightened Ryan's anxiety. New York Governor Thomas E. Dewey created a Crime Commission to examine the labor relations and gangster control on the New York waterfront. A series of witnesses and union officials confirmed that the ILA was riven with gangsters, that corruption in the form of kickbacks was common, and that Ryan ruled this mixture of trade union and criminal enterprise. The Crime Commission findings at last pushed the AFL to kick out the ILA from the established labor movement.

Ryan's days as union leader were numbered. He was first indicted for bribery after taking money from stevedores and shippers. The ILA leaders decided that the symbolic removal of Ryan from the presidency could help quieten calls for a new union to be formed. Correspondingly, Ryan accepted the inevitable and announced his retirement from the ILA in November 1953. His troubles were not over, however. He was convicted of taking bribes and fined $2,500 and sentenced to six months in jail. He appealed the case to the U.S. Supreme Court but lost. He paid the fine but managed to avoid jail time because of ill health. He continued to battle illness until June 26, 1963, when he died of cancer.

COLIN DAVIS

References and Further Reading

Davis, Colin J. *Waterfront Revolts: New York and London Dockworkers, 1946–1961*. Urbana: University of Illinois Press, 2003.

Kimeldorf, Howard. *Reds or Rackets: The Making of Radical and Conservative Unions on the Waterfront*. Berkeley: University of California Press, 1988.

Russell, Maud. *Men along the Shore*. New York: Brussel and Brussel, 1966.

See also **International Longshoremen's Association**

S

SACCO AND VANZETTI

When Nicola Sacco and Bartolomeo Vanzetti were arrested on June 1920, they were virtual unknowns, destined, in Vanzetti's words, to "die, unmarked, unknown, a failure." Charged with the April 15 robbery of a South Braintree, Massachusetts, shoe factory payroll that left two security guards dead, the two Italian immigrant anarchists faced hostility based on their identity and their political beliefs that ignited worldwide indignation. When they were executed 7 years later after a trial marked by a level of injustice that remains its central legacy, they were, in one journalist's words, "the two most famous prisoners in all the world."

Galleanisti and the Red Scare

The postwar Red Scare, the seismic reaction to the perceived threat of imminent revolution, imperiled the two anarchists. Sacco and Vanzetti were caught in a dragnet designed by a police chief named Michael Stewart who was certain that the robbery was the work of revolutionaries. Both men were armed when arrested, and convinced they were being held because of their politics, lied repeatedly under questioning.

They had ample reason to be fearful. Sacco and Vanzetti were followers of Luigi Galleani, the fiercely anti-organizational anarchist who led a small but passionately dedicated group of fellow radicals. Galleanisti believed that all institutions, even labor unions, were hopelessly corrupt and that true freedom would come only through wholesale destruction of existing political and economic structures. Galleani broadcast his ideas in his weekly *Cronaca Sovversiva* and published a pamphlet on manufacturing bombs.

Many of their defenders portrayed Sacco and Vanzetti as pastoral anarchists, gentle men with innocent ideals. To an extent this was true. Vanzetti's neighbors spoke glowingly of him, and the son of one of his landlords described him as a father figure. Sacco was a dedicated family man whose employer trusted him with the keys to his factory. But there was another side to them as well.

To them "the Idea"—their belief in anarchism— was not simply a philosophical stance. Considerable evidence points to Galleanisti's involvement in a series of bombings in May and June 1920, as well as other explosions before and after. Sacco and Vanzetti may not have been involved—the evidence is circumstantial at best—but clearly they had comrades who were. They eventually asserted that the night they were arrested, they were attempting to move incendiary literature; it may have been dynamite.

The Trial

The indictment for the crime was delayed by Vanzetti's trial for an attempted robbery in Bridgewater, Massachusetts, on Christmas Eve, 1919. His trial— Sacco was not charged because he was at work that night—was defined by contempt for Italian immigrants and a Red Scare mentality. Prosecutor

Bartolomeo Vanzetti (left) and Nicola Sacco, manacled together surrounded by heavy guard and onlookers, about to enter the courthouse at Dedham, Massachusetts where they will receive the death sentence for murder they committed seven years ago. Library of Congress, Prints & Photographs Division, NYWT & S Collection [LC-USZ62-124547].

Frederick Katzmann mocked and confounded defense witnesses as they struggled to testify in Italian. One young eyewitness identified Vanzetti by claiming, "The way he ran I could tell he was a foreigner." The judge, Webster Thayer, stated openly that he regarded anarchists to be capable of any criminal act. Despite weak evidence against Vanzetti, and indisputable proof the jury tampered with evidence, Thayer gave the anarchist an unusually harsh 12–15 years. More important—the reason he had been tried first for this crime—the scant evidence against him in the South Braintree case was now less important than the fact that he was now a convicted felon.

Over the course of the trial, which lasted from May 31 to July 14, little of the evidence should have stuck to either defendant. More than 50 people witnessed the crime. Only seven claimed to have seen Sacco, and just four identified Vanzetti at the trial. In every instance their testimony was faulty or manipulated or both. The material evidence broke down as well. The police claimed that they found Sacco's cap next to one of the murdered security guards, but the prosecution struggled to establish either that Sacco owned the cap or that it had been found at the crime scene. The police also claimed the gun they took from Vanzetti the night he was arrested

had belonged to one of the guards. But the prosecution could not prove the guard even had his gun the day of the crime—much less that Vanzetti had picked it up as the guard lay dying. In fact police records unsealed in the 1970s revealed that the police and prosecutor Katzmann knew they had the wrong gun and suppressed this evidence. Ballistics testimony was also suspect at best. Of the six bullets extracted from the security guards, Bullet 3 was the only one prosecutors even attempted to tie to the defendants. Though they claimed the bullet came from Sacco's gun, neither of their ballistics witnesses could argue this definitively. One—Massachusetts State Police Captain William Proctor—later filed a deposition admitting that he had prepared intentionally vague and misleading testimony with the prosecution.

Ultimately this case was defined not by the evidence, but by the misconduct of the prosecutor and the judge and by the dire presence of the anarchists' political beliefs in the courtroom. As in Vanzetti's first trial, the prosecutor was Frederick Katzmann and the judge—who made a special request to be assigned this trial—was Webster Thayer. Thayer, anxious to prove his mettle to the elite Boston Brahmin community, was openly hostile to the defendants and to Sacco's lawyer, a maverick defender of radical causes named

Fred Moore. The judge repeatedly committed judicial misconduct by attacking Sacco and Vanzetti outside his courtroom. Having rejected four appeals in one day, he boasted to a friend, "Did you see what I did to those Anarchist bastards the other day?" The anarchists' politics became a central focus in the courtroom as well. Much of Katzmann's case hinged on the defendants' "consciousness of guilt"; he argued the two had lied when they were arrested because they were guilty. This forced Sacco and Vanzetti to explain that they lied because they feared political persecution. Katzmann leapt at this opening, and Thayer provided him with remarkable leeway as he attacked the defendants for their political beliefs.

Katzmann also had help from the Department of Justice, which assisted the prosecution in numerous ways. For example it placed spies in a cell next to Sacco and on the Sacco-Vanzetti Defense Committee and tried to get one into Sacco's wife's house. It tracked anarchist groups' finances, trying—unsuccessfully—to uncover large infusions of cash. Its extensive involvement in the case, like Katzmann's prosecutorial interrogations and Thayer's comments outside of court, raised the question of exactly what the defendants were being tried for.

The Appeals

A quick verdict in the trial initiated the lengthy appeals process. After 6 long weeks, the jury took part of the afternoon of July 14, 1921 to convict Sacco and Vanzetti. Over 6 years, the defendants' various lawyers filed seven appeals. Vanzetti was represented first by local lawyers Jeremiah and Thomas McAnarney, Sacco by William Callahan and the flamboyant Moore. In late October 1924, William Thompson, a highly respected Boston lawyer, took over the defense; he was joined a year later by Herbert Ehrmann, who dedicated the next 40 years to vindicating his clients. In the last weeks of Sacco and Vanzetti's lives in August 1927, attorney Arthur Hill took over their case.

Because of byzantine legal codes in Massachusetts, later changed as a result of this trial, the judge sitting in the case heard all appeals. This rendered successful appeals all but impossible. Thayer quickly rejected four appeals that asserted tainted witnesses' testimony and a prejudiced jury foreman—and one based on his own judicial misconduct. The most heart-rending appeal came from a prison cell confession by a young Portuguese immigrant named Celestino Madeiros. Madeiros implicated a criminal gang operating out of Providence, Rhode Island. Ehrmann argued he

provided new and telling details about the crime. But because Madeiros, drunk and afraid, hid on the floor of the getaway car, he missed obvious details about the crime. Thayer rejected this appeal in October 1926, labeling Madeiros an unreliable criminal.

The Final Months: Protest, the Lowell Committee, and the Executions

By this time, protests against the proceedings had grown increasingly loud and persistent. They began slowly, confined to the Italian immigrant Left community. Anarchosyndicalist Carlo Tresca brought the case to a broader audience, urging his compatriot Elizabeth Gurley Flynn to use her influence in American Left and liberal organizations. Moore also did all he could to publicize the trial. Both Nicola and Rosa Sacco ended up furious at him, convinced he had misused defense funds. But Moore helped make their case an international issue, working largely through increasingly powerful Communist parties worldwide. As the defense campaign grew, organized principally around the Sacco-Vanzetti Defense Committee, it attracted prominent Boston Brahmin women like Elizabeth Glendower Evans, who sent Sacco and Vanzetti food and flowers, and tutored them in English. Poets Dorothy Parker and Edna St. Vincent Millay, hardly known as political activists, were arrested for protesting. Writer John Dos Passos marched and published a volume describing the injustice of the trial. Finally when future Supreme Court Justice Felix Frankfurter wrote a scathing expose of the trial and the conservative *Boston Herald* questioned the proceedings, the governor of Massachusetts took the unusual step of establishing a committee to review the case.

The committee, led by Harvard President A. Lawrence Lowell, appeared to conduct an exhaustive investigation. Its review took longer than the trial itself, but committee members had made up their minds before their work began. Lowell drafted the committee's findings before they heard closing arguments from the attorneys. Governor Fuller conducted his own investigation—it too tainted by his obvious bias—but had declared he would abide by the decision of the Lowell committee. When it issued its report on July 27, 1927, little stood between Sacco and Vanzetti and the electric chair.

By this point support for Sacco and Vanzetti had reached a fevered pitch. Governor Fuller received a petition with over half a million signatures collected worldwide. A wide array of renowned intellectuals and political leaders—among them H. G. Wells,

Marie Curie, Albert Einstein, John Dewey, H. L. Mencken, and Jane Addams—raised increasingly angry voices. Another appeal came from Alfred Dreyfus, who had endured a trial for espionage in a profoundly anti-Semitic atmosphere in France in 1894. Protests wracked cities around the world. There were protests and strikes in Boston and New York City, and in towns like Rochester, Indianapolis, Baltimore, Scranton, and Tampa. Workers led rallies and general strikes in every major city in Europe, in Japan, China, Argentina, Brazil, Chile, Mexico, and Panama and across North and South Africa.

It was all to no avail. When appeals to the most liberal Supreme Court justices to issue a stay of execution failed, Sacco and Vanzetti were doomed. Both calmly wrote letters and received visitors in their final hours. Sacco exclaimed, "*Vive Anarcismo!*" and "farewell, Mother" as the electricity surged through him. Vanzetti pointedly forgave "some of the people" who had sent him to his death and thanked the warden for caring for him during his internment. Both men were dead by a few minutes after midnight on August 23, 1927.

The Legacy of the Sacco and Vanzetti Case

The building of their legacy began immediately. The injustice of the case has provoked an outpouring of novels, poems, plays, and even operas. While artistic productions have shared an outraged certainty of their innocence, the case has been heatedly debated among scholars and on myriad websites. Broad early debates on the evidence, the judge and the attorneys, and the impact of the protest movement have funneled down to one bullet. Bullet 3 is the only piece of material evidence that has not fallen apart. Sacco and Vanzetti's detractors argue that ballistics tests over the years implicate Sacco's gun. Their defenders counter that the police lied about Vanzetti's gun and may have planted bullet three as well.

While the question of their guilt or innocence will probably never be resolved, the unfairness of their trial remains indisputable. In 1977, Massachusetts Governor Michael Dukakis acknowledged as much, declaring that because of the anti-immigrant and anti-radical fervor of the time, it had been impossible for Sacco and Vanzetti to receive a fair trial.

MICHAEL M. TOPP

References and Further Reading

Avrich, Paul. *Sacco and Vanzetti: The Anarchist Background*. Princeton, NJ: Princeton University Press, 1991.

Ehrmann, Herbert B. *The Case That Will Not Die: Commonwealth vs. Sacco and Vanzetti*. Boston, MA: Little, Brown and Company, 1969.

Felix, David. *Protest: Sacco-Vanzetti and the Intellectuals*. Bloomington: Indiana University Press, 1965.

Frankfurter, Felix. *The Case of Sacco and Vanzetti: A Critical Analysis for Lawyers and Laymen*. Stanford, CA: Academic Reprints, 1954 (1927).

Polenberg, Richard. *The Letters of Sacco and Vanzetti*. New York: Penguin Books, 1997.

Topp, Michael. *The Sacco and Vanzetti Case: A Brief History with Documents*. Boston, MA: Bedford, St. Martin's, 2005.

Young, William, and David Kaiser. *Postmortem: New Evidence in the Case of Sacco and Vanzetti*. Amherst: The University of Massachusetts Press, 1985.

See also **Communist Party; Flynn, Elizabeth Gurley; Immigration Restriction; Italians**

SADLOWSKI, ED (1938–)
United Steelworkers of America

Ed Sadlowski, the son of a Polish steelworker, once served as president of the United Steelworkers of America's (USWA) largest local union. Sadlowski was the subject of feature stories in the *Atlantic Monthly, Rolling Stone, Time, Newsweek,* and *Penthouse* magazines and appeared on the *60 Minutes* television program. Famed economist John Kenneth Galbraith even penned a very rare union-leader tribute in the pages of *Commentary*. The man many union members called Oilcan Eddie because of his working-class character was also a successful defendant in a Federal Department of Justice lawsuit and even had a U.S. Supreme Court case named after him, *Sadlowski v. United Steelworkers, 1982*.

Sadlowski earned his glossy props by being the lead player in one of the most important union election dramas in modern American history. In 1977 Eddie ran for the presidency of the one-million strong USWA. The campaign embodied the hopes and aspirations of thousands of union and political progressives. Sadlowski's candidacy rubbed raw the wounds of blue-collar workers from Buffalo to California and inspired college students and environmentalists seriously to consider that the labor movement could be an agent for social change. It was a heady expectation to project on the person of a rather young, self-educated Chicago steelworker, but Sadlowski had an impatient quality that fast-tracked him for union leadership.

Sadlowski was born in 1938 in a southeastern Chicago neighborhood. His grandfather participated in the big steel strike in 1909, and his father was a union organizer. In 1956, at the age of 18 Sadlowski began working at megagiant steel maker U.S. Steel's Chicago South Works. Three years later he was elected shop steward, and incredibly in 1962 at the tender age of 24, Sadlowski managed to craft together a multicultural leadership group to govern USWA Local 65. The South Works was not only the largest employer in Chicago, but one of the biggest steel mills in the country. The 8,000-strong membership of Local 65 was a polyglot of multiethnic and multiracial groupings. Sadlowski won the presidency of Local 65 by building a union coalition with the local's large number of Mexican-American workers. Once in office the brash Sadlowski quickly began to build a reputation for democratic and militant leadership. After only 6 years as local president, Sadlowski accepted a 1968 appointment as a representative to the District 31 staff. But 5 years later Eddie decided to leverage his nearly 20 years of toil in a steel mill to run for the USWA District 31 director post. His decision startled and offended the union's established bureaucracy.

Sadlowski's move to become the highest ranking officer in the union's largest district representing over 110,000 workers contradicted the accepted process of allowing the incumbent leadership to anoint the heir apparent. Samuel Evett was the candidate backed by the union's hierarchy and after a very tumultuous campaign appeared to have fended off the brash challenger by only 1,800 votes. District 65 was now safely once again under the control of a safe, career functionary. But appearances proved deceiving, because the Sadlowski campaign charged Evett and other district officials with massive vote fraud. A federal court agreed with the challenger and in 1974 ordered the election to be rerun. With over 300 federal investigators monitoring voting throughout the Chicago-Gary, Indiana, area, Sadlowski stomped the union's favorite son by nearly a 2-to-1 margin.

Sadlowski was now the elected leader of the largest district of workers within the nation's biggest union. The USWA represented over 1.4 million workers and in conjunction with the autoworkers union had set the national pattern for collective-bargaining agreements for millions of manufacturing workers since 1946. Economists, industrial relations experts, and national politicians had considered the steel industry the country's most important manufacturing sector. By the 1960s, steel companies were making money, and the quality of life for steelworkers had dramatically improved. All the economic indicators however were not so upbeat. Markets at home for steel products had been threatened by foreign steel imports, and prices for most steel products had not fairly represented consumer demand. In addition a persistent 3-year cycle of work stoppages had created a management

and union perception that the industry suffered economic loss each time a new round of contract talks began. In response to threats allegedly caused by strikes, the international union leadership, under I. W. Abel, agreed in 1974 to a very controversial Experimental Negotiating Agreement (ENA). In brief the ENA prohibited national strikes in exchange for a guaranteed 3% annual wage increase.

The ENA existed for two rounds of bargaining (1974 and 1977), and its benefits were widely disputed. But the economic effects of ENA aside, it was the way the deal was struck that most rankled union members. In accordance with the USWA Constitution, Abel signed the agreement without a rank-and-file ratification vote. To union leaders like Sadlowski, forfeiting the members' right-to-strike was an act of labor treason. In his and the eyes of other workers, the USWA had now come to exemplify "country club unionism where union executives feel more at home playing golf with corporate executives than they do talking to and working for workers" (Sadlowski letter, undated). Angered by the ENA, the loss of the strike weapon, and the erosion of contract rights and backed by a group of self-proclaimed union reformers organized as Steelworkers Fight Back, in 1977 Sadlowski ran for the international presidency of the USWA.

In 1976, Abel stepped down as union president, and after a tussle within the executive board, Lloyd McBride emerged as the Abel loyalists' choice to be the USWA's fourth international leader. Sadlowski had only been a district director for 2 years, but at age 38 he already spent a lifetime in steel mills and steel town bars. Campaigning on a platform of sweeping and visionary principles, he portrayed McBride as a "fat cat" union leader and pilloried what he believed was the prevailing notion that the union leadership was "comfortable partners with top corporate management." Depending on the work of about a dozen paid staffers and scores of volunteers, Sadlowski had significant support from basic steelworkers in California, Buffalo, Pittsburgh, Youngstown, Cleveland, and Chicago. His efforts were supported by nickel-and-dime and pass-the-hat contributions from workers in dingy union halls and fat donor checks from national figures like Jane Fonda, John Kenneth Galbraith, Ralph Nader, and Studs Terkel. Sadlowski also drew the enmity of the entire USWA officialdom, including Abel and AFL-CIO President George Meany. Frightened by his progressive political philosophy and critique of American capitalism, Sadlowski was attacked openly by McBride supporters as a Communist.

Sadlowski was also subject to a scurrilous charge from the union hierarchy that he would allow thousands of mill jobs to be eliminated. McBride took advantage of a freewheeling interview that Sadlowski did for *Penthouse Magazine* to mischaracterize badly the south Chicago firebrand as endorsing the use of technology to reduce the need for manpower in the steel mills. The selected use of words taken out of context appeared to represent a candidate for union president who was indifferent to job loss (E. Kelley, *Penthouse*, 1977).

Some commentators described the contest as a pivotal point for organized and unorganized labor. If McBride were to win, the nations largest industrial union would likely continue to function in a bureaucratic, nonadversarial, and concessionary manner. But if Sadlowski grabbed the top post, then one of the nation's most important unions would become more democratic, militant, and less conciliatory toward the mill owners. It was as if organized labor and the politics of work were held in the balance. In the end Sadlowski fell short of victory, receiving only 43.1% of the 578,141 votes cast. But a breakdown of the actual votes by locals revealed that Sadlowski won a majority of union votes from large basic steel locals (1,000 or more members) in the country. McBride however swept Canadian and southern locals and nearly all the small nonsteel producing units within the union.

Sadlowski's unsuccessful charge for the union leadership was a serious confrontation of conflicting views of unionism. The steelworkers, like other manufacturing union members in the 1970s, had experienced a creeping loss of economic security. Union ranks had grown agitated and impatient over corporate and union indifference to changing economic realities. McBride, rightly or wrongly represented appeasement and more-of-the-same. Sadlowski on the other hand was the "man of steel," perceived as confrontational and unorthodox. In retrospect perhaps the campaign was an historical moment when just as the country's right-wing political forces were about to assume dominance, organized labor in the United States could have embraced a more class-conscious, assertive form of unionism. But the philosophy, rhetoric, and campaign of Oilcan Eddie mostly add up to a question of what might have been. After all when he ran for president, he had been district director for only a brief time and had never negotiated a major contract, taken any initiatives on organizing, or proposed any dramatic health and safety measures. And while it took a bit longer to take form, the USWA did in the late 1980s construct an effective strategy for saving steelworker jobs and protecting negotiated benefits.

Following the McBride-Sadlowski race, the USWA in 1978 amended its constitution, imposing a blanket prohibition on financial campaign contributions from persons other than union members. The objection to outsider funding was instituted to avoid the type of insurgent political challenge that Sadlowski had constructed. The rule also marked the first attempt by a labor union to restrict financial support for candidates for union office. Charging that the edict restricts the free speech and associational rights of union members, Sadlowski sued the USWA in 1981. After wining at the federal, district, and appellate levels, Sadlowski faced a final test in front of the Supreme Court. But in 1982, the High Court found in a 5-4 decision that the union's new provision was legal and reasonable. As a result of the ruling, many other unions rushed to adopt constitutional bars that forbade candidates for union office from receiving financial campaign contributions.

After his 1977 race Sadlowski continued to serve on the union staff but never again ran for any union office. He retired in 1995. But in retirement Sadlowski remains a strong advocate for unionism. Sadlowski was appointed in 1995 to the Illinois Labor Relations Board by Chicago Mayor Richard J. Daley. His rich appreciation and knowledge of Chicago labor history led to his becoming active in the South-East Historical Society, promoting the preservation of a steel-industry culture on the city's southeast side. Sadlowski has also served as an occasional guest lecturer in the Labor Studies Program at Indiana University's Northwest Campus and as an instructor for the USWA. He currently continues to reside in the neighborhood he was raised in on the southeast side.

In the 1970s, Sadlowski was one of the Midwest's most notable and accessible labor union leaders, projecting an intoxicating and hopeful working-class spirit. At a time when U.S. labor too often kept an arms' length from social movements and such progressive struggles as civil rights, anti-Vietnam War resistance, women's rights, and environmental issues, Sadlowski's unionism embraced these social conflicts as part of a broad working-class fight for social justice.

ROBERT BRUNO

References and Further Reading

Bogdanich, George. 1973. "Never a Kind Word for Abel." *The Nation* 216, 19 (May 7).
Fanning, John. 1988. "Libelous Speech: A Survivor of United Steelworkers v. Sadlowski." *Catholic University Law Review* 38, 155 (fall).
Ignatius, David. 1977. "The Press in Love." *Columbia Journalism Review* (May/June): 26–27.
Kelley, Ed. 1977. Interview with Ed Sadlowski. In *Penthouse Magazine*. (Jan. 1977).
Moberg, David. "Steelworkers' Showdown." *Chicago Reader* 6, 16 (Jan. 21, 1977).
Nyden, Phillip. *Steelworkers Rank-and-File: The Political Economy of a Union Reform Movement*. New York: Praeger Publishers, 1984.

Cases and Statutes Cited

United Steelworkers of America v. Sadlowski, 457 U.S. 102, 1982 (Decided June 14, 1982).

SAILORS' UNION OF THE PACIFIC

Union legend states that the Sailors' Union of the Pacific (SUP) began on San Francisco's Folsom Street lumber wharves on March 6, 1885. Approximately 300 sailors gathered that night to discuss the problems they faced: Poor food, low wages, inadequate quarters, and the abusive practices conducted by labor brokers, known as "crimps." Representatives from the Steamshipmen's Protective Association, the International Workmen's Association, and the Knights of Labor led the meeting. Scandinavian and German sailors, engaged in trade on North America's Pacific Coast and influenced by Europe's socialist rhetoric, constituted the majority of attendees. The meeting ended with 222 sailors creating the Coast Seamen's Union (CSU), the precursor to the SUP.

While the CSU's leadership tended toward socialist ideologies, non-Socialists quickly filled the union's ranks, which led to struggles over the organization's course that continued into the twentieth century. This struggle first showed itself in regard to the place that Chinese sailors would assume in the union. While Socialists argued that Chinese sailors should join the union, the non-Socialist rank-and-file resented the Chinese's unfair competition and refused to consider them sailors or potential union members. Rank-and-file members rose to leadership positions early in the CSU's history, and men like Andrew Furuseth established increasingly conservative craft union attitudes to the labor organization. Union conservatism led to a close relationship between the CSU and later the SUP and the American Federation of Labor (AFL).

In 1886, the CSU participated in its first strike when the Ship Owner's Association created the "grade book" policy. This policy required sailors to present grade books containing an employment history and a list of qualifications to potential employers, but in order to obtain a grade book, sailors had to relinquish their union books.

The ship owners refused to abandon the policy and hired strike breakers, who quickly defeated the strike and forced union members to seek work elsewhere. The 1886 strike exposed the union's weaknesses, and in 1891 the CSU and the Steamship Sailors' Protective Union, founded in 1886, united to create the SUP. The new union included both coastal and deepwater Pacific sailors and strengthened the seamen's cause. The SUP supported the 1895 McGuire Act, which targeted the worst abuses against seamen, such as punishment for desertion and wage advancements and allotments, and while abuses continued, sailors had made progress. In the early twentieth century, the SUP joined the International Seamen's Union (ISU), an antimilitant craft union that maintained tight control over 19 maritime unions across the United States.

Under Furuseth's leadership, the SUP joined the City Front Federation in 1900–1901, along with San Francisco teamsters, longshoremen, engineers, marine firemen, freight handlers, and lumbermen, when employers locked the teamsters out after the teamsters refused to handle nonunion baggage. Over 26,000 men had walked off their jobs from July to October, but the strike ended in a stalemate after California Governor Henry T. Gage declared the lockout and strike over, and both sides agreed to end the struggle. The SUP broke with the City Front Federation in 1906 when the union confederation refused to support longshoremen during a lockout.

The SUP made considerable progress in 1915 when Congress passed the 1915 Seamen's Act. Senator Robert M. LaFollette pushed the bill through Congress, building on the McGuire Act's minor successes. The act included abolishing punishment for desertion in foreign ports, crews' rights to demand safety inspections on their vessels, and allowed sailors to collect damages for officer and owner neglect.

The SUP opposed U.S. entry into World War I, but the union and sailors benefited from the increase in shipping and the desperate need for more sailors to man the trans-Atlantic supply and troop convoys. After the war, Socialists, Communists, and members of the Industrial Workers of the World (IWW) gained some influence among sailors even as the postwar backlash against leftist radicals increased. These groups proved inept at securing the union's leadership however, and moderates continued to dominate the SUP. Division among sailors and employers' increasing attacks on labor in the antileftist environment caused the SUP to lose ground during the 1920s as owners used lockouts and blacklists to weaken the union.

The SUP entered the 1930s divided and broken, due largely to antiradicalism and ISU interference, but Franklin Delano Roosevelt's apparent pro-unionism inspired greater militancy among union sailors. In 1934, the SUP joined in the longshoremen's strike in San Francisco, Seattle, and Portland. On July 5, San Francisco police attempted to force open the ports, and fighting broke out in the streets. Workers burned several freight cars, and police used tear gas and guns, killing two strikers. California Governor Frank Merriam called out the National Guard to quell the strike and return order to the city. Angered by police violence and the National Guard's presence in the city, workers called a 3-day general strike in San Francisco. The strike ended on July 31 after both sides agreed to arbitration. The SUP participated in several small strikes after 1934, the most important being the 1936–1937 off-dock hiring strike. During the AFL's struggles with the CIO, the SUP leadership sided with the more conservative AFL in 1937. In 1937, the SUP was also expelled from the ISU for joining the Maritime Federation of the Pacific Coast, which united officers, seamen, longshoremen, and radio operators. Rank-and-file seamen across the nation grew weary of the ISU officials' tight control over their unions, and in the 1937–1938 labor board elections they supported the National Maritime Union (NMW), which sought to eliminate craft and regional divisions. After the labor board elections, the ISU virtually disappeared. Interunion rivalries however took a backseat after Japan attacked Pearl Harbor in December 1941.

During World War II, SUP members served in the navy and armed merchant marine, often with distinction. As with the First World War, the Second World War proved an economic and political boon for the SUP and its members. The Cold War also proved ultimately detrimental to left-wing activists, since it created another bout of overt antiradicalism, and leftist leaders and members were purged from the SUP.

After participating in the Oakland general strike in 1946 and the Wall Street employees strike in 1948, the SUP's largest postwar action occurred in 1962 when it joined with the Marine Firemen and the Cooks and Stewards in a successful strike against the Pacific Maritime Association in order to secure better benefits. Led by such activists as Harry Lundeberg, the SUP made great strides from 1950 to 1980 in securing better wages, obtaining comforts for men aboard ship (such as individual crew quarters, heating and ventilation, laundry services, and recreational facilities) and ensuring that employers followed the McGuire and 1915 Seamen's acts to the letter. Despite setbacks during Ronald Reagan's anti-union administration, the SUP's history is one of success and progress. During the 1980s, the SUP began working toward global unionization by cooperating with sailors from Asia and other Pacific Rim nations. This new global trend proved increasingly important after the Soviet Union's collapse and the ever-increasing interconnectedness of the world's markets. The SUP entered the twenty-first century poised to ensure that as trade increased and employer profits rose, the men and women who worked aboard seagoing vessels would reap the benefits of their labors.

JOHN GRIDER

References and Further Reading

Butler, John A. *Sailing on Friday: The Perilous Voyage of America's Merchant Marine.* London, UK: Brassey's, 1997.
Chapman, Paul K. *Trouble on Board: The Plight of the International Seafarers.* New York: ILR Press, 1992.
Kindleberger, Charles P. *Mariners and Markets.* New York: New York University Press, 1992.
Nelson, Bruce. *Workers on the Waterfront: Seamen, Longshoremen, and Unionism in the 1930s.* Chicago: University of Illinois Press, 1988.
Schwartz, Stephen. *Brotherhood of the Sea: A History of the Sailor's Union of the Pacific, 1885–1985.* Oxford: Transaction Books, 1986.
Standard, William L. *Merchant Seamen: A Short History of Their Struggles.* New York: International Publishers, 1947.
Taylor, Paul S. *The Sailor's Union of the Pacific.* New York: The Ronald Press Company, 1923.

Cases and Statutes Cited

McGuire Act
Seamen's Act

SAN JOAQUIN VALLEY COTTON STRIKE (1933)

In October 1933, thousands of cotton workers, predominantly Mexicans and Mexican-Americans, walked off their jobs on cotton plantations across the San Joaquin Valley. A violent 27-day strike followed, which ended in the final days of October with higher wages for the workers mandated by the federal government in what became an important test case of the New Deal's policies toward agricultural labor.

The San Joaquin Valley cotton strike was actually the largest single part of a longer strike wave that spread across California in 1933. Beginning in April in the fruit groves of the Santa Clara Valley and continuing through December, a total of 37 strikes involving 50,000 workers extended across the state into fruit, sugar beet, lettuce, grape, and cotton production, crippling large parts of California's massive agricultural industry. As the strikes continued to spread, it was apparent that migrant workers, predominantly Mexican and Mexican-American, were carrying the strike with them. Also increasingly important was the organizational work of the Cannery and Agricultural Workers' Industrial Union (CAWIU).

Work was first disrupted in the San Joaquin Valley in August when workers went on strike at the Tagus Ranch, one of the largest agricultural operations in the area, for higher wages during the peach harvest. Other growers in the area, fearful that this was the beginning of a general strike in the San Joaquin Valley, raised their wages and eventually pressured

Tagus to do the same, ending the strike and forcing the state of California and the growers to raise prevailing wages. Still this signaled the beginning of labor upheaval, and it solidified the position of the CAWIU and its locals throughout the valley.

By the time the cotton harvest began in early October, word of the strikes had spread among migrant workers who were ready to extend the walkout into the cotton fields. When wage rates were announced for the season, workers left the fields, and the union declared a strike on October 4. While workers walked off the job throughout the valley, the primary targets of the strike were the largest growers, who were able to pressure smaller operations into altering their wage scales.

In retaliation for the walkout, the large growers evicted migrant workers from their camps, hoping to starve them back to work, but the action had the opposite effect. Instead of pushing the workers back into the fields, this only strengthened the strike and left the growers with no one to pick their crops. The growers tried to import workers from Southern California and Texas but were unsuccessful in attracting sufficient numbers. Since cotton is a perishable item, this meant that the longer the strike lasted, the threat of losing all or most of a year's crop grew. As their attempts to recruit workers failed and the strike continued to spread, the growers turned instead to intimidation to combat the walkout. Vigilante groups were organized all across the valley to force the union out and to end the strike. With armed bands of growers now spread across the valley, workers also began to arm themselves, making a confrontation almost inevitable.

The confrontation came on October 10, when a group of these vigilantes arrived in the small town of Pixley to break up a union meeting. Seeing the shotguns held by the vigilantes, the crowd of workers began to cross the street to seek safety in the union hall. One of the vigilantes fired, leading to a scuffle in which one of the strikers was thrown to the ground and killed. The growers then opened fire on the crowd as they hurried into the union hall. When it was all over, three Mexican nationals were dead. With this escalation of the strike to open warfare, strikebreakers abandoned the fields, leaving the growers without even the skeleton crew they were forced to work with before October 10. In addition the federal governments of the United States and Mexico moved in to try and find solutions to the escalating tension and violence.

In 1933, the New Deal was still in its infancy and policy makers had yet to determine the extent to which they would deal with issues of agricultural workers. Rural labor had been left out of the National Industrial Recovery Act, and would also be ignored by subsequent legislation, such as the National Labor Relations Act (Wagner Act) in 1935. But in 1933, the federal government acted to bring an end to the strike by making the growers compromise with the workers and the union. George Creel, the western administrator of the National Recovery Administration, stepped in and threatened to withhold crop loans and payments from the Agricultural Adjustment Administration (AAA) if the growers refused to negotiate in good faith. With federal pressure and the ever-looming threat of losing an entire cotton harvest, the growers agreed to increase wages to 75 cents an hour. When the union balked at this agreement, wanting to hold out for more concessions from the growers, Creel ended federal relief to the workers and threatened to send one thousand workers from Southern California, leading the workers to accept the offer, thus ending the strike.

While the federal government never recognized the collective-bargaining rights of the CAWIU or the agriculture workers they represented, in this instance George Creel gave the union unofficial recognition that forced the growers to arbitrate. It is now clear that the San Joaquin Valley cotton strike marked the federal government's most sustained and successful effort to alter labor relations within agriculture. The San Joaquin Valley strike served to redouble the efforts of the organized agricultural interests to keep the federal government out of their relations with labor.

JOHN WEBER

References and Further Reading

Guerin-Gonzalez, Camille. *Mexican Workers and American Dreams: Immigration, Repatriation, and California Farm Labor, 1900–1939*. New Brunswick, NJ: Rutgers University Press, 1994.
McWilliams, Carey. *Factories in the Field: The Story of Migratory Farm Labor in California*. Berkeley: University of California Press, 1939.
Taylor, Paul. *On the Ground in the Thirties*. Salt Lake City, UT: Peregrine Smith Books, 1983.
Weber, Devra. *Dark Sweat, White Gold: California Farm Workers, Cotton, and the New Deal*. Berkeley: University of California Press, 1994.

Cases and Statutes Cited

National Industrial Recovery Act
National Labor Relations Act

See also **Agricultural Adjustment Act; California; Cannery and Agricultural Workers Industrial Union; Immigration Restriction; Mexican and Mexican-American Workers; Migrant Farmworkers; National Industrial Recovery Act; National Labor Relations Board**

SCHNEIDERMAN, ROSE (1882–1972)

Only 4 feet 9 inches tall, with flaming red hair, this diminutive Polish-Jewish immigrant was one of the most important figures in the history of the American labor movement. "The woman worker needs bread," Schneiderman (1882–1972) famously said in 1911. "But she needs roses too." Shortened to bread and roses, Schneiderman's best-known line became the rallying cry for the early twentieth century labor movement, symbolizing the desire of millions of industrial workers both for the basics—decent wages, safe working conditions, and reasonable hours—and for the extras that make life worth living, such as books, theater, art, and recreation. For more than half a century—as an officer of the United Cap and Hat Makers' Union, president of both the New York and National Women's Trade Union Leagues (NYWTUL), and as an official in state and federal agencies—Schneiderman worked tirelessly to improve the lives of working people.

Schneiderman possessed legendary skill as an orator. From 1904 through the 1950s, the militant trade unionist and women's rights advocate spoke on street corners from atop soapboxes, in lecture halls, and over the radio, impressing and persuading many who did not initially share her political views. In an age when political oratory was a leading form of entertainment, many described her as the most moving and effective speaker they had ever heard. Her powers as a speaker did not earn her universal acclaim. In the years after World War I, when the United States was in the grip of a national backlash against radicalism, enemies warned of her potential influence on the masses, dubbing her "the Red Rose of anarchy." Still Schneiderman's warmth and ability to persuade listeners would ultimately provide her entree into the highest circles of political power.

A close friend and advisor to Franklin and Eleanor Roosevelt, Schneiderman taught them much of what they knew about working people. Roosevelt's Labor Secretary Frances Perkins would later say that it was as a result of FDR's long conversations with Rose Schneiderman that he could plausibly present himself as someone who knew and understood the living and working conditions of America's industrial laborers. The only woman on FDR's National Recovery Administration Labor Advisory Board, Schneiderman played a key role in shaping the landmark legislation of the New Deal: the National Labor Relations Act, the Social Security Act and the Fair Labor Standards Act. As president of the New York Women's Trade Union League from 1917–1949, and as New York State secretary of labor from 1937–1943, Schneiderman also helped make New York State a laboratory for progressive labor and social welfare legislation.

Schneiderman identified strongly with Jewish causes throughout her career. Her speeches and letter-writing campaigns mobilized the resources of the labor movement and of famous refugees of Nazism, among them Albert Einstein, to help Jews escape from Europe during the 1930s and 1940s. During this period she also helped to raise funds to establish the Leon Blum Colony, a labor-Zionist settlement in pre-1948 Palestine.

Rose Schneiderman was born on April 16, 1882, into an observant Jewish family in Saven, Poland. Her father Samuel was a tailor. Her mother Deborah, like so many Jewish housewives in Eastern Europe during those years, did whatever she could to help support her little family. She took in sewing, baked *challah*, sewed uniforms for the Russian Army, treated the sick with herbal medicines she made herself, and tended bar at a local inn. Both of Schneiderman's parents were strong believers in educating girls. When Rose was four, her parents caused a stir in town by enrolling her in a *kheydr* (religious school). At six they moved to the city of Chelm so that Rose could attend a public school.

Rose was nine when the family immigrated to New York in 1890. She was 11 when her father died of meningitis, leaving Deborah pregnant and with three children to support. The bereft mother did the best she could, taking in boarders, sewing, and washing for neighbors and even working as a building superintendent—doing repairs in exchange for a free apartment for her family. For a time she was forced to place her three children in an orphanage. Still when she had saved enough to take them back home to live with her, Deborah Schneiderman insisted that her children stay in school rather than finding jobs themselves. She worked nights so that Rose could attend school during the days. But in 1895, when Deborah Schneiderman lost her night job, 13-year-old Rose was forced to leave school for good to help support her siblings.

Deborah Schneiderman wanted Rose to find a respectable job at a department store. She feared that factory work would sully her daughter's reputation and make it difficult for Rose to find a decent husband. The single mother who at times was forced to feed her children on charity food baskets was determined to see her four children make it into the middle class. Perhaps self-conscious about a childhood that was poor even by Lower East Side standards, Rose Schneiderman would latch onto her mother's obsession with respectability. That preoccupation lasted throughout her life, shaping her political choices, and ultimately drawing her away from immigrant socialism to an alliance with the Democratic party.

But respectability did not pay the rent. Then as now blue-collar jobs paid better than pink-collar retail work. After 3 years as a salesgirl, Schneiderman asked a friend to train her as a cap maker. Though her wages improved dramatically, Schneiderman chafed at the gender hierarchy she found in the garment industry. The best-paying, highest skilled positions were reserved for men, while women were concentrated in the worst-paying, least-satisfying jobs. When she complained several older women in the shop began to tutor her in the fundamentals of socialist trade unionism. They and the increasingly militant young Schneiderman interpreted that ideology through a decidedly feminist lens.

At 21 Schneiderman organized her first union local, convincing the women in her shop to join the fledgling United Cloth Hat and Cap Makers' Union. The leadership of the union, mostly East European Jewish immigrant men, were at first skeptical of the ability of young women to organize. But in spite of themselves they were impressed by Schneiderman. Within a year they and the shop-floor cap makers Schneiderman had organized made her the first woman elected to national office in an American labor union.

In 1905, Schneiderman organized a general strike of New York's cap makers. This brought her to the attention of the leaders of the NYWTUL, an alliance of middle-class reformers created to provide support to female workers attempting to unionize.

Schneiderman's talents as an organizer and speaker won her election as vice-president of the NYWTUL. German-Jewish philanthropist Irene Lewisohn offered to pay for Schneiderman to attend college, but reluctantly the young cap maker declined, saying that she could not in good conscience accept a privilege afforded to so few working women. She did however gladly accept Lewisohn's offer to pay her salary as an organizer. In 1908, Schneiderman became chief organizer for the NYWTUL, over the next few years helping to galvanize a wave of unrest and strikes among female workers that by the end of World War I brought 40% of all women in the garment industry into trade unions.

She began with a furious burst of organizing in Manhattan garment shops that laid the groundwork for the 1909 uprising of New York shirtwaist makers, the largest strike of female workers to that time. That strike, galvanized and led largely by East European Jewish women, breathed life into the tiny International Ladies' Garment Workers' Union (ILWGU) and gave the NYWTUL a national reputation. But it also generated tensions between working-class Jews like Schneiderman and her fellow organizer Pauline Newman and the middle-class Christian women, who in those years still dominated the league. League Secretary Helen Marot described Jewish women as too fervent, too militant, and too demanding and urged the league board to devote their resources toward American girls. In the years leading up to World War I, Schneiderman would resign and rejoin the league numerous times.

From 1914 to 1916, Schneiderman worked as general organizer for the ILGWU. However Schneiderman felt that the male leadership distrusted and undermined her efforts, and in 1917, she resigned that job as well to become chair of the Industrial Section of the New York Woman Suffrage party.

Schneiderman had begun working for female suffrage as early as 1907, speaking at rallies for the Equality League of Self-Supporting Women, whose membership was largely made up of professional women. In 1911, Schneiderman helped found the Wage Earners' League for Woman Suffrage—the first suffrage organization made up primarily of industrial laborers. In 1912, she embarked on a speaking tour through the Midwest to promote state-based suffrage referenda. Her campaign on behalf of the Industrial Section of the Woman Suffrage party in 1917 was instrumental in helping secure the vote for New York women that year.

By the time the United States entered World War I, Schneiderman was a nationally known figure in labor, feminist, and socialist politics. In 1917, Schneiderman was elected president of the New York WTUL, a post she would hold for 32 years. In 1920, she ran for the U.S. Senate on the Labor party ticket. Although she did not win (and had not expected to), Schneiderman used the campaign to articulate an industrial feminist agenda. Her broad platform called for the construction of nonprofit housing for workers, improved neighborhood schools, publicly owned power utilities and staple food markets, and publicly funded health and unemployment insurance for all Americans. During the late 1910s and early 1920s, Schneiderman was labeled a subversive by conservative politicians and was investigated both by New York State and federal agencies.

In 1921, as part of her foray into reform politics, Eleanor Roosevelt joined the New York WTUL. The immensely privileged society lady took an immediate liking to the sharp-tongued league president, and the two began a lifelong friendship. By the mid-1920s, Schneiderman was a regular guest both at Eleanor Roosevelt's New York apartment and at Franklin's Hyde Park estate. In 1926, Schneiderman was elected president of the National WTUL (she ran the league until her retirement in 1950). When FDR became New York governor in 1928, the immigrant labor activist became a close advisor.

In 1933, FDR brought Schneiderman to Washington as part of his National Recovery Administration. Four years later she became secretary of labor for New York State. In both posts Schneiderman fought race-based inequities in minimum wage legislation, pushed to extend social security benefits to domestic workers, and lobbied for equal pay and comparable worth laws to erase the gap in pay between men and women in the workforce. Still active in the WTUL, Schneiderman also tried to use state legislation to aid union drives among hotel maids, beauty parlor workers, and waitresses. During those same years, Schneiderman threw herself into efforts to rescue European Jews and to resettle them in either the United States or Palestine.

Schneiderman retired from public life in 1950, but she remained close with the women of the WTUL circle who had been both her professional and personal network throughout her life. Her partner of two decades, Irish immigrant labor activist Maud Swartz, died in 1937. Schneiderman never again entered into a long-term relationship. Schneiderman died on August 11, 1972, at the age of 90.

For more than 50 years, Schneiderman organized women to fight not just for economic independence, but also for the right to have meaning and beauty in their lives. Long before the women's movement of the 1970s declared that the "personal is political," Schneiderman's life and work embodied that philosophy. She attacked sex segregation in the workplace, tried to organize domestic and service workers as well as industrial laborers, and called for state regulation of food and housing prices as well as wages and hours. Recognizing that women's responsibilities to home and family were, and should be seen as, an inextricable part of the working-class struggle, Schneiderman called both for comparable-worth laws and government-subsidized day care, for workers' health care and health insurance for all mothers.

Schneiderman died just as the 1970s' women's movement was gaining strength. But many of her ideas were taken up by that movement, and they are still being debated in courtrooms, legislatures, and classrooms today. Those ideas and dreams, as much as the government protections that millions of American workers have enjoyed since the mid-1930s, are the legacy of Schneiderman.

ANNELISE ORLECK

References and Further Reading

Kessler-Harris, Alice. "Rose Schneiderman." In *American Labor Leaders*, edited by Warren Van Tine and Melvyn Dubofsky. 1987.
Orleck, Annelise. *Common Sense and a Little Fire: Women and Working-Class Politics in the United States*. 1995.
Schneiderman, Rose, and Lucy Goldthwaite. *All for One*. 1967.

Cases and Statutes Cited

Fair Labor Standards Act
National Labor Relations Act
Social Security Act

See also **International Ladies' Garment Workers' Union; Newman, Pauline M.; Women's Trade Union League**

SCOTTSBORO CASE

One of the most infamous and celebrated racial spectacles of the 1930s, the Scottsboro case, began on March 25, 1931, with a brawl between black and white hoboes on a freight train moving through northern Alabama. The blacks prevailed, expelling a number of whites from the train. One of the whites reported the incident to the stationmaster in Stevenson, Alabama, who contacted authorities further down the line in Scottsboro, Alabama, but the train had just left. The word reached the next town of Paint Rock, where a posse was deputized and ordered to apprehend all the African-Americans on the train and bring them back to Scottsboro. The deputized men searched the train and discovered nine young African-American men; they also discovered a white man and—to their considerable surprise—two young white women, Victoria Price and Ruby Bates, dressed in men's clothing, a mode of dress often adopted by women who rode the trains during the Depression.

Of the nine young men who quickly became known as the Scottsboro boys, four of them—Roy and Andy Wright, Eugene Williams, and Heywood Patterson—know each other from their home town of Chattanooga, Tennessee. Clarence Norris, Ozie Powell, Charlie Weems, Olen Montgomery, and Willie Roberson had come from different towns in Georgia and were thrown together on the train by circumstances. Olen Montgomery was completely blind in one eye and had very poor vision in the other; Willie Roberson was so debilitated by untreated venereal diseases that he could walk only with the assistance of a cane. Nonetheless within hours of their arrest, all nine of them were charged with rape.

Two weeks later on April 9, 1931, after four separate trials conducted in rapid succession before four separate all-white juries in the mountain Alabama town of Scottsboro, eight of the Scottsboro boys were found guilty as charged; presiding judge Alfred E. Hawkins immediately sentenced them to death.

The ninth defendant, 13-year-old Roy Wright, was sentenced to life imprisonment.

The Communist party USA, which had begun its first serious effort to organize in the Deep South in early 1930, had monitored the Scottsboro case from the beginning. From their base in Chattanooga, Tennessee, James Allen and Helen Marcy, editors of the Communist party's *Southern Worker*, alerted the New York office of the International Labor Defense (ILD). Communist party and ILD organizers attended the pretrial hearings and the trials. Seeking to mobilize pubic opinion, they sent pre-emptive telegrams to Judge Hawkins and the governor of Alabama, warning them against "legal lynching" and demanding that the defendants be protected from lynch mobs. Immediately after the verdicts were issued, the Communist party USA published a lengthy statement in support of the Scottsboro defendants in the *Daily Worker*; simultaneously, the ILD voted to defend them.

In the meantime the Chattanooga Minister's Alliance had appealed to the National Association for the Advancement of Colored People (NAACP) for assistance, but the NAACP responded cautiously, seeking more information before proceeding. Right after the Scottsboro verdicts, there were demonstrations of outrage in the United States and abroad. The ILD sprang into action by locating the families of the defendants, offering legal support, and other assistance. The NAACP officially entered the case in early May 1931, when Walter White, executive director of the organization, visited the Scottsboro boys at Kilby prison, trying to convince them that the NAACP should take the responsibility for their defense. These events set the stage for a bitter, acrimonious, and divisive public struggle between the ILD and the Communist party and the NAACP for the control of the case, with the ILD and the Communist party castigating the NAACP for its reformist ideology and legalistic tactics, and the NAACP accusing the ILD and the Communist party of recklessly endangering the lives of the Scottsboro boys by their emphasis on mass demonstrations and other extrajudicial measures in their efforts to free them. The bitterness engendered by this conflict decisively marked the early years of the Scottsboro campaign and would shape accounts of the case for many years to come.

Having persuaded the Scottsboro boys and their families to accept their support, the Communist party and the ILD launched a two-pronged offensive on their behalf. The ILD assigned Communist party and ILD lawyer Joseph Brodsky the task of pursuing its legal strategy in the early years of the campaign, filing for a stay of execution, pending appeals to the Alabama Supreme Court. Although the Alabama Supreme Court affirmed the convictions of seven of the Scottsboro defendants in March 1932, it reversed the conviction of Eugene Williams on the grounds that he was a juvenile at the time of his conviction. In May 1932, the Supreme Court agreed to review the Scottsboro convictions, thus setting the stage for its historic reversal of them in its November 1932 decision *Powell v. Alabama*, ruling that the Scottsboro boys had been denied counsel and therefore had suffered a clear violation of due process. *Powell v. Alabama* set the stage for the second round of Scottsboro trials in Decatur, Alabama, in March 1933.

In addition to their legal strategies, the ILD and the Communist party vigorously pursued the defense of the Scottsboro boys on the world stage, with street marches, large protest meetings, letter-writing campaigns, postcards and telegrams. Not only community leaders and union organizers joined the campaign, but many well-known artists, musicians, writers, and scholars as well. The Scottsboro mothers were enlisted to travel on national speaking tours on behalf of their sons. One of them, Ada Wright, the mother of two of the Scottsboro defendants, Roy and Andy Wright, toured Europe with J. Louis Engdahl, the national secretary of the ILD, on the eve of the Nazi take-over of Germany. News about the Scottsboro case outpaced European coverage of other events in the United States during the early years of the case. Images of the incarcerated Scottsboro boys circulated throughout the world, and they were the frequent subjects of songs, poetry, plays, fiction, political cartoons, and works of art.

For the March 1933 Scottsboro trials, the ILD secured the services of one of the most renowned lawyers in the country, Samuel S. Leibowitz. Buttressed by the dramatic repudiation of the rape charges by one of the two female accusers, Ruby Bates, Leibowitz relentlessly and aggressively sought to discredit the claims of Victoria Price. Nonetheless the all-white jury quickly found Heywood Patterson, the first of the Scottsboro boys to be retried, guilty and sentenced him to death. The presiding judge, James E. Horton, suspended Patterson's sentence in view of Joseph Brodsky's motion for a retrial however, then suspended the remaining trials indefinitely. Several months later in a dramatic and unexpected ruling, Judge Horton overturned Heywood Patterson's conviction and ordered a new trial—an act for which he subsequently lost his re-election bid for the judgeship he held.

A second Decatur trial began in November 1933, concluding with another conviction and death sentence for Heywood Patterson and a second conviction for Clarence Norris. The Alabama Supreme Court affirmed both convictions in June 1934. Several months later a major rift developed between Samuel

Leibowitz and the ILD when Leibowitz learned that two lawyers associated with the ILD had attempted to bribe Victoria Price. Leibowitz subsequently formed the American Scottsboro Committee, with the support of established black leaders and some white liberals and clergymen, in 1934.

In 1935, the United States Supreme Court agreed to review the convictions of Patterson and Norris, paving the way for the second major decision involving the Scottsboro case: In April 1935, *Norris v. Alabama* reversed the conviction of Norris (and effectively of Patterson), ruling that the exclusion of African-Americans from jury duty in Alabama deprived black defendants of the equal protection guaranteed by the Fourteenth Amendment.

In November 1935, the Jackson County, Alabama, grand jury, augmented by one black member, reindicted the Scottsboro boys. One month later in the spirit of the "popular front" that now characterized the political outlook of the Communist party, it joined with representatives of the NAACP. The American Civil Liberties Union, the League for Industrial Democracy, and the Methodist Federation for Social Service came together to form the Scottsboro Defense Committee—an organization that agreed on legal means, as opposed to mass organization, as the primary means to achieve freedom for the Scottsboro buys.

Meanwhile the State of Alabama pressed ahead with its determination to prosecute the Scottsboro boys. In January 1936, Heywood Patterson was tried for the fourth time and found guilty; this time however his sentence was 75 years. During the same month another Scottsboro defendant, Ozie Powell, slashed the neck of a deputy sheriff while being transported from the Decatur courthouse to the Birmingham jail. Powell was shot in the head; he survived, but suffered permanent brain damage.

In January 1937, the Alabama Supreme Court affirmed Patterson's most recent conviction In July 1937, Clarence Norris was tried for the third time, convicted, and sentenced to death. Andy Wright was convicted for the second time and sentenced to 99 years; Charlie Weems was convicted for the second time and sentenced to 75 years. Ozie Powell was convicted of assaulting the deputy sheriff and sentenced to 20 years. In a dramatic turnabout however, the Alabama authorities worked out an arrangement with the Scottsboro Defense Committee that led to the release of Eugene Williams, Olen Montgomery, Willie Roberson, and Roy Wright.

The remaining five Scottsboro defendants languished in prison, as the Scottsboro case periodically floated up and receded in public consciousness during the late 1930s and the 1940s. Charlie Weems was released in 1943, Ozie Powell in 1946. Clarence Norris and Andy Wright finally gained their freedom in 1944; Haywood Patterson escaped from Kilby prison in 1948. Taken together, the Scottsboro boys served a total of 130 years in prison, and their lives were destroyed by it.

Still the campaign to free the Scottsboro boys must be seen as a watershed moment in twentieth-century racial politics. As a campaign organized and orchestrated by the international Communist movement, it touched the lives of countless people, spanning the British Empire, Europe, Latin America, Asia, and the African continent. It placed the issue of racial injustice on the national and international agenda in ways that were unprecedented in the twentieth century. In the context of the United States, the sharp debates about the strategies and tactics necessary to confront effectively the legacy of racism in the United States, the appeal of the Scottsboro campaign to the ideals of interracial empathy and solidarity, and the insistence on mass organizing across racial lines all laid the groundwork for what would become the modern civil rights movement—as did the two landmark Supreme Court decisions that were a direct result of the Scottsboro case.

JAMES A. MILLER

References and Further Reading

Allen, James S. "Organizing in the Depression South: A Communist's Memoir." *Nature, Science, and Thought: A Journal of Dialectical and Historical Materialism* 13, 1 (2000).

Carter, Dan T. *Scottsboro: A Tragedy of the American South*. Baton Rouge: Louisiana State University Press, 1979. (revised edition)

Goodman, James. *Stories of Scottsboro*. New York: Pantheon, 1994.

Miller, James A., Susan D. Pennybacker, and Eve Rosenhaft. "Mother Ada Wright and the International Campaign to Free the Scottsboro Boys, 1931–1934." *The American Historical Review* 106, 2 (Apr. 2001): 387–430.

Murray, Hugh T., Jr. "The NAACP versus the Communist Party: The Scottsboro Rape Case, 1931–1932." *Phylon* 28 (1967).

Cases and Statutes Cited

Norris v. Alabama
Powell v. Alabama

SELLINS, FANNIE (1865?–1919)
President, United Garment Workers of America Local 67

Fannie Sellins is perhaps most widely known and celebrated because of the manner in which she died.

From 1909 to 1919, however, her life was dedicated to the cause of labor organization, a cause that carried her across the United States and placed her in the center of the turmoil that was American labor relations for that decade.

Little is known of Sellins's early life. In the 1910 census, she is listed as living in St. Louis, Missouri, a 45-year-old, widowed head-of-household with four children, three of them living at home. A dressmaker by trade, Sellins worked in her rented home in a St. Louis working-class neighborhood. She also served as president of the United Garment Workers of America (UGWA) Local 67, which had approximately 400 female workers.

On September 13, 1909, the clothing company of Marx and Haas locked out 1,000 of its employees, members of UGWA Locals 23 and 67. The company was possibly seeking to institute an open shop. The UGWA declared a national boycott of Marx and Haas, and Sellins began to make local, and then nationwide, tours to publicize the boycott and seek support for the striking workers. Highlights of the early part of the tour included visits to Chicago, where Sellins and a companion were assisted by Jane Addams of Hull-House in Chicago, and before the annual convention of the United Brotherhood of Carpenters and Joiners in Des Moines, Iowa. In October 1911, the UGWA and the company of Marx and Haas signed a closed-shop agreement with wage issues to be settled by negotiations.

Shortly thereafter in December 1911, the UGWA local attempted to organize the workers of the Schwab Clothing Company and again, Sellins went on a national speaking tour to urge the boycott of Schwab Company products. Seeking support at the 1912 convention of the United Mine Workers of America (UMWA) in Indianapolis, Indiana, Sellins made a plea that prefigured her involvement with mine workers, appealing for "a bond of sympathy" between mine and garment workers.

The labor confrontation between Schwab and the UGWA local intensified in the summer of 1912. In July 1912, UGWA Local 67 removed Sellins from its presidency in what one newspaper described as a "little family row." The Schwab strike and boycott were not supported by the national leadership of the UGWA because the federal court system had ruled union-organized boycotts as illegal. In August 1912, the UGWA reversed the decision of Local 67 and reinstated Sellins as president of the union, and the incoming general executive board appointed her organizer and labor promoter. Sellins's victory was bittersweet however, as she later remarked, "I have no home. My home was broke up during the big strike in St. Louis."

Sellins was to remain in St. Louis for another year, during which she entered the political arena. In the spring of 1913, the Socialist party of St. Louis nominated her for a seat on the board of education, along with Kate Richards O'Hare, the well-known socialist lecturer and organizer. Sellins received 6,826 votes, slightly less than the 6,896 received by O'Hare, and about 550 more than the socialist candidate for mayor.

Sometime in the late summer of 1913, while lobbying for the garment workers in West Virginia and Pittsburgh, Pennsylvania, Sellins's attention shifted to coal miners. In September 1913, she joined the effort of the UMWA to organize the West Virginia–Pittsburgh Company mine at Colliers, West Virginia. Sellins's activities with the striking miners were one of social welfare, the provision of clothing and food, and providing nursing services to the stricken families of miners. Her reasons for doing so were obscure. Sellins noted that "I couldn't tell you how I come to be among them (the miners).... I don't know myself."

The West Virginia–Pittsburgh Company mine in Colliers was located near the Hitchman Coal and Coke Company Mine, near Wheeling, West Virginia. In 1907, Judge Alston G. Dayton, of the U.S. Circuit Court for northern West Virginia, issued a restraining order preventing the UMWA from organizing the Hitchman mines. In January 1913, under this injunction, Dayton found the UMWA guilty of interfering with the Hitchman Company's individual employment contracts requiring its employees not to join a union and declared that the UMWA was an unlawful organization in restraint of trade. On September 14, 1913, the UMWA initiated a strike against the West–Virginia Coal Company mine at Colliers. The company also maintained that its individual employment contracts prohibited employees from joining the UMWA.

On September 29, Dayton issued a restraining order, repeating nearly verbatim his Hitchman injunction. After a mine guard was shot during a confrontation in October, Dayton issued a temporary injunction to replace the restraining order on December 1 and issued a contempt of court citation against 11 UMWA defendants, including UMWA organizer James Oates and Sellins. Dayton sentenced the defendants to up to 60 days in jail and personally chastised Sellins "...not to emulate Mother Jones."

On December 3, the UMWA held a rally in Wellsburg, West Virginia. At the rally Sellins defiantly displayed her oratorical skills, noting the poverty of the striking families in Colliers, and speaking of the children, "...that if it be wrong to put shoes upon those little feet, then I will continue to do wrong as long as I have hands and feet to crawl to Colliers."

On March 17, 1914, Sellins and the other strike leaders were found guilty of contempt of court and sentenced to 6 months in jail. Shortly thereafter the Fourth Federal Circuit Court of Appeals reversed Dayton's Hitchman injunction of January 1913. The appeals court also remanded the Colliers case to Dayton.

As a partial result of the Hitchman case being overruled, the West Virginia–Pittsburgh Coal Company and the UMWA reached a settlement in June 1914, but it did not include a contract for the UMWA. Bond was raised for the defendants, and they were released in July 1914, but Dayton again found the defendants guilty of inciting violence in April 1915. The court of appeals affirmed Dayton's decision in May 1916, and the U.S. Supreme Court refused to hear the case. In December 1916, based on an appeal from the defendants, President Woodrow Wilson commuted the sentences of the defendants to time served.

On December 10, 1917, a divided U.S. Supreme Court issued its *Hitchman Coal and Coke Company v. Mitchell* (John Mitchell, president of the UMWA) decision. The decision ruled that the Hitchman contract was valid and that injunctions were proper in preventing third-party interference in the contractual relationship between owners and employees. Until 1932, and the passage of the Norris-La Guardia Act, this ruling was part of established labor law.

After receiving President Wilson's clemency, Sellins in 1917 continued her organizing work in the Allegheny and Kiskiminetas River valleys in western Pennsylvania, known as the Alle-Kiske, near Pittsburgh and not far from Colliers. No longer just providing assistance to the families of striking miners, she was active in the front of the picket lines and was known for convincing potential strikebreakers not to work as replacements.

The entry of the United States into World War I and a subsequent mobilization brought a year-and-a-half of peace to the region, during which the bituminous coal operations signed a basic national agreement with the UMWA. With the Armistice of November 1918, however, came increased tension between coal operators and miners as the operators sought to escape government labor controls and end recognition of the UMWA and miners sought permanent recognition of the UMWA and increases in pay. In the spring of 1919, operators abrogated the 1917 agreement. Sellins again stepped into the fray taking place in western Pennsylvania.

On July 21, 1919, employees of Allegheny Coal and Coke Company, a subsidiary mine owned by the Allegheny Steel Company of Brackenridge, Pennsylvania, walked out on strike. Despite Sellins's efforts the company was able to hire other strikebreakers. Sellins continued to work toward preventing the collapse of the strike and also tried to organize unskilled workers in local steel mills.

On August 26, Sellins witnessed the beating of a miner by a deputy. Having photographs taken of the deputy who beat the miner, Sellins and a group of miners, women, and children moved toward Brackenridge to file a complaint. As the group began to move, a fight ensued between a miner, Joseph Starzelski, and deputies. The miner was killed, and Sellins, trying to get beyond a fence bordering the road, was gunned down, a bullet entering the left side of her face, and coming out her forehead. An Allegheny County Coroner's Jury ruled in September 1919 that Sellins' death was justifiable homicide. Both the Federal Bureau of Investigation and the U.S. Conciliation Service investigated the circumstances of Sellins's death, but it was considered beyond the purview of the federal government. In June 1924, three deputies were indicted for the killing but were acquitted.

Sellins and Starzelski were buried in Union Cemetery on August 29, 1919. An allegorical statue marks the grave. During the steel strike of 1919, small stickers of a postmortem photo of Sellins were distributed among steel workers. On seeing one of the stickers, Mother Jones commented, "I often wonder it wasn't me they got. Whenever I look at a picture of her I wonder it's not me lying on the ground."

Perhaps Mother Jones's comment was more than an acknowledgement of the dangers of the work of a labor organizer but instead a comment on the hardship of life as an organizer in early twentieth-century America. For Sellins was not always successful in her organizing activities, and at the same time, she lost her home in St. Louis, her freedom in West Virginia, and her life in Pennsylvania. To the end however, she was dedicated to her work as labor organizer.

JAMES G. CASSEDY

References and Further Reading

Cassedy, James. "A Bond of Sympathy: The Life and Tragic Death of Fannie Sellins." *Labor's Heritage* 4, 4 (winter 1992): 34–47.
Gibbons, Russell W. *Celebrating the Life of Fannie Sellins.* Pittsburgh, 1990.
Lunt, Richard D. *Law and Order vs. the Miners: West Virginia, 1907–1923.* Hamden, CT, 1979.
Meyerhuber, Carl J., Jr. "The Alle-Kiski Coal Wars, 1913–1919." *Western Pennsylvania Historical Magazine* 63 (July 1980).

Cases and Statutes Cited

Hitchman Coal and Coke Company v. Mitchell
Norris-La Guardia Act

SERVICE EMPLOYEES' INTERNATIONAL UNION

Having more than doubled its membership since 1980, the Service Employees' International Union (SEIU) is the fastest growing union in the American Federation of Labor-Congress of Industrial Organizations (AFL-CIO). In its four divisions—health care (the largest division, with 870,000 members), public employees, building service, and industrial and allied—the SEIU represents some 1.8 million working people across the United States, Canada, and Puerto Rico. Members of the SEIU work for public and private employers as, for example, nurses, doctors, building cleaners, police and corrections officers, librarians, social workers, and ballpark employees. From the union's earliest days, the SEIU has had a diverse membership. Today women are in the majority and some 20% of union members are African-American.

Early Days

The SEIU's origins go back to 1902 when janitors working in Chicago's apartment houses and downtown office buildings successfully organized a union. Three years later this first effort collapsed due to internal dissension and intense employer opposition. William F. Quesse, one of the union's early founders, led a second organizing campaign in 1912, launching Federal Union 14332, which represented Chicago's apartment, or flat, janitors. By 1917, the Chicago Flat Janitors' local had grown into a multiracial union with 6,000 members and had signed a citywide contract. Small locals among janitors in cities including Philadelphia, Boston, Seattle, and San Francisco had also been established. In April 1921, the Chicago union became Local 1 of the AFL-chartered Building Service Employees' International Union (BSEIU) and Quesse became the new union's first president. Most of the BSEIU's seven founding locals had fewer than 150 members, leaving Local 1 dominant.

Also in April 1921, Quesse and nine members of Local 1 were indicted in Chicago's circuit court on charges of conspiracy, extortion, bombing, and malicious mischief. Their trial ended in a hung jury, but a second trial resulted in guilty verdicts mainly on the conspiracy charge. It was not uncommon in the 1920s for union leaders to be convicted of criminal conspiracy for engaging in legitimate organizing and strike actions. Eventually a well-organized petition campaign that included some 60 letters from members of Chicago's real estate board, as well as strong support from Mayor William Hale Thompson, the city's Republican political boss and a union ally, resulted in a

pardon from the governor of Illinois. Quesse died in 1927 and was temporarily replaced as BSEIU president by Oscar Nelson, president of Local 1. At the international's next convention in March 1928, Nelson gave way to Jerry Horan, who had replaced him as president of Local 1. On the eve of the Great Depression, the BSEIU numbered some 7,000 members in 20 small locals across the nation.

Growing up in the 1930s

With the nation engulfed in hard times, many BSEIU locals failed, and even those that survived were forced to accept pay cuts as nonunion workers flooded the labor market. In 1929, to promote greater cooperation and unity among union locals, the international began publishing a journal, *Public Safety*. Despite the economic despair, international union membership rose by 10,000 during the Hoover administration. Nevertheless for the BSEIU and for the labor movement in general, the election of Franklin Delano Roosevelt as president in 1932 resulted in a fundamental turnaround in their fortunes. During Roosevelt's first term, the BSEIU doubled in size to reach a membership of 40,000. At the center of the international union's growth during these years was the emergence of a militant building trades union movement in New York City, spearheaded by the formation in 1934 of Local 32B.

By 1933, conditions among New York's building trades workers had reached bottom. Janitors had no paid holidays, vacations, life insurance, hospitalization, or other benefits. Yet even though labor was weak, the firing in March 1934 of Tom Young, a native West Indian elevator operator active in an independent union, stirred his 25 fellow workers to go on strike. Aided by James J. Bambrick, an organizer for the Typographers' Union, the strikers secured Young's reinstatement, and Young, using the momentum gained by this victory, helped establish Local 32B. Bambrick was elected the union's first president and Young its vice-president.

On November 1, 1934, Bambrick led 32B members out on strike against owners of buildings in New York's garment center. Three days later Mayor Fiorello LaGuardia helped negotiate a temporary agreement that granted the union's demand for a closed shop; all other basic issues were to be arbitrated. The Curran award issued in February 1935 maintained the closed shop, improved wage scales, and instituted maximum hours. The next year contract negotiations stalled after employers refused to meet with the union's negotiating committee. A 17-day strike marked by violence led the mayor to again intervene. An arbitrated settlement was reached that increased minimum wages but left hours the same. By 1936, although the number of building-service locals in New York had grown to include a 32K, most of the city's BSEIU members belonged to 32B.

The BSEIU's spectacular growth in the 1930s appears to have attracted the interest of organized crime. George Scalise, a former president of a Teamsters garage washers' local was appointed the BSEIU's fifth vice-president in 1935 by BSEIU President Jerry Horan. When Horan died unexpectedly in 1937, Scalise was chosen to replace him as president. Within the BSEIU Charles Hardy, Local 9's president, led the West Coast unions in opposition to Scalise. For his efforts Hardy faced suspension from office and an attempt to take control of his local. In April 1940, after a series of newspaper articles by the syndicated journalist Westbrook Pegler drew nationwide attention to Scalise's ties to organized crime, New York Attorney General Thomas E. Dewey's racket bureau indicted the BSEIU president. Convicted of embezzlement and forgery, Scalise was sentenced to from 10–20 years in prison.

Modernization

Two weeks after Scalise's indictment, the BSEIU annual convention in Atlantic City, New Jersey, elected William McFetridge, a flat janitor since 1923 and Quesse's nephew, to lead the union. To McFetridge the crisis confronting the union resulted from its weak internal controls and loose administration. McFetridge believed that New Deal legislation like the National Labor Relations Act not only helped sustain the labor movement but also imposed responsibilities on unions to adopt more businesslike practices. To this end McFetridge set out to modernize the administrative structure of the BSEIU.

Union leaders began by upgrading record keeping. The same 1940 convention that elected McFetridge president amended the BSEIU constitution to require the international to send quarterly financial reports to all unions. Local unions were mandated to send in membership lists and to report when new members paid their per capita dues. In 1942, McFetridge replaced *Public Safety* with *Building Service Employee*, a larger monthly publication that would be produced by the union's research department, itself newly created to provide the necessary wage, hours, and other information required by the War Labor Board. McFetridge also moved to distance the BSEIU from identification with organized crime by

suspending any local that appeared to be involved with racketeers.

Looking to professionalize union organizing, the BSEIU also developed regionally based "joint councils" that by providing trained, skilled people, and pooling resources both assisted and extended the international's influence over local unions. As technological advances displaced some BSEIU workers—self-service elevators did not require manual operators—the union added new members among airport workers, atomic plant workers, nonacademic school employees, and hospital employees. Having grown steadily through the 1930s, the BSEIU added an average of 10,000 members each year to reach a total of some 275,000 members by the end of McFetridge's 20-year presidency.

Although a longtime Democrat, McFetridge became the only labor leader to endorse the Republican candidate, New York's governor, Thomas Dewey, in the 1948 presidential election and was regarded as favoring the Republican Dwight D. Eisenhower in his two presidential campaigns. Although the records are silent on his reasons for endorsing Dewey, McFetridge may have encountered the presidential candidate when Dewey was prosecuting former BSEIU President Scalise. Dewey also seems likely to have solicited McFetridge's support in the election. In 1950, McFetridge became the thirteenth vice-president of the AFL and his union's first member on the federation's executive council, a position he retained after the AFL and the CIO merged in 1955. The *New York Times* characterized McFetridge as one of the more conservative leaders of the labor movement in the 1950s, and *Business Week* regarded him as the prototype of the modern union leader.

In 1960, McFetridge retired, and David Sullivan, who since 1941 had been the president of 32B, was his handpicked successor. Unlike the conservative McFetridge, Sullivan was a New Frontier and Great Society, liberal Democrat. Under his leadership the union became involved for the first time with the Committee on Political Education (COPE), the AFL-CIO's political action committee. In 1965, the BSEIU established a department on civil rights to promote the inclusion of nondiscrimination clauses in local union contracts; the international also required each local to establish a permanent civil rights committee. In 1963, Sullivan oversaw the relocation of BSEIU national headquarters from Chicago to Washington, DC. This change not only placed the international in the nation's political capital, but also reflecting Sullivan's desire to strengthen BSEIU ties with the labor federation moved it closer to the AFL-CIO's headquarters.

Under Sullivan the BSEIU moved more aggressively to organize employees in the public sector.

In 1961, the union's efforts were significantly bolstered when President John F. Kennedy signed Executive Order 10988, guaranteeing federal workers the right to organize and bargain collectively. The following year Milton Murray, former director of the CIO's Government and Civic Employees Organizing Committee, led the BSEIU's initial organizing campaign at Veterans Administration (VA) hospitals in Buffalo, New York. Successful after some initial difficulties, and having learned the importance of local contacts to organizing in new areas, the BSEIU, by 1965, represented VA employees in cities including Albany, Syracuse, Chicago, Milwaukee, and several on the West Coast, as well as in Buffalo. Reflecting the ongoing changes in the composition of the union's membership, the international at its convention in 1968, dropped "building" from its name to become the Service Employees' International Union (SEIU).

Moving Forward

By 1971, when George Hardy, who had been an international union vice-president since his father Charles died in 1948, replaced the retiring Sullivan, the SEIU had more than 430,000 members, an increase over the previous decade of more than 50%. Like Sullivan Hardy emphasized organizing and union growth. In his opening address to the 1972 SEIU convention, Hardy called for doubling the union's membership by organizing a half-million workers as soon as possible. To achieve this goal, he added 1 million dollars to the union's organizing budget. Hardy personally led a series of 35 weeklong organizing workshops that added 1,500 local and 70 international organizers to the ranks. To counter the increasingly sophisticated anti-union tactics employed by corporate consultants, the SEIU, under Hardy's leadership, produced a new organizing guide, its first stewards' handbook, and a strike manual.

Hardy made the SEIU a more active player in the growing field of health care organizing. Although its interest in health care organizing dates back to the union's earliest days, its first breakthrough came in 1941 when Local 250 signed a master agreement with San Francisco General Hospital. Through the 1950s and 1960s, Hardy and the BSEIU built on these efforts. By 1968, the second, third, and fourth largest locals in the international union were largely composed of health care workers. In 1974, the SEIU and 1199 National Union of Hospital and Health Care Workers cooperated to win a change in federal law that extended protection under national labor laws to workers in not-for-profit, voluntary hospitals. The

SEIU participated in more than 500 hospital elections during the next 5 years, adding over 30,000 health care workers to the union's membership. By the end of the decade, the leaders of the SEIU and 1199 agreed that the goal of organizing the health care industry nationwide would be better served by a united effort. However the proposed merger led to an internal war in 1199 after Leon Davis, its president, retired in 1982, and this delayed the unification of the two unions for 20 years.

The 1970s also saw the SEIU pay more attention to meeting the needs of female workers. In 1973, Karen Nussbaum, an office worker at Harvard University, started Nine to Five as an insurgent group of clerical workers. The new organization issued an "Office Workers' Bill of Rights" that among other basic reforms demanded equal pay and promotion opportunities, maternity benefits, and the right to refuse to do personal errands for the employer. In 1975, Nussbaum joined with the SEIU to charter Local 925. Although Nine to Five continued to function as a separate organization, Local 925 helped bridge the gap between organized labor and the women's movement. Focusing on organizing office workers in the Boston area, Local 925 had about 350 members by 1979.

In 1978, Nussbaum helped start Working Women–National Association of Office Workers. Concentrating on the banking industry, Working Women's efforts led the federal government to investigate sex discrimination in the nation's banks. But Working Women was not a union. Using Local 925 as the model, Nussbaum in 1981 again joined forces with the SEIU, this time launching District 925 to bring union representation and collective bargaining to an estimated 20 million office and clerical workers in the United States. District 925 contracts improved wages and working conditions for telephone operators in Boston after a 9-month strike in 1983; in 1994, after a 10-year campaign, District 925 won full collective-bargaining rights at the University of Washington. In 2001, the SEIU restructured District 925 into state organizations, while chapters of Nine to Five, National Association of Working Women, remained active across the United States.

Hardy retired in 1980, and John Sweeney, who had risen in the ranks to lead 32B in New York, was elected to replace him as president of the SEIU. One way that the SEIU expanded its membership under Sweeney was through the acquisition of independent public-employee unions, such as the 80,000-member California State Employees' Association in 1984. Two years earlier the SEIU joined with the United Food and Commercial Workers' (UFCW) Union to mount a corporate campaign against Beverly Enterprises, a company that operated nursing homes throughout the United States. Adopting a strategy that the Amalgamated Clothing and Textile Workers' Union had recently used against the textile manufacturer J. P. Stevens and Co., the SEIU and the UFCW attacked Beverly Enterprises by publishing studies assailing the quality of patient care at its nursing homes and by engaging in shareholder actions at the annual meetings of large Beverly stockholders like Chase Manhattan Bank. In March 1984, the SEIU and the UFCW agreed to abandon their corporate campaign in return for Beverly's permitting union elections free from company intimidation. Although a promising start, more than 20 years of failed negotiations, court suits, strikes, and other militant confrontations passed before, in February 2004, Beverly Enterprises and 1199P, the statewide SEIU health care workers' union, signed a contract covering 1,500 workers in 24 nursing homes in Pennsylvania. Beverly management's change of heart seems to have resulted from the SEIU's offer to use its political muscle in the state's legislature to oppose aid cuts to nursing homes. Nevertheless the breakthrough in Pennsylvania still left Beverly operating over 400 nursing homes without a union in 25 states and Washington, DC.

In 1985, in a return to its roots the SEIU launched Justice for Janitors, a campaign to organize office cleaners and custodians. First in Denver and Pittsburgh, and then spreading to other cities, including Los Angeles and Boston, the SEIU's Justice campaign won wage and benefit concessions for workforces that consisted mainly of non-English-speaking immigrants. The campaign in Los Angeles exemplified the SEIU's now more confrontational approach. As multinational contractors in the early 1980s began to exercise greater control over the building service industry in the City of Angels, that industry became largely nonunion. Building services were essentially outsourced to major contract cleaning-service firms. Seeking to keep their labor costs low, these firms hired immigrant Latinos for wages at or close to the minimum. To overcome the daunting obstacles of organizing among a scattered and highly vulnerable workforce, the SEIU reached out to rank-and-file leaders, many of whom had been involved in left-wing or union activities in their home countries. On June 15, 1990, the Los Angeles police attacked a peaceful march of Justice for Janitors strikers and supporters. Recorded on videotape the attack caused public outrage and brought pressure from Mayor Tom Bradley on the contractors resulting in an agreement. Each year since 1990, the SEIU joins with community activists to stage visible events on or around June 15. In 2002, an American Dream Tour began in Washington, DC, with a rally and a march on the Justice Department to protest Attorney General John Ashcroft's harsh immigration policies; the tour ended 3 days later in Boston just as contract talks covering more than 10,000 area janitors began between the cleaning contractors and the SEIU.

In the mid-1990s, Sweeney led an internal revolt within the AFL-CIO that resulted in the retirement of Lane Kirkland, the labor federation's longtime president. After Sweeney was elected in October 1995 to replace Kirkland as head of the AFL-CIO, he named Richard W. Cordtz interim president of the SEIU. Andrew Stern, a former social worker in Pennsylvania whom Sweeney had recruited to oversee the SEIU's organizing and field-service programs, successfully challenged Cordtz at the SEIU's next convention and was elected president. During his presidency Stern has continued Sweeney's emphasis on organizing, grassroots activities, and progressive politics. Yet in the new century, the SEIU president has also emerged as a leader of dissident unions (the Teamsters, the United Food and Commercial Workers, the Laborers' International Union of North America, and Unite Here) within the AFL-CIO that have challenged Sweeney's leadership of the labor federation. Representing more than one-third of the AFL-CIO membership, Stern and the other insurgents fault Sweeney for not getting union leaders to agree to spend up to half of the federation's budget on recruiting new members through field organizing, especially in the South and the West. Stern also proposes merging, for the purpose of consolidating their power, the current 58 AFL-CIO unions into 20, each devoted to a single sector of the economy. Moreover Stern insists that the only way for labor to counter the challenge posed by the globalization of capital is to build a multinational labor movement. In June 2005, the five dissident unions agreed to form the Change to Win Coalition to pursue their reform agenda. The following month the SEIU and the Teamsters withdrew from the AFL-CIO just before the labor federation began its fiftieth-anniversary convention. Meeting in St. Louis in September 2005, six other unions joined with the SEIU to found the Change to Win Federation. Announcing that "Organizing is our core principle," SEIU secretary-treasurer Anna Burger was chosen to be chairwoman of the new federation. Despite concern that dual federations would splinter an already weakened labor movement, the two groups have been able to find ways to work together. The SEIU and the American Federation of State, County, and Municipal Employees have signed a 2-year pact not to raid each other's memberships and have agreed to organize jointly some 25,000 California home health aides. For its part in one of the biggest unionization drives in the South in decades, the SEIU in November 2005 successfully organized 5,000 janitors in Houston, Texas. Nevertheless the concern remains that the split between the two labor federations will lead to wasted resources and an ugly struggle within the labor movement.

BRIAN GREENBERG

References and Further Reading

Beadling, Thomas, et al. *A Need for Valor: The Roots of Service Employee's International Union, 1902–1992.* Washington, DC: Service Employees International Union, 1992.

Fink, Leon, and Brian Greenberg. *Upheaval in the Quiet Zone: A History of Hospital Workers' Union, Local 1199.* Urbana: University of Illinois Press, 1989.

Jentz, John, "Citizenship, Self-Respect, and Political Power: Chicago's Flat Janitors' Trailblaze the Service Employees' International Union, 1912–1921." *Labor's Heritage.* 9, 1 (summer 1997): 4–23.

Waldinger, Roger, et al. "Justice for Janitors." http://proquest.umi.com

Cases and Statutes Cited

National Labor Relations Act

See also **American Federation of State, County, and Municipal Employees**

SEXUAL HARASSMENT

Feminist activists in Ithaca, New York, coined the term sexual harassment in 1975, in response to the case of Carmita Wood, a 44-year-old administrative assistant who had quit her job with a Cornell University physicist after becoming ill from the stress of fighting off his advances. When Wood's application for unemployment benefits was denied because she had willingly quit her job, she approached Cornell's Human Affairs Program. Lin Farley, Karen Sauvigne, and Susan Meyer, feminists on staff there, gave Wood's problem a name—sexual harassment—and formed Working Women United, the first grassroots organization devoted to publicizing and researching the issue. The first speak-out on sexual harassment was held in Ithaca in May 1975. An article on the speak-out appeared in the *New York Times* in August 1975; by the end of the decade, stories about sexual harassment had appeared in a broad range of national and local newspapers and magazines. A 1976 article in the women's magazine, *Redbook*, reported on the results of a survey of nine thousand readers and described the problem as pandemic, affecting women whether they worked in corporate offices or on

assembly lines. Another organization devoted to the problem, Alliance against Sexual Coercion, formed in Boston in 1976.

The feminist movement against sexual harassment reflected both liberal feminists' concern with employment discrimination and radical feminists' opposition to violence against women. Sexual harassment was understood to be a significant barrier to women's equality, both a cause and consequence of women's segregation in the labor force. Because of women's inferior employment positions, women were vulnerable to harassment while at the same time such harassment led women to change jobs or resulted in poor performance and absenteeism, which ensured that women stayed in lesser situations. If sexual harassment worked to keep women down in traditional jobs, it was also a way of keeping women out of nontraditional jobs, where harassment was especially virulent and pervasive. Building on their work in the antirape movement, radical feminists saw harassment as a similar form of violence against women, another expression of male dominance, and not as an individual man's expression of sexual interest. Sexual harassment was often described as economic rape, a term that highlighted the connections between patriarchy and capitalism.

Social recognition of sexual harassment as a widespread social problem increased in the second-half of the 1970s, but the search for legal remedies to sexually exploitative behavior in the workplace began even before the phrase sexual harassment existed. Legal theorists ultimately focused on Title VII of the Civil Rights Act of 1964, which prohibited sex discrimination in employment, as the most viable approach. In 1976, in *Williams v. Saxbe*, a case involving a woman who was fired after repeatedly resisting her supervisor's sexual advances, a federal district court ruled that sexual harassment was a form of sex discrimination.

The legal theories of Catharine MacKinnon were the most influential in establishing sexual harassment as a violation of Title VII. MacKinnon argued that such behavior was not just an injury to an individual woman, but a form of sex discrimination, since it reinforced all women's subordinate status in the workplace. MacKinnon identified two types of harassment: *Quid pro quo* and condition-of-work (later called hostile environment). In the former a woman must submit sexually or forego employment or an employment benefit. In the latter a woman is not promised or denied a benefit, but harassment is such a significant part of the work environment that her job becomes unbearable. In 1980, the Equal Employment Opportunity Commission (EEOC), the federal agency charged with investigating claims that employers have violated

Title VII, adopted MacKinnon's argument and description of the two different forms of harassment as part of their guidelines on what constituted sex discrimination.

In 1986, the Supreme Court held in *Meritor Savings Bank v. Vinson* that both the *quid pro quo* and hostile-environment forms of sexual harassment were forms of sex discrimination that violated Title VII. Feminists saw the court's recognition of the hostile environment claim as especially significant, since it is more pervasive and less clear-cut than *quid pro quo*. However feminists and scholars were disturbed by some aspects of the decision that addressed claims of hostile-environment harassment. First the decision failed to adopt the same standard of employer liability as for *quid pro quo*. Second the court determined that evidence of a woman's speech, clothing, and conduct were admissible. Finally a plaintiff would need to prove that the behavior was unwelcome and so "severe or pervasive" that it altered the conditions of her employment. This last qualification proved divisive as courts struggled to determine the degree of severity needed to be an actionable claim. Here the issue centered on men's and women's varying interpretations of what constituted harassing behavior. In acknowledging this difference, some commentators have argued for a subjective standard, generally known as the reasonable-woman standard, though this is a controversial position that subsequent Supreme Court decisions have not adopted.

Since *Meritor* sexual harassment law has continued to evolve. The Civil Rights Act of 1991 for example allows plaintiffs to receive punitive damages, while the decision in *Harris v. Forklift* (1993) held that it is not necessary to prove that one suffered severe psychological injury in order to make a hostile-environment claim.

A number of events in the 1990s drew national attention to the issue, while at the same time conservatives and civil libertarians began to criticize hostile-environment law as unduly restricting free speech and as a politically correct form of censorship. Many Americans first learned of sexual harassment during the nationally televised confirmation hearings of Supreme Court nominee Clarence Thomas in 1991. Anita Hill testified that Thomas had made unwelcome sexual advances to her when she worked for him. The hearings sparked heated and divisive discussion about the issue, including in the African-American community, where Hill's accusations raised issues of persistent racism, loyalty to the race, and the historic sexual exploitation of women of color. In the wake of the hearings, the Equal Employment Opportunity Commission (EEOC) saw a dramatic increase in the number of sexual-harassment complaints, and

commentators suggest that women voters who were angered by the way congressmen treated Hill contributed to the victories of many women in the congressional elections of 1992. The navy's Tailhook scandal in 1991, the 1995 resignation of Senator Bob Packwood over numerous allegations of sexual harassment, and media coverage of President Bill Clinton's relations with Paula Jones and Monica Lewinsky all kept the issue in the public's eye. The year 1998 saw the largest (as of this writing) sex discrimination settlement when the Japanese automaker Mitsubishi agreed to pay 34 million dollars to more than 450 women who maintained they were groped and subjected to lewd behavior at the Normal, Illinois, plant.

Although there is widespread support for legislation against *quid pro quo* harassment, the increased visibility has led some critics to assert that too much attention has been paid to the issue, transforming trivial, everyday occurrences into social outrages. Some commentators, including some feminists, feel that the focus on sexually hostile workplaces casts women as delicate, asexual, and in need of protection, a view that they believe encourages a victim mentality and trivializes actual sexual assault by comparing it to behavior that merely offends.

Historians and the History of Sexual Harassment

The behaviors we now associate with sexual harassment existed before such behavior was named and declared a form of illegal discrimination. Early scholarship on the history of women's experience in the labor force—whether as enslaved women, workers in factories, offices, stores, or as domestics in private homes—documented examples of unwanted pressure for sexual activity, demands for sexual acts to maintain employment, and work environments that were overtly sexualized, where suggestive comments and uninvited touching were an ordinary occurrence. In these works harassment was portrayed as an ahistorical phenomenon, an ever-present and largely unchanging reality of women's work, common to all women regardless of the nature of the work. More recently scholars have begun to examine how the experience of sexual harassment is historically specific, focusing especially on how the resistance to, and function of, harassment changes in different environments and historic moments. Historians have examined how harassment made work not only uncomfortable or unbearable for some women, but how men used it to protect their place in the labor hierarchy. Sexual intimidation and coercion reinforced gender differences and contributed to gender segregation in the labor force, thereby maintaining men's power and their status as skilled workers, leaders, and higher wage earners. While men used harassment as a way of shoring up cultural ideals of masculinity, women also used ideas about gender to resist unwanted sexual attentions. Women in offices and factories in the early twentieth century, for example, asserted that they were ladies even if they were working outside of their homes for wages. As ladies these women demanded to be treated with respect by their male coworkers and bosses. The continuing emphasis on gender history will no doubt lead to further study of the history of sexual harassment.

JULIE BEREBITSKY

References and Further Reading

Baker, Carrie N. "Race, Class, and Sexual Harassment in the 1970s." *Feminist Studies* 30, 1 (spring, 2004): 7–27.
———. "Blue-Collar Feminism: The Link between Male Domination and Sexual Harassment." In *In the Company of Men: Male Dominance and Sexual Harassment*, edited by James E. Gruber and Phoebe Morgan. Boston, MA: Northeastern University Press, 2005.
Bender, Daniel E. "'Too Much of Distasteful Masculinity': Historicizing Sexual Harassment in the Garment Sweatshop and Factory." *Journal of Women's History* 15, 4 (2004): 91–116.
Bularzik, Mary. "Sexual Harassment at the Workplace: Historical Notes." *Radical America* 12, 4 (July–Aug. 1978): 25–47.
Enstad, Nan. *Ladies of Labor, Girls of Adventure: Working Women, Popular Culture, and Labor Politics at the Turn of the Twentieth Century*. New York: Columbia University Press, 1999.
MacKinnon, Catharine. *The Sexual Harassment of Working Women*. New Haven, CT: Yale University Press, 1979.
Meyer, Steve. "Workplace Predators: Sexuality and Harassment on the U.S. Automotive Shop Floor, 1930–1960." *Labor: Studies in Working-Class History of the Americas* 1, 1 (2004): 77–93.
Segrave, Kerry. *The Sexual Harassment of Women in the Workplace, 1600–1993*. Jefferson, NC: Mcfarland, 1994.
Stein, Laura W., ed. *Sexual Harassment in America: A Documentary History*. Westport, CT: Greenwood Press, 1999.

Cases and Statutes Cited

Civil Rights Act
Harris v. Forklift Systems, Inc., 510 U.S. 17 (1993)
Meritor Savings Bank v. Vinson, 477 U.S. 57 (1986)
Opportunity Act of 1972 and the Civil Rights Act of 1991, 42 U.S.C. Sec. 2000e
Title VII of the Civil Rights Act of 1964, as amended by the Equal Employment
Williams v. Saxbe, 413 F. Supp. 654 (D.D.C. 1976), *rev'd in part and vacated in part*, 587 F/2d 1240 (D.C. Cir. 1978)

See also **Gender**

SHANKER, ALBERT (SEPTEMBER 14, 1928–FEBRUARY 22, 1997)
President, American Federation of Teachers

Albert Shanker, president of the American Federation of Teachers (AFT) from 1974 to 1997, was one of the most important labor leaders in the United States in the late twentieth century. He played a prominent role in the upsurge in public-sector unionism during the 1960s and 1970s. He also came to symbolize the split between the old and new left for his leadership of the New York City teachers' union during the infamous Ocean Hill-Brownsville strikes of 1968. Thanks to that strike, and his famous "Where We Stand" articles, Shanker rose to national prominence. In addition to his role as a labor leader, Shanker became a leading figure in the movement for school reform during the 1980s and 1990s. Central to his concerns throughout his career was his desire to empower teachers, both economically and professionally.

Albert was born in New York City to parents Morris and Mamie Shanker, Jewish immigrants from Russia. Like many New York Jews of his generation, he was exposed to organized labor and left-wing politics at an early age. His mother for instance was a member of the Amalgamated Clothing Workers. While still in high school, he subscribed to *Partisan Review*, and he became an active member of the Student League for Industrial Democracy while attending Columbia University, and belonged to the Trotskyite Young People's Socialist League.

After obtaining a bachelor's degree in 1949 from the University of Illinois at Urbana-Champaign, Shanker entered graduate school at Columbia University. By 1952, after having pursued a doctorate in philosophy for 3 years, he had run out of patience and money. In order to support himself, he began teaching math in the New York City public school system as a permanent substitute. He then joined the Teachers' Guild, one of dozens of organizations representing New York City schoolteachers at the time. He soon became a member of the union's executive board, and in 1958 David Selden, future president of the American Federation of Teachers (AFT), would offer him a full-time position on the union staff as an organizer.

In 1960, the Teachers' Guild merged with the Secondary School Teachers' Association to become the United Federation of Teachers (UFT). That same year, 1960, would also see the UFT's first strike. In order to force the school board into holding a representation election as a prelude to collective bargaining, the UFT staged a 1-day walkout on November 7, 1960. The school board, under heavy political pressure, capitulated. In the election that followed, the

UFT won exclusive bargaining rights for all New York City teachers. Then when negotiations over a contract faltered, the UFT staged another 1-day strike on April 11, 1962. Again the strike resulted in a stunning victory for the UFT. Two years after helping negotiate its first contract, Shanker became president of the UFT in 1964 and remained its president until 1986. The local became the largest teachers' union in the United States and would be the basis for Shanker's power in the AFT.

These victories by the UFT played a key role in the great surge of union organization among governmental employees during the 1960s and 1970s. From 1961, when Shanker's union first won collective-bargaining rights in New York City, to his death in 1997, membership in the AFT swelled from 71,000 to almost 1 million. More than just helping to expand his own organization however, the success of the AFT in gaining bargaining rights in New York and other cities in the early 1960s inspired unionization efforts by other governmental employees across the nation. Most directly the challenge presented by the AFT to the National Education Association (NEA) forced that organization, which had previously eschewed collective bargaining as being unprofessional, to transform itself into a full-fledged union. Today with over 2 million members, the NEA is the nation's largest union, and teaching has become the most heavily unionized occupation in the United States. Even more broadly the pressure of teacher strikes and militancy in combination with the example of President Kennedy's Executive Order 10988, which was issued in 1962 and which granted collective-bargaining rights to federal employees, would prompt a majority of the states to enact collective-bargaining laws for state, county, and municipal employees in the 1960s. This would result in a dramatic expansion of public-employee unionism from about 5% of public workers in the early 1960s to about 36% in 2004. By 2004, about 4% of all union members in the United States would be public-sector workers. As private-sector unionization rates plummeted in the late twentieth century, the expansion of public-sector unionism would represent the sole bright spot in an otherwise bleak picture for organized labor. While the sheer number of new union members added to organized labor's ranks by public-sector unions was in itself impressive, equally striking was the type of workers: For the first time white-collar employees were joining unions in large numbers.

The most dramatic and for many observers defining moment of Shanker's career came in 1968 during the Ocean Hill-Brownsville strikes. Like the rest of the AFT leadership, Shanker had actively supported the civil rights movement during the early 1960s.

For instance he participated in the March on Washington in 1963 as well as marches in Selma and Montgomery. As the integrationist goals of the early civil rights movement gave way to racial separatism and Black Power in the later 1960s however, Shanker's ideology and the interests of his union began to diverge sharply from those of the more radical civil rights leaders.

Dissatisfied with the slow pace of integration in New York City, and increasingly disillusioned with the assimilationist ideas of the mainstream, black activists advanced the idea of community control. They argued that the blacks should exercise greater authority over the schools where their children went, setting the curriculum, and establishing the standards for who would work in the schools. Community control ran directly counter to Shanker's ideas about professionalism. Not only did he believe that teachers should receive professional salaries, but that they should also have a, if not the, decisive say in how they performed their job and that professionals, not untrained laymen, should determine who was qualified to be a teacher.

In May of 1968, the board of the Ocean Hill-Brownsville demonstration school district dismissed 17 white teachers for allegedly being unsympathetic to the board's goals. Not only did this go against Shanker's ideas about professionalism, it violated the union's contract with the city and its responsibility to its members. In response to the firings, Shanker ordered the UFT out in a series of strikes in order to force the teachers' reinstatement. The strikes were marked by a number of racial incidents that pitted black New Yorkers against the predominantly Jewish UFT. This incident heralded a divorce between the Jewish and African-American communities and more broadly between the old Left, which was oriented toward class issues, and the new Left, which was more focused on issues of identity, whether that of race, gender, or sexual orientation.

Shanker's reputation as a liberal was badly damaged if not destroyed by the Ocean Hill-Brownsville strikes. Many on the Left viewed him as racially insensitive at best, a closet racist at worst. It was in response to such criticism that Shanker began writing the "Where We Stand" articles that first appeared as paid advertisements in the New York Times in 1970. In spite of this criticism, Shanker would continue to oppose racial quotas and preferences. For instance the AFT filed an amicus brief in the Bakke case in 1978 opposing racial quotas.

Shanker's support for U.S. involvement in Vietnam further alienated him from the Left. In fact it was his support for the war that elevated him to the executive board of the AFL-CIO in 1973 when then AFT

President David Selden refused the position because of his opposition to the war. Shanker became a strong supporter of George Meany and his anti-Communist foreign policy.

After Shanker became president of the AFT in 1974, he worked to make the union the pre-eminent spokesman for the teaching profession. He secured his place as a leader in school reform in 1983 when he endorsed the report of the President's Commission on Excellence in Education, *A Nation at Risk*, which deplored the state of America's public schools. While the National Education Association (NEA) worried that setting national standards for teacher competency and student achievement would have a disparate impact on minorities, Shanker endorsed the concept of high-stakes testing. In keeping with his ideas about professionalism, Shanker felt that teachers should be held to high standards. This was essential, he believed, in order for teachers to claim the prerogative of having the determining voice in how they performed their jobs. He also popularized the idea of charter schools, although he opposed school vouchers, both because of his ideological commitment to public education and the interests of his union. The idea of national standards in education has now become official government policy, in part due to Shanker's work.

LAWRENCE RICHARDS

References and Further Reading

Murphy, Marjorie. *Blackboard Unions: The AFT and the NEA, 1900–1980*. Ithaca, NY: Cornell University Press: 1990.

Podair, Jerald. *The Strike That Changed New York: Blacks, Whites, and the Ocean Hill-Brownsville Crisis*. New Haven, CT: Yale University Press: 2002.

Selden, David. *The Teacher Rebellion*. Washington, DC: Howard University Press: 1985.

See also **American Federation of Teachers; National Education Association; Ocean Hill-Brownsville Strikes (1968)**

SHARE CROPPERS' UNION (1930s)

The Share Croppers' Union (SCU), sometimes referred to as the Alabama Share Croppers Union, was a predominantly African-American organization composed of sharecroppers, agricultural workers, and tenant farmers. It was the largest Communist-led mass organization in the South. The SCU was founded in 1931 and disbanded in 1937, transferring its workers to other labor unions. At its peak the SCU claimed to have over 10,000 members.

Sharecropping

It is important to recognize the context in which the SCU was founded. Sharecropping is a system of farming in which laborers contract to farm a tract of land they do not own in return for a fraction of the profits generated by the tract's crops. Sharecropping was a major feature of the South during the Reconstruction Era (1865–1876) and is still used in many poor, rural areas of the world, including India.

Sharecropping developed in response to the emancipation of African-American slaves in the Deep South. Plantation farms relied on slave labor, while slaves relied on plantation owners for shelter, food, and basic necessities. After the Thirteenth Amendment abolished the institution of slavery, sharecropping enabled both sides to maintain their dependent relationship. However because the terms of sharecropping were very difficult and clearly in the plantation owners' favor, the arrangement cemented the subordinate status of African-Americans in the South. That is, sharecroppers were required to buy seed and farming implements from the plantation owner, generally at exorbitant prices or rates of credit, while receiving only a small share of the crop to sell. In short it was extremely difficult for sharecroppers to generate any profit, so they remained almost completely dependent on the plantation owners, just as they were as slaves. Because sharecroppers often had a difficult timing paying their debts, they lived under constant threat of eviction from white landowners.

Communist Party Influence

In 1928, at the Sixth World Congress of the Communist Internationale in Moscow, representatives recognized the "Negro nation" that existed in the South and drafted a resolution to encourage self-determination of laborers in the Black Belt of the South. The Communists wanted to liberate African-American farm laborers by seizing land from white owners and distributing it to landless peasants and to unite laborers all across the South. A group of advanced African-Americans would be trained to organize other poor southerners, both black and white, in a common struggle against white landowners.

The Communists' organizing efforts began in Alabama. In 1930, the American Communist party opened its southern headquarters in Birmingham and began organizing industrial workers (primarily in the steel and iron industry), publishing the *Southern Worker* newsletter, and supporting candidates for state and local offices. A decade-long agricultural

Sharecropper plowing. Montgomery County, Alabama.

depression that resulted in extremely low cotton prices made the sharecroppers especially fertile ground for the Communist organizers.

The Founding of the SCU

Ralph and Tommy Gray, African-American tenant farmers in Tallaposa County, Alabama, organized a small group of black sharecroppers and tenant farmers in spring 1931. In response to their request for assistance, the Communist party sent Mack Coad, an African-American steelworker from Charleston. Coad became the first secretary of the fledgling union, which gathered nearly 800 members in its early months. In addition to the broader goals of the Communist leadership, the SCU sought to demand better wages and working conditions, abolish share-cropping, and garner voting rights for blacks.

Fearing economic upheaval white landowners and government officials tried to prevent sharecroppers from joining and met the new union with violence. Several violent conflicts ensued. Two night police raids of union meetings in Camp Hill, Alabama, where officials confiscated union literature and membership lists culminated in a violent shootout between union members and a sheriff. The conflict left Ralph Gray dead and his house torched, forced many tenant farmers into hiding, and impelled Coad to leave Alabama. The union soon regrouped, led by Eula Gray, Tommy Gray's teenage daughter and an activist in the Young Communist League, and officially adopted the SCU name.

Growth of the SCU

By the summer of 1932, the SCU included over 600 members despite continued violent opposition from the police and lynch mobs. Al Murphy, an African-American Communist activist, took over the union and transformed it into an underground organization that met secretly. In December 1932, another wave of violence, instigated by SCU members fighting the seizure of a member's livestock by creditors, left three SCU members dead and several wounded, and five others imprisoned. Despite the violence, sharecroppers and farm laborers continued to join the union, especially after landowners took advantage of certain New Deal policies to evict sharecroppers on a mass scale. In summer 1933, the union claimed 2,000 members and by fall 1934, nearly 8,000. At this point the membership was still entirely African-American.

In winter 1934, Clyde Johnson, a white Communist and Minnesota native with extensive organizing experience, took over the SCU. Johnson steered the union away from its underground status and began working to make it a legitimate agricultural labor union. He edited and published the *Union Leader: A Voice of the White and Negro Farm Toilers of the South*, the SCU's first newsletter. The union was active in many ways, leading strikes by cotton pickers in three Alabama counties and organizing local committees, women's auxiliaries, and youth groups. The SCU continued to face violent opposition—a cotton workers' strike in 1935 left several strikers killed and dozens of union members assaulted and jailed. Around this time the SCU sought a merger with the newly formed Southern Tenant Farmers' Union, but their leadership declined because of the SCU's Communist influences.

By 1936, the SCU grew to over 10,000 members, spread from Alabama into neighboring Mississippi and Louisiana, and opened a public headquarters in New Orleans. By now the SCU was fighting not just the repression of the southern ruling class, but also the fast-occurring changes in the agricultural South, the most important being the increasing mechanization of cotton farming. With these rapid changes in sharecropping leading to the SCU's increasing irrelevance as a stand-alone body and the Southern Tenant Farmers' Union continuing to be uninterested in merging, Johnson led the effort to disband the SCU in 1937. Sharecroppers and tenant farmers were transferred to the National Farmers' Union, agricultural wage laborers to the Agricultural Workers' Union, an affiliate of the American Federation of Labor (AFL). However some SCU local groups remained in existence and continued to function into the period of World War II.

DAVID PURCELL

References and Further Reading

Dyson, Lowell K. *Red Harvest: The Communist Party and American Farmers*. Lincoln: University of Nebraska Press, 1982.
Kelley, Robin D. G. *Hammer and Hoe: Alabama Communists during the Great Depression*. Chapel Hill: University of North Carolina Press, 1990.
Rosengarten, Theodore. *All God's Dangers: The Life of Nate Shaw*. New York: Knopf, 1975.
Solomon, Mark I. *The Cry Was Unity: Communists and African Americans, 1917–36*. Jackson: University Press of Mississippi, 1998.

See also **African-Americans; Sharecropping and Tenancy; South**

SHARECROPPING AND TENANCY

The sharecropping and tenancy system arose in the South in the years immediately following the Civil War and emancipation. At first however planters employed the contract labor system, and Freedmen's Bureau officials often acted as the brokers in the arrangement. But neither freedmen nor planters were satisfied with the contract system. Freedmen were unhappy with the fact that they were required to work under the close supervision of planters or their representatives, often laboring in gangs just as they had as slaves. Planters preferred to regulate closely their laborers, but the contract system worked another kind of hardship on them. As cotton prices declined in the years after the Civil War, planters found it increasingly difficult to pay wages. It was in this context that the sharecropping and tenancy system arose: as a compromise. Planters no longer had to part with cash, and freedmen were able to move away from the old slave quarters and on to 25–40 acre slots. In some circumstances they were even free of the close supervision of the planters for whom they worked. Many freedmen withdrew their wives from the fields, something that planters resented but were unable to control, given their need for labor.

Much confusion surrounds the terms sharecropping and tenancy. When linked as two alternative forms of plantation labor, they both referred to working for shares of the crop. A more appropriate definition would be sharecropping and share tenancy (although the latter was also sometimes also known as a share renter), and they differed in important respects from a third category of tenancy, cash tenancy (sometimes called the fixed renter). Cash tenancy was for good reason considered separately, for in this circumstance, the farmer made a cash payment to rent land from the owner. Sharecropping and share tenancy however involved men (and on rare occasions women) of modest or no means. While sharecroppers typically had no more than their labor to bring to the bargaining table, share tenant farmers owned mules and implements. Because of these differences in material conditions, the law came to recognize the share tenant as having some legal standing in court.

The sharecropper was regarded as little more than a wage laborer who was paid a half of the cotton and corn crops he grew in exchange for his labor. The share tenant farmer however technically owned the crop he grew and paid a share of it—typically one-fourth of the corn and one-third cotton crops—to the planter in exchange for the use of the land. Even though the courts recognized the tenant farmer as owning the crop and thus having some standing in court, few tenant farmers actually took disputes to court, probably because they understood that planters had greater influence and the likelihood of winning a court contest with them was remote.

One other important difference existed between sharecropping and share tenant. Many white farmers in the years after the Civil War lost their farms and turned to tenant farming as an alternative. Because they had some means, they were more likely than freedmen to have mules and implements. Freedmen, who came out of enslavement with little more than the clothes on their backs, found it impossible to acquire property under the sharecropping arrangement and thus despite the myth of the agricultural ladder (whereby one was supposed to be able to move from sharecropping to tenancy to landowning), they remained sharecroppers. By the end of the nineteenth century, the overwhelming number of sharecroppers were black. Share tenant farmers on the other hand tended to be white.

Economists Richard Sutch and Roger Ransom suggest in *One Kind of Freedom* that sharecropping might have served the purposes of freedmen, might have allowed them to prosper but for the emergence of the commissary system and the institutionalization of debt peonage. Because returns on the crop were realized only once a year when they marketed their crop at the end of harvest, sharecroppers and share tenants both came to depend on advances from the planters for whom they worked. Planters charged exorbitant interests—sometimes as much as 50%–75%—for all such advances. When the crop was harvested in the fall and the debts were subtracted, many sharecroppers and share tenants found themselves barely able—or unable—to pay debts, and thus required yet another advance in order to make it through the next crop year. Some sharecroppers and tenants found themselves locked in an almost hopeless cycle of indebtedness. One thing that further complicated the situation for both tenants and sharecroppers was the emergence of laws that circumscribed the movement of tenants and sharecroppers who owed a debt to planters. Planters would send local law enforcement officials after sharecroppers and share tenants who departed owing a debt. Pete Daniel, in *The Shadow of Slavery*, calls this just another kind of slavery.

African-Americans meanwhile endured a number of other legal sanctions that grew more onerous as time went on, and these measures tended to reinforce their economic dependence on planters. In the years immediately following the Civil War, in the period when planters briefly regained power before the emergence of congressional Reconstruction, freedmen were required to carry a pass if not on the plantation. They were discouraged from seeking alternative forms of employment, and vagrancy laws further inhibited their movement from the plantations to towns and cities. The Ku Klux Klan, at least in its earliest incarnation, was oriented to the task of forcing freedmen to remain in place, working for planters. During congressional Reconstruction when blacks gained the ballot, the Klan's focus shifted to preventing freedmen (and white Republicans) from exercising their right to vote or hold office. In fact by the end of the century, the implementation of various disfranchisement measures further circumscribed the opportunities open to African-Americans and together with segregation, drove a wedge between black and white plantation laborers. To make matters worse, the racist rhetoric employed by white Democrats to champion disfranchisement and segregation statutes gave rise to a virulent racism that led to an increase in lynchings and night-riding activities against African-Americans. In this context it was unwise for black sharecroppers to challenge planters' assessment of what was owing to them at the end of the crop year. Ironically planters had to defend the right of African-American sharecroppers to remain on the plantations when landless white men began in the 1890s to try to drive them off so that they could gain a share tenancy. One courageous federal judge in the eastern district of Arkansas convicted white night riders of violating the Thirteenth Amendment right of African-Americans to employment, but the U.S. Supreme Court, in *Hodges v. U.S.* ruled that there was no such right guaranteed by the amendment. That ruling stood unchallenged until 1968. In the interim southern states passed night-riding laws, but it is impossible to determine whether they were enforced. Nevertheless by the beginning of the twentieth century, the options open to African-Americans were severely limited, and those who remained in the South were principally employed as sharecroppers.

Historians and economists debate the extent to which mobility was reduced as a result of debt peonage. There is clear evidence that those working for honest planters tended to remain in place voluntarily, but those employed by unscrupulous ones who were still able to break even at the end of the crop year, moved on seeking better opportunities elsewhere. Many African-American and white farmers moved from the older South (of South Carolina, Georgia, and Alabama) to the South on the western fringe, Mississippi, Arkansas, and Texas, as new lands there were coming into cultivation. Labor agents, hired by planters opening up new plantations there, enticed landless men with promises of opportunities on the abundant and fertile land. However most of these migrants found themselves once again engaged in sharecropping or share tenancy and rarely able to ascend the mythical agricultural ladder. Thus whenever they could pay out of debt at the end of the year, they continued to move, ever on the search for a better opportunity.

The sharecropping and share tenancy system persisted until after the mechanization of the cotton crop and the emergence of a scientific agriculture in the post-World War II period. Scientific agriculture typically means the use of chemicals to cut down on the need to weed the cotton in the summer months, one of the two labor-intensive aspects of premechanization cotton farming. In fact the sharecropping and share tenancy system began to erode in the 1930s when New Deal programs began to pay farmers to reduce production of certain crops. Cotton was one of the crops that farmers could elect to reduce acreage on, but they were allowed to put the land that would have grown cotton to other uses. Planters in the South began to move toward the cultivation of soybeans, a fully mechanized crop, and thus had little need for excess sharecroppers and share tenants. Many were evicted from plantations during the 1930s and made their way to southern, northern, or western cities, looking for work. The post-World War II period merely witnessed an acceleration of a process that had already begun. By 1960, the printed census of agriculture no longer even listed sharecropper as a separate category. Share tenancy still exists, but most tenants today pay a cash rent and are not regarded as agricultural laborers.

JEANNIE WHAYNE

References and Further Reading

Ayers, Edward L. *The Promise of the New South: Life after Reconstruction.* New York and Oxford, UK: 1992.

Brundage, W. Fitzhugh. *Lynching in the New South: Georgia and Virginia, 1880–1930.* Urbana, IL: 1993.

Cobb, James C. *The Most Southern Place on Earth: The Mississippi Delta and the Roots of Regional Identity.* New York and Oxford, UK: 1992.

Conrad, David Eugene. *The Forgotten Farmers: The Story of Sharecroppers in the New Deal.* Urbana, IL: 1965.

Daniel, Pete. *Shadow of Slavery: Peonage in the South, 1901–1969.* Chicago, IL: 1972.

———. *Standing at the Crossroads: Southern Rural Life since 1900.* New York: 1986.

Fite, Gilbert. *Cotton Fields No More: Southern Agriculture, 1865–1980.* Lexington, KY: 1984.

Kirby, Jack Temple. *Rural Worlds Lost: The American South, 1920–1960.* Baton Rouge, LA: 1987.

Kousser, J. Morgan. *The Shaping of Southern Politics: Suffrage Restriction and the Establishment of the One-Party South, 1880–1910.* New Haven, CT: 1974.

Litwack, Leon F. *Been in a Storm So Long: The Aftermath of Slavery.* New York: 1979.

Mandle, Jay R. *The Roots of Black Poverty: The Southern Plantation Economy after the Civil War.* Durham, NC: 1978.

Mertz, Paul E. *New Deal Policy and Southern Rural Poverty.* Baton Rouge, LA: 1978.

Powell, Lawrence N. *New Masters: Northern Planters during the Civil War and Reconstruction.* New Haven, CT: 1980.

Ransom, Roger, and Richard Sutch, *One Kind of Freedom: The Economic Consequences of Emancipation.* Cambridge, MA: 1977.

Reidy, Joseph P. *From Slavery to Agrarian Capitalism in the Cotton Plantation South: Central Georgia, 1800–1880.* Chapel Hill, NC: 1992.

Roark, James L. *Masters without Slaves: Southern Planters in the Civil War and Reconstruction.* New York: 1977.

Tolnay, Stewart E., and E. M. Beck. *A Festival of Violence: An Analysis of Southern Lynchings, 1882–1930.* Urbana and Chicago, IL: 1994.

Whayne, Jeannie. *A New Plantation South: Land, Labor, and Federal Favor in Twentieth-Century Arkansas.* Charlottesville, VA: 1996.

White, Walter. *Rope and Faggott: A Biography of Judge Lynch.* New York: 1929.

Williamson, Joel. *The Crucible of Race: Black-White Relations in the American South since Emancipation.* New York: 1984.

Woodman, Harold D. *New South—New Law: The Legal Foundations of Credit and Labor Relations in the Postbellum Agricultural South.* Baton Rouge, LA and London, UK: 1995.

Wright, Gavin. *Old South, New South: Revolutions in the Southern Economy since the Civil War.* New York: 1986.

Cases and Statutes Cited

Hodges v. U.S.

SHEFFIELD, HORACE (1914–1977)
United Auto Workers

Horace Sheffield, one of the first blacks to serve as an international representative for the United Auto Workers (UAW), played a major role in mobilizing support in the black community of Detroit for the strike against Ford Motor Company at the River Rouge plant in 1941. He also helped open up black representation on the International Executive Board (IEB) of the UAW and was a founding member of the Trade Union Leadership Council (TULC) in 1957. Although Sheffield identified with the moderate wing within the UAW—represented by Walter Reuther and his supporters—he presented a significant challenge to the Reuther coalition when they refused to add an African-American to the executive board.

Born in Vienna, Georgia, in 1914, Sheffield moved with his parents to Detroit, Michigan, 1 year later. After attending Detroit public schools, Sheffield got a job at Midland Steel when he was 17 years old. When he was laid off by Midland, he landed a job as a sander at the River Rouge plant on December 23, 1934. For several years he worked during the day and attended Wayne State and the Detroit Institute of Technology at night. By the time of the UAW organizing drive during the late thirties, Sheffield, imbued with youthful idealism, changed his career path. Although he had planned to enroll at the Detroit College of Law, he signed on as a volunteer organizer for the UAW in late 1940. His decision, opposed by his father, a foreman at the Ford Motor Company, led to a familial split and Sheffield's moving out of his father's house.

After the successful strike in 1941, Sheffield was elected a UAW committeeman at the Rouge foundry. Initially he was an inspector, then education director of the foundry, and finally he was assigned to monitor discrimination in the Ford employment office. Despite the fact that the vast majority of black leaders within the UAW identified with what was known as the left-wing caucus, Sheffield supported the Reuther faction, which was regarded as the right-wing caucus within the UAW. In November 1942, Sheffield became one of half-a-dozen black staff members on the international staff.

At the UAW Convention in Buffalo in 1943, black union leaders—those in the left-wing and those in the right-wing of the UAW—agreed the time was right to make the issue of a black board member a major topic of discussion. Initially the caucus of black delegates endorsed a resolution proposing the creation of a minorities' department headed by an elected black board member. When that proposal was rejected by the Reuther camp, the original proposal (known as the Tappes resolution because it was submitted by Shelton Tappes) was watered down to appeal to moderate white workers. Sheffield abandoned the Tappes proposal and the wishes of the majority of the black caucus, sided with Reuther's faction, and declared that the altered version of the Tappes resolution entailed dividing power unequally, giving a black board member less weight than a white board member. The convention rejected the Tappes proposal.

Sheffield spent the remainder of the forties and a good part of the fifties working within the Reuther circle and challenging the power of Communist-oriented black workers in Local 600. He helped shape and interpret the needs of the black community for UAW officials and leaders. But on the issue of black representation on the UAW's executive board, Sheffield had no success. The question of black representation on the UAW's executive board was raised regularly at UAW annual meetings, but it was not until the late 1950s that serious pressure was placed on Reuther to open up the all-white board to African-Americans. The challenge came from the Trade Union Leadership Council (TULC), organized largely by black activists, such as Sheffield, who had learned union politics inside Reuther's tent. Reuther therefore was not prepared when Sheffield charged him with hypocrisy on the issue of his civil rights practices. Although Reuther and international UAW unions had maintained a good record in the public arena, Sheffield exposed Reuther's resistance to all efforts to change the all-white board of directors, highlighting the UAW's contradictory civil rights practices.

The TULC brought the issue of black representation on the union's executive board to a head at the 1959 UAW convention. Reuther announced, as he had on many previous occasions, that he could not entertain a "black position" because that would amount to practicing Jim Crow in reverse. Moreover, he added, the time will arrive when a black would be qualified for such a position, implying that was surely not yet the case. Sheffield, along with other black unionists, could hardly contain his anger. Later he recalled that he decided the line had been drawn by 1959, and he was determined not to let anyone stop him. During a later interview, he declared that he was prepared to ignore even Jesus if he had tried to keep him from speaking up at the convention. As the cavernous convention hall fell silent, Sheffield reminded the audience that since 1943— for 16 years—black workers in the UAW had been promised representation on the international executive board. Black Americans, he told the crowd, were sick and tired of the issue of qualifications. Looking at the board members, he noted that he thought it was fairly obvious that one does not have to be a Rhodes Scholar to sit on the International Executive Board.

Sheffield, with the backing of the TULC, had thrown down the gauntlet. For the next several months, Reuther and his advisers prepared the way for the nomination of an African-American to the executive board of the UAW, which took place at the convention in 1962. Although Nelson Jack Edwards, not Sheffield, was the choice of the executive board, Edwards chose Sheffield as his administrative assistant. Sheffield spent the last years of his life operating as a political moderate, tempering the more militant voices coming from black autoworkers in the late sixties. He continued to be active in the TULC and was also one of the founders of the Coalition of Black Trade Unionists in 1972.

BETH TOMPKINS BATES

References and Further Reading

Hill, Herbert. "Interview with Horace Sheffield, July 24, 1968, Detroit, Michigan." In *Blacks in the Labor Movement*. Detroit, MI: Archives of Labor and Urban Affairs, Wayne State University.
Lichtenstein, Nelson. *Walter Reuther: The Most Dangerous Man in Detroit*. New York: Basic Books, 1995.
Stepan-Norris, Judith, and Maurice Zeitin. *Talking Union*. Urbana: University of Illinois Press, 1996.
United Auto Workers. "Proceedings of the Seventeenth Constitutional Convention." Atlantic City, NJ: October 9–16, 1959.

See also **Coalition of Black Trade Unionists; Tappes, Shelton**

SHERMAN ANTI-TRUST ACT

The Sherman Anti-Trust Act was the first government action taken to limit trust companies, which often monopolized certain industries and therefore segments of the economy. Passed in 1890, it was named after Senator John Sherman of Ohio, and made "every contract, combination in the form of trust or otherwise, or conspiracy, in restraint of trade or commerce among the several States, or with foreign nations... illegal." The Sherman Anti-Trust Act also placed a burden of responsibility on district courts and government attorneys to investigate possible trust violations and elucidated the possible consequences to violators. Due to the original wording of the Sherman Anti-Trust Act, which did not specifically refer to monopolies or trusts, the act was sometimes applied to stop striking. This provoked controversy and an assessment as to whether the Sherman Anti-Trust Act was actually antilabor.

Changes in manufacturing practices contributed to the act's passage. Starting in the late nineteenth century, large corporations integrated horizontally and vertically to form oligopolies and monopolies in their respective areas of industry. Some of the trusts that emerged in the late nineteenth and early twentieth centuries were Standard Oil, American Sugar Refining Company, American Tobacco Company, and United States Steel. However due to adverse court rulings, the Sherman Anti-Trust Act failed to regulate trusts until Theodore Roosevelt's presidency.

Roosevelt undertook a trust-busting campaign and overcame the Supreme Court ruling in *United States v. E. C. Knight* (1895), which impaired the enforcement of the Sherman Anti-Trust Act by exempting manufacturing corporations from the act's authority. However in 1904, the Supreme Court consented that Northern Securities Company, a railroad monopoly, should be dissolved because it dealt with interstate transportation. President Roosevelt continued to pursue antitrust suits, initiating more than 40 antitrust proceedings. Roosevelt's successor, William Howard Taft, also supported trust-busting. Under Taft's presidency there were twice as many antitrust suits as during his predecessor's terms.

The Sherman Anti-Trust Act was also used against labor movements. By including all organizations in its original wording, the act could be used against labor unions during strikes by claiming they unlawfully interfered with commerce. One of the most famous of such cases was the 1894 Pullman strike near Chicago, Illinois. Employees paid high rent for company-owned housing within the model town of Pullman and suffered from reduced wages simultaneously. Those conditions among others caused the workers at the Pullman Palace Car Company, a luxury sleeper railcar manufacturer, to strike. In doing so the strikers asked the American Railway Union (ARU) to boycott Pullman cars and to disconnect them from every train and depart without them. Once the ARU agreed, the General Managers' Association (GMA), formed by 24 railway companies to help combat the increasing power of labor unions, claimed only railway managers could determine which cars made up the trains and that they would fire any worker supporting the boycott. These actions resulted in 150,000 ARU members striking, causing rail traffic to halt and the intervention of the federal government on the side of the GMA. United States Attorney General Richard Olney obtained an injunction against the strikers, claiming the strike prevented mail delivery and violated the Sherman Anti-Trust Act by restricting commerce. Persuaded by Olney and fearful of violence, President Grover Cleveland authorized the use of U.S. marshals and federal troops to protect the trains operated by strikebreakers. Violence increased with the arrival of the troops; railroad property was attacked and burned, and fights broke out in the streets of Chicago between the authorities and strikers. The strike, which had started May 12, ended July 8, with the death of 34 people. The use of the injunction made striking illegal, seriously curtailing the powers of trade and labor unions.

Judicial rulings also limited workers' organizations. In *Loewe v. Lawlor*, also known as the Danbury Hatters' Case, the Supreme Court issued a 1908 ruling against unions. The Court, upholding the ideology that labor unions could be subject to antitrust laws, banned secondary strikes (strikes or boycotts performed in support of another strike), claiming they were conspiracies and violated the Sherman Anti-Trust Act. *Loewe v. Lawlor* enabled triple damages to be assessed against the unions and also held individuals accountable for monetary damages. This ruling among others asserted unions' subjectivity to antitrust laws.

In the Buck's Stove and Range cases, the Supreme Court ruled against the American Federation of Labor (AFL); its president, Samuel Gompers; and two other men associated with the AFL, John Mitchell and Frank Morrison. These cases resulted from an AFL boycott against Buck's Stove and Range Company. The AFL was supporting a strike that was already occurring at Buck's Stove and Range Company. The *American Federationist*, the AFL's periodical, called the company unfair and stated, "We Don't Patronize," resulting in damages to Buck's Stove and Range. The company, claiming the defendants had plotted a conspiracy to limit Buck's Stove and Range Company's interstate commerce, obtained an injunction against the AFL's boycott and also against verbal or written discussion of the strike. However the AFL violated the order, which resulted in Gompers, Mitchell, and Morrison being held in contempt of court and their imprisonment. The Supreme Court issued a 1908 ruling that upheld broad uses of injunctions against labor, debilitating organized labor's tactics of boycotts and strikes.

Such uses of the Sherman Anti-Trust Act resulted in criticism from organized labor, the People's party, and liberals in the legal domain. In 1914, during Woodrow Wilson's presidency, the Sherman Anti-Trust Act was amended through the passage of the Clayton Anti-Trust Act. The latter act banned such practices as price fixing but also exempted unions and farmers' organizations from prosecution under antitrust laws. This act, too, had organized labor critics. Since 1914, the United States Congress passed additional legislation aimed to strengthen the Sherman Anti-Trust Act's effectiveness, such as the Robinson-Patman Act of 1936 and the Hart-Scott-Rodino Antitrust Improvements Act of 1976. In June 2004, President George W. Bush signed into law the Criminal Antitrust Penalty Enhancement and Reform Act, which increased the maximum Sherman Anti-Trust Act penalties for corporations to $100 million, for individuals to $1 million, and for jail terms to 10 years. This most recent act also heightened incentives for corporations to self-report criminal activity and aims to enhance the antimonopoly policy.

HEIDI SCOTT GIUSTO

References and Further Reading

Chandler, Alfred D., Jr. *The Visible Hand: The Managerial Revolution in American Business.* Cambridge, MA: The Belknap Press of Harvard University Press, 1977.
Clayton Anti-Trust Act of 1914. Johnsen, Julia E. *Trade Unions and the Antitrust Laws, the Reference Shelf.* Vol. 13, no. 10. New York: H. W. Wilson, 1940.
"Labor Law. Application of Sherman Anti-Trust Act to Sit-Down Strikes." *Virginia Law Review* 1 26, 4 (Feb. 1940): 518–519.
Painter, Nell Irvin. *Standing at Armageddon: The United States 1877–1919.* New York: W. W. Norton, 1987.
Pate, R. Hewitt. "Assistant Attorney General for Antitrust, R. Hewitt Pate, Issues Statement on Enactment of Antitrust Criminal Penalty Enhancement and Reform Act of 2004." www.usdoj.gov/atr/public/press_releases/2004/204319.htm (June 23, 2004).
Sherman Anti-Trust Act of 1890. Taft, William Howard. *The Anti-Trust Act and the Supreme Court.* New York: Harper & Brothers, 1914.

Cases and Statutes Cited

Clayton Anti-Trust Act
Criminal Antitrust Penalty Enhancement and Reform Act
Hart-Scott-Rodino Antitrust Improvements Act
Loewe v. *Lawlor*
Robinson-Patman Act
Sherman Anti-Trust Act
United States v. *E. C. Knight*
U.S. Supreme Court Gompers v. Bucks Stove & Range Co., 221 U.S. 418 (1911). http://caselaw.lp.findlaw.com (1994–).

See also **American Federation of Labor; Boycotts; Gompers, Samuel; Pullman, George Morimer; Pullman Strike and Boycott**

SHOEMAKING

The nineteenth-century process of industrialization in the making of boots and shoes is a classic story of artisans turning into industrial workers. Based on the European guild system, the artisan shoemaker in the British North American colonies, whose patron was St. Crispin, practiced his skills, oversaw journeymen, and taught apprentices in a small shop adjacent to his household. In this shop in the seventeenth and eighteenth centuries, the master shoemaker cut out his own leather, shaped and sewed the cut pieces to size, and attached the sole. Sometimes the shoes and boots were made to order. More often in the late eighteenth century, the shoemaker sold the completed shoes to a merchant or took them by horseback to a marketplace. The master artisan owned his product, enjoyed a sense of economic independence, and expected to be treated as a respected and valued member of colonial society. His political rights established in the War of the American Revolution ensured—or so he believed—that independence.

As the new republic expanded geographically and cities and towns grew, artisan shoemaking faced the challenges of supplying new markets. Store merchants in towns found it profitable to lend shoemakers leather and guarantee a sale. Aside from custom-made riding boots, most shoes were durable work brogans or lighter shoes and slippers for women and children. But in taking leather from the merchant, the artisan lost ownership of the shoes he made. Paid for his skilled labor, masters and journeymen became dependent on their labor and on the wages it commanded. Markets and prices fluctuated, as did wages. The artisan sense of economic independence was eroding.

One solution might be to expand production in the artisan shop. At some point probably within the family of a shoemaker in Lynn, Massachusetts, a daughter or a wife was recruited to hand sew or bind the top of the shoe, called an upper. When completed the shoe binder passed the uppers to her husband or father working along with journeymen and apprentices in the shoe shop. In an effort to promote family economic well-being, a sexual division of labor was introduced into shoemaking, which lasted throughout the nineteenth century despite mechanization and centralization of production. In order to ensure a ready supply of bound uppers, merchants hired women in rural and town households to bind the cut leather as homework for very low wages. Shoemakers rarely bound their own uppers unless they had no alternative. The shoe merchant who was often called a shoe boss coordinated all of the steps in a central shop: The handing out of cut leather to shoe binders and delivering them to artisan shops.

Under supervision skilled men carefully cut the merchants' leather in those central shops located in towns. Here the merchants with capital to buy leather and market shoes decided on the wages for shoemaking and shoe binding. Many of the cheapest kinds of work shoes were sold to be worn by slaves in the cotton South. During the depression of 1837 when wages fell sharply and in the 1840s, organized protests by male and female workers arose against merchant control over the economic well-being of shoemaking families. The artisan's independence was fast disappearing. But none of the processes of shoemaking had yet been mechanized or put into a factory. The invention of the sewing machine and its adaptation to leather in 1852 was the first step toward centralization of production. Sewing machines, either hand-cranked or run by foot treadles, sewed the lighter leather of uppers. Shoe binders either rented sewing machines or their daughters moved into centralized shops as stitchers where sewing machines were run by steam power. The sexual division of labor begun in the shoemaker's family shifted to the shoe factory.

Meanwhile in order to expand production of shoes and control shoemakers' wages, merchant capitalists hired shoemakers in rural areas far away from the established centers of production, such as Lynn and Natick in eastern Massachusetts. Cut leather and machine-sewn uppers were delivered by wagons over rural roads. Wages continued to fall, especially during the hard times of the 1850s. Organized protest against low wages erupted in Lynn during the Great Shoe Strike of 1860, but home workers and former artisans battled unsuccessfully against the developing efficiencies of centralized, mechanized production, while shoe bosses cited the natural laws of supply and demand to justify their control over production and wages.

After the Civil War, during which boot and shoemaking centers in the Northeast flourished from Union Army contracts, more steps in the making of shoes were centralized and mechanized, drawing male workers away from their artisan shops into industry. For a time these men worked as teams "bottoming shoes." But each process became subdivided and as quickly as possible, mechanized and powered by steam engines. By late 1860s, the McKay stitcher was used—a sewing machine mounted above a moveable horn over which the sewn upper, inner sole, and outer sole were positioned after hand lasting by male "lasters" to the correct size. A curved needle penetrated and firmly sewed together all the layers of leather. Beating-out machines then leveled the sole. When the work of bottomers became mechanized in the 1870s, machines for trimming, edge setting, heeling, buffing, burnishing, and finishing replaced skilled men. As each machine was introduced, piece rates were cut.

As a result of intensified investment in factories and machinery, Lynn became the national center for the production of the popular lady's high-buttoned shoe. Competition over style and finish created skilled work and high wages for experienced women's shoe stitchers, especially in the fancy stitching on the vamp or on the button holes of the upper where perfection determined the value of the product. Similarly other towns in New England became known for the production of men's shoes and boots and of children's shoes. National markets for specific products were being subdivided.

Seasonal demand for different shoe styles created busy seasons of intense activity. Shoe workers faced furiously busy months, followed by weeks of idleness. All activity was governed by piece rates paid for each process finished. The negotiation over piece rates became the center of labor disputes. Shoe workers turned first to the Knights and Daughters of St. Crispin, then to the Knights of Labor (KOL) in defense of their rights and wages. Lowering piece rates meant far more intense effort to maintain a living wage for families or individuals. New systems of marketing shoes featured traveling salesmen called drummers who carried samples for display to buyers, then telegraphed the orders back to the factories. The depressions of the 1870s and the 1890s created pressure on piece rates and wages, while the development of competition in Philadelphia, in the cities of northern New York, in Ohio, and Missouri challenged the older centers of shoemaking to set national standards for quality and low-cost production.

In 1889, the final, exacting hand process of lasting, the hand shaping or "pulling over" the upper to fit the sole, by male lasters faced mechanization. A machine using moving, fingerlike metal pincers drew the upper smoothly over the molded last while another mechanism drove tacks in automatically. The lasters reported that machines seemed to whisper, "I've got your job." Leather cutters used metal dies to stamp out leather pieces, while skilled fancy stitchers used double-needled sewing machines for work on uppers. Desperate to produce novelties during the depression years, shoe manufacturers marketed shoes for both men's and women's wear with an extremely narrow needle or "razor" toe. Stitchers and lasters complained that this extreme style resulted in broken needles and ruined stock, delays that reduced their wages and caused them great physical strain. In addition the hard times during the depression of the 1890s convinced shoe workers throughout the Northeast to organize trade unions in the federated Boot and Shoe Workers' Union. Former artisans, who had once worked by hand, such as the lasters, had unmistakably become industrial workers.

New immigrant groups crowded a labor market formerly dominated by Yankees and Irish Americans. By 1910, migrants from the Middle East and from southern and central Europe where men controlled leatherwork filled American shoe factories and replaced women as fancy stitchers. Protective legislation that did not permit women to work at night or more than 54 hours a week did not apply to foreign-born men during the busy seasons. Style changes to low-cut oxfords for women's wear, which lowered the costs of production in Lynn. The production in the 1920s of novelty shoes with a maximum of style at a minimal price to be bought in the new department stores encouraged even more intensive competition and lowered wages. The 1930s depression and the reciprocal trade agreements of the New Deal dealt a serious blow to domestic manufacturing, while imported shoes, first from Europe and in the late twentieth century from Asia and Latin America, finished the American leather dress shoe industry. Other

nations, notably Italy and Spain, had preserved their artisan traditions to become the leaders of high-quality footwear in the twentieth century.

MARY H. BLEWETT

See also **Artisans; Knights of Labor; Knights of St. Crispin and the Daughters of St. Crispin**

SIGNIFICANT GAINS AND MISSED OPPORTUNITIES: 1950s AND 1960s

Beginning in 1950, organized labor in the United States faced a paradox it would fail to resolve over the course of the next two decades. More than any other period in United States history, the 1950s and 1960s marked the golden age of unionism, in which organized labor held unprecedented economic and political power and organizational stability. Workers, both union and nonunion, made significant material gains and won important rights and protections on the job, while millions of Americans benefited from the expansion of the liberal welfare state that organized labor supported. Yet at the same time, labor seemed to be constantly frustrated and on the defensive. During the 1950s and 1960s, organized labor failed to consolidate its political power and was unable to pass significant labor law reforms or expand its membership past its World War II peak. Organized labor was also out of step with the decades' great social movements—civil rights, youth counterculture, antiwar, and feminism—and increasingly allied with a liberal establishment in crisis. In addition not all workers shared in the postwar affluence, which was unevenly distributed across various regions and occupational sectors. Labor proved unable to respond effectively either to structural changes in the economy and managerial strategies that weakened labor's influence and undermined its greatest postwar achievement, collective bargaining in the economy's primary industrial and manufacturing sector.

During the late 1940s and early 1950s, organized labor established long-term collective-bargaining relationships with employers in the mass-production sector, including such major industries as automobiles, steel, rubber manufacturing, and electrical consumer parts and products. In May 1950, the United Automobile Workers (UAW), the nation's largest industrial union, and General Motors (GM), its largest corporation, signed a landmark 5-year contract, which *Fortune*, a leading business magazine, hailed as the "Treaty of Detroit" because it signified that big business had conceded organized labor's right to exist. The contract not only promised GM 5 years of industrial stability, but gave UAW members a wage increase and a host of fringe benefits, including a cost-of-living adjustment (COLA), a pension, and a health insurance plan. Through the rest of the decade, Ford and Chrysler, the other two members of the automobile industry's big three, along with major companies in basic industry, signed similar agreements with industrial unions. Such contracts not only included improvements in wages and benefits, but also explicitly defined workers' rights on the job and specific grievance and arbitration procedures to remedy any violations of those rights. The protection of these rights through collective bargaining, what one historian has termed "workplace contractualism," marked a major achievement for unionized workers who could now expect management to observe a binding "rule of law" in the workplace. Industrial relations experts welcomed collective-bargaining contracts in basic industry as an indication of the maturing relationship between capital and labor and the permanent solution to the labor question—the chronic class conflict that had plagued the United States since the beginning of the industrial revolution. These experts were convinced that industrial stability based on an expanding postwar economy and collective bargaining was destined to become the norm in all industries for decades to come.

Such optimism over the eventual triumph of collective bargaining supports the common assumption that the 1950s and 1960s marked a unique period of class accommodation, later termed the postwar accord. But what appeared to be a class compromise can best be viewed as a stalemate that reflected the prevailing balance of forces between capital and labor. Collective bargaining in basic industry attested less to management's acceptance of collective bargaining than to the strength of industrial unions in the postwar era. Industrial unions in basic industry had their roots in the rank-and-file insurgency in the mid-1930s that was bolstered by favorable New Deal labor legislation, most notably the 1935 Wagner Act, which declared workers' right to form unions free of employer interference. The Wagner Act also established the National Labor Relations Board (NLRB) to monitor union elections and investigate and penalize employers who engaged in "unfair labor practices," such as blacklisting union members or failing to negotiate in good faith with unions. Membership in labor unions increased from the 1930s through World War II, when compulsory union membership became government policy for military contractors. By 1945, the year the war ended, union membership peaked at more than 14 million members, representing 35% of the nonagricultural labor force.

In the immediate postwar years, management was determined to roll back labor's gains and squared off with labor in a massive postwar strike wave. Although forced to settle with unions, management successfully protected its control over production and pricing decisions. Employers, particularly those in competitive sector industries who belonged to the conservative National Association of Manufacturers, also turned to political activity to curb labor's power. Taking advantage of the Republican party's control of both houses of the U.S. Congress in 1947 and 1948, management secured the passage of the Taft-Hartley Act over Democratic President Harry Truman's veto. Taft-Hartley, a complex revision of the Wagner Act, placed severe restrictions on unions, including prohibitions on union picketing and boycott tactics, the right to intervene in union certification elections, and two provisions that would define labor politics in the late 1940s and 1950s: Section 14(b) that outlawed the closed shop and allowed states to pass so-called "right-to-work" laws that prohibited compulsory union membership. Within a year after the passage of Taft-Hartley in June 1947, 14 states enacted right-to-work laws; and in the early 1950s, three more states followed with similar legislation, making a total of 17 states that outlawed union security provisions. These right-to-work states were located in the South, the Western Plains, and intermountain West; all had politically weak labor movements; and all had relatively low levels of industrialization and union density when compared to other regions.

Another important Taft-Hartley provision, Section 9(h), required all union officials to sign affidavits declaring that they were not members of the Communist party or believed in any organization that advocated the overthrow of the United States government by force or illegal methods. Unions whose officials refused the sign the affidavits risked losing NLRB protections and left themselves open to raids on their membership by rival unions. The American Federation of Labor (AFL) and Congress of Industrial Organizations (CIO) leaders initially labeled Taft-Hartley a "slave labor" act and pledged to work for its repeal. Although union leaders also initially vowed not to sign the non-Communist affidavits, they eventually relented, ostensibly to preserve access to NLRB protections. By that time labor leaders in the CIO were ousting Communists from the ranks of organized labor.

As the federation of industrial unions that had spearheaded labor's rise in the 1930s and 1940s, the CIO was split between its liberal unions and its left-led unions, which contained Communist party members in its top leadership and a small but significant number of Communists among its rank-and-file. As union activists Communists had played an important role in organizing unions during the CIO's formative years, but their presence proved much more troublesome during the Cold War era. The Communists' presence provided antilabor employers and politicians with an easy target to taint the entire labor movement as subversives beholden to the Soviet party line and willing to wage political strikes to weaken the United States. When the mainstream union movement grew increasingly closer to the Democratic party and its Cold War containment policy, liberals viewed the Communist-led unions as an expendable liability. During the 1948 election, the CIO threw its support behind the Democrats, but left-wingers either stayed neutral or endorsed insurgent Progressive party candidate Henry Wallace. When Truman won a narrow election victory and the Democrats regained Congress, the CIO move decisively against its left wing.

In several unions the campaign against Communists gave liberals the opportunity to prevail in long-standing feuds over leadership and strategy. Such was the case in the UAW, in which a center-right coalition led by former-Socialist-turned-anti-Communist liberal Walter Reuther ousted Communists from the union's top leadership in 1946. The Communist question also reflected internecine disputes in state and local union councils, where anti-Communists used red-baiting to dispense of their rivals. In several cases, such as the United Transit Workers' Mike Quill and National Maritime Union's Joseph Curran, leaders renounced their ties to the Communist party, expelled Communists, and remained at the head of their unions.

In 1949 and 1950, the CIO's top leadership, led by its president Phillip Murray, an anti-Communist Catholic, and the UAW's Reuther, expelled or forced out 11 unions that they accused of Communist domination. The purge of the CIO's left-wing solidified the federation's political direction, but it would have profound consequences for the labor movement as a whole. While a small number of expelled left-led unions survived the purge, it fatally weakened most of the left-led unions, which became open targets for raids on their membership by rival CIO and AFL unions. The purge also committed the labor movement to a more moderate stance on civil rights. Left-wing unions, such as the Food, Tobacco, Agricultural, and Allied Workers (FTA), which enjoyed support among black tobacco workers in the South, became easy targets for red-baiting once they were ousted from the CIO. The late 1940s and early 1950s marked a missed opportunity for the large labor federations to champion an agenda that addressed the merged union and civil rights issues, particularly in the southern states, which had the lowest level of union density of any region.

The CIO's purge of left-led unions also put the labor movement firmly behind U.S. Cold War foreign policy. In 1950, the CIO left the left-wing World Federation of Trade Unions to join AFL in the anti-Communist International Confederation of Free Trade Unions. Both unions would work secretly with the federal government's Central Intelligence Agency to provide organizational and financial support for anti-Communist trade unions, first in Europe, and then throughout the globe.

The CIO's purge of left-wing unionists cleared the way for the reunification of the rival AFL and CIO, which combined represented over 12 million of the nation's 15 million union members. The two federations made tentative moves toward reconciliation as early as the late 1930s, but continual disputes over jurisdictional authority and deep-seated differences between the two federations' leaders prevented a formal reconciliation. One obstacle was removed when John L. Lewis, head of the United Mine Workers and founder of the CIO, pulled out of that federation in 1942, and later joined the AFL, only to pull out of that federation in 1947. With Lewis out of the way, the two federations grew closer politically. The AFL began endorsing the prolabor Democrats in the late 1940s, and both federations worked together during the Korean War to shape national wage policy in labor's favor.

By 1950, the two federations made the first overtures toward formal reconciliation. The movement stalled until November 1952, when Republican Dwight Eisenhower won the presidency, convincing leaders of both federations that a merger was necessary to strengthen labor's political clout, a need that became more apparent when Eisenhower staffed the NLRB with anti-union appointees. Also clearing the way for the merger was the death of each federation's president, the AFL's William Green and the CIO's Murray, within weeks of each other in November 1952. Their successors, George Meany, a New York plumber who worked his way up to secretary-treasurer of the AFL, and Reuther, the head of the UAW who narrowly won the CIO presidency, would eventually complete the merger, although not before clearing up questions of jurisdiction and corruption. The two federations cleared up the first questions when most of their unions signed a no-raiding pact in 1953. The second question, concerning corruption, reflected Reuther's opposition to a number of AFL unions that had ties to known gangsters, particularly the racket-ridden East Coast International Longshoreman's Association (ILA). In a bold move Meany overturned the AFL's tradition of local autonomy and expelled the ILA, paving the way for eventual reconciliation. Although additional questions over racial discrimination in the AFL craft unions remained, the two sides agreed to address this issue later, opting for what they termed the "short approach" to unity. In December 1955, the two federations officially agreed to a merger, with Meany, reflecting the AFL's superior numbers, assuming the role of presidency of the reunited AFL-CIO and Reuther assuming a secondary position as head of its new Industrial Union Department.

The AFL-CIO merger marked the beginning of what both critics and supporters of the labor movement would term the era of big labor. With its headquarters in Washington DC, the reunited AFL-CIO embarked on an aggressive lobbying campaign through its newly created legislative department, which pursued a prolabor agenda in Congress, almost always in concert with the liberal wing of the Democratic party, whose ties with organized labor grew stronger during the decade. The AFL-CIO played a role in state and local politics through its Committee on Political Education (COPE) that mobilized union members for elections, registered voters, endorsed local and state candidates, and collected voluntary campaign contributions from union members. Through its political activity, the AFL-CIO sought to protect and extend labor rights won in the New Deal era and to promote liberal welfare-state policies. Although the AFL-CIO had little success in strengthening union protections, it helped expand Social Security legislation and secure an increase in the minimum wage during the 1950s.

While the AFL-CIO merger certainly strengthened the labor movement by resolving chronic jurisdictional disputes between the two federations, it contained several important weaknesses that would become apparent by the mid-1960s. The reunited AFL-CIO reflected in many ways the personality of its president, Meany, a product of AFL-style business unionism who boasted that he had never called a strike or walked a picket line when he served as a union official in the New York plumbers' union. Meany represented a new style of labor bureaucrat: The industrial statesman, comfortable with power and content to pursue welfare-state reform while uncritically backing the U.S. Cold War foreign policy. In line with liberal Keynesian economists of the day, Meany was convinced that organized labor's goal was the achievement of higher wages and better contracts in an expanding postwar economy.

Meany's supporters praised his skills as an administrator and lauded the bureaucratic organization and stability he brought to the labor movement. Meany also upheld the ethical standards he first demonstrated when he expelled the Longshoremen, when in 1957, he ousted the Teamsters' union, which had supplanted the UAW as the nation's largest union, after revelations of criminal behavior on the part of its leaders. In many ways Meany's leadership reflected the goals and aspirations of the union rank-and-file, mostly white men in manufacturing, processing, and transportation industries who shared his moderate liberal politics, support for Cold War containment, and interest in material improvement.

Meany's critics, such as prominent labor journalist Daniel Bell, blamed him for what Bell termed labor's "loss of *élan*" and for its general failure to fulfill its role as a social movement. Led by aged bureaucrats or money-hungry racketeers, the labor movement was in danger of losing public favor and slipping into irrelevance. While Bell believed that Reuther was the only major labor leader capable of redirecting the labor movement as a social movement, by this time Reuther had shed his earlier quest for transforming the United States into a European social democracy and opted for a pragmatic approach in which he hoped that employers would eventually tire of matching union demands and turn over many welfare functions to the state. While Reuther would continue to worry that the labor movement had abandoned its political idealism, his plan never came to fruition and instead, as his critics would point out, the United States featured a two-tiered system, consisting of a generous set of benefits for workers in unionized, private industries and a relatively weak set of benefits from the public welfare system. The two-tiered system often undercut sympathy for organized labor because unionized firms passed on labor costs to consumers. Nonunion workers in effect subsidized union workers' increased wages and benefit packages by paying higher prices for union-made goods.

In addition neither Meany nor Reuther could ever figure out how to increase the number of well-paid unionized, blue-collar jobs, many of which would eventually fall victim to automation or plant relocation. Not only were corporations leaving the unionized Northeast and midwestern states for right-to-work states in the Sun Belt, but increasingly moving to low-wage, nonunion Asian and Latin American countries. By the 1960s, American foreign investment abroad was increasing at a rate of 12% annually, with capital funds directed toward new *maquiladoras*, no-tariff zones in Mexico and the Philippines that were first established in 1968. By the early 1970s, some of the largest firms, such as Ford, Kodak, and Procter and Gamble, employed up to one-third of their workforce in regions outside the United States, which contained a significant segment of the consumer goods and electrical-parts industries.

Organized labor's failure to expand its organizational frontiers in the face of such structural transformation of the U.S. economy constituted the primary complaint against the Meany-era AFL-CIO. Under

Meany's leadership the AFL-CIO unions remained strong in the construction trades, transportation, and mass-production industries that its constituent unions had organized during the 1930s and 1940s, but by the mid-1950s organized labor's membership peaked at 35% of the nonagricultural workforce. From that point organized labor would increase its membership, but because of a postwar job expansion, the percentage of union members would slowly decline to 27% over the next 15 years.

Much of the AFL-CIO's failure to expand its organizational frontiers can be attributed to management's postwar campaign against unions. By the 1950s, management had launched massive ideological campaign that touted the "free-enterprise" system as a patriotic alternative to unions. In concert with the free-enterprise campaign, a key source of employer resistance came from modern welfare capitalist firms, such as Eastman Kodak, Sears Roebuck, and IBM, which competed against unions for their workers' loyalties by promoting paternalism and a corporate communal ideal as an alternative to unionism. These modern manors tended to be stable, profitable corporations with progressive employment and benefits policies that followed closely the hiring, seniority, and promotional patterns found in unionized counterparts. Even unionized companies in basic industry began to compete with unions for workers' loyalties through a strategy called Boulwarism, named after General Electric Personnel Director Lemuel Boulware, which was designed to undercut collective bargaining by making a single take-it-or-leave-it offer, and then publicizing the reasonableness of the offer directly to the rank-and-file. Even large manufacturing firms that accepted unions were engaged in constant strikes with industrial unions over wages and work rules. During the 1950s and 1960s, the number of strikes reached their highest recorded levels, averaging from 285–350 per year. Most major industries experienced a strike during contract renewals, and other smaller industries were constant targets for work stoppages. The steel industry was shut down five times between the end of World War II and 1960, including a 116-day strike in 1959, in which steelworkers' militancy prevented management from weakening job protections in local contracts.

The number of strikes attested to both workers' determination to protect the collective-bargaining system but also to a renewed vigor on management's part to weaken organized labor. Some of the most fervent anti-union firms were found in the southern region of the United States. All southern states, with the exception of Louisiana, passed right-to-work legislation, and the region had the lowest level of union density and lowest wages in the nation. This regional wage differential threatened labor's wage scale in the North, particularly when textile plants began relocating to the South after World War II. Both the AFL and CIO failed to organize much of the region's textile industry in highly publicized campaigns, and the disastrous 1950 General Textile Strike damaged what little unions were left in textiles. Although unions made inroads in the southern lumber, paper, and oil industries, the textile industry's low union rate and the region's relatively large number of agricultural workers who lacked collective-bargaining rights ensured that the South remained hostile to unions throughout the 1950s and 1960s. Workers who did display militancy often encountered employers and their political supporters who used such crude tactics, as intimidation of union activists, injunctions, state troopers, and appeals to white workers' racism to break strikes. By the 1950s, southern boosters, touting the region's low union density and open-shop legal environment, were successfully luring numerous northern and foreign firms to the region to escape unions back home.

Another challenge to organized labor's power came from smaller, competitive sector employers who bitterly fought to rid their plants of labor unions. These employers sought to slash labor costs to compete with rivals and usually made producers' goods and unlike oligopolistic sectors, could not pass increased labor costs on to consumers. The most violent strikes of the 1950s occurred in this sector when anti-union employers moved to rid their plants of unions with classic union-busting tactics that harkened back to earlier bloody periods in United States labor history. In addition to fighting for their institutional existence in the competitive sectors, unions made few inroads into the expanding clerical and retail sectors of the economy. While the absolute number of workers in unions increased through the 1950s and 1960s from over 14 million in 1950 to over 19 million in 1973, the percentage of union workers fell from 31% to 27% over the same period.

Part of labor's failure to expand its organizational reach could be attributed to its declining public image, which suffered from public hearings conducted by the United States Senate's McClellan Committee, known by its nickname the Labor Rackets Committee, which lasted from 1957 to 1960. The McClellan Committee held a series of high-profile hearings that uncovered criminal activity among national and local officials of the Teamsters, Bakers, and other AFL trade unions. The hearings titillated the public with a dark portrait of organized labor that reinforced the sinister image depicted in 1950s labor *noir* films, such as *On the Waterfront* (1954) and *Slaughter on Tenth Avenue* (1957), and in Lester Velie's lurid articles in

Reader's Digest. The committee failed however to pin any charges of malfeasance on the mainstream labor movement and particularly Reuther and the UAW, the special targets of the committee's anti-union members, notably Arizona Senator Barry Goldwater.

The McClellan Committee succeeded in turning public attention to Jimmy Hoffa, then an obscure Teamster vice-president. Along with Meany and Reuther, Hoffa became one of the most recognizable union figures of this period and a symbol of blue-collar toughness. After he became the Teamster president in 1957, Hoffa spurned Reuther's idealism and Meany's industrial statesmanship and opted instead for a law-of-the-jungle approach that made improved contracts for Teamster members his sole concern. Possessing little regard for rank-and-file democracy or the union's tradition of local autonomy, Hoffa transformed the Teamsters into an effective centralized bureaucracy. He not only made the Teamsters the largest U.S. union by organizing workers in occupations outside the trucking and shipping industry, he took full advantage of the Interstate Commerce Commission's regulation of interstate trucking rates, which encouraged unionization by limiting price competition among shippers, and his own innovative picketing tactics to gain national contracts for his members. These contracts included increased wages, benefits, and provisions for job security, a primary concern for many truckers. Despite his achievements and the support among many Teamster members, Hoffa's questionable loans to mobsters from the Teamster pension fund and his willingness to overlook gangster-controlled Teamster locals made him a constant target for federal investigators, who eventually sent him to prison in 1967 for jury tampering.

A host of anti-union ideologues joined the crusade against organized labor, which they claimed was simultaneously infested with gangsters and Red officials who secretly served as agents for the Soviet Union. The campaign began in the late 1940s when right-wing propagandists for the shadowy Committee for Constitutional Government joined with such syndicated newspaper columnists as Westbrook Pegler to rail against the union shop, which these critics condemned as compulsory unionism and the first step toward a socialist state. The right-wing campaign against unions crested in 1957 with the publication of ex-New Dealer Donald Richberg's pulp paperback, *Labor Union Monopoly*, in which Richberg accused powerful and aggressive labor union leaders and their goons of waging "warfare on a competitive free economy" and thus "preparing the way for communism more effectively than the Communists themselves" (Richberg, *Labor Union Monopoly*, 175).

The right-wing assault on unions coupled with the McClellan Committee hearings gave congressional Republicans and conservative Democrats leverage to pass the 1959 Labor-Management Reporting and Disclosure Act (commonly known as the Landrum-Griffin Act for its congressional sponsors), the only major labor legislation during the 1950s. Landrum-Griffin reflected the right-wing's obsession with unions as corrupt, undemocratic organizations that needed tighter federal regulation. Landrum-Griffin bolstered Taft-Hartley's restrictions on union strike tactics and required unions to hold regular and democratic elections with a secret ballot, to keep accurate financial records, and disclose these records to the public. Landrum-Griffin also contained a bill of rights for workers putatively designed to protect workers from what the bill's authors assumed were dictatorial labor bosses, but it lacked any provision to protect black workers or women from discrimination by labor unions or from anti-union employers.

Despite organized labor's legislative failures, workers, and particularly white male workers in unionized mass-production industries, posted solid gains through the 1950s and 1960s, a testament to both the strength of organized labor and the expanding postwar economy. Beginning in 1947, a surging economy provided millions of jobs, boosted by a combination of a dynamic consumer sector, relatively little foreign competition, and rising military spending. From 1948 to 1972, when adjusted for inflation, the economy grew at an annual rate of 7%. Although the top-tenth of the population still held 40% of all wealth, the economic pie was getting bigger as total GNP increased 165% while population grew by only 66%. As a result of the postwar economic boom, real wages climbed steadily upward. From 1939–1959, workers in manufacturing industries saw their real income rise 62% from $39 to $64 per week, or $2,000 to $3,300 per year (in 1947 dollars). Unionized steelworkers for example wrested real wage increases of 110% from 1936 to 1959. More importantly for all workers these wage increases came as workers labored fewer days and fewer hours per week. By the 1960s, the 5-day, 40-hour week became standard throughout almost all sectors of the economy. Thanks to rising wages, the highest paid craft and industrial workers were able to purchase homes, automobiles, and such consumer durable goods as home appliances and television sets; and smaller segment even had enough discretionary income to take vacations, send their children to college, and to retire without fear of slipping into poverty because of union pensions, health insurance, and federal social security payments. Workers' rising standard of living led mainstream publications to proclaim that postwar affluence had eliminated the economic basis of class stratification and as a result, the United States had become a middle-class society.

Despite such pronouncements, workers' gains in the postwar era should not be exaggerated. Lacking guaranteed salaries, workers' earnings could fluctuate from year-to-year, and many lived in fear of lay-offs and strikes, which could quickly erode their hard-earned savings. Even the best-paid union workers lived amid some material instability. In 1952, the federal government determined that a "modest but adequate budget for a family of four" was 79 dollars per week at a time when the average steelworker was still earning only 78 dollars per week. In most cases workers supported middle-class consumption patterns through credit or time purchases or because both husband and wife worked for wages outside the home.

While workers made some significant material gains during the 1950s, they also began registering high rates of dissatisfaction, or alienation in the sociological parlance of the day. Studies in the 1950s showed that many factory workers hated their jobs and desired independence from the monotony of mass-production work. According to sociologist Eli Chinoy, except for a small group of union officials, many autoworkers looked forward to getting out of the factory and owning their own small business. Such problems persisted through the 1960s and early 1970s when they came to light in a famous study conducted by the United States Department of Health, Education, and Welfare, published in 1973, which concluded that "significant numbers of American workers are dissatisfied with the quality of their working lives. Dull, repetitive, seemingly meaningless tasks, offering little challenge or autonomy, are causing discontent among workers at all occupational levels" (*Work in America*, 1973). Given these findings it was not surprising that only 22% of blue-collar workers would recommend their job to their children. By the 1960s, increased educational and economic status for many working-class Americans meant that an interesting job was as important as a job that paid well.

For a significant number of workers, a job that paid well would have constituted an improvement. These workers who failed to benefit from the postwar boom were overwhelmingly black or Hispanic, and female, and concentrated in sectors of the economy—agriculture, public and domestic service—that were unprotected by federal labor or wage-and-hour laws. In his best-selling *The Other America* (1962), Michael Harrington estimated that as many as 50 million workers lived in conditions of "painful poverty" and family instability. These workers lived in areas experiencing industrial decline, such as Appalachia, or urban or rural migrant ghettos. More often poor workers, such as black agricultural and service workers in the South, were victims of racism that barred their entry into higher paid industrial jobs. Harrington's book launched liberals' discovery of poverty in the 1960s, and inspired President Kennedy and his successor, Lyndon Johnson, to launch the War on Poverty—supported by the AFL-CIO—that included a host of government programs designed to solve, with mixed success, what later came to be known as the underclass problem. Liberals and labor leaders also placed their faith in an expanding economy, which they hoped would open job opportunities for the poor and underemployed while expanding organized labor's membership base

As the 1960s opened however, union growth had stagnated in the industrial sector, but workers in other sectors of the economy would embrace the union ideal during the decade. Some of these workers were such elite labor aristocrats as airline pilots and professional athletes who converted their ineffective employee associations into strong labor unions. But the most dramatic growth in unionism came from public-sector employees at the federal, state, county, and municipal levels. The growth of public-sector unionism reflected the expansion of the postwar state, which grew to over 14 million jobs and accounted for over 19% of the nonagricultural workforce by the mid-1970s. The rise of public-service unionism was also remarkable given the numerous obstacles faced by public workers who desired unions; federal and most state labor laws refused to recognize the right of public workers to bargain collectively or to strike.

The rise in public-sector unionism reflected a change in public workers' consciousness, with many public workers rejecting the prevailing view that government work by its very nature constituted a low-paying form of civic service and instead viewed their jobs as work that deserved the same pay and benefits as similar employment in the private sector. The upsurge in public-sector unionism also testified to organized labor's political power during the 1960s. Public-sector unions received crucial support from liberal politicians dependent on union workers' votes in the urban centers and union-dense states outside of the Deep South. At the federal level, government workers in particular benefited from labor's support for Democratic John Kennedy in his narrow 1960 presidential election victory. In 1961, Kennedy issued Executive Order 10988, which legalized collective bargaining for federal employees and fostered a favorable environment for nonfederal public employees. While nonfederal employees belonged to a variety of trade associations, unaffiliated unions, and established AFL-CIO unions, the leading union to emerge among nonfederal workers in the postwar years was the American Federation of State, County, and Municipal Employees (AFSCME), an AFL-CIO affiliate. Starting in the 1950s with less than 100,000 members, AFSCME waged a vigorous campaign to gain collective-bargaining status. In 1958, AFSCME's efforts paid off when New York City Mayor Robert Wagner signed an executive order that granted collective-bargaining rights to the city's public-employee unions. Similar laws in other states and municipalities followed, allowing AFSCME to increase its membership, and by the early 1970s, it claimed over 600,000 members.

The most unexpected group to unionize during the 1960s was elementary and secondary schoolteachers, who also became the most militant of public-sector employees. Teachers' unions had their roots in early twentieth century occupational associations, but few of these associations engaged in collective bargaining until the 1960s. The transformation of teacher unionism benefited from the competition for members between the National Education Association (NEA), the largest teachers' union, which also included school administrators, and the smaller American Federation of Teachers (AFT), an AFL affiliate dedicated to collective bargaining and traditional trade union activity. By the end of the 1960s, thanks to the rivalry, the combined membership of the NEA and AFT stood at two million members.

The rise of teachers' unions also reflected the outlook of a new generation of teachers, including many feminists and college graduates radicalized by their campus experience. These teachers rejected the public-service model and instead viewed teaching as a legitimate middle-class career. Members of this new generation turned to unions to improve their pay, benefits, and working conditions. Unionized teachers also demanded better classroom conditions because of the increased burdens placed on them by middle-class parents who expected public schools to prepare their children for college and by administrators in urban areas, where teachers were expected to educate children in less than ideal circumstances. Teachers demonstrated a willingness to strike to achieve their demands, often defying state and municipal ordinances against such action. By 1967, public schools would witness almost 90 strikes involving 96,000 workers, a rate that exceeded any other public-service sector.

The drive for unions by workers at voluntary non-profit private hospitals paralleled the public workers as another group that experienced increased unionization from the late 1950s through the 1960s. As with public workers, hospital workers were excluded from federal and state labor laws and were likewise limited by a service ideology. Hospital workers were overwhelmingly members of those groups, African-American women and Hispanic men and women, situated on the margins of the postwar economy where they worked long hours for wages below the minimum wage. Organizational efforts in this sector melded the left-wing idealism of labor's upsurge in the 1930s with the burgeoning civil rights movement. In the late 1950s, left-wing organizers in New York's Retail Druggists' Local 1199 launched a drive to organize hospital workers that used strikes to win collective-bargaining contracts. As a key to its success, Local 1199 merged trade union demands with a civil rights consciousness, linking its demands for better wages and working conditions to black and Hispanic workers' drive for legal rights and dignity that stood at the center of the modern civil rights movement.

For most black workers the post-World War period opened with promise but ended with pessimism. During the early 1950s, black unemployment reached its lowest levels as black male workers claimed industrial jobs during the Korean War military expansion. In the postwar recession year of 1954, black unemployment rose to twice that of white unemployment, a common pattern during the postwar decades. Black workers faced several obstacles. Those who lived or migrated to the North encountered a shrinking job market, and many lacked the training to fill the skilled occupations. In turn trade unions openly discriminated against those blacks who possessed necessary skills or who sought entry to apprenticeship training. For the most part black women were excluded from all but the lowest paying jobs. Black workers who achieved some measure of affluence were those who had gained seniority in sectors organized by industrial unions or who labored in certain sectors of the South, such as the unionized lumber and paper industry and only then in families with at least two wage earners.

The rise of the modern civil rights movement promised to revive the civil rights unionism of the late 1940s. During the 1950s and 1960s, the AFL-CIO's official policy supported civil rights legislation and successfully lobbied in support of the landmark 1964 Civil Rights Act and the 1965 Voting Rights Act. But except for the UAW, which helped sponsor the celebrated 1963 March on Washington and the United Packinghouse Workers and consistently championed black workers' concerns, the AFL-CIO's leadership failed to grasp black workers' frustration and instead relied on the expanding postwar economy to provide opportunities for black workers. The AFL-CIO also did little to move its constituent unions toward racial equality; many craft unions still barred blacks from membership; others maintained *de facto* black unions, or in the case of more liberal former CIO unions that contained large number of African-American members, failed to promote blacks to leadership positions.

To address their lack of representation in labor's upper echelon, black union officials and activists, led by A. Philip Randolph, formed the Negro American Labor Council in 1960 but were rebuffed by Meany as dual unionists who did not speak for black rank-and-file. By the late 1960s, some black unionists, influenced by the growing militancy of the civil rights movement and increasing unemployment, established a series of "revolutionary union movements" centered on the Detroit automobile industry. Although the movements failed to attract a large number of supporters, they highlighted the growing discontent of black unionists with lack of progress and representation in union leadership positions. The same sense of frustration over the persistence of racial inequality led civil rights leader Martin Luther King, Jr., to address the problems of poverty and unemployment. In the 2 years before his death, King began working more closely with such unions as Local 1199 that merged collective bargaining with civil rights consciousness. His assassination in 1968 came during a campaign on behalf of striking Memphis sanitation workers; black public-sector employees who won a union contract after King's death brought public scrutiny to their cause.

Despite the AFL-CIO's lack of urgency on racial discrimination, most black workers in unionized sectors remained loyal to their unions and used legal action to break down racial barriers. Black workers benefited from the 1964 Civil Rights Act's Title IV provision that barred discrimination by both employers and unions. In several industries, most notably the southern paper and textile industries, black workers filed a series of Title VII lawsuits that ended segregated, Jim Crow unions and discriminatory promotion and seniority policies. By the close of the 1960s, black workers had made inroads into previously white-only occupations and unions, and black unemployment dropped below 4% nationally. Despite these gains black unemployment stood in double digits in northern manufacturing cities, which had previously provided high-wage entry-level jobs but were now losing plants to the Sun Belt or to foreign countries. The success of the civil rights movement underscored the most confounding paradox of the 1950s and 1960s. While workers were able to achieve legal protection against employment discrimination, neither their unions nor liberal politicians could find a way to increase the number of high-paying entry-level jobs. By the 1970s, despite the achievements of the civil rights movement, black unemployment had risen sharply, and black upward mobility began to ebb.

Hispanic workers also benefited from the civil-rights-conscious unionism of the 1960s. In the Southwest Mexican-American workers who labored in the region's nonferrous mining industry benefited from union campaigns in the 1940s, when the left-led Mine, Mill, and Smelter Workers combined trade unionism with an assault on discrimination in the company towns of New Mexico and Arizona. During the 1950s and early 1960s, these workers stayed loyal to Mine Mill even after its ouster from the CIO and continued to benefit from union contracts. Outside of mining most Mexican-American workers labored in the region's poorly paid service and agricultural sectors amid the worst job and living conditions in the United States. The plight of Mexican-American and Filipino farmworkers in California's Central Valley during the 1960s became the site of the decade's most high-profile organizing campaign spearheaded by the United Farm Workers' Organizing Committee (UFW). Led by the charismatic Cesar Chavez, who combined devout Catholicism and community outreach with trade unionism, the UFW united militant Filipino and Mexican-American farmworkers to improve conditions in the California agricultural fields. The UFW's campaign was unique because it attracted the support of Chicano activists, campus radicals, and liberals such as Robert Kennedy and Reuther, who saw the farmworkers' campaign as an opportunity for labor to renew its social activism while increasing its organizational scope. The campaign was most notable for the national grape boycott, the most novel strike tactic of the postwar era devised during the UFW's struggle against grape growers in Delano, California. Enthusiastic consumer response to the grape boycott helped the UFW win the first union contract in the California fields and eventually to gain legal protection for collective bargaining from the state of California. Much like the paradox faced by black workers, the UFW's campaign on behalf of farmworkers would stall in the 1970s, when it faced more determined resistance from employers and their political allies.

The 1950s and 1960s witnessed the increasing feminization of the workforce. During these two decades, women's participation increased from 24% to 42% of the total workforce, and the number of female workers doubled from 18 to over 30 million workers. By the 1970s, over half of all women were engaged in paid employment, with almost two-thirds working in full-time positions. Women's increased participation reflected the demand for labor in the burgeoning service sector and the rise in the number of women—single, married, or divorced—who needed to earn a living to support themselves or their families.

The demand for women's labor undercut the post-war domestic ideology that celebrated women's role as a wife, mother, and homemaker. Over half of the mothers with children were working by the end of the 1960s, and the same percentage of two-parent families had wives who contributed at least one-fourth of the total family income. Women's increased workforce participation also reflected the rise of second-wave feminism among women who came of age in the 1960s. Determined to pursue careers outside of the home, women began bearing fewer children, attaining higher education levels, and marrying husbands with more favorable attitudes toward working wives.

The major problem with women's work was that most women were concentrated in sex-segregated occupations—typists, telephone operators, secretaries, waitresses, maids, and hair stylists—which paid less than traditional male jobs. Few women had access to more lucrative jobs because craft unions barred women from apprenticeship programs or because supervisors in both public and private employment barred women from promotions to higher-level positions. Because more women were clustered in low-wage pink-collar jobs, their rate of pay relative to men's actually declined from the beginning of the 1950s to the 1970s from 64% to 59%. Women also faced gender-specific grievances and different job criteria than men, such as physical attractiveness, and different requirements, such as possessing so-called domestic skills. Unlike men women also faced the pressures of sexual harassment and doing double duty as housewives, which usually entailed an extra 30 hours per week of work.

During the 1960s, most women used individual strategies to address their grievances by moving off and on the labor market in response to family and personal considerations. But a significant number worked within unions to remedy their concerns. By 1954, women constituted a sizeable minority—three million or one-fifth—of all union members. A small percentage of women unionists worked in manufacturing industries and held membership in various industrial, garment, or textile unions, but most female union members were concentrated in the service unions, such as the Hotel Employees and Restaurant Employees, or Communication Workers of America. As union members women pushed for equal pay, fair job rates, and the end to sex-based discrimination in hiring while lobbying for a higher minimum wage. Female union members were split on the question of eliminating all gender distinctions on the job. Many opted for an approach that one historian has termed "labor feminism," which urged the elimination of sex-based policies on wages and promotions but favored those measures, such as maternity leave and opting out of certain shifts to take care of their children, that were specific to their position as women and homemakers.

Workingwomen drew on the example of the civil rights movement and turned to politics for government solutions. In the early 1960s, President Kennedy prohibited sex discrimination in the federal civil service and in 1963 signed the Equal Pay Act, which mandated equal pay for equal work. A year later Title VII of the Civil Rights Act barred sex discrimination by unions and firms with 15 or more employees and gave women access to the Equal Employment Opportunity Commission to file complaints against employers and unions. By the beginning of the 1970s, the National Organization for Women and other feminist organizations were directing women's political agenda away from labor feminism and toward sex-neutral policies, assuming that women would make more progress through measures that ensured fair competition within a strict meritocracy. By the beginning of the 1970s, these organizations gained two-thirds majorities in both houses of Congress for the Equal Rights Amendment, which barred all discrimination based on sex and was expected to achieve rapid ratification by two-thirds of the states. Although the Equal Rights Amendment would eventually fail, women posted impressive gains in the 1960s and the decade that followed. But as was the case with other rights-consciousness campaigns, women failed to close the wage gap, reach equity with men in higher-paying occupations, or eliminate gender-specific grievances.

As the 1960s came to a close, labor was stuck in the paradox that plagued it since the end of World War II. Unions still wielded impressive political power and could boast material improvements for its members. Bolstered by union gains and the expanding economy, the national poverty rate fell to an all-time low of 11% of the population by the mid-1960s. Through its support of President Lyndon Johnson's Great Society programs, organized labor could also point to some concrete legislative achievements, from national medical care for the elderly and the poor to increases in the minimum wage and social security and the establishment of the Model Cities Urban-Renewal Program.

But organized labor also faced serious political setbacks, best illustrated in its failure to repeal Taft-Hartley's Section 14(b) in 1965, a year in which pro-labor Democrats made up majorities in both houses of Congress. Although the repeal effort passed the House of Representatives by an 18-vote margin in July 1965, a filibuster led by Illinois Senator Everett

Dirksen, leader of the Senate's Republican minority, and backed by a coalition of conservative Republicans and southern Democrats twice prevented a full Senate vote on the repeal bill in October 1965 and February 1966. The defeat of several prolabor Senators in the 1966 midterm elections closed any repeal effort for the remainder of the decade.

The politics of the Vietnam War also presented organized labor with a dilemma. By uncritically backing the Johnson administration's escalation of the Vietnam War beginning in 1965, the AFL-CIO had committed itself to supporting a liberal Democratic administration waging an increasingly unpopular war. The AFL-CIO President Meany proved intransigently committed to the Vietnam War and continued to back the war through the late 1960s even as public opinion turned against the war. Meany's stance also pitted the AFL-CIO against the growing number of antiwar liberals, rank-and-file members, and intellectuals, who dismissed organized labor as a reactionary bureaucracy irresponsive to concerns over the war, but also opened the union to questions of racial and gender equality and the lack of democracy in AFL-CIO unions.

By the late 1960s, even the most established unions were split by internal dissension over the lack of democratic institutions and corruption, as was the case in the United Mine Workers and Teamsters. Similar dissension also split the AFL-CIO. In 1968, Reuther, frustrated with the AFL-CIO's uncritical support for the Democratic party's foreign policy, its failure to increase organizational efforts, and its lack of "social vision" on race and poverty, pulled the UAW out of the AFL-CIO to chart a course as an unaffiliated independent union, which represented more a valiant gesture than an effective strategy to direct the labor movement toward a more progressive course.

The dissension within labor's ranks reflected widespread political polarization during the second-half of the 1960s. Early in the decade organized labor had worked closely with young radicals in the emerging New Left, but by supporting the Vietnam War, and not pushing hard enough for civil rights and other social justice movements, labor lost the support of New Left youth and campus radicals, who increasingly viewed organized labor as part of the establishment wedded to a corrupt status quo. The AFL-CIO also lost support from a significant number of white union members who resented what they viewed as the excesses of the welfare state and the Warren Court, the youth counterculture and antiwar movement, and the radicalism of the civil rights movement, feminist and other group-liberation efforts. The white backlash against labor and liberalism posed problems for organized labor at the ballot box when enough working-class voters abandoned the Democratic party to deny Hubert Humphrey the presidency in 1968. Most southern white working-class voters cast their ballots instead for former Alabama governor and arch-segregationist, George Wallace, who ran as an independent candidate on an antiliberal, populist platform, while a number of northern backlash votes went to the eventual winner, Republican party candidate Richard Nixon. While Nixon had neither the political power nor intention of dismantling the welfare state or weakening existing labor law, a new breed of right-wing Republicans (many of them southern ex-Democrats) would first emerge, determined to curb unions' power by championing free-market policies. Economic expansion kept this New Right at bay during the late-1960s, but it would gain strength during the 1970s when the postwar boom ended.

During the 1970s, the combination of inflation, unemployment, and higher energy prices signaled the end of postwar expansion, and by the end of the decade, the AFL-CIO would begin waging a defensive action to preserve the gains it made during the boom years. However this outcome is clear only in retrospect, and it would be a mistake to view labor's eventual decline as inevitable. During the 1970s, organized labor would continue to exert its political influence; strengthen existing welfare-state provisions; and maintain collective-bargaining relationships in basic industry, the construction and building trades, and other unionized sectors of the economy. Even as the postwar boom ebbed, unionized workers showed their willingness to strike to maintain their share of national wealth, and new workers in government and the public sector would continue to join unions. Organized labor would have many of the same strengths and weaknesses in the 1970s that it possessed since the mid-1950s, but it would be these weaknesses that anti-union politicians and employers would exploit during the 1980s to bring the era of big labor to a close.

DAVID M. ANDERSON

References and Further Reading

Babson, Steve. *The Unfinished Struggle: Turning Points in American Labor, 1877–Present.* Lanham, MD: Rowan and Littlefield Publishers, 1999.

Bell, Daniel. *The End of Ideology: On the Exhaustion of Political Ideas in the Fifties.* Glencoe, IL: The Free Press, 1960.

Boyle, Kevin. *The UAW and the Heyday of American Liberalism, 1945–1968.* Ithaca, NY: Cornell University Press, 1995.

Brody, David. *Workers in Industrial America: Essay on the Twentieth-Century Struggle.* 2nd ed. New York, NY: Oxford University Press, 1993.

———. *In Labor's Cause: Main Themes on the History of the American Worker*. New York: Oxford University Press, 1993.

Chinoy, Eli. *Autoworkers and the American Dream*. 2nd ed. Urbana: University of Illinois Press, 1955, 1992.

Cobble, Dorothy Sue. *The Other Women's Movement: Workplace Justice and Social Rights in Modern America*. Princeton, NJ: Princeton University Press, 2005.

Cowie, Jefferson. *Capital Moves: RCA's Seventy-Year Quest for Cheap Labor*. Ithaca, NY: Cornell University Press, 1999.

Daniel, Cletus E. "Cesar Chavez and the Unionization of California Farm Workers." In *Labor Leaders in America*, Melvyn Dubofsky and Warren Van Tine, eds. Urbana: University of Illinois Press, 1987.

Draper, Alan. *Conflict of Interests: Organized Labor and the Civil Rights Movement in the South, 1954–1968*. Ithaca, NY: ILR Press, 1994.

Dubofsky, Melvyn. *The State and Labor in Modern America*. Chapel Hill: University of North Carolina Press, 1994.

Fink, Leon, and Brian Greenberg. *Upheaval in the Quiet Zone: A History of Hospital Workers' Union, Local 1199*. Urbana: University of Illinois Press, 1989.

Fones-Wolf, Elizabeth. *Selling Free Enterprise: The Business Assault on Labor and Liberalism, 1945–60*. Urbana: University of Illinois Press, 1994.

Freeman, Joshua B. *Working-Class New York: Life and Labor since World War II*. New York: The New Press, 2000.

Gabin, Nancy. *Feminism in the Labor Movement: Women and the United Auto Workers, 1935–1975*. Ithaca, NY: Cornell University Press, 1990.

Gall, Gilbert J. *The Politics of Right to Work: The Labor Federations as Special Interests, 1943–1979*. Westport, CT: Greenwood Press, 1988.

Gross, James A. *Broken Promise: The Subversion of U.S. Labor Relations Policy, 1947–1994*. Philadelphia, PA: Temple University Press, 1995.

Harrington, Michael. *The Other America: Poverty in the United States*. New York: Macmillan, 1962.

Jacoby, Sanford. *Modern Manors: Welfare Capitalism since the New Deal*. Princeton, NJ: Princeton University Press, 1997.

Kessler-Harris, Alice. *Out to Work: A History of Wage-Earning Women in the United States*. New York: Oxford University Press, 1982.

Korstad, Robert Rodgers. *Civil Rights Unionism: Tobacco Workers and the Struggle for Democracy in the Mid-Twentieth-Century South*. Chapel Hill: University of North Carolina Press, 2003.

Levy, Peter. *The New Left and Labor in the 1960s*. Urbana: University of Illinois Press, 1994.

Lichtenstein, Nelson. *The Most Dangerous Man in Detroit: Walter Reuther and the Fate of American Labor*. New York: Basic Books, 1995.

———. *State of the Union: A Century of American Labor*. Princeton, NJ: Princeton University Press, 2002.

Metzgar, Jack. *Striking Steel: Solidarity Remembered*. Philadelphia, PA: Temple University Press, 2000.

Minchin, Timothy J. *Fighting against the Odds: A History of Southern Labor since World War II*. Gainesville: University of Florida Press, 2005.

Murphy, Marjorie. *Blackboard Unions: The AFT and NEA, 1900–1980*. Ithaca, NY: Cornell University Press, 1990.

Rosswurm, Steve, ed. *The CIO's Left-Led Unions*. New Brunswick, NJ: Rutgers University Press, 1992.

Slater, Joseph E. *Public Workers: Government Employee Unions, the Law, and the State, 1900–1962*. Ithaca, NY: ILR Press, 2004.

Stebenne, David L. *Arthur J. Goldberg: New Deal Liberal*. New York: Oxford University Press, 1996.

Stein, Judith. *Running Steel, Running America: Race, Economic Policy, and the Decline of Liberalism*. Chapel Hill: University of North Carolina Press, 1998.

Sugrue, Thomas J. *Origins of the Urban Crisis: Race and Inequality in Postwar Detroit*. Princeton, NJ: Princeton University Press, 1996.

Zieger, Robert H. *American Workers, American Unions, 1920–1985*. Baltimore, MD: The Johns Hopkins University Press, 1986.

———. *The CIO, 1935–1955*. Chapel Hill: University of North Carolina Press, 1995.

Cases and Statutes Cited

Civil Rights Act
Equal Pay Act
Labor-Management Reporting and Disclosure Act
Taft-Hartley Act
Voting Rights Act
Wagner Act

See also **Affirmative Action; American Federation of Government Employees; American Federation of Labor-Congress of Industrial Organizations; American Federation of State, County, and Municipal Employees; American Federation of Teachers; American Postal Workers' Union; Anticommunism; Beck, David; Black Lung Associations; Civil Rights Act of 1964/Title VII; Cold War; Collective Bargaining; Communist Party; Davis, Leon; Delano Grape Strike; Equal Pay Act of 1962; Foner, Moe; GI Bill; Hoffa, James P.; Hoffa, James R.; House Un-American Activities Committee/Dies Committee; Huerta, Dolores C.; Immigration and Nationality Act of 1965; International Brotherhood of Teamsters; March on Washington Movement; McCarran-Walter Act (1952); McClellan Committee Hearings; Meany, George; Memphis Sanitation Strike (1968); Miners for Democracy; National Education Association; National Federation of Federal Employees; National Right to Work Committee; New Left; Operation Dixie; Service Employees' International Union; Shanker, Albert; Slichter, Sumner; Steel Strike (longest and largest) 1959; Taft-Hartley; Teamsters for a Democratic Union (1976); United Mine Workers of America; Waitressing and Waiting/Food Service**

SINGLE TAX

The single tax was the brainchild of social reformer Henry George, and it became one of the most popular, if unconventional, reforms for the inequalities of

American capitalism in the late nineteenth and early twentieth centuries. Many workingmen flocked to the banner of the single tax, as did a host of middle-class reformers. This ability of the single tax to bridge often antagonistic political opponents was one of its strengths, as well as one of the reasons for its ultimate decline by World War I.

Born in Philadelphia in 1839, George ended up in California during the 1860s. Rather than finding economic opportunity on the frontier however, George personally experienced great deprivation. A printer by trade, he became politically active in anticorporate agitation and ultimately came to the conclusion that powerful economic interests were monopolizing land, destroying economic opportunities for ordinary people. George first formulated his single-tax philosophy in an 1871 pamphlet, which he followed with his 1879 masterpiece, *Progress and Poverty*. A blend of Jeffersonian democracy, evangelical Protestantism, and populist economics, that book became one of the greatest bestsellers in the nineteenth-century United States.

Even during the late nineteenth century, when complicated issues of taxation and government finance were much more matters of public discussion than they are today, the single tax was fairly esoteric. While proponents formulated different specific, pragmatic ways of putting the single tax into effect, the basic goal was always the same: To end the unjust land monopoly supposedly at the root of economic inequality. Single taxers for example pointed to land owners who bought a block in a developing city, and then watched the property value of that block skyrocket through the rise of population and the general development of the economy—not through any effort of the owner.

This economic windfall should therefore, single taxers argued, belong not to the land's owner, but to the community as a whole. Complete confiscatory taxation of increased land value would eliminate unjust gains in real estate speculation and force the broad sale of land held by monopolists, thus encouraging industry and providing all male households with the opportunity to own a homestead. The proposed tax was single because, its advocates proclaimed, it would provide all the money needed for government coffers. And in any case single taxers argued that all other taxes (including income and inheritance) were immoral and unproductive because they took money and property away from the workers and business owners who had earned them through their own labor.

During the late nineteenth century, George and his allies forged a potent set of alliances to fight for the single tax. The most pitched battle occurred when George ran for mayor of New York City in 1886. While not all supporters of George were single-tax devotees, many of the workingmen who formed the foundation of his campaign were Irish immigrants for whom the single tax provided a potent appeal in its invocation of land for the hungry masses. George finished a close second in that race, behind Democrat Abram Hewitt but ahead of Republican Theodore Roosevelt.

George died in 1897, and much of the punch of the single-tax movement died with him (even though his son, Henry George, Jr., was elected to Congress from New York City in 1910 and 1912). Yet agitation did not cease, with many cities and states continuing to be convulsed with battles for the single tax. With strong labor support, a single-tax mayor took office in Seattle in 1912; the Georgeites obtained victory in Pueblo, Colorado, in 1913; and the Industrial Workers of the World stronghold of Everett, Washington, witnessed two single-tax electoral triumphs during the teens. The most powerful labor movement in the country, in San Francisco, proudly advocated the single tax, as did the nation's most powerful socialist movement, in Oklahoma.

The most significant movement for the single tax during the early twentieth century arose in Oregon. A powerful combination of American Federation of Labor (AFL) unionists and radicals sympathetic to the cause of small business joined forces to advocate various shades of Georgeism. Using the initiative of the direct-democracy device that allowed voters to propose and vote on laws and newly enshrined in Oregon, such single taxers as William U'Ren put their question to citizens in every election from 1908 to 1916. Yet only one election could be viewed as even a partial victory for the single tax. Despite significant support for the reform in plebeian Portland neighborhoods, these radical measures generally went down to increasingly bigger defeats. Oregon labor leaders continued to advocate the single tax through the 1920s, but they no longer viewed it as the backbone of their campaign to eliminate "disemployment" and promote greater economic equality.

Single taxers were always part of an eclectic world of reform politics, with especially strong roots in the movements opposing imperialism and racial inequality. Many proponents went on to mainstream political success; pro-union Cleveland Mayor Tom Johnson was a devoted Georgeist, as was Louis Post, assistant secretary of labor in the administration of Woodrow Wilson. Yet the mass of politicized workers became increasingly disenchanted with the reform during the course of the Progressive Era. Leaders of the AFL became much more likely to withdraw support for the utopian single tax in favor of the pragmatic income tax, while Socialists—always, at best, grudging in their acceptance of *petit bourgeois* Georgeism—became more uniform in their hostility. In an era that saw the simultaneous rise of polarized class politics and mass consumerism, a reform that promised to bring together working-class and middle-class producers seemed increasingly anachronistic.

The single tax may today appear to be at best confusing and at worst a dangerous panacea. Yet the basic impulse behind the reform—to prevent the immoral accumulation of wealth—resonated powerfully with Americans of various social classes during the tumultuous period of the late nineteenth and early twentieth centuries.

ROBERT D. JOHNSTON

References and Further Reading

Johnston, Robert D. *The Radical Middle Class: Populist Democracy and the Question of Capitalism in Progressive Era Portland, Oregon.* Princeton, NJ: Princeton University Press, 2003.

Scobey, David. "Boycotting the Politics Factory: Labor Radicalism and the New York City Mayoral Election of 188[6]." *Radical History Review* 28–30, (1984): 280–325.

Thomas, John L. *Alternative America: Henry George, Edward Bellamy, Henry Demarest Lloyd, and the Adversary Tradition.* Cambridge, MA: Belknap Press of Harvard University Press, 1983.

See also **George, Henry**

SIT-DOWN STRIKES (1937)

After the National Labor Relations Act was passed by Congress in July 1935, unions anticipated a more congenial atmosphere for organizing workers. These expectations were raised even higher by the landslide win by President Franklin D. Roosevelt in the election of 1936—a victory that labor had helped to achieve and from which labor organizers benefited by telling reluctant workers "the President wants you to join the union." Businessmen on the other hand hoped that the Supreme Court would overturn the act, as they had the National Industrial Recovery Act (NIRA). Many unorganized workers during this era were reluctant to join unions largely because of the precarious situation that many of these new labor unions caused by the lack of recognition of these unions as bargaining agents for their members; this meant that union members often had less job security than nonunion workers, since union activists were often targeted for harassment and dismissal by company representatives. The sit-down strikes that took place in 1937 inspired workers to overcome these

doubts and join unions—particularly those unions under the umbrella of the new Congress of Industrial Organizations (CIO)—in unprecedented numbers.

A strike is by definition the withholding of labor by workers, usually characterized by workers leaving their place of work and forming a picket line at the entrances to discourage other workers from entering the place of work until grievances are satisfactorily settled. A sit-down strike on the other hand is characterized by worker occupation of the workplace, usually to prevent the replacement of strikers by other workers. The sit-down strike tactic allows strikers to ensure that production is halted in the factory. The tactic also allows a small number of militant strikers to ensure that production is halted—an important consideration when many workers are reluctant to join unions and even more reluctant to go out on strike. The United States Supreme Court, in *NLRB v. Fansteel Metallurgical Corp.* in 1939, ruled sit-down strikes illegal; the sit-down strike by that time had largely been abandoned by labor unions and so had little effect.

The first use of a sit-down strike in the United States happened in 1906 during an Industrial Workers of the World (IWW) strike against Westinghouse. The sit-down strikes of 1937 were the result of the success that rubber workers in Akron, Ohio, experienced in using the tactic in 1936. In January of that year, workers at the Firestone plant halted work after a union activist was suspended for a week without pay. The strike quickly spread to both the B. F. Goodrich and the Goodyear facilities in Akron; Firestone management relented and reinstated the activist with back pay for the time he was off. This led to a larger job action in February 1936, when Goodyear discharged 137 tire builders who had engaged in a quickie sit-down strike (that is, a strike engaged in by a relatively small number of workers intended to force management to settle a shopfloor dispute immediately). The rubber workers responded on a massive scale; 5,000 pickets faced down the Akron police force sent to re-open the plant despite an injunction forbidding mass picketing. The effectiveness of the strike eventually led Goodyear to accept terms favorable to the union—including re-instating those workers discharged, agreeing to limit the company's discretion on increasing hours, and other concessions. The success of this tactic in Akron resulted in more than 50 subsequent sit-down strikes in the city's rubber plants before the end of 1936.

The most famous of the 1937 strikes actually began in the final days of 1936. Workers at the Cleveland Fisher Body plant, in response to General Motors' (GM's) decision not to bargain with the then-president of the UAW, Homer Martin, seized control

Sit-down strikers in the Fisher Body plant factory number three. Library of Congress, Prints & Photographs Division, FSA/OWI Collection [LC-USF34-040027-D].

of the plant on December 28, 1936. The UAW officials in Flint feared that workers in Cleveland "had jumped the gun," and attempted to wait in calling members out on strike until after the first of the year, when a new, union-friendly governor—Frank Murphy, elected in November 1936—was sworn into office on the first day of 1937. In order to stay in control of the membership, and to prevent General Motors from removing important dies used to make car bodies to a safer location, union officials found that they had to jump the gun a bit themselves and gave the go-ahead for the planned seizure of the plant. The Flint sit-down strike began on December 30, 1936, when a small group of union activists shut down the assembly line at the Fisher Body Plant Number 1. The infant United Auto Workers (UAW) had been working intensively to organize workers in Flint, first under the direction of Wyndham Mortimer, the former president of UAW Local 9 at the White Motor Company in Cleveland, and later under Robert Travis, who helped organize and lead UAW Local 14, which had successfully struck GM's Chevrolet Transmission Plant in Toledo, Ohio, in April 1935. The Toledo walkout resulted in a small gain in the hourly rate paid workers, but more importantly for workers was the fact that GM had recognized and bargained with the union. These gains were negated later in the year however when GM moved a substantial amount of machine tools out of the factory

in Toledo, and into a solidly nonunion plant in Saginaw, Michigan. Despite this setback, Local 14 continued to represent workers at GM's Toledo facility—but it made it readily apparent that the continued viability of the union could be ensured only by organizing workers in the company's two Michigan strongholds, Flint and Detroit.

The sit-down strike tactic allowed for a relatively small number of strikers to shut down production at the two plants in Flint. Many workers chose to stay home and wait out the struggle—not an unwise decision in a town where the local government and largest employer were as closely intertwined as was the case in Flint. The relatively small number of active strikers gave the forces arrayed against them the impression that the strikers could be removed by force if the occasion warranted it, particularly at Fisher Plant Number 2, which was held by approximately 100 strikers. Such an attempt was made on January 11, 1937, and it was defeated by the strikers at Fisher Number 2—assisted by UAW picketers and the members of the Women's Emergency Brigade—in an altercation that has entered union lore as "the Battle of the Running Bulls" (bulls being a slang term for police in this era). This battle prompted city and county officials, corporate representatives, and union officials to call on newly elected Governor Frank Murphy to bring in the Michigan National Guard to restore order, which was done on the following day. Significantly the guard was not used to break the strike but to keep order in the streets around the two plants. The stalemate between the corporation and the union continued until February 1, when the union was able to seize another plant in Flint, Chevrolet Plant Number 6, after fooling the company and city officials into believing that another plant would be the target by planting misinformation with a suspected company spy within the union. Another week-and-a-half passed before GM grudgingly accepted the UAW as the sole bargaining agent for its "employees who were members of the union."

The effect of this seemingly limited victory by a fledgling member of a fledgling labor organization—the CIO—was momentous. The UAW was able quickly to organize most of the rest of the GM factories as well as those of the Chrysler Corporation. The effects of the strike were felt outside of the automobile industry as well. United States Steel granted recognition to the Steel Workers' Organizing Committee, which was the predecessor of the United Steel Workers. The successful sit-down strike against the largest corporation in the world also inspired workers in Woolworth stores, pencil makers, sailors, tobacco workers, janitors, rug weavers, pie bakers, hotel and restaurant workers, garbage collectors, newspaper pressmen, and opticians to sit-down to get their own grievances addressed. There were 477 sit-down strikes in the United States in 1937; 279 called by CIO affiliates, 100 by AFL affiliates, and the remainder called by workers or unions unaffiliated with either body. The textile industry witnessed the largest number of sit-down strikes, with 80; the automobile industry by comparison, had only 45. Sit-down strikes were widely supported by the general public in January and February of 1937. As they became increasingly popular with workers as a way to address grievances however, this public support eroded. Sit-down strikes also became less popular with workers during the year, so that by the month of December there were only four sit-down strikes. The sit-down strike was not only popular in the United States however; it was also used in the 1930s in France, where Indian textile workers seized a mill in Pondicherry, as did tobacco workers in Greece; miners in Wales, Scotland, Yugoslavia, Hungary, Poland, and Spain all stayed underground during the decade.

Although the sit-down strike was increasingly unpopular with workers in the United States during the second-half of 1937, it was still a tactic in the arsenal of unions until the *NLRB v. Fansteel* Supreme Court decision in 1939, when a majority of the justices decided that the tactic was "out of bounds" and an illegal usurpation of private property. Despite this ruling however, workers through the years have used elements of the sit-down in quickie strikes over shopfloor disputes.

GREGORY M. MILLER

References and Further Reading

Bernstein, Irving. *The Turbulent Years: A History of the American Worker, 1933–1941*. Boston, MA: Houghton-Mifflin, 1969 Dollinger, Sol, and Genora Johnson Dollinger. *Not Automatic: Women and the Left in the Forging of the United Auto Workers' Union*. New York: Monthly Review Press, 2000. www.historicalvoices.org/flint/
Fine, Sidney. *Sit-down: The General Motors Strike of 1936–1937*. Ann Arbor: University of Michigan Press, 1969.

Cases and Statutes Cited

National Industrial Recovery Act
National Labor Relations Act
NLRB v. Fansteel Metallurgical Corp.
NLRB v. Fansteel Supreme Court

SKIDMORE, THOMAS (1790–1832)
Working Men's Parties

Thomas Skidmore was one of the leading figures of the Jacksonian era Working Men's parties, which were organized in Philadelphia, New York, Boston, and 70 other locations in the late 1820s. Born in Newton, Connecticut, in 1790, Skidmore was a precocious learner and began a 5-year teaching career at his local school at the age of 13. In 1819, Skidmore settled down in New York City as a machinist. He maintained an active interest in practical science and worked on several projects and inventions. In 1829, Skidmore began a career of political activism and became a driving force in the New York City Working Men's party. Despite some initial electoral success under his stewardship, Skidmore lost a series of faction fights and was forced out of the party. He died at the age of 42 in the cholera epidemic of 1832.

The primary thrust of Skidmore's political activity lay in his advocacy of the abolition of inheritance and the complete equalization of property. He also fought those who, in his view, were attempting to water down the Working Men's party's program or like Robert Dale Owen, were pushing ideas and proposals that were not strictly related to the interests of working people. Skidmore's redistributionist ideas dominated the Working Men's platform in the 1829 local elections, in which the movement garnered 31% of the vote and elected two state legislators. Despite this initial success, politicos Noah Cook and Henry

Guyon, assisted by Owen, accused Skidmore of being too radical and forced him and his followers out of the party in late 1829. Not long after Cook and Guyon expelled Owen as well. Skidmore attempted to lead a dissident group, but the movement wrecked on the shoals of factionalism.

Aside from his political leadership during the tumultuous second-half of 1829, Skidmore's chief contribution to labor was intellectual. He wrote three books, *The Rights of Man to Property, Moral Physiology Exposed and Refuted*, and *Political Essays*. The latter merely recapitulated the ideas of his first work, while *Moral Physiology Exposed* was an attack on Robert Dale Owen's work, *Moral Physiology*. The issues that tore the New York Working Men's party apart were several, but among them were Skidmore's proposal to equalize all property and Owen's advocacy of free love and contraception. Owen considered Skidmore's ideas far too radical, while Skidmore, in *Moral Physiology Exposed*, attacked Owen for wanting to destroy the family with his support for free love, contraception, and compulsory boarding schools for children.

The Rights of Man to Property! is Skidmore's most important work, and its title underscores Skidmore's intention to transcend the intellectual limits of his hero, *Rights of Man* author Thomas Paine. Paine, along with Thomas Jefferson, had been one of the leading English speaking theoreticians and revolutionaries of eighteenth-century radicalism. Skidmore confronted the radical legacy more directly than did most of his contemporaries and attempted to transcend its categories and formulate a new basis for radical social analysis.

Skidmore contended that Jefferson's understanding of natural rights remained fundamentally flawed by its failure to recognize the importance of the right to property. Criticizing Jefferson for his use in the Declaration of Independence of the phrase "life, liberty, and the pursuit of happiness," Skidmore argued that "man's natural right to life or liberty, is not more sacred or unalienable, than his right to property." Indeed, Skidmore insisted, the right to property is "essential and indispensable in the pursuit of happiness." Skidmore's argument for the recognition of the rights of man to property rested largely on his contention that political equality cannot exist in conjunction with social injustice. Pointing to the power granted by great wealth, Skidmore asserted that "he who commands the property of a State, or even an inordinate portion of it, . . . can feed me, or starve me; give me employment, or bid me wander about in idleness; is my master; and it is the utmost folly for me to boast of being anything but a slave" (T. Skidmore, *The Rights of Man to Property*, 1829).

Ironically for one who so valued property rights, Skidmore's conceptual framework was oriented toward a critique of private property and a set of proposals that included state expropriation of all property. Skidmore called for a constitutional convention that would abolish all debts and assume ownership of all property, real and personal, in the name of the newly reconstituted state. This was the first step in what Skidmore called the "general division." The government was to inventory all this property, assign it value, and total these values. Each adult citizen (male and female, regardless of race) would then be credited an equal share, or dividend, of this total, and with this share buy property back from the state at an enormous auction. The general division would thus be complete; and all adult citizens would possess equal amounts of property. To ensure the permanence of this equality, Skidmore proposed that inheritance be eliminated and the property of the deceased be distributed annually in the form of a patrimony to all those who attained the age of majority in a given year. The patrimony would prevent the accumulation of wealth over generations, and each would be assured an equal opportunity to attain wealth and comfort. Skidmore also advocated the establishment of state funding for child raising and the abolition of banks, corporate charters, and private charity. The well off, Skidmore reasoned, could use the latter to circumvent the abolition of inheritance by disposing of their property to their children shortly prior to death.

Skidmore's work represents the first American synthesis of egalitarian and producerist ideas, that is, that strand of ideas proceeding from the proposition that the producer of wealth is entitled to the whole of that wealth rather than the portion that wage labor represented. He synthesized the two by fusing the artisanal hostility to accumulated, unearned wealth with the egalitarian impulse to equalize property holdings. The terms of this synthesis formed the framework for the type of socialism that animated farmer and worker movements in nineteenth-century America. He provided an urban version of agrarian radicalism and thus brought to the struggles of artisans and laborers the vitality of a tradition that had its roots in the English revolution. The feeling that the abundance of land in the United States might somehow serve as part of the solution to the social question remained never far from view in nineteenth-century radical movements. The first of these movements was the Working Men's Movement, and it was Skidmore who provided early leadership and provocative ideas to that movement.

MATTHEW S. R. BEWIG

References and Further Reading

Hugins, Walter. *Jacksonian Democracy and the Working Class: A Study of the New York Workingmen's Movement, 1829–1837.* Stanford, CA: Stanford University Press, 1960.

Laurie, Bruce. *Artisans into Workers: Labor in Nineteenth-Century America.* New York: Hill & Wang, 1989.

Pessen, Edward. *Most Uncommon Jacksonians: The Radical Leaders of the Early Labor Movement.* New York: SUNY Press, 1967.

Skidmore, Thomas. *The Rights of Man to Property.* New York: Burt Franklin, 1964. (reprint, 1829)

———. *Moral Physiology Exposed and Refuted.* New York: Skidmore & Jacobs, 1831.

———. *Political Essays.* New York: Skidmore & Jacobs, 1831.

Sumner, Helen. "Citizenship (1827–1833)." In *History of Labour in the United States,* edited by John R. Commons et al. Vol. 1. New York: Macmillan, 1918.

Whitman, Alden. *Labor Parties, 1827–1834.* New York: International Publishers, 1943.

Wilentz, Sean. *Chants Democratic: New York City and the Rise of the American Working Class, 1788–1850.* New York: Oxford University Press, 1984.

SLAVE CODES
See **Slavery**

SLAVE REBELLIONS

Demographic realities and power relationships in the mainland British colonies and later, following independence, in the United States, militated against the type of large-scale slave revolts and conspiracies that erupted in South America and the Caribbean. The presence of a heavily armed white majority in every state except South Carolina (and, toward the very end of the antebellum period, Mississippi), the lack of an impregnable hinterland in which to create Maroon colonies from which runaways could besiege plantations, the relatively dispersed nature and small size of slaveholding, and the fact that the landlord class was in residence (not absentee) combined to make massive slave rebellions far less common than day-to-day resistance or individual acts of violence. In the years after the American Revolution, as harsher forms of colonial patriarchalism began to metamorphose into paternalism—a complex and ongoing process of negotiation and brutality that many scholars regrettably reduce to a simplistic model of accommodation—slaves achieved enough living space to build stable families and rich spiritual communities. Given the odds against success, it is hardly surprising that the handful of slaves bold enough to rise for their freedom found their rebellions reduced to unsuccessful conspiracies and their fellows doomed to die in combat or on the gallows.

Despite persistence by historians to force a uniformity of vision and goals on rebel leaders, insurgent slaves in the eighteenth and nineteenth centuries differed from one another fully as much as white revolutionaries in the same era. Jemmy, an Angolan who led an agrarian uprising near Stono River, South Carolina, tried to hasten his African followers across the border into Spanish Florida. Caesar Varick, who only 2 years later conspired to burn New York City, lived in one of North America's largest urban centers with a common-law Irish wife. Gabriel, a young, secular rebel who had turned away from African traditions, hoped to remain and work in a more egalitarian Virginia. Denmark Vesey, an aged free black who bought his freedom the year before Gabriel died, expected to achieve a limited exodus for his family and followers out of Charleston to Haiti. Vesey and his chief lieutenant, "Gullah" Jack Pritchard, an East African priest, fused African theology with the Old Testament God of wrath and justice, whereas Nat Turner relied on Christian millennial themes and hoped to bring on the day of jubilee for black Virginians. Beyond their obvious abilities as leaders and their equally obvious desire to breathe free, bond rebels in the United States fit no simple pattern.

If slave rebellions in North America correspond to any one model, it is that they proliferated during times when the white majority was divided against itself in crippling ways. Colonial insurgents in South Carolina and New York City turned to violence at a time when their masters were at war with France and Spain. Gabriel, the most politicized of all the slave rebels, formulated his plans during the divisive election of 1800, when Federalists and Republicans threatened to take up arms against one another. The rebels in the Tidewater area of Virginia, despite the memory of the repression that followed Gabriel's death, began to organize again during the chaos of the War of 1812. Having read of the Missouri debates in Charleston newspapers, Vesey prayed that northern whites would prove tardy in riding to the rescue of their estranged southern brethren. Slaves near Natchez, Mississippi, began to plan for their freedom in 1861, following the outbreak of the Civil War.

Most of all enslaved rebels, who well knew what they were up against and rarely contemplated suicidal ventures, plotted for their freedom only when safer avenues had been closed to them. For most of the seventeenth century for example, when the high death rate in the southern colonies made inexpensive white indentured servants far more numerous than costly African slaves, enterprising bond persons relied more on self-purchase than the sword. The economic possibilities in early Virginia produced more run-aways than rebels; the practice of buying one's own body even produced several black entrepreneurs—such as Anthony Johnson, a former slave who became a wealthy planter and who named his estate Angola after the land of his birth. It was only after landless whites and hard-used white indentured workers under the command of Nathaniel Bacon burned Jamestown in 1676 that southern planters made a concerted effort to replace white servants with African slaves. The comprehensive Virginia Slave Code of 1705, the first of its kind on the English colonial mainland, crushed the hope of industrious slaves that they might be upwardly mobile. Only then as North American racial walls rapidly hardened did desperate slaves turn to physically hazardous paths toward freedom. During the last days of Queen Anne's War in April 1712, a determined band of 25 Africans and Native Americans burned several buildings in New York City and killed nine whites. (Unfree labor had been legalized in New York by the Duke's Law of 1665.) Having made a commitment to unfree labor, equally determined whites revenged themselves on the rebels. Several rebels committed suicide before they could be captured, but those taken alive were broken on the wheel and hanged in chains as a warning to future rebels.

In the early eighteenth century, even though the constant threat of war between Britain and its continental neighbors provided endless opportunities for daring slaves, mainland revolts rarely posed much real danger to the slaveholding regime. Because the Atlantic slave trade was at its peak, every colony included large numbers of native Africans who sought to escape from bondage by building isolated Maroon communities. Most runaways fled into the hinterland, where they established Maroon colonies and tried to recreate the African communities they had lost. Even the two most significant rebellions of the period—that of Stono, South Carolina, in 1739 and the subsequent attempt to burn New York City in 1741—were led by Africans who dreamed only of ending their own bondage, not of ending unfree labor in general. Aware of Spanish promises of freedom in colonial Florida, enslaved soldiers under Jemmy, many of them Christians from the Kingdom of Kongo, tried to escape across the border. To the north, New York City bondmen planned to torch the wooden city and flee to French Canada, which was then at war with the rebels' masters. The price of failure was high. New York authorities ordered Caesar Varick and 12 of his followers burned alive; 18 others were hanged—two of them in chains—and 70 more bondmen were banished from the colony.

The American Revolution alternately discouraged and stimulated slave rebellions. Although the British invasion and the animosity between patriots and Tories presented slaves with a unique opportunity to organize, most slaves chose instead to take advantage of the dislocation of war to escape with their families into the growing cities or behind British lines. (The Revolution was the one time in North American history when as many female slaves as males ran away.) Because the aggressive bondmen who cast their lots with the military forces of King George were precisely the sort of bold, determined slaves who normally tended to organize slave conspiracies, the bloody fighting in the southern states after 1778 actually diminished the prospect that a mainland counterpart of Toussaint Louverture would rise out of the tobacco and rice plantations.

Nonetheless, as Eugene D. Genovese suggests in his influential study, *From Rebellion to Revolution* (1979), the age of revolution, and especially the slave revolt in Saint Domingue in 1791, marked a change in patterns in black resistance. The Caribbean rebels under the leadership of Boukman and Louverture sought not only to destroy the power of their Parisian absentee masters, but also to join the societies in which they lived on equal terms. For black Americans determined to realize the egalitarian promise of the American Revolution, the news from the Caribbean reminded them that if they dared, the end of slavery might be within their reach. Whereas Jemmy and his African recruits hoped only to escape the chains of colonial South Carolina, the slave Gabriel of Virginia, born in the year 1776, wanted to join political society on equal terms. Gabriel and his lieutenants, who instigated the most extensive plot in Virginia history, hoped to force the white patriot elite to live up to its stated ideal: That all men were created free and equal. Leading a small army of slaves in Henrico County, the young blacksmith planned to march into Richmond under a banner emblazoned with the words death or liberty. He assured one supporter that poor white people, who had no more political power than the slaves, would also join them in the struggle for equality. Although trial testimony makes little mention of events in Saint Domingue, white authorities, like Governor James Monroe, harbored no doubts that Louverture's victories had an enormous "effect on all the peoples of colour" in the early national South.

In several cases bondmen who had been carried from revolutionary Saint Domingue by their masters participated in North American slave revolts. In 1792, slaves on Virginia's eastern shore proposed to "blow up the magazine in Norfolk and massacre its inhabitants." Norfolk County had a white majority, but Northampton and Elizabeth City counties, just across the Chesapeake Bay, had an enslaved majority. Although the rebel leader Caleb, a favored servant and driver, was evidently American-born, several of his recruits were Haitian refugees, and all—according to the trial testimony—had been inspired by the example of Saint Domingue. Two decades later in 1811, one of the most extensive conspiracies in the history of the United States erupted in southern Louisiana, only a few miles upriver from New Orleans. Slaves led by a mulatto driver named Charles Deslondes announced their intention of marching on the city "to kill whites." Contrary to myth Deslondes was not Haitian-born, but many of his recruits were. Reliable eyewitness accounts placed the number of rebels at 180 to 500.

The limited evidence available from slave trials also indicates that rebellion was the occupation of skilled slaves and men who understood the power of cash. Field hands of course could be found tangled up in the court proceedings that followed slave conspiracies, but they rarely were the instigators of the plots. When the occupational status of enslaved rebels can be obtained, it is clear that skilled slaves found their way into courts in numbers that far exceeded their statistical ratio in the overall slave community. Of the 135 slaves and free blacks put to trial by Charleston magistrates in 1822, occupations may be had for 41 of the defendants. Four were carpenters, four were coopers, two were blacksmiths, and five were rope makers. The others were painters, cooks, stone masons, wheelwrights, ship caulkers, and draymen; not a single man, so far as the extant evidence indicates, waded Carolina's rice fields. Similarly enslaved artisans took the lead in organizing rebellions across the Americas. In the fall of 1736 in British Antigua, two black carpenters orchestrated an islandwide conspiracy. Among the rebels executed were 13 carpenters, eight coopers, two masons, three domestics, and even three fiddlers, but of the 49 men banished from the island, only six were unskilled field workers.

After Gabriel's execution and the death of 25 of his followers in the fall of 1800, slave rebellions on the eastern seaboard became both less common and less politically conscious. Slaves who worked along the rivers in southern Virginia and Halifax County, North Carolina, under the leadership of Sancho, a ferryman, formed a highly decentralized scheme to rise on Easter Monday of 1802. But Sancho, despite having been involved in Gabriel's plot, shared little of Gabriel's dream of a multiracial republic. The lack of an ideological dimension appeared even when the dislocation brought on by the War of 1812 and a second British invasion of the Chesapeake once more gave bondmen in Virginia an opportunity to rise for their liberty. Gloucester County authorities jailed 10 slaves in March 1813, and the following month found rebels in Lancester County and Williamsburg "condemned on a charge of conspiracy & insurrection." By the late summer and early fall, rumors of revolt unnerved inhabitants of Norfolk and Richmond as well.

If the relative ease with which white authorities crushed these isolated rebellions did not extinguish the desire for freedom, it nonetheless reminded leaders in the slave community that the determined white majority in the American South presented insurgents with a formidable obstacle. Vesey of Charleston, perhaps the most pragmatic of all the rebel leaders, realized that Gabriel's dream of forcing mainland elites to accommodate blacks' aspirations for freedom and economic justice was impossible. Vesey plotted therefore not to end slavery in South Carolina, but instead to lead a mass escape from Charleston to the Caribbean, where he had lived and worked as a boy. Hoping to take control of the city on the night of July 14, 1822, Vesey's recruits—many of them Africans—intended to slaughter the inhabitants of the city and seize bank reserves before fleeing to Haiti, an embattled black republic sorely in need of capital and skilled labor. If Vesey, a prosperous free man, doomed those who remained behind to renewed repression by whites, he can scarcely be faulted: He understood that his followers had virtually no hope of bringing down the peculiar institution in South Carolina.

Even Vesey's unsuccessful exodus, which may be regarded more as mass flight than a revolution, indicated the difficulties of planning an effective strategy amid large numbers of ever-vigilant whites. Like virtually all rebel leaders in the United States, Vesey recognized the danger of openly recruiting in the countryside. Word of the Charleston plot probably reached several thousand slaves—which is not to say that even half that number committed themselves to the struggle—and there was always a danger that a black Judas would hear the whispers and inform the master class. White authorities had long ago perfected the art of dividing the slave community by offering a tempting reward—freedom—to those who would turn their coats. Like Jemmy and Gabriel before him, Vesey, whose army had more officers than soldiers, planned to rise quickly and present the low-country black majority with a *fait accompli*. The victorious armies would not be recruited nor armed in advance but raised by the captains as they marched.

Ironically the bloodiest slave revolt in the United States took place in the decade after Vesey's failure, at a time when rebellion—as opposed to other forms of resistance—had become virtually suicidal. The slaves in Southampton County, Virginia, who rose with Turner in 1831 shared neither Gabriel's trust in a second American Revolution nor Vesey's hope of fleeing to the Caribbean. Although Turner may have hoped to establish a Maroon colony in the vast Dismal Swamp, his plot gave little evidence of planning or rational preparation. Most likely the messianic Turner hoped that God would protect and guide his army as the Lord had guided the Israelites. At least 57 whites perished in the revolt, but local militiamen easily routed the ill-equipped rebels; three companies of federal artillery together with seamen from two warships in the Chesapeake reached Southampton only 3 days after the insurrection began.

Although the secession of the southern states in the winter of 1860–1861 presented militant blacks with precisely the sort of division that rebel leaders typically tried to take advantage of, the Civil War channeled black resistance into patterns acceptable to the politicians of the free states. During the first year of the conflict, as Confederate soldiers repulsed northern invasions, militant slaves across the cotton-growing South saw few options but to pull down the rebel government from within. The plot in Natchez, Mississippi, still shrouded in mystery, stands as but one example of collective resistance during the months before the Confederate debacle at Antietam Creek. Rumors of black resistance spread in New Orleans and Columbia, South Carolina. Seven slaves swung from the gibbet in Charleston in April 1861. The Confederate Brigadier General R. F. Floyd urged the governor of Florida to declare martial law in the hope of eradicating a "nest of traitors and lawless negroes."

Most slaves however, understood, as Herbert Aptheker suggested in his definitive work, *American Negro Slave Revolts* (1943), that "the Army of Lincoln was to be the Army of Liberation." Aged slaves with long memories counseled patience and waited for the arrival of northern forces. Following the Emancipation Proclamation, northern freemen and southern runaways, eager and willing to fight, donned blue uniforms in the name of liberty for blacks. Despite the Confederates' threat to execute black soldiers as slave insurgents, thousands of bondmen fled the countryside, planning to return and liberate their families. By the end of the war, 180,000 African-Americans (one out of every five males in the republic) had served in Union forces. Those former slaves who marched back toward the plantations of their birth singing "General Gabriel's Jig" rightly understood themselves to be a part of the largest slave rebellion in the history of the United States.

In recent years it has become fashionable for scholars to dismiss black rebelliousness as white paranoia or even Machiavellian attempts on the part of white authorities to advance their political careers, shut down troublesome black churches, or unite whites across class lines. One historian has argued that a series of slave plots—New York City in 1741, Antigua in 1736, and the Chesapeake in the 1790s—more approximated "witchcraft scares than slave revolts," while another, severed white heads notwithstanding, suggests that "evidence cannot sustain a credible interpretation that the Stono Revolt was a slave rebellion." Even conceding the problematical nature of testimony extracted from incarcerated bondmen by vengeful whites however, such denials ultimately silence too many black voices and memories. In later years men who knew Vesey, from enslaved carpenter Robert Nesbitt to Minister Morris Brown to black abolitionist Thomas Brown, discussed their memories of 1822, often from the safety of the free north, far from the reach of vengeful authorities. Perhaps then this debate is not about the evidence but rather about what modern historians wish to read into the evidence; the explanation for these theories lies not so much in a determination to make Vesey go away, but instead to make any evidence of black rebelliousness disappear.

DOUGLAS R. EGERTON

References and Further Reading

Aptheker, Herbert. *American Negro Slave Revolts*. New York, 1943.

Egerton, Douglas R. *Gabriel's Rebellion: The Virginia Slave Conspiracies of 1800 and 1802*. Chapel Hill: 1993.

———. *He Shall Go Out Free: The Lives of Denmark Vesey*. 2nd ed. Lanham: 2004.

Frey, Sylvia R. *Water from the Rock: Black Resistance in a Revolutionary Age*. Princeton: 1991.

Genovese, Eugene D. *From Rebellion to Revolution: Afro-American Slave Revolts in the Making of the Modern World*. Baton Rouge: 1979.

Greenburg, Kenneth S. "*Nat Turner: A Slave Rebellion in History*." In *History and Memory*. New York: 2003.

Hoffer, Peter Charles. *The Great New York Conspiracy of 1741: Slavery, Crime, and Colonial Law*. Lawrence: 2003.

Parent, Anthony S. *Foul Means: The Formation of a Slave Society in Virginia, 1660–1740*. Chapel Hill: 2003.

Wright, Donald R. *African Americans in the Colonial Era: From African Origins through the American Revolution*. Wheeling: 2003.

Cases and Statutes Cited

Duke's Law
Virginia Slave Code

SLAVE TRADE

Interest in the history of the Atlantic slave trade to the United States has been stimulated in recent years by the availability of new digitalized data sets and by a revival of debates about African cultures and identities. These discussions have moved beyond prior discussions of African survivals and acculturation to new discussions of the process of creolization and cultural exchange. A prominent role has been played by historians trained in the history of Africa, whose findings have been welcomed in some cases and challenged in others by historians working within the tradition of slave studies in the United States. Both groups of historians have emphasized the history of slavery in the eighteenth century, long neglected in favor of the antebellum period. Beyond the Atlantic slave trade, there has also been a new focus on the internal slave trade within the United States in the antebellum period, which was linked to the emergence of the cotton kingdom and provided powerful ammunition to the anti-slavery movement in the decades preceding the civil war.

In light of these developments in the recent historiography, this article focuses on three main themes. The first is the new possibilities to map and analyze the slave trade to what became the United States on the basis of shipping data and what it can tell us about the Africans imported as slaves. The second theme is the debate about African and later African-American identities and their relationship to the slave trade and new debates about African contributions to agrarian systems and the process of creolization. The rice-growing region of the Carolinas plays a prominent role in these discussions. Finally recent research on the internal slave trade adds a dynamic element to antebellum slavery by focusing on the expansion of the cotton frontier after 1790. The internal slave trade also played a key role in political debates about slavery and strongly shaped abolitionist discourse in the final decades of American slavery.

Patterns of the Atlantic Slave Trade

The availability of detailed shipping records permits historians to examine the connections between the main slave-importing regions of the United States and specific African regions. Historians have more or less agreed on a total slave trade from Africa of about 12 million, with the future United States accounting for 5%–7% of total imports, or in round numbers around 600,000–700,000 slaves, including imports from the Caribbean. Out of this total we have more detailed shipping records of around 300,000 slaves imported from Africa, with indications of regional African origins for 215,000. What we can say about this last group is the focus of some recent debates about the African impact on the United States. The slave trade to the Chesapeake, a tobacco-exporting region, and the low country of the Carolinas and Georgia, a region of rice plantations, accounted for

the vast majority of slave imports. In the past one predominant idea was that slave cargoes consisted of randomized crowds of Africans from diverse tribal backgrounds and that the horrors of the middle passage further stripped these victims of any meaningful connection with their African homelands and their cultural identity. Their sale and dispersion to plantations completed the process and delivered atomized workers ripe for acculturation to their new masters. Data from shipping records does not support these generalizations, which have also been criticized for their misleading assumptions about the extreme diversity and isolation of African cultures. Most slave ships purchased their entire cargoes in one or two ports in one African region and delivered hundreds of slaves with similar material cultures, speaking related languages and sharing many general beliefs. Secondly slave-importing regions drew on commercial networks that led them to import slaves from the same African region time after time.

For the United States as a whole, certain patterns stand out when slave imports by region are compared to the overall patterns of the Atlantic slave trade. The African regions from Senegambia to the Gold Coast were privileged in the slave trade to the United States in that the percentages imported from these regions significantly exceed those predicted by their share in the slave trade as a whole. At the same time west central Africa, centered on the Congo River basin, was the single largest source of slaves, even though the percentages imported were lower than that region's overall role in the slave trade. The most likely explanations for these patterns are geographical proximity, with a preference for the shorter routes from West Africa to the United States, and the patterns of British African commerce. But regional preferences cannot be excluded when slave imports are broken down by exporting or importing regions.

Senegambia is the most striking example, since imports to the United States are four times larger than the share of Senegambia in the slave trade as a whole. This may reflect a preference for slaves from the Gambia River, the main British supply region in Senegambia, who were valued in the rice plantation regions of the Carolinas. The same over-representation in imports to the United States applies to a lesser degree to Sierra Leone, the Windward Coast, and the Gold Coast. There are also clear regional preferences within importing regions in the United States. Two-thirds of all slaves imported from the Bight of Biafra (in what is today southeastern Nigeria) went to Virginia, with the result that one-in-four slaves imported into Virginia came from that region. The Carolinas imported 80% of the slaves from Sierra Leone and 83% of the slaves from west central Africa. Because of the large number of slaves from west central Africa overall, this meant that about one in every three slaves in the Carolinas came from this African region, whose languages and cultures were closely related. Cultural connections between slaves may have played a greater role in resistance and rebellion than the literature has allowed to this point.

These patterns give credibility to the exploration of links between such events as the Stono rebellion of 1738 in South Carolina and the import of thousands of Kongolese slaves, as argued by John Thornton, or the search for West African influences in the shouts of Afro-Baptism or west central African patterns in slave burial sites, as presented in works by Robert Farris Thompson and others. In the world of work, it means that enslaved Africans would have found it easier to forge links across the cultural divides in the slave population as three or four groups rather than as a randomized crowd. This suggests that Africans could draw on common understandings of the rights of bondsmen and slaves in their own societies in their struggles with their masters. The constant battle of slaves to gain rights over provision grounds and time to work for themselves is a good example. While this can be seen in purely economic terms as a trade-off, with the master supplying all provisions or allowing slaves some time off in exchange for lower costs, the cultural expectations of slaves played a role. Planters showed a consistent preference for centralized control but gave ground on this issue time and again. The paternalism of masters may have been forged as much by the expectations of slaves as by any other factor.

From Creolization to Cultural Exchange

Sidney Mintz and Richard Price's influential study, *The Birth of African-American Culture*, first published in 1976, argued that slave cultures, however tied to Africa, were essentially Creole, born in the New World in the crucible of slavery. Because no single African culture could survive under the conditions of plantation slavery, slaves combined cultural elements from various African societies at the same time as they adopted new languages and adapted to the conditions imposed by slavery. The results were hybrid, syncretic cultures that were African-American. Their interpretation inspired considerable research and bypassed previous debates about African survivals and acculturation by seeming to reconcile key points from both schools. Because their formulation suggested that creolization began immediately and reflected the harsh conditions imposed by slavery, it echoed arguments about the stripping away of African culture. At the

same time such African-derived features of religions as Santería in Cuba or Vodun in Haiti were highlighted, as was syncretism with Catholicism.

Creole cultures and religions seemed much more evident in Brazil and the Caribbean when compared to the United States. This was explained in a number of ways: by the different demographic balance between black and white; by the relatively small size of American plantations and the slave communities that resided on them; by the austere culture of Protestantism compared to Catholicism, with no saints to identify with African spirits, few visual representations, and little ritual; and by the early ending of the slave trade from Africa to the United States, especially when compared to Brazil or Cuba. Whatever the merits of these arguments, recent research has shown that the difference between the United States and other slave regions was one of degree, not of kind. The creolization thesis, as formulated by Mintz and Price, has also been criticized for its assumption that creolization began almost immediately. James Sweet's research on Brazil has shown that specific African religious practices were transplanted to the Americas and survived for generations before giving way to syncretic African ones, a step that preceded their gradual fusion with Brazilian Catholicism. The whole process took centuries. While nothing quite comparable occurred within the boundaries of the United States, slaves' reluctance to embrace Christianity until late in the eighteenth century and their self-identification as African point to similar trends. Further research on the process of conversion and slave religion may reveal that the exceptionalism of the United States reflects lack of scholarly attention to African cultures more than a true divergence from other regions. Recent research on Islam in the Low Country has already moved in this direction.

The rice-growing regions of the Carolinas and Georgia have been the focus of most research that argues for significant African influence based on a cultural exchange that brought not just labor but African technologies and agricultural know-how to the rice plantations. This region has attracted scholarly attention for multiple reasons, many of which point to a strong African imprint. The rice plantations were distinctive for the task system of labor management that granted slaves more autonomy from absentee planters and their agents. Culturally the region is marked by the distinct Gullah dialect, a rich folklore, the early presence of Islam, and by a distinctive Afro-Baptism. As Peter Wood pointed out in a pioneering study of the region, the Low Country was also demographically the most African region in the United States. At the root of all of this, many scholars have pointed to what they have identified as West

African systems of water management (dykes and drainage systems), African tools for processing and winnowing rice (mortar and pestles, fanner baskets), all parts of a larger agrarian system brought from the rice coast of West Africa to plantation America. Scholars have pointed to the preference of South Carolina rice planters for slaves from the Gambia and Sierra Leone and to the fact that 80% of Sierra Leonean and 60% of Senegambian slaves (where shipping records permit identification) went to the Carolinas. Since the Carolinas also imported a high percentage of west central African slaves (where rice was not a crop), the arguments that are most convincing are based on an analysis of agrarian practices. Planters in the Carolinas may have later improved on the West African technologies brought by West African slaves, but the foundation of rice cultivation was built on an African base.

There is no consensus in the literature on whether the task system reflected the bargaining power of African slaves, whose knowledge and skills gave them leverage, or the fear of absentee whites and their agents of the deadly fevers that raged in the Low Country during the planting season. In either case an African exchange is central to the explanation based as much on labor negotiations by slaves and ecology as by a preference for slaves who brought knowledge of rice cultivation, always a minority. Arguments about African rice cultivation need to avoid the pitfalls of studying the survival and transmission of specific traits or even a rice complex divorced from the history of slavery and disease. The fevers feared by European on the Carolina coast were strains of malaria and yellow fever imported with slaves when mosquito larvae traveled as stowaways in water casks from the African coast and combined with the blood-borne parasites brought to the Low Country by African slaves. The absenteeism of the task system imposed a hybrid agricultural system, neither African nor European, but one controlled by slave owners. European self-interest promoted a physical separation from the fields and swamps, where masters pampered by their house slaves sent poorer whites to oversee their plantations on the coast. The task system was forged by disease, by accommodations between masters and slaves over tasks and provision grounds, and by the geographic separation of masters and slaves into white towns and black Low Country.

The Internal Slave Trade

The slave trade within the boundaries of the United States has attracted considerable attention in recent discussions of American slavery. While the United States is notable for the relatively small size of the direct slave trade with Africa, compared to Brazil or the Caribbean, the internal slave trade was the largest of any slave society in the Americas. In the period from 1790 to 1860, it is estimated at somewhere from 800,000 to a million slaves. It reached a peak in the decades from 1820–1860, when over 200,000 slaves were transferred from the upper South and the Low Country to what became known as the Deep South or the cotton kingdom and frontier regions further west. Ira Berlin has aptly called the internal slave trade a second middle passage, a term that focuses attention on the human suffering of slaves and on the political ramifications of the internal slave trade.

The broad outlines of the internal slave trade are well-known. The first region to become a major exporter of surplus slaves was the tobacco-growing region of the upper South, which was faced by declining profits, a shift to wheat cultivation and mixed farming, and the natural growth of its slave population. The Low Country entered the slave trade as an exporter somewhat later. The internal slave trade was greatly stimulated by the emergence of cotton as a new cash crop in the period after 1790, fueled by the adoption of new strains of cotton, new technologies (cotton gin), and the enormous demand for cotton in the industrializing textile industry led by Great Britain. The cotton frontier in the Deep South was the destination for the vast majority of slaves. The emergence of sugar plantations in Louisiana also fueled the demand for slaves. The slave system of the antebellum South, long the central focus of studies of American slavery, was built on this vast trade in slaves from the old plantation regions to the cotton belt and the sugar fields.

The internal slave trade played a central role in political debates about slavery in the antebellum period and strongly shaped abolitionist discourse about the evils of slavery. The expansion of the cotton kingdom into new territories in the West sparked heated debates about the future of slavery, whose fate was tied to the settlement of the frontier. The expansionism of southern planters and their political and legal victories, most notoriously the Fugitive Slave Law and Dred Scott, united diverse groups in opposition to slavery. Antislavery won new converts among native whites and immigrants who had little interest in the plight of southern slaves but wanted to save the West for free, white settlement. In abolitionist circles the most powerful moral and religious arguments against slavery focused on the slave trade. An earlier generation of English abolitionists had turned the middle passage into a symbol, using it to focus on the buying and selling of human flesh, the separation of families, and the horrors of human degradation. The internal slave trade provided some of the most powerful ammunition against apologists for slavery. The forced march of thousands of slaves overland, the separation of children from fathers and mothers, and the indignities of the slave auction, made a mockery of planters' paternalism and their claims that slaves were part of a larger family. In many ways the domestic slave trade was an even more powerful symbol than the middle passage from Africa. The victims of the second middle passage were American-born and Christian, with deep roots in the country. Their sale and shipment to the Deep South broke up slave communities with ties to the land and to kin that had been built up over generations. Fear of sale contributed to the resistance of runaways and the slave rebellions of Nat Turner and Denmark Vesey. The horrors of the second middle passage became the bread-and-butter of the radical abolitionists, who denounced slavery as a sinful evil and a stain on the nation's honor.

JAMES SEARING

References and Further Reading

Berlin, Ira. *Generations of Captivity: A History of African-American Slaves*. Cambridge, 2003.

Carney, Judith A. *Black Rice: The African Origins of Rice Cultivation in the Americas*. Cambridge, 2001.

Deyle, Steven. *Carry Me Back: The Domestic Slave Trade in American Life*. New York: Oxford University Press, 2004.

Eltis, David, Steven D. Behrendt, David Richardson, and Herbert S. Klein. *The Trans-Atlantic Slave Trade: A Database on CD-ROM*. Cambridge, 1999.

Gomez, Michael A. *Exchanging Our Country Marks: The Transformation of African Identities in the Colonial and Antebellum South*. Chapel Hill, 1998.

———. "Muslims in Early America." *Journal of Southern History* 40 (1994): 671–710.

Littlefield, Daniel C. *Rice and Slaves*. Baton Rouge, 1981.

Mintz, Sidney W., and Price, Richard. *The Birth of African-American Culture: An Anthropological Perspective*. Boston, MA: Beacon Press, 1992. (reprint, 1976)

Morgan, Philip D. *Slave Counterpoint: Black Culture in the Eighteenth-Century Chesapeake and Low Country*. Chapel Hill, 1998.

Sweet, James H. *Recreating Africa: Culture, Kinship, and Religion in the African-Portuguese World, 1441–1770*. Chapel Hill, 2003.

Thompson, Robert Farris. *Flash of the Spirit*. New York, 1983.

Thornton, John K. *Africa and Africans in the Making of the Atlantic World, 1400–168.0* Cambridge University Press, 1992.

———. *The Kongolese Saint Anthony: Dona Beatriz Kimpa Vita and the Antonian Movement, 1684–1706*. Cambridge, 1998.

Walsh, Lorena S. *From Calabar to Carter's Grove: A History of a Virginia Slave Community*. Charlottesville, 1997.

Wood, Peter H. *Black Majority: Negroes in Colonial South Carolina from 1670 through the Stono Rebellion*. New York, 1974.

See also **African-Americans**

SLAVE TRADE, DOMESTIC

In many respects the story of the domestic slave trade, or the buying and selling of enslaved American workers, is also the story of the early United States, and it is quite difficult to understand the growth of the latter without appreciating the significance of the former. While the buying and selling of human slaves had always been a part of American society, the nature of this traffic changed over time. In the seventeenth and eighteenth centuries, most slaves sold in British North America were imported from Africa or the West Indies, although by the mid-eighteenth century a small, locally based domestic trade had also developed. Following the American Revolution, this changed. The slave trade became an indigenous operation, annually transporting thousands of enslaved men and women from the upper South to the lower South and transferring an even greater number locally from one owner to another. Some of the reasons for this transformation were ironic outgrowths of the Revolution itself, such as the closing of the African slave trade in 1808. Others, like the invention of the cotton gin in the 1790s, simply coincided with these events. What is important is that the emergence of this new trade went hand-in-hand with the birth of American liberty.

The impact that this new traffic in human commodities had on the southern states and on the early American economy cannot be overemphasized. For one thing the magnitude of this trade made it a common form of commerce. From 1790–1860, Americans transported from the upper South to the lower South more than 1 million African-American slaves, approximately two-thirds of whom arrived there as a result of sale. Twice as many individuals were sold locally. During this period slave sales occurred in every southern city and village, and "coffles" of slaves (gangs held together in chains) could be found on every southern highway, waterway, and railroad. The domestic slave trade, in all of its components, was very much the lifeblood of the southern slave system, and without it, the institution would have ceased to exist.

This important new trade proved essential for the creation of the cotton kingdom. Primarily it transferred slave labor from those parts of the South where there was deemed to be excess to those areas where slaves were most in demand. Changes in agricultural production during the mid-eighteenth century meant that most southern slave owners, especially those in the Chesapeake, found themselves with a surplus of human property. Not only did this lead to a drop in slave prices, but following the Revolution, it also made many in the upper South question the future of the institution of slavery itself. By the early nineteenth century, this changed with the explosion in the international demand for cotton. As more and more land was opened up or turned over to the production of cotton, an almost insatiable demand for enslaved workers developed in the new cotton states of the old Southwest. And because the nation had closed off all outside sources of supply in 1808, this demand could be met only through a redistribution of the existing slave population. Recognizing that planters in the new cotton states were willing to pay hundreds of dollars more per slave than were owners in the older states, thousands of southern speculators transported hundreds of thousands of bonds people from the upper South and seaboard states to the markets of the Southwest.

In addition to fueling southern expansion, the domestic trade also solidified the region's commitment to the institution of chattel slavery. Because the demand for slaves was always greater in the lower South than elsewhere, planters there drove up the price of slaves throughout the South. In other words the market value of an enslaved worker in a place like Richmond was no longer dependent on local demand, but on what someone in New Orleans was willing to pay. As a result from 1800–1860, the price of enslaved workers throughout the South more than tripled. While this rise in slave prices made it increasingly difficult for those who wished to purchase, it played a crucial role in the economy of the upper South. What was formerly seen by those in Virginia, for example, as excess property now became a major source of capital that could be mortgaged to produce even more wealth. And it also became the upper South's most infamous export. By linking the South's two main subregions in a common economic concern, the interregional trade raised the value of slave property for everyone who owned it and put to rest any doubts that white southerners in the upper South may have had about the future of the institution. Even more important, it turned slave property into one of the most valuable forms of investment in the country, second only to land.

Yet while the domestic slave trade brought great wealth to those who held human property, and to the nation itself, it had a devastating impact on those southern workers who found themselves being bought and sold like things. For these individuals the domestic trade was not just an economic transaction. For the enslaved each sale was an action with potentially devastating and lifelong consequences. Millions of working men, women, and children found themselves torn from their families and friends against their will through sale or having those they loved taken from them by this process. Many African-Americans vividly remembered the traumatic effect that this trade had on their lives decades later. Even for those who were never sold, the threat of sale was pervasive, and they never knew for sure whether or not they, too, would one day be sold and forcibly taken away from their loved ones and homes. For most American slaves, little could be done to prevent the threat and actuality of sale. Yet many did resist. Even those who had never struck out against slavery before fought back when sale forced them to confront the reality of being torn away from family and loved ones.

While most were unsuccessful in their attempts to prevent a sale, their collective efforts to resist the trade did make the system run less smoothly than slave owners would have liked. Moreover for years white southerners had argued that their "peculiar institution" was based on a nonmarket relationship, radically different from that between a factory owner and his employees. Unlike the free-labor North, where the bond between an employer and employee was simply commercial and workers could be abandoned at will, they argued that in the South a special relationship existed between an owner and a slave and the workers were supposedly taken care of for life. For self-proclaimed masters, this meant looking after their charges, or their people, as they liked to call them. Not only did they have to provide them with a lifetime of food and shelter, but they also cared for their personal lives. In return the supposedly grateful slaves would perform whatever labor their beloved masters required. The extraordinary efforts to which enslaved workers went to resist the domestic slave trade however, be it through violence, flight, manipulation, or memory, were some of the most telling pieces of evidence for anyone who wished to notice that the paternalistic fantasy that the slaveholders had created was all just one big lie. The ramifications of that lie and of the trade that sustained it can still be felt in American society today.

STEVEN DEYLE

References and Further Reading

Bancroft, Frederic. *Slave Trading in the Old South.* Columbia: University of South Carolina Press, 1996. (reprint, 1931)

Deyle, Steven. *Carry Me Back: The Domestic Slave Trade in American Life.* New York: Oxford University Press, 2005.

Gudmestad, Robert H. *A Troublesome Commerce: The Transformation of the Interstate Slave Trade.* Baton Rouge: Louisiana State University Press, 2003.

Johnson, Walter. *Soul by Soul: Life inside the Antebellum Slave Market.* Cambridge, MA: Harvard University Press, 1999.

Rothman, Adam. *Slave Country: American Expansion and the Origins of the Deep South.* Cambridge, MA: Harvard University Press, 2005.

Tadman, Michael. *Masters and Speculators: Masters, Traders, and Slaves in the Old South.* Madison: University of Wisconsin Press: 1989.

See also **African-Americans; Civil War and Reconstruction; Slave Trade; Slavery**

SLAVERY

Slavery, the historian Kenneth Stampp has written, "was above all a system of labor" (K. Stampp, *The Peculiar Institution*, 1956). Although it became a means for one people to dominate another and begat an ideology of racism, the purpose of slavery from its origins during the seventeenth century until its demise during the Civil War was to produce staple crops and other goods for the benefit of slaveholders. The organization of slave labor varied widely from place to place and over time in colonial North America and the United States and shaped the contours of slave society.

Africans lived in North America nearly a century before English settlers established slavery as the solution to the labor problem in colonial Virginia. To be sure Elizabethan England entertained harsh notions about Africans from the outset of colonization. Travelers to Africa returned to spread word that the inhabitants were uncivilized strangers to proper government and the Christian God. One writer condemned Africans in the mid-1550s as "a people of beatly lyvynge, without a god, law, religion, or common wealth." Yet partisans of this view had to contend with a strong crosscurrent of opinion that imagined Europeans, Africans, and Native Americans living in harmony in the New World, one sheepfold, as the Reverend Samuel Purchase wrote in 1614, "without any more distinction of Colour, Nation, Language, Sex, Condition" (B. Wood, *The Origins of American Slavery*, 1997). In the early 1600s, when the English began colonizing North America, a clear conception of racism was still over 150 years in the future.

Until the last-quarter of the seventeenth century, the status of Africans in the colonies was varied. Many were slaves. A census of Virginia in 1619 recorded 32 African-Americans, although their status is unknown (B. Wood, 1997). In August some 20 more Africans arrived from Angola as slaves, captured from a Portuguese slave ship by Dutch and English privateers preying on ships in Spanish America, where the slaves were headed for sale. Delivered to Virginia instead, the slaves were likely put to work growing tobacco, which English settlers had begun to grow for export 2 years previously.

Tobacco required constant tending and created a steady demand for laborers in Virginia and Maryland. It took several months merely to get the crop properly planted, beginning in winter when field laborers hoed the soil into beds, planted them with seeds, then hoed the beds into hills 3 feet apart. Seeding the beds, to take just one task for example, was back-breaking labor, requiring men and women to bend over as many as 6,000 times a day to drill a hole in the soil with a stick or finger. In summer work gangs went over the fields again and again to hoe and plow the soil to keep it loose and allow roots to spread, then to pick worms off the plants, and to trim the plants down to eight hardy leaves. Harvest began in the fall when field laborers knocked down the stalks, piled them up to wither a few days in the sun, then stripped the leaves, and hung them in the tobacco house to cure. The leaves were then tied into bundles and pressed into barrels, or hogsheads, weighing up to 1,300 pounds, which slaves then rolled to a creek or cart and hoisted onto a wagon or boat for transport to market for sale.

Other Africans labored in indentured servitude, an exacting form of bondage in its own right. Servants were bought and sold, whipped, and worked for no pay. Until the 1680s, most laborers in the Chesapeake were indentured servants, English colonists in the main who had their passage paid to the New World in return for several years of unpaid labor. Slaves and servants, African as well as English, were in much the same condition, often made common cause, and ran away together. Once servants completed their indenture however, they gained their freedom. Indentured servitude was a way station to freedom for Europeans and many Africans.

The free African population grew through the middle of the seventeenth century. Slaves leveraged the demand for labor to negotiate favorable arrangements—to work on their own account for example and eventually bought their freedom. In 1651, Francis Payne paid for his freedom by giving his owner 1,650 pounds of tobacco and two English indentured servants. In 1668, 29% of all African-Americans in Northampton County, Virginia, on the eastern shore of the Chesapeake Bay were free (T. Breen et al., *"Myne Owne Ground": Race and Freedom on Virginia's Eastern Shore*, 1980). Some were prosperous small tobacco planters, owners of substantial property in slaves, indentured servants, and land.

By the turn of the century however, slavery was becoming the predominant system of labor in the Chesapeake and the exclusive condition of Africans. In the mid-1660s, Virginia finally adopted laws to define the status of slaves as a life-long condition, imposed exclusively on people of African descent, inherited from generation to generation. Subsequent statutes, consolidated in slave codes of 1705, closed off most avenues to freedom for bond people, and stripped them of means of resistance.

African slavery had several advantages from the planters' standpoint over other solutions to the colonial labor problem. Virginia planters could not extend servants' terms of indenture indefinitely, for servants had legal standing to invoke the much-vaunted "rights of Englishmen." Colonists enslaved thousands of Native Americans although the precise number is unknown. Yet native people, familiar with the American terrain, in close proximity to their countrymen, formidable adversaries in warfare, were difficult to keep in slavery. Africans, wrenched from their homelands across the Atlantic Ocean, lacked the legal rights or formidable allies to resist enslavement on foreign terrain. African slaves rapidly replaced English indentured servants on the plantations of the Chesapeake after 1680. The population of African descent in the region grew from 4,000 that year to 31,000 in 1710 (42% of all Virginians) (B. Wood, 1997).

Meanwhile African slavery grew apace in low-country Carolina, conceived as a haven for planters from Barbados and the only colony in British North America founded with legal provisions for slavery. Carolina's *Fundamental Constitutions*, written in 1669 by the philosopher John Locke with idealistic provisions for religious tolerance and representative government, also granted land to colonists who brought slaves to the colony. Settlers, guaranteed the right to property in man, eagerly imported African slaves.

Colonists resorted to slavery early and employed it extensively in the North, although not on so vast a scale as in the South. Indeed the first laws on slavery in North America were enacted in the "Massachusetts Body of Liberties" in 1641. In the countryside most slaves worked on small farms, often side-by-side with their owners, in iron furnaces, tanneries, and other manufacturing enterprises, as well as on large agricultural estates. Towns and port cities also had large concentrations of slaves who worked for artisans, merchants, and other prosperous colonists as maritime, domestic, and craft laborers, one-seventh (14.4%) of the population in New York by 1703 and one-sixth in Philadelphia by 1710 (Nash, *Many Thousands Gone*, 1998). Urban elites deployed their people as emblems of status and wealth, fitting out their carriages for example with a livery of lavishly attired Africans.

In the Low Country Carolinians experimented with cattle raising, cotton, and coffee before seizing on rice by 1730 as a viable staple with a ready market, mainly to feed slaves producing sugar in the West Indies. By the mid-eighteenth century, rice plantations extended from Cape Fear, North Carolina, 35 miles inland and south to the St. Johns River in Florida. Knowledge and skill in the methods of rice cultivation by slaves from the Grain Coast of West Africa—Senegambia, Sierra Leone, and Liberia— were crucial to a shift, beginning in the 1750s, from inland swamps to tidal rivers that transformed the Low Country into the wealthiest region in colonial North America, the so-called rice kingdom.

Rice plantations, described by one observer as a "huge hydraulic machine," were places of heavy labor. Slaves dug ditches, trenches, 6-foot banks, and canals 15 feet wide to connect plantations to the tidal rivers that bisected the Low Country, rising and falling as much as 3 feet daily, to flood and drain the rice fields. At the beginning of the crop year in February, slaves extended and repaired the network of earthworks, gates, and sluices. In March and April laborers broke ground in the fields, hoeing, digging trenches, and sowing seeds. As the rice plants matured, slaves returned to the fields with hoes repeatedly between floodings. They opened the floodgates, first in mid-May, and again in July. At harvest slaves cut the plants with sickles, bound them into bundles, took them to barns, threshed the rice with flails, removed the husk, sifted the grains, and packed them.

African-Americans transferred rice-growing practices from the Grain Coast to the Low Country. Slaves sowed seeds with a protective casing of mud, covered them with a step of the heel, separated the hull from the grain by grinding it with mortar and pestle and winnowing it in fanner baskets. They reproduced tools from West African material culture, such as short- and long-handled hoes and reconstituted a familiar sexual division of labor, where men dug earthworks and women hoed the fields and processed the harvested rice.

Labor-intensive rice production made the Low Country the seat of the largest plantations in North America. It required a large force of slaves to maintain the latticework of waterways and to produce enough rice to make the outlay in capital pay. The slave population grew with the rice crop. Slaves were a majority of the population in South Carolina as early as 1708, 60% by 1720 (P. Morgan, *Slave Counterpoint*, 1998). During the 1740s, when about one-half of Virginia slaves lived on units with 10 bond people or less, over half in South Carolina lived on plantations with at least 30 (P. Morgan, 1998).

Colonial North America relied on the trans-Atlantic slave trade during the eighteenth century. A majority of slaves came from Africa to Carolina and Virginia by 1700, to the North by midcentury. Of all the slaves imported to South Carolina from 1749–1765, fully 54% came from Senegambia and Sierra Leone on the Grain Coast (D. Richardson, *Slavery and Abolition*, 1991). Charleston was the largest port of entry for Africans to North America, while the leading ports of embarkation in the African trade were in New England.

Slavery was thus deeply entrenched in every region of colonial North America by the beginning of the eighteenth century. The slave population in North America increased 10-fold from a mere 7,000 in 1680 to 70,000 in 1720 and to 246,000 in 1750 (I. Berlin, 1998). Colonists had committed themselves to the African trade to obtain slaves, lucrative staple crops for them to produce, and laws to protect the rights of slaveholders. To be sure slave labor varied from place to place sufficiently to distinguish the character of slavery in different regions. Slavery in the mid-Atlantic and New England colonies was extensive, but not the predominant system of labor. The Low Country and the Chesapeake by contrast were *bona fide* slave societies, dependent primarily on slave labor, which left its mark on every aspect of social organization and became the lens through which people—free and enslaved—saw themselves and their society.

In the Low Country the terms of slave labor laid the foundation for the most independent slave culture on the North American mainland. Here slaves tended the staple on the basis of task labor. In contrast to gangs, where slaves worked owners' crops sunup to sundown, slaves in Carolina worked until they completed an assigned task at their own pace. Neither owners nor overseers nor drivers were free to define what amounted to a day's work at will because the daily task for a particular job—a quarter of an acre for hoeing, half an acre for digging trenches—was customary regionwide and changed little over time. Men and women working deliberately could complete their task by midafternoon. The division between the time field laborers owed owners and what belonged to themselves afforded field laborers a rare control over their work.

Bond people devoted much of their own time to working on their own account. Families worked garden plots to grow rice, potatoes, cabbages, and other garden truck, which they used to supplement their diets as well as to trade and accumulate property. Women performed much of the labor in garden patches, although men did their part here, and fished,

hunted, and produced baskets, pipes, and other handicrafts.

The relative independence of slave labor in the Low Country also laid the foundation for a distinctly African slave culture. A steady stream of Africans met the pressing need for workers in the rice fields, where they persisted as a majority in the slave population until the 1740s. Over the course of the eighteenth century, slaves developed their own Creole language, Gullah, which combined the grammar, syntax, and lexicon of several West African languages as well as English. Low Country slaves forged a similar synthesis of African and Anglo-American religious practices as well. Low Country people shared African beliefs that a dead person's spirit would harass the living if his/her death were not properly observed. Funerals therefore included many rites to propitiate the spirits, such as leaving food, water, and various personal effects on a fresh grave to tide over the deceased on the journey to the spirit world. Of all the regions of mainland North America, the Low Country most resembled the slave societies of the West Indies and South America in its large plantations, a majority slave population, Creole language, and profoundly African ways.

Although the North was not a slave society, labor shaped slave culture nonetheless. Slaves' employment as farmhands, artisans, and domestic servants on smallholdings concentrated in cities, towns, and fertile rural areas gave a particular geography to their collective life. Its focal point was public spaces—grog shops, taverns, town squares, and graveyards—and public occasions—holidays, elections, and funerals—where slaves could gather in numbers. Black New Englanders in towns like Newport, Rhode Island, Hartford, Connecticut, and Boston, Massachusetts, made an annual rite of colonial election days and held a canvass to select their own king or governor, who appointed a retinue of sheriffs, justices of the peace, among other lieutenants. Festivities were announced with beating drums, complete with speeches, lobbying, processions of men and women decked out in powdered wigs, cocked hats, and fine dresses, accompaniment by banjos, fiddles, and tambourines. In New Jersey and New York, slaves appropriated Pinkster, a celebration of the Christian holiday Pentecost, for the election of an African-American monarch.

Even here in the northern colonies, the enslaved population grew and moved toward the center of production during the mid-eighteenth century. As late as the 1740s, slaves comprised 15% of all workingmen in Philadelphia, 30% in New York City (I. Berlin, 1998; G. Nash, *Urban Crucible*, 1979). Artisans owned an increasing proportion of urban slaves, who worked as rope spinners, sail makers, bricklayers, tailors, carpenters, and blacksmiths. As urban slavery shifted from domestic service in the households of the mercantile elite to the workshops of craft laborers, a growing proportion of all slaves worked in the countryside, especially on farms along rivers that formed the sinews of commerce in the diverse northern economy, the Connecticut River valley in New England, the Hudson in New York, and the Delaware in Pennsylvania, where about one in every 10 families in Chester County southwest of Philadelphia owned slaves.

Slavery was shaken during the American Revolution, but its foundations ultimately emerged in the new republic stronger than ever at their keystones of law and ideology. Slavery was a profound contradiction in the patriot's enterprise. Slaveholders stood out prominently among the foremost revolutionaries, including Thomas Jefferson, George Washington, James Madison, George Mason, Henry Laurens, even Ben Franklin. "How is it," asked Samuel Johnson, the London man of letters, "that we hear the loudest *yelps* for liberty among the drivers of negroes?" (D. Davis, *The Problem of Slavery in the Age of Revolution*, 1975). It was the labor of slaves, the widespread ownership of human property, and the shared experience of mastery, with all its struggles and perquisites, that enabled colonial planters to conceive of Americans as distinct and independent and as a nation of equals.

Yet many slaves gained their liberty during the revolution. Some gained their freedom by military service in the Revolutionary War, to the patriot army in the North, mainly the British army in the South. In 1777, Connecticut accepted slaves in its revolutionary regiments, and Rhode Island offered bond people freedom in return for military service. In 1775, some 800 slaves enlisted in a Tory Ethiopian Regiment, organized by colonial governor of Virginia, Lord Dunmore, and served with the slogan, "liberty to slaves," emblazoned across their chests. In the South as well, slaves served the patriot army as spies, guides; built fortifications and performed other military labor. Virginia, Maryland, and Delaware all authorized the enlistment of slaves in patriot ranks by the end of the war. According to the best estimates, from 18,000–25,000 slaves seized on the disorder of the Revolutionary War to leave their owners and seek their freedom behind British army lines. Many of these men and women, perhaps up to 50% or 60%, died of disease or wounds or were captured and re-enslaved. The rest evacuated with the British at the end of the war in 1782–1783, resettling elsewhere in British America and England or insinuated themselves into the free black population of the new republic.

Many Americans resolved the contradiction between slavery and liberty in favor of freedom after independence. The northern states enacted laws for gradual emancipation—Pennsylvania in 1780, Connecticut and Rhode Island in 1784, New York in 1799, and New Jersey in 1794. These measures freed no one enslaved at the time the statute was enacted and applied exclusively to slaves born after the date the emancipation law was adopted, who gained their freedom well into adulthood, at age 28 in Pennsylvania, for example. Even in Massachusetts, where in 1783 the state supreme court declared slavery contrary to the new state constitution, it took many years for slaves to gain their freedom in practice. Thus under the niggardly terms of northern emancipation, this was a long, slow process designed to last 20 years or more. Yet slaves hastened gradual emancipation mightily by compelling owners to free them ahead of legislative timetables in hard bargaining, often initiated by runaways who made the negotiations a condition of their return. Many bond people agreed to work for some period of years or on their own account to accumulate the means to purchase their freedom.

In the Chesapeake thousands of slaves gained their freedom by manumission. Some slaveholders, their scruples about the contradiction between slavery and revolutionary liberty sharpened by a revival of religious piety, the Great Awakening, freed their own bond people. Yet even these slaves gained their freedom at masters' convenience, gradually, often on an owner's death. Robert Carter III freed some 500 slaves over the course of 20 years, manumitting his bond people by the dozens annually starting in 1791 (L. Morton, *Robert Carter of Nomini Hall*, 1941). Despite the limitations of the emancipatory impulse during the revolutionary era, a new class of free black people grew dramatically from 59,000 to 183,000, about 9 out of 10 living in the North and upper South (I. Berlin, 1998).

Yet the Revolution also gave impetus to another resolution of the contradiction between liberty and slavery, a new ideology of racism. The question of how a nation devoted to the proposition that all men are equal, as the Declaration of Independence would have it, could practice slavery cried out for an answer, and Thomas Jefferson provided it: Perhaps Africans were not men at all. Instead, he suggested in *Notes on the State of Virginia*, they fit somewhere in the scheme of creation between white people and "orangootans." Jefferson argued in effect that all men are created equal, but some people are not men. Jefferson's notion bordered on heresy, for it was conventional wisdom in the Anglo-American world that in "the great chain of being," all the peoples of humankind were equally good, and to say otherwise cast aspersions on God's creation. Racism, a belief in the immutable inferiority of some peoples to others, has origins in the liberal principles of the American Revolution.

The Constitution moreover laid a new legal foundation under slavery in the new republic. Although several delegates expressed their misgivings about human bondage to the Constitutional Convention in Philadelphia during the summer of 1787, planters, South Carolinians especially, forced a compromise and gained four clauses recognizing slavery. Southern states increased their power in the federal government from a clause in Article I, Section 2 counting slaves as three-fifths of a person for purposes of apportioning seats in the House of Representatives. The three-fifths clause thus inflated slaveholders' influence in the House, where the size of each state's delegation depended on the size of its population; and in the Electoral College, where the selection of the president was decided and the number of votes cast by each state was equal to the size of its delegation in Congress. Other clauses prohibited Congress from abolishing the African slave trade before 1808 (Article I, Section 9), provided for the return of fugitive slaves who crossed state lines (Article IV, Section 2). Perhaps the strongest buttress the founders erected for slavery was the restriction on Congress solely to exercise those powers "enumerated" in the Constitution, which prohibited the House and Senate from subsequently claiming the authority to abolish slavery. The founders' unease over slavery was implicit in their refusal to introduce the word slavery into the Constitution, preferring instead such euphemisms as persons "held to Service or Labor" (D. Nieman, *Promises to Keep*, 1991).

Over the next seven decades, slavery expanded explosively across the United States. Slaves carved plantations out of the wilderness across a belt of black loam soil from central Georgia, west across Alabama, Mississippi, Louisiana, to east Texas. Some of the largest slaveholdings in the black belt were along the banks of major rivers, which facilitated the marketing of staple crops—the Tombigbee River along the border of Alabama and Mississippi, the Mississippi River from New Orleans to Memphis, and the Red River in Southern Louisiana. As many as one million slaves migrated to the Deep South in a second middle passage, larger than the first middle passage from West Africa to North America. The number of slaves leaving the upper South waxed and waned with the fortunes of the staple economy.

Slave labor in the burgeoning cotton kingdom was inextricably bound up with the rise of industrial capitalism, as southern slaves became the leading producers of the raw material for textile factories in the North and England. Cotton, requiring 200 days without frost and the modest equipment of hoe, plow, and seeds, could grow on small upcountry farms as well as large black belt plantations. King cotton was a harsh taskmaster. The annual routine began in winter, when slaves prepared the ground for planting, knocked down the stalks from last year's crop, and turned the soil to pile up into rounded beds. In April slaves began to plant, plowing the crests of the beds, drilling seeds into the dirt, and covering them by drawing a harrow or small plow over the bed. Through July slaves went over each row with their hoes, digging up some of the new plants until only two remained every few feet, chopping out weeds and grass with hoes and plows. When the blossoms began hatching into bolls, cultivation ended, and the crop was "laid by." Cotton stained if it fell to the ground or was strafed by heavy rain, so slaves went into the fields as soon as the bolls opened, usually in late August and early September. An adult slave was expected to pick up to 200 pounds each day, every day from September to Christmas. Cotton rose to become the leading staple in the South in tandem with a shift in production to the old Southwest. By 1834, three states that entered the Union after 1790—Louisiana, Mississippi, and Alabama—accounted for over half the cotton produced in the South.

Slaves produced a range of other crops during these years. Slaveholders, planters with 20 bondmen or more as well as yeomen, strived to protect themselves from the vagaries of the market by raising their own food crops. Indeed slaves planted more acreage in corn than cotton. Different regions moreover specialized in different staples—tobacco in middle Tennessee and Kentucky, hemp in Kentucky and Virginia, and sugar in southern Louisiana.

Sugar production required the most demanding work routine of any crop in the Americas because it combined agricultural and factory labor. Slaves had to grow the sugar cane, then refine it, extracting the juice from the cane and turning it into granulated sugar. Raising cane was especially arduous in the United States, where it required compressing a 15-month growing season into just 9 months. The fieldwork began in January when slaves set fire to the fields to burn the dregs of the previous crop. Slaves prepared beds in the bare earth with deep-running plows, pulled by six-mule teams, then planted two small stalks every 4 inches or so and went back over the rows, hoeing dirt over the stalks 3 inches deep. The canes shot up quickly after the sprouts broke through the ground. Slaves hoed around the stalks, chopping out grass and weeds, three times before cutting the cane. Men and women entered the rows three abreast, wielding 15-inch knives tapered at the ends and wide in the middle like a new moon and cut each cane with three swift blows, severing the leaves from the stalk, the green tops from the cane, then the cane at the root.

The factory labor took place in sugar mills, hulking buildings, some 50 feet wide and 100 feet long. Inside rows of rollers stretched past towering boilers. Mill workers had to process the cane quickly to maximize the quantity and quality of sugar. They pushed cane onto wooden belts moved by metal chains into iron rollers over a brick pier to crush the stalks into a thick juice. The juice slithered down into filters, removing impurities, and turning the liquid clear before it was piped into the iron boilers and into coolers. When the sugar met the air, clear liquid suddenly jelled into pure white grains. Keeping the mills going into the night required a small army of slaves to perform a variety of tasks and develop a range of skills, from the children who toted the cane into the mill, the men who cut wood to keep the fires lit under the boilers, to the sugar master who chose the precise moment to strike or quicken, the sugar. Coordination—between the laborers supplying the cane and wood to the mill and those tending the sophisticated equipment inside—was the hallmark of sugar production.

Slaves also reconstituted their prerogatives to work on their own account across the South during the antebellum period. Low Country bond people, building on colonial foundations and with the advantage of task labor, established independent production on the best terms in the South and a widespread progression in the accumulation of property. Families used their earnings from vegetable produce and handicrafts to acquire and trade poultry, eggs, and pigs, and then parlayed trade in these goods into more valuable livestock, such as horses and mules, which slaves used to increase their volume and control of independent production. Although planters struggled to assert control over this commerce, slaves, especially slave women, were a formidable presence in urban markets in Charleston and Savannah

Elsewhere in the South ownership of livestock and other productive property was limited mainly to slaves who hired their own time and to artisans, drivers, and other slaves who worked outside the fields. Nonetheless field laborers on many farms and plantations cultivated garden patches, raised poultry, and produced handicrafts. Slaves also contended for payment for work on Sundays to trade in town and buy what they pleased, while owners struggled to keep their people from raising staple crops, trading off the home place, and the slaves' enterprise in

general within confines consistent with good order. Despite these pressing constraints, slaves made and traded goods extensively, brightened their wardrobes, meals, and celebrations, and forged networks of work and exchange that undergirded family ties.

The destruction of slavery during the Civil War built on wartime transformations in the terms of work. Relations of labor changed from the outset of the conflict as slaveholding men enlisted in the Confederate army and field slaves came under the supervision of slaveholding women, elderly men, and young boys. The South's strategy of provoking British recognition of the Confederate States of America by withholding cotton from the international market prompted a gradual shift from staple to food crops and a reduction in field labor. Slaves increased the volume of their production and trade on their own account in 1861 and 1862. The terms of independent production improved further still wherever the Union army advanced, as African-Americans found a ready market for their goods and services in Union troops.

Slaves' withdrawal of their labor was critical to turning the Civil War into a war for emancipation. As early as May 1861, within weeks of President Abraham Lincoln's Inaugural Address, confining northern war aims to restoring the Union, slaves began making their way to Union outposts. Slaves demanding freedom met the Union army wherever it advanced throughout the war. By taking this step slave men and women forced Union authorities to choose between returning bond people to their owners, who were bound to employ them in the Confederate war effort, or employ them in the Union cause. Federal authorities adopted a policy declaring fugitive slaves contraband of war and put these so-called contrabands to work building fortifications, digging trenches, transporting supplies. Finally on September 22, 1862, President Lincoln announced his intention to issue an Emancipation Proclamation. Although it applied solely to areas not under Union occupation, thus freeing slaves where the North lacked the power to enforce the edict and exempting areas under federal control, Lincoln had turned the Civil War into a war against slavery.

The final proclamation, issued New Year's Day 1863, included a new provision to enlist slaves in the Union army. By the end of the war, 179,000 African-Americans enlisted, including 79% in slave states, and comprising 21% of all black men of military age. Another 17,000 black men served in the Union Navy, including about 65% from the slave states, approximately 20% of the navy's total manpower (J. Reidy, *Prologue*, 2001). They proved their mettle in battle with dispatch in three pitched battles in

1863—in Louisiana at Port Hudson on May 2 and Milliken's Bend on June 7, in South Carolina at Fort Wagner on July 18. Black men, organized into separate regiments, fought in over 400 engagements, including such legendary battles as the Wilderness, Cold Harbor, the Crater, and marched victorious into South Carolina and Richmond. The North, eagerly putting black soldiers to work in the Union war effort, compelled them to struggle to serve the army on equal terms however. They were excluded from the ranks of commissioned officers (lieutenant or above), assigned more than their fair share of military labor, and paid a mere $7 monthly, which was well below the $13 received by white troops and put their pay on a par with military laborers. The latter included thousands of other men who built fortifications, transported supplies by mule team, tended the sick in army hospitals, among other employments, and a relatively small number of women who also worked as nurses, cooks, as well as laundresses.

The shift from slavery to free labor also began in earnest during the Civil War under the auspices of the Union Army. The largest wartime experiment in free labor was the least promising from the feed people's point of view. In the Mississippi Valley, 750,000 field workers toiled away on plantations under army regulations providing for wages of just $2 per month in southern Louisiana and $7 in Mississippi and Tennessee. At Davis Bend, the plantations of Confederate President Jefferson Davis and his brother on the Mississippi River, freed people worked land collectively in companies and colonies and gained a modicum of self-government in a court presided over by judges elected from their own ranks. In the Low Country, General William T. Sherman issued Field Order 15 on January 16, 1865, setting aside the Sea Islands off the coast and a stretch of plantations south of Charleston 30 miles inland for the settlement of freedmen and according every family's "possessory title" to 40-acre plots. Forty thousand freed people raised food crops instead of commercial staples on the so-called Sherman Reserve, seeking independence from the market and for their communities, before the land was ordered returned to its original owners by President Andrew Johnson in October 1865. By the end of the Civil War, former slaves had begun an epoch-making transition to wage labor.

ANTHONY KAYE

References and Further Reading

Berlin, Ira. *Many Thousands Gone: The First Two Centuries of Slavery in North America.* Cambridge, 1998.
Breen, T. H., and Stephen Innes. *"Myne Owne Ground": Race and Freedom on Virginia's Eastern Shore, 1640–1676.* New York, 1980.
Carney, Judith A. *Black Rice: The African Origins of Rice Cultivation in the Americas.* Cambridge, 2001.
Creel, Margaret Washington. *"A Peculiar People": Slave Religion and Community-Culture among the Gullahs.* New York, 1988.
Davis, David B. *The Problem of Slavery in the Age of Revolution, 1770–1823.* Ithaca, NY: 1975.
Frey, Sylvia. *Water from the Rock: Black Resistance in a Revolutionary Age.* Princeton, NJ: 1991.
Hodges, Graham Russell. *Root and Branch: African Americans in New York and East Jersey, 1613–1863.* Chapel Hill, 1999.
Kulikoff, Allan. *Tobacco and Slaves: The Development of Southern Cultures in the Chesapeake, 1680–1800.* Chapel Hill, 1986.
Melish, Joanne Pope. *Disowning Slavery: Gradual Emancipation and "Race" in New England, 1780–1860.* Ithaca, NY: 1998.
Mintz, Sidney W. *Sweetness and Power: The Place of Sugar in Modern History.* New York, 1985.
Morgan, Philip D. *Slave Counterpoint: Black Culture in the Eighteenth-Century Chesapeake and Low Country.* Chapel Hill, 1998.
Morton, Louis. *Robert Carter of Nomini Hall: A Virginia Tobacco Planter of the Eighteenth Century.* Charlottesville: University Press of Virginia, 1941.
Nash, Gary. *The Urban Crucible: Social Change, Political Consciousness, and the Origins of the American Revolution.* Cambridge, MA: Harvard University Press, 1979.
Nash, Gary B., and Jean R. Soderlund. *Freedom by Degrees: Emancipation in Pennsylvania and Its Aftermath.* Oxford, 1991.
Nieman, Donald G. *Promises to Keep: African-Americans and the Constitutional Order, 1776 to the Present.* New York, 1991.
Piersen, William D. *Black Yankees: The Development of an Afro-American Subculture in Eighteenth-Century New England.* Amherst, 1988.
Pybus, Cassandra. "Jefferson's Faulty Math: The Question of Slave Defections in the American Revolution." *William and Mary Quarterly* 62 (Apr. 2005): 243–264.
Reidy, Joseph P. "Black Men in Navy Blue during the Civil War." *Prologue* 33, 3 (2001): 154–167.
Richardson, David. "The British Slave Trade to Colonial South Carolina." *Slavery and Abolition* 12 (1991): 125–172.
Sitterson, J. Carlyle. *Sugar Country: The Cane Sugar Industry in the South, 1753–1950.* Louisville, 1953.
Sluiter, Engel. "New Light on the '20 and Odd Negroes' Arriving in Virginia, August 1619." *William and Mary Quarterly* 54 (Apr. 1997): 395–398.
Stampp, Kenneth M. *The Peculiar Institution: Slavery in the Ante-Bellum South.* New York: Alfred A. Knopf, 1956.
Tomich, Dale. *Slavery in the Circuit of Sugar.* Baltimore, 1990.
White, Shane. *Somewhat More Independent: The End of Slavery in New York, 1770–1810.* Athens, 1991.
Wood, Betty. *The Origins of American Slavery: Freedom and Bondage in the English Colonies.* New York: Hill and Wang, 1997.

See also **Abolitionism; African-Americans; Civil Rights; Emancipation and Reconstruction; Slave Rebellions; Slave Trade; Slave Trade, Domestic; South**

SLICHTER, SUMNER (1892–1959)
Economist

Sumner Huber Slichter was a renowned economist who served on the staff of the Commission on Industrial Relations (1913–1915), taught at Princeton University (1919–1920) and Cornell University (1920–1930) but spent the bulk of his career at Harvard University (1930 until his death). Originally recruited by the Harvard Business School, he subsequently joined their Economics Department and the Littauer School of Public Administration when it was founded. Slichter worked in the tradition of institutional economics, offering courses on collective bargaining, problems of industrial relations, problems of economic balance, and the economic aspects of public administration. In 1940, he was named the Lamont University Professor, one of the most prestigious posts on the Harvard faculty. He was the first member of the faculty to receive that honor.

There are few if any professors who had greater impact on industrial relations than Slichter at the peak of his career, although he is seldom read or even cited by labor historians today—except for a 1948 article in which he declared that the United States was becoming a "laboristic" state, a contention he subsequently disavowed.

While George W. Taylor, William H. Davis, and former members of the second National War Labor Board's staff, such as John T. Dunlop and Clark Kerr, served as the principal arbitrators for corporations and unions in the mid-twentieth century, it was Slichter who provided the benefits of collective bargaining for unions, management, and the public, while nonetheless critiquing the system. "Slichter was our guru," Kerr remarked in a 1992 interview with this author.

In three major works published in 1921, 1941, and 1960, Slichter explored the ways in which managerial policies in such areas as hiring, seniority, wages, unions, and grievances hurt or benefited corporations. In 1941, he founded the Harvard Trade Union Program. It offered midlevel trade unionists, principally from the building trades and the railroad brotherhoods, an entire year to live in Harvard dormitories (or houses) with undergraduates and graduate students and take classes not only on collective bargaining but also in the liberal arts. A much-abbreviated version of the program continues to this day. In 1946, Slichter was selected by the governor of Massachusetts to chair a tripartite committee on labor-management relations in the state. The committee unanimously recommended that Massachusetts recognize public employees' right to join unions but prevent strikes and lockouts through arbitration. The Slichter Commission, as it was called, laid the groundwork for similar programs by other states and municipalities in later years.

As early as 1928, Slichter began to publish articles in the *New Republic* and the *Atlantic Monthly*. After his magnum opus, *Union Policies and Industrial Management*, a distillation of 20 years of research on trade unions' practices and co-operation in the railroad and garment industries, appeared in 1941, he began publishing articles on industrial relations and the U.S. economy virtually every month in the *New York Times Magazine, Saturday Review, Harper's Magazine, Nation's Business, Fortune, Harvard Business Review*, the *Commercial and Financial Chronicle*, the *Christian Science Monitor*, the *Atlantic Monthly*, and the *New Republic* while also publishing in the *Quarterly Review of Economics*, the *American Economic Review*, and other scholarly journals. From November 1952 until his death, he sent his personal analysis of the business outlook in the United States every month to the *Nihol Keizai Shimbun*, Japan's major business newspaper, and 300 prominent figures in American business, finance, economics, and government. During the latter 1940s, Slichter also gave lectures on collective bargaining and the future of the U.S. economy at universities and to business and union organizations, which were collected and published in book form by major commercial publishers. In 1940, he was elected president of the American Economic Association. Thus he had a wide audience, an extraordinary accomplishment for a man who was neither a compelling speaker nor a theoretician. Indeed he suffered from a speech impediment early in his career

Unlike John R. Commons, with whom he studied at the University of Wisconsin, or Richard Ely, Slichter was never inspired by the social gospel, a popular agitator, or devoted to social reform. Rather he approached economics from the perspective of science and business. Born and raised in Madison, Wisconsin, when that city was the citadel of the Progressive movement, Slichter was the son of a noted mathematician who became dean of the University of Wisconsin's Graduate School and did consulting work for the U.S. Geological Survey and the railroads on the flow of underground waters. One of his brothers became director of Geophysics at the University of California; another went into chemical engineering and then business; the third, into geology and then owned a steel foundry. Both of Slichter's sons also became professors of science.

Viewing himself as an expert who could benefit the general public through research, Slichter devoted his career to investigating trends over time in wages, the labor force, productivity, prices, sales, profits, company and union practices, and related matters. He reached conclusions quite different from many of his contemporaries. For example while the majority of professional economists (like the American people generally) believed that the United States had reached maturity by 1929, Slichter felt absolutely certain that the American economy would grow rapidly after the depression of the 1930s. The depression would not have continued so long, he believed, if the Roosevelt administration had recognized the needs of corporations, particularly their need for venture capital. Similarly while many of his contemporaries, like most other Americans, feared that depression would resume after Japan and Germany surrendered, Slichter offered evidence to prove that the U.S. economy would boom after the war.

In a 1941 essay entitled "The Development of National Labor Policy," Slichter warned of a disjunction between the Wagner Act and other recently enacted labor laws and actual practices of unions. He publicly advised union and corporate leaders to alter their behavior lest the federal and state governments intervene. None took his admonition. Instead the U.S. Congress passed the Taft-Hartley Act in 1947, and state governments had competed with each other to offer similar acts restricting unions.

An expert on trade unions and the U.S. economy who was supportive of collective bargaining yet friendly to business and financial leaders, Slichter acquired clearer insight into union-management relations and their place in the political economy than other experts of his time or many of the labor historians who have studied those subjects.

In at least one area however, he erred significantly. That was his predictions about inflation. Throughout the 1950s, Slichter repeatedly criticized conservative politicians and economists who were anxious about rising wages and prices. He argued that steady but moderate wage and price increases were not only inescapable but desirable in modern industrialized societies. There is no need to worry about "creeping inflation," he declared often. Even if Slichter was correct in the short run, the history of the U.S. economy during the 1970s, when wages and prices exploded and productivity stagnated, demonstrated the falsity of that contention.

RONALD W. SCHATZ

References and Further Reading

Dunlop, John T., ed. *Potentials of the American Economy: Selected Essays of Sumner H. Slichter*. Cambridge, MA: Harvard University Press, 1961.

Healey, James J., E. Robert Livernash, and Sumner H. Slichter. *The Impact of Collective Bargaining on Management*. Washington, DC: The Brookings Institute, 1960.
Slichter, Sumner H. *The Turnover of Factory Labor*. New York: D. Appleton & Co. 1921.
———. *Toward Stability: The Problems of Economic Balance*. New York: Henry Holt, 1934.
———. *Union Policies and Industrial Management*. Washington, DC: The Brookings Institute, 1941.
———."The Challenge of Industrial Relations: Trade Unions, Management, and the Public Interest*. Ithaca, NY: Cornell University Press, 1947.
———. *Trade Unions in a Free Society*. Cambridge, MA: Harvard University Press, 1947.
———. *The American Economy: Its Problems and Prospects*. New York: Alfred A. Knopf, 1948.
———. *What's Ahead for American Business?* Boston, MA: Little, Brown, 1951.
———. "Argument for 'Creeping' Inflation." *New York Times Magazine* (Mar. 8, 1959): 23ff.
Slichter, Sumner H., Wesley C. Mitchell et al., "The Development of National Labor Policy." In *Studies in Economics and Industrial Relations*. Philadelphia: University of Pennsylvania Press, 1941.

Cases and Statutes Cited

Taft-Hartley Act
Wagner Act

SMITH-CONNALLY ACT

The Smith-Connally Act, or the War Labor Disputes Act of 1943, was a piece of temporary labor legislation passed during World War II over the veto of President Franklin D. Roosevelt, which limited the right of workers in key industries to strike and authorized the president to take control of firms in the event of strikes that threatened the war effort. The bill was primarily a response to a spring 1943 strike by John L. Lewis's United Mine Workers of America (UMWAA) that violated the labor movement's wartime no-strike pledge. In addition to its provisions relating to wartime strikes, the Smith-Connally Act also included the first legislative prohibition on campaign contributions by labor unions.

Lewis and the UMWAA had generated considerable popular hostility when the union struck twice after the outbreak of World War II, first in 1939 and again in 1941. Nevertheless the striking coal miners returned to work on 7 December 1941, immediately after Pearl Harbor. Indeed the UMWA joined practically all labor unions in agreeing to a no-strike pledge after the U.S. entry into the war. But the UMWA's acceptance of the no-strike pledge was a short-lived affair. The notoriously volatile Lewis was a staunch isolationist who grew increasingly hostile to Roosevelt during the 1940s. And in the spring of 1943, Lewis led the miner's union out on strike again.

By 1943, the UMWA's agreements with bituminous coal mine owners had expired, and Lewis demanded a 2-dollar wage increase to compensate workers for the time it took them to travel from the entrance of the mine to the work site, travel time for which they had not previously received any pay. The matter was referred to the War Labor Board, but Lewis refused to appear before the board, and the union went out on strike. President Roosevelt responded by seizing the coal mines and attempting to force the UMWA and the mine owners to come to an agreement. No agreement was reached however, and Lewis led the miners out on strike a second time on 11 June 1943, this time against the federal government, who were at that point running the mines. Roosevelt responded by threatening to ask Congress for the ability to draft striking miners. This temporarily ended the strike, but UMWA walked out again in October. This time an agreement was reached, and the coal miners received a wage increase of $1.50.

While Lewis did succeed in winning a wage increase for the miners, his actions also led to the passage of the Smith-Connally Act, which greatly limited the ability of workers in key wartime industries to strike. The War Labor Disputes Act was passed by Congress on 25 June 1943, immediately after the second time Lewis led the miners out on strike. President Roosevelt vetoed the law, but Congress overrode his veto. This can be accounted for largely because of the great popular hostility that erupted in the wake of UMWA's violation of the no-strike pledge. A Gallup poll in 1943 showed that Lewis was one of the most unpopular men in America, with 87% of respondents reporting an unfavorable view of the labor leader.

While the Smith-Connally Act was a temporary wartime measure that expired 6 months after the end of hostilities, it set a precedent for future labor legislation in two important respects. First, the act included an unprecedented legislative restriction on unions' campaign contributions. Smith-Connally prohibited unions from making any direct campaign contributions to candidates for any political office. This restriction had applied to corporations after the passage of the Tillman Act in 1907, but it had not previously covered unions. This was also the only provision of the Smith-Connally Act that was retained after the end of the war, and it was eventually incorporated into the 1947 Taft-Hartley Act. And second, Lewis's role in the passage of the War Labor Disputes Act would be repeated 4 years later in the run up to Taft-Hartley. Both acts were largely responses to strikes by the UMWA against coalmines that had been seized by the federal government, and both are generally seen as having hurt labor despite the success of the strikes that inspired them.

AARON MAX BERKOWITZ

Cases and Statutes Cited

Smith-Connally Act
Taft-Hartley Act
Tillman Act

SOCIALIST LABOR PARTY

In the first decade of the twenty-first century, the Socialist Labor party (SLP) is the longest surviving Marxian socialist party in the United States. Founded approximately 130 years ago, the roots of the SLP can be traced back to the second convention of the Workingmen's party, held in Newark (New Jersey) in 1876. At this gathering the organization definitively threw its support behind increased political activity, renounced those militants who believed that socialism could be obtained only through trade union work, and changed its name to the Socialistic Labor party of North America, which was later shortened to the Socialist Labor party. During the first 2 years of its existence, the group experienced substantial success with the launching of 24 newspapers that provided either direct or indirect support to the party. With SLP-backed candidates obtaining approximately 100,000 votes in the local elections of 1877 and 1878, three representatives and one senator were elected to the Illinois State House of Representatives and aldermen obtained seats on the Chicago and St. Louis city councils in the latter of the 2 years. By the beginning of 1880, the SLP had declined dramatically, with members engaged in rampant factionalism between moderate and anarcho-internationalist groups during much of the following decade. The moderates believed that the socialist revolution should not be hastened but would gradually emerge over time while the anarcho-internationalist position was that the SLP should do everything that it could to encourage the revolution during the immediate present.

The major ideological influence in the SLP was and still is (through the present day) that of Daniel DeLeon, a rigid, dogmatic, and sectarian Marxist. Joining the party in 1890, he was already a seasoned Socialist who became immediately active in the SLP's educational wing before becoming the permanent editor of the *People*, the party newspaper, in February 1892. Assuming the paper's editorship launched DeLeon into a leadership role that he never relinquished. Using an authoritarian style, he sought to remake the SLP through Americanizing the party, promoting the party press, establishing a party-controlled trade union arm, resolving the financial difficulties facing the party, and unifying and controlling the faction-ridden SLP. Of these five objectives, DeLeon was able to achieve only a modicum

Morris Hillquit. Library of Congress, Prints & Photographs Division [LC-DIG-ggbain-18322].

of success with the last one, basically through the expulsion of political opponents who refused to toe the DeLeonist line.

As a Marxist party, the SLP sought to become active in the established trade union federations, specifically the Knights of Labor (KOL) and the American Federation of Labor (AFL). The SLP was able to obtain control of New York City's District Assembly 49, the largest in the KOL, in 1884, and the national organization for a period of time in 1886. In addition the party combined with Western delegates to elect James R. Sovereign as KOL president in 1893. However by 1895, with the loss of control of District Assembly 49 and differences emerging between DeLeon and Sovereign, SLP influence had been dramatically weakened in the KOL. Although the party wielded significant influence at the 1893 and 1894 AFL conventions, as indicated by delegate support for planks advocating the municipal ownership and the nationalization of key industries as well as the collective ownership of the means of production, at the 1895 convention, the SLP's influence in the AFL was on

the wane. At this time DeLeon was engaged in the creation of the Socialist Trade and Labor Alliance (STLA), the party's trade union arm.

With the establishment of the STLA on December 13, 1895, at a mass meeting held in New York City's Cooper Union, many labor unions joined the new combination with the alliance's strength residing in District Assembly 49 and the four bodies of the New York City United Central Labor Federations, an unaffiliated union, formed by the SLP in 1889. Refusing to recognize the legitimacy of the KOL and the AFL unions, the new federation sought to form dual unions in already organized industries. Concentrating its recruitment efforts in the manufacturing and mining industries, the STLA's organizational structure mirrored that of the KOL in allowing trade, mixed local, or district assemblies within the combination.

Although formally endorsing SLP electoral tickets and candidates as well as the creation of a socialist cooperative commonwealth, the STLA's major activities—engaging in strikes and boycotts—were strikingly similar to that of the AFL unions. While the organization claimed a membership of 30,000 at the time of its July 1898 convention, due to internal dissension within the alliance over the next few years, by the time of its absorption into the revolutionary syndicalist Industrial Workers of the World in 1905, only 1,450 members remained.

By the late 1890s, the SLP was experiencing a rampant factionalism that would eventually lead to an organizational split. The controversy largely focused on what the party's relationship should be to Eugene V. Debs's group, Social Democracy, and his Social Democratic party (SDP) after it was formed in 1898. DeLeon's opposition, known as the Kangaroos, was made up of party sections sympathetic toward working with the SDP. Comprising approximately 50% of the SLP membership, suspension of these dissident sections began in the summer of 1899. Since these expelled members still considered themselves to be Socialist Laborites, they began to publish a newspaper also titled the *People*. Holding its own SLP national convention in late January 1900, the expellees nominated its electoral ticket—Job Harriman for president and Max Hayes for vice-president—and formed a Committee of Nine, with veteran New York socialist Morris Hillquit as leader, to confer with the SDP.

At the SDP convention held in Indianapolis, beginning on March 6, 1900, Debs was nominated for president and Harriman for vice-president, a ticket that was immediately accepted by Hillquit's committee. Shortly thereafter a meeting of the two groups' Committee of Nine resulted in the SDP and the Hillquit-led SLP merging to form the Socialist party of America (SPA). Within several years, the SPA eclipsed the fading DeLeonite SLP in both membership and support, becoming the leading socialist party in the United States during the first two decades of the twentieth century.

The subsequent success of the SPA indicates that a more flexible tactical approach toward promoting socialism—advocating both reform and revolution—could appeal to significant segments of farmers and industrial workers in the early twentieth-century United States. However the SLP's disdain for advocating reforms under capitalism was probably not the primary reason for its lack of long-term success. Rather it was the centralization of authority in the DeLeonite-controlled national office that was the major obstacle toward building a broader based socialist movement.

VICTOR G. DEVINATZ

References and Further Reading

Buhle, Paul. *A Dreamer's Paradise Lost: Louis C. Fraina/ Lewis Corey (1892–1953) and the Decline of American Radicalism in the United States*. Atlantic Highlands, NJ: Humanities Press, 1995.

Girard, Frank, and Ben Perry. *The Socialist Labor Party, 1876–1991*. Philadelphia, PA: Livra Press, 1991.

Kraditor, Aileen S. *The Radical Persuasion, 1890–1917: Aspects of the Intellectual History and the Historiography of Three American Radical Organizations*. Baton Rouge: Louisiana State University Press, 1981.

Quint, Howard H. *The Forging of American Socialism: Origins of the Modern Movement*. Columbia: University of South Carolina Press, 1953.

Seretan, L. Glen. *Daniel De Leon: The Odyssey of an American Marxist*. Cambridge, MA: Harvard University, 1979.

White, Charles M. *"The Socialist Labor Party in America, 1890–1903."* Ph.D. dissertation, University of Southern California, 1959.

See also **DeLeon, Daniel**

SOCIALIST PARTY OF AMERICA

Founded in 1901, the Socialist party of America (SPA) represented an influential political expression of homegrown, working-class radicalism. In its heyday the party's vision of dismantling capitalism at the ballot box and at the point of production gained a significant foothold within the ranks of organized labor and through the appeal of third-party politics. The resultant movement culture of the SPA would serve to spark a number of electoral and grassroots successes while shaping the reform impulses of the Progressive Era.

The birth of the SPA can be traced to an amalgam of native-born and immigrant Socialists, small-craft and industrial workers, members of the American Railway Union (ARU), Social Democracy of America, the Socialist Labor party (SLP), and former Populists and Gilded Age radicals. With Eugene V. Debs as the party's standardbearer, the SPA ran colorful campaigns in every presidential election from 1904 to 1920, when Debs received close to a million votes while running from his prison cell in Atlanta, Georgia. The 1910s represented the high watermark for the party in both national elections, as Debs received 6% of the popular vote and in state and municipal campaigns, as Victor Berger of Wisconsin and Meyer London of New York's Lower East Side were each elected to Congress in 1910 and 1914, respectively. At its peak the party counted some 118,000 members who found a voice through a socialist press that included well over 300 English and foreign language daily, weekly, and monthly publications. such as the *Appeal to Reason*, the *International Socialist Review*, the *National Rip Saw*, and the *Jewish Daily Forward*. Frequent contributors included Clarence Darrow, Carl Sandburg, Upton Sinclair, and Jack London.

Despite a generation-long project among labor and social historians to expand our understanding of political and cultural movements, the concept of failure has been central to most accounts of the socialist movement in the United States. Scholars both sympathetic and hostile have generally accepted the failure of socialism in the United States as a given. In this debate organized resistance to capitalism has been characterized either as foreign to the nation's liberal consensus or the victim of state-orchestrated repression. Unfortunately, neither explanation affords an accurate understanding of the imprint socialist ideology—and SPA activity in particular—left on the lives of its believers and detractors, as well as on institutional politics.

While the SPA ultimately failed to secure a permanent place in national political life, it did enjoy electoral success in hundreds of communities and exerted considerable influence in national, state, and local trade union bodies. By 1912, over 1,200 Socialists held public office. The party dominated municipal government in Milwaukee for close to 30 years and influenced and shaped local political life in such disparate cities as Schenectady (New York), Bridgeport (Connecticut), Reading (Pennsylvania), and Girard (Alabama). In 1914, Oklahoma elected five Socialists to the state assembly, one to the state senate, and more than 130 county and township officials; and in 1918, voters in the state of Wisconsin sent 22 Socialists to the state legislature. In Florida the party counted one state legislator, citrus farmer A. J. Pettigrew from Manatee, and at various junctures assumed majority control of the municipal governments of St. Augustine, Lakeworth, and Gulfport.

In several instances American socialism animated the regional character much more than standard portrayals or assumptions have long suggested. While the party's intellectual base was located in New York and the Northeast generally, the SPA made significant strides in the Midwest, Far West, and Deep South, where economic diversity, complex ethnic and racial composition, and political and cultural traditions helped shape distinct regional identities of the party. In Milwaukee, in the logging and mining camps of the West, or among immigrant workers in the urban Northeast, SPA organizers appealed to regional codes and cultural variants while building the party and the movement.

In the American Southwest, collective protest took the form of an agrarian radicalism informed by socialist rhetoric of class struggle rather than old populist and Farmer's Alliance appeals to property rights, reduced freight rates, and a fair price. The party would exert significant influence in the heartland, particularly in Oklahoma, building on the region's populist heritage while appealing to farmers and tenants not to defect to the Democratic party. Similarly in Louisiana, a radical agrarian tradition yielded to limited socialist influences in the northern section of the state where People's party strongholds existed in the 1890s. Elsewhere in the state, an alliance between farmers and laborers broadened the base of party support and created an atmosphere that gave birth to the Brotherhood of Timber Workers (BTW), a biracial union in the state's pine region, and aided the Industrial Workers of the World (IWW). Throughout the South, particularly among unions of carpenters, machinists, and miners and in the central labor unions and trade federations of Tampa, Birmingham, Jacksonville, Augusta, Chattanooga, and Atlanta, socialist organizers were active. On the heels of intensified racial and class disfranchisement, antidemocratic terror, and single-party rule that marked the post-Populist era, the southern wing of the Socialist party accomplished in the trade union movement what it largely could not achieve through traditional political avenues. From 1903–1918, southern party members captured over 30 leadership positions in national, state, and local American Federation of Labor (AFL) bodies.

The Socialist party's construction of an alternative political culture found its greatest success in the trade union movement, and by the turn of the century, workers in several important occupations embraced the SPA as a vehicle for industrial and political deliverance. For many craft workers, the espousal of socialism seemed consistent and complementary with membership in an AFL trade union. Indeed SPA members controlled the state federation of labor in Illinois, Pennsylvania, and Georgia at various junctures in the years 1912–1919. Through these bodies party activists routinely urged greater cooperation between labor and farmers, supported the organization of workers across race and ethnic lines and advocated municipal ownership.

Socialists' ability to push for industrial unionism within the AFL however was long complicated by a pronounced right-and-left split in the party over whether to radicalize and transform the AFL through a strategy of "boring from within" or break ranks and embrace the IWW's industrial philosophy of "one big union." Debs, a proponent of industrial unionism since his experience in the Pullman Strike of 1894, consistently sided with the vision of the IWW, but other prominent and influential members of the national party resisted any break from the entrenched, politically connected, and numerically superior AFL. Some, led by Max Hayes, editor of the *Cleveland Citizen*, sought to radicalize the traditionally conservative federation by challenging Samuel Gompers's presidency at the 1912 AFL convention, reasoning that if leadership positions could be captured by Socialists, the policies and ideology of the AFL might be changed without dividing workers. As a result the right wing of the party used a tactic of boring from within in its effort to capture the AFL for socialism. Ultimately this tactical split led to a mass expulsion of the party's left wing in 1912 and anticipated the bitter factionalism of the postwar years.

But it was the Socialist party's almost singular political opposition to the war in Europe that posed the greatest challenge to the party as massive repression from the federal government and vigilante forces in the form of "true Americanism" were unleashed. Using the Espionage and Sedition Act, the Justice Department imprisoned party workers (including Debs, for an antiwar speech he delivered in Canton, Ohio), shut down socialist publications, and indicted Victor Berger as he campaigned for the U.S. Senate in the state of Wisconsin. Similarly vigilante activity cast a dark mood over party activity in the Midwest and South. In the end federal suppression and red-baiting in the face of the Bolshevik revolution would combine with bitter ideological disputes within the Socialist party to render it a shell of its prewar strength. In 1919, the party split into three, resulting in the formation of the Communist Party of America and the Communist Labor party.

The SPA would enjoy a brief resurgence in the early 1930s under the leadership of Norman Thomas. Responding to a range of frustrations sharecroppers held toward President Roosevelt's Agricultural Adjustment Act, the SPA attempted to broaden its organizing reach by embracing the biracial organizing efforts of the Southern Tenant Farmers' Union (STFU). By the late 1930s, many in the party ranks however began to drift into New Deal politics and industrial unionism of the emergent Congress of Industrial Organizations (CIO). The subsequent outbreak of war in Europe, the fight against fascism, and the postwar red scare combined to recalibrate dramatically left political life in the United States and cast the party into something of its wilderness years. Ultimately with the advent of the New Left, the SPA ceased to be a significant vehicle of American radicalism, save for Michael Harrington's short-lived efforts in the 1970s to push socialist principals within the Democratic party through the Democratic Socialists of America (DSA).

Prominent members of the party included IWW leader Big Bill Haywood, civil rights leader and founder of the Brotherhood of Sleeping Car Porters A. Philip Randolph, poet Carl Sandburg, birth control advocate Margaret Sanger, and disability rights activist and author Helen Keller.

BRAD PAUL

References and Further Reading

Booth, Douglas. "Municipal Socialism and City Government Reform: The Milwaukee Experience, 1910–1940." *Journal of Urban History* 12(1985): 51–74.
Buhle, Mari Jo. *Women and American Socialism, 1870–1920.* Urbana: University of Illinois Press, 1981.
Critchlow, Donald T., ed. *Socialism in the Heartland: The Midwestern Experience, 1900–1925.* Notre Dame, IN: University of Notre Dame Press, 1986.
Davis, Colin, "Eugene V. Debs: From Conservative Unionist to American Socialist." In *The Human Tradition in American Labor History*, Eric Arnesen, ed. Scholarly Resources, 2003.
Ginger, Ray. *The Bending Cross: A Biography of Eugene Victor Debs.* Kirksville, MO: Thomas Jefferson University Press, 1992. (reprint, 1949)
Green, James. *Grass-Roots Socialism: Radical Movements in the Southwest, 1895–1943.* Baton Rouge: Louisiana University Press, 1978.
Johnpoll, Bernard. *Pacifist's Progress: Norman Thomas and the Decline of Socialism.* Chicago, IL: Quadrangle Books, 1970.
Johnson, Daniel J. "No Make-Believe Class Struggle": The Socialist Municipal Campaign in Los Angeles, 1911." *Labor History* 41 (Feb. 2000): 25–46.
Judd, Richard W. *Socialist Cities: Municipal Politics and the Grass Roots of American Socialism.* Albany: State University of New York Press, 1989.
Laslett, John H. M., and Seymour Martin Lipset. *Failure of a Dream? Essays in the History of American Socialism.* Berkeley: University of California Press, 1984.
Miller, Sally. 3 ed. *Race, Ethnicity, and Gender in Early Twentieth-Century American Socialism.* New York: Garland, 1996.
Murray, Robert K. *Red Scare: A Portrait of National Hysteria, 1919–1920.* New York: McGraw-Hill, 1955.
Pittenger, Mark. *American Socialism and Evolutionary Thought.* Madison: University of Wisconsin Press, 1993.
Preston, William, Jr. *Aliens and Dissenters: Federal Suppression of Radicals, 1903–1933.* Urbana: University of Illinois Press, 1994.
Salvatore, Nick. *Eugene V. Debs: Citizen and Socialist.* Urbana: University of Illinois Press, 1982.
Shore, Elliot. *Talkin' Socialism: J. A. Wayland and the Role of the Press in American Radicalism, 1890–1912.* Lawrence: University of Kansas Press, 1988.
Weinstein, James. *The Decline of Socialism in America: 1912–1925.* Westview Press, 1984. (reprint, 1967)

Cases and Statutes Cited

Agricultural Adjustment Act
Espionage and Sedition Act

See also **Berger, Victor L.; Debs, Eugene V.; Industrial Workers of the World**

SOCIALIST TRADE AND LABOR ALLIANCE

The Socialist Trade and Labor Alliance (STLA), founded in December 1895, was a union movement attached to the Socialist Labor party (SLP). The SLP was the successor of the first Marxist group in the United States. In the 1880s and early 1890s, it attracted a significant following among German and Jewish immigrants, particularly in New York City. In the period before 1896, the SLP made various attempts to work within both the American Federation of Labor (AFL) and the Knights of Labor. In 1894, members of the SLP successfully sponsored a number of socialist planks at the AFL convention and helped get Samuel Gompers replaced by John McBride of the miners as the main leader of the AFL for one year. In 1895, the SLP gained control of Knights of Labor District Assembly 49 from New York. When in 1895, District Assembly 49 was barred from entry into the Knights of Labor General Assembly and the AFL reelected Gompers and turned resolutely toward bread-and-butter unionism, the SLP became increasingly dissatisfied with the strategy of working within existing unions.

Shortly after it was rejected by the Knights of Labor, District Assembly 49 became the backbone of the new Socialist Trade and Labor Alliance (STLA). According to the SLP's figures, the new federation brought the majority of the remaining Knights of Labor with them. The new assembly began with about a hundred locals in the New York area in 1896, and by July of 1898, the STLA claimed to have issued 228 charters and to have about 15,000 members. It had grown out from the New York area into Pennsylvania,

New England, and elsewhere. Although the STLA was not officially endorsed by the SLP until July of 1896 at its convention, that party formed the nucleus of the STLA from the beginning and encouraged its members to join. However the STLA also attracted many workers not affiliated with the SLP.

Like the AFL the STLA was not an industrial union, and it organized workers by trade. Despite this similarity Gompers and the AFL attacked the STLA from the beginning as a dual union and a divisive force within the workers' movement. The STLA replied that the AFL was hopelessly corrupt and was useless to the working class while it stood for cooperation between labor and capital. The STLA's official position was that workers could not win any real gains under capitalism and that they really needed to organize to elect SLP candidates. In order to attract workers however, the STLA had to fight for immediate gains, and it led a number of relatively important strikes.

In July of 1898, Daniel De Leon, the main leader of the SLP, charged the two main officials of the Central Labor Federation with corruption for accepting advertising for Republican and Democratic candidates. In response the Central Labor Federation withdrew from the STLA. Up to that point the alliance had extended its influence and membership well beyond the SLP, and while its basic political orientation was determined by the SLP, many of its leaders were not in the SLP. As a result while SLP members formed its core, its newspapers sometimes expressed different views from those of the SLP. After the Central Labor Federation withdrew, the STLA's membership and influence declined rapidly, and it became essentially an arm of the SLP, with the bulk of its members and all of its policies decided by that organization.

SAMUEL MITRANI

References and Further Reading

Girard, Frank, and Ben Perry. *The Socialist Labor Party, 1876–1991; a Short History.* Philadelphia, PA: Livra Books, 1991.

Seretan, L. Glen. *Daniel DeLeon, the Odyssey of an American Marxist.* Cambridge, MA: Harvard University Press, 1979.

See also DeLeon, Daniel; Dual Unionism; Socialist Labor Party

SOCIALIST WORKERS' PARTY

The Socialist Workers' party (SWP) was for many years the largest and most influential Trotskyist organization in the United States. Founded in 1938, the SWP was the outgrowth of 10 years of splits and mergers between left-wing organizations. The earliest Trotskyist organization in the United States, the Communist League of America, had been founded in 1928 by expelled members of the Communist Party USA, including James P. Cannon and Max Schachtman. During the early 1930s, the Communist League merged with A. J. Muste's American Workers' party, and then in 1936, the membership of the Communist League joined the Socialist party *en masse*. This union with Norman Thomas's Socialists was short lived however, and the Trotskyists withdrew only 2 years later, forming the SWP in the process.

Most of the SWP's history has been consumed with ideological disagreements and the frequent splintering of the party. The earliest split occurred only 2 years after the party's founding, when Schactman led almost half of the membership out of the organization after a dispute over the nature of the Soviet Union. Another major split in the early 1950s, along with the outbreak of the Cold War and the rise in anti-Communist sentiment, reduced the SWP to a small shell of a few hundred members.

The SWP remained a marginal party of the Left, although some scholars have argued that the party played an important role during the New Left period. Pointing to SWP involvement in the black liberation, women's liberation, and antiwar activities, these scholars hold that the SWP was instrumental in bringing thousands of young activists into the New Left. Nevertheless the SWP, like other parties of the American Left, was unsuccessful in its major political and organizational goals. The SWP, like other American Trotskyist organizations, was most influential in terms of the numbers of writers and intellectuals who passed through the organization. While few remained Trotskyists, and many became neoconservatives after their break with Trotskyism and the Left, the large number of influential figures who were at one time SWP members is impressive. The party's ranks included such figures as Hal Draper, Irving Howe, C. L. R. James, Sidney Lens, and Staughton Lynd.

The SWP, like other Marxist parties, attempted to work with and influence the American labor movement. In this they were much less successful than their Communist rivals. While some SWP members did obtain leadership positions within unions, and some workers were recruited into the party, on the whole the SWP obtained little or no influence within the labor movement. The most successful labor campaign among American Trotskyists occurred before the founding of the SWP, when Trotskyite activists managed to organize a militant Teamsters' union in

Minneapolis. But other than this beachhead, the SWP made few other inroads with workers during the 1940s, 1950s, and 1960s. Largely this was a result of the insularity and infighting that dominated the party during these years. When the party began to recover as a result of the rise of the New Left, new efforts were made to bring the SWP closer to the working class. The most important of these was the attempted "proletarianization," whereby members were strongly encouraged to get factory jobs to proselytize for Trotskyism on factory floors and in unions. This tactic was largely unsuccessful however, and few new working-class members joined the party. However because the SWP has continued to emphasize proletarianization, a large number of its members did go to work in industrial jobs, and many obtained rank-and-file union positions.

One of the most influential aspects of the SWP's history may be its prosecution under the Smith Act in 1941. The Smith Act, which criminalized advocating the violent overthrow of the U.S. government, was used to prosecute 28 members of the SWP and the SWP-led Minneapolis Teamsters' Local 544. In the end 12 members were convicted of violating the act and served from 12–16 months in prison. Ironically the leadership of the Communist party vigorously supported the Smith Act prosecutions of their Trotskyist rivals only to find themselves prosecuted under the same law after the end of World War II. This case was particularly important because it was the first major government prosecution of radicals after the end of the first Red Scare.

Today the SWP is smaller and less influential than at any point in its history. During the course of the 1980s, the party moved further and further away from Trotskyism, and the party no longer considers itself a Trotskyist organization.

AARON MAX BERKOWITZ

References and Further Reading

Breitman, George, Paul Le Blanc, and Alan Wald. *Trotskyism in the United States: Historical Essays and Reconsiderations.* Atlantic Highlands, NJ: Humanities Press, 1996.

Cases and Statutes Cited

Smith Act

SONS OF LIBERTY

Unlike the Sugar Act, the Stamp Act generated a political storm in 1765. Nearly every rank in society was caught up in the tempest—unskilled workers, artisans, small farmers, planters, and merchants; blacks as well as whites, women as well as men. Before the protest was over, upper-class community leaders had assumed direction of the colonial resistance movement.

As secret organizations formed in the American colonies to protest the Stamp Act of 1765, the Sons of Liberty took their name from a phrase used by Isaac Barre in a speech against the Stamp Act in Parliament. They were organized by merchants, businessmen, lawyers, journalists, artisans, and others who would be most affected by the Stamp Act. The leaders included John Lamb and Alexander McDougall in New York and Samuel Adams, James Otis, and Paul Revere in New England. These societies, including those in the Carolinas, Virginia, and Georgia, kept in touch with each other through committees of correspondence, supported the nonimportation agreement, forced the resignation of stamp distributors, and destroyed stamped paper. They also participated in calling for the Continental Congress of 1774.

In Boston in the summer of 1765, a group of shopkeepers and artisans who called themselves the Loyal Nine began preparing for agitation against the Stamp Act. As that group grew, it came to be known as the Sons of Liberty. Comprised mainly of artisans and tradesmen, it grew fast.

The first widely known acts of the sons took place on August 14, 1765, when an effigy of Andrew Oliver, the distributor of stamps for Massachusetts, was found hanging in a tree on one of the city's streets along with a large boot with a devil climbing out of it. Before the evening a mob burned Oliver's property on Kilby Street, then moved on to his house, where they beheaded the effigy and stoned the house as its occupants watched in horror.

The Sons of Liberty first formed in New York City in the fall of 1765. One of its aims against the Stamp Act was to enforce nonimportation agreements. If discovered the merchants would force the guilty merchants to make humiliating public confessions. New York's sons were also active in encouraging resistance through committees of correspondence.

Signing their name, *Vox Populi*, the Sons of Liberty sent warnings against using stamps required by the Stamp Act, telling those distributors to take care of their houses, persons, and effects. Crowds thus forced those men to resign, and then destroyed any shipments of stamps. In New York processions involving hundreds of residents shouted liberty and paraded through the streets nearly every night in late 1765. The sons gained widespread support and popularity among the city's craftsmen, laborers, and sailors. Wherever they existed they posted notices reading "liberty, property, and no stamps" and took the lead in enforcing the boycott of British imports.

The 10 weeks from August 14 to November 1, 1765 were the most disorderly period of colonial opposition to British authority. The Sons of Liberty directed their violence against property however and invariably left avenues of escape for their victims. No one was killed or tarred and feathered, although some stamp distributors had their pride wounded. By September 1765, leaders of the sons recognized that unless they prevented violence, their cause would be discredited. Thereafter they directed public demonstrations with firm, disciplined hands, sometimes organizing hundreds of protesters like a small army. They also forbade their followers to carry weapons even when facing armed adversaries.

Violence did erupt in Newport, Rhode Island. A gang of seamen led by John Webber, an English sailor, rampaged against the provincial stamp distributor. He then turned against the merchants, publicly humiliated the sheriff, and seemed on the verge of plundering the town until the authorities subdued him.

In the early months of 1766, there was such chaos that many of the royal governors had gone into hiding. The sons had displaced the royal government in nearly every colony. The Stamp Act Congress had concluded its business, but there was little hope that its petition to England would be heard. Correspondence between the various groups began toward the mutual support and the cause.

After the repeal of the Stamp Act in early 1766, the Sons of Liberty waned in most of the colonies. However the movement was revived with the passage of the Townshend Acts in 1767 and remained a fixture of American resistance up to the time of independence. It was then that the Sons of Liberty played a particularly prominent role in developing the First Continental Congress (1774). New York's sons, notes Roger Champagne, proved to be the best organized, most capably led, and most effective band of extremists. These Liberty Boys played a major role in shaping colonial public opinion against the British government. During the Stamp Act crisis, Isaac Sears, John Lamb, Joseph Allicocke, and Alexander McDougall all effectively bridged the distance between aristocrats and the general populace by successfully forging alliances to defeat British policies.

The Sons of Liberty resurfaced to resist the Tea Act that Lord North tried to implement against the colonists' wishes. The leaders engaged in subversive acts that Greenville responded to swiftly and decisively by closing the city's port to all trade until the tea was fully paid off. Parliament followed that up by imposing stiffer measures known as the Coercive or Intolerable Acts. But these reprisals against the sons only emboldened the colonists even more.

A new framework for popular patriot politics emerged as the sons and Committees of Correspondences elaborated a coherent set of democratic political ideals. Mechanics in Philadelphia, New York, and Boston lead the anti-British agitation by adapting established campaign techniques; they coordinated and galvanized opposition to the Quartering Act and supported nonimportation. Such activities, notes Sean Wilentz in *Chants Democratic*, continued once the Intolerable Acts were imposed. The formation of an independent Mechanics' Committee to replace the Sons of Liberty in 1774 ensured the survival of what Alfred Young contends was the city's militant, anti-British, increasingly democratic brand of popular Whiggery. As Gouverneur Morris once observed, with the sons' help, "the mob had indeed, begun to think and reason."

TIMOTHY C. COOGAN

References and Further Reading

Boyer, Lee R. "Lobster Backs, Liberty Boys, and Laborers in the Streets: New York's Golden Hill and Nassau Street Riots." *N-YHSQ* 57 (1973): 281–308.

Champagne, Roger J. "Liberty Boys and Mechanics of New York City, 1764–1774." *Labor History* 8, 2 (spring 1967): 115–135.

Davidson, Philip. *Propaganda and the American Revolution, 1763–1783*. Chapel Hill, 1941.

Dawson, Henry B. *The Sons of Liberty in New York*. Poughkeepsie, NY: 1859.

Foner, Philip S. *History of the Labor Movement: From Colonial Times to the Founding of the American Federation of Labor*. Vol. 1. New York: International Publishers, 1972.

Lynd, Staughton. "The Mechanics in New York City Politics, 1774–1785." *Labor History* 5 (fall 1964): 225–246.

Maier, Pauline. *The Old Revolutionaries: Political Lives in the Age of Samuel Adams*. New York, 1980.

McKee, Samuel, Jr. *Labor in Colonial New York: 1664–1776*. New York, 1935.

Morais, Robert M. "The Sons of Liberty." *The Era of the American Revolution*, Richard B. Morris, ed. New York, 1939.

Morgan, Edmund, and Helen S. *The Stamp Act Crisis: Prologue to Revolution*. Chapel Hill, 1953.

Wilentz, Sean. *Chants Democratic: New York City and the Rise of the American Working Class, 1788–1850*. New York: Oxford University Press, 1986.

Cases and Statutes Cited

Coercive Acts
Quartering Act
Stamp Act
Sugar Act
Tea Act
Townshend Acts

SONS OF VULCAN

The Sons of Vulcan began as a secret organization of Pittsburgh iron puddlers in 1858. Despite the advantages of being high-skilled workers, the organization remained underground because of the negative attitude toward trade unionism in Pittsburgh at that time. Because of a favorable tariff bill and the demand created by the outbreak of the Civil War, the Sons of Vulcan came out in the open in 1862. Puddler Miles Humphrey served as the union's first president.

As the demand for iron remained strong after the Civil War ended, membership increased rapidly. By 1865, the union represented puddlers in five different states. At this point manufacturers did their best to resist the expansion of the union. What was essentially a fight to the death occurred in the Pittsburgh area that same year, and the Sons of Vulcan won. As part of their victory in 1865, the union introduced the sliding scale to the iron industry for the first time. Designed by Humphrey and other Sons of Vulcan leaders, the sliding scale meant when the price of iron bars increased, wages went up as well. However if the price dropped, the union puddlers had 2 months to adjust to the coming wage drop. This system stayed in place in the iron industry well into the twentieth century.

In 1867, the ironmaster-turned-politician Abram Hewitt struck out at the Sons of Vulcan, calling puddlers "the most ignorant men we have." Such an attack was a sign of the union's growing strength. By 1873, the union had 83 lodges located in 12 states. It was widely regarded to be one of the strongest organizations in the entire labor movement. The Pittsburgh district, where most steel in the United States was made, was the strongest region represented in the union, too.

The Panic of 1873 marked the beginning of the decline of the union's power. In 1874, iron makers called a lockout that threw 40,000 people out of work nationwide. The manufacturers wanted to reduce the rates of the sliding scale because of the low price of iron. The union agreed to a revision, but the two sides could not work out the exact terms. Convinced that the lockout was an attempt to seize control of an industry that the puddlers considered to be "our trade," the dispute dragged on for months. In the spring of 1875, a few puddlers returned to work. They were joined by nonunion apprentices and African-American strikebreakers imported directly from Richmond, home of the largest ironworks in the South. Despite these setbacks the first ironworks around Pittsburgh broke ranks in April 1875 and agreed to re-employ Sons of Vulcan under the previous sliding scale. Within a few weeks all the manufacturers signed. At this point the puddlers' skills remained essentially irreplaceable, so employers felt compelled to capitulate.

However the 1874–1875 strike had put a big scare into the puddlers. They came to realize that they had to align their interests with the interests of other iron-making unions in order to protect their position in a changing industry. In fact it is no coincidence that Andrew Carnegie was planning and erecting the first successful Bessemer steel mills around Pittsburgh at precisely this time. Bessemer steel was a decided improvement over the iron rails used for the nation's burgeoning railways. Besides being more productive than iron mills, Bessemer steel mills did not require puddlers. Therefore the Sons of Vulcan feared for their future.

This is why the Sons of Vulcan were the primary organizers of the Amalgamated Association of Iron and Steel Workers in 1876. This merger of craft unions also included the United Brotherhood of Iron and Steel Heaters, Roughers, and Rollers, and the United Nailers. The members had come to recognize that in times of trouble, workers in every part of the mill had to band together to coordinate their response. Nevertheless antipathies continued to exist between these trades, which would threaten this amalgamation in the future. The puddlers who had been the Sons of Vulcan however were the largest and strongest of the constituent unions in this new organization, contributing approximately 85% of the union's original membership. Therefore it should come as no surprise that Joseph Bishop, the former president of the Sons of Vulcan, became president of this new organization.

JONATHAN REES

References and Further Reading

Fitch, John A. *The Steel Workers*. Pittsburgh, PA: University of Pittsburgh Press, 1989. (reprint, 1911)
Krause, Paul. *The Battle for Homestead 1880–1892: Politics, Culture, and Steel*. Pittsburgh, PA: University of Pittsburgh Press, 1992.

SORGE, FREDERICK (1828–1906)
International Workingmen's Association

Frederick Sorge was a key figure in bringing Marxism to the United States, both as a trusted correspondent of Karl Marx, as an organizer of the International Workingmen's Association in the United States, and as a pioneering historian of the American labor movement. The son of a broad-minded Protestant clergyman, Sorge was born in 1828 in the German state of Saxony. Probably radicalized as a student in Halle, he participated in the 1848 liberal uprising and fought with Friedrich Engels in the battle of Baden. Like thousands of others made refugees by the failed revolution, Sorge moved through Switzerland, the Low Countries, England (where he met Marx) before landing in New York in 1852 and making a home in Hoboken, New Jersey.

In the United States Sorge fell in with the large community of German "forty-eighters" and like them continued liberal activism through the Republican party and the election of Abraham Lincoln. Steadily moving toward more class-oriented politics, Sorge joined the Communist Club of New York City, which in 1867 affiliated as Section 1 of the International Workingmen's Association (IWA; First International).

By this time Sorge's career as a music teacher and some shrewd investments in boarding houses allowed him a comfortable living and plenty of time for organizing work. As president of Section 1 of the IWA, Sorge initially attempted to recruit Yankees or native-born, English-speaking members who, he understood, would have to adopt the organization for it to make inroads in the United States. However he came to regret this tactic as the IWA was overrun by Yankee reformers, like Victoria Woodhull, whose universal-program included women's rights, spiritualism, land reform, racial equality, besides restoring to labor its full measure, and inaugurating the cooperative commonwealth. Fearing that such enthusiasms would alienate the true American workers, a prospect that seemed promising when the largest U.S. labor federation, the National Labor Union, voted to affiliate under the IWA's banner, Sorge seized control of the organization and expelled the Yankee reformers, thus saving and destroying the organization at the same time.

The demise of the IWA in 1876 and the Lassallean turn of its successor, the Socialist Labor party, seemed to temper Sorge's revolutionary ambitions. In the following years he devoted most of his time to the cause of the 8-hour day and trade union organizing, though he kept up his regular correspondence with Marx until Marx's death in 1883. At the urging of Engels, who visited his home in 1888, Sorge undertook to write a history of American labor, which was serialized in the Marxist journal *Die Neue Zeit* over a period of nearly 5 years. Sorge died in 1906 at his home in Hoboken.

TIMOTHY MESSER-KRUSE

References and Further Reading

"Friedrich A. Sorge's Labor Movement." In *The United States: A History of the American Working Class from Colonial Times to 1890*, Philip S. Foner and Brewster Chamberlin, eds. Westport, CT: Greenwood Press, 1977.

Friedrich A. Sorge's Labor Movement in the United States: A History of the American Working Class from 1890 to 1896, translated by Kai Schoenhals. Westport, CT: Greenwood Press, 1987.

SOUTH

From the early period of European settlement, the colonies along the southeastern coast of North America drew on different populations to satisfy their labor demands. The early settler population included substantial numbers of English and Irish indentured servants who initially found themselves working alongside smaller numbers of Native Americans and Africans, all held in various degrees of "unfreedom" ranging from temporary indenture to slavery for life. In the unstable conditions of midseventeenth-century Chesapeake, this "equality of misery" bred both resentment and solidarity among those at the bottom of an unstable economy constructed around the export of tobacco for sale on the world market. An insatiable demand for new sources of labor combined with elite fears of rebellion among the "giddy multitude"—anxieties briefly realized during the multiracial Bacon's Rebellion in 1676—to encourage a hardening of racial lines and a growing dependency on the forced labor of African slaves. The racial stratification introduced to sustain this sharp division between the free and the unfree, formally inscribed in southern law and custom from the colonial period, would dramatically undermine the power and influence of southern laborers and encourage racial antagonisms that continue fundamentally to shape American working-class history 3.5 centuries later.

Southern slavery provided the foundations for a hierarchical society hostile to popular democracy. The plantation-based elites in whose hands power was concentrated resisted attempts to tamper with the existing social and economic order and were generally opposed to industrial development. The divergence between an industrializing North and an agrarian South became increasingly apparent in the decades between Revolution and the late antebellum period, and at the outbreak of the Civil War, the South could boast of only a small handful of industrial islands in a sea of cotton and other agricultural commodities. Dominated by a master class obsessed with fears of servile insurrection and equipped with a powerful police apparatus, slaves enjoyed few opportunities to assert their collective power. Their resistance was marked mostly by individual acts of rebellion, punctuated occasionally by short-lived collaborative plots and insurrections. By the late antebellum period, white wage workers had managed to establish craft guilds in some southern cities, but their bargaining power was constantly undermined by slaveholders and by urban employers who resorted increasingly to slave labor to frustrate free laborers' attempts to win better wages and conditions. Such circumstances reinforced the racial animosity that pervaded southern society and rendered unlikely any possibility for collaboration across the color line.

Emancipation and Reconstruction

Those prospects were transformed by the Civil War itself, which did away with slavery, bestowed formal legality on collective action by former slaves, and made possible for the first time since the late seventeenth century, meaningful collaboration between black and white free laborers. At the center of the struggle over Reconstruction was the fundamental clash between the freed slaves' aspirations to build a new order free from exploitation and humiliation and their ex-masters' determination to retain as much of the prerogative they had enjoyed under slavery as possible. In that confrontation black workers displayed a remarkable capacity for collective organization—most visibly in the Republican-sponsored Union or Loyal League Movement, which swept across much of the South and which at the peak of its influence fused the workplace militancy of a grass-roots trade union with the broader political aspirations of its black, overwhelmingly working-class membership. Such was their influence that in many places, the Ku Klux Klan organized as a direct response to the activity of these leagues and societies. Sometimes under cover of the Republican party apparatus, at other times independent of, or in opposition to it, black workers engaged in a series of offensive strikes aimed at expanding their rights and improving their working conditions.

Planters feared that emancipation and the introduction of the free-labor system advocated by northern Republicans would bring an end to their control over their mostly black agricultural workforce, and they responded to freed people's assertiveness in the immediate postwar period with harsh brutality and attempts to resurrect slavery in all but name. Federal officials in Mississippi and Alabama reported that freedmen were drifting into the cities from the countryside with their "ears cut off by their former masters for their assertion of their freedom," and similar outrages were reported from across the South as unrepentant Confederates attempted to reestablish their domination. Their outrages provoked a reaction in the North, shifting power to radicals in the Republican party and placing federal power behind freed people's attempts to carve out new lives free from such humiliation. Where federal intervention or negotiation could not produce an outcome acceptable to freed people, they resorted to strikes—in the rice swamps and the cotton and sugar cane fields; along the docks in Jacksonville, Mobile, New Orleans, Galveston, Charleston, and Savannah; and in shipyards along the Atlantic and Gulf coasts.

The threat of physical coercion temporarily abated by radical ascendancy, black agricultural workers began to restructure their working lives—withdrawing women and children from field labor, shortening their working hours, and abandoning the old gang-labor system in favor of arrangements more amenable to their aspirations to become independent landholders. Deprived of their old authority, planters in parts of the South began searching for an alternative source of labor: Chinese coolie labor was imported into South Carolina, Louisiana, and Mississippi in substantial numbers in hopes that it could be "compelled to labor the year round," and in places Italian and German immigrant colonies were established, but most of these experiments were short-lived and from the landowners' perspective, unsuccessful. By the late nineteenth century, most planters had reconciled themselves to the reality that African-Americans would continue to provide the bulk of plantation labor for the region.

The Reconstruction period also saw the first tentative efforts at interracial collaboration. The end of the war brought the emergence of the National Labor Union (NLU) and widespread agitation for the 8-hour day. Meeting in Baltimore in August 1866, the NLU committed itself of the "grand and ennobling idea that the interests of labor are one; that there should be no distinction of race or nationality." In reality the NLU's deeds lagged considerably behind its rhetoric. Despite considerable interest on the part of African-Americans, the NLU balked at making an energetic attempt to bring black workers into its organization. It was not until 1869 that its leaders became convinced of their folly, and even then they recommended the organization of black workers into a separate Colored National Labor Union (CNLU). In its statement of purpose, the CNLU declared that "any labor movement based upon...discrimination and embracing a small part of the great working masses of the country, while repelling others...will prove to be of little value." It appealed to the "'poor white man' of the South, born to a heritage of poverty and degradation like his black compeer," to "overcome the prejudices now existing" in order to build a labor movement that could win gains for all working men and women.

For various reasons the potential embodied in the early period of the NLU was never realized. With the struggle over Reconstruction dominating political life in a racially polarized South, it was almost inevitable that the CNLU assemblies would be transformed into adjuncts of the Republican party. Tensions had surfaced between state-level Republican leadership that came to assume prominent positions in the black labor conventions held throughout the South and black workers who though loyal to the Republicans, wanted an organization that would fight to improve their wages and working conditions. Some of their actions revealed a fusion between political aspirations and economic concerns that had been common in the Union League agitation: Savannah dockworkers fought not only to raise their wages but also to repeal the odious poll tax; rice field hands in the South Carolina low country resorted to strike action in 1876 not only to reject the wage concessions demanded by local planters, but also to mobilize against the conservatives' return to state power.

Though some effective grassroots local assemblies would outlive the early period of consolidation under the leadership of Republican politicians and party operatives, the general assault on radical-led state governments took its toll on black workers' organization, and the racial polarization that accompanied the overthrow of Reconstruction throughout the South crushed whatever fragile possibilities for interracial collaboration might have existed several years earlier. The onset of economic crisis in 1873 dealt a staggering blow to the NLU throughout the United States and this combined with the restoration of white supremacy after the election of 1876 brought the decline of the NLU and a setback to the wave of working-class organization that had followed the conclusion of the war.

The Knights of Labor and Working-Class Inter-Racialism

Ironically the same economic difficulties that had brought about the decline of the NLU led later that decade to a revival of labor organization under the leadership of the Knights of Labor, a formerly secret society with obscure origins in Philadelphia in the late 1860s, but whose membership and profile in American industrial life rose dramatically in the context of the nationwide railroad uprising (known as the "great upheaval") that erupted in 1877. By 1880, hundreds of local knights' assemblies had been established across the South, with substantial numbers of black workers pledging their loyalty to the organization.

In the practical work of attempting to lay the foundations for organization among southern workers, the knights exhibited in more developed form all the contradictory positions on the race question that had earlier characterized the NLU. The radical impulse behind its enduring motto "An Injury to One Is an Injury to All" left open the possibility of collaboration across the color line, but the situation on the ground was more complex, suggesting a continual negotiation between egalitarian principle and accommodation to local and national prejudices and to the racism prevalent among much of their white membership. Variations ranged from the more typically segregated local assemblies to genuine attempts at biracial and interracial structures. Workers occasionally struck together across the color line, as they did in the 1881 New Orleans Cotton Yard strike, but more often black workers were left to face their employers and local and state authorities on their own, and on some occasions blacks found white workers positively hostile to assertions of black militancy. The peak in the knights' influence nationally, and in its stature among southern laborers, occurred in 1886, when membership reached 700,000 workers. In addition to launching its historic agitation for the 8-hour day, the organization was preparing for a confrontation with Jay Gould, railroad tycoon and the most prominent employer of the age, who seemed to epitomize the arrogance and contempt of capital for labor.

The year 1886 was a watershed in one other important respect. In October of that year, the knights held their annual convention in Richmond, Virginia, the former capital of the Confederacy, and a minority of delegates, including New York Painters' Assembly No. 49, determined to take a stand against race prejudice and for the rights of African-American workers. On their arrival in Richmond, the New York delegation was informed that one of their members, African-American delegate Frank J. Ferrell, would not be permitted to stay in the hotel they had arranged in violation of segregation laws, whereon the delegates canceled their reservations and approached convention organizers urging them to make a stand. After negotiations organizers consented to having Ferrell introduce knights' General Master Workman Terence W. Powderly in the opening ceremony. Ferrell's presence on the stage and the attendance at a Richmond theater later that evening of the entire New York delegation without respect for segregation caused a near riot in Richmond and an uproar in the southern white press, which declared it an outrage for "visitors in a southern community to attempt to ride rough shod over the social laws [and] traditions…of their entertainers."

Conversely the knights' willingness to defy southern racial custom under the glare of the national press in Richmond raised their stature in the eyes of African-Americans throughout the United States. The crusading black editor T. Thomas Fortune wrote in his *New York Freeman* that the events proved "there is one great organization in the land which recognizes the brotherhood of all men and has the courage to practice what it preaches," and he and other prominent African-Americans urged blacks to join the knights *en masse*. By 1887, there were reportedly some 400 all-black locals through the South and over 60,000 black workers enrolled in the order nationally. In the South they were strongest in industrial and urban centers, like New Orleans, Louisville, Richmond, and Birmingham, but the knights met with an enthusiastic response among rural workers as well, especially in Georgia and the Carolinas.

A number of observers stirred by the knights' work in the South less than a decade after the restoration of white supremacy concurred with the overly optimistic assertion of one labor journal that the organization had "broken the walls of prejudice," but the reality was less flattering. Powderly had won acclaim for his defiance in Richmond, but there and throughout his leadership of the knights, he had been careful to draw a distinction between economic agitation and social equality, conceding the thrust of the segregationist position. He favored separate black and white knights' locals moreover, and he was less than energetic in responding to correspondence from black workers appealing for practical aid. The knights had always shown ambivalence toward industrial militancy—workers engaged in some of the most militant confrontations in American labor history were under its banner, but the organization was formally opposed to strikes. Throughout the South the movement had given birth to a variety of class-based political insurgencies, such as the Greenback-Labor parties, but this development too flew in the face of a formal policy of political abstention.

The crucial impediment to a more rigorous interracialism in the 1880s came from outside the workers' movement however. The knights met with relentless hostility from both rural- and urban-based employers and particularly from those who resented any tampering with their black-labor supply. In South Carolina newspapers called for a lynch law against white organizers attempting to organize African-American field hands, and white organizer Hiram F. Hover was shot by a white mob in Warrenton, Georgia, in 1887 for his efforts in organizing black farm laborers. In their campaign to limit the knights' appeal, South Carolina authorities introduced legislation that harkened back to the conspiracy laws of the old South and appropriated funds for resurrecting the state militia, disbanded since Redemption. Southern knights found themselves drawn into three bitter strikes in the late 1880s: a bruising showdown with Gould's Texas and Pacific railroad, another with Arkansas cotton planters and their vigilantes in 1886, and a third bloody confrontation in the Louisiana sugar parishes in 1887. The knights' defeat in all three of these, in which Powderly had offered only tepid support, combined with the repressive atmosphere after the Haymarket affair to extinguish yet again hopes for organizing the South. Individual assemblies survived, attaching themselves in some cases to the emerging Populist movement or where they existed, to affiliates of the fledgling United Mine Workers, but as a real force in the South, the knights were finished.

The AFL and Racial Exclusion

The knights' main rival, the American Federation of Labor (AFL), had been founded in 1881 but consolidated only in 1886, and from the beginning its commitment to an exclusive craft unionism limited its appeal in the South to relatively small groups of skilled white, male workers in the building trades and on the railroads. Samuel Gompers, who presided over the AFL, maintained throughout his career that the organization did not discriminate on account of race, and by the early twentieth century, a number of affiliated unions had hired black organizers and taken other steps to organize African-American workers, but these feeble measures coincided with wide-scale displacement of blacks from skilled trades throughout the region, and for the most part lily-white or white-dominated labor councils reached out to blacks only as a means of protecting the livelihood of their white members, consigning them to segregated, all-black federal labor unions.

In general Gompers and the AFL leadership tolerated racial exclusion and discrimination on the part of affiliated locals, offering as a rationalization the excuse that national AFL leaders could not violate the autonomy of local unions. Outside the AFL the railroad brotherhoods pursued an even more flagrantly racist exclusionism, and through their organization, black workers throughout the South were pushed from skilled engineer positions into the dirtiest, most dangerous, and lowest paying jobs as firemen and common laborers. Economically marginalized and feeling little or no loyalty to a labor movement that formally and informally excluded them, black southerners felt little compunction about lending their efforts to breaking strikes called by the craft unions.

The only prominent exceptions to the AFL's disastrous accommodation to segregation at the end of the nineteenth century were to be found on the docks and in the mines and to a limited extent, in the southern lumber industry. Black longshoremen either dominated work at the ports or enjoyed such strength in numbers there that a policy of outright exclusion was simply unviable. Galveston dockworkers had cooperated across the color line in 1877 and again in 1898, and a long period of racial conflict on the New Orleans docks—punctuated briefly by a general strike in 1882—gave way in 1907 to an impressive interracial strike involving 10,000 black and white workers backed by the local Central Labor Council. In the coal-mining districts around Birmingham and southern Tennessee, a resilient interracial tradition with roots in the Knights of Labor galvanized miners during important strikes in the 1890s and the first decade of the twentieth century.

The IWW in the South

On the docks and in the mines, interracial cooperation developed within industrial unions formally affiliated with the AFL, but in the lumber industry, it was the Industrial Workers of the World (IWW) that went furthest in attempting to forge cross-racial unity. Founded in Chicago in 1895 by a coalition of left-wing radicals and industrial unionists convinced of the ineffectiveness of the AFL's craft exclusionism, the IWW stood from its inception for "[admitting] the colored worker on the same basis as the white," speaking out against the prevailing racist temper of the times, and committing itself to organizing the "one big union" on the principle of industrial unionism. After a difficult beginning, the IWW launched a concerted effort to recruit black workers into its ranks from 1910 onward, pushing beyond the narrow economism typical of the official labor movement previously. Its leaders spoke out against the brutal lynching of African-Americans so common in the South and openly defied segregation, distributing pamphlets directed at winning the loyalty of African-American and Mexican workers and seeking to subvert the powerful legacy of white supremacy among its white membership. "Labor organized on race lines will drown," it

reminded them. "Only organized along *class* lines will it swim." "If you are a wage worker," it promised lumber workers, "You are welcome into the IWW, no matter what your color." Labor historian Philip Foner asserts that the IWW was "the only federation in the entire history of the American labor movement that never chartered a single segregated local."

The IWW organizers made substantial inroads in two important sectors of southern industry. Its Maritime Workers' Union established locals in Galveston, New Orleans, and Baltimore, with the New Orleans local playing an influential role in the local labor movement from 1910 onward. Its most impressive success however came in the notoriously anti-union southern lumber industry, which employed more workers than any other in the region, a majority of whom were African-American. The Brotherhood of Timber Workers (BTW) was established in 1911 by a group of IWW organizers and Socialist party sympathizers headquartered in southwest Louisiana, and they rapidly recruited members throughout the region's sawmills and logging camps before being faced with a determined campaign against them led by some of the most powerful employers in the South. By early 1912, more than 20,000 lumber workers—half of them African-Americans—were locked into a bitter struggle against the South's lumber barons, who resorted to blacklists, race-baiting, and armed vigilantes to crush attempts at organization. Abandoned by the AFL, the BTW affiliated with the IWW, and its leading organizer Big Bill Haywood visited the region to address interracial mass meetings. Despite mounting a sustained and impressive display of interracial solidarity, the BTW finally went down to defeat in the face of orchestrated mob violence in February 1913.

Despite the optimistic predictions of the region's industrial boosters from the 1880s onward, the new South remained predominantly an agricultural region through the first-half of the twentieth century, and aside from a modest foothold in the skilled trades, organized labor remained confined mainly to port cities and to the male-dominated extractive and manufacturing industries well into the twentieth century. There were two notable exceptions to this trend. Black women had been engaged in domestic service in the homes of southern whites, and later in commercial laundries, from the 1870s, and in spite of the difficulties of organizing in these circumstances, they had on occasion engaged in collective action. In the wake of emancipation, whites throughout the region had complained about widespread insubordination among black domestics. In Richmond black women refused to "cook [or] do the washing for the white people" in protest of new laws segregating public transportation.

In Florida whites suspected that blacks had organized "a kind of secret society [that met] regularly [to] fix their own prices for doing housework, cooking, washing, etc." The strike launched by dockworkers in Galveston in 1887 extended to include black domestics, and in 1881 black washerwomen in Atlanta had struck *en masse* against the multiple indignities they faced in their working lives.

The other source of employment that drew in female workers in large numbers was the southern textile industry. Founded under public guise of a philanthropic exercise to rescue poor whites from poverty, the textile industry was saturated in paternalism and racial exclusion from the outset. With an infinite supply of desperate white southerners fleeing the countryside for the employer-dominated mill villages winding their way southward from the Carolina piedmont through to northern Alabama, southern textile mills proved difficult to organize.

World War I and the Great Migration

Just as textile employers enjoyed a monopoly on labor within the mill villages, southern employers generally enjoyed near-exclusive command over their labor supply, and particularly over black workers deprived of the most basic democratic rights, from the end of Reconstruction through the period of the First World War. But U.S. entry into the war brought a profound disruption to labor relations in the South. The availability of relatively well-paid industrial work sent black and white laborers northward in the hundreds of thousands, making skilled labor scarce, raising the value of unskilled labor across the South, and providing laborers with a degree of leverage in negotiating wages and conditions they had not known previously. Employers attempted to shape federal intervention in the region's economy and during the war enjoyed the support of the government in suppressing industrial militancy and containing wage demands, but workers also attempted to make the best of the extraordinary conditions brought about by the war. Despite the employers' efforts, workers' frustrations exploded in a wave of strike activity in the postwar period as they did elsewhere across the United States, though usually without success. The repression unleashed by government and employers against this postwar militancy overwhelmed the fragile roots of union organization in much of the South—handicapped as it was by racial exclusion in some of the region's most important industries—and the 1920s saw a further steady retreat on the part of organized labor in the South.

The Depression and Southern Workers

The stock market crash in October 1929 found organized labor at a low ebb across the United States and nowhere more than in the former slave states. There every advantage enjoyed by northern employers was enhanced and every weakness among laborers magnified. While the Depression Era would not bring a complete turnaround in these conditions, the 1930s did give rise to two critical developments: The rise of industrial unionism and the first sustained attempt to confront the racial divisions that had paralyzed southern labor. The first major confrontation of the period developed in the nearly all-white textile industry, where workers embarked on a series of spontaneous strikes in 1929 to protest against the stretch-out— mill owners' attempts to boost productivity dramatically while reducing millworkers' pay. The most dramatic confrontations came in Elizabethton, Tennessee, and Gastonia, North Carolina, where fierce, lethal violence broke out among workers and national guardsmen, local police, and company security. In Elizabethton workers responded with fury to the kidnapping of union officials by local businessmen, while the Communist-led National Textile Workers' Union pointed to the official violence in Gastonia to expose the absence of basic democratic rights for workers in the South.

The fledgling Communist party (CP) had met with little success in attempts during the late 1920s and early 1930s at forming revolutionary alternatives to the lily-white, narrow craft unions approved by the AFL, but importantly for its southern work, its organizers had insisted that durable organization could be built only on the basis of black and white unity and a forthright reckoning with the legacy of racial division. This would prove an important asset when by the mid-1930s more favorable conditions opened the door to the Congress of Industrial Organizations' (CIO's) industrial unionism in the South, and a substantial number of CP organizers brought their experience and their antiracist convictions into the new work of organizing basic industry. Under pressure from black trade unionists, like A. Phillip Randolph, the AFL itself had experimented fitfully with organizing black workers, but its successes were even more limited, and in the thirties its slightly improved record owed much to efforts to keep pace with the infectious appeal of the CIO's industrial crusade.

The Depression years brought widespread misery to southern workers, but it also compelled federal intervention when the Roosevelt administration recognized the region's poverty as the "nation's number one economic problem." The South's backwardness, manifested in widespread destitution, acted as a drag on the U.S. economy as a whole, Roosevelt's advisors warned, and fundamental reform became a matter of national urgency. Ultimately however the New Deal program left an ambiguous legacy across the region. Sharecroppers and agricultural laborers found their hopes dashed under Roosevelt's AAA program, which paid large landowners to leave productive land fallow but offered little or nothing to tens of thousands of laborers left without work or compensation of any kind. As a result fierce struggles would break out when planters attempted to drive unemployed laborers off their holdings in Arkansas and Alabama. Organized into the Southern Tenant Farmer's Union and the Alabama Sharecroppers' Union, these laborers were led by left-wing radicals associated with the Socialist and Communist parties.

The South's industrial workforce experienced similarly mixed results under the New Deal. Though employers would continue to mount stiff resistance and often to prevail in industrial confrontations, workers buoyed by the protective elements of the NRA responded enthusiastically to new opportunities for unionization, and the first dramatic manifestation of this came in the textile industry, where some 200,000 southerners joined a 3-week long national strike in 1934 in a renewed attempt to combat the stretch-out. Led this time by the AFL-affiliated United Textile Workers' Union, whose strategy of looking to the Roosevelt administration did not reflect the determination of rank-and-file strikers and ultimately failed to bear fruit, the 1934 general strike went down in defeat, leaving a bitter legacy of betrayal among textile workers and reinforcing a widespread sense of ambivalence toward trade unionism. In legislative terms the NRA codes reinforced the wage differentials that had penalized southern workers and black workers concentrated in low-paid, unskilled positions in particular.

World War II and the Rise of the CIO

The CIO's industrial unionists recognized the importance of organizing the South even before they had deserted the AFL, but translating that impulse into an effective campaign proved difficult. Organizers in a range of industries documented the difficult conditions existing in the region, where they faced staunch opposition from employers and the Ku Klux Klan. The newly independent CIO had expressed its resolve to organize the South at is first convention in 1937, but a concerted effort would not be undertaken until the end of that decade, after it had consolidated gains

in basic industry in the North. In areas where interracial unions like the United Mine Workers of America (UMW) had held onto some semblance of organization through the 1920s, as in the Birmingham district, their support for the organizing efforts of vulnerable workers unlikely to prevail on their own proved crucial. Northern Alabama was described by one observer as a "strike hatchery" by the late 1930s, and with the miners' assistance, area sawmill workers succeeded in organizing a rare foothold for lumber unionism. Other hopeful signs emerged from the tobacco industry, where an overwhelmingly black workforce showed increasing militancy from 1936 onward; and by the end of the decade the CIO, with growing support among black workers and civil rights organizations, had accumulated a modest record of success in organizing southern industry.

The outbreak of World War II thus occurred against the backdrop of mixed results for the labor movement in the South: A vibrant current of principled inter-racialism had emerged—thanks largely to the CP and its organizers and publicly endorsed by a layer of southern liberals—and established a presence in the new unions; but large sectors of southern industry remained unorganized, and on the whole white supremacy remained firmly entrenched among broad layers of white southerners, including white workers. In some ways war mobilization brought results similar to those that had prevailed during the First World War—the reduction of unemployment through vastly increased labor demand and attempts by both workers and employers to manipulate the negotiating apparatus set up by federal authorities to enhance their position. In the South once again, employers exerted themselves to preserve the status quo against the winds of change, but with the pall of the Depression lifted, workers felt increasingly confident to assert themselves, and the CIO managed to win unionization in southern steel plants, in the tobacco industry, and in other important sectors that it had been unable to organize in the 1930s. Black workers in particular sensed that the wartime emergency provided an opportunity to strike out against exclusion and workplace inequality. Barred from employment in key defense industries and suffering widespread discrimination throughout the American economy, they responded enthusiastically to A. Phillip Randolph's call for a "march on Washington" in July of 1941, called off only after Roosevelt agreed to issue an executive order banning discrimination in defense industries.

The establishment of the Fair Employment Practices Committee (FEPC) grew directly out of the March on Washington Movement (MOWM), and its establishment polarized the South. Black workers looked to it for support in their struggles against the hostility they faced from racist employers and unions alike. With its modest efforts opposed at every turn by southern Democrats, the AFL bureaucracy, and the Railroad Brotherhoods, the FEPC conducted public hearings in Birmingham, but employers throughout the region vowed defiance against any attempts to compel them to hire black workers. The fruits of that opposition became evident in June of 1943, when white shipyard workers launched vicious race riots to protest black workers' promotion into semiskilled labor in shipyards in Beaumont, Texas, and Mobile, Alabama. In the tense national atmosphere punctuated by fierce race rioting, the CIO came under withering and wholly legitimate criticism from the National Association for the Advancement of Colored People (NAACP) for not adopting a more forthright campaign against racism, but unlike the AFL, it formally endorsed the FEPC's efforts and established a Committee to Abolish Discrimination, undertaking an energetic campaign to win its membership to solidarity across the color line in its early years. "Today CIO unions are found in every Southern state and are growing steadily in the region's basic industries," Lucy Randolph Mason pointed out in 1945. "Among the many hundreds of thousands of CIO members there are a vast number of Negro workers."

Postwar Organizing

On the basis of the modest inroads they had made in the South, both the AFL and the CIO launched campaigns to organize the South in the immediate postwar period. From the outset the AFL's campaign was laced with race-baiting and strident anticommunism, its potency enhanced in the new Cold War context. The CIO, too, became tentative in the face of a growing conservative backlash, and when it launched Operation Dixie with great fanfare in 1946, CIO organizers determined from the outset that they would pursue a respectable campaign purged of left-wing influence. Against the backdrop of increasing polarization between the national CIO's left and right wings, steelworkers' organizer Van Bittner embarked on a defensive campaign, attempting at every juncture to avoid a confrontation with Jim Crow and pinning his hopes for success on organizing groups of white workers far less receptive to unionization than southern blacks.

In responding to the CIO challenge, the AFL committed substantial resources to organizing black southerners, and though neither campaign could claim gains sufficient to turn the tide in favor of organized labor in the region, in the end even the moribund AFL won more workers to unionization than the faltering CIO effort, including substantial numbers of African-Americans. Under Bittner's direction, the CIO launched raids against some of the most vibrant left-led unions in the region, including United Tobacco Workers' Local 22 and Birmingham's Mine, Mill, and Smelter Workers' Union. By the time the AFL and CIO merged in 1955, the crusading zeal that had fired the rise of industrial unionism in the mid-1930s and offered hope for a vibrant inter-racial labor movement had expired, and former CIO unions in parts of the South were reported to be upholding segregation laws in their union halls. Indeed the new federation purged those left-led unions that had stood at the forefront of interracial unionism, and southern workers would have to navigate the convulsive years ahead without the guidance and support of a labor movement committed to principled inter-racialism.

Labor and Civil Rights at the Crossroads

Ironically just as black workers' legal challenges to workplace inequality began to bear fruit in the late 1950s a number of key industries—steel, shipbuilding, lumber, even textiles—began to enter into sharp decline. The civil rights movement that emerged into public view with the Montgomery Bus Boycott in 1955 had been gestating among black southerners for decades and particularly since the end of World War II. Black workers, many of them veteran trade unionists and some who had received their training in the labor movement, played a key role in initiating and building the movement at its grass roots. Often behind the scenes, and occasionally more visibly, black workers managed to fuse their workplace struggles with increasingly militant public agitation. Black industrial workers played a prominent if unacknowledged role in the Reverend Fred Shuttlesworth's Alabama Christian Movement for Human Rights. Some of the energetic young radicals attracted to Student Nonviolent Coordinating Committee (SNCC) extended their early voting rights work to organizing black and white workers in the Mississippi Delta to fight for better wages and access to health care. Most dramatically Memphis sanitation workers fed up with dangerous working conditions and pitiful wages engaged in a determined strike that would result in deployment of the national guard and draw Martin Luther King, Jr., into the epic confrontation that would end in his assassination. A year later

Charleston hospital workers attracted widespread support when they launched a 113-day strike to protest the firing of 12 of their colleagues for demanding a union.

Sections of the labor movement, particularly the remnants of the left-led United Packinghouse Workers, would play an active role in the civil rights movement, and others, including the United Automobile Workers (UAW), would provide it with critical financial support, but within the South itself, a weak and politically timid labor movement could do little to counter the racist sentiment taking hold of its white membership in the increasingly polarized South. Some white workers influenced by the White Citizen's Councils and the Klan and outraged by organized labor's tepid support for black advancement attempted to organize breakaway unions. The Southern Federation of Labor, organized in direct response to the Supreme Court's *Brown* decision tried unsuccessfully to establish a segregated regional alternative to the AFL-CIO. In Virginia white members in one of the largest textile workers' locals in the country pooled their unions' dues to subsidize private schooling for their children rather than consent to integration. A similar wave of white defiance occurred in reaction to the 1964 Civil Rights Act, with walkouts launched to protest the dismantling of in-plant Jim Crow facilities or black promotion to white positions. It was this backlash against black advance that drove white workers to abandon the Democratic party in the South and led to the resurgence of the Republicans, a shift with profound consequences for national politics.

In some respects the post-civil rights era South is unrecognizable from the politically monolithic, economically stagnant, overwhelmingly agrarian region it was even as late as half-a-century ago. The Sunbelt South boasts a diversified economy with an upwardly mobile urban middle class, and cities like Atlanta, Houston, and Miami are today metropolitan powerhouses on a par with their counterparts elsewhere in the United States. This new prosperity has been unevenly experienced of course, and the decline of basic industry has reinforced the low-wage characteristic of the southern economy at the same time that public services have been drastically reduced. Recent years have seen a massive influx of immigrant laborers, mainly from Central America, who now play a key role in the food-processing and construction industries. While the South has shed some of its distinctiveness, the region retains the legacy of fierce anti-unionism. None of this, from the vantage point of the early twenty-first century, looks particularly southern any longer. In important ways the South, long the beneficiary of the race-to-the-bottom among American manufacturers seeking cheap labor, is now itself a victim of a global capitalist economy offering even lower production costs abroad—a transformation that confronts the region's workforce with unprecedented challenges and perhaps new opportunities as well.

BRIAN KELLY

References and Further Reading

Arnesen, Eric. "Biracial Waterfront Unionism in the Age of Segregation." In *Waterfront Workers: New Essays on Race and Class*, edited by Cal Winslow. Urbana: University of Illinois Press, 1998.

———. "Up from Exclusion: Black and White Workers, Race, and the State of Labor History." *Reviews in American History* 26, 1 (Mar. 1998): 146–174.

———. "Following the Color Line of Labor: Black Workers and the Labor Movement before 1930." *Radical History Review* 55 (winter 1993): 53–87.

———. "'Like Banquo's Ghost, It Will Not Down': The Race Question and the American Railroad Brotherhoods, 1880–1920." *American Historical Review* 99, 5 (Dec. 1994): 1601–1633.

———. *Waterfront Workers of New Orleans: Race, Class, and Politics, 1863–1923*. Urbana: University of Illinois Press, 1994.

Berlin, Ira. *Many Thousands Gone: The First Two Centuries of Slavery in North America*. Cambridge, MA: Harvard University Press, 1998.

Clark-Lewis, Elizabeth. *Living in, Living out: African-American Domestics in Washington, DC, 1910–1940*. Washington, DC: 1994.

Draper, Alan. *Conflict of Interests: Organized Labor and the Civil Rights Movement in the South, 1954–1968*. Ithaca, NY: 1994.

Du Bois, W. E. B. *Black Reconstruction in America 1860–1880*. New York: Free Press, 1998. (reprint)

Foley, Neil. *The White Scourge: Mexicans, Blacks, and Poor Whites in Texas Cotton Culture*. Berkeley: University of California Press, 1998.

Foner, Eric. *Reconstruction: America's Unfinished Revolution, 1863–1877*. New York: Harper and Row, 1988.

Foner, Philip. *Organized Labor and the Black Worker, 1619–1981*. New York: Praeger, 1974.

Green, James. *Grass-Roots Socialism: Radical Movements in the Southwest, 1895–1943*. Baton Rouge: Louisiana State University Press, 1978.

Griffith, Barbara S. *The Crisis of American Labor: Operation Dixie and the Defeat of the CIO*. Philadelphia, PA: Temple University Press, 1988.

Fitzgerald, Michael W. *The Union League Movement in the Deep South: Politics and Agricultural Change during Reconstruction*. Baton Rouge: Louisiana State University Press, 2000.

Hahamovitch, Cindy. *The Fruits of Their Labor: Atlantic Coast Farmworkers and the Making of Migrant Poverty, 1870–1945*. Chapel Hill: University of North Carolina Press, 1997.

Hahn, Steven. *A Nation under Our Feet: Black Political Struggles in the Rural South from Slavery to the Great Migration*. Cambridge, MA: Harvard University Press, 2003.

Hall, Covington. *Labor Struggles in the Deep South and Other Writings.* Chicago, IL: Charles H. Kerr Publishers, 2000.

Hall, Jacquelyn Dowd, and James Leloudis et al. Like *a Family: The Making of a Southern Cotton Mill World.* Chapel Hill: University of North Carolina Press, 1997.

Halpern, Rick. "Organized Labor, Black Workers, and the Twentieth-Century South: The Emerging Revision." In *Race and Class in the American South since 1890,* edited by Rick Halpern and Melvyn Stokes. Oxford, UK: Berg Publishers, 1994.

Honey, Michael. *Black Workers Remember: An Oral History of Segregation, Unionism, and the Freedom Struggle.* Berkeley: University of California Press, 2000.

Hunter, Tera. To *"Joy My Freedom": Southern Black Women's Lives and Labors after the Civil War.* Cambridge, MA: Harvard University Press, 1997.

Huntley, Horace, and David Montgomery, eds. *Black Workers' Struggle for Equality in Birmingham.* Urbana: University of Illinois Press, 2004.

Janiewski, Dolores E. *Sisterhood Denied: Race, Gender, and Class in a New South Community.* Philadelphia, PA: Temple University Press, 1985.

Jones, Jacqueline. *Labor of Love, Labor of Sorrow: Black Women, Work, and the Family from Slavery to the Present.* New York, 1985.

Jones, William P. *The Tribe of Black Ulysses: African-American Lumber Workers in the Jim Crow South.* Urbana: University of Illinois Press, 2005.

Kahn, Kenneth. "The Knights of Labor and the Southern Black Worker." *Labor History* 18, 1 (1977): 49–70.

Kelley, Robin D. G. *Hammer and Hoe: Alabama Communists during the Great Depression.* Chapel Hill: University of North Carolina Press, 1990.

Kelly, Brian. *Race, Class, and Power in the Alabama Coalfields, 1908–1921.* Urbana: University of Illinois Press, 2001.

———. "Sentinels for New South Industry: Booker T. Washington, Industrial Accommodation, and Black Workers in the Jim Crow South." *Labor History* 44, 3 (winter 2003): 337–357.

Kessler, Sidney H. "The Organization of Negroes in the Knights of Labor." *Journal of Negro History* 37, 3 (July 1952): 248–276.

Korstad, Robert Rodgers. *Civil Rights Unionism: Tobacco Workers and the Struggle for Democracy in the Mid-Twentieth-Century South.* Chapel Hill: University of North Carolina Press, 2003.

Kuhn, Clifford M. *Contesting the New South Order: The 1914–1915 Strike at Atlanta's Fulton Mills.* Chapel Hill: University of North Carolina Press, 2001.

Letwin, Daniel L. *The Challenge of Interracial Unionism, 1878–1921.* Chapel Hill: University of North Carolina Press, 1998.

———. "Labor Relations in the Industrializing South." In *The Blackwell Companion to the American South,* edited by John B. Boles. London, UK: Blackwell, 2002.

Lichtenstein, Alex. *Twice the Work of Free Labor: The Political Economy of Convict Labor in the New South.* New York: Verso, 1996.

Marshall, F. Ray. *Labor in the South.* Cambridge, MA: Harvard University Press, 1967.

Minchin, Timothy J. *What Do We Need a Union For? The TWUA in the South, 1945–1955.* Chapel Hill: University of North Carolina Press, 1997.

Mohl, Raymond A. "Globalization, Latinization, and the Nuevo New South." *Journal of American Ethnic History* 22, 4 (summer 2003): 31–66.

Morgan, Philip D. *Slave Counterpoint: Black Culture in the Eighteenth-Century Chesapeake and Low Country.* Chapel Hill: University of North Carolina Press, 1998.

Nelson, Bruce. "Organized Labor and the Struggle for Black Equality in Mobile during World War II." *Journal of American History* 80 (winter 1993): 952–988.

Norwood, Stephen H. "Bogalusa Burning: The War against Biracial Unionism in the Deep South, 1919." *Journal of Southern History* 63 (Aug. 1997): 591–628.

Ortiz, Paul. *Emancipation Betrayed: The Hidden History of Black Organizing and White Violence in Florida from Reconstruction to the Bloody Election of 1920.* Berkeley: University of California Press, 2005.

Rachleff, Peter. *Black Labor in Richmond, 1865–1890.* Urbana: University of Illinois Press, 1989.

Rodrigue, John C. *Reconstruction in the Cane Fields: from Slavery to Free Labor in Louisiana's Sugar Parishes, 1862–1880.* Baton Rouge: Louisiana State University Press, 2001.

Rosenberg, Daniel. *New Orleans Dockworkers: Race, Labor, and Unionism 1892–1923.* Albany: State University of New York Press, 1988.

Salmond, John A. *Gastonia 1929: The Story of the Loray Mill Strike.* Chapel Hill: University of North Carolina Press, 1995.

Simon, Bryant. *A Fabric of Defeat: The Politics of South Carolina Millhands, 1910–1948.* Chapel Hill: University of North Carolina Press, 1998.

Spero, Sterling D., and Abram L. Harris. *The Black Worker: The Negro and the Labor Movement.* New York: Athenum, 1931.

Trotter, Joe William, Jr. *Coal, Class, and Color: Blacks in Southern West Virginia, 1915–32.* Urbana: University of Illinois Press, 1995.

Woodward, C. Vann, *Origins of the New South, 1877–1913.* Baton Rouge: Louisiana State University Press, 1971.

Worthman, Paul B. "Black Workers and Labor Unions in Birmingham, Alabama, 1897–1904." *Labor History* 10 (summer 1969): 375–406.

Worthman, Paul B., and James R. Green, "Black Workers in the New South, 1865–1915." In *Key Issues in the Afro-American Experience,* edited by Nathan I. Huggins, Martin Kilson, and Daniel M. Fox. New York: Harcourt Brace, 1971.

Zieger, Robert H., ed. *Organized Labor in the Twentieth-Century South.* Knoxville, TN: 1991.

See also **Emancipation and Reconstruction; National Labor Union; Slavery; Union League Movement**

SOUTH ASIANS

South Asian Americans (those who trace their ancestry to the South Asian countries of India, Pakistan, Bangladesh, Sri Lanka, Nepal, Bhutan, and the Maladives) are comparatively small in number (1.9 million in the 2000 census or 0.67% of the total U.S. population), but they have made a distinctive mark with their outstanding contributions to the American economy. The general impression is that they are highly paid, well-qualified professionals, but there is also a growing number employed in low-wage industries as waiters, newsstand workers, retail clerks, taxi drivers, and domestic servants.

An overwhelming number of South Asian Americans are from India—1.7 million or 89%—compared to 9% from Pakistan and 1% each from Bangladesh and Sri Lanka. The remaining three groups number less than 10,000. The majority of South Asian immigrants arrived after the passage of the 1965 Immigration Reform Act, which gave preference to highly skilled professionals, such as doctors, engineers, and scientists. They were followed in the 1980s by sponsored relatives who lacked the English language proficiency and technical skills of the earlier group and moved into lower sectors of the economy as small-scale entrepreneurs in retail and service industries or on the factory floor. The 1990s saw a fresh wave of immigration of hi-tech workers for the computer and information industries. By the turn of the twenty-first century, South Asians were to be found in a wide range of occupations, from the most sophisticated to the most menial. However their heavy concentration in certain areas, for example, as taxi drivers or in the hotel-motel industry, led them to organize effectively against racist practices and exploitative conditions.

The history of activism among South Asian American labor can be traced to an earlier, smaller immigration from 1900–1910, when more than 7,000 workers, mostly Sikhs, migrated from Punjab in British India to the Pacific Northwest. They were peasants who came to work the lumber mills and railroads in British Columbia and Washington State, and they eventually settled down as a farming community in California. Employers eager for cheap labor welcomed the industrious Sikhs but also used them to undercut other workers. There were no female immigrants, so the men lived in crowded camps on the outskirts of town. The Sikhs encountered fierce prejudice and organized violence from a white population, especially the Asiatic Exclusion League, which was already inflamed with hatred for the Chinese and Japanese who had arrived earlier. Prohibited from owning land, marrying white women, or becoming citizens, the Sikhs fought back by maintaining ethnic solidarity, marrying and raising families with Mexican women, setting up elaborate and complicated land-lease partnerships with whites, and moving the courts aggressively whenever they felt cheated. A dramatic example of success among this first group of immigrants was the Punjabi farmer Dalip Singh Saund, who became a member of Congress and served three terms from 1957–1963.

Immigration from South Asia shut down completely after 1917 with the Barred Zone Act and did not pick up until after World War II, when Indians were granted citizenship rights in 1946. The 1965 Immigration Act was a watershed for South Asian immigration. The United States, suffering a severe labor shortage of skilled personnel due to the demands of the Vietnam War and Cold War competition with the Soviet Union, dropped its racist criteria in immigration policy for the first time in history and encouraged the immigration of qualified professionals from Asia. Thousands of South Asians, educated in western-style engineering and medical institutions and facing limited opportunities in the homeland, immigrated to the United States, particularly to the major metropolitan centers of the Northeast and Midwest where jobs were plentiful in the manufacturing and healthcare industries.

Though they climbed the economic ladder comparatively swiftly and settled in middle-class white suburbs, South Asian Americans encountered obstacles at work that forced them to organize into professional associations to help redress their grievances. Thus the American Association of Physicians of Indian Origin (AAPI) was formed in 1982 to fight discrimination in residency requirements. With a membership of 35,000 physicians and 10,000 medical students in 1994, AAPI became a powerful lobbying force, actively monitoring policy changes that could affect the practice of its members. Similarly associations of engineers, scientists, journalists, and the like were formed to serve the common interests of South Asians in the professions.

The immigration of nonprofessionals from Asia in the 1980s and 1990s saw their rapid growth in other niche markets, especially in the franchise industry. By the year 2000, about 90% of Dunkin' Donuts franchises in the Midwest were owned and operated by South Asians, with Ismaili Muslims or Khojas claiming a significant share of the market. Gujaratis (from the western Indian state of Gujarat), most with the common surname of Patel, control an estimated 65% of budget hotels and 40% of all hotels and motels nationwide. They built up their businesses through chain migration of family members who supplied round-the-clock labor needed for the upkeep of motels. South Asians also experienced discrimination and hostility from competitors and were denied insurance as high-risk clients. They fought back by organizing and forming their own association in 1989, called the Asian American Hotel Owners Association (AAHOA), an advocacy group to champion the rights of Asian American hoteliers.

It was not until 1998 that South Asian taxi drivers, mostly Muslims from Pakistan and Bangladesh, founded the New York Taxi Workers Alliance

(NYTWA). With over 5,000 taxi drivers and spirited leadership from cofounder and director Bhairavi Desai, the union fought to change discriminatory and excessively punitive rules and regulations by the Taxi and Limousine Commission (TLC) and to protect drivers' rights to due process. On May 13, 1998, the NYTWA organized one of the most stunning strikes in the history of the labor movement when over 45,000 licensed taxi drivers withheld their labor for 24 hours. Since New York taxi drivers represent more than 90 countries, the victory was both a triumph of interethnic solidarity and a reaction to oppressive conditions in the taxi industry. Other South Asian workers' movements in New York include Worker's *Awaaz*, first organized to assist domestic workers but later broadened to include other workers in seeking fair compensation, reasonable working hours, and safe conditions, and *Andolan*, which organizes low-wage female workers to fight against the injustices of abusive employers. The growth of grassroots labor activism in the New York area stems in part from the higher proportion of low-wage South Asian workers in this region compared to other parts of the United States.

PADMA RANGASWAMY

References and Further Reading

Leonard, Karen Isaksen. *Making Ethnic Choices: California's Punjabi Mexican Americans*, Philadelphia, PA: Temple University Press, 1992.

Mathew, Biju, and Vijay Prashad, eds. "Satyagraha in America: the Political Culture of South Asians in the U.S." *Amerasia Journal* 25, 3 (1999/2000).

Rangaswamy, Padma. *Namaste America: Indian Immigrants in an American Metropolis*. University Park: Pennsylvania State University Press, 2000.

Cases and Statutes Cited

Barred Zone Act
Immigration Reform Act

SOUTHEAST ASIANS

According to U.S. Census figures, in 2000 Filipino Americans constituted the largest Southeast Asian group in the United States, with an estimated population of 1,864,120. The estimated 1,110,207 Vietnamese Americans made up the second largest group of Southeast Asians. Cambodians were a distant third with 178,043. Two groups originating in Laos, the Hmong and the ethnic Lao, were almost as numerous as the Cambodians, with 170,049 and 167,792 individuals, respectively. Census figures in 2000 showed 110,851 people of Thai origin in the United States.

The census also estimated 37,167 Indonesians and 10,711 Malaysians at the end of the twentieth century.

Among the Southeast Asian groups, only the Filipinos had a long history in the United States. Nearly all the others had arrived in the United States in significant numbers only since the second-half of the 1970s. The Vietnamese, Cambodians, and people from Laos began to arrive after 1975, as refugees following American involvement in wars in their countries. During the two decades from 1951 to 1970, only 4,998 people from these three countries migrated to the United States, according to data from the U.S. Immigration and Naturalization Service. The smaller numbers of Thai, Indonesians, and Malaysians came as part of a general increase in immigration from Asia to the United States that began in the 1970s following a change in American immigration policy in 1965. Even among Filipino Americans, newcomers tended to predominate at the opening of the twenty-first century, as nearly 70% of all Filipinos to reach America from 1930 to 2000 came in the 1980s and 1990s.

Beginnings of Southeast Asian Labor: Filipinos in Agriculture

Filipinos began to arrive in the United States after the Americans seized control of the Philippines in 1898 in the Spanish-American War. From 1910 to 1920, the Filipino American population grew from under 3,000 to over 26,000, and it increased to four times the latter number during the 1920s. Most of this growth was a result of the demand for Filipino labor in the agriculture of Hawaii and on the West Coast of the mainland.

In 1906, the Hawaii Sugar Planters Association (HSPA) hired attorney A. F. Judd to travel to the Philippines to recruit field workers and to make legal arrangements for bringing the workers to Hawaii. By 1925, Filipinos made up about half of all plantation workers in Hawaii. Five years later an estimated three out of every four agricultural workers in Hawaii were Filipinos.

Farmers in California and canning factories in Alaska also started to recruit Filipino workers in large numbers. An estimated 45,000 Filipinos reached the West Coast of the mainland United States during the 1920s. Improved transportation and refrigeration had made it possible to grow fruits and vegetables on large farms in one part of the nation for export to all other regions. The resulting demand for cheap agricultural labor on the West Coast resulted in a rapid growth of the Filipino population on the mainland, from 5,603 people in 1920 to 45,372 in 1930. Filipinos worked as migrant laborers, following the harvest seasons of crops around California and the other West Coast states of Oregon and Washington.

The migration of Filipino agricultural workers to the United States decreased after 1935, as the Philippines began to move toward political independence. Still Filipinos in the United States continued to work in farming in fairly large numbers until the end of the 1960s, and they were involved in major labor movements in Hawaii and California. In the early 1920s, Filipino labor activists in Hawaii organized several major strikes. Lettuce pickers in the Salinas Valley in California formed the Filipino Labor Union (FLU) in 1933, and the FLU staged a strike the following year. In 1966, under the leadership of Filipino American Larry Dulay Itliong, the largely Filipino Agricultural Workers' Organizing Committee (AWOC) joined with the National Farm Workers' Association (NFWA) to create one of history's broadest labor alliances. Known as the United Farm Workers' Organizing Committee and later simply as the United Farm Workers (UFW), this union extended the NFWA's ongoing strike and boycott against California grape growers.

Southeast Asian Labor after World War II: Filipinos in Medicine

Following World War II, the Filipino American population began to shift from primarily male to primarily female. Much of this demographic shift was due to the arrival of women from the Philippines married to American men stationed on military bases. An additional reason though was the increase in Filipino nurses in the U.S. labor market. The Exchange Visitor Program, established as part of the U.S. Education Exchange Act of 1948, enabled foreign nurses to come to the United States for 2 years of study and professional experience. Filipino nurses, with their American-style educations and English-language skills, were able to take advantage of this opportunity in much larger numbers than nurses from other countries, and Filipino nurses frequently remained beyond the stipulated 2 years. Numbers of nurses from the Philippines grew from 7,000 in 1948 to 57,000 in 1953.

Filipinos continued to be a prominent part of the American medical profession. As demand for doctors in the United States increased, the number of Filipino physicians in the United States grew, so that physicians from the Philippines were arriving in this country at the rate of over 700 per year by the early 1970s.

This number decreased after 1976, when Congress passed legislation requiring medical personnel, and other professionals, to have job offers from American employers before arrival. However numbers of Filipino nurses continued to increase as recruiters in the U.S. health care industry began actively seeking nurses in the Philippines. Filipino nurses in the United States increased from an estimated 10,500 in 1970 to close to 100,000 by 2000, with nearly 1 out of every 10 Filipino Americans in the labor force employed in nursing by the latter year.

The Late Twentieth Century: Diversification

Southeast Asians from countries other than the Philippines began to become a recognizable part of American labor history only during the 1980s. As newer Southeast Asians entered the American labor force, they tended to be over-represented in retail trade. By 1990, about one-fourth of all Americans of Southeast Asian ancestry were in retail, and this continued to be the case through 2000. The retail concentration was particularly high among the Thai, with about 38% of Thai Americans in the labor force in retail trade in 2000. Thai Americans were notable for their heavy over-representation in restaurant work. Just under one out of every five Thai Americans worked in eating and drinking establishments by 2000.

Connected to the high rates of employment in retail and such occupations as small stores and restaurants, self-employment increased rapidly among people from Southeast Asia from 1980 to 2000. In 1980, a little over 4% of all employed people of Asian nationality who were born in Southeast Asia were self-employed. By 2000, this had grown to 7%. The Vietnamese and Thai were the most likely to be self-employed, since an estimated 10% of all Vietnamese Americans and 9% of all Thai Americans in the labor force were self-employed in 2000.

The Southeast Asian groups that had arrived in the United States as refugees generally had higher levels of unemployment than those that had arrived as immigrants, probably because many of the latter had come to the United States specifically for work. In 1990, for example, unemployment rates for the refugee groups ranged from about 8% for the Vietnamese, Lao, and Cambodians to about 17% for the Hmong. In that same year, unemployment rates were under 6% for Thai and Indonesians and under 5% for Filipinos. A decade later unemployment among the Hmong had gone down to just over 8% while the rate continued to hover at about that same level for Lao and Cambodians. Vietnamese unemployment rates however had gone down to below 6%, approximately equal to that of the Thai and only slightly above the rate of Filipinos, Indonesians, and Malaysians.

By 2000, most of the nonrefugee groups enjoyed median household incomes that were close to or even above those of other Americans. The refugee groups had also experienced substantial upward mobility in income and professional status. However many also experienced difficulties as a result of their positions in the American labor force. The self-employed Vietnamese Americans often operated small stores in economically disadvantaged neighborhoods. This made them subject to robberies and even murders. While some Thai Americans operated restaurants or worked in professional jobs, others labored on the margins of the American economy. Some of the most serious labor market problems involving Thai people in the United States came to light in August 1995, when United States Immigration officials staged a raid on a garment factory in El Monte, California. Surrounded by barbed wire, the factory held 72 workers from Thailand, kept in virtual slavery by co-ethnic employers. In a number of other cases, immigration officials in the United States have found Thai women brought illegally to the United States and forced to work as prostitutes.

DANIELLE HIDALGO and CARL L. BANKSTON, III

References and Further Reading

Bankston, Carl L. III. "Filipino Americans." *Asian Americans: Contemporary Trends and Issues*, edited by Pyong Gap Min. 2^d ed. Thousand Oaks, CA.: Sage Publications, 2005.

Bankston, Carl L. III, and Danielle Hidalgo. "Southeast Asia: Laos, Cambodia, and Thailand." In *The New Americans: A Guide to Immigration since 1965*, edited by Mary Waters and Reed Ueda. Cambridge, MA: Harvard University Press, 2006.

Rumbaut, Ruben G. "Vietnamese, Lao, and Cambodian Americans." In *Asian Americans: Contemporary Trends and Issues*, edited by Pyong Gap Min. 2^d ed. Thousand Oaks, CA.: Sage Publications, 2005.

SOUTHERN TENANT FARMERS' UNION

Denied coverage under the National Labor Relations Act, isolated in small groups in the countryside, working seasonally, impoverished, and thus unable to afford union dues, racially divided, oriented toward either subsistence or independent land ownership, farm and plantation workers have been notoriously difficult to organize into unions. Until the California organizing victories of Cesar Chavez's United Farm

Workers (UFW) in the 1960s, their scattered successes remained of limited duration, especially in the Deep South, with its legacy of slavery, racism, and hostility to organized labor. One of the most dramatic examples of organizing farm workers however occurred on the cotton plantations of northeast Arkansas during the 1930s, under the auspices of the interracial Southern Tenant Farmers' Union (STFU).

Galvanized by the 1934 visit of Socialist Norman Thomas to the Arkansas delta, local Socialist party members H. L. Mitchell and Clay East began to organize black and white tenants and sharecroppers to form the STFU. Encompassing roughly 6,000 square miles of fertile river bottom squeezed between the St. Francis and the Mississippi rivers to the north and west of Memphis, the delta was characterized by highly concentrated land ownership, a single-minded devotion to cotton production, a black majority, and an extremely high rate of farm tenancy and indebtedness. In the STFU strongholds of Poinsett, Crittenden, and St. Francis counties, for example, 80%, 88%, and 95%, respectively, of all farmers were tenants working someone else's land rather than as independent owners in 1930. Forty years earlier 75% of farmers in this region of the Deep South had owned the land they worked.

The STFU began with the modest goal of helping both black and white sharecroppers and tenants claim a fair share of the government payments made to cotton farmers under the Agriculture Adjustment Act's (AAA's) crop-reduction program. In an effort to boost cotton prices, Franklin Roosevelt's New Deal agricultural program directly compensated planters for taking land out of cultivation. Although crop reduction contracts obligated cotton planters to share AAA payments with the families who worked their land, they often pocketed the government check and illegally evicted their tenants and sharecroppers instead. Displaced and cheated plantation workers filed grievances with the Cotton Section of the AAA, but to little avail. In 1934, for instance, the AAA received 477 complaints from cotton workers in Arkansas, but canceled only 11 planter contracts. In response to these abuses and the government's failure to correct them, the STFU rapidly grew into an interracial social movement that challenged the power wielded by large landholders over indebted sharecroppers, tenants, and small farmers of both races in the rural South.

The union's first significant victory came in the harvest season of 1935, when it called out Arkansas cotton pickers in a successful strike. Led by a motley coalition of socialist organizers, Christian social activists radicalized by the Great Depression, and African-American preachers (who made up half of the union's executive board), like Edward Britt

McKinney, the STFU combined the fervor of religion with a faith in union solidarity that cut across racial lines. Supported by the national office of the National Association for the Advancement of Colored People (NAACP) and Rheinhold Niebuhr's Committee on Economic and Racial Justice, by 1936 the STFU enrolled 25,000 members, two-thirds of them black, in Arkansas, Missouri, Oklahoma, and Texas.

Declaring itself open to "laborers, share-croppers, renters, or small landowners whose lands are worked by themselves," the STFU organized the men and women who bore the brunt of the collapse of the cotton economy during the 1930s. The union embraced several goals, some practical, others utopian. First it defended the rights of tenants and sharecroppers to AAA payments and secure tenure on the land and lobbied in Washington for agricultural programs that would respect the interests of the South's millions of farm-tenant families. Second the union hoped to organize seasonal and itinerant agricultural day laborers in the cotton fields to demand a fair wage. More ambitiously however STFU organizers sought to break the dependency engendered by the crop-lien system, which kept sharecroppers and tenants perpetually in debt to their landlords. In this they aimed at nothing less than a radical transformation of the southern plantation system and envisioned a new rural social order based on widespread smallholding land ownership, government-backed loans, and the development of cooperative farms.

Black and white workers in the South had on occasion cooperated before the 1930s, most notably in labor struggles on the docks of the Gulf Coast, the coalmines of Alabama, and the piney woods of Louisiana and east Texas. But the STFU brought black and white sharecroppers together for the first time since the Populist movement of the 1890s. The union's commitment to inviting both races into the same labor organization reflected a widespread tendency in the 1930s, as the new industrial unions sponsored by the Committee on Industrial Organizations (CIO) shook off the American Federation of Labor's (AFL's) entrenched habit of racial exclusivity that had denied African-Americans the opportunity to participate fully in the American labor movement. In the view of the planter class, the STFU's bold racial egalitarianism proved as threatening as its economic program, since open violation of the rural South's laws and customs of segregation undermined the system of white supremacy on which the impoverishment of rural workers depended.

The embrace of an interracial union movement in the segregated rural South subjected STFU partisans to violent repression by planters and their allies, resulting in tentative federal investigations of the wholesale violation of sharecroppers' civil rights. But inter-racialism created internal tensions as well, since not all white tenants proved ready to abandon racial privilege, and not all black sharecroppers easily placed their trust in whites, some of whom had helped suppress an attempt at black farm union organization in Arkansas a generation before in the Elaine massacre of 1919. Mitchell insisted that in the STFU, "There are no 'niggers' and no poor white trash..., only Union men" (H. L. Mitchell, *Mean Things Happening in This Land*, 1979), but some segregated locals persisted. Nevertheless where blacks and whites worked and lived in close proximity, they joined the same organization. Even then however some blacks charged that the STFU's African-American members bore the brunt of repression while whites reaped the benefits of organization.

The STFU also suffered factional division over the nature of its relationship to the industrial union movement. Hoping to gain the backing of the powerful new unions in the CIO, and to benefit from their access to the National Labor Relations Board (NLRB), in 1937 the STFU affiliated itself with the United Cannery, Agricultural, and Packing Workers of America (UCAPAWA). We wanted to be a union," H recalled of the STFU many years later. "We wanted to be in the mainstream of organized labor." UCAPAWA, which drew together workers in the fields and packing sheds of California's San Joaquin Valley, the fish canneries up and down the Pacific Coast, and the citrus groves of Florida, seemed the natural home for the cotton pickers of the STFU. But the CIO was designed for workers who toiled in factories and mines, earned wages, met in union halls, and paid dues. The STFU members remained rooted on the land, farmed on shares, met in rural churches, and certainly never had enough cash to support their organization. These were the factors that had shaped the union's basic character, its organizing strategy, its emphasis on protest, its appeal to the conscience of the nation, and its religious fervor, but they sat quite uneasily within UCAPAWA. "Fish cannery workers on the West Coast do not have the same problem as cotton workers in the South," proclaimed the STFU in an open letter to its friends explaining its reasons for breaking with UCAPAWA in 1939, after only 18 months of affiliation. The STFU and UCAPAWA had quarreled over questions of procedure, finance, autonomy, and jurisdiction. During this brief but troubled stint as part of UCAPAWA, the STFU never really could accommodate itself to its role as part of a CIO union.

A closely related source of internal turmoil for the STFU was the division between Communist and Socialist party approaches to the problems of agricultural workers. The Communist party, and the leadership of UCAPAWA, argued that that farm labor unions should be divided by tenure: One organization for day laborers and sharecroppers, whom they saw as rural industrial workers, and another for small farm owners and tenants, who retained a modicum of independence from the owners of large plantations. In contrast the Socialist-led STFU nurtured a deep commitment to organizing people who worked the land, whatever the particulars of their relationship to capital. This ideology, predicated on what STFU organizers believed was the essential fluidity of rural class relations and oriented toward the goal of petty proprietorship, remained central to the STFU's philosophy, political program, and status as an organization. It ultimately proved irreconcilable with the Communist party's program of division by land tenure and its view of sharecroppers and tenants as an agricultural proletariat. Ultimately the bitter feuds over CIO affiliation and Communist influence in the STFU split the union, and many African-American members chose to remain in UCAPAWA.

Together the challenges of inter-racial organizing, the uneasy alliance with an industrial union movement oriented toward the needs of production workers, and the contentious disputes over communism fatally weakened the STFU by the end of the decade. In addition the latter part of the 1930s saw the rapid dispersal from the land of the very people the union sought to organize. Rural poverty, soil depletion, evictions, and mechanization drove many southerners out of agriculture during the Depression. By World War II the STFU served its dwindling membership primarily as a labor recruiter rather than as a union or a social movement, as southern agricultural workers began to enter wartime industries in large numbers. Renamed the National Farm Labor Union (NFLU) in 1946, the union affiliated with the AFL. Although in its new incarnation the NFLU took on the struggles of farm workers in California and Louisiana, it never fully recaptured its identity as a radical social movement. Nevertheless the STFU's original vision of an inter-racial movement of the rural poor set an important precedent for the wave of change that swept the South during the 1960s. In retrospect Mitchell admitted that "the ordinary trade unionist never understood the STFU. We were a mass movement, something like the civil rights movement thirty years later" (H. L. Mitchell, *Mean Things Happening in This Land*, 1979).

Indeed the STFU prefigured important aspects of the synthesis of the civil rights and labor movements that characterized some of the most dynamic organizations of the 1960s. First it drew on the latent political activism of the black church, which breathed life into the union gospel through the community standing and stirring oratory of local preachers like E. B. McKinney and the union songs set to gospel music by the union's unofficial bard, John Handcox. Secondly the union's socialist and Christian leadership, if not always its constituency, embraced nonviolence on both tactical and philosophical grounds. Finally in order to defend itself against repression and publicize the sharecroppers' plight, the STFU recruited more privileged advocates from churches, universities, and civil liberties' organizations far beyond the confines of the rural South. In this the STFU foreshadowed tactics that would re-emerge in the movements of the civil rights era, embodied in the struggles of the UFW, the Student Nonviolent Coordinating Committee, and the Memphis sanitation workers strike of 1968. Like their predecessors in the STFU, the grassroots activists in these social movements understood that the nation's disinherited, isolated, faced with repression, and often written out of labor law and state protection, had to rely on public sympathy and the active support of progressives and concerned clergy to secure social justice.

ALEX LICHTENSTEIN

References and Further Reading

Grubbs, Donald H. *Cry from the Cotton: The Southern Tenant Farmers' Union and the New Deal*. Chapel Hill, 1971.
Kester, Howard. *Revolt among the Sharecroppers*. Knoxville, 1997. (reprint, 1936)
Mitchell, H. L. *Mean Things Happening in This Land: The Life and Times of H. L. Mitchell, Co-Founder of the Southern Tenant Farmers' Union*. Montclair, 1979.
Whayne, Jeannie M. *A New Plantation South: Land, Labor, and Federal Favor in Twentieth-Century Arkansas*. Charlottesville, 1996.
Woodruff, Nan Elizabeth. *American Congo: The African-American Freedom Struggle in the Delta*. Cambridge, MA: 2003.

Cases and Statutes Cited

Agriculture Adjustment Act
National Labor Relations Act

See also **American Federation of Labor; Mitchell, H. L.; United Farm Workers of America**

SOUTHWEST

The Knights of Labor swooped into Texas and Indian and Oklahoma Territories in 1882, organizing coal miners, railroad shop men, and disparate groups of workers and farmers. On the Galveston docks skilled white longshoremen who compressed cotton in the holds of ships failed in their 1883 boycott of black longshoremen who took part of the work. By 1885, black and white longshoremen, members of the knights, threw themselves in front of bales to persuade black dockhands to strike, and a settlement was worked out. It was the beginning of a long and fragile biracial alliance on the wharves, rare in a southern state. Apparent success in the 1885 railroad strike on Jay Gould's lines was earned by men weary of 12-hour days for $1.15, 7 days a week. It brought much growth nationwide, and Texas discontent reached a peak in 1886 with 75 strikes—but it was a false dawn for labor as shown in the railroad-provoked Great Southwest Strike in 1886. Food provided by sympathetic farmers prolonged the strike. The dramatic climax came April 3, when 10 federal and state deputies under the command of gunslinger Jim Courtright, who was wanted for murder in New Mexico Territory, shot it out with five strike sympathizers south of Fort Worth. Three days later the knights swept the Fort Worth city elections, including one member who was elected mayor. Yet the collapse of the strike—smashed by court injunctions, strikebreakers, and special deputies—revealed the lack of significance of the earlier triumphs. And the scattered political victories in 1886 drove the Texas knights more into political cooperation with the Farmers' Alliance and later the Populists and in the direction of establishing agrarian assemblies.

The railroads meanwhile offered jobless miners free transportation to Indian Territory, hauling in so many eastern and southern Europeans that wages were depressed to as low as $30 a month in their dreary company towns. The Krebs mines were the most dangerous in the nation, since they were particularly dusty and the men often had to work while stooping in water. Over 1,600 men died in Oklahoma mines from 1873–1969. The showdown came in 1894 when the company slashed wages 25%, provoking a strike. Backed by the Choctaw Nation's eviction notice, federal troops routed 2,000 miners and their families without warning, herded many of them into boxcars, and dumped them at the Arkansas state line. Despite some political and economic successes in various communities, the knights went down in Indian Territory with the failure of the coal strike in 1894, and in Texas with the collapse of the Populists and the last two railroad assemblies in Dallas and Houston in 1896.

The knights arrived in New Mexico in the mid-1880s, and many of its members were associated with the Santa Fe Railroad. Key assemblies around Las Vegas however were soon infiltrated by the masked, night-riding *Gorras*, a band of Mexican-Americans defending their small plots of land from the encroachment of Anglo ranchers. Besides cutting fences, the *Gorras* destroyed thousands of Santa Fe Railroad ties because the workers were not paid enough to cut and haul them. The knights and the *Gorras*, in their independent People's party, won an upset election victory over the Republicans in San Miguel County, 1890, but sharp division in the ranks over the use of violence and fusion with the Democrats ruined their political efforts in northern New Mexico by the time of the 1894 elections.

Arizona Territory was isolated from national trends, not plagued by an excess of labor, and dominated by mine owners who were small operators and maintained a fairly close relationship to the miners. During the 1890s, the lowest wage in the Globe-Miami mines, using Anglo and European hands, was $3 a day while the Mexican workers in Clifton-Morenci made no more than $2 for a 10-hour shift. But discontent was rare until Anglo miners in Globe in 1896, protesting wage cuts and the employment of Mexicans, organized the first Western Federation of Miners (WFM) local in the territory, and it prevailed after a company lockout.

The Southwest was knit together by the Santa Fe Railroad system, which was partially shut down by the American Railway Union (ARU) in July 1894, during the Pullman boycott. The ARU was trying to organize one big railroad union, but court injunctions and U.S. Marshals kept the stoppage brief. Also the operating crafts and machinists had contracts with the Santa Fe, and most of them—even many who were also ARU members—believed they had to honor those contracts.

State courts invariably ruled for employers, illustrated when railroad construction hand Henry Wilson sued his former employer for not providing his back pay as provided by the Texas Judge J. Simkins ruling in 1892 that the law was unconstitutional class legislation and wrote: "Unquestionably, so long as men must earn a living for their families and themselves by labor, there must be, as there always has been, oppression of the working classes."

Progressive Era and Collapse

Railroading and mining were the two leading industrial professions in most of the Southwest, and the Santa Fe line was struck again, this time by machinists and other shop men, in 1904–1905. The unions resented the hiring of nonunion workers as well as work rule changes, especially piece-rate payment. The company had strikebreakers ready for over a thousand who walked out, and the machinists were finished after a few months. During World War I the federal government forced the Santa Fe to raise wages and engage in collective bargaining.

Phelps Dodge (PD) was the biggest of the mining companies, and the most consistently depressed industrial work force in the Southwest were its coal miners in New Mexico, most of whom were Mexicans and Italians. In the Dawson mines, opened in 1902, 385 were killed in tremendous explosions in 1913 and 1923. The United Mine Workers (UMW) tried to organize in the very early days, but organizers were barred from entering town, and the merest whisper of unionism was forbidden. Company-owned housing made it a classic slum-ridden company town. There were waves of layoffs caused by technological improvements in the 1920s and the Depression in the 1930s.

Indian Territory and Texas coal miners fared better, winning strikes in 1903 that secured numerous benefits. It led to the organizing of every craft in Thurber, Texas. During the Progressive Era the miners were a third of the membership of the Oklahoma State Federation of Labor (OSFL), and the miners and carpenters were the two largest unions in Texas. For some two decades after 1903, miners and operators prospered.

The OSFL, the railroad brotherhoods, the social progressives under Kate Barnard, and their agrarian ally, the Farmers' Union, dominated the writing of the new Oklahoma State Constitution, 1906–1907, which provided child-labor, 8-hour, and employer liability provisos regarding mines and the abolition of both convict labor and the fellow-servant doctrine, among others. Enabling legislation for these provisos along with other reforms, for example, forbidding railroads from using blacklists and requiring the 8-hour day for all public workers, passed during the progressive heyday, 1907–1910. Oklahoma's unions claimed 21,285 in 1907. The same coalition and similar provisos prevailed in Texas during Thomas Campbell's terms as governor, 1907–1911.

Dominated by the railroad and mining industries, but pushed by their respective unions, New Mexico also adopted similar legislation, beginning with statehood in 1912. The initiative, referendum, recall, direct election of U.S. senators, an anti-injunction measure, and several others previously mentioned were enacted by Arizona's progressive coalition of labor, agrarians, and small businessmen. The Arizona State Federation of Labor, representing some 7,000 union members at its founding in 1912, was perceived as having control of Arizona politics, 1910–1916. The state's first elected governor, George P. Hunt, was a former copper miner and labor supporter. In the 1910s, only the Arizona unions were keenly concerned about the incursion of labor from Mexico, but that sentiment gained ground

in Texas at the time. Texas was a one-party, Democratic state, but in all four states the effective political alliances were with the Democrats.

Traditional craft unions also sprang up in southwestern cities. There were scores of locals representing the building and printing trades, tailors, musicians, barbers, cigar makers, brewery workers, oil workers, blacksmiths, theatrical stage hands, coopers, butchers, telephone operators, among others. Some struggled to stay alive, for example, the retail clerks, street railway employees, laundry workers, and unskilled hands in the directly affiliated federal labor unions. In a number of communities where there were railroad shops or mines, their unionization inspired the organization of many other crafts.

In 1915, with wartime demand raising copper prices, Arizona miners enjoyed a flurry of success, especially when the WFM called out some 5,000 at Clifton-Morenci, where the wages were lowest. Governor Hunt called in the National Guard to keep strikebreakers out. The men got a wage increase, abolition of the differential wage scale, and standing grievance committees. Hunt's action was hailed as a model settlement by some media, but PD responded by taking control of every aspect of Arizona life, buying newspapers and sheriffs, seducing legislators, and bullying union leaders. Hunt was defeated by fraud in 1916, and by the time he was reinstated, the companies had broken the WFM and destroyed the progressive movement in the state. In 1917, PD faced a strike at Bisbee led by the Industrial Workers of the World (IWW) and the Mine, Mill, Smelter Workers (MMSW, the former WFM). Twelve hundred miners were loaded into boxcars and hauled to a desert stockade in New Mexico. Over half the deportees were citizens, and some were war veterans. Company unions replaced the real unions. The MMSW in Arizona, and New Mexico as well, were wracked by internal schism and constituted only a shell of unionism.

Though the Texas State Federation reached its peak of pre–World War II membership with 55,000 in 1920, World War I and its aftermath of red scare and renewed open-shop drives ended progressivism and sent southwestern labor into decline. The largely peaceful Galveston longshoremen's strike in 1920 was suppressed by martial law, highlighted by the attempt of three Texas National Guard lieutenants, out of uniform, to kidnap the editor of the *Houston Press* 40 miles outside the martial law zone. The state then adopted the Open Port law, 1921, which virtually required governors to break up strikes and impose open shops wherever disputes interfered with the shipment of goods.

Organizing drives in the oil fields of Texas and Oklahoma in 1917 were subverted by wartime charges of radicalism and serving German interests. Masked vigilantes seized 17 IWW members from the police—in the Tulsa Outrage–whipped them repeatedly and tarred and feathered them. Most of the oil companies soon granted wage increases and other benefits similar to union demands as part of the open-shop movement, and oil unionism was dead until the early 1930s. Texas coal miners, facing a declining market and huge wage cuts, were locked out in 1921 and soon dispersed. Oklahoma's coal operators abrogated their contract with the UMW in 1924, slashed wages by a third, and imposed the open shop. The demise of the UMW was a severe blow to the Oklahoma labor movement. During the war the Amalgamated Meat Cutters of Oklahoma City and Fort Worth had prospered under federal mediation, but the packers, facing renewed international competition after the war, slashed wages and imposed company unions. The nationwide strike of 1921–1922 was broken in large part because of the availability of numerous unskilled and semiskilled workers from the swollen ranks of the unemployed. Most of the strikebreakers were black, and one each was killed in the two cities. The defeat of the nationwide shop men's strike, 1922, was a body blow to the railroad union movement in the Southwest.

Southwestern building trades and retail locals in the burgeoning cities from Phoenix to Beaumont were the targets of the Open Shop Association. Texas and Oklahoma oil booms in the 1920s spurred much construction, and the building trades—all almost entirely Anglo—held on to their membership and jobs better than other unions in the less than prosperous 1920s.

Labor's political clout vanished. A revived farmer-labor movement did elect J. C. Walton governor of Oklahoma, 1922, but he got so caught up in a literal war against the Ku Klux Klan that he neglected to push his farm-labor agenda, which included an 8-hour day for all labor and a minimum-wage law for women. Klansmen and others impeached Walton and removed him from office in November 1923. The finances of the Oklahoma State Federation of Labor became so depleted that for several years it was unable to pay the salaries of the president and secretary.

Hard times deepened labor's gloom. By the early 1930s, in the desperate years of the Depression, labor backed repatriation efforts. State and local governments took the lead in shipping some half-a-million people of Mexican ancestry to Mexico, though some were American citizens. In Arizona Anglo packing shed workers and black hands in the cotton oil mills and cotton compresses were among those who joined the cannery workers union, 1937–1939, but there were too many available workers, and the union lacked the power and the money of the Associated Farmers of Arizona. The mostly Mexican coal miners in the Gallup, New Mexico, fields became affiliated with a Communist-controlled splinter group that rejected the UMW. Their strike in 1933 raised wages, but the killing of the sheriff brought fierce retribution, including deportations and long prison sentences. In Texas Southwestern Bell engaged in mass layoffs, given with 15 minutes' notice, typified by rampant favoritism and age discrimination. Female operators sometimes fainted at the switchboards from the extreme summer heat. On passage of the federal minimum wage law in 1938, American Telephone and Telegraph (AT&T) was forced to raise wages throughout the Southwest. Oklahoma chain-store clerks worked 16 hours a day for as little as $9 a week. Waitresses worked for their meals and shared tips with employers. Over 300 thousand were unemployed by 1933, some 42% of all workers in the state.

Revived Unions, 1930s–1970s

Traditionally repressed groups benefited slightly from the New Deal and the war. In the Dawson, New Mexico, coal mines many futile strikes broke out in the 1930s, but the length of the national strikes in 1943 finally yielded a closed-shop contract, 1945, including a retirement plan and portal-to-portal pay. Only 4 years later the last major customer, the Southern Pacific, switched to oil, and the Dawson mines soon closed. The dreary history was much the same in Van Houton, 1903–1949; Sugarite, 1912–1941; Gardiner, 1911–1939; Brilliant, 1917–1953; and Madrid, 1893–1954. The Southern Tenant Farmers' Union operated in eastern Texas and Oklahoma and elsewhere in the South. It made the nation conscious of the low living standards associated with cotton production, and Oklahoma passed the first landlord-tenant relations bill in the United States in 1937, promoting equitable rental contracts and arbitration. Even after winning a 1938 strike over wages, over 10,000 San Antonio pecan shellers lost their jobs because it was the only industry in the country that was forced to mechanize by the passage of the minimum wage law. Low wages and poor living conditions persisted for central Arizona's Yaquis through World War II. Many lived in tents or cardboard shanties and slept on their floors. Many joined building trades unions during the war and got back pay, but it still did not raise their wages to the level of Anglos or Mexicans

The New Deal's Wagner Act, 1935, triggered widespread organizing efforts. Mine, Mill launched organizing drives throughout the region. In Oklahoma the zinc and lead operators retaliated by raising wages and launching a company union. The new National Labor Relations Board (NLRB) ordered the company union disbanded, and the MMSW eventually won a contract. At Bisbee in 1941, after PD fired 35 union members, the NLRB reinstated them. The company challenged the NLRB's authority before the U.S. Supreme Court, which devised the "Phelps Dodge rule." It became a touchstone in American labor law—companies could not refuse to hire workers on account of union membership. Organized labor not only played a key role in raising wages above the poverty level for minorities in unionized communities but also abetted their political awakening. When the MMSW organized PD at Clifton in 1942, the number of Mexican-Americans on the town council soared from zero, where it had been since the turn of the century, to an average of three for the next two decades.

The oil workers union advanced through Texas and Oklahoma with several successful strikes, but it was not until World War II, when the federal government ensured peaceful collective bargaining that virtually all refineries were organized. The wartime Fair Employment Practice Committee found both the union and the companies discriminatory in dealing with black workers, and they began their gradual change at that time. Texas locals took the lead in the nationwide refinery strikes in 1945 that preserved take-home pay even as working hours were cut after the war. Oil workers were the biggest of the Congress of Industrial Organizations (CIO) unions in both states in the 1940s and 1950s.

In the maritime industry in the 1930s, sailors aboard U.S. vessels suffered from damp, vermin-infested quarters, rotten food, and harsh discipline. Rank-and-file sailors, a number of whom were Communists, rebelled against the shippers in the strikes of 1936–1937 After considerable violence in several Texas ports, the CIO's National Maritime Union (NMU) brought about a quick and dramatic transformation of seamen's living and working conditions. During World War II Communist NMU leaders pressured employers and the government to end the Jim Crow hiring practices in Texas ports. Communist rhetoric was radical, but in negotiations they tended to conduct themselves just like other CIO officials. The union grew prodigiously in the war. The casualty rate among merchant seamen during the first-half of 1943 was proportionately greater than in the armed services. A successful postwar strike was followed in 1950 by the purging of Communists from the NMU.

After the Wagner Act was upheld by the U.S. Supreme Court in 1937, the Bell companies officially severed their relationship with the company unions.

The unions soon became truly independent, led by the Southwestern Telephone Workers. The fractured bargaining system was dissolved in 1947 with the establishment of the Communications Workers of America, which was forced to strike that year, primarily over AT&T's refusal to recognize the new union.

The largely Hispanic MMSW workers in Hanover, New Mexico, accused of communism, fought off injunctions in their 1950 strike against Empire Zinc by putting wives and sisters on the picket lines and blocking strikebreakers from getting into the mines. They wanted payment for all time spent underground, which was common in the other mines in the district. In the 1951 settlement, the union did not score much more than a moral victory, but the unusual confrontation inspired some leftist Hollywood writers and directors to make the 1953 movie, *Salt of the Earth*, which was targeted in the hysteria of the McCarthyite era and banned from being seen in the United States.

From 1939 to 1953, union membership in Texas grew—in thousands of members—from about 111 to 375, in Oklahoma from 34 to 87, in Arizona from 16 to 56, and in New Mexico from 9 to 25. The revived unions energized corporations and political leaders into cracking down on organized labor. In 1947, Texas banned all union security measures, thereby entrenching the open shop in the name of right to work. The Arizona electorate approved an open-shop constitutional amendment in 1948 while New Mexico, the least industrialized southwestern state, defeated one in 1948. The United Auto Workers (UAW) represented nearly 9,000 members at Temco and Chance Vought in Texas in 1956, but under the state right-to-work law also represented over 2,400 in the bargaining units who opted not to join the locals. Labor exercised occasional political clout, as shown in the elections to Congress, 1950s–1970s, of the Udall brothers, Clinton Anderson, Ralph Yarborough, and Fred Harris.

A collective-bargaining breakthrough with the big four copper companies, including PD, came in 1967 after the United Steel Workers absorbed the MMSW. The idea that companies of similar size producing similar products should be pressed into similar contracts—pattern bargaining—had become the postwar norm in the auto and steel industries. But in the nonferrous metals, the various craft unions had preserved their individual strongholds, and the companies had played off the unions against each other. The Steelworkers united with the crafts for bargaining, and when the companies rejected the uniform contracts, an industrywide strike of some 60,000 shut down copper, lead, zinc, and silver mining and refining in the United States, centered in the Southwest. The companies did not employ strikebreakers, since inexperienced workers could easily ruin machines and themselves in the dangerous mines and smelters. In 1968, the companies agreed to their first pattern contract.

Hard Times Again

In 1979, the UAW waged an intense campaign to organize the new General Motors plant in Oklahoma City. Oklahoma business leaders financially supported plant workers who were campaigning against the union, but the UAW won the representation election overwhelmingly. While it was blow to the Oklahoma establishment, it was a more typical of the post-1973 era of higher fuel costs and intensive global competition when Oklahoma voters adopted a right-to-work constitutional amendment in 2001. The UAW has not organized any of the growing number of foreign-owned auto plants built in the United States, and Toyota is confident that its new truck plant announced in 2003 in San Antonio will be nonunion. Toyota is taking aim at the big three truck market in the Southwest and will benefit from a large labor pool on the struggling south side of the city.

On striking PD in Morenci, the Steelworkers inadvertently launched one of the milestone events in the retreat of organized labor in the 1980s. The other copper companies had agreed to a basic wage freeze for 3 years, but PD—facing collapsed copper prices and stiff international competition—wanted more. Over 2,300 workers struck in 1983 rather than accept a much-reduced package of wages and benefits. The governor reluctantly called out the national guard to protect strikebreakers, whose jobs were guaranteed against replacement by strikers. While President Ronald Reagan's firing of the Professional Air Traffic Controllers (PATCO) in 1981 was a landmark loss for labor, PATCO was a public-sector union whose members were legally barred from striking. It was the PD strike of 1983–1984 that provided the private-enterprise model for creating an open-shop environment, overt company strikebreaking through the tactic of permanent replacement. Many companies followed.

Many mines, smelters, steel mills, and packinghouses shut down because of foreign competition and obsolete operations. Railroads, newspapers and publishers, petrochemical plants, and auto and aircraft factories cut jobs by the thousands, replacing workers with machines. The open shop returned to the building trades, hit by the application of industrial technologies to construction as well as competition from skilled immigrants. The old mining base as well as the newer manufacturing enterprises in much of the Southwest gave way to service-sector jobs, especially low-wage ones.

Unions in the Southwest began focusing on public employees, teachers, and service-sector jobs, for example, those in hotels and hospitals. Many of these workers have been intimidated over the decades, but attitudes can be changed, and few of their jobs can be moved. The Service Employees' Union is establishing building service unions, many of whose members are Mexican immigrants looking for ties with labor. Many southwestern public workers and teachers are forbidden to engage in collective bargaining or strikes, but unions always at least install grievance machinery. Teachers and state, county, and municipal employees have learned that they can engage in consultation agreements in lieu of collective bargaining if need be. The growth rate of these unions has surged since the 1970s.

GEORGE N. GREEN

References and Further Reading

Allen, Ruth. *Chapters in the History of Organized Labor in Texas.* Austin: University of Texas Bureau of Research in the Social Sciences, 1941.
Byrkit, James. *Forging the Copper Collar: Arizona's Labor-Management War of 1901–1921.* Tucson: University of Arizona Press, 1982.
Federal Writers' Project of Oklahoma. *Labor History of Oklahoma.* Oklahoma City: A. M. Van Horn, 1939.
Foster, James C., ed. American *Labor in the Southwest.* Tucson: University of Arizona Press, 1982.
Joyce, Davis D., ed. *An Oklahoma I Had Never Seen Before.* Norman: University of Oklahoma Press, 1994.
Kern, Robert, ed. *Labor in New Mexico.* Albuquerque: University of New Mexico Press, 1983.
Obadele-Starks, Ernest. *Black Unionism in the Industrial South.* Texas A&M University Press, 2000.
Rosenbaum, Jonathon. *Copper Crucible: How the Arizona Miners' Strike of 1983 Recast Labor-Management Relations in America.* Ithaca, NY: ILR Press, 1995.

Cases and Statutes Cited

Phelps Dodge Corporation v. National Labor Relations Board, 313 U. S. 177–212 (1941).
San Antonio and A. P. Rye Co. v. Wilson, 19 S.W. 910–914 (1892).
Wagner Act

SOVEREIGN, JAMES R. (30 MAY 1854–1920s?)
Knights of Labor

James R. Sovereign served as the Knights of Labor's national leader during the economic depression and social upheaval of 1893–1897. A product of farm life and a stonecutter by occupation, Sovereign both personified and advocated the merging of the urban, industrial labor movement of the 1880s and 1890s with the rising agrarian protest among farmers. Sovereign played a central role in articulating the mutual concerns of farmers and workers by allying the Knights of Labor with the National Farmers' Alliance. He also attempted to redirect and focus the protests of workers and farmers into political action by campaigning for a third national political party, The People's (or Populist) party, during elections in 1892, 1894, and 1896.

Sovereign was born on 30 May 1854, in Cassville, Wisconsin. Sovereign's early experiences help to explain his labor ideology. When Sovereign was 2 years old, his parents left him with paternal grandparents on their farm 7 miles west of Elgin, Illinois. Sovereign stayed until 16, when his grandfather's death and grandmother's relinquishment of the farm left him homeless. He migrated to Kansas to drive cattle from Texas, then worked heavy-construction jobs. By spring 1872, Sovereign moved to his father's farm near Cresco, Iowa, where he resumed high school at age 18. Four years later, he married Caroline Saucer. The couple had six children.

In 1874, Sovereign took up the craft of a marble cutter and carver and ended up in Muscatine, Iowa, by 1880. In 1881, he joined a Muscatine local assembly of the Knights of Labor, which first appeared in Iowa in 1878. Sovereign left stonecutting in 1884 to recruit new knights and edit a local knights' newspaper, the *Industrial Leader*, in Dubuque, Iowa. Due in part to Sovereign's organizing, Iowa knights grew from 41 local assemblies and 3,200 members in 1885 to 233 local assemblies and 30,000 members across 86 counties and 228 communities.

Sovereign's subsequent election as state master workman coincided with dramatic changes in Iowa's economy and population. Both the value of manufactured goods in Iowa and the number of wage workers outside of agriculture increased by 60% from 1875–1895. During the 1880s, the rural population shifted toward the cities and towns to increase the urban population by 50%. In response to these changes, the Iowa knights secured through legislation a new Iowa Bureau of Labor Statistics in 1884 and new coal mine safety and health regulations. The knights state organization provided data and drafted legislation to the point where their political platform became the Bureau of Labor Statistics' recommended legislative reforms. As the leader of Iowa knights, Sovereign was poised to make the jump into state government. In 1890 and again in 1892, Governor Horace Boies appointed Sovereign as Iowa Commissioner of Labor Statistics.

Although the knights' national leader Terence Powderly had initiated cooperation with the National Farmers' Alliance in December 1889, the knights' losses of membership from failed strikes of 1886–1890 weakened them. Powderly's nonpartisan political stance also attenuated the ability of workers and farmers to obtain economic reform through a unified political agenda. In Iowa a convention of Knights of Labor members, trade unionists, Greenback party loyalists, and Iowa Farmers' Alliance supporters formed the Iowa People's party (Populists) on 3 June 1891. Discontent with Powderly grew until the November 1893 national meeting of the knights, when he resigned and an unstable coalition of Midwestern Populists and New York Socialists under Daniel DeLeon elected Sovereign grand master workman.

Sovereign lacked Powderly's broad administrative and leadership abilities. When he reneged on a promised editorship for Socialist Lucien Sanial, Socialists quit the Knights, abandoning their effort to move the Knights toward Marxism. A return to Masonic-style secrecy in 1895 alienated Catholics. More significantly though, Sovereign suspended the coal miners' National Trade Assembly 135, strong in Iowa, and glassblowers Local Assembly 300, which had funded the national office during crises. During the Pullman Strike and Boycott, he allied the knights with Eugene Debs's American Railway Union, but his call for a national sympathy strike was limited by other knights to Chicago alone. Later he testified against participation in future strikes: Words that would follow him. In July 1897, he joined Debs and AFL President Samuel Gompers in West Virginia during a United Mine Workers' strike but was privately seen as a liability by AFL leaders. That November Henry Hicks replaced Sovereign as head of the national knights. Sovereign moved to Idaho, where he witnessed military abuses during the 1899 Coeur d'Alene miners strike. He also spent time farming and selling insurance in Sulphur Springs, Arkansas, around 1900, but subsequently resumed newspaper editing in Ferry County, Washington, near the Colville Indian Reservation, where he died during the 1920s. Keller, Washington, residents erected a monument in Sovereign's honor in 1931.

MARTIN TUOHY

References and Further Reading

Fink, Leon. *Workingmen's Democracy: The Knights of Labor and American Politics*. Urbana: University of Illinois Press, 1983.

Goodwyn, Lawrence. *Democratic Promise: The Populist Moment in America*. New York: Oxford University Press, 1976.

Journal of the Knights of Labor (21 Dec. 1893).

Kaufman, Stuart B., and Peter J. Albert, eds. *The Samuel Gompers Papers*. Vol. 3: *Unrest and Depression, 1891–94*. Urbana and Chicago: University of Illinois Press, 1989.

Kaufman, Stuart B., Peter J. Albert, and Grace Palladino, eds. *The Samuel Gompers Papers*. Vol. 4: *A National Labor Movement Takes Shape, 1895–98*. Urbana and Chicago: University of Illinois Press, 1991.

Phelan, Craig. *Grand Master Workman: Terence Powderly and the Knights of Labor*. Westport, CT: Greenwood Press, 2000.

Register (Grundy, Iowa), 13 November 1931.

Scharnau, Ralph. "Workers and Politics: The Knights of Labor in Dubuque, Iowa, 1885–1890." *Annals of Iowa* 48 (1987): 353–377.

———. "The Knights of Labor in Iowa." *Annals of Iowa* 50 (spring 1991): 861–891.

Weir, Robert. *Beyond Labor's Veil: The Culture of the Knights of Labor*. University Park: Pennsylvania State University Press, 1996.

———. *Knights Unhorsed: Internal Conflict in a Gilded Age Social Movement*. Detroit, MI: Wayne State University Press, 2000.

See also **Knights of Labor**

SOVEREIGNS OF INDUSTRY

The Order of Sovereigns of Industry was a labor reform organization that first appeared in Massachusetts in 1874, committed to "reconciling the interests of labor and capital" through cooperative consumption and production. William Earle, its founder, was a small fruit grower and organizer for the Patrons of Husbandry from Worcester, Massachusetts. Having found the Grange too limited in focus, he decided that American producers needed a more inclusive organization, one that would incorporate all working people. He issued a call to interested parties and in January of 1874 established the first council of the Sovereigns of Industry.

The sovereigns proposed to fight the middlemen, speculators, and monopolists who encroached "upon the liberties or rights of individuals" by charging extortionate prices for necessary goods. Their principal method was cooperation, primarily cooperative consumption, through which members would "purchase of such merchandise as we consume...[cheapen] production of such goods as we can produce with our labor, [and]...best *reconcile the interests of labor and capital*, which have been rendered antagonistic by the prevailing systems of trade." Their goal was to guarantee equal rights and "equal privileges under the social systems of the land," where producers would receive their proportionate share of the wealth and capital a suitable return for the risk of investment ("Declaration of Purposes," *Sovereigns of Industry Bulletin*, November 1875).

The Sovereigns of Industry came into existence during the depression of the 1870s, a period of economic and trade union decline, and yet it attracted a rapidly expanding membership. During 1875 and 1876, as many as 40,000 people from 18 states joined the organization. New England, and especially Massachusetts, was home to the greatest concentration of members, while in Pennsylvania the sovereigns organized over 11,500 members and 78 councils. The national organization could support a newspaper, the *Sovereigns of Industry Bulletin*, and fielded lecturers to spread their message.

In the process of expansion, the sovereigns absorbed an array of skilled workers, trade unionists, and labor reformers of all stripes. Only a few months after he founded the order, Earle sought to merge his organization with the Industrial Congress, the feeble descendant of the National Labor Union. Though the congress rebuffed his appeal, the order did absorb a number of trade unions. In Philadelphia the first council of the sovereigns absorbed many of the leaders of the failed International Workingman's Association Section 26 and included Fourierists, such as Albert Brisbane, as well as leading members of the Knights of Labor. One well-known Fourierist member, John Orvis, was also a former Brook Farm resident, labor reform editor in the 1840s, and long-time promoter of cooperative stores.

This diverse membership agreed on the importance of cooperation but seemed to have less confidence in the national leadership's analysis of the labor problem. In fact considerable disagreement arose over the proper role and usefulness of trade unions, the role of the state in labor reform, and the very nature of the antagonism between labor and capital. John Shedden, for example, a Yorkshire-born veteran labor activist from Philadelphia who was to become the organization's president in 1878, believed in the irreconcilable interests of labor and capital as did many trade unionists. He however rejected the utility of such trade union tactics as the strike. Strikes, Shedden argued, recognized the legitimacy of the wage system, which he believed should be entirely transcended.

Despite various dissenting opinions, the sovereigns approached cooperation earnestly. Being a hierarchal organization with local or subordinate state and national councils, the order contracted on each level with wholesalers and manufacturers for membership discounts. Local councils established cooperative grocery stores largely on the Rochdale model, and state councils purchased goods in bulk from manufacturers at a reduced price. In 1876, Earle estimated that the total yearly trade was $3,000,000. From the proceeds and experience they gained from these ventures, the sovereigns expected to fund and operate cooperative industries. Clearly many, not only Shedden, hoped to transcend the wage system entirely.

The sovereign's rapid success lasted only a few years. By 1878, the order was already collapsing. In part its problems stemmed from the decision to run its stores on the Rochdale model that forswore extending credit to consumers. To ensure the security of their cooperatives and save members from the trap of debt, the order denied its members credit and forced them to seek help elsewhere as the economy worsened. Prices also were falling, and this made successful negotiations for discounts with manufacturers difficult if not impossible to achieve. As the organization failed to deliver on its promise of inexpensive goods, membership rapidly declined, and by the end of the decade, the Sovereigns of Industry had completely disappeared.

STEVEN LEIKIN

References and Further Reading

Bemis, Edward. "Cooperation in New England." In *History of Cooperation in the United States*, edited by Herbert Adams. Baltimore MD: Johns Hopkins University Press, 1888.

Chamberlin, Edwin M. *The Sovereigns of Industry*. Westport, CT: Hyperion Press, 1976. (reprint, 1875)

Commons, John. *History of Labor in the United States*. Vol. 2. New York: MacMillan Company, 1936.

Ford, James. *Co-operation in New England: Urban and Rural*. Philadelphia, PA: Press of Wm. F. Fell Co., 1913.

Leikin, Steven. *The Practical Utopians: American Workers and the Cooperative Movement in the Gilded Age*. Detroit, MI: Wayne State University Press, 2004.

Messer-Kruse, Timothy. *The Yankee International: Marxism and the American Reform Tradition, 1848–1876*. Chapel Hill: University of North Carolina Press, 1998.

SPIES, AUGUST (1855–1887)
Anarchist

August Vincent Theodore Spies was born in Landeck, Germany, in 1855. The son of a forester, Spies became an avid reader and student of German history and philosophy before he left for the United States in 1872, where he would embark on a career as an anarchist agitator, organizer, orator, publisher, and, ultimately as a martyr to the revolutionary cause.

Spies traveled around the United States after he arrived, working odd jobs and discovering that many wage earners were, in his view, distressingly passive and deferential to their employers. He arrived in Chicago in 1874 or 1875, settled in the German North Side, and found work in his acquired trade, as an upholsterer. After the bloody repression of the

railroad trainmen's strike in 1877, Spies volunteered for the German workers' militia, armed groups organized in Chicago to protect workers from the police, and participated in the socialist movement.

In 1881, Spies played a leading role within a group of young, mostly German-born Socialists who abandoned electoral politics and embraced revolutionary activity. The Chicago militants were inspired by the exiled German anarchist Johann Most, who advocated the use of arms and dynamite in the violent struggles he believed were necessary to bring about a social revolution.

However Spies and other socialist revolutionaries in Chicago did not employ the violent tactics Most espoused. Indeed they remained faithful to the teaching of Karl Marx, who insisted that only the mass mobilization of the working class could create a labor movement powerful enough to overthrow the capitalist order. In 1883, Spies joined other revolutionary labor organizers in Pittsburgh where they issued a famous manifesto calling workers to act on their duty to rebel against oppressive rulers.

By this time Spies and his comrades had taken control of Chicago's influential socialist newspaper, *Arbeiter Zeitung*, a daily published in German that would, under Spies's direction, reach a circulation of nearly 20,000—making it by far the most widely read radical newspaper in the nation's history. Spies was equally active as a leader of the International Working People's Association (IWPA), which established branches in most of the city's working-class districts in 1885. Spies also participated in creating the Central Labor Union, a body of trade unions led by socialist revolutionaries, which soon rivaled the size of the established Trades and Labor Assembly.

By this time Spies and the Chicago revolutionaries had begun to call themselves anarchists because they believed in creating a cooperative society without centralized state control and because they believed direct action, rather than electoral action, was required to make the social revolution—action that would inevitably provoke violent repression by armed forces determined to defend the ruling order. Having completely abandoned electoral activity, Spies and the anarchists boldly advocated preparing for violent activity by urging their followers to arm themselves and to make dynamite bombs for use in confrontations with police and the militia.

While Spies waged this war of words against the capitalists and their minions, he was swept up in the tide of labor militancy that welled up across the country in March and April of 1886, as workers struck over a wide range of issues, mostly notably the 8-hour day. Acting on a proposal by the Federated Trades and Labor Organization that all workers leave their jobs on May 1 to gain an 8-hour day, Spies and his anarchist comrades organized a variety of work groups in Chicago who gained the 8-hour day, sometimes without having to take a pay cut.

When May Day came to Chicago, more than 30,000 workers left work, including many who were mobilized by the anarchists. Spies was at the center of the storm of strikes that hit Chicago. Despite the dire predictions of the press and the fear that the anarchists would resort to violent tactics, the strikes remained nonviolent until the night of May 3 when Chicago police killed four strikers at the McCormick Works.

Spies had given a speech to these workers just before the shootings, and he was outraged over the events he witnessed. He then published a militant editorial telling workers to arm themselves to battle the police. He also publicized a rally to be held on May 4 at the Haymarket to protest the shootings. Spies opened up the meeting that night calling for calm, but later the police marched on the assembly, a bomb was thrown into their ranks, and a bloody riot erupted in which at least seven policeman and three civilians were fatally wounded.

Spies and the anarchists were blamed for the whole bloody affair and accused of hatching a conspiracy to attack the police at the Haymarket and in other areas, as a means of launching the revolution. August Spies was arrested, charged with being an accessory to the murder of the first policeman to die, and identified as the ringleader of an alleged anarchist conspiracy. Along with six other anarchist workers, he was tried in the summer of 1886 and sentenced to death by hanging.

In a final appearance before the court, Spies delivered a much-quoted speech. After declaring himself a good citizen and an innocent person willing to die for his ideas, Spies angrily told the court, "If you think you can stamp out the labor movement, then hang us!" But, he added, "Here you will tread upon a spark, but here, and there, and behind you and in front of you...flames will blaze up. It is a subterranean fire. You cannot put it out."

Even more memorable were Spies's last words as he stood bound and hooded on the gallows on November 11, 1887. The covering over his head could not prevent Spies from uttering his last, free words: "The time will come," he said, "When our silence will be more powerful than the voices you strangle today."

Spies's final words became his epitaph and are inscribed at the base of the famous monument at Waldheim Cemetery in Forest Park, Illinois, that was dedicated to Spies and the four other Haymarket martyrs who died in 1887.

JAMES GREEN

References and Further Reading

Avrich, Paul. *The Haymarket Tragedy*. Princeton, NJ: Princeton University Press, 1984.

Foner, Philip S., ed. *The Autobiographies of the Haymarket Anarchists* (1886). New York: Humanities Press, 1969.

Green, James. *Death in the Haymarket: A Story of Chicago, the First Labor Movement and the Bombing That Divided Gilded Age America*. New York: Pantheon, 2006.

Nelson, Bruce C. *Beyond the Martyrs: A Social History of Chicago's Anarchists, 1870–1900*. New Brunswick, NJ: Rutgers University Press, 1988.

Parsons, Lucy, ed. *Famous Speeches of the Eight Chicago Anarchists in Court*. New York: Arno Press, 1969. (reprint, 1910)

Roediger, David, and Franklin Rosemont, eds. *The Haymarket Scrapbook*. Chicago, IL: Charles H. Kerr, 1986.

SPIES, LABOR

In 1935, a Cincinnati streetcar worker sent a letter to Senator Robert M. LaFollette begging him to send investigators to ferret out labor spies in the streetcar union. Spies "report everything that goes on at the meeting" to the boss, he wrote, and "It is hell to have to be afraid to work like that." Worse, workers suspected that their union officers were the double agents. Fearing the letter would fall into the hands of the spies and he would be "discharged without any kind of hearing," he signed his letter only "A member of this union." In mills, mines, and department stores, labor spies attended union meetings, ran for union elections, and looked out for agitators and signs of industrial unrest. Private detective agencies supplied undercover operatives to American industry from the mid-nineteenth century through the late 1930s, when the LaFollette Committee's public hearings exposed undercover detectives and embarrassed employers, effectively squelching the practice. The secretive nature of labor espionage precludes reliable assessments of its scope. Trade unionists and historians have argued that labor espionage and strikebreaking retarded unionization and revealed anti-unionism unique to American employers. But workers readily took jobs as labor spies, suggesting that workers' willingness to inform on each other should be incorporated into the history of class formation and working-class consciousness.

Origins

Labor espionage originated on the railroads in the 1850s. Railroads ballooned into huge employers in the nineteenth century, with dispersed workforces of conductors and engineers operating with marginal supervision by a thin layer of managers. Theft proliferated. Workers scalped tickets and stole freight, while conductors simply pocketed cash fare payments in a practice so widespread it acquired its own slang, "knocking down." Railroads searched endlessly for technologies, from fare boxes to ticket punches, that could thwart conductor thefts.

Allan Pinkerton marketed a creative solution. Few localities had standing police forces or detective squads, and the weak U.S. state meant that U.S. Marshals focused on protecting government property and the mails. While European employers turned to state police forces to surveil and suppress workers, the United States developed a characteristically privatized labor-discipline system. Pinkerton had been freelancing as a postal inspector in Illinois, and he approached the Chicago-area railroads in 1855 with a proposal jointly to sponsor a railroad-checking business; Pinkerton would supply detectives to report on the "habits and associations of the employees." Within a few months Pinkerton's agents had caught a conductor on the Chicago & Burlington Railroad with a pocketful of ticket receipts. Railroad contracts made up a substantial portion of Pinkerton's detective business for decades thereafter.

Undercover railroad surveillance was called "spotting." Spotters rode trains, posing as regular passengers while they surreptitiously noted the conductor's fare receipts and counted heads on the train car. Spotters also reported on conductors' demeanors and service to passengers, recording whether conductors kept their cars and uniforms clean and treated passengers courteously. Thus spotters functioned as surrogate supervisors, serving as the eyes of management. Conductors despised spotters and developed strategies to foil them, from marking their shoes with chalk to alert other workers to attacking them on the platform. As streetcar service grew in cities, spotters popped up to surveil streetcar conductors as well; department stores hired spotters to watch store clerks as early as 1869.

Spotting seems to have spawned labor espionage. The Philadelphia and Reading Railroad, already using Pinkerton spotters, called on Pinkerton in 1873 for help when violence erupted in the road's Pennsylvania coalmines. Pinkerton sent James McParlan, an experienced spotter, to work as a miner and infiltrate the miners' ranks. Two years later McParlan revealed himself and accused his astonished coworkers of membership in the Molly Maguires, helping send several to the gallows. The tremendous publicity surrounding the Molly Maguire trials apparently helped advertise the notion of using undercover operatives among workers to identify agitators and detect unrest. Once the technology of labor espionage was created, it could be deployed for multiple uses. Thus detectives posing as railroad passengers could just as easily pose as miners or conductors.

Growth and Practices of Industry

Detective agencies proliferated after the 1877 railroad strike. Few barriers to entry slowed the industry's growth: An aspiring detective needed only an operative and a client to get started. Pinkerton marketed his services with a steady stream of books and pamphlets, helping attract new entrants to the detective business, and former Pinkerton operatives opened their own agencies. Reliable assessments of the growth of the labor-spy business are hard to produce; detective agencies often provided general investigative services in addition to labor spies, and many added professional strikebreaking as well. After Pinkerton strikebreakers fired on steelworkers in Homestead in 1892, congressional hearings investigating the use of private strikebreakers led Pinkerton publicly to renounce labor spying and strikebreaking, although this renunciation lasted a few years at best. Open-shop movements in the early twentieth century and after World War I drove demand. New York City had 75 detective agencies by 1904; Chicago had 58 by 1918. In 1936, the LaFollette Committee counted 230 agencies nationwide and estimated their employment from 40,000–135,000. Large agencies included Thiel's, the Railway Audit and Inspection Company, Corporations Auxiliary, and the William J. Burns Agency (whose proprietor became the director of the Federal Bureau of Investigation from 1921 to 1924).

Agencies tended to use a standard set of practices. Solicitors visited employers to drum up business and if retained arranged for the employer to hire an undercover operative under an assumed name. Operatives were directed to apply for a job in the factory or mine and report to work regularly, all the while observing coworkers closely. If a union already represented workers, operatives were to join the union and seek elective office, to get access to membership lists and union strategy; in nonunion workplaces operatives looked for signs of trouble and identified potential organizers. Operatives prepared daily reports for the agency, which abridged and compiled findings for employers. Employers could fire agitators, develop blacklists, and strategize to avert strikes with the information thus obtained.

The defects in this system were obvious to workers and employers alike. Agencies had incentive to exaggerate and foment trouble to create demand for their services, and operatives could easily fabricate reports from a barstool. Skeptical of its labor spies, General

Motors retained several detective agencies to surveil each other's operatives in the 1930s. Despite the problems with labor espionage, employers lured by the promise of insider information continued to hire spies, and LaFollette's 1936 investigation revealed that firms like Standard Oil, Quaker Oats, Ford, and Montgomery Ward all hired labor spies.

Labor journalists and progressives regularly published antispy polemics beginning in the late nineteenth century. These polemics followed a generic pattern of announcing the existence of the labor-spy system, revealing the tactics used by spies, describing particular instances of espionage, and attributing worker quiescence to fear and mistrust bred by the spies. Well-publicized exposures of labor espionage included the Interchurch World Movement's report on the 1919 Steel Strike. Former spies sometimes wrote their own accounts, including Charlie Siringo of the Pinkertons, who described his infiltrations into the Western Federation of Miners at length.

State Intersections

Gradually a state surveillance apparatus grew alongside the private-detective agencies. While state governments built national guard forces to break strikes, federal and local police agencies created detective squads that investigated radicals, whether Communist or trade unionist. Many of these antisubversive units popped up during World War I, like the Bureau of Investigation and the Army's Military Intelligence Division; federal agents infiltrated the IWW and tailed researchers investigating the 1919 Steel Strike. In the 1920s, the line between state and private surveillance of workers blurred as detective agencies and government agencies shared information and operatives moved between public and private payrolls.

Union Strategies

Workers employed various tactics to discover spies in their ranks, from following suspected spies to see whether they met with handlers or mailed fishy letters to publishing photographs of exposed detectives in union newspapers to alert other locals to watch out.

The extreme secrecy and clannishness trade unions sometimes displayed can be attributed in part to fear of detective infiltration.

Two ideas for battling labor spies recurred. Most often unionists proposed licensure. Wisconsin trade unionists seem to have originated the idea to require

all detectives to obtain state-issued licenses, thus automatically precluding the anonymity spies required. Wisconsin passed a licensure law in 1925. Detectives easily skirted the law by closing their Wisconsin offices and sending agents in from nearby states. Another favored tactic was state-sponsored investigations; the Homestead hearings, the Commission on Industrial Relations, state hearings in Wisconsin in the early 1920s and Pennsylvania in 1928 all explored the phenomenon and proposed limitations on private detectives. Only in Wisconsin did legislation emerge from the hearings.

In general though labor espionage ranked low on unions' list of priorities. Union legislative agendas rarely mentioned labor espionage, and only rarely did union leaders speak about the problem. The American Federation of Labor's (AFL's) aversion to state intervention in labor relations may be one reason; the relative importance of other issues, like the injunction and the yellow-dog contract, may be another.

Workers as Spies

A third reason may be unions' anxiety about exposing their own members. While polemicists and unionists presented the labor-spy problem as one of professional detectives infiltrating workplaces, evidence suggests that most workplace operatives came from the ranks of workers. Investigators' files hold hundreds of letters soliciting work as an informant from machinists and garment workers. In 1936, one detective agency estimated that 70% of its operatives were workers who supplemented their wages with informant's stipends, not professional detectives. In this light labor espionage looks not just like a vast conspiracy of employers and detectives, but also as a shortage of solidarity. Workers who spied are a sign of the limits of class consciousness.

Collapse of Industry

New Deal progressives never publicly raised these questions however when the LaFollette Committee convened in 1936 to investigate labor spies and strikebreaking in a bid to build public support for the imperiled Wagner Act. Workers who spied were presented as dupes who had been tricked by cunning detectives into inadvertently betraying fellow workers. By shaming corporations using spies, and revealing the predilection of spies to embellish reports, the LaFollette Committee helped damp demand for labor espionage. Further the new National Labor Relations Board (NLRB) could readily investigate allegations of labor espionage and penalize employers, as the board interpreted the act to ban labor spying. The Supreme Court upheld this interpretation in *NLRB v. Fansteel* in 1939.

In the late 1930s, detective agencies complained to government investigators that lawyers had taken over the work of fighting unions, since attorney-client privilege shielded their consultation from public scrutiny. The NLRB investigators continued to discover labor spies at work through the early 1940s, but the number dwindled swiftly. Employers turned to more sophisticated strategies to fight unions, like welfare capitalism and human resources techniques.

JENNIFER LUFF

References and Further Reading

Howard, Sidney. *The Labor Spy*. New York: Republic Publishing Company, 1924.
Huberman, Leo. *The Labor Spy Racket*. New York: Modern Age Books, 1937.
Lukas, J. Anthony. *Big Trouble*. New York: Simon and Schuster, 1997.
Morn, Frank. *The Eye That Never Sleeps: A History of the Pinkerton National Detective Agency*. Bloomington: Indiana University Press, 1982.
Norwood, Stephen H. *Strikebreaking and Intimidation: Mercenaries and Masculinity in Twentieth-Century America*. Chapel Hill: University of North Carolina Press, 2002.
Smith, Robert Michael. *From Blackjacks to Briefcases: A History of Commercialized Strikebreaking and Union-busting in the United States*. Athens: Ohio University Press, 2003.

Cases and Statutes Cited

NLRB v. *Fansteel*
Wagner Act

See also **Fansteel v. U.S.; LaFollette Civil Liberties Committee; Railroad Strikes (1877)**

SPRINGER, MAIDA (1910–2005)
International Ladies' Garment Workers' Union

Once touted as the pride of the International Ladies' Garment Workers' Union (ILGWU), Maida Springer was a pioneer in struggles for social, political, and economic equality and justice for workers, women, and people of African descent. Beginning as an active volunteer for the ILGWU in 1932, Springer moved on to hold various union offices, including educational director, staff member of the Dress and Waistmakers'

Joint Board, business agent, and labor organizer. After 1955, her activism turned increasingly toward the African continent, where she served as a critical adviser to many of the burgeoning and struggling labor movements through her promotion of labor exchange programs and trade schools. She connected her struggle for civil and economic rights at home to the broader Pan-African movement for independence.

Born on May 12, 1910, in Panama, Springer immigrated to the United States where her early political outlook was forged in the cauldron of black protest politics of the World War I era. Weekly she heard Marcus Garvey's Universal Negro Improvement Association hammer the message of black pride and unity and street orators, such as A. Philip Randolph and Frank Crosswaith, inveigh against police brutality, lynching, and the widespread discrimination and exclusion African-Americans experienced. Springer brought the sensibilities forged in these childhood lessons to bear on her labor activism.

Just before the Depression forced her to join the wage labor force, Springer heard a speech by Randolph that transformed her thinking about organized labor. Randolph cast the problem of labor union exclusion in a new light by pointing out that white workers paid a price for their racism with lowered wages. This analysis awakened Springer to a new vision of organized labor as an institution capable of improving the lives of all workers. Randolph would become her lifelong mentor in her work for labor and civil rights and African labor development.

A serendipitous trip to England in 1945 as the first black woman to represent American labor abroad served to fuse Springer's domestic activism with an international purpose. Influenced by Pan-African luminaries George Padmore, Ras Makonnen, Jomo Kenyatta, and Una Marson, she committed herself to the task of orienting American labor toward an investment in the struggles of African workers to organize strong unions and free their countries from the yoke of colonialism.

Known affectionately on the continent as "mama Maida," Springer began more extensive work in Africa with her 1960 appointment as an American Federation of Labor-Congress of Industrial Organizations (AFL-CIO) international representative. Serving as a vital labor consultant, she brought attention to East Africa, where she helped the fledgling Tanganyikan labor movement withstand the combined effort of industry and the colonial government to render it ineffective. She advised the Ethiopian labor movement in the country's first labor-management agreement, involving a sugar plantation union. She provided the same services for Liberian labor in the country's first tripartite National Industrial Relations Conference. With her special interest in structuring programs designed to increase skill level, Springer oversaw numerous labor education programs. The Institute of Tailoring and Cutting, a Kenyan trade school that was established in 1963 primarily through her determined will, continues to operate in Nairobi.

Springer's work on behalf of Africa served to bolster the reputation of the AFL-CIO on the continent. As a close ally of many African labor and political leaders, including Julius Nyerere, Tom Mboya, and Rashidi Kawawa, Springer used her connections in labor, academic, and progressive circles in the United States to publicize the African perspective of colonialism. Many of the AFL-CIO anticolonial resolutions have the imprint of her influence.

In contrast Africans largely viewed the activism, policies, and personnel of the International Confederation of Free Trade Unions (ICFTU), the non-Communist world labor body to which the AFL-CIO belonged, as paternalistic, ineffective, and compromised by colonial sympathies. After the AFL-CIO agreed to direct its African activities through ICFTU channels only, Western labor's influence in Africa fell off dramatically. As African nations gained their independence and sought to disentangle from their colonial past and Cold War constrictions, Springer saw her influence wane further. Most of the new governments forced the disaffiliation of African labor centers from the ICFTU, viewing the organization as a threat to nation-building policies, including the incorporation of labor movements into one-party states.

In the mid-960s, Springer returned to the ILGWU as the general organizer for the Southeast region. She also traveled to the West to assess the prospects for organizing Mexicans and Asians into the garment industry in California. The pervasive racism among white union members throughout the country often dismayed her. Still she occasionally showed her trademark humor in the face of untenable barriers to organizing. When asked by southern white labor leaders how they could stop the practice of segregated bathrooms among their membership, Springer quipped, "Turn off the water in the white bathroom and let nature take its course."

Springer returned to the international affairs arena in the 1970s, first as a staff member of the African-American Labor Center, an AFL-CIO auxiliary, and then as an AFL-CIO consultant in international affairs. Her work included serving as coordinator of drought relief for the 17 affected West African countries in the Sahel and traveling extensively in Africa to provide various forms of aid to unions and assess needs.

Recognized as a role model, Springer acceded to the requests of labor centers to help bring more women into the labor movement and increase their levels of activism. In 1977, she helped to coordinate the first Pan African Conference on the Role of Trade Union Women, which served as a forum to discuss the struggle for equal rights and the economic and social conditions and impediments women faced. From 1977 to 1981, she served as coordinator for the establishment of the women's bureau of the Turkish Federation of Labor. In 1979, in Indonesia she participated in putting together a seminar for female workers designed to increase female activism. In many parts of the world, Springer found that the concerns of women were similar. They wanted equal opportunity, equal pay for equal work, day care provisions, family planning, an end to employer verbal abuse, and 8-hour days with no forced overtime.

In addition to her international work, Springer dedicated herself to domestic civil rights activism. At Randolph's behest she served as an organizer for the 1940s March on Washington Movement. As Midwest director of the A. Philip Randolph Institute in Chicago, Springer worked on expanding voter education and registration from 1969–1973. From 1970–1974 she served as a vice-president of the National Council of Negro Women, which had rural cooperative projects with women in the southern United States and in countries in Africa, Latin America, and the Caribbean.

In the few years of life left to Springer, she again extended her services to Africa by helping to raise money for the Maida fund, a program administered through the AFL-CIO's Solidarity Center. The fund helps child agricultural laborers leave this dangerous and exploitative work and return to school.

Springer's marriage in 1928 to Owen Springer produced one child, Eric Winston Springer. In 1965, she married James Horace Kemp, who would serve as president of the National Association for the Advancement of Colored People and was a prominent Chicago labor leader. Maida Springer died on March 29, 2005.

YEVETTE RICHARDS JORDAN

References and Further Reading

Murray, Pauli. *The Autobiography of a Black Activist, Feminist, Lawyer, Priest, and Poet.* Knoxville: University of Tennessee Press, 1987.

Orleck, Annelise. *Common Sense and a Little Fire: Women and Working-Class Politics in the United States, 1900–1965.* Chapel Hill: University of North Carolina Press, 1995.

Richards, Yevette. *Maida Springer, Pan-Africanist and International Labor Leader.* Pittsburgh, PA: University of Pittsburgh, 2000.

———. *Conversations with Maida Springer: A Personal History of Labor, Race, and International Relations.* Pittsburgh, PA: University of Pittsburgh, 2004.

———. "African and African-American Labor Leaders in the Struggle over International Labor Affiliation." *International Journal of African Historical Studies* 31, 2 (1998): 301.

———. "Race, Gender, and Anticommunism in the International Labor Movement: The Pan-African Connections of Maida Springer." *Journal of Women's History* 11, 2 (1999): 35.

Springer-Kemp, Maida. "'We Did Change Some Attitudes'; Maida Springer-Kemp Recounts Her Years at the International Ladies' Garment Workers' Union." In *Rocking the Boat: Union Women's Voices, 1915–1975*, edited by Bridgid O'Farrell and Joyce L. Kornbluh. New Brunswick, NJ: Rutgers University Press, 1996.

STANDARD OF LIVING
See **American Standard of Living**

STEEL AND IRON

Steel was the iconic industry of the Industrial Age—mammoth, smoky caldrons of fire and flame producing a miracle metal that could be shaped into anything and everything, from rails to I-beams, battleships to thumb tacks. The sheer size of its workforce and its central importance to the U.S. economy in the twentieth century made its labor struggles iconic as well. The industry and its workforce have fallen on hard times in the last few decades, and the industry as it exists today is a very different one than existed from 1880 to 1980. But for those 100 years, steelworkers were at the center of creating something like a (now apparently temporary) working-class republic. The rise of unionism in steel in the 1930s and 1940s transformed not only the lives of steelworkers, but it was a leading force in changing the rules of the game in American society for most of the second-half of the twentieth century.

When Iron Becomes Steel

Iron is an ancient metal, dating back to 3,000 B.C. or before. Steel is an alloy of iron and carbon, produced by burning iron at such high temperatures that it liquefies and in the process not only introduces small amounts of carbon, but also makes possible the removal of various impurities, such as silicon, phosphorus, and sulfur. When exactly iron becomes true steel is a matter of some definitional debate, since iron-working has almost from its very beginning, accidentally at first, involved some admixture of carbon. The Damascus steel that amazed European crusaders in the blades of Muslim warriors, and which was widespread in the Middle East from 900 to 1600 A.D., is thought to have derived from India's wootz steel, dating from 300 B.C. But in today's terms this steel—so visibly and practically different from iron in its time—is classified as wrought iron by metallurgists.

Steel becomes modern, true steel only when it can be reliably produced in large quantities—that is, only when the science of metallurgy is capable of precisely controlling the amounts of carbon and other alloys to produce a specific steel for specific purposes. Today's high-carbon steel, for example, is especially hard but brittle. Low- and medium-carbon steels are softer but more amenable to being shaped into sheets and structural forms. Adding other metals produces different kinds and qualities of steel. Chromium steel for example combines hardness, strength, and elasticity, while nickel steel has the tensile qualities of high-carbon steel without the brittleness.

Centuries of trial-and-error experimentation and repetition by iron masters in small shops eventually led in 1709 to the blast furnace that used coking coal to turn iron ore into large batches of pig iron. Puddling furnaces, developed about the same time, allowed rough variations of the carbon content in this wrought iron. But modern steel became unambiguously steel only in the 1850s with the invention of the Bessemer Converter in England, which finally allowed for the relatively precise control of the iron's carbon content. The Bessemer breakthrough was short-lived, being replaced in the 1860s by the open-hearth process for cooking iron into steel. Breakthroughs in rolling-mill technology during those same decades produced the modern integrated steel mill by 1870—one where a blast furnace turns iron ore into pig iron, which is then turned into steel by an open hearth, or today a basic oxygen, furnace. Molten steel is then poured into basic forms called blooms, which are then passed through a series of rolling machinery that shapes the steel into various forms as it gradually cools. With only minor variations, this was the industry of the 1870s in the United States, and it is the industry of the integrated portion of the U.S. industry today.

As steel mills increased their scale in the late nineteenth century, what had been craft-based small-scale production was transformed into mammoth workplaces full of relatively unskilled workers tending massive machines and moving raw materials and finished product from one place to another. The mechanization of steelmaking paradoxically produced a very labor-intensive process, and the workforce was divided between the craft occupations—some of them ancient, some of them less than a decade or two

At the lower level of the blast furnace. Drawing of the slag, steelworks, Homestead, Pa. Library of Congress, Prints & Photographs Division [LC-USZ62-69676].

old—and industrial grunts. The craft workers tended to be of English and German descent, while the much more numerous unskilled jobs were held by more recent immigrants from Eastern and southern Europe. As the metallurgists perfected their control of carbon content, so steel management sought to master its control of a polyglot workforce.

The Nonunion Era

Craft unions appeared simultaneously with the new steel industry of the late nineteenth century. In 1876, several of these unions—including the Sons of Vulcan, the Iron and Steel Roll Hands' Union, and the Associated Brotherhood of Iron and Steel Heaters, Rollers, and Roughers—merged into the Amalgamated Association of Iron and Steel Workers. Until 1892, these unions had substantial workplace power because they possessed craft knowledge and skills that management depended on. But as the noncraft part of the steel workforce grew in importance, the craft unions disdained them as members—partly because

the view of unions then was that they could work only based on craft power, partly because craft workers blamed unskilled workers for the degradation of their crafts in the transforming process they were undergoing, and partly because the unskilled workers were of different nationalities, religions, and traditions.

In the late 1880s, in the Pittsburgh area, then the center of American steel, the amalgamated was on the defensive at most non-Carnegie mills, and it had successfully enlisted the support of some of the unskilled immigrant workers, thereby winning some important local mill victories even as they still denied unskilled workers membership in their unions. This was the period during which Andrew Carnegie was buying and building mills, consolidating a haphazard industry under his control, and Carnegie was at first ostentatiously friendly with the amalgamated, accepting the iron scale for wages at all his plants until he faced stronger competition and the collapse of rail prices (then the principal steel product) in the late 1980s. Carnegie's approach changed dramatically in a showdown in Homestead, Pennsylvania, in 1892.

As Jonathan Rees has shown, the amalgamated was "never as strong in any other mill as it was in

Homestead and never as strong in any other district as it was in Pittsburgh" (J. Rees, *Managing the Mills,* 2004). The union also had substantial support among unskilled workers and the townspeople, including elected officials. By taking on the union at its strongest point, Carnegie Steel ensured that a victory in Homestead would rid it of the union in all its other mills. Under the leadership of former coke magnate Henry Clay Frick, Carnegie locked out the work force, declaring it would no longer run union in Homestead. After some initial victories against Pinkerton guards, Homestead steelworkers eventually succumbed as the State of Pennsylvania seized control of the town and eventually escorted scabs into the mill.

But Homestead was just the most dramatic of the losses the amalgamated suffered in 1891 and 1892. It lost a series of strikes in eastern Pennsylvania in 1891, and most of the non-Carnegie firms in the Pittsburgh area were abandoning union scale, as had several Carnegie mills. As Rees explains, "Many steel manufacturers besides Carnegie Steel took on the union in the summer of 1892 because companies throughout the industry perceived the Amalgamated Association as vulnerable . . . By August, there were more non-union mills up and running across the country than at any time in the previous twenty years" (J. Rees, *Managing the Mills,* 2004). The nonunion era in steel had begun, and it would last, with only minor interruptions, for nearly half a century.

Though the amalgamated maintained a membership in many mills after 1892, and it sought to rebuild itself more than once, it was eventually defeated in all subsequent struggles. When U.S. Steel was formed in 1900 by merging a variety of companies into Carnegie Steel, the amalgamated had contracts at several of the mills, and for the next decade, it mounted various plant-level strikes to maintain recognition. It took U.S. Steel almost a decade to eliminate the union, but by 1909 it had. Labor strife continued at U.S. Steel and other companies after 1909, and despite the virtual nonexistence of the amalgamated, labor actions heated up during the years of war production, beginning in 1914. In 1916, for example, there were 72 strikes in the industry. In most cases however, striking skilled workers were simply replaced, often by less skilled workers who increasingly showed that they could do the job. The increased organizing of the full-production war years culminated in the Great Steel Strike of 1919—great for its size, not its result, which was another resounding defeat.

By 1919, there were two dozen different unions, of which the amalgamated was but one, that claimed to represent some segment of the steel workforce, a combined dues-paying membership of 100,000 out of some 500,000 steelworkers during these peak production years. With leadership from the Chicago Federation of Labor and the decidedly tepid approval of the American Federation of Labor (AFL), this group of unions formed a national coalition and called a national strike across the industry beginning on September 22. A total of 250,000 steelworkers struck on that first day—more than twice the existing membership and clearly enough to disrupt production substantially, causing both economic pain for the companies and political problems for the war presidency of Woodrow Wilson. The strike's organizers had hoped for federal government arbitration of a settlement. When President Wilson made clear that was not going to happen, the organizationally weak but still symbolically prestigious amalgamated pulled its skilled workers off the picket lines in November. Though it varied greatly from mill to mill, there were fewer strikers with each passing week. By January 8, 1920, the unions admitted the obvious and declared the strike officially over.

Though another bitter defeat that would chill union organizing in steel another decade or more, the 1919 strike crafted a weapon that steelworkers would eventually use to change the economics of the industry—an industrywide strike that was as much political as economic, bringing the question of steel wages and conditions to the citizenry as a whole by halting steel production across the economy and thus not only strangling company profits, but also goading politicians to intervene between companies and workers who might otherwise destroy each other, the industry, and all it meant to the American economy then. What is more, the strikers in 1919 tended to be the foreign-born lesser skilled workers, not the craft aristocrats of old, and the idea that all steelworkers should act as one, whether in one union or a coalition of unions, took root in this core industry.

The Union Era, 1937–1983

The organization of the steelworkers in the mid-1930s by the Committee for Industrial Organizations (CIO) is well-known. At first the steelworkers seemed recipients of favorable external events, not themselves agents of their own destiny. The National Labor Relations Act was passed in 1935, encouraging the formation of labor unions as official government policy. The CIO was formed, over AFL objections, in 1936 to organize steel, auto, rubber, and other manufacturing workers on an industrial basis, with everybody in a given industry belonging to one big union. Rubber workers in Akron and autoworkers at

General Motors in Flint, Michigan, established the breakthroughs in 1936 and early 1937, from which the steelworkers benefited. Organizers from the United Mine Workers braved the slings and arrows of the Coal and Iron Police in steel company towns, and rank-and-file steelworkers worked quietly if at all to organize themselves department by department, mill by mill, sometimes using the company union structures that were in some cases leftover from the welfare capitalism of the 1920s and in others, hastily constructed mechanisms for avoiding the new legal environment. Seemingly out of nowhere, without a fight yet being mounted, U.S. Steel ([USS] in control of about half the industry) abandoned more than three decades of the fiercest anti-unionism and in March 1937 recognized the CIO's Steel Workers' Organizing Committee (SWOC). At the time somewhat less than 20% of steelworkers at USS had joined the union

When steelworkers finally did enter the fight on their own behalf in the Little Steel Strike of May 1937, they lost one last time—against the smaller but still huge steel companies of Bethlehem, Republic, Inland, and Youngstown Sheet & Tube. Direct, unalloyed repression had always been strongest in steel, and 13 workers were killed and scores more injured in the strikes that dotted Pennsylvania, Maryland, Illinois, Indiana, Ohio, and New York. But the tide was turning, and as production for World War II took off by 1940, SWOC renewed its organizing mill by mill, finally achieving a breakthrough with a series of successful strikes at Bethlehem Steel in February and March of 1941. By 1942, when SWOC officially became the United Steelworkers of America (USWA), the new union represented a commanding majority of all those who worked in steel.

The war years, during which unions traded membership security agreements for a no-strike pledge for the duration of the war, were years of internal organization, the time when most steelworkers learned their unionism, developed new leadership at the plant and department levels, and established a daunting number of committees, standing and ad hoc, to address the numerous issues the union chose to address from job classification schemes to the annual union picnic. The organization that emerged from the war was unlike anything seen before in steel.

With former miner Philip Murray the head of both the USWA and the CIO, the steelworkers were the main act in the massive 1945–1946 strike wave. With more than a million CIO workers already on strike in auto, meatpacking, and electrical equipment, on January 21, the steelworkers emptied the steel industry of workers, with 800,000 walking out of all steel, steel-related, and even some nonsteel plants. The entire industry simply stopped. Unlike all previous steel strikes, including the massive effort in 1919, everybody went out together regardless of occupation, employer, ethnicity, or location. And after the federal government forced what many saw as an inadequate wage increase to keep up with postwar inflation, they all went back together as one. The 18.5-cents-an-hour increase they won (nearly double what the steel companies had offered) then became the standard for settling all the CIO strikes and many AFL ones as well.

Over the next decade steelworkers' capacity to go out together and come back together across the entire industry not only bludgeoned the steel companies into something like a 50% increase in real wages, it made steel wages and benefits (and company profits and practices) national political issues every 3 years, with the general public broadly supportive because whatever the steelworkers won generally improved the prospects of all other workers, union and nonunion. Depending on the year, from 500,000 to 600,000 steelworkers shut down the industry with regularity—in 1949, 1952, 1955, 1956, and 1959. When the steelworkers won partial company funding of health insurance in the 1949 strike, they were among the first to have it, but the benefit became standard in most workplaces in the following 20 years. Something similar happened with private company-funded pensions, also first won in the 1949 strike. Though other unions were often the innovators of a new benefit or contract provision, the massive nationwide steel strikes made just compensation and higher standards of living for all workers consistent popular demands that the government (at all levels) was expected to help in achieving. For a quarter-century beginning in the late 1940s, real wages for all production and nonsupervisory workers (about 80% of the private-sector workforce) increased by nearly 70% until 1973, when they began a decline from which they have yet to recover.

Eventually the nationwide strikes wore out both the companies and the union, and after 1959 they took action to avoid them (including with a formal agreement in 1973) while still continuing to improve steelworkers' living standards and working conditions into the 1980s. The 40 years from 1941 to 1981 were prosperous ones not only for steelworkers, but for the industry as well. A well-managed oligopoly, the industry had substantial ability to raise its prices in a growing economy, and it was one of the few profit-making steel industries in the world in the postwar period. Until the 1970s, steadily rising real wages across the economy fueled further economic growth, but then as both nonunion wages and economic growth stagnated, the economics of the industry changed for the worse. About half the industry was lost in the worst economic recession in postwar U.S.

history in the early 1980s. After a dramatic wave of mill closings from 1977–1983, the industry was thoroughly restructured. After a few years when a renewed stability had seemed to be restored, a new stream of closings and then bankruptcies were followed by a second restructuring of the industry in the early years of the new century.

We can date the close of the union era with the 1983 concessions' contract, the last industrywide contract and indeed the last time the union even tried to negotiate on an industrywide basis. The character and financial condition of the various companies varied so widely that the union had to reorganize completely its postwar bargaining approach, treating each company's situation differently without putting wages (now defined as the broader "employment costs") into competition. Far from disappearing the USWA has probably played a stronger and more decisive role in the integrated part of the industry in the last 20 years than in the previous twenty. But that part of the industry is now but a part, and no longer the whole.

Globalization and Minimills: Workers on the Defensive

The American steel industry at the dawn of the twenty-first century produces about 100 million tons of steel a year (in net tons shipped), an amount that is 60% greater than its peak production during World War II and larger than in any year prior to the 1970s, when the industry first reached the 100-million-ton level. It is of course no longer a growth industry, but it is far from dead as a metal and an industry. What have been lost are jobs, hundreds of thousands of union jobs, and the communities that were built around the wages and benefits steelworkers received for doing those jobs.

Imports killed some of these jobs, since they now fulfill 20%–30% of American demand for steel in any given year. But minimills took many more, revolutionizing steel production within the United States in a new nonunion sector. Minimills produce steel from used steel, the ubiquitous scrap that has accumulated, and goes on accumulating, after a century of industrial production. Using electric furnaces to melt and reprocess scrap, minimills skip the entire front end of the integrated steelmaking process (the blast furnace and pig iron). With the development of continuous-casting (now used in integrated production as well), they also skip the blooming process. As a result these steel mills are much smaller (thus, minimills), with smaller workforces, and they can be located almost anywhere, as they increasingly have been

since the 1970s. Today about half of U.S. steel production comes from minimills. The workers in these mills are almost all nonunion, and they generally have wages and benefits that track union standards in the integrated sector at a 15%–25% distance.

What remains of the integrated sector is now the other half of the industry. This half is still strongly union, and after two decades of some of the most complicated and difficult negotiations in the history of collective bargaining, these workers have real wages that are roughly comparable to what steelworkers in 1980 had achieved.

Together these two halves of the steel industry employ about 100,000 wageworkers versus a rough average of some 500,000 a year from World War II into 1980. It may seem unfair to compare the productivity of this two-part industry with the days when there was only the integrated part, since minimills produce steel that somebody long ago had already produced. But today's steelworkers, union and nonunion combined, each produce about 1,000 tons of steel a year versus 138 tons in World War II, 200 tons in 1965, and 300 tons in 1980. The vast majority of steel jobs were lost to these productivity increases.

The steelworkers' union has fought a valiant defensive battle to preserve wages and standards in the integrated industry, and it has mobilized its members politically and in a series of fierce rearguard strikes that has kept a union presence in any mill that ever had one. It has not yet mounted a serious effort to organize the minimills. After losing more than half its membership (including many in other industries like copper, aluminum, and can), the union has more recently been gathering other manufacturing unions under its banner, with the Rubber Workers and Paper Workers the largest of a series of mergers. It has reconstituted itself as a broad manufacturing union now, with a longer official name reflecting its current complexity. By common agreement of this more industrially diverse membership however, the union will continue to be referred to as United Steelworkers, reflecting a labor struggle that continues into a third century and a metal known for its durability, resilience, and toughness.

JACK METZGAR

References and Further Reading

Brody, David. *Labor in Crisis: The Steel Strike of 1919.* Urbana: University of Illinois Press, 1987.
Brody, David. *Steelworkers in America: The Nonunion Era.* New York: Harper & Row, 1960.
Brooks, Robert R. R. *As Steel Goes . . . Unionism in a Basic Industry.* New Haven, CT: Yale University Press, 1940.

Bruno, Robert. "USWA-Bargained and State-Oriented Responses to the Recurrent Steel Crisis." *Labor Studies Journal* 30, 1 (spring 2005).

Clark, Paul, Peter Gottlieb, and Donald Kennedy, eds. *Forging a Union of Steel: Philip Murray, SWOC, and the United Steelworkers.* Ithaca, NY: Cornell University, 1987.

Fitch, John A. *The Steel Workers.* Pittsburgh, PA: University of Pittsburgh Press, 1989. (reprint, 1910).

Fonow, Mary Margaret. *Union Women: Forging Feminism in the United Steelworkers of America.* Minneapolis: University of Minnesota Press, 2003.

Hoerr, John P. *And the Wolf Finally Came: The Decline of the American Steel Industry.* Pittsburgh, PA: University of Pittsburgh Press, 1988.

Metzgar, Jack. *Striking Steel: Solidarity Remembered.* Philadelphia, PA: Temple University Press, 2000.

Needleman, Ruth. *Black Freedom Fighters in Steel: The Struggle for Democratic Unionism.* Ithaca, NY: Cornell University Press, 2003.

Rees, Jonathan. *Managing the Mills: Labor Policy in the American Steel Industry during the Nonunion Era.* Dallas, TX: University Press of America, 2004.

Stein, Judith. *Running Steel, Running America: Race, Economic Policy, and the Decline of Liberalism.* Chapel Hill: University of North Carolina Press, 1998.

Cases and Statutes Cited

National Labor Relations Act

STEEL STRIKE (1959)

On July 15, 1959, more than 500,000 steelworkers—from Buffalo to Birmingham, from Baltimore to Oakland, California, with Pittsburgh, Cleveland, Gary, Chicago, and the Minnesota iron range in between—struck 12 steel companies, shutting down more than 90% of steelmaking in the United States. They did not return to work until November 6, when the U.S. Supreme Court upheld President Dwight D. Eisenhower's right to force them back to work with a Taft-Hartley injunction.

Half-a-million workers on strike for 116 days makes the 1959 steel strike the largest single work stoppage in U.S. history. A few other strikes have involved as many or more workers, including the 1946 steel strike when 800,000 walked out, and many have lasted longer. But combining mass and length in what was then called "man days idled," no other strike in U.S. history comes close.

The strike was engineered by U.S. Steel and the other steel companies with the aim of reversing the momentum the steelworkers' union had gained in collective bargaining with similarly massive, but shorter strikes in 1946, 1949, 1952, 1955, and 1956. With each of the earlier strikes, the union had won some new benefit as well as real wage increases totaling nearly 100% in the 18 years prior to 1959.

The 42-day strike in 1949, for example, forced the steel companies to fund a pension plan and partially to fund health insurance. The 34-day strike in 1956 completed the union's immediate postwar bargaining agenda when it won supplemental unemployment benefits, which ensured that steelworkers received about 80% of their wages when they were laid off.

Though some of their public rhetoric suggested otherwise, the steel companies were not focused on taking away any of these gains. While also aiming to slow the growth of wages, their primary target in 1959 was "rigid union work rules" protected by Section 2-B, the "Local Working Conditions" part of the Basic Steel Contract. Particularly offensive was a "past practice" clause the union had won in 1947 and had then used in the grievance-and-arbitration system to expand greatly its shop-floor powers. The U.S. Steel head Roger Blough claimed that 2-B restricted management's right to manage, protected featherbedding and other forms of loafing on the job, and even more broadly, forced "labor practices which impair the competitive principle [and] are incompatible with a free society."

Chafing under the burden of "rigid union work rules" was a common management complaint during what Mike Davis has called the "management offensive of 1958–1963." As in steel, most unions had acceded to formal management rights clauses in the late 1940s, but had then used their grievance and shop-steward systems gradually to erode the authority and discretion of front-line and then higher levels of management. Blough spoke for management in general when he described this grievance-by-grievance process as "glacierlike forces" that had to be reversed. In many workplaces, as in steel, a key issue involved union restrictions on management's ability to eliminate jobs when it installed new technology.

Also common during this time was the long strike as a management strategy. In 1959 alone, coal miners in Kentucky and West Virginia were on strike for 129 days, wholesale and retail bakers in New York City for 102 days, copper workers at Kennecott for 173 days and at Phelps Dodge for 238 days. As the U.S. economy had been growing through 1957, companies had given unions more than they thought they could sustain when the worst economic recession of the postwar era hit in 1958. Coming out of that recession, workers' finances had been weakened by long lay offs, and many workers were therefore less capable of sustaining long strikes.

A long-strike strategy was particularly appealing in steel for two different reasons. One had to do with a pattern that had clearly emerged with the regularity of postwar steel strikes. Buyers of steel products, such as auto companies, engaged in frenzied buying prior to contract deadlines, stockpiling steel for use during the strike. With relatively short strikes (the 58-day strike in 1952 being the longest), demand for steel would fall precipitously after a strike, as buyers continued to draw down their stockpiles. Led by U.S. Steel Labor Relations chief R. Conrad Cooper, the companies sought to stimulate buyers' stockpiling in 1959 and to concentrate production (and profits) in the first-half of the year, leaving them in position to outlast the steelworkers in a prolonged economic war of attrition in the second-half. This part of the strategy succeeded brilliantly, since the companies compiled a profitable year despite the strike, and they never really faced economic pressure to settle the dispute.

The second reason for a long-strike strategy was that the steelworkers' union did not and could not pay strike benefits during steel strikes; even very modest payments to 500,000 workers who were no longer paying dues would bankrupt the union in a matter of weeks. An additional advantage the companies thought they had was that by 1959, there was a well-organized and bitter rank-and-file opposition to the steelworkers' union president, David J. McDonald. The logic was that months without paychecks would further split the ranks from the leadership, thereby weakening the union to renegotiate its work rules. This part of the strategy failed miserably.

A long-strike economic war of attrition is a contest of competing solidarities. Rank-and-file steelworkers began the strike reluctantly, with a clear majority telling reporters that they preferred continued work to a wage increase. The companies' June proposal, attacking 2-B and accompanied by loose language from Cooper about reversing "the mistakes of the last 18 years," forced a resigned unity but little enthusiasm. Having struck every 3 years for more than a decade, steelworker families had systematically prepared for a possible strike, with many building up stockpiles of their own based on the plentiful opportunities for overtime during the first-half of the year. The union had well-oiled machinery for striking, including an internal welfare system that addressed hardship cases among strikers based on local union treasuries. But the union also reached out to merchants, banks, charitable agencies, and local and state governments that in most steel towns were highly cooperative, both out of genuine sympathy for the strikers and for more pragmatic reasons given the steelworkers' previously demonstrated capacity for organizing politically and commercially to reward its friends and punish its enemies. The first months of the strike were relatively easy for most steel families, but by October most were hurting, and the union's internal welfare system was straining to meet all the hardships. According to extensive

week-by-week reporting in the *New York Times* and *Wall Street Journal* however, the mood among the ranks had hardened by then. As the situation became more desperate, reporters found an anger and an *élan* that had previously been absent.

When President Eisenhower's injunction forced steelworkers back to work in November, they were angry, not relieved. Though a smaller steel company, Kaiser, had broken ranks and settled with the union on its own, the other 11 companies showed little sign of weakening. The Taft-Hartley process however required the companies to submit a final offer that the steelworkers had to vote up or down by the end of the 80-day cooling-off period in late January. The companies' proposal was a long way from its June demands of no wage increase and a gutting of Section 2-B; it offered a package worth about 30 cents an hour over 30 months and to submit its issues with 2-B to an impartial arbitrator. The economic package was outsized compared to other labor contracts at the time, but the union leadership required even more in order to make up for wages lost during the strike, and they dismissed out-of-hand submitting anything in 2-B to the whims of an arbitrator.

As a late January vote of the rank-and-file approached, both the union and the companies conducted opinion polls among steelworkers, and they both showed enormous 9-to-1 majorities against the final offer and for going back on strike when the cooling-off period ended. With the Eisenhower administration aware of these results and claiming that a renewed strike would threaten national security, it leaned (gently in public, heavily in private) on the companies to settle, and on January 6 they did. The final package was worth 39 cents an hour over 30 months, and 2-B would be submitted to a union-management committee for further study.

The 1959 steel strike, the last industrywide strike, was a decisive victory for the steelworkers, and the steel companies would never again challenge the union. It also blunted, though it did not end, the larger management attack on union power, with Mike Davis aptly calling it "the Eastern front" of the Management Offensive. *New York Times* labor reporter A. H. Raskin saw the strike as part of a dangerous change in postwar labor relations, "a struggle over basic power relationships," not a "conventional bread-and-butter quarrel" but "a conflict profounder than any fought by unions and employers since the bloody strikes of the Thirties." The final settlement, Raskin said, "marked a rout of the major companies in what they considered a crusade to re-establish the lost prerogatives of management.... A management victory would have meant a general reassessment of the bargaining relationships built up in most major industries in the quarter-century since the New Deal." That reassessment would be delayed another quarter-century in no small part because of the extraordinary solidarity the steelworkers displayed in the second-half of 1959.

JACK METZGAR

References and Further Reading

Davis, Mike. "The Fall of the House of Labor." In *Prisoners of the American Dream*. London, UK: Verso, 1986.

Libertella, Anthony F. "The Steel Strike of 1959: Labor, Management, and Government Relations." Ph.D. dissertation, Ohio State University, 1972.

Livernash, E. Robert. *Collective Bargaining in the Basic Steel Industry*. Washington, DC: U.S. Department of Labor 1961.

Metzgar, Jack. *Striking Steel: Solidarity Remembered*. Philadephia, PA: Temple University, 2000.

Cases and Statutes Cited

Taft-Hartley Act

See also Steel and Iron

STEELE v. LOUISVILLE AND NASHVILLE RAILROAD COMPANY (1944)

In December 1944, the U.S. Supreme Court's ruling in *Steele v. Louisville and Nashville Railroad Company* squarely addressed the issue of the discriminatory treatment of African-American railroad workers by the all-white railroad brotherhoods that both excluded them from union membership and used their institutional power to negotiate contracts that were explicitly harmful to blacks' job rights. Although failing to overturn the brotherhoods' whites-only membership policy, the Court found an implicit "duty of fair representation" in labor law that accorded formal, legal recognition on the unions, requiring them to represent black workers covered by their "craft or class" without prejudice.

The context for the decision was the long-standing tradition of racial exclusion and discrimination in the railroad industry and its dominant unions. For decades before World War II, African-American workers in the railroad-operating trades (firemen, brakemen, and switchmen, in particular) had confronted a sharply discriminatory labor market as well as considerable hostility from their white counterparts. Allowed access to these positions only in the South, they were everywhere excluded from membership in the all-white railroad brotherhoods, which

used their strength and legal recognition as trade unions to negotiate contracts that favored white employees at black workers' expense. "For the past fifty years," civil rights attorney Charles Hamilton Houston observed in 1949, the white railroad brotherhoods "have been using every means in their power to drive the Negro train and engine service worker out of employment and create a 'racially closed shop.'" Whites' hostility toward blacks assumed a variety of forms, including strikes calling for the dismissal of black employees and outbreaks of violence, particularly in hard economic times. During the 1910s and especially after World War I, contracts became whites' most effective technique for limiting blacks' access to key jobs and fixing their percentage in the workforce.

In the years following World War I, it was evident that many black railroaders were losing ground in the labor market, and by the Great Depression, their status in the industry had reached a crisis point. Black firemen and trainmen had decreased in number from their historic high in 1920 of about 6,505 and 7,609, respectively, to 2,356 and 2,857 in 1940. So bad did the situation appear that John T. Clark of the St. Louis Urban League privately admitted in 1934 that the "story of the Negro in the railroad and transportation industry is most pathetic." There was little question that by the start of World War II, racial discrimination in the operating sector of the railroad industry, a long-established fact of life, was increasing. Despite growing shortages of labor, the white brotherhoods refused to relax their staunch opposition to the employment of black firemen and brakemen; for their part railroad managers and officials of the federal War Manpower Commission and Office of Defense Transportation responsible for labor procurement maintained an antiblack stance as well.

The plight of black railway firemen particularly deteriorated under the Southeastern Carriers' Conference Agreement of 1941, which one federal investigator later called the "ultimate in all discriminatory agreements" aiming at the "total elimination of colored men as firemen." The previous year the all-white Brotherhood of Locomotive Firemen and Enginemen (BLFE) informed some 21 railroads of its intention to negotiate even more restrictions for black workers. Their proposed agreement would reserve all diesel jobs for promotable men, a category restricted to whites; in addition promotable men would be given preference on all new or changed runs, and the percentage of nonpromotable men would be limited to 50% on each railway division. With officials of the National Mediation Board (NMB)—the federal agency overseeing railroad labor relations—playing a key role, the parties signed a contract in February 1941.

Almost overnight black workers found themselves confronting demotions and furloughs.

Southern black firemen turned to the courts for redress. In the late 1930s, two southern, independent railroad associations, the International Association of Railway Employees (IARE) and the Association of Colored Railway Trainmen (ACRT), had retained noted civil rights attorney Charles Hamilton Houston to represent them in legal matters. Houston was not a labor law specialist when he began his legal work on their behalf, but he needed little introduction to southern black railroaders' plight: His father, the prominent Washington, DC, attorney, William Houston, had served as general counsel for the independent Railway Men's International Benevolent Industrial Association after World War I. After graduating from Harvard Law School, Charles worked with his father in the firm of Houston & Houston and joined the Howard University Law School faculty, where he would serve as the vice-dean. In that capacity he transformed legal education with the aim of training a new generation of black attorneys committed to social activism in the legal realm. From 1935 to 1938, Houston served as special counsel for the National Association for the Advancement of Colored People before returning to private practice. Although he had only occasionally addressed labor issues before, the ACRT and the IARE retained him in 1939. Houston would now launch a campaign against employment and union discrimination that would engage a good portion of his energy until his death in 1950. The 1941 Southeastern Carriers' Conference Agreement, which Houston believed to have been "born in iniquity and conceived in sin," made for a convenient target.

Bester William Steele, a 54-year-old veteran employee of the Louisville and Nashville Railroad in Birmingham, Alabama, put himself forward as a plaintiff for the IARE. As a result of the new agreement, Steele lost a desirable job in the passenger pool in 1941, replaced by a white fireman who possessed less seniority. Out of work for 16 days, he was next assigned to a more difficult and less-remunerative position in local freight service, where he was again displaced by a junior white fireman and assigned to work on a switch engine. Angered by the unfair treatment, Steele turned to his union, the Birmingham chapter of the IARE, of which he was general chairman. For Steele and other IARE officers, the 1941 agreement and the subsequent legal challenge to it became an organizing tool to generate publicity and enthusiasm among black railroaders. Over the next decade of legal maneuvering, Steele remained a committed activist, representing his men not just in court, but in negotiations with company and white brotherhood officials as well.

Houston filed suit in Alabama court in August 1941. Over the next 3 years, the Steele case made its way through the judicial system. On January 13, 1944, only months after Steele and other black railroaders had publicized their plight by testifying at the federal Fair Employment Practice Committee hearings on discrimination in the railroad industry, the Alabama Supreme Court upheld a lower court's dismissal of Steele's suit. As in earlier rulings, the Alabama court found no constitutional questions or federal action involved. Where Steele's attorneys argued that the white brotherhood "was under a duty to give the minority employees, non-members of the Brotherhood, notice of any action to be taken which would in any manner detrimentally affect their seniority rights," the court found no such duty at all.

Then in December 1944, the U.S. Supreme Court dramatically reversed the lower court's decisions, as well as its own previous stance in cases of racial discrimination under the 1934 Railway Labor Act. In two related cases concerning railway trade unions and racial discrimination in employment—*Steele v. Louisville & Nashville Railroad Company* and *Tunstall v. Brotherhood of Locomotive Firemen and Enginemen*—the court held that the Railway Labor Act that governed union-management relations in the railroad industry implicitly imposed a "duty of fair representation" on the exclusive bargaining agent—in this case, the BLFE. Under the provisions of the Railway Labor Act, the BLFE had been "clothed with power not unlike that of a legislature which is subject to constitutional limitations on its power to deny, restrict, destroy or discriminate against the rights of those for whom it legislates and which is also under an affirmative constitutional duty equally to protect those rights." As the exclusive bargaining agent, the union had to serve as the representative of all members of its craft or class (in this instance locomotive firemen), the minority as well as the majority, nonmembers as well as members. That means that like it or not, the BLFE had to represent fairly the black workers in the class or craft of firemen that it excluded from membership. The court made it clear that the Railway Labor Act did not require the union to admit blacks to membership; indeed it could legally establish its own membership guidelines that explicitly prohibited African-Americans from joining. Yet the act imposed "upon the statutory representative … at least as exacting a duty to protect equally the interests of the members of the craft as the Constitution imposes upon a legislature to give equal protection to the interests of those for whom it legislates." The U.S. Congress had "seen fit to clothe the bargaining representative with powers comparable to those possessed by a legislative body," the court argued, but it had also "imposed upon the representative a corresponding duty . . . to exercise fairly the power conferred upon it in [sic] behalf of all those for which it acts, without hostile discrimination against them." Congress had not intended to "confer plenary power upon the union to sacrifice, for the benefit of its members, rights of the minority of its craft." Discrimination "based on race alone" was "obviously irrelevant and invidious." Such reasoning led the court to conclude that the 1941 contract was unquestionably discriminatory.

The ruling was widely hailed by supporters of civil rights. "[E]very single proposition we have advocated for five years was adopted by the United States Supreme Court," Houston privately but enthusiastically declared. For the black weekly the *Pittsburgh Courier*, the decisions had forever outlawed the nefarious practices of the "unholy alliance of reactionary employers and prejudiced rail unions." The decision was "another milestone in the legal struggle to break down discrimination against Negro Americans," declared NAACP special counsel Thurgood Marshall. The white head of the Fair Employment Practice Committee (FEPC), Malcolm Ross, insisted that the Steele case would in time "be recognized as a Dred Scott decision in reverse," while the white director of the FEPC's San Francisco Office, Harry Kingman, concluded that Houston's accomplishment was "worth many hundreds of the individual cases with which we deal in field operations." As a consequence Houston should be considered "one of the most famous and respected attorneys in the nation."

These assessments and predictions overstated the impact of these decisions. Houston himself realized that considerable legal effort would be required to make the ruling a reality. Moreover he understood clearly the limitations of his victory: The white brotherhoods were still legally free to bar black railroaders from union membership. The issue of racial exclusion in unions had been consciously left off Houston's legal agenda on the grounds that it "may be best that we do not bite off too much at one time." His purpose rather was to lay the groundwork for future challenges. But for Houston's clients—the IARE and the ACRT—the membership issue was hardly a priority; they exhibited little interest in merging into the much larger, more powerful, and hostile white brotherhoods, instead preferring an approach that would allow them to bargain for themselves.

Through the Steele, Tunstall, and numerous other cases over the next 15 years, black workers won tangible if limited gains. As the court toppled barriers to employment and representation, the white railroad brotherhoods erected new ones, although they took pains to disguise their discriminatory intent. Following the Steele decision, Houston predicted accurately that there would be a rush to the courts by the remaining several thousand black firemen who were still suffering under the 1941 contract. Houston, still representing the ACRT and IARE, filed multiple suits, while the Provisional Committee to Organize Colored Locomotive Firemen—an organization formed by A. Philip Randolph in 1941 and supported heavily by his Brotherhood of Sleeping Car Porters—followed an identical path, similarly seeking injunctive relief against the 1941 contract and subsequent revisions. After considerable legal effort, black firemen had emerged more-or-less victorious in their legal struggles against the white brotherhood and various southern railroads to preserve their jobs and respect their seniority by 1952. An internal study conducted for the Provisional Committee in 1954 concluded that "the anti-discrimination injunctions are effective in practice" and found "No over-all patterns of discrimination." The cases of discrimination uncovered, Provisional Committee Attorney Joseph Rauh concluded with satisfaction, were "more or less isolated incidents rather than a pattern of systematic discrimination."

In effectively overturning discriminatory contracts, black railroaders achieved their occupational preservation: They held onto their jobs and secured respect for their seniority rights. But their judicial victories did not address hiring discrimination or the overall loss of jobs brought about by the contraction of the railroad industry. Given the decline in railroad employment in this period, few new black workers replaced their retiring predecessors. Black railroaders were "rapidly passing out of the operating departments" of the railroad industry," Randolph testified before congress in 1962. "In the South today, most of the railway yards have been practically transformed from black to white."

The final and ultimately insurmountable barrier to full black rights was union membership. Over the course of the 1950s, Randolph and his Provisional Committee spearheaded an unsuccessful legal effort to open the firemen's brotherhood and force the admission of African-Americans on the straightforward grounds that the BLFE could not, by definition, represent blacks fairly—that is, exercise its duty of fair representation—if it continued to exclude them from membership In *Oliphant et al. v. BLFE, et al.*, the Provisional Committee's attorneys argued that the BLFE continued to discriminate through its exclusion of blacks from membership. But the court accepted the white union's assertion that no discrimination had taken place, only "legitimate practices used by most unions for reasons other than discrimination." The intent of Congress in passing the Railway Labor Act was the promotion of industrial peace, a goal that would have been undermined had Congress required the admission of blacks into white unions. The white brotherhood was, it concluded, a private association, not a governmental agency. "To compel by judicial mandate membership in voluntary organizations where the Congress has knowingly and expressly permitted the bargaining agent to prescribe its own qualification for membership would be usurping the legislative function," it reasoned. Black workers who continued to feel that union exclusion undermined fair representation needed to look to Congress, not the courts, for change. The Sixth Circuit Court of Appeals upheld the district court's ruling, resolving any doubt about the BLFE's status as a "private association, whose membership policies are its own affair." The following year the Supreme Court denied certiorari. The Provisional Committee's test case in its long campaign to mandate union desegregation through the law had failed. Throughout the mid-1960s, the Supreme Court refused to address the issue of railroad union integration, effectively resolving one of the most significant remaining issues in favor of the white brotherhoods. Only with the passage of the 1964 Civil Rights Act would union membership exclusion and segregation become illegal under federal law.

ERIC ARNESEN

References and Further Reading

Arnesen, Eric. *Brotherhoods of Color: Black Railroad Workers and the Struggle for Equality*. Cambridge, MA: Harvard University Press, 2001.
Chick, C. A. "Some Recent United States Supreme Court Decisions Affecting the Rights of Negro Workers." *Journal of Negro Education* (spring 1947).
Eberlein, E. Larry. "Judicial Regulation of the Railway Brotherhoods' Discriminatory Practices." *Wisconsin Law Review* (May 1953): 516–536.
Herring, Neil M. "The 'Fair Representation' Doctrine: An Effective Weapon against Union Racial Discrimination?" *Maryland Law Review* (spring 1964): 113–165.
Klare, Karl E. "The Quest for Industrial Democracy and the Struggle against Racism: Perspectives from Labor Law and Civil Rights Law." *Oregon Law Review* 61 (Dec. 1982).
Malamud, Deborah C. "The Story of Steele V. Louisville & Nashville Railroad: White Unions, Black Unions, and the Struggle for Racial Justice on the Rails." In *Labor Law Stories* (Laura L. Cooper and Catherine L. Fisk, eds). New York: Foundation Press, 2005: 55–105.
McNeil, Genna Rae. *Groundwork: Charles Hamilton Houston and the Struggle for Civil Rights*. Philadelphia: University of Pennsylvania Press, 1983.

Cases and Statutes Cited

Bester William Steele v. Louisville & Nashville Railroad Company, Brotherhood of Locomotive Firemen and Enginemen, et al., December 18, 1944 (323 U.S. 192, 65 S.Ct. 226)

Civil Rights Act
Lee Oliphant et al. v. Brotherhood of Locomotive Firemen and Enginemen, et al., U.S. Court of Appeals, Sixth Circuit (Cincinnati), No. 13387, November 26, 1958, cited in 9 *FEP Cases* 446–449
Railway Labor Act
Tom Tunstall v. Brotherhood of Locomotive Firemen and Enginemen, Ocean Lodge No. 76, Port Norfolk Lodge No. 775, December 18, 1944 (323 U.S. 210, 65 S. Ct. 235)

See also **Brotherhood of Sleeping Car Porters; Fair Employment Practice Committee; Railroad Brotherhoods; Railway Labor Acts; Randolph, Philip A.**

STEVENS, URIAH (1821–1882)
Founder, Knights of Labor

Uriah S. Stevens was a skilled garment worker and founder of the Knights of Labor. He served as its chief leader as it moved from local to national significance from 1869–1879. The order's most decisive years came after Stevens had shifted his attentions to electoral politics. Still he left his own unique imprint on the organization in its early years.

Born August 3, 1821, in Cape May, New Jersey, Stevens initially hoped to join the Baptist ministry. When the 1837 economic panic hit however, he could no longer afford his religious training and instead entered an apprenticeship under a tailor. In 1845, Stevens moved to Philadelphia to practice his trade. Wanderlust apparently prompted an 1853 journey to Mexico, the Caribbean, Central America. After a 5-year stay in California, he made Philadelphia his home again and immediately threw himself into the abolitionist cause. Perhaps his travels played some role in inspiring his radical antislavery. Perhaps, too, his mother's Quaker roots contributed. At any rate he actively supported the Free Soil party in 1856 and the Republican party in 1860.

In 1862, Stevens helped to found the Garment Cutters' Association of Philadelphia. By 1869, Stevens's union was so weak that its members had voted to abandon it. Nine stubbornly refused to go their separate ways, and led by Stevens, they created a new organization, the Royal Order of the Knights of Labor.

Stevens's ideas shaped the distinctive character of the early knights in three ways. First he intended that the knights reject the exclusiveness of craft unionism and bring the various trades and indeed all labor into one big union. Only by combining could American workers move beyond the wage system, or what Stevens and other Gilded Age labor activists called "wage slavery," to a cooperative society, he believed. Stevens's broad-based approach was interracial as well, although he advocated separate assemblies of black and white workers. Second Stevens insisted that members engage in strict secrecy and intricate rituals. As a longtime member of various fraternal societies, including the Masons and Knights of Pythias, he understood that mystery and ritual cemented members' loyalty to a union, protected them from employer backlash, and encouraged stability. Finally Stevens was unique in the degree to which he saw the relationship between employer and employee in the Gilded Age through the prism of his religious worldview. Certainly many labor leaders drew on religious language and principles in articulating labor's grievances and vision, including Terence Powderly, the Catholic leader of the knights who succeeded Stevens. But in contrast to Powderly, Stevens saw the knights' "brotherhood of producers" as God-ordained and mandated, while Powderly tended to emphasize social and economic justifications for amalgamation.

Under Stevens's leadership, the order grew slowly, from a handful of members in 1869 to only 9,300 10 years later, and it remained limited to Pennsylvania and neighboring states. One reason for this was that members' longstanding culture of craft unionism proved resistant to Stevens's principle of brotherhood. Unskilled workers did not gain entry until the mid-1870s. Also employers' antilabor offensive in the aftermath of the 1877 railway strike made it extremely difficult to organize. Many unions fell apart under the pressure of blacklists, lockouts, and (because the late 1870s were depression years) intense labor competition. In addition the knights' strict secrecy impeded growth.

The movement to end secrecy gained ground in the late 1870s. Besides the concern about growth, the knights' mainly Catholic membership was also anxious about opposition from the Catholic church and the public's negative view of secret organizations in the wake of the trial and execution of accused Molly Maguires, a secret association responsible for assassinating mine owners in Pennsylvania. Stevens adamantly opposed any compromises on secrecy and rituals, because in his eyes these were essential to nurturing bonds among divided and demoralized workers. But compromises there were, most of which Powderly sponsored. Consequently Stevens permanently left office in 1879, and Powderly took his place as grand master workman.

Stevens also left the knights because like many labor activists, he was drawn as an individual to electoral politics during the depression of the late 1870s. In 1878, he was a delegate to the Greenback-Labor party convention and the party's nominee to represent Philadelphia in Congress. He lost the election. Stevens died in 1882. It is a measure of his stature in the order as well as his distance from it that in the late 1880s, Powderly's opponents, who shared little with Stevens's ideologically, nonetheless identified their cause with him.

THERESA A. CASE

References and Further Reading

McLaurin, Melton Alonza. *The Knights of Labor in the South.* Westport, CT: Greenwood Press, 1978.

Voss, Kim. *The Making of American Exceptionalism: The Knights of Labor and Class Formation in the Nineteenth Century.* New York: Cornell University Press, 1993.

Ware, Norman J. *The Labor Movement in the United States, 1860–1895: A Study in Democracy.* Glouchester, MA: Peter Smith, 1959. (reprint,1929)

See also **Knights of Labor**

STEWARD, IRA (1831–1883)
Eight-Hour Day Activist

Few labor leaders in American history have devoted themselves so doggedly to a single legislative reform as did Ira Steward. Born in 1831, a man of little formal education, he was a laborer's son who was sent to work as a machinist' apprentice as a youth, Steward nonetheless left his mark on the thinking of an entire generation of American labor leaders. Over the 30 years of his 8-hour campaign, there were few labor reform papers that did not publish something he had written. Practically everything Steward wrote was a weapon in his battle for the 8-hour day; indeed so persistently did he charge up this same hill that even his labor allies came to refer to him as the "8-hour monomaniac." In the end Steward was victorious, not in achieving his dream during his lifetime, but in placing the 8-hour demand and his justifications for it at the forefront of labor's agenda.

Steward did not set out to establish a new economic paradigm for the labor movement. He was a practical man who worked out his theories to attain a practical end: The reduction of the hours of labor. His first task was to persuade the membership of his own International Union of Machinists and Blacksmiths to embrace the cause. Skilled workers at the time were skeptical of short-hour demands, which in their minds could be purchased only at the cost of reduced wages. Rather than attempt to skirt these all-important bread-and-butter issues, Steward chose to attack them head-on, a tactic he may have learned from his long association with Boston's abolitionists. Accordingly he introduced his fellow machinists and blacksmiths to the bold slogan, "a reduction of hours is an increase in wages."

The linchpin on which the entire superstructure of Steward's argument rested was the idea that the general level of wages was determined by the "habits, customs, and opinions" of the workers themselves. The idea that wages rise to the level of culture and character of the worker has its roots in Thomas Malthus and John Stuart Mill, but the elaboration and popularization of it was clearly Steward's own accomplishment. Given shorter hours, Steward argued in a writing style that was plain, direct, and unadorned with jargon, workers collectively would cultivate their habits, wants, and desires and gradually demand increasing pay to meet these newfound needs. But there was an even greater reward than higher wages: With rising wages and greater consumption, the wheels of industry would turn more quickly to meet the growing demand. Capitalists would be encouraged to make their workplaces more productive by introducing new workers, machinery, and technologies; as output increased and unit costs fell, so would prices. Not only were shorter hours going to deliver higher wages, but they also promised to make those wages go farther in the market.

While his theory contained much hope and promise for the anxious workingmen of the Reconstruction years, Steward was careful also to point out the stumbling blocks strewn across the road to the 8-hour day. Chief among these was a corollary of his first principle—the ability of workers to demand greater wages depended on the ability of all workers to uplift their habits and character; a few stragglers in the line of progress could hold back all the rest. How many stragglers it took to hold back the mass of rising workers was unclear; at times in his writings it appeared as though a single degraded worker was enough. In listing his 8-hour principles, Steward emphasized that progress depended on unanimity. "Where all ask for more wages, there will be no motive for refusing, since employers will all fare alike." Such solidarity had been labor's dream since its inception. But by founding this consensus not on moral suasion or the perfection of labor's organizations, but on the hard rock of the material, intrinsic character of the workers themselves—what Steward termed the "habits, customs, and opinions of the masses" that were "the strongest power in the world"—Steward insisted that such unified action was possible at last. All must rise together, he warned, or none will rise at all.

American labor was ready for Steward's ideas. By 1863, Steward had convinced his own union and the Boston Trades Assembly to proclaim the 8-hour reform "the cardinal point to which our movement ought to be directed." That fall the most influential labor paper in the nation, *Fincher's Trades' Review*, jumped onto Steward's bandwagon, adopting a new masthead that read, "Eight Hours. A Legal Day's Work for Freemen."

Steward made a shaky alliance with the Radical Republicans and former abolitionists of the Bay State by founding the Boston Eight-Hour League in 1869. The league scored one important victory in its first year, successfully lobbying for the establishment of the Massachusetts Bureau of Labor Statistics, the nation's first. Steward's influence was evident throughout the bureau's first annual report (1870), a report that was largely written by his close associate, George McNeill, assisted by Steward's wife Mary Bowers Steward (a longtime activist in her own right, having been secretary of the Hopedale utopian community when she wed Ira), who for many years lent her clerical services to the bureau.

Over the following decade, Steward published many influential pamphlets and columns, including "A Reduction of Hours, an Increase in Wages" (1865), and "Poverty" (1873), which were reprinted in many newspapers and quoted from rostrums across the land. Steward embarked on the writing of a definitive book on the 8-hour question, which he planned on entitling, "The Political Economy of Eight Hours," but he died before it could be finished in 1883.

TIMOTHY MESSER-KRUSE

References and Further Reading

Glickman, Lawrence. "Workers of the World, Consume: Ira Steward and the Origins of Labor Consumerism." *International Labor and Working Class History* 52, 3 (1997): 72–86.

Messer-Kruse, Timothy. "Eight Hours, Greenbacks, and 'Chinamen': Wendell Phillips, Ira Steward, and the Fate of Labor Reform in Massachusetts." *Labor History* 42, 2 (2001): 133–158.

Roediger, David, and Philip S. Foner. *Our Own Time: A History of American Labor and the Working Day.* Westport, CT: Greenwood Press, 1989.

STOCKYARDS LABOR COUNCIL

The Chicago Federation of Labor (CFL) created the Stockyards' Labor Council (SLC) on July 23, 1917 after a meeting between William Z. Foster and Robert McQueen, both of the Railway Carmen, and Dennis Lane and Joe O'Kane of the Cattle Butchers' Local 87 at the CFL headquarters on July 15, 1917. The purpose of the labor council was to provide an organization to unify all unions with jurisdiction over stockyard employees under one organizing body. Martin Murphy, a hog butcher from Chicago, was elected president of the SLC, and Foster served as the organization's first secretary.

The success of the SLC would ultimately depend on its ability to cross craft, racial, and ethnic lines. Under the direction of a central organizing body, the SLC worked carefully to display a united front within the yards and worked carefully to avoid open competition with other stockyard locals. To facilitate this endeavor, each affiliated union appointed representatives to work directly with the labor council. This helped prevent rivalries and ensured no conflicts of jurisdiction. With the beginning of American involvement in World War I, the SLC worked closely with the already established Amalgamated Meat Cutters and Butcher Workmen (AMC) to mobilize public support and to organize the packinghouse industry. Although the AMC and the SLC officially remained separate entities, the SLC's recruitment of black workers eventually forced the AMC to reconsider its own treatment of African-Americans and immigrants in the industry and changed the way labor organizers in the industry would address race and ethnicity issues.

In addition to determining the most effective way to recruit new members, Murphy and Foster struggled with how best to gain the support of the other craft unions. Drawing on an endorsement from the CFL, the SLC was able to access the vast labor- organizing resources of Chicago and began its first mass-organizing drive in 1917. At its first meeting, an estimated 10,000 workers attended. Unfortunately after this first meeting very few of those in attendance joined the fledgling group, since some feared the reprisal of packinghouse officials while others remembered the failed 1904 packinghouse strikes and were unwilling to throw their full support behind the union effort.

The SLC did recover from these disappointing results and began a new round of organizing. Subsequent attempts did attract a number of new members, especially after news that the SLC had prepared a list of demands that included a wage increase, gender-equitable pay scale, and an 8-hour day for presentation to the packers. With these demands in place, the SLC next focused its efforts by organizing their members. Rather than organizing members into skill or company unions, the SLC organized people according to neighborhood locals to best avoid ethnic conflict. This strategy was especially successful among Polish and Lithuanian workers who provided some of the strongest support for the SLC.

In spite of the strong central European support, there were still serious concerns as to the best way to reach out to and organize African-American stockyard workers. This was difficult because a number of black civic, fraternal, and religious organizations relied on the philanthropic activities of the packinghouse owners to maintain the operations of their institutions. In return many African-American community leaders cautioned their members against becoming too involved with the SLC. For example one influential church leader lectured his congregation that the interests of African-Americans were tied to the economic development of the country and of the white interests that control it. The SLC officials also faced difficulties enlisting the aid of important black newspapers, since these organizations often cautioned workers to proceed carefully before dealing with the union. In addition to the resistance to the union movement by African-American institutions, black workers, especially new arrivals from the South, found greater opportunity by aligning themselves with the packers, especially as companies like Swift directed its operations to fire labor unionists and replace them with black workers in 1917–1918.

Moreover African-Americans still remained apprehensive toward the SLC because of the policy of creating neighborhood locals. Some saw these institutions as merely an extension of the Jim Crow unionism of the American Federation of Labor. Under this plan African-Americans would feel free to attend union meetings in white communities and white members would be encouraged to attend meetings in black communities. However instead of motivating interracialism, this plan advanced *de facto* segregation, since African-Americans rarely attended meetings in white neighborhoods, and white workers avoided meetings in black enclaves. Despite the latent racial tension, the SLC continued to reach out to African-American workers by hiring more black organizers and electing an African-American hog butcher, A. K. Foote, vice-president in 1917.

Over time, the SLC made slight inroads with African-American workers but still failed to attract the mass support of southern black newcomers coming North in search of employment and still distrustful of unionization. By November of 1917, both the SLC and the packinghouse owners continued to look for support among black workers in preparation for labor unrest that many thought was imminent. As the packers continued to court black civic and religious groups, the SLC members authorized their leaders to launch a nationwide strike. At this same time the coalition between the SLC and the AMC began to splinter. The AMC leadership refused to support the proposed strike, since such action, some believed, violated the World War I no-strike pledges. However this debate was rendered moot when the President's Mediation Commission interceded, since any strike within the yards would negatively impact wartime meat production. Instead employers and union officials agreed to allow a federal arbitrator, Judge Samuel S. Alschuler, to settle any dispute through binding arbitration for the duration of the war.

By the spring of 1919, the war in Europe concluded and the packers, and the SLC and other organizations within the stockyards seemed headed for a confrontation. With the end of binding arbitration imminent, the SLC sought to increase its organizational profile and membership totals by staging a series of mass meetings and rallies. These meetings were designed to pressure packinghouse owners into recognizing the union and to demonstrate to African-American workers, many of whom still were leery of unionization, that the labor council's rhetoric of interracial cooperation was genuine. In addition to the rallies, the SLC sponsored a parade and union picnic to highlight further its commitment to racial solidarity.

Much of the work done to improve race relations in the yards was undermined by a race riot in the summer of 1919. During the riot the SLC and the CFL tried to maintain peace among the workers and maintain the organization by holding a mass, interracial meeting to encourage the rank-and-file not to return to work until the unrest had been settled. This measure appeared to have been successful, since there were no major incidents inside the yards. The situation changed however when 49 homes occupied by Lithuanian workers were burned, leaving hundreds of residents homeless. Although rumors circulated that African-Americans committed the crime, evidence to the contrary suggested that Irish gangs set the fires to incite racial conflict between the two groups.

While the SLC was struggling with internal discord, new challenges from a former ally, the AMC, developed. Following the war the SLC and meat cutters wrestled over the question of renewing the arbitration agreement, which the AMC supported, or launching a strike in the yards, a position held by the SLC. This conflict reached its epoch in April 1919 as the AMC, without consulting the rank-and-file, signed a recognition agreement with the packers and established the District Council 9, who claimed jurisdiction over all the butchers in the stockyards. This move not only threatened to re-establish occupational and class divisions in the yards, but also caused considerable confusion, since both District 9 and the SLC claimed to represent the butcher workmen.

This conflict continued until 1920 when the CFL convinced District 9 and the SLC to participate in an election to determine which organization would represent their interests. The workers decided to retain the SCL, and in response District 9 refused to accept the results. Before this new situation could be rectified, allegations surfaced that SLC leader John Kikulski—himself a veteran organizer since the 1904 unionization drive; an activist in the Polish National Alliance; and publisher of the Polish language paper, *Glose Rabotnica* or *Labor's Voice*, had embezzled money intended to aid striking butchers in Detroit, Michigan. After the allegations surfaced, Kikulski resigned from the SLC, taking a large number of his Polish and Lithuanian supporters with him, and joined District 9, where he was soon to be elected president. Despite the fact that an SLC investigation revealed Kikulski's guilt, many of his Slavic supporters still remained loyal to him and to District 9. Without the strong support from immigrant labor in the yards, and after months of organizational struggles, the SLC resigned from the CFL in 1920 and ceased operations.

LIONEL KIMBLE, JR.

References and Further Reading

Barrett, James R. *Work and Community in the Jungle: Chicago's Packinghouse Workers, 1894–1922.* Urbana: University of Illinois Press, 1987.

Cohen, Lizabeth. *Making of a New Deal: Industrial Workers in Chicago, 1919–1939.* Cambridge, UK: Cambridge University Press, 1991.

Halpern, Rick. *Down on the Killing Floor: Black and White Workers in Chicago's Packinghouses, 1904–54.* Urbana: University of Illinois Press, 1997.

Herbst, Alma. *The Negro in the Slaughtering and Meatpacking Industry in Chicago.* New York: Arno Publishing, 1971.

Slayton, Robert A. *Back of the Yards: The Making of a Local Democracy.* Chicago, IL: University of Chicago Press, 1988.

STOKES, ROSE PASTOR (JULY 18, 1879–JUNE 20, 1933)
Activist and Writer

Rose Pastor Stokes was born Rose Harriet Wieslander in Augustowo, Poland, then part of the Russian empire and subject to the increasingly frequent and violent Jewish pogroms. Her parents, Jacob Wieslander, a boot maker, and Hindl Lewin, separated when Stokes was young, and she and her mother moved first to Germany before settling in London's East End slum with her aunt. There her mother found work in a garment factory, and Stokes briefly attended a free Jewish school, but her childhood was marked primarily by grinding poverty. One of her earliest memories was of her mother leading a strike in her London factory when the owner whitewashed the windows, blocking the workers' view. When Stokes was 10, her mother married Isaac Pastor, a peddler, who soon left his new family to seek his fortune abroad. Her mother, pregnant with Pastor's child, took in sewing, and Stokes left school to help her mother at home. After the birth of her stepbrother, Rose, her mother, and the new baby immigrated to the United States, meeting Isaac Pastor in Cleveland, Ohio, in 1890. But once again Stokes, though only 11, needed to help her family, and she found work in a Cleveland cigar factory. Over the next dozen years, Stokes toiled long hours for low pay making cigars in both sizable factories and small shops in the owner's home, known as a "buckeye." Although her formal education ended, it was in the cigar-making shops of Cleveland that Stokes first heard of socialism as a solution to the exploitative work conditions under which she and millions of others toiled. Absorbing what she could from the local public library and like-minded co-workers, Stokes also sought redress through trade unionism. As a female Stokes was relegated to the least skilled, lowest paid positions within the cigar industry, but when she and her coworkers applied for a charter from the Cigar Makers' Union, they were rejected on the grounds that they were unskilled.

Shortly after Stokes moved away from socialism for a time as she began writing for the New York City-based *Jewish Daily News* (*Yidisher Tageblatt*) while still working at her Cleveland cigar shop. In March 1903, the paper offered Stokes a fulltime position on its staff, and she moved to New York, quickly becoming an avid observer of the city's vibrant immigrant community on the Lower East Side. She wrote various articles, many of which focused on working women such as herself, and under the pen name of Zelda, Stokes also wrote a regular advice column, "Just between Ourselves, Girls," in which she encouraged her readers to be well-behaved, even docile workers, a far cry from her earlier sentiments while toiling in the cigar shops of Cleveland. In 1905, while interviewing several Lower East Side settlement workers and philanthropists, the young reporter met James Graham Phelps Stokes. Graham Stokes, as he was known, was a graduate of both Yale University and Columbia University's Medical College and belonged to a wealthy and prominent New York family. Despite his considerable wealth and social privilege, Graham Stokes was drawn to settlement work, part of the Progressive Era's response to the misery caused by industrial capitalism. The young couple were drawn to each other, and their 1905 marriage drew headlines for its "Cinderella-like" qualities. She was the immigrant Jewish cigar maker, he was old native-stock, Protestant, and wealthy. Despite these vast differences, the marriage worked, at least for the first 12 years during which both Stokeses were active Socialists. She was an especially popular speaker for the socialist cause before both working-class audiences and the more well-to-do. In socialism she saw the remedy for the exploitative conditions of labor and dire poverty that she herself had so long experienced. Yet it was her new-found position as the wife of a wealthy man that seemingly freed Stokes to express so eloquently her radical politics, as she did during the 1909 garment makers' strike known as the "Uprising of the 20,000" and again in the 1912 New York hotel waiters' strike.

Like many Socialists in 1917 who initially supported U.S. entry into World War I, both Graham and Rose Pastor Stokes resigned from the party, which remained steadfastly antiwar. But the Bolshevik revolution later that same year changed her thinking—and caused an irrevocable rift in the marriage. Stokes returned to the Socialist party, speaking out against the war and was soon charged with espionage. Although her conviction was eventually overturned, that her husband's uncle provided evidence against her further distanced Stokes from her increasingly conservative husband. They were officially divorced in 1925. By then Stokes had become a leader in the newly formed Communist party, though she was among only a handful of women to do so within its male-dominated hierarchy. She was present at the party's first American convention in 1919 and for several years after was a member of the central executive committee of the Workers' party, the above-ground arm of the Communist party that had been driven underground in the United States shortly after its formation. Throughout the 1920s, Stokes spoke passionately and wrote eloquently on the lesser status of working-class women under industrial capitalism. She was equally interested in working for racial equality and saw in the Communist party the solution to the impact of racism on African-Americans. At the Fourth Congress of the Communist International, held in Moscow in 1922, Stokes presented the "Thesis on the Negro Question," in which she argued that African-Americans had a particular interest and an important role to play in the revolutionary struggle. Her motion was accepted by the Fourth Congress and would be the guiding force regarding race within the Communist party for years to come. Although the 1920s were generally productive and personally fulfilling years, including a second marriage to fellow Communist Jerome Isaac Romain in 1927, Stokes's happiness was short-lived. Diagnosed with breast cancer early in 1930, Stokes followed up a mastectomy with special radiation treatments available only in Germany, where she died in 1933, shortly after Adolf Hitler came to power. She spent the last 3 years of her life bravely fighting her terminal disease while feverishly working when able to finish her autobiography. Although it lay unfinished at her death, the autobiography—its very title of *I Belong to the Working Class* summing up Stokes's perception of herself—remains a passionate and elegant account of one activist's efforts on behalf of workers everywhere.

KATHLEEN BANKS NUTTER

Selected Works

Stokes, Rose Pastor. *I Belong to the Working Class*. 1992.
———. Personal papers. New Haven, CT: Sterling Library, Yale University.
Zipster, Pearl, and Arthur Zipster. *Fire and Grace: The Life of Rose Pastor Stokes*. 1989.

See also **Communist Party; Jews; Progressive Era; Socialist Party of America**

STRASSER, ADOLPH (1849–1936)
Cofounder, American Federation of Labor

Adolph Strasser, leader of the Cigar Makers International Union and one of the cofounders of the American Federation of Labor (AFL), belongs to a group of largely forgotten American labor leaders whose influence on the course of mainstream unionism was considerable in the late nineteenth century. A close associate of Samuel Gompers in the early years of the AFL, he steered the cigar makers and parts of the New York labor movement away from ethnic unionism in the 1870s and away from socialism in the 1880s. By the end of the 1880s, he had become one of the foremost proponents of what came to be known as "pure and simple unionism."

Strasser was born in 1849 in Hungary and immigrated (probably via London) to the United States in 1872. While very little was known about his background even among his close associates, the multilingual Strasser (he spoke German and English) was active in the labor movement of New York City from the time of his arrival there. Strasser joined the First International soon after his arrival but was expelled from it after his role in the Tompkins Square riot was criticized by the leaders of the group. He then helped found the Social Democratic Workingman's party in 1873 and became its secretary. Strasser also belonged to an organization of like-minded immigrant Socialists from Central and Western Europe, the Economic and Sociological Club, where he met the young Gompers.

In 1874, Strasser became active in the cigar makers union. To counteract the politically passive and exclusionary craft union in that trade, he and a group of politically minded fellow workers (Gompers among them) founded the United Cigar Makers of North America in 1874, a union that welcomed workers of all ethnic backgrounds and varying skill levels. In 1875, the group became Local 144 of the Cigar Makers' International Union (CMIU) of North America. Gompers served as president, Strasser was vice-president of the local, and a year later, Strasser became president of the CMIU whose journal he also edited. Strasser and Gompers together soon gained a political profile as union leaders in the city when they founded the Amalgamated Trades and Labor Union of New York City in 1877 and found themselves leading a lengthy strike of New York cigar makers in the fall of 1877. Even though the strike was neither started nor initially approved by the union Strasser led, he became the *de facto* leader of the movement for better wages and working conditions in the tenement-based cigar trade in New York City. The strike brought out Strasser's strengths as a tough-minded but practical organizer, whose energy for the cause outweighed his relative political inflexibility.

After the loss of the strike, Strasser continued to lead the CMIU. His primary interest was in stabilizing the membership and providing a fixed set of benefits for union members even if that meant limiting membership to relatively well-paid workers in the trade. Strasser spoke out in the labor movement's fight against Chinese workers (which preoccupied the cigar workers on the West Coast), testifying before the Senate Committee on Education and Labor in 1883 as a supporter of pragmatic, depoliticized trade unionism.

By the time of Strasser's testimony before the U.S. Senate, he had already become a controversial figure in the New York City labor movement, where his home base lay. Strasser's increasing distance from grassroots socialist movements in the city and his focus on lobbying the New York State legislature to prohibit cigar making in tenements, alienated him from many immigrant constituents who favored a more political unionism. In 1882, members of Local 144 voted a slate of socialist candidates into leadership positions. When Strasser (with the support of Gompers) disqualified the newly elected president of Local 144 and declared the election invalid, the cigar makers' union split nationwide into the Cigar Makers' Progressive Union and the Cigar Makers' International Union.

During the 4 years of dual unionism in the cigar trade, Strasser remained president of the CMIU and together with Gompers and a small group of craft unionists started the Federation of Trades and Labor Unions (FOTLU) in 1882 to provide a lobbying arm for organized labor. The federation became the foundation for the AFL, which he helped found as well in 1886.

Opposition from Socialists, especially in New York City, continued to dodge Strasser even after the reunification of the cigar makers' union in 1886. In the late 1880s, his outspoken and inflexible manner continued to cost him support within the union and in the New York City labor movement where he continued to fight with Socialists and politically active Knights of Labor. When Strasser opposed a change in the constitution of the Cigar Makers' International Union in 1891 that would affect the election of the international president, he found himself in opposition to Gompers and resigned his presidency of the union.

In subsequent years Strasser worked as an organizer and speaker for the cigar makers and the AFL, making his base in Buffalo, New York. Much of his work during this latter time did not provide much visibility for this erstwhile union president. Strasser retired from union work in 1914 at the age of 65 and became a real estate agent. He moved to Florida in 1918 and died in Lakeland, Florida, in obscurity and poverty on January 1, 1936.

DOROTHEE SCHNEIDER

References and Further Reading

Cooper, Patricia. "Whatever Happened to Adolph Strasser?" *Labor History* 20, 3 (1979).
Gitelman, Howard. "Adolph Strasser and the Origins of Pure and Simple Unionism." *Labor History* 6, 1 (1964).

See also **American Federation of Labor (up to CIO merger); Tompkins Square Riot (1874)**

STRIKE WAVE (1919)

In 1919, more American workers than ever before took collective action to create a new and better way of living for themselves. Over four million employed workers, one out of every five, were involved in a strike, a proportion that has not been surpassed before or since. In this extraordinary and truly decisive year, it was often not just the basic terms of employment that were at issue. The famously conservative railway brotherhoods, as well as prominent dissidents in the largest American union, the United Mine Workers, advocated nationalization of their industries. A vast strike challenged the governance of the steel industry, the heart of the nation's economic and military preponderance. The chairman of the strike committee, John Fitzpatrick, an American Federation of Labor unionist supposedly working directly under the indubitably patriotic Samuel Gompers, declared at one point that "we are going to socialize the basic industries of the United States."

The year 1919 was supposed to be the year of a great reconstruction of American industrial society. At the turn of the century and during World War I, progressives and working-class activists in numerous different factories, union halls, and government offices had experimented with new kinds of organizations that they thought might bring about the dream of production guided by social needs. For at least a decade before the beginning of the war, reformers had brought to the forefront of American consciousness the labor question. This was the problem of how to maintain the viability of a democratic polity in the face of profound changes in the workplace caused by exponential industrialization and unrelenting corporate consolidation. Despite its continuing attraction to millions of immigrant workers, the United States at the turn of the twentieth century was the most violent nation on earth when measured in terms of the ferocity of its strikes and various other forms of open conflict between working people and their employers.

The ideology and practices of scientific management, the open shop, and "Fordism" were at best uneasily accommodated by an astonishingly diverse workforce. The new factory regime of the twentieth century depended on workers whose various experiences included peasant economies or craft production, workers' control and Taylorism, socialism and the Republican party, the Industrial Workers of the World (IWW) and the American Federation of Labor (AFL), collectivism and nativism, sharecropping and iron molding, racism and respectability, family economy and the boardinghouse, factory paternalism and anonymous machine tending. The most common form of worker resistance, quitting, was endemic. In 1919, there was a kind of coalescence of aims, an attempt to apply or re-interpret the meaning of American freedom and democracy in the workplace in ways that might profoundly alter the new economic order. However despite challenges, by the end of 1919 and the beginning of the next presidential administration, the dominance of large corporations over American life remained secure.

The immediate causes of the strike wave of 1919 came out of the crisis of World War I. For labor the war created unprecedented opportunities. By early 1915, war orders were pouring into U.S. industry, helping to pull the nation out of the sharp economic downturn that had begun in 1914. As American industrialists mobilized their plants for much higher levels of production, and the cutoff of immigration sharply increased the demand for labor, workers sensed a new power and flexibility. As progressives had envisioned, with American entrance into the war, state-coordinated planning boards took over large sectors of the economy. The federal government took over the railroads and telegraphs and threatened seizure of Chicago's giant meatpacking plants in response to labor unrest there.

Gompers, the head of the AFL, pledged his support of the war effort. He forced through the federation's executive council a resolution to respect existing standards of industry during the war. Partly as a

Strike leader at Gary, Ind., advising strikers. Library of Congress, Prints & Photographs Division [LC-USZ62-77539].

result of Gompers's efforts to gain legitimacy and positions for the AFL in the administrative arms of the government's war agencies, union membership increased by about two million during the war. Labor's influence within the Wilson administration was evident everywhere in Washington. A former mine workers' official, William Wilson, had been appointed the first secretary of labor. In 1917, Woodrow Wilson became the first president to appear before a convention of the AFL. He declared that while American troops fought for freedom abroad, the nation must ensure the freedom of labor at home. In April of 1918, the National War Labor Board (NWLB) was created; the influence of cochairman (with William Howard Taft) Frank Walsh made it the most prolabor agency the federal government had ever created. In July of 1918, the NWLB decided that Bethlehem Steel should recognize workers' shop committees elected under the board's oversight; in October the board asked U.S. Steel's chairman, Elbert Gary, to grant the 8-hour day to his employees. By the time it had ceased functioning in the summer of 1919, the board had issued over 200 decisions that ordered collective-bargaining agreements with employees and had created over 100 independent shop committees in nonunion plants. Although the federal government's influence in the arena of labor

relations began to dissipate following the armistice in November 1918, it was in the context of state intervention or sanction that new, often more inclusive forms of workers' organization gained a tenuous legitimacy in a number of different industries, most notably in meatpacking, steel, and electrical manufacturing.

The first major strike of 1919 did not fit neatly into the template of corporate compromise and the government-labor entente that had emerged during the war. The Seattle General Strike had its origins in a decision by the city's 35,000 shipyard workers to authorize a strike against the U.S. Government Emergency Fleet Corporation 2 weeks after the armistice. When 110 locals of the Seattle Central Labor Council endorsed a general strike in support of the shipyard workers, the hierarchy of the AFL internationals was vehemently against the new movement. The Seattle labor movement was strongly influenced by radicals from the IWW and Socialist party and had often issued resolutions in support of the Bolshevik revolution. A General Strike Committee ran city services efficiently during the strike itself. The mayor and state attorney general requested and received federal troops to help suppress the strike, which was now overlaid with anxieties, spreading across the nation's headlines, about Bolshevism and revolution. The unions themselves voted to end the peaceful strike, but nonetheless a challenge had been forcefully made to the postwar delineation of labor's freedom.

The tactic of organizing beyond the boundaries of traditional union jurisdictions and developing the potential for larger general or sympathy strikes was one of the most important characteristics of the 1919 strikes. In the public mind, the general strike was associated mostly with the IWW, but before the war, expansive "system federations" of unions had been formed on the railways by rank-and-file activists and militant AFL locals. In 1917–1918, both a Stockyards' Labor Council and a National Committee for Organizing Iron and Steel Workers were established by militant minorities representing federated AFL unions. In February of 1919, the United Textile Workers announced a national strike movement for the 48-hour week, and silk workers in Paterson, New Jersey, organized a coalition of immigrant societies to present strike demands. In April an outlaw railroad strike began in Chicago and spread rapidly south and west; Attorney General A. Mitchell Palmer had 23 strike leaders arrested. In response to the unrest, President Wilson appointed a Railway Labor Board, which awarded a wage increase. On July 4, New York City put 11,000 police on alert, and there were mobilizations of troops in Boston and Chicago for an anticipated general strike in support of Tom Mooney, a radical convicted for the bombing of a Preparedness Day parade in San Francisco in 1916. Three general strikes in Canadian cities also made a deep impression.

A vitally important factor in considering the outcomes of the largest strikes in 1919 was the growing antiradical mood of the country at the time. Since President Wilson was occupied to a large extent following the armistice with questions of foreign policy and the progress of freedom and self-determination abroad, an angry red-scare mentality combined with ugly manifestations of racism and nativism surfaced at home. Strikes, protests, and any manifestations of left-wing sympathy with the Bolshevik revolution were exaggerated by the press as representing dangerous threats to American freedom. The Seattle General Strike at the beginning of the year was widely described as being led by Bolsheviks and Wobblies. In March the Supreme Court upheld the conviction of Eugene Debs for violating the Espionage Act; and the socialist leader was sentenced to 10 years in prison. In the spring several bombings occurred that were allegedly instigated by radicals, and in April a Post Office official intercepted 36 bombs that were to be delivered to prominent Americans. In June a large bomb devastated the front of A. Mitchell Palmer's house in Washington. In August and September the Communist and Communist Labor parties were founded in

Chicago; both organizations immediately turned their attention to endorsing mass strikes across the nation.

The outcome of the Boston police strike in early September quite dramatically illustrated the political potential of swelling antilabor and anti-Communist sentiment. Public opinion was from the beginning quite unfavorable to the strike; looting, chaos, and dangerous Bolshevik-inspired mobs were widely anticipated if and when the policemen left their posts. Thousands of Bostonians were mobilized into citizen defense committees to maintain order. There was some isolated looting. The city's Central Labor Union refused to endorse the strike, and Gompers proposed the police return to work pending arbitration. Governor Calvin Coolidge however declared that "there is no right to strike against the public safety by anybody, anywhere, anytime." He called in the national guard, fired all the strikers, and hired replacements. Coolidge's actions were widely publicized and propelled his political career. On his western speaking tour to gain support for the League of Nations, President Wilson called the strike "a crime against civilization."

The Boston police strike was still in progress when the National Committee to Organize Iron and Steel Workers announced that U.S. steelworkers had voted for a nationwide strike to begin September 22. It was the Great Steel Strike that best represented the many forces at work in the industrial warfare of 1919. It was the largest single walkout the nation had yet witnessed, with over 250,000 workers eventually striking under the auspices of a committee of AFL-affiliated organizers. The national committee was a hybrid creature of craft and industrial unionists, with William Z. Foster, a former Wobbly and syndicalist at its head. Before sending out the strike call, the committee appealed unsuccessfully to Elbert Gary for a conference, then to President Wilson for mediation, declaring that Gary's "kaiserism" made a mockery of the democratic ideals of the war. Gompers himself turned against the strike when Wilson proposed a national industrial conference of labor, employers and the public to consider postwar labor issues. However Foster and his cadre of organizers had built up a strong momentum among the rank-and-file for action, and the strike went on as scheduled.

The fact that the steel strike was strongly supported by immigrant communities in and around the mills and that it was organized by Foster, an avowed syndicalist who made only a hesitant repudiation of his earlier radical writings when questioned by a Senate committee, raised the issue of Americanism in the labor movement quite sharply. There were at least 30 different nationalities represented among the strikers, many of whom were Eastern Europeans inspired by the overthrow of autocracy in their homelands. The dynamics of the strike also clarified racial divisions that had emerged during the "great migration" of over 450,000 southern blacks to northern cities during the war. In 1917, a vicious race riot had erupted in East Saint Louis as a result of union exclusion of blacks; in the summer of 1919 a large race riot broke out in Chicago that helped undermine the solidarity of the packinghouse and steel workers' organizations that had established a tenuous hold there. During the steel strike itself, the city of Gary was placed under martial law following riots by strikers against African-American strikebreakers imported by the steelmakers. Foster himself observed after the strike that blacks had not hesitated to work as strikebreakers because of the discrimination traditionally practiced by many of the AFL unions involved in the steel-organizing campaign and strike.

The steel strike was carried out quite effectively in its first weeks. The nature of the movement that Foster and the national committee had helped to build was illustrated by the fact that several large mills had struck before the official call was put out. It was largely a movement inspired by rank-and-file energy and resentments, but under the guidance also of Foster with his extraordinary organizing ability, the strike showed once and for all that a nationwide strike against mass-production industry was possible.

Six weeks after the beginning of the steel strike, John L. Lewis announced a nationwide strike of coal miners. A settlement known as the Washington agreement had been negotiated between the United Mine Workers of America (UMW) and the coal operators in 1917 that set wage increases, prohibited discharge of miners for union membership, and laid fines against wildcat strikers for the duration of the war or until April 1, 1920, whichever should come first. The operators however continued to hold the agreement in effect after the armistice, and steadily rising prices after the war overtook the miners' wage gains. Wildcat strikes continued after the war in many mines. After Lewis issued the strike call, President Wilson denounced the impending strike as unlawful and immoral, and Attorney General A. Mitchell Palmer gained an injunction prohibiting the UMW leadership from participating in the strike. Despite a decision by the UMW Executive Committee to call off the strike in the face of government pressure and escalating accusations of mob rule and Bolshevism against the strike in the press, numerous independent unions stayed away from the mines. The miners eventually gained a wage increase brokered by the Wilson administration, but Socialists, Communists, and independent district leaders continued to press the grievances of discontented miners through the early 1920s.

In October, as steel strikers and organizers were being violently dispersed in Pennsylvania, the Wilson administration convened a national industrial conference in Washington to consider the democratization of industry. Gary maintained at once that the conference had no jurisdiction or power to compel a settlement in the steel conflict. The conference deadlocked on the issue of union recognition; the employers by a narrow majority refused to accede to bargaining with outside representatives of the workers. Still according to historian David Brody, the industrial conference must be judged a partial success for labor. Negotiations and resolutions during the conference revealed an informal, near consensus of union men, the public, and many of the employers that workers must be entitled to collective bargaining with representatives of their own choosing. According to Brody the conference laid the conceptual and ideological groundwork for the Wagner Act of 1935.

The strike wave of 1919 died amid the furor of the Red Scare, with its identification of strikers, immigrants, and dissenters against the new industrial order as "un-American." As well the strike wave illustrated the limitations of the new unionism of the prewar era, with its broadening of the extent and scope of union action to include federations, local councils, common organizing campaigns, and strikes and extension of jurisdictions to include African-Americans, women, and the unskilled. State suppression, vigilante attacks, and divisions in the labor movement undermined the inchoate but vigorous movement for industrial democracy. A sharp depression in 1921 and a renewed open-shop drive by employers further weakened the labor movement. By the end of 1919, the new capitalism of Fordism, Taylorism, labor-management cooperation, and corporate welfare policies had gained a new momentum and legitimacy in American economic life.

EDWARD P. JOHANNNINGSMEIER

References and Further Reading

Brecher, Jeremy. *Strike!* Boston, MA: South End Press, 1997.

Brody, David. *Labor Embattled: History, Power, Rights.* Urbana: University of Illinois Press, 2005.

———. *Labor in Crisis: The Steel Strike of 1919.* Urbana: University of Illinois Press, 1987. (reprint, 1965).

McCartin, Joseph A. *Labor's Great War: The Struggle for Industrial Democracy and the Origins of Modern American Labor Relations, 1912–1921.* Chapel Hill: University of North Carolina Press, 1997.

Montgomery, David. *The Fall of the House of Labor.* Cambridge, UK: Cambridge University Press, 1987.

———. *Workers' Control in America.* Cambridge, UK: Cambridge University Press, 1979.

Murray, Robert K. *Red Scare: A Study in National Hysteria, 1919–1920.* New York: McGraw, 1964. (reprint, 1955)

Cases and Statutes Cited

Espionage Act
Wagner Act

STRIKEBREAKING

Although the United States was in the forefront among nations in introducing civil liberties, many American corporations employed private armies to break strikes and to prevent workers from organizing. Usually independent entrepreneurs supplied corporations with armed mercenaries and replacements for workers on strike, but Ford Motor Company built its own private army. Because many municipal police forces were too small to control crowds, and sometimes sympathized with workers who walked off the job, state authorities often used militia to suppress strikes. Believing even state militia insufficient, Pennsylvania in 1905 formed an elite paramilitary strikebreaking force, the State Constabulary. During the period prior to World War II, management often resorted to violence in breaking strikes.

After 1945, violent labor conflict declined although it never disappeared. Management increasingly turned to psychological manipulation and screening in the hiring process to prevent unionization. The Taft-Hartley Act of 1947, which organized labor denounced as a slave labor bill, provided management with significant new advantages in combating strikes and union-organizing drives.

Labor was usually readily available to employers seeking to replace strikers during the first four decades of the twentieth century. A significant proportion of the workforce experienced either seasonal or long-term unemployment. The various industries experienced slack seasons at different times of the year, so there were almost always many people without jobs. In addition those who were not young often found it difficult to obtain work in industry, because many employers believed they did not possess the necessary strength or endurance. Regular "fink markets" sprang up at clearly identifiable locations in larger cities, often where homeless men congregated.

The Emergence of the Strikebreaking Business

Supplying strikebreakers and armed guards to protect them and intimidate unionists became a very profitable business during the first decade of the twentieth century. The first U.S. national detective agency, established by Allan Pinkerton, pioneered in providing armed guards to management during strikes, first performing this service when miners walked out in Braidwood, Illinois, in 1866. The Pinkerton Detective Agency's armed guards contributed to Carnegie Steel's decisive victory in the 1892 Homestead, Pennsylvania, strike, which eliminated unionism from the steel industry for several decades. By 1891, Jack Whitehead had become the first to assemble a permanent band of strikebreakers that could be moved quickly over significant distances to meet employers' needs. His "40 thieves," skilled ironworkers and steelworkers recruited in Birmingham, Alabama, assisted in breaking several strikes in the Pittsburgh area from 1891–1901.

During the early twentieth century, new strikebreaking agencies formed large mercenary armies that they could transport on short notice almost anywhere in the United States and even outside it. Although largely composed of men hastily recruited to break particular strikes, the mercenary armies were built around a core of permanently employed men, both armed guards and workers.

James Farley was the first to establish strikebreaking as a big business and consequently amass a fortune. He specialized in breaking urban transit strikes, nearly monopolizing the business from 1903 until his retirement in 1907. Farley operated on a national basis, breaking strikes from the Atlantic to the Pacific, often arming his crews on the streetcars. His most dramatic successes occurred in the 1905 New York subway strike, which he broke in less than a week, the 1903 Richmond and Chicago strikes, the 1907 San Francisco streetcar strikes, and the 1905 Chicago teamsters' strike.

Middle-class Americans, feeling stifled and ignored in an increasingly bureaucratized and overcivilized society, celebrated the strikebreakers' display of traditional masculine attributes, like courage and aggressiveness, that appeared to have vanished with the frontier. The mass media described Farley as combining the executive ability of a modern business executive with the primitive masculinity of a gladiator. It claimed strike sympathizers had inflicted scars on him in violent assaults in which his life had been at risk, a claim the labor press denied as false. The professional strikebreaker's prominence in early twentieth-century labor conflict was reflected in Farley becoming a subject of controversy in the 1906 New York gubernatorial campaign and in Jack London's portrayal of him in his novel the *Iron Heel* (1907) as instrumental in helping the capitalists establish a dictatorship.

After Farley's retirement the leading urban-strikebreaking firms were directed by three of his former hirelings: James Waddell and Archie Mahon, who met while working for Farley during the 1905 New York subway strike formed Waddell & Mahon, and Pearl Bergoff established Bergoff Brothers. These firms merged after Mahon's death in 1914 as Bergoff Brothers and Waddell. Like Farley they drew on contacts with organized crime to recruit armed guards and strikebreakers. The new firms expanded to include railroad, shipping, and mining strikes in addition to mass transit. Bergoff Brothers and Waddell even sent strikebreakers to Cuba in 1916. These firms derived significant revenue from gambling operations they set up, where they housed strikebreakers, some of whom complained they were forced to participate in them.

The Baldwin-Felts Detective Agency and the Mine Wars

The Baldwin-Felts Detective Agency assumed charge of strikebreaking and labor espionage in much of the coal-mining territory of southern West Virginia and in parts of Colorado. It also became primarily responsible for law enforcement in many isolated mining counties, exercising tight control over company towns. The firm was formed in 1892 as a partnership between William G. Baldwin, who concentrated on railroad policing, and Thomas L. Felts, who provided armed guards to mining corporations. The mass media praised Felts, like Farley, for entrepreneurial skill that enabled him to amass great wealth and attributed to him the fearlessness of the nineteenth-century frontier gunfighter.

Baldwin-Felts guards often used violence in strikes and in driving labor organizers from the mining region. They watched for any sign of union sympathy among the miners, even intercepting mail, and during strikes evicted miners and their families from company housing. In both West Virginia and Colorado during the 1910s, they engaged in large-scale gun battles with union miners, in some of which both sides sustained significant casualties. There were many smaller skirmishes. Baldwin-Felts guards were often organized along military lines into companies and squads. In strikes in both states, Baldwin-Felts guards paraded machine guns to intimidate the miners and their families. In 1913, in West Virginia, they fired one from an armored-plated train at a miners' tent colony in a night attack.

During the 1910s, bloody and sustained armed conflicts erupted during strikes in the western Arkansas coal country (1914–1915) and in the forests of western Louisiana (1911–1913), where management also entered into arrangements with detective agencies to suppress strikes. In Arkansas the Bache-Denman Coal Company hired the Burns Detective Agency to help it open previously unionized mines with nonunion labor, precipitating violent skirmishes that culminated in a massive gun battle lasting several hours. Striking timber workers in Louisiana denounced the Burns and Pinkerton detectives who raided their union meetings and drove them from their homes as "black hundreds," after Russia's brutal and reactionary paramilitary gangs, and armed in self-defense.

Pennsylvania's Coal and Iron Police and State Constabulary

In Pennsylvania, the nation's leading coal-mining state in the early twentieth century, mine corporations established the coal and iron police, a private force to disrupt labor organizing and break strikes. The state permitted corporations for a small fee to hire uniformed armed policemen, whom they paid and supervised. Many coal and iron policemen had criminal backgrounds.

In the twentieth century's first three decades, coal and iron police were a prominent presence in Pennsylvania's coal-mining sections, watching railroad stations and stopping automobiles on the road to ensure that labor organizers did not come into contact with miners. Union miners often accused coal and iron policemen of depriving them of basic civil liberties and of sexually abusing the women in their communities, a charge they also leveled at Baldwin-Felts guards in West Virginia and Colorado.

In 1905, Pennsylvania's legislature, anxious to quell labor militancy, established the nation's first state police, an elite mounted force known as the State Constabulary. It was modeled on British constabulary stationed in Ireland, and its members even wore bobby-style helmets. The men recruited were rigorously trained in the use of firearms, hand-to-hand combat, and horsemanship. State Constabulary troops were posted at four barracks in the coal regions, deliberately isolated so they would not develop any relationship with workers. The State Constabulary immediately gained notoriety for using rough tactics during mining and streetcar strikes, including riding into crowds on sidewalks and aggressively beating people with their long hickory batons, causing trade unionists to denounce them as "black Cossacks." This epithet associated the State Constabulary with the mounted paramilitary force of

Europe's most despotic regime and its savage suppression of peaceful protest.

Municipal Police and State Militia

Municipal police and state militia considered strikebreaking among their most important assignments, and they developed innovative methods to disperse crowds of strike sympathizers. Police departments, which grew significantly in the major cities during the early twentieth century, acquired fleets of patrol wagons to move men quickly to protect strikebreakers and erected a network of signal boxes to report trouble from crowds immediately. Police often charged picket lines and when mounted sometimes trampled strike sympathizers when riding into crowds. Such tactics could quickly demoralize strikers, driving them back to work. In Detroit, the nation's largest automobile-manufacturing center, the United Automobile Workers' union (UAW-Congress of Industrial Organizations [CIO]) accused the police of collusion with management during strikes and repeatedly denounced it for assaulting pickets and failing to investigate the bombings of union offices and activists' homes.

When confronted by charging, club-wielding mounted policemen, strikers and their sympathizers sometimes defended themselves by aiming their picket signs at the riders' kneecaps, which caused some of them to fall from their horses. Alternatively, they might place ball bearings on the street, knocking the horses off their feet. In Detroit in 1938, the UAW-CIO vigorously protested the police commissioner's order banning pickets from carrying signs he claimed were used as weapons. The UAW-CIO insisted this order violated the Second Amendment's guarantee of the right to bear arms. The most serious atrocity police committed against strikers and their sympathizers was the Memorial Day Massacre during the Little Steel Strike in Chicago, when they shot dead 10 people who had been peacefully demonstrating, hitting seven in the back and three in the side.

Because municipal police often lacked the manpower to suppress picket lines and strike crowds effectively, state authorities sometimes assigned militia this task. State militia possessed both superior firepower and greater mobility. The appearance of the militia's heavy-weapons' units, equipped with Gating guns, often caused strike crowds immediately to melt away. Before automobiles came into wide use, cavalry enabled militia to patrol a much larger area in and around a city than police could. Colorado state militia, which had absorbed some Baldwin-Felts guards, during the 1913–1914 southern Colorado coal strike committed the most famous atrocity in American labor history, the Ludlow massacre, killing two women and 11 children when they shot up and burned a large miners' tent colony.

The College Student as Strikebreaker

College students represented an important source of strikebreakers during the early twentieth century because their youth and vigor made them especially qualified for heavy physical labor, they had ample free time to intervene in strikes, and their affluence and ignorance of working-people's conditions caused them to sympathize with management in labor disputes. From the turn of the century until the early 1920s, male college students were prominent in breaking urban transit, teamsters', railroad, shipping, and gas and electrical workers' strikes; and the Boston policemen's strike. Because corporate business had assumed financial control over colleges and universities by the early twentieth century, administrators and faculty, who undoubtedly influenced students, tended to be hostile to organized labor. Many of the nation's leading college presidents were known for their anti-labor views. Harvard's president Charles W. Eliot, for example, offered fulsome praise for the strikebreakers' courage. As a result the labor press repeatedly used "elite hero" as a synonym for strikebreaker. Faculty tenure was uncommon until the late 1930s, so professors who expressed sympathy for unions were often discharged.

College students were also drawn to strikebreaking because it provided a test of manhood in a period when upper- and middle-class men felt increasingly insecure in their masculinity. Bureaucratization resulted in a loss of autonomy and deprived men of the opportunity to behave in the rough and boisterous manner that had been equated with manly conduct. Administrators at the turn of the twentieth century were also forbidding students to engage in violent, mass-student rituals, like cane rush, because of the danger involved. But strikebreaking, which administrators endorsed even though it often resulted in violent confrontations, bonded masses of young men together and allowed them to perform feats requiring strength and daring.

Female collegians were much less likely than men to participate in strikebreaking, further associating it with rough masculinity. While most female students, like their male counterparts, tended to be conservative, their ability to explore the world outside the campus was much more restricted. Nor did they share men's attraction to violence.

Engineering students were particularly desirable as strikebreakers because they were often the only skilled replacements available to management. By the early twentieth century, engineering colleges had developed close working relationships with corporations that funded and benefited from their research. In 1921, a railroad company even placed a track and passenger car on the campus of the nation's leading engineering school, the Massachusetts Institute of Technology, so it could train students to replace its striking workers.

College-student strikebreaking declined in the 1930s but did not disappear, as working-class youth more sympathetic to labor came to constitute a large proportion of the student body, and the Depression lessened frivolity's appeal. Many collegians had considered strikebreaking a lark. The shift from a homosocial to a heterosocial leisure culture by the 1920s also reduced strikebreaking's appeal to college men, to whom it had constituted an important opportunity for male camaraderie.

African-American Strikebreaking

African-Americans, excluded from industrial occupations and many trade unions, emerged as another important strikebreaking force after the turn of the century, often transported long distances from the South to northern cities to take the place of strikers. Most of the African-American elite believed that the best strategy for black advancement required forging alliances with white business leaders and lacked sympathy for unionism. The black elite exercised significant influence in the black community through the black press and the black colleges and manual-training institutes. Strikebreaking appeared to offer blacks an opportunity to break the color bar in hiring in northern industry.

In addition many African-American men found strikebreaking appealing because it provided the best opportunity to escape the obsequiousness white society required of them. Blacks became increasingly subordinated after 1890, as the South elaborated a system of legal racial segregation and disfranchisement. During the first decade of the twentieth century, violent antiblack riots with significant casualties and destruction of property broke out in both southern and northern cities. African-American opportunities in military service, the only arena in which aggressive masculinity was tolerated in blacks, greatly diminished in the decades after the Civil War. But as strikebreakers black men, ordinarily expected to step aside when encountering whites, could brandish weapons, assume a posture of intimidation, and even shoot white strikers and sympathizers with the approval of employers and often the white public.

The importation of massive numbers of African-American strikebreakers, largely from the South, by professional strikebreaking firms, was an important cause of the defeat of the national packinghouse strike in 1904 and the Chicago teamsters' strike in 1905. Steel corporation officials also credited African-American strikebreakers with a critical role in breaking the 1919 steel strike, which involved 365,000 workers. Yet invariably blacks failed to gain a permanent foothold in industry through strikebreaking. As late as 1939 and 1941, sizable numbers of black strikebreakers were used in the Chrysler and Ford auto strikes, respectively.

The Decline of Strikebreaking during the 1920s

As union membership and work stoppages declined precipitously after the early 1920s, sharply diminished demand pushed the professional strikebreaking business into temporary decline. Pearl Bergoff even sold off his arsenal and commissary equipment, hoping instead to make money in Florida real estate. Streetcar strikes, which had paralyzed the principal means of transportation in numerous American cities during the first two decades of the twentieth century and provided substantial revenue for strikebreaking firms, became infrequent as automobile ownership spread. Once this alternative mode of transportation became widely available, streetcar men lost most of their leverage and were much less likely to walk out.

Strikebreaking in the Auto Industry

Because the auto companies and their parts suppliers, closely allied with municipal police, presented a powerful and solid front against unionization, the UAW-CIO, determined to gain recognition but aware it could probably not prevail in any conventional strike, developed an innovative new tactic, the sit-down. By occupying a plant, the union prevented police from breaking picket lines and ushering in strikebreakers.

To break a sit-down strike, auto management might drive out the occupiers with tear gas, as at Detroit's Yale & Towne plant in 1937, which ended in a stinging union defeat. Management also mobilized large squads of vigilantes to intimidate the strikers and their families physically, as in the 1937 General Motors (GM) sit-down in Flint, Michigan, and in the sit-down against GM parts suppliers in Anderson, Indiana. In both strikes procompany vigilantes violently attacked and injured UAW-CIO activists and destroyed union property. Management also spread rumors to demoralize those engaged in the sit-down, claiming their wives and children had fallen ill and that little support existed on the outside.

To counter these strikebreaking efforts, the UAW-CIO formed paramilitary units known as flying squadrons that shored up picket lines threatened with police or vigilante assault; communicated accurate information to sit-downers about developments outside occupied plants, including family news; and transported food and other necessary supplies to the sit-downers. Female relatives of UAW-CIO members established their own flying squadrons called the Women's Emergency Brigade, whose members donned military-style berets. They gained renown in the 1937 Flint sit-down strike for positioning themselves in the front ranks in clashes with armed police and bravely withstanding tear gas attacks. In other conventional strikes, like those at Federal Screw and American Brass in Detroit in 1938, the flying squadrons fought mounted police hand-to-hand.

Organized labor confronted well-armed mercenary armies not only in isolated mining and lumbering regions, but in the leading U.S. automobile-manufacturing metropolis, a heavily populated center of advanced technology. The Ford Motor Company's service department, led by former navy boxer Harry Bennett, who developed close ties with organized crime, became the world's largest private army during the late 1930s, committed to preventing unionization by spying on the labor force at work and in their neighborhoods, intimidating workers, and beating union activists, often severely. Many Ford servicemen were ex-convicts who had served prison time for violent crimes. The service department's strong-arm tactics ensured that Ford was the last of the big three auto manufacturers to be organized.

Because of the layout of Ford's massive flagship plant, River Rouge in Dearborn, just outside Detroit, neither a sit-down strike nor one that depended on establishing picket lines offered much prospect for success. When Ford, refusing to bargain, forced a strike in April 1941, the UAW-CIO prevailed because it used highly innovative tactics. Bennett had obstructed plant windows in the only two buildings facing streets to prevent transmitting food and supplies to strikers. He also placed machine guns on roofs. But the union shut down the plant by barricading roads serving it.

To break the strike Bennett tried to divide the labor force by provoking interracial violence. Ford, which had long made significant financial donations to black churches and had hired more African-Americans than the other auto companies, enjoyed strong support in Detroit's black community. The UAW-CIO countered Ford's appeal to blacks by arguing that Ford assigned them to the less desirable jobs and pointed to backing from prominent African-American activists Walter White and Paul Robeson, both of whom came to Detroit to persuade black workers to join the union. Bennett armed black workers who remained loyal to the company with clubs, knives, and crowbars and had them assault predominantly white pickets, hoping to provoke militia intervention to break the strike.

However a split within Ford management, pitting Bennett, whom Ford strongly encouraged to use violence against the strikers, against Ford's son Edsel, apparently joined by Ford's wife, Clara, who urged negotiations, along with the union's innovative tactics, enabled the UAW-CIO to win recognition and the best settlement that had yet been achieved in auto manufacturing.

Strikebreaking in the Post-World War II Era

After World War II employers resorted less often to violence in suppressing strikes, particularly outside the South. Working-class suburbanization lessened opportunities for confrontation. In a heavily bureaucratized and more androgynous society that delegitimatized anger, management increasingly relied on psychological manipulation to disrupt organizing and defeat strikes. The 1947 Taft-Hartley Act provided management with new advantages that made successful organizing and strikes less likely. The erosion of the nation's disproportionately unionized manufacturing sector, as a result of job loss to overseas competition and technological unemployment, contributed to the steady diminution in the percentage of organized workers after the mid-1950s, resulting in fewer work stoppages.

New union-avoidance firms, staffed by psychologists and lawyers, emerged to advise management on how to break strikes and defeat organizing campaigns. Proliferating during the 1970s, the consultants trained management to run anti-union propaganda campaigns that involved special meetings employees were required to attend, the showing of anti-labor videos, and home visits. The consultants defamed union activists by falsely accusing them of sexual or financial misconduct, associated unions with violence, and spread rumors that the plant would relocate if unionized.

In the more conservative climate of the 1980s, with unions weakened by the migration of jobs abroad, workers who went on strike often found themselves permanently discharged. In 1981, President Reagan fired striking air traffic controllers *en masse*. The threat of permanent job loss proved highly effective in intimidating workers from using the strike, their weapon of last resort. In a 1991–1992 strike, Caterpillar Tractor decisively defeated one of the nation's strongest unions, the UAW, by threatening permanent replacement.

Labor's prospects for prevailing in a strike became increasingly bleak after 1980. It failed miserably in its attempt to persuade Congress to pass legislation to prohibit companies from permanently replacing strikers. By the first decade of the twenty-first century, the American public accorded unions less legitimacy than at any time since the 1920s, and most workers considered a strike too risky to attempt.

STEPHEN H. NORWOOD

References and Further Reading

Arnesen, Eric. "Specter of the Black Strikebreaker: Race, Employment, and Labor Activism in the Industrial Era." *Labor History* 44, 3 (winter 2003): 319–335.

Norwood, Stephen H. *Strikebreaking and Intimidation: Mercenaries and Masculinity in Twentieth-Century America.* Chapel Hill: University of North Carolina Press, 2002.

Cases and Statutes Cited

Taft-Hartley Act

SWEENEY, JOHN J. (MAY 5, 1934–) President, American Federation of Labor-Congress of Industrial Organizations

John J. Sweeney is the fourth president of the American Federation of Labor-Congress of Industrial Organizations (AFL-CIO). Succeeding interim chief Tom Donahue, he began his term in 1995. Sweeney was swept into office at the head of a federation-wide reform wave. The so-called Sweeney revolution, which was led by New Voice reformers, pledged to recapture organized labor's spirit from the 1930s, organize the unorganized, improve the standard of living of all Americans, and become once again a force to be reckoned with in American politics. As the initial euphoria wore off, Sweeney had a very difficult time fulfilling his promises and keeping the AFL-CIO together. Recently five powerful unions—the Service Employees' International Union (SEIU), the International Brotherhood of Teamsters, the United Food and Commercial Workers, the Laborers'

International Union of North America, and the Union of Needletrades, Industrial and Textile Employees, and Hotel Employees' and Restaurant Employees' International Union (UNITE-HERE)—have bolted from the AFL-CIO's ranks to form their own federation, the Change to Win Coalition (CTWC). Weakened and beleaguered Sweeney presently is continuing his fight to advance the working class while presiding over a divided labor movement. It remains to be seen if he can overcome these obstacles as well as the conservative political mood of the nation.

Although he represented the candidate for change in the 1995 AFL-CIO presidential election, Sweeney's background is nearly identical to those of the previous federation leaders. With the exception of Lane Kirkland, all the AFL-CIO presidents grew up in the Bronx, New York, which Sweeney described as a "pack-a-lunch-and-take-the-subway-to-work" kind of place. Similarly all three have been the descendents of Irish immigrants. Moreover and again with the exception of Kirkland, George Meany, Tom Donahue, and John Sweeney were raised in staunchly pro-union families. Sweeney's father was a bus driver and a member of the Transport Workers' Union (TWU). His mother was a domestic servant. Like so many people of that generation and those circumstances, three things dominated his early life: the Catholic church, family, and unions. Without the church, Sweeney once wrote, there would be no redemption. Without the family, there would be no love. And without the union, there would be no food on the table.

Sweeney began working as a teenager. He found a job at the Gate of Heaven Cemetery in Westchester County. And he joined what eventually became the Service Employees' International Union, Local 365. After high school Sweeney went to college, first to Iona College in New Rochelle, where he majored in economics. Later he attended the Xavier Labor School in Manhattan. His higher education helped him frame his political and economic philosophy, which centers on the idea that economies should work for workers, and not the other way around. Somewhat surprisingly despite his union background and his proworker sympathies, after college Sweeney went to work for International Business Machines (IBM) as a market researcher. His stint at IBM lasted a short time, and he left it for a research job with the International Ladies' Garment Workers' Union. That post led in 1961 to another, the contract director of the Building Service Employees' Union, Local 32B. This job brought Sweeney into more politically powerful circles, since he worked directly with Tom Donahue, then a rising star in organized labor. As Sweeney and Donahue expanded Local 32B, they began to gain regional, then national attention. In 1976, Sweeney succeeded Donahue as Local 32B president, and soon after, he helped transform the Building Service Union into the Service Employees' International Union (SEIU), dedicated to helping all service workers of all backgrounds.

The rising fortunes of the SEIU stood in stark contrast to the rest of the labor movement. Although there were some positive developments in the 1970s and early 1980s, unionists in those years witnessed a wholesale decline in living standards and in the power of the labor movement. The problem was threefold. First in the early 1970s, the American economy entered a long slowdown. High oil prices, antiquated factory systems, and rampant inflation contributed to an overall dwindling of worker economic and consumer power. Second instead of working with organized labor to improve the situation, employers and politicians waged an all-out campaign to rollback pocketbook and fringe-benefit gains that unionists had won from the 1930s–1960s. As Sweeney has put it, the rich and powerful broke the social contract that emerged from the Great Depression. Many employers and politicians gave up the commitment to provide a social and economic safety net for the working class. Third the labor movement itself became decrepit. Under the direction of the elderly Meany, the AFL-CIO lost political ground while American workers were losing economic ground. In 1979, Meany finally retired, and Kirkland became the federation's president. Arguably the average American worker barely noticed the difference.

Kirkland was the quintessential labor bureaucrat insider. He was greatly sympathetic to union workers, but he traveled in the nation's highest political circles away from the daily grind of local union politics, organizing, and labor relations. Although Kirkland vigorously opposed Presidents Ronald Reagan and George H.W. Bush's antilabor agendas, his challenge to the conservatives was rather anemic. Kirkland's greatest achievements came on the world stage where he was instrumental in the democratization of Poland and the efforts to find stable, moderate, and anti-Communist governments in Central America. Closer to home Kirkland failed to stem the lowering tide for the American workers' standard of living. He did however bring more unity to the shrinking labor movement. By 1989, three major unions—the United Auto Workers, the Teamsters, and the United Mine Workers—had rejoined the AFL-CIO. But increased solidarity did not translate into renewed activism to stop the declining impact of the AFL-CIO.

For many in the labor movement, their patience with President Kirkland ran out in 1994. That year the Republican party launched its Contract with America campaign to capture the U.S. Congress. In those off-year elections, many conservative candidates espoused anti-union rhetoric and won. Once again the AFL-CIO seemed slow and unresponsive. Angered by labor's inability to answer the challenge, several union leaders publicly denounced Kirkland. Under mounting pressure in June 1995, the 73-year-old Kirkland resigned as AFL-CIO president. His lieutenant (and Sweeney's personal friend) Donahue was tapped to fill the vacancy until the October AFL-CIO Convention.

The 1995 convention was one of the federation's most contentious. After months of organizing, an insurgent group of unionists, who called themselves the New Voice, were making lots of noise. Influenced by New Left radicals, like Michael Harrington, leaders like , Sweeney, Rich Trumka, Ron Carey, and Linda Chavez-Thompson forged a coalition of organizations including the International Association of Machinists, the SEIU, the Teamsters, the UAW, and the United Mine Workers of America (UMW). The group handily defeated Donahue and elected 61-year-old Sweeney. Sweeney pledged to fulfill the New Voice promise of "giving American workers a raise" while fighting for "economic security and social justice." President Sweeney dramatically reshaped the AFL-CIO headquarters, rearranging its national budget so that more union dollars went toward organizing. He helped the federation extend itself by changing its public relations approach, which resulted in the creation of the AFL-CIO web site (www.aflcio.org) and refashioning the old *American Federationist* into the much flashier *Americans @ Work*. Finally Sweeney made an immediate impact on the 1996 presidential election, helping the mainstream prolabor candidate, Bill Clinton, get re-elected.

Unfortunately for Sweeney the AFL-CIO, and unionists generally, the second Clinton term was not a halcyon age for American workers. Rather the final years of the millennium constituted a missed opportunity. President Clinton made very little headway with this domestic agenda as his presidency became mired in the Monica Lewinsky scandal. Having a wounded liberal president was bad enough, but beginning in 1996 the Teamsters' Ron Carey, a staunch Sweeney supporter, became embroiled in his own political scandal that resulted in his ouster from office and the election of James P. Hoffa, son of the fabled Teamster president. Other problems soon followed. Significantly despite the pledges of New Voice union leaders and millions of dollars devoted to organizing, the membership of the AFL-CIO has failed to grow. In fact the number of union workers in the American labor force has declined since 1995. Of course one can point to large impersonal economic forces, such as automation, the transplanting of American manufacturing overseas, and the continued downsizing of the labor force as major factors in organized labor's woes. But there were other causes as well. Sweeney has presided over an era when American politics have turned decidedly to the right. These pressures on the AFL-CIO have been almost too much to bear, and the federation has once again begun to break.

An internecine fight broke out in 2004 when SEIU President Andy Stern publicly attacked Sweeney's leadership. Stern, Sweeney's protégé who had in fact succeeded his mentor as SEIU's chief in 1996, challenged the federation to do more organizing and work harder to foster unity, consolidation, and cooperation among smaller unions. Sweeney tried to placate his rivals by adopting a series of reforms, instituting reorganizations, and laying off headquarters' staff. The tactic failed to convince the leaders of five major unions—the SEIU, the Teamsters, the United Food and Commercial Workers, the Laborers, and UNITE-HERE—to remain in the AFL-CIO. On June 14, 2005, these five unions formed the CTWC and began a process to pull their 5 million members out of the federation. Virtually overnight the AFL-CIO's membership has shrunk by nearly 40%. Moreover the federation has also lost more than one-sixth of its operating budget. The SEIU and the Teamsters alone had contributed over $20 million to the AFL-CIO. Enfeebled and splintered the AFL-CIO has tried to reach out to CTWC without result. Consequently Sweeney has had to increase the dues of remaining unions. He also sent out Rich Trumka to try to drum up some local support. The AFL-CIO has been somewhat successful in obtaining solidarity charters with some CTWC locals.

While organized labor has been battling itself, the overall situation for American workers has become more precarious. In addition to more plant closures and layoffs, both union and nonunion workers have struggled as their health insurance and pension systems have faltered and in some cases failed. President George W. Bush's administration seemed quite unsympathetic to those issues. In fact President Bush worked diligently to weaken overtime and wage rules, made unfriendly appointments to major federal labor relations posts, and has done very little to stop the continuing de-industrialization of the United States. He also proposed substantial revisions to the old New Deal safety net, including a privatization plan for social security. The AFL-CIO itself wrestled to define a strategy to oppose conservative politicians and their plans. There have been some victories. In October 2005, under pressure from the AFL-CIO's Building and Construction Trades' Department, the Bush administration re-instated

Davis-Bacon wage protections that had been suspended in the wake of Hurricane Katrina. But advances like this have seemed fleeting. In 2005, the percentage of union workers in the labor force reached a nadir, 12%. And, traditional stalwart groups within the labor movement, such as African-Americans, are quickly becoming nonunion workers because of downsizing. Once again—as social commentators had done immediately before the advent of the New Deal—some critics have begun to question if unions, particularly the AFL-CIO, are still relevant to today's workers. The answer to that question rests in large measure with Sweeney.

ANDREW E. KERSTEN

References and Further Reading

Buhle, Paul. *Taking Care of Business: Samuel Gompers, George Meany, Lane Kirkland and the Tragedy of American Labor.* New York: Monthly Review Press, 1999.
Mort, Jo-Ann. *Not Your Father's Union Movement: Inside the AFL-CIO.* New York: Verso, 1998.
Puddington, Arch. *Lane Kirkland: Champion of American Labor.* Hoboken, NJ: John Wiley, 2005.
Sweeney, John J. *America Needs a Raise: Fighting for Economic Security and Social Justice.* Boston, MA: Houghton Mifflin, 1996.

See also **American Federation of Labor-Congress of Industrial Organizations; Kirkland, Lane**

SWINTON, JOHN (1830–1901)
Labor Journalist

John Swinton was perhaps the most influential and unique labor journalist of the late nineteenth century. A longtime journalist for established New York newspapers, including the *New York Times* and the *New York Sun*, Swinton founded his own newspaper, *John Swinton's Paper*, to champion labor issues in 1883. Though short-lived, running for fewer than 4 years, *John Swinton's Paper* was one of the first independent U.S. labor newspapers and a force that even propelled some labor issues into the halls of Congress.

Swinton was born in Salton, Hoddingtonshire, Scotland, with the good fortune of having a vicar for an uncle who tutored him in a firm knowledge of letters. When the family moved to Montreal, Swinton was learned enough to be apprenticed to a newspaper printer, beginning his lifelong press career at the age of 13. Following in the footsteps of many Scotch and Irish immigrants for whom Canada was just the first leg in a journey to the United States, the Swintons moved to New York in 1849.

After a brief flirtation with academia, taking classes at New York Medical College, Swinton continued in his destined trade. As a journeyman he traveled extensively, for a time securing a position as a compositor in a South Carolina printing office in Charleston, then moving on to Kansas just as it began to earn its bloody nickname; there he set the *Lawrence Republican*, then back to New York City again. Though there is no documentary evidence of Swinton's youthful ideological views, the facts of his early life do fit with the assertions of some biographers who claim that Swinton was deeply offended by the slavery he witnessed in South Carolina and expressed his feelings in his rush to the frontlines of abolitionism in Kansas.

Skilled and experienced in printing, intelligent and critically minded, Swinton secured a position as a reporter for the *New York Times*. Swinton gravitated naturally to the city's literary and radical haunts, spending much of his time at Pfaff's saloon on the corner of Broadway and Bleecker with his close friend Walt Whitman. Most of his war years were consumed scribbling away at the *Times* without a byline, but in a remarkably short time, he was promoted to an editor's desk.

In 1869, Swinton embarked on the assignment that would shape the rest of his life. He penned a nine-article investigative series on "Our Working Classes," which were either the result of his developing interest in the conditions of labor or were the occasion of his awakening to them. The following year Swinton continued his interest in labor issues, publishing a biting analysis of foreign contract labor entitled "The Coolie Question," in the *New York Tribune*. By the time the sharp depression of 1873 struck the nation and police wantonly beat protesters at Tompkins Square Park (which Swinton witnessed), Swinton had become a committed labor activist.

Swinton had the rare ability to exist in both the conventional world of journalism and the radical milieu of the labor movement. While working for the *New York Sun*, Swinton spearheaded the effort to force the New York State Assembly to investigate police actions at Tompkins Square, ran for mayor under the banner of the ephemeral Industrial Political party, an offshoot of the moribund International Workingmen's Association, and held court at the anarchist Justus Schwab's Lower East Side saloon.

In 1880, Swinton toured Europe and unlike many of his American predecessors on their first visit to the continent found that the experience made the squalor of U.S. conditions seem even worse by comparison. While in England Swinton spent a day with Karl Marx and interviewed him for the *New York Sun*. Swinton, knowing his subject's philosophical bent, asked, "What is?" Marx, Swinton observed, "Seemed as though his mind were inverted for a moment...[and] in a deep and solemn tone, he replied: 'Struggle'."

In 1883, he testified before the Blair Committee of Congress that was then documenting industrial conditions and later that October launched the project for which he is primarily remembered, opening one of the first independent U.S. labor newspapers, *John Swinton's Paper*. Looking back on his publishing venture later in life, Swinton described his newspaper as "ideal, idyllic, heroical, archetypal, rational, godly and inexpensive." At four pages of six columns selling for 3cents a copy, it reached its peak circulation of 10,000 after its first year. Though its distribution was never great, its influence was keenly felt largely because of the great respect Swinton himself had earned for the integrity of his reporting and his commitment to independence and honesty. For example in 1884, *John Swinton's Paper* began a long investigative series uncovering contract-labor abuses in New York City that prompted Congressman Martin A. Foran of Ohio to introduce an anticontract labor bill that passed the following year.

John Swinton's Paper took up many causes but always maintained its independence from them. It supported Henry George's candidacy for mayor of New York, though it criticized his economic principles. It was a strong supporter of the Knights of Labor and criticized its leadership. While many labor reformers, such as Wendell Phillips, preached racial internationalism, Swinton embraced a spread-eagled racial nationalism, especially on the issue of Chinese immigration.

The newspaper never turned a profit, and Swinton freely underwrote its losses from his own savings. Even after it was evident his newspaper was sinking into bankruptcy, Swinton's stern view of journalistic independence caused him to refuse all donations unless accompanied by a similar number of subscriptions. His last issue was dated Aug. 21, 1887.

Swinton, as was his talent, continued to write for larger New York newspapers while continuing to speak on labor platforms and support labor causes. Swinton was the featured speaker at the 1892 American Federation of Labor convention where he reviewed the "battalions that fought this year at Homestead, Buffalo, and Coeur d'Alene." In 1895, he edited a collection of writings by Eugene Debs, Samuel Gompers, and other labor leaders entitled, *A Momentous Question: Labor's Side of the Labor Question*.

Marx described him as a "well-meaning bourgeois" and had he lived in the twentieth century, he probably would have been described as a fellow traveler. Swinton was a man highly regarded by many who did not share his principles, including one powerful chief editor who eulogized him by saying, "He is the only man I ever knew who had no axes of his own to grind."

TIMOTHY MESSER-KRUSE

References and Further Reading

Debs, Eugene. *John Swinton: Radical Editor and Leader.* Berkeley Heights, NJ: Oriole Press, 1939.

Ross, Marc. "John Swinton: Journalist and Reformer: The Active Years, 1857–1887." Ph.D. dissertation, New York Univ., 1969.

Swinton, John. *John Swinton's Travels: Current Views and Notes of Forty Days in France and England.* New York: C. W. Carleton & Co., 1880.

Waters, Robert. *Career and Conversations of John Swinton: Journalist, Orator, Economist.* Chicago: Kerr & Co., 1902.

SYLVIS, WILLIAM (1828–1869)
National Labor Union

William Sylvis was the premier U.S. labor leader during the 1860s. He organized iron molders into the strongest union in the country, helped found the National Labor Union, pioneered new organizing methods, and pushed for such reforms as an 8-hour day, greenback currency, and expanded rights for women and African-Americans.

Sylvis, the son of an American-born wagon maker, learned iron making as an apprentice in his hometown of Armagh, Pennsylvania. In 1850, Sylvis married Amelia Thomas, with whom he produced four children. Two years later Sylvis moved his family to Philadelphia where he found steady work. After Amelia's death in 1865, Sylvis married Florrie Hunter, who bore him one child.

During the Panic of 1857, Sylvis joined a local iron molders union that was fighting a wage cut. The strike failed, but the union survived, and Sylvis, who distinguished himself as a picket organizer, was elected recording secretary in 1858. The next year Sylvis helped organize a national convention of iron molders. In 1860, the International Iron Molders' Union (IMIU), the result of this effort, elected Sylvis treasurer.

In the 1850s, Sylvis supported Stephen Douglas's wing of the Democratic party, which opposed African-American civil rights and equivocated on slavery. During the secession crisis of 1860–1861, Sylvis participated in the Committee of Thirty-Four, a northern trade union effort to avoid war by compromising on slavery. When the Civil War began, Sylvis, like most northern Democrats, abandoned compromise. He organized a company of Union volunteers and in 1862, served in a Pennsylvania regiment.

Meanwhile the IMIU had nearly disappeared because of a bad economy and military service by its members. In 1863, Sylvis, who had returned to Philadelphia, won election as president of the IMIU (an office he held until 1869) and set out on a nationwide recruiting drive. By 1865, Sylvis had added over 100 locals, organized 6,000 of the nation's 9,200 journeymen ironworkers, and made the IMIU the largest U.S. trade union.

Sylvis pioneered such organizational methods as centralized union government, membership cards, and high-dues payments to fund strikes. These tactics enabled the IMIU to boost molders' pay ahead of inflation, a major achievement given the general decline in workers' wartime purchasing power. Despite this success Sylvis's personal abrasiveness alienated some union members.

Centralization helped the IMIU survive the postwar recession and an 1866–1867 employer drive to break the union. The onslaught cost the IMIU one-fourth of its membership, but by avoiding union-crushing strikes and playing employers off against each other, Sylvis kept the IMIU alive.

Sylvis's faith in centralization informed his efforts to establish a national union federation. Although unable to attend the founding meeting of the NLU in 1866, Sylvis supported its labor reform agenda of shorter hours, cooperative enterprise, currency reform, and creation of a federal labor department. Elected NLU president in 1868, Sylvis recognized that the organization's weak control over affiliated unions limited its effectiveness in collective bargaining. Accordingly Sylvis used the NLU to advocate labor-reform issues, which he publicized on national speaking tours and in the *Workingman's Advocate*, the NLU's official newspaper, which Sylvis co-owned.

Sylvis linked the cause of labor's rights to expanding rights for African-Americans and women. Despite Sylvis's prewar support for racist Democrats and his postwar denigration of the Freedmen's Bureau and Radical Reconstruction, as NLU president he supported organizing African-American workers. In 1869, shortly after Sylvis's death, the NLU seated its first black delegates. Isaac Myers, a Baltimore ship caulker who founded the Colored National Labor Union in cooperation with NLU, praised Sylvis's support for African-American labor. However most NLU-affiliated unions, which were overwhelmingly white, ignored Sylvis's recommendations and excluded African-American members.

Likewise Sylvis's support for women's rights neither sparked a wave of female union organizing nor secured woman's suffrage. Notwithstanding these failures, Sylvis befriended Elizabeth Cady Stanton and defeated a campaign to deny her a seat at the 1868 NLU convention where she represented the New York Woman's Suffrage Association. The NLU refused to endorse woman's suffrage, but it did support inclusion of women in trade unions.

Sylvis's growing interest in such legislative remedies as 8-hour day laws and greenback currency persuaded him that an independent political party could better advance labor's cause than could trade unions, which he perceived as defensive organizations. Sylvis's movement toward third-party politics was cut short by his death on July 26, 1869. During the Civil War era, Sylvis turned the iron industry into the stronghold of organized labor and demonstrated the effectiveness of centralized, bureaucratic union government.

FRANK TOWERS

References and Further Reading

Grossman, Jonathan. *William Sylvis: Pioneer of American Labor*. New York: Columbia University Press, 1945.
Montgomery, David. "William H. Sylvis and the Search for Working Class Citizenship." In *Labor Leaders in America*, Melvyn Dubofsky and Warren Van Tine, eds. Urbana: University of Illinois Press, 1987.
Sylvis, James C. *The Life, Speeches, Labors, and Essays of William H. Sylvis*. New York: Augustus M. Kelley, 1968. (reprint, 1872)

See also **Civil War and Reconstruction; National Labor Union**

SYNDICALISM

Syndicalism was a political philosophy that rejected electoral politics as ineffective and corrupt, focusing instead on economic action. Syndicalists identified unions as the focal point of revolutionary activity. They argued that increasingly militant strikes would educate workers about their own potential and grow into general strikes that would ultimately bring production to a halt and enable them to abolish the political state. The state would be replaced by a federated set of syndicates, or unions, through which production and distribution would be organized. Tactically they advocated not only general strikes, but also direct action—activism in the streets and at the factory door—and the frequently misunderstood practice of sabotage.

Revolutionary syndicalism emerged as an ideology and set of practices in Europe at the end of the nineteenth century. The most important theorists were in France, where syndicalism first took root. Fernand Pelloutier articulated the rationale for opposition to electoral politics and antistatism at the end of the nineteenth century. Emile Pouget wrote on the general strike, direct action, and, infamously, sabotage. Georges Sorel, the most influential syndicalist theorist, argued the importance of a militant minority to lead workers to revolution, defended revolutionary violence, and explored the emotional appeal of consciously constructed myths to motivate masses of people. When syndicalists established themselves in the *Confédération générale du travail* (CGT), the most important federation of unions in France, they became a formidable presence in the labor movement. Syndicalism also gained a footing in Italy, infused by a sharper antistatist edge that revealed the influence of anarchist Mikhail Bakunin. Like in France, Italian syndicalists strove to capture the most powerful labor organizations in their country—the Chambers of Labor, which exerted enormous influence in the years surrounding World War I.

Syndicalism and the Industrial Workers of the World

The major vehicle for syndicalist ideas and practices in the United States was the Industrial Workers of the World (IWW), founded in 1905. Debate continues about whether the IWW, whose leaders referred to themselves as industrial unionists, was actually a syndicalist organization. The IWW was too amorphous and diverse an organization to unite under a single ideological mantle—its leaders even argued endlessly about the value of political action—but clearly they were aware of European syndicalist ideas. William Trautmann, a major contributor to the IWW's *Industrial Union Manifesto*, drew explicitly on syndicalist ideas. William Haywood traveled to Europe in 1908 and met with CGT leaders. At the very least the IWW was an organization in which syndicalism was one of several competing ideologies and which frequently used syndicalist practices.

Unlike in much of Europe, the IWW's embrace of syndicalism came from a rejection not of political parties, but of an exclusive and conservative labor federation. American Federation of Labor (AFL) leaders wanted to organize only that fraction of the working class that had valuable craft skills. The AFL virtually ignored largely unskilled southern and Eastern European immigrants, African-American workers, and women of all races and ethnicities. This meant that again unlike most European syndicalists, IWW leaders were advocates of dual unionism who sought to organize unskilled workers rather than working with existing craft unions.

Syndicalism was an ideal ideology for the disempowered and disenfranchised the IWW sought to organize, relying on strength of numbers and confrontational tactics. The IWW leaders, like other syndicalists, considered the union the agent of revolutionary activity and the general strike the means to that revolution. More importantly they drew heavily on syndicalist tactics when organizing workers, be they rugged western miners or immigrant workers in the East, or African-American workers in southern ports. They relied on direct action and especially on its malleability as a strategy in strikes and other confrontations. Up and down the West Coast, Wobblies battled restrictions on free speech, getting arrested reading the Declaration of Independence and overflowing jails to sap recalcitrant towns' resources. In Lawrence, Massachusetts, in 1912, the IWW devised moving picket lines to overcome court injunctions and led marches through the streets so strikers could see their numbers and hear their own voices. The Wobblies guided over 20,000 workers from more than 20 nations to victory in a seemingly unwinnable strike.

In this strike, the most important waged by the IWW on the East Coast, the impact of immigrant syndicalists on the radical union was clear. The IWW relied heavily in Lawrence on the syndicalist *Federazione Socialista Italiana* [FSI], whose members contributed their own notions of direct action. The FSI syndicalists suggested a children's exodus to remove sons and daughters of strikers from the hardship of the strike. They infused the IWW's efforts with the anarchist mentality characteristic of Italian syndicalism, pushing the organization to confront the state directly to free framed striker leaders.

Ultimately the strike in Lawrence and the strike by silk workers in Paterson, New Jersey, in 1913 exposed the strengths and limitations of syndicalist strategy in the United States. Syndicalist tactics were potentially very powerful—scorned textile workers not only in Lawrence, but also in textile towns across the Northeast, won pay increases. But no general strike erupted as a result of the strike, and employers in Paterson, fully aware of the IWW, banded together to defeat it.

The Lawrence strike had an additional unintended effect of squelching an effort to create an alternative syndicalist organization. William Z. Foster, eventually a leading American Communist, was among those who argued the IWW was not a truly syndicalist organization because it practiced dual unionism. The Syndicalist League of North America (SLNA) he created to "bore from within" the American Federation of Labor (AFL)—to try to take control of the largest labor federation in the United States—followed the model of French syndicalism much more closely than the IWW. Unfortunately for Foster, he launched his new organization at the moment of the IWW's success in Lawrence. At its peak the SLNA, which Foster called an educational institution rather than a union, had a couple of dozen branches, mostly in the West and Midwest, and around 2000 members.

Whether or not the IWW was a syndicalist organization, its detractors certainly saw it as one. As its notoriety grew, so, too, did its reputation for advocating sabotage and promoting violence. Though many regarded sabotage and violence as synonymous, sabotage as an oppositional tactic covered a very broad range of potential activities from the destruction of machinery to "soldiering on the job," when workers intentionally slowed down to control the pace of production themselves. Regardless the Socialist party in 1912 voted to expel any members who advocated the use of sabotage or violence—a move aimed squarely at IWW members. In broader terms IWW advocacy of sabotage contributed to an aura of potential violence that followed its members wherever they went.

The notion that the IWW was a potentially violent organization was not wholly a fabrication. Sorel provided a theoretical basis for the use of revolutionary violence. The IWW members did not shy from advocating violence in conflicts with armed defenders of capitalism. But most Wobbly exhortations to violence never moved beyond a rhetorical level, and most of the time when actual violence occurred, the Wobblies responded in self-defense—and got the worst of it. Especially once the United States entered World War I, and during the postwar Red Scare, vigilante groups and patriotic organizations frequently attacked IWW members.

World War I and Its Aftermath

World War I was a turning point for syndicalism in the United States in two ways. First the flexibility of syndicalist philosophy and its emphasis on the creation of emotion-provoking myths and on the utility of revolutionary violence led certain immigrant syndicalists far to the right. Though the IWW strenuously opposed the war, many syndicalists throughout Europe and in certain immigrant communities in the United States supported it. Some believed that an armed proletariat would eventually turn to revolution; others began to argue that only nationalism could galvanize revolutionary ardor. The FSI members for example split angrily over the war; most who favored intervention eventually returned to Italy and became Fascists.

Those who remained opposed to the war—including virtually the entire IWW—faced an enormous backlash. Many immigrant syndicalists were deported. The IWW was plagued with mass arrests and became little more than a defense organization. By 1919, over 20 states had passed criminal syndicalism laws—once again the organization was deemed syndicalist by its foes—to aid prosecution of IWW members.

Syndicalists also had to face the emergence of the powerful new revolutionary force of communism. Though many syndicalists initially greeted the Russian revolution with enthusiasm, disaffection quickly followed as Lenin centralized power in the Soviet Union. It soon became clear moreover that Communists and syndicalists striving to organize workers would be ideological foes far more often than they were allies.

Syndicalism, especially if defined broadly as a set of tactics, survived the war in various ways. A number of the new unions, like the Amalgamated Clothing Workers of America and the International Ladies' Garment Workers' Union, had syndicalist members and emphasized direct action and the general strike. One historian discerned syndicalist impulses among San Francisco dockworkers in the 1930s, and one could make a similar argument for many CIO unions in their early militant days. But over the decades syndicalist tactics were sapped of the revolutionary vigor that had made the philosophy so potentially valuable to workers and that had created so much fear in its opponents.

MICHAEL M. TOPP

References and Further Reading

Dubofsky, Melvyn. *We Shall Be All: A History of the Industrial Workers of the World*. Chicago, IL: Quadrangle Books, 1969.

Foster, William, and Earl C. Ford. *Syndicalism*. Chicago, IL: Charles H. Kerr Publishing Company, 1990.

Kimeldorf, Howard. *Battling for American Labor: Wobblies, Craft Workers, and the Making of the Union Movement*. Berkeley: University of California Press, 1999.

Preston, William. *Aliens and Dissenters: Federal Suppression of Radicals, 1903–1933*. Urbana: University of Illinois Press, 1995.

Salerno, Salvatore. *Red November, Black November: Culture and Community in the Industrial Workers of the World*. Albany, New York: State University of New York Press, 1989.

Sorel, Georges. *Reflections on Violence*. Boston, MA: Cambridge University Press, 1999. (reprint, 1908)

Topp, Michael M. *Those without a Country: The Political Culture of Italian American Syndicalists*. Minneapolis: University of Minnesota Press, 2001.

See also **Amalgamated Clothing Workers/ UNITE; American Federation of Labor; Anarchism; Congress of Industrial Organizations; Dual Unionism; Foster, William Z.; Haywood, William; Industrial Workers of the World; Italians; Lawrence Strike (1912); Paterson (NJ) Silk Strike (1913); Textiles; World War I**

T

TAFT, PHILIP (1902–1976)
Labor Scholar, Historiographer

During the era when organized labor became "Big Labor," Philip Taft became the leading representative of the primary mode of U.S. labor historiography, the "Wisconsin School" of labor history. He gained scholarly prominence by adapting the school's analytical framework to the changes in organized labor brought about by the New Deal and the Congress of Industrial Organizations (CIO). Taft's persistent emphasis on the realities of institutional development, as manifested in changing union organization and operation, was well suited to comprehending the labor movement's experience with unprecedented organizational restructuring and expansion.

Taft's apprenticeship in labor scholarship began in 1928, with his enrollment in the labor studies program offered by the University of Wisconsin's Economics Department. Taft quickly embraced the program's unconventional practice of economics, with its emphasis on the empirical investigation of organized labor's experience with American capitalism. Underlying Taft's positive response was his own decade-long experience as a laborer in America's mobile workforce. Taft proceeded to make the Wisconsin School approach into his own. Narrating how unionists actually built and administered their own organizations became the enduring characteristic of his scholarship.

At Wisconsin, Taft worked closely with Selig Perlman, whose influential *A Theory of the Labor Movement* was published the year that Taft enrolled.

Taft conspicuously launched his career in 1935 when he coauthored with Perlman the fourth and final volume of the series that placed the Wisconsin School at the head of American labor scholarship, *History of Labor in the United States*. Like many of his fellow Wisconsin graduates, Taft worked in public administration. His service record included the Wisconsin Industrial Commission, the Resettlement and Social Security Administrations, and the War Labor Board. During his lengthy residence with Brown University's Economics Department (1937–1968), his involvement with the practice of labor relations continued. However, his primary career commitment was to research and teaching.

True to his Wisconsin training, Taft's extensive research record included investigations into contemporary unionism as well as historical union development. His contemporary focus was on the problems unions faced as independent institutions with distinctive modes of organization and operation. He examined existing union structures—the AFL's trade union autonomy, the CIO's organizational expansionism, and AFL-CIO rivalry—to assess their impact on the conduct of union functions: institution building, internal union governance, organizing policy, collective bargaining strategy, and public policy. His interest in these relationships endured throughout his career, with major studies published in 1954 and 1975.

Taft's best-known publications were histories: a two-volume history of the AFL (1957, 1959) and a single-volume survey of organized labor in the United States (1964). His historical analysis centered on the same union structures and functions but reversed the lines of influence. Taft detailed how the demands of solving everyday operational problems generated a structural core of "business unionism" common to successive versions of American unionism. Highlighted in his account was a pattern in which the ideological positions of unionists were repeatedly eclipsed by the problem-solving activities of unions. Taft's stress on the pervasiveness of business unionism—Taft's preferred terminology—re-iterated the Wisconsin School emphasis on job-conscious unionism. At the same time, he located the origins of this unionism in an institutional logic instead of the ideological conflict featured in Perlman's history. With this interpretive move, he established the continuity between the AFL and CIO. Taft thereby overcame the historiographical dilemma confronting the Wisconsin School, the analytical impasse generated by Perlman's equation of job-conscious unionism with AFL trade unionism.

Despite his objections to Perlman's adherence to outmoded theory in the face of changing historical reality, Taft remained bound to Perlman's theory in ways that limited his own historical reconstructions. Taft's treatment of business unionism as the essence of unionism led him to reduce the history of American unionism to the history of business unionism. Because his treatment of unions as institutions minimized their intersection with nonunion institutions, he similarly narrowed the bounds of institutional analysis.

Taft's significance is tied to his role in two historiographical transitions, since he twice served as a central figure in defining the relationship between one generation of labor historians and the next. In the first instance, he led economists in adapting the Wisconsin School's analytical framework to the changing realities fostered by New Deal reforms. Conversely, when historians responded to postwar social reform movements by broadening their empirical reach to include previously excluded workers and institutions, Taft held fast to the analytical boundaries set by his mentors. His adherence to Wisconsin School realism was grounded in the school's enduring quarrel with the reality-defying abstractions of mainstream economics. Despite the reasons behind his position, the limits of Taft's adaptability were momentous for the practice of labor history, marking the end of the Wisconsin School's interpretive hold over the field.

RONALD APPLEGATE

Selected Works

The A.F. of L. from the Death of Gompers to the Merger. New York: Harper & Brothers, 1959.

The A. F. of L. in the Time of Gompers. New York: Harper & Brothers, 1957.
History of Labor in the United States, 1896 to 1932, vols. III and IV, with others. New York: Macmillan, 1935.
"On the Origins of Business Unionism." *Industrial and Labor Relations Review* 17 (October 1963): 20–38.
Organized Labor in American History. New York: Harper & Row, 1964.
Rights of Union Members and the Government. Westport, CT: Greenwood Press, 1975.
The Structure and Government of Labor Unions. Cambridge, MA: Harvard University Press, 1954.

References and Further Reading

Barbash, Jack. "Americanizing the Labor Problem: The Wisconsin School." In *Labor Economics and Industrial Relations: Markets and Institutions,* edited by Clark Kerr and Paul D. Staudohar. Cambridge, MA.: Harvard University Press, 1994, pp. 41–65.
Brody, David. "Philip Taft: Labor Scholar." *Labor History* [Philip Taft commemorative issue] 19 (Winter 1978): 9–22.

See also **Commons, John Rogers; Historiography of American Labor History; Perlman, Selig**

TAFT-HARTLEY ACT

The Taft-Hartley Act, or the Labor Management Relations Act of 1947, was the first large-scale revision of a major New Deal program. Passed during a period of increasing hostility to labor as a result of the post-World War II strike wave, Taft-Hartley placed a number of restrictions on labor union practices. The Act's partisans argued that the bill would help equalize the playing field between labor and management, though its opponents instead labeled it a "Slave Labor Act." The Act survived a veto by President Truman and six decades of lobbying for its repeal, and most of its provisions are still in effect.

Origins of the Act

Almost immediately after the passage of the Wagner Act in 1935, which set up the National Labor Relations Board (NLRB) in an attempt to protect workers' efforts at creating and joining unions, groups like the National Association of Manufacturers (NAM) and the Chambers of Commerce began to lobby for a revision of federal labor policy. These groups argued that the NLRB and the Wagner Act were biased in favor of workers, pointing to the list of restrictions on the actions of management that were included in the 1935 act without any comparable restrictions on the actions of labor unions. Numerous Republicans and southern Democrats proposed revisions to the Wagner Act in the ensuing decades, most of them aimed at restricting certain union practices, such as the closed shop, a situation where union membership becomes a precondition for hiring, and secondary boycotts, which is when a union refuses to deal with any firm that purchases goods from the target of a boycott.

These attempts at labor reform came to naught until public opinion turned sharply against the labor movement in the immediate aftermath of World War II. While the strike wave that occurred in 1945 and 1946 was considerably smaller than the one which followed the first World War, it nevertheless was large enough to renew cries for reining in the power of the labor movement. Even prominent Democrats who had been largely prolabor, such as Harry Truman, became increasingly disillusioned with parts of the labor leadership when figures like John L. Lewis led their workers out on strike not just against employers, but even against the government.

The Republicans won back control of both houses of Congress in 1946, at least partially as a result of a wave of antilabor sentiment in the wake of the strike wave. The new Republican leaders of Congress seized upon this new public mood and quickly went to work to craft a bill aimed at reforming federal labor policy. This effort was led by Representative Fred A. Hartley Jr. of New Jersey and Senator Robert A. Taft of Ohio. Both men headed the Labor Committees of their respective houses of Congress, and both moved quickly to hold hearings and draft bills amending the Wagner Act.

Both bills were largely similar, though the Hartley bill was considerably more harsh. After the Taft-Hartley Act was passed, Hartley claimed that he had intentionally made his bill more extreme so that when a compromise bill was agreed on in the end, it would seem more moderate. Regardless, the compromise bill agreed upon by both houses of Congress ended up including most of the provisions that had long been called for by the NAM and other anti-union organizations. Moreover, it was immediately criticized by both the AFL and the CIO, along with a number of northern Democrats, liberals, and labor economists.

Despite this opposition, the bill sailed through both houses of Congress with overwhelming majorities, garnering votes from both Republicans and southern Democrats. President Truman decided to veto the bill, but his veto was overridden by Congress, and the Act was passed. While most at the time viewed Truman's veto as having resulted from an actual opposition to the Taft-Hartley Act, some scholars have disputed this view. In fact, Truman had become increasingly wary of some of the most powerful labor leaders, especially John L. Lewis, and actually had pushed for some labor legislation to increase his authority over unions that strike against the national interest. As a result, some have suggested that Truman vetoed the bill precisely because he knew his veto would be overridden. That way, he would be able to garner the appreciation of the labor movement while still achieving substantive labor reforms and increasing his authority to intervene in strikes.

Taft-Hartley's Provisions

The Taft-Hartley Act contained a number of revisions to federal labor policy. The major revisions fall into three main categories: first, the creation of a category of unfair labor practices to match the pre-existing set of unfair management practices instituted by the Wagner Act; second, limitations and restrictions on union security clauses in contracts; and third, institutional changes to the National Labor Relations Board. In addition, there were a number of minor changes covering a variety of topics, including the eligibility of supervisors to join unions and the status of Communists in positions of union leadership.

One of the stated goals of the drafters of the Taft-Hartley Act was to equalize the powers of labor and management. To accomplish this, the Act included a list of union practices that were to be outlawed as a counterweight to the list of unfair management practices already in effect. The most important of these restrictions was a ban on jurisdictional strikes, strikes that were called for the purpose of forcing an employer to give work only to members of a given union, and secondary boycotts. Both of these tactics had become popular among certain powerful unions, particularly the Teamsters.

Of more importance to the labor movement as a whole, Taft-Hartley placed restrictions on many popular union security practices. The closed shop was banned under Taft-Hartley, and it was made more difficult for unions to institute a union shop, where employees are forced to join the union after they are hired, and automatic dues checkoff, where the employer removes union dues directly from an employee's paycheck. Moreover, under Taft-Hartley, individual states could pass "right-to-work" laws, which would outlaw the practice of the union shop entirely.

Taft-Hartley also acted to restructure the NLRB, dividing its authority in two by creating a General Counsel, which was meant to be independent from the rest of the Board. This Counsel had the ability and the obligation to seek injunctions against both employers and unions who violated the Act. This division of powers was intended to separate the prosecutorial from the decision-making aspects of the NLRB's work and to potentially dilute the supposed pro-union bent of the Board.

Finally, the Act included a number of miscellaneous provisions. These included empowering the president to intervene in strikes that threatened a national emergency, requiring union leaders to sign affidavits stating that they were not supporters of the Communist Party, and explicitly excluding supervisors from protection from the NLRB. While these provisions did not form the basis for the contemporary opposition to Taft-Hartley, some have taken on increased importance in later years, both rhetorically and practically. The anticommunist affidavits, for instance, were not a major sticking point for most of the staunchly anticommunist AFL and CIO unions, although later scholars critical of the Act have placed a great deal of importance on it. And the provision excluding supervisors from NLRB bargaining units quickly became a powerful anti-union tactic for companies, allowing them to reclassify large segments of their employees as supervisors, thus making them ineligible for union membership.

Consequences of the Act

Despite the heated rhetoric surrounding its passage and the frequent attempts to repeal it over the last six decades, the Taft-Hartley Act had surprisingly few ramifications for the American labor movement. The unions that many thought would be most affected by the new list of unfair labor practices, such as the Teamsters, continued to flourish after the passage of the law. Union strength and the incidence of strikes were largely unaffected by the passage of the law, and outside of the South, where "right-to-work" laws were quickly enacted, union security provisions continued to flourish in most unions. Some have pointed to the South as the area hardest hit by Taft-Hartley, arguing that the "right-to-work" provisions were responsible for the low rates of unionization throughout the region. However, the labor movement was weak in the South even before Taft-Hartley.

Nevertheless, hostility toward Taft-Hartley continues to this day. Congressional efforts to repeal the Act were almost successful under the Carter and Clinton administrations, and Ralph Nader has used repeal of the Act as one of his campaign platforms in at least two presidential elections. Certain sections of the law have been amended or deemed unconstitutional by the Supreme Court, particularly the

provision mandating anticommunist affidavits. Nevertheless, most aspects of the law remain in effect.

AARON MAX BERKOWITZ

References and Further Reading

Dubofsky, Melvyn. *The State and Labor in Modern America*. Chapel Hill: University of North Carolina Press, 1994.

Lee, R. Alton. *Truman and Taft-Hartley: A Question of Mandate*. Lexington: University of Kentucky Press, 1966.

TAPPES, SHELTON, (1911–1991)
First Recording Secretary, United Auto Workers Local 600

Shelton Tappes, an African-American autoworker and the first recording secretary of United Auto Workers (UAW) Local 600, the largest local in the world in 1941, was born March 27, 1911, in Omaha, Nebraska. During the 1930s, Tappes, who participated in labor activities supported by the left, became one of the leading labor organizers within the black community of Detroit. As a member of the UAW's Negro Ford Organizing Committee, he was in the vanguard of black labor leadership, holding the position of chairman of the foundry at the Ford's River Rouge plant during the Rouge strike in April 1941. After the successful strike, Tappes was part of the Ford negotiating committee for the first union contract between the UAW and Ford Motor Company.

Tappes's early schooling, including high school and one semester on scholarship at the University of Nebraska, was in Omaha. He moved with his family to Detroit in 1927 and got his first job as an auto worker at the Briggs plant working in the wet-sanding department in 1928. During the Depression years, Tappes participated in social protest actions carried out by the Communist Party. While he was never a member of the Party, his curiosity pulled him toward educational programs and other activities sponsored by the Communists. For example, he participated in fund-raising for the Scottsboro Boys and Angelo Herndon, activities that were sponsored by Communist-affiliated groups such as the International Labor Defense.

In 1936, Tappes was hired to work in the foundry at the River Rouge plant of Ford Motor Company. Soon after, he became part of the early UAW organizing efforts through his work with the UAW Negro Ford Organizing Committee, which met every Sunday morning. The committee consisted of ministers, attorneys, and workers from Ford, Dodge, Murray, and Packard auto plants. Committee members fanned out through the black community to disseminate information about the importance of the UAW to African-American workers. The experience taught Tappes the skills that made him indispensable as a union organizer for the UAW. After the successful strike at the River Rouge plant in the spring of 1941, Tappes was elected first recording secretary of UAW Local 600, the largest and most militant local in the country, a position he held until 1946. As the leader of Local 600 and the left-leaning faction identified with George Addes and R. J. Thomas, Tappes initiated activities and goals for what soon became a "Negro" caucus in the UAW. He placed what was considered one of the most important issues among black workers on the table in 1943 when he proposed the appointment of a black representative on the International Executive Board (IEB) of the UAW at the Buffalo convention. The "Tappes" resolution did not succeed, but the issue of black representation galvanized black trade unionists to unite around common grievances within the union. Tappes also worked with the interracial Metropolitan Detroit Council on Fair Employment Practices and the Citizens Committee for Jobs in War Industry, two groups devoted to combating bias in the defense industry.

In 1945, Tappes lost the endorsement of the progressive, or left, caucus, which cost him the election for recording secretary. Soon after Walter Reuther became president of the UAW, he eliminated many black staff positions, which further weakened Tappes's influence. Increasingly, Tappes distanced himself from the Communist-tainted wing of the progressive black caucus. In 1950, Tappes applied for a position on the Ford Department staff of the UAW, which was once all white. Reuther hired Tappes—knowing full well that he had never voted for him—because of the high regard he had among black workers. Tappes signed on first as international representative for the UAW and was appointed assistant to William Oliver, the director of the Fair Employment Practices Department (FEPD), a few years later. Tappes once compared the role of the FEPD under Oliver to that of a fire station: rather than initiating changes in employment practices, the FEPD restricted its activities to putting out fires when the bell rang.

In 1957, Tappes joined with other black moderates within the UAW leadership circle to form the Trade Union Leadership Council (TULC) for the purpose of not only promoting African-Americans to higher positions but increasing the responsibilities of those already on the UAW's paid staff. The TULC was largely responsible for getting Nelson Jack Edwards

on the IEB in 1962, which was the culmination of the resolution introduced by Tappes in 1943.

Tappes retired in 1976 and was in the process of organizing around issues related to aging when he died on April 19, 1991.

BETH TOMPKINS BATES

References and Further Reading

Hill, Herbert. "Interview of Sheldon Tappes, October 27, 1967, and February 10, 1968." In *Blacks in the Labor Movement*. Detroit: Archives of Labor and Urban Affairs, Wayne State University.

Lichtenstein, Nelson. *Walter Reuther: The Most Dangerous Man in Detroit*. New York: Basic Books, 1995.

Stephan-Norris, Judith, and Maurice Zeitlin. *Talking Union*. Urbana: University of Illinois Press, 1996.

See also **Sheffield, Horace**

TEACHING

Teaching takes place in families, churches, organizations, and workplaces around the globe, but the occupation called teaching typically refers to the labor performed by an adult in a schoolroom of young people. Locally controlled in the United States, this work concerns the transmission of socially valued knowledge, skills, and habits. Teaching involves three core tasks: planning and delivering instruction, creating opportunities for students to practice their learning and expand their knowledge, and assessing student performance. Whether in public or private schools, these tasks have remained remarkably stable over time. Social, political, and economic developments, however, have influenced when and where schools were established, how they are organized, who became teachers, and how teachers approach these tasks.

Teaching in Early America

Schooling varied considerably among the colonies. Only in New England towns did anything resembling public education exist. Believing that widespread literacy would foster a godly, lawful community, the Puritans established one-room schools sustained by local taxation. Few schools existed in the southern colonies where settlements were sparse and distant. Wealthy planters hired itinerant tutors to instruct their children for a few months of the year, while other people educated their children themselves. Limiting access to knowledge was crucial to the maintenance of the slave system, and by the eighteenth century, southern colonies made teaching slaves illegal. New England-style district schools spread to the Middle Atlantic and western states, but very few opened in the southern states until after the Civil War. Churches maintained charity schools for the urban poor, and private academies and denominational schools also provided work for teachers. In large communities, a schoolmaster might have as many as one hundred pupils, and in small ones, an enrollment of 10 or 15. Schools were generally ungraded, though in large cities pupils were more likely to be separated by age and achievement into two groups: elementary and grammar schools.

Colonial schools were usually taught by men; some were barely literate, others college educated. Many communities valued evidence of good character over academic achievement when selecting a teacher. The common practice of boarding the schoolmaster with local families suggests that teaching was a single man's occupation, but some communities provided a house for the schoolmaster and his family, loath to employ transient unmarried men of questionable character. Occasionally, school boards hired women who needed income to teach young children and girls, or to teach during the summer when men were needed in the fields. Some widows also operated private "dame schools" out of their homes.

With school terms ranging from as little as two to 10 months a year, teaching was seldom regarded as a full-time, lifelong occupation. For the most part, men regarded teaching as temporary employment, which they would happily abandon if a better opportunity arose. Many taught to support themselves while preparing for a higher-status profession. Others pieced together a living by moving from one short-term school to another. Some supplemented teaching with work in the church or local government, while others farmed or engaged in other productive labor. This was not unusual in early America; only a small number of men specialized in a single occupation.

Comparatively free from direct supervision, teachers were nonetheless appraised by laypersons in the community. Ministers, local politicians, prominent citizens, and parents visited schools to hear the students read, examine their written work, check on attendance, and generally evaluate the teachers' work. Teachers were also expected to maintain the schoolhouse, keeping it clean and supplied with firewood. These visits, sometimes unannounced, influenced a teacher's continued employment and funding for the school.

Teachers typically received a combination of wages and perquisites in exchange for their labor. Perquisites might include room and board; the use of land, a house, or a horse; or the right to charge tuition for teaching additional subjects or for teaching pupils from outlying areas. Because teachers' pay came from the public purse, some communities awarded school employment to individuals unable to support themselves, such as physically handicapped men or widows. Schoolmasters generally earned more than common laborers, about the same or a little less than artisans, and much less than ministers, physicians, and lawyers. Schoolmistresses' pay was exceptionally lower.

Teaching Becomes Women's Work

Agricultural patterns continued to shape rural teaching in the nineteenth century, but rapid urban and industrial development spurred changes in city schools. Both working people and middle-class reformers agitated for more and better schooling. Reformers argued that the nation needed to educate and assimilate the immigrant masses, while leaders of the antebellum working class demanded public education as a measure of the nation's commitment to building a workingman's republic. The resulting mid-nineteenth-century common school movement increased the availability of education for urban youth, and in the process, fostered the expansion and feminization of the nation's teaching force.

In pursuit of greater operating economies, city school boards began to reconfigure school work in ways that made teaching less attractive to men. As teaching became more regimented, more time-consuming, and less rewarding in the 1830s, the number of male teachers in industrial states like Massachusetts began to decline. Lengthening the school year and standardizing the school day, school boards inhibited teachers from pursuing other employment while teaching. They also placed large numbers of teachers under the supervision of one principal-teacher, sharply reducing the number of positions in which men could exercise an accustomed degree of autonomy. By separating students into grades, school boards economized on salaries paid for teaching the lower grades, assumed to require less skill and knowledge, and they began to fill these positions with women. Besides encouraging men to seek other employment, these changes stratified school employment in ways that resembled domestic relations within the household, with women in charge of children yet accountable to a patriarchal figure, making women's employment in schools seem more natural than it had previously appeared.

The movement for women's education made this vast source of labor available for teaching. Whereas colonial literacy rates show a significant disparity between men and women, the gap closed after the Revolution. Enlightenment and republican ideals inspired tremendous improvements in women's education without conferring equal citizenship. The Revolutionary generation continued to deny women equality, but it ascribed to them new political obligations as the wives, mothers, and educators of citizens. Private academies flourished, and the training women received widened their prospects to include teaching.

Founders of female academies, like Catharine Beecher and Emma Willard, popularized teaching as a respectable work for young women that was not a departure from traditional female roles but rather preparation for their obligations as wives and mothers. Previously, women's work outside the home diminished the status of women, as well as the status of the men in their families, but in the nineteenth century, a few years of teaching became understood as a temporary stage in a woman's life, devoted to the service of others. Since women employed as teachers were presumed to be dependent on their fathers and expected to become dependent on a husband, and since they had few alternatives for wage-earning work, school boards rationalized paying women between 50% and 70% less than men.

Seeking to produce larger numbers of qualified teachers, U.S. educators adopted a European innovation: the normal, or teacher-training, school. The reformer and politician Horace Mann secured funding for the first state normal school in Lexington, Massachusetts, in 1839. Other states followed, using public funds to open more than 100 state normal schools and many more city and county normals by the turn of the twentieth century. Unlike in Europe, normal schools in the United States enrolled mostly women, offering two to four years of advanced education and pedagogical training in exchange for a pledge to teach. The growth of normal schools in the 1870s brought the daughters of farmers and mechanics into teaching, and in subsequent decades, city normal schools inadvertently fostered greater ethnic diversity among teachers, opening the occupation to a growing number of native-born daughters of immigrants, especially Irish-American and Jewish-American women. Despite the very low cost of attendance, only a minority of nineteenth-century teachers attended normal schools. As long as the need for trained teachers outstripped availability, normal training represented a means to advance to a more desirable position in a city school, especially one of the new high schools. It did not become a requirement for entry into teaching in most states until the twentieth century. More common was a few days' attendance at regional teachers' institutes, held once or twice a year. Led by administrators and experienced teachers,

institutes offered brief courses of study to enhance teachers' skills.

Nineteenth-century efforts to improve the work of teachers also included the formation of voluntary organizations. Men founded the earliest state teachers' associations as well as the American Institute of Instruction and the National Teachers Association, later renamed the National Education Association (NEA). Attracting mostly male educators, these national associations attempted to influence policy making in education and create a more self-regulating profession. Female classroom teachers began to form their own associations for mutual aid and economic protection in the 1870s.

The process of obtaining employment in teaching varied, but for most of the nineteenth century, laypersons, not educational professionals, hired teachers. Positions were sometimes advertised, but local authorities often awarded desirable positions to family members and friends. In both rural and urban schools, nepotism and patronage appear common, but employment in teaching almost always entailed some form of examination. Typically, the local minister or a school board member examined prospective teachers. Usually the examination was conducted privately, but some communities staged it as a public competition. Examiners might ask candidates about teaching methods or discipline, and perhaps quiz them on spelling or arithmetic. Some examiners concentrated on evaluating a prospective teacher's character. Others attempted to assess their mastery of academic subjects, while some simply tried to gauge whether the candidate had the strength to keep the big boys in line or haul firewood in the winter. Examinations for urban schools and high schools were more likely to emphasize academics. If successful, teachers received an official certificate, authorizing them to teach for one year in the district where the examination took place. Toward the end of the nineteenth century, examinations included written, graded tests in a range of subjects, and certification covered teaching throughout the county for a longer period of time.

Just as hiring practices varied, so did the terms and conditions of employment. No regulations governed teachers' pay or workplaces. Instead, gender and region factored strongly, with most city teachers earning two to three times what rural teachers did, and men earning two to three times what women doing similar work earned. Both urban and rural school facilities ranged from modest to uncomfortable. Common complaints included overcrowded classrooms, inadequate heating, and unsanitary facilities. Throughout the nation, but especially in cities and across the impoverished post-Civil War South, the cost of providing public education exceeded authorities' expectations. After emancipation, southern blacks crowded into makeshift schools in church basements, abandoned buildings, and under tree arbors. Local governments' miserly provisions for black schools hastened their employment of blacks as teachers, paying them a small fraction of what white teachers in white schools earned. Abysmal pay and facilities in segregated schools persisted until well into the twentieth century, but for black women, teaching represented the very best of a limited range of employment options.

Though seldom prestigious, teaching offered women unprecedented opportunities in the nineteenth century. While male teachers often complained of poor pay and demeaning supervision, family life accustomed women to labor with little or no remuneration and close supervision. Teaching offered women the means to live apart from family and even migrate, earn a small income, and maintain social respect—opportunities seldom experienced by middle-class women but taken for granted by middle-class men. Normal and academy-trained teachers figured prominently among those who migrated to teach on the frontier, overseas, and in the post-Civil War South. Although their migrations were likely influenced by spiritual and moral beliefs, most historians agree that a sense of mission was not the only factor. Self-supporting income, the prospect of useful labor, opportunities for higher learning, and often a desire to escape social constraints attracted women to pursue teaching opportunities near and far from home. Female domestic and factory workers sometimes earned more than women who taught, but the personal independence associated with teaching kept schools supplied with an educated, committed workforce. After the Civil War, women teachers reported working for much longer periods of their lives. Though available statistics are limited, average teacher tenure in cities like Boston extended to nearly 20 years. By 1900, teaching had become a means for women to postpone and, in some cases, reject marriage.

Teaching in Modern America

As the U.S. population exploded at the turn of the twentieth century, schools no longer looked like independent local enterprises but more like parts of a vast, nationwide bureaucracy structured by gender. Between 1870 and 1900, the nation's schools expanded dramatically; the number of teachers more than tripled. Women filled most of these teaching positions; they also composed the majority of elementary school principals and even attained the superintendency in several cites and states and many counties. Curtailing women's occupational advancement through teaching, however, were two related developments. First, existing political systems of school governance came under attack, and second, male educators re-asserted authority over education with a new centralized bureaucracy. Together, these developments consolidated a class of male administrators with authority over a predominantly female teaching force.

Criticism of the ward-based system of school governance in large cities precipitated the transfer of authority from local school districts to a central superintendency. Progressive-era reformers argued that local control fostered graft and patronage rather than efficient systematic education. They contended that ward politics had no place in the schools and that rational scientific planning would better facilitate the goals of public education. They succeeded in restructuring public education along corporate bureaucratic lines, creating new positions of administrative authority for a rising cadre of educational professionals, few of whom were women or long-serving classroom teachers. Centralization improved some of the terms of teachers' employment, but it also raised the specter of teachers becoming subject to industrial conditions of work.

With centralization, employment relations between teachers and public schools formalized. States took over responsibility for certification, introducing a range of certifications to reflect various levels of teacher training and moving away from examinations as a means of establishing qualifications to teach. Written contracts of employment also replaced oral agreements, giving teachers more security but also subjecting them to extensive new professional and moral regulation. Written rules prohibiting teachers from dancing, drinking, and dressing immodestly date from this era.

In cities like New York and Chicago, women teachers' associations rallied to defend the ward system, preferring the locally controlled, politicized schools they knew to the impersonal, "factoryized" schools they feared. Centralization portended to distance teachers from decision making in education. It also altered the relationship between teachers and their communities, frustrating teachers who saw their already limited authority diminished by these new relations of employment. Teachers regarded some reforms favorably, for example, efforts to replace the dubious oral examination with more definitive certification requirements. But accustomed to promotions based on seniority, many teachers objected when school authorities proposed to use standardized tests of merit to determine promotions, worried that test performance would matter more than years of classroom performance.

Several local teachers' associations developed into teachers' unions during these years. Formed to protect teachers' interests and provide mutual aid, these local associations grew more militant as centralization reconfigured relations between school authorities, teachers, and the communities they served. No longer beholden to school authorities as they had been under the ward system and yet alienated within these new bureaucracies, organized teachers developed a sharper sense of class identity and felt freer to make economic demands on their own behalf. Among the most influential early teacher organizations was the Chicago Teachers' Federation, which at the height of its power claimed more than half the elementary school teachers in the city as members. It affiliated with the Chicago Federation of Labor in 1902 and became Local 1 of the American Federation of Teachers (AFT) in 1916. Teacher activism peaked in the first decades of the twentieth century when the cost of living surged ahead of teacher salaries. But activism seldom reached small town and rural teachers, and the majority of city teachers remained more likely to join conservative professional and protective associations than unions.

Organized teachers, especially AFT members, suffered through the anti-union backlash and red scare of the World War I era. Even though most teachers were native born, white, female, and middle class, critics questioned their patriotism and professionalism. Entrusted with the responsibility to Americanize their pupils and blamed for soldiers' poor performance on intelligence tests, organized teachers were accused of being neither adequately trained nor sufficiently loyal. Superintendents urged teachers to join the more professional NEA, and legislatures around the country required teachers to sign loyalty pledges and passed laws to remove teachers who made any "treasonable or seditious" acts or statements. Thousands of teachers were suspended or discharged, or had their licenses revoked for violating loyalty regulations. Dutiful work was no longer enough; teachers were now enjoined to display their professionalism and loyalty as well.

Following this period of punitive regulation, the nation faced a serious teacher shortage. In the 1920s, the proportion of men in teaching declined to less than 15%, while opportunities in better-paid clerical and sales jobs enticed women to leave the classroom. School authorities' first response was to raise salaries and lower entry requirements, but some states experimented with raising standards to require normal school graduation for elementary teachers and bachelor's degrees for secondary teachers. These higher requirements for entry into teaching produced favorable results, leading other states to follow suit and soon creating a surplus of teachers. World War II brought another shortage, and again by raising entry requirements to require bachelor's degrees in most states, the schools attracted more wage earners into teaching.

As states raised hiring qualifications for new teachers, teachers grew more likely to identify as professionals rather than dependent servants of the community. Educational research and pedagogical innovations also contributed to teachers' sense of expertise. Although teacher activism declined during WWII, teachers demonstrated greater confidence in the value of their work and more impatience with poor remuneration in the following years.

Mid-Twentieth-Century Transformations

Teaching at mid-century was marked by numerous struggles over pay and discrimination. Faced with spiraling inflation after WWII, teachers in several cities resorted to strikes. Throughout the 1940s and well before *Brown V. Board of Education*, black teachers fought for equal pay with whites in school districts across the South, while white women teachers finally achieved pay equity with men in most urban schools in the 1950s. But even when these struggles succeeded, many still felt shortchanged because their salaries did not keep pace with inflation. Teachers' battles for gender and race equity and a fair standard of living persisted, while another form of employment discrimination, against married women as teachers, came to an abrupt end at mid-century without much of a struggle at all.

Prejudice against married women as teachers derived from two deeply rooted ideas in American society: first, that women's labor belongs to their husbands, and second, that public employment is akin to charity. School authorities doubted that women could serve their families and the schools without slighting the latter, and assuming married women did not need to earn income, they were also wary of putting them on the public payroll. During economic downturns in the late nineteenth century, some school boards passed regulations that required women teachers to resign when they married. About 5% of female teachers were married at the turn of the twentieth century when New York teachers launched a successful attack on prohibitions to married women's employment in schools. School authorities re-instated marriage bars during the Great Depression but dropped them again during WWII.

Several factors ensured that marriage bars would not return. War-related employment and higher wages in other lines of work reduced the pool of candidates interested in teaching, while the postwar marriage and baby boom increased demands on already limited school resources. At the same time, cultural concerns about sexual deviance raised anxieties about a teaching force composed largely of spinsters. As women won political rights, made economic demands, and lived independently of men in the twentieth century, critics had begun to question the influence of spinster teachers over children, charging that they made boys effeminate and girls more interested in teaching than marriage. In the 1940s, educators reversed their opinion on the employment of married women, suddenly arguing that motherhood enhanced teachers' success. Intense policing of gendered behavior and appearance among school employees followed, precipitating a sharp decline in single women teachers from 69% in 1940 to less than 30% of teachers in 1960. According to the historian Jackie Blount, this exodus of single women took place while married women entered teaching at twice the rate they entered the general workforce.

Schools also began to work hard to recruit male teachers as role models for boys, especially at the high school level. The baby boom triggered some growth in elementary schools, where most women continued to be employed, but high schools nearly doubled in size between 1957 and 1979. Anxious to attract more men to the work, school authorities promised career paths that failed to measure up to recruits' expectations. Frustrated city high school teachers fueled the resurgence of teacher unions in the 1960s, with aggressive demands for improved school conditions for all and better terms of employment for teachers. Participating in public demonstrations and standing on picket lines in defense of their social and economic rights did not feel unprofessional, disloyal, or self-interested to this new cohort of young male breadwinner-teachers as it did to many women teachers. Rather, in the context of the civil rights movement, these new male teachers regarded their activism as part of the broader movement for social justice.

Many teachers now identify as agents in the struggle against social inequality. Since the mid-twentieth-century battles over desegregating schools, diversity in the nation's classrooms has once again soared with multiple races, religions, ethnicities, and languages represented. Historically, Americans' strong support for public education derives from the belief that schooling provides all youth with equal opportunities. Attempting to make that dream become real continues to both motivate and frustrate individuals who pursue careers in teaching.

Receiving an education has long represented empowerment and social mobility for disadvantaged youth. For many minority groups in the twentieth century, pursuing a career in teaching has signified both personal social advancement and a commitment to help others follow. Teaching became associated with class advancement when educated blacks won positions in the segregated schools of the post-emancipation South and used those positions to claim rights and create a black middle class. Teaching shaped another trajectory of social mobility when the native-born daughters of Irish and Jewish immigrants secured jobs in urban schools in the early twentieth century. Their entry into the predominantly white, middle-class teaching force hastened the assimilation of those racialized groups, but it did not spur recruitment among other minority groups. Indeed, the race and gender of the teaching force has remained remarkably constant over the last 150 years. At the turn of the twenty-first century, women compose 72% of teachers, and only 13% of teachers are people of color. Asian, Hispanic, and Native Indian teachers remain rare. The nation's teaching force is not nearly as diverse as the student body.

A Profession, an Occupation, or a Vocation?

Scholars debate whether teaching should be understood as a profession. Nineteenth-century educators aspiring to professionalism sought to define the work of teachers as an important service to society, requiring specialized knowledge and autonomy in the performance of the work. Their interpretation of professionalism, however, soon reflected the emerging gender division of labor in schools between administration and classroom teaching. Male professionalism emphasized independence and expertise in decision making, while female professionalism stressed altruistic classroom service. Since then, some sociologists have described teaching as a semi-profession or a helping profession, attempting to reconcile a degree of classroom autonomy with a vocation in which practitioners are expected to sacrifice material rewards for the intrinsic satisfaction of serving others.

Rejecting these models of professionalization, some scholars identify teaching as a white-collar occupation. The historian Marjorie Murphy described teachers as "the aristocracy of labor." Indeed, urban teachers have shared much in common with workers in commerce and industry. Teachers may exercise some independence in the classroom, but they are dependent on school board members, superintendents, and taxpaying parents, among others, for their income and continued employment. As schools have grown more bureaucratic in the twentieth century, teacher autonomy has declined and the regimentation of classroom work has increased. Since the late nineteenth century, teacher activists have repeatedly protested how principles of business and industrial production have infiltrated the schools.

The mission of education, however, continues to distinguish relations of employment in teaching from those in commerce and industry. At the turn of the twentieth century, organized teachers recognized the distinctiveness of their work when they disagreed among themselves about a rather simple question: Who was their employer? Did they serve the public, or did they work for the school superintendent? Some teachers believed that all school workers were employed by the public and together had a professional responsibility to cooperate in the service of the public good. Others, influenced by the industrial conflicts of the turn of the twentieth century, questioned that vision of cooperative service, insisting that professionalism was an ideology that obscured the subordination and exploitation of teachers. These teachers tended to see the superintendent, not the public, as the teachers' employer, and a process of conflict and negotiation, rather than cooperation, as the dominant form of relations between them. These two perspectives continue to influence present conceptions of teachers' responsibilities. They offer historical insight into the current spectrum of opinions that locate teaching somewhere between the poles of an exploited service occupation and a professional, socially mobile pursuit.

KAREN LEROUX

References and Further Reading

Blount, Jackie M. *Fit to Teach: Same-Sex Desire, Gender, and School Work in the Twentieth Century*. Albany: State of New York University Press, 2005.

Cuban, Larry. *How Teachers Taught: Constancy and Change in America's Classrooms, 1890–1980*. New York: Longman, 1984.

Elsbree, Willard S. *The American Teacher: Evolution of a Profession in Democracy*. New York: American Book Company, 1939.

Grant, Gerald, and Christine E. Murray. *Teaching in America: The Slow Revolution*. Cambridge, MA: Harvard University Press, 1999.

Herbst, Jurgen. *And Sadly Teach: Teacher Education and Professionalization in American Culture*. Madison: University of Wisconsin Press, 1989.

Hoffman, Nancy. *Woman's "True" Profession: Voices from the History of Teaching*. Old Westbury, NY: Feminist Press, 1981.

Lawn, Martin, and Gerald Grace, eds. *Teachers: The Culture and Politics of Work*. London: Falmer Press, 1987.

Mattingly, Paul H. *The Classless Profession: American Schoolmen in the Nineteenth Century*. New York: New York University Press, 1975.

Murphy, Marjorie. "The Aristocracy of Women's Labor in America." *History Workshop Journal* 22 (1986): 56–69.

Rousmaniere, Kate. *City Teachers: Teaching and School Reform in Historical Perspective*. New York: Teachers College Press, 1997.

Sklar, Kathryn Kish. *Catharine Beecher: A Study in Domesticity*. New York: Norton, 1973.

Tyack, David B. *The One Best System: A History of American Urban Education*. Cambridge, MA: Harvard University Press, 1974.

Warren, Donald, ed. *American Teachers: Histories of a Profession at Work*. New York: Macmillan, 1989.

See also **American Federation of Teachers; National Education Association**

TEAMSTERS FOR A DEMOCRATIC UNION

Teamsters for a Democratic Union (TDU) is a reform caucus within the International Brotherhood of Teamsters (IBT). Its main goals are union democracy and militancy in collective bargaining. TDU was formed in 1976 from Teamsters for a Decent Contract (TDC). Teamsters belonging to the International Socialists (IS) created TDC in August 1975. TDC's goal was for the Teamsters to achieve a good Master Freight Agreement in 1976. TDC's activism led the Teamsters' president, Frank Fitzsimmons, to call a four-day official national strike against the freight companies. This resulted in a substantially improved Master Freight Agreement. However, TDC's success infuriated the Teamsters' leadership, and a group of Teamster thugs attacked the only convention delegate that TDC managed to elect during the 1976 IBT national convention.

The IS, while pleased with the work done by TDC, was disappointed that TDC did not lead to the formation of a broad rank-and-file leadership. Nevertheless, the success of TDC in helping the Teamsters achieve a good Master Freight Agreement resulted in the IS deciding to form a permanent reform movement within the Teamsters: Teamsters for a Democratic Union.

TDU believes in militancy and fighting against concessions in collective bargaining agreements. While for the first few years of existence TDU struggled to gain major victories, it engaged in collective struggle, whether through such actions as strikes, union elections, and contract campaigns. These battles paved the way for TDU's future successes.

Its first major victory occurred with the 1983 National Master Freight Agreement where the Teamsters president, Jackie Presser, agreed to a rider that would have allowed freight companies to pay lower wages and benefits to employees hired after layoffs. This would have resulted in rehired Teamsters receiving a lower wage compared with other employees, which would have adversely affected over one third of Teamsters under the Agreement, as they were currently unemployed. TDU managed to obtain a copy of the Agreement, which led to it publicizing the Agreement and its likely undesirable effects. TDU's campaign was successful, as the Teamsters' membership overwhelmingly rejected the rider.

TDU continued the fight against concessions during the 1980s, with an increasing number of Teamsters supporting its campaigns. However, IBT presidents continually defied the wishes of the members. For example, in 1987, Presser imposed the United Parcel Service (UPS) contract despite the members rejecting it, and in 1988, the acting president, Weldon Mathis, enforced the freight contract regardless of the fact that Teamster members once again voted against a national contract. Nevertheless, the rank and file gained enough strength, in part through agitation led by TDU, to ensure that future Teamster presidents accepted members' wishes.

In addition to its goal of militancy in collective bargaining, TDU also called for an end to discrimination against minorities. While TDU's members are mostly white males, this has not stopped it from adopting a progressive agenda in relation to minorities. For example, at its first national convention, TDU passed a resolution stating that employers use racial discrimination to divide and weaken the rank and file. It claimed that the only way it can be successful is to implement and support policies that end discrimination. Likewise, its current "Rank-and-File Bill of Rights" states that TDU opposes discrimination in all forms and supports affirmative action. TDU formed a "Women and People of Color Committee" as part of its efforts to eliminate discrimination against minorities. The Committee focuses on highlighting issues of race and gender on the job and in the union and encouraging leadership among these groups, but very few members of minorities have joined the group. Nevertheless, in both policies and practices, TDU is attempting to end discrimination against minorities. It was, however, to gain its greatest success in its attempts to democratize the Teamsters.

TDU and the Democratization of the Teamsters

TDU's main goal, as its name implies, is to democratize the Teamsters and for the rank and file to have an important role in the union. TDU's founding constitution stated that the purpose of TDU is to form a national unified movement of rank-and-file Teamsters that is committed to fight for rank-and-file rights on the job and in the union. Beginning in 1976, TDU had success in its efforts to democratize the Teamsters. This was despite its small size; in 1979, TDU had 6,000 members compared with approximately 2 million IBT members. TDU proposed new bylaws that would have allowed the rank and file to elect union stewards and business agents. While TDU was not successful in most situations (in part because any change required a two-thirds majority), it was successful on some occasions. These included, among others, Flint Local 332 in 1976 and Detroit Local 299 in 1980. Democratizing Teamster bylaws is still one of TDU's main goals; its current Rank and File Bill of Rights states that there should be elections for all business agents and stewards. Likewise, there should be a special election for vacancies in office, and local union committee members should also be elected. TDU's greatest success occurred with the democratization of the Teamsters.

In 1986, the United States government began investigations into the Teamsters through the Racketeer Influenced and Corrupt Organizations Act (RICO). The government believed that the Teamsters were corrupt and had ties with the Mafia. Indeed, from 1957 to 1990, every president of the Teamsters, save Billy McCarthy, has been convicted and sentenced for a federal crime. While the government considered placing the Teamsters under trusteeship, TDU argued that the government should monitor Teamster elections, with members being allowed to directly elect the president and other leading union officials. TDU campaigned around the country, held rallies, gathering signatures in support of direct election for the Teamsters' leadership. At times, the organization managed to persuade their locals to adopt the TDU's position. The campaign was ultimately successful. In March 1989, the government and the union reached an agreement. The RICO charges were dropped in return for the democratization of the Teamsters, including allowing the rank and file to elect national leaders. There is little doubt that without the RICO charges, the democratization of the Teamsters would not have occurred as quickly as it did. Nevertheless, TDU's national campaign against trusteeship and for Teamster members to directly elect the top union officials influenced the government.

TDU decided not to field a candidate for the Teamsters presidential election in 1991. Instead, it endorsed Ron Carey, who was president of Teamsters Local 804 in Queens, New York, because he supported its goals of union democracy and militancy in collective bargaining. TDU organized meetings in support of

Carey; its members provided places for Carey to stay as he toured the country, and passed out literature, made phone calls, organized rallies, and got out the vote. TDU's efforts were successful. In December 1991, Carey was elected as president of the Teamsters.

Under Carey's leadership, the Teamsters supported many of TDU's goals, and the Teamsters became a progressive union. Carey increased the organizing budget, while at the same time reducing union officials' salaries. He also increased education for stewards and rank-and-file members, and put emphasis on contract campaigns, local unions, and shop-floor organizing.

TDU, however, was not entirely happy with Carey's presidency. It was disappointed that Carey refused to discontinue a union pension plan for union officers (many were already covered by at least one other retirement fund), especially as the plan cost the Teamsters one seventh of its annual revenue. Likewise, TDU was frustrated because Carey did not authorize mail-out ballots in local officer elections. It believed that mail-out ballots would result in increased voter turnout, thus giving the rank and file a greater role in the union.

Nevertheless, TDU's independence suffered under Carey's presidency. It was afraid to criticize him, as it thought this would give the Old Guard grounds to attack Carey's reforms. Thus, under his presidency, TDU and its newspaper (*Convoy Dispatch*) became completely identified with Carey.

TDU's Role in the Successful 1997 UPS Negotiations/Contract

Apart from helping to democratize the Teamsters and moving the union to the left, TDU played an important role in the successful strike against UPS in 1997 (the UPS agreement is the United States' largest collective bargaining contract). As the 1993 UPS contract failed to meet member expectations, the Teamsters implemented many new campaign tactics well in advance of the 1997 negotiations. The union decided to implement TDU's idea for a contract campaign. TDU argued that bargaining happens at the bargaining table, but an equally important front is in the workplace through a contract campaign in which members support the Teamsters bargaining committee and attempt to unite all Teamsters.

In preparation for the negotiations, Carey formed a 50-person UPS bargaining committee, which included several TDU members. Indeed, TDU played an active role. In addition to the idea of a contract campaign, TDU had a long involvement on the shop floor at UPS. TDU had trained workers to fight their

bosses. In locals where officials were hostile to Carey (that is, the Old Guard), TDU members led the way.

Following the breakdown in negotiations, the Teamsters went on strike. Lasting 15 days, the strike was ultimately very successful, with the union achieving the majority of its demands. The victory was hailed as one of labor's greatest successes since the 1940s.

TDU Under Hoffa Jr.

The 1997 UPS negotiations were Carey's last major triumph. Instead of relying on the rank and file during his successful 1996 re-election campaign, as he did in 1991, Carey hired political consultants. However, the consultants—the November Group—implemented an illegal fund-raising scheme on Carey's behalf. While Carey was eventually cleared of all charges, during the investigation, the Justice Department forced Carey to step down as president and the Teamsters to conduct a new presidential election. The election led to James P. Hoffa Jr.—Jimmy Hoffa's son—defeating the TDU-backed candidate Tom Leedham to become president of the Teamsters.

This did not stop TDU from engaging in militant activity. During the protests against the World Trade Organization in 1999, unions had a separate protest from other antiglobalization protesters. However, it was a Teamsters local, whose president is a member of TDU, that was the most militant. Teamsters Local 174 in Seattle broke from the official union protest to join the protest by environmentalists, students, anarchists, and members of the general public. Other TDU members from different locals joined it.

Not surprisingly, however, TDU's influence declined under Hoffa Jr.'s leadership. Unlike the 1997 UPS agreement, the 2002 agreement was a disappointment to many, especially part-time workers (unlike the 1997 rank-and-file campaign, the 2002 negotiations were conducted from the top, with little member involvement). This was because there was only a 50-cent increase in starting pay for part-time workers, there was no increase in the daily guarantee (three and a half hours), and UPS workers in the Central States Pension Fund, which is the largest pension fund, received no increase.

TDU campaigned against the contract. However, a clear majority of UPS workers ratified the contract (72.1%), although voter turnout was only 38%. This was the lowest voter turnout in UPS history and the first time it had fallen below 50%. However, following member dissatisfaction with the collective bargaining agreement—in particular, that there was no pension increase in the Central States—according to TDU there has been a dramatic increase in membership (however, the actual size of membership is unknown, as TDU does not release its membership numbers).

While TDU started from humble beginnings, its influence is without question. Indeed, it is arguably one of the most successful union reform caucuses in U.S. history. TDU had an important role in two of the three biggest events in U.S. labor since the late 1980s: the election of Ron Carey as president of the Teamsters and the 1997 UPS strike (the other being the election of John Sweeney as president of the AFL-CIO. However, a case can be made that TDU also had a role in that. If it were not through the election of Carey, it is doubtful that Sweeney would have gained office). Thus, TDU has been at the forefront of major change within the U.S. union movement and is one of the most influential union reform movements in U.S. history.

MICHAEL SCHIAVONE

References and Further Reading

Brenner, Aaron. "Rank-and-File Teamster Movements in Comparative Perspective." In *Trade Union Politics: American Unions and Economic Change, 1960–1990s*, edited by Glenn Perusek and Kent Worcester. Atlantic Highlands, NJ: Humanities Press, 1995, pp. 110–139.
Convoy Dispatch (TDU newspaper).
La Botz, Dan. *Rank-and-File Rebellion: Teamsters for a Democratic Union*. London: Verso, 1990.
Teamsters for a Democratic Union Web site. www.tdu.org.
Tillman, Ray M. "Reform Movement in the Teamsters and United Auto Workers." In *The Transformation of U.S. Unions: Voices, Visions, and Strategies from the Grassroots*, edited by Ray M. Tillman and Michael S. Cummings. London: Lynne Rienner Publishers, 1999, pp. 137–166.

See also **Carey, Ronald; Fitzsimmons, Frank E; Hoffa, James P.; International Brotherhood of Teamsters; United Parcel Service Strike (1997)**

TELEPHONE OPERATORS UNION

During the 1910s, the Telephone Operators Union (TOU) dramatically improved telephone operators' working conditions, wages, and self-esteem, and significantly increased women's influence in the labor movement. At its peak in 1919, the TOU, with 18,000 members, had organized locals in over 30 states and several Canadian provinces, extending from the Atlantic to the Pacific coasts, and from Edmonton, Alberta, to the Panama Canal Zone. New England was the most heavily organized region, with 4,000 operators in the Boston local alone.

Telephone operators confronted formidable obstacles in organizing. The nationally integrated Bell companies, which provided most of the nation's telephone service, commanded enormous financial resources, and the Bell system could undermine union support by extending conditions and benefits the TOU had achieved to areas where it had not penetrated. Low wages made it difficult for operators to sustain a union or build strike funds. Companies could easily replace these semiskilled workers if they walked out. The TOU could not maintain a stable membership because company policy required that an operator resign her position when she married. Operators were almost entirely young women in their teens or 20s, inexperienced in union administration and bargaining. Male telephone workers—repairmen, cable splicers, and installers—whose skills gave them much more leverage in strikes, were reluctant to support the operators and sometimes deliberately undermined them.

The TOU was first organized in Boston in 1912, where a strong central labor union, a long-standing tradition of social activism dating back to abolitionism, and a vigorous women's movement provided a favorable environment for the emergence of a viable female labor organization. Boston was a principal center of the settlement house movement and of the Women's Trade Union League (WTUL), which provided critical assistance in establishing the TOU. The TOU also drew on an emerging youth culture that emphasized peer relationships, forged in high schools that most operators attended. The high school promoted a group consciousness and administrative skills through student government, as well as training in writing, beneficial to labor organization. The TOU promoted solidarity among its youthful membership with festive parades and dances. During the 1919 New England telephone strike, operators at a mass rally in Boston took to the stage to perform the shimmy.

Discontent over low wages, mandatory split shifts that often extended the working day over 15 hours, arbitrary discharge, and physical abuse by chief operators led a group of operators to seek help from the Boston WTUL secretary, Mabel Gillespie, who advised them to organize a union and present carefully formulated demands. She called in the chief organizer of the International Brotherhood of Electrical Workers (IBEW), American Federation of Labor (AFL), to assist in the campaign. In May 1912, having firmly established their local, the Boston operators initiated organizing among the male telephone workers.

After New England Telephone Company management made clear its unwillingness to negotiate, the operators voted overwhelmingly to strike. The Company immediately began importing hundreds of

Telephone operators at Aberdeen proving grounds. Aberdeen, Maryland. Library of Congress, Prints & Photographs Division, FSA/OWI Collection [LC-USF34-064182-D].

operators from other Bell subsidiaries throughout the East and Midwest, many of whom it housed at Boston's most luxurious hotel. After protracted negotiations, Boston's 2,200 operators stunned the Company by voting down a settlement that provided annual bonuses rather than wage increases. Back at the bargaining table, a group of young women, facing much more experienced and better-educated managerial officials, won highly favorable terms, including union recognition, wage increases, and a significant reduction in split shifts. The TOU also gained an eight-hour workday, which became universal throughout the Bell system, and established a six-hour day as a goal. During the next several years, the TOU spread outside New England, developing especially strong locals in Montana and along the Pacific Coast.

In its early years, the TOU mounted a vigorous campaign for equal rights within the IBEW, which initially chartered the operators as sublocals subsidiary to male locals, and restricted their voting rights at conventions. The operators modeled their struggle for equality within the IBEW on the vibrant women's suffrage campaign in which many of them were active. In 1917, the operators won full convention representation, and the next year the IBEW granted them an autonomous department, with control over finances. The Telephone Operators Department (TOD), IBEW,

became, in effect, the first national trade union led by women.

Telephone operators' militancy intensified after the telephone service was placed under government control and operation in August 1918, as a one-year war measure. Postmaster General Albert Burleson, the government official assigned jurisdiction, was hostile to unionism and discarded the collective bargaining procedure in use since 1913. Burleson announced that government employees were prohibited from striking. When neither New England Telephone nor the government acted on their wage demands, New England's union operators voted to strike, ignoring pleas from the IBEW leadership not to do so.

The April 1919 New England telephone strike resembled the garment workers' Uprising of the 20,000 a decade earlier in its spontaneity and rejection of male authority. It completely shut down telephone service in five New England states, although the male telephone workers did not join it until its third day. The strike was marked by street riots in Boston, as large crowds assaulted college students who volunteered their services as strikebreakers. The operators settled on very favorable terms, and most important, protected their right to bargain collectively.

Victory in the 1919 New England telephone strike precipitated a wave of national organizing among operators, resulting in the formation of over 50 new TOD locals outside New England in the next several months. The TOD, although severely handicapped by lack of funds, even managed to establish 11 locals in the Deep South, where women's unionism was almost unknown. Major operators' strikes occurred in several southern cities during 1919, as well as in St. Louis, Cleveland, and along the Pacific Coast.

The TOD was determined to promote women's labor leadership and heighten operators' self-esteem by involving the rank and file in the burgeoning post-World War I workers education movement. This movement offered young women workers the opportunity to acquire both a broad cultural education and the writing and speaking skills necessary to administer union locals and negotiate with management. Telephone operators flocked to night classes at Boston Trade Union College, which assembled arguably the most impressive faculty of any workers' school. Sizable operator delegations were enrolled at Bryn Mawr Summer School for Women Workers in Industry, the principal residential workers' school for women. Union operators also attended the National WTUL Training School in Chicago.

The TOD devoted considerable effort to enhancing worker dignity, combating unfavorable stereotypes of operators in the mass media. It pressed for higher wages, in part to permit operators to live independently of their families. The TOD also pioneered in countering the prevailing images of the sexes in trade union iconography, which depicted workers as brawny men and women as maternal figures. Its emblem, the "Weaver of Speech," presented the woman as a worker performing a task critical to commerce: the telephone operator held in her hands the lines through which the entire nation communicated.

The TOD declined sharply during the early 1920s as telephone management initiated a campaign to install company unions, part of a larger anti-union campaign that significantly weakened the labor movement. By 1923, TOD membership outside New England had largely evaporated, and the New England telephone men had seceded from the IBEW to form a company union. New England Telephone began plans to introduce the dial system, which threatened job loss and would greatly reduce union leverage. Boston's local, the TOD's largest, was torn by factional strife. With New England Telephone refusing to consider a wage increase, the TOD president, Julia O'Connor, who had directed the 1919 New England walkout, led the operators out on strike in June 1923 for higher wages and the seven-hour day. Although many operators refused to heed the call, the strikers put up a determined fight, paralyzing service in many of the region's major cities. As in 1919, violent conflict between prostrike crowds

and strikebreakers erupted on several occasions. The strike was broken after a month, and its leaders and many operators were permanently blacklisted.

After the failure of the strike, the TOD was in effect destroyed, although it maintained a skeletal existence under O'Connor until 1938. Telephone operators' unionism did not return to New England for nearly 50 years. Three of the nation's most prominent women labor activists during the next several decades—Julia O'Connor Parker, Rose Finkelstein Norwood, and Rose Sullivan—began their careers as leaders of the operators' union in Boston. Through them, the TOD continued to advance workers' interests long after its demise.

STEPHEN H. NORWOOD

References and Further Reading

Norwood, Stephen. *Labor's Flaming Youth: Telephone Operators and Worker Militancy, 1878–1923*. Urbana: University of Illinois Press, 1990.
———. "Reclaiming Working-Class Activism: The Boston Women's Trade Union League, 1920–1950." *Labor's Heritage* 10, no. 2 (Summer 1998): 20–35.

See also **Women's Trade Union League**

TENNESSEE CONVICT UPRISING (1891–1892)

Between July 14, 1891, and late August 1892, over a thousand Tennessee miners rose up in arms to protest the use of convict laborers in the State's coal mines. Most of the miners were white, while a majority of convicts were black. The miners targeted three coal companies in east Tennessee: Briceville, Coal Creek, and Oliver Springs, and one in mid-Tennessee, Tracy City. The largest of the companies, Tennessee Coal, Iron and Railroad Company (TCIR) in mid-Tennessee, leased convicts from the State of Tennessee; the smaller east Tennessee companies subleased convicts from the TCIR to work in their respective coal mines. The "Convict Wars" (the name given by contemporaries to the rebellion) took place amidst America's turbulent labor struggles of the 1890s, a period in which workers throughout the country challenged the waxing power of large-scale corporations, portrayed increasingly by unions as fostering unjust workplaces and perverting America's democratic ideals.

Over the course of this 13-month-long rebellion, the miners coupled military actions with vigorous political efforts in an attempt to undermine the convict lease system. They asked supportive government officials to intervene legally on their behalf and compelled the governor to call a special session of the legislature to debate the convict lease system. Continuing a legal strategy begun in the late 1880s, the miners brought a number of cases to the courts seeking to secure their rights as workers and to limit the reach of convict laborers into the east Tennessee mines. When all these efforts failed, the miners established a formal political alliance with the Farmers Alliances in an effort to secure the election of legislators committed to ending Tennessee's convict lease system. These political actions were interspersed with four distinct attacks on the prison stockades and suggest two important points: that the miners viewed the attacks as a form of political petition, and that they saw political and economic actions as two sides of the same coin. This worldview was particularly noteworthy at a time when major labor federations, like the American Federation of Labor, frequently disengaged from political lobbying and adopted a strategy that relied primarily on economic negotiations with company employers.

The miners' sustained political engagement with the State of Tennessee offers numerous indications of their political sensibilities and cultural outlook. The men who opted to work in Tennessee's coal mines in the late nineteenth century came from the areas surrounding Anderson and Grundy County, where the majority of farms were worked by their owners. As the population of these rural communities grew, younger sons, who did not inherit property, sought work in the nascent postbellum Tennessee coal mines. When they came to the east Tennessee coal towns, many of them bought houses and began to call the towns home. None of these mining sites were traditional company towns where the coal companies owned not just the mine, but also the land in the town and the local store, and thus could dictate rents, housing allotments, and the cost of mining and household supplies. Rather, many of the families who came to live in the mining towns viewed themselves as homeowners with a serious stake in the future of the mines and the surrounding towns. This perspective was shared by both the miners and the shopkeepers who came to service these communities.

In petitioning against the use of convict labor in the mines, the men of east and mid-Tennessee repeatedly spoke in the phraseology of homeownership. Were the coal companies to replace them with convict laborers or to force them to accede to lower wages by threatening to replace them with unfree miners, the miners argued that they would lose their homes, not just their jobs. The local shopkeepers, who joined the miners in the Convict Wars, likewise realized that if the miners were to lose their jobs to convict laborers, their businesses would suffer greatly. Thus, the miners and their local supporters positioned themselves politically and ideologically as family men who had

economic stakes in their communities—not as itinerants who moved from mining camp to mining camp with only a commitment to the next paycheck.

At the same time that the miners portrayed themselves as upstanding propertied citizens—and certainly not of the "school of the commune or nihilist," as Shapiro has noted in her larger study, *A New South Rebellion*—they depicted the companies as behaving in unpatriotic, "un-American" ways. The miners' leaders made clear that as a group they favored competitive capitalism but objected to what they believed were unfair interventions into the marketplace. They were particularly irked by the state government's decision to lease convicts to privately owned coal companies, thereby enabling the companies to impose onerous and unjust contracts on the miners. Should miners refuse to accede to company demands, the coal company owners could easily threaten to fire recalcitrants and replace them with convicts.

The Convict Wars ended in August 1892. During the miners' fourth attack on convict stockades, four militiamen were killed, some in murky circumstances. This loss of life turned public opinion against the miners. Faced with diminished public support and a much larger contingent of militia whom state officials had brought in from all over Tennessee, the miners capitulated. The aftermath of the rebellion continued to be felt in Tennessee's mining districts and in the state capital over the next few years, particularly in the form of court battles between the State of Tennessee and the coal operators over who should bear the costs of the rebellion and between the State of Tennessee and the miners. Although the rebellion had boosted labor organization in the Tennessee coalfields, especially the nascent United Mine Workers of America, its aftermath decimated these organizations as labor leaders faced a succession of rebellion-related prosecutions. Convict leasing continued in the State of Tennessee until the convict lease contract between Tennessee and the TCIR ended in December 1895.

KARIN A. SHAPIRO

References and Further Reading

Ansley, Fran, and Brenda Bell. "Miners' Insurrection/Convict Labor." *Southern Exposure* 1 (1974): 144–159.

Daniel, Pete. "The Tennessee Convict War." *Tennessee Historical Quarterly* 34 (1975): 273–292.

Hutson, Andrew C. Jr. "The Coal Miners' Insurrection of 1891 in Anderson Country, Tennessee." *East Tennessee Historical Society Publications* 7 (1935): 103–121.

Hutson, Andrew C. Jr. "The Overthrow of the Convict Lease System in Tennessee." *East Tennessee Historical Society Publications* 8 (1936): 82–103.

Shapiro, Karin A. *A New South Rebellion: The Battle against Convict Labor in the Tennessee Coalfields, 1871–1896.* Chapel Hill: University of North Carolina Press, 1998.

TEXTILE WORKERS UNION OF AMERICA

The Textile Workers Union of America (TWUA) emerged in 1939 in the wake of the upsurge in industrial unionism spurred by the newly formed Congress of Industrial Organizations (CIO) and the passage of the National Labor Relations Act in the midst of the Great Depression. The TWUA's immediate predecessor was the Textile Workers Organizing Committee (TWOC), which had attempted to organize the southern textile industry for the CIO in 1937. The TWOC had hoped for success despite the failure of the United Textile Workers (UTW) to organize southern mill employees in the massive, bloody General Textile Strike of 1934. In 1937, the TWOC won some early victories, securing nine contracts covering some 5,000 workers out of the 65,000 people who signed union pledge cards. Suspicion of union organizers, however, ran deep among many workers, who remembered the hostility, blacklisting, and humiliation they had recently experienced after having their hopes raised so high. But just as deep ran the mill hands' antagonism toward the working conditions they endured, particularly the hated "stretch-out," which required what they considered to be superhuman effort for little reward. The 1937 campaign stalled from a combination of intense, often violent opposition from businesspersons and local political and religious leaders and the deep recession that hit the entire country late that year. In 1939, activists from the TWOC along with many remaining UTW locals formed the TWUA-CIO, whose goal was the organization of the nation's textile industry, which meant a primary focus on southern cotton mills.

The textile industry presented many obstacles to TWUA organizers. "Textiles" included cotton, wool, silk, rayon, and nylon mills, as well as dye plants, hosiery mills, and rug and carpet factories. Each sector had its own history and internal squabbles. Historically, skilled workers in northern textile plants had organized their own unions, excluding the bulk of less-skilled operatives, who in the twentieth century were largely immigrants from Southern and Eastern Europe. Skilled hands often viewed the TWUA's goal of organizing all workers into a single union with skepticism. In addition, the textile industry was decentralized, with hundreds of companies, none of which had a market share of over 3%. The largest sector in textiles, cotton yarn and fabric, had shifted its base from the North to the South in the previous 50 years. By World War II, southern mills turned out nearly 80% of the nation's cotton textiles. But in 1946, there were over 1,000 individual cotton mills in North Carolina alone. Cannon Mills, the largest single southern textile employer, had 41,000 employees in 20 mills scattered throughout the region. The TWUA faced a formidable challenge. Organizing any particular plant required enormous expenditures of time and money, but success would mark only slight progress toward the larger goal of a unionized industry.

These challenges were compounded by the TWUA's meager finances. Although the union claimed to have 275,000 members in 1939, only a small percentage of them paid dues, and the TWUA began operations with a net deficit of $200. The TWUA had only 84 organizers on staff in 1939 and sought to cut its budget. Since the TWOC had spent nearly $2 million in its 1937 campaign, TWUA officials were understandably concerned about how they might pay for a new southern campaign.

Wartime Gains and Operation Dixie

World War II altered the organizing dynamic. Wartime government expenditures revived the textile industry, creating markets for whatever mills produced. To ensure labor peace, the federal government's National War Labor Board encouraged unionization, offering the automatic checkoff of union dues in return for no-strike pledges in union contracts. The TWUA gained over 120,000 new members during the war, its total membership reaching 450,000 in 1945. Broken down by region, however, the union's success had its limits. The TWUA had organized just over 40,000 southern workers during the war, reaching a total of 70,000 union members out of 600,000 textile workers in the region. Fewer than 10% of North Carolina's 200,000 mill workers were under contract. The vast majority of TWUA membership remained in the North, where tight wartime labor markets and government orders made unionization worth the price for even antiquated mills that would otherwise not be competitive. Most textile workers, however, lived in the South and were unorganized.

This imbalance affected the TWUA's goals. To pay for southern organizing efforts, the TWUA had to ensure the survival of northern mills. Increased southern wages would reduce the incentive for northern mills to relocate. Southern workers hardly opposed wage increases, but their main concerns were the pace of production, the stretch-out, and arbitrary supervisors. The speedup and stretch-out were directly related to wages, it turns out, because most textile workers were paid on a piece rate—a certain amount of money per unit of production—not by the hour. Sidestepping this complexity, TWUA organizers emphasized the North-South wage differential.

The TWUA's major southern organizing campaign after the war was Operation Dixie, which began in 1946. Although the union won a number of elections, Operation Dixie ultimately made little headway in organizing the region. Memories of the repression that followed earlier organizing efforts certainly affected mill workers, but the wartime and postwar boom also had resulted in a doubling of textile workers' wages between 1941 and 1946, whether or not workforces were unionized. This undercut arguments that only unionization would boost wages. In addition, anti-union forces exploited racial fears, noting that the CIO supported the principle of racial equality. In truth, the TWUA violated its principles in the South and did not challenge the color line in textiles that had long prevented blacks from obtaining production jobs. But fears of union civil rights activism made the predominantly white textile labor force wary. In the emerging Cold War climate, anti-union activists also linked the TWUA with Communism. Although the TWUA leadership was staunchly anticommunist, the historic Communist presence within the CIO, mainly among organizers and leadership in specific unions, provided a kernel of truth to the charge.

Unrealized Promise

Established TWUA locals could bring enormous, positive changes in the lives of workers. Unionized mill hands enjoyed secure access to their jobs, had some protection against burdensome workload increases, and could defend themselves against supervisors. Grievance procedures allowed workers to file official complaints, with the possibility of third-party arbitration if necessary. Grievance procedures hardly ensured workplace justice, but they represented an enormous increase in power for southern workers. These benefits could not be understood or realized, however, until mills were organized with signed contracts, something that precious few southern workers ever experienced.

Mill owners continued to oppose organizing efforts with impunity and to resist new demands by organized workers. In 1951, the TWUA called on unionized southern mills to strike for increased wages, cost-of-living allowances, medical insurance, and pensions. But unionized southern mills were still a small percentage of the region's textile industry, and targeted companies refused to concede, arguing that granting these demands would make them uncompetitive. Unwilling to risk their livelihoods, union members crossed picket lines in droves.

The failed 1951 strike further reduced the TWUA's slim credibility in the region and ignited a struggle between George Baldanzi and Emil Rieve for control of the organization. Baldanzi eventually left to join the UTW, which fought the TWUA over the remaining southern locals. Meanwhile, the northern textile industry finally collapsed, unable to survive in a competitive market after a burst of prosperity during the Korean War. The southern textile industry also suffered from intense competitive pressures in the 1950s. Many plants closed, some of them unionized, because of foreign competition and shifts in domestic industrial markets toward synthetics and plastics. A reeling textile industry did not bode well for the TWUA.

The TWUA limped along, but with little influence on the declining industry. The union focused its energy on organizing the giant J. P. Stevens Company plant in Roanoke Rapids, North Carolina. The union received a boost from the Civil Rights Act of 1964, which opened production jobs to African-Americans, who were more inclined than whites to join unions. Still, most white workers were reluctant to join an organization that included blacks. Nevertheless, the TWUA won an election at the Roanoke Rapids mill in 1974 but was unable to wrest a meaningful contract from the obstinate employer. In 1976, the TWUA merged with the Amalgamated Clothing Workers to form the Amalgamated Clothing and Textile Workers Union, with the goal of combining resources to force Stevens to bargain in good faith.

In the end, the TWUA never realized its ambitious early agenda, but given the overwhelming obstacles the union faced, it is not clear what strategies might have produced more positive results. The domestic textile industry was unstable and in decline throughout most of the union's history. There is plenty of evidence that most textile workers wanted better lives and working conditions, but the risks of joining a union, especially in the South, were real, and the benefits were impossible for organizers to demonstrate in advance.

DANIEL CLARK

References and Further Reading

Brattain, Michelle. *The Politics of Whiteness: Race, Workers, and Culture in the Modern South.* Princeton, NJ: Princeton University Press, 2001.

Clark, Daniel J. *Like Night and Day: Unionization in a Southern Mill Town.* Chapel Hill: University of North Carolina Press, 1997.

Daniel, Clete. *Culture of Misfortune: An Interpretive History of Textile Unionism in the United States.* Ithaca, NY: ILR Press, 2001.

Draper, Alan. *Organized Labor and the Civil Rights Movement in the South, 1954–1968.* Ithaca, NY: ILR Press, 1994.

Flamming, Douglas. *Creating the Modern South: Millhands and Managers in Dalton, Georgia, 1884–1984.* Chapel Hill: University of North Carolina Press, 1992.

Griffith, Barbara S. *The Crisis of American Labor: Operation Dixie and the Defeat of the CIO.* Philadelphia: Temple University Press, 1988.

Hall, Jacquelyn Dowd, James Leloudis, Robert Korstad, Mary Murphy, Lu Ann Jones, and Christopher Daly. *Like a Family: The Making of a Southern Cotton Mill World.* Chapel Hill: University of North Carolina Press, 1987.

Hodges, James. *New Deal Labor Policy and the Southern Cotton Textile Industry, 1933–1941.* Knoxville: University of Tennessee Press, 1986.

Minchin, Timothy J. *"Don't Sleep with Stevens!": The J. P. Stevens Campaign and the Struggle to Organize the South, 1963–80.* Gainesville: University of Florida Press, 2005.

———. *What Do We Need a Union For?: The TWUA in the South, 1945–1955.* Chapel Hill: University of North Carolina Press, 1997.

See also **Congress of Industrial Organizations; National War Labor Board (WWII); Operation Dixie; Textiles; United Textile Workers**

TEXTILES

The domestic textile industry had its origins in the eighteenth century, grew fitfully during periods of war, boom, and recession, reached its peak in the mid-twentieth century, and appeared to be on the verge of extinction in the early twenty-first century. The cotton textile industry initially competed primarily with wool for dominance in the American economy, but both experienced severe competition from foreign producers, particularly those in Great Britain. Entering the twentieth century, cotton was by far the largest sector in textiles, and the industry had begun a massive regional shift from the North to the South. Even under the heading of cotton textiles, the industry included many different processes, including spinning, weaving, and the dying of cloth. In addition, unlike other major industries, textile production was decentralized, with hundreds of companies entering a relatively competitive marketplace. The early twentieth century saw the development of synthetics like nylon and rayon, which diversified the industry and competed with cotton. Beginning in the late 1940s and peaking in the 1990s, domestic textile mills reeled more than ever from foreign competition, with most succumbing by the turn of the century. Hundreds of thousands of jobs disappeared with them, disrupting the lives of workers and their communities. Ironically, this had happened before with the southern migration of the industry. Textiles had always been a volatile industry, and textile workers struggled throughout to make the best of often dismal circumstances.

Origins

By exposing the long-standing industrial dependence of the colonies, the American Revolution prompted the development of many domestic industries, including textiles. One impediment was technological expertise, which the English had and Americans coveted. It is not easy to convert bolls of raw cotton into usable fibers. Dirt, seeds, and debris must be removed before the fibers can be straightened and twisted into yarns. No hand processes could compete with machines designed to perform these tasks. State-sponsored efforts, local ingenuity, and the knowledge imported with immigrants like Samuel Slater overcame these technical deficiencies to launch relatively large-scale wool and cotton textile production in the late eighteenth century. The development of the cotton gin—which removed seeds from short-staple cotton and allowed the expansion of cotton production—and slavery, beyond the coastal South, increased potential domestic textile production. Although most American cotton still went to British mills, plenty stayed in the United States.

Conflict with Great Britain in the early nineteenth century inadvertently boosted the domestic textile industry. By curtailing trade with Great Britain, Thomas Jefferson's Embargo Act of 1807 diminished the supply of cheap, imported fabric. In the next three years, the number of American textile mills increased from 15 to 87, mainly in the Northeast from Rhode Island to Massachusetts. These yarn-producing mills tended to be rather small, were powered by river currents, and relied on rural farm families, including children, for labor.

The War of 1812 provided further impetus for domestic textile manufacturing. Most notable was the construction of a large cotton textile mill in Waltham, Massachusetts, for a group of investors led by Francis Cabot Lowell. This "Waltham System" mechanized the weaving of cloth, using new power looms, as well as the spinning of yarn. For the first time, all operations would be housed under the same roof. Highly capitalized, with absentee owners and hired managers, the Waltham Mill began operations in 1814, providing coarse fabric to clothe slaves in the South.

Unlike earlier textile factories, the Waltham Mill employed mostly young, single, native-born women from farm families that were experiencing difficult circumstances. Textile employment lessened the economic burden for these families while allowing daughters new opportunities to be productive, and even to earn a dowry. Most of the young women expected mill work to be a brief phase in life, not a career. Mill owners adopted a paternalistic stance toward their workers, in part to assuage parents' fears that the new factory and dormitories would be corrupting dens of vice and immorality. In the early years of rapidly increasing production and profits, the more generous side of paternalism often prevailed, despite a work regimen that averaged 12 hours a day, six days a week. Signs of future tensions appeared, however. Mechanization required scrupulous quality control, hence close supervision, and certain stages of production still required high levels of skill, which left a significant degree of control outside management's domain.

Market Shifts and Labor Transitions

The Waltham experiment began to unravel in the 1830s. As hundreds of competing mills were built and new technologies allowed increased production, competition forced all textile companies to search for ways to economize. In moves that would prove to be the source of textile labor conflict for generations, mill managers increased the speed of production, assigned workers more machines to tend, and lowered wages, which were usually "piece rates," a certain amount of money for a set amount of production. The process continued for many years. Workloads in 1854 in Lowell, Massachusetts, were nearly double those in 1840. As early as 1834, 800 women left their jobs in Lowell, protesting a 12.5% wage cut. Although they did not succeed in having their pay restored, the women frightened management and offered a stinging critique of a labor system that denied these native-born daughters what they considered to be their American birthright of fair wages and humane treatment. Another larger strike in 1836 concerned increases in prices charged by the Lowell management for room and board in company housing. This time the women succeeded in the short run, but the textile industry floundered along with most of the national economy for several years beginning in the late 1830s. This recession prompted the beginning of a long-term trend, the hiring of immigrants to perform the increasingly arduous textile jobs. In 1836, only 4% of textile workers were immigrants; by 1860, the total had risen to 60%. Most were Irish, fleeing famine conditions, with a number of French Canadians as well.

Given the combination of harsh competition and an increasingly immigrant labor force, textile managers no longer attempted to justify their operations as paternalistic efforts to improve the intelligence and morality of workers. Companies no longer invested as heavily in housing for workers, especially for Irish immigrants, who generally lived in slum conditions.

For a while, employers offered segregated housing to native-born and immigrant workers. Many of the remaining native-born workers used the old paternalistic language to their advantage, arguing that limiting the workday to 10 hours would contribute greatly to their overall health and welfare. Referring to textile operatives as "wage slaves," the Lowell Female Reform Association worked to change conditions and accused mill owners of violating their rights as Americans. But in a hotly competitive market, they could not prevent speedups, increased workloads, and decreasing piece rates. Even if market conditions had been favorable, the deep divisions within the labor force would have been difficult to overcome. By the Civil War, the textile industry had grown considerably, and it was notorious for hard labor and low wages.

War, Peace, and Migration

Whereas the Civil War ultimately proved a boon for many northern industries, cotton textiles suffered considerably. No longer was there a supply of raw cotton from the South. As a result, cotton mills sat idle and workers scrambled for alternative employment. For many years, cotton textiles had been far more popular than wool, as cotton was more comfortable in summer and easier to wash. During the Civil War, however, woolen manufacturing increased dramatically to fill the void. When cotton supplies resumed after the war, northern cotton textile manufacturing resumed, but monumental changes were imminent.

The future of textile manufacturing was in the South. There had been some small-scale production of cotton yarns in the South before the Civil War, accounting for nearly 6% of the nation's total. The war, however, had convinced many southern business leaders and politicians that increased industrialization was necessary to boost the region's fortunes. Given the proximity of enormous supplies of cotton, textiles appeared the obvious choice to lead the way. The cotton mill crusade began in earnest in the 1880s, after the serious depression of the 1870s ended. The number of southern cotton mills increased from 161 in 1880 to 400 in 1900. By the 1890s, a number of southern businesspersons who had prospered from brokering tobacco and cotton crops looked for what they hoped would be safer investments, given the farm revolts and reform movements in this era. Most of the capital invested in these southern mills came from local investors in the communities where the factories were built. Some northern investment was involved, mainly from machinery companies, but these were primarily local, civic ventures with the goal of boosting the economic power and the image of individual towns.

Textile workers in the South were drawn from the ranks of poor farm families, caught in the whipsaw of increasing crop production, decreasing prices, and often hopeless debt. Most mills were in the Piedmont region of the South, where rivers emerged from the mountains to provide the water power necessary to operate machinery. Workers, then, tended to be from these upland areas and southern Appalachia. Since slavery had not been widespread in this part of the South, most potential workers were white, and with the increasing rigidity of segregation, virtually all production jobs were reserved for whites only. African-American males could find textile employment only as janitors, yardmen, or in the undesirable, dirty job of breaking open compressed bales of cotton as they entered the manufacturing process. African-American females had little chance of finding jobs in textiles. With few exceptions, this color line held until the Civil Rights Act of 1964.

Since many jobs were open to women and children, white workers often came to the mills as families. Indeed, mill owners often required a certain number of family members to work in the mills as a condition for obtaining housing in the company-owned mill villages. Just like the founders of the Lowell mills, most southern textile executives insisted that mill employment would be an uplifting experience for workers, teaching them solid work habits. In addition, mill owners emphasized their support for churches and recreational opportunities in the villages. For their part, most workers initially refused to commit fully to factory labor and often disappeared for long stretches during planting and harvesting seasons. As late as 1906, a regional survey concluded that whenever prices for tobacco and cotton rose, mill owners reported a scarcity of labor. In addition, daily absenteeism bedeviled managers, especially in departments that employed mostly women, who had to care for children, tend house, and do the shopping as well as hold down full-time jobs.

Meanwhile, the northern textile industry focused on woolens and high-quality cotton yarns, conceding the market for coarser yarns to southern producers. Many northern firms, however, began to invest in southern mills once the erstwhile competitors became established. Although the appeal of the South for investors was cheap labor, there is little evidence that northern textile workers were living a life of material ease. Local investigations showed that many mill employees, especially the large numbers of young women workers, suffered from malnutrition and exhaustion. Housing conditions were decrepit for the mostly immigrant labor force, which now consisted of dozens of nationalities. Labor conflicts rocked northern textile communities in the 1910s.

Perhaps the most famous strike occurred in Lawrence, Massachusetts, in 1912, when the American Woolen Company cut wages in response to a state law limiting the workweek to 54 hours for women and children. Leaders from the radical Industrial Workers of the World successfully organized the diverse and divided workforce, which struck fear in the hearts of Lawrence city officials and played into the hands of southern boosters who advertised a complacent, docile, native supply of labor. Although the strike resulted in a short-term victory for workers, their unity across ethnic lines could not be sustained. The strike also revealed long-standing divisions between skilled and unskilled textile workers. Skilled workers, like highly prized loom fixers, tended to be native-born, male, and committed to less radical craft unions. In times of conflict, they were often at odds with the masses of production workers. A similar dynamic took place in the silk mills of Paterson, New Jersey, in 1913, resulting in a defeat for strikers there.

War, Peace, and Depression

World War I provided some temporary relief for the industry and its workers. Government war spending kept mills humming and profitable. Mill production expanded considerably. Southern mill owners complained, however, that many employees failed to take advantage of this opportunity to maximize earnings, preferring instead to work as many hours as necessary to meet their basic needs and to take the rest of the week off. In any event, the conclusion of the war brought hardship all around. Government contracts ended, profits slumped, and the boll weevil decimated much of the nation's cotton supply, driving up production costs in textiles. Wartime labor scarcity had boosted wages in both the North and the South, and workers did not readily accede to managements' desperate efforts to remain competitive by demanding wage reductions and workload increases while offering intermittent employment at best. The postwar re-adjustment took several years, culminating in northern mills in 1922 with a series of hard-fought strikes, which proved to be Pyrrhic victories for workers. Although northern mill employees preserved their wartime wages and forced employers to observe the 48-hour workweek, these triumphs only increased both the competitive advantage of southern mills and the incentive for northern mills to relocate. Between 1923 and 1933, 40% of New England's textile factories closed, and nearly 100,000 of the 190,000 workers employed in that region lost their jobs.

Southern textile workers also fought postwar wage reductions. Strikes occurred throughout the region, beginning in 1919 and lasting into 1921, when the bottom fell out of the market for textiles. The American Federation of Labor's United Textile Workers (UTW) offered whatever financial support it could—which was meager—to groups of striking workers. In the end, workers and their organizations could not overcome the powerful economic forces arrayed against them, but their actions in the postwar strike wave gave pause to even the staunchest promoters of southern cotton textiles. No one could be so sure anymore that native-born, white mill hands were contented and docile compared with their immigrant counterparts in the North.

From 1922 on, the southern textile industry was essentially in a state of depression. Stiff international competition, new, more revealing fashions that required less cloth, and rising competition from synthetics combined to undercut demand for domestic cotton textiles. Mills operated when they received orders, which happened so unpredictably that mill workers had to learn to survive without steady industrial paychecks. This made it more difficult for managers to summon a full labor force when the opportunity arose. Since buyers often backed out of contracts, mills frequently accumulated large, unsold inventories of yarn and cloth and were forced to find ways to economize. In most cases that meant lowering wages. Later in the 1920s, a number of companies found that there were limits to what workers would accept. In 1927, the Harriet Mill in Henderson, North Carolina, was one of the first southern mills to experience intense labor conflict when the company refused to restore a previous wage reduction when the mills appeared to be temporarily profitable. This was followed in 1929 by large strikes in many southern communities that often involved armed troops and violent encounters. Most notable were conflicts at a rayon mill in Elizabethton, Tennessee, and at cotton mills in Gastonia and Marion in North Carolina. The UTW once again offered marginal assistance in Henderson, Elizabethton, and Marion, while the Communist-led National Textile Workers Union vied for leadership in Gastonia. In each case, however, the combination of a poor economy, insufficient strike funds, hunger, and hostility from business leaders, state and local politicians, and local clergy proved insurmountable for workers.

While the textile industry, both in the North and the South, had entered a version of the Great Depression in the early 1920s, conditions worsened after the 1929 stock market crash as the rest of the nation joined in the misery. The only relief in the early 1930s came during the first year of Franklin Roosevelt's New Deal, when the National Recovery Administration's (NRA) textile code allowed mill owners to collaborate to establish production quotas and wage scales. In hindsight, however, it appears that the rush of business at this time was prompted by anxious customers hoping to buy as much as possible before the codes went into effect. Lax enforcement of the codes, or at least the assumption that other mills were cheating, motivated many mill owners to break their own codes of competition, and the textile industry plummeted even deeper into depression.

Mill workers, however, were emboldened by the NRA's Section 7(a), which declared it illegal for employers to resist the efforts of their employees to form unions. Textile workers throughout the country rose up in 1934 to challenge their dismal conditions of labor, with most focusing on the "stretch-out," the assigning of more and more work to individual employees with the goal of cost cutting. Nearly 400,000 workers participated in what amounted to a general strike late that summer. Many angry workers joined the ever-fledgling UTW. Mill owners responded by firing union activists, hiring vigilantes, and successfully convincing state and local authorities to support private property rights by any means necessary, including deadly force and violence. The strike ended disastrously for workers. The strongest union supporters were permanently blacklisted from the industry, and others were forced to adopt an air of humility and obedience to keep their jobs. The memory of resounding defeat in the 1934 General Strike affected all future organizing efforts in the South. This somber aftermath contributed to the myth that southern workers were docile and anti-union, but that attitude was largely a result of the concrete lessons learned in 1934 about the tremendous risks inherent in challenging the economic order.

War and Peace, Boom and Bust

World War II rescued the textile industry. By September 1940, well before Pearl Harbor, the federal government was purchasing half of the nation's production of cotton goods, including over $1 million worth of North Carolina textiles each week. Throughout the war, most textile mills throughout the country could sell virtually anything they produced, with most goods going to support the troops. Before the war, farsighted mill managers, at least the few who either had financial reserves or who were able to obtain loans, had invested in "long-draft" spinning technology, which eliminated several stages of the production process and reduced labor costs while also improving yarn quality. WWII masked the significance of this technological breakthrough by allowing even antiquated mills to earn profits, but the future was clear. Only those mills that invested in state-of-the-art equipment stood a chance to compete once government contracts no longer drove the market.

The war also seemed to provide a favorable climate for union organizing in textiles. A shortage of labor, particularly in the South, along with record demand for production appeared to give workers an upper hand in organizing campaigns. Moreover, the federal government's National War Labor Board encouraged unionization as a means of eliminating work stoppages that threatened war production. Indeed, early in the war, the newly formed Textile Workers Union of America (TWUA), an affiliate of the CIO, gained over 120,000 new recruits, with membership peaking at 450,000 in 1945. Broken down by region, however, southern TWUA membership in 1945 composed only 42,450 of the newly organized, and just 70,000 of the 600,000 textile workers in the region. TWUA leaders were in a bind. Most of their dues-paying members were in the North, but three fourths of textile workers were in the South. Northern union members were primarily interested in raising wages in the South to protect jobs in the North. Southern workers, however, were still mainly interested in combating the stretch-out. TWUA leaders favored northern interests, which hurt the union's chances in the South. But given the powerful forces in opposition to unionization in the South, it is difficult to know whether or not any organizing strategy could have proved successful.

The southern textile industry withstood the CIO's Operation Dixie, which was a concerted effort beginning in 1946 to organize the main industry in the region. As usual, organizers in textiles faced hostile mill managers, local leaders, and state officials, who attacked the CIO for favoring racial equality and harboring Communists. The decentralized nature of the industry also proved to be a major obstacle. Although there were major textile companies, in 1947 the largest firm sold only 3% of the nation's production. Even the largest companies were so only because they owned a number of relatively small mills. This made it extremely difficult to organize, because companies could shift production to other facilities in the chain. Success at a single mill, therefore, often made little long-term impact. This was quite unlike other major industries, like automobiles, in which a small number of corporations controlled virtually the entire domestic market.

The wartime and postwar boom in textiles lasted only until 1949, when foreign competition resumed and the industry began a long-term decline. Exports of U.S.-produced textiles decreased dramatically in this period, and even the domestic market suffered from imports. In addition, industries that had once relied on cotton textiles began shifting to synthetics and plastics. This undercut many of the investments in technology that mill managers had gambled on in the early postwar years. The Korean War offered a temporary respite, but deep recessions in 1954 and 1958 forced the closure of dozens of textile mills, mostly nonunion, and gave managers incentive to intensify their efforts to squeeze more effort out of workers and to install new machinery that might sharpen their competitive edge. Declining production and quality of domestic cotton crops also hurt the textile industry during the 1950s, as cotton was the largest single contributor to production costs. With no control over cotton costs, mill managers sought to cut costs by increasing workloads and speeding up production.

Last Gasps

The Civil Rights Act of 1964 created new opportunities for African-Americans to enter the textile labor force. Indeed, companies began to hire blacks for production jobs, and African-American textile workers increased from about 5% of the labor force to between 25% and 30%. Black workers also appeared to be much more inclined than whites to support unionization campaigns, like the decades-long effort to organize the J. P. Stevens Company. White workers, however, were often reluctant to join organizations that included blacks as equals, and this obviously hindered unionization efforts. Moreover, the number of textile jobs continued to decline because of increasing mechanization and the loss of market share to foreign competition. In short, blacks finally gained access to the region's largest industry in the midst of a long-term collapse that would only accelerate in succeeding decades.

The northern textile industry fared no better in this era. Unable to compete with the southern United States, let alone the rest of the world, northern manufacturers either invested in southern companies or went out of business. TWUA membership in the North shrank from 132,000 in 1950 to 20,000 in 1970.

Many domestic textile companies moved operations to Asia and Latin America during the 1980s and 1990s. The loss of American textile jobs escalated with the passage of the North American Free Trade

Agreement in 1994. Between 1997 and 2002, 236 textile plants closed in North and South Carolina alone, with a loss of more than 75,000 jobs. The remaining workers in textiles were mostly recent immigrants, many of them Latino. Textile employment in the early twenty-first century offered rock-bottom wages and grim prospects. In the end, it is difficult to locate the "golden years" for the domestic textile industry. From the 1830s onward, textiles suffered the ravages of intense competition and offered difficult, uncertain livelihoods to its workers, who struggled against overwhelming odds to improve their situations.

DANIEL CLARK

References and Further Reading

Carlton, David. *Mill and Town in South Carolina, 1880–1920*. Baton Rouge: Louisiana State University Press, 1982.

Clark, Daniel J. *Like Night and Day: Unionization in a Southern Mill Town*. Chapel Hill: University of North Carolina Press, 1997.

Daniel, Clete. *Culture of Misfortune: An Interpretive History of Textile Unionism in the United States*. Ithaca, NY: ILR Press, 2001.

Dublin, Thomas. *Women at Work: The Transformation of Work and Community in Lowell, Massachusetts, 1826–1860*. New York: Columbia University Press, 1979.

Dubofsky, Melvyn. *We Shall Be All: A History of the Industrial Workers of the World*. Chicago: Quadrangle Books, 1969.

Flamming, Douglas. *Creating the Modern South: Millhands and Managers in Dalton, Georgia, 1884–1984*. Chapel Hill: University of North Carolina Press, 1992.

Gilman, Glenn. *Human Relations in the Industrial Southeast: A Study of the Textile Industry*. Chapel Hill: University of North Carolina Press, 1956.

Griffith, Barbara S. *The Crisis of American Labor: Operation Dixie and the Defeat of the CIO*. Philadelphia: Temple University Press, 1988.

Hall, Jacquelyn Dowd, James Leloudis, Robert Korstad, Mary Murphy, Lu Ann Jones, and Christopher Daly. *Like a Family: The Making of a Southern Cotton Mill World*. Chapel Hill: University of North Carolina Press, 1987.

Hodges, James. *New Deal Labor Policy and the Southern Cotton Textile Industry, 1933–1941*. Knoxville: University of Tennessee Press, 1986.

Minchin, Timothy J. *"Don't Sleep with Stevens!": The J. P. Stevens Campaign and the Struggle to Organize the South, 1963–80*. Gainesville: University of Florida Press, 2005.

———. *What Do We Need a Union For?: The TWUA in the South, 1945–1955*. Chapel Hill: University of North Carolina Press, 1997.

Mitchell, George Sinclair. *Textile Unionism in the South*. Chapel Hill: University of North Carolina Press, 1931.

Newby, I. A. *Plain Folk in the New South: Social Change and Cultural Persistence, 1880–1915*. Baton Rouge: Louisiana State University Press, 1989.

Prude, Jonathan. *The Coming of Industrial Order: Town and Factory Life in Rural Massachusetts, 1810–1860*. New York: Cambridge University Press, 1983.

See also **Gastonia Strike (1929); Industrial Workers of the World; Lawrence Strike (1912); National Union of Textile Workers; National War Labor Board (WWI); National War Labor Board (WWII); Operation Dixie; Textile Workers Union of America; United Textile Workers**

THIRTEENTH AMENDMENT

Approved by Congress in January 1865, and officially ratified by the states in December 1865, the Thirteenth Amendment to the U.S. Constitution provides that "neither slavery nor involuntary servitude, except as a punishment for crime" shall exist in the United States, and that Congress has power to "enforce this article by appropriate legislation." A great Civil War achievement, the amendment resulted not just from Union defeat of the Confederacy, but also from politics. Though Congressional Republicans first proposed an antislavery amendment in December 1863, a revised version failed in the House of Representatives in June 1864. After the fall 1864 presidential election, subsequently, President Abraham Lincoln intensely lobbied Congress for Republican and crucial Democratic support, finally gaining the amendment's acceptance.

Fluid politics invested the Thirteenth Amendment with ambiguities about labor rights. Avoiding radical language about "equality" that suggested social leveling, Republican sponsors adopted moderate words from the 1787 Northwest Ordinance permitting "neither slavery nor involuntary servitude." Democrats read this terminology merely to abrogate chattelism, ownership of one human being by another, but Republicans interpreted it to eliminate all forms of coerced labor, leaving labor "unfettered and free." In Section Two authorizing "appropriate legislation," moreover, Republicans embraced the abolitionist theory that the Constitution mandated positive federal action to realize freedom, provoking debate as to how far Congress could go to protect free labor in the states.

The post-Civil War struggle over southern reconstruction pushed Republicans toward even broader views of the Thirteenth Amendment. When southern planters imposed "Black Codes" harshly restricting ex-slaves' labor rights with vagrancy, apprenticeship, and entire contract regulations, federal officials in the Freedmen's Bureau responded by assisting freed people to negotiate voluntary and "fair" labor contracts commensurate with northern visions of free labor. Moreover, under authority of Section Two, Congress enacted the Civil Rights Act of 1866 both to annul Black Codes and to expand protection against "badges of servitude" impairing marital, property, and civil rights, as well as free labor, liberties soon secured in the Fourteenth Amendment.

Thereafter, lawmakers and jurists blunted the Thirteenth Amendment's radical potential and construed it narrowly. True, in 1867, Congress banned "debt slavery" in the Anti-Peonage Act. That same year, Chief Justice Salmon Chase's circuit court ruling in *In Re Turner* liberated an ex-slave from an apprenticeship agreement regarded as virtual slavery. Yet, the U.S. Supreme Court, beginning with the *Slaughterhouse Cases* (1873), limited the amendment just to abolish chattel servitude. In *Hodges v. U.S.* (1906), consequently, the Court denied congressional authority under the Thirteenth Amendment to stop mob obstruction of black employment, ruling that such was a state matter.

On occasion, labor organizers claimed that the Thirteenth Amendment liberated workers as well as slaves, but courts rejected that view. When, in 1972, Curt Flood challenged major league baseball's reserve clause on Thirteenth Amendment grounds that it subjected him to involuntary servitude, the U.S. Supreme Court dismissed that argument. Today, the Thirteenth Amendment remains a rarely cited and neglected part of constitutional law regarding labor rights.

DONALD W. ROGERS

References and Further Reading

Belz, Herman. *A New Birth of Freedom: The Republican Party and Freedmen's Rights, 1861–1866.* Westport, CT: Greenwood Press, 1976.

Hyman, Harold M., and William M. Wiecek. *Equal Justice under Law: Constitutional Development, 1835–1875.* New York: Harper & Row Publishers, 1982.

Schmidt, James D. *Free to Work: Labor Law, Emancipation, and Reconstruction, 1815–1880.* Athens: University of Georgia Press, 1998.

Tsesis, Alexander. *The Thirteenth Amendment and American Freedom.* New York: New York University Press, 2004.

VanderVelde, Lea S. "The Labor Vision of the Thirteenth Amendment." *University of Pennsylvania Law Review* 138, no. 2 (December 1989): 437–504.

Vorenberg, Michael. *Final Freedom: The Civil War, the Abolition of Slavery, and the Thirteenth Amendment.* New York: Cambridge University Press, 2001.

Cases and Statutes Cited

Flood v. Kuhn, 407 U.S. 258 (1972)
Hodges v. U.S., 203 U.S. 1 (1906)
In Re Turner, 24 F. Cas. 337 (C. C. D. Md. 1867)
Slaughterhouse Cases, 83 U.S. 36 (1873)
Anti-Peonage Act of March 2, 1867, c. 187, 14. stat. 546
Civil Rights Act of April 9, 1866, c. 31, 14 Stat. 27
Fourteenth Amendment, U.S. Constitution, ratified July 9, 1868
Northwest Ordinance of July 13, 1787, in *Constitutional Documents and Records, 1776–1787*, Vol. 1, edited by Merrill Jensen, Madison: State Historical Society of Wisconsin, 1976, pp. 168–174.
Thirteenth Amendment, U.S. Constitution, ratified December 6, 1865

THOMAS, NORMAN (NOVEMBER 20, 1884–DECEMBER 19, 1968)
Socialist Party

Norman Mattoon Thomas was America's best-known Socialist from the late 1920s through the late 1960s. He ran as presidential standard-bearer for the Socialist Party six times.

Thomas was born in Marion, Ohio, on November 20, 1884, the descendant of a line of Presbyterian ministers on his father's side and Presbyterian missionaries on his mother's side. Showing great intellectual promise from an early age, Thomas graduated as valedictorian of his class at Princeton in 1905. After several years of volunteer service in slum neighborhoods of New York, Thomas attended Union Theological Seminary and was ordained a Presbyterian minister in 1911, taking on the pastorship of a church in East Harlem.

The First World War radicalized Thomas. An opponent of the war, he helped found the pacifist Fellowship of Reconciliation (FOR) and the National Civil Liberties Bureau, predecessor of the American Civil Liberties Union (ACLU). In 1918, declaring that "these are days when radicals ought to stand up and be counted," he joined the beleaguered Socialist Party. In 1922, he became codirector of the League for Industrial Democracy (LID), a post he would hold through 1937.

Thomas was an eloquent orator, and starting in 1924 when he ran for governor of New York State on the Socialist ticket, he put his talent to good use as a spokesperson for American Socialism. Eugene Debs had been the Socialist Party's candidate for president of the United States many times between 1900 and his death in 1926, winning as much as 6% of the vote in the 1912 election; with Debs gone, Thomas stepped up to take his place.

In the 1920s, the Socialist Party was a shadow of the organization that had existed before government repression and internal splits had decimated it in 1919–1920. In 1928, when he first ran for president, Thomas received only 267,000 votes, a quarter of Debs's vote in 1912. But with the onset of the Great Depression at the end of the decade, the Socialists' prospects improved dramatically. Thomas made a much stronger run for president in 1932, garnering

881,000 votes. The Socialists were disappointed that they had not broken Debs's old record, but the increased vote seemed to bode well for the future. So did the influx of new recruits, many of them college students but also labor organizers including Walter and Victor Reuther in Detroit.

As it turned out, 1932 marked the end rather than the beginning of a Socialist renaissance. The presidential victor that year, Franklin Delano Roosevelt, secured the loyalty of working-class voters with programs like Social Security. Many people said that Roosevelt was "carrying out" the Socialist platform; Thomas would respond that the president was carrying it out "on a stretcher." The Socialists also faced stiff competition in the later 1930s from a vigorous Communist Party and suffered from debilitating faction fights. When Thomas again ran for president in 1936, his vote declined to a mere 187,000 and would never again reach even that low total in the succeeding elections (1940, 1944, and 1948) in which he stood as a candidate for the Socialists.

As war returned to Europe in 1939, Thomas opposed American entry on the side of the Allies, joining the conservative isolationist America First Committee. After Pearl Harbor, Thomas became a reluctant supporter of the war effort, though he criticized the internment of Japanese-Americans during the war and the dropping of the atomic bomb on Hiroshima and Nagasaki that brought the war to an end.

The Cold War years were difficult ones for Thomas. The Socialist Party continued its decline. While Thomas was an outspoken critic of the Communist Party in the United States, he was dismayed by the assault on civil liberties in the McCarthy era. He offered critical support to the United Nations in the Korean War but opposed the arms race between the United States and the Soviet Union. Seeing little point in running losing races for the presidency, he turned his energies to writing, publishing four books in a dozen years, including *A Socialist Faith* in 1951, *The Test of Freedom* in 1954, *The Prerequisites of Peace* in 1959, and *Socialism Re-examined* in 1963. In the 1960s, he began to draw crowds of eager listeners on college campuses again and was outspoken as a supporter of civil rights and as an opponent of the war in Vietnam. He died on December 19, 1968.

MAURICE ISSERMAN

References and Further Reading

Fleischman, Harry. *Norman Thomas: A Biography, 1884–1968.* New York: Norton, 1969.
Swanberg, W. A. *Norman Thomas: The Last Idealist.* New York: Scribner's, 1976.

TOBIN, DANIEL J. (1875–1955)
President, International Brotherhood of Teamsters

During his long tenure as the president of the International Brotherhood of Teamsters (IBT) from 1907 to 1952, Daniel J. Tobin hewed publicly to a conservative union philosophy while at the same time working steadily to build the size and power of the Teamsters organization. While he came into office as a reformer, by the 1930s he was frequently criticized for being complicit in the growing role of organized crime in his union.

Born in County Clare, Ireland, Tobin immigrated to the United States at the age of 15 and eventually came to work as a teamster in Boston. He joined the newly organized Teamsters Union in Boston at the turn of the twentieth century and soon won election to office in his local union. In 1907, he was elected to the presidency of the Teamsters Union as part of a reform effort to unseat the controversial incumbent Cornelius P. Shea. In the first years of his presidency, Tobin worked to bring stability back to a union troubled by local secession movements, many of which had resulted from opposition to Shea's leadership. At the same time, Tobin's unwillingness to accept improper practices by local leaders led to new secession movements, most importantly by a group of 14 locals in Chicago. Tobin himself received a life-threatening beating in 1909 when he tried to speak directly to members in one troubled local in New York City. In this initial period of turmoil, the union's membership and finances declined. While the IBT had been formed in 1903 with 50,000 members, by 1909, membership had dropped to 30,000.

Over the next two decades, Tobin oversaw a period of steady resurgence for the IBT. By 1930, the union had 90,000 members and its financial health was quite good. Tobin husbanded the union's resources carefully by urging local unions to pursue a cautious strategy in dealing with employers and requiring them to avoid sympathy strikes. He championed the ideals of craft unionism (organizing workers into particular unions according to their skill or occupation) and in the 1930s took a strong stand against efforts to move the American Federation of Labor (AFL) toward an aggressive organizing strategy based on industrial unionism (organizing workers by their workplace). All the while, however, he steadily worked to expand the Teamsters' jurisdiction to include a host of occupations besides the union's traditional drivers. By bringing stable hands, dairy workers, and warehousemen, among others, into the union, Tobin increased the organization's membership and its strategic power.

He essentially created an industrial union even as he proclaimed the virtues of craft organization. He maintained control over what became a sprawling organization by cultivating a group of powerful regional leaders, among whom were Dave Beck and James Hoffa, who served as international representatives. Appointed to their posts by Tobin and answering to him, these men dominated the locals in their area, overseeing strike efforts, leading organizing campaigns, and resolving intra-union disputes.

As the head of one of the largest and most powerful unions in the AFL, Tobin assumed a prominent role in the labor movement. He served as treasurer of the labor federation from 1917 to 1928 and was one of its vice presidents from 1933 until he died. Tobin sat among the inner circle of national union leaders who shaped the AFL's policies. While he spoke out against the formation of the Committee for Industrial Organization, by the early 1940s, he became a leading voice within the AFL executive council, urging efforts to heal the breach within the labor movement. Tobin also took an active role in national Democratic Party politics. An avid admirer of Franklin Roosevelt, Tobin was the head of the Labor Bureau of the Democratic National Campaign Committee during presidential elections from 1932 to 1944. His prominent support for Roosevelt spurred hopes that Tobin might be appointed secretary of labor, but the president instead chose to appoint Frances Perkins.

During the 1930s and 1940s, the Teamsters grew dramatically, and by 1940, the union had 450,000 members and had become the nation's largest union. At the same time, it attracted increasing controversy over the role of organized crime in some of its local affiliates, especially in New York and Chicago. One critic in 1940 labeled it "the most racketeer-ridden union in America." Although Tobin loudly proclaimed his own integrity, his apparent inability or unwillingness to root out corruption in these locals drew criticism. By the time of his retirement in 1952, he was depicted as out of touch with his membership and disinterested in their conditions.

DAVID WITWER

References and Further Reading

"The I.B.T.C.W.H. of A." *Fortune Magazine* 23 (May 1941): 97–102, 135–42.
Leiter, Robert. *The Teamsters Union: A Study of Its Economic Impact.* New York: Bookman Associates, Inc., 1957.
Witwer, David. *Corruption and Reform in the Teamsters Union.* Urbana: University of Illinois Press, 2003.

See also **International Brotherhood of Teamsters**

TOMPKINS SQUARE RIOT (1874)

From the end of the Civil War in 1865 to the early 1870s, organized labor experienced a growth in real wages. But in 1873, the nation was hit with a severe industrial depression, which lasted nearly six years. With the Depression of 1873, wages dropped dramatically and most national labor unions collapsed. Hunger and unemployment ravaged both urban and rural areas. By 1877–1878, some three million workers were unemployed and perhaps 20% of the nation's working class was without work. Of the roughly 30 national labor unions in existence in 1873, there were but nine still alive in 1877. In New York City, the depression was particularly acute. During the winter months of January–March 1874, some 90,000 unemployed and homeless workers found but a temporary respite from life on the streets by moving among the city's police stations—which allowed the homeless to stay for one or two nights in any given station house.

In the midst of this suffering, workers intensified their call for public works employment and other forms of government intervention to aid the suffering. This movement, according to the historian Herbert G. Gutman, had expired in major cities across the country except New York. In New York, workers organized themselves into ward committees and created a Committee of Safety in late 1873. Foremost on the agenda of this movement of workers and the unemployed was pressuring the city government to take immediate action to relieve the distress of the unemployed. To that end, the Committee called for a large demonstration to take place in Tompkins Square on January 13, 1874. The Committee printed and distributed handbills urging workers to come to the rally by stating: "Winter is upon us, and nearly all employment has been suspended. Cold and hunger are staring in our faces. Nobody can tell how long the misery will last. Nobody will attempt to help if we don't do something ourselves. Now is the time to meet and consider how we are to get work, food, clothing, and shelter." In the meantime, it advised unemployed workers to simply take food and bill the city.

The mayor of New York, William Havemeyer, initially agreed to speak to the gathering at Tompkins Square, but quickly the city's response to the planned demonstration became one of organized repression, and the city's newspapers, almost without exception, condemned the call for a demonstration and the Committee of Safety as communistic and a danger to the natural order of civil society. City authorities and the police met to plan how best to deal with the demonstration. They decided to quell the demonstration as soon as it took place. On the morning of January 13, 1874, thousands of workers, employed and unemployed, began gathering in Tompkins Square. The Square had been donated to the city by John Jacob Aster. Covering 10 acres, it served as a social space for the mostly poor immigrants who lived in abutting tenements. By 11 a.m., seven thousand people jammed the square and adjacent streets. No violence had taken place and not a single speaker had yet addressed the assembly. The police had been at work even earlier. By 6 a.m., two thirds of the entire New York City police force was on hand in the area of the Square and City Hall—some 1,600 officers, including detectives. Led by the police commissioner, police charged into the rally and began indiscriminately clubbing people; pandemonium ensued. The thousands of men, women, and children who had filled the Square and the area around it fled in all directions—with the police still pursuing them and clubbing anyone they came across. Among the thousands of people running from the police attack was Samuel Gompers, who in the following decade would become president of the American Federation of Labor. Indeed, Gompers wrote that he avoided being clubbed by jumping into a cellar doorway and that the police were engaged in "an orgy or brutality." Not everyone ran from the police, at least not at first. In one spot, a group of German workers fought back, but to little effect. Violent disorder in the streets surrounding the Square continued off and on for a few hours. By the end of the melee, 46 workers were arrested and jailed. Most were under 40 years of age, with just over half of the arrested composed of German immigrants. Only 10 of the arrested were native-born.

The reaction of the city's elite to the conduct of the police was overwhelmingly supportive, with few exceptions. A religious weekly labeled the unemployed "fools" and their leaders little more than "ruffians." The New York Herald opined that only brute force could instill in workers a respect for those "who have plenty when [they] have nothing." Mayor Havemeyer stated that "nothing better could have happened .... It is often easier to cure an evil than to arrest its progress when it is under way." The response of the city's elite was clear: municipalities had no responsibility for the unemployed, and any efforts by them to agitate for public relief would be dealt with severely. Organized labor attacked the city's police department: the Tailors' Union, the United Cigar Makers' Union, the United Order of American Bricklayers, and the United Cabinetmakers' Union, among others, denounced the action of the police as that found among tyrannical European monarchies; such conduct was hostile to the very foundations of liberty in a republic.

In the wake of the crushing of the demonstration at Tompkins Square, the movement of unemployed workers and its allies in organized labor disintegrated.

The Committee of Safety lost much of its support and opted for taking action in electoral politics by forming the Industrial Political Party. With a platform calling for government ownership of railroads, suffrage for all free citizens, and free secular education through college, for example, organized labor repudiated the Party as being too radical. Trade unions affiliated with the New York State Workingman's Assembly and the Workingman's Central Council formed their own political party, but both parties collapsed. Nonetheless, the agitation of the unemployed movement and trade unions helped fuel the formation of a labor party that put forth the newspaper editor John Swinton as its mayoral candidate in the fall 1874 municipal elections. This effort, though, received few votes. Not until the decade of the 1880s would workers' organizations recover from the devastating consequences of the Depression of 1873–1879.

DAVID O. STOWELL

References and Further Reading
Foner, Philip S. History of the Labor Movement in the United States. Vol. 1. New York: International Publishers, 1947.
Gilje, Paul A. Rioting in America. Bloomington: Indiana University Press, 1996.
Gutman, Herbert G. "The Tompkins Square 'Riot' in New York City on January 13, 1874: A Re-examination of Its Causes and Its Aftermath." Labor History 6, no. 1 (1965): 44–70.

TOWNSEND, WILLARD (1895–1957)
African-American Labor Leader

From the mid-1930s until his death in 1957, Willard Townsend emerged as one of the most prominent African-American labor leaders in the country, second only to A. Philip Randolph of the Brotherhood of Sleeping Car Porters. From his base in the union of red caps that he helped to found and then lead, Townsend relayed his visible position into a platform promoting black unionization and attacking discrimination in the labor movement, the economy, and the broader society. Although the labor journalist George McCray exaggerated when he observed in 1942 that Townsend was "fast becoming the most powerful Negro leader in the country," he was right to call attention to the union leader's growing importance as a national figure and political commentator in the realm of race, labor, civil rights, and the economy.

Townsend was born in Cincinnati, Ohio, in 1895, the son of a local building contractor. During World War I, he served with the U.S. Army in France as a first lieutenant in the 372nd Infantry. Upon returning to the United States after the war, Townsend matriculated at the University of Toronto and then the Royal Academy of Science to pursue a medical education. The young veteran, like so many other black students, sought employment in the railroad industry to earn money to pay for his schooling. In Townsend's case, the job of dining car waiter on the Canadian National Railroad afforded him flexible employment during weekends and summers in the mid-1920s, until the company discharged its black workforce during an economic downturn. Townsend then took to the road, teaching at a black religious high school in Texas before securing a variety of unskilled jobs in Chicago. By 1930, Townsend worked as a red cap (a station porter responsible for carrying passengers' baggage to and from trains) at the Northwestern Railroad Terminal.

The upsurge in unionization that swept so many sectors of the American economy during the 1930s extended to the ranks of black railroad service workers. As A. Philip Randolph was securing union recognition and then a pathbreaking contract for the Pullman porters in his Brotherhood of Sleeping Car Porters, African-American dining car waiters and station red caps were also organizing their own craft unions. Townsend was initially at the forefront of red cap unionization in Chicago, contributing to the establishment in 1937 of a small, interracial Brotherhood of Railroad Depot, Bus Terminal, Airport and Dock Red Caps, Attendants and Porters, which affiliated with the American Federation of Labor (AFL) as a federal local (a union attached directly to the Federation with no formal connection to larger international unions). The fragile alliance between the small number of white red caps and the larger number of black red caps did not last: when Townsend was elected to the union's presidency, many white members disaffiliated and instead joined the all-white Brotherhood of Railway Clerks. Racial problems—in this instance manifested in the union's second-class status as a federal union within the AFL—prompted the now largely black union to leave the AFL, opting instead for an independent status as the International Brotherhood of Red Caps (IBRC).

The union Townsend led confronted numerous obstacles in its early years. Jurisdictional claims by the all-white clerks' union led to efforts to subordinate black red caps in various terminals into segregated, auxiliary unions with few rights. In the late 1930s and early 1940s, Townsend and the IBRC crusaded against the clerks and their racial policies, insisting that red caps deserved equal union rights and the opportunity to select democratically their own bargaining agent.

In numerous union elections, the IBRC bested the clerks among black employees. But before they could even compete in union elections, red caps had to establish their eligibility to draw upon the services of the National Mediation Board and the National Railroad Adjustment Board, the federal agencies responsible for labor relations in the railroad industry. The 1934 Railroad Labor Act initially did not apply to red caps, who, unlike Pullman porters and dining car waiters, were not formally recognized as railroad employees. Station managers claimed that unlike other service workers, red caps were independent contractors. Townsend's union devoted considerable effort to persuade the Interstate Commerce Commission (ICC) that, contrary to employers' claims, red caps were bona fide railroaders. The union's "March Forward to Job Legality" campaign was successful by September 1938 when the ICC rejected employers' claims and ruled that red caps were covered under the law. With that single move, the IBRC invoked the National Mediation Board's services and proceeded to win numerous union representation elections. With union recognition quickly followed contracts that established grievance procedures, seniority rights, and other nonmonetary gains. As a largely unskilled and easily replaceable labor force possessing little workplace bargaining power, however, red caps found that modest wage gains came only slowly.

When the red caps union—now called the United Transport Service Employees of America (UTSE)—ended its independent status and affiliated with the Congress of Industrial Organizations (CIO) in 1942, Townsend joined the CIO's executive board, a move that afforded him a high-profile platform from which to carry on his campaign to organize black workers and oppose white unions' racial policies. As the highest-ranking African-American within the CIO, he quickly emerged as a prominent proponent of wartime civil rights and a sharp critic of American race relations. The violent race riots of 1943, he declared, were "grave symptoms of a disease that is gnawing at the vitals of our democracy." During the war, he spoke out in defense of Japanese-Americans, and during and after the war, he condemned restrictive covenants in real estate and federal agencies' roles in fostering segregation in new housing, denounced white trade unions' discriminatory practices, and attacked the widespread discrimination in the realm of employment. Townsend remained a fierce advocate of black trade unionization, the racial inequities in the labor movement notwithstanding. Racial problems were "workers' problems," Townsend argued, and the "labor movement" was the "only vehicle" to achieve "those things we have aspired and hoped for." "Aggressive unionism becomes the major force for the extension of the rights and progress for the Negro race," he insisted. "It is the only segment of our society where Negroes and whites have been able to work together in common purpose."

At the same time A. Philip Randolph was promoting his March on Washington Movement, however, Townsend adopted a skeptical stance, decrying the Fair Employment Practice Committee created by President Franklin Roosevelt to placate Randolph as underfunded and ineffective. Townsend's critique was, to an extent, on the mark. But it is likely that his rivalry with Randolph played some role in his coolness toward Randolph's various projects. Part of the tension was personal, with each leader vying for influence, but part of the tension was also organizational. Townsend was allied with the CIO and Randolph with the AFL. While Randolph did not deny the AFL's racist policies (choosing to fight those policies from within), Townsend was harshly dismissive of the Federation and energetic in his praise for the CIO.

Townsend also directed criticism against the Communist Party (CP) and its allies in the labor movement, charging that Party members sought to "use Negroes in labor to further their ideology" and placing his UTSE at the service of the CIO in jurisdictional battles with a left-led union in the late 1940s and early 1950s. Like other black social democrats and liberals after World War II, Townsend indicted American racial practices for providing ammunition to the Communists. "We say 'Communism is no good!!' 'Communism is dangerous," he insisted. "Yet we do everything in this country to make the Negro Communist-conscious. Bad housing, discrimination, the whole list of grievances that cause him to seek an emotional escape." In speeches and his regular column in the pages of the African-American weekly the *Chicago Defender*, Townsend invoked the intensifying Cold War as a spur to civil rights reform, charging that American race relations and practices weakened the United States in its contest with the Soviet Union for the allegiance of nonwhites in the decolonizing world.

In the final decade of his life, Townsend continued to promote his vision of black unionization and his critique of racial inequality. With the merger in 1955 of the CIO and the AFL, Townsend, like Randolph, served on the new AFL-CIO's executive board. At the same time, he continued to lead the UTSE during its period of slow decline as falling numbers of railway passengers and management cost-cutting measures reduced the number of red caps dramatically. Townsend died of a kidney aliment in Chicago in 1957.

ERIC ARNESEN

References and Further Reading

Arnesen, Eric. *Brotherhoods of Color: Black Railroad Workers and the Struggle for Equality*. Cambridge, MA: Harvard University Press, 2001.
———. "Willard S. Townsend: Black Workers, Civil Rights, and the Labor Movement." In *Portraits of African American Life since 1865*, edited by Nina Mjagkij. Scholarly Resources, 2003, pp. 147–163.
Townsend, Willard S. "One American Problem and a Possible Solution." In *What the Negro Wants*, edited by Rayford Logan. 1944. Reprint, Notre Dame, IN: University of Notre Dame Press, 2001, pp. 163–192.

See also **Fair Employment Practice Committee; International Brotherhood of Red Caps/United Transport Service Employees of America; March on Washington Movement; Randolph, A. Philip**

TRADE UNION UNITY LEAGUE

The Trade Union Unity League (TUUL), founded in Cleveland in August 1929, was the most significant industrial union federation to emerge in the United States between the birth of the Industrial Workers of the World (IWW, 1905) and the formation of the Congress of Industrial Organizations (CIO, 1935). As a member of the Communist Red International of Labor Unions (RILU, or the *Profintern*—the Russian acronym for the organization), its history was closely linked to the history of the Communist Party USA (CPUSA) and the vicissitudes of policy directives from Moscow. Yet, in its struggle to carve out a militant union movement in a nation dominated by craft unions, the TUUL charted a course not dissimilar to that of the syndicalist Industrial Workers of the World, in which many of its leaders had first honed their organizing skills. Though it never recruited vast numbers of workers and was only in existence between 1929 and 1934, in those five short years it kept alive the ideal of industrial unionism. The TUUL's challenge to the American Federation of Labor (AFL) in the late 1920s and early 1930s helped inspire support for an internal rebellion in the AFL that ultimately led to the formation of the independent Congress of Industrial Organizations.

Origins: The Trade Union Educational League (TUEL)

The TUEL emerged specifically out of another Communist-dominated organization, the Trade Union Education League (TUEL), founded by the syndicalist and soon-to-be Communist William Z. Foster in 1920. The TUEL sought to build a democratic, industrial, rank and file-centered union movement by steering conservative AFL and independent unions to the left. It rejected the IWW mold of independent, dual unionism even as it accepted the former organization's emphasis on syndicalist, shop-level organization. The TUEL's official organ, the *Labor Herald*, continually criticized the IWW's strategy for growing industrial unionism, condemning those "who still think that it is a 'revolutionary' act to draw a handful of militant workers outside of the masses, unite them on a dogma, and call it a revolutionary union." Its founding declaration clearly enunciated its mission: to take on "the reactionaries, incompetents, and crooks who occupy strategic positions in many of our organizations," and "to replace them with militants, with men and women unionists who look upon the labor movement not as a means for making an easy living, but as an instrument for the achievement of working class emancipation."

The TUEL attempted to bring about a universal "amalgamation of the trade unions" by forging alliances, organizing unity conferences, winning control of disparate local unions as well as city and state labor federations (such as the powerful Chicago Federation of Labor), and providing leadership for several local and regional industrywide strikes. By September 1923, eight international unions, 14 state federations of labor, and a number of central labor bodies had gravitated into the orbit of the TUEL. Yet the organization's growing influence was soon stifled by the persistent hostility and attacks of conservative regional and national craft union leaders, which led to a growing disaffection among many TUEL organizers with the policy of "boring from within." Thus, it was not surprising that many of the organization's leaders and rank-and-file members were quite responsive to new directives from the Communist International (Comintern) and the Moscow-based Profintern—directives that came in 1928 and that ironically encouraged a return to dual unionism.

Organizing Revolutionary Trade Unions

Even earlier, there were signs that TUEL members were charting a more independent and militant course—encouraged to do so by the Profintern head Alexei Losovsky. In 1927, in the midst of a failed TUEL-supported challenge to the dominance of John L. Lewis in the United Mine Workers (UMW), Losovsky wrote to William Foster, "THE QUESTION OF SETTING UP AN INDEPENDENT UNION MUST BE RAISED, otherwise you will

never escape from this vicious circle." A year later, the Comintern finally encouraged League members to abandon their "boring from within" strategy. This was at the start of the so-called "Third Period," when the Comintern and the Profintern, anticipating a widespread crisis in world capitalism and the birth of a revolutionary labor movement, encouraged its members to create independent, Communist-led, revolutionary unions and to engage in mass strikes. Losovsky now condemned American trade unions, and particularly the AFL, as "schools of capitalism," incapable of stimulating revolutionary change. His comments were echoed by Earl Browder, the managing editor of the Communist newspaper *The Labor Herald*—and soon to be the head of the CPUSA—who declared in 1929: "Today the workers must be prepared for the actual organization of revolutionary trade unions separate from and fighting against the class-collaborationist, social reformist A. F. of L., organizationally and politically."

The TUUL placed its emphasis on building mass industrial unions and on interethnic and interracial organizing (it immediately established a "Negro Department"), and came forward with political demands that anticipated (but went further than) much of the unemployment relief, social insurance, and labor legislation of the New Deal. Beginning in 1928 and in 1929, when the TUUL was formally established, the organization helped organize between 40,000 and 60,000 workers and built more than a dozen unions: the National Miners Union (NMU), the National Textile Workers Industrial Union, the Needle Trades Workers Industrial Union, the Auto Workers Union, the Marine Workers Industrial Union, the Agricultural Workers Industrial League (later the Cannery and Agricultural Workers Industrial Union), the Packinghouse Workers Industrial Union (also known as the Food and Packinghouse Workers Industrial Union), the Tobacco Workers Industrial Union, the Shoe and Leather Workers Industrial Union, the Laundry Workers Industrial Union, the Metal Workers Industrial League, the Tobacco Workers Industrial Union, and the Sharecroppers Union.

The TUUL was involved in a number of major conflagrations during the years of its existence. In 1929, the TUUL-affiliated National Textile Workers reluctantly led a bloody strike of thousands of textile workers in Gastonia, North Carolina—begun when management fired five union activists. A year before the official founding of the TUUL, in 1928, Communist leaders—after years of failed efforts to gain influence within John L. Lewis's United Mine Workers Union—decided to establish their own National Miners Union. In 1931, now affiliated with the TUUL, it took on the leadership of a strike that the

UMW had first called in Harlan County, Kentucky. The violent response of mine owners, the NMU's strong opposition to racial discrimination, and union leaders' overt support and identification with the Soviet Union (widely publicized by their opponents) made it difficult for the union to make headway among the many white, religious miners of Harlan County.

Elsewhere, the TUUL was far more successful. Its Food Workers Industrial Union organized New York cafeteria and restaurant workers; its members became major players within the AFL's Hotel Employees and Restaurant Employees union in New York. In the electrical industry, it helped build the foundations of the independent United Electrical Workers Union—actively organizing in industrial centers like Schenectady, New York (where GE had one of its largest works). The TUUL's Marine Workers Industrial Union helped lead the West Coast longshoremen's strike of 1934 and rejuvenated the moribund International Longshoreman's Association in San Francisco. The TUUL also enjoyed modest success in Michigan's steel and automobile industry, but perhaps its most successful efforts lay in organizing the unemployed—in Detroit, Los Angeles, New York, Chicago, and throughout the nation.

Legacies

In 1935, with the formation of the newly formed Committee for Industrial Organization (soon to become the Congress of Industrial Organizations) and with another shift in Communist Party policy, the life of the TUUL ended and the locus of industrial union struggles shifted to the newly established CIO. Communist trade unionists were instructed to enter the CIO industrial unions or to work within existing AFL unions to promote general labor unity and industrial unionism. John L. Lewis, who years earlier had purged his United Miners Workers of CP members, now embraced Communists and welcomed them into the CIO. Some, like Lee Pressman, became major national leaders in the organization (Pressman was its general counsel). Other TUUL activists became local and regional leaders in many of the newly emerging CIO unions of the late 1930s. They brought with them many of the organizational skills and much of the left labor culture that had characterized the TUUL. As the historian Edward P. Johanningsmeier noted, "the TUUL helped to establish a new type and style of Communist unionism, more suited to the organization of African-Americans, women, and mass-production workers."

GERALD ZAHAVI

References and Further Reading

Barrett, James R. "Boring from Within and Without: William Z. Foster, the Trade Union Educational League, and American Communism in the 1920s." In *Labor Histories: Class, Politics, and the Working-Class Experience*, edited by Eric Arnesen, Julie Greene, and Bruce Laurie. Urbana: University of Illinois Press, 1998.

Foner, Philip Sheldon. *The TUEL, 1925–1929*. Vol. 10 of *History of the Labor Movement in the United States*. New York: International Publishers, 1994.

———. *The TUEL to the End of the Gompers Era*. Vol. 9 of *History of the Labor Movement in the United States*. New York: International Publishers, 1991.

Johanningsmeier, Edward P. *Forging American Communism: The Life of William Foster*. Princeton, NJ: Princeton University Press, 1994.

———. "The Trade Union Unity League: American Communists and the Transition to Industrial Unionism: 1928–1934." *Labor History* 42, no. 2 (May 2001): 159–177.

Saposs, David Joseph. *Left Wing Unionism: A Study of Radical Policies and Tactics*. New York: International Publishers, 1926.

See also **Congress of Industrial Organizations; Foster, William Z.**

TRANSPORT WORKERS UNION

The Transport Workers Union of America (TWU) is one of two main unions in the United States—the other is the Amalgamated Transit Union (ATU)—that represents mass transit workers. It also represents groups of airline, railroad, utility, and university employees. The TWU grew out of an effort in the early 1930s to unionize subway, elevated train, trolley, and bus workers in New York City, later expanding to become a national union.

The Founding of the TWU

From the days of horse-drawn trolleys through World War I, the urban mass transit industry had turbulent labor relations. Transit workers, poorly paid and required to work inordinately long hours, banded together in periodic efforts to better their conditions. Employers vigorously resisted unionization, leading to strikes notable for their intensity and violence. Workers sometimes succeeded in improving wages and conditions and establishing ongoing organizations, but their victories often proved short-lived. By the 1920s, the Amalgamated Association of Street Railway Employees (later renamed the ATU), an affiliate of the American Federation of Labor (AFL), managed to build stable organizations on some transit lines. However, in much of the country, including New York, most transit workers lacked union representation and continued to work extraordinarily long hours for low pay.

The Great Depression worsened the already difficult working conditions in the transit industry. In New York, companies eliminated benefits, laid off hundreds of workers, and reduced hours and pay rates for those who remained. The cutbacks led to employee unrest and discussion of the possibilities for collective action. This sentiment crystallized through the efforts of the Communist Party (CP), which in 1933 declared transit one of its "concentration points" for organizing in the New York area. Though the Party had only a few members working in the industry, its organizers soon made contact with a scattering of workers interested in forming a transit union, who in turn began pulling together small groups of activists.

Irish workers played a particularly important role in the organization of the TWU. In the early 1930s, nearly half of New York's transit workers had been born in Ireland. Some had been active in the republican movement during the Irish independence struggle and subsequent civil war. The republican veterans who joined the nascent union effort proved critical to its success. With an unusual degree of political experience, widespread respect among Irish workers, and in many cases a left-leaning inclination, they served as a link between the CP and Irish workers and took key positions in the union as it emerged.

The TWU was formally founded in April 1934 as an independent union, with the head of the Communist organizing effort, John Santo, as its initial leader. When the CP decided to move its union forces into the AFL, the TWU attempted to affiliate with the Amalgamated Association, but the groups could not agree on terms. Instead, in February 1936, the TWU affiliated with the International Association of Machinists (IAM). By then, the TWU had restructured its leadership, with the Irish-born transit worker Thomas H. O'Shea chosen to serve as the group's first president but soon replaced by another Irishman, who like O'Shea had been active in the republican movement, Michael J. Quill.

The TWU's initial clandestine effort soon led to open recruiting and a series of clashes with employers, including several short strikes at car barns and a power plant. In the spring and summer of 1937, the union won a series of representation elections and signed contracts with every major private transit company in New York City, giving it a membership of nearly 30,000 and beginning the process of upgrading pay, benefits, and working conditions for its constituency.

Becoming a National Union

Just before its sweep of representation elections in New York, the TWU left the IAM to accept a national union charter from the Committee for Industrial Organization (CIO) that gave it jurisdiction over "all workers employed on or about passenger transport facilities, excluding steam railroad systems." The union set up a national structure, headquartered in New York, while converting its New York group into an affiliate, Local 100. In October 1937, at the TWU's first national convention, delegates elected Quill international president, Douglas MacMahon, another New York transit worker, vice president, and Santo secretary-treasurer. Later that year, Local 100 elected Austin Hogan, an Irish-born Communist, as its president.

It took a while for the TWU to become a national union in more than name. Upon joining the CIO, the TWU established locals of bus, trolley, and taxicab workers in a number of small cities and towns. But its efforts to move into larger cities failed. Then, just prior to World War II, it began winning a series of organizing drives, including among bus and taxicab workers in Omaha, transit workers in Columbus, Ohio, and track workers in Chicago. Its biggest victory came in Philadelphia in 1944, when it beat out the Amalgamated Association and another group to become the representative of 9,200 employees of the Philadelphia Transit Company (PTC), who became the core of Local 234. After the war, the TWU's expansion continued with new locals in Louisville, Houston, and San Francisco.

The TWU also began moving beyond mass transit. During the early 1940s, a variety of groups affiliated with the union, including truck drivers in New Orleans, gas workers in Brooklyn, and maintenance workers at Columbia University. More important, the TWU began organizing the rapidly growing passenger airline industry, beginning with Pan American Airways maintenance workers in Miami. In the immediate postwar years, the TWU's Air Transport Division signed up airline mechanics, navigators, radio operators, flight attendants, fleet service workers, guards, and commissary workers employed by Pan Am and American Airlines. By 1948, only 35,000 of the TWU's 68,000 members belonged to its original New York local.

The TWU's expansion helped stabilize it as Local 100 confronted a threat to its very existence. When the union began, the entire New York transit industry was privately operated, except for one subway line. However, in 1940, New York City took over the two privately operated subway systems as well as some bus and trolley lines, integrating the properties into a single system. The city takeover forced the TWU into a prolonged fight to maintain collective bargaining and union grievance procedures in what became a civil service operation. While the New York mayor, Fiorello La Guardia, did not forbid city workers from belonging to unions, he ruled out signing contracts with them, granting exclusive representation rights, or allowing municipal employees to strike. It took until the mid-1950s for Local 100 to regain the right to exclusive representation and to negotiate signed contracts with the New York City Transit Authority, which ran the public transit lines. Its success helped pave the way for the unionization of other New York City workers in the years that followed.

Political Re-Orientation

During its first 15 years, the TWU generally aligned itself on international affairs, national labor issues, and electoral politics with the Communist-led left. Though there were never a large number of Communists in the union, they were disproportionately represented in its leadership. TWU members generally held more conservative views than their leaders, but by and large they supported the officers who had played central roles in organizing the union and in its collective bargaining advances, to the frustration of Catholic anticommunists who targeted the union.

The situation changed with the onset of the Cold War. As anticommunist pressure grew inside and outside of the labor movement, the TWU president, Quill, decided to distance himself from the CP. Most other left-wing leaders of the union remained allied with it. A resulting civil war for control of the union culminated at its December 1948 convention, when Quill and his allies defeated the left. Many key leaders, including Santo, Hogan, and MacMahon, were pushed out of the union, which Quill steered toward more mainstream liberal politics.

During the 1950s, the TWU continued to grow, though modestly. In 1954, it absorbed the CIO United Railway Workers Organizing Committee, which became its Railroad Division. It also continued to organize airline and mass transit workers and eventually began signing up school bus drivers as well.

Most TWU contracts were settled without strikes, but the union did not shy away from militant action. The railway and airline industries were covered by the federal Railway Labor Act, which restricted the right to strike. Nonetheless, the union did occasionally lead walkouts in those industries. The most disruptive came

in 1960, when the TWU, in alliance with another labor group, led 40,000 Pennsylvania Railroad maintenance workers out on strike, shutting down the huge railway for the first time in its 114-year history.

TWU transit locals operated under a variety of state labor laws—New York State outlawed public employee strikes—and with differing degrees of militancy. Some locals rarely, if ever, struck. By contrast, Local 234 struck frequently when its contracts with the PTC (and later with the Southeastern Pennsylvania Transportation Authority, which took over the PTC lines) expired. From 1946 to 2005, there were over a dozen major transit strikes in Philadelphia, including a 42-day walkout in 1978 and a 40-day strike in 1998.

In New York, Local 100 repeatedly threatened to strike the subway system and did hold occasional walkouts against privately run bus companies, but the first citywide transit strike did not occur until 1966. New York transit wages, though improved over the years, remained low, especially for the more skilled workers, who saw their standard of living slip behind workers doing equivalent jobs in the private sector. At the same time, as more African-Americans took transit jobs, many felt that they were not being given sufficient roles in the union leadership or access to the best-paid jobs. As various subgroups with the union became dissatisfied, the local fragmented. With Quill determined to re-unify Local 100 through a militant struggle and a rich contract and an incoming mayor, John Lindsay, committed to breaking the pattern of ties between the TWU and city leaders, no agreement could be reached. On January 1, 1966, TWU members walked off their jobs, all but paralyzing the city. Four days into the strike, Quill, Matthew Guinan, who had succeeded Hogan as the Local 100 president, and other TWU leaders were jailed for defying a court injunction. In jail, Quill suffered a heart attack. After 12 days, the strike ended with a settlement favorable to the union. Two weeks later, Quill died.

The Next Generation

After Quill's death, members of the founding generation of the TWU continued to hold leadership positions. But a transition already was under way to a younger generation of leaders, who soon found themselves facing a variety of challenges. In New York, the shifting racial, ethnic, and later gender makeup of the workforce, along with deteriorating job conditions as a result of the city's mid-1970s fiscal crisis, sparked the formation of a series of rank-and-file opposition groups. Their militancy led to a second citywide transit strike, lasting 11 days, in 1980.

In the airline industry, the TWU lost members as a result of dissatisfaction among flight attendants and industry turmoil following the 1978 Airline Deregulation Act. As the women's movement of the early 1970s began influencing female airline workers, who faced a variety of discriminatory obstacles, flight attendants belonging to the TWU grew dissatisfied with how it represented them. In 1976, Pan American flight attendants left the TWU in favor of an independent group. Later, Pan American and Eastern Airlines went bankrupt and dissolved, costing thousands of TWU members their jobs. But through ongoing organizing, the TWU added members at other airlines. By 2005, the union represented nearly 50,000 airline workers at over two dozen companies.

Even as the demographic profile of the TWU membership and its leaders changed, the union retained its traditions of militancy, lively, sometimes fractious internal politics, and an unusually strong representation of left-wing voices. In Local 100, new rank-and-file dissident groups began organizing in the 1980s, growing in strength from year to year and merging under the umbrella of the New Directions caucus. In 2000, the New Directions candidate for Local 100 president, Roger Toussaint, a Trinidadian-born track worker, defeated the incumbent and another candidate. Though New Directions fractured after sweeping aside the old administration, under Toussaint, Local 100 took a more aggressive stance in collective bargaining, including conducting a three-day citywide transit strike in 2005. Toussaint portrayed himself as reviving the spirit of Mike Quill, highlighting the continuities in the history of the TWU, which from its start aggressively fought to upgrade the working and living standards of transportation workers, even if that required occasionally inconveniencing the public.

JOSHUA B. FREEMAN

References and Further Reading

Freeman, Joshua B. *In Transit: The Transport Workers Union in New York City, 1933–1966.* Philadelphia: Temple University Press, 2001.

Lichtenstein, Alex. "Putting Labor's House in Order: The Transport Workers Union and Labor Anti-Communism in Miami during the 1940s." *Labor History* 39, no. 1 (1998): 7–23.

Marmo, Michael. *More Profile than Courage: The New York City Transit Strike of 1966.* Albany: State University of New York Press, 1990.

See also **American Federation of Labor; Communist Party; Quill, Michael J.**

TREVELLICK, RICHARD F. (1830–1895)
Labor Leader

Richard Trevellick, a Civil War-era labor leader who headed several trade unions and labor reform organizations, was an effective spokesman for a wide range of causes including shorter hours, greenback currency, temperance, and equal treatment for African-Americans.

Trevellick was born in 1830 to a Methodist farm family on the Scilly Islands near southwest England. Trained as a ship carpenter, at age 21 Trevellick took a job on the dry docks of Southampton, England, beginning a decade of global travel that introduced him to principles of labor reform. From 1852 to 1855, Trevellick prospected for gold and labored in shipyards in Australia and New Zealand. In these colonies, Trevellick joined in his first campaign for the eight-hour day. Following a brief stint in Peru's navy, Trevellick worked for a Panama-based mail company. In 1857, he moved to New Orleans. Building on past associations, Trevellick joined a temperance society and the local ship carpenters union, of which he quickly became president. In 1858, he led an eight-hour day strike. That year, Trevellick married Victoria, his landlady's daughter, with whom he raised five children. Opposed to slavery and the South's secession from the Union, in 1862, Trevellick moved his family to Detroit, Michigan.

Trevellick quickly moved up the ranks of Detroit's Ship Carpenters and Caulkers Union to become its president. In 1864, he helped organize a citywide trade assembly that claimed 5,000 members. The trade assembly influenced city politics and gave organized labor a stronger role in the city's economy. Its effectiveness whetted Trevellick's interest in building a national trade federation. In 1865, Trevellick won the presidency of the national ship carpenters union and led a successful strike against a Buffalo, New York, dry-dock company.

Despite leading several strikes, Trevellick disliked the tactic because better-funded employers usually prevailed. He preferred arbitration, boycotts, and legislative solutions to labor's concerns. The quest for shorter hours fit this strategy. In 1866, Trevellick led the Michigan Eighth-Hour League in a campaign for a state law shortening the workday. That same year, Trevellick quit the shipyards to work full-time as a labor reformer. He helped launch the National Labor Union (NLU) in 1866, and he headed a state-level counterpart, the Michigan Labor Union. Appointed as the NLU's Washington lobbyist, in 1868, Trevellick helped persuade Congress to mandate an eight-hour-day law for federal employees.

However, the law proved nearly unenforceable as did state-level eight-hour laws passed during the same period.

In 1869, the NLU elected Trevellick as its president, a post he held until the organization died in 1872. As NLU president, Trevellick advocated organizing African-American workers on the grounds of white economic self-interest; if African-Americans went unorganized, he argued, then they would break strikes and lower wages in competition with unionized white workers.

Although Trevellick organized approximately 50 unions during his lifetime, he pushed the NLU toward politics and away from trade-union activism. The National Labor Reform Party, the fruit of this effort, fared poorly in the 1872 presidential election, garnering less than 1% of the total vote. This weak showing reflected the persistent attachment of workers to the established parties and increasing fragmentation among reformers over issues related to class and race. The shift toward politics drove trade unions away from the NLU and contributed to its demise.

Like many contemporary labor reformers, Trevellick believed that credit and currency reform would alleviate labor's exploitation. As a member of the NLU and as a supporter of the Greenback-Labor Party in the late 1870s, Trevellick supported an end to private banking and the replacement of gold-backed currency with interest-bearing greenbacks. These reforms would lower interest rates and increase credit and thereby promote prosperity for both labor and capital. The Panic of 1873, the longest recession prior to the Great Depression of the 1930s, spurred interest in the broad-ranging economic change promised by credit and currency reform. In 1874, Trevellick attended a meeting to organize the new Greenback-Labor Party, which was dedicated to structural economic changes that neither Democrats nor Republicans would support. Trevellick chaired Greenback national conventions in 1878 and 1880. In 1878, Greenbackers won state and local offices but garnered no more than 3% of the vote in presidential contests from 1876 to 1884.

In 1878, Trevellick signed up with the Knights of Labor as an organizer and lecturer, a position he held for the rest of his life. He died in 1895. Trevellick was one of several leaders who helped revitalize and expand the labor movement after the Civil War.

FRANK TOWERS

References and Further Reading

Hicks, Obadiah. *Life of Richard F. Trevellick, the Labor Orator.* 1896. Reprint, New York: Arno Press, 1971.

McLaughlin, Doris B. *Michigan Labor: A Brief History from 1818 to the Present.* Ann Arbor, MI: Institute of Labor and Industrial Relations, 1970.
Montgomery, David. *Beyond Equality: Labor and the Radical Republicans, 1862–1872.* New York: Alfred A. Knopf, 1967.

See also **Civil War and Reconstruction; Greenback-Labor Party; National Labor Union**

TRIANGLE SHIRTWAIST FIRE

The Triangle factory occupied the top three floors of the modern Asch Building on the corner of Washington Place and Greene Street in New York City's fashionable Greenwich Village. Constructed in 1900, the Asch Building was thoroughly modern in design and safety. Saturday, March 25, 1911, began as a typical Saturday at the Triangle factory. At 4:00 p.m., workers on the eighth floor (the factory occupied the eighth, ninth, and tenth floors) heard the watchman ring the bell, signaling quitting time. The young women raced for their pay envelopes and then off to the dressing rooms to begin what was left of their weekend. Five minutes after the bell rang, a fire was discovered under worktable 2 near the Greene Street windows, and it spread rapidly. The fire most likely started as the result of a discarded cigarette thrown carelessly on a pile of "cut-aways"—scraps of cloth that were saved and sold to scrap cloth dealers. It was common for Triangle to accumulate over a ton of scrap before it was carted away, creating a serious fire hazard. While it is impossible to know the exact amount of cloth on hand, there had not been a pickup for nearly three months. It is likely that over a ton of scrap cloth, plus much more uncut cloth, was on hand. The presence of that amount of cloth caused the factory to go up in flames within minutes.

The fire started on the eighth floor and a warning was given to the executive offices on the tenth. No one notified the workers on the ninth, many of whom jumped out the windows rather than burn. The vision of young women jumping to their death was a sight many New Yorkers would never forget. The *New York Times* reported that "girls rushed to the window and looked down at Greene Street 100 feet below them. Then one poor, little creature jumped. There was a plate of glass protection over part of the sidewalk, but she crashed through it, wrecking it and breaking her body into a thousand pieces. The crowd yelled 'DON'T JUMP!' But it was jump or be burned—the proof of which is found in the fact that fifty burned bodies were taken from the ninth floor alone."

The city was thoroughly unprepared to cope with a fire of this magnitude. The *New York Times* stated, "Mostly all there was to do was to determine if life was extinct in the bodies on the pavement and cover them over." At the time of the fire, New York's Fire Department had at its disposal the latest in firefighting technologies. It had one of the nation's first fully motorized units—still in an experimental stage. The Asch Building was located in one of the city's few new high-water-pressure areas. The Fire Department dispatched to the scene one of its newest pump engines, as well as the new hook and ladder companies. When Fire Company 20 arrived with the city's largest hook and ladder, witnesses recalled that the crowd screamed for them to "raise the ladder!" But "the ladder had been raised . . . it was raised to its fullest point. It reached only to the sixth floor." "The [fire]men did the best they could," according to Battalion Chief Worth, "but there was no apparatus in the department to cope with this kind of fire."

In the fire's aftermath, emotions in the city's working-class communities ran high. To middle-class guardians of law and order, however, the scene at the fire's site was that of a mob. All the city's major newspapers reported that police pushed the extremely large crowds gathered in front of the building into nearby Washington Square Park. Police re-inforcements were needed to "hold back" the crowds, which gathered for many reasons: some were morbidly curious for the grisly details of the fire, others were searching for family and friends, and many were simply shocked.

The families of the victims spent most of the week following the fire arranging for burials. As is common in tragedies with a social subtext, these funerals became a catalyst for protest. The Women's Trade Union League (WTUL) and the International Ladies' Garment Workers' Union (ILGWU) made most of the burial arrangements. The cloakmakers' union announced that its members would symbolically work only a half day on the day of the mass funeral for the remaining unidentified victims and turn out in mass for the service. Other unions declared similar intentions. The 146 young women who died in the blaze were honored in one of the largest displays of class solidarity the city had ever experienced. In 1909, this very factory was the site of labor unrest. At the time, the ILGWU was a weak union, with a tiny membership. But the women in the shirtwaist industry gave it life. By 1910, the ILGWU was the largest union of garment workers in the country.

While families buried their kin separately, the union planned a mass service for the final seven victims who were not claimed by family because they could not be positively identified. The city would not release the unidentified bodies. So, without bodies to bury or a permit to assemble, the activists decided on a mass public funeral—what the *Call* declared would be the "greatest demonstration of workers ever seen here . . . when the Triangle's victims are laid to rest." Over 30,000 marchers followed the empty hearses under the Washington Square Arch in Greenwich Village, just two blocks from the site of the fire. They followed the carriages to the Twenty-Third Street Pier, where they watched the bodies as they were ferried across to Brooklyn. A crowd of nearly 10,000 met the ferries in Brooklyn.

"Who is responsible?" the editors of the socialist *Call* had asked after the fire. Because the trial of the Triangle owners had been so unrewarding, and no agency seemed to take responsibility, the paper warned that workers should set their sights higher. Individuals were certainly at fault, but it was the economic and political system that permitted them to do what they did and get away with it.

The fire, more than many other events, made visible the plight of the working class to the public at large. The middle class was forced to view the conditions workers toiled under. They were appalled at the unsanitary and unsafe conditions and began to demand action. Middle-class reform groups pressed for change.

Yet, the lasting legacy of the fire was the work that young Tammany upstarts such as Alfred E. Smith and Robert F. Wagner accomplished, through the Factory Investigating Committee (FIC). The FIC existed for four short years, but in the process, it redefined the role of the state and labor. Wagner and Smith were transformed as well from local politicians to national leaders. They introduced new laws into the state, making it one of the most progressive in the nation. And in the end, they cemented the relationship between workers and the Democratic Party that would find its fuller expression during the New Deal.

RICHARD A. GREENWALD

References and Further Reading

Greenwald, Richard A. *The Triangle Fire, the Protocols of Peace, and Industrial Democracy in Progressive Era New York (Labor in Crisis)*. Philadelphia: Temple University Press, 2005.

Stein, Leon. *The Triangle Fire*. New York: Carroll and Graf, 1962.

Von Drehle, Dave. *Triangle: The Fire That Changed America*. New York: Atlantic Monthly Press, 2003.

See also **International Ladies' Garment Workers' Union (ILGWU) (1900–1995); Women's Trade Union League**

TRUMKA, RICHARD L. (1949–)
President, United Mine Workers

A third-generation miner born and raised in the Monongahela River community of Nemacolin, Pennsylvania, Richard L. Trumka, at the time of his November 1982 election to the presidency of the United Mine Workers (UMW), became the youngest leader of any American labor organization.

Working summers in the mines while in college, Trumka was 20 years of age when the 1969 murder of the UMW reformer Joseph "Jock" Yablonski in Clarksville—a town but 10 miles distant from Nemacolin—profoundly altered the union and the young student's life. The killing of Yablonski, along with his wife and daughter, had been ordered by the then UMW president William "Tony" Boyle to silence his union election rival. Instead of quelling opposition, Yablonski's death led to a surge of activism against the corrupt administration that resulted in the federal Labor Department invalidating the election, Boyle's conviction, and a victory by the Miners for Democracy (MFD).

After graduation from Pennsylvania State University in 1971, Trumka studied law. Although in college during the height of the Vietnam War, Trumka drew more on the UMW traditions and Catholic New Deal legacies of southwestern Pennsylvania than on currents of New Left activism. Upon finishing law school at Villanova in 1974, Trumka worked in the union's legal department for the MFD reformer Arnold Miller, whose UMW presidency was accompanied by democratic upsurge, unsanctioned strikes, and internal infighting. In the end, Miller proved unequal to the task of organizational consolidation and resigned in 1979. As a result of a leadership vacuum, the former Boyle loyalist, Sam Church, whose forces retained strength on the UMW's International Executive Board (IEB), became president.

Disappointed with the circumstances and the looming return of the old guard, Trumka left his staff position in 1978 and returned to the mines. In June 1981, he won election to the IEB, unified his Pennsylvania base, and organized a geographically balanced slate against Church. Alarmed by the coalition arrayed against him, Church turned to conservative Republicans to try to retain his presidency and attacked Trumka for alleged "leftist" connections. Almost in tandem with Church, the Republican chairman of the Senate Labor Committee announced the Committee would investigate "subversives" in the union. The accusations made little difference, as Trumka, who pledged to rejuvenate the UMW, bested Church by a 2-to-1 margin. Commenting on the victory, one labor lawyer said, "[the killing of] Jock Yablonski made Rich Trumka's victory possible."

Facing daunting tasks, which included the increased use of alternative energy sources, imported foreign coal, and nonunion western surface mining—combined with adversarial political power in Washington—Trumka turned to approaches favored by John L. Lewis when he built the CIO. Using Lewis's very words, Trumka vowed "No backward steps" in contract bargaining. As did Lewis during the heady years of the CIO, Trumka hired a coterie of able and experienced working-class activists, and by 1984, the new UMW leader concluded a national agreement without making a single concession.

When Trumka settled the contract with the Bituminous Coal Operators Association (BCOA) without a major disruption, it won him great prestige. Typically, one newspaper headline asked whether Trumka was "The next labor giant?" Trumka prepared well, winning modest gains for his members in an era typified by union retreats in other industries. Nevertheless, he encountered trouble corralling recalcitrant companies like A. T. Massey, which refused to sign the BCOA agreement. Even there, however, Trumka found ways to pressure companies like Massey. Owned by Royal Dutch/Shell, Massey imported South African-mined coal. The UMW launched a boycott against the company and joined the battle against the apartheid regime, which won the UMW new friends in the social movements.

Innovative tactics such as boycotts aimed at energy titans like Shell, and the use of selective strikes that played one company off against another, cemented Trumka in place as the UMW head. A further test came in 1987 when the Pittston Company, as had A. T. Massey, announced its refusal to honor the BCOA agreement then being negotiated. Characteristically, Trumka's union planned meticulously before striking Pittston in 1989. Building labor unity and using tactics of plant takeovers and mass mobilization inspired by the civil rights movement, the UMW gained nationwide support. Against a background of labor defeats elsewhere during the 1980s and in the face of hostile political authority that used arrests and injunctions in an attempt to subdue the organization, the union stood its ground. When $65 million in fines was levied against the union by a state judge, the UMW waged a write-in campaign against the judge's son, unseating the Virginia state representative. In the end, UMW solidarity prevailed, gaining additional health coverage for Pittston miners while limiting the company's ability to contract out, which initially provoked the strike. Federal intervention helped end the mounting conflict when it became apparent that the UMW would match Pittston's tactics of escalation.

Despite victories against long odds, Trumka's UMW experienced less success in unionizing western coalfields in right-to-work states where operators often paid surface miners above UMW minimums to keep the pits from being organized. Combined with large-scale mechanization and a downturn in coal usage because of steel-industry decline, membership of active UMW miners dropped precipitously, with the organization losing anywhere between a third to as many as half of its members. Moreover, while Trumka harnessed labor power to achieve contractual gains, he was unable to effect a merger with the Oil, Chemical and Atomic Workers in 1988 that would have increased UMW membership and fused the two energy unions in their common battles with energy giants. The reversal proved to be a portent of Trumka's future difficulties in trying to marshal cooperation within the AFL-CIO.

Still, few could equal Trumka's achievements. During his 13-year UMW tenure, he concluded three agreements with the shrunken BCOA, enhancing his reputation as a militant union leader. When dissatisfied labor leaders ousted Lane Kirkland from his AFL-CIO leadership post and defeated his designee in 1995, Trumka was the overwhelming favorite in one rank-and-file poll to serve as the new head of the federation. Instead, that position went to John Sweeney, the head of a much larger union. Trumka won the post of secretary-treasurer. Believing in the need to bolster other reformers if labor was to grow once more, Trumka supported the 1996 re-election of the progressive Teamster president Ron Carey. When some said Trumka raised money for Carey's campaign illegally, his name became linked with a criminal investigation. He denied involvement, and Carey, while later barred from Teamster office by the Labor Department, was exonerated in a court of law.

Ultimately, the Sweeney-Trumka team, despite repeated efforts to change and revitalize the labor movement, could not exert the level of control over the Federation that they had exerted within their respective unions. Hence, they were unable to reverse the decline of union membership and influence or prevent self-styled reformers from leaving the AFL-CIO at the group's fiftieth anniversary convention in 2005.

THOMAS M. GRACE

References and Further Reading

Buhle, Paul. *Taking Care of Business: Samuel Gompers, George Meany, Lane Kirkland, and the Tragedy of American Labor*. New York: Monthly Review Press, 1999.
Dubofsky, Melvyn and Warren Van Tine. *John L. Lewis: A Biography*. Urbana: University of Illinois Press, 1986.
Geoghegan, Thomas. *Which Side Are You On?: Trying to Be for Labor When It's Flat on Its Back*. New York: Farrar, Straus, & Giroux, 1991; New York: The New Press, 2004.
Green, James. *Taking History to Heart: The Power of the Past in Building Social Movements*. Amherst: University of Massachusetts Press, 2000.
Heineman, Kenneth J. *A Catholic New Deal: Religion and Reform in Depression Pittsburgh*. University Park: Pennsylvania State University Press, 1999.
Laslett, John H. M., ed. *The United Mine Workers of America: A Model of Industrial Solidarity?* University Park: Pennsylvania State University Press, 1996.
Lichtenstein, Nelson. *State of the Union: A Century of American Labor*. Princeton, NJ: Princeton University Press, 2002.
Moody, Kim. *An Injury to All: The Decline of American Unionism*. New York: Verso, 1988.
Mort, Jo-Ann, ed. *Not Your Father's Union Movement: Inside the AFL-CIO*. New York: Verso, 1999.

See also **Boyle, W. A. (Tony); Carey, Ronald; Kirkland, Lane; Lewis, John L.; Sweeney, John J.; United Mine Workers of America; West Virginia Mine War (1920–1921)**

TRUTH, SOJOURNER (1797–1883)
Abolitionist, Women's Rights Advocate, Reformer

Born Isabella Baumfree in Ulster County, New York, sometime around 1797, Sojourner Truth was the child of enslaved parents who were owned by a wealthy Dutch patroon in the Hudson Valley. Her early life was marked by slavery's brutish handicaps and associated hardships—hired out to a parade of demanding masters. The young Isabella was especially maltreated by English masters until she became bilingual, learning English as well as her native Dutch. She became a valued worker in the household of John Dumont, a New Paltz farmer. While living on Dumont's estate, Truth gave birth to five children between 1810 and 1827, fathered by a fellow slave named Thomas. She left her children with her husband and fled to freedom, emancipating herself when her master failed to free her following his promise to honor New York's emancipation statute. In 1827, she took refuge with a couple named Van Wagener, adopted their name, and as Isabella Van Wagener successfully sued to have her son Peter returned to her, as he had been illegally sold away to Alabama.

As Isabella Van Wagener, Truth migrated to New York City in 1829, where she earned her living as a domestic, and became involved in a religious cult, settling into the household of Elijah Pierson in 1831.

Truth later removed with the Piersons to "Zion Hill," a community near Ossining, New York, living under the spell of the "prophet" Matthias. After scandals and arrests following Pierson's mysterious death in 1835, the group disbanded and Truth returned to Manhattan. She left behind her old identity and took the name Sojourner Truth—to signify her powerful conversion—striking out for parts unknown in June 1843. She spent the summer and autumn months of 1843 traversing Long Island and Connecticut, singing and preaching, offering spiritual counseling to listeners.

By the winter of 1843, she joined another utopian experiment when she became one of a handful of blacks to join the community run by the Northampton Association of Education and Industry. Truth befriended the Manhattan abolitionist David Ruggles, a community resident, and Frederick Douglass, another prominent black abolitionist and lecturer, who was a regular visitor to the commune. Through her contacts at Northampton, Truth was befriended by William Lloyd Garrison (a brother-in-law of the community's founder, George Benson), who wrote a warm endorsement of her authorized autobiography, which was penned by Olive Gilbert and published in 1850.

Following the collapse of the Northampton co-operative in 1846, Truth took out a mortgage on one of the houses within the abandoned community. She went on the road to support herself as an abolitionist lecturer and to pay off her $300 mortgage and the $500 printing bill for her memoir. During the 1850s Truth used the offices of the Salem (Ohio) *Antislavery Bugle* as her midwestern headquarters during extensive lecture tours throughout Indiana, Missouri, and Kansas. She was often paired on the platform with Frederick Douglass or Parker Pillsbury. But she maintained her own separate career as well and opened her own performances with a song, ending with a pitch to the audience that they might purchase a copy of her autobiography for sale, offering as a motto, "I sell the shadow to support the substance."

By 1857, Truth had paid off the mortgage on her Massachusetts house. She then gave this home to her daughter Sophia, and she moved with three of her daughters to Michigan, settling in a spiritualist community called Harmonia, located six miles from Battle Creek, the town that was her permanent home for the rest of her life.

Truth became a familiar face at women's rights conventions, making a notable speech in Akron, Ohio, in 1851, where she challenged a male speaker's concerns that women were too delicate for equality, allegedly responding with a speech that began, "Aren't

I a woman?" Nearly six feet tall and with a deep, booming voice, detractors claimed Truth was too powerful a speaker to be a woman, and claimed Truth was a man in disguise. This controversy fueled an impromptu demand at a meeting in Indiana in 1858 that she demonstrate she was not a sexual imposter. Truth bared her breast on the occasion of this public challenge, offering a scathing speech that indicated that it was not her shame but her tormentors who shamed themselves with this "test." She was a powerful critic of those who preached women's inferiority and consistently pointed out women's abilities and exploited talents as laborers.

When the Civil War broke out, Truth crossed Michigan to raise funds for soldiers. Her career was celebrated in a profile written by Harriet Beecher Stowe, published in the *Atlantic Monthly* in April 1863 (and incorporated into the 1875 and subsequent editions of Truth's memoir). She also appeared prominently in Elizabeth Cady Stanton's *History of Women's Suffrage* (1881). For years she was associated with the catchphrase, "Ain't I a woman?" taken from a recorded white recollection of her speech at a convention. Truth might have uttered the phrase, "Aren't I a woman?" but "Ain't I a woman?" demonstrates the mythmaking of the era, whereby whites racialized and re-invented to conform to stereotypes. This catchphrase and its association with Truth was popularized in feminist revivals of the 1960s, before scholarship in the last decades of the twentieth century called into question the accuracy of this imagery. Truth's career was intertwined with the folklore of early feminism and embellished by white women's interest in demonstrating Truth's emblematic exceptionalism.

She gave stump speeches for Lincoln's re-election while moving East in the summer and fall of 1864 and was greeted at the White House by Lincoln himself on October 29. Following the war, Truth was tapped as a "counselor" for freedpeople, and settled in Arlington Heights, Virginia, to work for the government. She became enamored with plans for a "negro state" and campaigned for government resettlement of blacks onto western lands. These ideals never materialized with government programs, but African-Americans spontaneously mounted their own campaigns, and migrant groups, known as Exodusters, moved onto lands in Oklahoma and Kansas to form independent communities.

Truth was both witness to and an agent of change for both women and blacks during her lifetime. Although her legacy as been obscured by myth and symbolism, her legendary contributions cannot be diminished. Her remarkable voice and accomplishments continue to remind Americans of the complexity of race, gender, and class in shaping the American narrative. Truth's death on November 26, 1883, was the occasion for the largest funeral ever held in Battle Creek, Michigan, before she was finally laid to rest at Oak Hill Cemetery.

CATHERINE CLINTON

References and Further Reading

Bernard, Jacqueline. *Journey toward Freedom: The Story of Sojourner Truth*. 1967. Reprint, New York: Feminist Press, 1990.

Painter, Nell Irvin. *Sojourner Truth: A Life, a Symbol*. New York: W. W. Norton, 1996.

Sterling, Dorothy, ed. *We Are Your Sisters: Black Women in the Nineteenth Century*. New York: W. W. Norton, 1984.

Washington, Margaret, ed. *Narrative of Sojourner Truth*. New York: Vintage, 1993.

Yellin, Jean Fagan. *Women and Sisters: The Antislavery Feminists in American Culture*. New Haven: Yale University Press, 1989.

TUBMAN, HARRIET (1825–1913)
Underground Railroad Worker, Reformer

Harriet Tubman became one of the best-known crusaders for black equality during the nineteenth century and was one of the most effective combatants in the fight to end slavery. Harriet Tubman was born to enslaved parents in Dorchester County, Maryland, in 1825 and given the name Araminta by her parents, Harriet Green and Ben Ross. From roughly the age of six until early adolescence, Araminta Ross was hired out to masters, several of whom allowed brutish punishment—including being struck on the head by an iron weight, a near fatal injury that left her permanently scarred. Following the death of her owner and threat of sale by his widow, Araminta decided to escape, making her way to Philadelphia in the fall of 1849.

She left behind a free black husband (John Tubman) and took the freedom name of Harriet. As Harriet Tubman, she moved from fugitive to liberator with her involvement in the Underground Railroad (UGRR). Working closely with both Thomas Garrett of Wilmington, Delaware, and William Still of Philadelphia, Tubman executed a series of raids into slave territory (beginning in 1851) and facilitated the flight of scores, perhaps even hundreds, of slaves. She was known as a "conductor," someone who moved escaped slaves from a safe house ("depot") to the next "station" on the "liberty line," as these clandestine activities were described. But Tubman's bold technique was extremely rare, as she was one of a small cadre of underground railroad agents who became "abductors," those who ventured behind enemy lines to extract slaves and guide them to safety. Her fame as a liberator grew, and she became known popularly as Moses. Slave owners on the Eastern Shore of Maryland began to organize against losses caused by fugitive escapes, and especially the phenomenon of mass escape, with which Tubman, as Moses, became associated.

Tubman worked as an unpaid agent of the UGRR during the decade leading up to the Civil War, supporting herself by wage labor as a cook and domestic in Philadelphia and Cape May, New Jersey. All of her earnings subsidized efforts to liberate first her own family members, and then other enslaved African-Americans. She secured additional financing from abolitionists and philanthropists such a Gerrit Smith. At times, escaped slaves themselves would offer her money with a request that a family member be rescued. Tubman received donations from as far away as Scotland to support her clandestine, dangerous operations. After meeting with John Brown in Ontario in April 1858, Tubman devoted time and energy in support of his insurrectionary plans. She was unable to accompany Brown on his raid in October 1859 and mourned his death by hanging on December 2, 1859. His martyrdom inspired her to participate in (or perhaps even engineer) her first public rescue of a fugitive slave—Charles Nalle of Troy, New York, who was slated for return to slavery in Virginia in April 1860. An antislavery mob attacked his captors, which resulted in the death of several rioters. Nalle was liberated from a judge's chambers and sent to safety in Canada.

Tubman's activism and example were highlighted during speeches she offered at conventions in Boston during May and June of 1860. When the Civil War erupted a year later, Tubman believed it symbolized the moving of the Underground Railroad "above ground."

Tubman volunteered as an unpaid worker at Ft. Monroe, Virginia, where she nursed and assisted the fugitive slaves, dubbed "contraband" by the Union general Benjamin Butler. In 1862, the governor of Massachusetts sent her to assist freedpeople in the occupied regions of the south Atlantic coast centered around Port Royal, South Carolina, characterized by the historian Willie Lee Rose as "rehearsal for reconstruction." Tubman became indispensable to the medical staff of the federal army, posted as far south as Fernandina, Florida, to nurse Union soldiers who were "dropping like flies." She taught freedwomen laundry skills and assisted Union physicians until her other talents were tapped by military leaders.

By the spring of 1863, both the Massachusetts abolitionist Thomas Wentworth Higginson (head of a black regiment, the First South Carolina Volunteers) and James Montgomery, a former ally of John Brown in the Kansas border wars, urged Union command to take advantage of Tubman's skills as a scout and spy. She infiltrated enemy territory and collected intelligence for the military commander, Union General David Hunter. During the Combahee River Raid on June 2, 1863, over 750 slaves were liberated off Rebel plantations by federal troops. Valuable Confederate property was confiscated or destroyed during the inland invasion, which went off without a hitch due to Tubman's effective planning. The African-American soldiers were under the command of Montgomery but clearly followed Tubman's lead on this successful operation.

Following her retirement from the army in 1865, Tubman returned to her home in upstate New York, where she settled into the role of activist and philanthropist. She solicited funds for Freedman's Aid and veterans' benefits, while remaining active in the women's suffrage movement and other important reform campaigns. Tubman sought compensation from the government, petitioning at first for back wages and then for a soldier's pension, a campaign that continued for over 30 years. She was awarded a monthly stipend of $8 for widows—as she had remarried in 1869 the veteran Nelson Davis, who died in 1888. After a series of petitions, in 1899, she was granted $20 per month, a lifetime pension, in recognition of her war work. Tubman died on March 10, 1913, in the Harriet Tubman Home, a charitable institution she had established to shelter and care for the needy within her Auburn, New York, community.

CATHERINE CLINTON

References and Further Reading

Bradford, Sarah. *Scenes in the Life of Harriet Tubman.* Auburn, NY: W. J. Moses, 1869.

Clinton, Catherine. *Harriet Tubman: The Road to Freedom.* New York: Little Brown, 2004.

Conrad, Earl. *Harriet Tubman.* Washington, DC: The Associated Publishers, 1943.

Humez, Jean. *Harriet Tubman: The Life and the Life Stories.* Madison: University of Wisconsin Press, 2003.

Larson, Kate Clifford. *Bound for the Promised Land: Harriet Tubman, Portrait of an American Hero.* New York: Ballantine, 2004.

U

UNDERCLASS

Media coverage of Hurricane Katrina in 2005 not only focused attention on the devastation of the Gulf Coast region, particularly New Orleans, Louisiana; but more than any other recent event, it also brought the interlocking issues of race and class to the center of public debate. Poverty-stricken African-Americans—members of the so-called urban underclass—comprised the largest and most visible segment of those who, unable to evacuate the rising floodwaters, crowded on rooftops and in sports arenas for days without food, fresh water, medical attention, or a timely federal response. Residents of the poorest wards in the nation's ninth poorest major metropolis, many had existed on the economic and social margins of U.S. society long before the disaster hit.

Over the past three decades, the underclass has emerged as a key metaphor for poverty in the United States, though it remains ill-defined. In popular accounts it refers to the most socially and economically isolated elements of the urban working class—the underemployed and chronically unemployed, menial laborers, ex-convicts, female-headed households receiving means-tested welfare programs, high school dropouts and young delinquents, drug users and dealers, public-housing tenants, violent career criminals, and hustlers. In the conventional wisdom, the underclass is distinguished not simply by its indigence, but more importantly by its deviant, self-defeating, and dependent behaviors. Typically associated with African-Americans and Latinos, who comprise a disproportionate share of the poor, the term is freighted with moral assumptions about race, gender, class, and poverty.

Both liberals and conservatives have trafficked in underclass discourse. For liberals it has served a compassionate, yet condescending agenda: Because of their economic and social circumstances, the black and brown urban poor lack appropriate (white) middle-class values and therefore need proper education and stewardship as well as better structural opportunities. Conservatives on the other hand have used the concept of the underclass to explain away social inequality through attention to individual and group deficiencies. Their focus has been primarily on strategies of punishment and containment. Both liberal and conservative perspectives however view the black working-class poor from the outside and regard them from the standpoint of being different or more precisely, defective.

Although value-laden discourses about the dangerous classes and undeserving poor are hardly new, the historical context that gave rise to the underclass debate was certainly distinct. One immediate antecedent was the culture-of-poverty thesis elaborated in the mid-1960s by anthropologist Oscar Lewis. In *La Vida* (1965), his study of a Puerto Rican family in San Juan and New York City, Lewis argued that those mired in such a culture were qualitatively different from those who were merely poor. The former experienced high rates of illegitimate birth and often lived in unstable marriages or informal common-law unions. Female aggression and male emasculation were also commonplace, often leading to female-headed households. Distrustful of mainstream institutions, dogged by feelings of social inferiority, and strongly present-oriented, this segment of the poor were trapped in a way of life that perpetuated itself across generations.

Daniel Patrick Moynihan's widely circulated Labor Department report, *The Negro Family: The Case for National Action* (1965), emphasized the role of matrifocal households in generating a "tangle of pathology" among the poor; in this he owed intellectual debts to both Lewis and sociologist Charles S. Johnson. Responding directly to the successes and evolving demands of the civil rights struggle, Moynihan observed that an economic gap was growing between African-Americans and most other groups, which he attributed to the deterioration of the black family. The central cause of this crisis was the rising rates of female single-parenting households, which begat increases in dependency on Aid to Families with Dependent Children (AFDC). He maintained that the legacies of slavery, and contemporary patterns of male unemployment and low-waged work, had undermined the status of black men in the household and community, creating a matriarchal structure out of step with the rest of society.

Such beliefs about the social maladjustment and cultural deprivation of the black, urban poor underlay President Lyndon B. Johnson's Great Society programs aimed at inner-city communities. Hence job training and educational initiatives reflected an assumption that poverty, far from being endemic to the functioning of U.S. capitalism, could be abated by better preparing unemployed workers for opportunities. Johnson-era antipoverty programs responded most directly to the black, urban working-class riots of the period. Indeed the economic and social conditions of inner-city communities were a matter of federal emergency, since the participants in these rebellions—young, male, frequently jobless, and often high school dropouts—were potential recruits of emerging black-nationalist and radical organizations.

The National Advisory Commission on Civil Disorders, initially convened for the purpose of determining the role of black-power activists in fomenting the uprisings, concluded in its report that the riots stemmed not from organized conspiracies. Rather the disturbances originated in a web of grievances that included unemployment and underemployment, overcrowded and squalid housing, poor educational facilities, exploitation by inner-city merchants, irregular municipal services, police abuse, and an unresponsive city hall. In forthright language that acknowledged the existence of a distinct black working-class poor, the Kerner Commission reported: "Our Nation is moving toward two societies, one black, one white—separate and unequal." However the commission's recommendations for massive social reforms came at a moment of Republican retrenchment of Great Society programs, conservative reaction against progressive political movements, and the Oval Office's preoccupation with the war in Vietnam. The commission report was ignored, even maligned, as Richard M. Nixon won the White House on a domestic platform of law and order. Granted the Nixon administration promoted the Office of Minority Business Enterprise, the Small Business Administration, and a proposal for a national guaranteed annual wage as palliatives to urban rebellion; yet retrenchment in poverty programs, and benign neglect on matters of race, were the order of the day.

Scholars have credited Swedish sociologist Gunnar Myrdal with coining the term underclass, which he used to describe the various urban and rural populations across the world who were being economically and socially dislocated by changes in global capitalism. By the latter part of the 1970s, other scholars had begun theorizing about a qualitatively new and persistent poverty. Chief among this cohort was William Julius Wilson, who argued that de-industrialization, and the ascendance of a highly skilled technological service sector, had undermined job prospects for unskilled and semiskilled black workers. "Given the internationalization of the economy, the automation of both manufacturing and service industries, and the hyper-mobility of capital," concluded Creigs C. Beverly and Howard J. Stanback, "the economy, left to its current devices, no longer has the capacity to periodically absorb a significant share of the black population" (*The Black Scholar*, 1986). In *The Black Underclass: Poverty, Unemployment and Entrapment of Ghetto Youth* (1980), Douglas G. Glasgow rendered an even bleaker assessment of the new postindustrial economy: Many among the black poor in fact held jobs, but remained "vocationally obsolete" and worse yet, fundamentally unwanted by society. In Wilson's view this was exacerbated by the growing spatial concentration and isolation of the black poor, particularly from more stable black families, whose flight from the nation's inner cities weakened neighborhood institutions and communal values. Thus he highlighted a widening divide between a secure black middle class that had benefited from civil rights reforms and a disorganized black majority.

At the same historical moment, another definition of the underclass emerged among social scientists and journalists. Centering less on cultural deprivation, and racism and other structural causes, it credited defective behavioral patterns for the existence of the black urban poor. This included a disrespect for work, educational achievement, and playing by the rules and a fixation on immediate gratification, sexual and otherwise. Ken Auletta's *The Underclass* (1982), based on a series of articles for the *New Yorker*, helped to popularize this view. Perhaps the main avatar of this position was Charles Murray, whose book *Losing Ground: American Social Policy, 1950–1980* (1984), connected the underclass to a cycle of dependency created by War-on-Poverty programs themselves. Rather than expanding, or even maintaining, social welfare programs for the poor, he argued, repealing them would stimulate a work ethic lacking among recipients. This trend was inextricably linked to a rightward shift in U.S. politics during the 1980s, characterized by the presidency of Ronald Reagan. Hence behavior-oriented interpretations of the underclass became the dominant discourse and the most influential in shaping subsequent policies, including the draconian welfare reform implemented during the administration of President William Jefferson Clinton.

In recent years some scholars have objected to continued use of the term underclass altogether. They argue foremost that it contains implicit racist sentiments and tends to overlook the realities of racial oppression in limiting economic opportunities for African-Americans and Latinos. This is particularly germane to most women of color, whose access to livable wages has been minimal; the addition of children and single parenthood simply compounds their exclusion on the bases of race, gender, and class. Moreover critics maintain, the discourse of the underclass has a distinctly patriarchal, antifeminist character. Taking as its point of departure the male-headed, two-parent household, such rhetoric devalues the importance of women being able to maintain autonomous households with or without a male breadwinner.

Detractors also contend that the underclass conceptually lumps together diverse groups of people with equally diverse circumstances, needs, and motivations. It assumes for instance that the inhabitants of public housing are homogeneous simply because they share similar statistical profiles; unemployment or female-headed households may stem from a number of factors. To the extent further that so-called underclass behavioral traits can be ascertained, they cannot reasonably be assumed to be either static or reflective of attitudes. More to the point they reveal little about the presence of any distinct population. That is, drug abuse, divorce, teenage fertility, female single-parenting households, educational underachievement, and

the pursuit of immediate gratification exist broadly across social strata. This being the case, they can hardly be construed as the cause of poverty.

Underclass discourses also misrepresent the history of black urban communities by drawing a causal link between the exodus of middle-class role models on the one hand and the moral and cultural degradation of those left behind. As scholars like Mary Pattillo-McCoy have maintained, middle-class families by and large did not flee black communities in the post-civil rights period. Nor did they ever singularly exercise the leadership and cultural authority romanticized by sociologists like Wilson. As well trumpeting black, middle-class success imbibes African-American professionals with the feeling, in Glasgow's words, that "exceptional individual capacity alone led to their success and that they thus need not identify too closely with the plight of the underclass" (*Black Picket Fences*, 1999). At the same time, it elides the matter of racial discrimination as experienced by black, middle-class professionals.

These objections aside, the term underclass persists as an archetype according to scholar Michael Zweig, precisely because it is vague and serves ideological purposes. The concept removes the poorest segments of the black working class from the mainstream of life and culture. Meanwhile it also legitimates political assaults on the working class by itself through the mobilization and exploitation of racial antipathy. As exemplified by welfare reform, the war on drugs, and a growing "prison-industrial complex," this has justified a range of punitive social policies that threaten the social safety net and civil liberties for all. Finally the underclass discourse narrows the range of discussion about welfare and dependency, limiting it to those programs targeted to the poorest citizens. Indeed public- and private-welfare benefits were responsible for most of the class mobility among Americans in the three decades following the Second World War. As illustrated by the Hurricane Katrina crisis, the rhetoric of the underclass obscures the widening inequities in wealth in U.S. society, the retreat of the federal state from a commitment to guaranteeing social welfare, continuing patterns of urban development, and their marginalizing effects on urban, working-class communities.

CLARENCE LANG

References and Further Reading

Auletta, Ken. *The Underclass*. New York: Vintage, 1982.
Banfield, Edward C. *The Unheavenly City: The Nature and Future of Our Urban Crisis*. Boston, MA: Little, Brown, 1968.

Beverly, Creigs C., and Howard J. Stanback. "The Black Underclass: Theory and Reality." *Black Scholar* (Sept.–Oct. 1986): 24–32.

Darity, William A. Jr., and Samuel L. Myers, Jr., et al., eds. *The Black Underclass: Critical Essays on Race and Unwantedness.* New York: Garland Publishing, 1994.

Gans, Herbert J. "Deconstructing the Underclass: The Term's Dangers as a Planning Concept." *Journal of the American Planning Association* 56 (summer 1990): 271–277.

Glasgow, Douglas G. *The Black Underclass: Poverty, Unemployment, and Entrapment of Ghetto Youth.* New York: Vintage, 1981.

Katz, Michael B., ed. *The "Underclass" Debate: Views from History.* Princeton, NJ: Princeton University Press, 1993.

Lewis, Oscar. *La Vida: A Puerto Rican Family in the Culture of Poverty—San Juan and New York.* New York: Vintage, 1965.

Moynihan, Daniel Patrick. *The Negro Family: The Case for National Action.* Washington, DC: U.S. Department of Labor, 1965.

Murray, Charles. *Losing Ground: American Social Policy, 1950–1980.* New York: Basic Books, 1984.

Pattillo-McCoy, Mary. *Black Picket Fences: Privilege and Peril Among the Black Middle Class.* Chicago, IL: University of Chicago Press, 1999.

Reed, Adolph Jr. "The Underclass As Myth and Symbol: The Poverty of Discourse about Poverty." *Radical America* 24 (Jan.–Mar. 1990): 21–40.

Wilson, William Julius. *The Truly Disadvantaged: The Inner City, the Underclass, and Public Policy.* Chicago, IL: University of Chicago Press, 1987.

Zweig, Michael. *The Working-Class Majority: America's Best Kept Secret.* Ithaca, NY: Cornell University Press, 2000.

UNEMPLOYED LEAGUE (1930s)

In response to extraordinary unemployment during the early 1930s, groups from across the political spectrum worked to relieve the suffering of the unemployed and to use their dissatisfaction to build a larger movement for social change. The Unemployed League, led by A. J. Muste (1885–1967) and his allies, was a counterpart to the Communist- and Socialist-driven movements of the jobless. Muste was one of the most important leaders of twentieth-century American pacifism and worked to unite pacifists, labor unions, and civil rights groups. In 1929, Muste called the Conference for Progressive Labor Action (CPLA) to reform the American Federation of Labor (AFL) from within. In 1930, the CPLA, with support from the Seattle Labor College, built the first Unemployed League in the nation in Seattle. The Seattle League claimed 12,000 members in that city in 1931, and 80,000 members across Washington State by the end of the next year. In 1932, Musteite organizers from Brookwood Labor College began to establish leagues in rural areas and small towns in Ohio, West Virginia, Kentucky, North Carolina, and Pennsylvania. These smaller communities formed the core of league influence, while Communist and Socialist groups made more headway in urban areas. Local leagues worked with varying success until 1936, when Muste distanced himself from leftist organizations and league organizers began to work for any of a number of burgeoning labor-oriented and civil rights groups.

The Unemployed League, like Muste himself, used diverse methods and had a changing relationship to Socialist workers' committees and Communist unemployed councils. Originally the Seattle Unemployed League promoted self-help strategies and was derided for it by leftist activists. However by 1933, unemployed leagues began to include direct action along with a dual emphasis on connecting the unemployed to the increasingly militant labor movement and reforming the state's role in providing direct relief and a safety net for the unemployed and elderly. Throughout their history, local unemployed leagues built rank-and-file membership through on-the-ground responses to individual grievances, such as hunger, unfair relief administration, and evictions.

Leaders searched for ways to knit together the disparate unemployed organizations. A number of gatherings from 1932–1936 succeeded in creating only regional organizations and only for a few years. In the end efforts to create a truly national unemployed organization suffered from ideological factionalism and a crumbling rank-and-file base. Members joined resurgent labor organizations or disappeared among the ranks of Americans receiving public relief.

Although the Unemployed League was short lived, its local branches were part of an important broad-based movement that tied grassroots collective action to the labor movement. In 1934, leagues members took part in three pivotal labor clashes: The Toledo Electric Auto-Lite strike, the Minneapolis Teamsters' strike, and the West Coast longshoremen's strike. The league also demanded many of the legislative changes that Congress eventually passed in more-or-less limited ways during the New Deal. Unemployed leagues, for example, anticipated the New Deal's attempts at government relief, public works, unemployment and retirement insurance, and child labor laws.

JEFFREY HELGESON

References and Further Reading

Bernstein, Irving. *The Lean Years: A History of the American Worker, 1920–1933.* Baltimore, MD: Penguin Books, 1970.

Folsom, Franklin. *Impatient Armies of the Poor: The Story of Collective Action of the Unemployed, 1808–1942.* Niwot: University Press of Colorado, 1991.

Lorence, James J. *Organizing the Unemployed: Community and Union Activists in the Industrial Heartland.* Albany: State University of New York Press, 1996.

Phillips, Kimberley L. *Alabama North: African-American Migrants, Community, and Working-Class Activism in Cleveland, 1915–45.* Chicago: University of Illinois Press, 1999.

Piven, Frances Fox, and Richard A. Cloward. *Poor People's Movements: Why They Succeed, How They Fail.* New York: Vintage Books, 1979.

See also **Brookwood Labor College; Communist Party; Muste, A. J.; Socialist Workers' Party; Strike Wave (1934)**

UNEMPLOYMENT

The term unemployment is commonly associated with the percentage of the labor force without work in a particular geographic region, the so-called unemployment rate. By this very coarse measure, the unemployment rate in the United States has been lower than in similarly industrialized regions, like Western Europe and Canada, for most of the twentieth century. This is often attributed to the flexibility and dynamism of American labor markets and to the significance of self-reliance in the national culture. The accuracy of this assessment notwithstanding, there is a great deal more to American unemployment than statistical representations of mobility and individualism. Attendant insecurity and hardship have of course always been a part of working people's everyday experience of unemployment, and these factors have been popularly understood to reflect collective economic health at least since World War I. Nonetheless it took the dislocations of the Great Depression to make it both an acceptable policy object and the key indicator of social welfare today.

Although economic historians have developed estimates for specific times and places at earlier times, reasonably consistent measures of U.S. unemployment are available from only 1929. These data demonstrate the historical volatility of the U.S. labor market and the employment experience of many American workers. In 75 years the national unemployment rate has ranged from 25% (May 1933) to 1% (October 1944) and moved from 4%–11% in the years hence. Most estimates of pre-1929 unemployment suggest it was generally higher and more volatile still, especially seasonally. Yet these measures are only the tip of the iceberg. The history of unemployment in the United States involves the relation between the contentious history of the concept itself, and the manner in which this history has helped shape U.S. unemployment policy. The first includes the various theoretical explanations of unemployment

in a capitalist economy; the second the efforts by various actors to naturalize, politicize, and manage the facts of joblessness.

What Is Unemployment?

There are important differences between being unemployed in this *de jure* sense and being without employment. The unemployment rate reported in the popular media represents slightly different measures in different countries. In the United States the rate is published monthly by the U.S. Bureau of Labor Statistics, based on data gathered through the Current Population Survey. These data have been collected by sample surveys since 1940 and are used to calculate the government's formal definition of level of unemployment: The percentage of respondents (16 years of age and older) who have not worked for any wages in the last week, yet who are able and available to work and have actively looked for employment in the last 4 weeks. If the respondent has a job but did not work in the survey week because he/she was ill, on vacation, working part-time, on strike, on parental leave, or dealing with other personal obligations, the respondent is considered employed. Those who meet the unemployment criteria together with all those with jobs, full or part-time, constitute the Civilian Labor Force (CLF).

Who Is Unemployed?

These measurement criteria have been standard in the United States since the Depression, yet they exclude many who are voluntarily and involuntarily jobless. For example if a person has not sought employment because he/she is a homemaker, a full-time student, in prison, discouraged (that is, has not looked for work in the last 4 weeks), or for reasons of mental or physical disability, the person is designated neither employed nor unemployed and thus outside the CLF. The CLF participation rate, which represents the CLF as a proportion of the (legally resident, nonincarcerated, nonarmed forces) population 16 years of age and older, thus suggests the scale of disparity between unemployment and being unemployed: Since consistent data were first collected in 1948, the CLF participation rate has slowly risen from around 59% to approximately 66% in 2005.

A history of unemployment in the United States that stayed within the bounds of the CLF would thus

Parade of unemployed. Library of Congress, Prints & Photographs Division [LC-USZ62-22194].

tell a very different story than one that did not. On the one hand since 1929, the earliest point at which large-sample data are available at the national level, there are some broad patterns in unemployment as measured by the unemployment rate. Nonwhite groups are statistically more likely to be unemployed, and the unemployment rate among African-Americans and American Indians has almost always been twice that of white workers. Workers under 20 years of age and new immigrants are also far more likely to be unemployed, and women of all heritages and ages have until very recently been more highly represented among the unemployed. These groups are also more vulnerable to economic cycles than white men, the differential in relative unemployment increasing with downturns and decreasing with upturns in the national economy. On the other hand beyond the populations for which unemployment data are collected, historical and sociological studies are the best source of evidence. These indicate that women, youth, and people of color are even more disproportionately represented among those excluded from the CLF by statistical stipulation.

Why Is There Unemployment?

While theories of unemployment try to explain both *de jure* unemployment and being unemployed, the distinction between the two is based in liberal economic theory, which constitutes at the most general level the first of two types of unemployment theory appropriate to the capitalist United States. The first is comprised of a diverse set of economic explanations that has shaped virtually all American unemployment policy since the phenomenon was recognized as worthy of regulatory attention. The second theoretical form is associated with radical political economy and founded in Karl Marx's theory of the reserve army of labor.

Aside from the long-standing problem of seasonal unemployment, which afflicts some service and resource sectors in particular, liberal economists recognize three different types of unemployment, all of which can exist in a labor market simultaneously: frictional, cyclical, and structural. Frictional unemployment is joblessness associated with individual, sectoral, or economywide transition. It is temporary and inevitable in a dynamic economy, the result of workers looking for new jobs (search unemployment), industrial restructuring that induces a shift of labor from one sector to another, and so forth. Cyclical unemployment is a product of the business cycle in capitalist economies. As economies expand, workers enter the labor market and joblessness decreases; contraction leads to lay-offs and increased unemployment. Structural unemployment exists because of large-scale market failures or because of the failure of the labor market to match workers and jobs effectively. This may be due to formal institutions, like government regulations, education systems, and firm organization; informal institutions like fair wage norms; or less apparently malleable market structures, like geography, and information asymmetries.

The theoretical differences among liberal economists—neoclassical, institutional, and Keynesian—are not based on the accuracy of these explanations, about which they generally concur. They also agree that some level of unemployment is natural in capitalist economies. They disagree however on the proportion of unemployment that is attributable to each of the three and thus the relative proportion of involuntary and voluntary unemployment among potential participants in the labor force. This distinction is the basis of the unemployment/being unemployed divide, for the latter is seen as a choice, and addressing it less a legislative obligation.

Institutional and Keynesian approaches, which have most influenced the field of labor history, argue that a significant part of U.S. unemployment is a product of macrostructural inefficiencies, all of which are long-term, and only some of which are remediable. Although frictional unemployment is natural, joblessness or job loss in excess of temporary adjustment is involuntary and thus politically relevant. Neoclassical economists, whose influence has increased considerably in political and intellectual circles since World War II, acknowledge the import of cyclical unemployment and the forces of technological change. They nonetheless emphasize the voluntary nature of much nonfrictional unemployment by assuming that unemployment often represents a rational response to the work-leisure trade-off. From this perspective, a large part of joblessness is attributable to the greater marginal utility of leisure or homemaking in the face of constrained intertemporal choice: people are unemployed because when they consider their options over time, the expected benefits of being unemployed outweigh those that a job would provide. Female workers provide a much-cited example: The higher frequency with which they enter and exit the labor force relative to men, by this logic reflects optimization decisions regarding potential household or personal utility. This explanatory frame means that neoclassical theory usually associates a much greater part of joblessness with the natural rate of unemployment than the institutionalist, Keynesian or radical alternatives.

Radical theories of the reserve army of labor under capitalism—also fundamental to the practice of many labor historians—begin from the premise that the regulatory distinction between official unemployment and being unemployed is essential for the maintenance of social relations under capitalism. Radical economists are generally uninterested in the frictional-cyclical-structural explanations except to the extent that the reserve army is structurally critical to profit making. Instead they argue that the significance of unemployment lies not in its voluntary or involuntary nature, but in its function in the relations of production. In contrast to liberal economists, they suggest that the size of the U.S. labor force at any one time is endogenous to capitalist economies, that is, determined by the system of production itself, not by individual exogenous decisions to enter or exit the labor market. The relevant divide is therefore not between those inside the CLF and those outside it, but between those with jobs and those without. Unemployed workers serve as wage-depressing potential competition for the employed and as a ready source of labor, especially for short-term and low-wage work.

How Should We Deal with Unemployment?

The mechanisms identified as the cause of unemployment determine the form and extent of the policy response. The history of U.S. unemployment policy reflects the shifting hegemony of political economic theories and related conceptions of state intervention in the market. Prior to the Great Depression, in an era of faith in classical *laissez faire* liberalism, there was no national unemployment policy, either to mitigate its impacts through relief or to alter its macroeconomic effects. Limited relief was administered privately at the local and regional level. The crash of 1929 precipitated a revolution in unemployment policy, however, when President Herbert Hoover's failure to respond adequately to unemployment—a reluctance to break liberal taboos regarding government intervention and the extension of federal powers—helped cost him the election of 1932.

Franklin Roosevelt established the first federal unemployment program, the Civil Works Administration (CWA), in his first year after Hoover's defeat. In the spirit of the pragmatic institutionalism then dominant in U.S. economics departments through the work of scholars like John Commons, the Roosevelt administration believed the unemployed were victims of forces they could not control and were entitled to some relief and insurance against similar crises in the future. The object of the CWA was not primarily Keynesian, that is, to stimulate demand by injecting cash into the economy. Rather in combination with new legislation limiting the length of the workweek and banning child labor, the government intended to create jobs that would allow individual workers to weather what was still expected to be a short-term crisis. Later New Deal programs, like the Civilian Conservation Corps and the Works Progress Administration, served similar ends.

The persistence of the Depression pushed the government to pass the Social Security Act in 1935, which established the first national system of unemployment relief. The program of cash payments the act legislated was administered independently by each state, with funds and minimum program requirements provided by the federal government. The act also created the welfare system of Aid for Families with Dependent Children (AFDC, terminated by welfare-to-work legislation of 1996), and the social security retirement reserves, neither of which were part of its unemployment program. The act was part of a suite of legislation, including the Fair Labor Standards Act, and the National Labor Relations Act, to protect wageworkers' earnings and jobs from an unemployment threat that was increasingly believed to be permanent.

This set of statutes, founded as they are with an emphasis on involuntary unemployment, remains the core structure of extant worker protections. Yet it has weakened over time through policy shifts reflecting dominant political economic modes of explanation. In employment policy this sea change was effected during the clash between labor and capital in the years immediately following World War II. The prosperity and high levels of employment the United States enjoyed in the latter stages of the war, combined with the political power enjoyed by organized labor at war's end, stimulated popular demand for a permanent extension of New Deal state intervention in the labor market. The federal government and many states debated legislation that mandated full-employment programs, which would guarantee work for all who wanted it. Where such efforts succeeded however, the full-employment provisions as enacted were toothless. The federal Full Employment Act of 1946 requires the federal government to provide full employment but sets neither benchmarks nor criteria by which this endeavor might be organized or measured.

As such the policy interpretation of full employment has been progressively reshaped in ways that contrast sharply with New Deal institutionalism. Monetarist-neoclassical theory, increasingly dominant in policy and scholarly circles, attributes a significant proportion of unemployment to the realm of private decision making at the household level, beyond the appropriate reach of policy. Unemployment, formerly the key indicator of national economic health, has thus been displaced by inflation, which neoclassical theory explains as inversely related to unemployment: Decreasing unemployment leads to increasing inflation. Neoclassical theory consequently de-emphasizes employment policy in favor of monetary policy and emphasizes the maintenance not of some socially acceptable level of employment, but of a constant and reasonable rate of inflation: this is sometimes called the "non-accelerating inflation rate of unemployment" (NAIRU), estimated at around 6% at the end of the twentieth century. This explanatory shift is visible in the gradual dilution of unemployment and welfare services, such as was encoded in the workfare of the Clinton administration's Personal Responsibility and Work Opportunity Reconciliation Act of 1996. The unabated attack on inflation, beginning in earnest during Eisenhower's presidency, has since become the principal tool of both employment and fiscal policy in the post-World War II United States.

GEOFF MANN

References and Further Reading

Auerbach, Alan J., and Laurence J. Kotlikoff. "The Nature and Costs of Unemployment." In *Macroeconomics: An Integrated Approach*. 2nd ed. Cambridge, MA: MIT Press.

Bregger, John E., and Cathryn S. Dippo. "Overhauling the Current Population Survey: Why Is It Necessary to Change?" *Monthly Labor Review* 116, 9 (1993): 3–9.

Brown, Clair. "Unemployment Theory and Policy, 1946–1980." *Industrial Relations* 22, 2 (1983): 164–185.

Commons, John. *Institutional Economics: Its Place in Political Economy*. Madison: University of Wisconsin Press, 1959. (reprint, 1934)

Friedman, Milton. "Nobel Lecture: Inflation and Unemployment." *Journal of Political Economy* 85, 3 (1977): 451–472.

Garraty, John A. *Unemployment in History: Economic Thought and Public Policy*. New York: Harper & Row, 1978.

Keyssar, Alexander. *Out of Work: The First Century of Unemployment in Massachusetts*. Cambridge, UK: Cambridge University Press, 1986.

Marglin, Stephen A. *Growth, Distribution, and Prices*. Cambridge, MA: Harvard University Press, 1984.

Marx, Karl. *Capital*, translated by Ben Fowkes. Vol. 1. New York: Vintage, 1977.

National Bureau of Economic Research. "NBER Macrohistory: Vol. 8. Income and Employment." www.nber.org/databases/macrohistory/contents/chapter08.html

Nickell, Stephen. "Unemployment and Labor Market Rigidities: Europe versus North America." *Journal of Economic Perspectives* 11, 3 (1997): 55–74.

Rosenbloom, Joshua L. *Looking for Work, Searching for Workers: American Labor Markets during Industrialization*. Cambridge, UK: Cambridge University Press, 2002.

United States Dept. of Labor, Bureau of Labor Statistics. "Overview of BLS Statistics on Employment and Unemployment." www.bls.gov/bls/employment.htm

Cases and Statutes Cited

Fair Labor Standards Act
Full Employment Act
National Labor Relations Act
Social Security Act
Work Opportunity Reconciliation Act

See also **Aid to Families with Dependent Children (AFDC); Coxey's Army; Great Depression: 1930s; Strikebreaking; Underclass; Welfare Rights; Workfare; Works Project Administration**

UNEMPLOYMENT, INSECURITY, AND THE DECLINE OF LABOR: 1970s

In the turbulent 1960s, the concerns of organized labor and working people rarely held center stage. The civil rights' crusade, the escalating antiwar demonstrations, and the women's liberation movement were in the vanguard of social and political change. American workers had come to be regarded as affluent and content members of consumer society. It was widely believed that despite the dissatisfaction associated with factory work, high wages enabled workers to enjoy a lifestyle once reserved for the middle class. American society had presumably become a middle-class society in which the vast majority of the population participated as equals.

At the close of the decade however, the notion of the prosperous, suburban, middle-class worker was questioned. Unemployment rose appreciably, and wages failed to keep pace with soaring prices. In 1970, the typical American worker earned $9,500. This figure actually placed blue-collars closer to the working poor than to the affluent middle class. A rising discontent with working and living conditions was evident in the growth of rank-and-file militancy. The blue-collar blues caused a flurry of working-class studies that tried to determine the economic and social problems of workers. The debate centered on the alleged middle-class status, hawkishness, and political conservatism of the American worker.

The widely discussed blue-collar blues—often trivialized by the mass media—were a clear indication of the downward trend in workers' economic gains and the deterioration of working conditions. From 1966–1973, strike activity rose 40% over the relatively low level of the 1959–1966 years. The number of workers involved in walkouts rose steadily from just under a million in 1965 to 2.5 million in 1971. This strike wave reached a climax in 1970, when over 66 million days were lost due to strikes. Among the strikes of 1970 that best reflected the rank-and-file's discontent were the General Motors walkout; the wildcat strike of 40,000 coal miners in West Virginia, Ohio, and Pennsylvania; and the national wildcat strike by postal workers and teamsters.

The 1970 walkout against GM was an expensive triumph for autoworkers. The conflict cost the United Automobile Workers (UAW) about $160 million and almost bankrupted the union while the powerful multinational corporation lost millions of dollars in its attempt to resist the union's demands. At the end of the conflict, the UAW recovered the unlimited cost-of-living allowance that it had relinquished in 1967 and established the 30-and-out retirement principle, though not at any age, as the workers demanded.

Employees of the U.S. Postal Service are legally prohibited from striking. In 1970, however, pressured by inflation and tedious work conditions with no significant upgrading opportunities, postal workers in New York City walked off their jobs. Within days the strike spread across the country, closing down postal service in at least 200 cities. The strike lasted 2 weeks, and the postal workers won an immediate 14% wage increase as well as an improved upgrading system. Even before the wildcat postal strike ended, members of the International Brotherhood of Teamsters began walking off their jobs as the National Master Freight Agreement expired on April 1. Teamster President Frank Fitzsimmons asked workers to resume their activities, but many teamsters remained on strike for a long time, thus forcing their union leader back to the bargaining table.

In June 1970, 40,000 coal miners started an unauthorized strike in West Virginia, Ohio, and Pennsylvania. This was an attempt to address problems that the United Mine Workers of America under President Tony Boyle refused to deal with. The workers demanded hospital and pension benefits for miners forced out of work because of disabilities. Although the move received the full support of the working miners, the demands were not won. Similarly the 1973 Lordstown auto strike in Ohio became the epitome of the young workers' rebellion against technology and the rank-and-file's rising concern over working conditions. There were wildcat strikes in Detroit auto plants in 1973 at the time as the UAW negotiations with the big three automobile manufacturers—the General Motors Corporation, the Chrysler Corporation, and Ford Motor Company. Yet they did not signal permanent escalation in rank-and-file militancy.

After the summer of 1973, the leaders and the rank-and-file both went into retreat. From 1974 onward, the number of strikes diminished considerably: Higher unemployment rates and the growing threat of layoffs and plant shutdowns had a strong disciplinary effect. Drastic changes in the structure of industry as well as the workforce soon followed, as management adopted a more aggressive attitude toward their workers. Corporations started to move their fixed capital in manufacturing to regions where wages were lower and unions less influential. Antilabor consultants were hired to contest organizing campaigns, and in violation of the Wagner Act, union organizers were fired in an attempt to intimidate workers.

American business's determined assault on organized labor was eventually successful. According to the statistics of the National Labor Relations Board, the number of employer unfair labor practice charges tripled from 1960–1980, and the number of workers ordered to be re-instated because of illegal dismissals rose fivefold in the same period. The result was a drastic decline in union membership from 27% of private-sector workers in 1973 to 22% in 1979. Industrial unions would never recover the political and bargaining leverage that they had enjoyed in the 1945–1968 period.

The Unraveling of the Labor-Liberal Alliance

The 1968 presidential election signaled the end of the labor-liberal alliance that had sustained the New Deal order for over 30 years. Nevertheless Richard Nixon's margin of victory was extremely slim: 43.4% of the electorate voted for the Republican candidate compared to 43% who supported the Democrat and labor candidate Hubert H. Humphrey. The third-party candidate, George Wallace, eventually received the vote of only 13.6% of the electorate, his support having faded considerably from his high-water mark of almost 20%. According to nationwide data, 50% of blue-collar workers voted for the Democratic party ticket, 41% of white-collars, 34% of professionals and businessmen, and 39% of farmers.

If organized labor contributed to Humphrey's almost miraculous comeback, it was because unions fed into their members' fears of what a Nixon or Wallace administration could mean to the ordinary worker. Working-class voters had helped to transform a sure Democratic defeat into a very narrow loss. It was the tactical approach of business unionism rather than a revitalized labor movement that almost took Hubert Humphrey to the White House. Millions of voters, however, no longer felt it necessary to remain loyal to the Democratic party now constituted a highly volatile electorate. Moreover the Vietnam War remained one of the most divisive issues in American society.

In 1970, Nixon's decision to send U.S. ground troops into Cambodia further polarized American public opinion on the war. Violent protests broke out immediately after the president's announcement, and there was serious unrest at a number of colleges and universities. But it was Kent State University in Ohio that made the shocking headlines on May 4, 1970. During a campus antiwar demonstration, the Ohio National Guard shot and killed four students and wounded another 12. The murder of peace demonstrators prompted more protest and eventually led to a violent physical confrontation between students and workers.

On May 8, 1970, about 200 flag-waving construction workers armed with hammers and lead pipes attacked a group of demonstrators who had gathered in New York's Wall Street district to honor the memory of the students killed at Kent State University. After the assault, the hard hats—as the mass media would call them—invaded City Hall, and then left to break into Pace College and attack some students there. The construction worker soon became the symbol of American labor: The hard hat was the middle American, the member of the silent majority who had finally decided to speak his mind. It would prove very hard for construction workers—and for organized labor in general—to recover their image as law-abiding citizens after the mass media had portrayed them as believers in God and country and intolerant of dissent.

The May 1970 events marked a turning point in organized labor's stance on the Vietnam War. A large number of leaders and rank-and-filers decided either to break openly with the American Federation of Labor-Congress of Industrial Organizations' (AFL-CIO's) top bureaucracy's position or to embrace a prowar position by participating in patriotic demonstrations. Numerous unions made public statements against the war and distanced themselves from the official AFL-CIO's support of the war. But it was the New York hard hats' prowar demonstrators that made the headlines. The White House strategists would skillfully exploit this incident during the congressional election. Workers, they argued, backed Nixon on grounds of patriotism, support for law and order, and against the left-wing extremists in the Democratic party.

During the 1970 congressional campaign, the Republicans managed virtually to eliminate the Vietnam War as a political issue. But once the peace issue was obscured, the state of the economy assumed considerable importance. This was precisely what Nixon feared might prove the grand old party's undoing. A postelection Gallup survey showed that in 1970 blue-collar workers had voted even more strongly for Democratic candidates than in previous elections. It was evident that the business-dominated Republican party was finding it very difficult to win over a blue-collar majority. It was also apparent however that the Democrats could easily lose the blue-collar vote if they ignored the workers' needs.

In 1971, Nixon's priority was to reverse the economic downturn. The administration's New Economic Policy (NEP) relied on three key measures: Tax cuts for business and individuals to stimulate the economy and bring down unemployment rates; a 4.7 million-dollar cut in federal spending along with a 90-day freeze on wages and prices to cool off the inflationary spiral; and the termination of the dollar-gold convertibility to protect the dollar and the U.S. economic position in the international scene. George Meany and other labor leaders were outraged at what they considered a highly discriminatory program that favored big business at the expense of workers. Wages were frozen, but there was no freeze on interest rates, profits, stocks, land prices, capital gains, and dividends.

Despite organized labor's harsh criticism of Nixon's NEP, the president's strategy to stimulate a pre-election economic boom in order to capture the blue-collar vote worked. By September 1972, the Nixon administration and the labor leaders that had formally adopted a neutral position in the presidential race were developing an increasingly cordial relationship. There were two cases in point: The International Brotherhood of Teamsters and the building and construction unions. The teamsters, who endorsed Nixon, were pleased by the administration's opposition to antistrike legislation in the transportation industry. The construction workers for their part applauded the president for his opposition to racial quotas in hiring.

The Democrats' self-destructing behavior also increased Nixon's chances for re-election. They nominated as their presidential candidate George McGovern, a liberal senator whom conservatives tagged as the proponent of the three A's: "Acid, Abortion, and Amnesty." It was not difficult for Nixon to portray McGovern as the candidate of a small minority. Many citizens probably shared the Democratic candidate's criticism of the tax system, the welfare system, and economic policies, but his proposals did not seem workable. In order to build a truly national base, McGovern needed to move toward the center. Yet the Democratic candidate could not jettison those positions that had rallied his ideological partisans.

Nixon's efforts to court the silent majority eventually paid off. The nation's blue-collar workers—who made up a third of the electorate and since the 1930s represented the core vote of all Democratic presidential candidates—went for Nixon over McGovern by the ratio of 57% to 43%. Moreover for the first time since the early 1930s, a majority (54%) of members of labor union families voted the Republican ticket.

Political analysts concluded that having captured 62% of the votes, Nixon had finally succeeded in his quest to create a new Republican majority.

Over a 2-year period, Nixon had in fact violated every single tenet of the conservative dogma, particularly deep deficits in the federal budget, militant opposition to major Communist powers, and nonintervention in the economy. In 1972, a well-known conservative won the re-election by presenting his party as the party of reform. While Nixon promised to bring the country together under the banner of the new majority, McGovern's new populism picked up the rhetoric of class, which fostered division rather than unity and consensus.

The AFL-CIO's decision not to back McGovern had deepened the rift within the labor leadership. It was impossible to predict that a year later organized labor would call for the impeachment of the president. In 1972, only 53% of the voters were familiar with the Watergate charges, and only 3% thought it important enough to list among their major concerns. The 1972–1973 economic downturn exacerbated Nixon's problems in office, but it was the Watergate affair that destroyed his administration and eventually led to his resignation in August 1974.

In the months that followed, the recession deepened, and public confidence in the government's ability to manage the economy collapsed. President Gerald Ford, furthering Nixon's conservative agenda, offered no measures to halt the recession. In the midst of an economic disaster, both the UAW and the AFL-CIO leadership directed their efforts toward the 1974 congressional elections. Rank-and-filers were unlikely to think that Congress could do much for them, but union leaders viewed the 1974 electoral returns as encouraging. The Democrats made sizable gains, picking up 43 House seats, four Senate seats, and four governorships. The disastrous state of the economy and the widespread job insecurity explain why Republicans lost so many votes. Nevertheless the labor-liberal alliance would never be reconstructed.

Old Expectations in a New Political and Economic Reality

After the Nixon and Ford administrations, liberal Democrats were hopeful that Jimmy Carter's election in 1976 would restore the New Deal agenda in the White House. However the former governor of Georgia came out of the most conservative wing of the Democratic party and had little in common with liberal Democrats like Hubert H. Humphrey, George McGovern, or Edward Kennedy. Faced with one of the worst economic crises in the history of the United States, Carter endorsed many of the fiscal and economic policies that his successor, Ronald Reagan, would espouse.

By 1977, the combination of rising prices, persistent unemployment, and a stagnant economy came to be known as stagflation. Carter's proposed remedy included a minimum-wage bill, the creation of 200,000 jobs through public-works programs, 425,000 new slots in public-service employment, training programs, and a major youth program. These measures were well-received, but they would soon come to haunt Carter's economic advisers. The emphasis on unemployment and recovery pursued a combination of policies that accelerated the inflationary spiral. The cost of living leaped up at double-digit rates; the value of savings eroded; prices of meat, milk, and heating oil skyrocketed. In 1979, the annual rate of inflation hit 11.3%, and the administration appeared powerless to deal with it.

Despite the election of sympathetic senators and representatives to Congress and a friendly Democrat to the White House, organized labor was incapable of delivering any of the important public-policy initiatives it had proposed. The defeat of the Labor Law Reform Bill of 1977–1978 ended labor's most ambitious effort to strengthen American workers' eroded collective-bargaining rights under the National Labor Relations Act. The bill proposed to increase the penalties on companies that violated the law and to eliminate intricate appeal processes that business used to evade holding or accepting the results of union elections.

Labor law reform had become critical in holding together the fragile alliance between the Carter administration and organized labor. The House quickly passed the bill in 1977, but it got held up in the Senate in the winter and spring of 1978. With time on their side, the National Association of Manufacturers, the Chamber of Commerce, and the Business Roundtable, among others, quickly mobilized against the bill. Organized labor tried to defend its proposal, but it lacked the resources available to business interests. In the end the administration and its labor allies failed to obtain the 60 votes needed in the Senate to stop a filibuster by the bill's opponents. After the fifth ballot, Majority Leader Robert Byrd recommitted the bill to the Senate Human Resources Committee where it died.

In the wake of the 1978 legislative defeats, the new UAW President, Douglas Fraser, wrote a lengthy letter of resignation to the Labor/Management Group, a national committee chaired by former U.S. Secretary of Labor John Dunlop. The letter, which was widely circulated, became a kind of call to action for a renewed U.S. labor movement. Fraser attempted to create a new coalition called the Progressive Alliance that would unite labor with the movements of the sixties. The AFL-CIO turned its back on his initiative, and Fraser's call went practically unheeded. The 1980 presidential election would find organized labor as divided as ever.

Three days after the U.S. embassy takeover in Iran, Senator Edward Kennedy of Massachusetts announced his candidacy for the Democratic presidential nomination. Fraser and other leaders of industrial unions, together with many consumer, civil rights, and community-organizing activists, backed Kennedy's challenge to President Carter. For his part Lane Kirkland—who had succeeded Meany in November 1979 just 2 months before the AFL-CIO president's death—endorsed Carter's re-election along with many other Democratic politicians. Carter eventually won the nomination, but he was forced to make many concessions to Senator Kennedy. The Democratic party's split paved the way for Ronald Reagan's landslide and final triumph of the so-called new Republican majority.

The broader labor-Democratic alliance had been breaking down throughout the late 1960s and 1970s. In these years, although the Democratic party managed to win large majorities in several congressional elections, it did not always prove to be prolabor. As the U.S. economy began sliding into a sustained crisis and industrial relations appeared as a critical matter for government policy, unions were asked to restrain their collective-bargaining demands, and Congress turned a deaf ear to the unions' policy proposals. Furthermore the 1972 Democratic party's decision to adopt affirmative-action goals for its internal party deliberations also signaled the weakening of the labor-liberal alliance and the beginning of a new trend in American politics. The Democratic party would never recover its old commitment to economic planning and labor law reform, two key goals of the progressive industrial unions in the immediate post-WWII period.

In the early 1970s, as traditional industrial unions began to decline, the public-sector unions representing government workers and teachers increased their numbers dramatically. This was an important breakthrough for women, blacks, and Latinos, since they constituted a majority in these unions. In 1974, faced with organized labor's powerlessness and indifference, 1,200 women from all over the United States created the Coalition of Labor Union Women (CLUW), whose mission was to organize the unorganized, promote affirmative action, and increase women's political participation. John Sweeny's ascendancy as head of the Service Employees' International Union (SEIU) also marked an important power shift within organized labor. Through aggressive organizing campaigns, especially among the working poor, SEIU eventually became one of the largest unions in the country. The American Federation of State, County, and Municipal Employees (AFSCME) also began to grow. By 1979, 38% of the workers in the public sector were unionized and seemed to be pushing the U.S. labor movement in a new direction.

MARÍA GRACIELA ABARCA

References and Further Reading

Appy, Christian. *Working-Class War: American Combat Soldiers and Vietnam*. Chapel Hill and London: University of North Carolina Press, 1993.

Carter, Dan T. *The Politics of Rage: George Wallace, the Origins of the New Conservatism, and the Transformation of American Politics*. New York: Simon and Schuster, 1995.

Collins, Robert M. *More: The Politics of Economic Growth in Postwar America*. New York: Oxford University Press, 2000.

Fink, Gary M., and Hugh Davis Graham, eds. *The Carter Presidency: Policy Choices in the Post-New Deal Era*. Lawrence: University Press of Kansas, 1998.

Foner, Philip S. *US Labor and the Vietnam War*. New York: International Publishers, 1989.

Gallup, Alec, and George H. Gallup, eds. *The Gallup Poll Cumulative Index: Public Opinion, 1935–1975*.

Gordon, David M., Richard Edwards, and Michael Reich. *Segmented Work, Divided Workers*. Kansas: University Press of Kansas, 1998. (reprint, 1982)

Levison, Andrew. *The Working-Class Majority*. New York: Coward, McCann and Geoghegan, Inc., 1974.

Mattusow, Allen J. *Nixon's Economy: Booms, Busts, Dollars, and Votes*. Lawrence, Kansas: University Press of Kansas, 1998.

Moody, Kim. *An Injury to All: The Decline of American Unionism*. London, UK: Verso, 1988.

Schulman, Bruce J. *The Seventies: The Great Shift in American Culture, Society, and Politics*.

Cases and Statutes Cited

National Labor Relations Act
Wagner Act

UNION LEAGUE MOVEMENT

The Union League, or Loyal League, was the Republican party's organizational vehicle for securing the black vote during early Reconstruction. It also served to mobilize laborers against slaverylike conditions on southern plantations.

The league originated as a northern patriotic organization backing the Lincoln administration. As a secret society it had a ritual featuring oaths to support loyal candidates. With the end of the Civil War, the Republican patronage officials running the league turned attention to the ex-Confederate states. It initially secured a following among up-country Unionists,

absorbing local networks of draft resisters and anti-Confederate groups, like North Carolina's Red Strings. It became the political expression of the most intransigent white opponents of presidential Reconstruction. With enactment of Military Reconstruction in March 1867, congressional Republicans used this existing body to appeal to the newly enfranchised freedmen.

Agents of the Bureau of Freedman, Refugees, and Abandoned Lands, northern missionaries, native Unionists, and other Republican activists swore in vast numbers of freed people. Though white outsiders were the prominent organizers, local leadership was often African-American. League speakers offered basic instruction on politics and voting. It proved difficult for opponents to interdict the technique of holding nighttime meetings at secluded locations. An explosive politicization of rural freed people resulted in the summer and fall of 1867, as hundreds of thousands reportedly flocked to league councils and similar local groups. The general appeal was that conservatives essentially re-imposed slavery through the black codes. Though organization's Republican sponsors had narrow political goals, leagues generated martial drilling and other spontaneous militant actions throughout the countryside. Talk of land redistribution reportedly circulated freely as well.

The mobilization of the freed people had social roots in the plantation crisis. After emancipation large landowners resumed production under slavery-like conditions. In the leading crop of cotton, these included gang labor, tight supervision under overseers, women and children in the workforce, and even physical coercion if possible. The black codes wrote these practices into law. The freed people resisted, contributing to disastrous crops in the years after the war. Enfranchisement thus came at a crucial moment as the centralized plantation system gave way to decentralized tenant farming—especially family-based sharecropping. Labor force frustration with the survivals of slavery-fed insurgency and the politicization of the freedmen in turn undermined centralized management. It thus likely influenced the timing at least of the widespread transition to tenant farming.

The league mobilized virtually the entire black population, and so it contributed to the speedy approval of Reconstruction constitutions in most of the ex-Confederate states. But the organization was rapidly dismembered by the terrorist Ku Klux Klan and its offshoots in early 1868. In this climate the league's Republican sponsors concluded that the secret organization had served its purpose, though vestiges of the organization survived locally and as a paper organization at the national level. Though transient the

Union League created a tradition of Republican voting, and it also encouraged lasting changes in the plantation system.

MICHAEL W. FITZGERALD

References and Further Reading

Fitzgerald, Michael W. *The Union League Movement in the Deep South: Politics and Agricultural Change during Reconstruction*. Baton Rouge and London, 1989.

Foner, Eric. *Reconstruction, America's Unfinished Revolution*. Oxford, 1988.

Hahn, Steven. *A Nation under Our Feet: Black Political Struggles in the Rural South, from Slavery to the Great Migration*. Cambridge, 2003.

Cases and Statutes Cited

Military Reconstruction Act

UNION SUMMER

Union Summer is the American Federation of Labor-Congress of Industrial Orgnizations' (AFL-CIO's) 5-week long internship program for those who demonstrated an interest in and wanted to gain union-organizing skills. Started in the summer of 1996, Union Summer sent cadres of college or college-age students to sites across the United States where they worked with local union members in a variety of ways. Participants received a weekly stipend and free housing at their site. They also participated in an initial orientation and education sessions. Typical tasks included visiting, surveying, and educating workers, organizing, and joining pickets and other demonstrations, and building union and community partnerships. The program did not require prior experience with unions. Ideally though, the AFL-CIO hoped that participants would use their experience to contribute further to the labor movement, be it through student-labor coalitions or as union organizers or researchers.

Union Summer began as a prototype based on the Freedom Summer of 1964, where a thousand college students went south to register black voters. The AFL-CIO President John Sweeney saw the nation's youth as an untapped pool that could assist in his efforts to reinvigorate the labor movement through widespread organizing. In that vein Union Summer was only a part of the labor organization's creation of a new organizing department and expansion of its Organizing Institute, which trained full-time organizers. Sweeny earmarked $20 million for the organizing initiative, some of which went to Union Summer. Union Summer interns also represented the changing face of labor with more than half being females and minorities, many of whom were the targets of new organizing drives. Most significantly though, U.S. youth had education and progressive enthusiasm that the AFL-CIO felt it needed to harvest.

Since its inception approximately 3,000 individuals have participated in Union Summer. As of 2004, the program accepted 200 applicants from a pool of over 600, each to participate in one of two 5-week cycles. In its first year Union Summer sent over 1,000 activists to 22 cities for 3 weeks each. During that time the program claimed to have registered over 3,000 voters, handed out 100,000 leaflets, participated in nearly 250 demonstrations, and spoken to almost 45,000 workers either at home or on the job. Over time, interns have helped win contracts for hotel and resort workers, joined the picket lines during the Detroit newspaper strike, and convinced a New York-based garment company to stop using sweatshop labor. Union Summer graduates created the student-labor action group United Students against Sweatshops, which led the charge against university contracting with sweatshops to produce collegiate wear. Others led the Harvard Living Wage Campaign, a successful student-worker coalition that led to wage increases for Harvard's nonacademic workers.

Despite these successes questions remain about the use of those outside of the labor movement to reinvigorate stagnant union growth. On the one hand students possess a number of skills the average worker may not, including time, flexibility, computer knowledge, and research abilities. They also assume less risk than workers, since they have little to lose by supporting a union. Some argue that these skills balanced with personal modesty and an open-mind can lead to productive and truly cooperative relationships between union members and outside supporters. This argument also holds that union members themselves must also be willing to sublimate personal gain, perhaps as elected officials for the local or international, for the good of the membership. Only then can bottom-up democracy thrive in any union. Indeed a study of the first Union Summer in 1996 demonstrated that unions committed to strategic organizing were able to incorporate interns most successfully.

On the other hand, others contend that outsiders, such as the Union "Summer-istas" and former student organizers lack the requisite first-hand knowledge of those who actually work on the shop floors and are used by unions as professional substitutes for membership-bred leaders. Unions who use this approach overemphasize the education and other skills of students to the point where staffing the union becomes more important than rank-and-file involvement in the growth of the union. Union democracy and culture thus suffers for lack of workplace leadership and organization.

The 1996 study found that unions that struck a balance between site-specific education of their interns, an active membership, and open students had the most success in their local campaigns. The information gathered also suggested that the more direct exposure to social injustices, the more likely the Union Summer participant to continue involvement with the labor movement. Recognizing the factors important for success, the AFL-CIO altered the Union Summer program over the years to a more selective, longer internship for older students that was geared toward keeping interns involved in the movement beyond their summertime experience.

LINDSEY ALLEN

References and Further Reading

Bunnage, Leslie, and Judith Stepan-Norris. "'Outsiders Inside the Labor Movement: An Examination of Youth Involvement in the 1996 Union Summer Program." In *Rebuilding Labor: Organizing and Organizers in the New Union Movement*, edited by Ruth Milkman and Kim Voss. Ithaca, NY: Cornell University Press, 2004.

Compa, Lance. "More Thoughts on the Worker-Student Alliance: A Reply to Steve Early." *Labor: Studies in Working-Class History of the Americas* 1, 2 (2004): 15–22.

Early, Steve, "Thoughts on the 'Worker-Student Alliance' – Then and Now." *Labor History* 44, 1 (2003): 5–13.

"Union Summer Q&A." www.alfcio.org/aboutunions/ unionsummer/qapage.cfm (2004–).

See also **American Federation of Labor-Congress of Industrial Organizations**

UNITED AUTOMOBILE WORKERS
See **Reuther, Walter**

UNITED BREWERY WORKERS

The National Union of Brewery Workmen (later International Union of United Brewery, Flour, Cereal, Soft Drink, and Distillery Workers of America) began an important union of the early American Federation of Labor (AFL) era that made the transition from craft to industrial unionism early on. A mostly German-American organization, it had a strong socialist core membership during its first half-century. While industrial change had an impact on the union, it was Prohibition that posed the most massive threat to its members and helped the union seek alliances with unionized workers in related industries. The union survived after World War II and joined the Teamsters' Union in 1972.

Despite its roots in an ancient craft and its American history going back to colonial times, beer brewing was an increasingly mechanized, capital-intensive industry from the mid-nineteenth century on. From 1870–1890, the industry consolidated rapidly until it was dominated by a few large breweries at the turn of the twentieth century. By the 1880s, refrigeration, electricity, and introduction of scientifically controlled fermentation processes had made beer brewing one of the high-tech industries of its time.

Both workers and owners in the brewing industry had roots in Germany, with a minority coming from

Brewery. Workers inspecting beer vats. Library of Congress, Prints & Photographs Division, Theodor Horydczak Collection [LC-H822-T01-1745].

England and Ireland as well. Trained as craftsmen under the formal system of apprenticeship rules in central Europe, brewery workers in the U.S. post-Civil War era entered a workplace that was still governed by traditional European work hierarchies and practices. Eighty-hour workweeks, physical disciplining of workers, and financial dependency on boardinghouse keepers resulted in social isolation for the workers and contributed to mounting tensions in the industry. They erupted in two strikes in Cincinnati in 1879 and in New York City in 1881. The short-lived unions that resulted from these conflicts in each city dissolved after a few months due to blacklisting by employers.

But the brewery workers resumed organizing soon thereafter, mostly in secret. In many cities, such as Cincinnati, Chicago, Detroit, St. Louis, and Philadelphia, they joined the Knights of Labor (KOL) as local assemblies in the early 1880s. In New York City the reconstituted union went public in 1886, encouraged by the brewery owners who hoped that harmonious labor relations would give them an advantage in their struggle for a wider market.

Amid a lively national labor movement, the National Union of Brewery Workmen was organized in August of 1886 in Baltimore, comprising locals from New York, Newark, Baltimore, Philadelphia, Detroit, and St. Louis. The headquarters of the union was in New York City, and the head of Local 1 of New York, Louis Herbrand, became its first secretary. Virtually the entire membership of the early union was German-speaking. President Herbrand spoke only rudimentary English, and the union's paper, the *Brauer Zeitung* was published exclusively in German until 1917.

From this early period and through much of the first-half of the twentieth century, the basic structure and political orientation of the union remained similar. The union had no president, just a national secretary who was elected by all members. The union's board was also elected by members in a direct vote. Conventions were held every 3 years. The headquarters of the union, through most of its existence was in Cincinnati. The union offered relatively scant member benefits but low dues. Membership was open to all workers in breweries regardless of craft background or skill level. It was the heavily German culture of the brewery workers that limited its attractiveness to workers from a wider array of backgrounds.

The National Union of Brewery Workmen was chartered by the AFL 7 months after its founding. As the AFL became a more viable organization toward the late 1880s, the brewery workers' ties to the KOL became weaker during the late 1880s, mainly because of the KOL's widespread support of the

temperance movement. The union grew quickly within the next 2 years comprising 35 locals in 1888 with a membership of around 5,000. Local 1 of New York alone had 1,800 members. That year however brewery owners all over the country began a concerted campaign against the union, canceling contracts, locking out striking workers, and blacklisting union members. Within months the national union had shrunk to 1,800 members nationwide, with only 26 locals. Formerly mighty Local 1 had only 125 members.

A slow period of recovery commenced in the early 1890s when aided by the AFL, the National Union of United Brewery Workmen rebuilt its membership base slowly. A national boycott of the most powerful and largest breweries in the early 1890s forced Anheuser Busch of St. Louis and Pabst of Milwaukee to recognize the union and introduce the 12-hour workday. From St. Louis and Milwaukee the union spread to organize other locations in the Midwest, and in 1902 it finally achieved a contract for the workers in New York City. By the early twentieth century, employers and workers once again cooperated more closely.

As labor relations stabilized for the union nationwide, the political differences between the brewery workers' union and the AFL became more pronounced. From the beginning the brewery workers' union had had a large socialist membership, and its most prominent leaders were always articulate Socialists, such as Ernest Kurzenknabe, William Trautmann, Oscar Ameringer, and later Karl Fellner. True to its principles, the union had always organized all workers in breweries regardless of their craft background, and this policy brought them into conflict with the craft-oriented AFL and such unions as the firemen, the stationary engineers, and the teamsters. After a lengthy investigation and consultations, the AFL ordered the brewery workers to refuse admission to firemen and other skilled workers if a craft union existed in their trade. The brewers did not comply, and their charter was revoked by the AFL in 1907. After much debate the brewery workers union was re-admitted a year later.

By the second decade of the twentieth century, it was Prohibition rather than jurisdictional disputes or labor conflicts that began to dominate the union's agenda. Cooperation with the brewery owners on this topic was important to the union. Because of the special predicament of their industry, the brewery workers found themselves relatively isolated within the U.S. labor movement in the early twentieth century, since neither the socialist movement nor the AFL took an anti-Prohibition stance.

The union survived Prohibition as a small organization that incorporated flour, cereal, and soft drink workers during World War I. After the passage of the Twentieth Amendment, the industry revived in the 1930s. Membership recovered, but jurisdictional disputes also revived, this time mostly with the teamsters' union. As a result of continuing disputes, the brewery workers were suspended from the AFL in 1941 and remained an independent union until 1946 when they joined the CIO. In 1972, the International Union of United Brewery, Flour, Cereal, Soft Drink, and Distillery Workers of America joined the International Brotherhood of Teamsters as a separate conference.

DOROTHEE SCHNEIDER

References and Further Reading

Laslett, John M. *Labor and the Left: A Study of Socialist and Radical Influences in the American Labor Movement.* New York, Basic Books, 1970.

Schlueter, Hermann. *The Brewing Industry and the Brewery Workers' Movement in America.* Cincinnati, OH: 1910.

UNITED BROTHERHOOD OF CARPENTERS AND JOINERS OF AMERICA

Since its founding in Chicago in 1881, the United Brotherhood of Carpenters and Joiners of America (UBCJA) has stood among the strongest unions in the American labor movement. The role it has played however has been complex. Most historians of the union have divided its history into two distinct eras: the nineteenth century (personified by the leadership of Peter J. McGuire), in which the brotherhood was infused with social democratic ideals and positioned itself at the forefront of the labor movement; and the twentieth century (personified by the leadership of William L. Hutcheson), in which the union became a model of business unionism. Throughout its entire history the brotherhood has fought to achieve the best possible working conditions and wage rates for its members while remaining steadfast in its refusal to subordinate the interests of the national union to any other entity. Yet the union has also continually had to respond to technological, economic, social, and political developments.

The Founding of the UBCJA

The immediate impetus for the formation of a national carpenters' union resulted from successful organization at the local level. As the nation recovered from the economic depression of the mid-1870s, carpenters in cities across the country organized unions in order to secure better wages and to halt the spread of subcontracting and piecework. It quickly became apparent however that success brought problems that independent local unions could not mitigate. After St. Louis carpenters successfully struck for higher wages in the spring of 1881, carpenters from cities with lower wage rates flooded the city. In order to preserve their gains, St. Louis carpenters urged outsiders to stay away from their city and issued a call for a national convention.

The driving force behind the movement for a national organization of carpenters was Peter J. McGuire. An indefatigable organizer who devoted his life to working-class causes, McGuire harmonized trade union principles with socialist beliefs. Although his primary allegiance was to his craft, McGuire was at the forefront of the 8-hour movement, a founding member of the American Federation of Labor (AFL), a founding member of the Social Democratic party of North America, and campaigned for the Greenback party. With McGuire as their general secretary from 1881–1902, the brotherhood would also play a central role in the late nineteenth-century labor movement. Along with resolutions demanding shorter hours, equal pay during lean winter months, and the elimination of subcontracts and piecework, the brotherhood's founding convention also issued wider calls for united action among all building trades unions, abolition of convict labor, and elimination of unfair monopolies. Under McGuire's leadership, the union's membership grew from approximately 2,000 in 1881 to 167,000 by 1903.

McGuire's influence over the direction of the brotherhood was not universal. For example the union's founding convention in Chicago was nearly torn apart by two factions that disagreed as to the degree of power that the national union was to assume. The protectionists, who most closely embodied McGuire's vision, desired a national organization that would provide benefits, regulate itinerant members, coordinate strike activities, and support local struggles for better working conditions and higher wages. The benevolents on the other hand envisioned a national organization whose sole function was to provide death and disability benefits for union carpenters. McGuire and Gabriel Edmonston brokered a compromise that enabled the union to pursue both paths, but debates over the role of the central union and its relationship with its locals would reoccur throughout the brotherhood's early history. In fact the issue was not fully resolved until 1916, when the national union, under the new leadership of William L. Hutcheson, took decisive action against 61 New York locals after they initiated a strike in defiance of the general executive board.

Consolidation and Jurisdictional Disputes

Over the course of its history however the brotherhood's most serious battles were fought with external foes. One of its first challenges was to consolidate its representation of the woodworking trades, which involved bitter campaigns against the Amalgamated Society of Carpenters and Joiners and the Amalgamated Wood Workers' International Union. To the brotherhood, the Amalgamated Society was a dual union pure and simple. Established as a branch of the British union, the society was concentrated in New York, Philadelphia, and Chicago. After a controversial battle that generated intense debate within the AFL, the society was forced to merge with the more powerful brotherhood in 1912.

The wood workers posed a different type of threat. Chartered by the AFL in 1890, the wood workers claimed jurisdiction over all factory and mill workers. As traditional carpentry work increasingly moved indoors during the first decade of the twentieth century, the wood workers' membership grew and the brotherhood protested. After a lengthy dispute that tested the patience of the AFL, the brotherhood absorbed the wood workers in 1912. By encompassing mill and factory workers, one historian of the brotherhood has suggested, the union adopted a unique blend of craft and industrial unionism. The brotherhood's industrial appeal had strict limits however, as the 1930s would attest. This time staking claim to lumber and sawmill workers in the Pacific Northwest, the UBCJA engaged in a bitter and violent fight with the Congress of Industrial Organizations' (CIO's) International Woodworkers of America. Although the brotherhood succeeded in organizing some of these workers, this time it was compelled to coexist with its CIO rival.

While the brotherhood consolidated the woodworking trades, it also aggressively pursued jurisdictional disputes that arose from technological developments in construction. This issue rippled throughout the building trades, and the industry's unions devoted considerable energy to adjudicating interunion disputes. When it became clear that local building trades councils were incapable of resolving jurisdictional battles, the largest construction unions joined together to remedy disputes on an industry-wide basis. In 1903, they organized the Structural Building Trades' Alliance, which evolved into the AFL's Building Trades' Department (BTD) in 1908. Although it was instrumental in the BTD's formation, the brotherhood undermined the BTD's authority whenever it objected to the department's actions—which it often has in matters concerning jurisdiction and representation. On several occasions, most recently in 2001, the brotherhood left the department in protest—and in some cases the AFL altogether—only to later return.

The most contentious UBCJA jurisdictional disputes emerged in the early twentieth century as metal increasingly replaced wood in doors, window frames, and trim. Worried that new specialty unions would usurp their membership and strength, the brotherhood updated its jurisdictional claim from anything made of wood to include any work that once required wood. This policy soon led to long, drawn-out conflicts with the Wood, Wire, and Lather International Union and the Sheet Metal Workers' Union. In 1903, an agreement between the UBCJA and the lathers' union broke down when the brotherhood claimed jurisdiction over the installation of a new type of lathing material. The rivalry would not be fully resolved until 1979, when the UBCJA absorbed the lathers' union. The dispute with the sheet metal workers began in 1908 over the installation of metal trim and was not resolved until the two unions hashed out a compromise in 1926. Although these were two of the most significant jurisdictional disputes, the UBCJA would challenge numerous other unions in much the same way throughout the twentieth century.

Business Unionism and Defending the Closed Shop

As the UBCJA consolidated its power in the early twentieth century, it moved toward business unionism. In addition to strengthening the national organization *vis-à-vis* its locals, the brotherhood governed its craft through closed-shop agreements and the union label. The closed shop cultivated shared interests with union carpenters and contractors, while the union label extended urban strength to the hinterland and would cause the boycott to become a vital organizing tool. Particularly under the guidance of William Hutcheson, who led the union from 1915 to 1951, the UBCJA was sensitive to any interference in this craft economy. In the first-half of the twentieth century, the union expended considerable resources fighting injunctions in jurisdictional disputes and boycotts. During World War I Hutcheson approved a strike for carpenters working in shipbuilding when the Wage Adjustment Board stipulated that they should be paid less than regular carpenters. Although the brotherhood lobbied hard for passage of the Davis-Bacon Act, Hutcheson even criticized the New Deal for being too invasive—although most local leaders and rank-and-file members welcomed Roosevelt's relief measures and government-sponsored construction projects.

The open-shop movement of the 1920s and the Great Depression of the 1930s posed more serious challenges to the UBCJA and to building trades unions more generally. In the 1920s, local chambers of commerce, employers, corporations, and citizens' committees across the country attacked the closed shop and union label with "the American plan." The brotherhood battled against the offensive—most dramatically in San Francisco, where the national organization invested hundreds of thousands of dollars in a violent strike in 1926. But such efforts were unsuccessful, and as a result, the UBCJA's national membership declined from 400,000 in 1920 to 345,000 in 1928. The brotherhood's membership continued to decline during the Great Depression. Mass unemployment reduced membership rolls to a low of 242,000 in 1932. By 1933, less than a third of those members were able to find work as carpenters.

The brotherhood gradually recovered by securing work for its members on New Deal and World War II construction projects, and the union prospered during the postwar years thanks to the federal government's investment in defense work and heavy construction. Indeed the postwar construction boom ushered in a golden age for building trades unions. By 1969, 80% of construction work was performed by union labor, and the brotherhood's membership peaked at 850,000 in 1973. From 1945–1969, wages for union carpenters increased by 72%.

Amid this prosperity however, new problems arose. By the end of the 1960s, the decade's spiraling building costs inspired attacks on union strength in the construction trades. Arguing that high labor costs posed the greatest threat to the building economy, large open-shop groups, most notably the Business Roundtable and the Associated Builders and Contractors, launched determined campaigns to weaken prolabor legislation and open up the building trades to nonunion contractors and workers. These efforts were aided by the steady decline in federally funded construction projects throughout the 1970s. Because of the union's preference for work on these larger projects during the postwar decades, the brotherhood allowed nonunion workers to gain a foothold

in suburban residential construction during the 1960s. In addition technological changes—particularly the increased use of prefabricated materials that needed to be installed only at the job site—also undermined the union's ability to regulate the labor market through its apprenticeship and training programs. Largely as a result of these factors, in the early twenty-first century, less than one-third of construction work in the United States is performed by union labor.

The brotherhood has fought to oppose the advance of the open shop as well as its own declining membership. Since World War II, the UBCJA has increased its political activity (it had eschewed partisan politics at its founding convention) to fight antilabor legislation and politicians. In 1973, it launched two (unsuccessful) campaigns against the open shop—the Coordinated Housing Organization Program and the Voluntary Organizing Committee. More recently the brotherhood has restructured its approach to organizing, training, and politics in order to revitalize its position within the industry. Since becoming UBCJA president in 1995, Douglas McCarron has made organizing the union's top priority. Under his leadership the union reduced its national headquarters staff from 250 to 18, increased its organizing staff from 50 to more than 700, and constructed new training facilities—including a new national training center in Las Vegas, Nevada—to adapt better to technological developments in the industry. So far these changes appear successful, and membership is on the rise—reaching 525,000 by the end of 2005. The UBCJA's focus on organizing has also helped to diversify the union. While the brotherhood never did rank among the most racially exclusive unions of the building trades, by the time the civil rights movement targeted construction unions in the 1960s, the UBCJA leadership and rank-and-file consisted mostly of white males. In response to civil rights protests, pressure from the federal government, and the need to combat declining union membership, the union has increased its minority membership and beginning in the 1970s and 1980s, has opened its ranks to women.

McCarron has also urged organized labor to employ a bipartisan approach to politics instead of blindly supporting the Democratic party, and he has personally lobbied President George W. Bush on a number of issues concerning the building industry. The union's revamped leadership ultimately led to a clash with the AFL-CIO over organizing and political spending—in addition to recurring jurisdictional disputes. In 2001, the UBCJA broke with the AFL-CIO over these issues and in June 2005 joined Change to Win, a coalition of seven labor unions committed to organizing the unorganized who have also disaffiliated with the AFL-CIO.

JOHN J. ROSEN

References and Further Reading

Brooks, Thomas R. *The Road to Dignity, a Century of Conflict: A History of the United Brotherhood of Carpenters and Joiners of America, AFL-CIO, 1881–1981.* New York: Atheneum, 1981.
Christie, Robert A. *Empire in Wood.* Ithaca, NY: Cornell University Press, 1956.
Galenson, Walter. *The United Brotherhood of Carpenters: The First Hundred Years.* Cambridge, MA: Harvard University Press, 1983.
Schneirov, Richard, and Thomas J. Suhrbur. *Union Brotherhood, Union Town: The History of the Carpenters' Union of Chicago: 1863–1987.* Carbondale and Edwardsville: Southern Illinois University Press, 1988.
Internet Source: www.carpenters.org/home.html

Cases and Statutes Cited

Davis-Bacon Act

See also **Hutcheson, William L.; McGuire, Peter J.**

UNITED CANNERY, AGRICULTURAL, PACKING, AND ALLIED WORKERS OF AMERICA

The United Cannery, Agricultural, Packing, and Allied Workers of America (UCAPAWA) emerged from the revolt in the American Federation of Labor (AFL) that launched the Congress of Industrial Organizations (CIO). At its head stood an intense and energetic organizer named Donald Henderson. As a young economics instructor at Columbia University and a member of the Communist party, Henderson had served as the unofficial advisor to a left-wing student movement that mushroomed in response to the Depression and the rise of fascism in Europe. The instructor's activities did not go unnoticed, and in early 1933, he became one of a number of conspicuous radicals who lost their jobs because of their political convictions. Despite student protests, Henderson left academia. Joining the labor movement, he dedicated himself to organizing the country's agricultural workers.

Henderson initially worked in southern New Jersey with the Cannery and Agricultural Industrial Union, which was affiliated with the Trade Union Unity League, the Communist party's counter to the AFL. When the party abandoned its strategy of dual unions in 1935, Henderson became president of the National Committee for Unity of Agricultural and Rural Workers, a loose coalition of small locals affiliated with the AFL. Unable to persuade the AFL to charter an international union of agricultural workers and increasingly drawn to the CIO's industrial union structure, Henderson and representatives from locals throughout the country met in Denver in July 1937 to form UCAPAWA, which promptly received a charter from the CIO.

From the beginning UCAPAWA represented a veritable rainbow of American workers. Mexican sugar beet workers from the Rocky Mountains; black sharecroppers from Arkansas and Missouri; cannery and farm workers from New Jersey; laborers from the Florida citrus groves; Filipino, Chinese, and Japanese cannery workers in Washington—these were only a few of the dozens of occupations and nationalities involved. In addition to the challenges involved in molding this multicultural constituency into a forceful international union, UCAPAWA faced an almost insurmountable organizing task. Agricultural labor was notoriously difficult to organize: Workers were migratory because of the seasonal nature of the industry; the relatively unskilled nature of the work created an oversupply of labor; most agricultural laborers came from minority groups that lacked social or political clout; and because labor represented a high percentage of the cost of production, employers fought hard to keep unions out. Yet despite these difficulties, UCAPAWA enjoyed some early success, thanks in part to active organizing by established locals and the financial support of the CIO. By 1937, Henderson could report a membership of over 120,000 workers in more than 300 locals.

Like a number of CIO presidents, Henderson relied heavily on activists affiliated with the Communist movement. Many of the UCAPAWA officers and organizers in the early days shared Henderson's political sympathies. Some had become unionists as a result of their politics; others had been drawn to communism as a result of their organizing experiences. They saw little difference between being good trade unionists and loyal party members. Other UCAPAWA leaders, while not party members, saw themselves as participants in a radical cultural and political project in which the party played an important, but not necessarily a defining role.

The UCAPAWA entered the South when the Arkansas-based Southern Tenant Farmers' Union (STFU) affiliated with the new international. Organized in 1934 by black and white sharecroppers and tenant farmers under the leadership of storekeepers Clay East and H. L. Mitchell, the STFU focused public attention on the plight of southern farmers. Infighting between Communist party leaders and the local Socialists who served as the organization's principal administrators, as well as personality and ideological conflicts between Henderson and Mitchell marred the alliance from the start. The STFU and UCAPAWA also differed over a fundamental issue: Whether agricultural workers could best be served by a protest organization or a trade union. Despite its name the STFU functioned more like the former; it was loosely structured, had an uncertain membership, and depended on outside sources for financial support. Mitchell contended that sharecroppers and tenant farmers were too uneducated to keep records and too poor to pay regular dues. Henderson argued that agricultural workers could be taught the rudimentary procedures for running the locals and that union members had to support their own organization.

In its early years UCAPAWA focused on organizing migrants, particularly in California. But employer resistance, the exclusion of agricultural workers from the provisions of the Wagner Act, and the seasonality of farm labor made it virtually impossible to establish permanent, self-supporting locals. Finding itself increasingly rushing to the aid of wildcat strikers who had no chance of winning collective-bargaining agreements, UCAPAWA temporarily abandoned its efforts in the fields and focused on the fisheries, canneries, and processing plants, where workers' stability made them better candidates for unionization.

By the early 1940s, this strategy had paid off, and UCAPAWA was setting an example for the union movement across the United States. Local 3 represented workers at a variety of food-processing plants in the Los Angeles area, a majority of whom were Mexican women. In Camden, New Jersey, UCAPAWA broke through at the fiercely anti-union Campbell's Soup Company to organize Local 80. Filipinos and other Asian Americans represented a majority of the cannery workers in Seattle, Portland, and San Francisco who made up Local 7. Even in Memphis, Tennessee, one of the South's most staunchly anti-union cities, UCAPAWA Local 19 organized hundreds of low-paid workers—most of whom were African-American—in the large cotton seed oil plants and in dozens of small companies.

In 1941, UCAPAWA decided to target tobacco-manufacturing workers. Among its charter members were a small number of cigar worker locals in New York and Florida, but the main impetus came from tobacco workers in Richmond, Virginia. In 1937, black stemmery workers struck at a local leaf-processing firm and with the help of organizers from the Southern Negro Youth Congress (SNYC), a youth group led by young radicals who had worked on

the campaign to free the Scottsboro Nine, organized an independent Tobacco Stemmers' and Laborers' Union (TSLU). Within a few years the union had agreements with a number of the city's smaller firms, and affiliation with the CIO provided the financial support needed to tackle the large manufacturers. The CIO awarded UCAPAWA jurisdiction over tobacco workers, and in 1942, the TSLU became UCAPAWA Local 24. Building on this base, the union started organizing among tobacco workers throughout the South.

Labor shortages and the active participation of the National Labor Relations Board and the War Labor Board in labor disputes greatly enhanced the bargaining power of American workers during World War II. As a result UCAPAWA membership swelled. The most dramatic campaign occurred in Winston-Salem, North Carolina, at the plants of the R. J. Reynolds Tobacco Company. A sit-down strike in 1943 led to the rapid organization of an overwhelming majority of the company's approximately 8,000 African-American workers as well as several hundred whites. That same year several thousand of the city's leaf house workers also joined Local 22. During the same period, workers at American Tobacco Company's cigar plants in Charleston, South Carolina, Trenton, New Jersey, and Philadelphia joined the union. This influx of tobacco-manufacturing workers led the union to change its name to Food, Tobacco, Agricultural, and Allied Workers of America (FTA) in December of 1944.

Local 22 became the jewel in the crown for FTA. In the heart of the Jim Crow South, this militant, black-led local with women in key leadership positions captured the imagination of the Communist Left. The Winston-Salem local registered thousands of black voters, revitalized the local National Association for the Advancement of Colored People (NAACP), and spearheaded the election of a minister to the Winston-Salem Board of Aldermen, the first African-American to defeat a white opponent in the South since the turn of the century.

Although it was still small compared to most AFL and CIO affiliates, UCAPAWA had nonetheless shown that it could organize among the nation's most vulnerable workers. It had also shown that women and minority groups were capable of playing an important role in the labor movement. In fact the union's active recruitment and promotion of women, blacks, Mexicans, and other ethnic minorities to positions of leadership was unprecedented among American trade unions. Among UCAPAWA's vice-presidents and executive board members in the mid-1940s were Luisa Moreno, a Latina organizer in Southern California; the Reverend Owen Whitfield, a former African-American sharecropper from Missouri: Moranda Smith, Local 22's dynamic leader; and Armando Ramirez, a Cuban-born cigar maker. The union's Washington office was overseen by Elizabeth Sasuly, who served as legislative director from 1939–1950.

The postwar conservative attack on unions, led by the National Association of Manufacturers and its member corporations along with conservatives in both the Republican and Democratic parties cut deeply into FTA's strength. A forced strike wave in 1945–1946; the mechanization and automation of labor-intensive production processes; anticommunism; and the federal government's retreat on the rights of workers, women, and minorities—these were among the factors that put FTA on the defensive.

The Republican party's capture of both houses of Congress in 1946 allowed business interests to pass the Taft-Hartley Act, a piece of landmark legislation that prohibited unions from contributing to political campaigns; expanded employers' ability to dissuade workers from joining unions; and put the internal workings of unions under closer scrutiny. Taft-Hartley also required union officers seeking access to National Labor Relations Board (NLRB) services to file affidavits declaring that they were not members of the Communist party, and it allowed states to write their own laws governing union security and gave those laws precedence over federal regulations. Anxious to maintain labor's electoral support and convinced that Taft-Hartley went too far, Truman refused to ratify the measure. Undeterred, proponents marshaled the votes to override the president's veto.

Both CIO and AFL officials had been outraged by the affidavits' provision, which infringed on their civil liberties and put Communists and non-Communists alike in an untenable position. Initially most international leaders—including CIO President Phillip Murray—stood on principle, and the left-led unions urged the federation to wage an all-out fight for repeal, to shun the weakened NLRB, and rely on solid organization and the support of the rank-and-file. The CIO leadership however was unwilling to risk mass demonstrations, and within months most of the federation's international unions had capitulated. The FTA along with the Mine, Mill, and Smelter Workers, the United Electrical Workers, and other left-led unions refused to comply. That decision meant that when FTA's contracts expired, the union would have to rely entirely on its own clout to bring companies to the bargaining table.

Throughout its history the CIO had accommodated a wide range of political views, and FTA had always stood firmly on the federation's left wing. And until 1947, the CIO was united behind FDR's vision of world peace based on the continuation of the U.S. wartime collaboration with the Soviet Union as well as a renewal and expansion of the New Deal. The mounting antagonism between the two superpowers however dragged the federation into the international arena, bringing its factional rifts into sharp relief.

The FTA refused to go along with the conservative swing in foreign affairs. It did not endorse the Marshall Plan, the Truman doctrine, or the building attack on the Soviet Union. In December of 1947, former Vice-President Henry Wallace announced that he would run for president on the ticket of the newly formed Progressive party. That decision brought the deep conflicts in the labor movement to the surface, precipitating an ideological split that would have far-reaching reverberations. The clash came to a head when the CIO's executive board met in January 1948 and voted to maintain an officially nonpartisan position, which in practice meant strongarming dissidents into supporting the Democratic party candidate.

Ignoring the CIO's directives, FTA's executive board endorsed Wallace, one of only five CIO unions to do so. In the end Wallace got few votes, and even FTA officers voted for the victorious Truman when it seemed that the Republican candidate might win. But the Progressive party campaign dealt the CIO's fragile unity a final blow. In its wake the CIO's executive board moved not only to curb the political autonomy that international unions and even locals within international unions had always enjoyed, but also to isolate and undermine FTA and other left-wing unions. It did so chiefly by insinuating unions sympathetic to the national CIO leadership into election campaigns where rival organizations competed for representation even if the raiding unions had little affinity with the workers involved.

In 1949, the CIO Executive Board charged FTA with forwarding the interests of the Communist party rather than those of the CIO. The evidence consisted primarily of FTA's criticisms of Truman's foreign policies. The charges also mentioned the union's support for Wallace as an additional link that helped to prove the union's adherence to the party line. The only charge related to FTA's trade union record was that it had lost members over the previous few years. The FTA's membership had declined, but the charge of underperformance failed either to take account of its commitment to organizing the most vulnerable of workers or to demonstrate that the CIO's mainstream internationals could or would do better.

In the summer of 1949, FTA announced that its officials would comply with the Taft-Hartley Act and sign the anti-Communist affidavits. It had little choice. Few of its locals had the economic muscle to win contracts with no federal protection, and raids by the AFL and CIO unions were taking a devastating toll. President Donald Henderson resigned his post as president and became national administrative director. The NLRB however refused to accept affidavits from other union officers as long as Henderson remained on the staff. Finally Henderson admitted that he had once been a member of the Communist party and signed an affidavit. The NLRB again recognized FTA as a legitimate union under the terms of the Taft-Hartley Act. But that was too little too late, since the union lost elections in plant after plant across the United States, including in Winston-Salem.

In a last-ditch effort to keep FTA alive, Henderson arranged a merger with two left-wing unions based in New York to form the Distributive, Processing, and Office Workers of America (DPOWA), which held its founding convention in New York City in early October 1950. Some of the locals lived on, but many were destroyed by employers and raiding CIO and AFL unions.

ROBERT KORSTAD

References and Further Reading

Honey, Michael. *Southern Labor and Black Civil Rights: Organizing Memphis Workers.* University of Illinois Press, 1993.

Korstad, Robert Rodgers. *Civil Rights Unionism: Tobacco Workers and the Struggle for Democracy in the Mid-Twentieth-Century South.* University of North Carolina Press, 2003.

Ruiz, Vicki L. *Cannery Women, Cannery Lives: Mexican Women, Unionization, and the California Food Processing Industry 1930–1950.* University of New Mexico Press, 1987.

Cases and Statutes Cited

Taft-Hartley Act
Wagner Act

See also **Communist Party; Southern Tenant Farmers Union; Taft-Hartley Act**

UNITED ELECTRICAL, RADIO, AND MACHINE WORKERS OF AMERICA

The United Electrical, Radio, and Machine Workers' Union was founded in 1936 as a result of the grassroots worker-organizing surge that also established the Congress of Industrial Organizations (CIO), of which it was a charter union. Initially it represented workers in the eastern United States where the industry was concentrated but grew into a feisty union that expanded geographically and has withstood enormous political and economic strains. While it was once the third largest U.S. industrial union, factionalism, the Cold War, and then capital flight continually whittled away the union's numbers and power. Still it bequeathed an alternative model of union struggle that continues to inspire current union activists.

The disparate origins of the union and the legacy of radicalism in the electrical industry contributed to the unique development and decentralized structure of the union. In the early twentieth century, skilled machinists and toolmakers, some of them influenced by socialism and other forms of radical insurgency, faced the twin tools of scientific management and political repression, which weakened their ability to control conditions on the shop floor and establish strong unions. After World War I, the industry leaders General Electric and Westinghouse established control though company unions and corporate welfare programs. While these promised increased benefits for cooperation with the production regime, only a small segment of workers benefited from these promises. The oligopoly, like much of the appliance and radio industry, relied on wage rates produced by a political economy that depended on a constant surge of young workers, including significant numbers of young women, and high turnover to reduce costs. Workers resumed their efforts to organize as conditions plummeted in the 1930s. Among radio workers, NRA-era organizing established federal labor unions directly affiliated to the American Federation of Labor (AFL). This group, led by James Carey, sought to form a coalition to take on the industry and rebelled when the AFL sought to force them into a skilled trades union but without equal voting rights. At GE and Westinghouse, workers sought to take over company unions by running for office on union-oriented platforms. Another group of workers in the machine industry, affiliated with the International Association of Machinists, grew dissatisfied with that union's lackluster representation, joined the (UE) in 1937. Enrolling working people across the United States and Canada employed at such companies as GE, Westinghouse, General Motors Electrical, RCA, and Sylvania, as well as numerous independent shops, the UE attained a peak membership of 700,000 during World War II.

The structure set up at the founding convention and elaborated in the next 10 years directed the UE toward a grassroots style of unionism. The UE created a structure and recruited leadership that embodied more of the qualities of the decentralized local movements that gave life to the CIO than most other CIO internationals did. Each local union of the UE was relatively autonomous from the district and national office. District directors were elected by the district convention or through direct election, not appointed. The officers of the international were prohibited from making more than the highest paid worker. All union negotiation committees were elected; contracts were ratified by referendum; and strikes were called and concluded with membership votes. The UE shop steward system sought vigorous representation on the shop floor. Official policy suggested a shop steward for every company foreman. Its culture of organizing and representation encouraged group grievances and shop-floor activism, working to rule, on-the-job slowdowns, and other forms of collective action inherited from the early twentieth-century radical organizing tradition. A recent study shows that more UE contracts empowered workers on such issues as the right to strike, management prerogatives, and grievance procedure than those of the USWA and UAW, the other large CIO unions.

A variety of ideological perspectives flourished and competed for the loyalties of members from the outset of the union's history, but the Left held the prime leadership positions at the national level. Carey, who became the first president of the organization, was a relatively conservative Catholic who believed in industrial unionism but was deeply influenced by notions of collaboration and efficiency. A significant number of leaders were radicals who were or had been members of the Communist party, Socialist party, or Industrial Workers of the World. The UE's constitution ensured the right to membership regardless of political beliefs, and this provision created a culture that allowed leftists to protect their positions. Julius Emspak and James Matles, the two other leading officials in the early years, had been associated with the Communist party but sought to hide their radical affiliations in order to ensure the survival of the union. But in District 8, headquartered in St. Louis, open Communist party member William Sentner was directly elected by the membership. Because it grew to represent so many workers, it was the most important union in the CIO influenced by radical perspectives.

Among the CIO unions, the UE was an important advocate for female workers' rights. In part this was due to the significant number of female workers in the electrical and machine-manufacturing field, but the influence of feminism within the Communist party, which in turn influenced a significant number of the union's leaders, also contributed to this development. During World War II, the union not only fought for equal pay for female workers, but also argued in a landmark War Labor Board case that most of the

jobs that women held were paid at artificially low rates, a challenge that preceded the women's rights struggle for comparable-worth demands by decades. One of the UE's staffers in the immediate postwar era was Betty Friedan, who by the 1960s was a leading advocate of the middle-class feminist movement of the 1960s. But in the context of the UE's culture, Friedan's pamphlets for the union placed working-class women at the center of an argument to change a workplace regime that undervalued women's work.

International politics and the resurgence of the right wing in the postwar era was a significant factor in the development of the union's politics and its factional rifts. Critics within and outside the union argued that the leadership conformed to the Communist party line on foreign policy issues. The right wing originated the argument that continued to influence political and scholarly discussion of the union for a generation: That the union was not a legitimate trade union, but rather a front for Soviet power in the United States that sacrificed workers interests to those of Moscow's. Later scholarship would point out that there was little evidence for these views. For instance when the Communist Party (CP) opposed U.S. involvement in World War II, the UE had not authorized any strikes. The UE's no-strike pledge during World War II was in line with the CIO's. It was no matter. In a culture unique in the Western World where radicals hid their political affiliations from workers, the idea that a secret cabal was in control of the union made the union particularly vulnerable. The high degree of local autonomy that characterized the union also made it practically impossible for autocratic style and repression of rebels, which in this case meant the right wing. Carey after 1940 became the spokesman for this group. Carey was ousted from the presidency in the union largely because he had alienated even the right wing by union negotiations' blunders. But by then he had been appointed secretary of the CIO, from which position he sought to keep the leadership of the UE from influence in the direction of the federation.

After the war an internal faction, the UE members for Democratic Action (UEMDA), sought to oust the Left from leadership. But without outside assistance, this group would not have met much success. Catholic anticommunism was an important influence among many workers in the faction, and labor priests who sought to purge the Left of influence in the UE played a major role in formulating policy, though they sought to avoid publicity. Father Charles Owen Rice of Pittsburgh used his contacts around the country to bring the UEMDA together and coordinated the first meeting. (Rice later expressed deep regrets for his involvement in purging the labor movement of its most militant members). The Association of Catholic Trade Unionists provided the largest and best-organized group for the UE right wing; across the country the Catholic church intervened strenuously on the UEMDA's behalf. Another influence was that of Socialists whose factional disputes with the CP Left in other unions accelerated their anti-UE agenda. Socialist involvement helped mitigate the concerns of those who worried about Catholic church involvement and made liberals more comfortable with the idea that the purge was not a reactionary movement. However despite critical press support for the right-wing campaign, the internal movement was mostly unsuccessful between 1946 and 1949. If not for the influence of state repression and CIO efforts to purge the union, the internal efforts would not have been successful. The CIO refused to halt raids by other affiliates, especially the United Auto Workers. The UE's effectiveness was drained by these efforts, which escalated after the passage of the Taft-Hartley Act in 1947, whose non-Communist affidavit provisions prevented the UE from being placed on union election or decertification ballots. The issue came to a head when the UE demanded that the CIO stop the raiding and boycotted the 1949 convention in response. The CIO in turn expelled the UE and nine other unions they accused of being controlled by the CP. It also set up a rival union, the International Union of Electrical Workers (IUE), and appointed Carey as its leader. The CIO spent over a million dollars in campaigns to aid the IUE in wresting workers away from the UE. The UE held onto much of its base in machinery, but the heavy-manufacturing sector split between the two unions. Other unions also continued raiding, and this lent itself powerfully to arguments for relenting in order to become a legitimate union. Throughout all of this the state apparatus of repression, including FBI, House Un-American Activities Committee (HUAC), and other agencies, kept up a steady drumbeat of attack, joined by a style of yellow journalism that was difficult to counter. When critical union elections were held or strikes were taking place, government investigations of Communists' influence in UE often coincided. The accusations gained more salience as the electrical and machine industry became the heart of the defense industry in the postwar. The union's presence in the industry was considered a "dagger at the heart of our industrial system" according to the Senate's Internal Security subcommittee. By the 1950s, the Atomic Energy Commission ordered GE to refuse to accept the UE as a bargaining agent in any of its plants. As early as 1954, many were taking the initiative to defect to other unions. By 1960, the UE's membership fell to 58,000.

The weakened state of the union and the fact that the power was split between two unions made it difficult to bargain against GE and Westinghouse or to combat the capital flight that dogged the union in the postwar era. Many predicted the demise of the UE, but it survived and continued to articulate an understanding of global capitalism that was different than most of the AFL-CIO unions. But the UE continued to express an alternative union that won respect among some quarters from the 1960s to the present. In the 1960s, it was at the forefront of an argument about a shorter hours movement. It was host to labor cartoonists Fred Wright, Mike Konopacki, and Gary Huck, whose work epitomized an anticorporate culture that the UE refused to accept. It devoted significant parts of its budget to organizing and education and sought to educate its members to the workings of global capitalism and the need to unite across borders. It initiated cross-border organizing with Mexican workers in the Frente Autentico del Trabajo (FAT), collaborating in organizing and educational projects. It was a major force behind the organization of the Labor party, arguing that the AFL-CIO alliance with the Democratic party had failed American workers. It sought a community-based style of organizing in contrast to the trendy blitz organizing of the AFL-CIO, which by the early twenty-first century produced some results in the Chicago-Wisconsin corridor.

ROSEMARY FEURER

UNITED FARM WORKERS OF AMERICA

The United Farm Workers of America (UFW) represents the most significant and enduring effort to unionize agricultural labor in the United States. Organizing farm workers presented special challenges for the labor movement. Workers were predominately nonwhite, seasonal, migrant, oftentimes from another country, undocumented, and marginalized. The ethnic and racial composition of the workforce has changed, including over time Chinese, Japanese, Filipinos, Hindus, Arabs, African-American, and displaced migrants from the Dust Bowl, among others. Since the 1940s, the majority of farm workers have been Mexican and of Mexican heritage. Regardless of ethnic background, agricultural workers experienced low wages, poor working conditions, inferior housing, limited benefits, poverty, and racism. Despite fierce opposition from employers, workers protested and joined unions to improve their circumstances. By and large the efforts were short-lived, often not surviving beyond the harvest period. Emerging in the 1960s, more than a century after the earliest agricultural discontent, the UFW has managed to survive over 40 years of efforts to defeat it.

Early Labor Protests

Although attempts to organize agriculture did occur in the nineteenth century, they met with harsh resistance and were brief. Chinese labor was critical to the agricultural development of California. Racially, culturally, and linguistically distinct, the Chinese were identified as a cheap and docile labor source. Rejected by the white-dominated labor groups that supported skilled workers, the Chinese formed their own associations and engaged in strikes. During the depression of the 1870s, they experienced intense racism from broad sectors of society, including the Workingmen's party, which became a strong advocate for anti-Chinese legislation in California. This agitation culminated in the imposition of local and state restrictions and the passage of the Chinese Exclusion Act in 1882 by the Hayes administration. Growers searched for another compliant group of workers to replace them. Vulnerable and separated from the rest of society, the Japanese also encountered the same exploitation and hostility. Like the Chinese, they also organized associations and engaged in labor militancy, using strikes, slowdowns, and other tactics to improve their conditions. These actions were localized and did not create a permanent political base to achieve their goals beyond the harvest season. As in the case with the Chinese, Japanese labor protests encountered racist resistance in California and at the national level. In 1907, the administration of Theodore Roosevelt and the government of Japan concluded the Gentlemen's Agreement to restrict the immigration of skilled and unskilled laborers to the United States.

Another wave of labor protests erupted in the years prior to U.S. involvement in World War I. This labor strife centered around the struggles of the predominately white hops workers who rose up to achieve better conditions. In contrast to the Chinese and the Japanese, the well-known Industrial Workers of the World (IWW or Wobblies) orchestrated this uprising. The memorable 1913 Wheatland strike, deaths, and trial led to a government investigation and improvements in the fields. In addition to wage increases, workers called for the provision of drinking water, better sanitation in the camps, decent housing, and an 8-hour day. Better conditions proved temporary with the subsequent repression of the IWW and the onset of World War I.

The U.S. entry into the war created a labor shortage and consequently large-scale immigration of laborers from Mexico, who came to make up over 50% of migratory workers. Growers perceived them as a seasonal and an easily controllable work force and argued for the restrictions imposed by the Immigration Act of 1917 to be lifted to fill their insatiable need for labor. During the 1920s, agricultural landowners also began to recruit Filipino workers to satisfy their persistent demands for an abundant and submissive workforce. Filipinos were young, single, male, and could compete with Mexican workers in the event of labor unrest. Despite growers' beliefs that a competitive, ethnically divided workforce would quell labor troubles, Mexican and Filipino workers did strike for higher wages, better conditions, and the eradication of the derided contract-labor system. Growers preferred this arrangement because it removed them from dealing directly with workers and from being held responsible for workers' compensation and complaints. Workers objected to the system because it made them dependent on an intermediary who charged workers a fee for employment, housing, transportation, and other items and held a great potential for abuse and fraud. Increasing militancy in the late 1920s convinced growers to take action and call for stricter enforcement of immigration laws and quotas, and then to repatriate and later deport troublesome workers. As the impact of the Great Depression of the 1930s grew and mass unemployment created a surplus agricultural labor, these tactics accelerated.

Labor Protest during the Depression

The Depression decade recorded the most widespread outbreak of labor militancy in agriculture up to that point in U.S. history. A number of organizations participated in the upsurge of protest, including the Cannery and Agricultural Workers' Industrial Union (CAWIU), an affiliate of the Communist party. The CAWIU provided the leadership for the majority of the strikes in the early 1930s. Contrary to other labor organizations during this time, it was willing to work with migrant, nonwhites, including Mexican-heritage, Filipino, and black workers and organize on an industrywide basis. Directing over 20 strikes, including the well-known 1933 cotton strike in the San Joaquin Valley, which drew some 18,000 workers, the union not only pressed for better wages, but also for an end to the labor-contractor system; decent housing, drinking water, and camp sanitation. It faced vehement opposition from growers and their

Agricultural workers bunching carrots, Yuma County, Arizona. Library of Congress, Prints & Photographs Division, FSA/OWI Collection [LC-USF33-013258-M4].

allies, who resorted to such tactics as eviction, strike-breakers, harassment, arrests, and violence. Employers coordinated these activities through the formation of the Associated Farmers, a collection of vigilante groups whose goal was ruthlessly to suppress labor activity. The protracted turmoil caused state government to launch an investigation and to press for reforms. Although red-baiting, the lack of a union leadership well grounded in the nature of agriculture, and its relative isolation from the trade union movement in California weakened the CAWIU, it did achieve significant gains and provided an example of strategies for future organizers.

The CAWIU prepared the way for the emergence of another organizing campaign led by the United Cannery, Agricultural, Packing, and Allied Workers of America (UCAPAWA), an affiliate of the Committee for Industrial Organizations (CIO) during the late 1930s. The UCAPAWA's activities occurred in a more positive environment toward labor, ushered in by the passage of the National Labor Relations Act (NLRA) in 1935 during Franklin Delano Roosevelt's first term in office. The law guaranteed workers the right to join unions and to engage in collective bargaining with their employers. It prohibited employers from interfering with unionization efforts, from forming company unions, from showing preference toward one union over another, and from discriminating against union members. The act established the National Labor Relations Board (NLRB) to oversee the election process and to investigate violations of the

law on the part of both employers and unions. The NLRA primarily benefited the industrial labor movement; it intentionally excluded agricultural workers. Nevertheless it provided tacit approval for their union aspirations. Even with this encouraging development, the establishment of a permanent farm labor union encountered great difficulty. The UCA-PAWA achieved its greatest success with cannery and packing-shed workers but faced a greater challenge with field workers. Spontaneous strikes, which the union felt compelled to support, drained its resources. Its white, urban, educated, and more traditional leadership struggled to relate to its multicultural constituency, including Dust Bowl migrants and Mexican and Filipino workers. And despite the example in the industrial sector, agricultural employers felt no legal constraints to cease their activities to resist unionization. Growers evicted striking workers from labor camps, obtained antipicketing injunctions, harassed and assaulted workers, imported strikebreakers, created blacklists of union supporters, refused to negotiate with union representatives, and rebuffed mediation offers by government agencies. Finally the outbreak of World War II undermined union efforts.

The *Bracero* Era, 1942–1964

World War II caused a labor shortage and the imposition of a labor system that dominated agricultural labor relations for over 20 years. Beginning in 1942 as a wartime measure, the so-called *bracero* (field-hands) program, an international agreement between Mexico and the United States, authorized the temporary importation of Mexican citizens to work during the intensive harvest season. The agreement stipulated procedures for the recruitment, employment, and return to Mexico of these guestworkers. In the initial agreement the United States, reimbursed by growers, paid for *braceros'* roundtrip transportation and living expenses in transit. Prevailing wage and piece rates, already established in the area, determined the compensation for the temporary workers. Separate clauses addressed meals, housing, and medical care. Ten percent of the *braceros'* earnings were transferred to an account in the Agricultural Credit Bank in Mexico, available when the worker returned to Mexico. Other provisions protected workers from discrimination and abuse. Significantly the agreement stated that *bracero* workers could not replace domestic workers, could not be used to depress wages, and could not be used as strikebreakers in the event of a labor dispute. Although this arrangement was intended as a temporary emergency measure, in fact the general outlines of this program remained in place long after the war. Public Law 78, passed in 1951 during the Truman presidency, institutionalized the program on a more permanent basis. It was renewed until 1964. The *bracero* program demonstrated the most long-term, systematic cooperation between government and growers in U.S. history. It provided tremendous benefits for agribusiness; it worked to the great disadvantage of domestic workers and labor unions during the time it was in effect.

The domestic farm labor force endured severe consequences as a result of the *bracero* program. This arrangement displaced non-*bracero* workers who had been leaving the migrant stream to establish more permanent residences and more stable employment in rural towns. Some moved to urban areas in search of work. Those who stayed found increasing competition for their jobs and a depressed wage scale. Working conditions declined with the introduction of the short-handle hoe and production quotas. Growers lacked incentives to improve living conditions. Threatened with replacement, domestic workers increasingly found it difficult to lodge complaints about their treatment.

The *bracero* program seriously undermined the unionization efforts of domestic farm workers. In contrast with the militancy of the 1930s, this period witnessed a decline in labor organizing activities. But even with the growers holding an advantageous position, there were some union initiatives mounted immediately after the war. The National Farm Labor Union (NFLU), chartered by the AFL in 1946, launched a union drive. Led by H. L. Mitchell, the union organized several notable strikes against major agribusiness companies, such as DiGiorgio, where workers demanded a raise of 10 cents per hour, seniority rights, and union recognition. The workforce included domestic workers, undocumented laborers, and *braceros.* Although initially supportive of the walkout, under pressure from their employer, *braceros* and undocumented laborers returned to work, and the strike was broken. Another job action in 1949 involving several thousand cotton pickers was significant for the participation of a young César Chávez on a roving picket line. The protest won its modest demand that a wage cut be rescinded. The labor dispute illustrated the impact of the *bracero* program on depressing wages in agriculture. Although the NFLU achieved only moderate success in the fields, it helped focus attention on the deleterious impact of the *bracero* program on domestic farm laborers. Union staff, such as Ernesto Galarza, collected evidence of its damaging consequences and helped create the pressure for the termination of Public Law 78 that regulated the program.

Toward the end of the *bracero* era, the AFL, which had merged with the CIO (Congress of Industrial Organizations), financed another organizing effort. Established in 1959, the Agricultural Workers' Organizing Committee (AWOC) carried out hundreds of strikes from its founding until the mid-1960s. It accomplished this feat while confronting several obstacles.

First it faced ambivalence from the AFL-CIO, which preferred a status quo in agricultural labor relations that favored protecting existing collective-bargaining agreements in the distribution, packing, and processing of agricultural products to the detriment of field workers. Second the top leadership of AWOC consisted of individuals who had no expertise in organizing farm laborers. Despite these difficulties AWOC kept the focus on the destructive *bracero* program and the increasing farm labor discontent it fomented. The AWOC was joined in its attack on the program by a growing alliance that went beyond the mainstream labor establishment to encompass religious organizations, liberal political groups, and the emerging civil rights movement. This broad coalition finally ended the *bracero* program in 1964 during the administration of Lyndon Johnson. Although AWOC left a mixed legacy, it proved to be a critical factor in the resurgence of farm labor activism in the mid-1960s.

The Revival of Farm Labor Activism in the 1960s

The struggle to unionize California's farm workers entered a new stage in the early 1960s in Delano, California. This grassroots fight, ideologically linked to the civil rights movement, started with the founding of the National Farm Workers' Association (NFWA) by the charismatic César Chávez and his passionate associate and former AWOC member, Dolores Huerta. The two colleagues had acquired valuable leadership skills and experience in connection with the Community Service Organization (CSO), a Mexican-American self-help group that had surfaced in the heightened civic mindedness and civil rights consciousness that developed in southwestern barrios in the aftermath of World War II. When the cautious and urban-based CSO declined to back an initiative to organize farm workers, Chávez and then Huerta left the group to devote themselves to addressing the problems of agricultural laborers. The two intended to spend years building a strong membership base before directly confronting agribusiness.

The 1965 Delano grape strike interrupted their careful planning. Although the Delano strike marks the emergence of the NFWA, it was actually prompted by a predominately Filipino AWOC local, led by Larry Itliong, Ben Guines, and Andy Imutan. A veteran labor activist, Itliong had participated in several strikes during the 1930s and had also served as a vice-president of a UCAPAWA local. When the AWOC leaders asked the NFWA to honor their walkout, the NFWA membership voted to support it. As the protest grew, it became increasingly clear that the NFWA enjoyed stronger backing. Consequently the two organizations merged into the UFWOC (United Farm Workers' Organizing Committee) in 1966.

Even with the two entities joining forces, the combined effort confronted the staggering power and resources of agribusiness. Initial actions had yielded important contracts with winery grape growers, like Schenley and Almaden, and a contract with a major table-grape producer, DiGiorgio, which was soon lost when the company chose to sell its holdings in order to negate the agreement. Although the UFWOC won the enthusiasm of the farm worker population, it was apparent that harvest strikes and picketing would not be able to overcome the financial resources and influence of corporate agriculture. It was evident that the table-grape industry would use all of its clout to resist unionization. Such entrenched power called for a more creative response and a massive demonstration of strength to challenge it. Framing its struggle in the broader context of a social movement and forging its links with civil rights protest and the philosophy of nonviolence espoused by Mahatma Gandhi and Martin Luther King, Jr., the union mobilized to reach a nationwide audience. The UFWOC promoted marches, demonstrations, rallies, masses, and fasts to capture the attention of the public. The union leadership issued urgent pleas to students, church groups, civil rights activists, and women's organizations, as well as to urban unions to support a national grape boycott.

Labor, religious, community, student, civil rights, and political advocates responded by volunteering to staff donated office space to mount an effective boycott. Striking farm worker families also packed up their meager belongings and headed to boycott centers that were springing up across the United States and then spreading to Canada and even Europe. Often traveling as family groups in caravans, the experience transformed agricultural laborers, many of whom experienced the civic and political life of the nation for the first time. The public appeals of farm worker men, women, and children picketing at grocery stores struck a responsive chord with middle-class consumers, especially housewives, who saw these activities as part of the broader struggle enveloping the country. At the same time *La Causa*, the farm worker cause, became an important symbol and expression of Mexican-American civil rights.

The convergence of so many reformist constituencies applied extraordinary pressure on agribusiness, culminating in the historic grape contracts in 1970. The agreements gave union recognition to the UFWOC, raised wages, improved working conditions, provided benefits, regulated pesticide use, and established the union hiring hall to replace the debased labor-contractor system. The UFWOC had little time to relish its achievement before it faced a strike by restive lettuce workers in northern California. The conflict became increasingly violent with the intrusion of the International Brotherhood of Teamsters (IBT) into the dispute, a strategy that growers had also employed in the UFWOC's early years. The teamsters negotiated "sweetheart" contracts on more favorable terms with the vegetable industry. Table-grape growers also saw this tactic as a means to undermine the union, called the United Farm Workers of America (UFW), when it became a chartered affiliate of the AFL-CIO in 1972, whose 3-year contracts were due for renewal in 1973. Gallo winery also balked at renewing its contract. A violent confrontation ensued as assaults, mass arrests, and deaths filled newspapers and TV reports. The union intensified the boycott to compel a solution to the turmoil. The upheaval prompted state government to mediate a settlement between growers and the UFW. Under the sponsorship of Governor Jerry Brown, the Agricultural Labor Relations Act (ALRA) became law in 1975.

The passage of the ALRA introduced a new era in labor relations in agriculture. Similar to NLRB founded 40 years earlier, the Agricultural Labor Relations Board (ALRB) was established to supervise secret-ballot elections, to be held quickly, and to adjudicate violations of the law, grievances, and unfair labor practices. The union focused its resources on organizing workers. After 5 months of operation, the ALRB had conducted 423 elections involving the UFW, the teamsters, as well as the no-union option, and nearly 1,000 charges of unfair labor practices. Although the UFW was successful in winning a majority of the campaigns, growers frequently used the legal process to hold up certifications of the UFW as the collective bargaining agent for their employees. These delays led to innumerable frustrations on the part of the union and workers whose elections were left unresolved, sometimes for years. Furthermore as part of the compromise legislation, the UFW had given up its most effective tool against corporate agriculture, the secondary boycott.

While the ALRA did reduce the violence in the fields, it also hindered organizing efforts. Furthermore the UFW faced escalating internal discord regarding strategy and criticism of Chávez's rigid leadership style. The presidential election of Ronald Reagan in 1980s and later the governorship of George Deukmejian in California, both strong proponents of corporate agriculture, signaled a shift toward a more antilabor stance. In this unfavorable environment, the union looked to direct mail, computer-generated mailings, and the establishment of a radio station to restore its declining membership and sagging fortunes.

The Post-Chávez Era

The UFW suffered a startling blow with the sudden death of Chávez in 1993, during his return to San Luiz, Arizona, to testify in a legal suit against growers. The unexpected demise of Chávez at age 66 raised questions regarding the survival of the union after 30 years of his leadership. Contrary to fears of its collapse, Chávez's passing revitalized the union, since his son-in-law, Arturo Rodríguez, succeeded him. A native of Texas, his father was a sheet metal worker and his mother a schoolteacher. The college-educated Rodríguez met and married Linda "Lu" Chávez while organizing the boycott in Detroit, Michigan. After assuming the presidency, he initiated

an effort to reverse the decline in union membership. On the first anniversary of Chávez's death, he coordinated a march to Sacramento commemorating the momentous 1966 pilgrimage led by the revered leader. He also launched an aggressive legislative and organizing campaign to unionize farm workers. His efforts resulted in over 25 contracts for workers in mushroom, rose, citrus, strawberry, wine grape, and vegetable companies. The contracts covered workers in California and also in Washington State and Florida. Under his leadership, the UFW continued to lobby against a renewed guest worker program and for amnesty for undocumented farm workers and their families. Although having less membership than its peak achieved in the 1970s, the UFW currently claims over 25,000 members.

Despite its hopeful beginning, in the view of some critics, the UFW has not fulfilled its earlier promise. The unionization of farm workers in the twenty-first century has not found a receptive audience in the conservative era of Republican President George W. Bush. The ALRA continues to impede field organizing. And legislative gains are achieved by persistent and drawn out compromises that do not contain the drama of a strike or boycott. While falling short of the highest expectations, the UFW has won important benefits for agricultural workers, including wages in 2000 that ranged from $7 to $8, well above the federal and state minimum wages of $5.15 and $5.75, respectively. The activism of the UFW forced growers to maintain higher wages as a means to forestall union organizing. While improvements in negotiating contracts, obtaining better working conditions, adequate health insurance, and the enforcement of existing laws require attention, the UFW has defied the odds and outlasted all other previous unionizing efforts in agriculture.

MARGARET ROSE

References and Further Reading

Dunne, John Gregory. *Delano: The Story of the California Grape Strike.* New York: Farrar, Straus & Giroux, 1967.
Griswold del Castillo, Richard, and Richard Garcia. *Cesar Chavez: A Triumph of Spirit.* Norman: University of Oklahoma Press, 1995.
Jenkins, J. Craig. *The Politics of Insurgency: The Farm Workers Movement in the 1960s.* New York: Columbia University Press, 1985.
Levy, Jacques. *Cesar Chavez: Autobiography of La Causa.* New York: W. W. Norton & Company, Inc, 1975.
London, Joan, and Henry Anderson. *So Shall Ye Reap: The Story of Cesar Chavez and the Farm Workers' Movement.* New York: Thomas Y. Crowell Company, 1970.
Majka, Linda C., and Theo J. Majka. *Farm Workers, Agribusiness, and the State.* Philadelphia, PA: Temple University Press, 1982.

Matthiessen, Peter. *Sal Si Puedes: Cesar Chavez and the New American Revolution*. New York: Random House, 1969.

Meister, Dick, and Anne Loftis. *A Long Time Coming: The Struggle to Unionize America's Farm Workers*. New York: MacMillan, 1977.

Rose, Margaret. "'From the Fields to the Picket Line: Huelga Women and the Boycott,' 1965–1975." *Labor History* 31, 3 (summer 1990): 271–293.

——. "Gender and Civic Activism in Mexican American Barrios: The Community Service Organization, 1947–1962." In *Not June Cleaver: Women and Gender in Post-war America, 1945–1960*, edited by Joanne Meyerowitz. Philadelphia, PA: Temple University Press, 1994.

——. "'Woman Power Will Stop Those Grapes': Chicana Organizers and Middle-Class Female Supporters in the Farm Workers' Grape Boycott in Philadelphia, 1969–1970." *Journal of Women's History* 7, 4 (winter 1995): 6–36.

——. "Dolores Huerta: The United Farm Workers Union." In *The Human Tradition in American Labor History*, edited by Eric Arnesen. Wilmington, DE: Scholarly Resources Inc., 2004.

Taylor, Ronald B. *Chavez and the Farm Workers: A Study in the Acquisition and Use of Power*. Boston, MA: Beacon Press, 1975.

Cases and Statutes Cited

Agricultural Labor Relations Act
Chinese Exclusion Act
Immigration Act
National Labor Relations Act

See also **Agricultural Labor Relations Act (1975); Cannery and Agricultural Workers' Industrial Union; Chávez, César Estrada; Delano Grape Strike; Huerta, Dolores C.**

UNITED FOOD AND COMMERCIAL WORKERS' UNION

With just under 1.4 million members, the United Food and Commercial Workers' Union (UFCW) is the largest private-sector union in the American labor movement and the nation's third largest labor organization. Formed in 1979 by the merger of the Retail Clerks' International Union and the Amalgamated Meatcutters and Butcher Workmen, the UFCW's experience reflects many of the complex challenges that have confronted the labor movement over the last three decades.

The merger of the retail clerks (735,000 members) and the meatcutters (500,000 members) occurred at a time of increasing union consolidation, with the newly formed UFCW representing the largest merger to date in American labor history. The merger was prompted by growing consolidation in the meatpacking industry that had diminished the ranks of the meatcutters and undercut the union's effectiveness. These developments had led the United Packinghouse Workers of America

(UPWA), a militant Congress of Industrial Organizations (CIO) union that had organized most of the nation's packinghouse workers during the 1930s, to merge with the meatcutters just a decade earlier, while the retail clerks had also absorbed several smaller unions prior to the merger. The merger was regarded as a way to unify two unions that often had common employers, were facing industries bent on consolidation and reducing union bargaining power, and had frequently battled each other in disputes over jurisdiction. William Wynn, the retail clerks' leader, assumed the presidency of the new union, which also included workers employed in health care and manufacturing and subsequently added smaller unions that represented barbers and beauticians, insurance agents, chemical workers, and retail employees.

Although the differences can be exaggerated, the merger of the retail clerks and the meatcutters brought together two distinctive union cultures. The clerks were very much within the craft tradition of American unionism, negotiated mostly on a local market basis, and often tangled with other unions over jurisdiction. Their leadership structure was largely staff driven and not oriented toward extensive rank-and-file involvement. In contrast, the meatcutters union, and especially its packinghouse division, were more steeped in an industrial union approach. They bargained master and pattern agreements and coordinated centralized bargaining with rank-and-file participation on both the shopfloor and in strike actions. As the larger partner in the merged union, the clerks occupied the new organization's major leadership positions, and their approach to union governance dominated.

The new union was quickly tested amid a determined employer offensive to gain concessions in bargaining during the 1980s. In the wake of the breaking of the air traffic controllers' strike in 1981, a steep recession, and rising competitive pressures, many private-sector unions faced demands for contract concessions from their employers. The UFCW was one of the unions most severely affected by these developments, and it was directly challenged by employers in the meatpacking industry. Since the end of World War II, meatpacking had largely been governed by master and pattern agreements encompassing most of the industry's major employers, and workers enjoyed wages and benefits that were superior to those of most manufacturing workers. By the early 1980s, however, the meatpacking industry was reeling from a series of structural changes that threatened to undermine the union's ability to maintain the standards it had fashioned over three decades of collective bargaining.

Employers began to specialize by product and introduced technological changes that required less skill and fewer workers. New entrants to the industry were determined to cut labor costs and operate non-union whenever possible. Due to consolidations and mergers, the industry began to fragment, with new plants dispersing into rural areas that lacked union traditions and were harder to organize. As a result meatpacking employers insisted on wage and benefit freezes, threatened to close plants, and attempted to free themselves from master and pattern agreements. In a strategy that it later acknowledged amounted to one of "controlled retreat," the UFCW leadership often agreed to concessions in an effort to keep plants open, stabilize the industry, and retain national and regional agreements. However many workers, especially those from old UPWA locals, began to question this strategy as demands for concessions from meat packers mounted. This disagreement exploded on the national stage in 1985 during a bitter strike at the Hormel Company in Austin, Minnesota.

The strike waged at Hormel by UFCW Local P-9 became one of the defining labor events of the 1980s. Hormel, which had built a new plant in Austin in 1982, sought major wage, benefit, and contract language concessions from the union. Led by its militant new president, Jim Guyette, Local P-9 rejected this offer, one that had been accepted by other UFCW locals representing Hormel workers. Instead the union hired Ray Rogers, the labor strategist whose corporate campaign had pressured textile giant J. P. Stevens to grant union recognition, to help it launch a multipronged attack on Hormel. The corporate campaign against a bank that had connections to Hormel had a limited effect however, and P-9 went on strike in August 1985. Although the UFCW's national leadership approved the strike, it questioned the efficacy of the corporate campaign and accused P-9 of undermining unity within the union's packing-house division by going it alone.

The strike not only divided the UFCW but also prompted fierce debate within the broader union movement. Local P-9 succeeded in mobilizing its membership, actively sought and received substantial support from unions and community organizations throughout the country, and sent out roving pickets who were able to persuade some workers at other Hormel plants not to go to work. Meanwhile the American Federation of Labor-CIO top leadership sided with the UFCW, while union President William Wynn and P-9's Jim Guyette, along with others from both sides, engaged in a vitriolic public debate about the local union's strategy and its implications. In P-9's view it was offering an alternative approach for the entire labor movement that had the potential to counter concession bargaining by widening the field of battle and making employers pay a social and economic price for their actions. The UFCW leadership saw P-9's actions as badly timed amid a hostile political and economic climate and feared that the corporate campaign and strike would nullify efforts to keep national bargaining intact. After striking workers were arrested at Hormel's headquarters in March 1986, the UFCW's leadership placed P-9 under trusteeship, removed its leaders, and settled the strike largely along the lines of the company's prestrike offer. Two decades later the Hormel strike continues to generate controversy in labor circles, especially following what many observers cite as an ongoing decline in wages and working conditions in meatpacking and the UFCW's uphill struggle to re-establish its bargaining power in the industry.

The UFCW has also faced similar challenges in the supermarket industry where the bulk of its membership resides. During the 1980s and beyond, the industry has experienced numerous mergers and consolidations, penetration of the market by foreign-owned firms, and the rise of powerful new competitors in the form of superstores and discount warehouse clubs. Seeking to control labor costs and counter rising nonunion competition, supermarkets pressed during the 1980s for two-tier wage and benefit arrangements and gained reluctant union approval for these arrangements in many cases. The UFCW still retains bargaining power in many urban markets, but the supermarket labor force has bifurcated into a small group of full-time workers with good wages and benefits and a much larger cohort of part-time workers whose circumstances are less favorable and whose ranks turn over frequently. The looming presence of Wal-Mart, which as the nation's largest corporation is rapidly expanding its retail grocery capabilities while staunchly resisting unionization, has exerted a profound influence on collective bargaining and has emerged as the UFCW's most formidable adversary.

These circumstances have accelerated over the last 5 years and resulted in some major UFCW supermarket strikes. The most notable was a 2003 work stoppage involving nearly 70,000 workers in southern California that was the longest in the union's history. Citing Wal-Mart's plans to build superstores in the region, Safeway, Kroger, and Albertson's sought major concessions on health care and establishment of a two-tier wage and benefit structure for new employees, steps the companies claimed were needed to enhance their future competitiveness. After the union struck Safeway, the employers locked the remaining workers out. The union established spirited picket lines that attracted considerable public support and was able to affect Safeway in particular by pressuring the company through sympathetic pension fund holders. The strike did succeed in preserving health care benefits for incumbent workers, but the union ended up accepting a two-tier system for new hires. The strike garnered widespread public attention, highlighted Wal-Mart's profound influence on the collective-bargaining process, and underscored how health care has emerged as the defining labor-management issue of early twenty-first century labor relations. Yet the strike was widely regarded as a setback for the UFCW, and some critics charged that the union's tactics lacked the scale and aggressiveness needed to defeat a group of determined employers. Perhaps not coincidentally Douglas Dority, who had succeeded William Wynn as the union's president in 1994, announced his retirement just days after the walkout's conclusion.

The union has had some notable successes however both in organizing new workers and waging high-profile campaigns against some of the nation's most prominent corporations. Against considerable odds the UFCW has made consistent efforts to organize in the South over the last three decades, especially in the poultry- and fish-processing industries. It won an especially significant victory in 1986 by organizing Delta Pride, a Mississippi-based facility that ranked as the largest catfish-processing plant in the world and employed a workforce of mostly African-American women. In the nation's expanding poultry industry that is dominated by such large corporations as Tyson Foods and Perdue Farms, the union has engaged in a broad outreach strategy by supporting "poultry justice alliances" that bring together workers, farmers, environmental, and community organizations in seeking more responsible corporate behavior. This growing commitment to alliances with community organizations resulted in an important triumph in 2002, when the UFCW joined with an Omaha, Nebraska, community affiliate of the Industrial Areas Foundation to organize workers at a ConAgra meatpacking plant, many of whom were Latino.

These initiatives recognize the growing diversity of the workforce in the UFCW's key jurisdictions and the need to mobilize broadly based community support on behalf of workers who often perform dangerous jobs under trying conditions. The union has focused on several issues in this regard. It has been a leading advocate for better safety and health conditions for workers in industries like meatpacking and chicken processing where increased line speeds have often led to high injury and accident rates. The union has also pursued an aggressive legal strategy in filing or supporting litigation charging such companies as Perdue and Tyson with wage and hour violations. These cases have resulted in settlements totaling millions, providing direct benefits to workers while spotlighting employment policies that subvert the law.

The UFCW's most critical struggle however is with Wal-Mart, the world's largest corporation, whose power and influence have profoundly affected economic, labor, and community relations on a global basis. Since the late 1990s, the UFCW has devoted increasing attention to Wal-Mart, aligning itself with community efforts to halt its expansion, publicizing the company's relentless and often illegal opposition to unions, and attempting to organize Wal-Mart workers. These efforts have yielded limited results however. The union's first organizing success, an election victory in 2000 at the meat department of a Texas Wal-Mart, was blunted by the company's decision to close the department a week after the vote. And in 2004, a victory at a Wal-Mart in Quebec resulted in the company's announcement to shut down the store a year later.

Under its new president Joe Hanson, a meatcutter who replaced Douglas Dority in 2004, the UFCW is reshaping its Wal-Mart strategy. In 2005, Hanson and the UFCW joined other major unions in leaving the AFL-CIO and forming Change to Win, a new labor federation that has pledged to commit millions to organizing and providing the UFCW with both resources and technical assistance to bolster its efforts at Wal-Mart. Whether or not this alliance with some of the labor movement's most visionary unions will prompt broader changes in the UFCW's organizational culture remains to be seen. It is certain however that the future prospects of both the UFCW and the American labor movement will hinge on the union's ability to build a social movement capable of organizing at Wal-Mart and restoring private-sector unionism to a place of power and authority in U.S. social and economic affairs.

ROBERT BUSSEL

References and Further Reading

Adams, Larry T. "Labor Organization Mergers 1979–84: Adapting to Change." *Monthly Labor Review* (Sept. 1984): 21–27.

Harrington, Michael. *The Retail Clerks*. New York: John Wiley, 1962.

Horowitz, Roger. *"Negro and White, Unite and Fight!" A Social History of Industrial Unionism in Meatpacking, 1930–90*. Urbana: University of Illinois Press, 1997.

Kaufman, Phil R. "Consolidation in Food Retailing: Prospects for Consumers and Grocery Suppliers." *Economic Research Service/USDA, Agricultural Outlook* (Aug. 2000): 18–22.

Manheim, Jarol B. *The Death of a Thousand Cuts: Corporate Campaigns and the Contemporary Attack on the Corporation*. Mahwah, NJ: Lawrence Erlbaum Associates, Publishers, 2001.

Milkman, Ruth. "Supermarket Workers' Union Fails in California." http://reclaim_democracy.org/articles_2004/supermarket_union_failur... (2004).

Perry, Charles R., and Delwyn H. Kegley. *Disintegration and Change: Labor Relations in the Meatpacking Industry*. Philadelphia: University of Pennsylvania, Industrial Research Unit, 1989.

Schleuning, Neala J. *Women, Community, and the Hormel Strike of 1985–86*. Westport, CT: Greenwood Press, 1994.

UNITED GOVERNMENT EMPLOYEES

The United Government Employees (UGE), an independent union founded in 1936, fought for a variety of causes on behalf of its African-American members who were employees of the federal government and District of Columbia. It emerged during a period of active union organizing among African-Americans by such groups as the Congress of Industrial Organizations (CIO), and the Negro Labor Committee, formed by African-American Socialist Frank Crosswaith and others in 1935. The UGE competed for membership with the United Federal Workers of America-CIO, which also encouraged African-Americans to join, unlike its American Federation of Labor counterpart, the American Federation of Government Employees (AFGE). The AFGE locals expressed apathy, and often hostility, toward black membership during the 1930s and 1940s. Although UGE's members represented workers in all occupations, it had a strong following among employees in the lowest government grades. One of its first initiatives was an effort to increase the pay of various low-wage workers, including custodians. Within a year it succeeded in raising their salaries from a minimum of $1,080 per year to $1,200. In 1938, it supported a minimum wage of $1,500 a year for all federal and district workers, along with automatic promotions, extension of the merit system to employees in New Deal emergency agencies, an appeal board for civil servants, equal pay for equal work regardless of creed, color, or race, and the appointment of African-American administrators to the Civil Service Commission as well as to the executive office of the president. In 1939, the union lobbied President Franklin D. Roosevelt to appoint an African-American to the Supreme Court.

The latter objectives reflected the priorities of UGE's founder and president, Edgar G. Brown, who was a Negro affairs specialist in the Civilian Conservation Corps. Brown, a Chicago native and World War I veteran, was the only president of UGE and his personality guided the organization. Flamboyant and outspoken, Brown avidly supported the New Deal and President Roosevelt during the 1930s. He became part of the black cabinet, a group of African-American administrators in the Roosevelt administration who met regularly and was very active in Chicago politics, unsuccessfully running for numerous local and national offices from the 1920s to the early 1950s.

Brown and his union focused on the need of the federal government to hire more African-Americans in prominent positions, and to raise the pay and improve the working conditions of the lowest paid federal workers, many of whom were African-American. It also saw its mission as helping other poorly paid workers. For instance the union advocated training for domestic workers, taking 31 women from federal relief roles and teaching them home economics and domestic management in an effort to elevate their marketable skills. Intense lobbying by UGE President Brown resulted in a provision dedicating money to this program as part of a $3.7 billion work-relief measure passed in 1938. The UGE also pushed for nondiscrimination policies and put its weight behind the establishment of a training program for African-American pilots during World War II.

Like other general government unions, such as the National Federation of Federal Employees (NFFE) and AFGE, UGE did not favor use of the strike. It had significant membership among Works Progress Administration (WPA) workers, but when WPA workers struck in 1939, UGE leaders refused to sanction the work stoppage. Instead UGE President Brown called a national conference in Chicago for all WPA workers to discuss pay scales, especially regional wage differences, hours, as well as race and political discrimination within the agency. It likewise demonstrated no interest in supporting collective bargaining, preferring, again like NFFE and AFGE, petitions and lobbying Congress. Indeed as president of UGE, Brown testified in front of Congress over 75 times on issues ranging from police protection in DC to wage increases to poll taxes from 1937–1944.

Over 300 people attended UGE's first anniversary ball held in November 1937, and by the time of its 1940 convention, UGE claimed 30,000 members in over 30 states. In 1940, the union called for all-black military divisions, the construction of ships for all-black crews, training programs for black pilots, and black advisers in various agencies, including the War Department and Civil Service Commission. By 1944, however, the union seems to have folded, perhaps because of lack of money and/or membership support. The UGE's infrastructure did not appear to be very strong, and it never provided much evidence that it had as many members as claimed. Like the National Negro Council, of which Brown was also president, UGE largely seemed to be Brown's organization.

Brown and UGE's support for President Roosevelt defined much of its early work, but over time Brown's political allegiances shifted. In April 1940, Brown attended a CIO conference as a UGE representative. There he found himself booed for defending President Roosevelt's foreign policies and civil rights track record. By 1943, however, he expressed frustration at what he perceived to be President Roosevelt's failure to live up to his promise of racial equality. Brown then threw his support to the Republican party. Although a number of factors contributed to this shift in political loyalty, the failure by Congress to provide a nondiscrimination clause in an economic stabilization measure and President Roosevelt's appointment of James Byrnes as director of the Economic Stabilization Board seemed to provide the impetus for Brown and UGE's break with the Democratic party. Thereafter Brown became a Republican activist, campaigning for Republican candidates and running himself as a Republican candidate for Chicago alderman. Curiously in 1941, former UGE organizer Andrew Wicketts established a new organization for black workers, the National Employees' and Tenants' Union, which was fiercely loyal to President Roosevelt. There is no evidence however that Wicketts built this union to counter Brown and UGE's increasing criticism of the Roosevelt administration. During the short life of UGE, Brown remained focused on UGE's mission to represent federal workers and promote racial equality within the civil service. The UGE succeeded in raising awareness of race discrimination in the federal government and publicizing the plight of many of the civil service's most poorly compensated workers.

MARGARET C. RUNG

References and Further Reading

Hayes, Laurence J. W. *The Negro Federal Government Worker: A Study of His Classification and Status in the District of Columbia, 1883–1938.* Vol. 3. Washington, DC: Howard University Studies in the Social Sciences, 1941.

King, Desmond. *Separate and Unequal: Black Americans and the U.S. Federal Government.* Oxford, UK: Clarendon Press, 1995.

Krislov, Samuel. *The Negro in Federal Employment: The Quest for Equal Opportunity.* Minneapolis: University of Minnesota Press, 1967.

See also **Randolph, A. Philip; United Public Workers of America/United Federal Workers of America**

UNITED HATTERS, CAP, AND MILLINERY WORKERS' INTERNATIONAL UNION

The United Hatters, Cap, and Millinery Workers' International Union (UHCMW) was founded in 1934 when the two leading international unions in the headwear industry amalgamated. These two unions, the craft-oriented United Hatters of North America (UHNA) and the largely Jewish and socialist Cloth Hat, Cap, and Millinery Workers' International Union (CHCMW), had been engaged in jurisdictional warfare on and off for almost two decades. The newly formed UHCMW, led by right-wing Socialist Max Zaritsky, would come to wield a disproportionate degree of influence within the American labor movement considering the union's relatively small size. Zaritsky would play an important role in the founding of the Congress of Industrial Organizations (CIO) (although he and his union never left the American Federation of Labor [AFL]), and the UHCMW was frequently cited in the 1940s and 1950s as a model of responsible, anti-Communist, progressive unionism.

The United Hatters of North America was founded in 1896, when the national unions of Hat Makers and Hat Finishers amalgamated. The hatters drew on a long tradition of craft unionism, stretching back to the earliest hatters' unions in the 1820s. The hatters engaged in two major campaigns, the first in opposition to prison labor and the second in favor of the right of unions to encourage the boycotting of nonunion goods. In the late nineteenth century, prison labor became an increasing threat to a number of trades, including that of hat makers. Because of the low wages paid to convicts, many hat makers came to rely on prison labor over traditional sources of labor, leading to widespread unemployment among hatters. The hatters' unions responded with both economic and political measures, calling for boycotts on hat manufacturers who used convict labor and running their own candidates for political office throughout New England on an antiprison labor platform. These campaigns were largely successful, and by the mid-1880s, many states had passed laws banning convicts from making hats.

The hatters' campaign in favor of the boycott however was a resounding failure. In 1902, a local of the UHNA went on strike at the D. E. Loewe & Co. plant in Danbury, Connecticut. The hatters called for a boycott on Loewe's products, and many unions from around the country joined the effort. Then in 1903, Loewe sued the hatters under the Sherman Anti-Trust Act, arguing that the call for a boycott was a conspiracy to restrain trade. The Danbury hatters' case wound through the courts for the next 12 years until it was finally settled by the Supreme Court in 1915. The Court found in favor of Loewe, awarding over 200,000 dollars in damages to the hat manufacturer. This decision placed severe limits on the activities of unions until labor unions were explicitly exempted from the Sherman Anti-Trust Act by the Norris-LaGuardia Act in 1932.

The Cloth Hat, Cap and Millinery Workers are particularly interesting because despite their long history of socialist activism, they proved remarkably resistant to a series of takeover attempts by left-wing organizations. Among the radical Jewish immigrants who worked in the cloth cap industry, the Marxist ideas of German radical Daniel DeLeon were quite popular, but the leadership of the CHCMW repeatedly opposed giving DeLeon and his followers control over the union. This resistance to left-wing leadership re-emerged after the founding of the Industrial Workers of the World (IWW). Initially friendly to the idea of the Wobblies, the CHCMW quickly turned against the radical union and was even forced to defend itself against an IWW dual union. Most importantly however was the staunch anti-Communist leadership of the self-avowed Socialist Max Zaritsky. Zaritsky, who served as a leader in both the CHCMW and the UHCMW from 1911 until his retirement in 1950, violently opposed efforts by Communists to take control of union locals in the hat industry. This anti-Communist orientation would continue even after Zaritsky's retirement, and the UHCMW would go on to take such rather extreme anti-Communist positions as opposing the visit of Soviet Premiere Nikita Khrushchev to the United States in 1959.

The decline of the U.S. hat industry during the 1960s caused a dramatic decline in the UHCMW's membership. By the 1980s, the union had less than one-fifth of its membership during the 1940s, and in 1983, the UHCMW joined the Amalgamated Clothing and Textile Workers' Union, which has been succeeded by UNITE!-HERE.

AARON MAX BERKOWITZ

References and Further Reading

Bensman, David. *The Practice of Solidarity: American Hat Finishers in the Nineteenth Century*. Urbana: University of Illinois Press, 1985.

Green, Charles H. *The Headwear Workers: A Century of Trade Unionism*. New York: United Hatters', Cap and Millinery Workers' International Union, 1944.

Robinson, David B. *Spotlight on a Union: The Story of the United Hatters', Cap and Millinery Workers' Union*. New York: Dial Press, 1948.

Cases and Statutes Cited

Norris-LaGuardia Act
Sherman Anti-Trust Act

UNITED MINE WORKERS OF AMERICA

Throughout much of its long history, the United Mine Workers of America (UMWA) has been one of the largest and most powerful labor unions in the United States and Canada. The union was among the first to work actively against racism among its members, organize its workers without regard to their craft, and use the legal system and politics to defend its gains in the workplace. The UMWA achieved such significant advancements for mineworkers as the 8-hour day (1898), collective-bargaining rights (1933), health and retirement benefits (1946), and federal coal mine safety and health standards (1969). The union produced many of labor's most significant leaders: John Mitchell, John L. Lewis, Mary "Mother" Jones, William B. Wilson, John Brophy, William Green, Philip Murray, and Richard Trumka.

In the 1930s, the UMWA under the leadership of Lewis led the campaign to organize industrial workers who had been neglected by the craft-based American Federation of Labor (AFL). Lewis and other leaders created the Congress of Industrial Organizations (CIO) as an alternative to the AFL. The CIO quickly organized thousands of workers in the auto, steel, rubber, chemical, and other industries. Therefore the beginnings of many major unions and their leaders have their roots in the UMWA.

In the nineteenth century coal became the major fuel used in homes and much of American industry. Because of the abundance of coal in many sections of the country, there has been an overproduction throughout much of the industry's history. This overproduction has led to periodic economic downturns during which workers lost their jobs, were required to work in unhealthy conditions, and were forced to take pay cuts.

During the early years of the coal industry, miners had a great deal of autonomy in hours worked and amount of coal mined. That autonomy was an issue between miners and mine owners from 1865–1925. Attempts to curtail miner independence as well as disagreements over hours of work and wages were a major impetus for the founding of unions. Coal miners lived in isolated communities where they were at the mercy of mine owners. They were forced to live in company houses, buy goods at company stores, were paid in script rather than cash, and were often cheated in how their coal was weighed. These isolated workers quickly realized that they had to unite for their protection. In order to improve their work conditions, living conditions, and wages, miners created unions. Miners organized first at the local level, then into regional organizations, and finally in large national organizations like the UMWA. Early unions included the American Miners' Association (1861), Workingmen's Benevolent Association (1868), Miners' National Association (1873), the Amalgamated Association of Miners of the United States (1883), and the National Federation of Miners and Mine Workers (1885).

The UMWA was founded in Columbus, Ohio, in January of 1890 through the merger of the National Progressive Union of Miners and Mine Laborers (organized 1888) and National Trade Assembly No. 135 of the Knights of Labor. John B. Rae, a leader of the knights from Pennsylvania was elected as the first president. Rae served for 1 year and was succeeded by John McBride, who served for 2 years before becoming president of the AFL. The union established the *United Mine Workers' Journal* as a vehicle to unify and educate miners and affiliated with the AFL.

The union's constitution barred discrimination based on race, religion, or national origin because the miners realized the destructive nature of those practices and the common divisive practice used by mine owners of playing ethnic groups off against each other. The founders of the union believed that miners and employers could work together to resolve disputes at the bargaining table. The Declaration of Principles adopted by the UMWA's first convention stated that disagreements should be settled by all means short of a strike. The union was forced to resort to strikes in 1894 and 1897 when economic conditions led to dramatic wage cuts and the owners were unwilling to bargain.

Early in its existence the UMWA adopted the tactic of working with state and national governments to secure safety laws and other codes to improve the lives of miners. Many miners also became active in politics. The UMWA worked through existing political parties and refused to support a Labor party like the one in England.

Throughout most of the nineteenth century, a majority of miners were immigrants from the British Isles who had been coal diggers before they came to the United States. By the time the UMWA was founded, there was an increasing number of workers from southern and Eastern Europe in the states near the Atlantic seaboard and a large percentage of the miners in southern states were African-Americans. As time passed members of other nationalities entered

the mines: Workers from Germany, France, Belgium, Greece, Finland, and Mexico composed significant segments of miners. The immigrants brought with them different religions and styles of life, and they lived in communities that were divided by race and religion. African-Americans in particular were often segregated from other workers. The coal operators attempted to exploit ethnic and racial differences, so union leaders worked to achieve solidarity among all groups as a means of challenging the operators. The union was not always successful in its efforts, but it did attempt to bring all miners into the union on an equal basis. Eventually members of these individual groups moved into leadership positions in the union.

The integration of African-American miners into the union was more difficult because of prevailing social conditions in the country and because African-American miners were often used as strike-breakers by the operators. African-American miners faced particularly difficult situations in the South where they were often given the most dangerous and lowest paid jobs and were denied leadership positions. In some cases African-American miners created their own locals that were separate from the white workers. Although the union tried to create solidarity among all workers, the operators were able to exploit prevailing social conditions in order to defeat the union during strikes in the early 1900s. African-American miners were eventually integrated into the union, and many assumed leadership positions at the local and national levels.

The union worked to achieve a common wage for all miners. Its actions led to the creation in 1886 of the Interstate Joint Agreement, which set wage rates for the Central Competitive Field, consisting of Indiana, Illinois, Ohio, and western Pennsylvania. The agreement broke down from 1889–1898 because of rivalries between the Knights of Labor and the National Federation of Miners and Mine Laborers. The UMWA re-instituted the agreement in 1898, and it was renewed each year until the 1920s. That agreement required all miners to honor the contract. Those who did not were eliminated from the union. This practice led to a belief in the sanctity of the contract and ensured that all union locals and districts were under the control of the International Executive Board (IEB). The need for unity among workers in mines led to the Scranton Declaration of December 1901, in which the AFL agreed to allow the UMWA to organize all workers in and around the mines no matter their job. The AFL unions were organized based on the worker's craft, so the UMWA was the only major union in the federation that was allowed to practice this form of industrial unionism.

Early presidents served brief terms before accepting other positions. Mitchell was the first president to serve for an extended period of time. Mitchell became president in 1898 when he was only 28 years old and successfully led the miners until 1909. He also was the first strong leader who was deeply revered by the miners during his term and after he left the presidency. Mitchell oversaw the expansion of the union across the United States and into Canada, often overcoming difficult local situations to establish the organization. One of the organizers he relied on was the woman known as the miners' angel, Mary Harris "Mother" Jones, one of the most colorful individuals in the history of labor. He also developed a system of national collective bargaining that became a model for many industries, and under his leadership the union won the 8-hour day.

Although the bituminous miners were organized under the Central Competitive Field, the anthracite workers in Pennsylvania remained unorganized although a series of unsuccessful organizing efforts had been led by a miner named John Fahy. These efforts were unsuccessful because operators were unwilling to deal with unions. The poor working conditions led to a series of strikes from 1897–1902 during which the UMWA organized the workers. The Lattimer Massacre of striking miners in 1897 also helped build solidarity among miners because they shared anger and frustration because of actions of the coal companies. Those feelings inspired miners to join the union as a vehicle to oppose the companies. Strikes in 1900 led to an increase in wages, but not a recognition of the union. They were successful in building solidarity among miners that was crucial in later strikes. Continued frustration led to a walkout in 1902 that became one of the most famous in American history. At the end of a 5.5-month strike, mine owners under strong pressure from President Theodore Roosevelt accepted arbitration from a presidential commission. The commission raised wages and reduced the number of hours of work, but it did not recognize the union. The mine owners did however negotiate with the UMWA, and most workers became members. Mitchell led the union during the strike, and the victory only enhanced his reputation with the miners. In 1920 the anthracite operators officially recognized the UMWA as a bargaining body.

From 1908, when Mitchell stepped down as leader, to World War I the union faced divisive internal disputes and vicious battles with operators. Some of the fights with mine owners led to violence, such as the Ludlow Massacre in Colorado in 1914. The union also had to deal with serious health and safety issues caused by new mining methods and technologies. Because of the internal and external pressures, the union did not grow until World War I when the need for coal dramatically increased.

In 1919, Lewis became acting president of the union. He immediately found himself involved in a confrontation with the federal government. The union had made a no-strike pledge during World War I, but strikes in 1919–1920 led to the creation of the Bituminous Coal Commission by the federal government. That body awarded the miners a significant wage increase. Many miners were not happy with the raise, but Lewis called off the strike rather than lose a fight with the government. Lewis learned that the government had the power to either help or hinder the union in its goals, a lesson that he remembered in future dealings with political leaders. He also learned that a militant rank-and-file membership could help a union leader in his fight with politicians and leaders of the coal industry. The difficult problem however was to channel the workers' militancy in the desired direction. In 1920, Lewis was elected president and held the position until he retired in 1960.

Once he became president, Lewis worked to consolidate all power in the national office. He eliminated strong opponents from the union and appointed his supporters to the presidency of the union's districts in violation of the union constitution. In 1926, John Brophy challenged Lewis for the presidency. In a highly questionable election, Lewis defeated Brophy. He was never again seriously challenged, and he so dominated the union that there was no strong leader to replace him when he retired.

During the 1920s and 1930s, Lewis faced a difficult situation in keeping the union intact. An immense surplus of capacity and declining demand for coal led to layoffs among miners and forced the union to accept wage reductions. Lewis affiliated himself with Secretary of Commerce Herbert Hoover in an attempt to gain support from the federal government to aid the mineworkers. He supported Hoover's election to the presidency in 1928 and his bid for re-election in 1932.

With the election of Franklin D. Roosevelt in 1932, Lewis sensed an opportunity to re-energize the union. He and his advisers were largely responsible for the addition of Section 7a to the 1933 National Industrial Recovery Act (NIRA) that gave unions the right to organize. The union organized virtually all miners in the country within a year. The UMWA became the largest and wealthiest union in the country.

Lewis began calling on the leadership of the AFL to organize industrial workers in mass-producing industries. He realized that those workers were ready for organization and that their large numbers would greatly enhance the power of labor in the country. The AFL leadership balked, so Lewis and the other union leaders met in 1935 and formed the organization that became the CIO, with Lewis as its president. In 1937, the CIO was expelled from the AFL. In 1937, the CIO conducted a series of successful massive organizing efforts. Many of the organizers and most of the money came from the UMWA.

Lewis backed Roosevelt's re-election in 1936 but eventually broke with him for a variety of reasons, including a disagreement over foreign policy, and supported Wendell Willkie in 1940. Lewis publicly announced that he would resign as head of the CIO if Roosevelt were re-elected. After the election he resigned and was replaced by Murray, the president of the United Steelworkers, and a former UMWA vice-president. In 1942, the UMWA withdrew from the CIO.

The UMWA refused to take a no-strike pledge during World War I or World War II. A strike in 1943 forced the government to seize and operate the mines. After World War II, Lewis led a series of strikes that cost the union large amounts of money because it violated an injunction barring the union from striking. In 1946, the UMWA rejoined the AFL but left in 1947.

In 1946, Lewis created a national emergency that again caused the federal government to seize the mines. Lewis forced the government to create the UMWA Welfare and Retirement Fund, a benefit that coal companies refused to grant. The government also implemented safety codes that the operators had to accept once control of the mines was returned to them. A strike in 1950 led to a significant change that created a trust fund that administered the welfare and retirement funds. In the past the funds had been tied to the length of the contract; they now became permanent. Those retirement and health care benefits continue into the present and are seen as one of Lewis's most significant achievements. In 1969, the union helped pass the federal Coal Mine Health and Safety Act that implemented changes in mining practices that threatened miner safety and provided funds to compensate workers suffering from black lung disease.

The 1950 strike was the impetus for the creation of the Bituminous Coal Operators' Association (BCOA), a national association of operators. After that date all contract negotiations would be with this one body. Lewis worked with the leadership of the BCOA to implement changes in collective bargaining so there would be fewer confrontations. Lewis became a labor statesman who helped create the National Coal Policy Conference as a vehicle for the industry to deal with politicians and the public with a united front. He even invested UMWA funds in coal companies.

Lewis remained as president until 1960 and was replaced by his long-time, vice-president, Thomas Kennedy. Kennedy died in 1963, and he was succeeded by William Anthony "Tony" Boyle. Lewis died in 1969, but he still is revered by union members today.

Boyle was a weak leader who dominated the union through threats of violence, bribery, control of the union's hierarchy, and manipulation of the union's election machinery. He remained close to the leaders of the coal industry and lost touch with the rank-and-file, especially on issues of health and safety. In 1969, he was challenged by another member of the union hierarchy, Joseph A. "Jock" Yablonski. In a highly corrupt election, Boyle defeated Yablonski, then had Yablonski murdered. Yablonski became a labor martyr.

Yablonski's followers organized in a group called the Miners for Democracy (MFD). The MFD worked to have the 1969 election invalidated, and a new election was held in 1972. Arnold Ray Miller, a Yablonski supporter, defeated Boyle in that election. Miller immediately set out to reform the union. He replaced Boyle's appointees, stopped Boyle's pension, and reduced the salaries of union officials. In 1972, Boyle and other union officials were convicted of making illegal political contributions with union funds. Boyle was convicted of Yablonski's murder in 1974 and spent the rest of his life in jail.

Miller made significant attempts at returning democracy to the union, in reforming the collective-bargaining process, and on issues of health and safety, but eventually his administration bogged down in internal disputes. Miller resigned in 1979 and was replaced by his vice-president, Sam Church. Church was unable to re-energize the union and was defeated in 1982 by Richard Trumka.

Trumka entered office at a difficult time. The Reagan administration was not friendly toward labor, there was a downturn in the use of coal, and the number of nonunion miners continued to grow rapidly, so the union faced difficulties in negotiations with the industry. The Trumka administration made changes in the bargaining process to put pressure on the BCOA through the use of selective strikes and negotiations with independent operators separately from the BCOA. The tactic was successful. The union also undertook a highly publicized strike against the Pittston Company in 1989 that involved the use of many innovative tactics. The union continued to face serious health and safety issues, issues of the environment, and changes in the membership as many female miners became members of the union. As in the past these new members were welcomed as equals.

In 1989, the UMWA re-entered the AFL, and Trumka became a member of the federation's executive council. In 1995, Trumka was elected secretary-treasurer of the AFL and was succeeded by Cecil Roberts. Under Roberts' leadership the union faces a long-term reduction in the number of miners and the percentage of miners who belong to the union. Since World War II, increasing automation, the popularity of other energy sources, and the growth in nonunion mines has cut the number of UMWA from approximately 500,000 in 1945 to 240,000 in 1998, and the numbers continue to decline. In addition to those problems, the UMWA increasingly has to fight massive conglomerates whose coal-mining operations are a small part of their holdings. These changes in the industry will force the UMWA to create new approaches to unionism. The union has also been active in international affairs.

The UMWA has a rich legacy of adapting to changes in American society and the coal industry. Although the history of the union has not always been one that miners could view with pride, the UMWA has improved the lives of workers in one of the most dangerous professions in the country. The union has been a leader in workers' rights, health and safety, political change in the country, and an innovator in union management relations. The UMWA has been led by powerful leaders who had a significant effect on the history of the United States. The miners have traditionally responded with great loyalty to the union and its leaders. The union faces a difficult future, but based on its past history, its leaders will continue to work to improve the lives of miners and their families.

RICHARD J. JENSEN

References and Further Reading

Armbrister, Trevor. *Act of Vengeance: The Yablonski Murders and Their Solution.* New York: Saturday Review Press, 1975.

Blatz, Perry K. *Democratic Miners: Work and Labor Relations in the Anthracite Coal Industry, 1875–1925.* Albany: State University of New York Press, 1994.

Brophy, John. *A Miner's Life.* Madison: The University of Wisconsin Press, 1964.

Clark, Paul F. *The Miners' Fight for Democracy: Arnold Miller and the Reform of the United Mine Workers.* Ithaca, NY: Cornell University, 1981.

Coleman, McAlister. *Men and Coal.* New York: Farrar and Rinehart, 1943.

Dubofsky, Melvyn, and Warren Van Tine. *John L. Lewis: A Biography.* New York: Quadrangle/The New York Times Book Co., 1977.

Finley, Joseph E. *The Corrupt Kingdom, the Rise and Fall of the United Mine Workers.* New York: Simon and Schuster, 1972.

Fox, Maier B. *United We Stand: The United Mine Workers of America, 1890–1990.* Washington, DC: United Mine Workers of America, 1990.

Jones, Mary Harris. *The Autobiography of Mother Jones.* Chicago, IL: Charles H. Kerr Publishing Company, 1974.

Laslett, John H. M. *The United Mine Workers of America: A Model of Industrial Solidarity?* University Park: The Pennsylvania State University Press, 1996.

Lewis, Ronald L. *Black Coal Miners in America: Race, Class, and Community Conflict, 1780–1980.* Lexington: University Press of Kentucky, 1987.

Long, Priscilla. *Where the Sun Never Shines: A History of America's Bloody Coal Industry.* New York: Paragon House, 1989.

Moore, Marat. *Women in the Mines: Stories of Life and Work, 1920–1994.* New York: Macmillan/Twayne, 1996.

Phelan, Craig. *Divided Loyalties: The Public and Private Life of Labor Leader John Mitchell.* Albany: State University of New York Press, 1994.

Zieger, Robert H. *John L. Lewis: Labor Leader.* Boston, MA: Twayne Publishers, 1988.

Cases and Statutes Cited

Coal Mine Health and Safety Act
National Industrial Recovery Act

UNITED OFFICE AND PROFESSIONAL WORKERS OF AMERICA

From the late 1930s to late 1940s, the United Office and Professional Workers of America (UOPWA) provided an important union base for office workers, an ever-larger and increasingly female workforce that the labor movement had mostly ignored.

While clerical work was originally a male preserve and stepping-stone to business success, beginning in the late nineteenth century, corporate consolidation, mechanization, scientific management, and feminization transformed the nature of office jobs. At the end of World War I, women were already nearly half of all office workers in the United States; clerical work would become only more feminized and mechanized in subsequent decades. By the 1930s, offices had become an increasingly stratified world, with male managers overseeing largely female, white-collar workers performing routine tasks. Whether private secretary or typing-pool member, clerical workers, especially women, often endured low wages, little autonomy, and few opportunities for advancement.

Labor leaders and organizers traditionally viewed clerical workers as too closely identified with management to unionize. The fact that so many were women also discouraged interest from union leaders, who generally believed that women were less organizable than men. The UOPWA represented a breakthrough, though a temporary and limited one, in the labor movement's quite limited history of organizing the clerical labor force.

From AFL to CIO

In 1904, the American Federation of Labor (AFL) began chartering clerical unions as federal locals directly affiliated to the federation, many of them for trade unions' own office employees. By 1919, there were at least 40 office worker locals within the AFL. One of the most important was the Bookkeepers, Stenographers, and Accountants' Union (BSAU), Local 12646. The BSAU was formed in New York City in 1909 and claimed 3,000 members by the early 1920s. The AFL temporarily exiled the left-leaning BSAU and then expelled 23 of its members in the 1920s for Communist links. Despite the federation's enmity, BSAU proved more durable and influential than other office worker locals.

During the Great Depression, the growth in white-collar unionism that began in the 1920s quickened and so did local union leaders' requests that the AFL charter a national union for office and professional workers. The AFL leaders ignored these requests however. As a result at the 1936 AFL convention, BSAU president Lewis Merrill and others took matters in their own hands by organizing a National Committee of Office and Professional Workers. The AFL suspended the group and threatened expulsion, but the dissidents left before the federation could evict them. On May 30, 1937, 14 of the AFL's white-collar unions, including BSAU, and nine independent unions formed the United Office and Professional Workers of America International, with some 8,600 members. Merrill was elected president. UOPWA quickly secured a charter from the newly organized Congress of Industrial Organizations (CIO). (That same year, the CIO also chartered the United Federal Workers and the State, County and Municipal Workers, unions for government office workers along with other public employees.)

The AFL responded by continuing to charter federal locals of office workers—150 by 1942—and then finally offering them an international charter. In 1945, the AFL established the Office Employees' International Union (OEIU, later renamed the Office and Professional Employees' International Union). The OEIU largely relied for its appeal to clerical workers on simply being an anti-Communist alternative to the left-leaning UOPWA.

Organizing Successes

While UOPWA's jurisdiction was potentially broad, the CIO restricted its ability to organize clerical employees in manufacturing, where nearly 1 in 7 workers was an office-based employee in 1938. Bowing to the wishes of some of its large industrial unions, including the United Steel Workers and United Rubber Workers, the CIO decided that the office workers of manufacturing firms whose factory workers were unionized should be represented by those same industrial unions. After UOPWA was thus forced to give up some of its newly organized members in steel and rubber, the major industrial unions proceeded to do little to organize offices under their jurisdiction. The clerical labor force of large manufacturers then remained largely unorganized. The UOPWA went after office employees of smaller manufacturers, where there were no other CIO unions with which to jostle. But it also looked to other sectors with substantial clerical workforces, most of which had no history of unionization of any kind: Banking, insurance, nonprofits, graphic arts, publishing, and advertising. The UOPWA managed some considerable organizing successes in the late 1930s and early 1940s.

The UOPWA put particular effort into wooing agents and clerical workers in the insurance industry. Building on earlier failed efforts of BSAU to organize at the Metropolitan Life Insurance Company in New York City in 1927, UOPWA concentrated on the three insurance giants: Metropolitan, John Hancock Mutual Life Insurance, and Prudential Insurance Company of America. Aggressive organizing campaigns resulted in successes at all three. During the late 1930s and early 1940s, UOPWA gained bargaining rights for employees of Metropolitan and Hancock in and around New York City. The UOPWA enjoyed an even greater breakthrough at Prudential on February 1, 1943, when it signed a national agreement covering workers in more than 30 states.

By the 1940s, UOPWA had also established a small but notable foothold in the nonunion world of banks and had organized at a broad array of other firms, including Arthur Murray Dance Studios, CBS Radio, Maidenform Brassiere Company, and Remington Rand. The UOPWA represented 6,500 private-agency social workers organized in locals of the Social Service Employees' Union. The UOPWA found fertile ground, too, in some of the large factorylike offices of credit bureaus, direct-mail houses, and directory and catalog publishers. In 1941, a major campaign in New York City targeting the direct-mail industry brought 4,000 workers under a

UOPWA contract. At the end of 1937, its first year, UOPWA had claimed a membership of 22,000 in 40 locals; by 1943, it had almost doubled in size to 43,000 members in 118 locals. While the wartime ban on strikes that most unions adopted, UOPWA included, dampened the militancy that fed the union's growth, a postwar surge of organizing swelled UOPWA membership by half again from 1946–1948, when it claimed 75,000 members. Though its strongest base was in New York City, UOPWA had locals in cities all over the United States.

Though UOPWA did more to improve the lot of working women than most other unions could have claimed at the time, there were limits to its progressiveness, as historian Sharon Hartman Strom has shown. Trying to represent both higher-status professionals and lower-level clericals in the same industry and even workplace, as UOPWA did in many cases, led to a pattern of privileging largely male professionals' goals and needs over those of largely female clericals. Though in social work locals the professionals were often female and low-paid themselves and eager to make common cause with their colleagues, in insurance locals, at the other extreme, male agents insisted on organizing separately from clerical coworkers and rarely supported them in dealing with management. The UOPWA was perhaps less compromised in its stance against racism. The UOPWA not only supported racial equality in principle, like many other CIO unions, but organized black insurance workers and struggled to integrate direct-mail houses.

Internal Disputes and Taft-Hartley

Growing internal disputes and militant anticommunism in the post-World War II years brought UOPWA's precipitous demise. The UOPWA had always included a substantial left-wing group in its membership, especially in New York and other large cities, and its leadership generally supported Communist causes. During the later 1930s' popular-front era and the war years, Communists' cooperative ethos kept ideological friction to a minimum. After the war however leftist influence increasingly brought conflict and controversy within UOPWA, while the larger labor movement's tolerance of Communists evaporated. In 1946, UOPWA President Lewis Merrill, who had long-standing Communist links himself, began to criticize what he considered undue Communist influence within the union. When Merrill resigned the following year for health reasons, James H. Durkin, whose support for the party line was firmer, replaced

him. The hardening leftist stance of the leadership, just as national anti-Communist sentiment was growing, alienated more conservative elements of the membership.

But it was the Taft-Hartley Act of 1947 that signaled the beginning of the end for UOPWA. The act required union leaders to sign affidavits saying they were not members of the Communist party; if they refused, they forfeited their union's rights under the National Labor Relations Act. The UOPWA leaders would not sign. The UOPWA leaders angered the CIO and many members further by endorsing the left-wing, third-party candidacy for U.S. president, Henry Wallace in 1948.

The UOPWA was among the 11 unions singled out for expulsion as the CIO purged its left-led internationals. The CIO suspended UOPWA in 1949 and in 1950 permanently expelled it for "Communist domination." By that time disgruntled members were already leaving as UOPWA became vulnerable to raiding by other CIO and AFL unions. The staunchly anti-Communist United Paperworkers' Union of the CIO, for instance, created an insurance division to accommodate defectors from UOPWA's insurance locals, while AFL sought to move them into its new Insurance Agents' Council. As membership dwindled, UOPWA's leftist leadership came under investigation.

In October 1950, UOPWA merged with two other left-led unions that had been kicked out of the CIO, the Food, Tobacco, Agricultural, and Allied Workers and the Distributive Workers' Union in October 1950. The merger created the Distributive, Processing, and Office Workers of America, which endured only for 4 years, when the Distributive Workers re-entered the CIO fold.

The demise of UOPWA left office workers either without unions at all or with representation by more conservative white-collar unions, such as the OEIU, dominated by male professional workers and their agenda. It was not until the 1970s that office worker organizing revived significantly in the private sector. When it did, it was the women's movement more than the labor movement that provided the spark.

KATHLEEN M. BARRY

References and Further Reading

Clermont, Harvey J. Organizing the Insurance Worker: A History of Labor Unions of Insurance Employees. Washington, DC: Catholic University of America Press, 1966.
Feldberg, Roslyn L. "'Union Fever': Organizing among Clerical Workers, 1900–1930." Radical America 14, 3 (May-June 1980): 53–70.

Kocka, Jürgen. *White-Collar Workers in America, 1890–1940: A Social-Political History in International Perspective*, translated by Maura Kealey. Beverly Hills, CA: Sage Publications, 1980.

McColloch, Mark. *Whit- Collar Workers in Transition: The Boom Years, 1940–1970*. Westport, CT: Greenwood Press, 1983.

Mills, C. Wright. *White Collar: The American Middle Classes*. New York: Oxford University Press, 1951.

Strom, Sharon Hartman. "'We're No Kitty Foyles': Organizing Office Workers for the Congress of Industrial Organizations, 1937–1950." In *Women, Work, and Protest: A Century of Women's Labor History*, edited by Ruth Milkman. Boston, MA: Routledge & Kegan Paul, 1985.

Waters, Elinor. "Unionization of Office Employees." *Journal of Business* 27, 4 (Oct. 1954): 285–293.

Cases and Statutes Cited

National Labor Relations Act
Taft-Hartley Act

See also **American Federation of Labor-Congress of Industrial Organizations; Clerical Work and Office Work; Taft-Hartley Act**

UNITED PACKINGHOUSE WORKERS OF AMERICA/PACKINGHOUSE WORKERS' ORGANIZING COMMITTEE

The meatpacking industry contributed significantly to the growth and development of several midwestern cities, especially Chicago, in the late nineteenth and early twentieth centuries. Yet most meatpacking workers had little power and were generally poorly paid for their labor before the 1930s. The fact that oligopoly characterized the industry by the late nineteenth century contributed to workers' difficulties. The so-called big five, consisting of Armour, Swift, Cudahy, Wilson, and Morris, which then became the big four in 1923 with Armour's purchase of Morris, exerted tremendous power over the industry and workers' conditions, particularly in the large stockyard cities where these companies had most of their packing plants. Divisions among workers along skill, ethnic, and racial lines also stymied early labor organizing efforts. From the 1880s to the early 1920s, the Knights of Labor, the American Federation of Labor's (AFL's) Amalgamated Meat Cutters and Butcher Workmen (AMCBW), founded in 1897, and the Stockyards Labor Council in Chicago, all faced these organizing challenges. Corporate power and packing workers' internal divisions were significant causes of failed meatpacking strikes in 1886, 1894, 1904, and 1921–1922. In addition the growing packing plants outside the Midwest's large cities,

many of which were in Iowa and Minnesota and owned by independent packers, such as Morrell, Hormel, and Rath, were largely unorganized before the World War I era.

By the early 1930s, successful union building in the meatpacking industry required organization across racial and ethnic lines in the major cities' packinghouses and successful recruitment of the growing numbers of packinghouse workers in the rural Midwest. The CIO's Packinghouse Workers' Organizing Committee grew out of three major organizing efforts in Austin, Minnesota, Cedar Rapids, Iowa, and Chicago. Austin, the small-town headquarters of Hormel, experienced one of the most successful independent union movements of the 1930s. The Independent Union of All Workers (IUAW), formed in 1933, grew out of the sense of isolation, frustration, and poverty that workers in this small city perceived during the depths of the Great Depression. Jay Hormel, son of founder George A. Hormel, also exerted heavy paternalist pressure on workers. A core group of militants, particularly Joe Ollman, a Trotskyist hog splitter, and Frank Ellis, a foreman in the hog-casings department and former Industrial Workers of the World (IWW) member, guided the IUAW's growth. The IUAW garnered support once Hormel mandated a paycheck deduction policy for pensions, life insurance, and the Community Chest in July 1933. Success in a November 1933 strike, partly due to Minnesota's Farm-Labor party Governor Floyd Olson's support for binding arbitration, spurred the IUAW's ability to gain affiliates in several communities in southern Minnesota, eastern South Dakota, North Dakota, and much of Iowa. Before narrowly agreeing to join the Congress of Industrial Organizations (CIO) movement in 1937, the IUAW had consolidated its power in the Hormel plant, published a weekly paper, organized a variety of cultural activities, and organized workers in several other Austin businesses.

In Cedar Rapids, AMCBW Local 206, organized in August 1933, aggressively bargained with Wilson to gain a written contract in 1934 and even went on strike in May 1934, but the company refused to negotiate with an international representative. The local then broke from the AMCBW in January 1935 to form the Mid-West Union of All Packing House Workers (MUAPHW). Lack of seniority recognition and irregular employment were major concerns of Milo Barta and Lewis Clark, the two most important union pioneers in Cedar Rapids. They recruited heavily among the many Bohemian workers in the Cedar Rapids plant. Led by the aggressive, ambitious, and strongly anti-Communist Clark, the MUAPHW attempted to organize affiliates throughout the Midwest beginning in early 1935. Barta and Clark

Apple packinghouse worker. Camden County, New Jersey. Library of Congress, Prints & Photographs Division, FSA/OWI Collection [LC-USF34-026636-D].

recruited MUAPHW members from packinghouses in Des Moines, Waterloo, Mason City, Davenport, Ottumwa, and Omaha. Their greatest success outside Cedar Rapids was probably in Omaha.

In Chicago radicals, especially Communists, paved the way for the eventual emergence of the Packinghouse Workers' Organizing Committee on October 27, 1937, as the cementing force among the new union movements. The AMCBW continued to organize, but increasingly its membership strength was in smaller packing plants and among retail butchers. Herb March, a Young Communist League organizer from Brooklyn, arrived in Chicago in 1933 and led Communists' colonization efforts in the major packing plants. By 1934, there were at least five different unions in Chicago's packinghouses, including the Packing House Workers' Industrial Union and a revived Stockyards' Labor Council led by Arthur Kampfert. Communist organizers successfully unified Polish and other East European immigrants with African-Americans and Mexicans in the industry. Union leaders built on white and black workers' shared grievances over their employers' poor industrial relations practices during the 1920s and 1930s. Many of the leading radical organizers were black, such as Henry Johnson, an organizer for the steel

workers before moving to packing, who passionately and persuasively argued for racial equality. Johnson and others were also keenly aware of the important strategic positions that many blacks held in crucial departments, particularly on the kill floors. March, Kampfert, Johnson, and others joined forces to pull Chicago meatpacking workers into the newly formed CIO. By fall 1937, the CIO issued charters to nine Chicago locals with a membership of 8,200. Chicago's locals along with the former IUAW affiliates, including the large John Morrell and Company union in Ottumwa, Iowa, and the MUAPHW groups, formed the core of the new Packinghouse Workers Organizing committee (PWOC).

Organization during the PWOC Era

From 1937 to the formation of the United Packinghouse Workers of America on October 16, 1943, Chicago and nearly all the major packinghouse cities in the Midwest became CIO strongholds. In Chicago blacks and whites worked together in the PWOC to make significant changes, with blacks often assuming crucial leadership positions. By 1939, African-Americans were presidents of nine of 15 Chicago PWOC local unions, and by 1943, all of the city's major plants were organized, and most had collective-bargaining agreements. No small part of this success was the union's efforts to equalize white and black workers' wages. Blacks' wages were almost equal to whites' wages by 1940 and were much better in this respect than nearly any other industry in the North.

Organizing efforts in Kansas City, the nation's second-largest packing center, followed a pattern similar to Chicago's. Socialists and Croatians formed the activist union-building core of Kansas City's workers in the 1930s. As in Chicago the Armour plant in Kansas City was organized first during 1936 and 1937 before the CIO local won a National Labor Relations Board (NLRB) certification election in August 1937, actually predating the Armour-Chicago CIO local's election by over a year. Although the PWOC-CIO then organized and won elections at other Kansas City plants, they did not succeed at the Swift plant. There unlike the case in Chicago, the National Brotherhood of Packinghouse Workers (NBPW), the former Swift company union, won certification and represented workers.

Omaha's packing community was composed mostly of native-born East Europeans and blacks. African-Americans were recruited into the CIO movement during the late 1930s but less aggressively than in either Chicago or Kansas City. Anticommunism was rampant among Omaha packing union leaders and white ethnics in general, and radical organizers, unlike the case in Chicago and Kansas City, were not well-received. Nonetheless the Armour packing plant was organized first, and a CIO local won a certification election there in fall 1939. At Swift the PWOC won a tight election against the NBPW in August 1941, and Cudahy's PWOC local was granted a contract in 1941 based on a union membership card count.

The PWOC organized virtually all the major plants in the other midwestern stockyard cities during the late 1930s and early 1940s. As was true in Chicago, Kansas City, and Omaha, new immigrants and blacks worked together to build local unions in East St. Louis and Milwaukee. In these cities the only major non-CIO affiliated packing work force was the Swift plant in East St. Louis. There, the AMCBW won a tight certification election against the NBPW in December 1941. In the stockyard cities that had growing numbers of black workers and few new immigrants or smaller numbers of both groups, the PWOC was also successful. African-American workers' support for the CIO in Indianapolis was especially significant. In fact the PWOC defeated the AMCBW in July 1941 in Indianapolis's Kingan plant after the AMCBW

had initially been given a contract in June 1937, and the PWOC won a certification election there in April 1938, largely due to the PWOC's ability to sway blacks to its racial-equality platform. The UPWA then continued to win certification away from the NBPW in such cities as south St. Paul through the end of World War II. By 1951, the UPWA-CIO had signed master contracts representing 60,000 workers in 70 of the big four's 99 plants.

After the union movements in the rural midwestern segment of the industry began in 1933 in Austin and Cedar Rapids, other smaller packing communities were rapidly organized. Before the 1930s, unionism had played only a minor role in these workers' lives, chiefly during and immediately following World War I. Two of the earliest NLRB certification elections in the packing industry, resulting in victories for the PWOC, occurred in Ottumwa, Iowa, in October 1937, and Mason City, Iowa, in November 1938. The IUAW originally organized Ottumwa's Morrell workers, and then the city's packing workers pursued IUAW-style community organizing by forming affiliates at the Ottumwa Steam Laundry, Barker Ice Company, and Swift poultry plant. Although not the first CIO packinghouse union movement, Ottumwa's workers received the first CIO charter in the industry. Then United Packing House Workers Local Industrial Union No. 32 became PWOC Local 1 in 1939. By 1943, local affiliates of the PWOC-CIO represented workers in not only Austin, Cedar Rapids, Ottumwa, and Mason City, but also Albert Lea in Minnesota; Des Moines, Fort Dodge, and Waterloo in Iowa; and Topeka, Kansas. The AMCBW represented meatpacking workers in Dubuque, Iowa, Sioux Falls, South Dakota, and Madison, Wisconsin.

The United Packinghouse Workers of America's Achievements

From 1943–1968, the UPWA significantly improved packing workers' lives in their workplaces and communities. The union's master contracts with the big four and major independent packers typically provided workers with departmental (but not plantwide) seniority, paid holidays, vacation time, guaranteed work hours and days, severance pay, clothes-changing and tool-repairing time—crucial benefits given the extreme temperature variations and brutal working conditions—and largely equalized wages for workers who did the same jobs not only in the same plants but across the country. In the late 1940s, meatpacking's average wages had improved tremendously but still lagged behind the average for all manufacturing and were considerably lower than auto workers'. However calculated on a weekly basis, because of the relatively long hours clocked by meatpacking workers compared to workers in such industries as auto, packinghouse employees earned more money on average than other workers beginning in 1946. By the mid-1950s, meatpacking workers' wages were 11 cents per hour higher than the average manufacturing wage nationwide.

The transformation of packing workers' status from poor people to a respected and prosperous working class was especially notable around the rural Midwest's packing cities. Unlike the larger stockyard packing cities that really experienced only a 10–15 year period of prosperity before they started to shut down, the smaller packing communities' workers generally experienced 30–40 years of prosperity. Cheri Register's memoir of growing up in post-World War II Albert Lea, Minnesota, as a packinghouse worker's daughter illuminates what this meant. Her father, Gordy Register, a millwright in the Wilson plant from 1943–1974, saw his hourly wages increase nearly eightfold, and the family was able to buy a new house west of town. Greater affluence and community respect transformed the status of families like the Registers.

The UPWA's contracts generally signaled more stable and improved workplace conditions. The industry's two major postwar strikes, one in 1946, which involved both the UPWA and AMCBW, and the other in 1948, which included the UPWA only, affirmed unionism's hold on the industry. Hormel's guaranteed annual wage for Austin workers was one of the most acclaimed contracts of the period. Although the guaranteed annual wage probably contributed to Austin workers' tractability, packing workers often continued to struggle, particularly after the 1948 strike, against employer initiatives aimed at exercising greater control over their jobs. At the Morrell-Ottumwa plant, Local 1 contested the company's initiatives to restructure job loads based on industrial engineering studies. From 1949–1951, in particular, the local used wildcat strikes to combat such changes. In 1951 alone, workers walked out on 88 separate occasions. Although union building improved many elements of packinghouse work, the industry itself was not much safer than it had been when Upton Sinclair described it in the *Jungle*. Even in the late 1950s, when meatpacking's overall wage and benefit levels peaked relative to manufacturing industries in general, the injury frequency rate was still twice that of manufacturing as a whole.

The UPWA was also a major driving force behind several community reform movements, such as the Back of the Yards Neighborhood Council in Chicago,

founded in March 1939. But the UPWA's most ambitious effort to improve workers' lives was probably its aggressive antidiscrimination and civil rights program that was implemented in all its plants but which made the greatest headway in the major stockyard cities that employed most of the industry's black workers, particularly in Chicago. The UPWA's progressive agenda following the 1948 strike that stemmed from its locals' democratic shop-floor cultures promoted antidiscrimination and civil rights efforts. The antidiscrimination and civil rights program was then established at the union's 1950 national convention under the leadership of UPWA Vice-President Russell Lasley. The program had three interrelated concerns: Breaking down all-white plant departments; ending discriminatory practices in the communities, especially in terms of restrictions against blacks' access to bars, restaurants, and public facilities; and facilitating work with other civil rights community organizations, such as the NAACP. In Chicago especially changes in application procedures helped to eradicate plant-wide segregation. There UPWA members also helped African-Americans move into new neighborhoods and public housing. In Kansas City UPWA efforts gradually eroded many local Jim Crow customs and resulted in the opening up of Kansas City, Kansas's, main retail district to black shoppers.

The UPWA's antidiscrimination programs created considerable tension in locals where whites were unwilling to adopt them. Among the major stockyard cities, this was most notable in Omaha, where some white union leaders believed the antidiscrimination program was part of a leftist agenda, and anticommunism among many workers, especially those with Czech and Polish backgrounds, was common. Indeed tensions between Communists, particularly from Chicago, such as Herbert March, and anti-Communists had existed since the 1930s and were a central part of the UPWA's history through the 1950s. Omaha-Armour local president Nels Peterson was one of the most outspoken anti-Communists in the UPWA and became a strong opponent of the antidiscrimination program in the city.

The UPWA also attempted to make women's workplace equality a central feature of its social agenda. Although never so prominent as antidiscrimination, during the 1950s women's activism focused particularly on ending men's and women's wage differentials. Ending discrimination against pregnant women workers became an important UPWA goal in the 1950s that resulted in women receiving unpaid leave for up to 1 year, and half-pay for up to 8 weeks, under the union's sick-leave provisions. Cultural pressures against women's participation in the union, especially at the local level, were probably the greatest difficulty that women faced in securing further gains. Another problem was the introduction of new technologies in the 1950s and 1960s that eliminated jobs in many traditional women's departments. The UPWA's reliance on departmental seniority meant that women had difficulty gaining jobs elsewhere in the plants against more senior men. Attempts to bump less senior men often created tensions. Women in many UPWA-organized plants used Title VII of the 1964 Civil Rights Act to challenge workplace biases. Although the UPWA tried to respond to these challenges by creating a new job-classification system, women in some plants, especially in the smaller cities of the Midwest, sued the union for sex discrimination. The legal challenges of the mid-to-late-1960s showed not only the union's shortcomings in recognizing women's equality, but also demonstrated considerable differences among women in terms of their own perceptions of gender equality. Older women were often satisfied with their situations and unwilling to support their younger colleagues' protests.

During the post-World War II era, Iowa's UPWA was at the forefront of several larger political efforts. The CIO unions in Iowa, especially the large Waterloo-Rath and Ottumwa-Morrell UPWA locals, worked with the Iowa Farmers' Union, led by President Fred W. Stover, a strong social democrat and Henry A. Wallace supporter, on a variety of cooperative efforts. Lee Simon, the UPWA's farm relations' director, also encouraged political collaboration in the early post-World War II years. Particularly in Iowa counties with meatpacking and other significant manufacturing, farmers and laborers voted together for Democrats in increasing numbers. Democrat Herschel Loveless, a former railroad worker, Morrell employee, and mayor of Ottumwa, won the gubernatorial race in 1956 and 1958. Democrat Harold Hughes, a former trucker, won the governor's office and then a U.S. Senate seat in the 1960s. With Democratic majorities in the state legislature for much of the 1960s and 1970s, working people benefited from improvements in workmen's and unemployment compensation, industrial development, greater school aid, property tax relief, abolishment of the death penalty, improvements in state government organization and planning, increased highway patrol and traffic safety programs, and more state facilities for the mentally ill and physically handicapped.

The closing of almost all the big four's plants in the larger midwestern cities during the 1950s and 1960s, due partly to the emergence of Iowa Beef Packers (IBP) and its aggressive cost-cutting measures, brought a sudden halt to the tremendous improvements that unionism had made in workers'

lives. These plant closings were particularly devastating to African-American workers. While the UPWA was generally successful in securing transfers for workers who chose to relocate to other plants—though a strike against Armour in 1963 was necessary to enforce this—many black men and women who did not transfer and lost their packing jobs entered labor markets that were not only much less receptive to racial equality but also demanded more formal education than many had received. Shutdowns of big four and major independents' plants in the rural Midwest accelerated during the 1970s and early 1980s after the UPWA merged with the AMCBW in 1968 to form a new AMCBW, AFL-CIO. Despite constant battles over plant shutdowns, through the late 1970s, the AMCBW was able to maintain the strong commitment to master agreements that had resulted in considerable economic benefits for meatpacking workers from the 1940s on, one of many prominent UPWA legacies.

WILSON J. WARREN

References and Further Reading

Brody, David. *The Butcher Workmen: A Study of Unionization.* Cambridge, MA: Harvard University Press, 1964.
Deslippe, Dennis A. *"Rights, Not Roses": Unions and the Rise of Working-Class Feminism, 1945–1980.* Urbana: University of Illinois Press, 2000.
Fink, Deborah. *Cutting into the Meatpacking Line: Workers and Change in the Rural Midwest.* Chapel Hill: University of North Carolina Press, 1998.
Galenson, Walter. *The CIO Challenge to the AFL: A History of the American Labor Movement, 1935–1941.* Cambridge, MA: Harvard University Press, 1960.
Halpern, Rick. *Down on the Killing Floor: Black and White Workers in Chicago's Packinghouses, 1904–54.* Urbana: University of Illinois Press, 1997.
Horowitz, Roger. *"Negro and White, Unite and Fight!" A Social History of Industrial Unionism in Meatpacking, 1930–90.* Urbana: University of Illinois Press, 1997.
Rachleff, Peter. "Organizing 'Wall to Wall': The Independent Union of All Workers, 1933–37." In *"We Are All Leaders": The Alternative Unionism of the Early 1930s,* edited by Staughton Lynd. Urbana: University of Illinois Press, 1996.
Register, Cheri. *Packinghouse Daughter: A Memoir.* St. Paul: Minnesota Historical Society Press, 2000.
Street, Paul. "Working in the Yards: A History of Class Relations in Chicago's Meatpacking Industry." Ph.D. dissertation, State University of New York at Binghamton, 1993.
Stromquist, Shelton, and Marvin Bergman, eds. *Unionizing the Jungles: Labor and Community in the Twentieth-Century Meatpacking Industry.* Iowa City: University of Iowa Press, 1997.
Warren, Wilson J. *Struggling with "Iowa's Pride": Labor Relations, Unionism, and Politics in the Rural*

Midwest since 1877. Iowa City: University of Iowa Press, 2000.
———. *"Tied to the Great Packing Machine": The Midwest and Meatpacking*. Iowa City: University of Iowa Press, 2006.

Cases and Statutes Cited

Civil Rights Act

UNITED PARCEL SERVICE STRIKE (1997)

On August 3, 1997, the teamsters launched a 15-day strike against United Parcel Service (UPS) and won one of labor's biggest victories in years. The key to the union's success was a year-long contract campaign followed by a strike strategy that involved a national mobilization of popular support.

Like most large corporations these days, UPS is a global company with huge assets that would allow it to withstand the lost profits from a strike in order to win concessions from its union workforce. In 1997, the corporation made over a billion dollars in profits a year. However unlike many multinational corporations, UPS is not diversified. The UPS makes its money from one business, delivering packages. Ninety percent of its profits derive from its U.S. operations. As well it would have been very difficult for the company to hire scabs to continue production and break a strike as is increasingly common in major U.S. strikes. Since UPS employed 185,000 union workers, hiring scabs as replacement workers would have been a formidable task. All of this made the company potentially vulnerable to a teamsters strike.

The company's strategy was to count on the union imploding on itself. The company was counting on divisions erupting between part-time and full-time workers that would end the strike. The part-timers work in the warehouses getting packages ready for delivery. Their wages were half those of the full-time workers. The full-timers tend to be truck drivers who deliver the packages. The two groups of workers had very different contractual priorities. The company was counting on internal union divisions erupting and dividing the workforce. The union was sharply divided between reformers who supported newly elected president Carey and the old guard unionists who controlled many of the UPS local unions and who had opposed Carey in the last union election. The company sought to use the weakness in the union's finances to pressure striking unionists to cross their picket line by the thousands, thereby causing the strike to collapse. The company knew that the union's

treasury was low and that it could not long afford to pay strike pay to 185,000 workers. And the strike pay, while the workers received it, was just $55 a week and did not cover workers' bills.

However the company badly miscalculated. The teamsters remained unified throughout the contract campaign and the strike. In the end the teamsters won the 2-week strike and got just about everything they wanted. In the course of the strike, two separate polls showed that two-thirds of the American people supported the striking unionists. This type of support for strikers is unprecedented in the last 30 years. It is reminiscent of the support unions had from the public in the 1930s.

The union did not win because of a brilliant strike strategy during the 15-day strike, although the strike was extremely well-organized and well-led. The teamsters won because of the contract campaign they had successfully carried out for nearly a year prior to the strike. They won because they had worked systematically to involve the membership in every stage of the contract campaign. They won because they had transformed the internal life of their union.

The union began by surveying its members. Just asking the members what they thought when they had not been asked in previous contract negotiations had a big impact. Next the union began to establish a Member-to-Member Action Network among its 206 local unions. The network recruited hundreds of union members who were not local union officers or stewards to each stay in regular touch with 20 members, giving them information about the progress of negotiations and the union's stance, answering their questions, listening to their views, and publicizing the union's mobilizations.

The union produced and distributed a series of videos on the company's demands and the union's need to respond. As well the union set up and regularly updated a website to keep the members notified of the status of negotiations. While this is not uncommon today, in 1997 this was noteworthy. Corporations use the Internet to monitor their global operations. Virtually every social movement, most notably the student antisweatshop movement and the global justice movement, uses the Internet to organize and share information. The Internet is a valuable tool in the struggle for social change. Political parties use the Internet for publicity and fundraising. Yet the labor movement has been slow to use this tool fully.

The union's Education Department organized training throughout the UPS locals on how to set up the action network. Nineteen staffers, including a number of rank-and-file workers brought temporarily off their jobs to be union staffers, worked full-time on helping the local unions build the network. These rank-and-file workers also became spokespersons for the union at national press conferences and rallies.

Workers began to hold meetings on breaks to talk about the action network and to build member support for the contract campaign. The UPS spent more than $1 million on newspaper advertisements, but the teamsters put all their money into organizing the members.

Whenever a union negotiates a contract, the bargaining committee has dozens of issues to propose to management. As a result of surveying the membership, the teamsters knew what the UPS workers' top priorities were in the contract negotiations. Among those priorities the union chose one issue to make its central, public campaign theme: The demand that part-time workers be offered full-time jobs with full-time pay and benefits. Sixty percent of the UPS workforce were part-time workers, and not by choice. The part-timers earned less than half of what the full-time workers made—starting pay was just $8.00 an hour. There were UPS workers who had been employed by the company for many years but were still forced to work part-time hours. There were part-time workers who often worked 30 or more hours a week but were not considered full-time by the company.

The union made this issue its theme. The two positions could not have been clearer or more counterposed: 60% of the company's workers were part-time, and the company was determined to increase that number substantially. The union was just as determined that things would move in the opposite direction, away from part-time and toward far more full-time jobs.

The union talked about the part-time issue as one that affected not just UPS workers, but all U.S. workers. The union's slogan became "A part-time America just won't work." The slogan and the campaign theme appealed to American workers, millions of whom work low-wage, part-time jobs. According to the 2000 census, roughly 17% of the U.S. workforce, or 23 million workers, hold part-time jobs. Two-thirds of these workers are women.

Thirty percent of the 135 million U.S. workers (as of 2000) held nonstandard positions—part-time, temporary, or independent contractor positions. Only 6% of part-time and temporary workers get employer-paid health care. Temporary work alone is skyrocketing; the number of temporary workers rose 535% from 1982 to 1997, and in 1997 (since surpassed by Wal-Mart) the largest private employer in the U.S. was the temporary employment agency Manpower.

So in 1997, there was a ready audience in the country sympathetic to a union struggle around the issue of part-time work. The union's contract campaign became an attack on corporate greed, not just on UPS. United Parcel Service, with its policy of moving full-time jobs to part-time, was portrayed as a symbol of everything that was wrong with the corporate United States. The union reinforced its campaign by releasing research reports on the crisis of part-time work and how it affected all Americans.

As Rand Wilson and Matt Witt, who served as director and coordinator of the teamsters' Communication Department before and during the UPS strike, have wrote: "From the beginning, the union's contract campaign at UPS was designed to build broad public support that would be needed to either win a good contract without a strike or win a strike if that became necessary. For nine months, union communications stressed that the campaign was not just about more cents per hour for Teamsters members, but about the very future of the good jobs that communities need. Teamster members, in turn, emphasized the same message when talking to the news media and to family, friends, and neighbors." The UPS spokesperson John Alden captured the popularity of the union's campaign theme when he later told *Business Week*, "If I had known that it was going to go from negotiating for UPS to negotiating for part-time America, we would've approached it differently."

Beginning in the fall of 1996, the union's action network carried out a series of actions to mobilize the membership in the contract campaign. A petition was signed by 100,000 workers in support of the demand for more full-time jobs. The UPS drivers gave out union flyers to customers and explained that they did not want to strike but hoped the customers would understand that they were fighting for full-time, good paying jobs for all the workers. The union held T-shirt days, button days, and sticker days. The union had actions where all the workers were encouraged to file grievances. For example 5,000 grievances were filed in a short period over safety issues. Plant gate rallies, each with a different theme, were called virtually every month. There were family day rallies. There were "blow the whistle on UPS" rallies protesting the company's contracting out of union jobs to low-wage, nonunion contractors. There were rallies for the part-time workers. Special educational materials were distributed with a focus on safety. The "don't break our backs" information was sent to the local media across the country, explaining the unfairness of forcing workers to lift 150-pound packages and noting that UPS pays out $1 million a day in workers' compensation. The teamsters 1997 UPS contract campaign was in short a model campaign. It demonstrated what labor could achieve when it has the vision and the strategy to educate, organize, and mobilize the members in support of workers' rights.

In their article on the UPS contract campaign and strike, Wilson and Witt sum up the keys to the teamsters' success. They asserted that the UPS contract campaign succeeded because first it was a movement of the workers—not just the union officials; second because it was a movement for all workers—not just for the union's members; and third because it was a social movement of workers and their supporters—not a bureaucratic-run organization, not a union run like a business, not a top-down run union, and not a union in bed with management.

STEVEN ASHBY

References and Further Reading

Ryan, Charlotte. "It Takes a Movement to Raise an Issue: Media Lessons from the 1997 UPS Strike." *Critical Sociology* 30, 2: 483–511.
Witt, Matt, and Rand Wilson. "Part-Time America Won't Work: The Teamsters' Fight for Good Jobs at UPS." In *Not Your Father's Union Movement: Inside the AFL-CIO*, Jo-Ann Mort, ed. London and New York: Verso, 1988
———. 1999. "The Teamsters' UPS Strike of 1997: Building a New Labor Movement." *Labor Studies Journal* 24, 1 (spring).

See also **International Brotherhood of Teamsters**

UNITED PUBLIC WORKERS OF AMERICA/UNITED FEDERAL WORKERS OF AMERICA

The roots of the United Public Workers of America/United Federal Workers of American (UPWA/UFWA) belong in the New Deal. In 1932, the American Federation of Labor (AFL) chartered a new government employee union, the American Federation of Government Employees (AFGE) to rival the newly independent National Federation of Federal Employees (NFFE). The AFGE received a boost in 1933 with the establishment of a host of New Deal agencies that attracted young, left-leaning union sympathizers to government jobs. These workers joined the AFL union, hoping in many cases to mimic the goals and objectives of the private-sector labor movement.

From 1933 to 1935, a number of AFGE lodges began to agitate for the use of more aggressive tactics than their conservative leaders felt comfortable supporting. Employees were especially concerned with negotiating grievances, which often involved disputes over promotion practices and policies. The National Recovery Administration's (NRA) AFGE lodge for instance found itself in frequent conflict with NRA head Hugh Johnson over hours and promotions. Tension between the union lodge and Johnson escalated over a promotion grievance that led to the dismissal of an employee. When the AFGE lodge persisted in asking for a meeting with Johnson, the NRA chief fired the AFGE lodge president, John Donovan. His firing inspired picketing of NRA headquarters, resulting in a split between AFGE rank-and-file and its leadership, which supported Johnson's decision. Another rift emerged when several agency lodges banded together in a Committee against False Economy to protest President Franklin D. Roosevelt's 1937 budget cuts. In 1936 and 1937, AFGE leaders expelled numerous lodges, including those in the Securities and Exchange Commission, the Social Security Board, the Works Progress Administration, Labor Department, Interstate Commerce Commission, and Agriculture Department for alleged Communist ties and for engaging in actions deemed embarrassing or illegal to the national leadership.

Members of these locals turned to the newly established Committee (later Congress) of Industrial Organizations (CIO) for assistance. In June 1937, CIO head John Lewis agreed to charter a new union, the United Federal Workers of America. Lewis appointed Jacob Baker, a former assistant administrator of the Federal Emergency Relief Administration, as president. Eleanor Nelson, an economist in the Women's Bureau, president of AFGE Lodge 12, and daughter of a former Republican congressman from Maine, became secretary-treasurer. At their 1940 convention, UFWA delegates elected her to the executive board, and in 1944 she became the first female president of a CIO union.

Membership and Objectives

The original core of the UFWA therefore consisted of the ousted AFGE lodges. By August 1937, the union boasted 4,200 members. A year later organizing campaigns brought the number of members to 14,000 in 131 locals scattered across the nation. Although the organization forbade strikes and adhered to President Roosevelt's policy denying collective-bargaining rights for public employees, it actively sought the creation of formal agency-based grievance procedures and employer-employee policies, as well as recognition of the right of the union to represent employees and to negotiate with agency administrators. Indeed the union considered its grievance work a form of collective bargaining. Collective bargaining as practiced in the private sector had long been considered anathema in the federal civil service because taxpayers, through their representatives in Congress, paid the salaries of government workers. President Roosevelt had made a distinction between public- and private-sector employment and reiterated his opposition to public-service collective bargaining in a letter he wrote in 1937. The UFWA President Baker, along with the presidents of NFFE and AFGE, was present at a meeting in which Roosevelt discussed the contents of this letter.

Nevertheless UFWA's constitution reflected its commitment to private-sector union tactics and ideals. Its 1944 constitution listed as its objective the promotion of "rights of Federal employees equal to those of employees in private industry," and noted that it was the "right of all people in the United States in both public and private employment to organize into unions of their own choosing for purposes of bargaining collectively with their employers." In addition to the traditional support public-service unions gave the merit system, creation of a classification system for the field service, salary increases, retirement plans, and a 5-day work week, UFWA committed itself to pushing promotion from within, opposing racial discrimination, supporting women's issues, and seeking a general civil service appeals court for aggrieved employees. It innovated in making presentations to the Bureau of the Budget to advocate for agency appropriations.

As part of its effort to promote the labor movement, the UFWA established a Federal Workers' School in 1937. For $2 ($2.50 for nonmembers), students could take a course on topics ranging from union organizing to principles of economics to contemporary literature to group singing. Among the instructors were Dr. Caroline Ware, associate professor of social economy and social history at American University and wife of New Dealer Gardiner Means.

From its founding through the 1940s, the union continued to press its employee-rights agenda and to advocate for women and African-American workers. It worked to organize messengers, many of whom were African-American, and welcomed African-American workers of the United Cafeteria Employees union into its ranks in 1942. Its recreation committee refused to use segregated facilities, and in 1943, the union organized a Conference on Negro Discrimination in the Federal Service. A year later, largely at the behest of Nelson, the union held a national Conference of Working Mothers to address childcare and other matters. The Office of Price Administration, which had large numbers of female and African-American employees, had a lodge particularly active in promoting civil rights. Black employees successfully used the union to initiate an unprecedented racial

discrimination grievance against a branch chief. Similarly in the late 1940s, the union represented black workers denied promotional opportunities in the Bureau of Engraving and Printing in a multiyear case brought before the Fair Employment Board (a civil service successor to the Fair Employment Practices Committee).

UPWA/UFWA and Anticommunism

The union's militancy and association of many of its members with left-wing causes and organizations led to numerous allegations that the UFWA-CIO was a Communist organization. In 1939, Congress passed the Hatch Act, which included a provision denying federal employment to individuals belonging to organizations supporting overthrow of the government. It followed with appropriation bill riders refusing wages to employees deemed subversive. These initiatives along with others led by various congressional committees were aimed at undermining the UFWA-CIO, a union that many conservatives and white Southerners found troublesome.

Among CIO unions, the UFWA/UPWA had a reputation as a leftist organization. In the 1930s and 1940s, it attracted young, progressive-thinking federal workers, many of whom sympathized with socialist and Communist ideals. Although it was never controlled directly by the Communist party, UFWA/UPWA members shared a common agenda with the party, especially in the area of worker and black civil rights. Some UFWA/UPWA members and supporters held membership in the party, some did not. After passage of the Hatch Act in 1939, which severely curtailed the political activities of federal employees, UFWA hired lawyer and Communist party member Lee Pressman to press a constitutional challenge to the law. Albert Bernstein began organizing for the union in the 1930s and joined the party in the early 1940s, although he never considered himself a devout member. Thomas Richardson, who became a vice-president in the union, was also a party member. Prior to joining the federal government and the UFWA/UPWA, he had worked with the Southern Negro Youth Congress, an organization with close ties to the Communist party. Richardson's sister, Marie, also active in the union and a party member, went to jail in the 1940s for falsifying an application for temporary federal employment because she signed a loyalty oath even though she was a party member. Many UFWA/UPWA members did not join the party but sympathized with Communist ideals and worked closely with party members on issues of mutual concern. Typical of this type of union member was Coleman Young, the future mayor of Detroit. Active in the labor movement, he worked as an organizer for UPWA in 1940s. He publicly denied allegations that he belonged to the Communist party but openly voiced his sympathy for Communist aims and admitted to working closely with party members. While party members who belonged to the union strengthened its internal commitment to progressive aims in the areas of worker, black, and women's rights, they made the union the target of vigorous anti-Communist ttacks.

Allegations of Communist ties grew with the union's re-organization in 1946. Facing falling membership and in an effort to shore up resources, UFWA leaders agreed to a merger with the CIO's State, County, and Municipal Workers of America. The newly formed United Public Workers of America (UPWA) claimed over 70,000 members and was headed by Abram Flaxer, formerly with the State, County, and Municipal Workers. At the April convention creating the new union, members clashed over a foreign policy plank. Eventually the union adopted a resolution calling on the United States to end its isolation of the USSR and to withdraw troops from Greece, China, the Philippines, India, and other nations deemed friendly to the United States. Resolutions also supported disarmament, the work of the United Nations, and the continuation of rent and price controls, then a controversial issue facing President Harry Truman.

The UPWA critics focused on the Soviet resolution and on what they considered the UPWA's endorsement of the right to strike against government. State, local, and municipal workers had a longer tradition of striking, and thus the convention had adopted a more flexible strike provision than the unequivocal no-strike policy adopted by other federal service unions. Consequently the union stipulated that while UPWA supported a no-strike policy, it recognized that when all other methods of negotiation failed, a strike could be called but only if members had obtained permission from the UPWA president and its governing body.

After the merger federal employee membership continued to stagnate, with 20,000 federal worker members in 1947, 15,000 of whom were employees in the Panama Canal zone. In 1948, the union moved its headquarters from Washington, DC, to New York City and soon reduced the number of vice-presidents from six to one. Caught up in the postwar Red Scare, the UPWA spent much of its energy fighting allegations of Communist party influence. President Truman's Federal-Loyalty Security Program, created in 1947, intensified scrutiny of the union. In 1950, the CIO expelled the UPWA for its alleged ties to the Communist movement. Two years later Senator Pat McCarran's Internal Security subcommittee labeled UPWA President Flaxer a "fanatic" Communist and linked other top officials to the Communist party. The union folded that same year. During its 15-year existence the union served as the most progressive voice among federal worker unions. Its focus on interracial organizing, race discrimination, women's issues, and collective bargaining distinguished it from other government unions, but it also made it more difficult for the union to survive the postwar anti-Communist movement.

MARGARET C. RUNG

References and Further Reading

Bernstein, Carl. *Loyalties: A Son's Memoirs*. New York: Simon and Schuster, 1989.
Gall, Gilbert J. *Pursuing Justice: Lee Pressman, the New Deal, and the CIO*. Albany: State University of New York, 1999.
Hanson, Rhonda. "United Public Workers: A Real Union Organizes." In *The Cold War against Labor*, edited by Ann Fagan Ginger and David Cristiano. Vol. 1. Berkeley, CA: Meiklejohn Civil Liberties Institute, 1987.
Johnson, Eldon. "General Unions in the Federal Civil Service." *Journal of Politics* 1 (Feb. 1940): 23–56.
Mosher, Frederick C. *Democracy and the Public Service*. New York: Oxford University Press, 1968.
Spero, Sterling D. *Government as Employer*. New York: Remsen Press, 1948.
Zieger, Robert H. *The CIO, 1935–1955*. Chapel Hill: The University of North Carolina Press, 1995.

Cases and Statutes Cited

Hatch Act

See also **American Federation of Government Employees; Anticommunism; Lewis, John L.; National Federation of Federal Employees; United Government Employees**

UNITED RUBBER WORKERS OF AMERICA

When the United Rubber Workers of America met in Pittsburgh in 1995, the delegates should have been celebrating the union's sixtieth anniversary. Instead they were deciding on the union's future. By a slim three-vote margin, the delegates agreed to merge with the United Steelworkers, thereby giving up the URW's long, proud, independent, militant history within the labor movement. The delegates had little choice. With membership decreasing and finances

Buffalo, New York. Recently employed women being sworn into the rubber workers union at a Sunday meeting. Most of them have never worked before and know little about trade unionism. Library of Congress, Prints & Photographs Division, FSA/OWI Collection [LC-USW3-028180-D].

wrecked by a crippling strike during the so-called "War of '94," the rubber workers bowed to the inevitable, hitched their future to the larger steelworkers' union and banked on the trend toward unions that cut across industries.

The United Rubber Workers of America organized in the heart of the rubber industry—Akron, Ohio—in 1935. The union faced formidable odds: Meager financial resources, inexperience, and powerful corporate opponents committed to destroying any independent labor organization. For almost 50 years rubber companies had crushed attempts by labor to organize. In 1887, the Knights of Labor tried unsuccessfully to organize the rubber workers in New Jersey. In the early years of the twentieth century, the American Federation of Labor (AFL) faced similar results when it tried to organize the rubber workers in the East. Strikers in Trenton, New Jersey, were fired and blacklisted. The union did not recover. By the end of 1905, the AFL's executive board revoked the charter of the Amalgamated Rubber Workers of North America. In 1913, labor discontent moved into Akron in the biggest labor dispute the city had ever seen—and the rubber companies were ready for it. According to author Harold Roberts, the 1913 strike, led by the Industrial Workers of the World,

was a "landmark in the technique of strike breaking." After the Firestone workers walked off the job, rubber workers from across the city joined them. Rubber companies, with the support of community citizen committees and law enforcement, began tactics that were similar to those associated with the Mohawk Valley formula of the 1930s. The 1913 strike failed.

During the Depression, times were hard for the rubber workers in Akron and across the nation. Unemployment was high; rubber companies were not interested in negotiating for better conditions. But a new president—Franklin Delano Roosevelt—thought he had a New Deal to benefit workers and industry alike. In 1935, the Wagner Act encouraged collective bargaining and protected workers as they negotiated.

The United Rubber Workers came from this environment. Although the rubber companies were opposed to any worker organization except their own, the rubber workers were ready to press their case. The AFL sent union organizer Coleman Claherty to Akron with orders to organize the rubber workers. But the AFL soon discovered that the rubber workers had minds of their own. When the AFL tried to dictate the new union's leadership and constitution, the proud, independent rubber workers refused to go along, electing Sherman Dalrymple, one of their own, as their first president. Frustrated with the AFL's continuing commitment to crafts as opposed to industrial unions, the United Rubber Workers of America (URW) formally affiliated with the (CIO) in 1936.

A constitution and a leadership did not guarantee rubber worker union success. Rubber companies were still reluctant to negotiate. The rubber workers however were innovators when it came to organizing—and striking. The rubber workers introduced the sit-down strike to the labor movement in 1934 when General Tire workers in Akron sat down on the job until the company agreed to re-instate the workers, consider seniority in layoffs, and meet with union representatives. The maneuver did not bring union representation—nor did the 1936 Goodyear sit-down strike.

In late 1936, the URW was pushing hard to organize the Goodyear plant in Gadsden, Alabama. The URW President Dalrymple directed the organizing personally but was beaten by a crowd of Goodyear supporters and became "the highest ranking labor leader to be so violently attacked in the 1930s," according to the URW historian Bruce Meyer. Dalrymple would not be the last URW representative to be beaten in Gadsden. That plant would not be organized until 1941.

Benefiting from World War II production demands, the United Rubber Workers thrived during the 1940s. Membership grew from 55,000 in 1940 75,000 in 1941—or about half of the industry's workers. By the end of 1941, the union had 93,000 members, 63% of all rubber workers. By 1945, the union had 190,000 members in 222 locals. That same year the union expanded its jurisdiction to include cork, linoleum, and plastic workers and officially became the United Rubber, Cork, Linoleum, and Plastic Workers of America, although the press and rubber workers continued to use the URW name.

In 1945, Dalrymple retired, and Leland Buckmaster, president of powerful Firestone Local 7, was elected president. At the negotiating table, Buckmaster achieved the first master contract, which established pattern bargaining across the big four (Firestone, B. F. Goodrich, Goodyear and U.S. Rubber). Membership was increasing—up to 209,000 in 1947. Nonetheless Buckmaster ran into trouble with the union's executive board, which attempted to remove him from office, but the membership would have none of it. Buckmaster remained president until his retirement in 1960.

That year the URW turned to its organizing director, George Burdon, for leadership. Burdon's tenure as president was brief. A new vice-president, the charismatic Peter Bommarito, had his eye on the top spot. Running as an expert in contract negotiations, Bommarito, "the bomber," easily swept into office in 1966.

Bommarito's 15-year reign was marked by adversarial dealings with the rubber companies, strikes (143 in 1973 alone), and substantial decreases in union membership (from 178,000 in 1978 to 132,141 in 1982). Nonetheless Bommarito brought genuine financial gains to the membership. Wages increased, pensions improved, and as a result of the bitter strike of 1976, the cost-of-living allowance was put in place. Bommarito was also committed to improving the health of the rubber workers. The URW was the first union to hire a full-time industrial hygienist.

By the end of his tenure, Bommarito was also facing the harsh realities of shifts within the tire marketplace. In 1980, Firestone announced it was closing five tire factories and its synthetic latex plant. Milan "Mike" Stone, Bommarito's handpicked successor who was elected in 1981, had to deal with the plant closings, the layoffs, and the steadily declining membership. Part of this was due to imports. Aggressive foreign tire producers were making inroads into the lucrative North American replacement-tire market. Moreover foreign manufacturers were buying out American tire makers. Bridgestone acquired Firestone; Germany's Continental AG bought out GenCorp's General Tire; the French giant Michelin bought out the merged BFG and Uniroyal.

But the bigger reason was the shift in demand away from bias-ply tires to the new radials. The U.S. and Canadian tire plants had been slow to convert to radial tire production—that required updating and retooling old factories. In the end rubber companies found it cheaper to close factories and construct new ones. From 1975–1986, 30 of the 65 tire plants in the United States closed; all but one had been organized by the URW, costing 30,000 members their jobs. During the same time period, five new factories were constructed; URW could not organize any of those plants. To keep plants open, Stone agreed to concessions, and it was those concessions that ultimately led to his defeat as the URW president in 1990.

In 1990, the URW wanted a leader to "energize them, activate them, and make them feel like a union again," wrote Meyer in his history of the URW. Kenneth Coss, the grandson of an organizer for the steelworkers' union, seemed to fill the bill, and he soundly defeated Stone.

But Coss was unable to stem the downward spiral. Membership continued to decline (from 104,721 in 1990 to 91,304 in 1993); tire plants continued to close; companies wanted more concessions. Then came the War of 1994. There were a number of URW strikes that year: Against Dunlop, Pirelli Armstrong, and Yokohami Tire; but it was the crippling, extended, bitter strike against Bridgestone/Firestone that led to the merger with the steelworkers.

Bridgestone/Firestone was losing money and refused to accept the master contract approved by Goodyear without some concessions in wages and benefits. Local URW workers were in no mood to compromise, and Coss could not convince the local leaders to keep their members on the job. In July 1994, Bridgestone/Firestone workers walked out. In August the company put in place its final best offer and began hiring. In December the company started hiring permanent replacements. Finally in May 1995, the URW—worried that the replacement workers would vote to decertify the union—ordered its members back to work with no conditions. Only a minority of the strikers got their jobs back.

Four days later, the URW's executive board voted to merge with the steelworkers. All that was needed was a two-thirds vote of the membership, which was not necessarily assured. The URW members complained about the loss of identity and the increased dues. In the end however the merger was approved 617 to 304, three votes more than needed.

The United Rubber Workers is now a part of the Rubber and Plastics Industry Conference of the United Steelworkers' Union, a small part of a giant union. Ron Hoover, who has a 40-year history with the rubber industry, is now head of the conference, replacing John Seller, another long-time URW member. Little is left of the URW's identity in its hometown of Akron or nationally. An abbreviated version of the union's history is located on the steelworkers' website (http://uswa733.freeservers.com/urw_history.htm), many layers below the home page. The United Steelworkers of America (USWA) is now the organizer, the settler of strikes, and the negotiator of the master contracts in the rubber industry; but the rubber workers are only one small part of the union's constituency.

KATHLEEN L. ENDRES

References and Further Reading

Drown, Stuart. "URW under Siege, Missing the Signs Left Union Behind." *Akron Beacon Journal* (8 Jan. 1995).

Love, Steve, and David Giffels. *Wheels of Fortune: The Story of Rubber in Akron.* Akron, OH: University of Akron Press, 1999.

Meyer, Bruce M. *The Once and Future Union: The Rise and Fall of the United Rubber Workers, 1935–1995.* Akron, OH: University of Akron Press, 2002.

Nelson, Daniel. *American Rubber Workers and Organized Labor, 1900–1941.* Princeton, NJ: Princeton University Press, 1988.

Roberts, Harold S. *The Rubber Workers: Labor Organization and Collective Bargaining in the Rubber Industry.* New York: Harper & Bros., 1944.

Sabath, Donald. "Obstacles May Mar URW Vote to Join USW." *Cleveland Plain Dealer* (1 July 1995).

———. "Rubber Union to Merge with Steelworkers." *Cleveland Plain Dealer* (12 May 1995).

Thurber, John Newton. *Rubber Workers' History (1935–1955).* Akron, OH: Public Relations Department, United Rubber, Cork, Linoleum & Plastic Workers of America, 1956.

United for a Better Tomorrow: 40 Years of Dedication. Akron, OH: Exchange Printing Co., 1975.

Cases and Statutes Cited

Wagner Act

UNITED STATES EMPLOYMENT SERVICE

Although Congress did not formally create a federal employment service until 1933, the origins of the U.S. Employment Service (USES) lie in Progressive Era reform efforts to establish publicly funded and administered labor exchanges. Public employment exchanges began at the state level, with one of the first opened in Ohio in 1890. By 1917, 20 states had at least one publicly funded employment office. At the federal level, the first foray into employment services began in 1907, when Congress established the Division of Information within the Bureau of Immigration and Naturalization. This division advertised job opportunities to recent immigrants as a means of settling recent arrivals in communities across the country.

In 1915, the term U.S. Employment Service had come into informal usage, and a year later, the first secretary of labor, William B. Wilson, created USES to address war emergency needs. During and immediately after the Great War, USES functions expanded, and in March 1919, it boasted 854 offices, 4,079 employees, and 3,075 volunteers. Nevertheless the agency lacked formal congressional approval, largely because of disagreements over whether to create a centralized national office that operated separately from state-level offices or a federal office that shared authority with, and coordinated activities of, state offices.

During the 1920s, USES experienced significant funding cuts, operating as an information-clearing house with a skeletal staff. Pressure to expand, reinvigorate, and reorganize USES began as unemployment rose in 1929. President Herbert Hoover preferred to use administrative rather than congressional authority to revamp USES and pocket-vetoed a measure passed by Congress in March 1931 that would have given USES permanent status, streamlined and clarified its functions, and coordinated its efforts with state offices.

After the election of President Franklin D. Roosevelt in 1932, Senator Robert Wagner (D-NY) and Representative Theodore Peyser (D-NY) re-introduced employment service legislation. With strong support from the American Federation of Labor (AFL) and Secretary of Labor Frances Perkins, the Wagner-Peyser Act was signed by President Roosevelt on June 6, 1933. The AFL had become a strong advocate of public-employment exchanges, criticizing private, for-profit exchanges as ineffective and exploitative. The AFL President William Green encouraged local unions and state-level federations to lobby for the law and perceived it as part of a larger program aimed at addressing widespread unemployment.

The USES authorized under the Wagner-Peyser Act replicated the federal approach built into many of the New Deal programs. Although USES had permanent status and a home in the Department of Labor, the agency shared authority with states. Officials used matching federal grants to encourage state offices, which carried out the actual placement work, to affiliate with USES. States accepting these grants agreed to abide by federal standards. If a state refused to establish a public-employment service, USES had the ability to establish an office directly. As it had done previously, USES continued to collect and distribute information on employment. In its first year it had 125 affiliated state offices and in its second year, over 2000. By the end of the decade, all 48 states, along with Hawaii, Alaska, and Washington, D.C. had public-employment offices linked to USES.

Despite strong support for the legislation from the AFL, union members and leaders remained wary of USES's potential as a strikebreaker. They worried that employers would use state offices to procure replacement workers during work stoppages, as seemed to have occurred during agricultural strikes in the 1930s. In 1939, USES officials adopted a rule—later weakened—mandating that all affiliated state offices refrain from supplying workers to firms engaged in labor disputes, defined as any controversy involving terms or conditions of employment, including conflicts over unionization.

During World War II, the Roosevelt administration centralized USES functions and placed the agency within the War Manpower Commission. Both labor and civil rights groups preferred this national system to the previous federal system. Labor leaders believed that centralization would facilitate a national economic plan for maintaining full employment. Although National Association for the Advancement of Colored People (NAACP) leaders objected to USES's capitulation to employer requests for employees from specific racial groups, they recognized that decentralization had allowed state officials to discriminate blatantly against black job seekers by continuing that practice, as well as opening separate offices for black and white applicants and referring

blacks only to menial, unskilled jobs. The AFL leaders agreed with the NAACP regarding centralization, but they did not support the NAACP's call for Washington, DC to discontinue operating separate employment service offices for black and white applicants. Congress of Industrial Organizations (CIO) leaders, on the other hand, joined the NAACP in objecting to this practice and helped organize pickets of the DC offices.

In 1946, decentralizers succeeded in returning USES to its federal structure. From then on USES's mission became increasingly entangled with the distribution of unemployment benefits, and then in the 1960s, with job training. After passage of the Social Security Act in 1935 establishing unemployment insurance, some factions insisted that recipients of benefits be required to register with the employment service, and they mandated that state employment service offices be combined with unemployment-compensation offices. Once USES returned to its decentralized organization after the war, it saw its funding increasingly come from unemployment compensation taxes, thus linking it more firmly to this program.

Throughout the 1950s and 1960s, USES came under frequent criticism from all sides of the political spectrum for its rather poor placement record and oversight of state offices. It made fewer placements in 1957 than it had in 1947, and whereas only 17% of its job referrals were short-term in 1947, they increased to 30% in 1957. In the 1960s and under the Great Society, reformers sought to tie the service more closely to job training. This stress accompanied a decoupling of the unemployment-compensation program from the USES, which was largely accomplished by 1964. Nevertheless USES found itself in the middle of new debates over its role in welfare-to-work programs. Amendments to the Wagner-Peyser Act, including the 1982 Job Training Partnership Act and the 1998 Workforce Investment Act, continued to stress training and coordination with welfare-to-work programs, as reflected in USES's administrative placement within the Labor Department's Employment Training Administration. The 1998 act also focused on the creation of one-stop state-level employment services that once again tied the work of USES to unemployment insurance claims. In the latter part of the twentieth century, USES's increasing identification as an agency furnishing low-wage jobs to low or unskilled workers from economically disadvantaged groups tended to weaken its connection to organized labor. It also separated USES's mission and functions from a national economic policy, which was the original intent of its framers in 1933.

MARGARET C. RUNG

References and Further Reading

Breen, W. J. *Labor Market Politics and the Great War: The Labor Department, the States, and the first U.S. Employment Service, 1907–1933*. Kent, OH: Kent State University Press, 1997.
"Comprehensive Adult Programs." www.doleta.gov/programs/adult_program.cgm#le (2005).
King, Desmond. *Actively Seeking Work: The Politics of Unemployment and Welfare Policy in the United States and Great Britain*. Chicago, IL: University of Chicago Press, 1995.

Cases and Statutes Cited

Job Training Partnership Act
Social Security Act
Wagner-Peyser Act
Workforce Investment Act

See also **Department of Labor; Great Society; Perkins, Frances**

UNITED STATES INDUSTRIAL COMMISSION (1898–1902)

Established in 1898 by President William McKinley, the federal United States Industrial Commission in 1898 investigated corruption and greed in railroad pricing policy, industrial monopolies, and the impact of immigration on labor markets. The commission continued its work after McKinley's assassination in 1901 and provided his successor, Theodore Roosevelt, with recommendations to pursue more aggressive antimonopoly policies.

Andrew L. Harris, a former Ohio governor known as the farmer-statesman, led the commission's list of predominantly political participants. Two labor leaders sat on the commission: M. D. Ratchford, president of the United Mine Workers and F. B. Sargeant, leader of the Brotherhood of Locomotive Firemen. The high-profile targets of investigation were oil, railroad, and steel tycoons John. D. Rockefeller, Andrew Carnegie, and Charles M. Schwab. A growing contingent of businessmen and civic leaders complained that the trusts squashed healthy economic competition through hostile buyouts or by peddling political influence with state and local governments. Small businesses and farms could not compete against the new billion-dollar corporations like U.S. Steel or Standard Oil. Official protests or legal recourse against the trusts were dismissed or easily overridden by their political and judicial cronies who made decisions at the state and local levels.

While Congress focused primarily on the railroad and steel industries, the commission's final report revealed insights into other economy-related policy, including prison labor, transportation, the Chicago labor disputes of 1900, agriculture, mining, manufacturing, education, foreign legislation affecting U.S. labor, and comparisons to European industrial models. The final report consisted of 19 volumes of investigations, studies, hearings, and legislative recommendations undertaken from 1899 to 1902.

At the end of the nineteenth century, poverty, the issues of economic depression, and competition from immigration generated considerable public concern. It appeared to many that the nation's wealth and the chances for opportunity were concentrated in the hands of an elite group of men, including Carnegie and Morgan, who appeared to amass an enormous amount of cash and land wealth through the powerful trusts they controlled at a time when many American workers lived in poverty. In addition the unprecedented influx of immigrants at the turn of the century enabled companies to take advantage of cheap labor and ignore dangerous working conditions.

Armed with the commission's findings Roosevelt revived the moribund Sherman Anti-trust Act of 1890 and the Interstate Commerce Act of 1887 to curtail monopolies he believed to be in possession of too much power. In effect this gave the federal government and specifically the office of the president stronger regulatory powers over corporations. During his presidency Roosevelt supported investigations into antitrust suits against the beef, oil, sugar, tobacco, and steel industries and continued his attacks on the railroad barons. In 1902, he urged Congress to create a Bureau of Corporations to regulate big business. Then he brought suit against J. P. Morgan's Northern Securities Company, an act that dismayed the corporate world. The action against Northern Securities initiated a period in which Roosevelt brought more than 40 legal cases against trusts. In a 1904 decision, the Supreme Court invoked the Sherman Antitrust Act and ordered the Northern Securities Company to dismantle its railroad holdings. The Supreme Court also found Standard Oil Company in violation of the Sherman Antitrust Act. Deemed guilty of strangling trade through buyouts and predatory undercutting of competitors' pricing, Standard Oil was also ordered to fragment its corporate empire.

Roosevelt's use of the commission's findings broadened executive power in dealing with labor-management issues, yet the policy had mixed results. While business railed against his strong-arm tactics, labor complained that his reforms did not go far enough in addressing the rights of workers. However the commission supported labor's right to arbitration, which stated that "the rule of local and national trade unions, almost without exception, provides for conciliatory negotiations with employers before a strike may be entered upon."

MARTA M. KNIGHT

References and Further Reading

Cornell University Library. "Kheel Center for Labor Management Documentation and Archives." www.ilr.cornell.edu/library/kheel. Internet. Accessed November 2005.

Kaufman, Stuart B., Peter J. Albert, and Grace Palladino, eds. *The Samuel Gompers Papers*, Vol.5 : *An Expanding Movement at the Turn of the Century, 1898–1902*. Chicago: University of Illinois Press, 1996.

Mowry, George Edwin. *The Era of Theodore Roosevelt, 1900–1912*. New York: Harper, 1958.

United States. Industrial Commission Reports, Vols. 1–19, 1899–1902. Washington, DC: United States Government Printing Office, 1902.

Cases and Statutes Cited

Interstate Commerce Act
Sherman Anti-trust Act

See also **Gompers, Samuel; Sherman Anti-Trust Act of 1890**

UNITED STEELWORKERS OF AMERICA

The United Steelworkers of America was a union of workers in basic steel and related industries. In the mid-twentieth century it represented the vast majority of such workers. Through mergers it also came to represent workers in many other industries, such as aluminum and rubber. The union was formed in May 1942, when a convention of the steelworkers' Organizing Committee and the Amalgamated Association of Iron, Tin, and Steel Workers reformed themselves into the new union.

Before the Union

In the first three decades of the twentieth century, the steel industry was generally able to keep unions out. Workers' defeats in major strikes in 1892, 1901, and 1919 guaranteed nonunion status. The Amalgamated Association (the AA) carried on with a few thousand members in tiny, specialized parts of the industry but did little to organize the mass of steelworkers.

The coming of the Great Depression and the New Deal changed things. The Depression undermined workers' trust in the steel industry's managers. The National Industrial Recovery Act gave workers the right to organize unions. There was considerable conflict in 1933, 1934, and 1935. Some workers joined independent or Communist unions. The biggest group joined the AA and formed an activist wing (the Rank-and-File Movement) that far outnumbered the forces behind the faint-hearted elected officials. However the officials were able to prevail in a cautious course, and tens of thousands of disillusioned steel workers streamed out of the union. At the same time most steel companies tried to forestall unions by setting up company-dominated employee-representation plans (ERPs), which nominally included nearly all of the workers in the main companies.

The Steelworkers' Organizing Committee

In late 1935, John L. Lewis, the president of the United Mine Workers (UMWA), intervened to help the steelworkers. Lewis wanted to see a strong movement of industrial-style unions, especially in the steel industry. He believed in industrial unions in principle and believed such a movement would help his own union. Lewis led several other union leaders to set up the Committee on Industrial Organizations (CIO) in late 1935 to promote industrial unionism. A few months later Lewis was able to strong-arm the AA into joining the CIO. In June 1936, the CIO set up the Steelworkers' Organizing Committee (SWOC) to organize the steelworkers. The miners gave the organizing committee $500,000 to get started.

Formally the SWOC leadership was a committee made up of several union leaders, some from the mineworkers and some from other CIO unions. The chairman was Philip Murray, a vice-president of the UMWA. In reality the leadership committee rarely met and left most decisions up to Murray. Although Murray was willing to encourage democracy at the local union level, he kept the main power in SWOC firmly in his own hands. He could appoint district leaders, hire organizers, approve or turn down proposed contracts, and veto proposed strikes.

He began the job of staffing the union by appointing three regional directors. Clinton Golden was put in charge of the East (including Pittsburgh). He was a labor intellectual, organizer, and former government bureaucrat. The UMWA officers Van A. Bittner and William Mitch were appointed to oversee the Midwest and Canada, and the South, respectively.

The union cast a wide net to find its organizers. Many came from the UMWA. Roughly one-third came from the Communist party (CP) after Lewis and the CP's leaders came to an understanding. The full-time organizers were supplemented by part-time

Representatives of steel talks leaving White House after session. Left to right: Arthur J. Goldberg, general counsel, United Steel Workers; Philip Murray, president, USW; John Stephens, vice president, U.S. Steel; Ben Morrell, Jones & Laughlin; David J. McDonald, Secy. Treas., USW; and Charles White, President, Republic Steel. Library of Congress, Prints & Photographs Division [LC-USZ62-100673].

workers from inside the mills, including many leaders from the ERPs. The organizers worked both inside the mills and in steelworkers' communities. They tried to gain support for the union in ethnic organizations and neighborhood churches. They also promoted President Roosevelt's re-election.

The SWOC followed a policy of being racially and ethnically inclusive but met a lot of skepticism in the black community. Here the UMWA's reputation as a racially inclusive union proved to be a big asset to its offspring. In many locals the union leaders encouraged racially mixed slates to run for office. Blacks often served as vice-presidents. The SWOC also hired many black organizers.

The results were mixed. Despite widespread sympathy, actual members were hard to come by. In early 1937, the SWOC claimed to have 125,000 members, but that was a very soft figure. The tide turned in SWOC's favor after U.S. Steel voluntarily signed a written contract in March 1937. The U.S. Steel managers had been impressed by the autoworkers' sit-down strike against General Motors in January and February. They were also worried by the National Labor Relations Board (NLRB) rulings against the company's ERPs. The contract mostly restated the current arrangements, but it gave a 10-cent-an-hour raise, and allowed the SWOC to represent its members in grievances and negotiations, with binding arbitration as a final (but voluntary) step.

Although the contract was not strong, getting any written agreement at all was seen as an advance. For a few months the organizing staff was flooded with new members and new locals. By October the claimed membership was over 535,000. The SWOC was able to win recognition at Jones and Laughlin Steel after a short strike.

The happy period came to an end with the little steel strike. Several steel companies including Bethlehem, Republic, Youngstown Sheet and Tube, and Inland decided to resist the union. Republic locked out workers at plants in Canton, Ohio, where the union was strong. The union struck Republic in protest, and the struggle soon spread to plants of all four companies. The SWOC was not so strong in the little steel companies as at U.S. Steel, and so the little steel companies decided to keep their plants operating during the strike. This led to considerable violence among union workers, procompany workers, and police.

The most famous episode took place at Republic Steel's plant in South Chicago. On Memorial Day 1937, the union held a large rally to protest police harassment of pickets. When the workers marched toward the plant entrance, they were blocked by Chicago police. The police fired on the marchers, and then charged and beat them. Ten union supporters were killed, and at least a hundred more were wounded.

Republic workers met with police violence or pro-company mobs in Canton and Massillon, Ohio, and Monroe, Michigan. Bethlehem Steel helped organize procompany mobs in Johnstown, Pennsylvania. By late June the strike was defeated in most locations. Many pro-union workers were fired, and SWOC spent several years struggling in the NLRB and in court to win their re-instatement. The only slightly bright spot for SWOC came in Indiana Harbor (in East Chicago, Indiana). The governor of Indiana was able to negotiate an end to the strike that involved *de facto* recognition of the union's right to represent its members at Inland and Youngstown Sheet and Tube.

After the defeat of the little steel strike, the union went into a slump, mostly due to the Roosevelt recession of 1938 to 1940. While the union still claimed to represent hundreds of thousands of workers, many of those workers were laid off for weeks or months. In 1940, there were fewer than 180,000 dues paying members. The union leaders cut the staff and took the opportunity to get rid of many of the Communists and leftists.

The World War II Era

World War II and the economic boom that came with it gave the union the chance to finish organizing the steelworkers. In 1940, Van Dittner was put in charge of the effort to organize Bethlehem Steel, the second largest steel company. This campaign bore fruit in early 1941 with successful strikes at Bethlehem's plants at Lackawanna, New York, and Bethlehem, Pennsylvania. The company agreed to hold elections at all its plants, and SWOC won. The other little steel companies agreed to NLRB-administered card counts that the union generally won. The contract negotiations for these companies dragged on until after the United States was in the war.

The union also used its new-found strength to improve its contracts with U.S. Steel, to win NLRB elections at several U.S. Steel plants, and to persuade big steel to take grievances to binding arbitration.

By the spring of 1942, Murray felt that the organization of the steelworkers was nearly complete.

The union claimed over 650,000 members. In response to rank-and-file complaints, a convention was called, and SWOC was transformed into the United Steelworkers of America. The union was open to all steelworkers. Its top-down internal structure and governance revealed its descent from SWOC and the United Mine Workers. The president still had the power to appoint staffers. The International Executive Board, made up of the national officers and the district directors could veto proposed strikes, negotiate contracts, and control the local unions' finances. Unlike most unions, the USWA's national officers and district directors were to be elected by the membership except that in 1942, they were selected by the convention.

Expansion during the war led the union into new areas. It began organizing locals of white-collar steel employees and plant guards. In 1944, the Aluminum Workers of America merged into the USWA. Further in 1940, Murray replaced John L. Lewis as the president of the CIO, while keeping his post as head of the SWOC.

The energy and growth of the era was reflected in a spurt of books and ideas in the early 1940s. In 1940, *Organized Labor and Production: Next Steps in Industrial Democracy* was published by Murray and Morris Cooke (though Murray basically just lent his name to the venture). The book argued that business would operate better with strong unions as cooperative partners. In 1942, Murray proposed a similar scheme when he suggested that American industry should be governed by a series of industrial councils made up equally of business and labor representatives to increase war production. Very little came of Murray's plan.

Also in 1942, Clinton Golden and Harold Ruttenberg (the USWA's director of research) published the *Dynamics of Industrial Democracy*. The book advanced the same theses as Murray and Cooke's book but in more detail. Most famously *Dynamics* described and justified a steel union local that tried and expelled one of its founding members when he criticized the way the officers were cooperating with company management. It seemed as if one could not achieve industrial democracy if there were too much union democracy.

There was a lot of dissent because once the United States entered the war, the CIO unions pledged not to strike. The union lost its strongest weapon against management. Even striking in violation of the pledge was considered a bad idea because it would alienate the government and public opinion.

The union made up for its weakness by winning favors from the government bodies running the war effort. In 1942, the national War Labor Board handed down a decision that defined the contents of the union's contracts with the little steel companies. The union won the right to maintenance of membership, which put new hires into the union and made it hard for them to leave later. There was also a modified dues check-off. The contracts included the so-called little steel formula that put a wartime cap on all workers' wage increases in the name of limiting inflation. After the union won those (usually meager) raises for most of its members, it concentrated on winning such nonmonetary benefits as vacations. In 1943, the USWA pushed the government into enforcing a mandatory 6-day workweek in most areas as one way to raise incomes. Workers flocked to the union to gain representation in government councils. However workers also went on wildcat strikes as a way to defend themselves in ways the union could not agree with. Union officials spent a lot of effort trying to end wartime strikes.

Postwar Prosperity

The 30 years after the war saw the USWA reach its maximum size and power. It grew to over 1.4 million members and was a power in several industries. In the early postwar years, the key challenges involved trade union issues. The union wanted to expand on wartime gains with union shops and dues check-offs. For the members the biggest issue was winning a raise to overcome the inflation of the period. The union struck in early 1946, and 750,000 workers stayed out for 26 days. The workers won a hefty raise. One of the union's gains from this strike was that it forced the companies to finish the reclassification and rationalization of tens of thousands of jobs to promote equal pay for equal work. Another union gain from the 1946 strike was the *de facto* emergence of pattern bargaining (that is, industrywide bargaining). Later the union went on big strikes five more times in 15 years in 1949, 1952, 1955, 1956, and 1959. The strikes were substantial and culminated in the 1959 strike, which lasted 116 days. Though the workers felt that they did not win high enough raises, their standard of living improved. Workers also won improvements in health insurance, pensions, and supplemental unemployment benefits (SUB pay). The union was also able to eliminate the wage differential between the South and the rest of the country. The postwar strikes were largely nonviolent, and the settlements usually involved significant intervention by the federal government.

The long 1959 strike led to a decade of settlements without strikes. In 1973, the USWA and the major steel companies agreed to the Experimental Negotiating Agreement (ENA). This guaranteed an annual 3% wage increase and regular cost-of-living raises. In return the union agreed ahead of time not to strike. This settlement brought major improvements in wages but also led to a lot of dissension by rank-and-file activists.

Postwar Problems

The union faced several problems after the war. The most immediate was what to do about the Communists in the union. They had helped build the union and held offices in many major locals. With the growing Cold War the anti-Communists in the USWA leadership felt that was unacceptable. After the Taft-Hartley Act banned Communists from holding union offices, some district directors began to hold trials of officers suspected of being Reds. In 1948, the USWA convention voted to ban Communists from holding union office. A couple years later the CIO expelled several Communist-led unions. The USWA began raiding and red-baiting the Mine, Mill, and Smelter Workers' union and severely weakened it. In 1967, the remnants merged into the USWA.

The issue of rank-and-file democracy and dissidence also emerged. When Murray was alive, dissent was usually muted. Murray died in late 1952 and was replaced by David J. McDonald. McDonald had been one of Murray's chief aides but had never been a steelworker. Some workers felt that McDonald was too distant, too friendly to management, and lived too opulently. They accused him of practicing tuxedo unionism. In 1956, a group called the Dues Protest Committee arose to call for lower dues. In the 1956 elections they ran Donald C. Rarick, a grievance man, for the international presidency. McDonald beat the unknown candidate by 2 to 1, but the fact that a virtual unknown could win so many votes indicated serious rank-and-file unhappiness.

By 1964, unhappiness with McDonald had spread to the top ranks of the leadership. I. W. Abel, the union's secretary-treasurer ran against McDonald on a platform of increased militancy and rank-and-file input. Abel won in 1965.

A more liberal dissident came forth in 1973. Ed Sadlowski, a staff man in the Chicago-Gary district, ran for district director against the candidate favored by the national leadership. Sadlowski also called for greater militancy and rank-and-file power. Sadlowski lost the 1973 election, but won the court-ordered rerun. In 1977, Sadlowski ran for USWA president on a militant program. He was beaten by Lloyd McBride, the official candidate.

Another long-term problem for the union was the issue of racial justice. Initially the union had upheld multiracial unity and had opened up some jobs to black workers. That process continued during World War II with union approval. However as the union grew stronger, the issue grew tougher to deal with. Many white union members did not want to open up their jobs to black workers. As the union developed seniority rules, it often ended up approving seniority systems that pushed blacks into low-paying, dead-end jobs. In the basic steel industry, this took the form of having seniority systems based on a worker's service in a small department rather than his plantwide service. These systems minimized disruption at times of layoffs, but they also kept workers penned up in particular departments. When workers were slotted into low-wage departments, it was nearly impossible for them to move to better jobs, no matter how much seniority they had. The companies used these rules to discriminate against black workers, often with the consent of union locals. The union tried to evade these issues by supporting civil rights in national politics and ignoring equal rights in the mills.

During the 1960s, a wave of black protest broke out in the steel mills and the steel union. Many suits were filed in court, and some included the union and the companies as codefendants. Much of this black militancy was channeled through the National Ad Hoc Committee, a nationwide group of black workers inside the union created in 1964. The racial issues were largely resolved in 1974 with the approval of a consent decree between the union, the steel companies, and the federal courts. The decree called for measures to defeat past discrimination and to pay black workers something to make up for potentially lost wages. Most importantly the consent decree made it easier for all workers to move from one department to another.

Another civil rights issue was getting a black voice into the top union councils. In 1976, the USWA created a new office, vice-president for human affairs. The union picked Leon Lynch, a black staffer, for the job. In the 1977 elections both slates fielded blacks for the post.

Industrial Decline

Just as many of the union's problems were being dealt with, the steelworkers and their union were hit by de-industrialization. From the late 1970s onward, the steel industry shut down many factories and drastically cut employment at the remaining mills. Union membership dropped from about 1.4 million in 1979 to 490,000 in 1991. The losses were especially sharp for female and minority workers. The steel industry insisted that the union make substantial concessions in wages and benefits. After some initial resistance, the union agreed. To sweeten the pill, a variety of labor-management cooperation schemes were tried in an effort to raise productivity. In addition the steel companies had forced the union to end pattern bargaining by the mid-1980s.

By the early 1990s, the remaining mills were operating far more profitably and efficiently with a much smaller workforce. In the early 2000s, another wave of mergers and shut-downs hit what was left of the industry.

The USWA responded to the harsh industrial climate by merging with other, smaller, unions. The most notable was a merger with the United Rubber Workers in 1995. On its 2005 web site, the union claims 850,000 members in the United States and Canada. Its official name was the United Steel, Paper and Forestry, Rubber, Energy, Allied-Industrial and Service Workers' International Union.

JAMES C. KOLLROS

References and Further Reading

Bernstein, Irving. *Turbulent Years*. Boston, MA: Houghton-Mifflin, 1969.
Brooks, Robert R. R. *As Steel Goes Unionism in a Basic Industry*. New Haven, CT: Yale University Press, 1940.
Clark, Paul F., Peter Gottlieb, and Donald Kennedy, eds. *Forging a Union of Steel: Philip Murray, SWOC, and the United Steelworkers*. Ithaca, NY: ILR Press, 1987.
Dickerson, Dennis C. *Out of the Crucible: Black Steelworkers in Western Pennsylvania 1875–1980*. Albany: State University of New York Press, 1986.
Hinshaw, John. *Steel and Steelworkers: Race and Class Struggle in Twentieth-Century Pittsburgh*. Albany: State University of New York Press, 2002.
Hoerr, John P. *And the Wolf Finally Came: The Decline of the American Steel Industry*. Pittsburgh, PA: University of Pittsburgh Press, 1988.
Metzger, Jack. *Striking Steel: Solidarity Remembered*. Philadelphia, PA: Temple University Press, 2002.
Needleman, Ruth. *Black Freedom Fighters in Steel: The Struggle for Democratic Unionism*. Ithaca, NY: ILR Press, 2003.
Reuter, Mark. *Sparrows Point: Making Steel*. New York: Summit Books, 1988.
Rose, James D. *Duquesne and the Rise of Steel Unionism*. Urbana and Chicago: University of Illinois Press, 2001.
Serrin, William. *Homestead: The Glory and Tragedy of an American Steel Town*. New York: Times Books, 1992.
Stein, Judith. *Running Steel, Running America: Race, Economic Policy, and the Decline of Liberalism*. Chapel Hill: University of North Carolina Press, 1998.

Cases and Statutes Cited

National Industrial Recovery Act
Taft-Hartley Act

See also **Amalgamated Association of Iron and Steel Workers; American Federation of Labor-Congress of Industrial Organizations; Civil Rights; Communist Party; Industrial Democracy; Labor-Management Co-operation; Lewis, John L.; Memorial Day Massacre; Significant Gains and Missed Opportunities, 1950s and 1960s; Ruttenberg, Harold; Sadlowski, Ed; Steel and Iron; Steel Strike (1959); Taft-Hartley Act; United Mine Workers of America; World War II**

UNITED TEXTILE WORKERS

The United Textile Workers (UTW) originated in 1901 primarily among the skilled, white, male workers in the New England textile industry along with scattered remnants of the National Union of Textile Workers in the South. Skilled workers in the textile industry had specialized jobs, including fixing weaving looms, operating mule spinning frames that turned out high-quality yarn, and sharpening blades on carding machines that separated and straightened cotton fibers early in the production process. These skills had not yet been broken down into smaller tasks, thereby subject to replacement by machines. Relatively difficult to replace, skilled workers had some leverage when bargaining with mill owners. The UTW belonged to the American Federation of Labor (AFL), which had been formed in the 1880s to protect the interests of skilled workers in many occupations. In 1901, the UTW's membership was roughly 10,000, less than 2% of the industry's workforce. Most textile employees were relatively unskilled women and children, who were either recent immigrants from southern and Eastern Europe in the North, or from white, Piedmont farm families in the South. Blacks were excluded from textile production jobs in the South.

Not necessarily seeing themselves as having common interests despite working in the same industry, UTW members were often reluctant to unite with other skilled workers. Unity was made more difficult because the textile industry was highly unstable in the early twentieth century. Textile production was a decentralized sector of the economy, far more competitive than most core industries. This was true in the North but even more so in the South, which had hundreds of independent mills. The industry had begun a long migration from North to South, with low-labor costs the major comparative advantage for southern mills. Anything that increased labor costs in the North, like unionized skilled workers, met harsh opposition from northern mill owners. After an unsuccessful strike by skilled workers in Augusta, Georgia, in 1902, the UTW gave up on the South for over a decade and focused on the North, making relatively strong progress, especially among weavers in rug and carpet mills.

Conflicts developed within the union however when locals negotiated with the national leadership over dues. Expanding union membership and influence required resources, but locals with large numbers of dues-paying members often resented paying for campaigns in other regions, especially when many locals barely collected any dues. Lack of money bedeviled the UTW throughout its existence, especially when existing or potential members went on strike and needed financial assistance.

The UTW also experienced competition from rival unions. Some UTW members defected in the 1910s to the National Amalgamation of Textile Operatives, which fought against skill dilution from both mechanization and fraternizing institutionally with other trades. The radical Industrial Workers of the World (IWW) competed with the UTW, most famously during a strike in Lawrence, Massachusetts, in 1912. The IWW hoped to represent all textile workers, skilled and unskilled, native-born and immigrant, a goal that anticipated industrial unionism in the 1930s, but one that most UTW members opposed in the 1910s. Indeed UTW leaders applauded the federal government's crackdown on the IWW after World War I. Nevertheless craft unionists gained no favor with mill owners, who strongly resisted the UTW.

A Brief Heyday

World War I marked the heyday of the UTW. The wartime combination of labor scarcity and abnormally high demand for textiles placed workers in a strong bargaining position. Government emphasis on democracy, including industrial democracy, resonated with mill workers. The UTW membership skyrocketed by nearly 70,000 during the war and in the immediate postwar years, peaking in 1920 at about 105,000, or roughly 10% of the nation's textile labor force. Significantly most new recruits were relatively unskilled, white women and young men, obviously not the original membership profile. Strikes erupted throughout the textile industry when the war ended as industrialists, faced with a completely different economic environment, sought to reverse what they saw as the peculiar and temporary increases in wages and job security their workers had enjoyed.

It seems a pity that some of the spinning frames are so large that the children cannot operate them. Catawba Cotton Mills. Location: Newton, North Carolina. Library of Congress, Prints & Photographs Division, National Child Labor Committee Collection [LC-DIG-nclc-01536].

Both northern and southern workers resisted retrenchment. Most strikes began without the blessing of UTW leaders, who knew that the union could not replace strikers' earnings and who realized that lost strikes could poison future prospects for textile unionization. Nevertheless the UTW had to be involved, or it would risk being perceived as irrelevant to, or even opposed to, workers' desires. The UTW organizers reached several tentative agreements with southern mill owners in 1919, which angered business leaders but gave hope to thousands of workers. By the end of 1919, the UTW claimed 43 chartered locals in North Carolina alone and a record number of dues-paying members. Although worker support for unionization was real, dues collection was often wildly exaggerated. In any event when the textile market turned down in 1921, the UTW could not protect its membership. Grudgingly the UTW struck to protest rollbacks in wages and working conditions, but its leadership knew that the union's prospects were dim. The UTW was somewhat more successful in the North, especially in a 1922 strike wave that halted most New England textile production. Significantly these strikes limited the number of hours per week for textile laborers. But ironically these victories increased the competitive advantage of southern mills and helped spur the movement of the industry

in that direction, which undercut the UTW's prospects where they looked brightest.

Futile Efforts

The UTW gained a fair amount of publicity but few positive results through its participation in a strike wave that swept southern textile communities from the late 1920s through 1934. In 1927, UTW organizer Alfred Hoffmann proved to be a popular motivator when he assisted mill workers in Henderson, North Carolina, attempt to re-instate a 3-year-old wage cut. Hoffmann offered $125 for strike relief and claimed to have recruited 600 members. His contribution however could hardly replace the mill's $9,000 weekly payroll. The strike faltered when workers could not pay their bills and the company evicted selected union activists.

Two years later the UTW attempted to lead a strike at a German-owned rayon plant in Elizabethton, Tennessee. Strikers, mostly young women, received more relief assistance from their families small merchants than from the chronically impoverished union. As strikebreakers appeared from the countryside, the UTW tried to settle the conflict long before most mill workers seemed ready. Better to cut losses than fight to the finish, the UTW appeared to say, and the message received by many workers was that union activists might not be worthy of trust.

Also in 1929, the UTW found itself in the midst of an enormous strike in Gastonia, North Carolina, one complicated by the presence of the Communist-led National Textile Workers' Union (NTWU). Although the UTWA presented itself as the moderate, anti-Communist alternative to the NTWU, business leaders, clergy, and government officials failed to make the distinction and fought hard, including the use of state troops, to defeat the strike while conveying the impression that all labor conflict was subversive. Later that year in Marion, North Carolina, textile workers received vague assurances of assistance from UTW organizers and walked out in protest over the stretch-out. The UTW representatives led a contingent to meet with mill owner R. W. Baldwin, who sneered at them. With the clever use of a staged incident, the company received support from the national guard, and the strike soon ground to a halt, again with no lasting gains for the union's efforts.

The same story repeated itself but on a much larger scale during the 1934 general textile strike. Spurred by Franklin Roosevelt's New Deal support for labor organizing, some 400,000 workers, North and South, struck in the late summer, primarily to oppose the hated stretch-out system. The UTW rode the back of this tiger, unable to provide adequate relief for such a vast number of strikers and also unable to diminish the formidable powers aligned against them. Hunger, mass firings, and violence eventually smashed the general strike and with it, the long-term prospects of the UTW.

By the end of the decade, the original UTW had been refashioned as first the Textile Workers' Organizing Committee, and then the Textile Workers' Union of America, affiliated with the Congress of Industrial Organizations (CIO). In 1939, however, a group of disaffected textile unionists reorganized the UTWA-AFL, but they were never again a major factor in textile unionism. The UTW existed into the 1970s, occasionally locking horns with the Textile Workers of America (TWUA) and serving in the 1950s as a harbor for disgruntled former TWUA leaders who hoped to challenge the CIO union. All this occurred however in the context of a declining industry and increasingly dim prospects for organization in textiles under any union. Always underfinanced, and never willing or powerful enough to challenge the military might of the state, the UTW crumbled before formidable opponents throughout its troubled history, yet no union in textiles has fared considerably better. This is tragic because

hundreds of thousands of textile workers clearly wanted more control over their working lives.

DANIEL CLARK

References and Further Reading

Carlton, David. *Mill and Town in South Carolina, 1880–1920.* Baton Rouge: Louisiana State University Press, 1982.

Daniel, Clete. *Culture of Misfortune: An Interpretive History of Textile Unionism in the United States.* Ithaca, NY: ILR Press, 2001.

Fink, Gary. *The Fulton Bag and Cotton Mills Strike of 1914–1915: Espionage, Labor Conflict, and New South Industrial Relations.* Ithaca, NY: ILR Press, 1993.

Gilman, Glenn. *Human Relations in the Industrial Southeast: A Study of the Textile Industry.* Chapel Hill: University of North Carolina Press, 1956.

Hall, Jacquelyn Dowd, James Leloudis, Robert Korstad, Mary Murphy, Lu Ann Jones, and Christopher Daly. *Like a Family: The Making of a Southern Cotton Mill World.* Chapel Hill: University of North Carolina Press, 1987.

Hodges, James. *New Deal Labor Policy and the Southern Cotton Textile Industry, 1933–1941.* Knoxville: University of Tennessee Press, 1986.

Marshall, F. Ray. *Labor in the South.* Cambridge, MA: Harvard University Press, 1967.

McLaurin, Melton Alonza. *Paternalism and Protest: Southern Cotton Mill Workers and Organized Labor, 1875–1905.* Westport, CT: Greenwood Publishing Corporation, 1971.

Mitchell, George Sinclair. *Textile Unionism in the South.* Chapel Hill: University of North Carolina Press, 1931.

Newby, I. A. *Plain Folk in the New South: Social Change and Cultural Persistence, 1880–1915.* Baton Rouge: Louisiana State University Press, 1989.

Pope, Liston. *Millhands and Preachers: A Study of Gastonia.* New Haven, CT: Yale University Press, 1942.

Salmond, John. *Gastonia 1929: The Story of the Loray Mill Strike.* Chapel Hill: University of North Carolina Press, 1995.

Tipppett, Tom. *When Southern Labor Stirs.* New York: Jonathan Cape and Harrison Smith, 1931.

See also **American Federation of Labor-Congress of Industrial Organizations; Gastonia Strike (1929); National Union of Textile Workers; Textile Workers' Union of America; Textiles**

UNITED TRANSPORT SERVICE EMPLOYEES OF AMERICA

See **International Brotherhood of Red Caps/United Transport Service Employees of America**

UPRISING OF THE 20,000 (1909)

The Uprising of 20,000, the largest strike of female workers in U.S. history started in 1909. This 14-week general strike had profound effects on the union

Two women strikers on picket line during the "Uprising of the 20,000" garment workers strike, New York City. Library of Congress, Prints & Photographs Division [LC-USZ62-49516].

and reform movements of the day. The strike started when Rosen Brothers factory refused to pay the negotiated price and sought to renegotiate the rate. The 200 workers walked out demanding a just price. The workers turned to Local 25, the shirtwaist makers' local of the International Ladies' Garment Workers' Union (ILGWU) and the United Hebrew Trades (UHT) for assistance. Yet in the face of insurmountable odds, and after a 5-week struggle, Rosen Brothers settled with the union. The workers gained union recognition, a 20% piece-rate hike, and, more importantly, a shop-floor committee to give workers a democratic voice. The first significant victory for Local 25 was achieved, and with it, workers streamed into the union and strike talk spread.

As the Rosen Brothers' strike was being settled, strike fever spread to other shops throughout the city. These strikes were unorganized and spontaneous in that workers went out first, then like the Rosen strike, contacted and joined the union. Two of these strikes, at the Leiserson and Triangle shops, were the two biggest shops.

By mid-October it appeared to union leaders that unless something drastic was done the strikes at Leiserson and Triangle would be lost. Both firms hired thugs to disrupt pickets and kept their factories open with scab labor. Under these circumstances, Local 25 and the UHT began to contemplate a general strike. However it was a risk. Local 25 had approximately 500 members and only $4 in its treasury. Still the

workers were driven by a hyperpassion for unionism that just might sustain a call for a general strike. Local 25's 15-member executive board (including four women, one of whom was Clara Lemlich) met to discuss the idea of a general strike. At a general meeting of the local on October 21, the union voted for a general strike and appointed a committee of five (three men and two women) to put it into effect. As talk of a general strike spread from shop to shop, picket-line violence, police brutality, and use of thugs hired by shop owners increased. The union was in a precarious position.

Early in the strike middle-class reform women became increasingly visible. Many seeing these mainly young immigrant women strikers as sisters in the larger women's rights struggle ran to the picket lines in a show of feminist solidarity. Others operated under an older sense of *noblesse oblige*, an effort to protect these fragile young female strikers. Middle-class female reformers, whatever their motivation, stepped up their activity as the strike wore on. The focus of these reformers' activities was the New York Women's Trade Union League (WTUL). The national WTUL was founded at the American Federation of Labor's (AFL's) Boston convention in 1903 by the noted socialist William English Walling, labor organizer Mary Kenny, and Hull-House's Jane Addams, along with others. The WTUL saw itself as filling a necessary void. The leaders believed in labor unions as a democratic necessity. But unions had ignored women workers. The WTUL's goal was to aid local and national unions in organizing women. It quickly established branches in Boston, Chicago, and New York (NY). The NYWTUL therefore saw the 1909 strike as its opportunity.

On the night of November 22, an overflow crowd had to be directed to other halls throughout the city, Beethoven Hall and the Manhattan Lyceum among them. "For two hours," the *New York World* reported, "attentive audiences were cautioned to use deliberation, to be sober in their decision, but to be loyal to each other, and when they did decide to strike to stand by their union until all demands were granted."

After listening for 2 hours, Lemlich rose to speak. She was a member of Local 25's executive board, a leader of the Leiserson strike, and an equally fiery Socialist. Rising and taking the floor, she said: "I am a working girl, one of those who are on strike against intolerable conditions. I am tired of listening to speakers who talk in general terms. What we are here for is to decide whether we shall or shall not strike. I offer a resolution that a general strike be declared—now." What Lemlich wanted was action, not words. With that, "the big gathering was on its feet," according to the *New York World*: "Everyone shouting an emphatic affirmative, waving hats, canes, handkerchiefs, anything that came handy. For five minutes, perhaps, the tumult continued; then the chairperson, B. Feigenbaum [of the *Jewish Daily Forward*], made himself heard and asked for a seconder of the resolution. Again the big audience leaped to its feet, everyone seconding."

The next day 15,000 shirtwaist makers walked out. The first few days were simply chaotic as thousands of workers tried to crowd into Clinton Hall, Local 25's headquarters, to join the union. Clinton Hall had the atmosphere of a religious revival meeting. In one corner workers were dancing; in another, signing union cards; and in yet another, talking strategy. Local 25 sent strike committees from location to location trying to settle all the strikes shop by shop. By November 26, 2,000 workers had settled and returned to work, but another 1,200 had walked out on strike.

The 70 large manufacturers that dominated the trade, led by Triangle and Leiserson, however, stayed firm. Rather than go it alone or attempt to negotiate with the union, the owners of Triangle, Max Blanck and Isaac Harris, circulated a letter in early November to all shirtwaist manufacturers suggesting the formation of an Employers' Mutual Protective Association "in order to prevent this irresponsible union in gain[ing] the upper hand . . . [and] dictating to us the manner of conducting our business." According to most newspaper accounts, by the evening of

November 24, 2 days after the call for a general strike, more than 20,000 workers remained on strike.

Following Triangle's call, the new Association of Waist and Dress Manufacturers (the association) met on November 25 and 26 at the Broadway Central Hotel. It elected I. B. Hyman as chair and Charles Weinblatt as secretary and legal counsel. Declaring open war on the union, Samuel Floersheimer, speaking for the association, stated that any contract signed with the ILGWU or Local 25 was not "worth the paper it was written upon . . . [for] the men connected with the union are a lot of irresponsible black guards." The organization further called for all manufacturers who had already signed contracts to openly break them and lock out their workers. Firms then that joined the association, according to Floersheimer, would be striking a blow for liberty. Yet few small shops took this advice. During this brief chaotic period, these settled firms were doing a brisk business picking up the orders left unfilled by the larger shops, and they were not going to jeopardize it for the larger shops or for any matter of principle.

Large manufacturers hired private security agents, mainly to keep their factories open with mostly non-union Italian labor. In their circular letters, these agencies included the names of known gangsters, thugs, and toughs. These services performed two main functions: To disrupt picketing and break the morale of the strikers, and to allow the use of scabs to keep their production going. On August 12, before the general strike, Rosen Brothers hired detectives to remain inside the shop. During an altercation in front of the shop, several picketers were badly beaten. The *Jewish Daily Forward* published photos of the girls and the names of the toughs. These detectives all had lengthy criminal records.

Increased violence against young and teenaged women, coupled with the injustice of the court system, finally worked to the strikers' advantage, since it gained the waist makers public support among the middle class. By the end of October, the police had arrested 77 strikers; by January 1, the number had reached 707.

On October 23, the police arrested Margaret Johnson, a middle-class ally and member of the WTUL, for picketing. With this, the activity of the WTUL increased. One incident that sparked a sustained controversy was the arrest of Mary Dreier on November 4. Working-class women had demanded that their allies in the WTUL fully participate in the strike by scheduling themselves for picket watches around the clock. Dreier, a socially prominent woman and WTUL president, had been persuaded to picket in an effort to protect the strikers. Many working-class members of the WTUL believed that the mere presence of the middle-class women would be enough to end the violence or more specifically, to shield them. Picketing peacefully in front of the Triangle factory, Dreier tried to convince some of the scabs not to cross the lines. One of their escorts called her a dirty liar. With that, Dreier approached a police officer and said, "You heard the language that man used to me. Am I not entitled to your protection?" The policeman replied that he could not be certain that she was not a liar. When a scab then accused her of assault, it was Dreier who was arrested. She was brought to the Mercer Street station, but when the police discovered who she was, they released her immediately. The arrest of Dreier brought heightened press coverage and a more intense WTUL effort to end police brutality and legal injustice.

Negotiations to end the strike began as early as the strike's second month but without much success. While much is known about the picketing, curiously little is known about the process of negotiation. What made this strike different from others were not just the number, age, and gender of the strikers, but the style of bargaining that developed. Early on both sides created elaborate new organizational structures for collective bargaining. In addition individuals and groups outside the New York garment industry and union shaped the bargaining process. The forces behind the new structures were led by men from within the union and elite women and men from without. One reason given for the need for this new, more bureaucratic structure was the youth and gender of the strikers. The strikers' inability to overcome the biggest stumbling block, combined with the manufacturers' absolute refusal to deal with the union, led many to believe that the details of bargaining should be handled by professionals—union leaders and reformers.

On December 6, a break in the stalemate came in the form of John Mitchell, ex president of the United Mine Workers, and Marcus M. Marks, president of the Clothiers' Association. Both of these men embodied a new spirit of industrial relations. They saw labor relations as involving more than just workers and managers. They argued and used their collective influence to gain a position for the public at the bargaining table. Acting on behalf of the National Civic Federation (NCF), Mitchell and Marks offered their services to help break the deadlock and end the strike. Their solution called for a six-member board of arbitration, each side choosing two members and the four choosing the remaining two, that would represent the public's interest. They argued that the current situation would hurt both sides and "prove only which side is stronger, not which side is right."

The union quickly responded to the NCF call and appointed union adviser Morris Hillquit and Mitchell as their chosen representatives. Management however refused the services of the NCF, announcing that they would have nothing to do with the union.

On February 15, the ILGWU called off the New York general strike. In reality it had all but ended at least 2 weeks before. Yet the union declared the strike a victory, and in many ways, it was. What was gained came from individual shop contracts with small and medium-sized shops, not the industrywide agreement that was hoped for. Of the 320 contracts signed, 302 recognized the union. Membership in the local went from 500 members in August to over 20,000 by February. The union had also survived to fight another day. To be sure without an industrywide agreement, these shop agreements were weak. However the strikers were able, at least for the present, to end the most noxious features of their servitude and begin to claim their rightful place as industrial citizens.

RICHARD A. GREENWALD

References and Further Reading

Carpenter, Jesse Thomas. *Competition and Collective Bargaining in the Needle Trades, 1910–1967*. Ithaca, NY: ILR Press, 1972.

Dye, Nancy Schrom. *As Equals and as Sisters: Feminism, the Labor Movement, and the Women's Trade Union League of New York*. Columbia: University of Missouri Press, 1980.

Greenwald, Richard A. *The Triangle Fire, the Protocols of Peace, and Industrial Democracy in Progressive Era New York, Labor in Crisis*. Philadelphia, PA: Temple University Press, 2005.

Orleck, Annelise. *Common Sense and a Little Fire: Women and Working-Class Politics in the United States, 1900–1965*. Chapel Hill: University of North Carolina Press, 1995.

V

VAN KLEECK, MARY (1883–1972)
Social Researcher and Reformer

In a career that spanned over 40 years—from the high tide of Progressive Era optimism to the low-water mark of McCarthyite cynicism—Mary van Kleeck's work, mostly at the Russell Sage Foundation, encompassed social settlements, women and labor, workers' rights, social insurance, and economic planning—work fueled by Christian idealism disciplined by reason and science.

Van Kleeck was born in Glenham, New York, the daughter of an Episcopal minister, a common vocation in her family. In 1892, following her father's death, the family moved to Flushing, New York, where Mary attended public schools. At Smith College, from which she graduated in 1904, she already demonstrated what would become a lifelong involvement with social investigation—the YWCA's "industrial work"—inflected by the social gospel. The missionary zeal of the enterprise is captured well in her writing. In a 1917 book on the millinery trade in New York City, she wrote, "To the social reformer today,—and by social reformer we mean every man and woman who has a vision of what the social order ought to be and who believes that it can be made like that vision,—to recognize an evil is to set about changing it. Nothing socially disastrous is inevitable. Such faith, however, if it is to be fulfilled, must be particularized. It must apply wherever the conditions of modern industry press heavily upon the workers,—in an artificial flower factory and in the mammoth steel works, in subway construction, and in the making of a woman's hat" (*A Seasonal Industry*, p. 26).

A year after graduation, van Kleeck went to work at the College Settlement Association on New York's Lower East Side, where she joined and was mentored by women whose province of action encompassed such groups as the Women's Trade Union League, the Consumers' League of New York, and the New York Child Labor Committee—vital parts of a women's public culture that promoted cross-class alliances in pursuit of social justice for working people. The city was a laboratory for social investigators—its vast immigrant population filling the teeming tenements and finding employment in small- and medium-scale enterprises such as the garment trades as well as in homework—and van Kleeck began her work there with studies of child labor and of overtime by women workers.

In 1910, van Kleeck began her association with the Russell Sage Foundation, established in 1907, that lasted almost without interruption until her retirement in 1948. Charged by its benefactor with "the improvement of social and living conditions in the United States," the foundation underwrote important social scientific investigations, including a continuation of van Kleeck's studies of women workers. As the head of its Committee on Women's Work, van Kleeck, with her mostly female staff of investigators, undertook important studies of the bookbinding, artificial flower, and millinery trades in New York, exposing the problems caused by night work and seasonal unemployment, which led to legislative action by the State of New York. In 1916, her remit was expanded as the director of the foundation's new Division (later Department) of Industrial Studies to include studies of male workers. In these years she also taught at the New York School of Philanthropy and at the School for Social Work at Smith College, and returned to lecture at the YWCA's annual student conference at Silver Bay, Lake George (which she had attended as a Smith undergraduate).

Her growing reputation as an expert on women and work led to her recruitment during World War I to establish employment standards for women in war industries. In Washington, she served in the Ordnance Department of the U.S. Army, as a member of the War Labor Policy Board and then as the director of the Women in Industry Service of the Department of Labor (which became the Women's Bureau in 1920). She resigned in August 1919 and returned to her position at the Russell Sage Foundation.

Her service during the war secured her national reputation in labor matters. She was appointed to the President's Conference on Unemployment in 1921 and to the Committee on Unemployment and Business Cycles in 1922–1923. The 1920s also saw a new emphasis in van Kleeck's work that had already been evident before the war intervened. Through her studies of the sweated trades, she had concluded that government regulation of working conditions alone was inadequate to address the variety of problems that workers faced, especially irregularity of employment. Instead, adopting the ideas of Frederick W. Taylor on scientific management, van Kleeck (with others in the Taylor Society) began to interpret unemployment and underemployment as waste, something to be eliminated by the same technocratic approach that Taylor had used in ordering factory production processes. The insistence on a more rational industrial organization, she argued, would redound to the benefit of all—employer and worker alike.

Van Kleeck's advocacy of protective labor legislation and minimum-wage laws for women inevitably brought her into conflict with feminists supporting the Equal Rights Amendment in the 1920s, whose emphasis on individual freedom, sometimes asserting liberty to contract issues, imperiled the gains working women had made collectively ("Woman and Machines"). Under the onslaught of the Great Depression, however, van Kleeck acknowledged the need for a larger government role in relieving the economic distress facing all workers, authoring in 1934 an unsuccessful Unemployment and Social Security bill, sponsored by Congressman Ernest Lundeen of Minnesota, whose expansive coverage and funding out of general revenues rather than payroll taxes brought down the ire of supporters of more moderate schemes, including the American Federation of Labor (AFL) leadership.

The New Deal, in fact, bitterly disappointed van Kleeck, especially the Roosevelt administration's failure to challenge corporate power. Her interest in Taylorism and planning had led her during the 1920s to participate in some of the national planning initiatives of Herbert Hoover, but her idea of "social-economic planning" found greater resonance internationally through the International Industrial Relations Institute (where she met Mary Fleddérus, with whom she lived the rest of her life). Increasingly, it was the Soviet Union that attracted her attention—and eventually admiration—for its centralized planning and social ideals. Her six-week visit in 1932 only confirmed her convictions. Until her death, she remained a fierce defender of the regime and a sympathetic ally of the American Communist Party, attracting the attention of the FBI and Senator Joseph McCarthy's Committee on Government Operations.

Her contributions as a social researcher and advocate for reform have not received the attention they deserve. Lesser figures in her world have attracted the attention of biographers, but scholars have seemed uncertain what to make of someone who was a member of the Society of the Companions of the Holy Cross *and* an apologist for the Soviet Union. Van Kleeck would probably be disappointed, as she spent much of her retirement organizing her papers.

STEPHEN COLE

Selected Works

Artificial Flower Makers. New York: Survey Associates, 1913.

Creative America: Its Resources for Social Security. New York: Covici-Friede, 1936.

Technology and Livelihood: An Inquiry into the Changing Technological Basis for Production as Affecting Employment and Living Standards. New York: Russell Sage Foundation, 1944 (with Mary L. Fleddérus).

A Seasonal Industry: A Study of the Millinery Trade in New York. New York: Russell Sage Foundation, 1917.

"Women and Machines." *Atlantic Monthly* 127 (February 1921): 250–260.

Employees' Representation in Coal Mines: A Study of the Industrial Representation Plan of the Colorado Fuel and Iron Company. New York: Russell Sage Foundation, 1924 (with Ben M. Selekman).

Women in the Bookbinding Trade. New York: Survey Associates, 1913.

References and Further Reading

The largest collection of van Kleeck's papers is in the Sophia Smith Collection, Smith College; Wayne State University also has a significant collection of papers. An extensive vertical file of biographical materials can be found in the Tamiment Library, New York University. An obituary appeared in the *New York Times*, June 9, 1972, p. 41.

Alchon, Guy. *The Invisible Hand of Planning: Capitalism, Social Science, and the State in the 1920s*. Princeton, NJ: Princeton University Press, 1985.

———. "Mary Van Kleeck and Social-Economic Planning." *Journal of Policy History* 3 no. 1 (1991): 1–23.

———. "Mary Van Kleeck of the Russell Sage Foundation: Religion, Social Science, and the Ironies of Parasitic Modernity." In *Philanthropic Foundations: New Scholarship, New Possibilities*, edited by Ellen Condliffe Lagemann. Bloomington: Indiana University Press, 1999, pp. 151–166.

———. "The 'Self-Applauding Sincerity' of Overreaching Theory, Biography as Ethical Practice, and the Case of Mary Van Kleeck." In *Gender and American Social Science: The Formative Years*, edited by Helene Silverberg. Princeton, NJ: Princeton University Press, 1998, pp. 291–325.

Fisher, Jacob. *The Response of Social Work to the Depression*. Boston: G. K. Hall, 1980.

Glenn, John M., Lilian Brandt, and F. Emerson Andrews. *Russell Sage Foundation, 1907–1946*. New York: Russell Sage Foundation, 1947.

VIETNAM WAR

The Vietnam War (1965–1973) proved as much of an ordeal for U.S. organized labor and working people as for the country at large. Indeed, divisions over the war significantly weakened American unions, causing bitter fissures that lasted decades. U.S. labor's involvement in Southeast Asia, however, was deeper and more complex than is popularly understood.

The interest of U.S. trade unionists in Indochina, in fact, dates back to the 1940s. During the postwar period, strongly anticommunist elements had emerged in leadership positions in both the American Federation of Labor (AFL) and the Congress of Industrial Organizations (CIO). In the aftermath of World War II, both organizations sent representatives to Western Europe to rally anticommunist unionists against the communist threat.

In this context, neither the AFL nor the CIO raised much objection to the initial re-imposition of colonialism upon Indochina, a move supported by virtually all political sectors in France, including initially the Communist Party. By 1949, however, AFL and CIO officials, certain that Ho Chi Minh and his followers were dedicated agents of Moscow, grew increasingly worried that harsh French rule was aiding the Communist cause. U.S. trade unionists began to call for an end to colonialism and the formation of a noncommunist, nationalist government, respectful of the rights of workers. At the urging of the AFL international representative Irving Brown, in 1950, the newly formed International Confederation of Free Trade Unions (ICFTU) sent a delegation, including John Brophy of the United Mine Workers of America, to Southeast Asia. In Vietnam, the group met with a nascent movement organized by French Christian trade unionists. Over the next several years, American trade unionists forged ties with the Vietnamese movement, which soon took the name the Vietnamese Confederation of Christian Labor (CVTC), under the leadership of Tran Quoc Buu, a nationalist previously allied with the Viet Minh.

During the dangerous days following the division of Vietnam in 1955, U.S. labor provided valuable assistance as the CVTC worked to relocate thousands of trade unionists fleeing the North. That same year, Jodie Eggers, formerly of the CIO International Woodworkers of America, arrived in Saigon to serve as the U.S. Operations Mission's labor advisor. Eggers quickly became a tireless advocate for the CVTC. American trade unionists meanwhile leaned on U.S. government officials to protect the CVTC as the Ngo Dinh Diem administration grew increasingly oppressive.

In 1961, Irving Brown traveled to Vietnam to size up the situation for himself. While he was dismayed by Diem's heavy-handedness, he quickly came to appreciate the CVTC as an independent force with much potential. In his report to the AFL-CIO, Brown was so laudatory of the CVTC that he touted it as a potential "paramilitary" force. After his return, from his offices in Paris, Brown began encouraging dissident Vietnamese. Meanwhile, in Saigon, Buu actively conspired against Diem.

In the aftermath of the 1963 coup against Diem, however, Buu went into hiding temporarily to avoid the threat of arrest from Saigon's new leaders. Eventually, Brown returned to Vietnam in mid-1964 to press directly South Vietnam's new leadership to recognize the rights of labor. Brown also made connections with USAID in Saigon, hoping to harness funds for AFL-CIO-sponsored programs to aid the CVTC.

While Buu's organization remained vulnerable, it increasingly took more of a public posture and drew closer to its American sponsors. In turn, the AFL-CIO, committed deeply to the anticommunist cause in Southeast Asia, began planning a permanent presence in Saigon to aid the CVT (which dropped the designation "Christian" from its name in 1964). The CVT, U.S. trade unionists hoped, might be transformed into a vehicle for much-needed reform in South Vietnam. Thus, when President Lyndon

Johnson, who had bonded closely with U.S. labor leaders, decided to intervene militarily in 1965, the AFL-CIO strongly applauded the move, offering its "unstinting support."

Yet from its beginnings, the war proved a source of painful controversy and tension for American labor. In the fall of 1965, antiwar protesters disrupted the AFL-CIO convention. Although a majority of delegates supported the war, dovish voices also were heard on the convention floor, including the United Auto Workers (UAW) official Emil Mazey, who decried South Vietnam as "a corrupt military dictatorship" unworthy of American support.

As the war progressed, so too did antiwar sentiment among trade unionists. In February 1966, the Executive Council of the Amalgamated Clothing Workers of America (ACWA) officially questioned the "burden of expense" of the war and complained that "the sons of workers. . .are being drafted first for military duty." A few smaller unions, such as New York City Hospital Workers Local 1199, took similar positions. Meanwhile, polls showed union members often less likely than the general public to support escalation of the war—perhaps a reflection of the "working-class" roots of many of those fighting in Southeast Asia. An internal poll taken by the Communication Workers of America in the summer of 1966 showed 56% of respondents favoring withdrawal or negotiations in Vietnam, while only 40% supported the status quo or escalation. Yet concurrently, some trade unionists insisted that Johnson take a tougher line in Vietnam and with America's allies who traded with North Vietnam. The presidents of the three major AFL-CIO maritime unions, in early 1966, sent Johnson a blistering letter threatening to boycott vessels of foreign nations trading with North Vietnam. The Johnson administration arranged a compromise, but positions on both sides were hardening and opponents were increasingly talking past each other. When antiwar trade unionists held a public meeting in Chicago in the fall of 1967, Meany assailed the gathering as "planned in Hanoi."

Wedded to the war, AFL-CIO leaders moved forward with plans for a permanent Federation presence in Saigon to be sponsored by AID dollars. But the Tet Offensive dealt a sharp blow to such plans. Even before the actual Viet Cong attacks, the CVT entered crisis mode when Saigon authorities violently broke a strike by CVT-affiliated electrical workers. As the dust from Tet settled, it became clear that U.S. organized labor faced shifting political terrain at home and mounting challenges in Vietnam.

In 1968, Walter Reuther pulled his United Auto Workers out of the AFL-CIO in part due to the Federation's uncompromising stance on Vietnam.

The violent and tumultuous presidential campaign that year saw the Vietnam War play an ever more divisive role as well. In the end, the AFL-CIO spent unprecedented funds and energies supporting the doomed candidacy of prowar Vice President Hubert Humphrey.

While most trade unionists were distrustful of President Richard Nixon, his struggle to find "peace with honor" won the support of large segments of the rank and file and the AFL-CIO leadership, who also needed Nixon's support for its newly minted Saigon labor office (founded in 1968), the Asian American Free Labor Institute (AAFLI). But Nixon's brazen invasion of Cambodia in 1970 again divided the ranks. While Meany and virtually the entire AFL-CIO leadership praised the attack, Nixon's move deeply angered dovish trade unionists. Walter Reuther, in a statement made the day before his death, warned Nixon the invasion represented "a repudiation of your oft-repeated pledge to bring this tragic war to an end." The ACWA president, Jacob Potofsky, sharply denounced both the invasion and the war at his union's 1970 convention. Elsewhere across the country, grassroots coalitions such as the San Francisco Bay Area Labor Assembly for Peace began working closely with the mainstream antiwar movement.

Yet concurrently, the Cambodian invasion also invigorated hawkish trade unionists. In Lower Manhattan, hardhat construction workers attacked doves protesting the Cambodian invasion; related "hardhat" demonstrations quickly flared in other cities. Seeking political advantage, Nixon invited the leaders of New York City's construction trades unions to the White House.

Although the immediate tumult settled quickly, acrimony remained as the 1972 elections approached. Asked if he wanted to see Nixon defeated, Meany responded, "I don't want to see him defeated by somebody who is advocating surrender, I don't believe in surrender in Vietnam." The Democratic Party's nomination of dovish Senator George McGovern thus created a crisis for the Federation. For the first time, the AFL-CIO Executive Council, primarily reacting to McGovern's call for immediate withdrawal, voted not to endorse a presidential candidate. In response, some dovish trade unionists grew more aggressive. The Teamster general secretary, Harold Gibbons, in the spring of 1972, joined a delegation of antiwar trade unionists on a high-profile trip to Hanoi. That summer, peace-minded trade unionists formed Labor for Peace, an organization dedicated to pressing for immediate withdrawal. Still, the new organization remained divided as to whether to adopt militant measures and work directly with radical elements in the antiwar movement.

While the peace settlement in January 1973 ended the most immediate divisiveness, the AFL-CIO remained a vocal supporter of continuing aid to South Vietnam. Through AAFLI, the Federation continued its mentoring relationship with the CVT. As Saigon tottered, Meany cautioned that the end of the war would hardly bring peace. "While the fighting might stop, the killing would not," he warned. When the end came in late April 1975, Meany scrambled to ensure CVT officials were included among the evacuees. Buu and several hundred did escape, although thousands of those left suffered retribution from their country's new rulers.

By 1975, organized labor in the United States was a divided force, alienated from its former liberal allies and facing the most severe economic downturn since the Depression. Acknowledging some of the lost ground, Meany appeared on the *Dick Cavett* television show. Referring to his support for Johnson and Nixon on Vietnam, he confessed, "If I'd known then what I know now, I don't think we would have backed them."

EDMUND F. WEHRLE

References and Further Reading

Appy, Christian. *Working-Class War: American Combat Soldiers and Vietnam*. Chapel Hill: University of North Carolina Press, 1993.
Boyle, Kevin. *The UAW and the Heyday of American Liberalism, 1945–1968*. Ithaca, NY: Cornell University Press, 1995.
Foner, Philip. *U.S. Labor and the Vietnam War*. New York: International Publishers, 1989.
Freeman, Joshua. "Hardhats: Construction Workers, Manliness, and the 1970 Pro-War Demonstrations." *Journal of Social History* 26 (1993): 725–744.
Gordon, Jerry. *Cleveland Labor and the Vietnam War*. Cleveland, OH: Greater Cleveland Labor History Society, Orange Blossom Press, 1990.
Jeffreys-Jones, Rhodri. *Peace Now!: American Society and the Ending of the Vietnam War*. New Haven, CT: Yale University Press, 1999.
Morgan, Ted. *A Covert Life: Jay Lovestone: Communist, Anti-Communist, and Spymaster*. New York: Random House, 1999.
Wehrle, Edmund. *"Between a River and a Mountain": The AFL-CIO and the Vietnam War, 1947–1975*. Ann Arbor: University of Michigan Press, 2005.

VOLUNTARISM

Voluntarism refers to the American Federation of Labor (AFL) strategy of securing gains through collective bargaining instead of through legislation. It reflects the primacy of economic over political struggle as the best strategy for workers to pursue their self-interest. According to voluntarist principles, the benefits workers can achieve through their own voluntary organizations are superior to those they can achieve politically because unions are more familiar with the needs of workers than government, voluntarism requires workers to take initiative on their own behalf, and finally, legislation promotes "big government," which threatens workers' freedom and independence.

Voluntarists have a profound distrust of the state and believe that workers can only improve their circumstances through the strength of their own self-organization. Consequently, the AFL opposed welfare state measures, such as unemployment insurance and minimum wage laws, which would have undermined and competed with unions' own efforts on behalf of their members. While skeptical of benefits derived through legislation, voluntarists are not opposed to all political activity. Such activity may be necessary in order to prevent the government from restricting the ability of unions to pursue their members' interests, such as passing laws that restrict the right to strike and organize. Political activity may be necessary so that unions can achieve results outside of it.

The strength of voluntarism within the AFL, its reliance upon economic as opposed to political power, has been attributed to many factors. The AFL's voluntarism reflected the lowest common denominator of workplace solidarities around which workers could ally. Political unity beyond issues of wages and hours was precluded by ethnic, religious, and racial cleavages among workers. Its grip upon the AFL also has been attributed to the institutional structure of American government. The separation of powers among the different branches of government created multiple veto points for opponents to block social legislation. Unions adopted voluntarism because of the institutional roadblocks they encountered that defeated their legislative efforts. Finally, it is argued that voluntarism was so dominant because it served the interests of trade union leaders. Members would be more dependent upon their union leaders if their benefits were derived through economic and not political struggle.

As much as voluntarism may have "fit" certain conditions, its strength within the AFL rested upon the degree to which it coincided with the strategic interests of skilled workers who composed the AFL. Skilled workers are particularly attracted to voluntarism because their craft unions have market power they can employ in group conflict with employers. Craft unions can leverage the skills of their members in collective bargaining with employers. In addition, frequent political defeat did not give skilled workers much confidence that politics was a fruitful arena from which rewards could be obtained. Finally, skilled workers were reluctant to work through politics because their relatively small numbers would have required them to ally with unskilled workers in order to be politically successful. But skilled workers were intent on maintaining and not reducing distinctions between themselves and the unskilled. The contrast between the shop-floor power skilled workers possessed and the lack of political resources such workers could command focused their hopes and ambitions on collective bargaining and their union rather than on political action and the state.

The decline of voluntarism in the American labor movement coincides with the organization of unskilled workers into industrial unions under the banner of the Congress of Industrial Organizations (CIO) in the 1930s. The power of unskilled workers rested upon a different principle than skilled workers. Unskilled workers enjoyed the power of numbers. They could leverage this into political power to gain legislative relief, which was in contrast to their lack of market power due to their lack of skills. The voting power of millions of unskilled workers made CIO unions more apt to support welfare benefits and workplace protections through the government and not depend exclusively on collective bargaining to achieve them. The ideology of voluntarism faded within the labor movement as the power of industrial unions grew and the influence of craft unions declined within it.

ALAN DRAPER

References and Further Reading

Greene, Julie. *Pure and Simple Politics: The American Federation of Labor and Political Activism, 1881–1917*. New York: Cambridge University Press, 1998.

Hattam, Victoria C. *Labor Visions and State Power: The Origins of Business Unionism in the United States*. Princeton, NJ: Princeton University Press, 1993.

Marks, Gary. *Unions in Politics: Britain, Germany, and the United States in the Nineteenth and Twentieth Centuries*. Princeton, NJ: Princeton University Press, 1989.

Rogin, Michael Paul. "Voluntarism: The Political Functions of an Antipolitical Doctrine." *Industrial and Labor Relations Review* 15 (July 1962): 521–535.

See also **American Federation of Labor**

VORSE, MARY HEATON (1874–1966)
Journalist

As the foremost pioneer of labor journalism in the nation, and as a correspondent covering international events from 1912 through the 1940s, Mary Heaton Vorse produced impassioned reporting that exposed her audience to a wider vision of democracy. She was also an important strike organizer, feminist, suffragist, peace worker, and fiction writer. The issues raised by economic inequality, labor battles, gender conflict, and war and peace compose the core of her thought and work and address the fundamental questions of her age.

Vorse was born into a wealthy family that later disowned her, due to her Bohemian lifestyle. As an editor of the *Masses* and a founder of the Provincetown Players, she was a key member of the group of intellectuals and radicals centered in pre-World War I Greenwich Village. Twice widowed, she learned to write romantic short stories for the women's magazines in order to support her three children. Her struggle to balance the demands of motherhood with those of her profession became a central theme of her life. Her experience in the suffrage movement and in women's peace work also shaped her feminist vision. The 1911 Triangle Shirtwaist Company fire in which more than 100 female garment workers died because exit doors were locked brought Vorse into direct contact with the brutal conditions facing working-women.

Vorse began her labor reporting at the 1912 Lawrence, Massachusetts, textile strike, where she wrote of the terrible human cost imposed on the poor by uncontrolled profit making. For the next 40 years, she demonstrated her uncanny ability to sense the moment and find the center where action would occur. She went on to report labor battles at the 1916 Mesabi Range and at the Great Steel Strike of 1919.

Vorse believed that her work as publicity director for the Passaic, New Jersey, textile strike of 1926 revolutionized union tactics and prefigured tactics that contributed to the victories of the Congress of Industrial Organizations (CIO) in the late 1930s. She successfully solicited endorsements for the strike from recognized liberal leaders, artists, and intellectuals. When police attacked peaceful strike marchers as well as journalists and cameramen, liberal indignation about Passaic turned white hot. Her publicity helped to make Passaic a national sensation. She reported the southern labor struggles at Gastonia in 1929 and at bloody Harlan County in 1931, where she was run out of state by night riders. Vorse was present at every major unemployed march and farmers' strike and reported the Scottsboro Boys trial in the 1930s.

She was present at the crucial labor battle in Flint, Michigan, in 1937 and was wounded at Youngstown in the Little Steel Strike of 1937. Vorse was perhaps the oldest war correspondent in World War II. Her last big story to receive national attention was the 1952 expose of crimes in the waterfront unions. In her 80s she wrote of the danger of toxic waste dumps and of nuclear bomb stockpiles. In 1965, at age 91, one year before her death, she backed her local minister, who was one of the first to march against the Vietnam War.

Unlike most labor journalists, Vorse was often a strike participant, in the thick of battle, with intimate knowledge of union strategy combined with a fervent commitment to honest, accurate reporting. She provided the news coverage that bridged the gap between union leadership and the reading public. Her writing was remarkable for its emotional re-creation of the human drama within a context of factual detail. Under her hand, the workers become visible and noisy, and one feels the fear on the picket line or the strength of marching protesters. Vorse's unique contribution to the labor journalism of her time was her consistent attention to the special concerns of women. The immigrant wife, the starving children, the harsh tenement home—these constituted the raw material for her dramatic power to make the reality of labor history come alive. Her accounts found easy entry into major journals, yet she also wrote for intellectuals and reformers in journals like the *Nation* and the *New Republic*. Her biggest audience was the workers themselves, in her hundreds of dispatches to union newspapers, newsletters, and broadsides for the union press.

Vorse eluded political categorization. She rejected liberals' belief that reasoned appeals would cancel the capitalist repression of worker rights as an illusion. Nor did she share the faith of the Communists. She rejected Communist dictatorship earlier than many of her liberal and radical friends, but she also stood in opposition to the Cold War. For over 50 years she fought for economic democracy, world peace, and feminism—a union of ideas far too radical for most of her contemporaries to consider. Although Communists knew her to be unreliable and unreasonable, the FBI in 1944 placed her on the list of dangerous citizens to be jailed immediately on presidential order, and even maintained an active surveillance file on her until she was 82 years old.

Mary Heaton Vorse brought to the American public the intimate stories of the workers who fought for fair pay, decent hours, and the right to a union. Her appeal to every class of readers was a call for commonsense application of traditional national ideals—liberty, equality, and justice for all.

JOHN LEGGETT

WAGE LOSSES AND UNION DECLINE: 1980s THROUGH THE EARLY 2000s

The U.S. workers entered the 1980s facing a much less supportive environment than they had enjoyed for many decades. From World War II into the 1970s, a confluence of events had brought a steadily rising standard of living to most working families, although significant numbers of minorities and women did not share fully in the prosperity. Unscathed by the world wars, and sitting astride a mighty economic engine that had grown rapidly during the war, U.S. businesses from 1945 through the 1960s moved across the globe and established the United States as the center of a global economic empire.

A massive upsurge during the Depression era 1930s and a consolidation of newly won unions during World War II created a sizable U.S. labor movement. Unions represented large percentages of workers in industries like auto, steel, construction, telephone, long-distance trucking, and other important economic sectors. High unionization rates and a measure of political influence enabled workers to demand a share of the nation's growing prosperity. The New Deal coalition (workers, minorities, urban populations, Catholics, liberal intellectuals) had dominant influence in the country, and it facilitated union survival and a degree of social welfare for many working-class people.

Adjusting figures into 2003 dollars so that comparisons show the real change in the purchasing power, average weekly earnings in the United States grew from $340.01 in 1947 to $547.82 by 1973, an increase of more than 61%. Productivity grew at a similar pace during this 26-year period.

During this same period unions were able firmly to establish and improve a variety of benefits for their members beyond wage rates. Healthcare and pension benefits plans were the most important; since these were established and increased in unionized industries, they spread to nonunion segments of the economy in (usually less generous) forms.

Reversal of Labor's Fortunes: A Statistical Portrait

Compare the earlier experience to occurrences in the subsequent decades. From 1973 to 1996, while productivity grew about 40%, average weekly earnings (in 2003 dollars) actually declined 12% from $547.82 to $481.74 per week. By 2003, average weekly earnings had increased to $519.56 per week, still below what they were in 1973. Sometime in the 1970s, wages no longer rose in tandem with productivity; new wealth went to owners and financiers, not to workers.

The declining economic fortunes of American workers coincided with the shrinkage of their primary instrument for economic defense, unions. Unions had emerged from World War II in a strong enough position to retain the major gains they had made previously. Different statistical sources on union density (the percentage of the nonagricultural labor force that is in a union) in the immediate post-World War II years vary, but all give density figures from 31%–36% in the 1945–1955 period. All place peak union density from 33%–36%.

By 1973, union density was down to 24%. By 1980 it stood at 23%, and subsequently plunged rapidly. By 2000, it was down to 13.5%, and by 2004, it dropped to 12.5%. Thus by 2004, union density was barely more than one-third of what it had been 50 years earlier.

The overall decline in union density masked differing fortunes for unions in different economic segments. Heavily unionized industries like manufacturing and construction experienced extreme declines, as did the entire private sector. Public-sector unionization rates held steady. Table 1 illustrates the difference from 1973 to 2004.

By 2004, the union density in manufacturing was less than one-third of what it had been in 1973, and it had dropped 61% in the construction industry. The entire private sector experienced a similar decline from almost a quarter of all workers to only 8%. From 1973 to 1980, public-sector unionization continued a surge that had begun in the 1960s and then leveled off. By 2004, union density in the public sector was 4.5 times as high as in the private sector.

Changing union density rates were reflected in the size and prominence of various national unions. In the 1950s and 1960s, the prominent unions were industrial unions, like the United Auto Workers (UAW), the United Steelworkers (USWA), and the International Association of Machinists (IAM); or they were construction unions organized around a specific craft, such as the International Brotherhood of Electrical Workers (IBEW), the United Brotherhood of Carpenters and Joiners (UBC), or the United Association of Plumbers and Pipe fitters (UA).

Changes from 1980 to 2000 and beyond changed this picture. Public-sector and/or service-industries unions surpassed the old style unions in size and prominence. The UAW dropped from a 1.4 million

member peak in the 1970s to less than half that (654,657) by 2004. The USWA and the IAM, both over one million at their late 1970s to early 1980s peaks, were down to 535,461 and 610,605, respectively, by 2004. Meanwhile the Service Employees' International Union (SEIU), once an obscure and relatively small union representing doormen and janitors in a few large cities, grew to be the largest union in the AFL-CIO by 2004 (1,702,639 members), now representing public- and private-sector service and health-care workers. The American Federation of State, County, and Municipal Employees (AFSCME), the main union for nonfederal public-sector workers, grew from less than 100,000 in 1955 to 1,350,000 members by 2004. Consequently the center of gravity in organized labor shifted to public-sector and service-sector unions in this period.

Changing Demographic Profile of the U.S. Worker and U.S. Unions

Women increasingly entered the workforce after 1980. This became more necessary as men's wages stagnated and declined. From 1980 to 2003, the percentage of women participating in the workforce (that is, working or looking for work) jumped from just over 51% to over 61%, almost a 20% increase. Women also lessened the wage gap with men: In 1980, women on average earned just over 60% of what men made; by 2000, the percentage had jumped to 76%. While some of the improved percentage was due to real increases in women's wages, much of it could be attributed to losses in men's real earnings (that is, earning adjusted for inflation).

During this period unions enrolled increasing numbers of women in their ranks. By 2003, women comprised 43% of all union members, still below their 48%

Table 1   Union Density in Different U.S. Economic Sectors, 1973 to 2004

Sector	1973 Union Density (%)	1980 Union Density (%)	1990 Union Density (%)	2000 Union Density (%)	2004 Union Density (%)
All	24.0	23.0	16.1	13.5	12.5
All private nonagricultural	24.6	20.4	12.1	9.1	8.0
Private manufacturing	38.9	32.3	20.6	14.8	12.9
Private construction	39.5	30.9	21.0	18.3	15.4
Public sector	23.0	35.9	36.5	37.5	36.4

Source: www.unionstats.com.

share of the entire workforce but much improved over previous periods. Union membership definitely benefited women during this period; in 2004, female union workers earned an average of 34% more than female nonunion workers. This union wage advantage exceeded the 28% advantage for all workers in that year.

Immigrants also entered the U.S. labor force in massive numbers during this period. From 1980 to 2004, the percentage of the U.S. population that was foreign-born jumped from just over 6% to approximately 12%. Over 40% of the entire growth of the labor force in the 1990s was composed of immigrants, and this percentage increased to over 50% in 2000–2003.

Most immigrants came from Latin America or Asia. Some held high-income jobs in the United States, but most were confined to the lower rungs of the job market. Immigrants were overrepresented in the private household worker occupations (child care, house cleaning), in agricultural labor, in construction, and in a variety of leisure and hospitality and other low-wage service-sector occupations.

The influx of immigrants eventually prompted an historic shift in the stance of U.S. labor unions toward immigration. Since the 1920s, the official labor movement had usually taken the anti-immigrant side of political immigration debates. The AFL-CIO supported the 1986 Immigration Reform and Control Act (IRCA), which contained provisions to fine employers who knowingly hired immigrants who had entered the country without proper documentation and who therefore were in the country illegally.

In the years after 1986, both documented and undocumented immigration grew rapidly despite this provision. The law had no apparent impact on either legal or illegal immigration, and it was virtually never used to prosecute employers. Instead it locked undocumented immigrants into a perpetual illegal status, making them vulnerable to employer abuse. Immigrant workers demanding their rights (to be paid or to form a union, for example) found the employer could simply call the federal Immigration and Naturalization Service (INS) office to have the workers arrested and deported. This had a chilling effect on workers' assertion of their rights. This undermined worker rights in general in the country, especially in low-wage occupations.

In 2000, the AFL-CIO changed course and called for an amnesty for all undocumented U.S. workers, providing them with a path to citizenship. It also called for the repeal of the ineffective employer sanctions, to be replaced with a policy of full legal protection (including the right to unionize) for all workers in the country regardless of legal status. The federation also called for whistleblower protections and sanctions against employers who recruit workers from abroad for the purpose of exploiting them. Many of the largest efforts by unions to organize unorganized workers in the early 2000s involved immigrants in such industries as hotel and lodging, home health care and nursing homes, and construction.

African-American blue-collar workers fared rather poorly in the 1980s and 1990s, as those unionized industries in which they had gained a significant toehold were decimated through plant closings. Entire communities that were predominantly African-American, such as Detroit and Gary, Indiana, were devastated when massive plant closures and downsizing in the automobile and steel industries occurred. In 1982, a quarter of African-American workers were employed in factories; by 2000 this percentage had declined to 14%. By the 2000s, government employment became one of the main avenues for African-Americans to gain middle-income status, and the large percentage of African-Americans in the memberships of public-sector unions reflects this fact.

Changing Political and Social Environment and Response

The year 1980 was a major political turning point for the country and also for U.S. labor. In that year Ronald Reagan was elected president, espousing a free-market and antigovernment perspective that was very unfriendly to labor's interests. Reagan fired the nation's air traffic controllers at the nation's airports and destroyed their union in 1981. He also appointed leaders to the federal agency charged with interpreting and enforcing the nation's labor law, the National Labor Relations Board (NLRB), who had previously expressed contempt for, and opposition to, the very law they were to uphold. One compared union demands in the collective-bargaining relationship to organized criminal extortion of a business. The Reagan NLRB from 1980 to 1988 reinterpreted labor law in ways that made more and more union tactics illegal while making a wide variety of union-busting tactics by employers legal.

The labor movement was unprepared for the onslaught. In the decades preceding 1980, it had lost much of its attractiveness for many former allies who had helped it prosper in the 1930s through the 1950s.

The 1960s Civil Rights and later Black Power movements had challenged a number of unions to incorporate more African-Americans, both as members and as leaders. The predominantly white craft unions in the building trades initially opposed the pressure to integrate, causing considerable hostility from many in the black community. The building trades' unions did eventually change; by 2001, unionized construction workers were more likely to be African-American than were nonunion construction workers. In time unions became among the most integrated institutions in American society, but some unions' unfriendly initial adjustment to the revolution in race relations had at least temporarily separated the labor movement from some of its former allies in minority communities.

Likewise the modern women's movement originating in the 1960s and 1970s faced indifference or even opposition from some, although not all, unions. Previously all-male enclaves of the workforce often did not receive new female entrants with open arms— the skilled trades in manufacturing plants and the building trades' craft unions were prominent examples. Unions with already established female memberships, such as the Communications Workers of America (CWA) or the teachers' unions (American Federation of Teachers [AFT] and National Education Association [NEA]) made a much smoother transition to the growing centrality of women in the labor force.

The student and antiwar movements of the 1960s and 1970s had even more problematic relations with the organized labor movement. Cultural clashes over perceived moral deficiencies of the young activists regarding sexuality and drug usage and other aspects of youth culture and differences over the Vietnam War drove the labor movement apart from many of its former allies among university-educated people who considered themselves liberal or progressive. Likewise the environmental movement ended up in conflict with those unions that were primarily interested in jobs when there was a perceived trade-off between jobs and environmental protection. Middle-class progressives in all of these movements often developed an indifferent or even disdainful attitude toward organized labor as a result.

Consequently the labor movement faced the hostile political climate of the 1980s in a more isolated position than it had been in for many decades. Differences over racial, gender, lifestyle, Cold War, and Vietnam War issues had torn apart the New Deal coalition that had governed the country for the most part since the 1930s. In the 1980s and 1990s, the ascendant right wing consolidated a new enduring coalition of corporate and wealthy interests with religious, cultural conservatives and patriotic/militaristic elements among working-class people. By the early 2000s, nonunion, white, working-class males were voting heavily for political candidates (usually but not always in the Republican party) who attacked the living standards of working-class people. So did working-class members of the Christian right, even though doing so meant the transfer of wealth from them to the very richest segments of society.

Thus from 1980 into the 2000s, conservative Republican presidents with unfriendly relationships with organized labor ruled with the exception of 1992 to 2000, when centrist Democrat Bill Clinton was in office. Clinton also disappointed the unions by failing to push for substantive change in labor law to make union organizing easier, while he used all of his political influence to push the North American Free Trade Agreement (NAFTA) through Congress without enforceable labor standards to protect workers' rights. Clinton did appoint to the NLRB individuals who attempted to return it to its earlier role of facilitating union organizing under the National Labor Relations Act (NLRA) and did undertake a few other relatively minor prolabor initiatives, but his presidency was by no means a return to unabashedly prolabor measures.

The election and re-election of George W. Bush to the presidency in 2000 and 2004, respectively, represented a return to stridently antilabor politics. The post-2000 NLRB issued rulings so restrictive toward labor and permissive to antiunion business behavior that increasing numbers of unions refused even to use the agency to enforce labor rights. Bush also used the tragic airplane attack on the World Trade Center on September 11, 2001, in an attempt to deny unionization and collective-bargaining rights to increasing numbers of federal employees.

During the 1980s and 1990s, the AFL-CIO and most member unions responded to the hostile political climate by creating a close-knit insider role within the Democratic party. But they found this strategy to yield ever more meager results, both because Democrats lost control of the U.S. Congress in the mid-1990s and because many Democratic politicians distanced themselves from organized labor in an attempt to attract Republican-leaning nonlabor voters. In the second-half of the 1990s and in the early 2000s, organized labor's political apparatus did become more effective. Even as union density fell into the low teens as a percentage of the labor force, union families accounted for more than 20% of the vote in both the 2000 and 2004 elections, but it still was not enough to reverse the conservative antilabor tide.

Changing Economic Environment and Employer Responses

Changes in the U.S. economy also affected U.S. workers and their unions during this time. By the 1980s,

European and Japanese competitors had recovered fully from World War II devastation and had become major rivals of U.S. corporations. Imports penetrated key domestic markets where U.S. corporations were accustomed to uncontested control. In the 1960s and early 1970s, the U.S. market for apparel and electronic consumer goods had shifted heavily toward imported goods, and in the 1980s and 1990s, the same thing happened in durable-goods markets, such as automobiles, steel, and a wide variety of other manufactured products.

The U.S. manufacturers responded in ways detrimental to the interests of U.S. workers. They funded and supported heavily the rightward political trend in the country described in the last section, bankrolling antilabor politicians. They also demanded massive concessions from unionized workers. Concession bargaining became the watchword for unionized labor relations in numerous manufacturing plants, many of them located in the industrial Midwest. For a while in the 1980s, union workers' pay increases actually were lower than those for nonunion workers.

Companies also frequently closed unionized plants. Sometimes this was simply giving up when faced with competition from foreign or other competitors, but often companies re-opened facilities either in nonunion locations in the southern United States or abroad. The objective was lower labor costs, union avoidance, or both. Another favorite response was downsizing, where a plant's workforce was slowly reduced over a number of years as it was phased out of the company's production plans.

When closing proved impractical, companies sometimes attempted to destroy the unions representing their existing workforces. A favorite 1980s tactic was to provoke a union strike by demanding totally unacceptable measures during contract negotiations, hiring replacement workers, re-establishing production with the new workforce, refusing to accept returning strikers even if the union surrendered, and getting the strikebreaking workers to vote out the union 1 year later, when the law allowed a union-representation election to occur. Strikes, which had once been the main weapon of labor unions to win improvements in pay and working conditions thus became in the 1980s a way for employers to destroy unions.

When unions attempted to organize workers at nonunion establishments, employers almost always strongly opposed the organizing drive. Union busting became a massive industry, with numerous lawyers and specialists offering employers their services in helping employers remain union-free. One academic study in 1990 concluded that the total amount of money spent yearly on these union-busting activities at that time was approximately one billion dollars.

Employers also outsourced work by shipping it to foreign suppliers on an accelerating basis throughout the 1980s and 1990s. Originally this occurred primarily in industrial sectors that were more likely to be unionized, although by the 2000s, news accounts noted that even traditionally high-end and nonunion tasks, such as computer programming and engineering tasks, were being outsourced. In the 1980s and 1990s, the U.S. economy was hollowed-out—basic manufacturing moved abroad, leaving in the country those service jobs (such as those in healthcare and personal services) impossible to export.

This globalization of operations by U.S. corporations meant that they were less anchored in, and accountable to, a national U.S. economy. Bargaining power by U.S.-based unions declined correspondingly. The U.S. balance of trade also shifted: In 1970, the country actually exported $2.25 billion more goods and services than it imported. But by 1980, a small trade deficit of $19.4 billion mushroomed to almost $81 billion by 1990, over $378 billion by 2000, and over $617 billion by 2004. This meant the loss of millions of U.S. jobs, mostly in (frequently unionized) manufacturing industries. From February 1998–December 2004, the country lost 3.3 million manufacturing jobs.

To some degree unions responded by attempting to become more internationalist. Cross-border ties with labor movements abroad increased, and the AFL-CIO moved away from its previous foreign policy role of being a Cold War tool of the U.S. government, which had alienated it from many unions around the globe.

The deregulatory and free-market political trend of the period also affected the economic realities of such previously regulated industries as the airline industry. In 1978, airline industry deregulation allowed previously controlled ticket prices, schedule and service levels to be controlled by the market. In the following 25 years, ruinous fare wars and the entrance of low-cost, no-frills competitors, such as Southwest Airlines and JetBlue, caused periodic crises of overcapacity, destruction of some historic legacy carriers, like Pan Am and Eastern Airlines, and near-bankruptcy or bankruptcy for the industry's major players, like Delta, U.S. Airways, United Airlines, and American Airlines.

The airlines responded by demanding or forcing massive concessions from airline unions. In what had been one of the most heavily unionized industries in the country, the craft airline unions found themselves stripped of much of their power. By the early 2000s, unions were reeling backward in an industry hemorrhaging billions of dollars.

The economics of healthcare and pension coverage also changed during this period. In 1980, the United

States spent 8.8% of its Gross Domestic Product on healthcare; by 2000, this had risen to 13.3%, and to 14.9% by 2003. Employers responded by attempting to shift an ever-increasing share of healthcare costs onto employees. By 2000, battles over healthcare were the primary cause of contentious negotiations and work stoppages.

Employers also attempted to shift risk in pension-plan retirement income to employers by switching from defined-benefit plans guaranteeing a set retirement income for each year of employment to defined-contribution plans guaranteeing payment only into some type of investment, with the employee taking the risk for how the investment fared or how large the final monthly pension would be. In 1980, over 80% of private-sector pension plans were the guaranteed defined-benefit type; by 2005, this percentage was down to 40%. Meanwhile the riskier defined-contribution plans grew from under 20% of total plans in 1980 to around 60% by 2005. Unions managed to retain the more secure defined-benefit plans for 79% of their members (as of 2005), but it was increasingly difficult to resist the trend toward shifting the risk to the worker.

Major Labor Struggles, 1980 to 2000

In August 1981, 13,000 members of the Professional Air Traffic Controllers' Organization (PATCO) at the nation's airports went on strike in defiance of a 1955 law making such strikes illegal. Two days later President Ronald Reagan fired the 11,359 controllers who had failed to return to their jobs. The strike was broken, with public opinion polls showing popular support for the president's action. Seventeen months later PATCO called off the strike in complete defeat. The debacle was widely seen as a public declaration that U.S. employers could declare war on their unions with the federal government's blessing.

The remainder of the 1980s and 1990s featured numerous confrontations between employers and unions, with the unions attempting to resist assaults. In 1983, the Phelps Dodge copper mining company intentionally provoked a strike in its 30 mines in Arizona and the Southwest, promptly replacing them with permanent replacement workers. Despite community support and the involvement of the wives and families of many of the striking miners, the strike was crushed. One-and-a-half-years later, the United Steelworkers of America was decertified and driven from all 30 mines.

In 1984, the Oil, Chemical, and Atomic Workers (OCAW) Local 4620 faced a similar attempt by the

BASF Corporation in Geismar, Louisiana. An intentionally provoked strike was losing badly until the union changed tactics and began to run a corporate campaign against the company by allying with environmentalists, politicians, federal government enforcement agencies, foreign politicians and unions and companies against BASF in its various business and environmental affairs. Five-and-a-half years later, the union returned to the plant intact with a contract. BASF had been badly damaged by the corporate campaign, and the union's return was a belated victory.

In August 1985, Local P-9 of the United Food and Commercial Workers (UFCW) in Austin, Minnesota, went on strike and conducted a corporate campaign against the Hormel meatpacking company, which was demanding massive concessions. An incredible amount of solidarity from union members and sympathizers from around the country failed to turn the tide for the union however, and the strike went down in defeat when the national union forcibly removed the local's intransigent leadership, called the strike off in June 1986, and imposed a concessionary contract on the local in August 1986.

In 1987, the International Paper Company demanded massive concessions from its workers despite having made $407 million in profit that year. The 1,250 members of United Paperworkers' International Union (UPIU) Local 14 in Jay, Maine, went out on strike and were soon replaced. The local began a corporate campaign and attempted to get other locals of the company to join the strike once their own contracts expired. But solidarity fell apart, the strike was defeated 16 months later, and the union was destroyed.

From 1989–1990, the United Mine Workers' (UMW) union conducted a 10-month strike against the Pittston coal company that involved unprecedented family and community involvement and nationwide solidarity with the strikers. The settlement preserved benefits for retired and disabled miners and widows, a partial union victory.

From 1989 into 1991, the International Association of Machinists (IAM), supported by the pilots' and air flight attendants' unions, conducted a monumental battle with Eastern Airlines and its rogue owner, Frank Lorenzo, over massive demands for concessions that would have meant an end to the union. Lorenzo sold profitable parts of the company to other entities he owned or controlled at a fraction of their true value and eventually destroyed the company in his attempt to defeat the union. Lorenzo's reputation was so damaged by this behavior that he was later barred from reentering the airline industry.

In 1990, the SEIU Justice for Janitors' campaign in Los Angeles made national news. Instead of targeting individual employers, the campaign aimed to unionize all the janitors in the downtown Los Angeles area at once. An inventive multifaceted campaign aimed at building tenants, building owners, contractors, the public, and public officials reached a climax during a June 15 savage beating by the Los Angeles police of peacefully protesting janitors in the city's Century City complex, creating widespread condemnation. The union soon won a union contract covering multiple janitorial contractors in the downtown area. The 2000 movie *Bread and Roses,* starring Academy Award winner Adrian Brody, was based on this struggle.

In 1990, the Ravenswood Aluminum Company in Ravenswood, West Virginia, attempted to provoke a strike from USWA Local 5668, which represented its 1,700 employees. The union refused to strike, so the company locked them out and replaced them with nonunion workers. The union began a corporate campaign to convince customers to boycott its products and traced company control to Mark Rich, a fugitive from U.S. tax evasion charges living in Switzerland. Targeting Rich, the union eventually toppled the company's chairman and won a union contract in 1992.

Decatur, Illinois, had so many labor struggles in the 1990s that it became known as the war zone. From 1991–1998, the city's Caterpillar earthmoving equipment plant went through a series of strikes and confrontations over the company's attempt to force concessions from the UAW local. The long battle ended with a union contract heavily dictated by the company.

The Staley corn-processing plant in the same city experienced a major work-to-rule campaign (workers doing only as ordered) by the union, followed by a company lockout of union workers while operating with replacements from 1993–1995. An impressive solidarity campaign and a corporate campaign in support of the Staley workers failed to win the struggle, which ended when the national union (UPIU) forced the local to accept a concessionary contract. Few of the original strikers returned to work. Mutual recriminations between the national union and local militants ensued.

A strike followed by a national corporate campaign at the Bridgestone-Firestone tire company in Decatur in 1994–1996 ended much more successfully when the USWA got the company to offer a decent contract through a domestic-tire boycott and international labor-solidarity actions. However a subsequent rash of failures of Firestone tires on Ford Explorer vehicles caused the company to close the plant in 2001.

The teamster's union strike against the United Parcel Service Company in 1997 was a bright spot for organized labor. Strong internal preparation well before the strike plus a clear message about the need for well-paying full-time jobs rather than part-time ones rallied the public solidly behind the union and won its major demand for a larger percentage of UPS jobs to be full-time.

The company exemplifying the business model of the new era was Wal-Mart, which pursued a single-minded pursuit of lowest cost whatever the consequences. Stridently anti-union, Wal-Mart spread rapidly throughout the country (and the world), destroying small local competitors and eventually encroaching on the markets of unionized grocery store chains. Wal-Mart spent millions yearly to fight unions and even closed entire stores in Canada whose workers had chosen to unionize. The company also provoked opposition from environmentalists, global-justice advocates and movements, numerous neighborhoods concerned about traffic congestion, women's rights groups, minorities, and others. Together with these organizations and individuals, the labor movement in the early 2000s took part in a nationwide movement to expose the company as harmful to the American public. One ultimate goal of this growing anti-Wal-Mart campaign among others was the eventual unionization of this company, whose workers were paid so little and charged so much for healthcare benefits that many were forced to use government assistance to meet their basic living and health needs.

The preceding struggles garnered national media attention; some of them inspired books. Together they defined the major contours of labor relations in the 1980 to 2000 period. Usually employers won, although a few union victories were achieved. In general unions did best when they broadened their struggles to issues relating directly to the public good, developed multiple avenues of pressure over employers, created alliances with progressive community organizations, and aggressively organized.

New Responses to Labor Decline

Union decline stimulated a number of responses. Workers' centers, independent community-based organizations addressing low-wage worker issues, grew rapidly in the 1990s. By 2004, at least 133 such centers existed in 80 cities. Many work exclusively with immigrant workers; all relate to low-wage workers for whom conventional unionization is extremely difficult. Workers' centers provide services (especially legal representation for back wages and workers' rights), advocate for change in public policies, and organize for collective empowerment. They have been most successful at winning back wages and changing public policies, as well as developing leadership among traditionally marginalized workers.

The living-wage movement also addressed the needs of low-wage workers. From 1994 to mid-2005, at least 130 municipalities, counties, and other public entities passed living-wage requirements. These laws require service contractors (and often the government itself or others tied to public money/land, such as airports) to pay at least a living wage on work done for the public entity. Most laws set the living wage at or above the federal government's poverty level for a family of four, well above the federal minimum wage, and some require health care benefits or a cash equivalent or other benefits.

Most living-wage laws are won by a broad-based coalition of community and labor organizations. The coalitions usually include unions, churches or faith-based community social-justice organizations, civil rights groups, human-services providers, community-organizing groups, and the like.

The declining fortunes of organized labor also stimulated internal union debate about organizational behavior and strategy. Some unions attempted less adversarial relationships with employers. Widely publicized examples like the General Motors–UAW partnership at the Saturn auto plant in Tennessee and the AT&T–CWA partnership in the telephone industry seemed to hold promise. But lack of employer commitment to these partnerships undermined most of them by the end of the 1990s.

An alternative strategy aimed to make the labor movement more of a social movement. Involvement in living-wage campaigns and the national organization Jobs with Justice exemplified this perspective. A partial reflection of this approach was the election in 1995 of the New Voice slate led by SEIU president John Sweeney to top leadership of the AFL-CIO, toppling old-guard leadership seen as too timid, conservative, and unimaginative to lead.

Sweeney pledged to make organizing the unorganized labor's top priority and worked to rebuild relationships with former allies alienated by business union behavior. But despite exhortations few of the federation's national unions aggressively organized the unorganized, and union density after 1995 continued to slide, although more slowly.

In 2005, seven unions calling themselves the Change to Win coalition demanded a major structural change in the AFL-CIO and more emphasis on organizing. In the summer of that year, the three largest unions in the Change to Win coalition (SEIU, the teamsters, and the UFCW) left the federation, taking more than a third of its 13.5 million members with them. Thus the official labor movement entered the early years of the new millennium divided both organizationally and strategically.

The future of U.S. workers may depend on four factors: (1) Prospects for social movement activism addressing increasing inequality and worker marginalization; (2) political trends away from or toward a supportive atmosphere for worker interests; (3) unions' ability to transform themselves and their internal cultures toward aggressive organizing of the unorganized; and (4) the ability of U.S. workers and unions to create ties of solidarity with workers elsewhere in the world. Trends from 1980 into the new millennium have been primarily unfavorable, but similar periods in the nation's past were followed by labor upheaval and permanent institutional and legal gains for workers and their families.

BRUCE NISSEN

References and Further Reading

Bernstein, Aaron. *Grounded: Frank Lorenzo and the Destruction of Eastern Airlines*. Frederick, MD: Beard Books, 1999.

Brisbin, Richard A. *A Strike Like No Other Strike: Law and Resistance during the Pittston Coal Strike of 1989–1990*. Baltimore, MD: Johns Hopkins University Press, 2002.

Bronfenbrenner, Kate, Sheldon Friedman, Richard W. Hurd, Rudolph A. Oswald, and Ronald L. Seeber, eds. *Organizing to Win: New Research on Union Strategies*. Ithaca, NY: Cornell University Press, 1998.

Craypo, Charles, and Bruce Nissen, eds. *Grand Designs: The Impact of Corporate Strategies on Workers, Unions, and Communities*. Ithaca, NY: Cornell University Press, 1993.

Ehrenreich, Barbara. *Nickel and Dimed: On (Not) Getting by in America*. New York: Owl Books, 2002.

Fine, Janice. *Worker Centers: Organizing Communities at the Edge of the Dream*. Ithaca, NY: ILR Press, 2006.

Franklin, Stephen. *Three Strikes: Labor's Heartland Losses and What They Mean for Working Americans*. New York: The Guilford Press, 2002.

Getman, Julius. *The Betrayal of Local 14: Paperworkers, Politics, and Permanent Replacements*. Ithaca, NY: Cornell University Press, 1999.

Hurd, Richard W., Rudolph A. Oswald, Ronald L. Seeber, and Sheldon Friedman, eds. *Restoring the Promise of American Labor Law*. Ithaca, NY: ILR Press, 1994.

Juravich, Tom, and Kate Bronfenbrenner. *Ravenswood: The Steelworkers' Victory and the Revival of American Labor*. Ithaca, NY: ILR Press, 2000.

Levitt, Martin J. *Confessions of a Union Buster*. New York: Crown Publishers, 1993.

Lichtenstein, Nelson, ed. *Wal-Mart: The Face of Twenty-First-Century Capitalism.* New York: The New Press, 2006.

Mishel, Lawrence, Jared Bernstein, and Sylvia Allegretto. *The State of Working America 2004–2005.* Ithaca, NY: ILR Press, 2005.

Nissen, Bruce, ed. *Unions in a Globalized Environment: Changing Borders, Organizational Boundaries, and Social Roles.* Armonk, NY: M. E. Sharpe, Inc., 2002.

Pollin, Robert, and Stephanie Luce. *The Living Wage: Building a Fair Economy.* New York: The New Press, 2000.

Rachleff, Peter J. *Hard-Pressed in the Heartland: The Hormel Strike and the Future of the Labor Movement.* Cambridge, MA: South End Press, 1992.

Rosenblum, Jonathan D. *Copper Crucible: How the Arizona Miners' Strike of 1983 Recast Labor-Management Relations in America.* Ithaca, NY: Cornell University Press, 1998.

Shulman, Beth. *The Betrayal of Work: How Low-Wage Jobs Fail 30 Million Americans and Their Families.* New York: New Press, 2003.

Cases and Statutes Cited

Immigration Reform and Control Act

See also **American Federation of State, County, and Municipal Employees; American Federation of Teachers; Gender; Immigration; National Education Association; North American Free Trade Agreement (NAFTA); Service Employees' International Union**

WAGES FOR HOUSEWORK

Wages for Housework is a demand, a political perspective, and a Marxist-feminist organization founded in 1972 by Selma James, third wife of the Trinidadian Socialist C. L. R. James. It grew out of the 1970s debates over the relationship between feminism and the Left, and in the United States, it was most visible during that decade. Despite a small membership, the International Wages for Housework Campaign and its affiliate organizations—including Black Women for Wages for Housework, the U.S. Collective of Prostitutes, Wages Due Lesbians, and a men's support group called Payday—have had a significant influence on feminist thinking about unpaid work.

Wages for Housework emerged in response to the once-common socialist position that unionized (male) industrial workers were the vanguard of the working class, while housewives were politically unreliable, and feminism was bourgeois. In the *Power of Women and the Subversion of the Community* (1972), the founding document of the Wages for Housework campaign, James and Italian feminist

Mariarosa Dalla Costa criticized the orthodox Marxist position that the housewife's labor was unproductive and was merely a personal service to her family. Instead they argued, housework was productive labor in the Marxist sense that it produced surplus value and capitalist profits. The home and community functioned as a social factory in which women-housewives produced a unique and highly profitable commodity: The worker on whose labor power (ability to work) capitalism hinged. Marxists recognized the exploitation of the wage laborer as the foundation of capitalist society, but Dalla Costa and James argued that unwaged laborers were also exploited through the wage relation, although their exploitation was hidden because they were unwaged. Their definition of housework was not limited to chores, such as cooking, cleaning, and laundry, but encompassed the entire feminine role—serving, shopping, nurturing, looking attractive, and performing sexually—that enabled the wage laborer to work and live. Men did some housework, but all women were housewives, even when they worked at a paying job. By demanding wages for housework from the state, supporters sought to expose women's hidden labor so it could be separated from their nature and refused.

In *Sex, Race, and Class* (1974) and several later publications, James elaborated on the concept of the social factory as it applied internationally. International capital created a hierarchy of labor power and wage scales, she argued, but that hierarchy—of race, gender, age, and nation—appeared unrelated to class or capitalism because the work done by people at the bottom was unseen and unwaged. In calling for compensation for unpaid work and labor stolen over generations, Wages for Housework was essentially a demand for reparations, not unlike the campaign for slavery reparations.

In the 1970s, the demand for wages for housework sparked a spirited and astonishingly bitter debate. Leftists challenged the group's reading of Marx. Insisting that the creation of labor-power was not part of, but a precondition to, the capitalist labor process, they urged women and men to challenge capitalists at the point of production (for example, factories). But the most significant and heartfelt criticism came from feminists who feared that Wages for Housework would institutionalize women's place in the home. In focusing exclusively on the capitalist exploitation of women's labor, some feminists argued, James and Dalla Costa failed to acknowledge the benefit that individual men derived from housework. Wages for Housework thus reinforced the assumption that housework was naturally women's responsibility, making it more difficult to get men to share the chores and worsening the psychological pressures on housewives. In the heady days of 1970s feminism, many young women imagined that housework could be eliminated (or at least socialized) through child-care centers, cafeterias, and communal living. They worried that Wages for Housework would strengthen the very gender roles they were attempting to subvert and undermine their efforts to abolish the housewife role.

In its everyday work the Wages for Housework campaign did not lobby for direct government payments for caregiving but engaged in specific campaigns around issues of poverty and unpaid work. Members participated in several local welfare struggles and gained national visibility and an important early success at the 1977 National Women's Conference in Houston. Working with welfare rights activists, they killed a resolution backed by the Carter administration and got delegates to pass a substitute resolution that called for increased welfare funding. Delegates resolved that "the elimination of poverty must be a priority of all those working for equal rights for women.... [H]omemakers receiving income transfer payments should be afforded the dignity of having that payment called a wage, not welfare."

Wages for Housework also organized for prostitutes' rights. Prostitution exposed both women's poverty and their unwaged work, since most women became prostitutes because they were desperate for money, and prostitutes got paid for the sex work other women did for free. Prostitutes' collectives affiliated with Wages for Housework campaigned for better services so women could avoid prostitution and for the abolition of the criminal laws that made sex work unsafe.

Since 1980, Wages for Housework has lobbied vigorously for the inclusion of women's unpaid work in international economic measures. Using a much-quoted statistic—women do two-thirds of the world's work but receive only 5% of its income—Wages for Housework pressed its agenda at a series of conferences and won a significant victory at the 1985 U.N. Decade of Women Conference in Nairobi. Delegates called on governments to count women's unremunerated work in agriculture, reproduction, and household activities in the Gross National Product (GNP) and other economic measures. However little has come of the resolution.

Despite its relative invisibility and in the United States, limited political success, Wages for Housework has contributed to a significant change in attitude. The principle of counting women's unpaid work in the GNP has been endorsed by many economists, and many feminist welfare advocates now call for the recognition—and compensation—of women's

caregiving work. The growing attention to caregivers' economic rights owes much to the Wages for Housework campaign.

MOLLY LADD-TAYLOR

References and Further Reading

Dalla Costa, Mariarosa, and Selma James. *The Power of Women and the Subversion of the Community*. Bristol, UK: Falling Wall Press, 1972.

Edmond, Wendy, and Suzie Fleming, eds. *All Work and No Pay*. London, UK: Falling Wall Press, 1975.

James, Selma. *Sex, Race, and Class*. Bristol, UK: Falling Wall Press, 1975.

Malos, Ellen, ed. *The Politics of Housework*. Cheltenham, UK: New Clarion Press, 1995.

WAGNER ACT
See **National Labor Relations Board**

WAITRESSING AND WAITING/FOOD SERVICE

Waitresses and waiters are the stars in what William F. Whyte, in his 1948 study of labor in restaurants, called "the great American drama of food, hospitality, and personal service offered to the public every day by the restaurant industry." Food service was one of the great growth areas of the expanding service sector in the twentieth century, with an estimated 75 million meals served daily to American diners by century's end. More than two million waitresses and waiters dished out those meals. Of the more than two million, nearly 4 out of 5 were female. The growing ranks of women in the craft over the twentieth century evidenced the deep and, for waitresses, double-edged associations of food provision with feminine nurturing and sexuality. Life at the front lines of food service has rarely if ever been easy. For striving to meet customers' bodily needs and emotional longings, wait staff earned gratitude, admiration, and generous gratuities but perhaps more often suffered abuse, disdain, and stinginess from employers and customers alike.

The First Waiters and Waitresses

The modern restaurant emerged from its roots in taverns and inns in the first-half of the nineteenth century in the United States. Maturing first in post-revolutionary France, the practice of dining out for pleasure soon took hold in larger American cities alongside the ancient need to eat out while traveling. The luxury hotels that became fixtures in nineteenth-century cities fed wealthy travelers' desire for fine dining by opening posh restaurants on site. Independent restaurants, led by New York's famous Delmonico's, also whetted elite urbanites' appetite for lavish cuisine. But a greater spur to the food service industry came from workers' changing lifestyles over the late nineteenth and early twentieth centuries. With the growing separation of residential from commercial areas in cities, a swelling number of industrial and white-collar workers were no longer able to return home for a midday repast. In addition single men and women in cities began abandoning more traditional boarding arrangements for apartments and rooming houses, which did not include meals. By the early twentieth century, more informal restaurants, including cafés, diners, lunchrooms, cafeterias, and automats (with coin-operated food service), flourished as a result.

Waitressing and waiting of course emerged in tandem with restaurants, evolving from food serving in private households as well as taverns and inns. In the nineteenth century men predominated in restaurant table service, especially in finer restaurants, following European standards. Women, though food servers in the home and in boardinghouses, were marginalized in restaurant work due to Victorian moral strictures on women in mixed-sex commercial spaces, especially where liquor was served. The Victorian disdain for exposing women to liquor also made the more lucrative allied trade of bartending a male preserve. The female minority who worked in nineteenth- and early twentieth-century restaurants was widely suspected to be of dubious morality. The Harvey girls were a celebrated exception to the poor reputation of waitresses. The Harvey House chain, which served gourmet fare to southwestern rail travelers, employed a fresh-faced waitress workforce and cloistered them in dormitories.

Though only female food servers were suspected of loose morals, everyone in the occupation suffered from low status due to the job's association with servitude. Uniforms for many waitresses and waiters were basically the same as for domestic servants. The practice of tipping, which originated with household servants, encouraged the association of waiting tables with servitude and reinforced the status inequality between giver and receiver. Despite resentment and protest from servers themselves and critics who decried gratuities as un-American, tipping was firmly entrenched by the late nineteenth century. For better and worse, tips provided a major portion of most waiters and waitresses' income—and still do.

A Changing Workforce

Most waiters and waitresses historically were immigrants or children of immigrants from northern and central Europe. Large numbers of waiters claimed German, French, Italian, and Slavic roots, and many waitresses claimed English, Irish, German, and Scandinavian heritage. Employers were biased toward Euro-Americans because they wanted servers who spoke good English and whose appearance would not make customers ill at ease or provoke their ire. In some cities foreign-born food servers were in the firm majority in the late nineteenth and early twentieth century, as immigration to the United States generally swelled. In 1910, more than 55% of waiters in San Francisco and more than 71% in New York City were foreign-born. But as immigration dropped after restrictionist legislation in the 1920s, so, too, did the number of foreign-born waitresses and waiters.

Into the twentieth century, waiters and especially waitresses were more likely to be white as well as native-born. African-American men held a disproportionate share of early waiter positions, reflecting their role as household servants in the South and the shortage of white male labor. By the twentieth century however, the proportion of black waiters began to decline from 33% in 1910 to 12% by 1940. Black men's hold in the occupation slipped first due to more competition from white men but more so due to competition from white women after the First World War. Employers' preference for whites was more evident from the start in the waitress workforce. In 1910, less than 9% of waitresses were African-American and by 1940, a mere 4%. African-American food servers received significantly lower wages as a rule.

The most dramatic change in the restaurant food-server workforce in the twentieth century was its feminization. In the 1920s, women became the majority. By the 1970s, more than 90% of those waiting tables were women. Feminization reversed somewhat in the last decades of the twentieth century, but women were still nearly 80% of food servers by century's end. There were multiple causes for the gender shift. Older taboos about women serving men in commercial establishments dissipated (as did much of the moral stigma attached to waitresses). In particular prohibition of the liquor trade from 1920 to 1933 eliminated concerns over the impropriety of women serving alcohol. Perhaps more important was the rising number of family-style and other moderate-to low-priced restaurants. In these establishments employers favored women as a cheaper and friendlier labor source. Employers increasingly valued women for their presumed ornamental potential, too, as evident in the rise of sexually provocative uniforms in more daring eateries and an enduring bias toward younger, attractive hires. Though men maintained their predominance in the most expensive, formal restaurants, women became more numerous in higher-end table service as well. During the labor shortages created by the world wars and sporadic episodes of labor strife, many employers turned to women as a stopgap but then kept waitresses on permanently.

For women waitressing provided some important benefits, which helped put it in the top 10 female occupations by 1940. Employers did not require any prior experience or specific credentials, making waitressing one of few such options for young women. Though considered unskilled by outsiders, many waitresses found excitement and took pride in mastering their craft and belonging to a distinct sisterhood.

Exploitation and Unionization

Waiting tables was often exhausting work, with longer hours than other jobs, hectic stretches at peak times, and rock-bottom wages. Until World War II, most employers required wait staff to live on-site, and 7-day workweeks were common. Room and partial board helped offset low wages, but also reinforced the problem of long periods on call. Meals for servers were also typically the cheapest, least appealing food the restaurant had available and were often consumed in cramped, unsanitary backrooms. Uniform purchases and upkeep taxed already meager wages, as did the widespread practice of fines for breakage, unpaid checks, and various breaches of serving procedure. Tipping boosted waitresses' and waiters' income but lowered their status in many Americans' eyes. Worse, gratuities were at customers' whim and enabled employers to justify low wages; and waitresses' tip income tended to decline with age, despite growing experience and efficiency. While hard to quantify, waitresses have perhaps suffered more sexual harassment than any other group of female workers.

Waiters and waitresses countered these various forms of exploitation by unionizing. They succeeded in building durable, often powerful, labor organizations that significantly improved wages and working conditions for many for several decades. Waiters began organizing in the 1880s. In 1891, the American Federation of Labor (AFL) chartered the Waiters'

and Bartenders' National Union, later to become the mixed-sex Hotel Employees' and Restaurant Employees' International Union (HERE). By the First World War HERE had organized 65,000 workers. At the turn of the century, waitresses began to organize themselves as well, defying stereotypes that cast women as unwilling and unfit to unionize. Some waitresses joined mixed-sex locals with waiters, but many preferred craft- and sex-segregated locals of their own. Within two decades of the founding of the first waitress local in Seattle in 1900, there were 17 such locals on firm footing, and 70% of HERE's waitress membership belonged to separate locals. Waitresses' preference for separate organizations endured until the 1970s.

As in many other industries, the 1930s and World War II era brought dramatic union growth and a shift toward industrial- rather than craft-style organizing. The HERE mushroomed from around 25,000 members in the early 1930s to more than 400,000 in 1946, and to 450,000 at the start of the 1960s. Waitresses' presence in the union grew apace, with women constituting nearly half of HERE's membership at mid-century and the waitress locals surpassing those of waiters and bartenders in size and influence. During the postwar peak of union strength, about a quarter of waitresses in the United States were unionized. In longtime union stronghold Seattle, 90% were organized.

Waitresses' work culture enabled such remarkable union strength, and the two were mutually reinforcing. As historian Dorothy Sue Cobble has shown, waitresses developed a strong sense of craft solidarity based on shared experiences as restaurant insiders and demographic commonalities. Not only were waitresses relatively homogenous ethnically, they were also more often primary wage earners than other working women, heading households or living on their own; they were generally older, too, and more likely to be married than other female wage earners. Waitresses' work culture stretched across workplaces, promoting continuity and unity among workers who switched jobs frequently but tended to remain in the occupation for many years. Waitressing generally called for assertive behavior, which also helped foster union activism.

Though located within a male-dominated international, waitress locals within HERE enjoyed considerable autonomy and used it to forge a distinct working-class feminist agenda. They pursued gender equality when it made sense for waitresses; at other times they stressed gender difference when it was more beneficial, such as protective legislation for working women. Waitresses' work culture and union culture proclaimed their skills as worthy of respect as other crafts and promoted their entitlement to the male prerogative of a family wage adequate to support a household.

Job Boom, Union Decline

After midcentury the restaurant boom brought dramatic employment growth for waiters and waitresses but did not bode well for their unions. Growing incomes, leisure hours, and mobility made eating out a regular activity for middle- and lower-income Americans across the nation in the postwar years. Since the 1970s, the rising number of dual-income families and the upward creep of working hours for many have encouraged still more reliance on restaurants. In 1954, there were about 127,000 restaurants total in the United States with sales of about $7 billion. A half-century later there were 900,000 restaurants in the United States with sales topping $400 billion. Americans by then were spending nearly half their food budget at restaurants, and the restaurant industry had become the largest private employer in the United States, with 11 million workers in total and more than two million waiters and waitresses. Among them was a growing portion of part-time workers. While only one-fifth of waitresses and one-tenth of waiters worked part-time in 1940, by 1970 a majority of wait staff did. Not counting tips, wait staff earned the lowest average wages of any occupational group at the turn of the twenty-first century.

As the industry flourished waitresses' and waiters' unions struggled. The postwar boom saw restaurant density spread from older urban areas on the West Coast and in the Northeast to the Sunbelt (the Southwest and Southeast) and to suburbs throughout the United States, areas that tended to be more anti-union. Restaurant growth after World War II also depended in part on the rise of chains and eventually of multinational conglomerates like McDonald's, which fiercely resisted unionization. Part-time workers, with less sense of craft solidarity and occupational commitment than earlier generations, proved harder to organize. Some restaurant growth bypassed waitresses and waiters altogether with informal self-service restaurants and coffee shops and take-out. By the mid-1990s, the union's total membership was down one-third from its postwar peak to about 300,000. Its main growth area, offsetting losses elsewhere, was in casinos.

But if the heyday of union protection had passed for nearly all waitresses and waiters, they became even more representative of the changing workforce in the United States. In an economy increasingly reliant on selling services based on low-wage, insecure, and largely female labor, food servers were—and are—at the leading edge of employment trends and of struggles for dignity and respect in the service sector.

KATHLEEN M. BARRY

References and Further Reading

Cobble, Dorothy Sue. *Dishing It Out: Waitresses and Their Unions in the Twentieth Century*. Urbana: University of Illinois Press, 1991.

Donovan, Frances. *The Woman Who Waits*. Boston, MA: R. G. Badger, 1920.

Josephson, Matthew. *Union House, Union Bar: The History of the Hotel and Restaurant Employees and Bartenders International Union, AFL-CIO*. New York: Random House, 1956.

National Restaurant Association Website, Press Room. www.restaurant.org (2005–).

Owings, Alison. *Hey, Waitress! The USA from the Other Side of the Tray*. Berkeley: University of California Press, 2002.

Paules, Greta Foff. *Dishing It Out: Power and Resistance among Waitresses in a New Jersey Restaurant*. Philadelphia, PA: Temple University Press, 1991.

Pillsbury, Richard. *From Boarding House to Bistro: The American Restaurant Then and Now*. Boston, MA: Unwin Hyman, 1990.

Poling-Kempes, Lesley. *The Harvey Girls: Women Who Opened the West*. New York: Paragon, 1989.

Spradley, James P., and Brenda J. Mann. *The Cocktail Waitress: Woman's Work in a Man's World*. New York: Alfred A. Knopf, 1975.

Whyte, William Foote. *Human Relations in the Restaurant Industry*. New York: McGraw Hill, 1948.

See also **Hotel and Restaurant Employees' International Union; Sexual Harassment; Working-Class Feminism**

WALSH, MIKE (1810–1859)
New York State Politician

Mike Walsh was among the earliest U.S. working-class politicians. Born near Cork, Ireland, in 1810, he came as a child with his family to New York City. Walsh apprenticed as a lithographer and worked as a journeyman in New York and New Orleans. After his return from New Orleans, he turned his attention to forging a political career. He joined a volunteer fire company, a traditional stepping-stone for ambitious young men in the city. Handsome and charismatic, Walsh's angry oratory championing the city's workingmen soon attracted a coterie of followers, and in 1840 he formed the Spartan Association, a combination political club and street gang that at its height had almost 500 members. The organization included many respectable supporters but also enlisted neighborhood bullies and prizefighters whom Walsh used literally to strong-arm his way to political influence in the Democratic party. The Spartan Band, as it was called, forcibly expelled rivals from nominating caucuses, and on Election Day the Spartans would seize and destroy ballot boxes in precincts where rivals were strong. By the mid-1840s, the Spartans were a political power in every ward in New York. Walsh shrewdly steered his own course around the myriad city and state factions of the party, most of the time remaining independent of Tammany Hall. A Protestant, he considered himself a true American, and often allied his gang with native-born elements of the party against the Irish.

Walsh was in many ways the last of the Jacksonian labor radicals. The Spartan banner showed a workingman breaking the chains of ignorance and servitude and was inscribed, "Arise now, man, and vindicate thy right." Independent artisans, Walsh believed, were the backbone of the republic but were threatened by the increasing concentration of wealth in the hands of a few. His blazing rhetoric was a peculiar mixture of a republican attack on luxury and defense of virtuous producers combined with profane vilification of those who were the enemies of the working classes. Walsh's favorite causes were for the most part traditional Jacksonian ones, such as rotation in office, specie, abolition of imprisonment for debt, and an end to state-sponsored monopolies. Central to the elevation of the workingmen, Walsh believed, was the election to office of candidates who were true friends of labor. In 1841, Walsh attracted national attention when he and some of his supporters traveled to Rhode Island to join the abortive Dorr War.

Walsh's reputation as a tribune of the people was only part of the reason for his fame. A ceaseless and creative self-promoter, he shrewdly appealed to the city's young working-class male population by portraying himself as a man among men, a drinker, fighter, and hell raiser. Walsh suggested that those who belonged to the Spartan Band were real men who used their hands at work and were not afraid to use their fists in politics. His boisterous persona was enhanced by his well-publicized friendship with Thomas Hyer, American heavyweight prizefighting champion. One part of Walsh's critique of capitalism was that the sober, businesslike ethos of the age was suffocating the tavern-based artisan lifestyle he so loved. Walsh strongly defended traditional masculine revelry from criticism by clerics and temperance advocates.

The *Subterranean*, Walsh's famous newspaper, was founded in 1843 and boasted it was "independent in everything, neutral in nothing." Walsh's combative personality was reflected everywhere in its pages. Even by the no-holds-barred journalistic standards of the day, the *Subterranean* stood out. What caught popular attention was not Walsh's articulate defense of the rights of workingmen but the newspaper's vituperative attacks on those Walsh deemed hostile to labor, which seemed to include at one time or another anyone not named Mike Walsh. Its invective was personal and relentless: Antagonists were blockheads, scoundrels, and shysters (a word Walsh may have coined). One foe was "a beastly and polluted old vagabond," another "a lecherous lover of black wenches" (Walsh threw racial slurs around freely). Abolitionists and temperance supporters were favorite targets of abuse. Walsh's four arrests and trials for libel provided New Yorkers with continuing entertainment. When he was released from prison after an 1843 conviction, 50,000 (or so he claimed) of "the subterranean populace of New York" gathered in City Hall Park to greet him. Walsh never shied from writing about himself, and for the edification of *Subterranean* readers, he recounted his late night tavern jaunts and his attendance at cockfights and prizefights. An advocate of land reform, Walsh merged the *Subterranean* with George Henry Evans's *Working Man's Advocate* in 1844, but the alliance was short-lived. The constant libel suits eventually took their toll, and in 1847, the *Subterranean* ceased publication.

Walsh ran for the New York State Assembly in 1841 but was defeated. In 1846, he received the Democratic nomination for the state senate and won and was re-elected in 1847 and 1851. Boasting he was "the tool of no political clique," Walsh advocated protection for apprentices and a shorter workday, but he antagonized Albany legislators with his erratic habits and bombastic rhetoric and seems to have accomplished little. In 1852, Walsh was elected to Congress as the Tammany candidate. A supporter of John C. Calhoun in the 1840s, Walsh now allied with the prosouthern Hunker faction of the New York State Democratic party. He gave few speeches on serious issues and seems to have been regarded as something of a comical figure. His rhetoric elevating independent, native-born artisans was increasingly out of date by the mid-1850s as the city's factories filled with semiskilled immigrants, and in 1854 Walsh was defeated for renomination to Congress by future Tammany boss "Honest" John Kelly. Walsh retired from politics. Drinking too heavily to be steadily employed, he worked as a freelance journalist and engaged in speculations of various sorts, including a silver mine in Arizona. He collapsed and died on the street on March 17, 1859.

RICHARD STOTT

References and Further Reading

Ernst, Robert. "The One and Only Mike Walsh." *New York Historical Society Quarterly* 26 (1952): 43–65.

Walsh, Mike. *Sketches of the Speeches and Writings of Michael Walsh.* New York: Thomas McSpedon, 1843.

Wilentz, Sean. *Chants Democratic: New York City and the Rise of the American Working Class, 1788–1850.* New York: Oxford: 1984.

See also **Dorr War**

WALSH-HEALEY PUBLIC CONTRACTS ACT (1936)

Enacted under special political and constitutional circumstances as part of President Franklin D. Roosevelt's New Deal in 1936, the Walsh-Healey Act set minimum labor standards for manufacturers and "regular dealers" who provided "materials, supplies, articles, and equipment" to the federal government under contracts worth $10,000 or more. The act prohibited child and convict labor; fixed maximum work hours at 8 per day and 40 per week; banned "unsanitary and hazardous" work conditions; and most importantly, required contractors to pay at least the "prevailing minimum wage" as determined by the secretary of labor based on wages received by persons in similar work or in "similar industries or groups of industries currently operating in the locality," exempting clerical workers, subcontractors, and suppliers of farm perishables, originally produced goods, and commodities purchased on the open market.

The law originated in the U.S. Department of Labor early in 1935, when Secretary Frances Perkins directed departmental lawyers to draw up legislation to replace National Recovery Administration codes mandating maximum hours and minimum wages under the New Deal's troubled National Industrial Recovery Act. At the time Perkins and President Roosevelt hoped to counteract Depression-era employer proclivities to cut wages, reduce worker purchasing power, and subject workers to sweatshop conditions. When the U.S. Supreme Court's *Schechter v. U.S.* decision in May 1935 struck the National

Industrial Recovery Act down and raised doubts about the constitutionality of other federal laws regulating private-sector employment, the Roosevelt administration advanced Perkins's labor department bill covering publicly contracted work. Emulating the 1931 Davis-Bacon Act governing federally sponsored public-construction projects, administration officials reasoned that the national government had constitutional authority to regulate work conditions under which goods for its own use were manufactured.

First introduced in the U.S. Senate by Massachusetts Democrat David I. Walsh in June 1935, the labor department's public-contracts measure stalled in Congress until Democratic Massachusetts Congressman Arthur D. Healey proposed a revised House version in March 1936. Led by the National Association of Manufacturers, employers delayed the bill and persuaded Congress to raise Walsh's $2,000 contract threshold to $10,000, but the measure secured support from the American Federation of Labor as a public standard for collective-bargaining agreements in the private sector and from women's groups seeking relief for underpaid female workers. Most importantly the Roosevelt administration denominated the now-called Walsh-Healey bill as "must" legislation for its upcoming 1936 presidential campaign, reassuring working-class voters that the administration aimed to establish "a floor under wages and a ceiling upon hours." Congress finally approved the Walsh-Healey Act, and President Roosevelt signed it on June 30, 1936.

Determination of prevailing minimum wages emerged as the focal point of Walsh-Healey administration, especially after the Fair Labor Standards Act of 1938 superceded Walsh-Healey provisions on child and convict labor. The labor department issued its first wage determination in February 1937 for garment workers, and soon thereafter Secretary Perkins created the Public Contracts Division under L. Metcalfe Walling to extend minimum-wage findings to public contractors making textiles, hats and gloves, paper, steel, cement, and fertilizer. Manufacturers promptly disputed the labor department's use of the statutory term locality to designate regional minimum-wage differentials. Yet in *Perkins v. Lukens Steel Co.* (1940), the U.S. Supreme Court ruled that the Walsh-Healey Act did not grant employers legal standing to secure judicial review of such decisions, leaving the labor department to interpret locality as it saw fit. In contrast to the Davis-Bacon Act's designation of local cities, towns, and villages consequently, Walsh-Healey allowed the labor department to embrace an industrywide conception of locality, focusing more on competitive markets than on geography. By 1940, the department had prescribed minimum wages for public contractors in 30 industries covering almost 900,000 workers. Departmental investigation of Walsh-Healey violations in 1941 forced employers to pay more than $500,000 in fines and overtime.

Suspended during World War II, Walsh-Healey proceedings became very legalistic when administrators branched out to determine prevailing minimum wages in the coal, chemical, and rubber industries in the postwar years. The labor secretary now had to reconcile Walsh-Healey wage determinations with the Fair Labor Standards Act's minimum-pay requirements. Moreover a 1952 amendment to the Walsh-Healey law sponsored by Democratic Arkansas Senator J. William Fulbright applied the 1946 Administrative Procedure Act's judicial review and procedural requirements to Walsh-Healey wage determinations. This Fulbright Amendment made subsequent Walsh-Healey proceedings cumbersome, even though a federal circuit court in *Mitchell v. Covington Mills* (1955) sustained the labor department's industrywide definition of locality for textile manufacturers, and another in *Ruth Elkhorn Coals v. Mitchell* (1957) upheld the labor secretary's interpretation of open market for the coal industry. The circuit court ruling in *Wirtz v. Baldo Electric* (1964) requiring the labor department to open confidential wage surveys to competing employers, however, brought Walsh-Healey wage determinations virtually to a halt.

Over the 28 years of its active administration, the Walsh-Healey Act attracted increasing employer opposition but steadfast labor defense. Nonetheless analysts contend that the law had minimal effect on wage levels, though there were exceptions in industries like bituminous coal mining. Observers complain that Walsh-Healey wage administration became excessively bureaucratic over the years, compared at least to efficient wage proceedings under the Davis-Bacon law. In addition unlike Davis-Bacon's mandate for prevailing wages that administrators often pegged to union wage rates, the Walsh-Healey Act's standard of the prevailing minimum rarely increased wages, but only mirrored existing minimums in the marketplace. The high contract threshold of $10,000, moreover, excluded small suppliers prone to lower wages. Most important Walsh-Healey's functions were absorbed by subsequent legislation: Hours regulation by the 1962 Contract Work Hours Standards Act, safety and sanitation by the 1970 Occupational Safety and Health Act, and especially minimum wages by the broader 1938 Fair Labor Standards

Act. The Walsh-Healey Act remains in effect today, but commentators wonder about its future usefulness.

Donald W. Rogers

References and Further Reading

Brandeis, Elizabeth. "Organized Labor and Protective Labor Legislation." In *Labor and the New Deal*, edited by Milton Derber and Edwin Young. Madison: University of Wisconsin Press, 1957.

Christenson, Carroll L., and Richard A. Myren. *Wage Policy under the Walsh-Healey Public Contracts Act: A Critical Review*. Bloomington: Indiana University Press, 1966.

Martin, George. *Madam Secretary: Frances Perkins*. Boston, MA: Houghton Mifflin Company, 1976.

Morton, Herbert C. *Public Contracts and Private Wages: Experience under the Walsh-Healey Act*. Washington, DC: The Brookings Institution, 1965.

Thieblot, Armand J., Jr. *Prevailing Wage Legislation: The Davis-Bacon Act, State "Little Davis-Bacon" Acts, the Walsh-Healey Act, and the Service Contract Act*. Philadelphia, PA: Industrial Research Unit of the Wharton School, 1986.

Cases and Statutes Cited

Mitchell v. Covington Mills, 229 F. 2d 506 (D.C. Cir. 1955).

Perkins v. Lukens Steel Co. 310 U.S. 113 (1940).

Ruth Elkhorn Coals v. Mitchell, 248 F. 2d 635 (D.C. Cir. 1957).

Schechter Poultry Corp. v. U.S., 295 U.S. 495 (1935).

Wirtz v. Baldo Electric, 337 F. 2d 518 (D.C. Cir. 1964).

Administrative Procedure Act of June 11, 1946, c. 324, 60 Stat. 237.

Contract Work Hours Standards Act of August 13, 1962, PL 87–581, 76 Stat. 357.

Davis-Bacon Act of March 3, 1931, c. 411, 46 Stat. 1494.

Fair Labor Standards Act of June 25, 1938, c. 676, 52 Stat. 1060.

National Industrial Recovery Act of June 16, 1933, c. 90, 48 Stat. 195, declared unconstitutional on May 27, 1935, by the *Schechter* decision cited above.

Occupational Safety and Health Act of December 29, 1970, PL 91-596, 84 Stat. 1590.

Walsh-Healey Public Contracts Act of June 30, 1936, c. 881, 49 Stat. 2039.

WASHINGTON, BOOKER T. (1856–1915)
African-American Leader

Booker T. (Taliaferro) Washington was an African-American educator and author who is generally considered, along with W. E. B. DuBois, as one of the two predominant African-American leaders in the late-nineteenth and early-twentieth centuries. In regard to labor history, Washington is perhaps best-known for his belief that African-Americans were best served by focusing on industrial and vocational skills rather than fighting for equality and civil rights.

Washington was born a slave on a small farm in Franklin County, Virginia. After emancipation his family moved to Malden, West Virginia, where extreme poverty forced him, beginning at age nine, to work in salt furnaces and coal mines rather than attend school. At age 16, determined to get an education, Washington enrolled at the Hampton Normal and Agricultural Institute in Virginia, where he worked as a janitor to help pay expenses. Washington noted the centrality of work in his formative years in his autobiography, *Up from Slavery*: "There was no period of my life that was devoted to play. From the time that I can remember anything, almost every day of my life has been occupied in some kind of labour" (2003).

After graduating with honors in 1875, Washington taught in Malden for 2 years, then studied briefly at Wayland Seminary in Washington, DC, before joining the teaching staff at Hampton in 1879. In 1881, he was asked to found Tuskegee Normal and Industrial Institute, a newly proposed normal school for African-Americans in a small, rural Alabama town that was part of the black belt of the South. Washington considered Tuskegee to be his life's work. In his 34 years at the helm before his death in 1915, Washington grew the school from a one-room shanty with 30 students into an established university with 100 fully equipped buildings, 1,500 students, and a faculty of 200.

Washington firmly believed that African-Americans in the post-Reconstruction era were best served by focusing on self-reliance, hard work, and thrift. Washington believed that an industrial education was the key to escaping the difficult life of sharecropping and could lead to self-employment and ownership of land, homes, and small businesses. Thus in addition to a strong emphasis on personal hygiene and character building, his educational mission was focused on teaching industrial skills, trades, and crafts. "All of these teach industries at which our men and women can find immediate employment as soon as they leave the institution," he wrote. Tuskegee offered training in such areas as carpentry, printing, cabinetmaking, tinsmithing, farming and dairying; women were offered training in such domestic skills as cooking and sewing. In addition students helped supply the labor needs of the school and helped the Tuskegee expand by building new buildings and sleeping cabins.

As Tuskegee grew, so did Washington's influence. A strong network of Tuskegee graduates, employees, and Washington's associates, along with African-American social institutions that were influenced by Washington, became known as the Tuskegee machine. The Tuskegee machine impacted African-American hiring practices, collected and distributed philanthropic funds, worked to influence public opinion, monitored the press, and served as a center of African-American research. DuBois noted that few African-Americans were appointed to political positions without his consent. Washington was generally considered the most powerful African-American in the United States at this point.

A key point in Washington's ascent was a famous address at the Cotton States and International Exposition in Atlanta in 1895. Speaking before a predominantly white audience, Washington declared for African-Americans, vocational education and economic security were more important than social equality, traditional higher education, or political office. Washington offered that African-Americans would accept segregation and social inequality if whites would encourage their economic and cultural progress. Washington summarized his approach thusly: "In all things that are purely social we can be as separate as the fingers, yet one as the hand in all things essential to mutual progress" (Atlanta Compromise, 2003). This address became known as the Atlanta Compromise.

Washington's success and growing reputation were not without controversy however. Although his approach was hailed by white leaders, African-American critics took aim at his emphasis of work skills and economic independence over equality and civil rights, especially given the social backdrop of harsh Jim Crow laws, segregation and discrimination, regular lynchings of African-American men, and political disenfranchisement. African-American intellectuals, led by W. E. B. DuBois, viewed Washington as an accommodationist, whose pragmatic philosophy would condemn blacks to permanent subservience to whites.

Although Washington's views lost out to DuBois's more progressive and integrationist stances, he remains a historical giant for his emphasis on economic self-reliance and his founding of Tuskegee University.

DAVID PURCELL

Selected Works

Washington, Booker T. "The Booker T. Washington Papers." University of Illinois Press. www.historycooperative.org/btw/index.html.

———. *My Larger Education: Chapters from My Experience*. Amherst, NY: Humanity Books, 2004.

———. "The Atlanta Compromise." In *Ripples of Hope: Great American Civil Rights Speeches*, edited by Josh Gottheimer. New York: Basic Civitas Books, 2003.

———. *Up from Slavery*. Boston, MA: Bedford/St. Martin's, 2003.

Booker T. Washington works. "Documenting the American South." University of North Carolina. http://docsouth.unc.edu/index.html.

References and Further Reading

Bauerlein, Mark. "Washington, Du Bois, and the Black Future." *Wilson Quarterly* 28, 4 (2004): 74–86.

Harlan, Louis R. *Booker T. Washington in Perspective: Essays of Louis R. Harlan*, edited by Raymond W. Smock. Jackson: University Press of Mississippi, 1988.

———. *Booker T. Washington: The Wizard of Tuskegee, 1901–1915*. New York: Oxford University Press, 1983.

Verney, Kevern. *The Art of the Possible: Booker T. Washington and Black leadership in the United States, 1881–1925*. New York: Routledge, 2001.

Wintz, Cary D., ed. *African-American Political Thought, 1890–1930: Washington, Du Bois, Garvey, and Randolph*. Armonk, NY: M. E. Sharpe, 1996.

See also **African-Americans; Du Bois, W. E. B.; South**

WEBSTER, MILTON PRICE (1887–1965)
Brotherhood of Sleeping Car Porters

Milton Price Webster, a Pullman Sleeping Car porter, was a key figure in the formation and founding of the Brotherhood of Sleeping Car Porters (BSCP), the first national labor union of African-Americans that was recognized by the leaders of a major American corporation. As director of the Chicago district for the BSCP, Webster, working closely with A. Philip Randolph, the head of the brotherhood, helped build the BSCP from a small group of Pullman porters in 1925 into a major labor union that secured a contract with the Pullman Company in 1937, long known for its anti-union management policies. He served as first vice-president of the BSCP for the rest of his life. He was also an active participant in the historic March on Washington movement and was appointed by President Franklin D. Roosevelt to the Fair Employment Practice Committee in 1941. From 1925 until his death in 1965, Webster was a pioneer on the labor front fighting for the economic and civil rights of African-Americans.

Webster, born in Clarksville, Tennessee, in 1887, migrated north with his father when he was just a boy and began working as a Pullman porter out of Chicago during his teens. After working for the Pullman Company for almost 20 years, he was fired in the early twenties for his part in trying to organize porters in the Railroad Men's Benevolent Industrial Association. As a result of his connections with the black Republican machine in Chicago, he was able to land a job as a bailiff and also a position as Republican head of the Sixth Ward. He was not looking for work when Randolph approached him in the fall of 1925 about organizing a union to represent the interests of Pullman porters in negotiations with the Pullman Company.

Chicago was headquarters for the giant Pullman Company and over one-third of the porters were based in the area. Yet the fledgling union faced major resistance in the black community from middle-class leaders who felt the Pullman Company had done much more for black Chicagoans than any labor union. For the next several years, Webster and Randolph worked to break down resistance not just from managers of the Pullman Company but also from black leaders and the institutions they controlled. When Webster began trying to organize Chicago's Pullman porters, he declared that "Everything Negro was against us." After approaching 45 or 50

M. P. Webster, first international vice president, Brotherhood of Sleeping Car Porters. Library of Congress, Prints & Photographs Division [LC-USZ62-97539].

prominent citizens about endorsing the porters' union movement, only five agreed to speak at the first meeting, and only one showed up. If the brotherhood wanted its union to succeed, it had to win support from Chicago's black leaders.

Starting with a small network consisting of prominent clubwomen and a minister, Webster organized a Citizens' Committee to break down resistance within the community. In January 1928, he launched the first Negro Labor Conference in Chicago to challenge Pullman paternalism and educate the community about the politics of patronage. At that first labor conference, Webster asserted that Pullman porters and maids had a right to choose who represented their interests at work that was as basic as that guaranteed under the Fourteenth Amendment to the Constitution. By 1937, when Pullman officially recognized the BSCP, Webster and Randolph had also won the hearts and minds of much of black America.

In January 1941, when the United States economy was shifting its forces to defense production, Webster and Randolph began organizing black America to March on Washington in protest against discrimination in the job market and the armed forces. In June after President Roosevelt issued Executive Order No. 8802, prohibiting discrimination in defense industries and agencies of the federal government, the March on Washington was canceled. Shortly thereafter Webster was appointed to the Fair Employment Practice Committee (FEPC), the first federal agency in history to deal exclusively with job discrimination, and he spent the war years trying to put some teeth in the proclamations of Executive Order No. 8802. Webster, initially one of only two black members of the FEPC, distinguished himself on that body, keeping employers on the defensive with his hard questions and frontal attacks against job discrimination. His scrutiny of industrial relations influenced policy; his leadership helped break down stereotypes about the abilities of African-Americans held by white government bureaucrats; and his questioning white witnesses in southern cities challenged the racial status quo in a fundamental way.

After the FEPC folded in 1946, Webster devoted the rest of his life to the BSCP. He died of a heart attack during the American Federation of Labor-Congress of Industrial Organizations convention in Bal Harbour, Florida, in 1965.

BETH TOMPKINS BATES

References and Further Reading

Arnesen, Eric. *Brotherhoods of Color: Black Railroad Workers and the Struggle for Equality.* Cambridge, MA: Harvard University Press, 2001.

Bates, Beth Tompkins. *Pullman Porters and the Rise of Protest Politics in Black America, 1925–1945.* Chapel Hill: University of North Carolina Press, 2001.

Harris, William H. *Keeping the Faith: A. Philip Randolph, Milton P. Webster, and the Brotherhood of Sleeping Car Porters, 1925–1937.* Urbana: University of Illinois Press, 1977.

LeRoy, Greg. "The Founding Heart of A. Philip Randolph's Union: Milton P. Webster and Chicago's Pullman Porters Organize, 1925–1937." *Labor's Heritage* 3, 3 (July 1991): 22–43

See also **Brotherhood of Sleeping Car Porters; Randolph, A. Philip**

WELFARE CAPITALISM

The term welfare capitalism has been used to refer to the overall structure of Western and U.S. economies comprised of a varied mix of state- and private-welfare programs that provide a safety net of economic and social security to workers and that help stabilize and rationalize employment. Historically however welfare capitalism has generally been applied much more specifically and narrowly—as it will be here—to the private aspect of economic and social-welfare programs.

In practice welfare capitalism is historically associated with a specific and extensive movement of industrial reform emerging in the late nineteenth century and extending well into the twentieth. Profit-sharing and employee-representation plans were at the heart of its ideological formulation though in practice rare. More prevalent and characteristic in practice were such corporate-welfare services and provisions as company housing, free education in company kindergartens or grammar schools, recreational facilities and corporate athletic programs, company stores providing relatively inexpensive foodstuffs to employees, factory cafeterias, sickness and injury insurance wholly or partially subsidized by firms, and company-built hospitals providing free medical care. In essence as Louis A. Boettiger noted in 1923 in *Employee Welfare Work*, welfare capitalism included any "voluntary effort of the employer, in excess of the requirements of law, of the market, or of custom, directed toward the improvement of employment practices respecting working conditions, hours of work and wages, together with the general conditions of community life of the workers." As a movement welfare capitalism contributed considerably to the revision of traditional *laissez faire* capitalism and played both a transitional and supplemental role in the development of the welfare state.

As a collection of particular reforms and programs, welfare capitalism has been considered by some recent revisionist scholars as little more than fringe benefits, and—as a percentage of total corporate expenditures—hardly amounting to much at all. Yet the volume, intensity, timing of—and promotional activity associated with—corporate-welfare work suggests the rise of welfare capitalism represented far more than the sum of its parts. What most now refer to as job fringe benefits, certainly eroding in recent years, undoubtedly had their origin—in part—in welfare capitalism: Health insurance and medical care (in the United States far more dependent on employers than on the state), pensions, vacations, corporate gyms and athletic facilities. All were championed in the early years of the movement by one or another advocate. All became a part of the expectations of workers in many corporations as a result of a century of formal and informal negotiations between employers attempting to build an efficient, harmonious and loyal labor force and employees seeking to extract, expand, and preserve services and facilities.

The writing on welfare capitalism from the 1880s to the present is voluminous. Industrialists, magazine writers, churchmen, labor leaders, muckrakers, economists, and historians all wrote extensively on the subject, though few until recent decades employed the more academic term welfare capitalism. Most of those who wrote about the obligations of employers or industrial paternalism or welfare work wrote about a movement of labor-management reform motivated by sometimes idealistic, more often pragmatic, motives. Among them were increasing productivity and efficiency, reducing labor turnover, attracting a desirable grade of labor, advertising the business, reducing strikes, providing palliatives for low wages, averting state regulations, disrupting union activities, and warding off charges of corporate "soullessness." A few saw it in terms of pure philanthropy.

The history of welfare capitalism in the modern United States follows an evolutionary track, starting from the familial, intimate, and patriarchal regimes that arose in the nineteenth century to the large, bureaucratic, corporate-welfare firms of the late twentieth and early twenty-first centuries. The movement was neither static nor temporary, as some have suggested, but an evolving strain in modern capitalism itself—one that rose and fell, and reshaped itself as society, economy, and the state evolved. Welfare capitalism was first and foremost an ideology, expressing the ideas and ideals of reform-minded capitalists in the nineteenth and early twentieth centuries and possessing both conservative and liberal elements. Hardly unique to the United States, its origins lay in a variety of sources—some domestic, some foreign. In

Europe welfare capitalism was clearly tied to feudal paternalistic traditions and was adopted in societies where class conflict was a constant theme as an implement of social control—designed to ensure labor discipline and a stable social order. Pre-industrial and precapitalist traditions established long-lasting expectations and obligations that were associated with all forms of master-servant relationships, but with the coming of market capitalism, they came under great strain; welfare capitalism was one way of addressing such strain.

In the early nineteenth century such industrial experiments as the Lowell system, associated with Francis Cabott Lowell and the mills owned by the Boston Manufacturing Company, anticipated the growth of welfare capitalism. Convincing young women to leave their rural New England families and enter a highly suspect industrial community—and persuading their parents to let them do so—required special protections, enticements, and amenities: Boarding houses, strict supervision, schools, hospitals, churches, corporate-sponsored cultural events, and relatively generous wages. Through the middle of the century, the need to overcome Jeffersonian reservations about American industrial development—with its associated fear of the growth of an insurgent, dependent laboring class—fueled some of the nation's earliest experiments with corporate-welfare reforms. Industrial regimes became concerned not merely with enlarging corporate profits, but also, in varying degrees, employee welfare.

Yet overall the triumph of industrial capitalism and the ideology of *laissez faire* overwhelmed Jeffersonian fears and undermined industrial paternalism. The existence of plantation slavery further strengthened and promoted a faith in free-market capitalism in the industrializing North. In the mid-nineteenth-century United States, the celebration of free labor over slave labor and plantation paternalism fueled rejection of all paternalistic models of labor-capital relationships. This was reinforced by the success and expansion of the American industrial behemoth in the decades following the Civil War. *Laissez faire* capitalism was offered a new vocabulary and paradigm when conservative social Darwinist William Graham Sumner promoted and celebrated the inequality and struggle of the American marketplace as the most effective means of social and economic progress. Sumner gave voice to the inchoate views of a generation of mid-to-late-nineteenth-century American employers.

Still in the midst of the success of late nineteenth-century capitalism lay plenty of evidence of failure; the facile adherence of Americans to mobility ideologies and Horatio Alger myths was challenged by the obvious signs of poverty and destitution that accompanied industrial growth at the end of the century. In the context of a rapidly industrializing United States increasingly dominated by large monopolistic business firms and plagued by periodic bouts of economic recession and depression, dissident voices arose countering the message of Sumner and his ideological brethren. Social gospel proponents, Populists, labor unionists, Socialists, anarchists, and concerned liberals began to question economic orthodoxy and conservative strains of social Darwinism and looked for ways to reconcile industrial growth and efficiency with long-cherished democratic and egalitarian ideals and institutions. While Populists called for the nationalization of certain key economic sectors (to destroy the reign of corporate plutocrats) and the revival of Jeffersonian self-sufficiency in others, and socialists advocated the abolition of the wage system and the construction of a co-operative commonwealth, social gospel ministers called on businessmen to humanize their practices and to reconstruct the fellowship between social classes that was perceived to have existed in the U.S. pre-industrial past.

Of all the criticism leveled against corporate capitalism in the late nineteenth century, that which came from the Social Gospel movement had the greatest impact on the business community; after all it did not call on business leaders to abandon their leadership roles in society and in the economy. It did not challenge their power. It merely called for the application of fundamental Christian values and principles to social and economic affairs. Social gospel proponents Washington Gladden, Josiah Strong, Edward M. Sheldon, and Walter Rauchenbusch all sought, in the words that Gladden first penned in his *Working People and Their Employers* a year before the Great Railroad Strike of 1877, to "bring the truth of the New Testament to bear directly upon matters now in dispute between labor and capital." Gladden and his fellow clergymen called for the corporate assumption of a sense of guardianship and Christian obligation toward employees. Christian obligation included such things as care for the physical health and comfort of workers (providing medical facilities and care, and ensuring a safe workplace), polite and considerate treatment by supervisory personnel, and responsibility for the intellectual improvement of workers (company-built schools, teachers, cultural activities, libraries). But that was not the ultimate aim of most social gospel advocates. For many of them the ultimate goal was to pave the path for escape from the dependency of wage labor and to achieve a more egalitarian society overall, though not necessarily through socialism (though Gladden and other reform clergymen did promote worker cooperatives). As Gladden suggested, the aim of reform is to decrease the number of wage laborers, to promote their passage into the ranks of capitalists, and to give employees in general a more proprietary interest in the economic engines of the nation.

In many ways many of the social gospel debates around industrialization of the late nineteenth century recapitulated those of the early nineteenth century. Now it was not a nascent capitalism that promoted such debates, but a maturing and thriving one. The Social Gospel movement's advocacy of corporate paternalism (though often mixed with a warning to avoid overly intrusive and obtrusive initiatives) did encourage many businessmen to begin experimenting with various corporate-welfare schemes. Gladden and Josiah Strong both became very strong promoters and propagandists for welfare capitalism, encouraging employers—for humanitarian, practical, and public-relations reasons—to adopt corporate reforms. Strong in 1896 for example spoke to Procter and Gamble stockholders, praising the extensive welfare work undertaken by the firm (including one of the earliest profit-sharing plans in the country). He became involved in the work of the American Institute of Social Service, an outgrowth of Strong's League for Social Service, one of several organizations founded at the turn of the century that actively promoted welfare capitalism.

Initially many employers scoffed at the idea of private-welfare initiatives on behalf of their employees. For some besieged by trade unions and labor militants, it was difficult to abandon the Sumnerian view of industrial-labor relations as necessarily fraught with constant conflict. Welfare programs carried out in an obtrusively paternalistic manner also seemed to ignite hostile working-class reaction (the Pullman Strike of 1894 was in part blamed on precisely this factor) and hardly encouraged reform. Finally the depression decade of the 1890s posed an economic obstacle to the adoption of welfare programs. However with the recovery of the economy in the late 1890s and with labor conflicts continuing, more and more businessmen began to grow responsive to secular and religious welfare-capitalist advocates and looked to business-welfare schemes to assuage labor strife and ward off public criticisms of corporate abuses.

It was truly in the first decade of the new century that the movement toward welfare capitalism became a movement. In those years new advocates and critics arose, reviving once again the old conflict between democracy and corporate dependency and authoritarianism. The final years of the nineteenth and early decades of the twentieth centuries witnessed a large number of individuals and institutional efforts aimed at spreading employer-welfare work. Such individuals as Toledo's reform mayor "Golden Rule" (Samuel Milton) Jones, Edward Filene, the progressive Boston merchant, Harold Fowler McCormick of International Harvester, Clarence Hicks at International Harvester (also active in Colorado Fuel and Iron and Standard Oil), John D. Rockefeller, Jr., Gertrude Beeks (active in private, institutional, and government-work), and the Chicago newspaper editor Ralph Easley all took strong advocacy roles in the movement. In books, newspaper articles, magazine stories, and promotional publications, early twentieth-century advocates represented and promoted business welfarism in a variety of ways, suggesting the mix of pragmatic and ideological factors behind its growing popularity. When advocated by theologians, particularly social gospel ministers active in the League for Social Service, it was posed as a solution to the materialism and selfish corporate practices of *laissez faire* capitalism. Under the auspices of the National Civic Federation (NCF), welfare capitalism was a central element in a grand design: The rationalization and stabilization of the relationship between workers and managers. Both the League for Social Service (later the American Institute of Social Service) and the NCF actively and heavily promoted welfare work in the first two decades of the twentieth century, arguing for both its moral and practical benefits. The Department of Industrial Betterment of the League for Social Service, under the directorship of William Howe Tolman, initiated a decade-long promotional drive on behalf of welfare work in industry.

By far however a much more powerful and influential endorser of corporate-welfare work was the NCF, the institutional arm of the progressive corporate community—and one supported by such labor leaders as Samuel Gompers and John Mitchell. The organization's Welfare Department was established in 1904 to help forge an identity of interests between working people and their employers. From 1904 until World War I, the NCF with its Welfare Department were the nation's most aggressive advocates of welfare work. Representatives of United States Steel and International Harvester Corporation, two of the largest and most prominent welfare-capitalist firms in the country, often took the lead in such promotional work.

By the middle of the second decade of the twentieth century, scores of industrial firms took on welfare work. Estimates varied depending on the extent to which companies adopted welfare programs from 119 in 1905 to 1,500 to 2,000 companies in 1917. Among some of the most comprehensive programs were those adopted by Amoskeag Mills in New Hampshire; Remington Typewriter in Ilion, NY; General Electric in its various plants; Colorado Fuel and Iron in Pueblo, Colorado; Goodyear and Firestone Tire companies in Akron, Ohio; Plymouth Cordage in Plymouth, Massachusetts; Procter & Gamble in Cincinnati, Ohio; and Solvay Process in Solvay, New York. Solvay Process provided employees with a profit-sharing plan, discretionary bonuses, pensions, sickness and accident insurance, educational benefits (the company ran a half-time mechanic's school and occasionally assisted students in obtaining a college education with low-interest loans), a day nursery for infants, and numerous recreational and entertainment programs (many of the latter were made available to community residents, and not merely employees). A number of firms, like the Endicott Johnson Company in upstate New York, manufacturer of leather and shoes, adopted welfare work during or after the war and constructed incredibly comprehensive systems—building hospitals, sanitariums, athletic and recreation facilities; adopting profit-sharing plans; and providing support to surrounding working-class communities in the form of schools, church, and local charity funding. John Paterson, president of National Cash Register (NCR) and another of the pioneers in industrial welfare, provided employees and their families with kindergartens, libraries, an extensive recreation program (including a golf course, a children's playground with a wading pool, family camping grounds, tennis courts, a dance hall, a basketball court, and much more). He also, beginning in the 1890s, focused a great deal of attention on factory beautification and safety—increasing natural light through the extensive replacement of masonry walls with glass, using light-colored paints in interiors and on machinery, installing dust-collection systems, providing clean baths and restrooms for women, and adding on-site hospitals and first-aid stations. Some of the earliest implementations of welfare capitalism came in firms that employed large numbers of women, employees viewed as particularly vulnerable and requiring specialized services. The NCR, for example, employed many women and targeted many of its earlier welfare programs toward them; it organized a Woman's Century Club, a literary and social organization, and a Domestic Economy Department, which taught female employees cooking, sewing, housekeeping and domestic hygiene, basic nursing skills, and dancing.

Increasingly welfare capitalism began to be rationalized and bureaucratized; welfare departments were soon established in larger firms, and welfare secretaries were hired to staff them (often specially trained and highly educated young women from such colleges as Bryn Mawr and Smith). These changes constituted the foundations of modern personnel management. The professionalization of corporate-welfare work could be seen in the growth of specialized training; universities for example began to offer courses in practical industrial-welfare work as early as 1906, when the Chicago Institute of Social Science began to teach the subject. In 1908, Yale University provided a course in Industrial Service Work, and by 1916, over 150 engineering schools were offering such courses. State and federal agencies, too, began to employ trained employee-welfare personnel. The administrations of Theodore Roosevelt, William Howard Taft, and Woodrow Wilson all supported corporate-welfare work under various institutional and practical guises. The federal government in fact sent Gertrude Beeks to Panama to supervise welfare work among the Panama Canal workers.

World War I was an important catalyst for the movement's expansion; the need for rapid industrial mobilization and for increasing industrial productivity was in part answered by welfare capitalism's promise. The Advisory Commission of the Council of National Defense, created by Congress in 1916, soon established a Committee on Welfare Work that sought to convince employers to adopt welfare reforms as a means of stimulating efficiency and boosting production of war materials for the Allied powers. The war, too, had a profound effect on private industry's receptiveness to welfare capitalism. Responding to the disruption of a relatively stable prewar labor market, industries adopted and expanded welfare programs as a hedge against labor militancy and as a means of stabilizing employment. Contented workers, they believed, stayed with their employers and chose loyalty to the firm over loyalty to a union. Finally the Bolshevik revolution of 1917 fueled existing fears of domestic social revolution and expanding working-class radicalism and offered employers yet another incentive to adopt welfare capitalism.

In the 1920s, a decade that witnessed immense industrial expansion and consumerism, the doctrine of corporate welfare expanded even more dramatically than in the previous decade. The survival of Russian communism did offer a constant reminder of the threat of domestic revolution, but more significantly, an almost religious faith in industrial expansion and in the mutuality of interests between capital and labor propelled the movement forward. The notion of industrial democracy, stimulated by Woodrow Wilson's idealism and by Progressive reformers, began to take hold and expand, but in the realm of corporate United States, it was interpreted and applied in a conservative manner. Unlike trade union and socialist notions of industrial democracy—emphasizing independent and autonomous organizations engaged in collective bargaining with employers—businessmen looked for reforms that would give workers some voice in employee-employer relations but would essentially preserve management's right to manage and control. The solution was a variety of employee-representation plans and company unions. By 1923, according to one contemporary study, over 80 major firms had adopted one form or another of employee representation—often using elected employee committees and shop councils. Such half-way reforms, as union and socialist critics, and such progressive intellectuals as Walter Lippman, Herbert Croly, and Walter Weyl frequently pointed out, were hollow indeed. All too often shop councils and employee committees were easily intimidated, coerced, and controlled directly or indirectly by autocratic employers.

As welfare capitalism spread through the 1920s, as open shop movements grew, and as organized labor's ranks began to shrink, more and more strident criticism of welfare capitalism could be found in the labor and socialist press. Gompers's association with the NCF and the latter organization's heavy promotion of corporate-welfare work brought on him the wrath of the American Federation of Labor's (AFL's) left wing. But Gompers was by no means accommodating to the NCF's promotion of various welfare programs—and grew increasingly skeptical and finally downright hostile to welfare capitalism in general. As early as 1899, he had singled out profit sharing—an important element in corporate-welfare ideology and practice—as a ridiculous attempt to resolve society's most pressing social and economic problems. In 1908, he called International Harvester's profit-sharing plan a sham, since the firm had cut wages after initiating the plan. By 1916, there was little doubt that Gompers had come out squarely against corporate welfarism; the pages of the AFL's monthly publication, the *American Federationist*, were filled with critical articles on welfare work in industry. In the September 1923 issue of the periodical, Gompers asserted that the "paternalistic idea is the child of autocracy." Other issues echoed and elaborated on that charge. Welfare capitalism actively competed with unions for the loyalty of workers.

William Green, who succeeded Gompers to the leadership of the AFL on the death of the latter, continued Gompers's crusade against corporate paternalism, emphasizing corporate welfare's unfortunate encouragement of employee dependence. Throughout the 1920s, a decade of declining union membership, union leaders recognized in welfare capitalism a major threat to the continued existence of trade unions. New members were difficult to attract, and old members were difficult to hold. It is not surprising thus to find the AFL Executive Council and the officers of various railroad labor unions adopting resolutions in the mid-1920s condemning employer group-insurance plans as subversive to trade unionism.

Similarly Socialists repeatedly condemned industrial-welfare work as merely another weapon in capital's arsenal against labor—an attempt to buttress the traditional exploitative relationship between labor and capital with minimal and insignificant reforms. What socialist and Communist critics of welfare capitalism most feared was the movement's ability to destroy class consciousness and to cloud workers' recognition of the divergent interests of labor and capital. The socialist League for Industrial Democracy for example discussed industrial-welfare work extensively at its 1926 annual conference, and members echoed the previously summarized fears. Socialist Abraham Epstein, who attended that conference, published a study of welfare capitalism in that same year. He found, to his chagrin, that indeed class antagonisms were being effectively assuaged by corporate-welfare reforms.

While such critics as Epstein were sensitive to the class dimensions—and motives—behind welfare capitalism, recent scholars have examined some of the other aspects of the movement. In terms of questions of success and failure, they have refocused on the workers themselves rather than on trade union and socialist critics, asking what welfare capitalism meant to rank-and-file workers—and how workers were able to manipulate welfare regimes to maximize benefits and rewards. Certainly welfare capitalism contained many elements that went beyond motives of social discipline and control. It was also, as many scholars—and welfare-capitalism promoters—repeatedly pointed out, designed to boost industrial efficiency by enhancing labor incentives. Many employers undoubtedly adopted and abandoned welfare practices precisely for reasons of efficiency and productivity—and not because they were overly concerned about labor militancy or Bolshevism. The strongest advocates of welfare capitalism in the early twentieth century rarely missed an opportunity to remind their audiences that welfare capitalism paid off. Welfare capitalism paid off not only internally, because workers gave loyalty and willing and efficient labor to the firm, but also because consumers viewed the firm in more favorable light when its generous treatment of employees was widely publicized. The public relations functions of welfare capitalism have been emphasized by some scholars, most notably by the late Roland Marchand.

In terms of the persistence and long-term development of welfare capitalism, the scholarship is divided. Unfortunately few historians have examined welfare capitalism in detail beyond the Great Depression, and even fewer beyond World War II. Most scholars until recently argued that welfare capitalism died as a movement in the 1930s as a result of one or more of the following: The economic pressures that accompanied the Great Depression, the rise of industrial unionism and the adoption of New Deal labor reforms, and the growing competition of the welfare state. They pointed out that the government in the late 1930s even actively challenged some important features of many welfare regimes, like employee-representation plans and company unions. The National Labor Relations Board for example began to take on company unions, relying on Section 8 of the NLRA (calling corporate support of company unions an "unfair labor practice"). Similarly—though not as a result of government pressure, welfare work and welfare departments began to disappear. Personnel management departments began to take on more and more responsibilities formerly associated with welfare departments. Additionally as union membership began to expand as a result of support from the National Labor Relations Board in the 1930s, the National War Labor Board (NWLB) during World War II, and the continuing aggressive organizing drives of the Congress of Industrial Organizations (CIO) in the postwar years, former welfare benefits became items of negotiation in contract disputes. Unions began to bargain as much over welfare benefits, such as pensions, as they did over wages. This tendency was strongly reinforced by the Supreme Court's 1949 Inland Steel decision, which let stand a ruling of the Chicago U.S. Circuit Court that pensions were a proper matter for collective bargaining.

Increasingly though modestly scholars have slowly begun to probe more deeply into the fate of corporate welfare in the post-Great Depression era. Though many historians concur that the depression of the 1930s began to slow and reverse the tide of corporate welfare, as companies—often under great stockholder pressure—jettisoned all nonessential expenditures, including welfare work, there is extensive evidence—most recently marshaled by historians Sanford Jacoby and Jennifer Klein—that industrial welfarism came back to life after the Depression and expanded in tandem with the welfare state. Health insurance and pensions for example remained incredibly important sources of security for workers in the post-World War II era. Workers who had grown accustomed to them under welfare regimes had also come to recognize their limits during the Depression; because they retained the expectation that such benefits were a right of employment, they pressured employers to expand them—and many did. Some because they feared a growing welfare state and a mushrooming corporate tax burden, others because they sought labor loyalty and industrial harmony above all else.

The New Deal had provided workers with a rhetoric of economic justice and security. Growing expectations of basic economic security from government and private employers yielded a system in which public- and private-welfare systems coexisted and mutually limited one another. Some have even explained the absence of a national health care system in the United States as a product of the expansion of privately funded group-insurance plans widely adopted by American big business. Jennifer Klein for example argues that collective bargaining over workplace-based health insurance helped undermine a more aggressive pursuit of real and more comprehensive health security—one not tied to individual employers. The persistence of welfare capitalism only created "islands of security"—and in the final decades of the twentieth century, even these islands were becoming increasingly vulnerable.

Still the essential ideas and ideals behind welfare capitalism persist. Those same concerns—and contradictions—that lay behind the Lowell system, behind social gospel notions of labor-management cooperation, and behind the earliest NCF promoters of welfare capitalism continue to shape labor-management decisions in the nation's more enlightened corporations today. Even as U.S. capitalism in recent decades continues to swerve between seeking new and cheaper labor markets (corporate flight) and finding new ways to hold onto valued workers and increase efficiency, even as corporate contributions to pension plans decline, even as both public- and private-welfare systems come under fire, a significant number of progressive firms—often high-tech and heavily capitalized—continue to experiment with corporate-welfare reforms. Many have come to rely heavily on social and behavioral scientists to understand what their employees need and expect. They provide childcare for employees, medical benefits to same-sex partners, often generous vacation plans; they continue to offer profit-sharing plans and stock options; they make available to employees expanded educational opportunities. Lest we prematurely declare welfare capitalism dead, we might recall that even in its heyday, it was never the dominant movement within the U.S. business community. It was always a movement of a progressive minority, and it remains so today.

Perhaps most significant—from a global perspective—in the last four decades modern corporate-welfare firms have redefined the community of labor they serve. The nineteenth-century and early twentieth-century firms that once contributed benefits to their workers and to the immediate community of their host communities (in the form of schools, churches, recreation parks) have now become the national and global good citizens that establish charity foundations, fund hospitals and museums, sponsor concerts and athletic competitions, provide scholarships and grants, and offer relief services during national and international disasters (such companies as Microsoft, PepsiCo, EMC, Intel, and General Electric). These are expanded directions for welfare capitalism; such general service functions and actions have little directly to do with employee security and well-being, but they do have much to do with the public perception of the corporation and with the belief that a good corporate reputation is important in today's global marketplace. While it is ever more tempting to declare that welfare capitalism is once again dead, given the fundamentally fluid nature of corporate-labor relations and the ebb and flow of economic and ideological cycles, it would be wrong to exaggerate the demise of welfare capitalism and equally wrong to ignore how it has changed or how it might change in the future as global labor markets evolve.

GERALD ZAHAVI

References and Further Reading

Boettinger, Louis A. *Employee Welfare Work: A Critical and Historical Study*. New York: Ronald Press Co., 1923.

Brandes, Stuart D. *American Welfare Capitalism, 1880–1940*. Chicago, IL: The University of Chicago Press, 1976.

Brody, David. "The Rise and Decline of Welfare Capitalism." In *Workers in Industrial America: Essays on the Twentieth Century Struggle*. 2nd ed. Chicago, IL: Oxford University Press, 1993.

Gitelman, Howard M. "American Welfare Capitalism Reconsidered." *Labor History* 33, 1 (winter 1992): 5–31.

Harris, Howell John. "Industrial Paternalism and Welfare Capitalism: 'Where's the Beef?'—or 'Show Me the Money.'" www.dur.ac.uk/h.j.harris/IPWelfCapm2001.doc.

Jacoby, Sanford M. *Employing Bureaucracy: Managers, Unions, and the Transformation of Work in the 20th Century*. Revised ed. Mahwah, NJ: Lawrence Erlbaum Associates Publishers, 2004.

———. *Modern Manors: Welfare Capitalism since the Great Depression*. Princeton, NJ: Princeton University Press, 1997.

Klein, Jennifer. *For All These Rights: Business, Labor, and the Shaping of America's Public-Private Welfare State*. Princeton, NJ: Princeton University Press, 2003.

Licht, Walter. "Fringe Benefits: A Review Essay on the American Workplace." *International Labor and Workingclass History* 53 (1998): 164–178.

Mandel, Nikki. *The Corporation as Family: The Gendering of Corporate Welfare, 1890–1930*. Chapel Hill, NC: University of North Carolina Press, 2002.

Marchard, Roland. *Creating the Corporate Soul: The Rise of Public Relations and Corporate Imagery in American Big Business*. Berkeley: University of California Press, 1998.

Nelson, Daniel *Managers and Workers: Origins of the New Factory System in the United States, 1880–1920*. Madison: University of Wisconsin Press, 1975.

Tone, Andrea. *The Business of Benevolence: Industrial Paternalism in Progressive America*. Ithaca, NY: Cornell University Press, 1997.

Zahavi, Gerald. *Workers, Managers, and Welfare Capitalism: The Shoeworkers and Tanners of Endicott Johnson, 1890–1950*. Urbana: The University of Illinois Press, 1988.

WELFARE RIGHTS

The term welfare rights represents both the rallying call and the philosophy of a group of mostly female welfare recipients and their allies who began in the 1960s to demand higher grants, better treatment, a voice in welfare's administration, and ultimately the replacement of the American welfare system with a more generous and dignified guaranteed income program. Such activism culminated in a briefly influential national Welfare Rights movement in the late 1960s and early 1970s, while local activists and recipients continue to this day to organize, lobby, and protest under the banner of welfare rights.

Origins of a Welfare Rights Movement

A variety of factors encouraged welfare recipients to begin organizing in the early 1960s. In response to rising welfare rolls in the postwar years, state and local legislators and administrators placed restrictions on receipt of Aid to Families with Dependent Children (AFDC), the federal grant-in-aid program for poor children deprived of parental (usually male breadwinner) support. Residency requirements, employable-mother rules, and man-in-the-house and suitable-home tests were aimed at keeping rolls and costs down, ensuring a ready supply of low-wage workers, denying grants to nonwhite women, and protecting taxpayers from subsidizing indolent male breadwinners, immoral women, and illegitimate children. In the early 1960s, informal discussion of shared problems in local welfare offices or solo-parent groups sparked organizing. Most likely recipients and their occasional allies among social workers and religious organizations responded as well to an increasingly liberal political mood and the growing momentum of civil rights activism. While the first welfare rights groups formed before the Johnson administration declared a legislative war on poverty, federal antipoverty efforts, like Legal Aid (which provided disadvantaged communities with professional legal help) and community action agencies (which sought to include poor people in the administration and consolidation of social services), channeled organizers and resources into poor communities, furthering welfare rights organizing.

The AFDC recipients usually led local welfare rights groups, sometimes with financial, logistical and moral support from churches, and less often, liberal and radical groups. In the Los Angeles Watts area, Johnnie Tillmon, mother of six, applied her experience as a union shop steward to organizing fellow welfare recipients in her public-housing project. Washington, DC, leader Etta Horn, mother of seven, had a history of activism in church and the PTA. Local groups usually formed in response to specific problems: Detroit recipients organized to demand locks on public-housing mailboxes to prevent theft of welfare checks and to demand that local utility companies waive deposits for recipients, while grant cuts in Ohio sparked a coalition of recipients, church, and social welfare agencies to organize and lobby for more adequate benefits. Welfare rights groups advocated for individual applicants and recipients, publicized regulations in easy-to-read form, lobbied legislators, and conducted demonstrations. Special grants campaigns proved their most effective tactic. Welfare caseworkers rarely informed recipients that they were entitled to one-time special grants for household equipment, school clothing, or winter coats. Welfare rights groups publicized lists of available grants, gathered applications, and presented them *en masse* at local welfare offices, a tactic that was remarkably successful in achieving material rewards and recruiting members.

By 1966, some middle-class activists saw in local welfare rights organizing the potential for large-scale institutional change. In "A Strategy to End Poverty" in 1966, academics and social activists Frances Fox Piven and Richard Cloward estimated that for every AFDC recipient in New York, another person was eligible. They argued that by encouraging massive welfare enrollment, welfare rights organizing could precipitate fiscal and political crisis, which would finally force federal lawmakers to replace categorical public assistance with a federally funded guaranteed-income program. They shared their interest in welfare rights with George Wiley, who had been seeking to convince first the Congress of Racial Equality (CORE, a civil rights organization) and then the Citizens'

Crusade against Poverty (CCAP, a UAW-funded private antipoverty coalition) to commit to grassroots organizing among the poor. In 1966, Wiley set up a Poverty/Rights Action Center in Washington, DC, to pursue his model of an integrated grassroots movement for economic justice. He helped turn a welfare-recipient march in Ohio into a national media event and called a meeting of welfare-recipient activists from across the country, social workers, and organizers who decided to form a National Welfare Rights Organization (NWRO).

Welfare Rights as a National Movement

While not broadly representative of the country's AFDC recipients, the NWRO for a time provided welfare recipients with a national voice. Wiley with many friends and contacts acted as executive director from 1966 to 1972 and proved an adept fundraiser, collecting three million dollars from individual contributors, foundations, and churches (particularly the Interreligious Foundation for Community Organizing and the United Church of Christ's Welfare Priority Team) during his directorship. The NWRO also had brief success in recruiting members, growing from 5,000 dues-paying members in 1967 to over 24,000 at its height in 1969, or from 1%–2% of the AFDC population. While more than half of AFDC recipients were white, the NWRO was 85% African-American, 10% white, and 5% Latino, with a small proportion of Native Americans. The racial make-up reflected the organization's largely urban base, while its overwhelmingly female membership (98%) reflected its focus on the AFDC program. The NWRO was less successful in garnering powerful political allies. On a local level some unions, civil rights organizations, and civic and women's groups allied with welfare rights activists, and by the early 1970s, the NWRO boasted 3,000 middle-class members of its Friends network. Nationally though coalitions with other organizations proved tenuous at best.

The NWRO's four stated goals—adequate income, dignity, justice, and democratic participation—structured its activities. Theoretically it sought to replace AFDC and other categorical public-assistance programs with a guaranteed income at poverty level for all Americans. On a more practical level, its affiliates used sit-ins, demonstrations, and special-grant campaigns to pressure welfare departments. Their efforts resulted in a considerable liberalization of welfare and significant increases in AFDC rolls, which experienced their steepest increase (220%) during the decade of the NWRO's existence (1965–1975).

Scholars have estimated that in 1966, only one-third of those eligible were receiving AFDC, while by the 1970s, nearly 90% were. Lawyers proved the movement's most valuable allies, helping recipients to challenge and overturn a variety of restrictions, from residency requirements to substitute parent rules, to establish recipients' right to a fair hearing before termination or reduction of a grant and in general to establish a legal right to welfare.

At the same time welfare recipients demanded dignity—the end to invasions of privacy, better treatment from caseworkers, the right to control their own sexuality, and recognition of their important role as mothers. Several years before largely white, middle-class feminists articulated a demand for reproductive choice; welfare recipient activists insisted on their right to decide when to become parents, fighting both against involuntary sterilization and for access to birth control and abortion. Activists rejected society's denigration of poor, black women by drawing on their moral authority as mothers, holding Mother's Day marches and appealing to other women's organizations for support. Poor women's experience in the labor market—often in physically onerous, low-wage jobs that failed to bring them out of poverty—led welfare rights activists to vociferously oppose forced-work requirements. They insisted that society value their work as mothers and give them the right to choose whether to combine motherhood with wage labor. At the same time they insisted that many AFDC mothers wanted education, training, childcare, and good jobs. Over time childcare became a high priority for the organization.

The NWRO achieved the height of its influence during debate over the Nixon administration's Family Assistance Plan (FAP) from 1969 to 1972. The FAP would have replaced categorical public-assistance programs like AFDC with a very low guaranteed income for American families. Many liberals supported the plan: They wanted to establish the precedent of a guaranteed income and to extend federal aid to two-parent families, the so-called working poor. On the other hand the NWRO deplored the plan's low-benefit level, which would have meant reduced benefits for most of its members who lived in relatively high-benefit urban areas outside the South. It also opposed the FAP's forced-work provisions and its revocation of a host of legal rights the movement had only recently gained. The NWRO garnered some support, getting its own much more liberal guaranteed-income plan introduced into Congress and convincing several congressional families to participate in its Live on a Welfare Budget campaign. In the end many liberal organizations joined the NWRO's Zap FAP campaign, which combined with Nixon's abandonment and powerful conservative opposition, doomed the plan.

Various tensions between Wiley and other mostly male (and often white) staff members on the one side and recipient leaders on the other, along with welfare's unpopularity and crisis on the U.S. political left, led to the NWRO's demise. As legislatures began to crack down on welfare spending, Wiley hoped to broaden the movement to include low-wage and unemployed men, a way to neutralize racist and sexist attacks and return to his original vision of a broad, integrated poor people's movement. Recipient leaders feared this would dilute the needs of female AFDC recipients. Wiley resigned in 1972 to form the Movement for Economic Justice, and Tillmon became NWRO's executive director. The organization took on a more explicitly feminist cast, symbolized by Tillmon's article in a 1972 issue of *Ms.* Magazine, "Welfare Is a Women's Issue," in which she referred to AFDC as a "super-sexist marriage." While feminist organizations began to pay more attention to welfare and poverty during the 1970s, the NWRO folded in 1975.

Welfare Rights to the Present

Local welfare rights organizing continued however. Some former welfare rights organizers followed Wiley's lead, seeking through groups like Jobs and Justice to organize more broadly, while some professionals and academics, like those in the Center for Social Welfare Policy and Law, concentrated on welfare's legal dimensions. Hundreds of local recipient groups continued to lobby and protest into the 1990s (some of them formed the National Welfare Rights Union in 1987), ignored by the mainstream press. Their goals remain the same even as the political context changes: Adequate income, dignity, justice, and democratic participation.

MARISA CHAPPELL

References and Further Reading

Abramovitz, Mimi. *Under Attack, Fighting Back: Women and Welfare in the United States.* New York: Monthly Review Press, 1996.

Bailis, Lawrence N. *Bread or Justice: Grassroots Organizing in the Welfare Rights Movement.* Lexington, MA: Heath/Lexington Books, 1974.

Davis, Martha. *Brutal Need: Lawyers and the Welfare Rights Movement, 1960–1973.* New Haven: Yale University Press, 1993.

Davis, Martha, "Welfare Rights and Women's Rights in the 1960s." *Journal of Policy History* 8, 1 (1996): 144–165.

Kornbluh, Felicia. "A Right to Welfare? Poor Women, Professionals, and Poverty Programs, 1935–1975." Ph.D. dissertation, Princeton University, 2000.

———. "To Fulfill Their 'Rightly Needs': Consumerism and the National Welfare Rights Movement." *Radical History Review* 69 (1997): 76–113.

Kotz, Nick, and Mary Lynn Kotz. *A Passion for Equality: George A. Wiley and the Movement.* New York: W. W. Norton & Company, 1977.

Morrissey, Megan H. "The Downtown Welfare Advocate Center: A Case Study of a Welfare Rights Organization." *Social Service Review* (June 1990): 189–207.

Nadasen, Premilla. *Welfare Warriors: The Welfare Rights Movement in the United States.* New York: Routledge, 2004.

———. "Expanding the Boundaries of the Women's Movement: Black Feminism and the Struggle for Welfare Rights." *Feminist Studies* 28, 2 (2002): 271–301.

Piven, Frances Fox, and Richard A. Cloward. *Poor People's Movements: Why They Succeed, How They Fail.* New York: Pantheon Books, 1977.

Valk, Anne M. "'Mother Power': The Movement for Welfare Rights in Washington, DC, 1966–1972." *Journal of Women's History* 11, 4 (2000): 34–58.

West, Guida. *The National Welfare Rights Movement: The Social Protest of Poor Women.* New York: Praeger Publishers, 1981.

WEST VIRGINIA MINE WAR (1920–1921)

The West Virginia Mine War was a protracted struggle fought between miners, who sought to join the United Mine Workers of America (UMWA), and mine owners, who were determined to keep the union out of the southern West Virginia counties of Mingo, McDowell, and Logan. By unionizing and gaining recognition from the coal operators, miners collectively sought protection from the operators' control, wielded through the autocratic system of the company town and mine guards. As labor historian David Corbin notes, the miners engaged in "battles for timeless and universal values and principles: industrial democracy, social equality and political rights." The war involved numerous acts of violence committed by both sides and resulted in several declarations of martial law in West Virginia, as well as the occupation of its southern counties by federal troops. The duration of the miners' fight and the degree of violence make the events of 1920 to 1921 extraordinary; however in the end the coal operators' unity of purpose and domination of both local and state political machinery not only maintained an open shop in southern West Virginia, but forced the collapse of the union throughout the state. The mine war represents another case of the manipulation of legal systems by owners of capital during capital-labor conflict, as well as the proclivities of state and federal authorities to intervene to defend only the rights of property. The significance of the mine war lies in its dramatic expression of interracial, working-class solidarity: Rank-and-file miners demanded their right to join a union as the fundamental issue rather than the more traditional demands of wages or hours. Grassroots participation drove the direction and temper of the fight, as the union became the mode for political action.

The drive to unionize mine workers in the southern West Virginia counties of Mingo, McDowell, and Logan sits against the national backdrop of post-World War I economic conditions and the relative strength of the UMWA. On November 1, 1919, 425,000 mineworkers struck; the union's officials had called the national strike only in the face of its members' insistence. Miners in the bituminous and anthracite coalfields experienced inflationary pressures in the immediate postwar years that had eroded the wage gains and steady working time seen during the war. The national strike included unionized workers in the bituminous coal areas of the Central Competitive Field, which comprised those mines in Illinois, Ohio, much of western Pennsylvania, and the northern and central counties of West Virginia. The UMWA was weaker in the southern part of the state and had withdrawn its organizers with the country's entry into World War I in 1917, as the union and coal operators conformed to federal stipulations of the War Industries Board. The time was ripe then for organization of West Virginia's southern mines. Nationally as well as locally, miners considered their efforts integral to the war, and union miners demanded action from their leaders while nonunion miners sought their rights through union representation.

More than one-third of West Virginia's nonunion miners worked in Mingo and Logan counties, and when UMWA organizers were ousted from those counties in September of 1919, the first armed march of thousands of angry union miners formed just south of Charleston. The UMWA District 17 President Frank Keeney urged the miners to disband, having learned from West Virginia's Governor John J. Cornwall of his determination to call for federal troops. The aborted march was a prelude to the events of 1920–1921.

Medieval West Virginia

The civil war that erupted in southern West Virginia and the collective insurgency demonstrated by rank-and-file miners also must be understood within its locale, or "medieval West Virginia," as Mother Jones called it. Pro-union sentiment ran high in the counties of Mingo, McDowell, and Logan, and miners belonging to West Virginia's UMWA District 17, which covered most of northern and central part of the state, sympathized with the exploitation endured by miners of those southern counties, since District 17 had struggled for unionization and bargaining agreements just a few years earlier during Paint Creek-Cabin Creek Strike of 1912–1913. Then the anti-union coal operators had used blacklists, intimidation, and violence to resist the strike, to break previously signed contracts, and to drive all union sympathizers from their mines in the Kanawha and New River coalfields. Miners throughout West Virginia also remembered the Bull Moose Special, an armored short train, specially chartered by the Kanawha Coal Company and carrying the company's owner, local sheriff, armed guards, as well as a manned Gatling gun mounted to one of the car's roofs, which opened fire on a tent colony of striking miners and their families in February of 1913. Common experience of injustice and familiarity with mining life informed the local UMWA leadership. District 17 President Frank Keeney was a West Virginia native and mineworker who had participated in the strike of 1912–1913, as did organizer Bill Blizzard and the district's secretary-treasurer, Fred Mooney, and all pledged their support to organize the state's southern counties. Ninety percent of Mingo County's miners were quickly organized in the spring and summer of 1920 into 34 locals and District 17 began a strike on July 1.

Bituminous coal mining in southern West Virginia had recently and rapidly developed since the turn of the twentieth century. Coal operators in southern West Virginia paid notoriously low wages to its miners to offset these interior fields' disadvantage relative to the Central Competitive Field in transporting coal. During World War I, tonnage increased significantly as new transportation lines connected the mines with East Coast ports. After the war operators retrenched and formed associations jealously to guard their rights to set pay scales and working time, paid local law officers for extra protection, and attempted to assert total control over their workforces through the system of company towns. Coal operators were employers of miners as well as their landlords and store merchants; companies paid miners in scrip (redeemable only at company stores) and hired private police forces to guard their operations. The mine guards, called thugs by mining families, questioned any visitor to the company town; spied on worker gatherings; and beat, verbally harassed, and even murdered those sympathetic to union organization. Mine owners hired the Baldwin-Felts detective agency, and its guards assumed the power of the law: Detectives forced miners to sign yellow-dog contracts, maintained blacklists, and evicted families from company housing. By the fall of 1920, operators in Mingo County locked out union workers, and its guards then provided armed escorts for trainloads of arriving strikebreakers. If coal tonnage becomes the measure of the mine owners' success, then the operators had already won the war by December. Operators also waged a legal war by filing suits, gaining court injunctions, and aiding the numerous county and state prosecutions during and after the West Virginia Mine War, which would ultimately bankrupt UMWA District 17.

The Mingo County War

On May 19, 1920, 11 Baldwin-Felts detectives evicted union miners from company houses in the town of Matewan, Mingo County, on the West Virginia-Kentucky border. When questioned by local sheriff Sid Hatfield and Mayor C. C. Testerman, one of the Felts shot Mayor Testerman, and a gunfight erupted between Hatfield, the miners, and the detectives. The result of the Matewan Massacre was the deaths of three miners, the mayor, and seven detectives. For the next 16 months and until the Battle of Blair Mountain in early September of 1921, the violence made national headlines. Reporters from the *Nation, Leslie's Weekly,* and most notably, Winthrop D. Lane of the *New York Evening Post* described dynamited mines, hijacked trains, attacked tent colonies, murdered strikers, arrests, and beating in the renamed county of Bloody Mingo.

Sheriff Hatfield, though charged with murder, became a local hero. Most local law enforcement efforts antagonized the peace. Notorious in brutality was Sheriff Don Chafin of Logan County, whose determination to keep the union out was funded by the Logan County Coal Operators Association, enabling him to hire dozens of deputies and train and arm hundreds of the local middle-class, merchants, teachers, lawyers, to help defend mine owners' interests. The press condemned the law in West Virginia and exposed the state's anti-union tactics. The UMWA sponsored hundreds of tent colonies for evicted mining families, and operators flatly refused to recognize union representation; Governor Cornwall declared martial law in November of 1920—enforced by state police, a re-organized state national guard, and 250 citizens, or special police, supplied with arms by the coal companies.

A little more than 6 months later when the newly elected Governor Ephraim F. Morgan appealed for federal troops in May of 1921, President Harding refused until West Virginia's own resources proved inefficient. June saw renewed violence as a tent colony of 10,000 at Lick Creek was terrorized by state and special police who murdered a striker. In July state police jailed union leaders, closing the UMWA's office in Williamson, and on August 1, as Sheriff Hatfield and friend Ed Chambers climbed the McDowell County courthouse steps, Felts detectives murdered them both. Outraged miners gathered in protest as they had in 1919. Keeney urged them to wait for his call to mobilize, which came on August 20, and for several days miners streamed into Lens Creek, about 10 miles south of Charleston, to form a citizens' army. Their intent was to march south to Logan County, to hang Sheriff Chafin; and then move onto Mingo County, to free jailed miners, overthrow martial law, abolish the mine guard system, and complete the unionization of the southern counties. Thousands of union miners (estimates range from 7,000 to 20,000) from all over West Virginia joined the 60-mile, armed procession. They ignored Mother Jones who begged them to turn back but met with Keeney and U.S. Brigadier General Henry Bandholtz, sent by President Harding after increasingly frantic appeals from Governor Morgan. It was however a peaceful march until they reached the 25-mile ridge of Blair Mountain at the border of both Logan and Mingo counties. The miner's army met in a weeklong battle over 2,000 county defenders, including state police, Sheriff Chafin's local law enforcement with newly deputized citizens, Baldwin-Felts guards, and strikebreakers (who had been ordered to take up arms against the strikers or be fired). The press likened the terrain along 10 miles of the ridge to Belgium and the battles to those of World War I. They searched for the general of the miners army, described the lines of combat, skirmishes, and guerilla tactics, and surveyed the weapons of war that included rifles, machine guns, bombs. On September 1, 2,500 federal troops arrived along with General Billy Mitchell's air squadron, which never (fortunately) dropped its payload. Although some fighting continued until September 4, most miners returned to their homes at President Harding's direction, since their fight was not with the federal government. The largest armed conflict in American labor history was over.

Local grand juries handed down 1,217 indictments against Frank Keeney and 550 others that included murder and treason against the state of West Virginia, and over the course of several years, these cases were dismissed or dropped. Without a union wage rate, the coal industry expanded to its own detriment. Non-union mines undercut competition, union mines reverted to the open shop, and new production levels contributed to depressed coal prices. The UMWA collapsed in West Virginia: In 1922, when it formally ended the strike, its membership of over 40,000 had dropped by half, and by 1932, counted only several hundred union members.

RACHEL A. BATCH

References and Further Reading

Corbin, David A. "'Frank Keeney Is Our Leader, and We Shall Not Be Moved': Rank-and-File Leadership in the West Virginia Coal Fields." In *Essays in Southern Labor History*, edited by Gary M. Fink and Merl E. Reed. Westport, CT: Greenwood Press, 1977.
———. *Life, Work, and Rebellion in the Coal Fields: The Southern West Virginia Miners 1880–1922*. Urbana, IL: University of Illinois Press, 1981.
Corbin, David Alan, ed. *The West Virginia Mine Wars: An Anthology*. Charleston, WV: Appalachian Editions, 1990.
Jordan, Daniel P. "The Mingo War: Labor Violence in the Southern West Virginia Coal Fields, 1919–1922" In *Essays in Southern Labor History*, edited by Gary M. Fink and Merl E. Reed. Westport, CT: Greenwood Press, 1977.
Mooney, Fred. *Struggle in the Coal Fields: The Autobiography of Fred Mooney*, edited by J. W. Hess. Morgantown: West Virginia University Library, 1967.
Savage, Lon. *Thunder in the Mountains: The West Virginia Mine War, 1920–21*. Pittsburgh, PA: University of Pittsburgh Press, 1990.

See also **Blacklists; Company Towns; Collective Bargaining; Jones, (Mother) Mary Harris; Lewis, John L.; Mining, Coal; Miners for Democracy; National War Labor Board (WWI); Spies, Labor; Strike Wave (1919); Strikebreaking; United Mine Workers of America; World War I; Yellow Dog Contracts**

WEST, DON (1906–1992)
Cofounder, Highlander Folk School

Donald (Don) L. West, cofounder—with Myles Horton—of the Highlander Folk School in Monteagel, Tennessee, was born in 1906 to a poor mountain farming family in Devil's Hollow, near Elijay in Gilmer County, Georgia. He was a sharp and gifted poet and writer, a Congregationalist preacher who cultivated and practiced an early strain of liberation theology, and a political and labor radical—sometimes working as an organizer for the Communist party (CPUSA). Throughout his years as a student, teacher, preacher, writer, and political and labor activist, West celebrated the culture and history of progressive southern highlanders. He attempted in his life to accomplish the task of grafting Marxism-Leninism onto southern religious and cultural traditions.

West's rebellious youthful streak (which had led to two school expulsions) first found direction at Vanderbilt Seminary, where he studied under Alva Taylor. There he obtained degrees in education and religion. It was while at Vanderbilt that West was first introduced to Myles Horton. Horton and West soon became partners in a venture to help create a progressive, cooperative folk school—the Highlander Folk School. The school became a major center of radical and progressive activist training in the South (it was where Rosa Parks later obtained some of her training in nonviolent resistance). Yet as the school began to participate in labor-organizing drives in the South, a rift began to emerge between Horton and West. West, apparently drawing closer to the Communist party and further and further from Horton (due to growing ideological and personal divisions between them), decided to leave the school and chart his own path.

West's admiration of the aggressive organizing strategies of the Communist party led him into its orbit. He joined the party sometime in 1933–1934—though he had been gravitating toward it for some time. Already as a student at Vanderbilt in education and religion, an increasingly radical perspective was evident in his work. His thesis "Knott County, Kentucky: A Study" (1932) was a regional study of culture and class in the South and demonstrated clear socialist sympathies. By the early 1930s, he had already become acquainted with a number of Communist organizers, including Clyde Johnson, a Communist National Student League activist who had come down to Rome, Georgia, to assist in a student strike at West's former school, the Martha Berry School. In 1933, after a harrowing motorcycle ride on his 1932 Indian Chief up to New York City (the cycle ride twice almost killed him), he met with Clarence Hathaway, then editor of the Communist *Daily Worker* and a major party leader and Marxist theoretician. Hathaway quickly recruited West to take over the Angelo Herndon Defense Committee in Atlanta. Herndon was a young black Communist activist in Atlanta who had been arrested—under a pre-Civil War insurrection act—for organizing an inter-racial demonstration in the city for increased municipal relief for the unemployed. (Herndon received a 20-year prison sentence for his crime—but was freed as a result of effective legal action by the party.) But before

West was sent to Atlanta, Hathaway insisted he attend the Communist Party (CP) organizer's school at Camp Nitgedaiget (Yiddish for "no worries") in the Catskill Mountains, near Beacon, New York—one of a handful of proletarian camps operated by the party in New York (along with Camp Unity, Camp Wocolona, and Camp Kinderland). He spent 10 weeks there and met Hosea Hudson, a black organizer in-training while at the camp. The two began a life-long friendship.

West's experience with northern CP condescension toward southerners, and especially Appalachian southerners, at Nitgedaiget foreshadowed his future tensions with the party. West came to feel that though the party had some successes here and there—in Gastonia through its work with the International Labor Defense (ILD) and in several other areas, the main obstacle to party progress in that region lay not in the resistance of the culture or people to communism—not in the South as a conservative region—but with the party itself. Arguing that the southern mountain regions of Appalachia had a long tradition of abolitionism, West argued that the party simply failed to tap that culture of resistance effectively. In his organizing work in the southern Appalachians, in Atlanta, and in Kentucky (he served as general organizer for Kentucky Workers' Alliance—which represented public works employees and the unemployed), West brought with him an acute understanding of the dual legacy of the South: A racist slavocracy that nonetheless produced the earliest abolitionist movement.

For West the South's poor white trash were his people, and it was his mission to bridge their struggles with those of blacks. History, language, and religion were three of his weapons. His poetry and prose, characterized by his use of proletarian regional vernacular and a strong identification with the region's working class, were filled with historical allusions to a progressive past, one filled with struggle against injustice. In pamphlets and articles, he cultivated a regional chauvinism that allowed him to celebrate the heroes of his region at the same time as he confronted the injustices of the South. He considered Appalachia "a freedom loving oasis in a society dominated by the southern slavocracy," and saw himself continuing in the tradition of his grandfather, Old Kim Mulkey, who taught him that "everyone had a right to freedom no matter what color."

As a radical Congregationalist minister, West also clearly understood the transformative medium of religion. He was long-driven toward bridging a Christian and Marxist worldview. In the late 1920s, working his way through Lincoln Memorial University in Harrogate, Tennessee, West already felt the pull of his future calling as a minister. Inspired in his youth by a local preacher, Larkin Chastain, he turned to a class-conscious religion, one that drew on the image and symbol of Christ as a lowly carpenter. That emphasis would persist throughout his life. He would often explain and condemn war, racism, poverty, and capitalism in biblical terms. In "The Awakening Church," a column he published in the Birmingham *Southern News Almanac* from 1940–1941, he encouraged churches to be more aggressive in applying Christ's teachings to contemporary social and economic problems. He published a newsletter, the *Country Parson,* while in Meansville, Georgia. From 1942–1945, he served as superintendent of the Lula, Georgia, public schools.

West's career in the 1940s through the early 1990s, when he died, tracked a persistent regionalist course, but one influenced by broader historical and international developments. He continued to identify strongly with the Soviet Union and generally followed the Soviet line on political issues. In 1945, West received a Julius Rosenwald Foundation fellowship grant to attend Columbia University in New York (he also used the grant to attend the University of Georgia, and the University of Chicago). He decided not to pursue a formal Ph.D. program but to undertake independent study. Increasingly in those years, West, along with Rev. Fred E. Maxey from Leeds, Alabama, became more and more involved with fellow southern radical Claude Williams's Institute of Applied Religion. In 1946, he took a job as an assistant professor of literature and creative writing in the Department of Human Relations at Oglethorpe University (Atlanta) and published his poetry anthology, *Clods of Southern Earth* (1946). By this time he had achieved a national recognition as a people's poet. However West's growing involvement with left-wing politics led to his firing from Oglethorpe by reluctant University President Phillip Weldner, who was under pressure by the school's trustees. Preceding the 1948 national election, West had become more and more engaged in the Henry Wallace campaign and had also given his active support to the local defense of Rosa Lee Ingram. The Ingram case involved a white man who, while attempting to rape a black woman in her home, was shot and killed by her sons, aged 7 and 11. The all-white jury deliberated for only 30 minutes before finding the black family guilty and sentencing them all to death. The sentence was later reduced to life in prison after public protest. They were pardoned and released by President Jimmy Carter three decades later.

After the Wallace campaign, West kept a relatively low profile in Georgia but surfaced again in Dalton in support of local Chenille mill workers in 1955. There his work with a local church, the Church of God of the Union Assembly, and his publication of the *Southerner: A Voice of the People,* continued his earlier emphasis on religion as a class-conscious instrument of economic and social justice. He spent a great deal of time by himself in the 1950s, traveling occasionally to New York and continuing to write. His poetry reflected the repression and restricted quality of life imposed on Communists during the McCarthy era, with themes of love, separation, anxiety, and loneliness in evidence throughout (see *the Road Is Rocky,* 1951, for example). His daughters, Ann and Hedy West attended Berea College and Western Carolina College. West's wife, Connie, accepted a position in Baltimore teaching art in an elementary school and enrolled in an MA program at the Maryland Institute of Art, and in 1960, she was appointed art supervisor of Baltimore County. Though subpoenaed before various House and Senate investigative committees, West escaped the worst of the McCarthy and post-McCarthy era. In 1960, he obtained a job at the University of Maryland in College Park supervising student teachers and in 1962, served as the faculty adviser to the newly established Students for a Democratic Society (SDS) chapter on campus. That was a year before he retired to return to his beloved mountains, this time to Pipestem, West Virginia, where he had purchased 400 acres.

West came back to his dream of founding a folk-life school inspired by the Grundvigian philosophy he had studied in Denmark at the International People's College. In 1964, he and Connie founded the Appalachian South Folklife Center in Pipestem, West Virginia, dedicated to preserving and disseminating Appalachian mountain culture and folkways. They offered various practical courses to local residents, established the Mountain Freedom Press, set up a camp for Appalachian children (which also sponsored visits by northern urban kids), initiated several regional, modest economic-development projects, and put on annual music festivals that—in their heyday—drew more than 20,000 people from around the nation. The center, which exists today, created a food co-op and a clothing exchange, and sponsored group trips abroad by local Appalachian children. Don and Connie West finally made their dream in the region they both held sacred.

West died in Charleston, West Virginia, on September 29, 1992, 2 years after his wife passed away.

GERALD ZAHAVI

References and Further Reading

Biggers, Jeff, and Brosi, George, eds. *No Lonesome Road: Selected Prose and Poems.* Urbana: University of Illinois Press, 2004.
Byerly, Victoria M. "What Shall a Poet Sing? The Living Struggle of the Southern Poet and Revolutionary, Don West." Ph.D. dissertation, Boston College, 1994.
Dunbar, Anthony. *Against the Grain: Southern Radicals and Prophets, 1929–1959.* University Press of Virginia, 1981.

See also **Highlander Folk School/Highlander Research and Education Center**

WESTERN FEDERATION OF MINERS/ INTERNATIONAL UNION OF MINE, MILL, AND SMELTER WORKERS

The Western Federation of Miners

Few U.S. unions can match the militant and discordant history of the Western Federation of Miners (WFM). Formed by hard-rock metal miners in the 1890s, the WFM represented an authentic working-class response to the rise of industrial capitalism in the American West. Split by ideological dissension and ethnic divisions, the WFM shifted between radical socialism and business unionism during its volatile two-decade existence. Despite its internecine battles, the WFM's romantic legacy of militant unionism lingered long in the memories of western miners, smelter workers, and labor activists.

The WFM's roots lay in the development of lead and open-pit nonferrous metal mining and smelting in the Rocky Mountain West during the second-half of the nineteenth century. Miners' mutual aid associations and early unions first emerged in the 1860s, when highly capitalized enterprises and company towns, often controlled by absentee investors, replaced the mining camps and smaller placer operations that first extracted the region's gold and silver deposits. Local miners' unions enjoyed some success in dictating wages and working conditions around the region's mines and mills until the 1880s, when they faced stiff opposition from mine owners and their political allies. Clashes between miners and mine owners from the 1890s to the 1910s frequently ended up in armed warfare.

The WFM was first conceived in 1892 in the Coeur d'Alene, Idaho, mining district during a violent strike that united lead and silver miners and mill workers against their employers, organized as the Coeur

Man standing on back of coal car in tunnel. Library of Congress, Prints & Photographs Division [LC-USZ62-77538].

d'Alene Mine Owners' Association. Armed strikers shut down local milling operations to protest a wage reduction and the wretched living conditions in company-owned housing. In response the Mine Owners' Association imported strikebreakers, company spies, and eventually state and federal troops, who arrested the strikers and confined them to makeshift bullpens, which quickly became the symbol of class warfare in the West. The defeat convinced the Coeur d'Alene strikers that they needed to extend unionization throughout the West to combat the mine owners' substantial economic power and political influence.

The WFM was officially founded in 1893 when over 40 delegates from various Rocky Mountain states met in Butte, Montana, home of one of the West's strongest and most solvent miners' unions. Determined to establish a regional federation of local unions, the delegates' initial goal was the period's pure-and-simple business unionism, including union recognition, a closed shop, a fair wage, arbitration of industrial disputes, and improved mine safety laws. With only a quarter of the West's 30,000 miners belonging to unions, the WFM delegates also provided for the appointment of full-time organizers. With the exception of the Cripple Creek, Colorado, mining district, which became a WFM stronghold, the WFM floundered until 1896, when Edward Boyce, an Irish-born union officer from Coeur d'Alene, was named the union's president.

The WFM had affiliated with the American Federation of Labor (AFL) in 1896, but under Boyce's leadership, bolted from the federation a year later, frustrated with the AFL's political conservatism and craft unionism. The hard-rock mining industry contained a heterogencous mixture of skilled miners, craftsmen, semiskilled operatives, and unskilled laborers. This collection of workers constituted a transient and diverse labor pool, consisting of an Anglo-Irish elite, new immigrants from southern and Eastern Europe, Mexican-Americans, Native Americans, and Asian immigrants. Not surprisingly mine owners manipulated ethnic and skill divisions to prevent successful unionization. In response WFM leaders embraced industrial unionism—one union for all workers in the industry—to promote class solidarity among western miners and metal processors.

After leaving the AFL, WFM leaders backed several efforts to form a rival labor federation. In 1898, the WFM established the Western Labor Union, and when this organization faltered in 1902, they founded the more expansive American Labor Union. By this time the WFM had aligned with the Socialist party of America, moved its headquarters to Denver, Colorado, and appointed the Socialist William "Big Bill" Haywood as its secretary-treasurer. A year later Charles H. Moyer, a South Dakota miner, replaced Boyce as the union's president, marking the start of the WFM's most turbulent period. Beginning in 1902,

WFM unions in Colorado engaged in several violent and disastrous strikes that left the union in disarray by 1904. The Colorado mine wars, which demonstrated the mine owners' control of state political and police power, convinced the WFM's leadership of the pressing need for socialism and industrial unionism on a national scale.

The WFM's efforts at an anticapitalist federation of industrial unions culminated in 1905, when it spearheaded the formation of the syndicalist Industrial Workers of the World (IWW). Although the decision to align with the IWW split the WFM between anticapitalist radicals and trade union moderates, the WFM initially prospered from its association with the IWW and reached its organizational peak in 1907 with 40,000 members in nearly 200 union locals. That summer Moyer and Haywood were involved in a sensational trial after being forcibly deported from Colorado and made to stand trial for the assassination of former Idaho governor, Frank Steunenberg, a foe of miners' unions who had ordered troops into the Coeur d'Alene district during the mine wars of the 1890s. Represented by famed criminal attorney Clarence Darrow, Moyer and Haywood were eventually acquitted of the murder, but the two soon parted ways, with radical Haywood remaining with the IWW and the more cautious Moyer returning to the WFM, determined to steer it back toward the labor movement's mainstream.

In 1908, the WFM officially separated from the IWW as a first step toward reconciliation with the AFL, which it rejoined in 1911. The AFL in turn increased the WFM's jurisdiction to include all North American workers who labored in the nonferrous metals industry. At its annual convention in 1916, the WFM was renamed the International Union of Mine, Mill, and Smelter Workers (IUMMSW, or more commonly Mine-Mill), ostensibly to recognize the union's expanded geographical scope but also to distance the union from its radical WFM past.

International Union of Mine, Mill, and Smelter Workers

The WFM's name change did little to reverse the decline of unionism in the western metal-mining industry that began in the mid-1910s and persisted through the early 1930s. Split by competition with the IWW and chronic ethnic divisions, Mine-Mill easily fell victim to mine owners' open-shop movement, with the disintegration of the Butte Miners'

Union representing its most important casualty. When long-time president Charles Moyer was forced to resign in 1926, Mine-Mill was in organizational disarray; conventions were sparsely attended, and few union officers held full-time positions. The union limped through the first few years of the Great Depression when the nonferrous metals industry experienced a severe economic collapse and high unemployment levels prevailed. In 1933, Mine-Mill counted just 1,500 dues-paying members and a mere six active union locals.

Mine-Mill began its revival in the mid-1930s aided at the national level by New Deal labor legislation. In June 1933, inspired by the National Industrial Recovery Act's Section 7(a), delegates from Mine-Mill's remaining active unions promised an aggressive drive to take advantage of spontaneous organization among miners and smelter workers in the Butte-Anaconda district and throughout the West. By 1935, when Mine-Mill joined the insurgent Committee for Industrial Organizations (CIO, later renamed the Congress of Industrial Organizations), the union's membership had increased to 26,000 members in 132 union locals.

Like other CIO unions, Mine-Mill welcomed the passage of the 1935 National Labor Relations (or Wagner) Act that established the National Labor Relations Board (NLRB) to monitor union elections and restrict employers' unfair labor practices. Despite the passage of the Wagner Act, Mine-Mill encountered repeated jurisdictional disputes with AFL craft unions and never fully organized skilled workers in the nonferrous metals industry. In 1938, for the second time in its history, Mine-Mill left the AFL when the federation expelled the eight original CIO unions. Although hardly a dominant union in the CIO, claiming just 3% of its total membership, Mine-Mill would champion the CIO's brand of industrial unionism and liberal politics in the mountain West.

In 1936, 28-year-old Reid Robinson was elected Mine-Mill's president, signaling a new era for the union, one that would witness the resurfacing of the radical-moderate split similar to the one that had divided the WFM. The son of a Butte Mine-Mill union officer, Robinson had worked briefly in the copper mines before entering local union office in the early 1930s. Initially part of a conservative coalition, Robinson gradually advanced a left-wing Popular Front agenda that alienated his former supporters. Determined to maintain his independence from anti-Communist moderates on the union's ruling executive board, Robinson duplicated the CIO tactic of using handpicked Communist and other left-wingers on his office and organizational staff.

He also circumvented the board by establishing his own successful organizing projects at Connecticut brass refineries, southeastern iron ore mines, and the copper, gold, and silver mining and smelting districts in the western United States and Canada.

As Robinson increased the scope of his power, Mine-Mill officers and rank-and-file members red-baited Robinson and charged that the Communist party had taken control of the union, threatening the union's long tradition of rank-and-file democracy and local autonomy. Robinson's supporters responded that the metal industry's oligopolistic structure and New Deal labor relations regime necessitated a more centralized union bureaucracy. In retrospect Robinson (whose membership in the Communist party remains uncertain) posted several major achievements during his tenure. Mine-Mill not only retained its democratic procedures, including rank-and-file election of officers and ratification of contracts, but union membership increased from 20,000 to over 90,000. Not only did Mine-Mill organize much of the western metal mining industry during Robinson's presidency, but the union mended its chronic ethnic divisions, while also extending its reach into previously unorganized regions and industries.

During the first-half of the 1940s, the return of stability to the notoriously volatile metals industry along with the military draft shifted market forces in Mine-Mill's direction. By the end of World War II, Mine Mill had organized many of the 100,000 workers at the nation's top metal producers—Anaconda, American Smelting and Refining, American Metals, Phelps Dodge, and Kennecott. During its wartime organizing drive, Mine-Mill benefited from the United States Supreme Court's 1941 *Phelps Dodge* decision, which barred mine owners from firing union members. The *Phelps Dodge* decision not only helped Mine-Mill gain union recognition from the major metal producers in the American southwest, but aided the union's successful drive to organize the region's Mexican-American workers.

After World War II, Mine-Mill confronted the combined force of government repression, internal dissension, employer opposition, and repeated raids by other CIO and AFL unions. Robinson resigned from the union in 1947 amid charges that he solicited a loan from a brass company executive and was replaced by Mine-Mill's secretary-treasurer Maurice Travis, a Communist party member whom Robinson had first hired in 1944. Under pressure from anti-Communist moderates, Travis resigned the presidency after 1 year and returned to his post as secretary-treasurer. He was replaced by John Clark, a union officer from Great Falls, Montana.

Clark's critics claimed he was a front man for Travis and by association, the Communist party, but Clark held the union together during the Cold War era, when the federal government made Mine-Mill a special target. The union first came under government scrutiny when Mine-Mill's leadership refused to sign Taft-Hartley non-Communist affidavits until 1949, when Travis publicly resigned his Communist party membership and only because Mine-Mill risked losing NLRB certification. In 1956, the U.S. Justice Department indicted 14 Mine-Mill leaders on charges they had falsified their Taft-Hartley affidavits, a case that went through several trials and numerous appeals before it was dismissed by federal courts in the mid-1960s. The federal government's Subversive Activities Control Board branded Mine-Mill a Communist-infiltrated organization in 1962 and started proceedings to strip the union of its right to represent employees in the metals industry.

By this time Mine-Mill, which officially opposed the Truman administration's Cold War containment policy, faced bitter opposition from the labor movement's anti-Communist majority. In 1950, the CIO expelled Mine-Mill, as part of the federation's purge of 11 left-led red unions. In the wake of the expulsion, several CIO and AFL unions began raiding individual Mine-Mill local unions by urging dissidents to secede from the union and calling for repeated NLRB representation elections. The raiding increased after 1955, when the newly merged AFL-CIO gave the powerful United Steel Workers of America (USWA) exclusive jurisdiction over the nonferrous metals industry. The frequent raids and red-baiting caused Mine-Mill to lose many eastern unions, including those in the Connecticut brass refineries and Alabama iron mines, along with several important unions in its Rocky Mountain stronghold, most notably at Bunker Hill, Idaho, in 1960 and Anaconda, Montana, in 1962.

Although isolated from the labor movement's mainstream, and almost bankrupt from fighting the government in court and fending off rank-and-file secession movements, Mine-Mill remarkably managed to survive throughout the 1950s and early 1960s. Despite numerous controversies most rank-and-file members in the West remained loyal to the union. Many members recalled fondly the WFM's militant past and dismissed Cold War red-baiting as a routine anti-union tactic. Other members stood by Mine-Mill because of its ability to win contract improvements, contrary to the USWA's charges that mine owners preferred to deal with a weakened Mine-Mill rather than a more stable AFL-CIO union. Mexican-American members embraced Mine-Mill as a civil rights organization that helped them challenge the discrimination they routinely faced on the job and in the company towns located in southwestern United States.

The plight of Mine-Mill's Mexican-American members gained national attention through the 1954 film, *Salt of the Earth*, produced by members of the Hollywood blacklist who dramatized a 15-month strike by Mine-Mill zinc miners in Grant County, New Mexico. Although the film garnered favorable reviews, it suffered from opposition from the film industry unions, the Catholic clergy, and conservative citizens' groups. Nevertheless it was a unique Cold War-era film that compared the ethnic and class oppression suffered by Mexican-American workers to the gender oppression suffered by their wives, who served picket duty during the strike to circumvent a court injunction. Although few women worked in the metal-mining industry, with the exception of a brief period during World War II, members' wives exerted influence on Mine-Mill policy during the secessionist battles of the 1950s and 1960s, through their membership in the union's women's auxiliary.

The combined cost of contesting AFL-CIO raiding, government repression, and internal dissension spelled Mine-Mill's eventual demise. In the mid-1960s, a weakened Mine-Mill claimed just 26,415 members in 63 union locals, down from its peak of 114,000 members in 1948. Throughout the postwar era, Mine-Mill's leadership had looked for a possible merger with several other unions, but none of these efforts panned out until Albert Skinner replaced Clark as the union's president in 1963. Skinner, who acknowledged that western miners and smelters needed a united front against the major copper companies to achieve industrywide pattern bargaining, guided Mine-Mill to its 1967 merger with the USWA, dissolving the last remaining link to the WFM and its legacy of militant unionism in the mining West.

DAVID M. ANDERSON

References and Further Reading

Aiken, Katherine G. "'When I Realized How Close Communism Was to Kellogg, I Was Willing to Devote Day and Night': Anti-Communism, Women, Community Values, and the Bunker Hill Strike of 1960." *Labor History* 36, 2 (spring 1995): 165–186.

Cargill, Jack. "Empire and Opposition: The 'Salt of the Earth' Strike." In *Labor in New Mexico: Unions, Strikes, and Social History since 1881*, edited by Robert Kern. Albuquerque: University of New Mexico Press, 1983.

Dinwoodie, D. H. "The Rise of the Mine-Mill Union in Southwestern Copper." In *American Labor in the Southwest: The First One Hundred Years*, edited by James C. Foster. Tucson: University of Arizona Press, 1982.

Dubofsky, Melvyn. *We Shall Be All: A History of the Industrial Workers of the World*. Chicago, IL: Quadrangle Books, 1969.

Emmons, David M. *The Butte Irish: Class and Ethnicity in an American Mining Town*. Urbana: University of Illinois Press, 1989.

Hildebrand, George H., and Garth L. Mangum. *Capital and Labor in American Copper, 1845–1990: Linkages between Product and Labor Markets*. Cambridge, MA: Harvard University Press, 1992.

Jameson, Elizabeth. *All That Glitters: Class, Conflict, and Community in Cripple Creek*. Urbana: University of Illinois Press, 1998.

Jensen, Vernon H. *Heritage of Conflict: Labor Relations in the Nonferrous Metals Industry up to 1930*. Ithaca, NY: Cornell University Press, 1950.

———. *Non-Ferrous Metals Industry Unionism, 1932–1954*. Ithaca, NY: Cornell University Press, 1954.

Lingenfelter, Richard E. *The Hard Rock Miners: A History of the Mining Labor Movement in the American West, 1863–1893*. Berkeley: University of California Press, 1974.

Lorence, James J. *The Suppression of* Salt of the Earth: *How Hollywood, Big Labor, and Politicians Blacklisted a Movie in Cold War America*. Albuquerque: University of New Mexico Press, 1999.

Lukas, J. Anthony. *Big Trouble: A Murder in a Small Western Town Sets off a Struggle for the Soul of America*. New York: Simon and Schuster, 1997.

Mellinger, Philip J. *Race and Labor in Western Copper: The Fight for Equality, 1896–1918*. Tucson: University of Arizona Press, 1995.

Rosenblum, Jonathan D. *Copper Crucible: How the Arizona Miners' Strike of 1983 Recast Labor-Management Relations in America*. Ithaca, NY: ILR Press, 1995.

Suggs, George G. Jr., *Colorado's War on Militant Unionism: James H. Peabody and the Western Federation of Miners*. Norman: University of Oklahoma Press, 1991, 1972.

Cases and Statutes Cited

National Industrial Recovery Act
National Labor Relations Act

See also **Bisbee Deportation/Copper Strike (1917); Communist Party; Company Towns; Congress of Industrial Organizations; Film; Haywood, William D.; Industrial Workers of the World, 1950s–1960s; Phelps Dodge Copper Strike (1983–1984); Taft-Hartley Act**

WHEATLAND STRIKE/RIOT (1913)

The Wheatland strike grew out of several factors relating to the problem of farm labor in California and other regions of the American West. Farmers needed agricultural labor for harvesting, which could not be secured solely by using local seasonal wageworkers and family members. Therefore farmers needed to attract workers to their farms to work on a temporary basis. California farmers had been making use of seasonal and migrant agricultural labor for years before 1913. However the supply and demand of migrant workers grew steadily after the turn of the century. Farmers, who had to deal both with fixed operating costs and fluctuating market prices for their crop, treated labor as a variable cost.

Ralph Durst was co-owner and manager of a large farm and ranch that produced a series of crops, including hops, in Wheatland, California. In 1913, the price of hops fell. For Durst to continue making a profit, he chose to cut harvest labor costs. For the August harvest, he advertised in broadsides throughout the region and in a number of newspapers in California, Oregon, and Nevada for workers to journey to his farm to pick hops. Twenty-eight hundred men, women, and children answered his call. These workers represented the essential diversity of the California farm labor workforce. Cubans, Puerto Ricans, Mexicans, Hawaiians, Syrians, Japanese, Indians, Poles, Greeks, Italians, and Lithuanians made up the largest contingents of foreign-born workers; in all the workers spoke 27 different languages. The native-born workers included migrant, white, male workers, resident seasonal day laborers, and a number of local families who regularly participated in the harvest season in the valley.

When the workers arrived, they quickly discovered poor living and working conditions at the labor camp. They had to rent a campsite and buy food at the on-site grocery store. The toilet facilities and drinking water supply were inadequate. In his advertisements, Durst promised that the pickers would receive the going rate of $1 for 100 pounds of picked hops. But this was deceptive. He required excessively cleaned hops before weighing and had no hop pickers present on the inspection crew for harvested hops. He also withheld 10 cents per 100 pounds of picked hops. Pickers would receive this withheld pay at the end of the harvest. Workers ended up making less than $1.50 a day. Despite temperatures reaching over 110 degrees, workers did not have access to water in the fields. Durst did provide a powdered lemonade drink at a cost of 5 cents a glass.

The harvest commenced on July 29, and by August 1, labor discontent over the poor living and working conditions permeated the entire camp. Working among the hop pickers were current and former members of the Industrial Workers of the World (IWW), also known as Wobblies. With the participation of the vast majority of the workers, the Wobblies established a committee out of several mass meetings. The elected members included former Wobbly Richard "Blackie" Ford as chief spokesman for the hop pickers and current Wobbly Herman Suhr as the secretary of the committee. The committee approached Durst with a list of worker demands. These demands included a flat rate of $1.25 per 100 pounds of picked hops, drinking water in the

fields, inspection of picked hops by the pickers themselves, and improvement of camp toilets generally among other demands.

Durst would only agree to meet some of the demands. The workers' committee warned Durst that the hop pickers would strike if all of their demands were not fully met. Durst broke off the negotiations and ordered the strike committee to get their pay and leave the ranch. When Ford and the committee refused, Durst asked deputy sheriff Henry Daken to arrest Ford. Workers intervened on behalf of Ford when Daken could not produce a warrant. Later that day the workers organized a mass meeting in which Ford and Suhr urged the workers to strike in order to force Durst to address their grievances. In order to persuade as many as possible to join in the strike, speakers in German, Greek, Italian, Arabic, and Spanish addressed the crowd. With a show of hands the vast majority of hop pickers favored a strike.

Durst summoned Edward Manwell, the district attorney, and Marysville's sheriff, George Voss, who brought along a number of deputies, to arrest Ford and to break up the workers' gathering. When the party approached Ford, the workers again intervened on his behalf. A member of the posse fired a shot into the air to disperse the crowd. This had the opposite effect. Manwell, a deputy, and two hop pickers died in the ensuing violence and gunfire. Many in the crowd suffered bullet wounds from the 20 or so rounds fired during the melee. The crowd was unarmed, though by most accounts, the deaths of Manwell and the deputy resulted from members of the posse having their guns taken away and used against them.

After this initial outbreak of violence, the hop workers immediately left the ranch in all directions. Fearing more worker disturbances, Governor Hiram Johnson sent national guard units to the area. Eventually law enforcement officials arrested Ford and Suhr for murder. Two organizations emerged to help with the workers' defense, the IWW's Wheatland Hop Picker's Defense League and a coalition group, the International Workers' Defense League. Their primary purpose focused on generating public support for the men on trial and raising funds for their defense. However contributing to an anti-IWW atmosphere surrounding the trial, California's newspapers demonized the defendants and associated in the public's mind Wobblies with violence. Never in the course of the trial could the prosecutors demonstrate that Ford and Suhr either fired a weapon or encouraged others to use violence. Yet the conspiracy case against the defendants led to a second-degree murder conviction. Ford and Suhr received life sentences but were eventually released in the late 1920s.

Following the Wheatland strike and the convictions of Ford and Suhr, the IWW inaugurated a systematic effort to organize the state's farmworkers. Also in response to Wheatland, progressives in state government began to address the issues that led to the strike with the California Commission of Immigration and Housing (CCIH). Simon J. Lubin, Carleton Parker, and other officials of the CCIH instituted sanitation inspections of farm-labor camps throughout the state. These early efforts by both organized labor and state intervention on behalf of farmworkers began a long and continuing struggle to address the needs of California's agricultural laborers.

GREG HALL

References and Further Reading

Daniel, Cletus E. *Bitter Harvest: A History of California Farmworkers, 1870–1941.* Berkeley: University of California Press, 1981.

DiGirolamo, Vincent. "The Women of Wheatland: Female Consciousness and the 1913 Wheatland Hop Strike." *Labor History* 34 (1993): 236–255.

Dubofsky, Melvyn. *We Shall Be All: A History of the Industrial Workers of the World.* Chicago, IL: Quadrangle Books, 1969.

Foner, Philip S. *History of the Labor Movement in the United States.* Vol. 4: *The Industrial Workers of the World, 1905–1917.* New York: International Publishers, 1965.

Hall, Greg. *Harvest Wobblies: The Industrial Workers of the World and Agricultural Laborers of the American West.* Corvalis: Oregon State University Press, 2001.

Kronbluh, Joyce L., ed. *Rebel Voices: An IWW Anthology.* Chicago, IL: Charles H. Kerr Publishing Company, 1988.

McWilliams, Carey. *Factories in the Field: The Story of Migratory Farm Labor in California.* Boston, MA: Little, Brown, and Company, 1939.

Mitchell, Don. *Lie of the Land: Migrant Workers and the California Landscape.* Minneapolis: University of Minnesota Press, 1996.

Parker, Carleton H. *The Casual Laborer and Other Essays.* New York: Harcourt, Brace, and Howe, 1920.

WOMEN'S AUXILIARIES

While little is known about the activities of labor union auxiliaries in the United States, many assume that the violent clashes between the working-class wives of the United Automobile Workers (UAW) Women's Emergency Brigade and Ford's hired thugs during the 1936 Flint sit-down strike was the birth of the women's auxiliary movement. In fact the genesis of the movement actually dates back to the 1890s. As the influence and power of the Knights of Labor waned, working-class women found themselves isolated from the labor movement. Unlike the inclusive mission of the knights, the craft-driven American Federation of Labor (AFL) focused little energy on organizing female workers. Nor did the AFL's leadership struggle with issues of gender equity. And while many working-class women during the late nineteenth century engaged in wage labor outside the home, it was their activities as wives, mothers, and daughters, not their contributions as wage earners, that defined their identity.

Yet interestingly it was working-class women's role within the home as consumers, or mangers of their husbands' income, that motivated them to organize labor union auxiliaries. By organizing auxiliaries, women saw an opportunity to engage in the economic marketplace through the labor movement. While the unions representing their fathers and husbands were fighting for the 8-hour day and a family-wage, working-class women used auxiliaries to emphasize further the necessity of increased wages in order to achieve an American standard of living. While inherent in their argument was an embracing of the ideal of a male breadwinner, working-class women at times embraced militant rhetoric and action to achieve these goals. Furthermore while there is a dearth of published material on women's auxiliaries in the United States, there exists a tension within the historiography about the nature of their militancy as labor activists and women.

Some of the earliest auxiliaries were formed by the wives of workers in such unions as the International Association of Machinists (IAM), the Brotherhood of Railroad Brakemen (the union later changed the name to Trainmen), and the International Typographical Union. As early as 1888, Sophia J. Granger, the wife of the union's treasurer, led 25 wives, sisters, and mothers of the Brotherhood of Railroad Brakemen in Fort Gratiot, Michigan, to petition the brotherhood's convention to form a Ladies' Auxiliary. They succeeded and on January 23, 1889, the Grand Lodge of Ladies' Auxiliary to the Brotherhood of Railroad Trainmen was formed. Similarly in 1902, the Women's International Auxiliary to the International Typographical Union was organized in Cincinnati, Ohio, at the Golden Jubilee Convention of the International Typographical Union.

One early account of agitation among working-class wives took place in Oshkosh, Wisconsin. Woodworkers affiliated with the AFL were striking for wage increases and union recognition when the company attempted to bring in replacement workers. On June 23, 1898, a clash broke out between the strikers and their wives and the nonunion workers who showed up at the factory to work. According to the *Oshkosh Daily Northwestern,* the wives were among the most disorderly. With pouches filled with eggs, sand, and pepper in one hand and clubs in the other, the women chased the nonunion workers away from the mill. The plant remained closed until strikebreakers were brought in under policy protection. Several days after the plant re-opened using nonunion labor, nine women were arrested and jailed for attempting to keep the strikebreakers from entering the mill. The next morning, 40 women, all wives of striking workers, filled the mayor's office and demanded the release of the women and intervention in the labor dispute. According to the wives their husbands' wages were too low to live on without going into debt to feed their families. It was this issue—the standard of living—that drove the organization of the first auxiliaries and would continue to fuel their organization into the 1970s.

In other cases auxiliaries were born out of ancillary organizations. For example the Ladies Auxiliary to the Brotherhood of Sleeping Car Porters (BSCP) grew out of Women's Economic Councils (WECs). Organized by A. Philip Randolph in the mid-1920s, the WECs functioned to help wives encourage their husbands to join the BSCP. In 1938, however, the councils were transformed into full-fledged auxiliaries. No longer simply a cheering squad on the sidelines of the labor movement, the Ladies' Auxiliaries acted as "soldiers in aprons" bringing together consumer issues and labor issues. As with so many auxiliaries, the auxiliary membership believed that the union wife controlled her own sphere of domestic influence over the labor movement. Similarly in 1936, the AFL's Union Label Trades' Department formed the American Federation of Women's Auxiliaries League (AFWAL). Rather than focusing only on promoting the consumption of union made goods, AFWAL advocated the organization and centralization of women's auxiliaries throughout the AFL. Like the Ladies' Auxiliary to the BSCP, AFWAL encouraged union wives to use their influence politically as well as economically.

It is not a coincidence that one of the most well-known moments in auxiliary history—the attack of hired thugs on the UAW Women's Brigade during the Flint sit-down strike in 1937—overlaps with the formation of AFWAL or the founding of the Ladies' Auxiliary of the BSCP. The 1930s witnessed an explosion of auxiliary activity to accompany the fast and furious growth of the labor movement. While the AFL auxiliaries had been active for close to four decades in some cases, a new era of auxiliaries flourished as a result of industrial organizing through the CIO. The wives of UAW workers were encouraged by Walter Reuther to organize auxiliaries to assist in building union density in the auto industry by quelling anxiety among the wives of newly organized

workers. The confrontation between Ford's hired thugs and the auxiliary women on May 26, 1937, was just the beginning for the UAW Women's Auxiliaries. And like the AFL auxiliaries, the CIO auxiliaries organized a national coalition called the Congress of Women's Auxiliaries (CWA).

Across the country working-class housewives formed auxiliaries. For the most part auxiliary membership comprised women who did not identify as wage earners. It is difficult to discern what percentage of auxiliary members did not work outside of the home. However it is clear that many auxiliaries prohibited membership of women who were also members of the union to which the auxiliary was affiliated. For example the UAW prohibited participation of female UAW members in the auxiliaries. Meanwhile the BSCP did not discourage the participation of female union members from joining the Ladies' Auxiliary. In fact female participation in the Ladies' Auxiliary seemed to be encouraged by the male leadership of the BSCP. There was one significant exception to this division between wage-earning women and auxiliary women, the entry of the United States into World War II. During the early 1940s, auxiliary members heeded the call by the federal government and industry to join the ranks of wage earners. Among UAW auxiliary members, many women saw this as an opportunity to spread the gospel of unionization among the working class. For instance in 1943, Julia Katz, the CWA National Director, took a job as a burner in a Baltimore shipyard. According to a letter she sent to the CWA-affiliated auxiliaries, it appears that Katz joined the workforce as a patriotic gesture as well as an opportunity to build the labor movement. In her letter Katz wrote that she was working with women from across the country who have migrated temporarily to Baltimore for work. Katz expressed total joy in learning her trade, but the opportunity to build the labor movement was the dominant theme in the letter. The female workers' husbands "are members of the union and they will be 'union-men' too! At least I will try and make them so...I am persuaded that these very 35 women cannot achieve their needs without the organization of their mothers and mother-in-law and the wives and mother of all of their co-workers into auxiliaries . . . There is one thing about which I am certain; that is the fact that the auxiliary is a training-school for unionism."

By the 1940s, both the AFL and CIO affiliated auxiliaries reached their heyday. In fact almost as many women belonged to labor auxiliaries as to labor unions during this time. Throughout the 1940s and into the 1950s, union auxiliaries participated in a range of activities, including legislative campaigns.

Working-class housewives mobilized their membership in legislative battles to fight the high cost of living, often organizing in concert with other working and middle-class organizations to keep the Office of Price Administration active. While many auxiliaries sought equal pay and seniority rights for female workers within their unions, within the legislative context, the auxiliary leadership within the AFL and CIO clearly objected to the passage of the National Women's party Equal Rights Amendment (ERA).

The ERA was one of the most controversial issues between working- and middle-class women's groups. Joining forces with such groups as the American Association of University Women, the National Council of Jewish Women, and the National Trade Union League, the auxiliary leadership viewed the ERA as a threat to the protective labor legislation that had been gained during the Progressive Era. By erasing the inherent differences between men and women, many auxiliaries believed the ERA weakened women's role in the workplace. In the February 2, 1944, issue of the *CIO News*, Eleanor Fowler, the secretary-treasurer of the CIO Women's Auxiliaries, attacked the National Women's party writing, "The women's rights line [is] slick and dangerous . . . They [the NWP] don't bother to say that equality means to them elimination of minimum wage and maximum hours laws for women where men don't have the same protection. And that the equal rights amendment would immediately toss into the waste basket all the protective legislation for women which labor has struggled to achieve." In addition to the battles to save the Office of Price Administration (OPA) and defeat the ERA, auxiliaries also sought support among their membership for other key labor legislation.

Aside from their legislative activity, the CIO and AFL auxiliaries had little in common programmatically. For example in addition to legislative activity, AFL auxiliary members emphasized the importance of buying union-made products. A significant portion of their publications were dedicated to urging women to purchase union-made goods for the home as well as encouraging affiliated auxiliaries to compile lists of union-made goods. For example in a 1945 pamphlet entitled "A Heart-to-Heart Talk with Consumers," Mrs. Herman H. Lowe, president of the AFWAL, wrote, "Because about 90 cents out of every union-earned dollar is spent by the women members of the family, we are carrying on a continual campaign, through the American Federation of Women's Auxiliaries of Labor, urging women members of labor unionists' families to buy Union Label goods and to use Union services." This emphasis was never far from the programmatic work of AFL auxiliaries, since the national organization was tied

through organizational structure and leadership to the AFL's Union Label Trades' Department. In fact such historians as Dorothy Sue Cobble have argued that the AFL auxiliaries resisted expanding their mission beyond union label campaigns and community service, which has placed them in a historically more conservative framework than their counterparts in the CIO auxiliaries.

In contrast the CIO auxiliaries took up issues of gender and racial equality throughout the 1940s and 1950s. Unlike the AFL publications, the women's auxiliaries' column in the *CIO News* as well as individual auxiliary publications concentrated on a variety of social and economic issues affecting both union and nonunion families. Some of the reoccurring CIO auxiliary campaigns included the creation of childcare centers for working mothers, establishment of school lunch programs in public schools, and the ongoing struggles for racial equality through the Fair Employment Practice Committee (FECP). In fact the issue of purchasing union goods was an anomaly in the pages of CIO auxiliary publications.

In 1956, the sharp differences between the AFL and CIO auxiliaries dulled once the AFL and CIO merged to form a unified labor federation. Soon after the merger in 1957, the AFWAL and the CWA followed suit and formed the AFL-CIO National Auxiliaries. The *AFL-CIO Auxiliaries Reporter*, the new auxiliary publication, portrayed the merger as a new phase in the auxiliary movement: "This historic convention marks the beginning of a new, unified Auxiliaries Organization, the AFL-CIO Auxiliaries. It is an organization that is dedicated to and bound by the all-inclusive program of its parent body, the AFL-CIO. It embraces a program of Education; of Community Services; of Promoting the Union Label and Union-Made products; of Political Education and Activity; of Legislative Activity; and of Promoting the Good and Welfare of the Trade Union Movement." And for a while this new auxiliary federation did rejuvenate the work of the auxiliaries. The integration of the two auxiliary agendas brought much needed attention to political mobilization during the late 1950s and early 1960s. As the auxiliaries reorganized, many added political-action committees to their structure and urged their membership to increase their volunteer time to certain legislative campaigns and getting-out-the-vote efforts.

At the time of the merger, the CWA counted 12,000 members and the AFWAL claimed to have 15,000. It is important to note however that not all union auxiliaries, such as the Women's International Auxiliary to the International Typographical Union (WIA-ITU) and the Ladies' Auxiliary to the Brotherhood of Sleeping Car Porters (BSCP), were members of the national federations. In fact the AFWAL estimated that close to a million women belonged to AFL auxiliaries that had not yet affiliated with the federation. After the merger the AFL-CIO National Auxiliaries organized a membership campaign urging unaffiliated union auxiliaries to join. Many unions, including the WIA-ITU and the Ladies' Auxiliaries to the BSCP, agreed to join the national federation.

As the civil rights and women's movements continued to gain prominence, the mission and appeal of women's auxiliaries grew increasingly outdated. Not surprisingly by the mid-1960s, auxiliary membership and activity waned. The programmatic work of auxiliaries reverted back to a more community service-based focus. In some cases the auxiliaries discontinued, while other unions rewrote the membership rules to include the families of union members, thereby opening up membership to men and children for the first time. For example in the United Transportation Union (formerly the Brotherhood of Railroad Brakemen), the word ladies was eliminated from the name to reflect the changing membership. Currently the auxiliary has approximately 6,000 members in the United States and Canada that focus on such community-service efforts as fundraising for cancer research and seeing-eye guide dogs. While the mission of the remaining union auxiliaries is no longer directly tied to directly building the labor movement, the record remains clear that auxiliaries played a central role in helping to establish the American labor movement.

EMILY E. LaBARBERA TWAROG

References and Further Reading

Chateauvert, Melinda. *Marching Together: Women of the Brotherhood of Sleeping Car Porters*. Urbana: University of Illinois Press, 1997.
Cobble, Dorothy Sue. *The Other Women's Movement: Workplace Justice and Social Rights in Modern America*. Princeton, NJ: Princeton University Press, 2004.
Foner, Phillip. *Women and the American Labor Movement*. New York: The Free Press, 1979.
Lasky, Marjorie Penn. "'Where I Was a Person': The Ladies Auxiliary in the 1934 Minneapolis Teamsters' Strikes." In *Women, Work, and Protest*, Ruth Milkman, ed. London, UK: Routledge Press, 1985.
Levine, Susan. "Workers' Wives: Gender, Class, and Consumerism in the 1920s United States." *Gender and History* 3 (1991): 45–64.
Pfeffer, Paula F. "The Women behind the Union: Halena Wilson, Rosina Tucker, and the Ladies' Auxiliary to the Brotherhood of Sleeping Car Porters." *Labor History* 36 (fall 1995).

See also **Brotherhood of Sleeping Car Porters**

WOMEN'S BUREAU

Officially established within the Department of Labor by the U.S. Congress in 1920, the framework for the Women's Bureau emerged during World War I with the creation of the Women in Industry Service by Woodrow Wilson in 1918. During the war the Women in Industry Service devised wartime labor standards for workingwomen. In 1920, the newly created bureau's mandate proposed to investigate and improve the conditions of female workers. Although the bureau does not initiate legislation or possess any enforcement capabilities, it is the only federal agency that represents the needs of wage-earning women in the public-policy process.

Founded on the heels of the progressive movement, female reformers seeking to create a government agency to protect workingwomen through protective legislation influenced the bureau's inception. Mary Anderson, a Swedish immigrant boot maker who became president of the Stitchers' Local 94 and an organizer for the Women's Trade Union League led the bureau until 1944. Under Anderson's direction the coalition of women's groups that had advocated for the agency remained closely allied with it for decades. These groups included the League of Women Voters, the National Consumers' League, and the Women's Trade Union League. In its early years Anderson and her colleagues were forced to defend themselves from Red Scare accusations of socialist sympathies. A more enduring point of dissension revolved around the question of strategy that should be used to obtain women's rights. A minority of female activists led by the National Women's party believed that passage of an Equal Rights Amendment at the federal level would be in the best interests of all American women. Anderson and her associates however felt that this type of blanket amendment would in effect negate the existing state-based protective legislation and strike a harsh blow for workingwomen. Equality for women, they believed, could be achieved only by furthering protective legislation.

Some of the agency's most important work centers around the investigative reports that it publishes. The bureau has investigated multiple topics of concern to women, including conditions facing black women in industry, older women as office workers, and availability of childcare. Much of the bureau's work has focused on the wages, hours, and employment conditions for female workers. With the possible exception of the New Deal years, the Women's Bureau has suffered from a perpetual lack of funding.

The Women's Bureau and its leaders faced criticism as well. In 1924, the *Dearborn Independent* accused Anderson of being a Communist tool. That same year, Lucia Maxwell, a librarian in the Chemical Warfare Section of the War Department, created the so-called Spider Web chart, which listed the Women's Bureau and other women's organizations, including the Women's Trade Union League, as members of a vast conspiracy out to destroy the United States.

In 1936, Anderson's attempt to promote a charter of women's rights failed due to the division of various women's groups over protective legislation for women and the Equal Rights Amendment. The bureau spent much of the 1930s chronicling the low wages and unemployment of women during the Great Depression. Under Anderson's tenure, the agency successfully lobbied for women's inclusion in the Fair Labor Standards Act in 1938, which for the first time in U.S. history, set national standards for minimum wages and maximum hours for all workers. During World War II, working closely with the Congress of Industrial Organizations, the bureau identified the need for advanced skill training and more job opportunities for female wartime workers—80% of whom stated in 1944 that they wanted to retain their jobs once the war ended. It also conducted studies that revealed that the 100,000 children enrolled in federal day-care centers constituted only 10% of the children who needed such care.

Frieda Miller took charge of the Women's Bureau after Anderson retired in 1944. Although Miller empathized with trade union women, she shifted the bureau's emphasis from women in industry to women in agricultural and domestic work who remained excluded from the provisions of the Fair Labor Standards Act. In the wake of the New Deal, the bureau's support from a coalition of women's organizations began to slip away. One of its staunchest advocates, the Women's Trade Union League disbanded in 1950, and the influence of the National Consumers' League declined considerably. Eisenhower's appointee, Alice Leopold, took over in 1953 and redirected the bureau's efforts toward calculating and deciding the nation's most effective use of women's power. No longer a resource of advocacy for trade union women, Leopold cast the bureau as a bureaucratic data-collection agency that encouraged a partnership with business.

Esther Peterson who took the helm under Kennedy and her 1964 successor, economist Mary Dublin Keyserling, both shared an allegiance to labor and revived the bureau's reform interests and government regulatory participation on behalf of workingwomen. Peterson took the lead in convincing the government to address women's economic difficulties by initiating the creation of the President's Commission on the Status of Women. The Women's Bureau and its supporters, many of them members of the presidential commission, were instrumental in the Passage of the Equal Pay Act of 1963 mandating equal pay for equal work. The bureau also began to direct its efforts toward addressing the special needs of low-income and minority women. Keyserling's refusal to endorse the ERA contributed to its declining position. Although Nixon's Women's Bureau Director Elizabeth Duncan Koonz endorsed the ERA, the bureau's status declined further. It failed to ally successfully with the women's movements of the 1960s and 1970s. The bureau backed a 1982 employer-sponsored day-care drive and the 1993 passage of the Family and Medical Leave Act. Today the Women's Bureau operates in an informational capacity acting mainly as what Peterson called a staff arm of the United States Department of Labor.

KAREN PASTORELLO

References and Further Reading

Harrison, Cynthia. *On Account of Sex: The Politics of Women's Issues, 1945–1968*. Berkeley: University of California, 1988.

Laughlin, Kathleen A. *Women's Work and Public Policy: A History of the Women's Bureau, U.S. Department of Labor, 1945–1970*. Boston, MA: Northeastern University Press, 2000.

Women's Bureau. Washington, DC: U.S. Department of Labor, Record Group 86, National Archives and Record Center.

Women's Bureau website. www.dol.gov//wb/info

Cases and Statutes Cited

Equal Pay Act
Fair Labor Standards Act
Family and Medical Leave Act

WOMEN'S TRADE UNION LEAGUE

The Women's Trade Union League (WTUL, 1903–1950) was an organization founded by trade unionists and social reformers to organize wage-earning women into trade unions, as well as provide education and agitate for protective labor legislation.

Beginnings

Founded in 1903 during the annual convention of the American Federation of Labor (AFL), the WTUL was a coalition of middle- and upper-class female allies and working-class women with deep roots in the Progressive Era's efforts for social reform, especially as situated within the settlement house movement. As growing numbers of white women entered the industrial workforce at the start of the twentieth century, the often-horrific conditions under which they labored became increasingly apparent. Although certainly aware of the situation, the AFL continued to advocate for a family-wage, earned by a male wage earner at the same time it focused its energies on the organization of skilled male craft workers as it had done since its inception in 1886. Arguing that women tended to work only briefly before marriage for pin money, the AFL claimed it was not in their organization's best interest to allocate resources toward the organization of female workers. But wage-earning women like Pauline Newman, Leonora O'Reilly, Mary Kenney O'Sullivan, and Rose Schneiderman knew that growing numbers of women worked for much of their adult lives, both before and after marriage in low-paying jobs for long hours and often in dangerous conditions. These women needed union protection, too; however the AFL remained ambivalent at best regarding the organization of female workers. Thus women like O'Sullivan turned to middle-class social reformers, especially within the settlement house movement, to seek support and much needed assistance. At the same time nonetheless women like O'Sullivan, a former bookbinder and the first female organizer appointed by the AFL in 1892, knew full well the efficacy of union representation and sought an alliance that would bridge the gap between female workers and the trade union movement. In this spirit the WTUL was born.

During the 1903 AFL annual convention, held that year in Boston, O'Sullivan met with the wealthy settlement house worker William English Walling. Walling, later a cofounder of the National Association for the Advancement of Colored People (NAACP), had just returned from England where he was introduced to the British Women's Trade Union League. Founded in 1874 and first known as the Women's Protective and Provident League, the British WTUL had aggressively campaigned to bring significant numbers of British female workers into pre-existing trade unions by the early twentieth century. As a former factory inspector and resident of the University Settlement House in New York City, Walling was well-aware of the poor labor conditions faced by wage-earning women. Inspired by the British WTUL, he hoped to create a similar organization for working-women in the United States, and in O'Sullivan he found a willing partner. With the permission of her old friend and then president of the AFL, Samuel Gompers, O'Sullivan announced an organizational meeting from the convention floor. At that meeting, held in a Boston settlement house, several trade unionists and settlement house workers, both male and female, discussed the initial plans for an American WTUL and were soon writing a constitution and by-laws. Before the AFL annual convention ended, the WTUL had officers in place and a plan of action that included the establishment of branch leagues in New York, Chicago, and Boston.

The WTUL goal of being a cross-class alliance was reflected in its first selection of officers. The first national president of the WTUL was Mary Morton Kehew, a wealthy and progressive woman who was then also president of the Women's Educational and Industrial Union in Boston. Jane Addams, middle-class settlement house pioneer and cofounder of Chicago's Hull-House, was elected national vice-president. Representing wage-earning women were O'Sullivan as national secretary and Mary Donovan, a Lynn, Massachusetts, shoe worker as treasurer. Initial executive board members included the middle-class Lillian Wald, founder of the Henry Street Settlement House, and Leonora O'Reilly, a former garment worker and labor organizer, both from New York. Executive board members from Chicago in addition to Addams included her fellow settlement house worker Mary McDowell and labor organizer Ellen Lindstrom. However well-intended its efforts were to bridge the formidable class divisions between the wage-earning female members of the WTUL and their so-called allies, that is, the middle- and upper-class women who would eventually include such women as Eleanor Roosevelt, the organization would always be hampered by class tensions. So, too, would its tenuous relationship to the male-dominated trade union movement be a constant factor in its nearly 50 years of existence. The pattern was set at its founding. Perhaps in recognition of the ambivalence of the AFL membership at large to the organization of women, the WTUL chose not to ask the AFL for an official endorsement at the 1903 convention. Instead they asked the convention for a resolution regarding the appointment of a female organizer. The AFL sanctioned that decision but waited another 5 years to act. In any case official recognition of the WTUL did not come from the AFL until 1912. Nonetheless branches were organized in the targeted cites within a few months, and the WTUL on the national and local level was quickly involved in several major strikes across the country. Despite the ever-present class tensions within the organization and the ambivalent attitude of the AFL, the WTUL achieved much in its early years as it sought to improve the conditions of wage-earning women in the United States.

Early Years

From its founding up through the outbreak of World War I, the WTUL participated in a number of strikes, some small, some large, all involving significant numbers of female wage earners, many of whom were not trade union members. Throughout, despite its continued official distance from the AFL, the WTUL aimed to organize female workers into pre-existing AFL affiliates. The organization of female workers was the primary mission of the WTUL but so too was education—in part, this was the education of female workers regarding the benefits of trade unionism as well as the education of male trade unionists to the need for organization of female workers. Increasingly the WTUL turned also to lobbying for protective labor legislation aimed specifically at female workers at the same time its efforts in the struggle for women's suffrage accelerated. In 1906, the wealthy and well-connected Margaret Dreier Robins became president of the WTUL, which a year later in recognition of the growth of its local leagues that now included a fourth in St. Louis, renamed itself the National Women's Trade Union League (NWTUL). During Robins's presidency, which lasted until 1922, the NWTUL focused on its three-part approach—organization, education, and legislation. In varying degrees these three strands guided the WTUL as it went from strike to strike in its early years.

One of the largest strikes that the WTUL took part in occurred only a few months after its formation. During the summer of 1904, upward of 25,000 textile workers, more than half of whom were women, went on strike in Fall River, Massachusetts, protesting a series of wage reductions and speedups. Only approximately 20% of the entire workforce was organized into AFL-affiliated textile unions representing weavers and spinners, for the most part those who were considered skilled workers, the majority of whom were male, either native-born or English and Irish immigrants. However most Fall River textile operatives were classified as unskilled workers and were increasingly female and newer immigrants, primarily French Canadian and Portuguese, none of whom were yet seen as organizable by the AFL. Yet the misery associated with low wages and worsening work conditions crossed craft, gender, and ethnic lines, and it was into this void that the WTUL stepped, hoping to address the concerns of the 12,000 or so female textile workers on strike for several months during 1904. As it would in other times and places, the WTUL provided assistance on the picket lines, raised strike relief funds, and generated much publicity about the conditions of life and labor in the Fall River textile mills. In this its first labor action, the WTUL also engaged in what it referred to as a strike time experiment, sending 130 female textile workers on strike to work as domestic servants in Boston. In her capacity as NWTUL secretary and a leader in the New York League, Gertrude Barnum, the well-to-do daughter of a Chicago judge,

conceived of this experiment that was soon judged a failure—by most of the 130 women who took part and by working-class leaders in the league, such as O'Sullivan, now vice-president of the NWTUL. That this well-meaning ally would think that sending female textile workers to work as domestics for even lower pay and under potentially more exploitative working conditions, was indicative of the limitations of the WTUL in its early years. It was a somewhat more mature organization that took part in the massive strike of New York City garment workers in 1909–1910 known as the Uprising of the 20,000. Within the New York WTUL by this time, working-class members, such as Pauline Newman and Schneiderman, had joined their fellow garment worker and veteran trade union activist Leonora O'Reilly. And while Schneiderman would eventually be president of the New York branch, during the Uprising of the 20,000 it was still the middle- and upper-class allies, such as Helen Marot and Mary Dreier, sister of NWTUL President Margaret Dreier Robins, who led the organization. But their resources were sorely needed during this long and bitter strike. The WTUL, in New York and on the national level, worked hard to raise funds and generate publicity. In the city as the strike dragged on into the winter of 1909–1910, wealthy WTUL allies wearing furs joined the picket lines and were soon dubbed the mink-coat brigade. Some were even arrested and that, too, generated much press for the strikers, since many of the so-called mink-coat brigade were related by blood and/or marriage to the city's most prominent men. Just a year after the strike was finally settled, fire broke out in the Triangle Shirtwaist Factory in New York City; within a few minutes on that Saturday afternoon in March 1911, 146 workers, most of them young female immigrants from Italy and Eastern Europe, died in one of the worst workplace disasters in American history. The tragedy, which in part stemmed from the fact that the factory owners had locked the doors to prevent employee theft and keep union organizers out, made clear the need for improved work conditions in the city and on a national level. Working with other concerned social reform groups, such as the National Consumers' League, the WTUL pressed for and then took part in the state investigation that eventually did lead to improved worker-safety laws and the beginnings of better enforcement of those laws. In addition to these large strikes, the WTUL took part in countless other smaller labor actions across the country, primarily in or near those cities—New York, Chicago, Boston—where they had established branch leagues. Yet another strike of huge proportions, ultimately quite divisive for the WTUL, was the Bread and Roses strike in 1912, which involved more than 20,000 textile workers in Lawrence, Massachusetts. There it was the Industrial Workers of the World, not the AFL, that took charge of the strike, and when the AFL decided not to sanction this increasingly violent strike of primarily immigrant workers, the majority of whom were women, the WTUL split over what its stance should be. The WTUL cofounder O'Sullivan and some others felt strongly that the league should assist the strikers in whatever way they could even if it meant going against AFL policy. Robins, then president of the NWTUL, and her sister, Dreier, president of the New York League, felt otherwise and ordered the WTUL out of Lawrence in keeping with the AFL policy. In response O'Sullivan resigned in protest from the organization she helped form. Later that same year, 1912, the AFL finally recognized the WTUL as an affiliate.

Later Years

Throughout these strikes the WTUL also sought to meet its goals of organizing female workers, providing labor education, and lobbying for protective labor legislation, and it did so in a number of ways. In 1913, the WTUL organized more than 2,000 women into the newly created Boston Telephone Operators' Union at the same time it continued to organize female industrial workers. Providing education, especially that which focused on union activities, was also important to the league. Part of the educational effort was done through league publications, including their monthly newsletter, *Life and Labor*, which first appeared in 1911. Beginning in the 1910s, but especially during the 1920s, the WTUL sponsored yearly labor schools for female workers, including the Bryn Mawr Summer School for Women Workers. While always claiming that union representation was the best way to improve work conditions, the WTUL had, especially in the wake of the Triangle Factory fire, pressed for protective labor legislation. Branch leagues frequently sponsored investigations of workplace conditions, often doing so in cooperation with local unions and social reform groups, such as the National Consumers' League. These detailed investigations would then be presented to state legislative bodies, leading to the passage of several labor laws during the 1910s, such as the 1913 Massachusetts Minimum Wage Law for Women, the first of its kind in the nation. The NWTUL fought for minimum-wage laws for female workers across the country and succeeded in several other states in addition to Massachusetts, until all such laws were found unconstitutional by the 1923 Supreme Court decision *Adkins v. Children's Hospital of District*

of Columbia. In lobbying for protective-labor legislation, the WTUL increasingly came to realize the importance of women's suffrage and joined that mostly white, middle-class movement in earnest in 1911 when it formed the Wage-Earners' League for Woman Suffrage. Schneiderman and Newman, both veteran organizers for the International Ladies' Garment Workers' Union and active in the New York WTUL, were especially active in the WTUL women's suffrage campaign that finally achieved its goals in 1920 with the passage of the Nineteenth Amendment. However this unity around gaining women's suffrage was short-lived. The industrial feminism, as it was then called, of white, working-class women, such as in the WTUL, differed from that of many middle-class women on some key points. This became especially evident in the postsuffrage years when the WTUL opposed the Equal Rights Amendment as put forward by the National Women's party beginning in 1923, citing the danger the ERA would pose to the protective labor legislation the WTUL had fought so hard to achieve. Increasingly the WTUL turned to the federal government in its efforts to improve working conditions for women. After World War I several organizations, including the NWTUL, pushed for the creation of a Women's Bureau within the U.S. Department of Labor. When created in 1920, the first director was former shoe worker and long time Chicago WTUL leader, Mary Anderson. This collaboration with the federal government increased only during the 1930s when New York WTUL ally Eleanor Roosevelt's husband was elected president. Franklin Roosevelt's New Deal, the monumental legislative response to the onset of the Great Depression, brought many WTUL leaders to Washington, including Schneiderman. President of the NWTUL from 1926 until 1950, Schneiderman would be the only woman appointed to the National Recovery Administration's Labor Advisory Board when it was established in 1933, a position she held for the next 10 years.

In part it was this success in terms of labor legislation on the federal level that led to the eventual demise of the WTUL in 1950. In 1935, Congress passed the Wagner Act, which guaranteed all workers the right to organize; a year later, the Congress of Industrial Organizations (CIO) formed. From its inception the CIO actively recruited industrial workers, skilled and unskilled, including women, and union representation for female workers increased dramatically during the second-half of the 1930s and into World War II. The Fair Labor Standards Act of 1938 established a minimum wage and maximum hours for workers of either sex, though agricultural, food service, and domestic workers—all job categories in which women predominated—were initially excluded. Nonetheless the labor laws that the WTUL had worked so hard to achieve on a state-by-state basis over the years were now federal law. Financially, too, the WTUL had suffered along with the rest of the nation during the Great Depression as even those middle- and upper-class allies who gave so much support curtailed their contributions. This coupled with the changes on a national level led the organization formally to disband in 1950. In its almost 50 years of existence, the WTUL achieved much for wage-earning women while it sought to organize them into trade unions, provide education, and lobby for protective-labor legislation. Even after its demise the WTUL remained an example for later groups, such as the Coalition of Labor and Union Women, as the issues of female workers continue to be addressed.

KATHLEEN BANKS NUTTER

References and Further Reading

Dye, Nancy Schrom. *As Equals and as Sisters: Feminism, the Labor Movement, and the Women's Trade Union League of New York*. Columbia: University of Missouri Press, 1980.

Jacoby, Robin Miller. *The British and American Women's Trade Union Leagues, 1890–1925*. Brooklyn, NY: Carlson Publishers, 1994.

Kessler-Harris, Alice. *A Woman's Wage: Historical Meanings and Social Consequences*. Lexington: University of Kentucky Press, 1990.

———. *Out to Work: A History of Wage-Earning Women in the United States*. New York: Oxford University Press, 1982.

Norkov, Julie. *Constituting Workers, Protecting Women: Gender, Law, and Labor in the Progressive Era and New Deal Years*. Ann Arbor: The University of Michigan Press, 2001.

Nutter, Kathleen Banks. *The Necessity of Organization: Mary Kenney O'Sullivan and Trade Unionism for Women, 1892–1912*. New York: Garland Publishers, 2000.

Orleck, Annelise. *Common Sense and a Little Fire: Women and Working-Class Politics in the United States, 1900–1965*. Chapel Hill: University of North Carolina Press, 1995.

Cases and Statutes Cited

Adkins v. Children's Hospital of District of Columbia.
Fair Labor Standards Act
Wagner Act

See also ***Adkins v. Children's Hospital* (1918); American Federation of Labor; Coalition of Labor Union Women; Congress of Industrial Organizations; Lawrence Strike (1912); Minimum-Wage Laws; National Industrial Recovery Act; Newman, Pauline M.; Robins, Margaret Dreier; Schneiderman, Rose; Textiles; Triangle Shirtwaist Fire; Women's Bureau**

WOODHULL, VICTORIA (1838–1927)

Victoria Woodhull is known for her firsts—the first woman to run for president of the United States, the first to present an argument before the Judiciary Committee of Congress, the first to open a brokerage house in New York City—but her significance lies in brilliantly occupying the crossroads of American reform movements at the midpoint of the nineteenth century.

Victoria California Claflin was the seventh of 10 children born into the poorest family in Homer, Ohio. While her mother earned money selling the patent medicine she brewed at the hearth, her father exploited Victoria's precocious oratorical talents and took her at the age of eight on the revival circuit as a child preacher, then in imitation of the Fox sisters of Rochester, toured Victoria and her sister Tennessee as child spiritualist mediums, alternately starving and beating them to add effect to their trances. When at the age of 14 Victoria's health finally broke from her father's abuse, she was treated by a Dr. Canning Woodhull, a man exactly twice her age who cured her, then eloped with her.

Victoria was 16 when she gave birth to her first disabled child, Byron, and largely on her own, due to her husband's addiction to gin, morphine, and mistresses. She followed Dr. Woodhull to California, where she worked first as a seamstress, then as a bawdy theater actress and casual prostitute, but a few years later, when they headed back to the Midwest, the tables had turned, and Dr. Woodhull, unable to care for himself, followed her.

Her second child, Zulu, arrived in 1861 after Victoria had returned to working the spiritualist circuit and like her first was nearly killed by the botched delivery of a drunken Dr. Woodhull. Her life had become itinerant, with stays in Chicago (opening a short-lived clinic of magnetic healing), and then travels throughout the Midwest with her sister and the rest of the n Claflin clan as a traveling medicine show. In late 1865, Victoria left her family and struck out on her own, making a new start in St. Louis, where she fell in love with Colonel James Harvey Blood, a local war hero and spiritualist, who left his wife and two daughters to marry her. Blood was well-versed in reform politics, which proved to be the missing element of Victoria's latent radicalism. Together they set about to defy the conventions of an oppressive society, such as filing divorce papers just to protest the inequities of the institution of marriage.

Victoria rescued her sister Tennessee from her father, and they all moved to New York City where opportunity abounded, most importantly in the form of Cornelius Vanderbilt, whose deep interest in spiritualism encouraged him to underwrite some of

Victoria's new enterprises. Certainly a reputation as a sage could not have hurt her newly opened brokerage house, Woodhull, Claflin & Co., especially when they showed a tendency to end up on the winning side of highly leveraged bets (though this may have been more attributable to Vanderbilt's insider tips than to the aid of the spirit world). With her profits and expanding credit, Victoria moved into a large brownstone and showed a generosity that was later repaid in scandal. She accepted into her household her ne'erdo-well husband, Dr. Woodhull, who was practically an invalid and lived only a few years more. She welcomed as a permanent guest, Stephen Pearl Andrews, an obscure genius who invented shorthand, a universal language, an impenetrable theory of everything he called Pantarchy, and claimed to have started the Civil War by causing the secession of Texas. Over time she eventually housed most of the members of her large family, including her mother, who repaid her kindness by unsuccessfully suing to have Col. Blood evicted from the household and to assume ownership of Victoria's properties.

In April 1870, Victoria Woodhull announced that she was running for president of the United States (on her own Cosmo-Political party, which later changed its name to the Equal Rights party) in order to illustrate "the rights I already possess," observing the fact that while she was barred from voting by state law, she had a perfect right to hold the highest office in the land according to the qualifications stipulated in the U.S. Constitution. Though it began as a means of ballyhooing her campaign, the newspaper she started, *Woodhull & Claflin's Weekly*, soon expanded to champion the full myriad of reform movements then percolating through the nation.

Woodhull was viewed suspiciously by the other women's rights reformers who gathered in Washington, DC, for the 1871 National Women Suffrage Association, though she quickly became, for a short time, their hero when she secured an audience before the Judiciary Committee of the House and delivered a memorial arguing that the Fourteenth Amendment had established women's suffrage and that the continuing denial of the right of women to vote was therefore unconstitutional. Over the next year Woodhull became a notorious celebrity who packed halls with lectures on women's rights and free love, currency reform, cooperative economics, and "stirpiculture" (an early form of Eugenics). She also embraced the cause of radical labor reform and placed her newspaper at the disposal of the English-speaking faction of the International Workingmen's Association, and became the first American publication to reprint the *Communist Manifesto* (translated into English by Andrews). But her presence also proved to be one of the poles of controversy within the first U.S. Marxist labor organization and contributed to its ultimately splitting along ethnic and ideological lines.

In November of 1872, Woodhull published details of the scandalous affair between the nation's most famous Protestant minister, Henry Ward Beecher, and the wife of the well-known reformer and her intimate friend, Theodore Tilton. Arrested for publishing obscene material, a violation of the recently passed federal Comstock Act, she and her sister Tennessee were jailed twice though ultimately acquitted. However the legal ordeal drained them of their wealth and broke Victoria's health. In 1877, she and Tennessee sailed to England (a trip possibly paid for by the heirs of Vanderbilt to remove her from a pitched battle over his estate), where they both married wealthy aristocrats.

In 1892, Victoria resumed her interests in reform and with her daughter Zulu as coeditor, published the *Humanitarian*, which while more conservative than her old weekly, maintained her breadth of interests. Retiring from publishing in 1901, Victoria established her home as a bohemian salon that welcomed a long train of eccentric visitors to the dismay of the local villagers. She died near the beach in Brighton in 1927 at the age of 89.

TIMOTHY MESSER-KRUSE

References and Further Reading

Goldsmith, Barbara. *Other Powers: The Age of Suffrage, Spiritualism, and the Scandalous Victoria Woodhull*. New York: Alfred A. Knopf, 1998.
Stern, Madeleine B. *The Woodhull Reader*. Weston, MA: M & S Press, 1974.

Cases and Statutes Cited

Comstock Act

WORK ETHIC

The work ethic defies easy explanation. As a matter for academic investigation, the work ethic transcends strict disciplinary boundaries and has been the subject of scholarly debate in a variety of academic disciplines: Sociology, anthropology, economics, and political science, to name only a few. As a concept though, the scope of work ethic's influence reaches far beyond the boundaries of academic discourse and penetrates deep into American cultural life providing an important source of both popular mythology and individual identity.

Historically when scholars have discussed the work ethic, they have treated it as a uniquely Western phenomenon; however the idea of a work ethic is not endemic to one culture (for instance it is not uncommon to speak of the Confucian work ethic). When offering definitions of the work ethic, scholars and laypersons alike usually refer to a particular attitude toward work. To have a strong work ethic is to find intrinsic value in work, and usually this value is thought to transcend mere material considerations. The idea of the work ethic is irreducible to work itself; merely working is not sufficient evidence of a work ethic. Instead it is the way in which an individual approaches work that is important. Persons with a strong work ethic are lauded for their commitment to hard work and sacrifice and usually display a degree of self-discipline. Furthermore the work ethic is often considered a testament to a person's moral value, and those who fail to demonstrate such an ethic are often judged harshly.

The Work Ethic in Religion

Most commonly when scholars discuss an American work ethic, they are talking about a conception of the work ethic thought to be rooted in the Protestant tradition, and this Protestant work ethic was most famously explored in Max Weber's *The Protestant Ethic and the Spirit of Capitalism*, originally published in 1905. Protestantism, Weber explained, laid a unique foundation for the rise of industrial capitalism because it gave moral value to earthly activity, augmenting previous conceptions of religious devotion with a commitment to one's working life. Weber traces the Protestant work ethic to Luther's initial rejection of monasticism and his belief that even the layperson could lead the devoted life through the dedicated pursuit of an earthly calling. What begins with Luther however is made explicit by Calvin, and it is in Calvinism that Weber finds the most potent source of the modern work ethic. In Calvinism the role of the work ethic was threefold: First the work ethic was thought to provide the best evidence that a particular individual was among the elect and predestined for salvation. Second the absence of a work ethic could reveal to the community of believers the identity of those who were not so fortunate. Finally Calvinism more than any other Protestant sect justified working in pursuit of a profit and encouraged individuals to invest their profits back into their earthly pursuits.

Given Protestantism's role in the religious and cultural life of the early American colonies, it is not surprising to find the Protestant version of the work ethic so entrenched in the American identity. Whether expressed by colonial preachers, such as John Winthrop (1588–1649), John Cotton (1584–1652), or Cotton Mather (1663–1728), the idea of serving God through a commitment to one's own calling was quite consistent with the project of civilizing the new world in the face of overwhelming circumstances, and as the colonies blossomed, the work ethic provided an important standard by which to judge the commitment and character of the colonial citizen. The work of Mather is exemplary in this respect: Mather is among the first American Protestant ministers to accept the accumulation of wealth as consistent with the religious duty of a calling. In his *Bonifacius* (1710), he explains to good Christians that a life of riches can be a moral life as long as one remembers that those riches are a gift from God to the deserving and as good Christians, they are obligated to return a portion of these gifts to the community. At the same time Mather warned that damnation was sure to follow idleness. In an early expression of what has now become a popular response to poverty and unemployment, Mather advised fellow Christians against giving simple charity to one's less-fortunate neighbors; their salvation could be assured, he argued, only by finding them work and insisting that they keep it.

Although many scholars of the work ethic—Max Weber among them—saw the Protestant ethic as the source of mostly middle-class values and bourgeois business acumen, it must be noted that religious notions of the work ethic have been important elements in cultivating working-class consciousness as well. With the rise of American industrialism, both labor organizers and rank-and-file workers drew from religious traditions in an attempt to counter the capitalist attempts to increase their own wealth through the exploitation of labor. Gilded Age workers for instance turned to the work ethic to reclaim the intrinsic value of their own labor, and the gospel of wealth preached by industrialists was often met by the gospel of labor preached in both churches and union halls. Drawing as much from Christianity as they did from radical socialism, many American workers held firm in their belief that labor was a gift from God; to make one's livelihood through the sweat of his or her own brow was among the most significant earthly manifestations of God's magnificence. An economic system that allowed one person to benefit from another's labor, without appropriate recompense, was considered among the most aberrant forms of exploitation.

The Work Ethic in Politics

Whether religious or secular in origin, the concept of a work ethic had an important role to play in the politics of the revolutionary-era United States. For those who dreamed of a new social order free from monarchical reign, a positive attitude toward work served as an important distinction between citizens of the new nation and the British aristocracy who still viewed labor as a curse meant solely for the lower classes.

The importance of this ethic to the political history of the early republic cannot be overstated. Some of the earliest partisan divisions revolved around the role of work and the work ethic in American life. Whether it was Jeffersonian Republicans or Jacksonian Democrats, the strategy was often the same: Appeal to a common work ethic to paint the opposition as adherents to the old aristocratic order, a leisurely class whose wealth rested on the back of another's labor. The work ethic provided a valuable character trait thought to be common to the early nation's emerging middle-class of artisans, farmers, and small entrepreneurs. The work ethic was an outward sign of fitness for self-determination and distinguished the middle class of American citizens from both the aristocratic elite (who do not work) and the growing population of African slaves (who are not free).

At no time was this fact of American political life more relevant than in the years preceding the Civil War. The Republican party for instance built the work ethic and the accompanying concept of free labor into their ideological opposition to slavery. For Republicans one of the great sins of the southern aristocracy was the fact that they devalued the labor of blacks and poor whites alike. The South was damned not only morally but economically; in fact the two could not be disconnected. By disallowing free labor, the South betrayed the American promise of social mobility and stifled the rise of a vibrant middle class thought necessary for economic and moral progress. For many of the Republican faithful, this was the South's greatest sin.

Using the work ethic as part of a political strategy that paints another in a negative light is not limited to partisan politics; it has played a role in a multitude of political struggles, not the least of which has been the ongoing struggle between capital and labor. Some conception of the work ethic was often an important element of capital's various schemes of accumulating wealth. For instance Fredrick Taylor's system of scientific management was among other things a system aimed at increasing the productivity of individual workers by instilling in them a materialistic work ethic and rewarding productive work accordingly. Labor often responded to these attempts by employing its own interpretation of the moral value of work, one that was meant to raise the consciousness of alienated workers. Industrialism, labor often argued, betrayed the promise of the work ethic by failing to reward an individual for his or her own dedication to work: First industrial factory work stripped the worker of the ability to fulfill the promise of self-determination thought to follow from a strong work ethic. Second it betrayed the promise that a strong work ethic would be rewarded, and many within the labor movement claimed that industrial capitalism in fact robbed workers of their labor's ultimate value regardless of how hard they labored and how much they were paid for their labor; no compensation could equate to labor's intrinsic value.

The work ethic has also been used as an important element in the politics of discrimination and bigotry. Gender discrimination for instance has often revolved around the work ethic's interpretation as a masculine attribute. Contrary to women's lived experiences, women were often portrayed in the popular imagination as the intrinsically idle sex, capable of only the most mindless of employments. If the work ethic had everything to do with the sense of liberty and self-determination that characterized American masculinity, then it seemed to have little to do with the perceived dependency of womanhood.

In fact many of the most potent ethnic stereotypes have traditionally included the assumption that the group in question lacks a strong work ethic and as a corollary the ability to contribute to American society. Laziness was primary among the negative qualities that informed discrimination against African-Americans long after the abolition of slavery. Furthermore the discrimination against immigrants in the United States has always revolved around the perceived absence of a commitment to hard work. It is still common to see stereotypical depictions of immigrants and racial minorities that emphasize their supposed lack of a proper American work ethic.

The Work Ethic in Culture

As a core value of American life, the work ethic has been reinforced through a variety of cultural forms, all of which follow religion and politics in advancing the work ethic as a moral virtue, one usually thought to be necessary for social mobility. This was especially evident during the industrial revolution. In nineteenth-century children's literature, authors, such as Horatio Alger, Jacob Abbott, and Mari Edgeworth, all contributed popular stories that advocated the work ethic as central to moral character, and although it is easy to exaggerate the ways in which the themes of these works are similar, generally they all share a common concern: Their narratives teach the values of hard work and self-discipline by weaving stories around the multiple successes of the industriousness and the multiple failures of the slothful.

The literary and cultural fascination with the American West told a similar story. Westward expansion was interpreted as a testament to the hard work and commitment of the American character, and these attributes were further propagated by a genre of popular literature that told the stories, albeit fictionalized, of those who conquered this vast frontier. In his famous frontier thesis delivered to the American Historical Association in 1893, Fredrick Jackson Turner explained how the values of hard work and self-determination necessary to civilize the savage terrain of the American West were fundamental characteristics of the American self. Drawing on both the religious and political origins of the work ethic, this particularly American mythology paved the way for Herbert Hoover's eventual appeal to the rugged individualism of Americans in his 1928 presidential campaign.

The work ethic still remains an important part of the American cultural imagination, primarily through its relationship to the promise of the American dream. Pulling from many aspects of American culture, unbridled faith in the possibility of achieving this dream demands equal faith in the power of the work ethic, and although the American dream is often thought to be available to all, there is an accompanying belief that only the committed few can actually realize it. (In fact when Americans are asked, they regularly think hard work is more important than starting position when predicting one's ability to climb the socioeconomic ladder.) Harkening back to its Protestant roots, this contemporary work ethic is often employed to justify socio-economic inequality and disparity in wealth. The spoils of the American dream, it is argued, rightfully go to the deserving, and those whose dreams go unrealized have only themselves to blame. Like its predecessors this version of the work ethic is very individual in nature and is consistent with the priority of individualism in American culture.

G. V. DAVIS

References and Further Reading

Applebaum, Herbert. *The Concept of Work: Ancient, Medieval, and Modern.* Albany, NY: SUNY Press, 1991.
———. *The American Work Ethic and the Changing Work Force: A Historical Perspective.* Westport, CT: Greenwood Press, 1998.
Beder, Sharon. *Selling the Work the Ethic: From Puritan Pulpit to Corporate PR.* New York: Zed Books, 2002.
Bernstein, Paul. *American Work Values: Their Origin and Development.* Albany: State University of New York Press, 1997.
Foner, Eric. *Free Soil, Free Labor, Free Men.* New York: Oxford University Press, 1995.
Gutman, Herbert. "Protestantism and the American Labor Movement: The Christian Spirit of the Gilded Age." *American Historical Review* 72, 1 (1966): 74–101.
Mather, Cotton. *Bonifacius: An Essay upon the Good,* edited by David Levin. Cambridge, MA: Belknap Press of Harvard University Press, 1966.
Rodgers, Daniel T. *The Work Ethic in Industrial America, 1850–1920.* Chicago, IL: The University of Chicago Press, 1978.
Scott, Janny, and David E. Leonhardt. "Class in America: Shadowy Lines That Still Divide." *New York Times* (May 15, 2005): A-1.
Weber, Max. "The Social Psychology of World Religions." In *From Max Weber: Essays in Sociology,* edited by Gerth and Mills. New York: Oxford University Press, 1946.
———. *The Protestant Ethic and the Spirit of Capitalism,* Talcott Parsons, translator. New York: Charles Scribner's Sons, 1958.
Wood, Gordon. *The Radicalism of the American Revolution.* New York: Vintage, 1993.

WORKER MOBILIZATION, MANAGEMENT RESISTANCE: 1920s

American workers in the 1920s experienced a number of dramatic transformations. Labor militancy following World War I and hopes for an expansion of industrial democracy gave way to retreat and conservatism within the labor movement. In expanding mass-production industries, management steadily asserted its control. In the early years of the decade, workers launched a range of political efforts to advance more democratic interventions of government into the economy. By decade's end it was clear to many workers that the state reinforced conservative business goals and nativist policies. Sharing unevenly in the celebrated prosperity of the decade, workers initially participated in consumerism in ways that supported ethnic and racial identities. Mass culture increasingly threatened community control over consumption as the 1930s began. On the whole the twenties witnessed a growing shift away from worker efforts to democratize production and toward concerns about more equal participation in consumer culture.

Postwar Confrontations

World War I profoundly shaped the character of the decade that followed. It created new expectations for federal government interventions to advance industrial democracy even as the war led some officials to repress radicalism. Debates about patriotism and the meaning of immigration intensified during the conflict, generating new pressure in the years ahead for restrictions and support for a narrow definition of

Row of completed "Tin Lizzies" or Model T's come off the Ford assembly line. Library of Congress, Prints & Photographs Division [LC-USZ62-63968].

Americanism. Though the war accelerated demographic changes and opened up new possibilities for industrial unionism, the democratic promise of labor mobilizations faded in the immediate postwar years. Most unions retreated after 1922, and the federal government shifted its support toward employers who defused the radical potential of industrial democracy with company unionism and welfare capitalism.

The postwar strike wave from 1919–1922 ended in bitter disappointment for workers. The defeats of the Seattle General Strike and the steel strike by the end of 1919 coincided with government roundups of immigrant radicals across the United States. Defiant displays of working-class unity faced strong opposition from employers, city authorities, and state governments during this turbulent period. Rejecting working-class proposals to nationalize major industries, officials in the Wilson and Harding administrations committed themselves instead to bringing down prices and defending the existing social order. Employers and government officials frequently joined forces to mobilize the public against collective industrial action. Union membership had peaked in 1920 at over five

million workers, only to decline to 3.6 million just 3 years later.

Important examples of these trends in the immediate postwar period can be seen in the meatpacking industry. During World War I leaders of the Chicago labor movement had begun to organize racially and ethnically diverse packinghouse workers into an industrial union. Federal mediation briefly enhanced worker strength but limited strike possibilities. When meat prices began to fall in the early twenties, the big five packers revived an anti-union campaign and pledged to cut wages and increase working hours. The Harding administration did not renew federal wartime agreements. Packinghouse workers struck late in 1921, sparking an unequal confrontation. The packers were united by economic crisis and supported by local and state governments. Unionists were plagued with financial and organizational problems, fragmented by race, ethnicity, and skill, and without federal oversight. Police attacks against picketing workers generated high levels of violence and rioting in Chicago. Though Denver suffered no violent confrontations during the walkout, a district court judge ordered the imprisonment of local union leaders for calling a strike that threatened the public interest.

Shifting Management and Labor Relations

The defeat of major postwar strikes and the dismantling of wartime agreements paved the way for changes in management and labor relations during the 1920s. Bent on challenging wartime gains, employers in oligopolistic industries increasingly combined welfare capitalism with open-shop drives in order to combat unionization. Bethlehem Steel, Goodyear, General Electric, and International Harvest, among others, promised workers pensions, modest insurance plans, subsidized mortgages, and social programs. Southern textile mill owners built churches and hired sympathetic ministers. Welfare capitalism touched the lives of roughly four million workers at its height. Administering these limited programs were employee-representation plans or company unions. Although publicized examples predated the war, company unions were widely celebrated in the mainstream press. Touted by employers as a form of industrial democracy, company unions circumscribed the issues that workers could address. Mimicking bona fide trade unions, company unions stabilized labor relations by weeding out radicals and constraining worker protest.

Many of the organizational and management techniques that shaped mass-production industries during the decade began at the Ford Motor Company. Though others had experimented with assembly-line construction, Ford refined such techniques on a scale previously unmatched after 1913. By 1928, his River Rouge complex in Dearborn, Michigan, featured a continuously moving chain of production that could turn out 6,400 cars in one day. To lower turnover rates and discourage union organizing, Ford initially reduced working hours and increased wages to 5 dollars a day, double the prevailing wage for semiskilled workers in Detroit. Yet skilled workers increasingly gave way to semiskilled and unskilled machine tenders. The automaker imposed strict rules for shop floor behavior, created a sociological department to investigate workers' private lives, and maintained a private spy network to suppress union efforts and physically intimidate organizers. Throughout the decade the automobile industry stimulated a host of related businesses like steel, glass, rubber, and petroleum. These expanding sectors of the economy demonstrated particular hostility toward unions during the 1920s. Though industrial workers produced the goods that fueled the prosperity of the decade, they increasingly lost control and authority on the shop floor.

The technical and organizational changes that marked mass production during the 1920s were not uniformly experienced by workers. Agriculture was only partly changed by the introduction of mechanized harvesters and tractors. The African-Americans and Chicanos who harvested cotton, fruits, sugar beets, and vegetables endured difficult hand labor and oppressive management tactics. The construction industry, which enjoyed a decade of dramatic growth fueled by a surge in demand for new homes, also continued to rely on hand labor. Women's service and sales work at times centered on interactions with clients that managers could less directly supervise.

The 1920s saw a steady decline in strike activity. Americans had witnessed roughly 3,500 strikes per year from 1916–1921. By the end of the decade, that number had fallen to only 790 per year. The militant confrontations of the immediate postwar years gave way to more indirect and submerged worker challenges. A few dramatic strikes did punctuate the otherwise calm years of the late 1920s, but these reflected the militancy of diverse workers typically outside mass-production industries. Unionized Chicano farm workers in California tested the growing power of agribusiness. Unorganized textile workers in the South, the majority of them women, walked out to protest the stretch out, night work, and the oppressive hand of the employer in company towns. One group of African-American workers mobilized within the Brotherhood of Sleeping Car Porters to confront the oppressive management of the Pullman Company. But these protests achieved little in the short run even as they lay the groundwork for some successes in the 1930s.

The most influential labor federation in the 1920s, the American Federation of Labor (AFL), largely accommodated itself to management changes. Dominated by affiliated unions in coal, clothing, printing, public service, transportation, and construction, the AFL focused chiefly on the concerns of conservative craft unionists in local market sectors of the economy. The death of long-time AFL President Samuel Gompers in December 1924, created an opportunity for more conciliatory leadership under William Green. Promoting union-management cooperation, Green even oversaw the reversal of the AFL's long-standing opposition to scientific management. Though the federation "shifted from militancy to respectability," as historian Irving Bernstein has aptly noted (*The Lean Years*, 1960), talk of union-management partnerships achieved little for workers. The AFL struggled to respond to falling membership over the decade. Construction and transportation unions did maintain or even increase their membership rolls over the decade. But unions in mining and clothing manufacture lost significant numbers. Workers in these industries suffered from overcapacity, overproduction, and downward pressure on wages.

The AFL mostly ignored the growing service sector, which increasingly provided opportunities for female workers. At the start of the decade, more women worked in clerical or sales work than in manufacturing or domestic service. White women particularly gained new opportunities even as black wage-earning women remained largely confined to domestic service. Though wage earning promised a measure of economic independence, female workers struggled against discrimination by employers and within some unions. Labor force segmentation and expectations that marriage should end wage work for women constrained female ambition during the decade. Some working-women looked to the state to address economic inequalities.

Labor Politics

Despite long-standing suspicions of the state among AFL leaders, electoral politics captured the attention of a significant group of workers in the early 1920s. Mine and railroad union leaders were at the forefront of a progressive bloc advancing broad visions of government activism. The plan for government ownership of the railroads sketched by Glenn Plumb became a rallying point for a range of reformers urging ambitious social welfare programs. In 1922, members of the railroad brotherhoods, the stationary engineers, and the machinist unions organized a national Conference for Progressive Political Action (CPPA). Though rejecting calls for a third party, CPPA activists created local and state branches that worked to elect a number of progressive candidates in 1922 while helping to defeat several champions of the open shop in Congress.

Additionally the first years of the new decade witnessed a brief revival of independent labor politics. Unionists in Chicago and New York organized an independent labor party. Worker alliances with farmers also appeared promising. Building on the success of the Non-Partisan League in North Dakota, a number of farmer-labor groups in the Midwest and Far West called for public ownership of key industries and banks, public-works programs, legal protections for collective bargaining, and public housing.

The 1924 presidential campaign marked a high point of progressive labor and farmer activism during the decade. Farmer-labor coalitions, the CPPA, and even the AFL leadership joined forces to support

Wisconsin Senator Robert M. La Follette's campaign for the presidency. La Follette attempted to redefine the public interest in terms less hostile to labor while supporting collective bargaining and limits to court injunctions against striking unionists. Organizational and financial problems however plagued his campaign. In some communities divisive battles over the rise of the Klan and prohibition overshadowed this progressive challenge. Though Coolidge carried the election with 15 million votes, La Follette collected nearly five million. Ethnic voters in the late 1920s did not yet participate in electoral politics in ways that reinforced class critiques.

Governmental Interventions

Despite labor defeats at the polls, the role of government in economic life remained a contested issue. Often state action worked to the detriment of organized labor. Colorado and Kansas experimented with compulsory arbitration boards that narrowly defined the rights of the public in terms of uninterrupted production of basic consumer necessities. Court injunctions were widely used against striking workers during the decade, most notably during the nationwide railroad strike of 1922. U.S. Supreme Court decisions also constrained strike and picketing activity in such cases as *Duplex Printing Press Co. v. Deering* (1921) and *Truax v. Corrigan* (1921) illustrate. By the early 1930s, however, abusive injunctions against struggling coal miners ignited a successful movement to secure congressional support for anti-injunction legislation.

For female workers government action sparked intense debate during the 1920s. Growing judicial approval of sex-specific protective labor legislation raised important moral and political issues. Earlier Supreme Court rulings like *Muller v. Oregon* had affirmed state authority to set maximum hours for women on the grounds of their biological difference from men and potential maternity. Though such legislation could serve as an entering wedge to advance protections for all workers, it also threatened to isolate women from the laboring mainstream. By 1920, male unionists, many employers, the National Consumers' League, and officials in the U.S. Women's Bureau embraced protection.

Yet sex-specific protective labor law faced a key test during the decade. Following the success of the woman's suffrage movement in 1920, leaders of the National Women's party rallied support for an Equal Rights Amendment (ERA) to the Constitution. Successfully persuading Congress to introduce the measure in 1923, ERA advocates insisted that protective laws penalized female workers and legitimated a view of femininity that rested on maternity and biological weakness. Protection activists countered that the ERA would jeopardize hard-won gains to protect workingwomen. Working-class women remained divided by the debate. Some, like Fannia Cohn of the garment workers' union, argued that unionization rather than legislation offered the best protection for workingwomen as it did for men. But because of the obstacles to women's organization, Cohn felt that "it would be folly to agitate against protective legislation." In its 1923 *Adkins v. Children's Hospital* decision, the U.S. Supreme Court struck down a minimum-wage law for women in a blow to protection advocates. During the New Deal, however, the minimum wage campaign ultimately bore fruit with the Fair Labor Standards Act.

The federal government during the 1920s was not only a site of struggle over protective legislation for female workers. It also transformed the meaning of ethnicity and race with changes in immigration policy. The AFL leadership and many western affiliates had long called for restrictions on immigration to limit competition for working-class jobs. Fears of immigrant diversity, dissent in ethnic communities, and antiradical crusades during and after the Great War generated a growing consensus among native-born Americans for restriction. In 1921, and more conclusively in 1924, Congress approved dramatic restrictions on immigration from southern and Eastern Europe, while excluding outright any remaining immigration from Asia. The new quota system had a tremendous impact on the working class. Communities of southern and Eastern European immigrants became more settled and confronted steady Americanization pressure. The new national-origins system also transformed a formerly multi-ethnic nation into a white republic, separating white ethnicity from non-white race. Congress allowed Mexican immigration to continue however in order to provide cheap labor for western agribusiness. Escaping quota restrictions, Mexican immigrants soon confronted a new border patrol. With its changing immigration policy, the federal government created new links between citizenship and whiteness that would last for decades.

Working-class immigrants moreover could not assume that the state would protect their civil liberties. The trial of two Italian-born anarchists, Nicola Sacco and Bartolomeo Vanzetti, particularly highlighted the excesses of nativism and brought home to many immigrants the coercive power of the state. Accused of robbery and murder in Braintree, Massachusetts, Sacco and Vanzetti stood trial in 1921 as much for their political beliefs. Though their trial was marred by questionable evidence, the two men were convicted

of murder. Six years of appeals and a murder confession from another anarchist could not avert the execution of Sacco and Vanzetti on August 22, 1927. Crowds across the United States and around the world gathered in protest, and immigrant workers in a number of locations walked off their jobs.

Diverse Workers and Mass Consumption

Immigration policy and Americanization campaigns were not the only pressures on ethnic and racial identity among workers. The pervasive impact of mass culture threatened to lessen the salience of both. Cars, radios, movies, home appliances, commercial recreation, and sports all helped to integrate previously isolated groups into the mass cultural mainstream. But they did so in uneven ways, as workers sought to give their consumption an ethnic or racial cast.

Family income clearly shaped possibilities for participating in the consumer culture of the decade. Prosperity was not uniformly experienced, as unemployment and seasonal layoffs continued to plague many workers. Contemporary studies of income levels and consumer spending suggest that workers did not widely share in the consumption of consumer goods, with skilled workers participating more fully in the much-advertised prosperity. Middle-income Americans, rather than members of the working class, were most likely to buy goods on credit.

In her study of Chicago communities, Lizbeth Cohen argued that the impact of mass culture in immigrant neighborhoods depended on the social and economic contexts in which it developed. Chain stores did not widely penetrate working-class, immigrant communities at first. Movie theaters initially reflected the ethnic values of the local community, but the pressure of consolidation in the movie business worked to crowd out local theaters by the late 1920s. Hollywood increasingly appealed to middle-class audiences in the 1920s, shifting the target audience for many films away from the working class. Ethnic, religious, and labor organizations used local radio to reinforce community identities, until the pressure of commercialization became too great. Contacts with mass culture had the most profound effect on the children of new immigrants, worrying parents and religious leaders. But even mainstream mass culture did not always reflect the values of the Protestant middle class.

African-American immigrants in northern cities like Chicago participated more widely in mainstream commercial life but did so in ways that forged a new urban black culture. Black migrants continued to leave the rural and urban South in record numbers during the 1920s, a trend initiated during the Great War. From 1920–1930, over 800,000 headed north in search of economic opportunity and a measure of freedom. The discrimination they faced in residential, political, and industrial life worked to reinforce racial ties. Marcus Garvey's United Negro Improvement Association sparked a broad movement that stressed the importance of black-owned businesses and encouraged a new race pride. Black musicians and recording companies helped to define white mass culture in terms of jazz. While large enterprises like Victrola dominated the recording industry, local companies could reproduce music that reinforced racial and ethnic identities whether in black Chicago or Mexican-American neighborhoods in Los Angeles.

The focus on consumption during the twenties offered workingmen and women some political possibilities. Working-class cooperatives, boycott, and union-label campaigns could become tools for enhancing trade union influence or even restructuring the consumer economy in more democratic directions. But these campaigns often faltered without broad support from working-class housewives. They also suffered from racial exclusions that divided potential class allies.

Generally working-class Americans turned in the 1920s to consumption and leisure for a measure of compensation for the loss of influence on the job and harshness of work life. Even though the culture of consumption could still affirm community ties, industrial productivity increasingly outpaced the ability of many to consume. After the stock market crash of 1929, this problem became much harder for Americans to ignore.

R. TODD LAUGEN

References and Further Reading

Bernstein, Irving. *The Lean Years: A History of the American Workers, 1920–1933.* Boston, MA: Houghton Mifflin, 1960.

Bucki, Cecelia. *Bridgeport's Socialist New Deal, 1915–36.* Urbana: University of Illinois Press, 2001.

Cohen, Lizbeth. *Making a New Deal: Industrial Workers in Chicago, 1919–1939.* Cambridge, UK: Cambridge University Press, 1990.

Dumenil, Lynn. *The Modern Temper: American Culture and Society in the 1920s.* New York: Hill and Wang, 1995.

Frank, Dana. *Purchasing Power: Consumer Organizing, Gender, and the Seattle Labor Movement, 1919–1929.* Cambridge, UK: Cambridge University Press, 1994.

Hall, Jacquelyn Dowd, et al. *Like a Family: The Making of a Southern Cotton Mill World.* Chapel Hill: University of North Carolina Press, 1987.

Kessler-Harris, Alice. *Out to Work: A History of Wage-Earning Women in the United States.* Oxford, UK: Oxford University Press, 1982.

Meyer, Stephen, III. *The Five-Dollar Day: Labor Management and Social Control in the Ford Motor Company, 1908–1921.* Albany: State University of New York Press, 1981.

Montgomery, David. "Thinking about American Workers in the 1920s." *International Labor and Working-Class History* 32 (fall 1987): 4–24.

Ngai, Mae. "The Architecture of Race in American Immigration Law." *Journal of American History* 86 (1999).

Novkov, Julie. *Constituting Workers, Protecting Women: Gender, Law, and Labor in the Progressive Era and New Deal Years.* Ann Arbor: University of Michigan Press, 2001.

Stricker, Frank. "Affluence for Whom? Another Look at Prosperity and the Working Classes in the 1920s." *Labor History* 24 (1983): 5–33.

Cases and Statutes Cited

Adkins v. Children's Hospital
Duplex Printing Press Co. v. Deering
Muller v. Oregon
Truax v. Corrigan

WORKERS' ALLIANCE OF AMERICA

The Workers' Alliance of America was a nationwide, mass movement of relief workers, recipients of direct relief, and unemployed workers formed in the United States in 1935 and dissolved in 1941. The organization was initially created through the merger of Socialist-led groups of unemployed workers with the Musteite Unemployed Leagues. In 1936, the Communist-led Unemployed Councils were also folded into the Workers' Alliance, although non-Communist leaders retained a majority on the alliance's national executive board.

Workers' Alliance locals elected delegates to countywide or statewide organizations, which in turn elected delegates to nationwide annual conventions. For most of its existence, David Lasser (its non-Communist president) and Herbert Benjamin (its Communist secretary-treasurer) led the Workers' Alliance at the national level. The movement grew rapidly, prompting the *New York Times* to warn in 1938 that it was becoming "an enormous pressure group compared with which the American Legion and the farm lobbies may pale into insignificance." By 1939, the Workers' Alliance claimed several hundred thousand members, reportedly exercised an influence over about 1.5 million Americans and included a total of 1,521 locals in 45 states, the District of Columbia, and Puerto Rico. Nearly all of the organization's monthly income (about $4,000 on average in 1939) came from membership dues, initiation fees, charter fees, and the sale of organizational supplies and literature to members.

The Workers' Alliance fought for a permanent, practical, and adequate works program for the unemployed. In practice this meant additional funding for the Works Progress Administration (WPA), more WPA jobs, higher wages for WPA workers, and application of new federal labor laws to the WPA. The Workers' Alliance also sought to secure adequate relief for those not given WPA jobs. At its 1938 National Conference on Work and Security, the movement insisted that "the Federal government makes its contribution only in part when it provides a work program." Accordingly the Workers' Alliance called for the restoration of federal responsibility for general assistance, which was to be accomplished by adding another entitlement to the Social Security Act. However direct relief was seen as a necessary evil. As Lasser put it in 1939, the alliance's primary aim was to "secure work [for the unemployed]—and failing that, enough income to provide security for themselves and their families."

By 1939, three-quarters of Workers' Alliance members were WPA workers, for whom the organization served as a kind of labor union. However since the status of WPA workers as employees was contested, the Workers' Alliance had to struggle to bring into existence the very constituency that labor unions presuppose and represent. In other words the movement demanded not only higher wages and better working conditions for WPA workers, but also recognition of a new identity. As Lasser put it in 1936, "the WPA workers . . . want to be taken out of the twilight zone in which they are not on relief and yet have an essentially relief status. We WPA workers want to work and be treated as workers." Consistent with these claims, the Workers' Alliance sought to forge organizational ties to the American Federation of Labor (AFL) and the Congress of Industrial Organizations (CIO). By the late 1930s, the Workers' Alliance and CIO locals (sometimes joined by AFL locals) had set up unemployment committees in cities throughout the nation to plan and carry out joint actions on issues of common concern. In addition the Workers' Alliance, the AFL, and the CIO cooperated to protest WPA retrenchment in 1939. However cooperation was limited by organizational rivalry and competition. While the AFL's and CIO's willingness to recognize WPA workers as employees confirmed the claims of the Workers' Alliance, it also triggered a struggle over who would represent them.

Women made up roughly 20% of the alliance's membership in 1939. Although often consigned to women's work or relegated to women's auxiliaries, women participated in a broad range of movement activities, including picket lines, demonstrations, and fund raising. Women also assumed leadership positions as organizers, newspaper editors, elected officers, convention delegates, and executive board members at local and national levels. Like women, African-Americans were also active in the Workers' Alliance, forming an estimated 10% of its membership in 1939. Due largely to Communist influence, the Workers' Alliance aggressively advocated racial equality. The movement sought to organize black workers, fought to expand the political rights of southern blacks (particularly through the abolition of the poll tax), and forged growing ties to black civil rights organizations in the late 1930s. These efforts provoked brutal and often violent resistance in the South; Workers' Alliance members and organizers were harassed, tarred and feathered, prohibited from meeting, forced out of town, tear-gassed, jailed, beaten, and shot.

The demise of the Workers' Alliance is typically attributed to economic recovery or co-optation by the Roosevelt administration. Neither explanation is fully convincing. The Workers' Alliance was already in decline by 1939, when unemployment was still high (more than 17% of the civilian labor force). Moreover co-optation was symptomatic of a deeper underlying cause: The rise of an increasingly powerful coalition of Republicans and southern Democrats in Congress in the late 1930s. Concerned about the growing power of the Workers' Alliance and the threat its multiracial organizing might pose to the southern agrarian economy, congressional conservatives led an anti-Communist campaign to delegitimate and repress the movement. At the same time red-baiting and the 1939 nonaggression pact between Nazi Germany and the Soviet Union exacerbated tensions between Communist and non-Communist members of the Workers' Alliance, leading to a costly series of splits, purges, and defections from 1938–1940 External repression and internal conflict over Communist influence within the Workers' Alliance severely hindered the organization's capacity to mobilize resources. By the time the national executive board of the Workers' Alliance dissolved the organization in November 1941, it had dwindled to 200 branches in 25 states.

CHAD ALAN GOLDBERG

Cases and Statutes Cited

Social Security Act

WORKERS' DEFENSE LEAGUE

The Workers' Defense League (WDL) was founded in 1936 to protect the legal rights of workers. Ad hoc committees established in response to the violent repression of labor protests during the Great Depression served as precursors to the WDL. One such committee formed in Terre Haute, Indiana, in 1935, when Socialists protested the imposition of martial law during a labor strike and pressured city officials to release two jailed socialist leaders. Another temporary committee arose in 1936 following violence against organizing sharecroppers in Arkansas. A third precursor to the WDL formed in early 1936, when Socialists rallied public opposition against the kidnapping, torture, and murder of labor organizer Joseph Shoemaker in Tampa, Florida.

Several months after the Tampa rally, on May 28, 1936, the American Socialist party's executive committee voted to establish a permanent institution to coordinate similar activities addressing labor problems. Party leader Norman Thomas chaired an organizing committee whose members included lawyers Francis Heisler and Max Delson, the Reverend Aron S. Gilmartin, and David Clendenin. Clendenin, a Yale graduate spurred to social activism by the Great Depression, was particularly instrumental in the WDL's creation. As the organization's first secretary-treasurer, Clendenin was mainly responsible for establishing the WDL as an alternative to the largely Communist International Defense League (ILD).

Despite its socialist ties, the WDL pledged independence from all political parties. It established two nonpartisan goals: Providing legal aid to workers unfairly accused of violating the law and taking affirmative legal action against abusive employers and public officials. To achieve these goals, the WDL used litigation, education, independent investigations, picketing, protests, and mass mobilization.

The WDL, like the ILD, did not limit itself to particular categories of workers. Not only did it defend industrial laborers, but it also championed the rights of agricultural workers often ignored or marginalized by the organized labor movement. The WDL provided legal support to the interracial Southern Tenant Farmers' Union, founded with the help of Socialists in 1934 to assist farm workers in the Southeast. In the 1930s and 1940s, investigators revealed numerous instances of peonage and involuntary servitude in the South, including the infamous case of slave master Paul Peacher, who was eventually convicted under federal law. The WDL was particularly active in Florida, where it challenged both the unbridled power of sheriffs to arrest African-American workers and the various laws that forced allegedly idle men and women into employment. In Georgia WDL leader Frank McAllister investigated involuntary-servitude complaints and passed on information to the NAACP and to the U.S. Department of Justice for additional legal action.

As the origins of the WDL suggest, the WDL set out to intervene in far more than workplace disputes between employers and employees. In particular the WDL recognized the importance to workers' rights of First Amendment rights to free speech, press, and assembly. As a result, the WDL launched a successful legal campaign in the late 1930s to strike down local ordinances barring leaflet distributions in several states. The WDL also cooperated with other civil liberties organizations to address broader issues of civil rights. Along with the ACLU and the Congress of Industrial Organizations (CIO), the WDL was influential in successfully challenging the antilabor repression of free speech by Mayor Frank "I-am-the-law" Hague in Jersey City, New Jersey. Together with the NAACP, the WDL defended Odell Waller, an African-American sharecropper convicted of killing his landlord over a crop dispute who was eventually executed.

The WDL extended its work beyond the borders of the United States in the late 1940s. It created an International Commission of Inquiry into Forced Labor to investigate involuntary servitude in the American South as well as Communist countries and southern Africa. The WDL, backed by the American Federation of Labor (AFL), succeeded in persuading the United Nations to create a Commission on Forced Labor. In the 1950s, the WDL helped reform the Industrial Personnel Security Program, which had enabled employers to label union organizers security risks to evade federal restrictions on retaliating against union members and leaders. During this period the WDL continued to defend the legal rights of American workers not protected by other organizations. These workers included soldiers in the U.S. military, migrant farm workers, merchant seamen, and the unemployed.

As it matured the WDL continued to address the concerns of minorities and especially of minority workers. The WDL was the first organization to protest the internment of Japanese Americans during World War II, and in the 1960s, its Apprenticeship Program trained more than 30,000 minority youth in the building trades, helping them gain union membership and skilled jobs. In the 1990s, the WDL reaffirmed its commitment to ending forced labor by publicizing new cases of peonage among agricultural workers.

RISA L. GOLUBOFF

References and Further Reading

Fleischman, Harry. *Norman Thomas, A Biography: 1884–1968*. New York: W. W. Norton & Co., 1969.

Sherman, Richard B. *The Case of Odell Waller and Virginia Justice, 1940–1942*. Knoxville: The University of Tennessee Press, 1992.

Shofner, Jerrell H. "The Legacy of Racial Slavery: Free Enterprise and Forced Labor in Florida in the 1940s." *The Journal of Southern History* 47, 3 (1981): 411–426.

See also **International Labor Defense; Sharecropping and Tenancy; Socialist Party of America; Southern Tenant Farmers Union; Thomas, Norman**

WORKERS' COMPENSATION

Workers' compensation statutes govern the obligation of employers to compensate their employees for injuries arising out of and in the course of employment. Workers' compensation—known as workmen's compensation until the 1970s and 1980s—thus functions as an alternative to the common law of torts under which an injured employee could sue an employer in the event of an injury. Compared to tort liability, workers' compensation both simplifies and expands the basis for awarding compensation to employees—relying on work connection rather than fault as its test of liability—while at the same time benefiting employers by limiting damages to legislatively determined benefit rates instead of the significantly more generous jury-determined awards traditionally available in tort law.

The Origins of American Workers' Compensation Statutes

American workers' compensation statutes were enacted beginning in the second decade of the twentieth century. In the years after the Civil War, employees in American industry were injured and killed at rates that dwarfed those in comparable industrializing nations. Overall at the turn of the twentieth century, one worker in 50 was killed or disabled for at least 4 weeks each year because of a work-related accident. This crisis presented a paradox for free-labor thinking, the leading paradigm of American economic, political, and social life after the Civil War. Indeed such free-labor principles as competition among firms, which tended to drive down working conditions, and worker independence, which led employees to disregard safety procedures, appeared to be exacerbating factors in the industrial-accident epidemic. These and other failures of free-labor ideology and the mounting toll on the industrial army gave rise to a series of large-scale experiments in adapting the nineteenth-century law and politics to a new problem of industrial social policy.

Four leading approaches to the accident problem emerged in the United States. Judges, jurists, and legislatures developed the law of employers' liability as an attempt to set principles to govern the rights and duties of employers and employees in the event of work injuries. Workers themselves organized widespread systems of cooperative insurance that may have provided more compensation to injured employees than any other mechanism. Some of the most sophisticated employers developed early private programs of injury compensation. And social insurance advocates began to propose compulsory workers' compensation schemes along the lines of those that had been enacted in Western Europe beginning in the 1880s.

It was hardly inevitable that workers' compensation statutes would become the central American mechanism for compensating work-injury victims. Yet each of the alternatives to workers' compensation faltered in the years leading up to 1910. Notwithstanding a frantic series of legislative amendments, the common law of employers' liability seemed increasingly unable to deal with the mounting number of injured workers. Workers' cooperatives were ever more powerless to police against the proliferation of new, lower cost insurance associations that siphoned off the cooperatives' lowest risk members. Employers' contractual work-injury compensation systems in turn proved far more expensive than the common law of employers' liability, and so in many industries competition from cost-cutting competitors threatened to do in the welfare capitalist experiment in work injury compensation.

Drawing workers' compensation programs from transatlantic progressive policy dialogues, American reformers became convinced that workers' compensation was the best solution to the industrial-accident crisis. In place of tort law's tortured inquiries into the relative rights and duties of employers and employees, they reasoned, workers' compensation would substitute rational compensation based on the needs of injured employees and their families. Where the cooperative insurance societies generally failed to create financial incentives for employers to take safety precautions in the production process, workers' compensation would ensure that employers paid for the costs of the injuries arising out of their operations. And where the costs of employer-specific welfare capitalist plans often created prohibitive competitive disadvantages, compulsory workers' compensation statutes would force all employers in an industry to take on the added injury-compensation costs involved in moving from the common law of tort to workers' compensation.

Yet for all the virtues offered by workers' compensation, the question why workers' compensation statutes were enacted so quickly and with such unanimity in American states in the decades after 1910 has long posed a troubling problem for legal and political historians. Five leading interpretations have emerged. One school of thought contends that workers' compensation statutes were enacted on the basis of a Progressive Era idea of social justice. The corporate liberal school holds, to the contrary, that workers' compensation statutes were enacted to allow employers to avoid the increasing costs of tort lawsuits by shunting injured employees into a system in which payments were perhaps more common but were sharply capped at low-dollar values. A third approach, the prior-regulation approach, is agnostic as to the question of increased or decreased employer costs but associates the enactment of workmen's compensation statutes with the fact that work injuries—unlike sickness or old age—were governed by the law of employers' liability such that enacting workers' compensation statutes did not require the creation of a completely new regulatory regime where none had existed before. The fourth leading explanation—and perhaps the most influential in the literature—is the bargain theory. Under the bargain theory, workers' compensation statutes attracted constituencies sufficient to ensure enactment because they offered something for almost everyone. Employees gained by receiving simple and effective insurance against work accidents. Employers gained by receiving protection from the creeping possibility of high-verdict awards by juries.

Each of these four theories leaves much to be explained. The social justice theory cannot explain why so many sophisticated employers who often declined to support other social insurance reforms were supporters of workmen's compensation. The corporate liberal theory fails to account for the fact that employers' liability insurance rates increased (as they had been predicted to do), often sharply, in the early jurisdictions to enact workers' compensation statutes. The prior regulation theory does not explain why railroad employee injuries—the most heavily regulated injuries under the common law at the turn of the twentieth century—are still governed not by workers' compensation but by the law of employers' liability. And lastly the bargain theory fails to account for the fact that the first general workers' compensation statute in the United States—enacted in New York in 1910—included none of the benefits that the bargain is supposed to have provided. Indeed the New York statute—like several of the other earliest statutes—left employers exposed to potentially high-verdict tort suits by allowing the injured employee to choose ex-post between a lawsuit or a workers' compensation claim.

The fifth leading theory contends that progressive reformers set the agenda for legislation by drawing the workers' compensation model from European policy dialogues. Once on the table, workers' compensation provided benefits to employees whose post-injury recoveries seemed likely to increase, as well as to the sophisticated welfare-capitalist employers who had adopted their own internal work-accident compensation schemes. Only by enacting compulsory statutory compensation schemes could sophisticated firms raise the labor costs of their cut-rate competitors to match the costs they had voluntarily assumed through their private, contractual compensation systems.

In 1910, New York enacted the nation's first important compensation statute. Over the next decade, 42 of the 48 states followed suit. But enactment of the statutes was only the beginning of the story. In early judicial tests in Montana and (most importantly) New York in 1911 (*Ives v. South Buffalo Railway*) courts struck down workers' compensation statutes as unconstitutional takings of the employers' property. A combination of state constitutional amendment, popular outrage, and judicial retreat (for example, *Jensen v. Southern Pacific Co.*, *New York Central RR Co. v. White*) followed, making clear that workers' compensation was not necessarily unconstitutional. Yet the threat of judicial review had a powerful effect on the trajectory and character of workers' compensation in the United States.

The first American compensation statutes, like the workers' compensation program in the United Kingdom to this day, had allowed employees to elect between compensation claims and a lawsuit after being injured. Statutes enacted in the wake of the 1911 New York decision however were redrafted with a *quid pro quo* or exclusive structure in which the employer's obligation to compensate in the absence of fault was matched by the employee's inability to sue in tort for unlimited damages even where the employer had been at fault. Moreover as extra protection from unconstitutionality, statutes enacted after the 1911 New York decision typically adopted an elective or voluntary structure in which employers were subject to the statute only if they opted in or (depending on the state) declined to opt out. Both of these alterations had powerful effects on post-injury compensation. Absent the choice to sue at law, injured employees were left with capped compensation claims. Elective statutes in turn sharply constrained the ability of states to raise compensation benefit rates.

The Administration of Workmen's Compensation

The enactment of workers' compensation statutes coincided with a decline in industrial-accident rates and the end of the U.S. world-historic industrial accident crisis, although it is unclear how much of the progress was due to changed employer accident costs, to widespread public attention that workers' compensation brought to the industrial accident crisis, or to other factors. The success of workers' compensation programs signaled a shift from the free-labor ideology of the post-Civil War moment toward the actuarial categories and managerial models of the twentieth-century state. Where tort law had entailed individual inquiries into the boundaries of individuals' freedom of action, workers' compensation statutes aggregated accident cases and averaged the outcomes. Workmen's compensation thus seemed at times like a kind of entering wedge for a whole panoply of social insurance schemes, schemes that by the middle of the twentieth century would become the modern welfare state.

Compensation statutes also helped to rework many of the nation's legal and political institutions. Many of the reformers who would become leaders in the New Deal cut their teeth on workers' compensation reforms in the 1910s. Compensation statutes introduced the first mass system of administrative adjudication, replacing judges and juries with specialist administrators; they established the constitutional legitimacy of regulating the labor contract; and they supplied a model for the New Deal's programs of economic security and insurance. Workers' compensation statutes anticipated exceptions in New Deal programs for agricultural and domestic laborers. Workers' compensation prefigured the ways in which mid-century American social policy would rely heavily on such private entities as insurance companies, labor unions, and employer human resources departments as the administrative apparatus for implementing social policy. In addition workers' compensation (originally work*men*'s compensation) also set in place the gendered structure of mid-century American welfare state programs, providing benefits through predominantly male wages and often limiting death benefits to widows rather than widowers.

If compensation statutes were models for the twentieth-century administrative state, they foreshadowed its limits as well. Where the turn of the twentieth century had been characterized by eclectic experimentation and openness in the American law of work accidents, by the middle of the twentieth century, an interest-group politics of employers, insurers, plaintiff's lawyers, and labor unions seemed to lock down and ossify reform. Unions and employers for example quickly turned claims hearings from arbitrations of the needs of an injured worker into adversarial contests. Interest group politics also helped to prevent workers' compensation from serving as a model for

social insurance programs, like health insurance, as had been hoped by some of its proponents. In addition interest-group politics helped to ensure that work accident law in the United States would remain a patchwork scheme of overlapping state and federal systems, all existing alongside employers' liability tort schemes for railroad workers and seamen.

In the middle of the twentieth century, interest-group domination of workers' compensation policy also produced expansion in the scope of workers' compensation statutes. Agricultural workers and industrial diseases were brought within the scope of workers' compensation statutes for example as employers saw financial advantages in replacing tort law's open-ended damages awards with compensation programs' legislatively determined damages schedules.

And yet injured workers and their representatives at mid-century also found new ways to expand their post-injury remedies. In such areas of tort law as manufacturers' liability for defective products, the workmen's compensation principle that enterprises should pay for the damages arising out of their operations was yoked to a legal regime that allowed juries to award uncapped damages to injury victims. In addition the legislative dynamics of workers' compensation programs caused claimants' lawyers for the first time to assemble their own lobbying organizations. Those early claimants' lawyer organizations in turn gave rise to the modern American plaintiffs' bar, an institution that by the late twentieth century would be one of the most powerful political forces in the nation. Among other things the plaintiffs' bar has developed a successful practice of bringing tort suits against product manufacturers and other third parties for injuries on the job. Workers' compensation statutes insulate employers from suit because they are an injured employee's exclusive remedy against an employer. But third parties, such as product manufacturers, are not so insulated. And so in so-called third-party suits, which make up about one-half of all products' liability actions in the United States, many injured employees file workers' compensation claims against their employers while simultaneously pursuing high-damage-award product liability actions.

JEAN-DENIS GRÈZE and JOHN FABIAN WITT

References and Further Reading

Aldrich, Mark. *Safety First: Technology, Labor, and Business in the Building of American Work Safety, 1870–1939.* Baltimore, MD: Johns Hopkins University Press, 1997.

Eastman, Crystal. *Work-Accidents and the Law.* New York: Russell Sage Foundation, 1910.

Fishback, Price V., and Shawn Everett Kantor. *A Prelude to the Welfare State: The Origins of Workers' Compensation.* Chicago, IL: University of Chicago Press, 2000.

Larson, Arthur. *Larson's Workers' Compensation Law.* New York: Bender, 1952–.

Nonet, Philippe. *Administrative Justice; Advocacy and Change in a Government Agency.* New York: Russell Sage Foundation, 1969.

Rosner, David, and Gerald E. Markowitz. *Deadly Dust: Silicosis and the Politics of Occupational Disease in Twentieth-Century America.* Princeton, NJ: Princeton University Press, 1991.

Rosner, David, and Gerald E. Markowitz, eds. *Dying for Work: Workers? Safety and Health in Twentieth-Century America.* Bloomington: Indiana University Press, 1987.

Witt, John Fabian. *The Accidental Republic: Crippled Workingmen, Destitute Widows, and the Remaking of American Law.* Cambridge, MA: Harvard University Press, 2004.

———. "Speedy Fred Taylor and the Ironies of Enterprise Liability." *Columbia Law Review* 103 (2003): 1–43.

Cases and Statutes Cited

New York Central RR Co. v. White, 243 U.S. 188 (1917).

Ives v. S. Buffalo Ry. Co., 94 N.E. 431 (N.Y. 1911).

Jensen v. S. Pac. Co., 109 N.E. 600 (N.Y. 1915).

Act of June 25, 1910, ch. 674, 1910 N.Y. Laws 1945.

WORKFARE

Workfare is a federal program that requires those receiving welfare to work in exchange for their benefits. Workfare workers receive no wages, but they continue to receive the welfare benefits (such as subsidized housing, food stamps, or cash payments) for which they are qualified. Work assignments are commonly in the public sector, such as parks' maintenance, janitorial or hospital work, though corporate and non-profit employers also participate, often drawn by salary savings or tax incentives.

Workfare as a concept has a long history beginning with the workhouses and poor farms of the 1600s. However it took on renewed life in the last-half of the twentieth century. The U.S. Congress considered requiring work in exchange for benefits in the mid-fifties, but its advocates were outnumbered by those who sought to keep women (who comprised the majority of welfare recipients) at home. Workfare officially began in 1962 with the Community Work and Training Programs (CWTP) included in Aid to Families with Dependent Children (AFDC) legislation. The CWTP remained small, with only 12 states participating by 1967. Meanwhile the numbers of welfare recipients climbed dramatically. From 1960–1968, their numbers nearly doubled from 745,000 families to 1.5 million, and by 1972, they doubled again, as 3 million families received relief. Spurred by this growing population, welfare rights groups affiliated with the National Welfare Rights Organization demanded higher benefit levels, day care for working parents,

and medical benefits. Expanding rolls provided conservative politicians with an opening to attack welfare. The Nixon administration's Family Assistance Plan (1969) included a punitive workfare provision. Though it was defeated, in part by mobilization of welfare rights activists, its forced-work requirements were incorporated into AFDC.

Workfare differs from government jobs programs, such as the Works Progress Administration during the Great Depression or the Comprehensive Employment and Training Act (CETA) in the 1970s. Those voluntary programs created jobs for unemployed workers seen as deserving them—usually white men. In contrast workfare programs disproportionately affect women and people of color and assume that welfare recipients are unemployed due to lack of motivation, skills, or a work ethic. Most recipients' work lives however are marked with cycles of employment in low-wage jobs or the informal economy, alternating with periods on public assistance. Others are single parents working to raise their children at home.

The Personal Responsibility and Work Opportunity Reconciliation Act (1996) ended six decades of support under AFDC, which the act renamed Temporary Assistance for Needy Families (TANF). The new law, administered by states, ended the concept of welfare as an entitlement program and placed a 5-year lifetime limit on benefits, requiring adults to work after 2 years.

During the 1990s, TANF's workfare requirements enabled politicians to replace union workers with unwaged workfare workers. Tens of thousands of workfare workers performed the same jobs that cities, counties, and private employers had previously paid wages to union workers to perform. In this process of job restructuring, welfare recipients replaced waged workers, who often ended up on the welfare rolls themselves.

One of the largest workfare programs began in New York City in 1995. As attrition thinned the ranks of unionized city workers by some 20,000, their positions were filled with twice that number of part-time workers from the city's Work Experience Program. A similar dynamic occurred across the nation. In San Francisco 3,000 workfare workers labored in public transit and parks; in Los Angeles 25,000 worked in schools and hospitals; in Wisconsin tens of thousands were put to work under that state's plan to cut welfare rolls.

Organizing Workfare Unions

Workfare workers have a history of organizing unions. In 1973, welfare recipients in New York

City's Work Relief Employment Project (WREP) began organizing among the program's 10,000 workers—the vast majority of them African-American and Latinos—who labored at over 400 worksites. With financial support from community groups workers inaugurated United WREP Workers in February 1974. Its objectives included voluntary, adequately paying jobs, and collective-bargaining rights. Its organizing drew from traditional labor movement tactics, such as demonstrations, pickets, and collecting signatures in support of a union election. Support from trade unions was mixed, with some skeptical about the organizing, while others supported it both ideologically and materially. By late 1974, more than 30% of the workers had authorized United WREP Workers to represent them, and the union announced it would petition for an election. Shortly thereafter AFSCME District Council 37 convinced the state's labor board to add the workfare workers to its existing bargaining units.

Large-scale efforts to organize workfare workers re-emerged in the late 1990s with the explosive growth of workfare under TANF. The Association of Community Organizations for Reform Now (ACORN) set up organizing projects in New York City, Milwaukee, and Los Angeles, among other cities. In New York City ACORN organized demonstrations and filed collective grievances, winning improvements in conditions as well as a grievance procedure but no actual wages. When the city refused to recognize the union's 13,000 authorization cards, Jobs with Justice facilitated a symbolic election, resulting in a vote for ACORN representation of 16,989 to 207. While workfare participants were not covered under collective-bargaining laws, the process showed their desire for representation and put pressure on the city to curb workfare abuses.

In San Francisco People Organized to Win Employment Rights (POWER) was founded as an independent union in July 1998. Because its members did not have bargaining rights under state law, POWER used direct-action tactics, winning a grievance procedure, free public transportation, health and safety protections, and a 40% reduction in work hours. The city agreed to consult POWER before making any changes, recognizing it as workfare workers' *de facto* collective-bargaining agent.

In some cases workfare organizing deepened connections between traditional unions and community-based poor workers' unions. For instance the Communications Workers of America and ACORN launched a joint campaign in New Jersey in 1998, called People Organizing Workfare Workers, and gathered thousands of authorization cards that were used to pressure employers.

By century's end the number of people on workfare had declined. From 1996–1999, TANF rolls fell by over 50%, and some six million recipients lost benefits. Forcing the poor into workfare jobs without childcare, transportation, or education forced many off the welfare rolls; others were cut off after exhausting their limited period of assistance. Those workfare workers who remain continue to organize for their rights as both workers and as welfare recipients.

VANESSA TAIT

References and Further Reading

Abramovitz, Mimi. *Under Attack, Fighting Back: Women and Welfare in the United States.* New York: Monthly Review Press, 2000.

Mink, Gwendolyn. *Welfare's End.* Ithaca, NY: Cornell University Press, 1998.

Piven, Frances Fox. "The New Reserve Army of Labor." In *Audacious Democracy: Labor, Intellectuals, and the Social Reconstruction of America*, edited by Steven Fraser and Joshua B. Freeman. Boston, MA: Houghton Mifflin, 1997.

Reese, Ellen. "Resisting the Workfare State: Mobilizing General Relief Recipients in Los Angeles." *Race, Gender, and Class* 9, 1 (Jan. 31, 2002): 72–95.

Rose, Nancy E. *Workfare or Fair Work: Women, Welfare, and Government Work Programs.* New Brunswick, NJ: Rutgers University Press, 1995.

Simmons, Louise. "Unions and Welfare Reform: Labor's Stake in the Ongoing Struggle over the Welfare State." *Labor Studies Journal.* 27, 2 (summer 2002): 65–83.

Tait, Vanessa. *Poor Workers' Unions: Rebuilding Labor from Below.* Cambridge, UK: South End Press, 2005.

Cases and Statutes Cited

Comprehensive Employment and Training Act
Personal Responsibility and Work Opportunity Reconciliation Act

See also **Aid to Families with Dependent Children (AFDC); Living Wage; Minimum-Wage Laws; Poor People's Campaign; Unemployment; Welfare Rights**

WORKING GIRLS' CLUBS

In the 1880s, an increasing number of females in their late teens and early twenties left their parents' home to work in urban factories. The young, single, and increasingly immigrant, workingwomen struggled to find affordable housing and social outlets. Three general forms of clubs developed to address those needs. The first were associations and homes established by middle-class, white, female philanthropists who were concerned about the morality of girls living alone in the city. The second were cooperatives established by workingwomen, sometimes with the assistance of wealthy reformers, but managed by the working-women themselves. The third were clubs founded by black women to provide services for themselves, often requiring the assistance of middle-class women's associations. These clubs varied in their aims, organization, and services.

White women's Christian associations began to offer affordable housing to white, working girls in urban centers beginning in 1856. In 1884, New York philanthropist Grace Hoadley Dodge founded the Working Girls' Society to provide workingwomen with moral, health, and religious instruction. Several additional clubs followed in New York and other industrial cities in the East and Midwest. In 1885, the leaders of the clubs formed the national Association of Working Girls' Societies (AWGS) and published a magazine *Far and Near*. The clubs were typically tied to homes for working girls also established by middle-class philanthropists to provide female laborers with affordable housing, camaraderie, and a social outlet.

The number of working girls' clubs and the religious diversity of their sponsors grew through the late nineteenth century, but the membership increasingly comprised women working in vocations. The U.S. Department of Labor speculated in 1898 that the primary reasons factory workers did not reside in the clubs were the cost of the boarding clubs and their location far from the manufacturing districts. Some workers also objected to the moral regulation the patrons of the club imposed on the residents. Many of the factory workers therefore resided in tenements.

In 1892, settlement worker Jane Addams founded an alternative form of a working girls' club in Chicago. Though Addams had learned of the AWGS a year earlier when Dodge visited the Hull-House settlement, she founded Jane Club in response to requests by workingwomen who needed secure and affordable housing to enable them to organize and strike for better working conditions and higher wages. With the assistance of labor activist Mary Kenney (O'Sullivan), Addams acquired a house and paid the initial expenses but allowed the club to be managed as a cooperative by the members without moral education or behavior requirements.

Into the twentieth century laboring women developed a handful of similar cooperatives in other cities. These associations typically offered members insurance or mutual aid, recreation, educational opportunities, and sometimes housing. They comprised native-born and immigrant women, self-segregated by ethnicity.

African-American women who migrated from rural areas to work in cities during this period faced racial as well as economic restrictions in their search for housing. The existing working girls' clubs accepted only white women and most respectable boarding-houses were too expensive. Many single black women without means, whether they worked in a factory, office, or in the professions, thus resided in the cities' vice districts.

During the 1890s through the 1920s, a number of African-American women established clubs for themselves. In 1913, Jane Edna Hunter and a group of black female workers in Cleveland established the Working Girls' Home Association, later the Phillis Wheatley Association, which offered boarding, social activities, and assisted its members in securing employment. Other black working girls' clubs were established in Boston, New York, Buffalo, Providence, and Chicago. Some of these clubs sought assistance from local chapters of the National Association of Colored Women or from black churches. Sometimes the middle-class clubwomen and church members' efforts to impose their moral values on the residents caused tension between the groups; however many of the homes needed the financial support to remain viable.

During the height of the industrial revolution, white, black, religious, and ethnic working girls' clubs provided workingwomen in urban centers with essential services. For a few the clubs became places where women were also able collectively to organize and agitate for better working conditions and higher wages. Most required their members to adhere on some level to the moral values of their middle-class sponsors. Many of the clubs remained vibrant associations through the 1920s but were unable to survive the Great Depression. The few clubs that did survive adapted their services and continued to support working girls through the twentieth century.

GWEN HOERR JORDAN

References and Further Reading

Brown, Victoria Bissell. *The Education of Jane Addams* Philadelphia: University of Pennsylvania Press, 2004.

Ferguson, Mary. "Boarding Homes and Clubs for Working Women." *U.S. Department of Labor Bulletin* 3 (1898): 141–185.

Meyerowitz, Joanne J. *Women Adrift: Independent Wage Earners in Chicago, 1880–1930* Chicago, IL: University of Chicago Press, 1988.

Murolo, Priscilla. *The Common Ground of Womanhood: Class, Gender, and Working Girls' Clubs, 1884–1928.* Urbana: University of Illinois Press, 1997.

White, Deborah Gray. *Too Heavy a Load: Black Women in Defense of Themselves, 1894–1994.* New York: W. W. Norton & Company, 1999.

WORKING-CLASS FEMINISM

Working-class feminism has had a dramatic effect on the lives of men and women. Where once women were assigned to sex-segregated jobs under seniority and wage schemes separate from and unequal to those of men, they now expect to be able to vie with men for positions on an equal basis. The most important issues relating to women in the paid work force today, such as sexual harassment, pay equity, and pregnancy and family leave, were central concerns to working-class feminists who first openly challenged the old system beginning in the 1950s.

The origins of working-class feminism lie in the struggle of women to define their place in society over the course of the last 150 years. It first took significant organizational form when the coalition of working-class and reform women who championed Progressive Era protective legislation regulating women's working hours and conditions created a campaign to challenge workingwomen's status. To those women toiling in cotton mills and food-processing plants, in garment shops and laundries, and at other work sites, these measures provided welcomed relief. Unionists of all political stripes, including Communists who were influential in the labor movement in the 1930s and 1940s, steadfastly defended protective laws. They rejected the call of mostly upper class, professional women in the National Woman's party for passage of the Equal Rights Amendment (ERA). These workers and their allies accepted the limits on women's working hours and regulation of working conditions; by the 1960's wage-earning women chafed at the constraints protective laws placed on their ability to obtain overtime pay and work in higher-paying jobs as well as the second-class status in unions.

Most historians identify the 20 years following the end of World War II as crucial to the grounding of working-class feminism. The war, especially the introduction of women of all races into production jobs previously considered suitable only for men, had a limited effect on the rise of feminism: There was little popular support for gender equality in the 1940s. The demographic, economic, and technological transformations in the 1950s and early 1960s proved to be more significant. More women, especially married women with young children, entered the workforce in search of permanent employment. As part of the postwar consumer culture, they sought higher wages and greater opportunity; automation lessened the heavy-work requirements of designated male jobs, giving rise to a halting and uneven call that equality replace protection on the job.

As working-class women began to think differently about their status at work, the union hall, and at home, a cadre of union women activists—staff members and elected officers—joined together under the auspices of the U.S. Department of Labor's Women's Bureau, with business, religious, and civic leaders to form the Women's Bureau Coalition. Black and white women unionists dominated the coalition. It was during the early 1960s, with a sympathetic Democratic administration in office and Esther Peterson, longtime union staff member and head of the Women's Bureau, that women achieved their most impressive results. They played a crucial role in bringing about the Equal Pay Act of 1963, the formation of the president's Commission on the Status of Women, the expansion of the Fair Employment Standards Act to include low-paid and marginalized workers, and the enactment of a law providing for federal government support for day care. Even as female leaders maintained their support for protective laws, the results of these efforts pointed to a growing support for equality.

Female union leaders opposed passage of a provision banning sex discrimination in employment contained in Title VII of the Civil Rights Act of 1964. They believed, as did many others, that the new law should ban only racial discrimination, viewing the sex discrimination ban, originally introduced by a recalcitrant white southern Congressman, as a distraction. They were as surprised as union men when rank-and-file women filed a large number of complaints and lawsuits against their employers and unions based on the new law. No labor organization was immune to such charges, although the level and type of unfair treatment women experienced varied across and within unions according to membership composition, union politics, and industrial workplace organization. The women's action emboldened the largely middle-class liberal feminists in such organizations as the National Organization for Women (NOW), who in turn, lobbied reluctant government officials to enforce Title VII fully. Judicial rulings largely invalidated protective laws by the early 1970s.

Working-class unionists came together in scores on new groups to support gender equality. By the time the Coalition of Labor Union Women (CLUW), the largest and most influential of these groups, held its founding convention in 1974, most unions, as well as the American Federation of Labor-Congress of Industrial Organizations (AFL-CIO), had formally endorsed the ERA. Even so some union feminists remained skeptical of the amendment's equality standard. National leaders, like the Hotel Workers' Myra Wolfgang, budged little from the view that sweeping demands for equality were not in the best interest of workingwomen; others, notably activists and staff members with the United Automobile Workers, chafed at protective measures constraints and welcomed the ERA. Most working-class feminists fell somewhere between these two tendencies. They grappled with the tensions between the goals and strategies of equality and difference, understanding that the ERA would not solve many problems affecting workingwomen.

The CLUW members succeeded in establishing an effective, cross-racial organization that helped transform gender relations in unions and contributed to advancing liberal issues in the Democratic party. Their membership increased from 6,000 members in the late 1970s to 18,000 by the mid-1980s. They faced opposition from those who accused them of a too cozy relationship with union leaders. Other feminists and some civil rights leaders attacked them in the face of a severe economic downturn in the mid-1970s that threatened to undo affirmative action progress due to their defense of the seniority principle of "last hired, first fired."

As a result of the continuing prevalence of female-dominated employment sectors, working-class women in the late 1970s shifted their attention to advocating from a perspective of gender difference. They focused on pay equity or comparable worth, and on reproductive rights issues, such as working to help pass the Pregnancy Discrimination Act of 1978. In the 1980s and 1990s, as seasoned activists from industrial unions worked with younger unionists in unions representing service and government employees, they continued to address the central concern of power and gender relations with a practical feminism that recognized the unique experiences of wage-earning women.

DENNIS A. DESLIPPE

References and Further Reading

Cobble, Dorothy Sue. *The Other Women's Movement: Workplace Justice and Social Rights in Modern America.* Princeton, NJ: Princeton University Press, 2004.

Deslippe, Dennis A. *"Rights, Not Roses": Unions and the Rise of Working-Class Feminism, 1945–80.* Urbana: University of Illinois Press, 2000.

Fonow, Margaret Mary. *Union Women: Forging Feminism in the United Steelworkers of America.* Minneapolis: University of Minnesota Press, 2003.

Gabin, Nancy F. *Feminism in the Labor Movement: Women and the United Auto Workers, 1935–1975.* Ithaca, NY: Cornell University Press, 1990.

Kessler-Harris, Alice. *Out to Work: A History of Wage-Earning Women in the United States.* New York: Oxford University Press, 1982.

Milkman, Ruth. "Women Workers, Feminism, and the Labor Movement Since the 1960s." In *Women, Work, and Protest: A Century of U.S. Women's Labor History,* edited by Ruth Milkman. New York: Routledge & Kegan-Paul, 1985.

O'Farrell, Brigid, and Kornbluh, Joyce L. *Rocking the Boat: Union Women's Voices, 1915–1975.* New Brunswick, NJ: Rutgers University Press, 1996.

Weigand, Kate. *Red Feminism: American Communism and the Making of Women's Liberation.* Baltimore, MD: Johns Hopkins University Press, 2001.

Cases and Statutes Cited

Civil Rights Act
Equal Pay Act
Fair Employment Standards Act
Pregnancy Discrimination Act

See also **Coalition of Labor Union Women**

WORKPLACE HAZARDS, DISABILITY, AND INJURY

Workers in every occupation have long faced the threat of work-induced disabilities and illnesses. The particular kinds of hazards encountered by workers, however—as well as the kinds of injuries and illnesses produced—vary in relation to such technological developments as mechanization, beliefs about gender and race, and the legal climate. The impact of workplace hazards reaches well beyond the workplace, shaping working-class life, inspiring unionization, and affecting the lives of disabled workers themselves.

Changing Industries, Evolving Hazards

Workers in major industries have historically faced a heavy toll in injuries and accidents. During the early years of the railroad industry in the 1860s, accidents were so common that missing or crushed fingers signified an experienced brakeman or engineer. Coal miners encountered similar dangers in the 1860s: 6% of Pennsylvania miners sustained serious temporary disabilities, another 6% were permanently disabled, and another 6% died. Due to rapid mechanization and the increasing scale of industry, injury rates peaked in the late nineteenth and early twentieth centuries. By 1900, American workers were from three to five times more likely to die in accidents than their European counterparts, depending on their industry. This industrial accident crisis inspired the passage of workers' compensation laws and the safety movement in the 1910s, which helped halve industrial accident rates by the mid-twentieth century. Certain industries, such as meatpacking, remain dangerous today, however; roughly one-third of meatpacking workers develop an occupational injury or illness each year.

Seemingly lighter jobs—often those filled by women—have also long been physically taxing and injurious. Early twentieth-century servants complained of the painful feet, lower back problems, and varicose veins caused by 15-hour days and 7-day workweeks, while seamstresses and laundresses developed pelvic injuries from foot-powered treadles and irons. Ironically many of the early light industrial jobs that employers advertised as being especially suitable for women—and which offered women a means of avoiding the drudgery of household labor—involved high levels of exposure to toxic chemicals. Women thus made up a majority of the victims of many of the first occupational diseases to be identified: Phossy-jaw (necrosis of the jaw induced by white phosphorus) among matchmakers around 1900, radium poisoning among watch dial painters in the 1920s, and benzene poisoning in the 1930s and 1940s. The rise in repetitive-stress injuries and environmental illnesses in the late twentieth century testifies to the potential dangers lurking in the seemingly safe environs of offices.

The Paradoxical Impact of Mechanization

Technological developments and in particular, mechanization, have had dramatic and often paradoxical impacts on workers' safety. They have frequently produced startling increases in certain types of injuries and have even created new diseases. Both the mangles of early twentieth-century steam laundries and the die presses introduced at Ford Motor Company in the 1910s caused vast numbers of finger amputations, while textile workers risked being scalped if their hair became caught in power-operated shafts. The rise of mechanized drills in mining, granite cutting, and foundries in the 1920s, in turn, created silicosis, an incurable and often fatal lung disease caused by the inhalation of silica particles from rock. Similar epidemics of dust diseases—brown, black, and white lung—developed in mechanized textile mills, coal mines, and among asbestos workers, while the nuclear, chemical, and plastics revolutions caused radiation sickness and cancer.

Mechanization—and the accompanying growth in the scale of industry—has long been an integral part of employers' quest for productivity, a quest that has often had negative consequences for workers' safety. The sheer size of early twentieth-century steel plants, as well as the vastly increased productivity of blast furnaces, for instance, required railroad tracks across much of the plant floor as well as dozens of unguarded walkways high above the ground. Mechanized coal mines, by contrast, held many of the same hazards as before—explosions, cave-ins, and haulage car accidents—but their reliance on electricity, greater concentrations of explosive coal dust, and increased size made mass tragedies far more likely. A single open light brought into a gassy area in a Pennsylvania mine in 1902, for instance, caused an explosion that killed 112 men. Even unionized workers had little control over the vast array of new hazards presented by mechanization, although skilled workers sometimes had the option of making the difficult choice between safer working practices and higher productivity and wages.

Moreover mechanization has often tempted employers to try to push the pace of work beyond what human bodies can withstand. Starting in the late nineteenth century, steelworkers lost much of their traditional control over the speed and amount of work. As in many other industries, newly introduced "pushers" drove workers so hard that by 1907, one in four workers at U.S. Steel was injured each year. Speed-ups continue to cause injuries today: After the Hormel Meat Company fired many of its expert workers and increased line speed in the mid-1990s, over 70% of workers at a Nebraska plant developed carpal tunnel syndrome.

At the same time some technological advances—and certain types of mechanization—have significantly reduced workplace hazards. Overall electricity provided better light and removed the labyrinths of dangerous boilers, flywheels, pulleys, and belts on factory floors. Improved ventilation systems and drilling with water significantly reduced the scale of the silicosis epidemic by the 1950s. Moreover the rise of the safety movement in the 1910s—which began with the efforts of U.S. Steel, DuPont, and Ford to educate workers and redesign machines—inspired design engineers to incorporate guards, automatic shut-off and reversal mechanisms, and other safety devices into new machines. Better medical care has also gradually eliminated many of the permanent disabilities once caused by the everyday wear-and-tear of work: A broken leg for instance now rarely costs a worker the ability to walk.

Race, Gender, and the Legal Climate

Assumptions about race and gender have often placed certain groups in unsafe workplaces. In the infamous Hawk's Nest tunnel case in the 1930s, Union Carbide and Carbon specifically recruited migrant African-American laborers to drill through rock that consisted of nearly 99% pure silica (which the company planned to use in manufacturing). The company failed to inform workers about the dangers and refused to permit wet-drilling, provide masks, or ventilate the tunnel; instead managers relied on racism and the isolation of their workforce to hide the deaths of at least 500 workers and the disablement of many more from the public. Ironically the horrendous safety provisions revealed the company's avarice by greatly speeding up the course of silicosis among workers, who died after only a few months rather than a few decades. Likewise racism shaped how California farmer treated their workers during the Depression, reserving the relatively easy ladder crops for whites while confining Mexicans and Asians to the often literally backbreaking ground crops.

Women's supposed docility, dexterity, and hostility to unions, as well as the assumption that they needed clean, nonstrenuous work, made them an attractive workforce for many light industrial jobs. As previously mentioned many of these jobs involved exposure to dangerous toxins yet because early workers' compensation laws covered neither occupational diseases nor domestic nor farm workers, women made ill by their work rarely received compensation. Ironically concerns about how workplace hazards would affect women have at times limited their employment options. Early twentieth-century protective legislation, for instance, excluded women from many well-paid skilled jobs in the lead industry, but left men entirely unprotected from lead poisoning.

Changing legal and regulatory regimes have fundamentally shaped both the hazards faced by workers and the treatment of disabled workers. During much of the nineteenth century, injured and disabled workers struggled with, as John Fabian Witt argues in the *Accidental Republic* (2004), "a legal climate that made accidents cheap." In upward of 85% of cases, employers' liability law protected employers from paying compensation. The limited scope and weak enforcement of factory safety legislation—Iowa had only two inspectors for nearly 15,000 workplaces in 1903—likewise failed to push employers to invest in safety equipment. The advent of mandatory no-fault workers' compensation laws in the 1910s encouraged companies to invest in machine guards, ventilation systems, and other safety devices as cost-saving measures. Combined with the safety and efficiency movements, and more stringent safety and factory inspection laws, workers' compensation dramatically reduced accident rates by the late 1930s. Cost continues to help determine workplace safety however; in the late twentieth century, globalization began redistributing jobs to countries that lack basic safety provisions or effective workers' compensation programs, in effect redistributing the social burdens of dangerous workplaces.

Victims of occupational diseases have often had great difficulty winning compensation. Most states were slow to offer compensation for occupational illnesses. Moreover the difficulty of tracking victims and identifying the causes of diseases that can often take years if not decades to develop has made it easy for unscrupulous employers to resist paying ill workers. For instance although English doctors definitively linked brown lung with the high levels of cotton dust found in mechanized textile mills in 1705, stricken workers gained no compensation until the late 1970s. Instead company doctors diagnosed workers as having tuberculosis, lung cancer, bronchitis, or other noncompensable diseases. Since the establishment of the Occupational Health and Safety Administration (OSHA) in 1970, OSHA standards for cotton dust and carcinogenic chemicals, among others, have raised awareness about occupational diseases, while OSHA inspections have significantly reduced accident rates in certain industries.

Beyond the Workplace

The impact of workplace hazards has extended far beyond the workplace itself, shaping working-class communities, inspiring unionization, and of course affecting the lives of disabled workers themselves. Until the mid-twentieth century, work-induced injuries and illnesses were so frequent as to be considered a commonplace misfortune. When Crystal Eastman interviewed Pittsburgh workers for her famous treatise, *Work-Accidents and the Law,* she found that workers had trouble remembering even such major injuries as the loss of a finger or a crushed skull. In fact a fully functional body may well have been abnormal in many communities. The physical perfection of people in the Sears catalog shocked memoirist Harry Crews: "Nearly everybody I know [in rural Georgia] had something missing, a finger cut off, a toe split, an ear half-chewed away, an eye clouded with blindness from a glancing fence staple." Injuries have also shaped the membership of communities, especially in company towns. A North Carolina textile worker's refusal to return to work the day after losing two fingers in a carding room accident cost him not only his job but also his home. Moreover workplace hazards have often spilled over into surrounding communities: In the tristate region of Oklahoma, Missouri, and Kansas, notorious in the 1930s as the center of the silicosis epidemic, residents continue to struggle with respiratory diseases caused by tailings piles.

The fear of disability or death at work has long stimulated unionization and aided unionization campaigns. Cesar Chavez and the United Farm Workers Organizing Committee drew heavily on reports of farmworkers sickened by leukemia and other occupational diseases caused by heavy pesticide to attract union supporters and create negative press for growers, while the renowned union organizer Mother Jones found one of her most powerful rhetorical weapons in the deformed hands and breaker boys in coal mines. Supporting ill comrades could also become a central part of the union's identity, as in the Western Federation of Miners. To avoid dealing with company doctors, the union founded and ran a number of hospitals in the 1890s.

Ironically while the threats posed by workplace hazards and disabilities have often inspired unionization, unions have not always been very progressive on health and safety issues. Starting in the 1880s, the railroad brotherhoods joined railroad companies in excluding disabled workers from returning to regular employment and blaming them for causing their own injuries. Union locals also discouraged disabled members from remaining active; however the brotherhoods eventually established a union home for destitute members. More recently the United Mine Workers of America attempted to balance its budget on the backs of disabled miners and miners' widows, groups that union leaders viewed as politically expendable. After losing financial stipends and medical coverage in the 1960s, disabled miners and widows formed the Black Lung Association and helped successfully lead a 20,000-person wildcat strike in 1970 for union democracy, proper benefits, and federal black lung compensation. Starting in the 1970s, however, OSHA's work on health and safety standards inspired many unions to become more engaged in health and safety issues.

Workplace hazards have of course also affected the lives of those injured and their families. Disabilities were relatively common in most working-class communities until the mid-twentieth century, and disabled people seem to have found relative acceptance. Starting in the late nineteenth century, the growing interest of employers in efficiency, mechanization, and high productivity, and their related assumption that people with disabilities were inefficient workers, however, made it ever more difficult for disabled workers to find employment. Notably the Ford Motor Company actively hired people with disabilities, placed them in positions where they could be productive, and paid them equal wages, but many disabled workers were forced to turn to either low-wage, low-skill jobs in sheltered workshops or the informal labor market. While workers' compensation undoubtedly benefited disabled workers and their families, it provided further disincentives for employers to hire people with disabilities. The vocational rehabilitation movement, which

began in the 1910s, gradually educated employers about disabled workers' capabilities; as a result many employers temporarily hired people with disabilities during World War II. Many disabled people still struggle to find employment today, although the disability rights movement and the Americans with Disabilities Act of 1990 have significantly reduced barriers.

SARAH F. ROSE

References and Further Reading

Aldrich, Mark. *Safety First: Technology, Labor, and Business in the Building of American Work Safety, 1870–1939.* Baltimore, MD: Johns Hopkins University Press, 1997.

Asher, Robert. "Organized Labor and the Origins of the Occupational Health and Safety Act." *Labor's Heritage* 3, 1 (Jan. 1991): 54–76.

Crews, Harry. *A Childhood: A Biography of a Place.* New York: Harper & Row Publishers, 1978.

Derickson, Alan. *Workers' Health, Workers' Democracy: The Western Miners' Struggle, 1891–1925.* Ithaca, NY: Cornell University Press, 1988.

Longmore, Paul K., and David Goldberger, "The League of the Physically Handicapped and the Great Depression: A Case Study in the New Disability History." *Journal of American History* 87, 3 (Dec. 2000): 888–922.

Markowitz, Gerald, and David Rosner, eds. *Dying for Work: Workers' Safety and Health in Twentieth-Century America.* Bloomington: Indiana University Press, 1987.

Markowitz, Gerald E., and David Rosner. *Deadly Dust: Silicosis and the Politics of Occupational Health in Twentieth-Century America.* Princeton, NJ: Princeton University Press, 1991.

Rose, Sarah F. "'Crippled' Hands: Disability in Labor and Working-Class History." *Labor: Studies in Working-Class History of the Americas* 2, 1 (Mar. 2005): 27–54.

Williams-Searle, John. "Cold Charity: Manhood, Brotherhood, and the Transformation of Disability, 1870–1900." In *The New Disability History: American Perspectives,* edited by Paul K. Longmore and Lauri Umansky. New York: New York University Press, 2001.

Witt, John Fabian. *The Accidental Republic: Crippled Workingmen, Destitute Widows, and the Remaking of American Law.* Boston, MA: Harvard University Press, 2004.

Cases and Statutes Cited

Disabilities Act

See also **Bureau of Labor Standards; Occupational Health and Safety Administration (OSHA); Workers' Compensation**

WORKS PROGRESS ADMINISTRATION

The Roosevelt administration launched the Works Progress Administration (WPA) in 1935 to employ some of the millions of Americans left unemployed by the Great Depression. The WPA, as it came to be known, was one of the key programs of the second New Deal. Like the rest of the second New Deal, the WPA emphasized direct, interventionist solutions to the social problems of the Great Depression. The agency was headed by Harry Hopkins, who represented the more liberal, free-spending wing of the Roosevelt administration. Hopkins aimed to bring as many unemployed workers as possible into the WPA. The WPA was the largest of the New Deal relief efforts. In all approximately 13 million people worked for the WPA at some point, and the WPA employed three million workers annually. Every state and just about every county in the country hosted at least one WPA project.

Like the Civilian Conservation Corps (CCC) and the Public Works Administration, the WPA attempted to replace standard poverty relief (the dole) with a relief stipend earned through work. Yet the WPA was also a significant departure from earlier New Deal programs. Whereas the CCC was expressly limited to conservation work, and the PWA was limited to the construction and expansion of public works, the WPA undertook all kinds of work to occupy the unemployed. The bulk of WPA relief recipients went to work on construction projects—building schools, hospitals, libraries, and other public buildings. The Roosevelt administration also took the WPA in a new direction, hiring painters, dancers, actors, writers, and other artists in several divisions of the WPA. For the first time in U.S. history, the federal government became a major benefactor of the arts.

The Federal Theater Project, headed by Hallie Flannigan, hired actors, directors, and stage hands to put on live theater. During its 4-year existence, an estimated 30 million Americans saw a Federal Theater Project play. The Federal Art Project hired painters, sculptors, and other fine artists to produce new works and teach Americans about art. While the painting of the Federal Art Project has generally been perceived as subpar, several skilled painters, among them Jackson Pollock, participated. Art historians credit the New York branch of the Federal Art Project for helping to lay the groundwork for the abstract expressionist movement that took hold later in the century.

The Federal Writers' Project composed travel guides, recorded regional folklore, and wrote histories of the individual states. Several prominent American writers, among them Saul Bellow, Ralph Ellison, John Steinbeck, and Richard Wright, worked for the WPA. Perhaps the greatest historical legacy of the Federal Writers' Project was the compilation of the WPA slave narratives. Alan Lomax led teams of WPA writers as they interviewed thousands of former slaves about life in the antebellum American South.

The slave narratives continue to be a rich if sometimes controversial source about life for African-Americans before emancipation.

The National Youth Administration (NYA) focused on unemployed young people. In an age where many families depended on the wages of teenage and young adult workers for survival, the high unemployment rate amongst the young was especially troubling. Hundreds of thousands of young Americans found first jobs with the WPA, and many went to college with the proceeds.

While historians frequently criticize the New Deal for its record of accomplishment regarding African-Americans, the WPA was generally a model agency in hiring black workers. Because of its high degree of federal control, local governments had less power to deny jobs to African-Americans. Even in the South many black workers found steady, albeit low-paid employment in the WPA. Hopkins appointed Mary McLeod Bethune to head the National Youth Administration (NYA) Division of Negro Affairs, making Bethune the highest ranking African-American official of the New Deal.

The WPA did not succeed so well in bringing relief to the millions of unemployed American women. Many women did serve in the WPA, especially on sewing projects, producing clothing, blankets, and other items for poverty relief. Yet the gender rules of the American workplace remained in place for the WPA. For instance few women found employment on the WPA construction projects.

STEVEN DIKE-WILHELM

References and Further Reading

Harris, Jonathan. *Federal Art and National Culture: The Politics of Identity in New Deal America.* New York: Cambridge University Press, 1995.

Leuchtenburg, William. *Franklin D. Roosevelt and the New Deal.* New York: Harper and Row, 1963.

Watkins, T. H. *The Hungry Years: A Narrative History of the Great Depression in America.* New York: Henry Holt and Company, 1999.

WORLD WAR I

The United States was an active belligerent during the First World War for just 20 months. During that time no foreign troops set foot on U.S. soil, no trenches scarred its countryside, and no long-range artillery targeted its cities. Ultimately American casualties were but a fraction of those endured by other belligerent powers. And yet the war profoundly affected American workers and unions. The war produced a sudden and acute labor crisis in the United States. More than 3,000 strikes erupted during the first 6 months of U.S. participation in the war. Immediately following the war, the country was wracked by even more labor upheaval. No previous period of U.S. history has seen such intense and widespread labor conflict. Ultimately the World War I years altered the course of U.S. labor history, producing new patterns of workplace management, union organization, labor politics, and workforce composition that would affect American labor history long after the war.

In many ways modern American labor history began in the period of the Great War. To understand this and to appreciate how deeply the war changed things for American workers and unions, we must consider three factors: The context within which American workers encountered World War I, the surprising developments that unfolded during the war, and the impact of the war's end on workers and unions. Together these factors defined the legacy of the war for American labor.

Wartime Context

Because U.S. participation in the war was so brief, understanding its impact requires an acute appreciation for the fluid state of the nation, its workers, unions, and labor relations practices at the moment the U.S. entered the war. This in turn requires taking stock of both immediate and long-range trends that unfolded at the time of the war, setting the context for the way in which workers experienced the war.

The U.S. entry into the war changed the landscape of American labor relations in dramatic fashion. One of the changes first evident was the worker-friendly labor market that the war produced. Hostilities in Europe cut off the flow of immigrant labor to American industries. Military enlistments and the draft further drained the ranks of factory labor. Furthermore highly paid war production jobs pulled workers from less highly remunerated manufacturing jobs into war production plants, producing labor shortages in many industries. This turbulence broke down the boundaries of prewar labor markets. Drawn by the promise of factory wages, African-Americans left the agricultural South by the hundreds of thousands for jobs in steel mills, shipyards, and auto plants. As the East St. Louis riot of 1917 illustrated, black workers were often greeted by white hostility when they arrived in the North looking for industrial jobs. Other sources also fed the growing demand for labor. Women left their homes or their jobs in retail and service

industries for manufacturing employment. Mexicans also streamed northward across the boarder to fill job vacancies created by wartime conditions. Still labor shortages persisted.

Labor shortages gave workers an unprecedented opportunity to organize unions. For the first time in their working lives, many workers were thus able to address long-standing grievances. For more than a decade prior to the outbreak of the war, employers had waged a largely successful battle to make manufacturing industries open shop. Toward that end employers had used the stick of professional strikebreakers, blacklists, and yellow-dog contracts as well as the carrot of limited company benefits. Wartime conditions weakened employers' traditional anti-union weapons. Not only did labor markets favor workers, the role of employers' most reliable ally—the courts—receded and the executive branch of the federal government became more involved in shaping labor relations.

These short-range developments were in turn magnified by the three longer range developments that intersected on the eve of the war: Progressive Era reform politics and state building reached a high-water mark; the nation's labor movement entered a period of ferment and experimentation; and employers, policy makers, and progressive reformers began a search for a common solution to labor unrest and inefficiency.

The state's growth was perhaps the most evident of these changes. World War I dramatically expanded the role that the state played in the lives of Americans. But the war merely continued prewar trends in state building. From 1912–1916, progressive reformers had widened the capacity of the federal government to regulate the nation's economic life through new agencies, such as the Federal Trade Commission (1913), the Federal Reserve System (1914), and laws regulating working conditions on railroads and merchant ships. These initiatives were passed by Democratic majorities in both the U.S. House of Representatives and Senate and signed by Democratic President Woodrow Wilson. Democrats' embrace of reform-oriented state building marked a significant moment in U.S. political history. The Wilsonian Democratic party attempted to position itself as the nation's reform party, broadening its base beyond the solid South. The Democrats' reform agenda in turn opened the party to an alliance with the American Federation of Labor (AFL).

The AFL was itself in a state of flux on the eve of World War I. Founded on the clear principles of craft union organization, nonpartisanship in politics, and voluntarism (as opposed to statism), the AFL had seen its central premises put to the test in the years before the war. The labor federation was beset from two sides. On the one hand it was excluded from the nation's burgeoning mass-production industries and harassed elsewhere by employer opposition and hostile judicial interventions. On the other hand it felt pressured by the syndicalist Industrial Workers of the World (IWW), which mounted a significant challenge to the AFL after 1915 by seeking to organize unskilled workers who had been neglected by craft unions. These problems pushed AFL president Samuel Gompers and other union leaders into an alliance with Wilson's Democratic party. This was bad news for the Socialist party of America, which had long hoped to build an alliance with the AFL.

As the AFL underwent such changes, new problems and possibilities were also emerging in prewar workplace relations. The advent of mass production—perhaps best symbolized by the opening of Henry Ford's first assembly line in 1913—exacerbated tensions in the workplace. During the early twentieth century, manufacturers relentlessly drove to increase efficiency and their control over the work process by introducing new technologies, variable piece rates, bonus plans, and the scientific management theories famously expounded by Frederick Winslow Taylor. They succeeded in deskilling many elements of craft work, creating multitudes of semiskilled machine operatives to do the work once done by highly experienced all-around machinists, for example. But employers often found it difficult to retain semiskilled workers in whom they had invested considerable training costs. This very problem had led Ford to introduce his famous 5-dollar day, offering a premium wage to workers in return for loyalty to the company. With the same goals in mind, some other large-scale employers adopted welfare plans that included profit sharing and rudimentary health care and pension benefits.

The obvious need to find a solution to the nation's labor question prompted a wide range of reform minded actors to embrace the idea of industrial democracy prior to the war. The term industrial democracy was not new. Some early twentieth-century reformer, such as the progressive lawyer Louis D. Brandeis, had used it. But it was President Wilson's creation of the U.S. Commission on Industrial Relations (USCIR) in 1913 that placed the ideal of industrial democracy on the agendas of a broad range of reformers. Progressive labor lawyer and USCIR chairman, Frank P. Walsh, played a key role in that process. After 2 years of headline-grabbing USCIR hearings, Walsh issued a report that blamed the nation's labor troubles on autocratic management and argued that the "only hope for the solution" of labor conflict lay in "the rapid extension of the principles of democracy to industry." "Political freedom can exist only where there is industrial freedom," the Walsh report said, "political democracy only where there is industrial democracy." The USCIR thus primed Americans to later see industrial democracy as the solution to wartime labor upheaval. Once at war President Wilson's framing of U.S. intervention in Europe as a struggle to spread democracy made the achievement of industrial democracy a priority on the nation's wartime domestic agenda.

But what would industrial democracy look like? While Americans increasingly embraced the term during World War I, they meant a wide range of different things by it. To most progressives industrial democracy meant bargaining between management and workers represented either by unions or nonunion employee councils. To AFL leaders however industrial democracy was only possible where unions won formal recognition, closed shops, and collective-bargaining contracts from employers. To the enlightened management officials who began to embrace the term, it usually meant labor-management cooperation that gave unions no recognition or privileges. To wartime radicals the term became a synonym for socialism, syndicalism, or workers' control. Much of the wartime upheaval was bound up in sorting out which brand of industrial democracy would prevail.

War, Workers, and Unions

The U.S. entry into the Great War in April 1917 unleashed a wave of labor conflicts within the United States. As strikes spread so, too, did efforts to suppress them. Many states and localities enacted work-or-fight laws that threatened idle workers (including strikers) with being drafted into the army. Superpatriot groups, such as the American Protective League, launched "slacker raids" in working-class communities. But the most infamous episode of repression occurred in Bisbee, Arizona. When copper miners tried to organize in July 1917, more than 1,000 of them were rounded up at gunpoint by vigilantes and shipped into the New Mexico desert on cattle cars. In Bisbee and throughout the country, employers blamed the IWW for stirring up strikes. The Socialist party (SP), too, was singled out for attack due to its decision to formally oppose U.S. participation in the war. Gompers and the AFL on the other hand supported both U.S. participation in the war and Wilson administration attacks on the antiwar SP and IWW. In September 1918, the Justice Department rounded up more than 100 IWW leaders and later put them on trial for obstructing the war effort. The AFL leaders and a small group of prowar

Socialists meanwhile organized the American Alliance for Labor and Democracy (AALD) and used their new organization to attack the SP. By the end of the war, both the once vibrant IWW and SP were all but destroyed.

Yet the Wilson administration realized early in the war mobilization that repression alone would not establish the labor peace necessary to win the war. As wartime strikes spread, Wilson named Secretary of Labor William B. Wilson (a former official of the United Mine Workers union) to lead a mediation commission that would investigate the causes of strikes and recommend solutions. Secretary Wilson and his mediators in turn became convinced of the need for a broad federal policy that would protect workers' rights to organize during the war's duration. Other administration officials came to a similar conclusion. Labor mediators with the U.S. Shipping Board, Fuel Administration, and Railroad Administration experimented with plans that gave workers the right to elect representatives who would bargain with their employers. As the strike rate rose through the fall of 1917, the administration finally moved decisively to centralize such experimentation and adopt a national policy in favor of collective bargaining. In January 1918, the president named a committee of labor and business leaders to hammer out such a policy. The outcome of the committee's work was the creation of the National War Labor Board (NWLB), composed of five employers, five trade unionists, and cochaired by former Republican President William H. Taft and USCIR veteran Frank Walsh. From April 1918 through the end of the war, the NWLB implemented a war-labor policy that was destined to alter the course of the nation's labor history.

A set of principles guided the NWLB's intervention in wartime industrial disputes. The board proclaimed the right of workers to organize and bargain collectively. It called for equal pay for women working in jobs also done by men, and it set 8 hours as a nationally recognized workday in war industries. The NWLB did not force private employers to abandon the open shop and recognize unions, but it did obligate them to bargain with their workers. To promote collective bargaining in cases where employers refused to grant union recognition, the NWLB called for workers to elect shop-committee representatives who could bargain on their behalf. Employers were never enthusiastic about the NWLB or Wilsonian labor policies, but the AFL embraced them warmly. This was scarcely surprising, for such policies helped unions establish a strong foothold in steel mills, railroad shops, meatpacking plants, and electrical-manufacturing factories that organized labor had never been able to penetrate.

Yet few in labor or the government could have anticipated three unintended consequences that flowed from the administration's war labor program. First the very existence of agencies like the NWLB did not foster labor peace as much as they encouraged workers' to strike in an effort to win government intervention. Indeed the government program even helped equip strikers with a rationale for their militancy. Ultimately the NWLB admitted over 1,000 labor disputes to its docket before the war ended. Almost 90% of those cases originated in complaints by workers, most of which were brought to the board's attention when workers struck their employers. Militancy triggered government intervention, which in turn spread militancy. As one contemporary explained, the NWLB's decisions "looked so good to workers that they were stirred to instigate" disputes so as to "secure the good offices of the Board." At the same time the Wilsonian labor program allowed workers to justify their militancy in patriotic language as an attack on autocratic management. This was especially important for immigrant workers whose militancy might otherwise be suspect as evidence of their disloyalty. War workers shrewdly began referring to their employers as the "American Junkers," the "Kaiser[s] of industrial America," and the "American Hohenzollerns." They portrayed their challenges to their "Prussian" or autocratic bosses as efforts to secure the "de-kaisering of industry." And they argued that authentic de-kaisering could take place only when workers had joined unions that could bargain on an equal basis with their bosses. Joining the union was thus not merely a worker's right, but a *responsibility* in this "war to make the world safe for democracy." The rallying of the Machinists union in one war production center was simply "Wake up! Be real citizens!" As this slogan implied, union membership was thus portrayed as a prerequisite of full citizenship. With such rationales everywhere in 1918, it is not surprising that when one employee of the General Electric company was asked about the origins of his union sympathies, he could reply: "In a way, I didn't have any [union sympathies], only–I might say I had an American feeling, that is all...I didn't have much thought in the matter... of union stuff."

A second unintended consequence that flowed from the administration's war labor program was its unintentional empowerment of those workers who had been most subordinated prior to the war: Recent immigrants, African-Americans, and women. During the war each of these groups made considerable gains. Not only was their access to better paying jobs improved by labor shortages, but the war labor program also promised them a voice over the conditions under which they labored at a time when they lacked full citizenship rights outside of the workplace. Typically immigrants voted in shop elections without regard to their American citizenship. So did women at a time when they had yet to win the suffrage nationally. In a nation where the memory of the bloody 1917 East St. Louis race riot (in which white workers brutally attacked blacks who came to their city in search of war work), federal labor agencies offered African-Americans important avenues of appeal through which to challenge some injustices. Though federal labor policies generally left racial discrimination intact, blacks did benefit from minimum wages set in some war-related industries and from policies that opened their access to wage-earning jobs. "I am getting more to day then I ever made in all my past life," one black worker wrote to Washington, "I thanks you so mightily for seein to it." Ultimately the Wilsonian war-labor program raised the expectations of immigrants, women, and black workers who deserved—and could win—fairer treatment from employers and white male coworkers.

A third unintended consequence flowed from the impact of shop committees on the American labor movement. Although they were intended to allow collective bargaining without compelling employers formally to recognize unions, the election of shop committees ended up triggering union organization and contributing to the spread of industrial unionism within a labor movement dominated by craft unions. Developments in such previously anti-union industries as electrical manufacturing and steel demonstrated this. The largest U.S. electrical manufacturer, General Electric owned five large U.S. factories in 1917, none of which were unionized. No sooner had the NWLB been formed than GE workers organized a company-wide movement to create an inclusive union of all GE workers: The Electrical Manufacturing Industry Labor Federation. The election of NWLB shop committees in the GE plants fostered this organizing. Meanwhile in the nation's largest nonunion sector, the steel industry, a similar dynamic unfolded. Shop-committee elections at steel plants encouraged workers to organize unions. These initiatives in turn helped persuade the AFL to launch the National Committee to Organize Iron and Steel Workers in 1918. By September 1919, the steel-organizing committee comprised of numerous craft unions working in concert was strong enough to lead the largest strike to that point in the history of the U.S. steel industry. In a development that the designers of the war-labor program certainly did not intend, both the electrical- and the steel-organizing drives were led by militants far to the left of President Gompers of the AFL.

By the time the armistice was signed on November 11, 1918, much had changed for American workers and unions in less than 2 years time. More than a million workers joined the labor movement during the war, boosting AFL membership to roughly 3.2 million by the war's end. Many believed that postwar reconstruction would see labor consolidate and extend its gains. As one journalist saw it, the central issue for the postwar era was "how far can industrial democracy go?" Union leaders had good reason to hope that they could finish organizing the nation's manufacturing core. They were soon to be disappointed when this did not happen. When the Armistice was signed on November 11, 1918, unionization of the nation's basic industries was far from complete and panicked employers were already mobilizing to roll back both union gains and the government interference in their workplaces.

Legacy of Wartime Change and Postwar Backlash

Ironically for U.S. workers their wartime labor insurgency tended to dissipate each of the long-range trends that had presented the prewar era with such lively cause for labor reform. Whereas prewar progressives had entertained dreams of state building, the postwar era saw a violent reaction against all vestiges of statism. This backlash threw progressives on the defensive. Farmers who abhorred the administration's efforts to control wartime wheat prices and consumers who blamed the government for wartime inflation fed this trend. But it was the government's attempts at labor regulation that most energized the backlash among employers. By late 1918, industrialists railed against "that damn NWLB," and demanded what one employer called an end to interference by "petty government officials and shop committees." Conservative southern Democrats were just as irritated by Wilson administration labor reforms, seeing in them a potential threat to racial segregation. As a result Democrats were increasingly divided on the desirability of labor reform. Sensing an opening the Republicans coalesced after nearly a decade of internal turmoil and took back both houses of Congress in 1918. The reactionary Sixty-Sixth Congress sped the shutdown of such agencies as NWLB in 1919.

As support for labor reform dissolved, the AFL was divided over the proper way forward. Many in labor called for a peacetime version of the NWLB. As one left-winger shrewdly observed, the NWLB's shop committees had provided an "enormous stimulus to industrial unionism" by offering "the nucleus of a shop soviet through which workers may exert the full weight of their collective power." Not surprisingly conservative craft union leaders did not relish such thoughts. They sought to disengage from government policies that they blamed for fomenting a challenge to craft union predominance and weakening the AFL's traditional voluntarism. Whereas the wartime AFL had experimented with industrial organization and government regulation, the postwar AFL had second thoughts. Craft unionism and voluntarism were both resurgent within the AFL by the early 1920s as industrial union efforts in steel, meatpacking, and electrical manufacturing were destroyed, the NWLB was dismantled, and an effort to nationalize the nation's railroad under the Plumb Plan collapsed.

Contributing to labor's postwar conservatism was the hostile climate that developed in the United States in the aftermath of the Bolshevik revolution of 1917. During the strike wave of 1919, employers successfully linked labor militancy to the threat of communism. This linkage helped undermine support for the Seattle general strike, the Boston police strike, and the great steel strike of 1919. Complicating matters for labor was the fact that the Bolshevik revolution also provoked a split in the American socialist movement. Those loyal to the Russian revolution broke away from the SP and helped found the Communist party in 1919. Thereafter the American Left was itself deeply divided over the issue of communism.

These developments in turn gave employers the greatest amount of power to define the legacy of the Great War for American workers. Employers did this by breaking unions where they were able to do so. But this was not all. If they were to have postwar peace, many large-scale employers knew that they needed more than the absence of a union. As a pragmatic businessman put it, with "labor crying for democracy, capital must go part way or face revolution." Such employers understood that the war had significantly altered workers' expectations, encouraging them to demand a voice over their conditions of labor. Employers wanted to satisfy the demand for a voice, without giving up power in the bargain. Toward this end they sought to fashion the ideal of industrial democracy in their own image. They replaced NWLB shop committees and unions with company unions and representation plans. By 1921, AFL unions had been driven from electrical manufacturing and steel, and 700,000 workers were enrolled in company unions.

Although employers tamed industrial democracy after the war, reducing this ideal to a shadow of its prewar promise, labor relations were quite different than they had been a decade earlier. Employers had successfully beaten back government regulation and

mass unionization, but they could not destroy the memory of the wartime promise of industrial democracy. After the war even many anti-union employers admitted the legitimacy of workers' demands for a voice in determining the conditions of their employment even as they fought to make sure that unions would not be the vehicle for expressing that voice.

The war also changed the composition and the consciousness of the American working-class. It had contributed to the great migration of black workers to the North and triggered an ongoing influx of Mexican workers from the South. By cutting off immigration, giving rise to intense wartime loyalty campaigns, and drawing millions into military service, the war had also contributed to the Americanization of immigrant workers. All of these trends together with the rising expectations unleashed by the war left a lasting imprint.

Finally the war provided an indispensable experience for reformers and progressive trade unionists—one that they would later draw on. Although progressives and trade unionists were marginalized in the decade following the war, the Great Depression later provided them with an opportunity to resurrect experiments of the World War I years. As President Franklin Roosevelt's government invoked the precedents of World War I to justify his New Deal programs, reformers and trade unionists renewed their campaign for industrial democracy through the industrial union effort of the 1930s. Thus the Great War continued to influence the fortunes of American workers and unions long after its guns were silenced.

JOSEPH A. MCCARTIN

References and Further Reading

Breen, William J. *Labor Market Politics and the Great War: The Department of Labor, the States, and the First U.S. Employment Service, 1907–1933.* Kent, OH: Kent State University Press, 1997.

Conner, Valerie Jean. *The National War Labor Board: Stability, Social Justice, and the Voluntary State in World War I.* Chapel Hill: University of North Carolina Press, 1983.

Dubofsky, Melvyn. "Abortive Reform: The Wilson Administration and Organized Labor, 1913–1920." In *Work, Community, and Power: The Experience of Labor in Europe and America, 1900–1925*, edited by James E. Cronin and Carmen Sirianni. Philadelphia, PA: Temple University Press, 1983.

Dubofsky, Melvyn. *We Shall Be All: A History of the Industrial Workers of the World.* Chicago, IL: Quadrangle Books, 1969.

Greene, Julie. *Pure and Simple Politics: the American Federation of Labor and Political Activism, 1881–1917.* New York: Cambridge University Press, 1998.

Greenwald, Maurine Wiener. *Women, War, and Work: The Impact of World War I on Women Workers in the United States.* Westport, CT.: Greenwood Press, 1980.

Grubbs, Frank L. *The Struggle for Labor Loyalty: Gompers, the AFL, and the Pacifists.* Durham, NC: Duke University Press, 1968.

Haydu, Jeffrey. *Making American Industry Safe for Democracy: Comparative Perspectives on the State and Employee Representation in the Era of World War I.* Urbana: University of Illinois Press, 1997.

Jacoby, Sanford M. *Employing Bureaucracy: Managers, Unions, and the Transformation of Work in American Industry, 1900–45.* New York: Columbia University Press, 1985.

Kennedy, David M. *Over Here: The First World War and American Society.* New York: Oxford University Press, 1980.

Larson, Simeon. *Labor and Foreign Policy: Gompers, the AFL, and the First World War, 1914–1918.* Rutherford, NJ: Farleigh Dickinson Press, 1974.

McCartin, Joseph A. *Labor's Great War: The Struggle for Industrial Democracy and the Origins of Modern American Labor Relations, 1912–21.* Chapel Hill: The University of North Carolina Press.

McKillen, Elizabeth. *Chicago Labor and the Quest for a Democratic Diplomacy, 1914–1924.* Ithaca, NY: Cornell University Press, 1995.

Montgomery, David. *The Fall of the House of Labor: The Workplace, the State, and American Labor Activism, 1865–1925.* New York: Cambridge University Press, 1987.

Sarasohn, David. *The Party of Reform: Democrats in the Progressive Era.* Jackson: University of Mississippi Press, 1989.

See also **American Federation of Labor; Bisbee Deportation/Copper Strike (1917); National War Labor Board (WWI); United States Industrial Commission**

WORLD WAR II

World War II brought enormous changes to working-class life in the United States and to the fortunes of organized labor. Wartime labor mobilization incorporated more workers than ever before into a modern industrial working class, including many who had previously been relegated to the margins of the American economy. The trade union movement grew in size during the war, and labor union density reached a century high peak by 1945. And the wartime state intervened in labor-management relations to an unprecedented degree. All of these developments represented accelerations of trends inaugurated by the Depression and the New Deal and also proved to be harbingers of some important transformations to come in the postwar period.

Changing Composition of the Working Class

First and foremost the war helped put Americans back to work after a decade of depression and unemployment. When the war began in Europe in 1939, 10 million Americans remained out of work; by the time the United States entered the conflict in December 1941, that number had been reduced to four million. During the Great Depression mass unemployment seemed impervious to New Deal programs, never dipping below 14%; by the height of war production in 1944, this figure had been reduced to 1.2%, virtually a full-employment economy. From 1940–1943, the peak of wartime production, the employed private-sector civilian labor force increased by five million, a 12% expansion. Workers spent more hours at work as well: Average weekly hours in manufacturing jobs increased from 38.1 to 45 during the same period.

Officially rationing governed wartime consumption habits of basic goods, like gasoline, rubber, sugar, and meat. Nevertheless for many working-class Americans on the home front, the wartime economy meant the return of prosperity and expanded consumption. By mid-1942, 6 months after Pearl Harbor, one-third of the nation's economy was devoted to war production; and from 1939–1945, federal spending multiplied 10-fold. Full employment, overtime, incentive pay, deferred pension plans, and increasing numbers of industrial jobs put spending money in the working-class consumer's pocket for the first time since the 1920s. The combination of rising incomes, the entry of new workers into the labor force, wartime shortages, and admonitions to invest in war bonds, dammed up an enormous reservoir of spending power that would deluge the American economy in the postwar period, threatening inflation at first but eventually ushering in a rising tide of broad postwar prosperity.

The attraction of wartime jobs also encouraged American workers to move, drawing millions of laborers from rural, isolated, and the small-town United States to the burgeoning war-production facilities in the industrial heartland and on the Gulf and West coasts. Fifteen million Americans moved in search of work during the war. Many of these men and women left the most economically depressed sections of the country, the rural South and Southwest in particular. Four-and-a-half million people moved from rural to urban communities, and 1.6 million alone left the South. The nation's farm population dropped by 5.7 million during the war years. These changes permanently altered the nature of working-class life in the United States.

American workers also found themselves concentrated in production plants that drew together huge numbers of laborers. During the war the number of corporations employing 10,000 or more workers went from 13% to 30% of American companies. In the Douglas Aviation facilities in the Los Angeles basin,

100,000 workers built planes; in San Francisco Bay's Kaiser shipyards, 90,000 employees mass-produced liberty ships; the Willow Run bomber plant outside of Detroit employed 40,000 people. Such huge conglomerations of workers, many of them new to urban industrial life, led to housing shortages, transportation bottlenecks, and crowded and tense living conditions. Exacerbating these tensions was the entry into the industrial workforce of new recruits previously denied access to most production jobs: African-Americans and women.

African-Americans at Work

With the initial stirrings of wartime mobilization, African-Americans found themselves shut out of defense jobs by the combined resistance of employers and white workers just as they had been denied entry to decent industrial employment in peacetime. But in mid-1941, rallied behind the banner of black labor leader A. Philip Randolph and his Brotherhood of Sleeping Car Porters, the March on Washington Movement (MOWM) threatened a mass march on Washington unless the federal government pledged to open wartime defense jobs to black workers. The MOWM relied on the mobilization of working-class blacks, and President Franklin Roosevelt complied with Randolph's demand by establishing the Fair Employment Practice Committee (FEPC) by executive order. Though limited in scope—it could combat discrimination only in plants engaged in war work—and lacking enforcement powers, the FEPC was the first government entity devoted to combating employment discrimination and as such established an important precedent for the postwar civil rights movement. The FEPC helped blacks gain access to defense employment but proved largely unable to dislodge obstacles to black entry into skilled positions or to rectify unequal pay arrangements.

Still with the government's imprimatur on their wartime employment, over one million new black workers entered the workforce, two-thirds of them women. Wartime employment gains for blacks in manufacturing proved especially significant. Only 17% of black men worked in manufacturing in 1940, but by 1944 this figure had increased to 30%. The changes for black women, who previously had been employed primarily in domestic service, proved dramatic as well; by the end of the war, nearly 20% of employed black women worked in manufacturing.

Trade unions responded in a number of ways to the influx of black workers. By 1943, there were 500,000 blacks enrolled in the Congress of Industrial Organizations (CIO) unions and another 650,000 in the American Federation of labor (AFL), a dramatic increase over prewar levels in both federations. Some CIO affiliates, like the United Automobile Workers (UAW) or the United Electrical Workers, made efforts to quell the racial hostility of their white membership and to discipline workers who engaged in hate strikes against the promotion and upgrade of black workers or desegregation of previously all-white shop floors. It was here that a lasting alliance was forged between the nascent civil rights movement and the racially progressive forces inside the CIO, which helped set the stage for some postwar working-class based civil rights activism. In response to the mobilization of its African-American members, for example the CIO instituted a Committee on Racial Discrimination (CARD). On the other hand powerful AFL unions, like the Machinists and the Boilermakers, continued to discriminate against African-Americans. The latter union, which maintained a grip on many jobs in the rapidly expanding shipbuilding industry, relegated black workers to impotent auxiliary unions. Blacks for their part filed complaints against the Boilermakers with the FEPC and developed independent organizations to challenge union and workplace discrimination. In general, the war years marked a moment of opportunity and mobilization for black workers, but the basic barriers of employment discrimination were not breached, the efforts of the FEPC, the CIO's CARD, and black workers themselves notwithstanding.

Women at Work

The war conscripted male workers into military service—almost 30% of the male labor force in the Detroit area entered the military, for example—and thus opened up opportunities—and pressures—for women to enter the work force. When the United States entered the war in late 1941, one-quarter of the nation's women already worked for wages outside their own homes (although the figure for black women was far higher—38%—than for white). But only 15.5% of married women did so. The number of women employed expanded from 12 million in 1940 to 19 million by 1945, peaking at a female labor-force participation figure of 36%. This was not simply a market response to the huge labor demand stimulated by wartime output and labor shortage. Federal government agencies did much to encourage female labor-force participation, from recruitment and training (the War Manpower Commission) to propaganda (the Office of War Information) and even in a few rare instances, the provision of child care for female defense workers with young children (Federal Works Agency). Women also joined unions in new record numbers: Their ranks jumped from 800,000 to 3 million, representing nearly one-quarter of all organized workers by 1943.

Despite the ubiquitous image of Rosie the Riveter, the attractive, unmarried, can-do female-manufacturing worker who appeared in wartime propaganda, the female industrial-defense worker represented but a small percentage of the overall number of women who poured into the wartime labor force. At the peak of female employment, two million women worked in defense plants, but this never represented more than 10% of all female workers at the time. As the figure of Rosie suggested, shipyard employment was one of the largest categories of female industrial employment during the war (second only to aviation, in which one-third of all workers were female), but the total in this sector never exceeded 225,000, or less than 20% of workers in that crucial wartime industry. And only a small number of women broke into the skilled trades in any industry; less than 5% of war jobs classified by the government as skilled went to women and even fewer to African-American women, who were only hired into these positions late in the war if at all. Still at the peak of war production in 1943 and 1944, nearly half of all women entered the workforce for some period, and for the first time the number of married women in the workforce exceeded the number of single women.

The new role for women as industrial workers was simultaneously embraced and denied, understood as an act of patriotic duty and yet accommodated to the feminine ideals to which most of the society, including women themselves, continued to adhere. An article in the *Woman's Home Companion* could report with pride that "American women are learning how to put planes and tanks together, how to read blueprints, how to weld and rivet and make the great machinery of war production hum under skillful hands and eyes," yet insist at the same time that "they're also learning how to look smart in overalls and how to be glamorous after work. They are learning to fulfill both the useful and the beautiful ideal."

In general long-standing gender barriers and attitudes seemed impervious to the upheavals of the war. "The unprecedented relationships between men and women which wartime work entailed . . . were to be in large part reabsorbed into the dominant pattern of tradition," one woman who worked in a shipyard remarked with evident disappointment. The sudden change in the place of women in the labor market proved profoundly threatening to male coworkers, husbands (and prospective husbands), and postwar reconversion planners alike. Not only did women's war work erode divisions between male and female work, but it had material consequence as well: These jobs paid better than any work women had done before and provided them with the potential means of economic independence. Three-quarters of the women surveyed by the U.S. Women's Bureau in the last year of the war claimed they intended to remain in the labor force, most often out of economic necessity, to provide for their own support or that of other family members.

A combination of factors—returning servicemen eager for work and wives; government reconversion planning that favored men; a shrinking number of jobs as shipyards and aviation plants demobilized; the opposition of trade unions; and on the part of many if hardly all women, the desire to marry, bear children, and return to the home—drove women from the workforce at the close of the war. If one-quarter of the workforce in the auto industry was female in 1945, a year later the figure had shrunk to 1 in 12. In the last 6 months of 1945 alone, 1.32 million women were laid off from their defense jobs. At bottom male anxiety about maintaining the role as breadwinner and fear of female economic independence proved unshakeable.

Unions and the State

With the rapid growth of wartime employment in the sectors of the economy that had seen union gains during the organizing drives of the 1930s—steel, rubber, meatpacking, auto, electrical—organized labor gained five million new members during the war, an increase of 50%. Those sectors of the economy oriented to the production of war materiel grew exponentially. In the shipbuilding industry on the Pacific Coast, for example, the San Francisco Bay Area alone saw the number of shipyard workers increase from a mere 6,000 to 240,000 during the war, and many of these newcomers joined unions. By 1945, the UAW had surpassed one million members, from a 1939 starting point of 165,000. Over 700,000 steelworkers, 400,000 electrical workers, 225,000 meatpackers, and 200,000 shipbuilders helped fill the ranks of organized labor by war's end. By 1945, 35% of nonagricultural workers belonged to unions, and a remarkable 80% of the workforce in basic industry had been organized. Although these gains swelled union treasuries and enhanced labor's political clout, they also served to dilute the number of committed and experienced members and weakened union discipline. The new recruits paid dues, but few had experience with trade unions, and many proved reluctant to participate in union affairs. Others chafed at the union restrictions they encountered and found the no-strike pledge, enforced by the unions themselves, a hindrance to the expression of shop-floor grievances. Finally the new industrial unions of the CIO and the old-line craft unions of the AFL, especially in the metal trades, fought bitter jurisdictional battles over access to labor's potential new members.

The CIO in particular sought to bolster its position by working closely with government agencies. As the imperative of conversion to military production approached, leaders of the industrial union federation moved to establish joint labor-management councils to guarantee labor a seat at the table with big business and government in the event of wartime industrial mobilization. In 1940–1941, both Philip Murray, president of the CIO, and UAW Vice-President Walter Reuther proposed industrial-council plans that would make organized labor an equal partner in tripartite planning of production, investment, procurement, and labor supply. Reuther for example put forth an ambitious vision of an Aviation Production Board that would convert Detroit's industrial plant into a production unit capable of manufacturing 500 planes a day. But large corporations, the military, and even government wartime civilian agencies, like the National Defense Advisory Commission (NDAC), fended off these bold initiatives and ensured that organized labor would remain a junior partner in the organization of war production. Management resisted outside interference—whether from civilian boards, labor, or the state—with its prerogatives: As General Motors President and member of the NDAC William Knudsen put it: "We don't want any part of the Russian system over here."

If organized labor had limited success in influencing mobilization plans, in the arena of labor relations they did achieve a genuine involvement in tripartite dispute-resolution mechanisms during the war. In 1941, spurred by rapidly increasing labor demand and a desire to consolidate the organizational gains of the 1930s, workers took to the picket lines in unprecedented numbers. That year unions called 4,200 strikes, taking out a total of 2.3 million workers, many of them in coal, steel, auto, and electrical industries, the heart of the American industrial economy. This upheaval in the face of the growing threat of American involvement in the war led Roosevelt and his allies in the labor movement to establish a tripartite mediation board that would adjudicate labor-management disputes in defense industries. Once the United States entered the war however strike action took a backseat to patriotic production, and both the CIO and AFL agreed to a no-strike pledge for the duration.

In exchange the National War Labor Board (NWLB)—prior to Pearl Harbor, the National Defense Mediation Board—which consisted of 12 members, four each from labor (divided evenly between the CIO and AFL), business, and government provided unprecedented protection of union security. Of the many wartime administrative agencies designed to oversee war production—the War Manpower Commission, the War Production Board, the U.S. Employment Service—this was the only one in which organized labor proved able to gain some representation and wield some influence. Despite grumbling by rank-and-file workers about limited wage increases, restrictions on labor mobility and strikes, and limitations on overtime pay, the NWLB placated labor leaders by granting maintenance-of-membership clauses in many of the union contracts it approved. Under these agreements all newly hired workers in a union shop would be automatically enrolled in the union after a 15-day waiting period. For organized labor this proved an essential component of the wartime industrial-relations regime because of the enormous influx of new workers with no prior experience with unions into the defense industries. The union security thus gained proved instrumental in encouraging the growth of organized labor during the war.

Union security came at a price, however. In exchange for state-mandated expansion of their organizations, union leaders were expected to uphold the no-strike pledge embraced by both the CIO and AFL and to suppress unauthorized, or wildcat strikes. Furthermore the necessity of war production entailed increased overtime, production speed-ups, and shortcuts on workplace safety. The volatile combination of inexperienced workers, new machinery, long stretches of overtime, and ceaseless demand for increased output led to an epidemic of workplace accidents, with an especially terrible toll in the nation's coal mines. From 1942–1943, 3,000 miners were killed on the job, and over 500 were injured every week. Across the nation 80,000 workers had been killed by accidents by 1943, far less than American battlefield casualties up to that time. Finally while state-mediated collective bargaining helped unions secure recognition and contracts, the NWLB sought to check inflation and thus served as a brake on rising wages during a period of intense labor demand.

In particular despite the organizational gains instigated for unions by the NWLB, both workers and the labor movement expressed deep dissatisfaction with the board's little steel formula on wage increases. In an effort to restrain rapidly advancing wartime inflation, the NWLB laid down a policy in July 1942 that capped wage increases at about 3%, a figure the board claimed matched the gap between the increase in cost of living and wage gains over the past 18 months. This wage-stabilization formula essentially placed the burden of inflationary restraint on wage earners and proved immensely unpopular with rank-and-file workers. In order to mollify workers however, the NWLB granted frequent nonwage benefits in lieu of wage increases. In fact despite wage restraints, real pay for manufacturing workers did increase significantly during the war, setting the stage for a postwar consumption boom. But this can be attributed more to regular employment, grueling overtime, and more widespread access to skilled positions than growth in basic wage rates.

The combination of strict union discipline, dampened wage demands, and intensification of production eventually led to an outbreak of wildcat strikes. Despite the no-strike pledge, millions of workers continued to walk off the job during the war when dissatisfied; indeed the figure in 1944, when over two million workers engaged in 5,000 strikes, neared that of the strike-prone year of 1940. In the auto industry such strikes were especially widespread, with over half of all workers taking part in some form of work stoppage during that tumultuous year on the factory floor. The work stoppages of 1944 however had an average duration of less than 6 days, historically a very low number, and involved only half as many striking workers as did 1946, a year with a comparable number of strikes. Thus wildcats consisted of strikes of short duration and of relatively small groups of workers (43% brought out 100 workers or less), designed to resolve particularistic shop-floor grievances.

Union leadership was often enlisted in cajoling recalcitrant rank-and-filers back to work. Those leaders who refused to relinquish the strike weapon, most notably John L. Lewis of the United Mine Workers (which broke from the CIO during the war), found themselves hedged in by punitive legislation. Lewis had never shared the interventionist aims of Roosevelt's foreign policy, had opposed the militarization of the American economy and the corporatist labor policy of the war, and refused to endorse the president for a third term in the 1940 election. By 1941, Lewis took the miners out on strike and after a bitter battle secured a closed shop in the captive mines owned by the steel industry. Two years later in 1943, when he did so again in an effort to thwart the little-steel-formula cap on wages, a Republican-dominated Congress enacted in response the War Labor Disputes, or Smith-Connally Act, giving the president wide powers to seize defense plants (and the coal mines) threatened by strikes and mandating a 30-day cooling off period in essential workplaces threatened by a strike call. The act went well beyond the war crisis and attempted to clip labor's wings politically as well, forbidding union contributions to political campaigns. In order to evade these restrictions, the CIO created a political action campaign, the CIO-PAC, to register and educate working-class voters, back labor-friendly candidates, and serve as a counterweight to the emergent congressional alliance of antilabor Republicans and southern Democrats. Though the effects of Smith-Connally were not so drastic as labor feared, it proved a harbinger of postwar limitations of labor's rights embodied in the Taft-Hartley Act of 1947.

Conclusion

The impact of World War II left a mixed legacy for the nation's working class. Wartime mobilization created full employment, but victory over Japan in August 1945 instantly ushered in layoffs, as $24 billion in war contracts evaporated; 300,000 defense workers lost their jobs in Michigan alone after V-J day. Over the next 3 months as pent-up consumer savings stimulated inflation, real income dropped by an average of 15%, and the specter of unemployment returned as nearly 13 million men in uniform demobilized into the American labor market. Although many of the nation's most powerful corporations accepted the basic elements of collective bargaining over wages and benefits extended by the wartime state, they also sought to ensure that the growing influence of organized labor would not intrude on such managerial and corporate prerogatives as investment decisions, pricing policy, and basic control of production processes on the shop floor of the nation's factories. Declining incomes, fear of layoffs, the end of the no-strike pledge, and the re-assertion of corporate power generated a postwar strike wave that expressed accumulated grievances. In the 12 months following the end of the war, there were 4,630 strikes, involving five million workers.

Wartime work had incorporated millions of new workers into the industrial working class. But with the conflict over, the no-strike pledge, stepped up production, racial and sexual tension on the shop floor, and bitter interunion rivalries between the CIO and AFL, the wartime workplace was shot through with tensions that sporadically erupted into violent altercations and unauthorized work stoppages. These conflicts set the stage for postwar disputes about the place of women in the workplace, the civil rights of black workers, and the political influence of organized labor.

Finally historians continue to debate the nature of the corporatist settlement organized labor struck with business and the state during the war. The workplace contractualism bequeathed to the postwar social order by the NWLB was at one time regarded as a straitjacket for the rank-and-file, enlisting bureaucratic trade unions in quelling militant shop-floor tendencies.

ALEX LICHTENSTEIN

References and Further Reading

Archibald, Katherine. *Wartime Shipyard: A Study in Social Disunity*. Urbana: University of Illinois Press, 2006. (reprint, 1947)

Atleson, James B. *Labor and the Wartime State*. Urbana: University of Illinois Press: 1998.

Gluck, Sherna Berger. *Rosie the Riveter Revisited: Women, the War, and Social Change*. Boston, 1987.

Himes, Chester. *If He Hollers, Let Him Go*. New York, 2002. (reprint, 1945)

Lichtenstein, Nelson. *Labor's War at Home: The CIO in World War II*. Philadelphia, PA: 2004.

Milkman, Ruth. *Gender at Work: The Dynamics of Job Segregation by Sex during World War II*. Urbana: University of Illinois Press, 1987.

Miller, Sally M., and Daniel A. Cornford. *American Labor in the Era of World War II*. Westport, CT: 1995.

Reed, Merl A. *Seedtime for the Modern Civil Rights Movement: The President's Committee on Fair Employment Practice, 1941–1946*. Baton Rouge, 1991.

Cases and Statutes Cited

Smith-Connally Act
Taft-Hartley Act

See also **Brotherhood of Sleeping Car Porters; Fair Employment Practice Committee; March on Washington Movement; National War Labor Board; No-Strike Pledge; Randolph, Philip A.; Reuther, Walter; Rosie the Riveter; Smith-Connally Act; Taft-Hartley Act; United Electrical Workers of America; United Mine Workers of America; Women's Bureau**

WRIGHT, FRANCES (1795–1852)
Radical Reformer

Born in 1795, in Dundee, Scotland, Frances, or Fanny, Wright was a writer, orator, feminist, freethinker, and utopian Socialist who was one of the boldest radical reformers of her time. Though her prosperous father held radical and democratic views, she was orphaned at age two and was raised in London and Devonshire by Tory relatives, against whom she rebelled. At the age of 18, she left England to live with her uncle, James Mylne, a noted professor of moral philosophy at the University of Glasgow, who also espoused radical democratic ideas at a time

when to do so was to dissent from British orthodoxy. Though barred from attending the university because of her sex, Wright read widely and began writing. She soon became enamored of the republican United States, whose egalitarian founding principles were reflected in her own views. By 1818, when she set sail for New York, Wright's social and political philosophy was already fully formed. Influenced by Enlightenment rationalism, Mary Wollstonecraft's feminism, Paineite radicalism, Bentham's utilitarianism, and such utopian Socialists as Robert Owen and Saint-Simon, Wright devoted her career to democracy, feminism, the rights of workers and the poor, free thought, and racial equality. Although her career included more failures than successes, Fanny Wright brought immense publicity to the causes she espoused and influenced others to support labor and other progressive views.

In 1821, shortly after her return to Britain, she published the first serious study of the United States by a British woman, *Views of Society and Manners in America*. Openly sympathetic toward the democratic ideals of the new republic, the book won plaudits from several British intellectuals, including Jeremy Bentham, and sparked a friendship with the Marquis de Lafayette. Indeed when Wright returned to the United States in 1823, it was with Lafayette, who introduced her to James Madison and Thomas Jefferson, with whom she discussed her evolving communitarian scheme to achieve the gradual emancipation of slaves. Instead of returning with Lafayette, she became a naturalized U.S. citizen and set out to put her ideas into action.

Encouraged by Jefferson and Madison to pursue her experiment, in 1825 Wright used some of her inheritance to purchase a tract of land, which she named Nashoba, near Memphis, Tennessee, and 10 slaves. Believing that slaves needed training and education before they could succeed as free people, Wright's original intent was for her slaves to earn their freedom by working the land for 5 years, and then moving to another country. Though Wright advocated abolition of slavery, like many who believed in colonization, she could not envision a racially egalitarian United States. Instead her goal was the uplifting and emigration of the black population. Marriage laws and religion had no place at Nashoba, and when one of her white followers publicized this interracial free love philosophy, Nashoba lost financial backers and made many enemies. Wright's defense of racial and sexual equality outraged conventional opinion. Owing to the poor quality of the land and the prevalence of malaria and other diseases, Nashoba failed by early 1828. Although she eventually managed to resettle 30 ex-slaves in Haiti, the collapse of the Nashoba experiment surely caused Wright to question her belief in the value of communitarian solutions to social problems.

Undaunted Wright repaired to New Harmony with Robert Dale Owen, to assist him in editing the *New Harmony Gazette.* Her principal activity for the rest of her life however was as a public speaker. Defying the limits on women by appearing widely as a public lecturer, Wright became one of the first women publicly to address gender-mixed audiences on secular topics in the United States. To make matters even more controversial, Wright advocated radical viewpoints on sensitive themes, attacking slavery, the oppression of women, revealed religion, the rising influence of evangelical clerics, the exploitation of workers and the poor, and existing forms of schooling. Most shocking were her frontal assaults against traditional marriage and the subjugation of women. An electrifying speaker and a hero to fellow freethinkers, Wright became the object of vitriolic abuse, both physical and verbal. Several of her lectures were met with riots.

In 1829, Wright and Owen relocated to New York City, where they renamed their newspaper the *Free Enquirer.* Here Wright found an enthusiastic audience among the radical artisans of the city, many of whom shared her radical democratic views and anticlerical beliefs. Her lectures were attended by hundreds, and she played an important role in reviving the energy of the anticlerical and artisanal Left. Wright increasingly focused on the plight of urban workers, and promoted Owen's proposal for a system of state-sponsored free boarding schools as the key to abolishing class inequality. Though her ideas were influential among many artisans and her undoubted skill as a public speaker helped to energize radical politics in New York, Wright was never directly or formally involved in the Working Men's party of New York, though Owen did lead a faction for a time. After the failure of the Working Men's party, Wright left the United States for Europe, where she lived from 1831 to 1835.

On her return to the United States in 1835, Wright resumed her writing and lecturing, but some of her ideas were no longer quite so radical. Her advocacy of gradual emancipation and colonization seemed almost moderate in comparison to the rise of the immediate abolitionism of William Lloyd Garrison and others. In 1836, Wright positioned herself unusually close to the political mainstream by campaigning for Martin Van Buren and the Jacksonians' banking policies. Her feminism however remained radical and controversial, and she published several powerful statements regarding the universality of woman's oppression. In January 1852, having endured a bitter divorce, she slipped on ice and broke her leg. After suffering for 10 months with severe pain, she died.

Wright represented an important Atlantic crossing between the salon radicalism of Britain and France and the radical politics of the nineteenth-century United States, in particular the feminist, abolitionist, communitarian, and labor movements. Though her radical projects failed and her ideas lacked originality, Wright played an important role as a popularizer and publicizer of radical thought. Her most important legacy was to feminism, and her work on behalf of the Working Men's party helped to popularize that movement and some of its ideas for a time. More broadly her life stands as a testament to the radical potential of American egalitarianism—and to the contradictions confronting those who try to realize that potential in words and deeds.

MATTHEW S. R. BEWIG

References and Further Reading

Bartlett, Elizabeth Ann. *Liberty, Equality, Sorority: The Origins and Interpretation of American Feminist Thought: Frances Wright, Sarah Grimke, and Margaret Fuller.* Brooklyn, NY: Carlson Publishing, 1994.

Bederman, Gail. "Revisiting Nashoba: Slavery, Utopia, and Frances Wright in America, 1818–1826." *American Literary History* 17, 3 (2005): 438–459.

Born, Kate. "Organized Labor in Memphis, Tennessee, 1826–1901." *West Tennessee Historical Society Papers* 21 (1967): 60–79.

Earle, Jonathan H. *Jacksonian Antislavery and the Politics of Free Soil, 1824–1854.* Chapel Hill: University of North Carolina Press, 2004.

Eckhardt, Celia Morris. *Fanny Wright: Rebel in America.* Cambridge, MA: Harvard University Press, 1984.

Ginzberg, Lori D. "'The Hearts of Your Readers Will Shudder': Fanny Wright, Infidelity, and American Freethought." *American Quarterly* 46 (June 1994): 195–226.

Lane, Margaret. *Frances Wright and "The Great Experiment."* Manchester, UK: Manchester University Press, 1972.

Perkins, A. J. G., and T. Wolfson. *Frances Wright, Free Enquirer.* New York: Harper & Brothers, 1939.

Wilentz, Sean. *Chants Democratic.* New York: Oxford University Press, 1984.

Wright, Frances. *Views of Society and Manners in America.* London, UK: 1821.

———. *Course of Popular Lectures.* New York: 1829.

WURF, JERRY (MAY 8, 1919–DECEMBER 10, 1981)
President of District Council 37 (New York City) of the American Federation of State, County and Municipal Employees (AFSCME)

The most important public-sector union leader of the last-half of the twentieth century, Jerry Wurf helped turn public workers from a weak and neglected section of organized labor into one of the most dynamic groups within the American Federation of Labor-Congress of Industrial Organizations (AFL-CIO), eventually challenging and shaping the broader goals of trade unionism in the United States. Born and raised in New York City, Wurf was the son of Sigmund and Lena Tannenbaum Wurf, first- and second-generation immigrants from Central and Eastern European Jewish backgrounds. Wurf attended local public schools, where he excelled in the humanities, and in the early 1940s, enrolled at New York University where he received a degree in economics. During his high school years, he became a follower of American socialist leader Norman Thomas, joining the Young People's Socialist League (YPSL), an experience that introduced him to the art of political organizing and developing in him a broader interest in social concerns and civil liberties that would shape his political commitments for the remainder of his life.

Following graduation Wurf took a job as a cashier in a cafeteria and organized his workplace for the Hotel and Restaurant Employees' Union, Local 488, eventually working on the union's staff. Frustrated with the level of bureaucracy in the local, but wanting to remain involved with the labor movement, Wurf accepted a position as an organizer with District Council 37, New York City's section of the American Federation of State, County, and Municipal Employees (AFSCME) in 1947. Wurf soon emerged as a reformer within AFSCME, taking over as DC 37 president in 1952 and transforming a weak organization into one of the most powerful unions in the city. Wurf was a demanding leader whose hot temper and tendency to micromanage union affairs sometimes alienated staff members, but his single-mindedness also resulted in unprecedented success. As DC 37 head Wurf directed major organizing drives into unrepresented city departments and succeeded in challenging New York's labor-management policies. Wurf's ability to secure new rights for municipal employees helped gain AFSCME new members in New York, going from a scant 400 members in 1952, to 20,000 by 1960.

In 1960, Wurf married Mildred Kiefer, who joined the District Council 37 staff in the early 1950s. A committed activist involved in the workers' education movement, she was the source of many of the innovative ideas that marked AFSCME's growth in New York during these years, and she was Wurf's greatest inspiration in his work as a labor leader.

Wurf's success in New York City gained him recognition as one of AFSCME's most innovative leaders. Eventually a series of disagreements with AFSCME international founder and president, Arnold Zander, would launch him into a national campaign to restructure the union. Since AFSCME's founding in 1932, Zander had reigned as the union's undisputed chieftain, but by 1958 a series of internal disputes, centered on controversial increases in membership dues and undemocratic convention regulations divided many within AFSCME. Although not originally a leader of the reform section, Wurf reluctantly emerged as its most forceful spokesperson. Following the union's 1960 convention, a national reform organization emerged within AFSCME, the Committee on Union Responsibility (COUR). With Mildred Kiefer and a cadre of regional leaders, Wurf established COUR chapters across the United States and narrowly defeated Zander as international president in 1964.

Taking over as AFSCME international president, Wurf immediately set out to restructure and reform the union. Financial restructuring ranked high on Wurf's agenda, with measures taken to improve the union's financial status, which had long been supported by the AFL-CIO Industrial Union Department. By 1966, Wurf had realized most of his campaign promises, including the redrafting of the international union constitution, implementing more transparent election codes, placing limits on the international's ability to place locals in trusteeship, establishing a judicial panel to oversee the union's disputes, and expanding AFSCME's executive board from 13 to 18 members.

The initial period of Wurf's presidency was marked by a series of high-profile national organizing campaigns. The AFSCME along with other public-sector unions expanded membership by the thousands during the 1960s. By 1969, AFSCME led the way, gaining as many as 1,000 new members a week. The most famous AFSCME drive of this period occurred in 1968, when almost 2,000 African-American sanitation workers in Memphis went on strike for higher wages, better working conditions, and recognition of AFSCME Local 1733 as their official bargaining agent. Memphis city officials refused to recognize the union, resorting to violent anti-union measures. The AFSCME forged new alliances with numerous community- and church-based organizations in the city's African-American community, linking the workplace struggle of the sanitation workers to broader community issues and African-American civil rights. Seeing the struggle of the sanitation workers as central to the broader movement to secure better conditions for the nation's poor, civil rights leader Martin Luther King came to Memphis to aid the cause, where he was assassinated on April 4, 1968. Following King's death, with international attention drawn to the cause of the striking workers, Wurf went to Memphis where he helped to negotiate Local 1733's first contract.

1553

Through the late 1960s, Wurf was the most visible national spokesperson for the new form of social unionism championed by AFSCME, often making public appearances on national television and radio programs. Through these years Wurf spoke out often against the Vietnam War and the domestic policies of President Richard Nixon. In 1969, Wurf was named to the AFL-CIO executive council, signifying the new status of public-employee unionism and AFSCME within the U.S. labor movement. Wurf's independence often placed him at odds with federation President George Meany over national politics, foreign policy, and the position of public workers within the labor movement. Wurf broke publicly with Meany over his failure to support the formation of AFL-CIO Public Employees' Department as a national lobbying organ of the federation committed to the concerns of public workers. In response Wurf went outside the federation by linking with the independent National Education Association (NEA) in forming the Coalition of Public Employee Organizations (COPE) in 1971. Two years later Wurf organized a similar organization with other AFL-CIO public employee unions, linking with the International Association of Firefighters (IAFF) and the National Treasury Employees' Union to form the Coalition of American Public Employees (CAPE), a move that further distanced him from Meany. Rival public-sector union leaders, especially Albert Shanker, head of New York City's American Federation of Teachers (AFT) publicly fought with Wurf in the 1970s over agenda and policy issues, causing rifts between their organizations that hampered solidarity in a period of mounting government opposition to public-sector unionization.

Perhaps Wurf's most important contribution as a labor leader in the last-quarter of the twentieth century was his insistence that the labor movement be an instrument for broad social change. Political engagement was primary to this objective. Wurf envisioned AFSCME as an important force in shaping a progressive agenda within the national Democratic party, an aspect of his vision that continues to shape AFSCME's sense of purpose into the twenty-first century. In 1971, Wurf established the union's political arm, Public Employees Organized to Promote Legislative Equality (PEOPLE), which actively supported Democratic presidential candidate George McGovern in 1972 as well as Jimmy Carter's successful bid in 1976. The AFSCME's PEOPLE organization was one of the largest political-action committees in the United States in the early twentieth century. Disappointed with President Carter's economic, labor, and social policies, Wurf sided with Senator Edward Kennedy in his challenge to Carter in Democratic primaries in 1980. Despite increasing health problems, Wurf was the key organizer of the Solidarity Day demonstration in Washington, DC, in September 1981, where 260,000 labor and civil rights groups, led by a 60,000-member AFSCME delegation, protested against the social programs of the Reagan administration. Wurf died on December 10, 1981, and was replaced by Gerald McEntee, leader of Pennsylvania AFSCME District Council 13 as AFSCME international president. Wurf's legacy in the U.S. labor movement remains his call to link social causes with workplace issues and in the challenge continuously to organize new members in the lowest paid job categories.

FRANCIS RYAN

References and Further Reading

Bellush, Bernard, and Jewel Bellush. *Union Power and New York: Victor Gotbaum and District Council 37*. New York: Praeger, 1984.

Billings, Richard N., and John Greenya. *Power to the Public Worker*. Washington, DC: R. B. Luce, 1974.

Freeman, Joshua B. *Working-Class New York: Life and Labor since World War II*. New York, The New Press, 2000.

Goulden, Joseph C. *Jerry Wurf: Labor's Last Angry Man*. New York: Atheneum, 1982.

Maier, Mark H. *City Unions: Managing Discontent in New York City*. New Brunswick, NJ and London, UK: Rutgers University, 1987.

See also **American Federation of State, County, and Municipal Employees (AFSCME); McEntee, Gerald W.; Shanker, Albert**

Y

YABLONSKI, JOSEPH A. "JOCK" (1910–1969)
United Mine Workers

In 1969, Joseph A. "Jock" Yablonski challenged the president of the United Mine Workers of America (UMWA), William Anthony "Tony" Boyle, in a union election. Boyle defeated Yablonski and then ordered his death. Yablonski's supporters, known as the Miners for Democracy, mounted a campaign that led to the election being nullified in 1972. Boyle was defeated in an election in that same year and later was convicted of Yablonski's murder.

Yablonski was born in Pittsburgh on March 3, 1910, the son of Polish immigrants. He quit school at age 15 to work in the mines. He left the mines in 1927 and worked as a baggage handler for the Pennsylvania Railroad and as an appliance salesman for the West Penn Power Company. In 1930, he was sentenced to eight months in a workhouse for stealing money from a slot machine.

In 1933, his father died of injuries suffered in a mine. Yablonski took his father's job and began a career as a union leader. He became active in the UMWA and rose quickly in the union hierarchy. In 1934, he was elected to his local mine committee, became president of UMWA Local 1787, and was chosen as a member of the District 5 executive board, even though he was only 24 years old. In those roles, he was an outspoken advocate of mine safety and led several successful organizing drives.

In 1940, he supported the union's revered leader, John L. Lewis, in his campaign for Wendell Willkie for president. With Lewis's backing, Yablonski was elected to the UMWA's International Executive Board (IEB). In 1958, he became president of District 5 in Pittsburgh. That district was one of the few that elected its officers rather than having them appointed by the president. Yablonski's positions as a labor executive allowed him to live comfortably on one hundred acres of land in Clarksville, Pennsylvania.

Yablonski hoped to become president of the union but was not selected for the office when Lewis retired in 1960. Yablonski continued to be a member of the UMWA's hierarchy, but he upset Boyle by running for the union's vice presidency in 1964 without Boyle's approval. He was fired as District 5 president in 1966 as a result of his actions but remained on the International Executive Board. In April 1969, he became acting director of the union's lobbying wing, Labor's Non-Partisan League. He was fired from that position when he announced his candidacy for president.

Yablonski had been loyal to the union's leadership, but he finally became sufficiently frustrated to mount a challenge. Yablonski was the highest-ranking officer ever to challenge a UMWA president. He was an effective negotiator who had maintained contact with the rank-and-file miners. He had worked with Lewis and believed he had similar skills as a leader. If he could get his message to the miners, Yablonski believed that he could defeat Boyle. Unfortunately, he was not able to mount an effective campaign because of threats of violence and Boyle's manipulation of the union's election machinery. Yablonski lost the election by 74,000 to 41,000 votes. Boyle, however, was not simply content to win the election. He wanted to punish Yablonski for running against him. On December 31, Yablonski, his wife, Margaret, and his daughter, Charlotte, were murdered in their home. Their murders outraged miners and led to the creation of the Miners for Democracy.

After his death, Yablonski was the subject of a movie, *Act of Vengeance* (1986), and songs were written about him across the coalfields. Although he failed to win the election, Yablonski provided a vivid example of the power of labor martyrs to overthrow corrupt and inefficient union leaders and make reform possible in the UMWA.

RICHARD J. JENSEN

References and Further Reading

Armbrister, Trevor. *Act of Vengeance*. New York: Saturday Review Press, 1975.
Brown, Stuart. *A Man Named Tony*. New York: W. W. Norton, Inc., 1976.
Dubofsky, Melvyn, and Warren Van Tine. *John L. Lewis*. New York: Quadrangle/The New York Times, 1977.
Finley, Joseph E. *The Corrupt Kingdom*. New York: Simon and Schuster, 1972.
Hume, Brit. *Death and the Mines*. New York: Grossman Publishers, 1971.
Lewis, Arthur H. *Murder by Contract*. New York: Macmillan Publishing Co., 1975.
Peterson, Bill. *Coaltown Revisited*. Chicago: Regnery, 1972.

See also **Boyle, W. A. (Tony); Miners for Democracy; United Mine Workers of America**

"YELLOW-DOG" CONTRACT

As early as the 1840s, employers had required workers to pledge to abstain from union membership as a condition for employment, but "ironclad" contracts, as such arrangements were called, only emerged as a common anti-union tool beginning in the 1870s. By the 1890s, unionists used the term "yellow dog" as a means of expressing contempt for workers who agreed, orally or in writing, to this employer demand. Despite labor's widespread resistance to the "yellow dog," the courts consistently upheld the contract's legality between the 1880s and 1932.

Employers defended the contract on ideological grounds—it represented the freedom to run one's business unhindered by outsiders and to work for an employer of one's choosing. The contract was the antithesis of slavery, according to this formulation, because it recognized workers' right to their own labor; it did not compel the worker to sign. Unionists, however, pointed out that the term "contract" obscured the unequal bargaining position of workers and employers. The yellow dog violated workers' freedom of association, a liberty that, as one Illinois labor leader put it, defined "the essential difference between the free man and the slave." (Ernst, p. 264). Unionists recognized that the danger of the yellow dog went beyond its violations of workers' individual rights. The main purpose of the yellow dog was to deter union organizers, who, faced with a possible lawsuit for interfering with a contract, might well abandon their efforts in the early stages of a union's campaign. Indeed, in some industries in the early twentieth century, union activity became nearly impossible as employers increasingly turned to court injunctions to enforce the yellow dog.

The federal courts largely accepted employers' arguments and consistently overturned state laws that banned the yellow-dog contract. Not until 1898 did the practice meet with its first federal legal challenge The Erdman Act prohibited the yellow-dog contract in the railroad industry, where it was widely used, as part of a general effort by large majorities in Congress to offer some minimal recognition to the legitimacy of trade unions, specifically, the railway brotherhoods, as a means of avoiding major strikes.

The federal judiciary continued to rule against labor, notwithstanding the impressive congressional support demonstrated for some accommodation with trade unionism. In the 1908 case *Adair v. United States*, the Supreme Court declared the Erdman Act's provision against the yellow dog unconstitutional on the grounds that it violated the principle of freedom of contract. Using the same rationale, the court overturned a Kansas law against the yellow dog in 1915. *Adair* served as a precedent for other antilabor rulings. In cases involving the United Mine Workers' attempts to bring into its ranks West Virginia workers who had signed yellow-dog contracts, federal judges issued strong rulings against the UMW. The first, citing the *Adair* case, concluded that the UMW had conspired to "destroy others' vested contract rights" (Dubofsky, p. 47). The second case's judge suggested that all unions were illegal under the Sherman Anti-Trust Act and the Constitution. A circuit court overturned the latter decision, but the Supreme Court upheld it.

Judicial support for the legality of the yellow-dog contract reached its highest point with the 1917 Supreme Court case *Hitchman Coal & Coke Co. v. Mitchell*. The majority opinion held that the agreement gave operators a "property interest" in their workers. The UMW's efforts to organize infringed on this interest, it continued, and thus represented "unfair competition." The mine operators' victory in *Hitchman* opened the door to a slew of injunctions against the UMW for even endeavoring to persuade nonunion workers to join in the nonunion southern fields. These injunctions increasingly brought federal and state troops into labor conflicts on the side of mine operators.

The yellow-dog contract served as the basis for at least 10% to 15% of the injunctions issued between 1917 and 1932. During WWI, the federal government suspended yellow-dog injunctions because the National War Labor Board's guiding purpose was to secure workers' wartime cooperation by promising mediation of labor disputes. But in the 1920s, the practice peaked, especially in smaller, highly competitive industries in which unions had made inroads but did not dominate, particularly bituminous coal mining and the garment industry.

In the late 1920s, political momentum built for anti-injunction legislation, partly as a result of labor's long and vociferous objections to "government by injunction." The restiveness in labor's ranks grew and found support among Progressive reformers within both of the major parties and in the courts. These reformers and a significant sector of the public increasingly accepted the idea that unions had a role to play in serving the common good as preservers of order in industrial relations. The economic realities of workers, which often involved employment with a large corporation, belied the claim that employers and employees met on an equal plane to freely contract or not with one another. Ironically, large firms had sought to reform their workplaces by introducing scientific management, pension plans, and annual vacations. These firms often viewed the yellow dog as a relic from a more autocratic, unstable industrial era.

With public sympathy for unions expanding further in the early years of the Great Depression, the Norris-LaGuardia Act of 1932 easily passed in both houses of Congress. The Act deemed the yellow-dog contract unenforceable with the larger purposes of legitimizing collective bargaining in the eyes of the law and limiting the grounds upon which the courts could issue antilabor injunctions. Under this legislation, American workers generally received the rights and protections previously applied only to railway workers. The means to enforce this labor law and others came in 1935 with passage of the Wagner Act, a pivotal piece of New Deal legislation that survived the Supreme Court's and employers' hostility. While the 1947 Taft-Hartley Act amended Wagner, and labor's fortunes have changed radically since the 1930s, the ban on the yellow-dog contract remains in place.

THERESA A. CASE

References and Further Reading

Dubofsky, Melvyn. *The State and Labor in Modern America*. Chapel Hill: University of North Carolina Press, 1994.
Ernst, Daniel. "The Yellow-Dog Contract and Liberal Reform, 1917–1932." *Labor History* 30, no. 2 (Spring 1989): 251–275.
Forbath, William. *Law and the Shaping of the American Labor Movement*. Cambridge, MA: Harvard University Press, 1991.

YONEDA, KARL (1906–1999)
California Labor Activist

Karl Yoneda was a labor organizer and civil rights activist. He was born Goso Yoneda to Japanese immigrants in California in 1906 but changed his name to Karl in honor of Karl Marx. In 1913, his father took the family back to Japan. In 1926, after receiving a notice that he would soon be drafted into the Japanese Imperial Army, Yoneda returned to America. In 1935, he married Elaine Black, who was well known in California for being a labor organizer. Yoneda worked closely with his wife for the next 60 years on behalf of organized labor in California and in an effort to improve civil rights for Japanese immigrants.

Yoneda engaged in and organized frequent labor strikes. As a teenager he participated in a strike against the newspaper for which he worked as a delivery boy, after they lengthened routes but did not increase the pay. As a young man he joined the labor movement in Japan, participating in printers' and rubber workers' strikes. After returning to America, Yoneda became a labor organizer for the Trade Union Educational League, which was affiliated with the U.S. Communist Party, of which he was a member. In 1927, he joined the Japanese Workers Association. In 1931, he participated in a labor protest in Los Angeles, in which he was severely beaten by police officers. Two years later, Yoneda was arrested for staging a protest at a Los Angeles City Council meeting, where he was beaten again by police officers.

He wrote for and edited several labor and Communist publications. While in Japan in the 1920s, he published an underground newspaper for poor farmers. He became the publications director of the Japanese Workers Association in 1928. In the 1930s, he served as the editor of *Rodo Shimbun*, a Japanese-language Communist newspaper in SanFrancisco. He used this newspaper to attract more Japanese immigrants to organized labor as well as to the Communist Party.

1557

After Japan invaded China in 1931, Yoneda was instrumental in leading strikes against Japanese ships among Japanese-American longshoremen throughout California. He was successful in organizing long-shoremen in a massive dock strike in San Francisco in 1934. The police were ultimately called in to break the strike, which resulted in two strikers being killed and dozens more being wounded. Because Yoneda had organized the strike, police officers broke into his office at the *Rodo Shimbun* newspaper and destroyed the printing press and arrested a number of the newspaper's employees.

Yoneda worked as a longshoreman intermittently for many years, from the 1930s to the 1970s. He also served as a labor organizer for the San Francisco chapter of the International Longshoremen's and Warehousemen's Union (ILWU). He was an official representative of the San Francisco ILWU at many state and national meetings. And he represented the ILWU at several international meetings. He also founded the Alaska Cannery Workers Union in San Francisco, where the company's employment office was located. He eventually served as the vice president of the union.

Following the bombing of Pearl Harbor in World War II, President Roosevelt issued an executive order mandating the internment of almost 112,000 Japanese-Americans on the West Coast. Although Yoneda resented having his loyalty to America tested, he was deeply committed to defeating Japan. As a result, he organized a group of Japanese-Americans to build an internment camp at Manzanar, where they would live for the duration of the war. Yoneda's wife and son also lived at the camp. He formed the Manzanar Citizens Federation to lobby for improved living conditions and to support the war effort. Because Yoneda supported the U.S. government's war goals, he was frequently criticized and accused of being a spy for the government in the camp. In an effort to avoid further tensions at the camp and due to his desire to defeat Japan, he joined the military in 1942. He served in the Military Intelligence Service, translating Japanese documents and writing propaganda materials. During the course of the war, he received several medals for his service.

After World War II, Yoneda continued to work as a longshoreman and remained active in the ILWU into the early 1970s. Following his retirement in 1972, he wrote several important books and a number of articles on Japanese-American labor history. Yoneda also taught labor history at several California universities. He organized annual pilgrimages to the Manzanar internment camp and was also an active member of the Japanese American Citizens League. He continued to participate in various peace and social justice organizations until his death in 1999.

GENE C. GERARD

References and Further Reading

Friday, Chris. "Karl Yoneda: Radical Organizing and Asian American Labor." In *The Human Tradition in American Labor History*, edited by Eric Arnesen. Wilmington, DE: Scholarly Resources, 2004, pp. 129–152.

Streamas, John. "Karl Yoneda and Japanese American Resistance." *Nature, Society, and Thought* 4, no. 2 (1998): 489–497.

Yoneda, Karl. *Ganbatte: Sixty-Year Struggle of a Kibei Worker*. Los Angeles: UCLA Press, 1983.

Z

ZOOT SUIT RIOTS

Since the late twentieth century, there has been much talk about the greatest U.S. generation, those who grew up during the hard times of the Great Depression of the 1930s, fought in World War II, and witnessed the nation become a global superpower. This breed of Americans, it is believed, was more self-reliant, more resilient, and more patriotic. Yet their behavior during the Zoot Suit Riots of 1943 was less than honorable. During that summer white sailors and soldiers in uniform rushed into downtown Los Angles seeking out Mexican youth and attacked them on the streets. This was an era when race riots were started by whites, and their violent actions often went without reproach. In fact the Los Angeles newspapers praised the troops for their bravery and thanked them for "cleaning up the town."

As World War II raged on overseas, numerous battles erupted on the home front. In addition to Los Angeles, 1943 saw riots in Harlem, Detroit, and even Beaumont, Texas. Tensions leading up to the Zoot Suit Riots had been brewing since the previous summer. The 1942 Sleepy Lagoon case fueled a backlash against Mexican youth. When Los Angeles resident Jose Diaz was found murdered, 17 Mexican young men, ages 17 to 21, allegedly rivals of the Thirty-eighth Street gang, were put on trial for murder. The International Labor Defense (ILD) came to their aid, and during the 1940s, the Sleepy Lagoon case became the West Coast's version of the Scottsboro case, in which the ILD had defended seven black youth on trial in the South for raping two white women.

The ILD assembled a defense team that included Carey McWilliams, Alice Greenfield McGrath, and Harry Braverman. They also formed the Sleepy Lagoon Defense Committee, a group of supporters that read like a roll call of prominent figures in the Hollywood Left: Actors Charlie Chapman, Rita Hayworth, Katherine Hepburn, Lena Horne, John Howard Lawson, Canada Lee, Clifford Odets, Dalton Trumbo, and Orson Welles. Novelist Guy Endore wrote a pamphlet entitled *Sleepy Lagoon Mystery* to help promote the campaign.

During the trial a captain in the sheriff's office told a grand jury that Mexicans were biologically predisposed toward violence because of their bloodthirsty Aztec heritage. The judge refused to allow the youth to fix their hair or change their clothes, thus further strengthening the impression that they were dirty criminals. Twelve of the defendants were convicted of murder, and five were convicted of assault. In October 1944, the U.S. District Court of Appeals overturned the convictions citing a miscarriage of justice. In the meantime many of the young women who were also believed to be part of the Thirty-eighth Street gang spent longer periods of time in reformatory school, which some claimed was worse than jail. During this 2-year span, the newspapers sensationalized the case, helping to create the perception among Los Angelenos that a crime wave was spreading through the city, and the terms zoot suit, *pachuco*, and gang became synonymous with Mexican youth.

Starting on June 3, 1943, and for a week afterward, thousands of sailors and soldiers stationed in Los Angeles stormed downtown, entered movie theaters,

Washington, D.C. Soldier inspecting a couple of "zoot suits" at the Uline Arena. Library of Congress, Prints & Photographs Division, FSA/OWI Collection [LC-USF34-011543-D].

assaulted brown-skinned youth, both blacks and Mexicans, and left them bloody and naked in the streets. Writing for the *Nation*, Carey McWilliams claimed that these riots were the result of sensational newspaper headlines about the Sleepy Lagoon case and police misconduct. In fact during the first few days of the riots, no police officers were seen in the area of downtown Los Angeles. When they finally did arrive, officers arrested more than 300 people—most all of them black and Hispanic. Even the Communist party denied the racial foundation of the riots and claimed instead that they were provoked by Fascists to disrupt the spirit of wartime unity. Among the few local newspapers that criticized the actions of the white servicemen was the Spanish community newspaper *La Opiñion* and the *California Eagle*, the black-owned and prolabor newspaper run by Charlotta Bass. In the *Crisis*, the national publication of the NAACP, black novelist Chester Himes gave his firsthand account of the riots and harshly criticized the white soldiers, whom he called "uniformed Klansmen."

The precise time and location that ignited a week of riots is unknown, but the conflict was captured in the image of the zoot suit, a popular style of dress among black and Mexican youth. Believed to be derived from actor Clark Gable's long-tailed suits in *Gone with the Wind*, the zoot suit costume was made famous by swing jazz musician Cab Calloway. The name zoot suit came from the bebop language of the 1940s, and the outfit was also referred to as drapes or reat pleats. In his autobiography Malcolm X reminisced about donning a zoot suit when he frequented Harlem night clubs as an adolescent. During World War II cloth was being rationed for the American troops overseas. The wide shoulders and baggy pants of the zoot suit were considered an open affront to the war effort. Made of bright and gaudy fabric, these outfits were truly a symbol of defiance and an expression of the unwillingness by these youth to fight what many believed was a white man's war. In fact during the week of rioting, the Los Angeles City Council passed a resolution declaring the wearing of a zoot suit a misdemeanor.

To the rebellious youth of the subsequent Chicano movement in the late 1960s and early 1970s, this generation of Mexican-Americans and their zoot suits were venerated as radical ancestors. The *pachucos* of one era became the Chicanos of the next. This is most clearly expressed by playwright Luis Valdez in his 1978 *Zoot Suit*, a popular play that was adapted to the silver screen in a 1981 movie starring Edward

James Olmos. According to historian Mike Davis, today's Los Angeles gangs emerged from the Zoot Suit Riots, when Mexican-American youth formed gangs to fight back against their white attackers. Today it is not uncommon for young men at predominately Hispanic Garfield High School in Los Angeles to come decked out in colorful zoot suits, topped with wide-brimmed hats and with a long chain swinging at their side. For these kids the stylish zoot suiters of the 1940s were the darker-skinned members of the greatest U.S. generation.

BRIAN DOLINAR

References and Further Reading

Davis, Mike. *City of Quartz.* New York: Vintage, 1992.

Himes, Chester. "Zoot Riots Are Race Riots." *Crisis* (July 1943): 200–222.

Kelley, Robin. "The Riddle of the Zoot: Malcolm Little and Black Cultural Politics During World War II." *Race Rebels: Culture, Politics, and the Black Working Class.* New York: Free Press, 1994.

McWilliams, Carey. *The Education of Carey McWilliams.* New York: Simon and Schuster, 1978.

See also **Communist Party; International Labor Defense; Scottsboro Case**

INDEX

INDEX

INDEX

MAR - 8 2007

MEMORIAL LIBRARY

Q

R

Taft-Hartley Act on, 33, 341, 661, 776, 1353
U.S. Chamber of Commerce on, 776
Secondary School Teachers' Association, 1233
Seeger, Charles, 927
Seeger, Pete, music of, 928
Seeliger, Lloyd, 325
SEIU. *See* Service Employees' International Union
Selective Service Administration, Hershey and, 520
Self-Preservation and Loyalty League (SPLL), of Bogalusa Labor
    Conflict, 167
Sellins, Fannie (1865?–1919), 1224–1226
    arrest/conviction of, 1226
    of UGWA, 1225
    UMWA and, 1225
    Wilson, Woodrow's clemency for, 1226
Senior Executive Service (SES)
    CSRA and, 959
    NFFE on, 959
September 11
    airlines operation/service influence by, 48
    Bush, George W., and, 1474
    DHS creation after, 1147
Serra, Junípero, 200
Service Employees' International Union (SEIU), 204, 559, 604, 683,
    885, **1227–1231**
    AFL-CIO and, 220, 714, 1227, 1230
    African-Americans and, 729
    BSEIU change to, 714, 1227, 1229
    Change to Win coalition and, 1478
    COPE and, 1228
    diminished strength of, 729
    Foner, Moe, and, 461
    on janitor contracts, 730
    Justice for Janitors' campaign of, 729, 1230, 1477
    living wage support by, 813
    membership of, 731, 1227
    modernization and, 1228–1229
    New York City hospital strike, 1006
    1930s and, 1227–1228
    origins of, 1227
    RWDSU merger with, 1187
    Sweeney and, 225, 379, 714, 864, 1229–1230, 1344, 1345, 1406
    UFCW and, 1229
    UFM and, 729
    union density and, 1472
Service Workers' International Union (SWIU), 80
    Sweeney and, 80
Serviceman's Readjustment Act (SRA), GI Bill as, 518
Servitude, of barbers, 144
SES. *See* Senior Executive Service
"Settlement as a Factor in the Labor Movement, The" (Addams),
    17–18
Settlement house movement, 1513–1514
Seventy Years of Life and Labor: An Autobiography
    (Gompers), 539
Sex discrimination, 1535–1536
Sex, Race, and Class (James), 1479
Sexism, in A. E. Staley Strike, 3
Sexual harassment, 1231–1233
    EEOC and, 1231–1232
    feminist movement and, 1231, 1232
    history of, 1232–1233
    MacKinnon on, 1231
    of women, 1482, 1535
    Working Women United and, 1231

Shachtman, Max, 796
    CP and, 1284
    SWP and, 1284
Shadow of Slavery, The (Daniel), 1238
Shanker, Albert (September 14, 1928–February 22, 1997), 89, 1035,
    1036, **1233–1235**, 1554
    AFT and, 1233
    collective bargaining and, 1234
    MOWM and, 1234
    NEA and, 1235
    racial quota opposition by, 1234
    Vietnam war support by, 1234–1235
Shapiro, Karin, 317, 1367
Share Croppers' Union (SCU) (1930s), 824, **1235–1237**
    CP influence in, 1235–1236
    founding of, 1236
    growth of, 1236–1237
    Johnson, Clyde, and, 1237
    Murphy, Al, and, 1236–1237
    sharecropping and, 1235
Sharecropping and Tenancy, 1237–1239
    AAA on, 37, 914
    African-Americans and, 404, 1238
    contract labor system in, 1237
    Daniel on, 1238
    definition of, 1237–1238
    in Emancipation/Reconstruction, 402
    Great Migration and, 547
    Hudson and, 620
    Louisiana Farmers' Union and, 824–825
    mechanization influence on, 1239
    in New South, 1002
    origins of, 402
    populism/People's Party and, 1112
    Ransom on, 1238
    in Reconstruction Era, 1235
    STFU and, 914, 1301
    on sugar plantations, 402–403
    Sutch on, 1238
    on tobacco plantations, 402
    violence against, 1528
    WWII and, 915
Sharpton, Al, 1037
Shaw, Lemuel, 785, 787
Shea, Cornelius P.
    of IBT, 667–668
    Montgomery Ward strike and, 667
    of Teamsters Union, 229
Sheet Metal Workers, Hill, Herbert, on, 942
Shefferman, Nathan W., 164
Sheffield, Horace (1914–1977), 1239–1241
    Reuther and, 1240
    TULC and, 1239, 1240
    UAW black representation by, 1240
Sheldon, Edward M., 1491
Sheppard-Towner Maternity and Infancy Protection Act
    American Medical Association against, 239
    Children's Bureau and, 239
    on infant mortality, 239
    Kelley and, 739, 950
Sherman Anti-trust Act, 66, 76, 173, 260, 341, 605, 658, 675, 788,
    789, 949, 1001, **1241–1242**
    on blacklists, 163
    Clayton Antitrust Act and, 261, 1242
    Cleveland and, 1241